THE BIRTH OF THE PALESTINIAN REFUGEE PROBLEM REVISITED

Benny Morris' *The Birth of the Palestinian Refugee Problem, 1947–1949*, was first published in 1988. Its startling revelations about how and why 700,000 Palestinians left their homes and became refugees during the Arab–Israeli war in 1948 undermined the conflicting Zionist and Arab interpretations; the former suggesting that the Palestinians had left voluntarily, and the latter that this was a planned expulsion. The book subsequently became a classic in the field of Middle East history. *The Birth of the Palestinian Refugee Problem Revisited* represents a thoroughly revised edition of the earlier work, compiled on the basis of newly opened Israeli military archives and intelligence documentation. While the focus of the book remains the 1948 war and the analysis of the Palestinian exodus, the new material contains more information about what actually happened in Jerusalem, Jaffa and Haifa, and how events there eventually led to the collapse of Palestinian urban society. It also sheds light on the battles, expulsions and atrocities that resulted in the disintegration of the rural communities. The story is a harrowing one. The refugees now number some four million and their existence remains one of the major obstacles to peace in the Middle East.

Benny Morris is Professor of History in the Middle East Studies Department, Ben-Gurion University. He is an outspoken commentator on the Arab–Israeli conflict, and is one of Israel's premier revisionist historians. His publications include *Righteous Victims: A History of the Zionist–Arab Conflict, 1881–2001* (2001), and *Israel's Border Wars, 1949–56* (1997).

THE BIRTH OF THE PALESTINIAN REFUGEE PROBLEM REVISITED

Benny Morris

Ben-Gurion University of the Negev, Israel

CAMBRIDGE
UNIVERSITY PRESS

CAMBRIDGE UNIVERSITY PRESS
Cambridge, New York, Melbourne, Madrid, Cape Town,
Singapore, São Paulo, Delhi, Mexico City

Cambridge University Press
The Edinburgh Building, Cambridge CB2 8RU, UK

Published in the United States of America by Cambridge University Press, New York

www.cambridge.org
Information on this title: www.cambridge.org/9780521009676

First published 1988 (0521 330289)
Paperback edition 1989 (0521 338891)
Second edition 2004
6th printing 2012

A catalogue record for this publication is available from the British Library

National Library of Australia Cataloguing in Publication Data
Morris, Benny, 1948–.
The birth of the Palestinian refugee problem revisited.
2nd ed.
Bibliography.
Includes index.
ISBN 0 521 81120 1.
ISBN 0 521 00967 7 (pbk.).
1. Refugees, Arab.   2. Israel-Arab War, 1948–1949 – Refugees.   3. Arab-Israeli
conflict.   4. Jewish-Arab relations.   5. Palestinian Arabs.   I. Title. (Series : Cambridge
Middle East studies; no. 18).
956.04

ISBN 978-0-521-81120-0 Hardback
ISBN 978-0-521-00967-6 Paperback

To the memory of my mother, Sadie, and my father, Ya'akov, who, I am sure, had a hand in the creation of this work in more ways than I can imagine.

Contents

Acknowledgements

The original version of this book, published in 1988, was written during the years 1982–1986. I was helped financially only by the British Council. Their grant enabled me to carry out research in British archives and, later, to give a lecture at a seminar on refugees in Oxford University. I thank them. I would also like to thank Roger Owen, at the time a fellow of St Antony's College, Oxford, and now Professor of Middle Eastern Economic History at Harvard University, and Middle East historian Yehoshu'a Porath, professor emeritus of the Hebrew University of Jerusalem, for their solicitude and help in seeing this work through. I owe them both a large debt. The Senior Associate Membership I held in St Antony's College, for which I thank Professor Owen and the fellows and college officers, facilitated my research. I frequently bothered with questions the late Middle East expert and Israel Foreign Ministry official Dr Ya'akov Shimoni and he deserves special thanks for his patience and help. I would also like to thank Professor Yoav Gelber of Haifa University, who has always been generous with his time and knowledge.

Since 1997 I have been on the staff of Ben-Gurion University in Beer-sheba, Israel, and, over the years, have enjoyed the friendship and as-sistance of Professor Jimmy Weinblatt, formerly the dean of humanities and social sciences and currently the university's rector. I owe him a very large debt.

I also owe an immense debt to my friend Jeff Abel, who over the years helped me in no end of computer-related ways to produce this work, and in other ways as well.

I would also like to thank the staffs of the various archives from which, in several bouts of research, I culled the material for both the original 'Birth' and the current work: These include Yehoshu'a Freundlich and Yemima Rosenthal of the Israel State Archives; Doron Aviad of the Israel Defence Forces and Defence Ministry Archive; and the staffs of the Haganah Archive; the Public Record Office; the United States National

Archive; the United Nations Archive; the Middle East Centre Archive at St Antony's College, Oxford; the Central Zionist Archive; the Hashomer Archive; the Hashomer Hatza'ir Archive; the Kibbutz Meuhad Archive; the Labour Party Archive; the Labour (Histadrut) Archive; the Jabotinsky Institute; the David Ben-Gurion Archive; the Haifa Municipal Archive; the Tiberias Municipal Archive; and the archives of a number of kibbutzim, especially of Mishmar Ha'emeq, Hazore'a and Ma'anit.

My biggest debt, of course, is to my family – my wife Leah, and my children, Erel, Yagi and Orian – for holding up under the strain of my years' long commitment to completing the original 'Birth' and the current work.

Map 1 The United Nations Partition Plan, November 1947
(Based on Martin Gilbert, *The Arab–Israeli Conflict, its History in Maps*, new edn, London, Weidenfeld & Nicolson, 1976)

Map 2 Arab settlements abandoned in 1948–9 and date and main causes of abandonment
(*Note*: The map omits a dozen or so very small or satellite villages and small bedouin tribes or sub-tribes)
(Based on *Carta's Historical Atlas of Israel, The First Years 1948–61*, ed. by Jehuda Wallach and Moshe Lissak, Jerusalem, Carta, 1978, p. 139)

Map 3 Jewish settlements established in 1948–9
(*Note*: Several of the settlements established in 1948–9 were either dismantled or collapsed. Some changed their names. Others subsequently moved from the original sites to nearby sites)
(Based on The Survey of Palestine 1946 Map with additions by the Survey Department of the State of Israel, made available by the kind permission of the Hebrew University of Jerusalem's Geography Department and Map Collection)

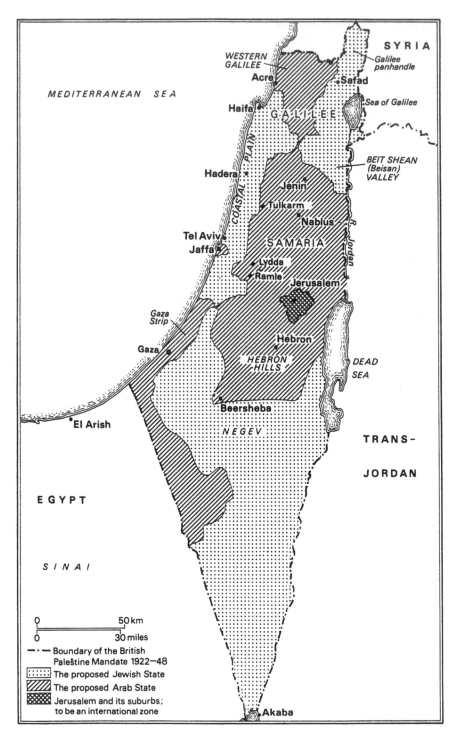

SYRIA

WESTERN
GALILEE
Acre
Safad
Galilee
panhandle

MEDITERRANEAN SEA

Haifa
GALILEE
Sea of Galilee

BEIT SHEAN
(Beisan)
VALLEY

Hadera
Jenin

Tulkarm

Nablus

Tel Aviv
Jaffa
SAMARIA

Lydda
Ramle

Jerusalem

Gaza
Strip

Hebron

Gaza
HEBRON
HILLS
DEAD
SEA

Beersheba

El Arish
NEGEV

TRANS-

JORDAN

EGYPT

SINAI

R. Jordan

COASTAL PLAIN

| 0 | 50 km |
| 0 | 30 miles |

Akaba

—·— Boundary of the British
       Palestine Mandate 1922–48
⣿ The proposed Jewish State
▨ The proposed Arab State
▦ Jerusalem and its suburbs;
   to be an international zone

MAP 1

MAP 2

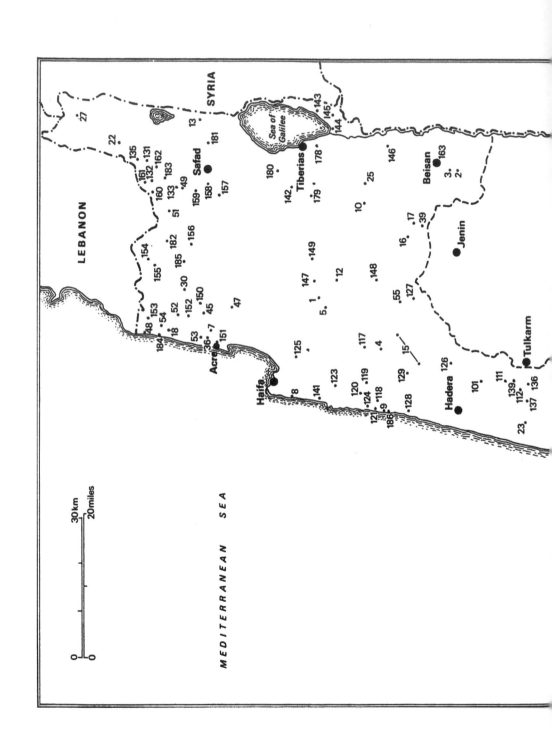

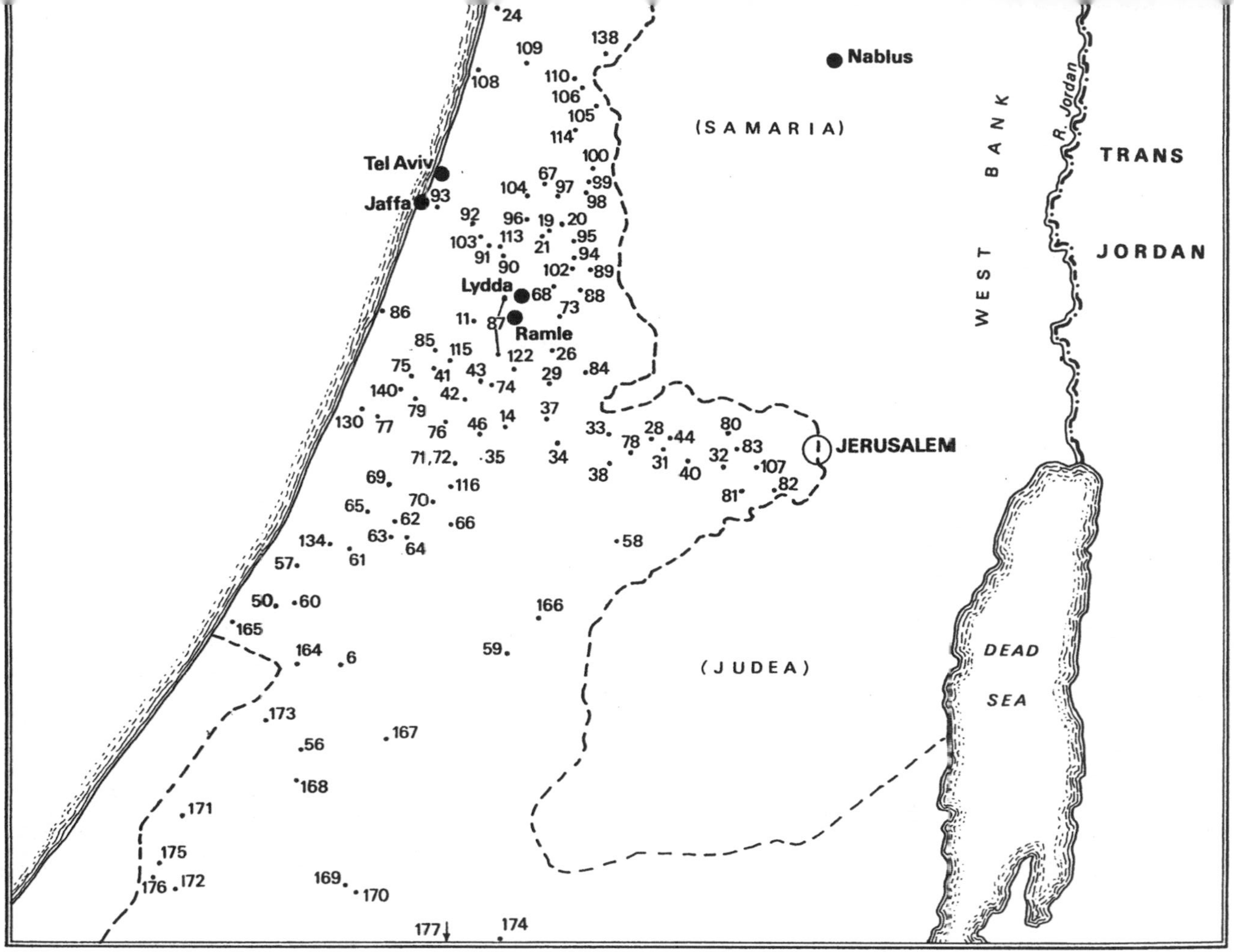

TRANS

JORDAN

R. Jordan

WEST BANK

DEAD SEA

(SAMARIA)

● Nablus

⊖ JERUSALEM

(JUDEA)

● Tel Aviv

● Jaffa

● Lydda

● Ramle

MAP 3

Key to Map 2

In the Key, the following codes are used for decisive causes of abandoment:

A Abandonment on Arab orders
C Influence of nearby town's fall
E Expulsion by Jewish forces
F Fear (of being caught up in fighting)
M Military assault on settlement
W Whispering campaigns - psychological warfare by Haganah/IDF

The lines between C, F and M are somewhat blurred. It is often difficult to distinguish between the flight of villagers because of reports of the fall or flight from neighbouring settlements, flight from fear of "being next" or flight due to the approach of a Haganah/IDF column. I have generally ascribed the flight of inhabitants on the path of an Israeli military advance to M, even though some villagers may have already taken to their heels upon hearing of the fall of a neighbouring village (which could go under C or F).
  Similarly the line between M and E is occasionally blurred.

Galilee Panhandle

1 Abil al Qamh - F, C, 10 May 1948
2 Zuq al Fauqani - W, M, 21 May 1948
3 Shauqa al Tahta - F, 14 May 1948
4 Sanbariya, al - May 1948 (?)
5 Khisas - W, C, E, 25 May 1948 / June 1949
6 Hunin - F, E, 3 May 1948 / September 1948
7 Mansura, al - W, 25 May 1948
8 Lazzaza - W, 21 May 1948
9 Zuq al Tahtanii - C, 11 May 1948
10 Khalisa, al - C, W, 11 May 1948
11 Madahil, al - F, 30 April 1948
12 Qeitiya - W, E, 19 May 1948 / June 1948
13 'Abisiyya, al - C, 25 May 1948
14 Dawwara - W, 25 May 1948
15 Salihiya, al - F, W, 25 May 1948
16 Muftakhira, al - F, 16 May 1948
17 Zawiya, al - M, E, 24 May 1948
18 Buweiziya, al - C, 11 May 1948
19 Na'ima, al - C, 14 May 1948
20 Hamra, al - F, M, 1 May 1948
21 Ghuraba - F, 28 May 1948
22 Khirbet Khiyam al Walid - F, I May 1948
23 Jahula - May 1948 (?)
24 Qadas - C, 28 May 1948
25 Malikiya, al - M, 28 May 1948
26 Nabi Yusha - M, 16 May 1948
27 Beisamun - W, 25 May 1948
28 Mallaha - W, 25 May 1948
29 Darbashiya, al - May 1948 (?)
390 Khan al Duweir - Not known
391 Manshiya, al (near Khalisa) - Not known

Upper Galilee

30 'Ulmaniya, al - M, 20 April 1948
31 'Arab Zubeih - F, 20 April 1948
32 Deishum - M, 30 October 1948
33 'Alma - M, 30 October 1948
34 Saliha - M, 30 October 1948
35 Fara - M, 30 October 1948
36 Husseiniya, al - C, 21 April 1948
37 Tuleil - late April 1948 (?)
38 Kafr Bir'im - E, early November 1948
39 Ras al Ahmar - M, 30 October 1948
40 Dallata - Not known
41 Marus - C, 26 May 1948 and M, 30 October 1948
42 Kirad al Ghannama - C, 22 April 1948 (later resettled, E 1956)
43 Kirad al Baqqara - C, 22 April 1948 (later resettled, E 1956)
44 Teitaba - May 1948 (?)
45 Safsaf - M/F, 29 October 1948
46 Qaddita - C, 11 May 1948
47 'Ammuqa - M, 24 May 1948
48 Qabba'a - M, 26 May 1948
49 Weiziya - May 1948 (?)
50 Mughr al Kheit - M, 2 May 1948
51 Fir'im - M, 26 May 1948
52 Ja'una - C, 9 May 1948
53 'Ein al Zeitun - M, 2 May 1948
54 Biriya - M, 2 May 1948
55 (Arab) Safad - M, 10–11 May 1948
56 Meirun - (?) C, (?) 10–12 May 1948
57 Sammu'i - C, 12 May 1948
58 Dhahiriya Tahta - C, 10 May 1948
59 Mansurat al Kheit - M, 18 January 1948
60 Sa'sa - M/E, 30 October 1948
61 Ghabbatiya - (?), 30 October 1948

Key to Map 3

The Hebrew name of the settlement is given first, followed by the former Arab name of the site or nearest site and the date of the settlement's establishment.

18 Sa'ar – Al Zib – August 1948

19 Be'erot Yitzhak – Wilhelma – August 1948

20 Bnei Atarot – Wilhelma – August 1948

21 Mahane Yisrael – Wilhelma – August 1948

22 Yiftah – near Jahula – August 1948

23 Nordiya – Khirbet Beit Lid – August 1948

24 Udim – Wadi Faliq – August 1948

25 Gazit – Al Tira – September 1948

26 Azariya – Al Barriya – September 1948 (re-established 1949)

27 Hagoshrim – Al Mansura – September 1948

28 Lehagshama (Beit Meir) – Beit Mahsir – September 1948 (re-established 1950)

29 Ameilim – Abu Shusha – September 1948

30 Ga'aton – Khirbet Jiddin – October 1948

31 Kesalon – Kasla – October 1948 (re-established 1952)

32 Tsova – Suba – October 1948

33 Harel – Beit Jiz – October 1948

34 Tal-Shahar – Khirbet Beit Far – October 1948

35 Revadim – Al Kheima – November 1948

36 Bustan Hagalil – Al Sumeiriya – December 1948

37 Mishmar-David – Khulda – December 1948

38 Tzor'a – Sar'a – December 1948

39 Nurit – Nuris – 1948

40 Ramat Raziel – Beit Umm al Meis – 1948

41 Ge'alya – north of Yibna – 1948

42 Beit Elazari – south of 'Aqir – 1948

43 Kfar Eqron – 'Aqir – 1948

44 Shoresh – Saris – 1948

45 Beit Ha'emek – Kuweikat – January 1949

46 Netiva – Al Mukheizin – January 1949

47 Yas'ur – Al Birwa – January 1949

48 Betset Bet (Kfar Rosh Hanikra) – near Al Bassa – January 1949

49 Sifsufa – Safsaf – January 1949

50 Mavki'im – Barbara – January 1949

51 Sasa – Sa'sa – January 1949

52 Kabrita (Kabri) – Al Kabri – January 1949

53 Lohamei Hageta'ot – Al Sumeiriya – January 1949

54 Beit Ha'arava (Gesher Haziv) – Al Zib – January 1949

55 Irgun Kaplan (Meggido) – Lajjun – January 1949

56 T'kumah – Al Muharraqa – 1949

57 Migdal-Gad (Ashkelon) – Al Majdal – 1949

58 Beit Nettef (Netiv HaLamed-Heh) – Beit Nattif – 1949

59 Al Qubeiba – Al Qubeiba – 1949 (re-established al Lachish, 1955)

60 Gei'a – Al Jiya – 1949

61 Hodiya – Julis – 1949

62 Ein Tsurim (Deganim) – Sawafir al Gharbiya – 1949

63 Massu'ot Yitzhak (Ein Tsurim) – Sawafir al Sharqiya – 1949

64 Shafir (Massu'ot Yitzhak) – Sawafir al Shamaliya – 1949

65 Giv'ati – Beit Daras – 1949–50

66 Arugot – Tall al Turmus – 1949

67 Nehalim – southeast of Petah Tikva – 1948

68 Ginaton – east of Lydda – 1949

69 Azrikam – Batani Gharbi – 1949–50

70 Yehiel (Kfar Ahim) – Qastina – 1949

71 Keren-Re'em (Bnei Re'em) – Masmiya al Kabira – 1949

72 Masmiya Bet (Masmiya Shalom) – Masmiya al Saghira – 1949

73 Kfar Daniel – Daniyal – 1949

74 Ganei-Yona – east of 'Aqir – 1949

75 Yavne – Yibna – 1949

76 Kidron – Qatra – 1949

77 Netivot – 'Arab Sukreir – 1949

78 Eshta'ol – 'Islin/Ishwa – 1949

79 Benaya – north of Bash-Shit – 1949

80 Beit Nekofa – Beit Naqubba – 1949

81 Ora – Al Jura – 1949–50

82 Manahat – Al Maliha – 1949

83 Beit Zayit – Khirbet Hureish – 1949

84 Mish'an (Mishmar Ayalon) – Al Qubab – 1949

85 Kefar Hanaggid – Al Qubeiba – 1949

86 Hatsofim Dalet – Al Nabi Rubin – 1949

87 Sitriya – Abu al Fadl – 1949

88 Hadid – Al Haditha – 1949

89 Nubalat (Beit Nehemia) – Beit Nabala – 1949–50

90 Tsafriya – north of Al Safiriya – 1949

91 Beit Dagan – Beit Dajan – 1948

92 Azor – Yazur – 1948

93 Abu Kabir – Abu Kabir – 1949

94 Beit Arif – Deir Tarif – 1949 (re-established 1951)

95 Tirat-Yehuda – Al Tira – 1949

96 Yehud – Al Yahudiya – 1948
97 Rantiya – Rantiya – 1949
98 Mazor – Al Muzeiri'a – 1949
99 Nahshonim – Majdal Yaba – 1949
100 Migdal-Yaffo – Majdal Yaba – 1949
101 Lehavot Haviva – west of Jatt – 1949
102 Kfar Truman – west Beit Nabala – 1949
103 Mishmar Hashiv'a – Beit Dajan – 1949
104 Magshimim – west of Rantiya – 1949
105 Yarhiv – east of Jaljuliya – 1949
106 Hak'ramim – Kafr Saba – 1949
107 Ein Kerem – 'Ein Karim – 1949
108 Reshef – Al Haram (Sidna Ali) – 1949
109 Tabsar (Khirbet Azzun) – 1949
110 Neve-Yamin – south of Kafr Saba – 1949
111 Ometz – Qaqun – 1949
112 Olesh – south of Qaqun – 1949
113 Sharir – Al Safiriya – 1949
114 Hagor – south of Jaljuliya – 1949
115 Zarnuqa – Zarnuqa – 1949
116 Talmei Yehiel – Masmiya al Kabira/ Qastina – 1949
117 Elyakim – Umm al Zinat – 1949
118 Ein Ayala – 'Ein Ghazal – 1949
119 Kerem Maharal – Ijzim – 1949
120 Geva-Carmel – Jab'a – 1949
121 Habonim – Kafr Lam – 1949
122 Ramot Meir – west of Na'ana – 1949
123 Ein Hod – 'Ein Haud – 1949
124 Tsrufa – Al Sarafand – 1949
125 Tel Hanan – Balad al Sheikh – 1949
126 Barka'i – Wadi 'Ara – 1949
127 Giv'at Oz – Zalafa – 1949
128 Ma'agan Micha'el – Kabara – 1949
129 Alona (Amikam) – Al Sindiyana – 1949–50
130 Nir Galim – 'Arab Sukreir – 1949
131 Dishon – Deishum – date uncertain but possibly 1949 (re-established 1953)
132 Porat – Fara – 1949
133 Shahar – near Safsaf – 1949
134 Nir Yisrael – west of Julis – 1949
135 Malkiya – Al Malikiya – 1949
136 Be'erotayim – Khirbet Burin – 1949
137 Burgta – Khirbet al Burj – 1949
138 Eyal – Khirbet Hanuta – 1949
139 Gan Yoshiya – south of Qaqun – 1949
140 Beit Gamliel – southeast of Yibna – 1949
141 Megadim – Bir Badawiya – 1949

142 Lavi – Lubya – 1949
143 Ha'on – Al Samra – 1949
144 Ma'agan – Samakh – 1949
145 Beit Katzir (Tel Katzir) – east of Samakh – 1949
146 Bashatwa (Neve-Ur) – Al Bashatiwa – 1949
147 Hasolelim – west of Saffuriya – 1949
148 Hayogev – Khirbet Beit Lid al Awadim – 1949
149 Tsipori – Saffuriya – 1949
150 Amqa – 'Amqa – 1949
151 Hayotzrim – Manshiya – 1949
152 Ben-Ami – Al Nahr – 1949
153 Betset (Shlomi) – Al Bassa – 1949–50
154 Shomera – Tarbikha – 1949
155 Yoqrat – Iqrit – 1949
156 Hossen – Sukhmata – 1949
157 Farod – Farradiya – 1949
158 Kfar Shamai – Sammu'i – 1949
159 Meiron – Meirun – 1949
160 Bar'am – Kafr Bir'im – 1949
161 Nir-On (Yiron) – Saliha – 1949–50
162 Alma – Alma – 1949
163 Beit She'an – Beisan – 1948
164 Erez – Dimra/Najd – 1949
165 Zikkim – Hirbiya – 1949
166 Beit Guvrin – Beit Jibrin – 1949
167 Beit Kama – southeast of Jammama – 1949
168 Beit Hagadi – south of Al Muharraqa – 1949
169 Gilat – 'Arab al Qudeirat – 1949
170 Tifrah – northeast of Khirbet Umm al Khrum – 1949
171 Beit Re'im – 'Arab al Hanajira – 1949
172 Magen – Sheikh Nuran – 1949
173 Mefalsim – southeast of Beit Hanun – 1949
174 Omer – east of Khirbet 'Amra – 1949
175 Ein Hash'losha – east of Khan Yunis – 1949
176 Nirim – east of Khan Yunis – 1949
177 Mash'a'bei Sadeh – east of Bir Asluj – 1949
178 Poriya – south of Tiberias – 1949
179 Sdeh Ilan – Kafr Sabt – 1949
180 Arbel – Khirbet Irbid – 1949
181 Elifelet – 'Arab Zanghariya – 1949
182 Alkosh – Deir al Qasi – 1949
183 Kerem Ben-Zimra – Ras al Ahmar – 1949
184 Tzahal – north of Al Zib – 1949
185 Me'una – Tarshiha – 1949
186 Doar – Tantura – 1949

Abbreviations

AAA – Antiquities Authority Archive
AFSC – American Friends Service Committee
AHC – Arab Higher Committee
ALA – Arab Liberation Army
AM – Agriculture Ministry (Israel)
BGA – David Ben-Gurion Archive
CAB – Cabinet Papers (Britain)
CIGS – Chief of Imperial General Staff (British Army)
CGS – Chief of General Staff (IDF)
CO – Colonial Office (Britain)
CP – Cunningham Papers
CZA – Central Zionist Archive
DBG-YH – David Ben-Gurion *Yoman Hamilhama* (the war diary)
DMZ – demilitarized zone
FM – Foreign Ministry (Israel)
FO – Foreign Office (Britain)
GSS – General Security Service (Shin Bet), Israel
HA – Haganah Archive
HC – High Commissioner (British in Palestine)
HHA – Hashomer Hatza'ir Archive
HHA-ACP – Hashomer Hatza'ir Archive – Aharon Cohen Papers
HHA-MYP – Hashomer Hatz'ir Archive – Meir Ya'ari Papers
HGS – Haganah General Staff
HIS – Haganah Intelligence Service
HIS-AD – Haganah Intelligence Service – Arab Department
HNS – Haganah National Staff
ICP – Israel Communist Party
IDF – Israel Defence Forces
IDF\GS – Israel Defence Forces General Staff
IDFA – Israel Defence Forces and Defence Ministry Archive

IJMES – *International Journal of Middle East Studies*
ISA – Israel State Archive
IZL – Irgun Zva'i Leumi (National Military Organisation or 'Irgun')
JA – Jewish Agency
JAE – Jewish Agency Executive
JA-PD – Jewish Agency Political Department
JEM – Jerusalem and East Mission
JI – Jabotinsky Institute
JM – Justice Ministry (Israel)
JNF – Jewish National Fund
JPS – *Journal of Palestine Studies*
KMA – Kibbutz Meuhad Archive
KMA-ACP – Kibbutz Meuhad Archive – Aharon Cisling Papers
KMA-IGP – Kibbutz Meuhad Archive – Israel Galili Papers
KMA-PA – Kibbutz Meuhad Archive – Palmah Archive
LA – Labour (Histadrut) Archive
LHI – *Lohamei Herut Yisrael* (Freedom Fighters of Israel or 'Stern Gang')
LPA – Labour Party (Mapai) Archive
MAC – Mixed Armistice Commission
MAM – Minority Affairs Ministry (Israel)
Mapai – *Mifliget Poalei Eretz Yisrael* (the Land of Israel Labour Party) (Yishuv)
Mapam – *Mifleget Poalim Meuhedet* (United Workers Party) (Yishuv)
MEJ – *Middle East Journal*
MES – *Middle Eastern Studies*
NA – National Archive (USA)
NC – National Committee
OC – officer in command
PIAT – projectile infantry anti-tank
PMO – Prime Minister's Office (Israel)
PRO – Public Record Office (London)
PS – Parliamentary Private Secretary
RG – record group
SAMECA – St Antony's College Middle East Centre Archive
SMC – Supreme Muslim Council
STH – *Sefer Toldot Hahaganah* (the history of the Haganah)
TJ – Transjordan
UN – United Nations
UNA – United Nations Archive
UNRWA – United Nations Relief and Works Agency for Palestine Refugees in the Near East
UNSCOP – United Nations Special Committee on Palestine
WO – War Office (Britain)
YND – Yosef Nahmani Diary

Introduction to revised edition

In 1988 CUP published the first edition of this work, which sought to describe the birth of the Palestinian refugee problem that, along with the establishment of the State of Israel, was the major political consequence of the 1948 war. The study examined how and why, over November 1947–October 1950, an estimated 600,000 to 760,000 Palestinian Arabs departed their homes, moving to other parts of Palestine (i.e., the West Bank and Gaza Strip) or abroad, primarily to Jordan, Syria and Lebanon.[1] There are today on the United Nations rolls close to four million Palestinian refugees (the Palestinian Authority says five million). About one third live in so-called refugee 'camps', which in reality are concrete-structured slum neighbourhoods on the peripheries of cities (Nablus, Gaza, Ramallah, Beirut, Damascus, Amman, etc.).

Perhaps curiously, little serious historiography had been produced, both in the four decades before the publication of the original version of this book or since, on why and how these Palestinians became refugees. Soon after 1948, several chronicles were published by Palestinian exiles, including 'Arif al 'Arif's *Al-Nakba, 1947–1952*[2] (the catastrophe 1947–1952) and Haj Muhammad Nimr al Khatib's *Min Athar al Nakba*[3] (following the catastrophe). About a decade after the event, Walid Khalidi, a Palestinian scholar, published two academic essays, 'The Fall of Haifa'[4] and 'Why Did the Palestinians Leave?',[5] that shed fresh light on aspects of the subject. The first major piece of research on the origin of the refugee problem, based mainly on open United Nations documentation and newspapers, was a doctoral study by an Israeli scholar, Rony Gabbay, *A Political Study of the Arab–Jewish Conflict: The Arab Refugee Problem (a Case Study)*,[6] published in 1959. Two decades later, a Palestinian scholar, Nafez Nazzal, published *The Palestinian Exodus from Galilee 1948*,[7] a path-breaking regional study but based almost completely on interviews in the Beirut-area refugee camps conducted in the early 1970s. A few years later, Israeli sociologist Baruch

1

Kimmerling's published *Zionism and Territory: The Socio-Territorial Dimensions of Zionist Politics*,[8] which contributed to understanding what had happened. During the decades after 1948, a number of Israelis and Palestinians produced serious essays and stories that illuminated the exodus, combining personal recollection and objective analysis – most prominently, Ephraim Kleiman's 'Khirbet Khiz'ah and Other Unpleasant Memories',[9] S. Yizhar's 'The Story of Khirbet Khiza',[10] and Elias Shoufani's 'The Fall of a Village'.[11]

All had suffered from the relative paucity of archival materials. In recent years, a number of young Israeli scholars produced MA and PhD theses and articles on the exodus in particular areas of Palestine and Yoav Gelber published *Palestine 1948: War, Escape and the Emergence of the Palestinian Refugee Problem*,[12] which in part dealt with the subject under discussion.

The Palestinian refugee problem and its consequences have shaken the Middle East and acutely troubled the world for more than five decades. Terrorist or guerrilla incursions into Israel by these refugees have helped trigger at least three conventional Arab–Israeli wars, in 1956, 1967 and 1982, and Palestinian terrorism, especially attacks on airline passengers and aircraft hijackings during the 1970s and 1980s, have caused chaos and instability worldwide. More recently, since 2000, Palestinian rebellion (the Second Intifada), largely powered by the refugee camps, has scuppered the Israeli–Arab peace process and destabilised the Middle East.

The centrality in the conflict of the refugee problem was convincingly demonstrated in the Israeli–Palestinian–American negotiations of July 2000–January 2001 ('Camp David' and after), when the refugees emerged as the single most important and intractable issue, with the Arabs insisting on their 'right to return' to their lost homes and lands and Israel rejecting that demand, arguing that its implementation would bring about the Jewish State's demise.

The question of what in 1948 turned hundreds of thousands of Palestinians into refugees has been a fundamental propaganda issue between Israel and the Arab states ever since. The general Arab claim, that the Jews expelled Palestine's Arabs with predetermination and preplanning, as part of a systematic, grand political–military design, has served to underline the Arab portrayal of Israel as a vicious, immoral robber state. The official Israeli narrative, that the Palestinians fled 'voluntarily' (meaning not as a result of Jewish compulsion) or that they were asked or ordered to do so by their leaders and by the leaders of the Arab states, helped leave intact the new state's self-image as the haven of a much persecuted people, a body politic more just, moral and deserving of the West's sympathy and help than the surrounding sea of reactionary, semi-feudal, dictatorial Arab societies.

The publication of the first edition of this book in 1988 provoked a great deal of anger and controversy. My conclusions appeared to satisfy no one (except the few who like their history complex and nuanced). The book failed to endorse either the official Palestinian or Israeli narratives and, indeed, tended to undermine both. I was vilified alternatively as a 'propagandist for the Palestine Liberation Organisation' and as a 'sophisticated Zionist propagandist'; more rarely, as merely a bad historian.

I embarked upon the research not out of ideological commitment or political interest. I simply wanted to know what happened. Often, at some point in their career, journalists get an urge to write 'a book' and I had decided on a history of the Palmah, the strike force of the Haganah, the main militia of the Jewish community in Palestine, and, later, of the Israel Defence Forces (IDF) in 1948. I had always wanted to do military history and nothing serious had been done on this subject. In late 1982 I was privileged to be given access to the still classified papers of the Palmah's headquarters by the association of Palmah veterans, 'Dor Hapalmah'. But a few months later, perhaps sensing trouble, the veterans abruptly withdrew this access, and I realised I would be unable to write the planned history. Yet I had seen and read batches of documents, often marked 'top secret', that shed light on the creation of the refugee problem. I felt that there might be a good story there. Serendipity would have it that my interest in the subject had been ignited a few weeks earlier when, as a reporter, I had been sent to cover the Israeli invasion and occupation of southern Lebanon. It was there, in the ruins of Rashidiye Refugee Camp, outside Tyre, in June 1982, that I first met and interviewed refugees, originally from al Bassa, in the Galilee.

Historians, like generals, need luck. 1982 proved to be a pivotal year in the Israeli archives. The government began opening large amounts of documentation on 1948 at the Israel State Archive (ISA). Simultaneously, local and party political archives began organising and releasing materials. When I added these to the material I had seen in the Palmah Archive (PA), and material I was later to see in British and American archives and the United Nations Archive, I had a solid documentary basis on which to write the contemplated study.

But a major problem remained: Arab documentation. Unfortunately, the Palestinians failed to produce and preserve 'state papers' from 1947–1949, and the Arab states – all dictatorships of one sort or another (military juntas, absolute monarchies, etc.) – refused and continue to refuse access to their papers from the 1948 war, which they regarded and still regard as a humiliating catastrophe. In the course of the research and writing, I did my best to illuminate this 'area of darkness' by culling heavily from Jewish or Israeli intelligence material and British and American diplomatic dispatches dealing with the Arab world and, specifically, with the evolving refugee problem. The intelligence and diplomatic material went some way towards filling out the picture of what was happening in the field, in the towns and villages of Palestine, in 1948. They were less enlightening about policy-making in the Arab capitals and military headquarters. But given the disarray, confusion and general absence of clear policy in those capitals concerning the evolving problem over November 1947 – June 1948, this paucity of information was not as important as at first seems. As it turned out, with regard to the refugees there was very little connection between what was happening in the field and what was discussed and, even, decided by the Arab leaders inside and outside Palestine.

I also made use of some Arab diaries, memoirs, and books based on interviews, to round out the picture. (A number of Israeli orientalists (though, strangely enough, no Arabs) later took me and the book to task for failing to cull Arab memoirs more thoroughly. But none was able to show how use of this ignored material would have substantially or even marginally altered or enhanced the picture that I was able to draw on the basis of the Israeli and Western archives.

After careful thought, I refrained almost completely from using interviews, with Jews or Arabs, as sources of concrete information. My brief forays into interviewing had persuaded me of the undesirability of relying on human memories 40–50 years after the event to illuminate the past. The clincher came when I asked Yigael Yadin, the famous professor of archaeology who in 1948 had served as the Haganah\IDF head of operations (and often de facto chief of general staff), about the expulsion of the Arabs from the towns of Lydda and Ramle. 'What expulsion?' he asked – about what had been the biggest expulsion of the war. He did not deny that an expulsion had taken place; he merely said that he could not remember.

I believe in the value of documents. While contemporary documents may misinform, distort, omit or lie, they do so, in my experience, far less than interviewees recalling highly controversial events some 40–50 years ago. My limited experience with such interviews revealed enormous gaps of memory and terrible distortion and selectivity born of 'adopted' and 'rediscovered' memories, ideological certainties and commitments and political agendas. I have found interviews occasionally of use in providing 'colour' and in reconstructing a picture of prevailing conditions and, sometimes, feelings. But not in establishing 'facts'.

The value of oral testimony about 1948, if anything, has diminished with the passage of the 20 years since I first researched the birth of the Palestinian refugee problem. Memories have further faded and acquired memories, ideological precepts, and political agendas have grown if anything more intractable; intifadas and counter-intifadas have done nothing for the cause of salvaging historical truth.

But, thankfully, the liberalisation of Israeli archival practices has led during the past decade and a half to the release of an enormous amount of archival material that was closed when I wrote the first version of this study. More specifically, the ISA has declassified almost all the Israeli Cabinet protocols for 1948–1949 and the IDF Archive (IDFA) and the Haganah Archive (HA), which were both completely closed to anyone not employed by the Defence Ministry, have opened their doors and declassified hundreds of thousands of documents, a true boon for historians. While the IDFA, HA and ISA continue to keep sealed a certain amount of sensitive documentation, enough has recently been declassified and made available – including much if not most of the IDF operational and intelligence material from 1948 – to warrant a fresh look at what brought about the refugee problem.

I have no doubt that the eventual declassification of the material still untouched or newly sealed by the IDFA declassifiers, and the materials stored in the still-closed Israeli intelligence archives at Gelilot, will supply further revelations and new insights. But enough has been opened to give a good idea of what at least the materials in the IDFA and HA can reveal about what happened. The newly-opened documentation very substantially enriches the picture, and our understanding, of what happened in various parts of Palestine during 1948 – what happened week by week and month by month in Jaffa and Haifa and Jerusalem, and in the countryside; and, on the other hand – and this is a paradoxical conclusion which won't sit well with either Israeli or Palestinian propagandists and 'black-or-white historians' – they substantially increase both Israeli and Palestinian responsibility for the creation of the refugee problem. For what the new documents reveal is that there were both far more expulsions and atrocities by Israeli troops than tabulated in this book's first edition and, at the same time, far more orders and advice to various communities by Arab officials and officers to quit their villages or to at least send away their women, old folk and children, substantially fuelling the exodus. I have added a great many passages based on this material to this edition.

The other major innovation here is the addition of a new chapter on Zionist thinking about 'Transfer' – i.e., the organised, compensated, mutually agreed shift, or one-sided expulsion, of Arab communities out of Palestine – a subject accorded only four pages in the 1988 edition. Over the intervening years, I have concluded that pre-1948 'Transfer' thinking had a greater effect on what happened in 1948 than I had allowed for and, hence, deserved deeper treatment and more space. An additional reason for this deeper treatment was criticism of my original handling of the subject by both Arab and Israeli scholars: Arab historians like Nur Masalha[13] argued that the pre-1948 Zionist 'Transfer' thinking was a pillar of Zionist ideology and was tantamount to a master plan – which was then systematically implemented in 1948. Masalha was eager to prove that Zionism was a robber ideology and Israel, an innately expansionist robber state. From the Israeli side, Shabtai Teveth,[14] David Ben-Gurion's biographer, and Anita Shapira,[15] an historian of Zionism, argued that the Zionist leadership – including Ben-Gurion – had never supported the idea of transfer and had never taken the idea seriously, and that, therefore, there was no connection between the occasional propagation of the idea in the 1930s and 1940s and what happened to the Palestinians in 1947–1949. Both were driven by a desire to clear Israel of the charge of premeditation in what befell Palestine's Arabs.

As readers of the new chapter will see, the evidence for pre-1948 Zionist support for 'Transfer' really is unambiguous; but the connection between that support and what actually happened during the war is far more tenuous than Arab propagandists will allow.

I have also tried, in this revision, to integrate fresh insights and evidence published by a number of Israeli historians during the past 15 years. Unfortunately, no worthwhile historiography on 1948, comparable to that of, say, Uri Milstein and Yoav Gelber, has been produced by Palestinians, though I have occasionally referred to the essentially anthropological 'village series' produced by Bir Zeit University Press during the past two decades.

The Arab exodus from the areas that became the Jewish State at the end of the war occurred over the space of 20 months, from the end of November 1947 to July 1949, with several small appendages during the following months and years. It occurred in the course of a war marked by radically shifting circumstances and conditions in the various areas of the country. The exodus of the rich from Jaffa and Haifa over December 1947 to March 1948 was vastly different from the mass urban flight of April and early May; indeed, the multi-layered flight from Jaffa was markedly different from that from Haifa; and both had little in common with the expulsion and flight from Lydda and Ramle in July or from 'Eilabun, Dawayima and Kafr Bir'im in October–November 1948. To describe and explain the exodus I have had to describe and explain events and circumstances during the war's various stages and in different areas. Where necessary, and this is truer of this edition than of its predecessor, I have gone into considerable detail. Fortunately or unfortunately, the devil is in the details and an historian cannot avoid the devil.

The study generally proceeds chronologically, from the United Nations General Assembly Partition Resolution (No. 181) of 29 November 1947 to the collapse of the Lausanne peace conference in September 1949. In examining the exodus, the study proceeds geographically, from area to area. But the chronological-geographical flow is interrupted by a number of horizontal chapters dealing with specific subjects ('Transfer' and 'Blocking the return of the refugees').

A major criticism of the 1988 edition, especially by Israelis, was that the book lacked 'context' — that I had not given sufficient weight to the Holocaust, which had ended less than three years before the events described, and, more importantly, to the events of the 1948 war itself, which had in many ways shaped and moulded Israeli decision-making and actions, at local and national levels. Some critics noted that I devoted little space to describing Arab massacres of Jews in the course of 1948 (there were three such massacres). My response to this is twofold. First, this is not a history of the 1948 war or a history of what the Arabs did to the Jews but a history of how and why the Palestinian refugee problem came about. In this context, what Jews did to Arabs, including massacres, played a role; what Arabs did to Jews was barely relevant. Second, where possible, I did try to describe the context of hostilities — specific battles — that resulted in Palestinian flight or expulsion. In any event, in this current edition I have slightly expanded the discussion of the varying contexts in which the refugee problem was created.

In general, it cannot be stressed too strongly that, while this is not a military history, the events it describes, cumulatively amounting to the Palestinian Arab exodus, occurred in wartime and were a product, direct and indirect, of that war, a war that the Palestinians started. The threat of battle and battle itself were the immediate backdrop to the various components of the exodus.

Throughout, when examining what happened, the reader must also recall the wider context — the clash of arms between Palestine's warring Jewish and Arab militias and, later, the armies of the Arab states and Israel; the intention of the Palestinian leadership and irregulars and, later, of most of the Arab states' leaders and armies in launching the hostilities in November–December 1947 and in invading Palestine in May 1948 to destroy the Jewish state and, possibly, the Yishuv (the Jewish community in Palestine) itself; the fears of the Yishuv that the Palestinians and the Arab states, if given the chance, intended to re-enact a Middle Eastern version of the Holocaust; and the extremely small dimensions, geographical and numerical, of the Yishuv (pop. 650,000) in comparison with the Palestinian Arabs (1.25 million) and the infinitely larger surrounding Arab hinterland, with tens of millions of people. At the same time, it is well to recall that, from late July 1948, it was clear to the Yishuv's leaders (and probably to most Arab leaders) that Israel had won its war for survival, at least in the short term, and that the subsequent IDF offensives were geared to securing the political-military future of the Jewish state in what continued to be a highly hostile and uncomfortable geopolitical environment and to rounding out its borders.

I believe this revised edition adds substantially to our understanding of what happened in 1948 and of the deep roots of Israeli–Arab enmity in our time.

ENDNOTES

1. While most of these dislocated people did not become 'refugees' in the strict sense of the word – they were not exiled from their country but rather they moved or were moved from one part of the country to another – the world has come to accept the usage 'refugee' to describe those dislocated from their homes who ended up outside the country and in other parts of Palestine, and their progeny. For shorthand's sake, we shall do the same.
2. Al Maktaba al 'Asriya, Beirut and Sidon, 1956–1960.
3. Al Matba'a al 'Amumiya, Damascus, 1951.
4. *Middle East Forum*, XXXV\10, Dec. 1959.
5. *Middle East Forum*, XXXV\7, July 1959.
6. Libraire E. Droz, Geneve, and Libraire Minard, Paris, 1959.
7. Institute of Palestine Studies, Beirut, 1978.
8. Institute of International Studies, University of California, Berkeley, 1983.
9. *Jerusalem Quarterly*, 40, 1986.
10. Sifriyat Poalim\Mishlat, Merhavia, 1949.
11. *Journal of Palestine Studies*, 1\4, 1972.
12. Sussex Academic Press, Brighton, 2001.
13. Masalha, *Expulsion of the Palestinians*; and Masalha, 'A Critique of Benny Morris'.
14. Teveth, 'The Evolution of "Transfer" in Zionist Thinking'.
15. Shapira, *Land and Power*, 285–86. Criticism of my original handling of the transfer issue was also broached by Efraim Karsh, 'Fabricating Israeli History, the "New Historians"'. But his criticisms are of such brazen mendacity and distortion – regarding what I wrote and what is in the documentation – that they are not worthy of detailed treatment. Readers may regard the new chapter on 'Transfer' as an implicit rebuttal of what the various critics have written.

1 | Background: a brief history

Modern Zionism began with the prophetic-programmatic writings of Moses Hess, Judah Alkalai, Zvi Hirsch Kalischer and Theodor Herzl and the immigration from Russia to Ottoman-ruled Palestine in the 1880s of Jews dedicated to rebuilding a national home for the Jewish people on their ancient land, the Land of Israel, in Zionist parlance. The immigrants were impelled both by the positive ideal and by the negative experience of oppression in Eastern Europe; a wave of pogroms had engulfed Russia following the assassination of Czar Alexander II in March 1881.

Simultaneously, during the last decades of the 19th century, Arab intellectuals in Syria, Lebanon and Egypt began to advocate a revival of Arab culture and cultural 'independence' from the Ottoman Empire. By the beginning of the 20th century, with the spread of the spirit of nationalism to the area, they began to think and talk about 'decentralising' Ottoman rule and, more hesitantly, eventual political liberation and the establishment of an independent Arab state.

The spread of Jewish settlement in Palestine resulted in friction between neighbouring Arab and Jewish communities. Townspeople and villagers resented the influx of Russian- and Yiddish-speaking, Allah-rejecting foreigners and began to fear cultural–religious subversion of their way of life and physical encroachment and even displacement.[1]

The First World War, which destroyed the Ottoman Empire, exacerbated regional nationalist hopes and fears and changed the face of the Middle East. The idea of national self-determination, trumpeted by the victorious Allies, fired the imaginations of the educated throughout the colonial world. Britain conquered Palestine in 1917–1918 and the League of Nations eventually sanctioned British Mandatory rule in the country (and in Transjordan and Iraq) and French Mandates in Syria and Lebanon; the imperial powers were charged with preparing the local inhabitants for self-government. But with regard to Palestine, the

British issued the Balfour Declaration undertaking to help establish in it a 'National Home for the Jewish People' while promising to safeguard 'the civil and religious rights' of its majority Arab inhabitants. The Mandatory charter, finally approved in 1923, stressed the historic connection of the Jewish people to the Land of Israel.[2]

Post-war troubles in Eastern Europe and the attractions of good British administration prompted new waves of Jewish immigration to Palestine. The contradiction between Britain's dual commitment to fostering Jewish self-determination and safeguarding Arab rights soon became apparent, and the inevitability of the clash between Jewish and Arab national aspirations became manifest.

The steady progress in the achievement of self-determination among the Arab peoples of the Levant; the reality of foreign, Christian imperial rule, albeit benign and constructive; the political separation of Palestine from (French-ruled) Syria-Lebanon; and the influx of Zionist immigrants with deeply held national aspirations, triggered a Palestinian Arab nationalist 'awakening'. But almost from inception, the Palestinian Arab national movement was rent into two camps, whose growth and polarisation was the chief characteristic of the politics of Arab Palestine in the 1920s and 1930s. One camp, assembled around the Husseini clan and the person of Haj Muhammad Amin al Husseini, from 1921–1922 the Mufti of Jerusalem and the head of the Supreme Muslim Council (SMC) and, from 1936, chairman of the Arab Higher Committee (AHC), soon demanded an immediate termination of the Mandate, the cessation of Jewish immigration and the establishment of an Arab state in all of Palestine, vaguely promising civil and religious rights for the Jews already in the country. The 'Opposition' camp, led by the Nashashibìs, another aristocratic Jerusalem clan, was generally more moderate, less insistent on immediate independence, and more conciliatory, at least in tone, towards the Yishuv (occasionally accepting Jewish Agency bribes in exchange for softening its criticism of Zionism). The 'Opposition' never really agreed to Jewish statehood in all or part of Palestine but during the late 1930s was willing to accept an at least temporary confederation of parts of Palestine with King Abdullah's Transjordan. But the Husseinis generally set the tone of Palestinian Arab politics – toward Zionism, Britain and Transjordan – and from the mid-1930s dominated the national movement.

Anti-Jewish Arab riots and pogroms in the towns of Palestine in 1920–1921 and 1929 demonstrated the growing hatred of the Palestinian masses – egged on by a mixture of real and imagined religious and nationalist grievances, and Muslim preaching – for the burgeoning Zionist presence. The most traumatic single event was the massacre of 66 ultra-orthodox (non-Zionist) Jews in Hebron by their Arab neighbours and visiting villagers in August 1929. Arab fears of displacement, heightened by the mass Jewish immigration from Europe of the mid-1930s (sparked by the rise of Nazism and the resurgence of Eastern European anti-Semitism) and Jewish land purchases for new settlement, and a sense that violence would turn the British around, led to the 1936–1939 Arab revolt.

The revolt began with sporadic acts of violence and a countrywide general strike. It was directed in the first instance against the British and, secondly, against what were seen as their Zionist wards. It spread from the towns to the countryside, and won for the Husseinis and their allies the unchallenged leadership of the national movement. From mid-1937, Opposition families became a target of Husseini terrorism and suppression; during late 1938–1939, the Nashashibis in effect collaborated with the British (and the Zionists) in helping to crush the revolt. But by its end, in spring 1939, the Opposition had expired as a serious political force. The crushing of the revolt vastly weakened Palestinian society, both militarily and politically, and paved the way for its defeat in 1948.

But the revolt persuaded Whitehall, beset as it was by the prospect of a multi-front war against Germany, Japan and Italy, of the advisability of maintaining tranquillity in the Middle East. Initially, the British had hoped that the dispatch to Palestine in November 1936 of the fact-finding Royal Commission headed by Lord Peel would propitiate the Arabs. But in July 1937, Peel tabled his report, proposing that the country be partitioned into a Jewish state (on 20 per cent of the land) and an Arab area (on more than 70 per cent) to be joined to Transjordan. A strip of land – including Jerusalem and Bethlehem with an outlet to the Mediterranean at Jaffa – was earmarked for continued British rule. But while the Zionist movement, after much agonising, accepted the principle of partition and the proposals as a basis for negotiation, the AHC flatly rejected them – and in September 1937 renewed the revolt. Whitehall swiftly distanced itself from the idea of partition and, while crushing the revolt (the message to the Arabs was that Britain was not to be messed with), took vigorous steps to appease the Palestinians and, through them, the Arab world in general.

The main step was the publication in May 1939 by Whitehall of a new White Paper on Palestine, amounting to a repudiation of the Balfour Declaration policy that had, with ups and downs, guided British policy since 1917. The new White Paper severely curbed Jewish immigration, in effect leaving millions of Jews stranded in Europe and about to fall victim to the Nazi extermination machine, and almost completely prohibited Jewish land purchases. It also promised the Arabs, who would remain in the majority, independence within 10 years. But the outbreak of the Second World War put moves toward independence on hold and Hitler's destruction of European Jewry added urgency, momentum and political thrust to the Zionist demand for Jewish statehood, on part or all of Palestine. For the first time, the movement forthrightly declared that nothing less than immediate, full Jewish statehood was its goal (the Biltmore Programme of May 1942). The gradual revelations about what had befallen European Jewry tended to mobilise public opinion and, progressively, governments in the West in favour of opening Palestine to Jewish immigration and, ultimately, of Jewish statehood.

The world war served the Palestinian Arab cause ill. While it tended to highlight the ultimate weakness of the Mandatory powers – Britain and France – and thus invigorated local nationalisms, ultimately helping Egypt, Iraq, Syria, Transjordan and Lebanon to gain their independence, the rebellious Palestinians, having just been crushed, became identified with the Axis cause. They had received a measure of political and financial support from the Axis states during the rebellion and, during the war years, Husseini and his protégés had supported a pro-Axis revolt in Iraq (1941). They had then moved to Berlin where they served the Nazi regime. Husseini himself had broadcast pro-Nazi propaganda and recruited Muslims in the Balkans for the Waffen-SS. At war's end, he was branded (by a Jugoslav commission) a 'war criminal' and fled to Egypt.[3]

Palestine's Jews, on the other hand, had rushed to the Allied colours to join the fight against the common Nazi enemy. The military experience garnered by the 28,000 Palestine Jewish volunteers who joined up was to stand the Yishuv in good stead in the trial of 1948. As well, the Yishuv's economy had transformed during the first years of the war into a vast workshop for the British Eighth Army; the technical and industrial skills and infrastructure acquired proved to be of great significance in 1948. In all, the Yishuv used the wartime interregnum in Arab-Jewish hostilities to prepare for the coming test of arms; the Palestinians, and, indeed, the Arab states (apart from Transjordan), did not.

The trauma of the revolt and Arab terrorism; the upsurge during 1944–1947 of anti-British Jewish terrorism by the Revisionist *Irgun Zvai Leumi* (IZL) (the National Military Organisation or 'Irgun') and *Lohamei Herut Yisrael* (LHI) (Freedom Fighters of Israel or 'Stern Gang'), bent on ejecting the British and attaining Jewish independence; the morally and politically embarrassing campaign by Britain during and immediately after the war to bar illegal Jewish immigration; the moral–political pressure exercised by the Holocaust and by the growing, pro-Zionist American involvement; and the economic cost of occupying Palestine and battling the Jewish terrorists – all by early 1947 had persuaded Whitehall that washing its hands of the whole mess represented the better part of valour, and it dumped the problem in the lap of the United Nations.

The United Nations Special Committee on Palestine (UNSCOP), set up in April, examined the situation and in September recommended a solution based on partition into two states, one Jewish and the other Arab. On 29 November 1947, the United Nations General Assembly, by a vote of 33 to 13 (10 members abstaining), endorsed partition, with the Jews to receive some 55 per cent of the country (much of the allotted area being desert) and the Arabs about 40 per cent; Jerusalem and Bethlehem, because of their unique, multi-denominational religious significance, were to constitute a separate enclave under international control. The Yishuv greeted the resolution with joy and its elected representatives immediately announced acceptance; the Palestinian Arab leaders, headed by the exiled AHC chief, Husseini, rejected partition and launched a three-day general strike, accompanied by a wave of anti-Jewish terrorism in the cities and on the roads. The Arab states, taking Husseini's cue, rejected partition and sent volunteers, arms and money to help the Palestinians. During January–March 1948 the Palestinians were reinforced by several thousand volunteers, most of whom assembled under the flag of the Arab Liberation Army (ALA); the Jews received financial and political support, and, at this time, a trickle of volunteers, from the Jewish Diaspora.

Within weeks the sporadic violence had snowballed into a full-scale civil war between the two communities. The British, adopting a neutral stand of non-interference, announced that they would terminate the Mandate and withdraw by 15 May 1948. While initially at least intending an orderly transfer of power, their actions over December 1947–May 1948 remained primarily geared to assuring a smooth, costless withdrawal, and one which would leave their position and prestige in the Arab world intact. Inevitably both the Jews and the Arabs accused them, in successive episodes, of partiality toward the other side.

During the first weeks of conflict it was unclear to most people that the two communities were indeed engaged in a war; rather, it seemed that they had merely embarked on a further bout of 'disturbances' à la 1929 and 1936. The Haganah stayed on the defensive, wishing not to annoy the British while it re-organised and armed for war; it knew that the real challenge would be posed not by the Palestinians but by the armies of the surrounding states. Until the end of January 1948, neither side had the upper hand. But in February and March, Arab ambushers inflicted major defeats on Haganah convoys along the roads, especially between Tel Aviv and (Jewish West) Jerusalem. It appeared to the Yishuv's leaders that, besieged, Jewish Jerusalem – with a population of 100,000 – might fall; there were similar fears regarding several clusters of Jewish rural settlements around Jerusalem and in western Galilee. The defeats and significant casualties suffered caused the Yishuv to rethink its strategy.

At the beginning of April, the Haganah switched to the offensive, at last unleashing a series of major counter-attacks. The British military pullout was well advanced and Ben-Gurion and the Haganah brass reasoned (correctly) that the British would not interfere. There was also a political context: In the second half of March, the United States had proposed that a United Nations trusteeship be imposed on Palestine, signalling a (possible) retreat from support for partition. Ben-Gurion feared that continued battlefield defeats would further undermine world endorsement of Jewish statehood. The start of the arrival of arms from Czechoslovakia at last made offensive action possible. Lastly, Ben-Gurion and the Haganah brass were moved by the prospect of the threatened invasion by the neighbouring Arab states. All realised that the Jewish state had to be consolidated by 15 May, its internal lines of communication and its border areas secured, its 'internal', Palestinian enemies neutralised or crushed and its armed forces freed for the coming contest; otherwise, the invaders might win. From the Haganah's point of view, it was a race against time.

Beginning with Operation Nahshon in the Jerusalem Corridor and the Battle of Mishmar Ha'emek during the first half of April, the local Palestinian militias (and their ALA supporters) were roundly defeated. Haganah troops successively conquered the Arab parts of Tiberias, Haifa and Safad and the towns of Beisan and Acre as well as eastern and western Galilee. Helped by the lack of Arab national organisation and supra-regional cooperation, the Haganah was able to pick off each village, each town and each region on its own, in staggered fashion. Palestinian military power was crushed and Palestinian society was shattered. The Palestinians would only reappear as political and military players on the Middle Eastern stage in the mid-1960s.

PALESTINIAN JEWISH SOCIETY

The keys to the Yishuv victory were its vastly superior motivation, a stronger economy, superior armaments, better military and administrative organisation, and its qualitative edge in manpower (better educated and militarily more experienced).

In the Yishuv – which in 1948 numbered 650,000 souls – liberal and social democratic parties had dominated the political arena from the beginning of the Mandate. The society was highly organised and highly ideological; despite many political and social differences, almost all were driven by a single-minded desire for immediate Jewish statehood. Their motivation was strongly reinforced in the 1930s and 1940s by the onset in eastern and central Europe of anti-Semitic oppression and, then, the Holocaust, which rendered supremely urgent the establishment of a safe haven, in the form of an independent Jewish polity, for the world's unwanted, assailed and endangered Jews.

Over the years, the Yishuv's leaders and political parties had managed to forge the institutional tools for achieving and perpetuating statehood. Its 'National Institutions' almost from the first were built with an eye to conversion into institutions of state.[4] By May 1948, it had a shadow government, with almost all the institutions (and, in some fields, such as agriculture and settlement, an excess of institutions) of state in place and ready to take over. The Jewish Agency (JA), with its various departments (political, finance, settlement, immigration), became the Provisional Government, the departments smoothly converting into ministries; the JA Executive (JAE) and, subsequently, the 'People's Administration' (*minhelet ha'am*) became the Cabinet; the Haganah became the Israel Defense Forces (IDF). By 1948, the Yishuv was in many respects functioning like 'a state within a state'; the National Council (*hava'ad hale'umi*) and the JA, together with municipalities, local councils and the Histadrut, the trades union federation, in coordination with the Mandate Government departments, provided the Yishuv with most essential services (health, education, social welfare, industrial development).

The Yishuv taxed itself, the funds going to various services and goals. The Histadrut taxed its members to provide health services and unemployment allowances; the Jewish National Fund (JNF) levied taxes for afforestation, land purchase and settlement infrastructure; special taxes were instituted to purchase arms and cover the costs of immigrant absorption. As well, the Yishuv received continuous financial aid from the Diaspora, with special, large-scale emergency funding during 1947–1949.

By 1948, the Yishuv had the tools to convert to statehood within days or weeks. Moreover, years of practical self-rule and preparation for statehood, while involving the usual struggles for power between and within parties, had thrust to the fore an exceptionally talented, self-sacrificing and committed leadership with expertise in politics, economics, settlement and defence. Headed, from 1930 on, by David Ben-Gurion and his Mapai party (the acronym of *Mifleget Poalei Eretz Yisrael*, the Land of Israel Workers Party), this leadership directed the struggle for statehood, with the right-wing Revisionists (who sought Jewish sovereignty over all of Palestine and Transjordan) and the various religious parties never garnering more than a minority of votes. Ben-Gurion, a pragmatist, from 1937 on, was willing (at least outwardly) to accept partition and the establishment of a Jewish state in only part of the country. In effect, he remained committed to a vision of Jewish sovereignty over all of Palestine as the ultimate goal of Zionism, to be attained by stages. But in the course of 1947–1948, he resigned himself to the inevitability of Jewish sovereignty over only part of Palestine.

The high quality of the national leadership was faithfully mirrored on the level of municipal and local government, in the *kibbutzim* (collective settlements) and *moshavim* (cooperative settlements) and in the Haganah. The rural settlements, most of them *kibbutzim*, were inhabited by the most politically advanced and committed elements of the Jewish population. They supplied much of the Yishuv's military and political leadership. Characterised by a pioneering, frontier spirit and demarcating the perimeters of the Yishuv, and having experienced Arab attacks over the decades, the *kibbutzim* were built with defence in mind – often on high ground, with trenches, bunkers and shelters. And they were psychologically prepared. When Israel was invaded after the British left, only a handful of *kibbutzim* fell to assault by the Arab armies; almost none were abandoned by their inhabitants. Like most *kibbutzim*, the Yishuv in macro saw itself as a community without choice – it was statehood or bust, and bust, given the depth of Arab enmity for Zionism, meant a possible repetition, on a smaller scale, of the Holocaust.

MILITARY PREPARATION

Following the riots and pogroms of 1920–1921 and 1929, and the revolt of 1936–1939, the Yishuv fashioned a highly organised, national underground militia, the Haganah. After a massive, covert arms acquisition campaign in the West following Ben-Gurion's assumption in 1946 of political direction of the organisation, and on the basis of his perception that the Yishuv had to make ready to defend itself both against Palestine's Arabs and a conventional attack by the surrounding states, the Haganah, by September 1947, possessed 10,489 rifles, 702 light machine-guns, 2,666 submachine guns, 186 medium machine-guns, 672 two-inch mortars and 92 three-inch mortars. (The Haganah had no military aircraft, tanks or artillery at the start of the 1948 war.) Many more weapons were purchased, or stolen, from the withdrawing British, during the first months of hostilities. Moreover, the Yishuv had a relatively advanced arms producing capacity. Between October 1947 and July 1948, the Haganah's arms factories poured out 3 million 9mm bullets, 150,000 mills grenades, 16,000 submachine guns ('Sten Guns') and 210 three-inch mortars.[5]

From November 1947, the Haganah, with some 35,000 members (a proportion of them women), began to change from a territorial militia into a regular army. Apart from a handful of fulltime 'shock companies' (the Palmah, established with British help in 1941 and numbering 2,000–3,000 troops), few of the units had been well trained by December 1947, and it was only gradually, over December 1947–May 1948, that the full membership was mobilised and placed in uniform on a permanent footing. Haganah members usually trained for 3–4 days a month, for the rest being fulltime civilians. But the organisation had a relatively large pool of British Army veterans and a highly committed, internally trained officer corps. By March–April 1948 it fielded still under-equipped 'battalions' and 'brigades'; by the start of June, it had become the 'IDF', an army, and consisted of 11–12 brigades, including artillery and armoured units, and an embryonic air force and navy.[6] By May 1948, the Haganah had mobilised and deployed 35,780 troops – 5,000–10,000 more than the combined troop strength of the regular Arab armies that invaded Palestine on 15–16 May (though the invaders were far better equipped and, theoretically, better trained).[7] The Haganah's successor, the IDF, by July 1948 had 63,000 men under arms.[8]

But, perhaps even more important than the numbers, which meant that by July 1948 one person in 10 (or one out of every 2–3 adult males) in the Yishuv was mobilised, was the Haganah's organisation, from its highly talented, centralised General Staff, with logistical, intelligence and operations branches, down to its brigade and battalion formations. By April–May the Haganah was conducting brigade-size offensives, by July, multi-brigade operations; and by October, divisional, multi-front offensives. By mid-May, it had thoroughly beaten the Palestinian militias and their foreign auxiliaries; by October–December, it had beaten the invading Arab armies.

PALESTINIAN ARAB SOCIETY

The Palestinian Arab defeat owed much to the society's shortcomings and divisions. Palestinian society was poor, agriculturally based, largely illiterate,[9] politically and socially primitive and disorganised, and deeply divided. The rifts in Palestinian society – between town and country, Husseinis and Nashashibis, Muslims and Christians, beduin and settled communities – were rooted in history.

In the mid-19th century, economic developments and Ottoman reforms triggered a measure of urbanisation and a population drift from the countryside to the towns. Palestine's towns, for centuries little more than overblown villages, during the last decades of the 19th century and first decades of the 20th began to grow as landless or poor fellahin left the villages.[10] In part, they were attracted by the economic benefits that flowed from newly developed commercial ties with Europe, via Jaffa and Haifa ports; in part, they were driven from the countryside by Ottoman taxation and indebtedness, and land purchases by Arab effendis (many from outside Palestine) and Zionists. In a general way, this process may have contributed to loosening the Palestinians' grip on or bonds with the soil in advance of the exodus of 1948.[11]

But it is well to recognise that there was also a parallel process at work during the 19th century, namely the immigration to Palestine of tens of thousands of Maghrebi (North African), Egyptian, Bosnian, Kurdish and Caucasian peasants and beduin tribes, either on their own volition or by Ottoman design. Many of these immigrants established new villages, particularly in the less populated lowlands of the Galilee and in the Coastal Plain. The names of some of the villages bore testimony to these immigrant waves; for example, there were a number of Kafr Misrs ('Misr' is Egypt in Arabic) and two 'Kirads' (indicating Kurdish origins). Later, the relative prosperity and order of Mandate Palestine drew thousands of additional Arab immigrants from the neighbouring countries, especially to the large towns.[12] In the 20th century, under British influence and the impact of the burgeoning, neighbouring Jewish society, the shift of centres of gravity from the countryside to the towns gained momentum.[13]

Nevertheless, while there was a large, growing urban component, Arab Palestine in 1947 remained essentially a peasant society. About half the Arab land was owned by small proprietors and much of the rest – worked by tenant farmers – was held by big landowners, who lived in the towns, many in Lebanon, Egypt or Syria. (About 50 per cent of Palestine's land mass – most of it in the Negev – was state land while Zionist organisations and individual Jews owned 6–7 per cent.)

By the end of 1947 there were one and a quarter million Arabs (about 1.1 million Muslims and 150,000 Christians), 65–70 per cent of them living in some 800–850 villages; about 30 per cent lived in cities and towns. Some 70,000 beduin were concentrated mostly in the northern Negev, their number steadily decreasing as they settled in villages and towns. While the vast majority of the labour force were village dwelling *fellahin*, a substantial number of town dwellers also worked in agriculture.[14]

While the rural majority and its agricultural economy remained largely primitive and inefficient, there were the beginnings, under British prompting, European cajoling and the influence of the neighbouring model of Jewish settlement, of innovation and modernisation, especially in the Coastal Plain. In 1922 there were some 22,000 dunams of Arab land producing citrus crops; in 1940 there were 140,000, mostly destined for export. In 1931 there were 332,000 dunams under orchards (apples, olives); in 1942 there were 832,000. By and large, however, agriculture in Arab Palestine remained geared to local consumption. The *fellahin* in 1947 had almost no tractors and used a primitive plough, a simple crop cycle and almost no irrigation or fertilisers. Jewish political leaders and settlement executives through the 1930s and 1940s spoke, with varying degrees of sincerity, of helping to reform Arab agriculture to increase its output which, in turn, would allow both the Arab and Jewish populations to increase while still coexisting peacefully on a constant, relatively small tract of land.

The Palestinian national movement took root mainly among the urban elite and middle classes, but over the decades of British rule, in which there was a major growth in education and literacy, the national idea began to filter down to the urban and peasant masses. The fact that each bout of anti-Zionist (and anti-British) rioting during the Mandate (1920, 1921, 1929, and 1936–1939) was larger than its predecessor reflected the growth and spread of political consciousness among the masses. In the course of the Mandate, in part as a result of improvements in education, the politicisation of the urban elites and growing middle class, and the threatening Zionist enterprise, villagers became increasingly politicised. Contrary to Henry Cattan's testimony before the Anglo-American Committee of Inquiry, in 1946, when he said that nothing had changed in this respect between 1920 and 1946, there was a measure of change in the level of political consciousness. But, by and large, the villager still maintained primary allegiances to family, clan and village; those were the focuses of his interest. Rural society was based on the village rather than the district or the country. And the experience of 1936–1939, in which villages were sucked into the maw of the revolt and devastated thereby, sufficed to cure many of political activism.[15] As late as the 1940s, for most villages and villagers politics and the national struggle were remote, playthings of sophisticated city folk. As one Arab memorialist from the Galilee village of Mi'ilya put it, 'The Mi'ilyan's world was his village – the land and the people. Matters of national or even regional politics were the concern of [only] one or two people in the village.'[16]

Most villages consisted of two or three clans, headed by notables, usually on the basis of wealth. The village headman (*mukhtar*) was often the head of the village's main clan. Clan power was largely determined by property (land). In many villages, land was owned collectively by the community. Many clans had a regional dispersion and influence, with groups of members scattered in a number of neighbouring villages. As a result of feuding or economic conditions, many villages over the decades had established satellite hamlets (*khurab*) a few kilometres away; many hill villages had *khurab* in the lowlands. In some areas, there were blocs or alliances of villages, based on extended clans inhabiting more than one village, or marital and other alliances between clans (*vide* the Zu'abiya villages in lower Galilee and the Bani Hassan near Jerusalem).[17]

The villages tended to be socially and politically self-centred and self-contained; economically, they were largely self-sufficient. The villager rarely visited the 'big city' (Haifa, Jaffa, Jerusalem) or his local town (Lydda, Ramle, Acre, Nazareth, Safad, Beisan) and seldom saw newspapers. Very few villagers could read and write, and most villages had only one radio, usually in the *mukhtar*'s house or in the village coffee shop, where the males would gather in the afternoons and evenings to play backgammon and to talk. Generally the villagers were politically ignorant. The fact of British rule and administration from 1917 to 1948, and the almost complete absence of local, district and national Palestinian political and administrative institutions, and the lack of democratic norms in the few that existed, meant that Palestinian rural society, beyond the village structure, was largely uninvolved in national affairs and unrepresented. Limited exceptions to this were the villages of the Samaria and Judea areas, whose leaders took part in the Palestinian congresses of the first years of the Mandate,[18] and many of whose young men participated in the rebellion of 1936–1939. The villages of the Coastal Plain, and Jezreel and Jordan valleys were not represented at these congresses and were largely uninvolved in the rebellion.

In general, rural interests were represented by the elite urban families, some of whom originated in the countryside and owned much of the arable land. The large landowners exercised a great deal of influence and power over *fellahin* and town dwellers alike.

Roughly a third of Palestine's Arabs lived in towns and cities. There were 17 wholly Arab towns – Beersheba, Khan Yunis, Gaza, Majdal (Ashkelon), Ramle, Lydda, Hebron, Bethlehem, Beit Jala, Ramallah, Tulkarm, Nablus (Shechem), Jenin, Shafa 'Amr (Shfar'am), Acre, Beisan (Beit Shean) and Nazareth. Some, such as Tulkarm, Jenin, Beisan, Majdal and Shafa 'Amr, were little more than overgrown villages serving as marketing centres and service stations for the surrounding hinterlands. In addition, there were five towns with a mixed population of Arabs and Jews: Jerusalem, Haifa and Tiberias, with Jewish majorities, and, predominantly Arab Safad and Jaffa.

In the first years of the Mandate, the Arab population possessed almost no motor vehicles; by 1945, they had more than 3,000, with a supportive infrastructure of garages and workshops producing spare parts. The enormous growth in transportation affected agriculture, commerce and industry. Commercial ties with Europe were channelled through chambers of commerce and an efficient banking network had developed in the towns by the end of World War II. The war was crucial; the credit of the largest Arab bank, the 'Arab Bank', grew between 1941 and 1945 eighteenfold, and deposits twentyfold. Industry, too, had begun to develop.[19]

Some 30–35 per cent of the urban Arabs were employed in light industry, crafts and construction, 15–17 per cent in transportation, 20–23 per cent in commerce, 5–8 per cent in professions, 5–7 per cent in public service and 6–9 per cent in other services. By the late 1940s, Palestinian Arab society was in the throes of rapid urbanisation. British rule and, particularly, the onset of World War II had triggered a small measure of industrialisation. Yishuv intelligence identified the beginnings of a change from 'the typical primitive workshop' economy to 'modernisation'. Sweet and chocolate factories and three glass factories were established; there was a significant growth of the textile industry; and a modern cigarette plant was set up in Haifa.[20] By the end of the Mandate, there were in Arab Palestine some 1,500 industrial workshops and small factories employing altogether 9,000 workers with an average of 5–6 employees per workshop. (By contrast there were 1,900 industrial workshops and plants in Jewish Palestine, employing 38,000 workers, an average of 19–21 workers per plant.) Other Arabs worked in Jewish-owned plants and in British-run plants and services. Altogether, the Arab proletariat numbered some 35,000, with 5,000 employed by oil companies and 8,000 in the government railway service. During the war, tens of thousands were employed by the government in public works and 30,000 in British Army camps (though most of these were laid off in the immediate post-war years).[21]

Palestinian Arab society was led by an elite of several dozen town-based families – the Nusseibehs, Khatibs, Khalidis, Nashashibis and Husseinis in Jerusalem, the 'Amrs, Tamimis and Ja'baris in Hebron, the Sa'ids, Bitars and Dajanis in Jaffa, the Shawas and the Husayns in Gaza, the Taji al Faruqis and Ghusayns in Ramle, the Tawqans, 'Abd al Hadis, Nabulsis, Shak'ahs and Tamimis in Nablus, the 'Abd al Hadis and 'Abushis in Jenin, the Khalils, Shukris, Tahas, Khayyats and Mahdis in Haifa, the Shuqayris and Khalifas in Acre, the Fahums, the Dahirs and the Zua'bis in Nazareth, the Tabaris in Tiberias and Khidras in Safad.[22] The families – collectively, the 'Ayan or notability – provided Arab Palestine's big landowners, politicians, judges, merchants, mayors, high civil servants, religious leaders, doctors, lawyers and intellectuals. Each family usually covered most or all fields, one member being a judge or a mayor, another a merchant and third, a professional. Their power, influence and connections were usually local rather than national; their obligations were to family, dependants, town and district, in that order. It was a highly regional, oligarchic structure. While the elite families exercised power over much of the rural and urban populations through direct and indirect economic and religious levers, they maintained a vital distance from the *fellah* and the urban worker; the vast socio-economic gulf was marked by resentment and mutual suspicion.

During the Mandate, a small middle class emerged – of professionals, officials and shopkeepers, some emerging from the urban and rural working classes. But, while aspiring to merge socially with the elites, and occasionally moving or marrying into them, the middle class remained too small and the traditional elitist structure too powerful to allow a real bourgeoisie to emerge and effectively challenge the 'Ayan's political and economic power.

In the late 1940s, 28 of the 32 members of the AHC were from the 'Ayan; the remaining four were bourgeoisie; none were peasants or proletarians. Some 24 were of urban extraction, and only four or five originated in the countryside. The wide gulf of suspicion and estrangement between urban and rural Arab Palestine was to underlie the lack of coordination between the towns and their rural hinterland during the hostilities. The elite families had no tradition of, or propensity for, national service and their members did not do military service with the Turks, the British or neighbouring Arab armies. Almost none of the military leaders of the 1936–1939 rebellion were from the 'Ayan. It was mainly a peasant rebellion, with the town dwellers restricting themselves largely to civil protest (demonstrations, riots and a general strike) and, at a later stage, to inter-factional terrorism.[23]

From the early 1920s, the 'Ayan split into two main camps, the *Majlisiyyun* and the *Mu'aridun* (Opposition) – that is, those supporting the Husseinis and the Husseini-controlled Supreme Muslim Council (*majlis*) and Arab Higher Executive (which preceded the emergence of the AHC), and those opposed to them, led by the Nashashibis. The towns and countryside split not so much along ideological lines as along lines of family loyalty and local affiliations. The struggle between the Husseinis and the Opposition was mainly over power and its economic spoils; the political–ideological differences were secondary, though the Nashashibis, with their rural allies in the Hebron, Nablus and Nazareth areas, tended to take a more moderate line towards Zionism and the Mandate. The Nashashibis often secretly met Jewish representatives and, in private, adopted a conciliatory tone. The rivalry between the two camps was to characterise Arab politics down to 1948 and the friction was to dissipate Palestinian strength at crucial junctures, including 1937–1939, when the Husseinis assassinated some of their opponents, and 1947–1948.[24]

During the 1930s, the elite families set up formal political parties. In 1935 the Husseinis established the Palestine Arab Party, which became the Arabs' main political organisation. Earlier, in 1934, the Nashashibis had set up the National Defence Party. In 1932 Awni 'Abd al Hadi of Samaria set up the Istiqlal Party, which was pan-Arab in ideology, and in 1935, Jerusalem mayor Dr Husayn Khalidi set up the Reform Party. The early 1930s also saw the establishment by Ya'qub Ghusayn of the Youth Congress Party and the Nablus-based National Bloc Party. The proliferation of parties tended to dissipate the strength of the Opposition. But the parties for the most part existed on paper and were powerless. All opposed Zionism and, in varying degrees, British rule, and aimed at Arab statehood in all of Palestine (though the Istiqlal did not espouse separate Palestinian statehood). The parties had no internal elections or western-style institutions, and no dues, and were based on family and local affiliations and loyalties. Families, clans and villages rather than individuals were party members, with semi-feudal links of dependence and loyalty determining attachment. Few 'Ayan families managed to remain neutral in the Husseini–Nashashibi struggle.[25]

All the parties, representing both over-arching factions, initially made common cause in 1936 in backing and leading the revolt. Differences were set aside and party activity was stopped. Representatives of the six parties constituted the AHC on 25 April 1936 to coordinate the struggle nationally. On the local level, the parties set up National Committees (NCs) in each town to run the strike and other political activities, but as the strike gave way to widespread violence, the traditional enmities re-surfaced, with the Nashashibis and their allies re-emerging as the Opposition. The Nashashibis came to represent and lead those Arabs who came to regard the revolt as fruitless. The Husseini response, of intimidation and assassination, decimated the ranks of the Opposition; terrorism, extortion, rapine and brigandage against villagers and town dwellers by the armed bands and the inevitable search and destroy operations against the rebels by the British military alienated much of the population. By late 1938–1939, it had grown tired of the fight. Villages turned against the rebels and, with Opposition and British intelligence backing, anti-rebel 'peace bands' were formed.

The outcome of the rebellion, apart from the political gains embodied in the 1939 White Paper, was that several thousand Arabs were killed, thousands were gaoled, and tens of thousands fled the country; much of the elite and middle class was driven or withdrew in disgust from the political arena. Husseini–Nashashibi reconciliation became inconceivable; implacable blood feuds were born, with telling effect for the denouement of 1947–1948.

In suppressing the rebellion, the British outlawed the AHC, arresting or exiling its members, some of whom fled to Germany and served the Axis during World War II. The Palestinians remained politically inactive during the war years, political parties and factions reconstituting themselves only 1944–1945. The AHC also re-emerged, with the Husseinis dominant. In early 1946 the rifts reappeared and in March 1946 the Arab League stepped in and appointed a new AHC composed only of Husseinis and their allies. Its leading members were Amin al Husseini (president), Jamal Husseini (deputy president), Husayn Khalidi (secretary), Ahmad Hilmi Pasha and Emil Ghawri. The Opposition was left out in the cold.

The neutering of the Palestinians in 1939 and during the war resulted in a peculiar division of power and representation, in which the Arab states represented the Palestinians and presented the Palestinian case vis-à-vis Britain and the rest of the world, with the Husseinis determining what was acceptable and (usually) vetoing any compromise. The Nashashibis, beaten, disbanded politically. Zionist efforts through 1942 to 1947 to revive the moderate camp – which the Jewish Agency always believed represented majority Palestinian opinion – were to no avail. Even as late as January–February 1948 senior JA Political Department and Haganah Intelligence Service (HIS) figures, such as Gad Machnes, Ezra Danin and Elias Sasson, hoped that the Opposition would reassert itself, restrain Arab militancy and wrest control of the masses from the Husseinis. But the Yishuv's Arab experts generally asserted that this was unlikely unless the Husseinis suffered major military defeat and Transjordan's King Abdullah supported the Opposition politically and with arms and money.[26]

The divide between the Husseinis and the Opposition had relatively clear geographical as well as familial–clan demarcations, both reflecting and intensifying the regionalism that had characterised Palestinian society and politics for centuries. Husseini strength lay in Jerusalem and its surrounding villages, rural Samaria and Gaza; the Opposition was strong in Hebron, the Galilee, Tiberias and Beisan, Nablus, Jenin and Haifa.

This regionalism meant perennial resistance in Haifa, Nablus and Hebron to the supremacy of Jerusalem in Palestinian life and the contempt of the highland inhabitants in Samaria and Judea for the Coastal Plain Arabs.

Another divisive element built into Palestinian society was the Muslim–Christian rift. The Christians, concentrated in the towns, were generally wealthier and better educated. They prospered under the Mandate. The Muslims suspected that the Christians would 'sell out' to the British (fellow Christians) or make common cause with the Jews (a fellow minority). Indeed, Christians took almost no part in the 1936–1939 rebellion. Sometime in 1946–1947, HIS compiled a list of prominent Christians 'with a tendency to cooperation with the Jews'. There are 'few such Arabs among the Muslims, and many among the Christians', wrote HIS.

> The reason for this is that the Christians suffered a great deal under the Muslims and see a blessing in Jewish immigration to the country and to the Middle East as a whole . . . But there are few willing to express their opinion publicly for fear of the reaction of the Muslims.[27]

As a measure of anti-Christian violence had accompanied the revolt, so the years immediately before 1948 were studded with expressions of Christian–Muslim antagonism and, occasionally, violence. The case of George Khoury Bakhut, of Shafa 'Amr, a small Christian–Druse–Muslim town near Haifa, was indicative. He was shot by a Muslim gunman on 8 February 1947 and died three days later. Muslim notables, including Haj Amin al Husseini from his home in Egypt, may have described the murder as 'personally motivated' but Shafa 'Amr Christians were 'certain' that the assassination was carried out by 'Muslim hirelings'.[28] According to one Haganah report, 'every Muslim boy in Shafa-'Amr knows that George was murdered because he was a land pimp for the Jews'.[29] The Christians demanded that the Muslims hand over the assassin, who had gone into hiding, threatening retaliation. Husseini invited the Greek Catholic Archbishop of Haifa, George Hakim, to Egypt to discuss the problem.[30] At their meeting, Husseini said 'there is no place now for a Christian–Muslim rift.'[31] But inter-communal relations in Shafa 'Amr hit rock bottom: 'The [mutual] boycott [between Christians and Muslims] is stronger than that between the Arabs and the Jews. Therefore the Christians are thinking of leaving Shafa 'Amr and building for themselves a new village';[32] others were thinking of moving to Haifa.

Eventually, the hubbub died down. But the event and its repercussions shed light on the nature and volatility of Arab inter-communal relations. The situation in Jaffa was less tense, but essentially no different. According to HIS, relations between the communities were

> not good, though outwardly appearances of coerced friendship were maintained. The relations between the lower and middle classes were worse

than among the rich. In fact, there was no contact (apart from commercial relations) between the communities . . . The Christians had participated in the 1936–37 disturbances under duress and out of fear of the Muslims. The Christians' hearts now and generally are not with the rioting, because most of them are in commerce and might be harmed . . .[33]

And in Haifa, a mere month before the passage of the UN partition resolution, a meeting of Haifa Christian notables had resolved to set up a Christian militia to

protect the lives and property of the Christians. Outwardly the call [for recruits] would be to prepare for attacks by the Jews, but in truth they want to defend themselves against attacks that the Muslims might launch against them if a situation of anarchy prevails during the withdrawal of the British army.[34]

Already in early November 1947, according to HIS, some Christians were 'trying to flee the country'. The reason was that

the Christians in Nazareth, among them most of the high officials in the district administration, live in fear for their property and lives (in this order) from the Muslims. The Husseini terror has recently grown worse and large amounts of money are extorted from the Christians.[35]

It is likely that the majority of Christians would have preferred the continuation of the British Mandate to independence under Husseini rule; some may even have preferred Jewish rule. All were aware of the popular Muslim mob chant: 'After Saturday, Sunday' (meaning, after we take care of the Jews, it will be the Christians' turn). To compensate, Christian community leaders repeatedly went out of their way to express devotion to the Palestinian national cause; indeed, a coterie of Christian notables was prominent in the Husseini camp (as, in the 1960s and 1970s, Christians would be prominent in the more radical Palestinian terrorist organisations, such as the Popular Front for the Liberation of Palestine, a world pioneer in aircraft hijacking). In 1948, as some Muslims had anticipated, the Christian community leaders, notably in Haifa and Jaffa, by and large were far less belligerent than their Muslim counterparts. Zionist leaders repeatedly tried to exploit the rift but at the last moment the Christians almost always shied away from advancing from conciliatory private assurances to moderate public action. During the first weeks of war, Christian–Muslim relations deteriorated against the backdrop of Jewish–Arab violence and Muslim suspicions that the Christians were collaborating or might collaborate with the Jews. HIS in Jerusalem reported:

The Christians continue to complain about bad behaviour by the Arabs [sic] towards them. Many of them wish to leave their homes. The gang members [i.e., Arab irregulars] indeed threaten to kill them after they finish with the Jews.'[36]

The Christians further complained that the Muslims were 'incapable of any sort of organisation and every activity turns into robbery. The only ones capable of organising are the Christians and they are denied access to these positions [i.e., positions of power].'[37]

There was a further rift in Palestinian society, between the settled communities and the beduin; each looked down upon the other. Centuries of beduin depredation had made the peasantry wary of the tribes. The beduin were the most apolitical segment of Arab society and were suspicious of Husseini manipulation. On the eve of the war, on 25 November 1947, a secret meeting of beduin sheikhs in Beersheba, including chieftains from the Taha and San'a tribes, resolved that

> the beduin of the Negev constitute an independent segment [of the population] and their sheikhs politically are not connected to any other element, and the beduins themselves will decide about the stand they will adopt regarding the development of events in Palestine, and will not take orders from above.[38]

This was a clear message to the AHC.

But what was to prove the fatal Palestinian Arab weakness was the fundamental lack of self-governing institutions, norms and traditions. Arab society was highly sectorial and parochial. It was backward, disunited and often apathetic, a community only just entering the modern age politically and administratively. In some fields (land-purchasing, militia organisation), its leaders tried to copy Zionist models, but the vast differences in the character of the two populations and levels of consciousness, commitment, ability and education left the Arabs radically outclassed. The moment the Yishuv quantitatively reached what proved a critical mass, the outcome – in hindsight – was ineluctable.

Before 1948, much of the Arab population had only an indistinct, if any, idea of national purpose and statehood. There was clarity about one thing only – the Jews aimed to displace them and they had to be stymied or driven out; they were less enthusiastic or united over wanting the British out. On the whole, save for the numerically small circle of the elite, the Palestinians were unready for the national message or for the demands that national self-fulfilment imposed upon the community, both in 1936–1939 and, far more severely, in 1947–1948. Commitment and readiness to pay the price presumed a clear concept of the nation and of national belonging, which the Arabs, still caught up in a clan-centred, a village-centred or, at most, a regional outlook, by and large lacked. As late as the 1940s, most of them still lacked a sense of separate national or cultural identity distinguishing them from, say, the Arabs of Syria. That sense certainly steadily matured during the Mandate, with the spread of education, literacy, newspapers and radios. But the process proved slow and failed to keep pace with the realities and demands of a swiftly changing historical situation. For the mass of Palestinians, the struggle to establish a state was a remote affair.

This absence of political consciousness and commitment (as well as the lack of educated personnel) provides a partial explanation for the failure to establish self-governing institutions. And even in the one field where the Arabs enjoyed 'self-governing' institutions based on some form of elections (albeit irregularly held, in 1926, 1934 and 1946, and with very limited, propertied suffrage) – the municipalities – they failed to function as well as the selfsame institutions in the Yishuv. Budgets give an idea of scope of operations. (Arab) Ramle, with a population of some 20,000 in 1941, had an annual budget of P£6,317. Jenin, a far smaller town, had a budget of P£2,320; Bethlehem, with a population of over 10,000, P£3,245; Nablus, with a population in 1942 of about 30,000, P£17,223; and Jaffa, with an overwhelmingly Arab population of about 70,000 in 1942, P£90,967. By comparison, all-Jewish Petah-Tikvah, with a population of 30,000, had a budget of P£39,463 in 1941; Tel Aviv, with 200,000, in 1942 had a budget of P£779,589.

The only functioning Arab national institution through the Mandate was the SMC, which until 1937 was presided over by Husseini and was to remain under Husseini sway until 1948. The SMC managed the *awkaf* (the Muslim trusts responsible for sacred properties) and the Islamic courts (the *shar'i*), maintained the mosques and appointed religious officials (such as imams and preachers), and ran a number of limited educational and social services (such as schools and orphanages). SMC members were appointed by the government. During the 1920s and 1930s, the Husseinis used the SMC's financial clout – principally coming from the government – to mobilise support against the Nashashibis; at the same time, SMC funds were withheld from Opposition centres such as Hebron. The SMC became politically marginal in the mid-1930s after the AHC was set up and after Haj Amin al Husseini was expelled from Palestine.

The only body that resembled a national 'government' (à la the JA) was the AHC. But it functioned only spasmodically, during 1936–1939 and 1946–1948, and its members – the Palestinian Arab 'Cabinet' – by and large operated from outside the counry during late 1937–1948. The Mufti was the nominal 'president' and the day-to-day running was in the hands of his cousin Jamal Husseini. During 1947–1948 the AHC had six departments that theoretically oversaw various areas of political endeavour: A Lands Department (headed by Mustafa Husseini), responsible for purchasing land and preventing Jewish purchases; a Finance Department (headed by 'Azzam Taunus), in charge of expenditure and fund-raising; the Economic Department (headed by Yassin al-Khalidi), responsible for commercial ties, imports and exports and the 'Boycott Committee' (headed by Rashid al-Khatib), which supervised the boycott of Jewish goods and services; the Department for National Organisation (headed by Rafiq Tamimi), responsible for sports agencies and paramilitary youth associations; the Department of Prisoners and Casualties (headed by Muhammad Sa'id Gharbiya and Salah Rimawi), responsible for caring for those killed, hurt or imprisoned while serving the nation and their families; and the Press Department (headed by Mahmoud Sharkas), an information or propaganda body responsible for media coverage and relations with journalists. This structure failed to cover other important areas of government (health services, education, transportation, foreign affairs, defence) and what was covered, was covered poorly, according to the HIS:

> In truth, chaos reigned in most of the departments and the borders between them were generally blurred. [Each] official interfered in his colleague's affairs, there was little [taking of] responsibility and public criticism was legion, while, moreover, the selection of the officials and departmental heads was improper [i.e., marred by corruption and nepotism].

By late January 1948 only one department – the Treasury – was still functioning.[39]

In effect, in most areas, the Palestinians remained dependent on the Mandate administration. Consequently, when the administration folded over winter and spring 1947–1948, and the towns, villages and roads were engulfed by hostilities, Arab Palestine – especially the towns – slid into chaos. Confusion and even anarchy characterised the distribution and sale of food, the delivery of health care and the operation of public transport and communications. Law and order collapsed. Palestine Arab society fell apart. By contrast, the Yishuv, under the same conditions of warfare and siege, and with far less manpower and no hinterland of friendly states, proved able to cope.

MILITARY PREPARATIONS

Nowhere was the pre-1948 organisational disparity between the two communities greater than in the military field. The Arabs began preparing for hostilities in the early 1930s. But the results were insubstantial and their worth was diminished by internal political feuding.

Three small *jihadiyya* (fighting societies) were established: *Al Kaff al Khadra* (the Green Palm) in the Hebron area, *al Jihad al Muqaddas* (the Holy War), led by Amin al Husseini's nephew, 'Abd al Qadir al Husseini, in the Jerusalem area, and *al Shabab al Tha'ir* (the Rebellious Youth) in the Tulkarm-Qalqilya area. All three planned or carried out anti-British attacks, albeit in a small way. More dramatic were the brief activities of Sheikh 'Izz al Din al Qassam around Haifa and in northern Samaria. After killing several Jewish settlers and a policeman, the band was cornered and Qassam was killed by the British in late 1935.

More important in the 'militarisation' of Arab Palestine was the establishment by the Husseinis of the *Futuwa* (youth companies), in which youngsters were trained in military drill and the use of weapons. The movement, modelled after the Nazi youth organisations,[40] never amounted to much though it supplied some of the political cadres who organised the general strike of 1936 and the terrorism later in the rebellion. The *Futawa* were re-established after World War II but never numbered more than several hundred youths under arms.

A larger organisation was the *Najjada* (auxiliary corps), set up in the post-war period, largely at Opposition initiative, with its centre in Jaffa. In summer 1946 it had 2,000–3,000 members and was led by Muhammad Nimr al Hawari; its officers were mainly Palestinians who had served in the British Army. The organisation lacked arms. In the run-up to the 1948 war, the Husseinis tried to gain control of the *Najjada*, in the process destroying it.[41] In the end, the Palestinians entered the war without a national militia.

During the 1948 War, Palestinian military power rested on a handful of mobile armed bands, each numbering several hundred irregulars, on town militias, and on individual village 'militias'.

The irregular bands – the most prominent of which were *al Jaish al Muqaddas*, led by 'Abd al Qadir al Husseini, in the Jerusalem hills area, and Hassan Salameh's, in the countryside around Lydda and Ramle – were mainly reconstitutions of bands that had been active in 1936–1939. They were lightly armed and dependent on (often unreliable) supplies from outside Palestine. They lacked logistical organisation and usually moved from village to village, imposing themselves on often reluctant inhabitants. Most were affiliated to the AHC and were often at loggerheads with neighbouring town militias, often led by Opposition figures, and ALA contingents. In ambushes on Yishuv convoys or attacks on settlements, bands were usually joined by local village militiamen in a *faz'a* (or alarm, as at Concord and Lexington at the start of the American Revolution). At the end of the day, the militiamen dispersed to their homes. Such *faz'as* were common during January–March along the Tel Aviv–Jerusalem road. But generally, each militia remained rooted to its village, intent only on defence against Jewish attack.

The individual village militias, with practically no military training, usually consisted of several dozen adult males who owned rifles. The rifles were of various vintages, sometimes of different calibres; the village might also own one or two light or medium machine-guns and a handful of pistols. There was usually very little ammunition and the militia had no logistical organisation for sustained action outside the village.

Exact figures about numbers and stocks of arms in these paramilitary organisations do not exist, but an idea of Palestine Arab military strength can be gained from figures relating to individual villages. Ghuweir Abu Shusha, by the Sea of Galilee, with a population of 1,240, in April 1948 reportedly had some 48 militiamen with 35–40 assorted rifles, and 20–50 rounds of ammunition per man. 'Ein Zeitun near Safad, with a population of 800, had 50–60 militiamen with 40–50 assorted rifles and one or two machine-guns, with 25–35 rounds of ammunition per rifle.

Safad, with about 9,500 Arabs, had 200–250 armed militiamen with 35–50 rounds per rifle. Al Khalisa, in the Galilee Panhandle, with a population of 1,840, had 35–40 armed militiamen, with 50–70 rounds per rifle.[42] In January 1948, according to HIS, the large village of Tira, south of Haifa, possessed 40 pistols, 64 rifles, four light machine-guns and a heavy machine-gun without ammunition; in nearby 'Ein Ghazal, with 3,000 inhabitants, there were, in mid-1947, a total of 83 weapons, including 23 obsolete rifles and 45 pistols.[43] In the main towns, the situation was proportionately no better.[44]

A close look in March 1948, well into the war but in an area until then unaffected by hostilities, by an (unnamed) British medical officer or official, gives an inkling of how things were:

> Spent Saturday afternoon and night and Sunday morning in the village of Ras al Ahmar [in northern Galilee] . . . This village of course is not very important, but if they are all organised like this one, then they won't get very far. They have no medical kit, no stretchers, no one who understands medical work. They have enough ammunition for one attack but no reserves, no leaders worth while.
>
> I asked them where they kept the mortars and artillery; they said Husseini will provide that when the time comes, as he will provide all the other things we need. There are enough guns at Nablus and Hebron, they said.
>
> In general the men of this [Husseini-aligned, Muslim] village behave like a bunch of school children, wanting a parade and to show off their weapons, and let me see how 'tough' they were and how ready they were to fight the Jews, and how sorry they were that there were no Jews [nearby] to kill.[45]

Under the Mandate, the Palestinians had relied on (mostly Jewish) government doctors and medical institutions; the lack of medical services was to plague the Palestinians through the ensuing war.[46]

Palestinian efforts to acquire weaponry during the last months of 1947 were hindered by the Husseini–Nashashibi divide, by poverty, and by a general unwillingness to contribute to the national cause, itself a reflection of the low level of political consciousness and commitment. From mid-1947, as the United Nations decision drew near, the Palestinian leaders began to levy taxes and 'contributions' to finance the impending struggle. Taxes were imposed on cigarettes (one mil per packet) and on bus tickets (five mil per ride). But, 'it appears that the Arab public was not participating enthusiastically and by 1.11.1947 only P£25,000 were raised. It was clear that such a sum could not suffice to finance the activities of the AHC, which steadily increased.'[47] During the first month of the war, HIS monitored dozens of cases of local Arab leaders and armed bands extorting 'contributions'; the will to give was absent. For example, on 29 December 1947 the mukhtars of 'Arab al Satariyya and

Yibna village in the lower Coastal Plain were reported to be exacting, 'with pressure and threats', P£5 per head to finance arms purchases.[48] The Palestine Arabs had no arms production capacity.

Despite the arrival of small irregular units from outside, matters did not greatly improve during the first months of the war. An Arab intelligence report from Damascus in late March 1948 stated that the urban militias had

> no more than a few old rifles and a very small number of machineguns and grenades. Were it not for the occasional intervention of the British Army . . . the ability of these forces to hold off the Jews, who are superior in number and equipment, must be in doubt.[49]

But it was in the realm of unity of command and control of armed forces, especially in the towns, that the Arabs were at the greatest disadvantage, as was to emerge starkly during the first months of the war. In the background, always, was the Husseini–Opposition divide, which had resurfaced during 1946–1947 as the resurrected Husseini-dominated AHC re-imposed its authority. During the period November 1946–April 1947 a veritable campaign of terror (à la 1937–1938) was unleashed against Opposition figures and those suspected of dealings with the Zionists: A Husseini-clan renegade, Fawzi Darwish Husseini, was murdered on 23 November 1946; Abu Ghosh clan members were attacked on 25 December; 'Ali Shahin was murdered in Jaffa in February 1947; and in April, attempts were made on the lives of Muhammad Yassin, Nimr Arsan, Zaki Safarini, and Muhammad Yunis al-Husseini. The Jaffa-based Arab newspaper *Falastin* denounced the last attempt as a reversion to 1937–1939 and subversive of national unity. There were also a number of Opposition retaliatory strikes, but they never amounted to much, and by November 1947 the Opposition was effectively cowed into silence.[50]

By the start of the fighting, Husseini domination assured a surface unity. Differences were temporarily buried and coalition NCs, as in 1936, were set up in each town, and in some villages. But divergent political outlooks and economic interests soon began to tell. On the national level, different militias and NCs were controlled by different bodies – the AHC, the Opposition, the Arab League Military Committee, the ALA, the Jordanian government, the Muslim Brotherhood (of Egypt). In some towns, such as Jaffa, there were several militias, each owing allegiance to a different master, who supplied its funds, arms and reinforcements. On the local level, in some areas, such as the Jerusalem hinterland, Husseini domination meant an aggressive, offensive strategy against the Jews. Elsewhere, where the Husseinis were weak, and where upper and middle class business interests prevailed, as in Jaffa and Haifa, Husseini aggressiveness was intermittently curbed. Throughout, there was lack of coordination and cooperation between the AHC and the Jaffa and Haifa NCs. AHC efforts to assert control through direct contacts with their supporters (imams, municipal officials, local militia leaders), bypassing the NCs, were only partially successful.[51]

Haifa and Jaffa were pointers to the more general problem that affected Palestinian war-making. The militias in each area and town in large measure operated independently of political control. This was especially the case in towns where there were large contingents of non-local irregulars, such as Jaffa. Militias in Jaffa, Haifa and Jerusalem continually ignored or defied instructions from their respective NCs and, occasionally, from the AHC or the Military Committee. In late January 1948, Jerusalem NC leader (and AHC) member Husayn Khalidi complained to the Mufti that 'Abd al Qadir al Husseini's irregulars were generally ignoring the local NC and acted without any coordination: 'Indescribable confusion is being created,' said Khalidi.[52] The British authorities believed that, in general, the NCs and the AHC managed to exercise only 'comparatively feeble authority' over the militias in the towns.[53]

In the countryside, each village tended to decide on a course and act alone, often fighting – and falling – alone. Occasionally, militiamen from one or more villages would – often with a band of irregulars – attack a Jewish settlement or convoy. But in general, the village mentality, which included a great deal of fatalism, was defensive. And the villages were not 'built' for war; they lacked trenchworks and bunkers. Nor were the inhabitants – unlike the *kibbutzim* – psychologically 'built' to withstand attack, which in 1948 often included mortar barrages and, occasionally, light air raids. The villages' stand-alone tendency and unpreparedness combined with regionalism to produce drastic results. The Haganah was able to overrun one area after another without having to face a coordinated trans-regional defence; and, in microcosm, to pick off village after village, one by one. In many areas, there was not even defensive cooperation between neighbouring villages, since their relations, as often as not, were clouded by historic feuds and rivalry over land or other matters.

In general, by the end of 1947 the Palestinians had a healthy and demoralising respect for the Yishuv's military power. A Jewish intelligence source in October 1947 described the situation in the countryside:

The *fellah* is afraid of the Jewish terrorists . . . who might bomb his village and destroy his property . . . The town dweller admits that his strength is insufficient to fight the Jewish force and hopes for salvation from outside [i.e., by the Arab states. At the same time, the] moderate majority . . . are confused, frightened . . . They are stockpiling provisions . . . and are being coerced and pressured by extremists . . . [But] all they want is peace, quiet.[54]

If it came to battle, the Palestinians expected to lose but, conceiving of the struggle as lasting for decades or centuries, they believed that the Jews, like the medieval crusader kingdoms, would ultimately be overcome by the Arab world.[55]

A British military intelligence assessment from July 1947 estimated that an embryonic Jewish state would defeat the Palestinian Arabs, even if they were clandestinely assisted by one or two of the Arab states.[56] The Arab League Military Committee, based in Damascus, in October 1947 reached similar conclusions:

A. The Zionists in Palestine – organisations and parties, political, military and administrative – are organisationally on a very high level. These institutions can immediately transform into a Zionist government possessing all the means necessary for governing.
B. The Jews today have large forces, in terms of manpower, armaments and equipment . . .
C. The Jews have enormous economic resources in the country and outside it . . .
D. The Jews have a great ability to bring reinforcements and equipment from overseas in great quantities.

As for the Palestinian Arabs:

A. Currently the Palestinian Arabs do not have enough forces (manpower, weapons and equipment), to withstand in any [acceptable] way the Zionist organisations.
B. In the areas where a Jewish majority is in control live today 350,000 Arabs – in isolated villages and blocks threatened with destruction, should the Zionists carry out wide-ranging operations.

A month later, two days before the passage of the UN partition resolution, General Ismail Safwat, the Iraqi chairman of the League Military Committee, reported to the Iraqi chief of staff that 'most of the [Palestinian] Arabs cannot today in any way withstand the Zionist forces, even though numerically the Arabs are superior . . .'[57] Thus all observers – Jewish, British, Palestinian Arab, and external Arab – agreed on the eve of the war that the Palestinians were incapable of beating the Zionists or of withstanding Zionist assault. The Palestinians were simply too weak.

Between December 1947 and mid-May 1948, Palestine witnessed a vicious conflict admixing elements of guerrilla warfare and terrorism between two highly intermingled communities. There were mixed neighbourhoods (in Jerusalem and Haifa); there were mixed towns, with a patchwork of distinct Arab and Jewish neighbourhoods (Jerusalem, Haifa, Safad, Tiberias); and in each rural district and along almost every road there was an interspersing of Arab and Jewish villages. The exception was in the core, hilly areas of Judea and (especially) Samaria, later known as 'the West Bank', where the population was almost exclusively Arab.

The civil war between the two communities was thus mainly fought in the mixed towns and mixed rural areas, mostly in the plains, in which the Jews were by and large demographically dominant. Each side could, and did, cut off and besiege the other's neighbourhoods, towns, villages and outposts. The Jewish half of Jerusalem, Jaffa and the Arab half of Haifa proved most vulnerable in this respect. But in the end, the Palestinians and the ALA failed to capture a single Jewish settlement, while the Jews, by mid-May, conquered close to 200 Arab villages and towns, including Jaffa, Beisan, Safad, Arab Haifa and Arab Tiberias. The general picture of Palestinian lack of arms and trained manpower, and a multiplicity of power centres, disorganisation and confusion reflected the lack of adequate preparation in the pre-1948 period.

THE ARAB WORLD

The Palestinian Arabs believed that succour would come from the Arab world around them, but the rifts within Palestinian society were matched by the rifts between the Palestinians and those who came to 'help' them. The Yishuv had financial help from Western, primarily American, Jewry; the Arabs, despite continuous efforts, enjoyed no such steady, reliable aid from the Arab states or the Muslim world. Indeed, the rejection by the Arab governments and armies of local and national Palestinian pleas for money, arms and reinforcements in late 1947 and early 1948 was merely a continuation of what had gone before. Cumulatively, it engendered among the Palestinians a sense of abandonment, which underlay their despair through 1948.

All told, some 5,000 Arab volunteers reached Palestine by March 1948. Most of them were from the urban slums (and, indeed, jails) of Iraq, Syria and Lebanon, organised as the ALA under Fawzi al Qawuqji. Militarily they were fairly useless, and throughout their sojourn in Palestine they were at loggerheads with local militias and populations. The ALA contingents rejected AHC, meaning Husseini, control and generally failed to coordinate their operations with the local bands or militia groups.

The Arab states, each pulling in a different direction and interested in a different area of Palestine, independently ran some of the bands (Egypt, for example, ran the Muslim Brotherhood volunteers in the south) and proved ungenerous in meeting the Palestinians' needs in money and arms. Most Arab leaders regarded Haj Amin al Husseini with antipathy, and had their own agendas.

Mid-way in the hostilities, the civil war gave way to the interstate Israeli–Arab war. On 14 May, the State of Israel was declared and the British left – and, on 15–16 May, the armies of Jordan, Syria, Egypt and Iraq invaded Palestine. Their declared aim was to help the Palestinians and, if possible, to thwart the establishment of the Jewish state and to occupy both Jewish and Arab parts of Palestine. The secretary general of the Arab League, 'Azzam Pasha, spoke of a massacre of the Jews akin to the Mongols' pillage of Baghdad in the 13th century. In Jordan's case, the principal aim of the invasion was to occupy as much as possible of Arab Palestine with the aim of annexation.

The war between Israel and the Arab states was protracted and bloody (about 4,000 of the Yishuv's 6,000 dead were killed after 14 May) and the Yishuv's leaders recognised that they faced a mortal threat. Indeed, on 12 May, three days before the invasion, Ben-Gurion was told by his chief military advisers (who over-estimated the size of the Arab armies and the numbers and efficiency of the troops who would be committed – much as the Arab generals tended to exaggerate Jewish troop strengths) that the 'chances' of winning were 'about even' (*'hashansim shkulim me'od'*).[58] And, indeed, the first 3–4 weeks of the invasion seemed, from the Yishuv's perspective, to be touch and go. During 15–18 May, the Jordanian army, the Arab Legion, fanned out across the Arab-populated hill country of Judea and Samaria, initially avoiding battle with the Jews. But clashes eventually developed in and around Jerusalem, focusing on the city itself and on the police fort and crossroads at Latrun, to the west, which dominated the Tel Aviv–Jerusalem road. The Syrian, Iraqi and Egyptian armies all crossed the international frontiers and attacked Jewish settlements in the areas allotted to the Jews by the UN, and the Egyptian Air Force bombed Tel Aviv.

The Arab armies initially had the advantage of tactical surprise and initiative and of heavy weaponry, including tanks, artillery and fighter aircraft. But all, save the British-led, -armed and -trained Arab Legion, had failed to prepare adequately, and were rapidly contained by the Haganah. By July, the initiative had shifted to the IDF and the war was characterised by a succession of Israeli offensives (interspersed with long UN-imposed truces). With Arab ammunition stocks slowly depleted (the British and French halted arms shipments in obedience to a United Nations embargo on the combatants) and with arms and ammunition pouring into Israel from private dealers and Czechoslovakia (which flouted the embargo), the IDF was on the offensive; by December 1948–January 1949, the Syrians, Jordanians and Iraqis were *hors de combat* and the IDF had isolated and crushed the Egyptian army. The Arab governments agreed to cease fire, and Israel and its four neighbours signed a succession of general armistice agreements over February–July 1949. The war was over. The Israelis, who had gained control of four–fifths of Palestine, were the chief winners; the Palestinians, without a state of their own and left under Israeli, Jordanianian and Egyptian rule, were the losers. The Palestinian refugee problem was the main expression of that defeat.

ENDNOTES

1. For a summary, see Morris, *Righteous Victims*, Chaps. 1 and 2.
2. After the Bar-Kochba Revolt of 132–135 AD the Romans renamed the province of Judaea 'Palaestina'. Palestine remained a province first of Rome and then Byzantium, until the Arab conquest in the seventh century. In the Ottoman centuries, there was no province or district of 'Palestine'; the various sub-districts (or sanjaks) into which historic Palestine was divided were parts of the province of Syria and, later, the province of Beirut (though in the last years of the Ottoman Empire Jerusalem and Jaffa and the area to their south enjoyed the status of an independent sub-district or mutasarri-flik). 'Palestine' was throughout used by the Christian world as a synonym for the geographically ill-defined Holy Land, which the Jews throughout called the 'Land of Israel'.
3. Lebel, *Haj Amin*, 193–202.
4. Horowitz and Lissak, *Origins*.
5. Pa'il, *Haganah*, 279–80.
6. Gelber, *Jewish Army*, 211–333; and Pa'il, *Haganah*, 241.
7. Pa'il, ibid., 285. To these Jewish numbers should be added the 2,000–3,000 members of the IZL and 300–500 members of the LHI. The number of Arab troops that invaded Palestine in May 1948 was around 25,000 (see, for example, Kimche & Kimche, *Both Sides*, 162, who speak of '24,000'); the number rose during the following weeks and months, as did the manpower of the IDF.
8. Pa'il, *Haganah*, 285.
9. In 1944–1945, only a third of Muslim children aged 5–15 attended school (as did close to 100 per cent among the Jewish and Christian populations). Rates of illiteracy were, of course, higher among those who had attained adulthood in Ottoman and early British Mandate days. They were also far greater among women. In 1945–1946, in the towns, 85 per cent of Muslim boys and 65 per cent of Muslim girls attended school; the comparative figures for the rural population were 65 and 10 per cent respectively. Only 432 of Palestine's 800 villages had schools by 1945–1946. Tests conducted in 1931 showed that 25 per cent of Muslim males and three per cent of Muslim females were literate, as were 70 per cent of Christian Arab males and 40 per cent of females (Miller, *Palestine*, 97–98).
10. Miller, *Palestine*, 86; and Seikaly, *Haifa*, 19–25, 38, et al.
11. Stein, 'One Hundred Years', puts it more starkly. He argues that this dispossession of *fellahin* and the steady population shift to the towns was among the causes of the Palestinian refugee problem, in that they served as a first stage in the separation of the peasants from their lands, psychologically and economically 'preparing' them for 1948. Thus, the 1948 exodus was, in his view, a late 'second stage' in a process that began a century or more before.
12. Grossman, *Arab Village*, 154–55, et al.
13. Miller, *Palestine*, 86.
14. Gabbay, *Political Study*, 6.
15. Miller, *Palestine*, 24–25.
16. Shoufani, 'The Fall of a Village', 120.

17. Grossman, *Arab Village*, 111; and Kark, *Jerusalem and Environs*, 279–286.
18. Porath, *Emergence*, 287.
19. Haganah economic warfare unit memorandum (p. 1 and title, missing), undated but from May or June 1948, HA 105\119.
20. Haganah economic intelligence memorandum, probably from May or June 1948, HA105\119.
21. Haganah economic intelligence memorandum, probably from May or June 1948, HA 105\119.
22. For a fuller list, see Shimoni, *Arabs*, 211–239.
23. Porath, *Palestinian Arab*, 162–273. See also Sayigh, *Peasants*, 47–51.
24. Khalaf, *Politics in Palestine*.
25. Shimoni, *Arabs*, 338, footnotes 5 and 6, gives a partial list of the family affiliations. The Husseinis enjoyed the fealty of the Dajanis and Abu Labans (Jaffa), the Suranis (Gaza), the Hassunas (Lydda), the Tamimis and 'Anabtawis (Nablus), the 'Abadins, 'Arafas and Khatibs (Hebron), the Tabaris (Tiberias) and the Nakhawis (Safad); and the Nashashibis, the loyalty of the the the Tawqans, Masris and Shak'ahs (Nablus), the Dajanis (Jerusalem), the Karazuns and Huneidis (Lydda), the 'Amrs and Tahabubs (Hebron), the Hanuns (Tulkarm) and the Fahums (Nazareth). Among the more prominent 'neutral' families through the late 1930s and 1940s were the Shawas (Gaza), the Nusseibehs (Jerusalem) and the 'Abushis (Jenin).
26. Entries for 22 Dec. 1947 and 19 Feb. 1948, DBG-YH I, 64 and 66 and 253–254; and Danin's and Sasson's statements, 'Protocol of the Meeting on Arab Affairs, 1–2 January 1948', KMA-IGP.
27. Unsigned, 'Arabs with a Tendency to Cooperation with the Jews', undated, HA 105\54. The memorandum names two Muslims ready to cooperate, for pecuniary gain.
28. 'George Antwan Bakhut is Dead', unsigned HIS report, 13 Feb. 1947, HA 105\195.
29. 'Hanoch-Hadamaska'i', 'The Situation between Shafa 'Amr's Christians and Muslims', HA 105\195.
30. 'Bishop Giorgius Hakim Went to Egypt on 15 February 1947', unsigned HIS report, HA 105\195; and 'Hanagid', 'Surrounding the Murder of George Bakhut', 19 Feb. 1947, HA 105\195.
31. HIS report, 17 Mar. 1947, HA 105\195.
32. 'Hanagid', 'The Shafa 'Amr Incidents', 7 Mar. 1947, HA 105\195.
33. 'Talmi', 'The Christians in Jaffa', 2 May 1947, HA 105\193 bet.
34. 'Subject: The Christian Arabs Worry about their Safety.' unsigned HIS report, 10 Oct. 1947, HA 105\195.
35. HIS-AD, 'Summary of a Conversation with Barkai, Nazareth District Officer (Afula) 5.11.47', HA 105\195.
36. 'Hashmonai', 'Group of Reports', undated but c.7 Jan. 1948, IDFA 500\48\\5.
37. 'Nir' to HIS-AD, 27 Jan. 1948, HA 105\195.
38. HIS, 'Subject: Meeting of Sheiks in Beersheba', 1 Dec. 1947, HA 105\194.
39. HIS, 'Subject: The Arab Institutions in Jerusalem Today; Organisation and Leadership (A Survey up to 25.1.48)', 28 January 1948, IDFA 500\48\\60.
40. Porath, *Palestinian Arab*, 76.

41. Shimoni, *Arabs*, 376–77.
42. Nazzal, *Exodus*, 30–31, 34, 39–40, and 46. These figures are based on recollections decades after the event.
43. Gelber, *Palestine*, 40.
44. See Levenberg, *Military Preparations*, for an overview of the Palestinian military preparations for the 1948 War.
45. Reproduced in 'Barak' to HIS-AD, 22 Mar. 1948, IDFA 900\52\\43.
46. Unsigned HIS report, 31 Dec. 1947, IDFA 500\48\\60.
47. Mordechai Abir, 'The Local Arab Factor in the War of Independence (the Jerusalem Area)' undated but from mid-1950s, IDFA 1046\70\\185.
48. HIS, 'Subject: Ahmad Abu Khattab and Muhammad Taha Najar', 29 Dec. 1947, unsigned, HA 105\23.
49. STH, III, part 2, 1362.
50. HIS-AD, 'The Arab Public's Reaction to the Internal Arab Terror (a Summary for the Period 1.11.46–20.4.47)', 16 May 1947, HA 105\102.
51. Entry for 22 Dec. 1947, DBG-YH I, 63.
52. Entry for 21 January 1948, DBG-YH I, 169; and Gelber, *Palestine*, 54.
53. HC to Secretary of State, 'Weekly Intelligence Report', 3 Jan. 1948, SAMECA CP III\1\3.
54. 'Pir'im', 'The Feeling Among Palestine's Arabs', 29 Oct. 1947, CZA S25–3300.
55. 'A.L.', 'A Conversation with Za'afer Dajani, chairman of the Jaffa Chamber of Commerce', 26 Nov. 1947, CZA S25-3300.
56. Untitled 7-page memorandum, examining Jewish and Arab military strengths and capabilities, signed illegibly by a lt. colonel, British Army general staff, 10 July 1947, SAMECA CP IV\4\65, General MacMillan, OC British forces in Palestine, minuted (for the HC's eyes): 'I think you would like to see this. I agree with the reasoning and deductions.'
57. *Behind the Screen*, 66–67 ('General Ismail Safwat's First Report Composed by the Military Committee and Presented to the [Arab] League Council on 9 Oct. 1947'), and 71 (Safwat to the (Iraqi) chief of general staff, 27 Nov. 1947).
58. ISA, *People's Administration*, 67 (protocol of meeting of 12 May 1948).

2

The idea of 'transfer' in Zionist thinking before 1948

In July 1948, about midway in the first Arab–Israeli war, Britain's Foreign Secretary, Ernst Bevin, wrote that 'on a long term view . . . there may be something to be said for an exchange of populations between the areas assigned to the Arabs and the Jews respectively.'[1] A few days later, he expatiated:

> It might be argued that the flight of large numbers of Arabs from the territory under Jewish administration had simplified the task of arriving at a stable settlement in Palestine since some transfers of population seems [sic] to be an essential condition for such a settlement.

But he then went on to argue that as there were only a handful of Jews living in the territory earmarked for Arab sovereignty in Palestine, there was no 'basis for an equitable exchange of population' and therefore Britain should pursue with the United Nations Mediator the possibility of a return of the displaced Palestinian Arabs to their homes.[2] By this time, 400,000–500,000 Arabs (and less than five thousand Jews) had been displaced in the fighting.

But the logic propelling Bevin's thinking, before he pulled on the reins, was highly persuasive: The transfer of the large Arab minority out of the areas of the Jewish state (as of the minuscule Jewish minority out of the Arab-designated areas) would solve an otherwise basic, insurmountable minority problem that had the potential to subvert any peace settlement. The selfsame logic underlay the analysis, a month later, of London's Middle East intelligence centre, the Cairo-based British Middle East Office:

> The panic flight of Arabs from the Jewish occupied areas of Palestine has presented a very serious immediate problem but may possibly point the way to a long term solution of one of the greatest difficulties in the way of a satisfactory implementation of partition, namely the existence in the

Jewish state of an Arab community very nearly equal in numbers to the Jewish one.

Previous examinations of this problem have always led to the rejection of transference of populations as a solution for the reason that the number of Arabs to be transferred from the Jewish state was 40 times as great as the number of Jews to be transferred from the Arab state. [But] this disparity has for the moment been largely reduced by the flight of Arabs from the Jewish state . . .

Now that the initial difficulty of persuading the Arabs of Palestine to leave their homes has been overcome by Jewish terrorism and Arab panic it seems possible that the solution may lie in their transference to Iraq and Syria . . . The project [of resettling the refugees in the Arab states] would have to be launched with utmost care. If it were put forward at the present stage the immediate reaction in all Arab minds would be that we had been working for this all along. But if it becomes obvious that through unwillingness on the part of either the Jewish [sic] or Arabs there is little or no chance of the displaced Arabs of Palestine being reinstated in their own homes, it might be put forward as a solution to the problem as it then appeared.[3]

Similar assumptions pervaded American thinking at the end of the war. The consul-general in Jerusalem, William Burdett Jr., no friend of Zionism, advised Washington in February 1949:

Despite the attendant suffering . . . it is felt security in the long run will be served best if the refugees remain in the Arab states and Arab Palestine instead of returning to Israel. Since the US has supported the establishment of a Jewish State, it should insist on a homogeneous one which [sic] will have the best possible chance of stability. Return of the refugees would create a continuing 'minority problem' and form a constant temptation both for uprisings and intervention by neighbouring Arab states.[4]

Such was the thinking in British (and some American) official circles by the second half of 1948, when the creation of the refugee problem was well under way. The same persuasive logic pertained already before the turn of the century, at the start of the Zionist enterprise. There may have been those, among Zionists and Gentile philo-Zionists, who believed, or at least argued, that Palestine was 'an empty land' eagerly awaiting the arrival of waves of Jewish settlers.[5] But, in truth, on the eve of the Zionist influx the country had a population of about 450,000 Arabs (and 20,000 Jews), almost all of them living in its more fertile, northern half. How was the Zionist movement to turn Palestine into a 'Jewish' state if the overwhelming majority of its inhabitants were Arabs? And if, over the years, by means of massive Jewish immigration, the Jews were at last to attain a majority, how could a truly 'Jewish' and stable polity be established containing a very large, and possibly disaffected, Arab minority, whose birth rate was much higher than the Jews'?[6]

The obvious, logical solution lay in Arab emigration or 'transfer'. Such a transfer could be carried out by force, i.e., expulsion, or it could be engineered voluntarily, with the transferees leaving on their own steam and by agreement, or by some amalgam of the two methods. For example, the Arabs might be induced to leave by means of a combination of financial sticks and carrots. This, indeed, was the thrust of the diary entry by Theodor Herzl, Zionism's prophet and organisational founder, on 12 June 1895:

> We must expropriate gently . . . We shall try to spirit the penniless population across the border by procuring employment for it in the transit countries, while denying it any employment in our country . . . Both the process of expropriation and the removal of the poor must be carried out discretely and circumspectly.[7]

This was Herzl's only diary entry on the matter, and only rarely did he refer to the subject elsewhere. It does not crop up at all in his two major Zionist works, *Der Judenstaat* (The Jews' State) and *Altneuland* (Old-New Land). Nor does it appear in the published writings of most of the Zionist leaders of Herzl's day and after. All understood that discretion and circumspection were called for: Talk of transferring the Arabs, even with Palestinian and outside Arab leaders' agreement, would only put them on their guard and antagonise them, and quite probably needlessly antagonise the Arabs' Ottoman correligionists, who ruled the country until 1917–1918.

But, in private, the Zionist leaders were more forthcoming. In 1911 Arthur Ruppin, head of the Zionist Organisation's Palestine Office, proposed 'a limited population transfer' of peasants to Syria; a year later, Leon Motzkin, one of the organisation's founders, declared: 'The fact is that around Palestine there are extensive areas. It will be easy for the Arabs to settle there with the money that they will receive from the Jews.'[8] For years, the Zionist advocate and novelist Israel Zangwill had been trumpeting the transfer solution to the Arab problem:

> We cannot allow the Arabs to block so valuable a piece of historic reconstruction . . . And therefore we must gently persuade them to 'trek'. After all, they have all Arabia with its million square miles . . . There is no particular reason for the Arabs to cling to these few kilometres. 'To fold their tents and silently steal away' is their proverbial habit: Let them exemplify it now.[9]

But most advocates of transfer kept their thoughts to themselves or restricted them to private letters and internal Zionist deliberations. Such was the situation in the waning days of Ottoman rule and so it remained during the first two decades of British government. Talking about transfer would needlessly alienate or at least complicate the lives of Palestine's new governors and perhaps put off potential Jewish supporters of Zionism as well.

To be sure, to some degree the praxis of Zionism, from the first, had been characterised by a succession of microcosmic transfers; the purchase of land and the establishment of almost every settlement (*moshava*, literally colony) had been accompanied by the (legal and usually compensated) displacement or transfer of an original beduin or settled agricultural community. The displaced Arabs more often than not resettled in another part of rural Palestine or moved to the burgeoning towns, though some moved across the Jordan, out of the country. One such displacement was graphically described by Haim Margaliyot Kalvaryski, a Zionist expert on Arab affairs and a key land-purchaser:

> The Arab question was revealed to me in all its seriousness immediately after my first purchase of land here, when I had to see to the first eviction [*nishul*] of the Arab inhabitants off their land to make way for the settlement of our brothers. For long afterwards I did not cease hearing the sad melody of the beduin men and women who gathered by the sheikh's tent that evening, before they left the village of Shamasin that is near Yama, which is [today] Yavniel [in eastern Galilee]. I sat in the tent and wrapped up the negotiation with Sheikh Fadul from Deleika. And the beduin men and women assembled around the fire prepared coffee for me and the rest of the guests. And at the same time they sang sad songs lamenting their bad luck, which was forcing them to leave the cradle of their homeland. These songs touched my heart and I realised how tied the beduin was to his land.[10]

Herzl, Motzkin, Ruppin and Zangwill, of course, had been thinking not of such mini-displacements but of a massive, 'strategic' transfer. But however appealing on the practical plane, the idea was touched, in most Zionists' minds, by a measure of moral dubiety. True, at least down to the 1920s or 1930s, the Arabs of Palestine did not see themselves and were not considered by anyone else a distinct 'people'. They were seen as 'Arabs' or, more specifically, as 'southern Syrian Arabs'. Therefore, their transfer from Nablus or Hebron to Transjordan, Syria and even Iraq – especially if adequately compensated – would not be tantamount to exile from the homeland; 'Arabs' would merely be moving from one Arab area to another.

Moreover, the transfer of ethnic minorities to their core national areas, was regarded during the first half of the 20th century as morally acceptable, perhaps even morally desirable. It also made good political sense. The historical experience in various parts of the globe during the 1920s and 1940s supported this view. The double coerced transfer of Muslim Turks out of Greek majority areas in Thrace and the Aegean Islands and of Christian Greeks out of Turkish Asia Minor during the early 1920s, a by-product of Greek–Turkish hostilities, at a stroke seemed to solve two long-standing, 'insoluble', minority problems, rendering future

Greek–Turkish relations more logical and pacific. 1947–1948 witnessed even larger (and bloodier) transfers, of Muslims and Hindus, between India and Pakistan, as these states emerged from the womb of history.[11] The world looked on, uncondemning and impervious. Indeed, the transfer of German minority groups from western Poland and the Czech borderlands to Germany at the end of the Second World War was positively lauded in most Allied capitals. In both the West and the Communist Bloc it was seen as both politically imperative and just. These minorities had helped to subvert the European order and a cluster of central and eastern European nation-states, at a mind-boggling cost in lives, suffering and property; it was just and fitting that they be uprooted and 'returned' to Germany, both as punishment and in order that they might cause no trouble in the future.

Still, the notion of transfer remained, in Zionist eyes – even as Zionist leaders trotted out these historical precedents – morally problematic. Almost all shared liberal ideals and values; many, indeed, were socialists of one ilk or another; and, after all, the be-all and end-all of their Zionist ideology was a return of a people to its homeland. Uprooting Arab families from their homes and lands, even with compensation, even with orderly re-settlement among their own outside Palestine, went against the grain. The moral dilemma posed was further aggravated during the 1930s and 1940s by the dawning recognition among many of the Zionist leaders, including Ben-Gurion and Zeev Jabotinsky, the leader of the right-wing Revisionist Movement, that Palestine's Arabs had brought forth a new, distinct (albeit still 'Arab') nationalism and national identity; Palestinian transferees might not feel at home in Transjordan or Iraq. For all these reasons, the notion of transfer was something best not mulled over and brought out into the open in public discourse and disputation; best not to think about it at all. Zionism might necessitate displacement of Palestinians, but why trouble one's conscience and linger over it?

Rather, the Zionist public catechism, at the turn of the century, and well into the 1940s, remained that there was room enough in Palestine for both peoples; there need not be a displacement of Arabs to make way for Zionist immigrants or a Jewish state. There was no need for a transfer of the Arabs and on no account must the idea be incorporated in the movement's ideological–political platform.

But the logic of a transfer solution to the 'Arab problem' remained ineluctable; without some sort of massive displacement of Arabs from the area of the Jewish state-to-be, there could be no viable 'Jewish' state. The need for transfer became more acute with the increase in violent Arab opposition to the Zionist enterprise during the 1920s and 1930s. The violence demonstrated that a disaffected, hostile Arab majority or large minority would inevitably struggle against the very existence of the Jewish state to which it was consigned, subverting and destabilising it from the start. Moreover, the successive waves of anti-Zionist Arab violence (1920, 1921, 1929 and 1936–1939) bludgeoned the British into periodically curbing Jewish immigration. Hence, Arab violence promised to prevent the gradual emergence of a Jewish majority. This was the significance of the British White Paper of May 1939, which the British delivered up at the end of, and in response to, the Arab Revolt of 1936–1939, the biggest outburst of Arab violence during the Mandate. The White Paper assured the Arabs – who at the time numbered about one million to the Jews' 450,000 – of permanent majority status (by limiting Jewish immigration to 75,000 over the following five years) while promising that majority 'independence' within 10 years. Palestine would become an Arab state with a large Jewish minority (whose future status and rights, needless to say, would be determined by the new Arab rulers).

Hence, if during the last decades of the 19th century and the first decades of the 20th century Zionist advocacy of transfer was uninsistent, low-key and occasional, by the early 1930s a full-throated near-consensus in support of the idea began to emerge among the movement's leaders. Each major bout of Arab violence triggered renewed Zionist interest in a transfer solution. So it was with the riots of 1929. In May 1930, the director of the Jewish Agency's Political Department and the chairman of the Jewish Agency Executive in Palestine, Colonel F. H. Kisch, proposed to the president of the Zionist Organisation, Chaim Weizmann, that the Jewish Agency should press the British to promote the emigration of Palestinian Arabs to Iraq, which is

> in urgent need of agricultural population. It should not be impossible to come to an arrangement with [King] Faisal [of Iraq] by which he would take the initiative in offering good openings for Arab immigrants . . . There should be suitable propaganda as to the attractions of the country which indeed are great for Arab immigrants – and there should be specially organised and advertised facilities for travel. We, of course, should not appear [to be promoting this], but I see no reason why H.M.G. should not be interested . . . There can be no conceivable hardship for Palestinian Arabs – a nomadic and semi-nomadic people – to move to another Arab country where there are better opportunities for an agricultural life – c.f. English agricultural emigrants to Canada.[12]

A few weeks earlier, Weizmann himself had suggested to British Colonial Secretary Lord Passfield that a solution to Palestine's troubles might lie across the Jordan: Palestine's troublesome Arabs could be transferred over the river.

> Lord Passfield observed that he was convinced he would have to consider a solution in that direction; but Iraq might present some difficulties . . . and they [i.e., the Iraqis] were very difficult people. My reply was: 'Of course, it isn't easy, but these countries [i.e., Transjordan and Iraq] have to be

developed . . .' Lord Passfield thought this a wide outlook and one to be taken into consideration very seriously. (I then said, supposing we were to create a Development Company which would acquire a million dunams of land in Transjordania, this would establish a reserve and relieve Palestine from pressure . . .)[13]

A year later, Kisch raised the subject again, saying that the movement had to adopt a clear policy in the matter. Responding, the veteran Zionist official Yaakov Thon wrote that from the movement's perspective, the ideal solution would be a transfer of Palestine's Arabs across the Jordan. But the movement's spokesmen, he added, could not say this openly.[14] Weizmann said similar things to Drummond Shiels, Passfield's under-secretary: Transferring Arabs out of Palestine would be 'a courageous and statesmanlike attempt to grapple with a problem that had been tackled hitherto half-heartedly . . . Some [of Palestine's Arabs] might flow off into the neighbouring countries, and this quasi-exchange of population could be fostered and encouraged.'[15]

But before 1936, sporadic talk and thinking about transfer was confined to tête-à-têtes behind closed doors and to internal departmental memoranda. The outbreak of the Arab Revolt in April 1936 opened the floodgates; the revolt implied that, from the Arabs' perspective, there could be no compromise, and that they would never agree to live in (or, indeed, next to) a Jewish state. Moreover, they were bent on forcing the British to halt Jewish immigration – and this, precisely at a time, when the Nazis threatened Europe's Jews with an unimaginably appalling future. Never had there been such need for a safe haven in Palestine.

To be sure, the Zionist leaders, in public, continued to repeat the old refrain – that there was enough room in the country for the two peoples and that Zionist immigration did not necessitate Arab displacement. Jabotinsky, the leader of the Revisionist movement, had generally supported transfer.[16] But in 1931 he had said: 'We don't want to evict even one Arab from the left or right banks of the Jordan. We want them to prosper both economically and culturally';[17] and six years later he had testified before the Peel Commission that 'there was no question at all of expelling the Arabs. On the contrary, the idea was that the Land of Israel on both sides of the Jordan [i.e., Palestine and Transjordan] would [ultimately] contain the Arabs . . . and many millions of Jews . . .' – though he admitted that the Arabs would become a 'minority.'[18]

But by 1936, the mainstream Zionist leaders were more forthright in their support of transfer. In July, Ben-Gurion, the chairman of the Jewish Agency Executive and de facto leader of the Yishuv, and his deputy, Moshe Shertok (Sharett), the director of the Agency's Political Department, went to the High Commissioner to plead the Zionist case on immigration, which the Mandatory was considering suspending:

Ben-Gurion asked whether the Government would make it possible for Arab cultivators displaced through Jewish land purchases . . . to be settled in Transjordan. If Transjordan was for the time being a country closed to the Jews [i.e., closed to Jewish settlement], surely it could not be closed to Arabs also.

The High Commissioner thought this a good idea . . . He asked whether the Jews would be prepared to spend money on the settlement of such Palestinian Arabs in Transjordan.

Mr. Ben-Gurion replied that this might be considered.

Mr. Shertok remarked that the Jewish colonising agencies were in any case spending money in providing for the tenants or cultivators who had to be shifted as a result of Jewish land purchase either by the payment of compensation or through the provision of alternative land. They would gladly spend that money on the settlement of these people in Transjordan.[19]

Three months later, the Jewish Agency Executive debated the idea. Ben-Gurion observed:

Why can't we acquire land there for Arabs, who wish to settle in Transjordan? If it was permissible to move an Arab from the Galilee to Judea, why is it impossible to move an Arab from the Hebron area to Transjordan, which is much closer? . . . There are vast expanses of land there and we [in Palestine] are over-crowded . . . We now want to create concentrated areas of Jewish settlement [in Palestine], and by transferring the land-selling Arab to Transjordan, we can solve the problem of this concentration . . . Even the High Commissioner agrees to a transfer to Transjordan if we equip the peasants with land and money . . .[20]

Already in May 1936 the British had promised to send a royal commission of inquiry which would determine the causes of the rebellion and propose a solution – if the Arabs ceased fire. By October the rebel bands had been badly ravaged and the Arab population had generally tired of the rebellion. Haj Amin al-Husseini suspended the hostilities and the Peel Commission arrived in Palestine. It toured the country, met outside Arab leaders and took testimony from British, Zionist and Palestinian Arab officials. In early July 1937, it submitted and published its report. The Peel Commission recommended the partition of Palestine between a Jewish state, comprising some 20 per cent of the country, and Transjordan, which would absorb most of the remainder (the residue, of less than 10 per cent, including Jerusalem and Bethlehem, was to remain in British hands). But even this failed to solve the perennial demographic problem: For even in the 20 per cent of the country where the Jews were concentrated and which was earmarked for Jewish sovereignty (the coastal plain and the Galilee) more than two fifths of the population was Arab. So Peel further recommended the transfer of all or most of the Arab population out of these areas.

The existence of these [Arab and Jewish] minorities [in the respective majority areas] clearly constitutes the most serious hindrance to the smooth and successful operation of partition . . . If the settlement is to be clean and final, this question of the minorities must be boldly faced and firmly dealt with.

The commission pointed to the useful Greco-Turkish precedent, in which about 1.3 million Greeks and 400,000 Turks were compulsorily exchanged or transferred in the first half of the 1920s. 'Before the [exchange] operation the Greek and Turkish minorities had been a constant irritant. Now the ulcer had been cleaned out, and Greco-Turkish relations, we understand, are friendlier than they have ever been before.' Formally, the commission spoke not of 'transfer' but of a 'population exchange' involving the removal to the Jewish state-to-be of '1,250' Jews from the Arab-populated areas and of the removal of '225,000' Arabs out of the Jewish state-to-be to the Arab areas. But, in effect, not an equitable exchange but a transfer of Arabs with a very small figleaf transfer of Jews, was what was envisaged. The commission preferred that the Arabs move voluntarily and with compensation – but regarded the matter as so important that should the Arabs refuse, the transfer should be 'compulsory', that is, it should be carried out by force. Otherwise, the partition settlement would not endure.[21]

The recommendations, especially the transfer recommendation, delighted many of the Zionist leaders, including Ben-Gurion. True, the Jews were being given only a small part of their patrimony; but they could use that mini-state as a base or bridgehead for expansion and conquest of the rest of Palestine (and possibly Transjordan as well). Such, at least, was how Ben-Gurion partially explained his acceptance of the offered 'pittance.'[22] But Ben-Gurion had another reason: 'The compulsory transfer of the Arabs from the valleys of the proposed Jewish state could give us something which we never had, even when we stood on our own during the days of the First and Second Temples . . . ,' Ben-Gurion confided to his diary. 'We are being given an opportunity that we never dared to dream of in our wildest imaginings. This is more than a state, government and sovereignty – this is national consolidation in an independent homeland.' Ben-Gurion deemed the transfer recommendation

a central point whose importance outweighs all the other positive [points] and counterbalances all the report's deficiencies and drawbacks . . . We must grab hold of this conclusion [i.e., recommendation] as we grabbed hold of the Balfour Declaration, even more than that – as we grabbed hold of Zionism itself . . . because of all the Commission's conclusions, this is the one that alone offers some recompense for the tearing away of other parts of the country [and their award to the Arabs] . . . What is inconceivable in normal times is possible in revolutionary times . . . Any doubt on our part about the necessity of this transfer, any doubt we cast about the possibility of its implementation, any hesitancy on our part about its justice, may lose [us] an historic opportunity that may not recur . . . If we do not succeed in removing the Arabs from our midst, when a royal commission proposes this to England, and transferring them to the Arab area – it will not be achievable easily (and perhaps at all) after the [Jewish] state is established . . . This thing must be done now – and the first step – perhaps the *crucial* [step] – *is conditioning ourselves for its implementation.*'[23]

The Peel report had, for the first time, accorded the idea of transfer an international moral imprimatur. At the same time, its publication triggered a profound and protracted debate in the Zionist leadership: Should the movement renounce its historic claim to the whole of Palestine and accept the principle of partition and the offered 20 per cent of the land? The controversy cut across party lines, with Ben-Gurion's own Mapai Party split down the middle. For the Revisionist right there was no problem; they claimed Transjordan as well as the whole of Palestine; partition was a non-starter. For the left, represented by Brit Shalom and Hashomer Hatza'ir, the Peel proposals were beside the point; they favoured a binational Arab–Jewish state, not partition. But for the moderate left and centre – the core and mainstream of the movement – the dilemma was profound. The culminating and decisive debate took place in the especially summoned Twentieth Zionist Congress in Zurich August 1937 (the Revisionists did not attend). Ben-Gurion mobilised the Peel transfer proposal in support of acceptance of partition:

We must look carefully at the question of whether transfer is possible, necessary, moral and useful. We do not want to dispossess, [but] transfer of populations occurred previously, in the [Jezreel] Valley, in the Sharon [i.e., Coastal Plain] and in other places. You are no doubt aware of the Jewish National Fund's activity in this respect. Now a transfer of a completely different scope will have to be carried out. In many parts of the country new settlement will not be possible without transferring the Arab peasantry . . . It is important that this plan comes from the Commission and not from us . . . Transfer is what will make possible a comprehensive settlement programme. Thankfully, the Arab people have vast empty areas. Jewish power, which grows steadily, will also increase our possibilities to carry out the transfer on a large scale. You must remember, that this system embodies an important humane and Zionist idea, to transfer parts of a people [i.e., Palestine's Arabs] to their country [i.e., Transjordan and Iraq] and to settle empty lands . . .

Ben-Gurion seemed to suggest that the transfer would be compulsory and that not the British but Jewish troops would be carrying it out. Other speakers at the Congress, including Weizmann and Ruppin, spoke in a similar vein, though all preferred a voluntary, agreed transfer, and some, such as Ussishkin, doubted that the whole idea was practicable; the British would not carry it out and would prevent the Jews from doing so. Many, including Berl Katznelson, the Mapai co-leader, opposed the gist of the Peel package, which was partition (while theoretically supporting transfer).[24]

In the end, after bitter debate, the Congress equivocally approved – by a vote of 299 to 160 – the Peel recommendations as a basis for further negotiation. The vote marked an in principle endorsement of the concept of partition. No specific mention was made in the resolution of the transfer proposal – though it was implicitly accepted as part of the package whose territorial provisions the Zionists sought to renegotiate (i.e., they wanted more than the 20 per cent offered).[25]

However, within weeks, the Peel recommendations were dead in the water. The Arabs, unappeased, renewed their revolt, and the British Government, taking fright, secretly voted against partition on 8 December 1937 and then appointed yet another ('technical') committee, ostensibly to look into the praxis of implementing the Peel proposals but in reality to bury them. The Woodhead Committee, set up in March 1938, presented its findings in November. It offered a handful of refashioned partition proposals, all with a much smaller Jewish state than proposed by Peel; the committee favoured the one with a Jewish state stretching from Tel Aviv to Zikhron Yaakov, comprising less than 10 per cent of Palestine's land mass (obviously unacceptable to the Zionists). The committee rejected Peel's compulsory transfer proposal as out of the question, suggested that voluntary transfer was 'impossible to assume', and concluded that a Jewish state with a large Arab minority would be dysfunctional. Hence, partition was unworkable.

But during the months of Woodhead deliberations, the Zionist leadership – unaware of London's secret, in principle, rejection of partition – roundly examined and debated the Peel proposals and the practicalities of their implementation. Transfer got a protracted, thorough airing. A 'Transfer Committee' of experts, chaired by Thon, then head of the Palestine Land Development Company, was established and investigated ways and means of implementing transfer – how many and which Arabs could or should be transferred? Where to? With what compensation? The problems were vast and the political circumstances were volatile (an ongoing Arab Revolt, a British Government whose support for the Peel recommendations was uncertain, a world drifting toward total war, when the problem of Palestine would surely be put on the back burner). The committee broke up in June 1938 without producing a final report.[26]

But simultaneously, the Jewish Agency Executive – the 'government' of the Yishuv – discussed transfer. On 7 June 1938, proposing Zionist policy guidelines, Ben-Gurion declared: 'The Jewish State will discuss with the neighbouring Arab states the matter of voluntarily transferring Arab tenant-farmers, labourers and peasants from the Jewish state to the neighbouring Arab states.' (As was his wont, Ben-Gurion at the same time endorsed complete equality and civil rights for the Arabs living in the Jewish State; some executive members may have regarded this as for-the-record lip service and posturing for posterity.)[27] Five days later Ben-Gurion laid his cards baldly on the table: 'I support compulsory transfer. I don't see in it anything immoral.' Ussishkin followed suit: there was nothing immoral about transferring 60,000 Arab families:

> We cannot start the Jewish state with . . . half the population being Arab . . . Such a state cannot survive even half an hour. It [i.e., transfer] is the most moral thing to do . . . I am ready to come and defend . . . it before the Almighty . . .

Werner David Senator, a Hebrew University executive of German extraction and liberal views, called for a 'maximal transfer'. Yehoshua Supersky, of the Zionist Actions Committee, said that the Yishuv must take care that 'a new Czechoslovakia is not created here [and this could be assured] through the gradual emigration of part of the Arabs.' He was referring to the undermining of the Czechoslovak republic by its Sudeten German minority. Ben-Gurion, Ussishkin and Berl Katznelson agreed that the British, rather than the Yishuv, should carry out the transfer. 'But the principle should be that there must be a large agreed transfer', declared Katznelson. Ruppin said: 'I do not believe in the transfer of individuals. I believe in the transfer of entire villages.' Eliezer Kaplan, the Jewish Agency's treasurer, thought that with proper financial inducement and if left impoverished in the nascent Jewish State, the Arabs might agree to a 'voluntary' departure. Eliahu Berlin, a leader of the Knesset Yisrael religious party, proposed that 'taxes should be increased so that the Arabs will flee because of the taxes'. There was a virtual pro-transfer consensus among the JAE members; all preferred a 'voluntary' transfer; but most were also agreeable to a compulsory transfer, preferring, of course, that the British rather than the Yishuv carry it out.[28]

In one way or another, Zionist expressions of support for transfer during 1936, 1937 and the first half of 1938 can be linked to the Peel Commission's work and recommendations. Not so Ben-Gurion's tabling of a new transfer scheme in early December 1938. Peel was now dead and buried. But in Germany, the Nazis had just unleashed the mass pogrom of *Kristalnacht*; in Palestine and London, the British, the Arabs and the Zionist leaders were preparing for the St James's Conference, soon to open in the British capital. The Zionist leadership was desperate to find a safe haven for Europe's Jews and to empty Palestine in preparation for their arrival. 'We will offer Iraq ten million Palestine pounds to transfer one hundred thousand Arab families from Palestine to Iraq', Ben-Gurion jotted down in his diary. On 11 December he raised the idea at a meeting of the JAE. The Iraqis, he said, were in urgent need of manpower to fill their empty spaces and to develop the country. But Ben-Gurion was not optimistic; he anticipated opposition from Saudi Arabia and Egypt. He was driven by a premonition of unprecedented disaster:

> The Jewish question is no longer that which was [the question] until now . . . Millions of Jews are now faced with physical destruction . . . Zionism [itself] is in danger . . . We now need, during this catastrophe that has befallen the Jewish people, all of Palestine . . . [and] mass immigration . . .[29]

Nothing came of these deliberations and plans. In November, the Woodhead Committee had scuppered any possibility of British endorsement of either partition or transfer; the St. James Conference of February 1939 produced only further deadlock; and in May, in a new 'White Paper,' Whitehall disavowed its commitment to Zionism itself, in effect supporting a continued, permanent Arab majority and Arab rule in Palestine within a decade.

But the idea of transfer, the golden *deus-ex-machina* solution to the Arab problem, continued to captivate the Zionist imagination. When deliberating transfer in the late thirties, the Zionist executives tended to think either in terms of a total transfer, which would leave the emergent Jewish state Arab free, or, should that prove impossible, in terms of particular categories of Arabs. Most often peasants and tenant farmers were mentioned, perhaps because their transfer would entail an accretion of land to the Zionist institutions. As well, cultivators were seen as 'highly transferable' because their (compensated) resettlement on land in Transjordan or Iraq would not necessitate vocational retraining or profound cultural acclimatisation. Moving the bulk of the Arab townspeople, on the other hand, would gain the Zionist enterprise little of value (only an 'improvement' in Palestine's demography) and would probably be much more problematic on the other, absorptive end.

In the absence of Anglo–Arab–Zionist agreement about a blanket transfer, proposals periodically surfaced regarding the selective transfer of this or that Arab religious or ethnic group. In March 1939, the leader of Syria's Druse, Sultan al-Atrash, proposed that the Yishuv buy up the dozen odd Druse villages in Palestine and that their 15,000 inhabitants be transferred to Jabal el-Druse in southern Syria. The envisioned voluntary transfer would benefit both the Druse and the Jews – and might serve as a model for further population transfers from Palestine, al-Atrash argued. Weizmann responded enthusiastically, launching a series of consultations with American Zionist leaders and French army officers and officials. He reported that the French – who ruled Syria – were in favour but Shertok, in Tel Aviv, was skeptical about the willingness of Palestine's Druse to move and ultimately quashed the negotiation. There the matter seemingly ended.[30]

But a seed had obviously been planted in Ben-Gurion's mind. In October 1941 he formulated a blueprint for future Zionist policy, in which he expatiated at length about the possibilities of transfer. He wrote that various categories of Palestinian Arabs were ripe for transfer:

> The Druse, several Beduin tribes in the Jordan Valley and the South, the Circassians, and perhaps also the Matawalis [Shi'ites living in northern Galilee] [would] not mind being transferred, under favourable conditions, to some neighbouring country.

Tenant farmers and landless labourers, too, could probably be transferred with relative ease, he argued. A transfer of the bulk of Palestine's Arabs, however, would probably necessitate 'ruthless compulsion'. But recent European history, he wrote, had demonstrated that compulsory transfer of populations was possible, and the ongoing world war seemed to underline the need and practicality of massive transfers to solve difficult minority problems. There would be massive transfers of population as part of the post-war settlement, he reasoned. But the Zionist movement must take care not to openly preach or advocate compulsory transfer of Arabs as this would be impolitic and would antagonise many in the West. At the same time, he wrote, the Zionists should do nothing to hamper those in the West who were advocating transfer as a necessary element in the solution of the Palestine problem.[31]

Ben-Gurion was obliquely referring to the proposal by Harry St. John Philby, an orientalist and adviser to King Ibn Saud of Saudi Arabia, to establish at the end of the war a Middle Eastern 'federation' of states, with Ibn Saud as its ruler. The plan also provided for a Jewish state in Palestine, transferring most of Palestine's Arabs out of the country, and the payment to Saudi Arabia of 20 million pounds sterling. Both Weizmann and Shertok were initially enthusiastic.[32]

Through the war years, Shertok and Weizmann remained steady proponents of transfer, flogging the idea to whoever would listen. One of Weizmann's interlocutors was Ivan Maiskii, the Soviet ambassador in London. The two met in London in late January 1941. Initially they discussed possible orange exports to Russia; Maiskii wasn't particularly interested. They then turned to a possible post-war settlement in Palestine. According to Weizmann, Maiskii said

> there would have to be an exchange of populations. Dr Weizmann said that if half a million Arabs could be transferred, two million Jews could be put in their place. That, of course, would be a first instalment; what might happen afterwards was a matter for history. Mr Maiskii's comment was that they in Russia had also had to deal with exchanges of population. Dr Weizmann said that the distance they had to deal with in Palestine would be smaller; they would be transferring the Arabs only into Iraq or Transjordan. Mr Maiskii asked whether some difficulties might not arise in transferring a hill-country population to the plains, and Dr Weizmann replied that a beginning might be made with the Arabs from the Jordan

Valley; but anyhow, conditions in Transjordan were not so very different from the Palestine hill-country . . . Dr Weizmann explained that they were unable to deal with [the Arabs] as, for instance, the Russian authorities would deal with a backward element in their population in the USSR. Nor would they desire to do so.[33]

Maiskii's report on the meeting contains a number of differences. Maiskii wrote that it was Weizmann who had raised the subject of transfer. Weizmann, according to Maiskii, had proposed 'to move a million Arabs . . . to Iraq, and to settle four or five million Jews from Poland and other countries on the land where these Arabs were'. The Soviet ambassador had expressed surprise regarding Weizmann's expectation of settling four or five million Jews on lands inhabited by only one million Arabs. Weizmann replied, according to Maiskii:

> Oh, don't worry . . . The Arab is often called the son of the desert. It would be truer to call him the father of the desert. His laziness and primitivism turn a flourishing garden into a desert. Give me the land occupied by one million Arabs, and I will easily settle five times that number of Jews on it.[34]

A few months later, an almost identical exchange took place between Shertok, visiting Cairo, and Walter Smart, the secretary for Arab affairs at the British Legation in Egypt. They spoke of possible massive Polish Jewish immigration to Palestine.

> I [Shertok] said . . . that the Land of Israel could accommodate a population of at least five million. But how many Jews? – he asked.
> I said: Three million Jews and two million Arabs. The Arabs increase thanks to Jewish immigration [which expands the economy that facilitates the absorption of Arab immigrants], but if we evict the Arabs there will be room for more Jews; and this will [also] benefit the Arabs.
> What will you do with them? [asked Smart].
> Syria, for example, will that country develop with such a small population, with its empty spaces? If several hundred thousand Arabs from the Land of Israel were transferred there, the Jewish people would provide funds, Syria would get an income. The same applies to Iraq.

During the visit, Shertok said similar things at his meeting with the American minister, Alexander Kirk.[35]

Nothing, of course, came of these meetings. But they give us an insight into the desperation growingly felt by the Zionist leadership as the news of the awful fate of Europe's Jews began to seep out – and into the measures they were willing to contemplate and propound to save their people.

And such thinking was not limited to the political leadership; it also characterised many of the officials who ran the Yishuv's 'state-within-a-state' institutions. Yosef Weitz, director of the JNF's Lands Department and a key land-purchasing and settlement executive, was characteristic if somewhat more articulate and blunt than most: 'It must be clear that there is no room in the country for both peoples', he confided to his diary on 20 December 1940.

> If the Arabs leave it, the country will become wide and spacious for us . . . The only solution [after World War II ends] is a Land of Israel, at least a western Land of Israel [i.e., Palestine], without Arabs. There is no room here for compromises . . . There is no way but to transfer the Arabs from here to the neighbouring countries, to transfer all of them, save perhaps for [the mainly Christian Arabs of] Bethlehem, Nazareth and old Jerusalem. Not one village must be left, not one [beduin] tribe. The transfer must be directed at Iraq, Syria and even Transjordan. For this goal funds will be found . . . And only after this transfer will the country be able to absorb millions of our brothers and the Jewish problem [in Europe] will cease to exist. There is no other solution.[36]

But solving the Jewish problem or the question of Palestine were far from priorities for the Allied leaders and generals during the world war; they had more pressing problems. Transferring Arabs to make way for Jews was hardly an urgent or, indeed, attractive proposition. Nonetheless, the news that gradually emerged during the second half of the war from Nazi-occupied Europe about the ongoing Holocaust certainly caused pangs of conscience among Western politicians and officials and underlined the urgency of a solution of the Jewish problem in Europe by way of a safe haven in Palestine. Pro-Zionist tendencies were reinforced. The Executive of Britain's Labour Party in April 1944 adopted a platform endorsing mass Jewish immigration to, a Jewish majority in, and a transfer of Arabs out of, Palestine as part of a Middle East peace settlement. '. . . In Palestine surely is a case, on human grounds and to promote a stable settlement, for transfer of population. Let the Arabs be encouraged to move out as the Jews move in. Let them be compensated handsomely for their land and let their settlement elsewhere be carefully organised and generously financed', stated the resolution, which was published in the Labour Party's volume, *The International Post-War Settlement*.[37] The publication of the resolution prompted a debate on 7 May in the JAE – not so much about the notion of transfer (all were agreed about its merits if not its practicality) as about how the Zionist leadership should react. Shertok, Israel's future first foreign minister and second prime minister, said: 'The transfer can be the archstone, the final stage in the political development, but on no account the starting point. By doing this [i.e., by talking prematurely about transfer] we are mobilising enormous forces against the idea and subverting [its implementation] in advance . . .' And he continued (prophetically): 'What will happen once the Jewish state is established – it is very possible that the result will be transfer of Arabs.' Shertok was followed by Ben-Gurion:

When I heard these things [about the Labour Party Executive's reso-lution] . . . I had some difficult thoughts . . . [But] I reached the conclusion that it is best that this remain [i.e., that the resolution remain as part of Labour's official platform] . . . Were we asked what should be our pro-gramme, I would find it inconceivable to tell them transfer . . . because talk on the subject might cause harm in two ways: (a) It could cause us harm in public opinion in the world, because it might give the impres-sion that there is no room [for more Jews] in Palestine without ejecting the Arabs . . . [and] (b) [such declarations in support of transfer] would force the Arabs onto . . . their hind legs.' Nonetheless, Ben-Gurion added: 'Trans-fer of Arabs is easier than any other type of transfer. There are Arab states in the area . . . and it is clear that if the Arabs [of Palestine] are sent [to the Arab countries] this will improve their situation and not the contrary . . .

The rest of the JAE members followed suit. Yitzhak Gruenbaum, who would be Israel's first interior minister, declared:

To my mind there is an Arab consideration in favour of transfer. That is, in the increase of population of Iraq by [additional] Arabs. It is the function of the Jews occasionally to make the Gentiles [goyim] aware of things they did not until then perceive . . . If for example it is possible to create artificially in Iraq conditions that will magnetise the Arabs of Palestine to emigrate to Iraq, I do not see in it any iniquity or crime . . .

Eliahu Dobkin, director of the Jewish Agency's Immigration Depart-ment, said: 'There will be in the country a large [Arab] minority and it must be ejected. There is no room for our internal inhibitions [in this matter] . . .' Eliezer Kaplan, who would become Israel's first finance minister, said: 'Regarding the matter of transfer I have only one re-quest: Let us not start arguing among ourselves . . . This will cause us the most damage externally.' Dov Joseph, the JA's legal adviser and soon to be Israel's justice minister, chimed in: 'I agree with Mr. Kaplan.' Werner David Senator said: 'I do not regard the question of transfer as a moral or immoral problem . . . It is not a matter I would refuse to consider . . .'[38]

Ben-Gurion returned to the transfer theme the following month, when he (unrealistically) proposed bringing one million Jewish immigrants to Palestine 'immediately'. The religious Mizrahi Party's Moshe Haim Shapira said that the matter would compel the Yishuv to consider trans-ferring Arabs. Ben-Gurion replied:

I am opposed that any proposal for transfer should come from our side. [But] I do not reject transfer on moral grounds and I do not reject it on political grounds. If there is a chance for it [I support it]; with regard to the Druse it is possible. It is possible to move all the Druse voluntarily to Jabal Druse [in Syria]. The other [Arabs] – I don't know. But it must not be a Jewish proposal . . .[39]

If the Second World War and the Holocaust in various ways quickened Zionist interest in transfer, they also, for a moment, resuscitated British support for a settlement based on partition and Jewish statehood in part of Palestine. In 1943 a special British ministerial committee submitted a proposal based on partition and in January 1944 the full cabinet endorsed the idea, with implementation left to the post-war era. In turn, this renewed advocacy of transfer in British and, perhaps paradoxically, Arab official circles.

In January 1943 a senior British Colonial Office official, the Duke of Devonshire, proposed the following trade-off: That Britain establish an Arab state in Libya, just conquered from the Italians, and that the Arab world, in exchange acquiesce in the establishment of a Jewish state 'in Palestine'. It was untrue, he added, that the Zionists had over the years displaced Arabs from Palestine but 'in any case . . . the Arab population in Palestine might be dealt with by an offer of assistance to migrate to Libya for those families who find conditions in Palestine unendurable'.[40]

Hard on the heels of the end of World War II, another prominent Englishman, General John Glubb, the Arabophile commander of Transjordan's army, the Arab Legion, became a prominent advocate of transfer (alongside partition of Palestine between a Jewish State and Transjordan). In July 1946, Glubb penned a memorandum entitled 'A Note on Partition as a Solution to the Palestine Problem'. In it he recommended partition 'because no other scheme offers any possibility of success'. He envisaged a Jewish state encompassing the Coastal Plain, the Jezreel Valley and the lower Jordan Valley. Glubb was uncertain about how to solve the problem of Jaffa, a large Arab town in the middle of the Jewish coastal area. One possibility, he wrote, was the transfer of its population 'somewhere else' over a 10–15 year period. As to the other Arab inhabitants in the Jewish state-to-be's areas, Glubb (rather hesitantly) recommended transfer:

> The best course will probably be to allow a time limit during which persons who find themselves in one or other state against their wishes, will be able to opt for citizenship of the other state . . . Some might, of course, opt for citizenship . . . without desiring to move into and reside in it. The great majority, however, would probably wish to move . . . A small proportion of the minorities could move by direct exchange . . . But . . . a large balance of Arabs would be left in the Jewish state. The Jews would want to get rid of them, and would soon find means of making the Arabs wish to move . . . It is not of course intended to move Arab displaced persons by force, but merely so to arrange that when these persons find themselves left behind in the Jewish state, well paid jobs and good prospects should be simultaneously open for them in the Arab state.[41]

Glubb seemed to be speaking of a 'voluntary' transfer reinforced by a number of tempting carrots. But in a follow-up 'Note', written apparently a few weeks later, Glubb appeared to move towards an acceptance of some measure of compulsory transfer as well.

> When the undoubtedly Arab and undoubtedly Jewish areas had been cleared of all members of the other community, work would begin on deciding the actual frontier . . . [In the frontier belt] every effort would be made to arrange exchanges of land and population so as to leave as few people as possible to be compensated for cash.[42]

In January 1947, as the United Nations partition resolution drew closer, Glubb refined his scheme. The Arabs in the Jewish-designated areas 'would have to be bought out and settled elsewhere', he wrote. But he added:

> The proposal for partition put forward in previous memoranda did not involve the forcible transfer of any of the population [Those wishing to move to the other state would be compensated.] . . . HMG or British troops will not be concerned with moving anybody – certainly not their forcible eviction from their homes. It is inconceivable that British troops be used to evict [Arabs] from their homes. Such things can be done by Germans or Russians . . . British troops are not capable of being frightful enough . . . [But] to attempt forcibly to transfer large blocks of Arabs by using Jewish troops would lead to civil war, and troops of the Arab states would refuse to do it. The inevitable conclusion therefore seems to be that large blocks of population cannot be moved, and hence that the only frontier which can in practice be implemented is one running approximately along the existing [demographic] front line . . .[43]

In effect, what Glubb was saying was that partition, between a Jewish state and Transjordan, was the only solution; that for partition to work, there would have to be a transfer of the Arabs out of the Jewish state (as of the far smaller number of Jews out of the Arab areas); and that the transfer would have to be voluntary and compensated because a compulsory transfer, by British or Jewish or Arab troops, was inconceivable and\or would merely lead to widespread hostilities.

But it wasn't only Zionist activists and British officials who during the early and mid-1940s swung around to acceptance of partition accompanied by a transfer of Arabs out of the Jewish state-to-be. So did senior Arab politicians – or at least that is what generally reliable British officials recorded them as saying at the time. In December 1944, Nuri Sa'id, Iraq's senior politician and sometime prime minister, told a British interlocutor that if partition was imposed on the Arabs, there would be a 'necessity of removing the Arabs from the Jewish state\thought it could be done by exchange . . .'. Sa'id assumed that the settlement would not provoke a violent Arab reaction but supported the idea – a small Jewish state in Palestine and transfer – only if it provided 'finality' to the problem. In a follow-up conversation, the British official heard similar things from Iraq's foreign minister, Arshad al-Umari: 'Arshad . . . repeated what Nuri had said . . . over [i.e., regarding] probable [Arab] reactions and also the necessity of removing the Arabs from the Jewish State.'[44] Nuri had put his position still more forcefully in a conversation with Alec Kirkbride, the British Resident in Ammam:

> Provided the partition was effected on an equitable basis, it might perhaps be best to lose part of Palestine in order to confine the Zionist danger within permanent boundaries . . . Nuri Pasha said that the only fair basis could be the cession to the Jews of those areas where they constituted a majority . . . [while] the Arab section of Palestine would be embodied in Transjordan.[45]

In Amman there was an understandable sympathy for a partition of Palestine between the Jews and Transjordan – and it quite naturally led to acceptance of partition's corollary, transfer. At a meeting in Jerusalem in February 1944 between Sir Harold MacMichael, the high commissioner, Lord Moyne, the Minister Resident in the Middle East, Kirkbride, and General Edward Spears, head of the British political mission in Syria and Lebanon, there was general agreement that 'partition offers the only hope of a final settlement for Palestine'. And, according to Moyne, Jordan's prime minister, Tawfiq Abul Huda, and Egypt's prime minister, Mustafa Nahas Pasha, both recognised that 'a final settlement can only be reached by means of partition' (though the Arab leaders, it was said, would not say so publicly).[46]

Abul Huda had informed Kirkbride directly of his position at two meetings, on 3 December 1943 and 16 January 1944. At the second meeting, Abul Huda – according to MacMichael – had said that 'he did not . . . see any alternative to partition . . .'.[47] Two years later, in July 1946, Kirkbride cabled London about meetings he had just had with King Abdullah and Transjordan's new prime minister, Ibrahim Pasha Hashim:

> [Abdullah] is for partition and he feels that the other Arab leaders may acquiesce in that solution although they may not approve of it openly . . . [Hashim said] the only just and permanent solution lay in absolute partition with an exchange of populations; to leave Jews in an Arab state or Arabs in a Jewish state would lead inevitably to further trouble between the two peoples. Ibrahim Pasha admitted that he would not be able to express this idea in public for fear of being called a traitor . . . [He] said that the other Arab representatives at the discussions would be divided into people like himself who did not dare to express their true views and extremists who simply demanded the impossible.[48]

A month later, Kirkbride commented:

> King Abdullah and Prime Minister of Jordan both consider that partition followed by an exchange of populations [meaning, as all understood, a transfer of Arabs out of the Jewish state-to-be] is only practical solution to the Palestine problem. They do not feel able to express this view publicly . . .[49]

What emerges from the foregoing is that the Zionist leaders, from the inception of the movement, toyed with the idea of transferring 'the Arabs' or a substantial number of Arabs out of Palestine, or any part of Palestine that was to become Jewish, as a way of solving the problem posed by the existence of an Arab majority or, down the road, a large Arab minority that was opposed to the existence of a Jewish state or to living in it. As Arab opposition, including violent resistance, to Zionism grew in the 1920s and 1930s, and as this opposition resulted in periodic British clampdowns on Jewish immigration, a consensus or near-consensus formed among the Zionist leaders around the idea of transfer as the natural, efficient and even moral solution to the demographic dilemma. The Peel Commission's proposals, which included partition and transfer, only reinforced Zionist advocacy of the idea. All understood that there was no way of carving up Palestine which would not leave in the Jewish-designated area a large Arab minority (or an Arab majority) – and that no partition settlement with such a demographic basis could work. The onset of the Second World War and the Holocaust increased Zionist desperation to attain a safe haven in Palestine for Europe's persecuted Jews – and reinforced their readiness to adopt transfer as a way of instantaneously emptying the land so that it could absorb the prospective refugees from Europe.

The bouts of Zionist reflection about and espousal of transfer usually came not out of the blue but in response to external factors or initiatives: In the early 1930s, Zionist meditation on the idea of transfer was a by-product of Arab violence and the frustration of efforts to persuade the British to allow Zionist settlement in Transjordan; in the late 1930s, it was triggered by the Arab revolt and the Peel Commission's recommendation to transfer the Arab population out of the area designated for Jewish statehood; during the early 1940s, thinking about transfer was stimulated by proposals by St. John Philby for a Middle East 'federation' and by the dire need for a (relatively) empty and safe haven for Europe's decimated Jews; and in 1944–1945, the talk was triggered by the British Labour Party Executive's decision to include transfer in its blueprint for a settlement of the Palestine question.

By the mid-1940s, the logic and necessity of transfer was also accepted by many British officials and various Arab leaders, including Jordan's King Abdullah and Prime Minister Ibrahim Pasha Hashim and by Iraq's Nuri Said. Not the Holocaust was uppermost in their minds. They were motivated mainly by the calculation that partition was the only sensible, ultimately viable and relatively just solution to the Palestine conundrum, and that a partition settlement would only be lasting if it was accompanied by a massive transfer of Arab inhabitants out of the Jewish state-to-be; a large and resentful Arab minority in the future Jewish state would be a recipe for most probably instantaneous and certainly future destabilisation and disaster.

The United Nations Partition Resolution of 29 November 1947 did not provide for population transfers and, indeed, left in the areas designated for Jewish statehood close to 400,000 Arabs (alongside some 500,000 Jews). Once battle was joined, it was a recipe for disaster – and for refugeedom for the side that lost. As it turned out, the Jews won and the great majority of the Arabs who had lived in the areas that became Israel fled or were driven out.

What then was the connection between Zionist transfer thinking before 1948 and what actually happened during the first Arab–Israeli war? Arab and pro-Arab commentators and historians have charged that this thinking amounted to pre-planning and that what happened in 1948 was simply a systematic implementation of Zionist ideology and of a Zionist 'master-plan' of expulsion.[50] Old-school Zionist commentators and historians have argued that the sporadic talk among Zionist leaders of 'transfer' was mere pipe-dreaming and was never undertaken systematically or seriously; hence, there was no deliberation and premeditation behind what happened in 1948, and the creation of the refugee problem owed nothing to pre-planning and everything to the circumstances of the war and the moment, chaos, immediate military needs and dictates, whims of personality, and so on.[51]

My feeling is that the transfer thinking and near-consensus that emerged in the 1930s and early 1940s was not tantamount to pre-planning and did not issue in the production of a policy or master-plan of expulsion; the Yishuv and its military forces did not enter the 1948 War, which was initiated by the Arab side, with a policy or plan for expulsion. But transfer was inevitable and inbuilt into Zionism – because it sought to transform a land which was 'Arab' into a 'Jewish' state and a Jewish state could not have arisen without a major displacement of Arab population; and because this aim automatically produced resistance among the Arabs which, in turn, persuaded the Yishuv's leaders that a hostile Arab majority or large minority could not remain in place if a Jewish state was to arise or safely endure. By 1948, transfer was in the air. The transfer thinking that preceded the war contributed to the denouement by conditioning the Jewish population, political parties, military organisations and military and civilian leaderships for what transpired. Thinking about the possibilities of transfer in the 1930s and 1940s had prepared and conditioned hearts and minds for its implementation in the course of 1948 so that, as it occurred, few voiced protest or doubt; it was accepted as inevitable and natural by the bulk of the Jewish population. The facts that Palestine's Arabs (and the Arab states) had rejected the UN partition resolution and, to nip it in the bud, had launched the hostilities that snowballed into fullscale civil war and that the Arab states had invaded Palestine and attacked Israel in May 1948 only hardened Jewish hearts toward the Palestinian Arabs, who were seen as mortal enemies and, should they be coopted into the Jewish state, a potential Fifth Column.

Thus, the expulsions that periodically dotted the Palestinian Arab exodus raised few eyebrows and thus the Yishuv's leaders, parties and population in mid-war accepted without significant dissent or protest the militarily and politically sensible decision not to allow an Arab refugee return.

It was at this point and in this context that some Yishuv leaders occasionally looked back and reflected upon the connection between what had already happened (by autumn 1948, some 400,000–500,000 Arabs had been displaced) and the transfer thinking of the 1930s and 1940s. 'In my opinion . . . there is no need to discuss a return of the refugees [so long as a renewal of hostilities is possible] . . .', said Yitzhak Gruenbaum, Israel's minister of interior, in September 1948.

> In the past we had a plan, that were we able to transfer the Arab population to [neighbouring] Arab states – we would have been ready to participate in the expense of their resettlement with assistance and financial help. Now, too, I see nothing wrong with this plan . . .[52]

ENDNOTES

1. Bevin to Kirkbride, 24 July 1948, PRO FO 816\139.
2. Bevin to chargé d'affaires, Amman, 28 July 1948, PRO FO 816\139.
3. BMEO to FO, 3 August 1948, PRO FO 816\139.
4. Burdett (Jerusalem) to Secretary of State, 5 Feb. 1949, PRO FO 371–75420.
5. Morris, *Righteous Victims*, 42.
6. In this context it is worth noting that at the end of the 1948 War, Israel had a population of some 750,000 Jews and 150,000 Arabs. By the year 2002, Israel's Arab minority still constituted some 20 per cent of the country's population (just over one million as compared with some five million Jews) – and this despite the fact that the Jews' natural increase had been supplemented during this 50-year period by the arrival of some two and a half million new immigrants!
7. Herzl, *The Complete Diaries of Theodor Herzl*, I, 88.
8. Morris, *Righteous Victims*, 140
9. Morris, *Righteous Victims*, 140. Prince Faisal, the de facto Arab ruler in Damascus, complained of this advocacy of 'the removal of the Arab population of Palestine by massive camel-trek' (see Morris, *Righteous Victims*, 141).
10. Segev, *One Palestine, Complete*, 98–99.
11. See Joseph Schechtman, *Population Transfers in Asia*, 1–50, which surveys the India–Pakistan exchange of population as part of its polemic arguing 'the [retroactive] case for [an] Arab-Jewish exchange of population' (pp. 84–141), meaning the transfer or expulsion of the Palestinian Arabs in 1948.
12. Kisch to Weizmann, 20 May 1930, Kisch Papers temporarily in author's keeping. It is worth noting that even before the 1929 riots, Kisch had been an enthusiastic advocate of transfer. In September 1928 he wrote about his meeting with the British director of the Lands Department in the Iraqi

administration. The official had highlighted Iraq's 'growing need for fela-heen' to develop its agriculture. 'This is what I have always been hoping and waiting for, having before now expressed the view that with the irrigation of Mesopotamia will be found the solution of the racial problem in Palestine', commented Kisch. 'Propaganda for an Arab emigration to Iraq cannot be made by us – except by the most indirect methods – but for the Iraq Gov-ernment to do so would be wonderful, and in the interests [sic] of both countries' (Kisch to Weizmann, 21 Sep. 1928, Kisch Papers temporarily in author's keeping).

13. Weizmann (London), 'Awaiting the Shaw Report', 6 Mar. 1930, *Letters of Chaim Weizmann*, Series B, 591–592.
14. Segev, *One Palestine, Complete*, 329.
15. Masalha, *Expulsion*, 32.
16. Teveth, 'The Evolution of "transfer" . . .', 16–21.
17. Jabotinsky, 'Round Table with the Arabs', *Ktavim*, 245. I would like to thank Dr Yoram Meital for directing me to this reference.
18. Katz, *Jabo*, 982. Jabotinsky testified on 11 Feb. 1937 in London.
19. 'Note of a Conversation between Mr D. Ben-Gurion and Mr M. Shertok and His Excellency the High Commissioner on July 9th, 1936 at Government Offices', HA, Yitzhak Ben-Zvi Papers, file 27. Ben-Gurion's views had ap-parently changed: During World War I and in its immediate aftermath, he had opposed transfer (see Simons, *International Proposals*, 16–17: 'It is not proper or possible to deport the country's present inhabitants').
20. Protocol of the Meeting of the Jewish Agency Executive, 1 Nov. 1936, CZA S100\20B.
21. Palestine Royal Commission Report, Cmd 5479 (London, July 1937), 389–91.
22. D. Ben-Gurion to Amos Ben-Gurion, 5 Oct. 1937, DBG Correspondence, IDFA. See also Shapira, *Land and Power*, 271.
23. Entry for 12 July 1937, David Ben-Gurion Diary, BGA. Emphasis in original.
24. See texts of speeches by Ben-Gurion, Ussishkin, Ruppin, etc. in CZA S5-1543. Weizmann also delivered a pro-transfer speech and tabled a spe-cific transfer proposal (but the text of his speech is not in the file; it is referred to in others' speeches). Following the Congress, the Zionist Organisation issued a laundered version of the speeches, in which most references to transfer were deleted (see *Twentieth Zionist Congress*). After seeing a copy of the Peel Commission Report, Weizmann met Colonial Secretary William Ormsby-Gore, in secret, on 19 July 1937, and wholeheartedly endorsed the transfer recommendation. 'I said', Weizmann reported, 'that the whole suc-cess of the [partition] scheme depended on whether the Government . . . [carried] out this recommendation.' Ormsby-Gore 'agreed that once Galilee was given to the Jews . . . the position would be very difficult without transfer' (see Weizmann, 'Summary Note of Interview with Mr Ormsby Gore, Colo-nial Office, Monday, July 19th, 1937, at 10:45 a.m.', Weizmann Archive. See also Simons, *International Proposals*, 19–23).
25. Interestingly, Jabotinsky, at least in public, continued to deny the necessity of transfer, if not actually to reject or condemn the idea. 'I never dreamt of demanding of the Arabs, [living] in a Jewish country, to emigrate from it. This could be a very dangerous precedent, which will be very harmful to

the interests of the Jews in the Diaspora . . . This whole matter of uprooting masses [of people] is nothing but foolishness' (Katz, *Jabo*, 1001, quoting Jabotinsky on 7 July 1937).

26. See documents, including protocols of the deliberations of the Transfer Committee, in CZA S25-247; and Katz, 'The Deliberations of the Jewish Agency Committee for Transfer of Population 1937–1938'.

27. Protocol of the Meeting of the JAE, 7 June 1938, CZA S100-24B.

28. Protocol of the Joint Meeting of the JAE and the Political Committee of the Zionist Actions Committee, 12 June 1938, CZA S100-24B.

29. Entry for 10 Dec. 1938, Ben-Gurion Diary, BGA; and protocol of JAE meeting of 11 Dec. 1938, CZA S100/25b. See also Simons, 'Supplement No. 1', 9.

30. See Ehrlich, *Lebanon*, 73 and 75–76. Sultan al-Atrash wasn't the only Arab interested in transferring Arabs from place to place. In Aug. 1941, Elias Sasson, head of the Arab Division of the Jewish Agency Political Department, reported that a certain Muhammad Haj Abdullah, a Muslim notable in southern Lebanon, had approached him with a proposal to sell to the JA the lands of Jabal 'Amal (roughly the area between the Litani River and the Palestine–Lebanon frontier), and transfer its Shi'ite inhabitants to Iraq. Sasson further reported that Lebanon's president, Bishara al-Khoury, thought that Jabal 'Amal's Shi'ites should be ejected and replaced by Maronites who had emigrated to the United States. Another senior Lenbanese politicial, Emile Edde, in 1946 reportedly proposed to Weizmann that Tyre and Sidon be handed over to Yishuv control and their 100,000 Muslim inhabitants be transferred (see Ehrlich, *Lebanon*, 118).

31. David Ben-Gurion, 'Outlines of Zionist Policy', 15 Oct. 1941, CZA Z4-14632. Here, too, Ben-Gurion took care to balance his obviously pro-transfer thinking by professions of liberal egalitarianism regarding the status of the Arab minority in the future Jewish state.

32. For a good summary of the Philby plan, see Porath, *In Search of Arab Unity*, 80–106.

33. 'Short Minutes of Meeting Held on Thursday, January 30th, 1941, at 77 Great Russell Street, London WC.1', unsigned, Weizmann Archive, 2271.

34. 'Meeting: I.M. Maiskii-Ch. Weizmann (London, 3 February 1941)', in *Documents on Israeli-Soviet Relations, 1941–1953*, 3–5.

35. Sharett, *Political Diary*, V, 234–235. During 1941, Shertok seems to have sounded out almost everyone he talked to about the possibilities of transfer (see, for example, his meeting with Egyptian journalist Mahmoud Azmi, Shertok, *Political Diary*, V, 246–247).

36. Entry for 20 Dec. 1940, Weitz, *My Diary*, II, 181. Weitz had been a leading member of the Jewish Agency 'Transfer Committee' of 1937–1938.

37. The passage is quoted in Simons, *International Proposals*, 185–207, which also discusses the resolution's formulation; and, partially, in Schechtman, *Population Transfers*, 118. The resolution also proposed the expansion of Palestine's area, in order to accommodate the expected Jewish influx, 'by agreement with Egypt, Syria or Transjordan'. See also Gorny, *British Labour Movement*, 178–79.

38. Protocol of the JAE Meeting of 7 May 1944, CZA S100-42B.

39. Protocol of the JAE Meeting of 20 June 1944, CZA S100-43B.

40. Duke of Devonshire to Secretary of State [for the Colonies], 27 Jan. 1943, PRO CO 733\443\10. It is worth noting that during the 1950s, Israel attempted to covertly engineer a (compensated) migration of part of its Arab minority to Libya.

41. Glubb, 'A Note on Partition as a Solution of the Palestine Problem', July 1946, PRO WO 216\207.

42. Glubb, 'A Further Note on Partition as a Solution of the Palestine Question', undated, PRO CO-537 1856.

43. Glubb, 'A Note on the Exact Siting of the Frontier in the Event of the Adoption of Partition', undated but with covering note Glubb to Kirkbride, 16 Jan. 1947, PRO FO 816\86.

44. 'Note on conversation with General Nuri Sa'id, the Iraqi Prime Minister and the Iraqi Minister of Foreign Affairs in Baghdad on 5th and 6th December, 1944', illegible signature, 18 Dec. 1944, PRO FO 921\149. Hamdi Pachachi, the Iraqi prime minister, took a different line, according to the report. He said that partition in Palestine would cause 'serious trouble' in Iraq.

45. Kirkbride to MacMichael, 28 Nov. 1944, PRO FO 921\149.

46. Moyne to Foreign Secretary Eden, 1 Mar. 1944, PRO FO 921\148. One could, of course, dismiss statements like Nuri Sa'id's, as a case of Arab leaders merely telling allied British officials what they believed these Britishers wanted to hear. My feeling is that these leaders genuinely believed that partition was likely if not inevitable and that for the settlement to work, there would have to be a transfer as well.

47. Note by Oliver Stanley, Colonial Secretary, and appended letter MacMichael to Stanley, 16 Jan. 1944, PRO FO 921\148.

48. Kirkbride to T. Wikeley, Eastern Department, FO, 29 July 1946, PRO FO 816\85.

49. Kirkbride to FO, 23 Aug. 1946 (No. 1387), and Kirkbride to FO 23 Aug. 1946 (No. 1364), both in PRO FO 816\85. Kirkbride left unclear where Abdullah and Hashim expected the Palestinian Arabs to be transferred to – Transjordan, Iraq, or elsewhere.

50. See Masalha, *Expulsion*, 175; and Finkelstein, 'Myths . . .', 67 et al.

51. See Shapira, *Land*, 285–286; and Teveth, 'The Evolution of "Transfer" in Zionist Thinking', 47–48 and 54–57.

52. Protocol of Israel Cabinet meeting of 12 Sep. 1948, ISA.

3 | The first wave: the Arab exodus, December 1947 – March 1948

The UN General Assembly resolution of 29 November 1947, which endorsed the partition of Palestine into two states, triggered haphazard Arab attacks against Jewish traffic. The first roadside ambushes occurred near Kfar Syrkin the following day, when two buses were attacked and seven Jewish passengers were shot dead.[1] The same day, snipers in Jaffa began firing at passers-by in Tel Aviv. The AHC, which flatly rejected the resolution and any thought of partition, declared a three-day general strike, beginning on 1 December, thus releasing the urban masses for action. On 2 December a mob, unobstructed by British forces, stormed the (Jewish) new commercial centre in Jerusalem, looting, burning shops and attacking Jews. Snipers exchanged fire in Haifa and attacks were launched on the neighbourhoods of Tel Aviv that adjoined Jaffa and its suburbs. Parts of Palestine were gripped by chaos; the escalation towards full-scale civil war had begun. As in 1936, NCs were set up in the Arab towns to direct the struggle and life in each locality, and bands of irregulars re-emerged in the hill country. The AHC reasserted itself as the leader of the national struggle.

Strategically speaking, the period December 1947 – March 1948 was marked by Arab initiatives and attacks and Jewish defensiveness, increasingly punctuated by Jewish reprisals. Arab gunmen attacked Jewish cars and trucks, from late December increasingly organised in British- and Haganah-protected convoys, urban neigbourhoods and rural settlements and cultivators. The attackers never pretended to single out combatants; every Jew was a legitimate target. The hostilities swiftly spread from a handful of urban centres to various parts of the countryside. The Haganah initially retaliated by specifically and accurately targeting the offending terrorist or militia group or village. But this often proved impossible and, in any case, failed to suppress Arab belligerence, and by February–March 1948 the organisation began to dispense with such niceties and to indiscriminately hit Palestinian traffic and villages, but still with relative restraint and in retaliation. At the same time, the IZL and LHI, acting independently, beginning already in early December 1947, reverted to their 1937–1939 strategy of placing bombs in crowded markets and bus stops. The Arabs retaliated by exploding bombs of their own in Jewish population centres in February and March (the bomb attacks against 'The Palestine Post', Ben-Yehuda Street and the National Institutions buildings in Jerusalem). The Haganah also on occasion inadvertently employed terror, as in the attack on Jerusalem's Semiramis Hotel in January 1948, but normally cleaved to a policy of hitting the guilty and, when not, at least limiting the violence in scope and geographically to areas already marked by Arab-initiated violence.

In January 1948, in line with Arab League resolutions in December 1947 supporting indirect intervention, volunteers (some of them Iraqi and Syrian soldiers and ex-soldiers), mostly under the flag of the newly formed Arab Liberation Army (ALA), began to infiltrate the country. That month, irregulars launched their first large-scale attacks on Jewish settlements with the aim of destruction and conquest – against Kfar Szold in the Galilee, and Kfar Uriah and the Etzion Bloc in the centre of the country.

During February and March, as the British stepped up their preparations for withdrawal and increasingly relinquished the reins of government, the battles between the Arab and Jewish militias, especially along the roads, intensified. Given the geographically intermixed populations, the presence in most areas of British forces and the militia-cum-underground nature of the opposing forces, the hostilities during December 1947 – March 1948 combined elements of guerrilla and conventional warfare, and terrorism. In the countryside, the Arabs gained the upper hand by intermittently blocking the roads between the main Jewish population centres and isolated communities, especially west Jerusalem, with its 100,000 Jews, the Etzion Bloc, south of Bethlehem, and the kibbutzim in western Galilee and the northern Negev approaches. The introduction by the Haganah of steel-plated trucks and buses in escorted convoys was more than offset, by late March, by improved Arab tactics and firepower. Moreover, the gradual British military withdrawal and continuing IZL-LHI attacks on British troops resulted in increasing British inability (and reluctance) to protect Jewish traffic. In a series of major successful ambushes in the last days of March, irregulars trapped and destroyed the Khulda, Nabi Daniel and Yehiam convoys, severely depleting the Haganah's makeshift armoured-truck fleet. Ben-Gurion feared that now-besieged west Jerusalem might fall.

These defeats along the roads, the start of the clandestine arrival of arms from Czechoslovakia, the increased efficiency and structural re-organisation of the Haganah, American signals of abandonment of partition, the unfolding British evacuation and the prospect of imminent invasion by the regular Arab armies prompted the Haganah to switch at the start of April to the strategic offensive. By then, the Arab exodus from Palestine was well under way. By the end of March 1948, some 100,000 Arabs, mostly from the urban upper and middle classes of Jaffa, Haifa and Jerusalem, and from villages in Jewish-dominated areas such as the Jordan Valley and the Coastal Plain, had fled to Arab centres to the east, including Nazareth, Nablus, and Bethlehem, or out of the country altogether.

Wealthy urban Arab families began to get the jitters already during the countdown to the partition resolution. Some families, it was reported, wished to leave Nazareth already in the first week of November 1947.[2] The actual flight began on the first day of hostilities. On 30 November Haganah intelligence reported 'the evacuation of Arab inhabitants from border neighbourhoods' in Jerusalem and Jaffa.[3] Jewish agents in Jaffa on 1 December 1947 reported the flight of families from several Jaffa border neighbourhoods, including Manshiya;[4] Arabs were also reported that day leaving the Jewish Quarter of Safad[5] and from Sheikh Muwannis and Jammasin, two villages bordering Tel Aviv, and Arab peddlers and stall-owners were driven out of a number of Jewish markets in the greater Tel Aviv area.[6] Within days, a similar process was under weigh in Jerusalem's Old City, where Arabs living in and around the Jewish Quarter were evacuating their homes (some of those bordering the quarter being taken over by Arab militiamen).[7] By 9 December, the Haganah Intelligence Service (HIS) was reporting that 'Arab refugees were sleeping in the streets [of Jaffa]' and 'wealthy families were leaving the [coastal] cities – heading inland. Rich people are emigrating to Syria, Lebanon and even Cyprus'.[8] Ben-Gurion's Arab affairs advisers informed him two days later that 'Arabs were fleeing from Jaffa [and] from Haifa. Beduins are fleeing from the Sharon [i.e., the Coastal Plain]'. Yehoshua ('Josh') Palmon and Ezra Danin, senior HIS Arab Department (HIS-AD) officers, told Ben-Gurion that Arabs were fleeing their villages to live with relatives elsewhere; ex-villagers resident in towns tended to flee back to their native villages. Palmon surmised that Haifa and Jaffa might be evacuated 'for lack of food'.'

Danin favoured economically strangulating the urban Arabs by destroying their buses, trucks and cars, cutting off the roads into Palestine and blockading Palestine's Arab ports.[9] Ben-Gurion was persuaded that the Arabs of Jaffa and Haifa, 'islands in Jewish territory', were at the Yishuv's mercy and could be starved out.[10]

By 11 January 1948, according to Elias (Eliahu) Sasson, the director of the Arab Division of the Jewish Agency's Political Department, Arab morale was low in all the main towns and their rural hinterlands. Sasson wrote to Transjordan's King Abdullah:

Hunger, high prices, and poverty are rampant in a frightening degree. There is fear and terror everywhere. The flight is painful, from house to house, from neighbourhood to neighbourhood, from city to city, from village to village, and from Palestine to the neighbouring countries. The number of these displaced persons is estimated in the thousands.[11]

YISHUV POLICY, DECEMBER 1947 – MARCH 1948

The Yishuv entered the war without a plan or policy regarding the Arab civilian population in its midst. To be sure, its leaders during the 1930s and 1940s had always taken for granted that the prospective Jewish state would have a substantial Arab minority and had always asserted that the Arab inhabitants would be treated fairly and as equals. But without doubt, come November 1947, they were unhappy with the prospect of having such a large Arab minority (some 400,000 Arabs alongside 500,000 Jews). As Yosef Nahmani, the director of the JNF office in eastern Galilee and a veteran Zionist defence activist, jotted down in his diary:

> In my heart there was joy mixed with sadness. Joy that the peoples [of the world] had at last acknowledged that we were a nation with a state, and sadness that we lost half the country . . . and . . . that we have 400,000 Arabs . . .[12]

But such was the card the international community had dealt the Zionist movement – and the movement would cope as best it could. Some leaders may have harboured thoughts about how, in the future, the Jewish government might engineer the departure of at least some of this unwanted, and potentially destabilising and hostile, minority. But they kept them to themselves. And, in any event, the Arabs allowed the Yishuv no hiatus in which to quietly ponder the problem – only a few hours separated the passage of the partition resolution from the start of Arab hostilities.

But during the first weeks of violence it was unclear to most observers, Jewish, British and Arab, that the two peoples, indeed, were now embarked on a war; most thought they were witnessing a recurrence of fleeting 'disturbances' à la 1920, 1929, or 1936. During December 1947 – January 1948, senior Mapai settlement figures (including Shimon Persky (Peres), Avraham Harzfeld, Levi Shkolnik (Eshkol), and Zalman Lifshitz (Lif), discussed the future Jewish state's settlement policy and produced a blueprint entitled 'Guidelines for a Development Plan for Agricultural Settlement in the Three Years 1949–1951'. It was assumed by the participants that their recommendations would serve as a basis for the state's policies. The discussions took little account of the surrounding violence or that a war, which might radically change everything, was gradually unfolding outside the room. The report they produced assumed that the partition resolution would be implemented as written.

At the meeting of 23 December, Yosef Weitz addressed the demographic problem. 'I have always been a supporter of transfer', he said.

> But today we won't raise the matter even in a hint. Nonetheless, I believe that in the future a certain part of the Arab population will emigrate of its own free will and through the will of the rulers of neighbouring countries, who will have need of them [i.e., of such immigrants]. The Beit Shean [Beisan] area for example, will in the future empty of its beduins, as they wish to join their tribes across the Jordan, and there are others like them in other areas.

Weitz assumed throughout that the Jewish State's borders would remain those laid down in the UN resolution.

Weitz added that the Jewish State 'would not be able to exist with a large Arab minority. It must not amount to more than 12–15 per cent [of the total population]'. But he envisioned the growth of the Jewish percentage – despite the Arabs' 'overly high' rate of natural increase – as attainable within 10–12 years through massive Jewish immigration. In all, both in the discussions and the final report (the 'Guidelines'), the participants assumed that (a) there would be no coerced expropriation by the state of Arab lands, (b) the state would allocate to the Arabs substantial water resources (20 per cent of the total), and (c) that the state's population, at least in its first years, would be 35 per cent Arab. Weitz's thoughts notwithstanding, a transfer of population was neither assumed nor endorsed.[13]

But throughout these first months of the civil war, there was also an underlying desire among Zionist officials and Haganah officers to see as few Arabs as possible remain in the country, and occasional concrete proposals designed to obtain this result were tabled. On 4 January 1948, Danin wrote: 'D[avid] Hacohen [a senior Mapai figure] believes that transfer is the only solution. I, for my part, agree . . .'[14] Tel Aviv District Haganah officer Zvi Aurbach's recommendation of early January 1948 was perhaps atypical in its forthrightness, but not in its intent: 'I propose . . . that Jaffa's water reservoir be put out of commission . . . and by so doing we shall force a large number of Arabs to leave the city.'[15] Similarly atypical, but telling, was Ben-Gurion's description on 7 February of his recent visit to Jerusalem:

> From your entry into Jerusalem through Mahane Yehuda, King George Street and Mea Shearim – there are no strangers [i.e., Arabs]. One hundred per cent Jews. Since Jerusalem's destruction in the days of the Romans – it hasn't been so Jewish as it is now. In many western [Jerusalem] Arab neighbourhoods – one sees not one Arab. I do not assume that this will change . . . [And] what has happened in Jerusalem . . . could well happen in great parts of the country – if we

[the Yishuv] hold fast . . . And if we hold fast, it is very possible that in the coming six or eight or ten months of the war there will take place great changes . . . and not all of them to our detriment. Certainly there will be great changes in the composition of the population of the country.[16]

Running through this passage is both an expectation and a desire.

But official policy assumed the continued existence of a large Arab minority in the state. This line was explicitly embodied in the JAE's draft statement of 12 December 1947:

Many thousands of Arabs will be living in the Jewish State. We want them to feel, right from this moment, that provided they keep the peace, their lives and property will be as secure as that of their Jewish fellow-citizens.[17]

Similarly, during January 1948 the Arab Department of the Histadrut, the powerful, Mapai-dominated trades union federation, distributed to 'the Arab workers' at least two leaflets calling for peace and cooperation among Jewish and Arab proletarians. The second leaflet stated that

the Arab worker, clerk and peasant in the Jewish state will be citizens with equal rights and duties . . . In this state there be no room for discrimination . . . Workers: Do not be led astray and pulled along like sheep after shepherds towards destruction.[18]

The overarching, general assumption, then, during the war's first weeks was that the emergent Jewish State would come to life with a large Arab minority. Certainly, the Yishuv did not enter the war with a master plan of expulsion. But developments over the following months – the most important of which were the unfolding Arab exodus itself and the Arab attacks on Jewish settlements, neighbourhoods and traffic – were to steadily erode this assumption. And the exodus itself was to be triggered not by an activation of some Jewish plan or policy but by constantly changing military and psychological realities on the ground in each sector along the time-bar. These realities were in some measure determined by changes in Haganah strategy and tactics, themselves by and large responses to Arab strategy, tactics and actions.

It is useful, in this respect, to look at the evolution of the Yishuv's military strategy and tactics during the first stage of the civil war. During the war's first days, it was agreed in the Defence Committee (va'ad habitahon), the Yishuv's supreme political supervisory body in defence matters, composed of representatives of the Haganah National Staff (hamate haartzi shel hahaganah) (HNS), the JA, the Histadrut and the National Council (hava'ad haleumi), and the HGS, that:

the outbreaks should not yet be seen as the start of planned, systematic and organised Arab aggression . . . The Arab population does not want a disruption of peace and security and there is still no decision [by the Arab leadership to go to war]. We judged these outbreaks as of a local character . . . [We decided] that we did not want our behaviour to aid the

AHC and the Mufti to suck into this circle [of violence] wider strata of the Arab population.

The Defence Committee and the Haganah commanders decided against 'widening the circle of violence'.[19] This line conformed to the drift of the committee's thinking during the first half of November 1947, before the eruption of hostilities. On 13 November the discussion focused on the Haganah's Plan B (*tochnit bet*), which assumed an attack on the Yishuv by the Palestinian Arabs with some assistance, in manpower and weaponry, from the neighbouring states. Ya'akov Dori, the Haganah's chief of general staff, said that the plan provided for Haganah retaliatory strikes against Arab perpetrators or potential perpetrators and against Arab targets identical to those attacked by Arab terrorists, such as road traffic. Galili, head of the HNS, a quasi-military body sandwiched uncomfortably between the JAE (and its defence 'minister', Ben-Gurion), the Defence Committee, and the HGS, which actually ran the Haganah, said:

> Our interest, if disturbances break out, is that the aggression [i.e., violence] won't spread out over time and over a great deal of space. From this perspective, the most important defensive measure is where we are attacked, there to retaliate; that will be the effective method of stamping out the fire.

Galili, in effect the Yishuv's deputy defence minister, added that if effective retaliation could not be carried out at the time and place of the original Arab attack, then the Haganah must have ready plans of attack against

> those . . . not . . . directly guilty . . . places . . . persons . . . villages . . . tending to [anti-Yishuv violence] . . . [But] the Haganah is not built for aggression, it does not wish to enslave, it values human life, it wants to hit only those who are guilty, it does not want to ignite, but to douse out flames . . . Occasionally, [moral values] are a burden on the Haganah's operations, and [i.e., but] we must take them into account.[20]

During the first week of hostilities, the committee continued to cleave to a policy of 'not spreading the conflagration' and against indiscriminate reprisal killings. As Ben-Gurion put it, 'we shall retaliate by hitting their vehicles, not passengers . . . If their property is damaged, perhaps they will be deterred'. Ben-Gurion, like Hapoel Hamizrahi Party's Moshe Shapira, was concerned lest over-reaction by the Haganah would push the Arab masses, until then uninvolved, to support Husseini and his gunmen. Yosef Ya'akobson, a citrus grove-owner and senior Tel Aviv Haganah figure, was concerned about Haganah destruction of groves, as proposed by Ben-Gurion, lest this lead to Arab retaliation in kind.

If Ben-Gurion, Galili and Shapira represented a moderate middle way, a crystallising harder line was already audible. Shkolnik (Eshkol) argued that perhaps on 30 November and 1–2 December it had been possible to hope that what the Yishuv faced was a brief, transitory eruption; but this was no longer tenable. 'From now on, if something happens, we [must] respond with full force, an eye for an eye, [if not] for the moment two eyes for one.' Eliahu Elyashar, a Sephardi notable from Jerusalem, argued that 'the Arabs don't want disturbances, they want quiet, but the Arab – his nature is like a primitive man's, if you make concessions, he thinks you are weak . . .' Events in Jerusalem had only whetted Arab appetites. Yosef Sapir, of Ha'ihud Haezrahi Party, declared: 'After several days [of Arab violence] have passed without response, we must not continue with this policy of restraint.'[21] But the committee adopted Ben-Gurion's line – to retaliate while 'avoiding harming people'.[22]

The Haganah's purely defensive, almost vegetarian, strategy was soon overtaken by events – and partially changed during the second week of December. As Arab attacks grew more numerous and spread to new areas, as Jewish casualties mounted, and as the feeling grew that the Husseinis were gaining control of the Arab masses despite – and perhaps because of – Haganah restraint, public pressure mounted for a switch to a more 'activist' strategy. There was also pressure from the Revisionist right, which was not represented in the JA, Defence Committee or Haganah command: The IZL's radio station, 'The Voice of Fighting Zion', on 7 December called on the Haganah to abandon defence and move over to the offence, both against the Arabs and the 'Nazo-British enslaver'.[23] The first expression of the hardening Haganah strategy was the HGS\Operations order of 9 December to the Alexandroni Brigade, responsible for the Coastal Plain from just south of Haifa to just north of Tel Aviv. The order called for 'harassing' and 'paralysing' Arab traffic on the 'Qalqilya-Ras al 'Ein-al-Tira-Wilhelma-Yahudiya' road. The units were ordered to hit vehicles or both passengers and vehicles.[24] Alexandroni sent out at least one unit, commanded by one 'Arik' (probably the young Ariel Sharon), which duly ambushed two vehicles. 'Arik' reported hitting them with Molotov Cocktails and the 'wounded Arabs were [burned] inside'; six appear to have died. The ambushers, he explained, recalled previous Arab attacks on Jewish convoys and were filled with 'hatred'.[25]

During the following months, HGS\Operations carefully modulated the brigades' operations against Arab transportation. Occasionally, it ordered strikes on specific days against traffic on specific roads;[26] sometimes, when the Jewish death toll from Arab ambushes mounted, it instructed the brigades to automatically retaliate along specific roads without further instructions;[27] occasionally, the order went out to attack all Arab traffic along all roads. These orders, precipitated by 'the increase in attacks on our transport in different parts of the country', were designed to 'quiet down the enemy's activities'. But, down to the end of March, they were invariably superseded, within a day or two, by orders to halt or suspend attack.[28]

Galili signalled the limited gear-change at the meeting of the HNS on 10 December 1947: 'The time has come for active defence [*haganah pe'ila*], reprisals and punishment.'[29] The meeting of the Defence Committee the following day was decisive. Galili said that the 'assumption that [the flames] would either die down or be extinguished' had not materialised. The Mufti's hold on the Arab public had grown stronger and the Opposition was paralysed. 'The fact that the events are getting worse necessitates a certain change in our . . . policy . . . [but] not an essential change . . .' Arab losses had not deterred further attacks and they were interpreting the lack of Haganah reprisals as a sign of weakness. Moreover, the world might begin to think that 'the Jews' strength is insufficient [to hold on] and inside the Yishuv [too] they will cease to believe that we can weather the storm'. People would come to doubt the Haganah's strength and perhaps shift their support to the more militant Revisionists. Galili proposed that the Haganah continue to defend itself 'in the classical way' but also retaliate against Arab targets, specifically attacking '[Arab] transportation . . . hitting the property of the responsible inciters [and] of the attackers . . .'.

Ben-Gurion pointed out that the disturbances were so far limited to the three big towns, Jaffa, Haifa and Jerusalem, and the northern Negev. The Arab rural communities were not engaged, and the Yishuv had to take care not to provoke them. He was worried lest Haganah retaliatory strikes lead to Yishuv–British clashes ('let us not rush into war with the English army'). Sapir said that 'a week ago we ruled [that in our reprisals we would] not hit people. I think we will have to change that'. Berl Repetor, of the militant socialist Ahdut Ha'avodah Party, called for more 'active' reprisals, while taking account of 'political-moral considerations'. Ya'akov Riftin, of the Marxist Hashomer Hatza'ir Party, stressed the moral aspect: 'We must maintain moral restraints on our responses. Our responses must be basically different from the Arabs' murders, morality must retain sovereignty [over our actions].'[30] The participants accepted Galili's recommendation to adopt this more 'active' defensive strategy.

As Jewish losses mounted, the policy-makers' and, in some localities, local Haganah commanders' hearts grew steadily harder. Two senior military advisers to Ben-Gurion, Yohanan Retner and Fritz Eisenstadt (Shalom Eshet), on 19 December argued that, with regard to 'each [Arab] attack[,] [we should] be prepared to reply with a decisive blow, destruction of the place or chasing out the inhabitants and taking their place'.[31] At the meeting of the Defence Committee the day before, specific offending Arab villages were named. Eliahu Elyashar urged the 'uprooting' of Abu Kabir, outside Jaffa, 'as a lesson to the rural communities'; and Binyamin Mintz, the leader of the orthodox Po'alei Agudat Yisrael Party, said with respect to a certain village in the Negev: 'If the possibility arises of evicting all its inhabitants and destroying it, this must be done.' (But Sapir, the mayor of Petah Tikva and a major orange-grove owner, argued against destroying whole villages, 'even small [ones] . . . This recalls Lidice – [and] here is food for thought.') Riftin also called for 'hardening the reprisals policy'. But the consensus, as expressed by Galili, fell short of the Retner-Eshet-Elyashar line. Galili summed it up by saying that 'it was not enough to hit huts, but people [too must be hit]. The intention is . . . that they should pay not only with property but with lives.' Abu Kabir, he said, should be 'severely punished' and, in general, the Haganah should act 'more drastically' in the course of defending a site or convoy (whereas after the fact, reprisals had to be more measured and softer). But he qualified this by saying: 'My intention is not, nor am I proposing, that from now on, wherever and in every case, Arab blood shall be shed freely.'[32]

From time to time thereafter, proposals were tabled to level this or that Arab village or string of villages – but they were almost always shelved. In late January 1948, the Haganah's Jerusalem District HQ apparently produced a document entitled 'Lines of Planning for Area Campaigns for the Month of February 1948'. It proposed a series of steps to assure security along the Jerusalem–Tel Aviv road and in Jerusalem itself. The measures included disrupting Arab traffic, 'destruction of individual objects (of economic value) . . . The destruction of villages or objects dominating our settlements or threatening our lines of transportation.' Among the proposed operations were:

the destruction of the small southern bloc [of houses?] of 'Islin . . . the destruction of the southern bloc of Beit Nattif . . . [a] destruction operation against Saris . . . Destruction operation against the villages of (a) 'Anata, (b) Shu'fat . . . the destruction of al-Jab'a' and, in the event of a British pullout, the 'conquest of al-Qastal' and various Arab neighbourhoods of Jerusalem (Qatamon, Sheikh Jarrah, Greek Colony, German Colony, etc.).[33] These proposals were not acted upon before April 1948 – but they were seeds that bloomed during the second stage of the civil war.

Perhaps the first operational result of the Defence Committee meeting of 18 December 1947 was the start of intensive but non-violent Haganah patrolling around and inside Arab villages in various parts of the country and the distribution of printed warning leaflets in Arabic. Both aimed to deter the villagers from joining the war. Initially, the circulars were distributed by the patrols during the third and fourth weeks of December in Jerusalem area villages and among northern Negev beduin. 'Ancient custom compels repayment and punishment [for crimes]. We too shall act according to this custom', read the leaflets to the beduin. The leaflets apparently made 'a great impression'[34] and on 4 January 1948, Yadin ordered that similar leaflets be distributed in other areas.[35]

The patrolling, at least in the Jerusalem area, also had beneficial results, according to the Haganah Etzioni Brigade's intelligence officer:

The political conflicts between the different Arab forces in the country, on the one hand, and the fear that our reconnaissance patrols have spread in a number of villages on the other, have brought and are bringing certain villages to make contact with neighbouring Jewish settlements and propose holding talks to reach peace agreements. There are villages that have already made peace agreements and there are villages with which talks are ongoing . . . Every intelligence officer or other officer directing patrols must take . . . into consideration [the opinion of local Jewish headmen] before deciding on sending out patrols. Regarding villages that have already signed peace agreements . . . – [patrols] should not be carried out.

The order detailed the villages with which agreements had already been reached or were being negotiated (al Qastal, Suba, Qatanna, Sur Bahir, al Maliha, and 'Ein Karim).[36]

On 18 December, the Haganah summed up the limited change of strategy thus:

During the first week of disturbances we implemented an aggressive defence at the moment and place of [Arab] attack and we refrained from sharp reprisals which would have aided the inciters. We called upon the Arabs to maintain peace . . . We had to examine whether the outbreak was local, incidental, and ephemeral . . . [But] the spread of the disturbances and terrorism has forced us to add to the aggressive defence . . . attacks on the centres of Arab violence. That's the stage we are in now. The reprisals in Karatiya, Balad al Sheikh, Wadi Rushmiya, Ramle and the Jerusalem-Hebron road must be seen in this light.[37]

The British quickly – indeed, somewhat prematurely – noted the Haganah's change of strategy, and claimed that the 'spontaneous and unorganised' Arab rioting might well have subsided had the Jews not resorted to retaliation with firearms. 'The Haganah's policy was initially of defence and restraint, which quickly gave place to counter-operations', wrote High Commissioner Alan Cunningham. He believed that the AHC was not initially interested in 'serious outbreaks' but that the Jewish response had forced the AHC to organise and raise the level of violence. Cunningham deemed some of the Jewish reprisals – such as the attack on an Arab bus in Haifa on 12 December 1947 – 'an offence to civilisation'. Cunningham did not differentiate between Haganah operations and those of the IZL and LHI.[38]

The gradual limited shift in strategy during December 1947 in practice meant a limited implementation of 'Plan May' (Tochnit Mai or Tochnit Gimel), which, produced in May 1946, was the Haganah master plan for the defence of the Yishuv in the event of the outbreak of new troubles similar to those of 1936–1939. The plan included provision, in extremis, for 'destroying the Arab transport' in Palestine, and blowing up houses used by Arab terrorists and expelling their inhabitants.[39]

The shift of the second week of December involved mounting retaliatory raids against militia concentrations and villages from which they had set out for attacks on settlements and traffic, with destruction of houses and killing of gunmen and unarmed or disarmed adult males; specific, limited but indiscriminate attacks on Arab transport in response to indiscriminate Arab attacks on Jewish transport; and active patrolling near and in Arab villages with the aim of deterrence. Villagers and townspeople who expressed a desire for peace were not to be harmed. There is no trace of an expulsive or transfer policy. In most of the operations, the troops were specifically ordered to avoid causing casualties among women, children and the old, and in most operations the troops tried to cleave to the guideline. A widely disseminated circular by the Haganah's northern brigade, 'Levanoni' (later split into the Carmeli and Golani brigades), stated:

> We must avoid as far as possible killing plain civilians [*stam ezrahim*] and to make an effort as far as possible to always hit the criminals themselves, the bearer of arms, those who carry out the attacks . . . We do not want to spread the disturbances and to unite the Arab public . . . around the Mufti and his gangs. Any indiscriminate massacre of Arab civilians causes the consolidation of the Arab masses around the inciters.[40]

This, in effect, was Yishuv–Haganah policy down to the end of March 1948.

Another element of the revised defensive strategy was planning for the assassination of Palestinian political and militia leaders, code-named 'Operation Zarzir'. In early January, the Haganah command ordered all units to target and kill specific Husseini-affiliated leaders. Galili instructed the units, without need for further approval, to assassinate, among others, Rafiq Tamimi, Hassan Salame, Emil Ghawri, Issa Bandak, 'Abd al Qadir al Husseini, Kamal Erikat, Sabri Abadin, Sheikh Muhamad Nimr al Khatib, Hassan Shibalak, and Abdullah Abu Sita. The units were ordered to make it appear, if possible, as the work of fellow Arabs and were forbidden to carry out the assassinations in places of worship or hospitals.[41] But, in fact, not much energy was invested in 'Zarzir' and only one assassination attempt was ever carried out – Sheikh Nimr al Khatib, a senior Haifa Husseini figure, was ambushed and seriously injured by a Palmah squad outside Haifa in January 1948.

The lobbying by various figures to adopt the destruction of villages, which necessarily entailed the eviction of their inhabitants, as part of the routine reprisals policy, was rejected by Ben-Gurion and the HGS. But two villages were levelled during the period November 1947 – March 1948; unusual circumstances accounted for both. The first instance followed a particularly savage Arab attack: on 9 January militiamen from the small village of 'Arab Suqrir ('Arab Abu Suwayrih) murdered

11 Haganah scouts on patrol outside Gan-Yavne. The local HIS man recommended: 'The village should be destroyed completely and some males from the same village should be murdered.'[42] The recommendation was endorsed by the director of the HIS-AD, Ziama Divon: 'The Arabs in the area "expect" a reprisal . . . A lack of response on our part will be interpreted as a sign of weakness.'[43] On 20 January, the appropriate operational order was issued: '. . . Destroy the well . . . destroy the village completely, kill all the adult males, and destroy the reinforcements that arrive.'[44] But as it turned out, the operation, in the early hours of 25 January, was bloodless. The Arabs had evacuated their womenfolk and children a few days before and the 30-odd men who had stayed behind to guard the village fled after getting wind of the approach of the raiders. The company-sized Haganah force 'found the village empty' and proceeded to destroy the houses, two trucks and the nearby well ('the village, apart from a few relics, no longer exists').[45] The operation apparently left a deep impression: 'The memory of "the night of the thunder",' wrote an HIS officer, 'will stay in the memories of the surrounding [Arab] villages a long time'. Moreover, the inhabitants of 'Arab Suqrir were angry that 'no village dared to come to their help and they asked how can the Arabs fight this way'.[46] (Some of the villagers apparently returned to the site soon after, and finally left at the end of March.[47])

In February, Haganah troops destroyed the village of Qisarya (Caesarea) and expelled its inhabitants (see below).

The main Haganah response to Arab attacks, down to the end of March 1948, remained the retaliatory strike, either against traffic or against specific villages. The reprisal policy was thoroughly aired in a protracted two-day meeting between Ben-Gurion and his military and Arab affairs advisers on 1–2 January 1948. The discussion was triggered, in some measure, by a series of unauthorised or ill-conceived Haganah attacks in which innocent civilians were killed. The guiding assumptions were to avoid extending the conflagration to as yet untouched areas, to try to hit the 'guilty', and retaliation as close as possible to the time, place and nature of the original provocation.[48] The resultant definition and refinement of Haganah policy was embodied in a two-page memorandum by Yadin sent to all units, entitled 'Instructions for Planning Initiated Operations', dated 18 January 1948. The targets for reprisals were to be selected from those enumerated in '*Tochnit May 1946*', but subject to two qualifications, namely (a) 'not to spread the disturbances . . . to areas so far unaffected . . .', and (b) there should be 'an effort to hit the guilty, while acknowledging the impossibility of [precise] individual targeting; to distinguish between [friendly and unfriendly] Arab villages'. The order outlined the methods of operation – sabotage, ambushes, etc. – and the types of objects to be hit: blowing up public and residential houses, 'identifying and killing gang leaders. Harassing a

settlement by firing at it and mining. Organising ambushes to hit transport to and from the settlement. Punitive operation against a village in
order to hit the adult male combatants.' All attacks required HGS approval. The memorandum gave special attention to attacking economic
objectives, including 'flour mills, storehouses, water pumps, wells and
waterworks, workshops . . .', and to attacks on Arab transportation in
retaliation for attacks on Jewish vehicles. 'On no account should holy
places, hospitals and schools be hit.' The brigade and city commanders were ordered to prepare plans and submit a list of objectives to the
HGS.[49]

Another result of the 1–2 January gathering was the appointment, at
Ben-Gurion's suggestion, of 'Arab affairs advisers' to each Haganah district, battalion and brigade headquarters.[50] The appointments were to
bear on the Haganah's – and the Yishuv's – policy towards the Arab population. On 20 January, Galili issued detailed instructions. The brigade
and urban district commanders were ordered to 'consult the adviser
in the selection of targets . . . and the method of [attack]'. When asking for the general staff's approval of a particular operation, the district
or brigade commander had to append the adviser's written opinion.[51]
In his 'Instructions for Planning Initiated Operations' of 18 January,
Yadin had ordered the brigade and city OCs to consult their Arab affair advisers before embarking on any operations not requiring further
HGS approval.[52] In the course of March, the advisers were also made
responsible for advising the regional Haganah commanders on how
to deal with Arab communities in their areas.[53] Among the advisers
appointed were Emmanuel ('Mano') Friedman (eastern Galilee), Yosef
Fein (Jordan Valley), Elisha Sulz (Beit Shean Valley), Tuvia Arazi (Haifa),
Amnon Yanai (Carmeli Brigade – Western Galilee), Shimshon Mashbetz
(Alexandroni Brigade – Hefer Valley), Giora Zeid (Golani Brigade) and
Shmuel Zagorsky (Golani Brigade).

But if there was a shift to more forceful retaliatory responses in many
areas, Haganah national strategy remained – and was to remain until
the end of March 1948 – one which would restrict as far as possible
the scope of the conflagration and to avoid reprisals in areas free of
hostilities. Initially, the motive was to avoid an all-out war between the
Jewish and Arab populations. Deliberately provoking violence in hitherto
quiet areas could bring the Yishuv into conflict with the British – the
last thing Ben Gurion wanted as he contemplated the countdown to
statehood – and probably eventual war with the Arab states as well.
Moreover, the Haganah, in February–March 1948, felt stretched enough
on the ground without adding new battlegrounds. Palmon on 1 January
1948 had put it this way: 'Do we want the Arab people to be united
against us, or do we want to benefit from . . . their not being united? Do
we want to force all the . . . Arabs to act against us, or do we want to
give them the opportunity not to act against us?' Allon agreed. 'There

are still untroubled places in the country. There is no need to hit an area which has been quiet for a long time . . . we must concentrate on areas where in effect we are at war.'

At the 1–2 January meeting, the heads of the Arab Division of the JA's Political Department had severely criticised the Haganah attacks in December on Romema and Silwan in Jerusalem, in the Negev, near Kfar Yavetz, and at Khisas, in the Galilee Panhandle. The criticisms had focused on Khisas, where, on the night of 18–19 December, Palmah troops had blown up a house, killing half a dozen women and children. Another handful of Arabs were killed in a simultaneous raid on a nearby mansion. Danin and Gad Machnes, a fellow Arab affairs expert, had charged that the Khisas attack had unnecessarily spread the fighting to a hitherto quiet area. They had hoped that Jewish restraint would enable the Arab Opposition leaders to frustrate Husseini-inspired Arab militancy. Ben-Gurion had cabled Shertok that the attack had been unauthorised and that the Haganah had apologised for the death of the civilians[54]; Danin blamed the local Haganah commander's desire to keep up his young fighters' morale.[55]

Yosef Sapir, in the Defence Committee, called for the 'severe punishment' of the officer responsible. Ben-Gurion responded that he agreed in principle, but thought that 'judicial' and 'disciplinary' matters were best left in the hands of the Haganah itself.[56] The attack was a reprisal for the shooting of a man ('Zalman') from Kibbutz Ma'ayan Baruch, itself a vendetta following the shooting of an Arab a few days before. Local Jewish leaders and Arab affairs experts had tried to prevent the attack on Khisas – but had been overridden by Yigal Allon. The HGS in Tel Aviv had had no advance knowledge of the operation.[57] The operational order had called for 'hitting adult males [or 'the adult males' – *pgi'ah be'gvarim'* or *'bagvarim*]' in Khisas and 'killing adult [or the adult] males in the palace of the Emir Faur', where the man responsible for Zalman's shooting was said to be hiding. 'The operation commander did not determine the number of those killed in the rooms [in Khisas]. There was indiscriminate fire. The house [in Khisas] was blown up with its occupants. A neighbouring house was partly destroyed.' In the attack on the mansion ('palace'), the raiders refrained from shooting women they came across. Following the raid, a large part of Khisas's population left their homes, neighbouring villages asked irregular bands to leave, and Khisas's inhabitants, according to Dayan, appealed to the Haganah to 'make peace'.[58] The implication was that, however unpleasant, the use of force, even if occasionally excessive, was in the long run fruitful. Danin, annoyed, wrote to Sasson: 'The army [i.e., the Haganah] does what it pleases despite our advice.'[59] Be that as it may, the raid apparently triggered some flight from surrounding localities: An Arab district officer in Safad, 'Yezdi', was reported on 19 December to have sent his mother and sister to Beirut to be out of harm's way.[60]

No one was disciplined or tried for Khisas. But the criticism had effect. Orders were immediately issued by the HGS to the brigades to refrain from unauthorised operations. On 19 December, for example, Alexandroni HQ instructed its units 'to carry out severe disciplinary measures regarding any violation [of orders] concerning reprisals. It must be emphasised that our aim is defence and not worsening the relations with that part of the Arab community that wants peace'.[61]

As to the Negev, Ben-Gurion, at the 8 January meeting of the Mapai Central Committee said that the Haganah had been largely responsible for 'spreading the fire' there; a Palmah unit had 'mistakenly' entered an Arab village, Shu'ut, provoking Arab fear and attack.[62]

Alongside such unauthorised or excessive operations, the Jewish response to Arab attacks also included some atrocities. The IZL and LHI showed little compunction in killing Arabs indiscriminately; for them, 'the Arab', any Arab, was the enemy and a legitimate target (as all Jews were in the eyes of most Arab militiamen). They never specifically targeted women and children, but they knowingly planted bombs in bus stops with the aim of killing non-combatants, including women and children. And the IZL and LHI also committed more discriminating atrocities. According to the Haganah, a squad of IZL or LHI gunmen on 10 February 1948 stopped an Arab truck carrying workers near Petah Tikva, took off the passengers, and killed eight and wounded 11 (apparently after robbing them).[63] Another ten Arabs, one of them a woman, were reportedly murdered ('probably') by IZL gunmen, in early February in a grove, where they apparently worked, near Abu al Fadl ('Arab al Satariyya), west of Ramle.[64]

The problem of killing non-combatants continuously exercised the Haganah commanders. Occasionally, indeed, raids were aborted out of fear that atrocities might result (as when a unit that set out to blow up buildings in Kafr 'Aqeb, north of Jerusalem, decided to withdraw when it heard 'the voices and screams of children' emanating from a house they were about to destroy[65]). But more common were cases of excessive behaviour. On 12 January 1948, militiamen from Kibbutz Ramat Hakovesh, contrary to explicit Haganah orders, shot at two Arab women, perhaps cultivating a field, nearby; at least one was injured and may have died. The matter was the subject of an internal investigation. No one appears to have been punished.[66] At the end of February, Haganah guards murdered an Arab peasant and his wife near Kfar Uriah, 'without any provocation', according to HIS.[67] On 24 January, four Palmahniks boarded a taxi in Tiberias and murdered the Arab driver (who may have been connected to irregulars).[68] Ben-Gurion was probably referring to such incidents when he criticised 'condemnable acts against Arabs' at a meeting of the Defence Committee in early February.[69]

The murder of the taxi-driver was subsequently investigated.[70] By early February, a senior Haganah officer recommended that the organisation set up 'an authorised' institution which could pass judgement in 'matters of life and death',[71] and in mid-February Galili ruled that Haganah units were forbidden to murder Arabs in order to gain possession of vehicles or other assets – even if these were 'destined for Knesset [i.e., Haganah] use'.[72]

However, these incidents were the exception. Haganah operations were usually authorised and effectively controlled by the general staff. Moreover, notwithstanding the British view of Haganah operations, the HGS, through December 1947 – March 1948, attempted to keep its units' operations as 'clean' as possible. While coming to accept the general premise that retaliatory strikes against traffic and villages would inevitably involve the death and injury of innocent people, orders were repeatedly sent out to all Haganah units to avoid killing women, children and old people. In its specific orders for each operation, the HGS almost always included instructions not to harm non-combatants, as, for example, in the attack on the village of Salama, outside Jaffa, in early January 1948, when Galili specifically forbade the use of mortars because they might cause casualties among non-combatants.[73]

On 8 January, Ben-Gurion said that so far, the Arab countryside, despite efforts to incite it, had remained largely quiescent. It was in the Yishuv's interest that the countryside remain quiet, and this depended in large measure on the Yishuv's own actions. 'We [must avoid] mistakes which would make it easier for the Mufti' to stir up the villages, he said.[74] Regarding the countryside, the Haganah's policy throughout February and March was 'not to extend the fire to areas where we have not yet been attacked' while at the same time vigorously attacking known bases of attacks on Jews and, in various areas, Arab traffic.[75] This policy also applied to the Negev. The JNF's Yosef Weitz, the chairman of the Negev Committee (the Yishuv's regional supervisory body), put it this way: 'As to the Arabs, a policy has been determined: We extend our hand to peace. Every beduin who wants peace, will be satisfied. But if anyone dares to act contrariwise – his end will be bitter.'[76] A few weeks earlier, on 12 February, the commander of the Negev Brigade, Nahum Sarig, instructed his officers:

(A) Our job is to appear before the Arabs as a ruling force which functions forcefully but with justice and fairness. (B) We must encourage the Arabs to carry on life as usual. (C) We must avoid harm to women and children. (D) We must avoid harm to friendly Arabs.

In praxis, this meant allowing Arabs to graze flocks in their own fields or public land but to prevent them from grazing on 'our fields' by hitting 'the flock with fire' while avoiding firing at the shepherd or confiscating the herd. Searches in Arab settlements should be conducted 'politely but firmly . . . If the search is a result of an attempt to hit our forces, you

are permitted to execute any man found in possession of a weapon.'
Searches of Arab cultivators in fields near Jewish settlements should
be conducted 'with emphatic politeness, preferably accompanied by an
explanation and encouragement to the Arab to continue his work . . .'.
Searches of Arab cars were also to be conducted 'politely but firmly'.
Only arms, military uniforms and identification cards, and stolen property were to be confiscated. If the arms were for self-defence (a single
pistol or grenade), they were to be confiscated and the driver or pas-
senger allowed on his way; if 'aggressive' (mines, machineguns, etc.),
the owner was to be detained for HIS questioning. Sums of money in
excess of PL100 were to be confiscated. Vehicles suspected of belonging to irregulars were to be confiscated or destroyed. If Arabs resisted
the search, force was to be use, including 'intimidation, blows and even
execution'.[77]

Though the Negev Brigade was the largest and strongest force in
the northern Negev, the area – given the brigade's shortage of vehicles
(especially tracked vehicles), the British military presence, the area's
size and the absence of roads, Arab hostility, and the dispersal of the
population, much of it beduin – was not under effective Zionist control.
But the Arab villagers and beduin tribes living in the largely Jewish-
populated Coastal Plain and, to a lesser degree, in the Jezreel and
Jordan valleys were during the first months of the civil war under effective
Yishuv control. For many of them, despite nearby hostilities and daily
apprehension, life during these months went on much as usual. A series
of documents from January 1948 from two of Haganah sub-districts
afford an insight into the nature of local Arab–Jewish relations at this
time.

A number of Arabs, who served as guards in the lower coastal plain,
continued to live and work in Jewish-owned groves (though 'some had
left the place out of fear'). One sub-district OC, 'Ephraim', commented:
'In my opinion there is no reason to fear leaving them for now in their
places of work.' They could belie what Husseini-supporting inciters were
saying; Arabs can live and work among Jews without coming to harm.
'If they are expelled from their work places, then most likely they will join
gangs because of lack of income and out of vengefulness because of
having been dismissed.' Moreover, he believed, Arab day-labourers from
neighbouring villages who were working in Jewish-owned farms should
be allowed to continue; this partly explained 'the relative quiet in the
area's villages'. (Local HIS officers concurred; Arabs should be allowed
to continue working in Jewish-owned groves.) But he cautioned against
Arabs being allowed freedom of movement in 'the built-up area and
near our settlements, especially at night', and recommended increased
Jewish patrols while avoiding 'careless provocative acts': 'The armed
patrols must initiate contact and converse with [the Arabs] as little as
possible when there is no one on the patrol who knows [Arabic]. If there

is someone who knows Arabic, the approach should be friendly.' But should local villagers initiate attacks, then all contact with Arabs would have to cease, the sub-district CO added.[78]

Until mid-January, apparently, Arab workers were still dorming in Jewish settlements. On 15 January, a Haganah commander issued a prohibition against Arabs cow-hands sleeping in Jewish settlements.[79] But Arab work in the Jewish areas continued, by order of Galili (who was a member of Kibbutz Na'an, in the same sub-district); such work was to be stopped in specific areas at specific times only if there was a crucial security need.[80] 'Ephraim' was annoyed by a report that in Ramatayim, a Jewish town in his sub-district, the local Haganah commander had 'forbidden Arabs of 'Arab Abu Kishk to buy in the settlement's shops and had destroyed Arab produce and had forbidden them from bringing it into town'. 'Ephraim' instructed that such actions should not be taken without approval from on high unless there was an immediate security need.[81]

Another sub-district OC, in the Coastal Plain, at the beginning of January ordered his deputies not to 'carry out a general stoppage of Arab work' in their areas 'until an order to the contrary was given'.[82] Indeed, in one or two areas, including the Samaria sub-district, Arab work in Jewish fields, vineyards and groves continued into April 1948. Only at the end of that month, 'Naftali' ordered a stoppage of Arab labour in Zikhron Ya'akov, Givat 'Ada and Bat-Shlomo – and immediately triggered protests that, in the absence of available Jewish laborers, the crops would suffer. The Arabs were not a security risk for now and if the situation changed, they would stop coming to work of their own volition, he argued.[83]

But different policies were in place in different areas; a lot depended on the specific security situation in each area and on the commanders involved. In Jerusalem, for example, orders were issued in early January forbidding the sale of goods by Jews to Arabs and shopkeepers were threatened with punishment.[84] Indeed, already in mid-December 1947, Arabs working in Jewish enterprises were warned by Haganah men – on order of the district intelligence officer – that if they continued, their lives would be in danger.[85]

By March, there were two principal, inter-related questions: how to deal with the remaining Arab communities in the Jewish areas and what to do with the property of those who had left.[86] Regarding property, the HGS and HNS were unhappy with ad hoc local arrangements. The property was falling victim to pillage and vandalisation by Jewish (and Arab) neighbours and military units. Some local Haganah commanders had appointed 'inspectors' of Arab property.[87] But a streamlined, national approach was called for. During the last week of March, the general staff set up a national 'Committee for Arab Property', comprised of Gad Machnes, an orange-grove owner, Ezra Danin, the veteran HIS hand from Hadera, and Yitzhak Gwirtz, a member of Kibbutz Shfayim. To-gether with David Horowitz, an assistant to JA Treasurer Eliezer Kaplan, it was to be responsible for the abandoned property.[88]

The murder by an Alexandroni Brigade roadblock of six Arabs on 1 or 2 March seems to have triggered a fresh look at the problematic issue of the remaining Arab communities.[89] A variety of local pressures, by settlements and military units, also came to bear. Just before 14 March, two horses were stolen from Shfayim and apparently taken to Tulkarm. Suspicion fell on Arabs still working in or near the settlement. An Arab collaborator named 'Ali Kassem chided the settlers for employing un-trustworthy Arabs and asked why they didn't kick them out. Immedi-ately afterward, shots were fired at houses in Shfayim and neighbouring Shavei-Zion and Rishpon from a nearby orange grove where about 150 Arabs were said to be living. There was need for 'clear orders about the status of the Arabs in the area', complained a kibbutz member.[90] In late March, the HIS issued an order completely forbidding the movement of Arabs inside Jewish settlements without special permission.[91] More sig-nificantly, Alexandroni officers complained that the quarantine imposed on the village of Sheikh Muwannis was being evaded at night by Arabs skirting Haganah patrols and roadblocks. Alexandroni's OC replied that the matter was being dealt with by the HGS.[92]

At the beginning of March, Galili ordered the Arab affairs experts to hammer out clear guidelines.[93] On the basis of their recommendations he issued the following blanket order, on 24 March, to all brigade OCs:

> Subject: The Arabs Living in the Enclaves.
>
> The behaviour of the Knesset [i.e., Haganah] toward the Arabs living in the area earmarked for the Jewish state or in continuous Jewish areas, in which the Arabs live in enclaves, stems from the Arab policy of the Zionist movement which is: Recognition of the full rights, needs and freedom of the Arabs in the Hebrew state without discrimination, and a striving for coexistence with freedom and respect.
>
> From this policy one may deviate in the course of battle only if security conditions and requirements necessitate this.
>
> The high command [i.e., the HGS and HNS] has appointed a committee which is responsible for determining in each place, together with the brigade OC or his representative, the rules of behaviour (matters of sup-plies, transportation, identity documents, etc.) with the Arab settlements in the continuous Jewish area, with the intention that security needs be stringently preserved as well as the wellbeing and needs of the Arabs living in the Jewish sector.

The members of the committee, henceforth known as 'the Committee for Matters Concerning the Arabs in the Enclaves', were Dayan, Machnes and Palmon, of HIS; Danin was added two days later.[94] These guidelines were immediately reflected in a complaint by the Alexandroni Brigade about a Palmah ambush in their area of jurisdiction. The ambush, in which three or four Arabs were killed, resulted in the evacuation of the inhabitants of Wadi Hawarith, a semi-sedentary beduin tribe south of Hadera. Alexandroni wrote:

> This morning a Palmah squad carried out an action near Kfar Hayim contrary to the general lines that we follow as a basis for our relations with the Arabs . . . This action caused great disaffection [hitmarmerut] among the Arabs in the area who were promised by [Haganah] spokesmen proper peaceful relations . . . On previous similar occasions we prevented the dissidents [i.e., the IZL and LHI] from carrying out actions against the Arabs with whom we are maintaining fair neighbourly relations . . . It is saddening that it was the Palmah that has disrupted us in [carrying out] this policy.[95]

The Haganah's difficulty during December 1947 – March 1948 was that while it sought to maintain quiet wherever possible, its reprisals, sometimes misdirected, sometimes excessive, tended to suck into the maelstrom more and more Arabs. Only strong, massive, retaliatory action, it was felt, would overawe and pacify the Arabs. But the reprisals often hit the innocent along with the guilty, bred anger and vengefulness and made additional Arab communities amenable to the Husseinis' militant-nationalist appeals, despite great initial reluctance to enter the fray.[96]

By and large, however, until the end of March, the Haganah's operations conformed to the general principle of restricting the conflagration, at least geographically, as much as possible. At the same time, Haganah reprisals tended to increase in ferocity as the months passed, as its units operated in increasingly larger formations and more efficiently, as Jewish casualties increased and as the Yishuv growingly realized it was engaged in a life and death struggle. But from December 1947 through March 1948 the organisation's policy remained constant: to defend against Arab attack and to retaliate in so far as possible against the guilty, while seeking to limit the scope of the conflict.[97] On 3 February, Ben-Gurion spoke of prospective Jewish settlement in the Negev. He said that those beduin tribes 'who live in peace with us, we will not fight them, we will not harm them, we will supply them with a little water, they will grow vegetables there, they will stay . . .'.[98] And three weeks later, Galili said:

> . . . There is great importance in choosing the objectives [for retaliation, we] must distinguish . . . between villages guilty of attacking us and villages that have not yet attacked us. If we don't want to bring about an alliance between the Arabs of the country and the foreign [irregulars] – it is important to make this distinction.

He hoped that eventually there would be friction, and possibly conflict, between the villagers and the foreign irregulars.[99] This line was appropriately reflected down the chain of command. At the start of March, Mishael Shaham, the HGS's transport security officer, wrote to Allon (after an incident involving Palmah soldiers): 'There is need to restrict transportation security details' behaviour and to prevent unnecessary provocations, something whose results are sometimes tragic, and raise a storm in villages that are still quiet . . .'[100] In part, this policy stemmed from moral considerations; in part, from Haganah weakness; in large measure, it was due to the belief, at least until the end of March, that the Haganah must hold its fire as the British would not allow a radical change in the Jewish–Arab military balance before their withdrawal from Palestine.

PALESTINIAN ARAB POLICY DURING NOVEMBER 1947 – MARCH 1948

Through the first months of the civil war, the JA and the Haganah publicly accused the Mufti of waging an organised, aggressive war against the Yishuv. The reality, however, was more nuanced, as most Zionist leaders and analysts at the time understood. In the beginning, Palestinian belligerency was largely disorganised, sporadic and localised, and for moths remained chaotic and uncoordinated, if not undirected. 'The Arabs were not ready [for war] . . . There was no guiding hand . . . The [local] National Committees and the AHC were trying to gain control of the situation – but things were happening of their own momentum', Machnes told Ben-Gurion and the Haganah commanders on 1 January 1948. He argued that most of the Arab population had not wanted hostilities. Sasson concurred, and added that the Mufti had wanted (and had organised and incited) 'troubles', but not of such scope and dimensions.[101] One senior HIS-AD executive put it this way:

> In the towns the feeling has grown that they cannot hold their own against the superior [Jewish] forces. And in the countryside [the villagers] are unwilling to seek out [and do battle with] the Jews not in their area. [And] those living near the Jewish [settlements] are considered *miskenim* [i.e., miserable or vulnerable] . . . All the villages live with the feeling that the Jews are about to attack them . . .[102]

A few days after the outbreak of hostilities, Galili asked HIS-AD to explain what was happening. HIS-AD responded:

> The disturbances are organised in part by local Husseini activists helped by incited mobs, and in part they are spontaneous and undirected . . . The AHC is not directing or planning the outbreaks . . . The members of the AHC is not responding clearly to local leaders about [the necessary] line of action. [They] are told that the Mufti has not yet decided on the manner of response [to the partition resolution]. The AHC and the local committees are beginning to organise the cities and some of the villages for defence . . .[103]

The Arab Division of the JA-PD thought that the Mufti himself wanted quiet and that this was the official Arab position; but some of his close associates, including Emil Ghawri, Rafiq Tamimi and Sheikh Hassan Abu Sa'ud, were organising the 'spontaneous' rioting and shooting.[104]

In part, the AHC's line was a response to the Arab public's reluctance to fight. Indeed, HIS-AD officers reported that 'most of the public will be willing to accept partition . . .'.[105] 'Tsuri', the HIS–AD officer in the north, reported that 'during the past few years, the Galilee villager, be he Ghawarni [i.e., resident in the Hula Valley swampland], Matawali [i.e., Shi'ite], or Mughrabi [i.e., of Maghrebi origin], lacked any desire to get involved in a war with the Jews'. In general, 'the Arab population of the Galilee is unable to bear the great and prolonged effort [of war] because of an absence of any internal organisation'.[106]

In fact, the lack of organisation and weaponry was not restricted to the North. General Safwat, chairman of the Arab League Military Committee, in March 1948 had warned more generally of Palestinian Arab factionalism, with the proliferation of armed bands owing no obedience to the 'general headquarters' and of villagers acquiring arms to defend themselves against other Arabs, not the Jews.[107] Husseini lacked the tools to launch a fullscale assault on the Yishuv and limited himself to sanctioning minor attacks (in part to pressure the Arab states to come to the Palestinians' aid), to tightening the economic boycott against the Yishuv and to organising the Arab community for *defence*.[108] Towards the end of December 1947, Husseini appears to have sent AHC member and Jerusalem NC leader Dr. Husayn Khalidi a letter explicitly stating that the purpose of the present actions was 'to harass (and only to harass)' the Yishuv, not fullscale assault.[109] He indicated that only at some unspecified future date the AHC would order a fullscale offensive though, meanwhile, preparations had to be taken in hand.[110] Khalidi didn't need any pressing. He himself was 'nervous, desperate and pessimistic'. According to HIS, Khalidi believed that in the disturbances of 1936–1939, 'the Arabs were . . . much readier, daring and willing to sacrifice. Now, by comparison, they demand payment for every action, are full of fear of the Jews and are constantly complaining.'[111]

Cunningham summarised matters fairly accurately five weeks into the war:

> The official Arab policy is to stand on the defensive against Jewish attacks until aggression is ordered by the national leadership. That widespread assaults on Jews continue and are indeed increasing illustrates the comparatively feeble authority of most of [the National] Committees and of the AHC . . . The latter is anxious to curb Arab outbreaks but probably not to stop them entirely and is known to be worried at [sic] its lack of control . . .[112]

Almost immediately, the Mufti's attention was drawn to Arab Haifa and Jaffa, the two largest Arab centres; both were highly vulnerable to attack and siege. In both, the NCs and the monied middle and upper classes whom they represented, sought quiet, lest the Jews be provoked into reprisals that could harm their persons and property. Indeed, in Jaffa the NC and the orange grove owners had within days initiated a short-lived truce with their Jewish neighbours.[113] But the local leaderships were unsuccessful in reining in the militia groups that often operated on the towns' peripheries.[114] Part of the Mufti's concern regarding the two towns no doubt stemmed from reports about the beginning of flight by their inhabitants. During the second half of December 1947 and January 1948, the Mufti or his close associates appear to have tried to shift the focus of hostilities to the countryside. But the villagers were not rushing to join up[115] (and, indeed, some of them sought to continue selling their produce to neighbouring Jewish towns[116]). Hassan Salame, one of the Mufti's main field commanders, discovered this at a meeting with local leaders in the area east of Jaffa. He asked that they organise attacks on Tel Aviv's Hatikva Quarter and Petah Tikva – 'but they all opposed the plan vehemently'.[117] He met a similar response from Ramle's NC. Its members argued that 'there was quiet in the area and until the Jews begin operations and Arab villages are attacked, they do not want to begin operations'. Lydda's NC responded similarly when asked to attack neighbouring Ben Shemen.[118]

The Mufti's main military lieutenant, 'Abd al Qadir al Husseini, responsible for the Judean Hills area, met a similar response at a meeting with the NC of Tulkarm: he enjoined them to collect money to purchase arms and to 'hurry up and engage in battle the Jewish settlements'. Hashim al Jayusi, the committee chairman, responded:

> We ask that you please leave the affairs of this district [for which 'Abd al Qadir was not responsible] to its inhabitants. We know the situation well . . . the western side of our district is open and undefended, and the Jewish settlements surround it on every side. If we begin provocations, the western villages will be lost.

He added that the people of Tulkarm 'did not want anyone's intervention [in their affairs] so that we don't fall subject to those crimes that occurred in the past ('36–'39) [the barely-veiled reference was to Husseini terrorism against fellow Arabs during the revolt]'.

'Abd al Qadir: I do not deny that crimes were committed such as the establishment of [kangaroo] courts and the theft of money.
Hashim: And the murders?
'Abd al Qadir: True, and we must avoid the recurrence of these crimes.'

Hashim repeated that he needed no advice, only arms, which so far, though paid for, had not arrived.[119]

'Abd Al Qadir was similarly rebuffed by Batir and neighbouring villages, which refused to allow him to use them as jump-off points for attacks on Jewish Jerusalem, 'for fear of retaliation'.[120] On the other hand, representatives of villages near Ramallah agreed to initiate certain operations.[121]

But the Mufti's policy regarding the countryside was also characterised by ambiguity. In late January, according to Haganah intelligence, he told a delegation from the village of Masmiya al Kabira, in the south, 'to keep quiet and not to clash with the Jews, unless attacked'. Similarly, Hajj Amin added: 'So long as help from the Arab states is not assured, one should avoid battle with the Jews.'

The change in Arab strategy, of trying to move the focus of violence from the towns to the countryside, had come about, Sasson explained to Ben-Gurion, because of pressure on the Mufti by the townspeople. Sasson advised that the Haganah step up the pressure on the towns so that the urban notables would sue for a cease-fire. Attacks on villages, Sasson felt, would lead nowhere as the Mufti would be indifferent to 'the death of *fellahin*'.[122]

During late January, February and March, the Haganah, mainly through a partial siege, maintained the pressure on the main towns; these put pressure on the Mufti. At the end of January, according to HIS, the AHC ordered all the NCs to maintain, for the moment, a truce and not to mount large attacks, pending new instructions.[123] By mid-February, the ALA, having promised the British to cease attacks, at least until their evacuation, was issuing similar orders – 'not to attack the Jews, but only to defend and organise . . . [for defence]'.[124] The ALA commander in the Qalqilya area, Sa'id Beq, in early March told an Arab interlocutor, Tawfiq Abu Kishk, that 'the ALA does not wish to attack and has no order at the moment to attack; it came to Palestine to defend the Arabs against Jewish aggression'. Sa'id Beq 'encouraged Abu Kishk to continue to maintain proper relations [*yahasim tkinim*] with his Jewish neighbours'.[125] Later that month Qawuqji himself told an Arab who was in close contact with the Yishuv that 'he could continue to live in peace [with the Jews] as had been the case until now'. He warned the locals not to initiate hostilities on their own bat.[126] Haifa's NC, long a bastion of anti-Husseini sentiment, on 22 February issued 'Communique No. 7', demanding 'a cessation of shooting, and a return of each man to his regular workplace . . .'.[127] The NC is unlikely to have issued the declaration without prior AHC approval.

Both the AHC and the ALA during February-March seemed to signal Palestine's Arabs that while low-level skirmishing by local militias and irregulars was fine and attacks on Jewish convoys, especially around Jerusalem, should be continued, a fullscale assault on the Yishuv was out of the question for the time being, though preparations for such an assault, to be unleashed just before or just after the British pullout, should be taken in hand.

JEWISH AND ARAB PEACE-MAKING EFFORTS, DECEMBER 1947 TO MARCH 1948

Side by side with the Haganah's policy during the war's first months of trying to restrict the violence, various Jewish bodies – including the Arab Division of the JA-PD, the Histadrut Arab Workers' Department, Mapam and local Jewish authorities – tried to maintain peace, or at least a cease-fire, in certain areas. In some measure, this was a carry-over from the efforts during the earlier part of the 1940s to achieve Jewish–Arab coexistence (which elicited limited, localised, and only occasionally favourable responses from the Arab side). In greater measure, these efforts were triggered by the outbreak of hostilities in November-December 1947. At the same time, the hostilities also engendered a significant upsurge in peaceful Arab overtures to Jewish neighbours, primarily by communities that felt isolated or under threat in predominantly Jewish areas and were keen on self-preservation.

In the course of the civil war, good neighbourly relations proved most long-lasting in the northern half of the Coastal Plain, and in the area to the east, adjacent to the northern Samaria foothills. Strenuous efforts were also made during the first months of the conflict by Jewish officials, led by Danin and Palmon, to keep the peace between the Yishuv and several Arab villages and beduin tribes in the area immediately north of Tel Aviv, and by Histadrut officials in the Jerusalem area.

In late August 1947, as war clouds gathered, a number of villages east of Hadera initiated a 'peace meeting' with their Jewish neighbours. The four and a half hour meeting was attended by about 70 Arab notables – including the mukhtars of Wadi 'Ara, Ar'ara and the Turkman tribe near Kibbutz Mishmarot – and 40 local Jewish leaders. The leaders of the largest village in the area, Baqa al Gharbiya, refused to attend. The Arab and Jewish leaders stressed their long-standing neighbourly relations and appointed a standing committee to settle disputes, should they arise.[128] The contacts led, on 22 October, to a visit by 60 children from Kibbutz 'Ein Shemer's school to the school in Khirbet as Sarkas, 'where they were received very well'. The visit reciprocated one by a class from Khirbet as Sarkas to 'Ein Shemer and Kibbutz Gan Shmuel earlier that month.[129] From the local Jewish leadership's point of view, the start of hostilities elsewhere in the country made the strengthening of contacts with Arab neighbours imperative. 'The order of the day is to strive for good neighbourly relations', the local Jewish authorities declared.[130] The Hefer Valley's leaders met, at the initiative of the mukhtar of the 'Arab al Shimali tribe, on 12 December 1947. The Arab notables declared that they wanted peace and a continuation of good relations, and asked for a promise that the Jews would not harm them and for 'the protection of the [regional] council'. The Jewish authorities said that the meeting had taken place despite attempts by emissaries from Tulkarm to 'incite' these Arabs against the Jews. The Jews would maintain peace so long as the Arabs did, said the council. Officials of the Arab Division had helped set up the meeting.[131] The Jewish leaders also made arrangements to provide neighbouring Arab villages with supplies, especially flour, in the event of a cut-off. Arab families living in (Jewish) Hadera had fled but Arab workers continued to come into town to work.[132]

Soon after the start of the hostilities, the somewhat dormant Arab Workers' Department of the Histadrut initiated contacts with Arabs in order to promote peace between neighbouring communities. The fraternity of workers of all nations lay at the core of the trade union federation's ideology. On 21 January 1948, the Histadrut distributed a poster addressed to 'all Arab workers' to live in peace with the Jews and to turn their backs on their leaders, 'who are leading you to destruction'.[133]

In the early months of the war, the desire for calm in certain areas took a number of forms. Several villages concluded formal peace agreements with neighbouring settlements or urban neighbourhoods. The notables of Deir Yassin on 20 January 1948 met with leaders of Jerusalem's Jewish Giv'at Shaul neighbourhood and agreed to mutual non-belligerency. Deir Yassin took upon itself to keep out bands of irregulars and if, nonetheless, some appeared, to inform Giv'at Shaul of their presence 'in daytime by hanging out laundry . . . (two white pieces with a black piece in the middle)' and 'at night Deir Yassin's people will signal three dots with a flashlight . . . and place three . . . [lanterns?]'. Similarly, patrols from Giv'at Shaul near Deir Yassin were to be armed with a mutually agreed password. Giv'at Shaul was responsible for the safety of Deir Yassin's vehicles passing through the neighbourhood.[134] The founder of the Arab Workers' Department, Aharon Haim Cohen, was instrumental in concluding this agreement as well as similar agreements that month and in February with the villages of al Qastal, Sur Bahir and al Maliha.[135]

During December 1947 and January 1948, the leaders of Sheikh Muwannis, Summeil (al Mas'udiya), Jammasin, 'Arab Abu Kishk and Jalil, met with Haganah representatives in the house of Avraham Schapira in Petah Tikva and expressed a desire for peace. They said that if they could not keep out the irregulars unaided, they would call on the Haganah. These overtures were apparently matched on the Jewish side in January and February by visits by Palmon and Danin to several villages, including Sheikh Muwannis and 'Arab Abu Kishk, where they asked the inhabitants to remain where they were and to accept Jewish protection and rule. The villagers agreed.[136] In one or two cases, agreements were reached between Jewish officials or Haganah officers and certain parts of a village population rather than the village itself. For example, in mid-January dozens of workers from Miska, in the Tulkarm

District, reached a non-belligerency agreement with their Jewish neighbours, in whose groves they were employed.[137]

During the war's first three months, more than two dozen Arab villages and tribes sent out feelers to Jewish officials to conclude local non-belligerency agreements. They were mainly motivated by fear of Jewish attack or reprisal; in some measure, by traditional economic ties they wanted to maintain. Among these villages were Qatanna, northwest of Jerusalem, which approached Kibbutz Ma'ale Hahamisha;[138] Wadi Hawarith, in the Coastal Plain, which approached Kfar Vitkin;[139] Manshiya, which approached Kibbutz Giv'at Haim, near Hadera;[140] Qisarya, whose notable Tawfiq Kadkuda, approached local Jews;[141] 'Ein Karim, west of Jerusalem, which approached leaders in the Bayit Vegan neighbourhood;[142] 'Arab Abu Kishk and the village of Jammasin, north of Tel Aviv, which jointly approached a Jewish police officer named 'Arieli' in the Ramat-Gan police station;[143] Ard al Saris, which approached the head of the Jewish regional council at Kfar Ata, Dr Bohm;[144] and Kafr Qari, which approached neighbouring Kfar Glickson.[145]

In the Beit Shean (Beisan) Valley, it was a British official who tried to bring together local Jewish and Arab representatives. The local HIS representative, Yehoshua Sulz, advised the regional bloc committee 'to grasp the offered hand', but other Haganah officers, while also interested in 'preserving the peace', advised that 'one must first clarify who it is who is demanding peace . . . We must demand that they send respected representatives and not children or nonentities. It is important that the Arabs not come from one family or one class alone . . .'[146]

Generally, matters were more straightforward: local Arab dignitaries approached and met with local Jewish representatives. On 7 January, for example, the mayor of Lydda, flanked by the mukhtar of Haditha, met in his office with the headman of Ben-Shemen, the neighbouring Jewish agricultural boarding school, an enclave in the Arab-populated area. The HIS-AD transcript of the meeting quotes the mayor as saying: 'We want peace with you and we have announced it in the town and its environs. But you know that there are people without sense and responsibility who might do silly things off their own bat.' He asked the Ben-Shemen headman not to post guards on the road but only inside the school compound. The Ben-Shemen headman, for his part, asked that the Lydda authorities allow Jewish automobiles to pass through the town unhindered. Shihadeh Hassuna, the head of Lydda's militia, then called and the mayor put Ben-Shemen's headman on the telephone. Hassuna said:

> We have spoken to all the mukhtars in the area and have warned them to avoid any harm to Ben-Shemen. You have sat among us now for many years and nothing [bad] has happened between us . . . your convoys will

not be touched. The local inhabitants, especially the older ones, want peace, but all sorts of strangers come to town, who act on their own and are difficult to control . . .

[Ben-Shemen] headman: Among us too there are elements who do not obey [orders] and act on their own and I cannot be responsible for them, as you cannot, as you say, be responsible for strangers.[147]

(As late as 19 March, Lydda's leaders were opposing attacks on Ben Shemen convoys.[148])

A similar discussion took place a week later between a local HIS-AD officer (probably David Karon) and the head of the NC in Tal as Safi, a large Arab village southwest of Jerusalem. The Arab notable, Haj Muhammad Khalil al 'Azi, promised to keep out 'strangers' and to keep Arab shepherds away from Jewish fields. Al 'Azi added, for good measure, that the Husseinis 'had no future' and 'control' would soon pass to Abdullah, king of Jordan. The local NC had ordered a group of beduins who had settled in Tal a Safi five-six years before to leave lest their grazing lead to clashes with the Jews.[149]

A few weeks later, Tal as Safi notables hosted a meeting between representatives of the Haganah and Hassan 'Abd al 'Aziz Mahana of Masmiyya al-Kabira, a large and influential village to the west. Mahana, a leading member of the village's main family, initiated the meeting. He promised that peace would reign in the area so long as the Mahana dominated the village and its environs. He asked that the guards in the Haganah convoys passing through 'not wave or point their weapons'. Mahana complained about both the Jewish and Arab leaderships who had brought about partition and the disturbances. The Mahanas, he said, had 'decided to strenuously oppose the Husseinis and build their political future on King Abdullah'.[150]

Tal as Safi and Masmiyya and their immediate Jewish neighbour, Kibbutz Kfar Menahem, were not (or not yet) at war. But between the Arab village of Sur Bahir and neighbouring Kibbutz Ramat Rachel and Jerusalem's southern district of Talpiyot shots had been exchanged. The leaders of Sur Bahir sought pacification and called for a meeting. Underlying their overture was a declining economic situation. In the past, much of their agricultural output had been sold to the Jews; now, there were no buyers for the surplus produce. At the same time, there was a lack of animal fodder; there was no outside work; and no Arab body was helping the village.[151] Mahmud Shihadeh, brother of the village's mukhtar, and two local flour-mill owners (whose business was affected by the hostilities), represented Sur Bahir; the Jews were represented by Moshe Isaacowitz, the headman of Ramat Rachel, and Elhanan Klein, of Talpiyot. The purpose of the meeting was 'to find a way to maintain a ceasefire between the Talpiyot bloc and the Arab villages of Sur Bahir and [neighbouring] Um Tuba. We [the Jews] said that we did not want a bloody conflict . . . The other side promised:

> A. That no action will be taken to the detriment of the bloc by the inhabitants of these villages.
> B. They will prevent, even by force, any strangers from entering the village in order to attack or incite [against the Jews] . . . If they do not succeed in preventing the strangers from entering, they will immediately inform Moshe Isaacowitz or Elhanan Klein . . .'

In return the Jewish representatives promised to allow the passage, possibly after inspection, through their area to and from Jerusalem of a specific Arab truck ('no. 282, a Dodge, with red cabin') and of 'children up to the age of five and women'.

The two Jews subsequently commented that:

> A. The motive of the inhabitants of these villages . . . is their desire not to be harmed by an end to the mutual non-belligerency. In principle, they are not opposed to the Arab hostilities.
> B. There is a feeling that they wish to gain time.
> C. There was a strong impression that the meeting was initiated by the flour-mill owners more than by the mukhtars, and we assume that Mahmud Shihadeh was paid by the mill-owners to arrange the meeting.
> The meeting ended with the arrangement of a follow-up meeting with Sur Bahir's and Um Tuba's mukhtars.[152]

The follow-up took place on 5 February; the two mukhtars (Haj Ahmad Shihadeh of Sur Bahir and 'Haj Mahmud of Um Tuba) and a number of other Arab dignitaries attended. The Jewish side was represented by Isaacowitz and an HIS officer called 'Yitzhar'. The meeting, according to Yitzhar's subsequent report, was 'very friendly' and characterised by 'a wish for good neighbourly relations'. The Arabs promised to keep strangers out. They said that in the past they had already kicked out strangers 'by force'. The Arabs asked for free passage on the road to Jerusalem passing by Ramat Rachel. The two sides agreed to allow ploughing by both Arabs and Jews in the fields lying between the villages and the Jewish area.[153]

During late March, April and May a driving force among villagers seeking a truce or peace with Jewish neighbours was the harvest: the villagers wanted calm in order to bring in their ripening crops. Such, at least, was one explanation proffered by an HIS-AD officer for the newfound willingness of at least some people in the village of Tantura, south of Haifa, to conclude a ceasefire in early May. (Another reason, in Tantura's case, was the fear generated by the fall of Arab Haifa a fortnight before.): 'Now is the harvest season and this is a good additional reason for "peace" with the Jews', he reported.[154] (Interestingly, at this time Jews from Zikhron Ya'akov 'on their own volition' approached Tantura's Arabs for an agreement on the harvest.[155]) The impending harvest also underlay the talks between the village of Qaqun and Kibbutz Hama'apil in early April. The Haganah's Arab affairs advisers in the area added, however, that 'to assure the existence of the ceasefire . . . Qaqun and Hama'apil should collect the harvest from their fields simultaneously'.[156]

On the eastern shore of the Sea of Galilee, too, Arabs contacted Jews to obtain assurances that their harvest would be unhindered by Jewish gunfire, implicitly assuring quiet in return.[157] On the edge of the Jezreel Valley, the mukhtars of the beduin tribe of Waft al Nasra (or Wafiya) approached the headman of Kibbutz Genigar and asked to negotiate a ceasefire to enable them to reap their crops.[158] A notable of 'Abisiyya, in the Galilee Panhandle, in late May asked the Haganah to allow him to remain in his village as, in his absence, fellow villagers were harvesting (and apparently taking for themselves) his crops; the Haganah 'advised him, nonetheless, to leave'.[159] The harvest was cited by Druse and Christians in the Shafa 'Amr-Ramat Yohanan area as a reason for not allowing or initiating hostilities.[160] The harvest was also cited by HIS officers as a reason for the willingness of certain villagers who had fled to return and accept Jewish government; the refugees from al Kheiriya, east of Jaffa, were mentioned in this connection.[161]

There was also a cluster of villages, south and southeast of Haifa, which had a special interest in a ceasefire: they wished to continue working in neighbouring Jewish settlements, their chief source of income. Such was the reason behind the repeated approaches to the Haganah in early May of the inhabitants of Sindiyana, Sabbarin and Fureidis, whose menfolk (still) worked in the fields and vineyards of Zikhron Ya'akov, Binyamina and Bat-Shlomo.[162]

The approach of 14–15 May and the pan-Arab invasion, auguring a substantial increase in hostilities, and the invasion itself, drove villages and clusters of villages in several areas to contact Jewish authorities to achieve a local armistice or to surrender and accept Jewish rule.

At the end of April or early May representatives of Tira, the large village south of Haifa, held ceasefire talks with Haifa Haganah officers. No agreement seems to have been reached. The villagers, headed by Sa'id al Dajani, agreed to mutual non-belligerency but refused to give up their arms, as the Haganah demanded.[163] In the Jerusalem area, representatives of the villages of Khirbet al Luz, Sataf, Suba and Um al Mis asked notables from Abu Ghosh, a village known to be friendly to the Yishuv, to mediate peace between them and the Haganah. (Abu Ghosh turned them down.)[164]

At the beginning of May the mukhtar of Zarnuqa, near Rehovot, visited the Qatra Police Station and announced that his village and neighbouring Mughar, Bash-Shit, Yibna and Qubeiba were all 'interested in surrendering'.[165] A week later, the head of the village's powerful Shurbaji clan, Ahmad al Shurbaji, proposed that the village hand over some of its weapons and ask for Jewish 'protection' (meaning surrender).[166] Jisr a

Zarqa (al Ghawarina), in the Coastal Plain, also said it wanted to surrender and receive Haganah 'protection'.[167] In early May the Alexandroni Brigade reported that the inhabitants of Kheiriya, Saqiya and Salama, just conquered in Operation Hametz, 'would willingly return to their villages and accept Jewish protection'.[168] The inhabitants of Kafr Lam and Sarafand, south of Haifa, who had abandoned their homes a few days before, were also reportedly interested in returning 'and accepting Jewish rule'.[169] In late May Mu'in Salah Khatib, identified as 'the biggest landowner' in the Druse villages of Isufiya and Daliyat al Karmil, approached HIS-AD and said that the two villages are 'ready to surrender and to hand over their arms'. He was also 'willing to hand over the few gang members' in the villages.[170] In late May, the Haganah reported an argument in the Galilee Panhandle village of Salihiya between youngsters and village elders. The youngsters did not want to assist the invading Syrian Army and thought it best 'to approach the Jews and hand over their arms and stay'. The elders, however, feared that if an Arab army nonetheless reached their area, they would be deemed traitors, 'and the village would be destroyed'.[171] In early June, the three militant villages of Jab'a, Ijzim and 'Ein Ghazal, south of Haifa, having witnessed the decline in Arab fortunes, were reportedly asking 'to open negotiations for surrender'. Similarly, 'the villages east of Acre and the Zebulun Valley' were reportedly 'ready to surrender'.[172]

The Haganah always had a problem with approaches for a truce or surrender. Often it was the initiative of only one faction or notable in a particular village: was the approach serious and credible? And even if the village mukhtar made the approach, was he fully authorised? Perhaps the move was merely tactical, designed to gain a temporary reprieve to allow the collection of crops or the arrival of a shipment of arms – after which the village would again join the militants? And what was the point in agreeing to a ceasefire with a particular isolated Arab community while in other areas, where Arabs had the upper hand, they rejected any thought of armistice and peace? After all, Haganah policy had to be determined by national, not local, considerations. So, often, such Arab approaches came to nought. By May, facing imminent invasion by the Arab states, the Haganah preferred not to take chances and leave Arab villages, whose sudden professions of acquiescence and loyalty were at best dubious, behind its front lines.

In any event, villagers usually preferred to avoid formal contact or agreements with the Haganah – acts that bespoke treachery in fellow Arabs' eyes; only a small minority are recorded as having made such approaches. But many more effectively refrained from initiating violence against Jews or refused, when asked, to join in; many actively prevented irregulars from entering or using their villages as bases. Occasionally, Arab villagers appealed to neighbouring villagers not to make trouble. The main consideration among the dozens of non-belligerent villages was to avoid Jewish retaliation against themselves.

In December 1947, the 'Arab al Basa beduins asked the Turkmans living in Mansi to refrain from attacking the Jews.[173] A few days later, the 'Arab al Jalad prevented an attack by 17 armed irregulars against the nearby Jewish settlement of Kfar Yona. The tribe said that 'first they would sell their lands and leave the site and [only] after this would agree and participate in such actions'.[174] The inhabitants of the large Druse villages on the Carmel, Isfiya and Daliyat al Karmil, from the start turned down Arab requests that they attack neighbouring Jewish settlements.[175]

In the Jerusalem District, there was widespread and persistent opposition by many villages to taking part in the hostilities; immediate self-interest won out over nationalism. Roving bands of Arab irregulars, sometimes led by 'Abd al Qadir al Husseini, were fairly regularly turned away, the villagers often refusing to put them up or give them supplies, let alone join in attacks. Al Maliha's mukhtar, Sheikh 'Abd al Fatah, had ordered the village militia to fire on any stranger who approached, 'Jew, Arab, or Englishman'.[176] In early January 1948, the inhabitants of Qaluniya chased away an armed band and prevented it from 'doing anything'.[177] Deir Yassin's inhabitants had a firefight with a roving band of irregulars who wanted to use their village as a base to attack west Jerusalem. One villager was killed and the village 'women burst into cries and screams'.[178] Just before 28 January, 'Abd al Qadir, at the head of a band of 400 armed men, encamped near Deir Yassin. Apparently they tried to recruit villagers. The village elders 'were opposed', and the band moved off to Beit Jala.[179] Deir Yassin's mukhtar was summoned by AHC representatives in Jerusalem to be questioned about the village's relations with the Jews. The mukhtar said that 'the village and the Jews lived in peace'.[180] A fortnight later, on 13 February, an armed band entered Deir Yassin bent on attacking nearby Giv'at Shaul. 'The villagers opposed this and the gang's reaction was to slaughter all the village's sheep . . .'[181] A month later, on 16 March, an AHC delegation composed of two men and (unusually) a woman visited the village and asked that it host a group of Iraqi and Syrian irregulars 'to guard the site'. The villagers refused and the delegation left empty handed.[182] Deir Yassin's notables registered a similar refusal on 4 April.[183]

To the north, in the village of Sabbarin in late January, the inhabitants rejected an appeal by visiting aides of 'Abd al Qadir al Husseini on a recruitment drive, and a fracas ensued.[184] In nearby Damun, southeast of Haifa, the son of the main local land-owner, Sadiq Karaman, paid the local ALA garrison P£5000 to leave.[185] A few weeks later, Sabbarin, Sindiyana and Fureidis agreed not to allow in any irregulars.[186] Sindiyana (and Bureika) also opposed the garrisoning of Bureika with ALA troops.[187]

The AHC strongly opposed local peace initiatives and agreements. The Mufti may at times have wanted a reduction in the scale of the conflict, but he opposed anything that smacked of peace with, or recognition of, the Yishuv. The AHC stymied a number of local peace efforts. In mid-January, for example, the British Galilee District Commissioner reported that the notables of the town of Beisan and the surrounding Jewish settlements were interested in 'an informal agreement of mutual restraint' but the AHC vetoed the idea.[188] By and large, however, as the fighting spread, suspicion and antagonism between neighbouring, and in some cases traditionally friendly, settlements grew and the possibility of concluding local peace agreements or maintaining local cease-fires receded. This was especially true in the centre of the country. In the south and north, some neighbouring settlements maintained effective cease-fires for months, primarily out of a mutual need to harvest crops. A similar state of non-belligerency, based on tacit or explicit understandings, prevailed with regard to the harvest of the citrus crop in the southern Coastal Plain during the war's first months.

By the end of March, there was a general sense of despair regarding continued Arab–Jewish contacts or amity, among the officials of the Histadrut Arab Workers' Department. One official, Avraham Ben-Tzur, on 26 March said that the villages along the border between the prospective Jewish and Arab Palestine states could serve as 'bridgeheads' of peace and cooperation. He mentioned a teacher in Khirbet as Sarkas as possibly embodying such hopes. And Eliahu Agassi, the department's director, spoke of the leaflets being distributed in the Hefer Valley–Samaria foothills area and of the joint Arab–Jewish supplies committee operating in the Hefer Valley. However, the general tenor of the meeting was pessimistic. At a follow-up meeting four days later, the officials spoke rather unrealistically of possible Jewish–Arab cooperation in the railways, radio station and oil refinery while conceding that Arab–Jewish coexistence in the countryside had broken down. They focused attention on one of the last districts in which Arabs were still living in a Jewish area – the Hefer Valley around Hadera – and planned a visit to the town the following week. Agassi said: 'Perhaps our visit could stop the exodus of the Arabs from the area.' Whether the visit took place is unclear.[189] What is clear is that within a fortnight, the Haganah, for strategic reasons, decided that no Arabs should remain in the Hadera area and those still there were expelled (see Chapter 4).

By the end of March, the Husseinis had managed to still the moderate voices in the Arab camp and had gained control over almost all of Arab Palestine. Most of the country was engulfed in warfare. The Haganah, especially on the roads, was sorely pressed and on the defensive. While some local truces remained in force, most Arab villages were now dominated by elements hostile to the Yishuv and many harboured active irregular units. And where the Husseinis were not in control, the locals, fearing the Mufti's wrath, preferred to have no truck with the Jews.

Palmon told a meeting of the executives of the JA-PD that contacts with the Arabs had been almost completely severed and that 'in general, the Arabs could be defined as united [behind the Husseinis] . . . Today, there is almost no area of the country where we can talk with the Arabs, even on local matters, to pacify and calm things down.'

Both Palmon and Danin thought that, in great measure, the situation was a product of ill-conceived Jewish military actions and over-reactions, and that by and large, the Arab affairs experts on the national level and in each locality had been, or were being, ignored by the military commanders. The situation was such, said Palmon, that in future, the Yishuv might find it difficult 'to prove that we weren't the aggressors' apart from the Jerusalem area, where the violence was clearly a product of Arab initiative. Danin added that 'as a result of several superfluous [Haganah] operations, which mainly hurt "good" Arabs who were in contact with us . . . the [Arab] mass exodus from all places was continuing. The Arabs have simply lost their faith [in our goodwill?].'

The situation had caused general demoralisation in the Political Department's Arab Division, whose ambivalent functions included both peace-making contacts and intelligence-gathering. Danin said that if things continued as they were, the Division 'should be closed down'. Ya'akov Shimoni, a senior division official, said that the Haganah commanders had concluded that 'war was war and that there was no possibility of distinguishing between good and bad Arabs'.[190]

THE FIRST STAGE OF THE EXODUS: DECEMBER 1947 – MARCH 1948

The hostilities of December 1947 to March 1948 triggered the start of the exodus of Palestine's Arabs. We shall first examine what happened in the cities, then in the countryside.

The cities

Haifa

The UN partition resolution had earmarked Haifa, with some 65,000 Arab and 70,000 Jewish inhabitants and a joint municipality, to be part of the Jewish state. Without doubt, this demoralised the Arab inhabitants. Their exodus began in early December 1947, with the start of hostilities. A British intelligence unit reported that both Jews and Arabs were evacuating the border areas between the two communities and moving to safer neighbourhoods. The unit commander, stressing, curiously, the movement of Jews rather than Arabs, commented that these initial shifts of population 'lead one to speculate on the eventual magnitude that this problem will present during the implementation of partition'. The first reported evacuation was of 250 Arab families from the Halissa quarter on 4 December.[191] By 10 December HIS-AD was reporting that 'a panicky evacuation is taking place from the [Arab] border neighbourhoods'.[192] Abandoning one's home, breaking a major psychological barrier, paved the way for eventual abandonment of village or town and, ultimately, of country. Danin and Palmon on 11 December noted the start of the flight from Haifa. Most of the Arab movement out of Haifa was due to the fighting – sniping and bombings – and fears of fighting that marked life in the border neighbourhoods. But a few Christian Arab families who lived inside or on the edges of Jewish neighbourhoods on Mount Carmel were intimidated into leaving their homes in mid-December by IZL threats and orders.[193] By 23 December, HIS was reporting that 'the economic condition in Haifa is – bad. Some 15–20 thousand Arabs, especially from the Hauran [Syria] and Egypt and many rich people, have left the city. Many shops and businesses have closed . . . The AHC demanded that the Haifa NC stop the flight . . . The Christians in Haifa live in fear of the Muslims . . .'[194]

The 14-member Haifa NC was established on 2–3 December, with Rashid Haj Ibrahim, a Muslim, in the chair. He was to lead the committee until its demise in late April 1948. From a letter he wrote to Husseini in May 1947, Haj Ibrahim emerges as violently anti-Zionist, even anti-Semitic. He wrote: Jews in Europe became symbols of 'baseness and cheating.' The 'Arab world faces destruction [because] . . . the Jews want to take over Egypt, because Moses came from there', and Lebanon and Syria 'because they built the Temple with Lebanese cedars, and they want Iraq because our forefather Abraham came from there and they [feel they] have a right to Hijaz because Ishmael came from there and they demand Transjordan, because it was part of Palestine and Solomon's kingdom.' He predicted – fairly accurately – that the Jewish state, if it emerged in Palestine, would establish a giant navy and giant air force, and build atomic weapons, with which to overawe the Arab world.[195] But from the start of hostilities in December 1947, Ibrahim was to preach and embody moderation and to relentlessly pursue a ceasefire in Haifa.

But Husseini agents and irregulars sporadically launched attacks on Jews, beginning on 7 December with ambushes against traffic moving through Wadi Rushmiya. From then on, there were almost daily exchanges of fire along the seam neighbourhoods, almost always initiated by Arabs. Beginning on 11 December, IZL operatives began to throw bombs at Arab crowds and buses. The first large Haganah reprisal, against the village of Balad al Sheikh, just east of Haifa, took place on 12 December (six Arabs were killed); other reprisals, against Tira and Hawassa, followed. By the end of the month, most of the inhabitants of the Halissa had evacuated, only a handful of men remaining to guard the neighbourhood; Wadi Rushmiya was also almost completely evacuated.

Most moved into Haifa's core Arab neighbourhoods (Wadi Nisnas and Wadi Salib) though some families left the country. The Lebanese and Syrian consulates in Haifa reportedly issued 8,000 entry visas during December, 'and many thousand left [the country] without visas and passports'.[196]

Some of the flight, no doubt, was due to the rapid deterioration in the economic situation. The price of a sack of flour rose during December from P£1.750 to P£6.500, 'and it is difficult to get it at this price as well. Most shops are closed all day. The vegetable market is closed and [public] transportation has almost completely stopped.'[197] 105 Arabs died and 248 were seriously injured in the violence that month.

From the first, the NC took note of the exodus and acted to stem it. Already on 6 December, Ibrahim forbade the members of the committee to leave town without NC approval[198] and on 14 December issued a 'warning' against the exodus.[199] Five days earlier, the NC decided to appeal to the AHC to instruct Palestinians not to leave without permission of their local NCs.[200]

It was this situation that prompted the NC, represented by the senior magistrate Ahmad Bey Khalil and 'Omar Taha, to seek and conclude a ceasefire with the Haganah on 28 December 1947.[201] But the ceasefire only held for a few hours. Late on the morning of 30 December, IZL gunmen threw bombs into an Arab crowd milling about the gate of the Haifa Oil Refinery. Six died and some 50 were injured. Immediately, a mob of Arab refinery workers, reinforced by Arabs who had survived the bombing, attacked their Jewish co-workers with sticks, stones and knives. Altogether, 39 Jews were murdered and 11 seriously injured in the hour-long pogrom.[202]

The Haganah massively retaliated on the night of 31 December 1947 – 1 January 1948, raiding the villages of Balad al Sheikh and Hawassa, in which many of the refinery's workers lived. The raiding units' orders were to kill 'maximum adult males'.[203] The raiders penetrated to the centre of Balad al Sheikh, fired into and blew up houses, and pulled out adult males, and shot them. According to the HGS, 'the penetrating units . . . were forced to deviate from the line agreed upon and in a few cases hit women and children' after being fired upon from inside houses. The Haganah suffered two dead and two injured. Haganah reports put Arab casualties variously at 'about 70 killed'[204] and 21 killed ('including two women and five children') and 41 injured.[205] Following the raids, many families fled the two villages to Nablus, Jenin and Acre.[206]

The raid was criticised in the Yishuv's Defence Committee. Riftin argued that many of the refinery workers had not participated in the pogrom; a few actually had protected Jews; but the raids on Balad al Sheikh and Hawassa were conducted indiscriminately 'and there is no knowing who was hit'. Moreover, the incident had been provoked by the IZL bomb attack. Ben-Gurion responded that 'discrimination is impossible. We are at war, and in war you cannot make individual differentiation . . .; between . . . villages, yes, but not between individuals.'[207]

Following this cycle of violence, the NC pushed to renew the ceasefire. Most Jewish and Arab employees had stopped going to work in mixed work places, including the municipality. At Arab initiative, a 'security committee' (with three representatives from each side) was established in the municipal and government offices and in the courts. At a meeting with Haganah representatives on 2 January, Arab notables, including Ahmad Bey Khalil, said that they had issued orders to avoid the recurrence of refinery-type incidents. Rashid Haj Ibrahim himself declared that 'the Arabs were interested in quiet in Haifa . . .'.[208] The NC was interested in 'a protracted truce'.[209] But Arab militants, and Husseini-affiliated politicians, such as Nimr al Khatib and Hassan Shibalak (both members of the Haifa NC), continued to foment violence.[210] Daily, there were ambushes and exchanges of fire. Following a bomb attack on a Jewish bus (which left four wounded), the Haganah blew up two houses and a garage and poured mortar and sniper fire into the Arab neighbourhoods; dozens were killed, including women and children and the militia leader Muhamad Hijawi and the deputy head of the National Bank, Muhamad Kanafani.[211] Arab public transport ceased, there was a shortage of goods and the flight from the city continued.[212] Businesses closed down, and shopkeepers began selling their stock to Jews at 25 per cent reductions in order to close up quickly.[213]

The British, for whom Haifa was pivotal to their plans for withdrawal from Palestine, stepped up their patrols and things calmed down. But the Jewish retaliatory strikes had severely shaken Arab morale; they sorely felt the Jews' topographical advantage (the Jews lived up Mount Carmel), and their superiority in organisation, arms and equipment.[214] 'The Haifa Arab public began to feel the weakness of its position and there were residents who began to emigrate from the city. Of course, this had a dampening effect on those who remained', recalled Nimr al Khatib.[215]

On 18 January, Ibrahim returned from a visit to Damascus, where his pro-truce stand had received significant endorsement. As he told the NC that day, Taha al Hashimi, the inspector general of the ALA, had supported his desire 'to refrain from incidents', given the local Haganah superiority. Hashimi and the Syrian president and war minister, with whom Ibrahim had met, had all 'agreed to our course of action . . . Hashimi had stressed that clashes in Haifa were to be completely avoided and [the Arabs were to] act only in a defensive manner.' But Ibrahim had failed to receive from the Mufti a similar endorsement of a ceasefire and proposed that a delegation travel to Cairo to try to pin Husseini down.[216] The NC meeting had been dominated by talk of Arab suffering and emigration.[217] The committee 'believed that Haifa needs quiet, or at least not to jump to the head of the [Arab] war [effort]' and that 'it is in their interest to maintain peace in Haifa as long as possible'.[218]

Meanwhile, Khalil, flanked by 'Omar Taha, and Haifa Jewish community representatives Ya'akov Solomon and Naftali Lifshitz renewed their meetings. Solomon demanded an open, public agreement. Khalil said that the NC had decided to send a delegation, headed by the Greek Catholic Archbishop George Hakim, to talk with the Mufti – and to threaten resignation if the Mufti's men continued to defy the NC's writ and launch attacks.[219] Meanwhile, a de facto truce began.

Hakim, accompanied by Sheikh 'Abdul Rahman Murad, the Haifa head of the Muslim Brotherhood, and Yusuf Sahayun, a Husseini supporter, left for Egypt on 20 January; according to HIS, 'Rashid [Haj Ibrahim] demanded that the delegation explain to the Mufti that many of the leaders of the city wanted to leave if explicit orders were not received to stop the terror in the city, and if their arguments were not accepted, then the leaders would leave the country and in the end Arab Haifa would empty of its veteran inhabitants.'[220]

Husseini's reaction to the delegation's appeal is unclear; probably it was deliberately ambiguous. According to one Haganah informant, the Mufti had said the problem was national, not local, and had ended the meeting by suggesting that the Arab struggle against the Jews and the British 'could [end by] destroying half the Arabs in Palestine'. The implication was that he opposed a ceasefire and 'his whole person bespoke war against the Jews to the bitter end. All his thought is focused on how to exploit the Arab peoples to reach this end . . . There is no talking [reason ? peace ?] to the Mufti.'[221] His only practical advice to the Haifa delegation had been 'to remove the women and children from the danger areas in order to reduce the number of casualties'.[222]

This advice conformed with the general guideline adopted by the Political Committee of the Arab League, meeting in Sofar, Lebanon, in September 1947, in preparation for the expected outbreak of hostilities in Palestine. The committee, in its unanimously adopted published resolutions, recommended that the Arab states 'open their gates to the absorption of, and care for, the babies, women and the old from among Palestine's Arabs – if events occur in Palestine that necessitate it'.[223] The resolution was adopted for two reasons: to try to avoid death and injury to Arab non-combatants, and especially to avoid violation of women, a desire deeply rooted in Arab tradition and mores;[224] and to free the adult males from the burden of dependents whose presence in prospective combat zones would hamper them in battle. As it turned out, this guideline, which during the first months of the civil war was endorsed and adopted (though by and large, especially in the towns, not acted upon) by the AHC and various NCs and village leaders, helped fuel the mass exodus from Palestine. As we shall see, in the course of the civil war, and in some areas also during the subsequent conventional war, dozens of villages, at the prodding of the AHC and NCs or off their own bat, evacuated women, children and old folk. The importance of these evacuations, underpinned and legitimised by the endorsement of the Arab states and the Palestinians' own governing institutions, cannot be exaggerated. By providing a model of behaviour and a pointer to assuring self-preservation, the evacuation of dependents had a crucial demoralising effect on the menfolk who stayed behind to fight or guard villages and towns, and at the same time ate away at their motivation to stay and fight; after all, they were no longer protecting their families.

At the meeting with the delegation, Husseini had apparently handed them a letter instructing the NC 'to oppose the exodus of families from Haifa, to avoid panic and to issue a call to those who had emigrated to return'[225] and had agreed to at least a temporary truce because 'the Arabs were in need of supplies . . . and mainly because the English were still in Haifa and the Arabs don't want to clash with them'.[226] Most likely, Husseini had conveyed a deliberate ambivalence, saying one thing and then its opposite, or, at least, different things to Hakim and Murad.

The delegation returned to Haifa on 26 January. Thereafter, for days, Hakim avoided contact with his Jewish interlocutors and, reflecting Husseini's ambiguities, the NC proved unable to agree on a clear line for or against a truce. Indeed, Murad told journalists that the delegation had only gone to plead for arms and men; there 'was no negotiation and would be no negotiation aimed at turning Haifa into a non-combatant city'; and 'the [Haifa] NC was only a branch of the AHC', implying that the Mufti's will overrode the NC's and that he wanted continued violence.[227]

Solomon and Lifshitz, who eventually met the notables, were debriefed by Arazi. He believed that the de facto truce would not hold for long; the Arabs' morale had risen following the entry into Palestine of ALA units. The NC would maintain non-belligerence only until the Arab militias were stronger or until the British withdrawal, but not thereafter.[228] Besides, the armed groups would continue to act without NC authorisation. Haifa's Christian notables were disheartened. As a result of the disagreement in the NC about an end to the violence, 'the rich Christians began to prepare to leave Haifa and the first was the merchant Amin Sahayun who moved his family with all their furniture in two large automobiles [trucks] to Lebanon. During the day many Christians said they will not stay in the town so long as Sheikh Nimr al Khatib's gangs rule it.'[229]

During January and early February, Haifa's economic condition worsened considerably:

> Hundreds of unemployed stayed at home because of the closing of the refinery and from fear of going to work elsewhere. The cost of living increased and it is difficult to obtain flour for bread. The exodus from the border neighbourhoods has resulted in the emptying of the Halissa Quarter and part of Wadi Salib. . . . The Christians refuse to pay for guards from outside [the city] . . . People began to barter goods for flour.[230]

The vegetable market remained closed, the large shops were closed, their owners having fled the city, and small shops and groceries were open only a few hours a day.

> Jaffa Street was completely closed and only two Christian merchants were selling the remainder of their wares and were about to depart for Lebanon. There were no building materials . . . and the Karaman [tobacco] factory works 8 hours [a day] instead of 16 before the disturbances.[231]

The irregulars remained unruly, initiating attacks on Jewish targets and drawing down Haganah retaliation – which generated further flight. Christian–Muslim tensions increased, with the Christians angered by the radical Muslim NC members like Nimr al Khatib, who called them 'traitors and pimps of the Jews'.[232] There was at least a grain of truth in the charge. As Yusuf Salim, a Christian notable, put it in early March:

> the Jews must think hard before they push the Christian community into the conflict between them and the Muslim world . . . The Jews must discriminate between Muslim and Christian property [and not blow up Christian houses] . . . The Christian community . . . is still not cooperating in [the Muslim] aggression . . .[233]

By early March, Haifa Christian morale had plummeted, mainly because of the entry of foreign (Muslim) irregulars into their neighbourhoods and the subsequent Haganah attacks, 'and every family capable of leaving had left for Lebanon'.[234] Some families began to send away their children. Already in early February, according to HIS, the AHC had ordered the removal of the women and children from Haifa and arrangements were under way for their transfer to Lebanon and Syria.[235] The NC endorsed the effort, on 23 March appealing to the AHC to speed up the transfer.[236] By 28 March, about 150 children, 'mostly Christian', had been evacuated, at least 50 of them to a monastery in Lebanon.[237] By mid-March, some 2,000 had been registered for evacuation and it was reported that during the following days, 'the women, the children and the old, on the AHC's instructions, would be evacuated from Haifa'.[238] And on 5 April a convoy of 15 vehicles, seven of them buses, left Haifa for Beirut; most or all of the 151 children on board were Christian;[239] a second convoy, with 200 children, mostly Muslims, may have left at this time for Damascus.[240] But altogether, only a very small minority of Haifa's children were evacuated before the fall and near-total abandonment of the city three weeks later;[241] disagreements between AHC officials in Jerusalem, the Mufti, and the NC; organisational difficulties, lack of funds and incompetence; Christian–Muslim rivalry; and the natural reluctance of parents to part with their young all played a part.[242] Husseini supported the evacuation of the non-combatants – but to sites inside Palestine, not out of the country. Hakim and the Haifa NC ignored his instructions.[243] Hakim and

Ahmad Bey Khalil's sister, Miriam Khalil, and Sahaj Nassir, who headed a body called the Arab Women's Organisation, were prominent in the operation.

During February–March there were repeated outbreaks of fighting, with almost daily Arab attacks on transport and sniping[244] and with Haganah reprisals inflicting serious casualties and undermining morale. The Jewish attacks usually were far more efficient and lethal.[245] Particularly effective were the Haganah's use of mortars. On 5 March, for example, it was reported that a single mortar bomb penetrated an Arab house 'and killed the five Arab occupants which [sic] included a woman and two children'.[246] On some days, the panic was such that Arabs seeking to leave were unable to hire a truck, and some paid P£50 for transport to Nazareth.[247] 'Every day tens of families are leaving the city, hundreds of houses stand empty', HIS reported – and this despite the fact that the abandoned houses were immediately pillaged by Arab militiamen and civilians.[248] The NC repeatedly issued communiqués against the robbers 'who are exploiting the situation to their advantage'.[249] But nothing seemed to help, not even the warning by the British GOC North to Ibrahim that he

> strongly disapproves of the increasing scale on which houses in Haifa are being evacuated of their inhabitants and thereafter fortified as strong points . . . In future, where he is satisfied that such buildings have been used for firing on the [British] security forces, it is his intention . . . to cause such buildings to be destroyed.[250]

But Arab abandonment of buildings continued, as did their pillage or occupation by irregulars. In mid-March, for example, HIS reported that the Greek and Armenian inhabitants of Kiryat-Eliahu had been ordered 'by the Arabs' to evacuate the neighbourhood 'for a fortnight'.[251]

Haganah reprisals tended to grow over the months in size and lethality. Dozens of Arabs were killed and wounded when Palmah agents at the end of February introduced a car bomb, with '300 kilograms of explosives', into an Arab garage suspected of being a weapons workshop.[252] On the night of 4–5 March, a Haganah unit raided Wadi Nisnas with orders to 'kill adult males'. They penetrated several houses, destroyed the furniture with Molotov Cocktails, and hit about 30 men, 'among them 19 sure kills'.[253] On 17 March, the Haganah ambushed an Arab arms convoy, accompanied by Arab Legion vehicles, from Lebanon near Kiryat Motzkin, blowing up two of the trucks. Among the dozen Arabs killed (and two Britons working for the Arabs) was Muhamad bin Hamad al Huneiti, the Jordanian commander of Haifa's militia. Two Haganah men were killed and two injured.[254] The ambush, which was followed by a series of sharp Haganah strikes in Haifa itself, severely shook Arab morale.[255] Once again, queues of Arabs formed outside the Lebanese and Syrian consulates, but the applicants were told that entry into these countries 'was prohibited'. 'Those with medical documents [i.e., conditions]' were also denied visas.[256]

General Safwat, vaguely responsible for the Arab forces in Palestine, ordered the Haifa area commander to attack Jewish targets on the Carmel and Jewish settlements around Haifa as a means of relieving the pressure on the Arab neighbourhoods.[257] But the orders were unrealistic; the Arab militias could barely protect themselves, let alone act in concert offensively. Indeed, notables, apparently headed by Hakim, renewed their efforts to achieve a truce. The Haganah commanders (and Ben-Gurion) repeatedly brushed them aside, arguing that a truce would not be honoured by the irregulars and would be used by the Arabs to stockpile weaponry. In any case, Haifa was a place in which the Haganah clearly had the upper hand; a local truce could work only to the Arabs' advantage. Ben-Gurion jotted down in his diary: 'The Arabs are still leaving Haifa' – seemingly making a connection between Haganah opposition to a truce and the idea that a truce might halt the exodus.[258]

The second half of March and the first half of April witnessed a further decline in the Arabs' economic situation. Medicines and doctors were reportedly in short supply. Haifa doctors were demanding 'at least P£1.5' per house call.[259] (In general, by early April the flight of doctors was acutely felt throughout the country and the Arab Doctors Association in Jerusalem and the AHC were demanding that doctors who had fled return, threatening those who refused with (unnamed) punishment.[260]) Bread and flour were scarce. The NC had requisitioned much of the flour allocated by the British authorities and given it to the militiamen. 'Many merchants had refused to give part of [their] flour and responded that the strangers [i.e., foreign irregulars] should receive their livelihood from the neighbouring countries', reported the Haganah. Some bakery-owners had fled to Safad and their bakeries had been confiscated by the NC. Nonetheless, militiamen complained that they were 'hungry'. British troops were selling sugar and wheat from the government warehouses to Arabs. The NC of Jenin had demanded that the government's food allocations to Haifa's Arabs – flour, eggs, rice, sugar – be reduced as only '8,000 people had remained in Haifa'. Haj Ibrahim had checked and said there were '35-40,000' Arab inhabitants left. Most other goods were said to be available.[261] The tobacco manufacturers – Karaman, Dik and Salti – had all removed most of their machinery to Cyprus and Egypt; construction goods merchants refrained from opening shop because 'there was no one to sell to'. 'The rich, [including] the big merchants, were busy converting their [Palestine pounds] to gold and dollars and transferring them to the neighbouring countries', reported the Haganah.[262] Telephones in the Arab sector often failed to work as the Jews had cut the lines.[263] The Haganah's Committee for Economic Defence concluded that in terms of 'speculation and the inability to properly organise [food distribution]', Haifa had become the most 'prominent' Arab town.[264]

The food shortages and the sense of military vulnerability and isolation caused by the Jewish settlements on the city's access roads certainly contributed to the demoralisation that underlay the exodus of the upper and middle classes; so did the concomitant breakdown of law and order. The irregulars robbed and intimidated the locals, terrorising those they had been sent to protect, in the words of Nimr al Khatib. He blamed equally the irregulars, the British, for doing nothing, and the civilians who had fled, leaving behind houses that invited despoliation.[265] 'Bands of robbers organised themselves . . . In March . . . waves of robbery and theft became frequent in Arab Haifa . . . From day to day, the feeling grew that Arab Haifa was on the verge of collapse. Anarchy and disorder prevailed in everything.' The situation was aggravated that month by the wholesale desertion and flight of the city's Arab constables, who usually took with them their rifles and ammunition.[266] Without doubt, the exodus was linked to Haganah reprisals, Arab attacks and fears of subsequent Jewish retaliation, but for the better educated, especially the civil servants and professionals, there were also constant long-term considerations. Ephraim Krischer, a Mapam activist, identified a general fear of future 'great disorder' as the main reason for this early stage of the exodus, adding more specifically, that Arab municipal and Mandate employees feared that 'in the Jewish state they wouldn't have any chance of advancement in their careers because precedence would be given to Jews'. This feeling was reinforced by the fact that most Arab officials lacked fluent Hebrew.[267]

Mapam's Arab Department, probably in part on the basis of Krischer's report, in March analysed the flight from Haifa. The department noted the Arabs' 'fears . . . for their future', both in the chaotic, transitional pre-State period and under Jewish rule, and pointed out that it was mainly 'Christians, professionals, officials' who were leaving. By 1 March, several mainly Christian districts were 'almost completely' empty. 'The flight is less marked in the eastern parts of town, where the poorer classes, who are under the influence of the extremists, are concentrated', stated the department. According to this analysis, the Christians were mainly worried about the transitional period, between the end of effective Mandate government and the start of effective Jewish government. They felt that they would then be 'between the hammer and the anvil, the Arab terrorist operations and Jewish reactions'.[268]

While the NC was clearly worried by the exodus, its efforts to stem it through most of December 1947 – early April 1948 appear to have been half-hearted and muted. In only one of the 12 communiqués issued by the committee over the period did it urge the Arabs to remain. On 12 December the committee warned against 'Fifth Columnists' spreading defeatism and influencing people 'to leave their properties and houses, which have become easy prey to the enemy who has seized and occupied them . . . Stay in your places', the committee urged. In none of the communiqués did the committee explicitly order the inhabitants not to leave. Over January–March 1948, the communiqués failed altogether to order or urge the populace to stay at home or in the city. Several, however, urged Arabs to 'stay at your posts' – referring, apparently, to militiamen and officials.[269]

It is only in the first half of April that we find the NC calling upon some of those who had fled to return. Indeed, on 1 April HIS was able to report that the remaining Arab notables were peeved at the municipal council members who had left 'and abandoned the Arab interests precisely when the government's powers were being transferred to the local authorities'. And it was Shabtai Levy, the city's Jewish mayor, rather than the Arab notables, who issued a public call to Arab councilmen to return.[270]

A few days later, Haj Ibrahim wrote letters to the absent NC members – George Tawil (in Beirut), Ahmad Kamal ('Anabta, near Jenin), Zaki Bey Tamimi (Damascus), Yusuf Sahayun (Alexandria) – demanding that they return,[271] and in the second week of April, according to Falastin, the NC called upon all shopkeepers who had fled to return and reopen their businesses, on pain of revocation of their licenses.[272] But by then, the cause of Haifa's Arabs was lost; too many had left and the town was about to fall. And as the situation worsened, the incentive to flee increased. On 12 April, for example, HIS in Haifa reported that the town's remaining Arab merchants had secretly decided to move their businesses and stocks to Jaffa (or to Egypt, Syria or Lebanon) for fear that they would be plundered by irregulars. Besides, the NC had imposed heavy taxes to finance the militiamen.[273]

The NC's failure to act strenuously to halt the exodus is easily understood. The committee lacked legal powers to curb emigration. More important, the pre-April 1948 exodus encompassed mostly the middle and upper classes – precisely the social strata from which the committee members were drawn. It was their relatives and friends, first and foremost, who were fleeing. Indeed, most of the NC itself had left. By 28 March, according to the Haganah, 11 of the 15 members had departed; efforts by chairman Ibrahim to lure them back had failed.[274] Indeed, Rashid Haj Ibrahim himself left Palestine in early April, never to return.[275] Those members who had remained behind were hardly in a position to vilify, condemn or punish would-be evacuees, however disruptive the exodus was understood to be to the Arab cause. The mass flight of the community leaders was to culminate, with telling effect, during the battle of Haifa on 21–22 April 1948.

Jaffa

Jaffa, an Arab city of about 75,000 inhabitants, had been earmarked by the UN partition resolution for Palestinian sovereignty. But it was to be an enclave inside the Jewish State, its land communications with the rest of the Palestinian State dependent upon the Jews. The inhabitants felt isolated and vulnerable. But as with Haifa, the exodus from the town was triggered by the start of hostilities, which were initiated by Jaffa's militiamen, who began sniping into neighbouring Tel Aviv on 30 November 1947. The following day, dozens of Arabs assaulted Jewish houses bordering on the northern Manshiya neighbourhood and an Arab mob in Abu Kabir, a neighbourhood to the west, attacked a Jewish car and murdered its three passengers. Jewish retaliatory strikes followed. The Haganah's Kiryati Brigade blew up a house in Abu Kabir on 2 December and the IZL torched several buildings four days later, killing at least two persons.[276]

Jaffa's inhabitants feared that worse was to come. The evacuation from Jaffa's border districts began already at the beginning of December. As with Haifa, the initial flight was from the peripheral neighbourhoods to the city centre. 'Families, with their belongings, are leaving Manshiya', reported Palmah scouts on 1 December.[277] A further reconnaissance, on 5 December, found that the evacuation of Manshiya was continuing and there was also flight from Jaffa's southern neighbourhoods, bordering on (Jewish) Bat-Yam and Holon.[278] On 2 December HIS reported that 'carts loaded with belongings [were] seen leaving' Abu Kabir for central Jaffa. The flight from the peripheral neighbourhoods inward no doubt sowed fright and flight-mindedness in the core areas.[279] Jewish behaviour contributed: on 5 December British observers reported an Arab beaten to death 'by a Jewish crowd' near the Mughrabi Cinema and Arab-owned shops and houses were set alight in the Carmel Market area[280] and in or near the Hatikva Quarter (all in southern Tel Aviv).[281] Uniformed IZL men toured neighbouring Petah Tikva and demanded that Jewish employers 'throw out their [Arab] workers'.[282] The British, too, marginally added to the displacement by warning Arabs living or working in Tel Aviv to leave for Jaffa.[283]

Jews in seam neighbourhoods were also displaced by the hostilities. By mid-January 1948, some 7,000 had been rendered homeless. Efforts by the authorities to persuade them to return home were unavailing.[284]

By 9 December, HIS was reporting:

> Economic conditions in Jaffa are bad. The price of flour has soared. Arab refugees sleeping in the streets of the city . . . Families of the well-to-do are leaving the cities – for the interior of the country. The rich are emigrating to Syria, Lebanon and even Cyprus.[285]

The Jaffa NC had requisitioned '42 hotels and brothels' to house the refugees.[286] Country folk who earlier had migrated to the town were now moving back to their villages.[287] By the end of December, HIS reported that some '60 per cent' of Jaffa's Christians had left.[288] The Jaffa Municipality was reportedly trying to persuade those who had fled to return and those encamped in the town centre to return to their homes in the peripheries, but to little avail.[289] On 23 December, HIS reported that '25,000' had fled Jaffa,[290] but on 1 February the Arab Division felt that the estimate that '15–20 thousand had left' was an exaggeration.[291]

The mayor, Yusuf Heikal, and Tel Aviv's mayor, Israel Rokah, on 7 December apparently agreed to issue a ceasefire call and to enable the inhabitants of the seam neighbourhoods from both sides to return home (though it appears the joint call was never actually issued).[292] The town's main militia commander, a moderate, Nimr al Hawari, tried to prevent hostilities and ordered his men to fire only when fired upon; they also suffered from a shortage of ammunition. But Hawari's reach was limited; in Abu Kabir, another militia leader, Abu Laban, ruled.[293] HIS identified three power centres in Jaffa – Hawari, Heikal, and local Husseini supporters, who were busy organising the violence in each neighbourhood. And armed extortionists had taken to the streets, intimidating people to contribute to 'the national cause'.[294] One Arab informant told HIS that the AHC 'had not intended the disturbances to reach the level they had reached . . . They made a mistake when they called for a three-day strike without taking account of the character of the Arab public.' Many were out of work and, hearing about the killings and arson in Jerusalem, 'an atmosphere was created conducive to such deeds in Jaffa as well'. The Jaffa mob ran amok and Hawari and Heikal were powerless.[295] Hawari, who may have been a HIS agent, and Heikal fell out. Hawari fled the country at the end of December.[296] Moderate and Opposition figures were afraid that the Husseinis would resume anti-Opposition terrorism à la 1937–1939.[297]

Most local notables, represented by the Jaffa NC, opposed hostilities against Tel Aviv, aware of their militias' inadequacy and fearful of Jewish retaliation. They were especially concerned about the orange crop in the surrounding groves, much of it destined for export through Jaffa. Initially, they even organised patrols in the peripheral neighbourhoods to prevent clashes.[298] Heikal, a protégé of Musa al 'Alami, a veteran Palestinian moderate, probably flew to Cairo in early December 1947 to obtain Husseini or Arab League permission to conclude a ceasefire[299] but the activists in the town were busy provoking incidents and undermining the NC.[300]

As in Haifa, by the third week of hostilities notables in southern Jaffa were trying to reach a ceasefire with Bat-Yam. A meeting took place on 16 December. The Arabs asked that the Jews refrain 'from shutting off their water and blowing up their houses'. The Jews demanded that the Arabs stop sniping at traffic. The Arabs 'promised to make sure that no one fired' and that night, 'for the first time, there was electricity in the Jibalya [neighbourhood]'.[301]

However, Husseini apparently opposed any local truce and, though aware that the city stood no chance of holding out in the long run, wanted it to continue to harass Tel Aviv as best it could, but with a minimum investment of external resources.[302] Apart from a lack of flour and oil,[303]

Jaffa seems to have suffered no severe food shortages during the first four months of the civil war.[304] One reason was the proximity of its satellite villages (such as Yazur and Kheiriya) and the access between them and the town; another was that the quick depletion of the population left those who remained with a surplus of food coupons and a surfeit of produce. But the high unemployment (compounded by fear of travelling to exposed work places[305]) meant that many lacked the wherewithal to purchase the available produce and, in addition, triggered fear among the middle classes – and an actual increase in cases – of 'theft and robbery'.[306] By March, the only major workplace still functioning was the harbour.[307] By April, there was a serious shortage of, and a black market in, petrol; long queues were the norm in petrol stations.[308] There was also a severe shortage of doctors and medicines. Telephone lines out of Jaffa were often down and postal services had completely collapsed.[309] By the end of January, the hospitals were overflowing with injured. Some were simply 'sent home'. There were no funds to pay doctors' wages.[310]

And there was an unwillingness to fight. One reason was the fear among Arab males that there would be no compensation or support for their widows and orphans.[311] People simply preferred to flee.

> The refugees have no illusions. They refuse to endanger themselves [by staying in or returning to] Jewish areas. Their flight is spontaneous, not organised . . . [It causes] fright. There is no . . . use preaching against the exodus. People are fleeing to Nablus, to Nazareth, even to Egypt.[312]

Haganah posters, threatening revenge and retribution, further undermined morale.[313] There was a 'general feeling' that Husseini 'wanted to sacrifice Jaffa in order to stir up the Arab world against the Jews and against partition'.[314] The efforts of the local NC and militia units to stem the floodtide of refugees – including the imposition of fines and property confiscations – failed.[315]

A major landmark in the town's demoralisation was the LHI's 4 January 1948 demolition of the town hall (saraya), which housed a militia headquarters, with a powerful car bomb, which left dozens of dead[316] Utilities and municipal services broke down. With the flight of middle and upper class families, businesses closed and unemployment became rife.[317] HIS reported:

> The town's main markets, that in the past were crowded, are today desolate, the coffee shops are empty and the cinema houses closed. Roadblocks, with barbed wire, have been set up in the centre of town [and] . . . on its borders. The people in Jaffa live in fear – of the Jews' bombs and internecine Arab attacks. Many Arabs, who lived on the peripheries . . . have left their places. It is estimated that from Manshiya alone fled three thousand families. Most moved to the old town, to the Nuzha and 'Ajami [neighbourhoods]. They took over the houses by force and these

houses are now crowded as in every room live more than ten people. Many families have left for Syria, Lebanon, Transjordan, Cyprus and Egypt.[318]

Trains to and from Jaffa stopped running.[319] Labourers stopped commuting to Tel Aviv, aggravating the unemployment. The local leaders became despondent. They put no trust in the contingents of foreign volunteers and many 'loudly proclaimed' that they wanted King Abdullah to conquer Palestine. At the same time, the Husseinis silenced Opposition figures.[320] The Lebanese consulate in Jerusalem reported that Heikal had said:

> that the situation in Jaffa has reached its worst [sic]. The Arabs he added were about to raise the white banners of surrender . . . for lack of ammunition and the general feeling [morale?] was completely broken down [sic] after the last big explosion [i.e., the *saraya*] . . . and if . . . the Jews wanted . . . they could conquer the whole town without great difficulties. The economic situation is so bad that it could not be described . . .[321]

An Arab informant told Sasson: 'There is no work. Whoever could leave, has left, there is fear everywhere, and there is no safety. Robbery and theft are common', and the NC had lost its authority and was expected to resign.[322]

Arab defeatism is well illustrated in telephone conversations from Jaffa, which were intercepted and recorded by IZL intelligence. Jaffa lawyer Sa'id Zain ad Din related to a friend or relative in Khan Yunis what had happened when the *saraya* was blown up. Two of his relatives had been injured and a whole street had been badly damaged. 'Why not move here?' asked the man from Khan Yunis. 'We will come soon', said Zain ad Din.

Two days later, the following conversation took place between 'Abdul Latif Qaddumi, an officer from a contingent of Nabulsi irregulars in Jaffa, and 'Abu Ahmad,' from Nablus:

> Abdul Latif Qaddumi: 'Where is Abu Fiad Qaddumi?'
> Abu Ahmad: 'He went to Nazareth.'
> Abdul Latif Qaddumi: 'I think I will soon return to Nablus.'
> Abu Ahmad: 'If your people in Jaffa don't know how to operate and allow the Jews to do to them as they wish, then leave them and come [back] here.'
> Abdul Latif Qaddumi: 'Indeed, they don't know how to operate here . . . I will leave them, let them do as they wish, and [I will] return to Nablus.

Throughout, the tapped conversations reveal an oppressive fear of the Jews and a sense that flight, with administrative chaos in its wake, was imminent.[323]

During the first months of the war, a number of militia bands had emerged in Jaffa; some were obedient to the AHC and Husseini, others were aligned to Heikal and other Opposition figures. There were also several groups of foreign irregulars, some belonging to the ALA (a contingent of Iraqis arrived in early February), others independent of it.[324] Bands of irregulars came and went. In March, for example, 75–150 Syrian volunteers abruptly pulled out of the city (after their commander was jailed for stealing provisions from a warehouse) and moved to Tulkarm; a platoon of Iraqis, under 'Abd al Jaber, left and garrisoned the abandoned British Army Wadi Sarar Camp.[325] An effort in early February by Hassan Salame to unify the militias was unsuccessful.[326] Emissaries from Jaffa tried to mobilise additional troops in the Hebron and Nablus area – but there were few takers, even though Jaffa was offering the princely sum of P£40 per month. One recruitment effort, in Hebron, yielded only '35 paupers'.[327]

Through January, and perhaps also early February 1948, important Jaffa notables sought a truce. But the Haganah was reluctant. As in Haifa, the Haganah had the upper hand and had no intention of letting Jaffa live in peace so long as the Arabs in other places, principally in Jerusalem, did not allow the Jews to live in peace. Moreover, the Jewish commanders believed, with justification, that concluding a truce with Jaffa's civilian leaders would not necessarily lead to a cessation of operations by the irregulars.[328]

And rifts among the Jaffa Arabs from the beginning subverted all efforts at peacemaking. In February, Ben-Gurion wrote to Shertok that Heikal, through a British intermediary, was trying to secure an agreement with Tel Aviv but that the new irregulars' commander, 'Abdul Wahab 'Ali Shihaini, had blocked him. The mayor had said 'that without agreement, Jaffa [would] be entirely destroyed'. According to Ben-Gurion, Shihaini had answered: 'I do not mind [the] destruction [of] Jaffa if we secure [the] destruction [of] Tel Aviv.'[329]

As in Haifa, the irregulars intimidated the local population, echoing the experience of 1936–1939. 'Most of the people who stayed with their commander, 'Adel Nijam ad Din, behaved towards the inhabitants like conquerors. They confiscated their weapons and sold them, imposed fines and stole, and confiscated cars and sold them . . . The inhabitants were more afraid of their defenders-saviours than of the Jews their enemies', wrote Nimr al Khatib.[330]

The fears of the Jaffa citrus merchants, that the Jews would block the export of the crop,[331] on which Jaffa's economy depended, mirrored those of their neighbouring Jewish compeers and were largely responsible for the British-mediated gentleman's agreement of December that the two sides should not hit each others' groves, citrus-carrying trucks and citrus-exporting facilities.[332] That agreement, acquiesced in by the local Tel Aviv Haganah chiefs under pressure from Jewish farmers and businessmen, was opposed by the HNS and was roundly debated at the meeting of 1–2 January 1948 between Ben-Gurion and his advisers. The representatives of the Arab Division, led by Machnes, himself an orange-grove owner, successfully opposed a complete blockade of Jaffa – as demanded by Yigael Yadin and Moshe Sneh. The debate ended with Ben-Gurion concluding that there was general agreement on the need to 'blockade Jaffa' but that the orange cultivators and shipments should be left alone.[333]

The Jewish grove-growers, represented by Yosef Ya'akobson (who was also a senior Haganah officer), through January continued to press for a formal ceasefire agreement around Jaffa, Rehovot, Nes-Ziona and east of Tel Aviv, but to no avail. Ya'akobson charged that the Haganah was murdering, terrorising and robbing orange-cultivators and looting Arab property. Moshe Dayan opposed an agreement, because this was an area in which the Haganah was stronger and also because the Arab irregulars could be supplied elsewhere in the country with food from this area, were it quiescent. Levi Shkolnik (Eshkol) argued that three months of quiet during the harvest would benefit the Yishuv, but Galili and Yadin countered that such a truce would favour the Arabs as 'Jaffa and Haifa were Arab weak points'. An agreement covering the Coastal Plain would free the Mufti of the pro-peace pressures emanating from the two towns. Ben-Gurion said that while in general he was for limiting the area of hostilities: 'I . . . do not believe that the agreement will be honoured . . . it will be disrupted.'[334]

But Arab notables, through British intermediaries, continued to press for a wider citrus agreement. Galili, with a touch of irony, proposed a ceasefire covering 'the whole area of citrus eaters', not just the areas of 'citrus cultivation'. He explained the minuses and pluses of the proposed agreement: the arrangement would not free Jewish troops and, conversely, would free Arab forces for operations in the countryside; would free the AHC from the pressure of the Jaffa notables; would shift the focus of hostilities to areas where the Haganah had no natural advantage; and would release Jaffa from being a Jewish 'hostage, something we have no interest in'. On the plus side, Galili said that Haganah policy had consistently been to limit the areas of conflagration; and the Yishuv was also interested in unhindered harvest and export of its citrus crop. Galili added that the Haganah was generally interested in quiet in the areas earmarked for Jewish sovereignty and in the Arabs not being harmed in these areas – 'this had value regarding our future relations with the Arabs . . . and this could serve [Jewish] propaganda [needs] . . .'. Moreover, the Haganah was interested in quiet that would enable it to arm and train.[335]

In the end, a formal agreement was never concluded. But neither was a complete blockade imposed on Jaffa, and the bilateral orange-picking and -exporting continued largely unhampered.

Between January and mid-April 1948, Haganah conquest of the town was out of the question; the British, it was understood, would prevent it. The Haganah restricted itself to a partial siege, limited reprisals and occasional harassment. It refrained from massive retaliation – save for the night of 12–13 February, when its units struck simultaneously at Abu Kabir, Jibalya and Tel a Rish, and the outlying village of Yazur. At Abu Kabir, 13 Arabs were killed, including the mukhtar, and 22 injured. Many of Yazur's inhabitants fled.[336] A second major attack on Abu Kabir was launched on 13 March; the objective was 'the destruction of the Abu Kabir neighbourhood', which during the previous weeks had been abandoned by most of its inhabitants and was guarded by several dozen militiamen. The Haganah shelled the neighbourhood with very noisy, Yishuv-produced mortars, 'Davidkas', and sappers blew up a number of houses.[337] 'The whole city was shaken and many of the inhabitants left their houses . . . The attack had a very depressing effect.'[338] The attack's demoralising effect reached as far afield as Gaza.[339] A further operation, on 24 March, against Jibalya, left six houses demolished and two dead.[340] By mid-April, Jaffa's inhabitants were also demoralised by events elsewhere in the country, principally Deir Yassin. A Jaffa inhabitant wrote to a friend or relation in Egypt that: 'The Jews are cruel. In Tiberias as in Deir Yassin they behaved barbarously and used axes to chop off hands and legs of people and children. They did awful things to women, but the writer cannot write about them out of shame.'[341]

These attacks, the general exodus and the withdrawal of the Iraqi and Syrian contingents prompted Heikal to make one last effort to save his city: he travelled to Amman to persuade King Abdullah to move Arab Legion units into Jaffa on 15 May or earlier.[342] By mid-April, HIS estimated that a full 50 per cent of the townspeople had fled.[343] The increasing efforts of the NC to stem the flow – including increased taxation against the evacuees (a tax on furniture, of P£12, was now added to the tax or ransom paid for each departee) – proved of no avail. Most of the important families had left – the Abu Khidras for Gaza, the Nabulsis and Dajanis for Egypt, the 'Abd al Wahims for Beirut, the Baidases for Nablus. Without doubt, the flight of the middle and upper classes served to further demoralise the remaining masses. There was large-scale unemployment and those still in the city engaged in theft and looting to maintain their families. Food, while available, had soared in price; a sack of flour cost P£14 (a month before it had cost P£7). Relations between the various remaining leaders and between the various militia groups were bad.[344]

Jerusalem

According to the partition resolution, Jerusalem, with about 100,000 Jews and 50,000 Arabs (or 85–90,000, if one includes the surrounding Arab villages), was to be an international zone, albeit one surrounded on all sides by the Palestine Arab state and Arab villages, which dominated the access roads. The Jewish population felt vulnerable and somewhat abandoned. Immediately following the passage of the resolution, the Jewish neighbourhoods, mostly in the western part of town, came under sniper fire from Arab quarters and, during the following months, the community was gradually strangulated by the blockade of the main road to Tel Aviv. By the end of March, despite the convoy system and occasional British military assistance, the city's Jewish districts were under almost complete siege. However, the Haganah and the smaller IZL and LHI units in the town were relatively well-armed and organised, and in the fighting which erupted, the Arab neighbourhoods along the 'seam' between the two communities and the semi-isolated Arab quarters in mostly Jewish western Jerusalem, repeatedly hit by raids and mortar fire, were the ones that collapsed and emptied of their inhabitants. (But Jewish 'seam' neighbourhoods also were partially evacuated: in early January 1948, for example, some 75 per cent of the residents of north Talpiyot and Mekor Hayim had evacuated and one-third of the residents of Arnona and central Talpiyot.[345])

Six weeks into the hostilities, on 10 January, Haganah intelligence tapped a revealing telephone conversation, between Dr Husayn Khalidi, the AHC and NC member, and an Arab merchant identified as 'Abu Zaki': 'Everyone is leaving me. Six [AHC members] are in Cairo, 2 are in Damascus – I won't be able to hold on much longer . . . Jerusalem is lost. No one is left in Qatamon, Sheikh Jarrah has emptied, people are even leaving the Old City. Everyone who has a cheque or a little money – is off to Egypt, off to Lebanon, off to Damascus', said Khalidi.[346] Khalidi's exaggerations regarding the extent of the flight were themselves symptomatic of the panic that had taken hold. Three days earlier, Haganah intelligence had reported that Arabs who turned to the authorities for arms were being turned away; there simply were none to hand out. In the Old City, the core of Arab Jerusalem, there were 'depression, despair and anarchy', and most of the population was unemployed. 'Some say that it were better to turn to [King] Abdullah or even that the British stay in the country.'[347]

Provisions were running out and the irregulars were paying for goods with worthless chits. Shopkeepers tried to hide their wares as they were being forced to pay 'taxes' of P£10 per day or the equivalent in goods.[348] Grocers were refusing to sell on credit.[349] Following the destruction of Beit Safafa's flourmill, the village – adjoining southern Jerusalem – reported that it had run out of bread, and by early January the price of flour in Jerusalem proper had increased fivefold (from P£1.20 per sack to P£6 per sack)[350] though other staples were plentiful.[351] That month, Jewish-made margarine was still available[352] and some Jews were reported bartering with Arabs bread and flour for sugar.[353]

But the massive unemployment caused a rash of thefts and robberies as the poor couldn't buy the produce in stock.[354] The government initially provided flour rations to each NC for distribution; but Arabs had robbed shipments of flour from government trains, so the high commissioner stopped the supply.[355] Apparently, there was also politically motivated discrimination in the distribution of the flour ration and some bakers were filling the bread with 'other, strange and bad, elements'.[356] The Arab inspector responsible for the flour distribution to retailers, Martin Hadad, apparently stole large quantities and went into business for himself – selling 'at inflated prices', some apparently to Jews.[357]

The NC had organised a fund-raising campaign to cover war costs, including guard duty in each neighbourhood. Christian Arabs often felt they were being over-taxed or subject to extortion. But some Arabs simply paid P£2-3 per month to be exempted from guard duty (harking back to corrupt practices under the Ottomans).[358] There were also gangsters among the guard contingents who exploited their position to rob and steal. HIS reported that occasionally they would start shooting to precipitate panic and flight; then they would plunder the houses just abandoned.[359] Irregulars also intercepted and robbed food shipments – as happened to one car-load of eggs and chickens bound for Jerusalem in early February.[360]

The arrival in the Old City during January–March of refugees from other neighbourhoods aggravated the situation. Food prices were such that on 27 February there was a demonstration in the Old City against the NC. The protesters were told 'to hold on a bit longer, until victory was achieved'.[361] In the southern neighbourhoods, by late March, the economic situation was mixed: on the one hand, there was a surfeit of produce in the shops because the foods traditionally destined for Jewish markets now remained in the Arab sector. Vegetable prices were extremely low (for example, '30 heads of lettuce sold for 10 mil') but most of the produce simply went unsold because people were too poor to buy. And no canned goods were available (these had all been bought up by the wealthy), and fish (traditionally from Jaffa) and meat were in very short supply. Price controls were anarchic as there were several different supervisory bodies – and militiamen from Hebron tended simply to take foodstuffs against empty promises of future payment. Textiles, which mostly came from outside Palestine, were scarce.[362]

In the course of the first four months of the civil war, transportation between Arab Jerusalem and the rest of Palestine was either completely blocked or severely curtailed. By early April, the Jerusalem–Jaffa and Jerusalem–Beit Jala bus lines had ceased functioning and buses to and from Hebron were down to two per day (nine before the war), with Bethlehem down to three per day (down from 12).[363] Inside the city, the number of passengers using public transport had fallen by 90 per cent.[364] In early April, Jerusalem was still suffering from severe shortages in bread, clothing and canned goods, and various types of petrol.[365]

The exodus of the Arabs from western Jerusalem can be said to have begun on 30 November, with the evacuation, in trucks, of three or four families from the mixed neighbourhood of Romema, which dominated the western entrance to the city and the beginning of the Jerusalem–Tel Aviv road. According to HIS-AD, the departees explained their evacuation as 'preparatory to [military] operations on the part of the Arabs'.[366] The same day, a group of Arabs apparently 'advised' Jewish residents 'to leave the area'.[367] A week before, the Arab inhabitants of a house in Ethiopia Street in downtown (west) Jerusalem had 'received instructions' – apparently from Arab authorities – to evacuate and move to an Arab area; hostilities were imminent.[368]

Hostilities began on 1 December, with Arab gunmen and stone-throwers attacking Jewish buses at the Jaffa Gate and Mahane Yehuda and with a mob attack, on 2 December, against the downtown New Commercial Centre, where dozens of shops and workshops were torched and looted, and 24 Jews were injured. British troops and police failed to intervene against the rioters but arrested 16 Haganah men who had.[369] That night, IZL men reportedly looted Arab shops in west Jerusalem[370] and a Jewish mob set fire to the Rex Cinema and adjoining Arab houses.[371] The following day, the IZL warned the mukhtar of Lifta, a suburb-village just west of Romema, that the village would be bombed if any Jews were harmed in Romema.[372] Around town, Arab snipers began firing into Jewish districts and, periodically, the Haganah replied. When asked, as by the inhabitants of Yemin Moshe, the Haganah ordered Jewish inhabitants in the seam neighbourhoods to stay put.[373]

On 4 December, some Arab families evacuated Lifta and several Jewish families evacuated the mixed, prosperous district of Talbiye, in the centre of west Jerusalem.[374] Lifta was apparently told by Arab authorities to evacuate its women and children and to prepare to house a militia company. A gang of some 20 oriental Jewish youths and a Jewish mob, consisting, according to Haganah observers, of 'some 200 persons, children and adults from oriental communities', rampaged in downtown west Jerusalem, torching Arab shops.[375] British police and Haganah men apparently tried to stop them. More Arab families were seen evacuating Romema.[376] In Jerusalem's Old City, some 1,500 of the Jewish Quarter's 3,500 Jewish inhabitants (almost all ultra-orthodox) fled in organised fashion to west Jerusalem while Arab families living in and around the quarter moved to Arab areas, many of their homes (and some Armenians' homes) being quickly garrisoned by Arab militiamen.[377] By the second week of December, firefights between the seam neighbourhoods and inside the Old City were a daily occurrence; Arab irregulars began ambushing traffic along the Tel Aviv–Jerusalem road; and IZL operatives began to throw bombs at Arab crowds inside the city.[378] Arab families were reported evacuating the Qatamon and Mekor Hayim neighbourhoods. The Mekor Hayim evacuees told Jewish interlocutors that they had been 'ordered' to do so, presumably by Arab authorities.[379] Jewish families in the southern Jerusalem neighbourhood of Talpiyot were 'advised' by Arab neighbours to evacuate their homes; they refused.[380]

The first mass evacuations of Jerusalem neighbourhoods took place in December 1947 – January 1948 from the suburb-villages of Lifta and Sheikh Badr, and the Arab area of Romema. Initially, Haganah patrols were ordered to patrol the outskirts of Lifta, not to enter the village, and to 'put up posters' (presumably warning the inhabitants against engaging in violence).[381] But the patrols occasionally sparked firefights with the village's militiamen,[382] and IZL and LHI operations, from the start, were more aggressive. Already in mid-December, irregulars from nearby villages had taken up positions in Lifta, to defend the site but also to harass neighbouring Jewish areas. The older villagers wanted peace but the youngsters, according to an HIS informant, 'were all activist'.[383] By the beginning of January, Lifta was suffering from a shortage of bread[384] and already on 28 December women and children were reported evacuating the village.[385] By 1 January, most of the villagers had apparently left (for Ramallah)[386], but armed irregulars or Arab Legionnaires were still in place. On or around 15 January, the villagers were ordered to return home[387] and apparently some, or most, did. A week later, the village was visited by 'Abd al Qadir al Husseini, who ordered the menfolk to stay put and 'the children, women and old' to leave.[388] Women and children were seen leaving.[389] The LHI raided the village and blew up three houses on 29 January.[390] By early February, all or almost all of Lifta's inhabitants were back in Ramallah (where they complained that the locals were 'mocking them' and that, in Lifta, they had been trapped between the irregulars, who used their homes to attack Jews, and the Jews, who destroyed their homes and killed them in retaliation).[391]

The cycle of violence that precipitated Romema's evacuation began with attacks on Jewish traffic leaving Jerusalem and the Haganah killing on 24 December of Atiya 'Adel, the owner, from Qaluniya village, of the petrol station at Romema who, using a motorcycle, doubled as a scout and informant for the Arab irregulars about Jewish convoys.[392] The following day, villagers avenged the attack by throwing a grenade at a Jewish bus. From then on, there were daily exchanges of fire in and around Romema (and Lifta) and the Haganah, IZL and LHI repeatedly raided the two sites. Romema was struck by two Haganah raids on the night of 26 December[393] and by the IZL (which destroyed a petrol station and coffee shop, killing at least five Arabs) on 27 December.[394] Some inhabitants apparently evacuated under British protection and in orderly fashion.[395] By the beginning of January, HIS reports spoke of Romema as empty[396] though some militiamen had apparently stayed and inhabitants kept returning, at least for brief visits, to inspect their property.[397] Threatening letters and telephone calls by the Haganah and LHI also, apparently, contributed to the neighbourhood's depopulation.[398] On

20 January, Israel Zablodovsky (Amir), the Haganah OC in Jerusalem, reporting to Ben-Gurion on the demographic changes in the city, said that in Romema, which had had an Arab majority, the Jews had intended to leave 'but the Haganah had not let them', and the Arabs had left. 'The eviction [*siluk*] of Arab Romema had eased' the Haganah's situation, he concluded.[399]

The inhabitants of Sheikh Badr (between the Knesset and Binyenei Ha'uma today) also evacuated their homes in mid-January, following one or more reprisal raids (provoked by Arab sniping), in which the house of the mukhtar, Haj Sulayman Hamini, was blown up by the LHI; other houses were destroyed in Haganah raiding. British intelligence reported that the Haganah had ordered Sheikh Badr's inhabitants to leave.[400] Many of the inhabitants left on 14 January.[401] Others handed over the keys to their houses to Jewish neighbours, presumably against a promise to protect their property.[402] But Jews from the poor Nahla'ot neighbourhood descended on Sheikh Badr and pillaged it. Haganah troops, perhaps fearing a re-occupation of the site by Arab irregulars, moved in and tried to drive away the Jewish 'thugs' ('twelve of them armed with knives') with shots in the air.[403] On 19 January British police escorted the last remaining Arab inhabitants out of Sheikh Badr, apparently to Lifta,[404] and moved in to guard the vacated houses. But as soon as they left, residents of the Nahla'ot returned, torching and pillaging what remained.[405] A number of left-wing intellectuals, including Hebrew University Rector Judah Leib Magnes and philosopher Martin Buber, possibly prompted by the events in Sheikh Badr, issued a call to Jerusalem's inhabitants to cease the plunder and the murder of Arabs.[406]

Talbiye, southeast of Rehavia, contained a mixture of prosperous Jewish and (mainly Christian) Arab families who had lived in relative harmony before 1948. The hostilities gradually undermined the coexistence, though for a time both groups tried to preserve it in face of the tide of belligerence washing over the city. At the start of January, a meeting of the neighbourhood's Arabs decided to boycott Arab peddlers, saying that 'they introduced conflict into the neighbourhood. They decided to call on the Jews to join them in this'.[407] They also proposed setting up a joint Arab-Jewish-British police station *in situ*.[408] But the Arabs came under growing pressure from Arabs outside, who 'informed [them] that they would take revenge against them if they kept up the good relations with the Haganah and [continued] giving [the Haganah] men tea'. When the Talbiye Arab housewives went shopping in the neighbouring German Colony area, irregulars from Hebron threatened them 'that the time would come when they would arrange [through provocations] that the Jews kill them . . . Many Christians want to leave their homes and the city but have been warned that if they do this, [other Arabs] will destroy their houses and steal all their possessions.' And Jews, too, occasionally intimidated the inhabitants, according to one HIS-AD report. Some families living in Karm al Ruhban, an area adjoining Talbiye to the west, were 'told' by Jews in early February to leave their homes. Specifically, a group of 10–13 Jews entered the home of George Mashbak, searched it and 'behaved rudely. Similarly, the Wahaba family received a warning to leave immediately.'[409] By 20 January, Zablodovsky was able to report that 'Talbiyeh is . . . increasingly becoming Jewish, though a few Arabs remain'.[410]

The Arab attack on 10 February on Yemin Moshe, a Jewish neighbourhood just east of Talbiye, proved decisive. The attack, possibly triggered by Jewish sniping at an Arab bus, was beaten off by Haganah fire and British troops, leaving more than a dozen Arab dead.[411] Either during the battle or immediately in its wake, Arab families were seen evacuating Talbiye with their belongings.[412] On 11 February, a Haganah car mounting a loudspeaker 'drove around Talbiye and warned the Arabs of Haganah retaliation. The Arabs began to flee.' The Arab national institutions opposed the flight and, using threats and persuasion, 'demanded that the inhabitants stay put and summoned the [British] Army. When the police arrived . . . they arrested the car's passengers.' The Arab authorities apparently feared that once established in Talbiye, the Haganah would push southwards, taking additional Arab, or partly Arab, neighbourhoods, such as the German Colony and Bak'a.[413] Some Talbiye Jews told their neighbours 'that they had nothing to fear' – but '60–70 [Arab] families left', only three remaining. The Arab authorities were highly critical, saying that the evacuation had been 'shameful and hurried'. Moreover, there was talk of taking revenge 'against the rich Arabs "who had cooperated with the Jews in Talbiye". All efforts to persuade the inhabitants to stay had failed and the feeling of shame is great.'[414] The AHC decided – and apparently publicised – that every Talbiye house abandoned by its owners would pass under its control and would be garrisoned by irregulars.[415] But additional families left during the following days[416] and while a number of families were reported to have returned (perhaps only temporarily to guard or pack and collect belongings),[417] in effect the neighbourhood had been evacuated. A few Arab males remained, 'sitting on their packed belongings and ready to leave at a moment's notice'. The Arab city OC had forbidden them to leave. The remaining Arabs sought to persuade the Haganah to agree to deem Talbiye a neutral, non-combat zone.[418] The Haganah apparently declined and they eventually departed.

Already by mid-January, 'a spirit of depression and panic' had gripped the Arab districts of Jerusalem, reported the Haganah; the mere rumour of a Jewish bomb led to panic flight from whole neighbourhoods. Even the non-prosperous were beginning to flee and the AHC was imposing heavy fines on the relatives of those leaving the country. Many Christians were saying out loud that 'Jewish rule was better than the rule of the [Husseini] extortionists'.[419] During December–February, many Arab residents in or near the largely Jewish neighbourhoods of Talpiyot and Mekor Haim, in southern Jerusalem, and the adjacent suburb village of

Beit Safafa, abandoned their homes, either as a result of Arab orders –
to get them out of harm's way or to free their home for incoming
militiamen[420] – or because of Jewish attack or fear of attack.[421] A major
precipitant to flight from the area was the Haganah raid on Beit Safafa
on 13 February, in which the regional militia leader, Mahmud al 'Umari,
was killed.[422] Beit Safafa was reportedly 'almost completely evacuated'
a few days later.[423]

During January, many inhabitants of the Sheikh Jarrah, Musrara
and Abu Tor neighbourhoods also evacuated.[424] The evacuation of
Sheikh Jarrah occurred in two stages, the first, in the first week of
January, spontaneously,[425] and the second, a week later, precipitated
by a Haganah raid in which 12 houses were torched[426] and an LHI raid
the following day.[427] The evacuation may have been partially coordinated with and assisted by the British, who wanted an end to hostilities
in and around the neighbourhood, which sat astride the main road out
of the city northward.[428] The departure that month from Musrara was
caused by fear of Jewish attack[429] and, later, its investment by a unit
of Syrian volunteers, who took over houses,[430] and from (largely Christian) Abu Tor, by the arrival of militiamen from Hebron, 'known for their
hatred for Christians'. The Hebronites 'extorted money and insulted the
residents', according to the Haganah.[431] By the end of March, 'almost
all' of Musrara's inhabitants had evacuated.[432]

Qatamon, another prosperous, almost completely Arab neighbourhood, was largely abandoned during the first four months of the civil war.
The neighbourhood's handful of Jewish inhabitants left during the war's
first weeks, either out of fear or under Arab intimidation.[433] The Haganah
reported Muslim Arabs leaving Qatamon already on 10 December[434]
and 'Lower Qatamon' empty – with the British assisting the evacuation –
by the beginning of January.[435] But the main precipitant to flight during
the first months was, without doubt, the Haganah raid on the night of 5–6
January, in which the Semiramis Hotel was blown up. The Haganah believed that several irregulars' commanders lived there and, possibly mistakenly, that the hotel served as the neighbourhood militia HQ.[436] Some
two dozen Arabs – who may have included several Iraqi irregulars[437] –
died in the explosion (as did the Spanish vice-consul, Manuel Allende
Salazar). The Mandate Government denied that the hotel had served as
an Arab militia HQ and condemned the attack as 'dastardly and wholesale murder'.[438] Cunningham called in Ben-Gurion for a dressing down;
he called it 'an offence to civilisation' and the Haganah perpetrators,
'murderers'. Ben-Gurion, 'clearly upset', said that the operation 'had
been carried out without central direction'.[439] The JA officially expressed
'regret at the loss of innocent lives' but criticised the government's public announcement, saying that it had failed to condemn similar Arab
outrages.[440] Ben-Gurion informed Cunningham that the Haganah officer responsible – deputy Jerusalem OC Mishael Shechter (Shaham) –
had been removed from command.[441]

The operation had a shattering effect on Qatamon's morale. It 'deepened the sense of insecurity . . . Many who previously spoke of the Palestine question and of defending the country to their last drop of blood pass in the street with bent heads and are ashamed to look their friends in the face.'[442] Immediately after the explosion, HIS reported that

> many families are leaving [Qatamon], some for Egypt, some for Lebanon . . . Many decided that . . . the Husseinis had pulled them into a maelstrom . . . The economic situation is very bad. There are no eggs, no bread, etc. The explosion of the houses in the area had instilled fear in all the people of Qatamon. They argue that the Jews are well-organised economically and the Arabs cannot withstand such organisation.[443]

Most of those fleeing were women, children and the old.[444] The Arab authorities tried to stem the flight[445] and many of the young men who had fled to the Old City returned to Qatamon.[446] Some veteran inhabitants held on: 'Whenever we saw people moving away, we tried to encourage them to stay', recalled Hala Sakakini. 'We would tell them: "You ought to be ashamed to leave. This is just what the Jews want you to do; you leave and they occupy your houses and then one day you will find that Qatamon has become another Jewish quarter!" '[447] But gradually, most of the neighbourhood emptied, families moving to the Old City or out of town altogether; a few moved to the southern end of Qatamon, around the Iraqi consulate, which was defended by an Arab Legion contingent.[448] LHI and Haganah raiders blew up additional Qatamon houses on the nights of 9 and 13 March.[449] By the end of March, only a handful of families remained, guarded by irregulars based in the San Simon Monastery, near the Iraqi consulate.[450]

The diary of Palestinian teacher and writer Khalil Sakakini, a resident of Qatamon and Hala's father, provides an insight into the state of mind of those still in the neighbourhood. On 16 March he recorded: 'God, I don't know how we will hold on against the Jews' aggression: They are trained, organised, united and equipped with the latest arms – and we, we have nothing . . .'[451] On 20 March he recorded:

> Since midnight yesterday the Jews are strongly attacking our neighbourhood . . . The shells from the guns, the bullets . . . Even [Lord] Kitchener [Britain's war minister in World War I] in all his wars perhaps did not hear what we heard last night . . . In this situation, what wonder that the inhabitants think of moving to another neighbourhood or another city . . . many . . . have migrated to the Old City, to Beit Jala, to Amman, to Egypt and elsewhere. Only a few with property have remained.[452]

By 13 April, shortly before he and his family fled Palestine, Sakakini wrote: 'Day and night, the heavy artillery shelling and firing of machine-guns . . . as if we were on a battlefield . . . We cannot get any sleep, and we say that when the morning comes we shall leave . . . Qatamon for somewhere else, or leave the country altogether.'[453]

The major precipitant of the flight of the bulk of the Arab inhabitants in western and southern Jerusalem were Jewish military attacks and fears of attack. A secondary factor, without doubt, were Christian–Muslim and (in part overlapping) Opposition–Husseini, tensions, with Christian and Opposition families – the majority in these neighbourhoods – assailed by Muslim militia suspicions, intimidation and extortion. The spectre of 1936–1939, in which Husseini gunmen had terrorised Opposition and Christian families, was prominently in their minds.[454] There was also a more general fear of the future.

By the end of the first stage of the civil war, southern and western Jerusalem had become almost completely Jewish. Most of those still there were Muslim militiamen and poor Muslim families. Some inhabitants had also fled from eastern and northern parts of the city.

THE BEGINNING OF THE EXODUS OF THE ARAB RURAL POPULATION, DECEMBER 1947 – MARCH 1948

The flight from the countryside began with a trickle, from a handful of villages, in December 1947, and became a steady, though still smallscale, emigration over January–February 1948. In March, in specific areas (for example, just north of Tel Aviv), the rural emigration turned into an exodus. In general, the emigration was confined to areas adjacent to the main concentrations of Jewish population and was due to Haganah (and, in small measure, IZL and LHI) retaliatory attacks and fear of such attacks, and to the orders of Arab authorities to evacuate whole villages or women, children and the old. Several communities were attacked or surrounded and expelled by Haganah units and several others were deliberately intimidated into flight by IZI operations. Intimidation by Arab irregulars also precipitated flight from several sites.

The Coastal Plain

The flight from the countryside during this period was most pronounced in the Coastal Plain, between Tel Aviv and Hadera, where the Jews were in the majority and which, according to the partition plan, was to be the core of the Jewish state.

According to HIS-AD records, the first villages to be wholly abandoned were neighbouring al Mukheizin and al Mansura, south of Rehovot, on 29 December.[455] Mansura's population, of about 100, fled to Na'ana and Qazaza, and al Mukheizin's, of about 200, to Qazaza and Masmiya. Both villages were evacuated following the Haganah reprisal against Qazaza on 19 December, in which two villagers were killed and several injured, and the mukhtar's house was partly demolished. Qazaza villagers had killed a Haganah officer, Yosef Teitelbaum, a few days before and on 16 December, fearing retaliation, had sent many of their women and children to safety in nearby Na'na. Following 19 December, more women and children were evacuated. 'The reprisal' – in the middle of a largely Arab area – 'left a strong impression . . . ,' reported HIS-AD.[456] (The last of Qazaza's inhabitants were expelled by the IDF seven months later, on 16 July.[457])

Women and children were also evacuated at this time from Khirbet Beit Lid (1 December),[458] Salama, outside Jaffa (6 December),[459] and Khirbet 'Azzun (Tabsar), just north of Ra'anana, on 21 December (the latter on orders from Nablus). Khirbet 'Azzun was instructed to maintain 'proper relations' with the Jews but 'only on the face of things. On the day when there will be a general [Arab] assault on the Jewish settlements, the whole population of the village will first be evacuated. Meanwhile, they must provide intelligence.'[460] The village had traditionally enjoyed good relations with its Jewish neighbours.[461] To the north, the men of Khirbet as Sarkas in January and February 1948 were repeatedly ordered by the AHC to move out their women and children – but they refused.[462] More inhabitants evacuated Khirbet 'Azzun, out of fear of Jewish operations, on 11 February.[463]

On 15 December 1947, the beduin tribe of 'Arab al Balawina, who lived in a number of encampments near Netanya, altogether some 350 souls, packed up and moved eastward, settling near Tulkarm;[464] they had been ordered already on 1 or 2 December by the authorities in Tulkarm to prepare to decamp.[465]

The first village to be fully evacuated in the Tel Aviv area was Summeil, just north of the city, on 25 December. The villagers moved to nearby Jammasin, probably causing demoralisation among their hosts.[466] Some villagers had evacuated Jammasin already on 1 December.[467] Arab authorities ordered traditionally friendly Jammasin to stop trading with the Jews;[468] no doubt the inhabitants felt trapped between a rock and a hard place. The village appears to have tried to keep out irregulars but within weeks 'small armed gangs' of outsiders were spotted in its alleyways by Haganah scouts, and on 2 January they began sniping at passing Jewish buses. The Haganah sent in a patrol. It encountered an Arab who asked whether it was dangerous to stay. The Jews responded 'that there was nothing to fear'. The Arab said that all the women, children and farm animals had been evacuated to 'Arab Abu Kishk, a large village to the north, and only troublemakers and militiamen had remained.[469] That day or the next, the remaining inhabitants began 'to leave in panic'.[470] The village mukhtar, along with the mukhtar of nearby Summeil, were reportedly in detention in Jaffa for trafficking with the Jews.[471] The remaining inhabitants left in March-April, moving to Kafr Qasim and Jaljulya.[472]

As we have seen, in the area immediately to the north, the large village of al Sheikh Muwannis, just north of the Yarkon River, and the large tribe of 'Arab Abu Kishk, living between the Yarkon and Herzliya-Ra'anana, had accepted Haganah protection during the first weeks of the war, and agreed to live in peace and keep out irregulars. The two communities – the Abu Kishk had migrated to Palestine from Egypt in the mid-19th century and by 1948 were largely *fellahin*, living in houses or huts, though many still lived in tents – had traditionally enjoyed friendly relations with their neighbours. (But relations had not always been easy. In 1946 three men from Sheikh Muwannis had raped a Jewish girl. Parallel to Mandate court proceedings, the Haganah had shot and wounded one of the attackers and then kidnapped and castrated one of the others (and then deposited him in a hospital[473]).) The start of hostilities in the area gradually undermined these relations. Inhabitants were seen leaving Sheikh Muwannis, which dominated Tel Aviv's airfield, Sdeh Dov, and the main Tel Aviv-Haifa coast road, already on 1 December 1947[474] but, by and large, the villagers stayed put, trusting in their agreement with the Haganah. The villagers rejected a request from Jaffa's AHC leader Rafiq Tamimi that they set up their own NC.[475] During January-February, shots were occasionally (and inconsequentially) fired from Sheikh Muwannis or its environs in the direction of Jewish houses. The villagers quickly proffered this or that explanation, and the Haganah kept its peace. Nonetheless, they agreed to move some inhabitants who were living, probably temporarily, in a plot of land just south of the Yarkon River. The Haganah allowed the villagers to fish in the river (which was adjacent to Tel Aviv).[476] Abu Kishk refused to allow entry to ALA irregulars, telling their emissary that 'the Arabs of the area will cooperate with the Jews against any outside force that tries to enter'.[477] The ALA area commanders in Qalqilya, Madlul Bek and Sa'id Bek, apparently knew of, and accepted, Abu Kishk's relations with the Jews ('given [Abu Kishk's] special position') and were themselves unenthusiastic about initiating hostilities. They had promised to inform Abu Kishk before any large scale ALA attack.[478] One notable, Tawfiq Abu Kishk, was instrumental in brokering a ceasefire between the settlement of Magdiel and the Arab village of Biyar Adas.[479] By mid-March, fearful that ALA units would enter the area, the Alexandroni Brigade imposed a 'quarantine' around Sheikh Muwannis, Abu Kishk and two smaller, satellite villages, Jalil al Shamaliya and Jalil al Qibliya[480] and Alexandroni even considered purchasing several houses in Sheikh Muwannis to house a small garrison.[481] It is possible that several houses on the edge of the village were actually occupied by Alexandroni.[482]

But Alexandroni's *cordon sanitaire* may have had an additional purpose: to protect Sheikh Muwannis from IZL and LHI depredations[483] – for on 12 March LHI gunmen kidnapped five village notables. The inhabitants, according to HIS-AD, thus 'learned that it was not sufficient to reach an agreement with the Haganah and that there were

"other Jews" [i.e., dissidents] of whom one had to beware and perhaps
of whom to beware of more than of the Haganah, which had no control
over them'.[484] Sheikh Muwannis was gripped by fear. On 22 March the
refugees from Summeil and Jammasin were seen evacuating Sheikh
Muwannis[485] and the Haganah's Arab affairs experts reported that the
villagers themselves 'wanted to leave but stayed in place because of
pressure by Jaffa's NC'. Sheikh Muwannis was said to be 'waiting for
orders' from the NC.[486] Haganah policy, as enunciated by Galili, remained unchanged – to leave in place and protect the Arab communities 'in the enclaves', inside Jewish-dominated territory.[487] And the
kidnapped notables appear to have been released already on 23 March
into Haganah hands and returned to Sheikh Muwannis.[488] But the confidence of the inhabitants of the swathe of villages north of the Yarkon
had been mortally undermined. During the following days, the inhabitants of Sheikh Muwannis and Abu Kishk began to evacuate and move
to Qalqilya and Tulkarm[489] after giving 'power of attorney' to Yosef
Sutitzky of Petah Tikva to negotiate Haganah protection for their abandoned properties.[490] Tawfiq Abu Kishk and his men held a large, parting
'banquet' with their Jewish friends on 28 March; 'the sheikh took his
leave from the place and the [Jewish] people with moving words'.[491] For
their part, the Yishuv's leaders almost immediately set about allocating
Sheikh Muwannis's lands for Jewish use.[492]

A few days later, the Abu Kishk leaders explained their evacuation as
stemming from '(a) the [Haganah] roadblocks . . . , (b) the [Haganah]
limitations on movement by foot, (c) the theft [by Jews?] of vehicles, and
(d) the last kidnapping of Sheikh Muwannis men by the LHI'.[493]

The neighbouring beduin tribe of 'Arab al Sawalima[494] and the inhabitants of Jalil al Qibliya and Jalil al Shamaliya, also departed. They
feared Jewish attack. Jalil notables asked Jewish neighbours to look
after their property and then hired Jewish vehicles, with Haganah approval, to transport their moveables, including one or two dozen rifles
and dozens of pistols, to the house of a nearby collaborationist effendi –
'Ali Qassim – for safekeeping.[495]

Within days, the evacuees from Abu Kishk and Sheikh Muwannis
and their environs were reported to be faring poorly in their encampments in the Qalqilya – Jaljuliya area: they had found no new sources
of income, their money was running out and their new neighbours were
treating them 'with hostility'.[496] Some, in light of rumours that their property was being pillaged or vandalised, were thinking of returning.[497] But
they didn't.

Further to the north, the first weeks of war were marked by flight,
generally eastward, out of the coastal plain, of several beduin tribes or
sub-tribes[498] – the 'Arab Balawina on 15–16 and 31 December 1947,[499]
the 'Arab al Malalha near Shefayim on 8 January,[500] the 'Arab Abu Razk
and 'Arab Abu Khadr on 31 January–1 February,[501] the 'Arab an Nuseirat

on 3 February and the 'Arab Shubaki near Herzliya on 11 February. The 'Arab 'Armilat and 'Arab Hawitat decamped on 15 February; 'Arab al Kabara, south of Tantura, on 17 February;[502] the small 'Arab al Sufsafi and Saidun tribes, who lived in dunes between Qisarya and Pardes Hana, in early February;[503] 'Arab Hijazi on 25 February; 'Arab al Kuz on 23 March; and 'Arab Amarir, 'Arab al Huk and 'Arab al Falk, all on 3 April. Most of them evacuated out of fear of Jewish attack. But 'Arab an Nuseirat reportedly fled because of Haganah 'operations' and 'Arab Shubaki after an attack on their encampment by the IZL.[504] Some of these tribes had always been seen by the Haganah as potential or actual troublemakers who would end up 'setting the whole area ablaze'[505] – and may well have been 'advised' by the Haganah to leave. The 'Arab ar Rumeilat encampments (near Netanya, Kibbutz Hama'apil and Kadima) evacuated following a Haganah psychological warfare operation.[506] One encampment of Abu Kishk tribesmen appears to have been expelled in an IZL operation.[507] On the other hand, the Arab al Nufei'at, southwest of Hadera, evacuated eastward, starting on 28 March, possibly after being warned by the Tulkarm NC of 'an impending Jewish attack'.[508]

In mid-February, the semi-sedentary Arabs of Wadi Hawarith, south of Hadera, were instructed by Madlul Bek, of the ALA, to evacuate their 'women and property to the Arab area'.[509] It is not clear whether they obeyed. A month later, after a Haganah ambush of a taxi resulted in the death of three or four Wadi Hawarith Arabs, the Wadi Hawarith began to leave, 'stressing that the Jews all along had promised them that nothing bad would happen to them [if they stayed]'.[510] The *Palestine Post* reported that they had been advised to leave by the British Samaria District Commissioner, E.R. Reeves, who had supplied the departees with a military escort.[511] The evacuation apparently lasted several weeks.[512] In early May, Alexandroni's Arab affairs advisers recommended that the Wadi Hawarith's homes be destroyed, all but those made of stone 'that may be made fit for human [i.e., Jewish] habitation'.[513]

Like the beduins, the Sharon villagers decamped over December 1947 – March 1948, mainly because of Haganah or IZL attacks or fear of such attacks. Al Haram (Sayyiduna 'Ali), on the Mediterranean coast, was evacuated on 3 February out of fear of Jewish attack.[514] Al Mirr was evacuated the same day, but some of its inhabitants returned on 15 February,[515] fleeing for the final time a month later.[516] Umm Khalid, east of Netanya, was evacuated out of fear on 20 March.[517]

As we have seen, Haganah policy until the end of March was non-expulsive. But there were one or two local, unauthorised initiatives. In early January, in the Hadera-Hefer Valley area, certain Jews apparently issued a 'severe warning' to their Arab neighbours 'to leave their present place of residence . . .'.[518] But it does not seem to have had effect, or immediate effect.

And there was one authorised expulsion. The inhabitants of Qisarya, south of Haifa, lived and cultivated Jewish (PICA) and Greek Orthodox church lands. One leading family evacuated the village on 10 January.[519] Most of the population left – apparently for neighbouring Tantura – immediately after the 31 January LHI ambush of a bus that had just pulled out of Qisarya in which two Arabs died and eight were injured (one of the dead and several injured were from the village).[520] The Haganah decided to occupy the site because the land was PICA-owned.[521] But after moving in, the Haganah feared that the British might eject them. The commanders asked headquarters for permission to level the village.[522] Yitzhak Rabin, the Palmah's head of operations, opposed the destruction – but he was overruled. On 19–20 February, the Palmah's Fourth Battalion demolished the houses. The 20-odd inhabitants who were found at the site were moved to safety and some of the troops looted the abandoned homes.[523] A month later, the Arabs were still complaining to local Jewish mukhtars that their stolen money and valuables had not been returned.[524] The Qisarya Arabs, according to Aharon Cohen, had 'done all in their power to keep the peace . . . The villagers had supplied agricultural produce to Jewish Haifa and Hadera . . . The attack was perceived in Qisarya – and not only there – as an attempt by the Jews to force them (the Arabs) living in the Jewish area, to leave . . .'[525]

But some evacuations were precipitated by Arab orders or advice. In late December 1947, the Arab guards in Jewish groves around Hadera were ordered by the regional NCs, reportedly fearing for their safety, to move out along with their families, and some reportedly left.[526] Jaramla was partially evacuated in early February 'on the order of the [Arab] gangs' and finally abandoned, out of 'fear', on 1 April.[527] The inhabitants of Bureika, southeast of Zikhron Ya'akov, were apparently ordered at the beginning of March by the AHC to evacuate so that the village might serve as a base for attack by irregulars on the Haifa-Tel Aviv road.[528] But most or all of the villagers appear to have stayed put.

FLIGHT FROM OTHER RURAL COMMUNITIES, DECEMBER 1947 – MARCH 1948

'There is a tendency among our neighbours . . . to leave their villages', Yosef Weitz wrote on 31 March 1948 to JNF chairman Avraham Granovsky (Granott). Weitz was writing after a visit to the North. He cited the departure of the inhabitants of (traditionally friendly[529]) Qumya in the Jezreel Valley.[530] The bulk of the inhabitants had left around

27 March. They had felt isolated and vulnerable; perhaps they had also received 'friendly advice' from their neighbours in Kibbutz 'Ein Harod. Some 15 men and a number of women stayed on for a few days. Most of them, and the village's movables, were trucked out by the British Army on 30 March and Haganah troops moved in.[531]

The Arab 'tendency' to depart was promoted by Weitz himself. Soon after the start of hostilities, he realised that the circumstances were ripe for the 'Judaisation' of tracts of land bought and owned by Jewish institutions (JNF, PICA) on which Arab tenant farmer communities continued to squat. Under the British, the Yishuv had generally been unable to remove these inhabitants, despite offering generous compensatory payments. Indeed, on occasion, Arab tenant farmers accepted compensation and then continued to squat. The conditions of war, anarchy and gradual British withdrawal in early 1948, Weitz understood, at last enabled the Yishuv to take possession. Often there was pressure by Jewish neighbours to remove the tenant farmers so that they could take hold of the land. Weitz related that at the end of March, settlers from Nahalal, the Beit Shean (Beisan) Valley and Kfar Yehezkeel had come to him to discuss 'the problem of our lands . . . and their liberation from the hands of tenant farmers. We agreed on certain lines of action . . .'.[532]

However, Weitz was not merely the voice of the Jewish settlements; he was an executive, an initiator of thinking and policy. His views on how to solve the tenant problem began to crystallise in early January. After meeting with JNF officials in the North, Weitz jotted in his diary:

> Is not now the time to be rid of them [he was referring specifically to tenant farmers in Yoqne'am and Daliyat ar Ruha]? Why continue to keep in our midst these thorns at a time when they pose a danger to us? Our people are considering [solutions].[533]

On 20 February, Weitz noted that beduin in the largely Jewish-owned Beisan Valley were beginning to cross the Jordan. 'It is possible that now is the time to implement our original plan: to transfer them there', he wrote.[534]

In March, Weitz, on his own initiative, began to implement his solution. First he tried, and failed, to obtain an HGS decision in principle to evict the tenants. Then, using his personal contacts in the settlements and local Haganah units, and HIS officers, he organised several evictions. At Yoqne'am, southeast of Haifa, he persuaded HIS officer Yehuda Burstein to 'advise' the local tenant farmers and those in neighbouring Qira wa Qamun to leave, which they did. Weitz and his JNF colleagues in the North then decided to raze the tenants' houses, to destroy their crops and to pay the evictees compensation.[535] At the same time, he organised with the settlers of Kibbutz Kfar Masaryk the eviction of the squatting Ghawarina beduin in Haifa Bay, and the eviction of small tenant communities at Daliyat ar Ruha and Buteimat, southeast of Haifa.[536]

Towards the end of March, Weitz began pressing the military-political leadership – Galili, Ben-Gurion and Shkolnik – for a national-level decision to expel the Arabs from the partition plan Jewish state area, but his continuous representations and lobbying met with resistance or deflection: The leaders either rejected, or were unwilling to commit themselves to, a general policy of expulsion.[537] Weitz was left privately to promote local evictions. On 26 March, for example, at a meeting with JNF officials, he called for the expulsion of the inhabitants of Qumiya and neighbouring Tira, arguing that they were 'not taking upon themselves the responsibility of preventing the infiltration of irregulars . . . They must be forced to leave their villages until peace comes.'[538]

The Haganah's strategy of forceful retaliation in the first months of the conflict resulted in the flight of a number of rural communities. Mansurat al Kheit (Mansurat al Hula), south of Mishmar Hayarden, was temporarily evacuated during a retaliatory strike on 18 January in which tents and huts were torched and farm animals killed. The raiders were ordered to 'eliminate' anyone who showed resistance.[539] Al Husseiniyya, to the north, was completely evacuated, as were neighbouring al 'Ulmaniyya and, temporarily, Kirad al Ghannama and Kirad al Baqqara, in mid-March following a Palmah strike against Husseiniyya on the night of 12–13 March. A number of houses were reportedly blown up and several dozen Arabs, who included members of an Iraqi volunteer contingent and women and children, were killed and another 20 wounded. The Palmah's Third Battalion lost three dead.[540] General G.H.A. MacMillan, OC British Army in Palestine, and Yosef Nahmani, the director of the JNF office in eastern Galilee, were both struck by the raid's particular 'brutality'. According to Nahmani's Jewish informant, Husseiniyya's mukhtar was executed after being reassured by the raiders that he would not be harmed.[541] The raid followed repeated Arab attacks on Jewish traffic nearby.

Elsewhere in the north, several villages were completely or partly abandoned out of a feeling of isolation and vulnerability to Jewish attack. Such was the case of Khirbet Khiyam al Walid, northeast of Safad, almost completely abandoned in the last week of March.[542] The inhabitants of al 'Ubeidiya, south of the Sea of Galilee, left for the Nazareth area on 3 March. Many of the inhabitants, especially the more prosperous, of nearby Samakh, left during the war's first months for similar reasons, as did all of the 'Arab al Bawati, northeast of Beisan, apparently after Haganah attack. In Western Galilee, al Mazra'a was temporarily abandoned on 6 February. Wa'arat al Saris, a small village near Kfar Ata, was abandoned on 12 February, after irregulars showed up.[543]

Three villages in the Jerusalem District, Kalandiya, Isawiya, and Beit Safafa, were temporarily abandoned during January–March – Isawiya on AHC orders,[544] and Beit Safafa following Haganah attacks,[545] but all were subsequently repopulated.

In the south, the hostilities around the Yishuv's water pipeline to its isolated Negev settlements resulted in March in the flight of beduin and semi-sedentary communities as irregulars blew up the pipeline and Palmah units retaliated.[546] The inhabitants of the small village of Shu'uth, near Kibbutz Gvulot, a satellite community of Khan Yunis, was temporarily abandoned by its inhabitants after they had murdered, on 9 December, six members of Gvulot (one of them a woman) who had mistakenly wandered into the village.[547] The inhabitants later returned to the site. In June 1948, many fled after a flourmill was destroyed, and the village was finally destroyed and abandoned during an IDF attack on 22 July. The orders had been to destroy the village and, apparently, kill the male inhabitants.[548]

THE ARAB AUTHORITIES' RESPONSES TO THE EXODUS, DECEMBER 1947 – MARCH 1948

The Arab reactions to the first months of the exodus were confused and uncoordinated – mirroring the confusion and lack of cooperation between the Arab states, between the states, the AHC, the NCs and the municipalities, between the various civilian authorities and the different armed bands, and between the various local militias and bands of irregulars.

The exodus at first appeared merely to reproduce what had happened in 1936–1939, when 25-40,000 Palestinians had temporarily fled the country.[549] As then, the evacuees who reached the Arab states during the first months of the war were mainly middle and upper class families, whose arrival was barely felt and was certainly not burdensome to the host countries. The rural evacuees from the Coastal Plain and the north mainly headed, at least initially, for Arab centres of population and villages to the east, inside Palestine (Nazareth and 'the Triangle'). Most of the evacuees probably regarded their dislocation as temporary.

Hence, until the end of March, the exodus had only a slight impact in the Arab states and troubled their leaders little, if at all. The states did nothing to precipitate flight from Palestine, but, feeling obliged to accept fellow Arab refugees from a holy war with the Jews, they also did nothing, initially, to bar entry to the refugees. Indeed, before the war, in September 1947, the Arab League Political Committee, meeting in Sofar, Lebanon, had resolved that 'the Arab states open their doors to absorb babies, women and old people from among Palestine's Arabs and to care for them – if events in Palestine necessitate this'.[550] Some Arab leaders may have begun to display a glimmer of concern.[551] But

Arab League decisions were binding and so it was only natural that during the war's initial months, the Arab states would by and large refrain from barring refugees from their territory, even though the AHC generally opposed the exodus and argued against giving refugees entry visas.[552]

On 8 January, the AHC issued a proclamation denying allegations that it had ordered the evacuation of civilians from certain areas, claiming that it had endorsed only the evacuation of children and the old from villages on the firing line. Women, the proclamation stated, should stay put and help their fighting menfolk.[553]

The problem was that not only dependants but army-age males were also leaving. But their numbers initially were too small to cause major concern, and it was only in the second half of March 1948 that the Arab governments began to address the problem. Around 22 March, the Arab governments apparently agreed among themselves that their consulates in Palestine would issue entry visas only to old people, women, children and the sick. Lebanon ordered that its borders be closed to Palestinians other than women and children.[554] In Haifa, it was reported on 23 March, the local Lebanese and Syrian consulates refused to give visas to 'the many' Haifa inhabitants who applied that day.[555]

But as seen from Palestine, the problem was far from marginal. Already in December 1947 we find the AHC and various NCs struggling against the exodus. There was especial concern about the flight of army-aged males. On 24 December an informant told the HIS that there was 'a secret directive [presumably from the AHC] . . . forbidding all Arab males capable of participating in the battle to leave the country. A trip abroad will require the personal permission of the Mufti.'[556] Rich families, mostly Christian, but also Arabs of 'lower classes', according to HIS, were also leaving. The AHC was 'doing its best to prevent trips abroad' and was forcing family members of those who had left for Syria or Egypt to pay 'very high taxes'.[557] In late January, British military intelligence noted that the AHC was worried by the phenomenon. Those who had left, the British reported, had been ordered by the Mufti to return home 'and, if they refuse, their homes will be occupied by other [foreign] Arabs sent to reinforce [defenses] . . .'.[558] The Haganah made propaganda capital in its Arabic broadcasts out of the flight of the wealthy – and the AHC 'Public Instruction Department', headed by Abdullah Rimawi, issued a disclaimer, saying that the 'Arabs emigrating abroad were not fleeing but merely joining the fighters' camp [i.e., being trained before returning to fight] or travelling on national business'.[559] (The AHC apparently was not worried about movement from one part of Palestine to another, only by departures from the country.[560])

The problem was, as HIS noted, that there were various loopholes (medical, economic, etc.) that could be exploited.

The Arab institutions are barring [the flight] of those wishing to settle abroad. [But] they are still not preventing the departure of those [claiming to] leave for other reasons, despite [the fact that] many of these are [in fact, would-be refugees], apparently because of a lack of an appropriate apparatus to check these cases.[561]

In each town, the NCs oversaw daily life, and in each neighbourhood its representatives or local militia groups put the guidelines into effect. By and large, the NCs, sometimes at AHC urging, sometimes independently, tried to combat the exodus, occasionally punishing departees by burning abandoned belongings or confiscating homes.[562] In Jerusalem's Musrara neighbourhood, for example, the local militiamen in early January 1948 forbade the inhabitants from evacuating and told them to 'guard their houses like the Jews [guard theirs]'.[563] A few days later, after the demolition of the Semiramis Hotel, an order went out to 'the youth of Qatamon to return to their places'. But few returned and the commander of the local militia threatened to resort to 'drastic means'. He further threatened with fines and corporal punishment parents who prevented their children from returning.[564] By late March, a fair number had been dragooned into returning[565] and no one was being issued a permit to leave. One person was allowed to take his family to Lebanon but was forced to pay P£1,000 to the NC and had to promise that he himself would return.[566] In Jerusalem's Talbiyeh neighbourhood, 'the Arab institutions tried every means of persuasion and threat to have the inhabitants stay but with no success'.[567] Indeed, the AHC decided that any house abandoned would 'pass into its control'[568] but the inhabitants 'were continuing to evacuate . . . .'.[569]

In Haifa, the NC already on 14 December 1947 decided to 'issue . . . a warning concerning movement out of the city'.[570] In January, the preacher Sheikh Yunis al Khatib 'attacked the rich who had fled the city out of fear that money would be demanded of them to finance those harmed [in the fighting]. He declared that according to Islamic law the property of anyone fleeing a jihad should be expropriated.'[571] In Jaffa, too, the NC imposed fines on would-be leavers, and threatened to confiscate the property of departees.[572]

Occasionally, NCs or the commanders of town militias also issued instructions to nearby villages on matters of flight and staying put. In early March 1948, for example, the Iraqi commander of Ramle, 'Abdul Jabbar, instructed the villagers of 'Arab Abu Rizik to return to their village 'and not to be frightened'.[573] On 27 February, Tulkarm's Opposition-dominated NC ordered the town's inhabitants, in the event of Jewish attack, to 'stay in their places'.[574] And in early March, the Tulkarm NC was said by HIS 'not to be interested in creating a refugee problem . . . in Tulkarm and the adjacent villages'.[575]

But just as often, NCs or ALA commanders ordered villagers to evacuate villages for this or that reason. Usually, as in the case of the ALA and Sabbarin in early March,[576] and Jerusalem and Beit Safafa at about the same time,[577] the militiamen wanted the villagers to evacuate so that their houses would be available to irregulars for bivouac or as positions. At other times, the evacuation was prompted by an unwillingness to leave communities under Jewish control, as with the order in December 1947 by the Tulkarm NC to the 'Arab al Balawina to 'be ready to leave their place at any moment'[578] and, in February 1948, to the 'Arab al Fuqqara 'to leave' ('but they refused')[579] and, more generally, to 'all the Arabs in the area . . . to leave their places, and it is being carried out'.[580] A similar order was issued by the Gaza NC to the Wahidat beduin.[581]

During December 1947 – February 1948, the Mufti and the AHC and most of the NCs did not mount a clear, consistent and forceful campaign against the exodus. The struggle against flight was at best lackadaisical. Perhaps some officials were not overly perturbed by a phenomenon that was still relatively small-scale. Perhaps, also, the Husseinis were not altogether unhappy with the exodus of many middle and upper class families who were traditionally identified with the Opposition. Moreover, the early exodus included Husseini-affiliated families and included many AHC members: to condemn them too strongly for fleeing might prompt backbiting within the Husseini camp. In general, the Palestinian leaders were quicker to condemn flight from villages than from the towns.

In addition, the AHC had only an infirm grip in many localities. The fact that the Mufti disapproved of flight was no assurance that local NCs or irregulars would do much to stop it. As we have seen, the local leaderships and militias often had their own set of concerns and priorities. In various areas, especially in the cities, NCs were hampered in halting the exodus by the fact that many of the evacuees were from among their own kith and kin. Indeed, NC members were prominent among the evacuees. Nonetheless, in general, the local leaderships and militia commanders, whether in obedience to the AHC or independently, discouraged flight, even to the extent of issuing formal threats and imposing penalties, but it all proved of little avail.

A major reason for the failure of the Arab institutions to stem the exodus was the provision endorsed by the states, the Mufti and some of the NCs regarding women, the old and children. Husseini at times explicitly permitted and even encouraged the evacuation of women, children and old people from combat zones or prospective combat zones in order to reduce civilian casualties – in line with pre-war Arab League directives. He may also have believed, mistakenly, that the departure of dependents would heighten the males' motivation to fight.

It was only in March 1948 that Husseini issued detailed, direct, personal orders to the NCs to halt the exodus. Husseini wrote to the NC of Tiberias:

> The AHC knows that a large number of Palestinians are leaving the country for the neighbouring 'sister' countries . . . because of the situation . . . The AHC regards this as flight from the field of honour and sacrifice and sees it as damaging to the name of the holy war movement and damages the good name of the Palestinians in the Arab states and weakens the aid of the Arab peoples for the Palestinian cause, and leaves harmful traces in the economy and commerce of Palestine in general.

> . . . The Arab governments have complained to the AHC in this matter.

> The AHC has studied this important question from all angles and has decided that the good of the nation requires the Palestinians to continue their activities and work in their own country and not to leave it except in the event of necessity for the general good such as [reasons of] political or commercial or medical importance, with the consent of the AHC in consultation with the national committees.

Husseini added that 'in areas where there was real danger to women, children and old people, they should leave the area for areas far from the source of the danger'. Those nonetheless wishing to travel out of the country should submit a request to their local NC, the NC would study it, and then pass it on, with a recommendation, to the AHC offices in Cairo or Jerusalem – and the AHC would then decide.[582]

A similar (or identical) order went out to Jerusalem's NC. The gist was: 'The Mufti knows that a large number of Arabs is leaving the country. He opposes this because this exodus creates a bad impression about Palestine's Arabs in public opinion in the Arab states.' Husseini wrote that only people with 'an important political, economic or medical reason' would be allowed to leave. In the event that there was danger in one part of Palestine, it was permissible to move women and children to other, safer parts, 'but on no account should Arabs be allowed to leave Palestine'.[583] On 29–30 March, HIS reported that 'the AHC was no longer approving exit permits for fear of [causing] panic in the country'.[584] On 31 March, a Galilee HIS officer was reporting: 'Every Arab leaving the country is regarded as a traitor and would be put on trial in Syria. Everyone wishing to leave the country had to obtain permission from the Arab [National] Committee in Haifa.'[585] The HIS surmised that it was this spate of orders that prompted Syria and Lebanon to close their borders to refugees toward the end of March.[586]

But the demand for visas from the Arab consulates in Palestine did not let up. The consulates, in cooperation with the AHC, reported Haganah intelligence, were trying to place obstacles on the path of would-be émigrés and to limit the number of visas issued. But the AHC was approving the issue of specific visas in return for bribes, some of the consuls complained.[587]

In general, NC members who had remained in Palestine regarded the exodus with misgivings. Their approach was perhaps embodied in an article in *Al Sarikh*, an Iraqi-financed Jaffa paper, on 30 March:

> The inhabitants of the large village of Sheikh Muwannis and of several other Arab villages in the neighbourhood of Tel Aviv have brought a terrible disgrace upon all of us by quitting their villages bag and baggage. We cannot help comparing this disgraceful exodus with the firm stand of the Haganah in all localities in Arab territory . . . Everyone knows that the Haganah gladly enters the battle while we always flee from it.[588]

In June 1948, HIS-AD accurately summarised the attitude and policies of the AHC toward the exodus during the first months of the war:

> . . . The Arab institutions tried to combat the phenomenon of flight and evacuation and to curb the waves of emigration. The AHC decided . . . to adopt measures to weaken the flight by restrictions, punishments, threats, propaganda in the newspapers, radio, etc. The AHC tried to mobilise the aid of neighbouring countries in this context . . . They especially tried to prevent the flight of army-age youths. But none of these actions was really successful . . . The actions of the preventive apparatus only led to displays of corruption and, in exchange for bribes, [the authorities] began to hand out [emigration] permits. With the mass flight [in April-May], this apparatus also collapsed and only here and there propaganda [against flight] was heard that [i.e., but it] failed to achieve any real result.[589]

The period between December 1947 and late March 1948 saw the start of the exodus of Palestine's Arabs from the areas earmarked for Jewish statehood and adjacent areas. The spiral of violence precipitated flight by the middle and upper classes from the big towns, especially Haifa, Jaffa and Jerusalem, and their satellite rural communities. It also prompted the piecemeal, but almost complete, evacuation of the Arab rural population from what was to be the heartland of the Jewish State – the Coastal Plain between Tel Aviv and Hadera – and a small-scale, partial evacuation of other rural areas hit by hostilities and containing large Jewish concentrations, namely the Jezreel and Jordan valleys.

The Arab evacuees from the towns and villages left largely because of Jewish – Haganah, IZL or LHI – attacks or fear of impending attack, and from a sense of vulnerability. The feeling prevailed that the Arabs were weak and the Jews very strong, and there was a steady erosion of the Arabs' confidence in their military power. Most of the evacuees, especially the prosperous urban families, never thought in terms of permanent refugeedom and exile; they contemplated an absence similar to that of 1936–1939, lasting until the hostilities were over and, they hoped, the Yishuv was vanquished. They expected the intervention, and possibly victory, of the Arab states.

Only an extremely small, almost insignificant number of the refugees during this early period left because of Haganah or IZL or LHI expulsion orders or forceful 'advice' to that effect. Many more – especially women, children and old people – left as a result of orders or advice from Arab military commanders and officials. Fears for their safety rather than a grand strategy of evacuation underlay these steps. And few were ordered or advised to leave Palestine; generally, the orders or advice were merely to move to safer areas within the country, where Arabs were demographically predominant.

Neither the Yishuv nor the Palestine Arab leadership nor the Arab states during these months had a policy of removing or moving the Arabs out of Palestine. With the exception of tenant farmers, the few expulsions that occurred were dictated by Jewish military considerations; the cases where Arab local commanders ordered villages to be wholly evacuated were motivated by both military and political considerations.

In general, before April 1948, the Palestinian leadership struggled, if not very energetically, against the exodus. The AHC and, by and large, the NCs opposed the flight. But there was no stopping it.

ENDNOTES

1. Traditionally, Zionist historiography has cited these attacks as the first acts of Palestinian violence against the partition resolution. But it is probable that the attacks were not directly linked to the resolution – and were a product either of a desire to rob Jews (see HIS-AD, 'The Attack on the Buses Near Petah Tikva on 30.11', 3 Dec. 1947, and 'The Attack on the Two Buses on 30.11.47', unsigned, 4 Dec. 1947 – both in IDFA 481\49\\62) or of a retaliatory cycle that had begun with a British raid on a LHI training exercise (after an Arab had informed the British about the exercise), that resulted in several Jewish dead (see '01203' to HIS-AD, 2 Dec. 1947, IDFA 481\49\\62). The LHI retaliated by executing five members of the beduin Shubaki clan near Herzliya ('Tiroshi', 'Subject: The Murder of 5 Members of the Shubaki [Family] Near Ra'anana', 20 Nov. 1947, HA 105\358: 'On 20.11 at 04:00 6–7 armed Jews, wearing [British] Army uniforms, came to 'Arab Shubaki near Herzliya. All the adult males were taken out of their tents, the armed men called out the names of five men who were taken to a place of concentration. The rest of the adult males were released; after this they fired on the 5'); and the Arabs retaliated by attacking the buses on 30 Nov. (see HIS, 'Tene Information Circular', 30 Nov. 1947, IDFA 900\52\\58).
2. 'Tene/Ayin' (HIS-AD), 'Summary of a Conversation with Barkai, Nazareth District Officer (Afula) 11.47', undated, HA 105\195. 'Tene' was the codename of HIS, 'Ayin' of its Arab Department.
3. HIS-AD to 'Hillel' (Israel Galili), 30 Nov. 1947, HA 73\98.
4. 'Ibrahim' to Haganah General Staff (HGS), 'Report of "Shahar" Reconnaissance in Jaffa 1.12.47', undated, HA 73\21; and 'HIS Information Circular', 1 Dec. 1947, IDFA 900\52\\56. "Shahar" was the codename of the Palmah's 'Arab Platoon', Arab-looking intelligence scouts.

5. Page of an unidentified Haganah logbook covering 2 Dec. 1947, HA 73\98.
6. HIS-AD to 'Dan' and Galili, 1 Dec. 1947, HA 73\98.
7. Unsigned, undated report, probably by HIS Jerusalem District, 'Report on the Situation in the Old City from 5/12 until 14.12.1947', IDFA 500\48\\61. The report noted that 'some 1,500' of the Jewish Quarter's Jews had also evacuated the Old City, moving to west Jerusalem; the trickle of individual evacuees had turned into 'organised mass flight'.
8. 'HIS Information Circular,' 9 Dec. 1947, HA 105\61.
9. Entry for 11 Dec. 1947, DBGY-YH I, 37–38
10. Ben-Gurion (TA) to Moshe Shertok (NY), 14 Dec. 1947, ISA\CZA, *Political and Diplomatic Documents*, 60; and protocol of meeting of Mapai Centre, statement by Ben-Gurion, 8 Jan. 1948, LPA 23 aleph 48.
11. Sasson to Abdullah, 11 Jan. 1948, *Political and Diplomatic Documents*, 145.
12. Entry for 30 Nov. 1947, Yosef Nahmani Diary (YND), Hashomer Archive.
13. Mapai, *On the Problems of Settlement and Irrigation in the State*, Tel Aviv, May 1948, 'Protocol of Meeting of the Committee on Settlement and Irrigation Matters, Second Meeting, Tel Aviv, Tuesday, 23/12/1947'; and Yossi Ben-Artzi, ' "To Conquer the State", Mapai's Settlement Plan . . . ', 224–25 and 235–36.
14. Danin to Sasson, 4 Jan. 1948, CZA S25-3569.
15. 'Shiloni' (Zvi Aurbach) to Galili, 4 Jan. 1948, HA 80\105\1 (Moshe Svirsky Papers).
16. Ben-Gurion, *As Israel Fights*, 68–69, text of Ben-Gurion's speech at the meeting of the Mapai Council, 7 Feb. 1948.
17. Text of statement, CZA S25-4148.
18. Histadrut, 'An Appeal to the Arab Working Classes', January 1948, CZA S25–9189. But the dissident organisations, the IZL and LHI, also distributed leaflets among the Arabs, and these were characterised by a more minatory tone (see 'Yavne' to HIS-AD, 26 Feb. 1948, HA 105\358).
19. Protocol of meeting of Histadrut Executive Committee (hava'ad hapo'el), statement by Galili, 10 Dec. 1947, Histadrut Archive.
20. Protocol of meeting of Defence Committee, 13 Nov. 1947, CZA S25-9343.
21. Protocol of meeting of Defence Committee, 4 Dec. 1947, CZA S25-9344.
22. Galili, 'Meeting of the [Haganah] N[ational] S[taff] – 7\12', undated, IDFA 481\49\\64.
23. Monitored text of broadcast, 7 Dec. 1947, HA 105\358.
24. Yadin, director of Haganah operations, to Alexandroni, 9 Dec. 1947, IDFA 922\75\\949. This order was dated a day or two before the adoption by the HNS and Defence Committee of the strategy change involved. But it was apparently only implemented after the political echelon had endorsed the change.
25. 'Arik' [Sharon], 'The Sharon [i.e., coastal area] Battalion Operations', 12 Dec. 1947, IDFA 922\75\\949.
26. Yadin to Allon, 28 Dec. 1947, IDFA 922\75\\1206.
27. See, for example, Galili to 'Sasha' (i.e., Yigal Allon, the Palmah's commander), 5 Jan. 1948, IDFA 922\75\\1206, ordering attacks on Arab water sources and transportation. The instruction proposes provoking Arab fire in order to justify Haganah retaliation (for example, by first 'sending [in] a temptation-convoy [*shayeret pitui*]').

28. Yadin to Allon and Giv'ati , 28 Jan. 1948; Yadin to all brigades, 23 Mar. 1948; and Yadin to Palmah, 26 Mar. 1948 – all in IDFA 922\75\\1206.
29. 'Meeting of the [Haganah] N[ational] S[taff] 10\12', IDFA 481\49\\64.
30. Protocol of meeting of Defence Committee, 11 Dec. 1947, CZA S25-9344.
31. Entry for 19 Dec. 1947, DBG-YH I, 58.
32. Protocol of meeting of Defence Committee, 18 Dec. 1947, CZA S25-9344.
33. Unsigned, 'Lines of Planning for Area Campaigns for the Month of February 1948', undated, and appended 'Plan After the British Evacuation', 25 Jan. 1948, IDFA 959\49\\202.
34. 'To the Arabs of the District of Gaza and Beersheba, to the Sheikhs and Notables', 19 Dec. 1947, CZA S25-4148; and Yadin to Allon, 24 Dec. 1947, IDFA 481\49\\35.
35. Yadin to Palmah, etc., 4 Jan. 1948, IDFA 481\49\\35. The new leaflets, from the Haganah to 'the Arabs of Palestine', dated 29 Dec. 1947, read: 'Listen and understand . . . evil does not breed good, murder [does not breed] security, robbery peace . . . Remember those killed, the injured, the orphans and the widows. Remember the dispossessed refugees . . . remember the unemployed, the hungry . . . remember the destruction and sabotage in the [Arab] towns and villages . . . Remember the women and babies, the old, the panic, the horror, the fear . . . Remember all this and know that we have declared, more than once, our sincere intention of peace and reconciliation . . . Don't force us to do the hard thing, and implement harsh measures in order to defend [our] lives and protect our entity and [our] continued building and prosperity' (CZA S25-9051).
36. 'Hashmonai' to general [distribution], 'Subject: Relations with the Neighbouring Villages', 24 Dec. 1947, IDFA 500\48\\60.
37. 'To Our Members, Daily Information Circular No. 10', unsigned but by an Haganah HQ, 18 Dec. 1947, HA 105\61. One house was blown up in Karatiya on the night of 9 Dec.; two nights later, the Haganah blew up a house in Wadi Rushmiya and fired shots into Balad al Sheikh, killing a number of Arabs; and on 12 Dec., Palmah troops destroyed eight parked trucks, two buses and a van in Ramle ('Reprisals', a logsheet, unsigned, undated, IDFA 6127\49\\93).
38. High Commissioner to Secretary of State, 'Weekly Intelligence Appreciation', 13 Dec. 1947, SAMECA CP II\3\147; and High Commissioner to Secretary of State, 15 Dec. 1947, SAMECA CP II\3\148. In DBG-YH I, 61, there is a list of Haganah, IZL and LHI operations up to 20 Dec. 1947.
39. Text of 'Tochnit May', STH III, 1939–43.
40. 'To our members', No. 21, 2 Jan. 1948, HA 105\61. Emphasis in original.
41. Galili to Allon, 5 Jan. 1948; and Yadin to Allon (handwritten note), undated – both in IDFA 922\75\\1206.
42. HIS, 'The Murder of the Eleven in Abu Suwayrih (near Gan Yavne)', 11 Jan. 1948, DBG Archive; and 'Na'im' to HIS-AD, 14 Jan. 1948, IDFA 481\49\\23.
43. 'Itai' to Yadin, 21 Jan. 1948, IDFA 481\49\\23.
44. 'Uri' to sub-commanders, 20 Jan. 1948, IDFA 1041\49\\9.
45. 'Report on "Operation 11"', unsigned, 25 Jan. 1948, IDFA 481\49\\23; and '000007' to HIS-AD, 26 Jan. 1948, HA 105\32.
46. '01127' to HIS-AD, 30 Jan. 1948, HA 105\32 aleph.
47. 'Na'im (Elitzur)' to HIS-AD, 31 Mar. 1948, HA 105\357.

48. DBG-YH, I, 102, footnote 16; and 'Protocol of the Meeting on Arab Affairs, 1–2 Jan. 1948', KMA, Israel Galili Papers.
49. HGS\Operations (Yadin) to brigades, etc., 18 Jan. 1948, IDFA 1196\52\\1. A major variant was distributed by the HGS to city OCs on 29 Jan. or 29 Feb. 1948, in which stress was laid on attacking Arab transport and forces operating against Jewish traffic ('Instructions for Planning Initiated Operations', 29 Jan. 1948 (or 29 Feb. 1948), IDFA 922\75\\1211.)
50. Entries for 2 and 3 Jan. 1948, DBG-YH, I, 106 and 108.
51. Galili to brigade and city OCs, 20 Jan. 1948, IDFA 1196\52\\1.
52. In IDFA 1196\52\\1.
53. 'Oded', Alexandroni, to sub-district OCs (*mefakdei-nafot* or *mafanim*) and battalion OCs battalions, ? Mar. 1948, and 'Oded' to sub-district OCs, 15 Mar. 1948, both in IDFA 2506\49\\91. Through the following months the advisers were often to complain that their advice was disregarded by the operational commanders.
54. Entry for 25 Dec. 1947, DBG-YH I, 97.
55. Danin to Sasson, 23 Dec. 1947, CZA S25-4057. See also STH III, 1415 and 1798 and *Book of the Palmah*, II, 123–124.
56. Protocol of meeting of Defence Committee, 25 Dec. 1947, CZA S25–9344.
57. Dan to Levanoni, 19 Dec. 1947, 6127\49\\93.
58. Pinhas to 'Ali, 22 Dec. 1947, 'Report on the Khisas Operation', IDFA 922\75\\1224; HM Minister, Damascus, to HM Minister, Amman, 16 Jan. 1948, PRO FO 816\115; and 'Magi' (i.e., Moshe Dayan) to Dan, 30 Dec. 1947, IDFA 481\49\\23.
59. Gelber, *Palestine*, 62.
60. Untitled, unsigned HIS report from 28 Dec. 1947, HA 105\358.
61. Alexandroni to battalions, 19 Dec. 1947, IDFA 2687\49\\35.
62. Statement by Ben-Gurion, protocol of meeting of Mapai Central Committee, 8 Jan. 1948, LPA 23 aleph 48.
63. ? to Alexandroni, 'Subject: Report on Situation in Petah Tikva', 11 Feb. 1948, IDFA 6400\49\\66.
64. HIS-AD, 'HIS Information', 25 Feb. 1948, IDFA 922\75\\1205.
65. 'Tzadik' to 'Hashmonai', 15 Feb. 1948, IDFA 500\48\\61.
66. 'Asaf' to OC Second Battalion, Alexandroni Brigade, 13 Jan. 1948; OC Second Battalion to OC Alexandroni Brigade, 14 Jan. 1948; OC Alexandroni to 'Menahem', 18 Jan. 1948; and 'Asher' to 'Menahem', 1 Feb. 1948 – all in IDFA 922\75\\949.
67. 'Yavne' to HIS-AD, 26 Feb. 1948, HA 105\32.
68. 'Shimon', 'Copy', undated, but with covering note 'Menahem' to 'Moshe', 30 Jan. 1948, IDFA 922\745\\1211.
69. Protocol of meeting of Defence Committee, 3 Feb. 1948, CZA S25-9346.
70. Palmah HQ to Galili, 6 Feb. 1948, IDFA 922\75\\1207.
71. Untitled, unsigned segment of memorandum outlining 'irregularities' in Haganah behaviour, including 'cases of execution of Arabs by security squads. Recently an Arab was executed near Rishon [Lezion]', IDFA 922\75\\1207. Parts of the document have been censored by IDFA officials.
72. Galili to OCs brigades, 16 Feb. 1948, IDFA 922\75\\1207; and 'Naftali' to staff officers etc., 27 Feb. 1948, IDFA 4663\49\\84.
73. STH III, part 2, 1362.

74. Statement by Ben-Gurion, protocol of meeting of Mapai Central Committee, 8 Jan. 1948, LPA 23\48.
75. Statement by Galili, protocol of meeting of Mapam Political Committee, 5 Feb. 1948, HHA 66.90(1).
76. Weitz, 'The Negev These Days', undated but probably from the end of March 1948, JNF files, 501–4.
77. Sarig, 'Instructions for Searches on the Roads, in Homes, and Grazing flocks', with appended detailed instructions for each type of search and treatment of shepherds, 12 Feb. 1948, IDFA 6809\49\\9.
78. 'Ephraim (Nishri)', to 'Menahem', undated but probably from early January 1948, 'Report on Arab Labour in the Sub-District, in Connection with the Security Situation', IDFA 410\54\\273; and 'Ephraim' to 'Menahem', 5 Jan. 1948 (mistakenly '5.1.47'), IDFA 410\54\\47.
79. 'Yehuda' in the name of 'Ephraim' to the 'Areas', 15 Jan. 1948, IDFA 410\54\\273.
80. 'Ephraim' to areas, 'These are the Orders of "Hillel" Concerning Arab Work in the Groves', 23 Jan. 1948, IDFA 410\54\\273.
81. 'Ephraim' to areas, 23 Jan. 1948, IDFA 410\54\\273.
82. 'Naftali' to 'Menahelei 'Anafim', 2 Jan. 1948, IDFA 4663\49\\84.
83. 'Naftali' to 'Oded', 28 Apr. 1948, and 'D.', 'Arab Labour', undated, both in IDFA 4663\49\\84.
84. 'Hashmonai' to Shadmi, Dromi, etc., 5 Jan. 1948, IDFA 2644\49\\402.
85. 'Hashmonai' to Shadmi, Dromi, Hetz, 23 Dec. 1947, IDFA 500\48\\60.
86. 'Oded' to 'mafanim', 2 Mar. 1948, IDFA 4663\49\\84.
87. See 'Hadari' to 'mahazim', 23 Mar. 1948, IDFA 244\51\\81; 'Naftali' to heads of municipalities and settlement mukhtars, 30 Mar. 1948, IDFA 4663\49\\84, and Alexandroni to battalions, etc., 28 Mar. 1948, IDFA 922\75\\1211.
88. Galili to Machnes, Danin and Gwirtz, 26 Mar. 1948, IDFA 481\49\\54, and Galili to brigade OCs, 29 Mar. 1948, IDFA 481\49\\50.
89. ? to Alexandroni, 1 Mar. 1948, and Alexandroni to 2nd Battalion, undated, both in IDFA 2687\49\\35; Galili to Machnes, 3 Mar. 1948, IDFA 481\49\\50; and Galili to Yadin, 4 Mar. 1948, IDFA 481\49\\50.
90. 'A Member of Shfayim Says', 14 Mar. 1948, IDFA 481\49\\50.
91. 'Ephraim' to areas, 24 Mar. 1948, enclosing an HIS guideline, IDFA 410\54\\99.
92. Alexandroni to OCs 2nd and 3rd Battalions, and the 'Asher' and 'Ayin' sub-district OCs, 14 Mar. 1948, both in IDFA 2323\49\\5.
93. Galili to Machnes, 3 Mar. 1948, IDFA 481\49\\50.
94. Galili to brigade OCs, 24 Mar. 1948, IDFA 922\75\\1219; and Galili to Machnes and Danin, 26 Mar. 1948, IDFA 481\49\\50.
95. Shemi (in the name of the OC), Alexandroni, to Haganah CGS, 25 Mar. 1948, IDFA 6127\49\\93.
96. Entry for 19 Feb. 1948, DBG-YH I, 253–35. Note especially Danin's statement. The same point was made by Aharon Cohen, head of Mapam's Arab Department, who tried to persuade the party leadership to influence Ben-Gurion to modify Haganah tactics so that the reprisals would hit only 'guilty' communities (see Cohen to Leib (Lova) Levite and Riftin, 13 Mar. 1948, HHA-ACP, 10.95.11(21)).

97. Protocol of meeting of Mapai Secretariat, 20 Mar. 1948, LPA 24\48.
98. Protocol of meeting of Defence Committee, 3 Feb. 1948, CZA S25-9346.
99. Protocol of meeting of Defence Committee, 24 Feb. 1948, CZA S25-9346.
100. 'Azarya' to Allon, apparently 3 Mar. 1948, IDFA 922\75\1218.
101. 'Protocol of the Meeting on Arab Affairs, 1–2 January 1948', KMA, Galili Papers.
102. Danin to Sasson, 13 Jan. 1948, CZA S25-9007.
103. HIS-AD to Galili, 4 Dec. 1947, HA 73\98.
104. Arab Division, 'In the Arab Camp', 7 Dec. 1947, CZA S25-9051.
105. For example, HIS-AD, 'Monthly Survey, November 1947' concerning the Arabs of 'the Galilee, South and Negev', 2 Dec. 1947, HA 105\228.
106. 'Tzuri' to HIS-AD, 30 Apr. 1948, HA 105\226.
107. Safwat's report of 23 Mar. 1948 to the chairman of the Arab League Palestine Committee, in Segev, *Behind the Screen*, 93, 100–101.
108. 'Protocol of Meeting on Arab Affairs on 9 March 1948', unsigned, 9 Mar. 1948, IDFA 8275\49\\126; and unsigned, 'The Responsibility of the Arab Higher Executive [i.e., Committee] for the Disturbances', 16 Dec. 1947, CZA S25-4148.
109. Unititled, unsigned report, HIS, 31 Dec. 1947, HA 105\123.
110. For example, 'Tiroshi', 'Khirbet 'Azzun', 23 Dec. 1947, HA 105\23; and Hashmonai, 'Information Circular', 4 Jan. 1948, IDFA 500\48\\60.
111. 'Yavne', 'Subject: Dr. Khalidi's state of mind', 4 Jan. 1948, HA 105\23. Khalidi also complained about the flight of the leadership class: 'It were better that all the Arab activists return to the country and help out here. Their sitting outside the country – has no value . . .'
112. Cunningham to Secretary of State, 3 Jan. 1948, PRO FO 816\115.
113. Arab Division, 'In the Arab Camp', 14 Dec. 1947, CZA S25-9051.
114. Arab Division, 'In the Arab Camp', 28 Dec. 1947, CZA S25-9051.
115. Arab Division, 'In the Arab Camp', 7 Dec. 1947, and Arab Division, 'In the Arab Public', 21 Dec. 1947, both in CZA S25-9051.
116. 'To Our Members', 21 Dec. 1947, HA 105\61.
117. Unsigned, 'Subject: A Meeting of Husseini Supporters with Hassan Salame, Miscellaneous', 19 Dec. 1947, HA 105\23.
118. '01217' to HIS-AD, 4 Feb. 1948, HA 105\72.
119. '01203' to HIS-AD, 19 Jan. 1948, HA 105\23 aleph.
120. 'Yavne', untitled, 4 Feb. 1948, HA 105\72.
121. '02204' to HIS-AD, 6 Feb. 1948, HA 105\23 bet.
122. Entry for 19 Jan. 1948, DBG-YH I, 163.
123. '31317' to HIS-AD, 2 Feb. 1948, IDFA 900\52\\25.
124. 'Tiroshi' to HIS-AD, 19 Feb. 1948, HA 105\215 aleph.
125. 'Tiroshi' to HIS-AD, 9 Mar. 1948, HA 105\54 aleph.
126. HIS-AD, 'Moshe H. Says', 11 Mar. 1948, HA 105\257.
127. Haifa NC, 'Communique No. 7', 22 Feb. 1948, HA 105\54 aleph.
128. Unsigned, 'Subject: Meeting of Jews and Arabs in Samaria', 5 Sept. 1947, HA 105\54.
129. Circular of the Settlement Bloc Committee of Samaria, 1 Nov. 1947, LA 235 IV, 2092.
130. Circular of the Settlement Bloc Committee of Samaria, 4 Jan. 1948, LA 235 IV, 2092.

131. Hefer Valley Regional Council Circular, 24 Dec. 1947, LA 235 IV, 2093; and Settlement Bloc Committee of Samaria Circular, 4 Jan. 1948, CZA S25-7089.
132. Danin to Sasson, 23 Dec. 1947, CZA S25-3569.
133. Text of poster, 21 Jan. 1948, CZA S25-9189.
134. HIS, 'Subject: Conditions of the Agreement Between Deir Yassin and Giv'at Shaul', 20 Jan. 1948, HA 105\72.
135. Report by A.H. Cohen, 11 Feb. 1948, HHA-ACP 10.95.11 (4).
136. STH III, part 2, 1375; entry for 10 Mar. 1948, DBG-YH I, 291; and interview with Yehoshua Palmon, 1984.
137. 'The Arab Workers in the Tel-Asher Grove' to the head of the Haganah, Tel Aviv, 16. Jan. 1948, HA 105\72.
138. '01104' to HIS-AD, 23 Dec. 1947, IDFA 500\48\\60.
139. 'Tiroshi' to HIS-AD, 'Subject: Local Arab Approaches for Peace with the Jews', 18 Dec. 1947, HA 105\72.
140. 'Tiroshi' to HIS-AD, 'Subject: Local Arab Approaches for Peace with the Jews', 18 Dec. 1947, HA 105\72.
141. 'Tiroshi' to HIS-AD, 22 Dec. 1947, HA 105\72.
142. Untitled, undated (but from first months of civil war), unsigned segment of a report, IDFA 500\48\\60.
143. '01123' to HIS-AD, 14 Jan. 1948, HA 105\72.
144. '01011' to HIS, 22 Jan. 1948, HA 105\72.
145. '01112' to HIS-AD, 25 Jan. 1948, HA 105\72.
146. Unsigned, untitled segment of Haganah report, from Jan. 1948, HA 105\72.
147. '01103' to HIS-AD, 7 Jan. 1948, HA 105\54 aleph.
148. 'HIS Information,' 19 March 1948, IDFA 922\75\1205.
149. '01207' to HIS-AD, 16 Jan. 1948, HA 105\72.
150. '01207' to HIS-AD, 4 Feb. 1948, HA 105\72.
151. 'Hashmonai' to general distribution, 22 Dec. 1947, IDFA 500\48\\60.
152. Unsigned, 'Subject: Meeting with the Arab Mukhtars', 18 Jan. 1948, IDFA 2644\49\\352.
153. 'Yitzhar' to 'Hashmonai', 5 Feb. 1948, IDFA 500\48\\60.
154. 'Tiroshi' to HIS-AD, 6 May 1948, HA 105\54 aleph.
155. 'Summary of Information [Reaching] Alexandroni Brigade (11.5.48), No. 8', IDFA 2506\49\\80.
156. Unsigned, 'Summary of the Meeting of Arab Affairs Advisers in Dora Camp 6.4.48', IDFA 2506\49\\91. An agreement was not reached, or, at least, long honoured. On 8 May an officer reported firing from Qaqun on Hama'apil agriculturists (Alexandroni, 'Brigade Bulletin', 8 May 1948, IDFA 922\75\\1205).
157. 'Tzuri' to HIS-AD, 'Subject: The Village of Argibat [i.e., Nuqeib] Near 'Ein-Gev', 10 May 1948, IDFA 1196\52\\1.
158. 'Hiram' to HIS-AD, 'Subject: The Beduin Tribes around Genigar', 16 May 1948, HA 105\54 aleph.
159. Segment of Haganah report from upper Galilee, unsigned, undated but from c. 20 May 1948, HA 105\54 aleph.
160. Hiram to HIS-AD, 'Subject: Events in the Ramat Yohanan Area', 1 Apr. 1948, HA 105\195.

161. 'Tiroshi' to HIS-AD, 'Subject: The Inhabitants of Kheiriya', 6 May 1948, HA 105\54 aleph.
162. 'Tiroshi' to HIS-AD, 'Subject: Echoes from the Villages Sindiyana, Sabbarin, and Fureidis', 6 May 1948, HA 105\54 aleph; and 'Tiroshi' to HIS-AD, 'Subject: Sindiyana Wants Peace', 11 May 1948, HA 105\54 aleph.
163. 'Hiram' to HIS-AD, 5 May 1948, HA 105\54 aleph.
164. HIS report from 11 May 1948, HA 105\54 aleph.
165. HIS report, 2 May 1948, HA 105\54 aleph.
166. Segment of HIS report, 10 May 1948, HA 105\54 aleph.
167. 'Tiroshi' to HIS-AD, 3 May 1948, HA 105\54 aleph.
168. Alexandroni to battalions, etc., 8 May 1948, IDFA 922\75\\1205. Regarding Kheiriya, see also 'Tiroshi' to HIS-AD, 'Subject: Inhabitants of Kheiriya', 6 May 1948, HA 105\54 aleph.
169. 'Summary of Information [Reaching] Alexandroni Brigade, (11.5.48), No. 8', IDFA 2506\49\\80.
170. 'Hiram' to HIS-AD, 23 May 1948, HA 105\54 aleph.
171. Segment of Haganah report from upper Galilee, unsigned, undated but from around 20 May 1948, HA 105\54 aleph.
172. IDF General Staff\Operations logbook, entry for 9 June 1948, IDFA 922\75\\1176.
173. 'Tiroshi' to HIS-AD, 'Subject: Among the Turkemans', 11 Dec. 1947, HA 105\195.
174. '02122' to HIS-AD, 16 Dec. 1947, IDFA 6400\49\\66.
175. 'Hiram' to HIS-AD, 23 Dec. 1947, HA 105\72.
176. '02104' to HIS-AD, 23 Dec. 1947, IDFA 500\48\\60.
177. A segment of an HIS-AD report from Jan. 1948, HA 105\72.
178. 'Tzadik' to 'Mat"hen' and 'Hashmonai', 'Report for 11.1.48', 12 Jan. 1948, IDFA 500\48\\61.
179. 'Tzadik' to 'Mat"hen' and 'Hashmonai', 'Report for 28.1.48', 28 Jan. 1948, IDFA 500\48\\61; and '02104' to HIS-AD, 'Subject: Refusal to Give volunteers to the Gangs', 1 Feb. 1948, HA 105\72.
180. '02104' to HIS-AD, 'Subject: Attitude of the AHC to the Connection between the Jews and Deir Yassin', 1 Feb. 1948, HA 105\72.
181. 'Yavne' to HIS-AD, 'Subject: Conflicts in Deir Yassin', 29 Feb. 1948, HA 105\72.
182. 'Hashmonai' to 'Yarkoni', etc., 23 Mar. 1948, IDFA 5254\49\\372. See also unsigned, 'Appendix to Letter 22941\6 from 11.9.52 Relating to: Deir Yassin Trial', IDFA 500\48\\29.
183. 'Yavne' to area OC, 'Urgent Arab Information Circular from 7.4.48', 7 April 1948, IDFA 500\48\\29.
184. '02112' to HIS-AD, 'Subject: Recruiting Arabs', 25 Jan. 1948 (misdated '25.12.48'), HA 105\72.
185. 'Hiram' to HIS-AD, 15 Apr. 1948, HA 105\257.
186. 'Tiroshi' to HIS-AD, 6 May 1948, HA 105\54 aleph.
187. Alexandroni Brigade, 'Brigade Bulletin', 10 May 1948, IDFA 2323\49\\6.
188. Galilee District Commissioner, 'Fortnightly Report for the Period Ended the 15th January 1948', 19 Jan. 1948, PRO CO 537-3853.

189. Protocol of meeting of Histadrut Arab Workers' Department, 26 March 1948, HHA-ACP 10.95.11 (4); and protocol of the Histadrut Arab Workers' Department, 30 March 1948, CZA S25-2968.
190. Protocol of meeting of JA-PD, 25 March 1948, CZA S25-426.
191. 317 Field Security Section, 6th Airborne Division, 'Report No. 57 for the Week Ending 10 December 1947', PRO WO 275–79; and 6th Airborne Division Logbook, entry 4 Dec.1947, PRO WO 275–52.
192. 'HIS Information', 10 Dec. 1947, HA 105\61.
193. 'Hiram' to HIS, 'Subject: Threats to Arabs by IZL Men', 18 Dec. 1947, HA 105\358, speaks of Christian families in Hassan Shukry and Hanevi'im streets being intimidated into flight. See also 'Report on the Situation in the Country', Danin to Sasson, 23 Dec. 1947, CZA S25-4057. Danin reported that Jewish refugees from Arab neighbourhoods of Haifa, 'apparently under dissidents' [i.e., IZL or LHI] guidance, had attacked Arab civilians whose homes were located between Jewish houses . . . took them from their homes roughly, with curses and blows, and sent them to their rioting brothers.' Quoting Arab sentiments, Danin wrote: 'If you [Jews] behave this way at the start [of hostilities], how will you behave when you have the power?' A British missionary report from Haifa at this time speaks of Jews terrorising two Arab families 'into giving up their house[s]' (S.P. Emery to the Bishop of Jerusalem, 13 Dec. 1947, SAMECA-JEM LXXI\2).
194. Untitled, unsigned HIS report, 23 Dec. 1947, HA 105\358. The figure '15–20 thousand' seems to me vastly exaggerated for this early in the civil war.
195. Ibrahim to Husseini, 27 May 1947, HA 105\252.
196. '01101' to HIS-AD, 'Subject: Haifa's Arabs during December 1947', 4 Jan. 1948, HA 105\67. On 31 December, the Haifa Heganah's bulletin stated: 'The stream of evacuees from the country continues. According to the "Near East Radio Station", 200 Arab families from Palestine have reached Lebanon, and according to AP – 2000 (the first number appears more reliable)', Haifa Haganah HQ, 'Lehavereinu', 31 Dec. 1947, HA 105\61.
197. '01101' to HIS-AD 'Subject: Haifa's Arabs . . .', 4 Jan. 1948, HA 105\67.
198. See Goren, 'Why . . .', 177.
199. See IDF History Branch, 'The ALA 31.12.47–23.9.55', undated but from late 1950s, IDFA 1046\70\\182, 7; and Goren, 'Why . . .', 178.
200. Goren, 'Why . . .', 178.
201. Tuvia Arazi to Sasson, 31 Dec. 1947, CZA S25-7721.
202. '01101' to HIS-AD, 'Subject: The Murder in the Refinery', 1 Jan. 1948, HA 195\23; and 'Report by the Yishuv Investigation Committee Concerning the Disaster in the Haifa Oil Refinery on Tuesday . . . 30.12.47', 25 Jan. 1948, CZA S25-4037.
203. Palmah logbook of operations, entry for 5 Jan. 1948, IDFA 661\69\\36.
204. '01011' to HIS-AD, 6 Jan. 1948, HA 105\32 aleph.
205. '00001' to HIS-AD, 'Subject: The Attacks on Balad al Sheikh and Hawassa', 9 Jan. 1948, HA 105\32 aleph. One HIS report ('01011' to HIS-AD, 'Subject: Balad al Sheikh', 6 Jan. 1948, HA 105\32 aleph) quoted an Arab informant as saying that 'whole families with their houses

disappeared . . . The Arab says that an indescribable panic ensued. The villagers ran about like lunatics in all directions to flee the village. The wounded too ran in the direction of the mountain and on the morrow were found dead . . .' The Haganah had not touched the beduin encamped in or near the village; they had had no part in the massacre.

206. 'Hiram' to HIS-AD, 'Subject: Balad al Sheikh', 7 Jan. 1948, HA 105\32 aleph.

207. Protocol of meeting of Defence Committee, 1 Jan. 1948, CZA S25-9345.

208. '01101' to HIS-AD. 'Subject: Detailed Report on the Meetings of the Security Committee of the Arab and Jewish Employees of the Municipality, Law Courts, and Government [Offices]', 7 Jan. 1948, HA 105\23.

209. Unsigned but HIS, 'Subject: Report on Events in Haifa on Wednesday 7.1.48', 8 Jan. 1948, IDFA 5942\49\\23.

210. '00001' to HIS-AD, 9 Jan. 1948, HA 105\23 aleph.

211. '01101' to HIS-AD, 18 Jan. 1948, IDFA 5942\49\\23. The Haganah had received British 'permission' and a promise of non-interference, prior to the attacks (see 'Hiram' to HIS, 19 Jan. 1948, IDFA 481\49\\62).

212. 'HIS Information, 18 Jan. 1948, IDFA 900\52\\58.

213. Entry for 5 Jan. 1948, DBG-YH I, 114.

214. Entry for 22 Jan. 1948, DBG-YH I, 177.

215. *In Enemy Eyes*, 12.

216. IDF History Branch, 'ALA 31/12/47-23/9/55', undated but from late 1950s, IDFA 1046\70\\182; Arazi to Sasson, undated but from 20 or 21 Jan. 1948, CZA S25-7721; unsigned report (possibly by Arazi), 18 Jan. 1948, HA 105\54 aleph; and Sasson to Arazi, 18 Jan. 1948, CZA S25-7721.

217. Eshel, *Haifa*, 326.

218. Entry for 22 Jan. 1948, DBG-YH I, 177; and Haifa District Commissioner, 'Report for the Period 16–23 January 1948', 3 Feb. 1948, PRO CO 537-3853.

219. Arazi to Sasson, undated but from 20 or 21 Jan. 1948, CZA S25-7721. According to HIS, the delegation had intended to demand the removal of the non-local irregulars from the city; otherwise, the NC would resign and 'Haifa would be evacuated' ('Hadad' to Sasson, 17 Jan. 1948, CZA S25-3569; and entries for 22 Jan. 1948, DBG-YH I, 171 and 177).

220. Unsigned HIS report, 21 Jan. 1948, IDFA 5942\49\\23. The idea of a massive exodus from Haifa was apparently in the air; other Haifa leaders also referred to it. One Haifa notable, Kamal 'Abd al Rahman, deputy chairman of the chamber of commerce, told his HIS contact that if the Mufti failed to take Haifa's 'special situation into account – not much time would pass before Haifa became a nest of gangs after its inhabitants left her' (HIS, 'Subject: Report on Events in Haifa on Friday 23.1.48', 25 Jan. 1948, IDFA 5942\49\\23.)

221. Arazi to Sasson, 31 Jan. 1948, CZA S25-7721.

222. 'Information from the Nagid' to HIS-AD, 9 Feb. 1948, ISA FM 2568\4.

223. *Behind the Screen*, 50.

224. Frances Hasso makes the point ('Modernity and Gender . . . Defeats', 492) that Arab fears of Jewish rape of their women 'contributed to the . . . exodus during . . . 1948 . . .'.

225. Goren, 'Why . . .'. 180.

226. Arazi to Sasson, 31 Jan. 1948, CZA S25-7721.

227. Arazi to Sasson, 31 Jan. 1948, CZA S25-7721.

228. Arazi to Sasson, 31 Jan. 1948, CZA S25-7721; and '01101' to HIS-AD, 'Subject: Report on Events Among Haifa's Arabs During January 1948', 2 Feb. 1948, HA 105\67. See also Gelber, *Palestine*, 21–22.

229. Unsigned HIS report, 'Subject: Report on Events in Haifa on Thursday 29.1.48', IDFA 5942\49\\23.

230. '01101' to HIS-AD, 'Subject: Report on Events Among Haifa's Arabs During January 1948', 2 Feb. 1948, HA 105\67.

231. 'Summary of Hiram information,' 10 Feb. 1948, IDFA 7249\49\\152.

232. HIS, 'Subject: Report on Events in Haifa on Monday 9.2', 11 Feb. 1948, IDFA 5942\49\\23.

233. 'Hiram' to HIS-AD, 7 Feb. 1948, HA 105\193 bet. A quarter or more of Haifa's Arabs were Christians.

234. 'Hiram' to HIS-AD, 11 Mar. 1948, HA 105\195.

235. 'Summary of Hiram Information', 10 Feb. 1048, IDFA 7249\49\\152.

236. Goren, 'Why . . .', 182.

237. 'HIS Information', 28 Mar. 1948, IDFA 900\52\\58; 'Hiram' to HIS-AD, 'Transfer of Children to Beirut', 14 Mar. 1948, HA 105'257; and excerpt from JA-PD Arab Division report, 16 Mar. 1948, HA 105\257.

238. Excerpt from HIS report, 17 Mar. 1948, HA 105\257.

239. 'Hiram' to HIS-AD, 12 Apr. 1948, HA 105\257; and unsigned Palmah Arab Platoon report, 'Report on Shahar Reconnaissance in Haifa', 10 Apr. 1948, HA 105\257.

240. 'Hiram' to HIS-AD, 'Evacuation of Children', 8 Apr. 1948, HA 105\257; and 'Hiram' to HIS-AD, 12 Apr. 1948, HA 105\257.

241. Haifa seems to have been the only town from which an orderly transfer of children was ever begun.

242. Goren, 'Why . . .', 181.

243. Gelber, *Palestine*, 81.

244. Carmeli to HGS, 'Subject: Report for the Period 14.2–12.3', 21 Mar. 1948, IDFA 6680\49\\3.

245. According to the Haganah, during the period 14 Feb.–12 Mar. 85 Arabs were killed and 95 wounded in Haifa, while there were 21 Jewish deaths (five of them Haganah men) and 63 wounded (four Haganah) (Carmeli to HGS, 'Subject: Report for the Period 14.2-12.3', 21 Mar. 1948, IDFA6680\49\\3). Six British soldiers were also killed.

246. A.J. Bidmead, Haifa CID, to Inspector General, 6 Mar. 1948, IDFA 900\52\\25. But an internal Haganah report for the same day ('Subject: Events in Haifa on 6.3', 7 Mar. 1948, IDFA 5942\49\\23) implies that the explosion was not caused by the Haganah.

247. HIS, 'Subject: Report on Events in Haifa on 21.2', 23 Feb. 1948, IDFA 5942\49\\23.

248. HIS, 'Subject: Report on Events in Haifa on Friday 27.2', 29 Feb. 1948, IDFA 5942\49\\23.

249. 'Hiram' to HIS-AD, 2 Mar. 1948, HA 105\102.

250. A.N. Law, Haifa District Commissioner, to Ibrahim, 4 Mar. 1948, HA 105\380.

251. 'Hiram' to HIS-AD, 18 Mar. 1948, HA 105\195.

252. Moatza to Knesset (Palmah HQ to HGS), 'Daily Report', 28 Feb. 1948, IDFA 922\75\\1066.
253. 'Yona' to 'Giora', 'Subject: Raid on Wadi Nisnas', 5 Mar. 1948, IDFA 5942\49\\10.
254. 'Ehud' to Carmeli, 'Report on Attack on Arms and Arab Commanders Convoy on 17.3.1948', 19 Mar. 1948, IDFA5942\49\\10.
255. Carmeli to HGS, 'Weekly Report on the Events in the Area between 20.3 and 26.3', 31 Mar. 1948, IDFA 7353\49\\46.
256. Unsigned, 'Subject: Report on Events in Haifa on Tuesday 23.3', 24 Mar. 1948, IDFA 5942\49\\23.
257. Safwat to OC Haifa area, 28 Mar. 1948, HA 105\127 aleph.
258. Entries for 10 and 30 Mar. 1948, DBG-YH I, 290 and 326.
259. See Committee for Economic Defence, 'Information on the Arab Economy, Bulletin No. 6', 17–19 Apr. 1948, HA 105\146.
260. See 'Avner' to HIS-AD, 12 Apr. 1948, HA 105\257; and 'HIS Information, 13.4.48', IDFA 7357\49\\7.
261. Committee for Economic Defence, 'Information on the Arab Economy, Bulletin No. 1', 11 Apr. 1948, HA 105\146.
262. Committee for Economic Defence, 'Information on the Arab Economy, Bulletin No. 3', 13 Apr. 1948, HA 105\146.
263. Committee for Economic Defence, 'Information on the Arab Economy, Bulletin No. 5', 14–16 Apr. 1948, HA 105\146.
264. Committee for Economic Defence, 'Information on the Arab Economy, Bulletin No.8, Summary of Information from 5 to 20 April', 26 Apr. 1948, HA 105\146.
265. *In Enemy Eyes*, 18.
266. *In Enemy Eyes*, 12, 17–18, and 20.
267. Krischer (Haifa) to Arab Department, Mapam, 10 Feb. 1948, HHA-ACP 10.95.10 (6).
268. Arab Department, 'Bulletin No. 2 (Information About Developments in the Arab Camp – from Our Special Sources)', 1 Mar. 1948, HHA-ACP 10.95.10 (6).
269. The Haifa NC communiqués – nos. 1–10 and no. 12 – are reproduced verbatim, in Hebrew, in *In Enemy Eyes*, 55–66. Khalidi, in 'The Fall of Haifa', 22–32, argued that the NC manfully and continuously struggled to halt the exodus. The evidence does not bear this out and is ambiguous.
270. 'Hiram', 'Daily Information Circular', 1 Apr. 1948, IDFA 5942\49\\23.
271. 'Hiram' to HIS-AD, undated but c. 5 Apr. 1948, HA 105\257.
272. Committee for Economic Defence, 'Information on the Arab Economy, Bulletin No. 3', 13 Apr. 1948, HA 105\146.
273. 'Hiram' to HIS-AD, 12 Apr. 1948, HA 105\379.
274. Eshel, *Battles*, 342.
275. Gelber, *Palestine*, 82.
276. Giv'ati Brigade HQ, 'Operations Logbook, 1.12.47–115.48', HA 73\98.
277. 'Ibrahim' to Palmah HQ, 'Report of Shahar Reconnaissance in Jaffa 1.12.47', HA 73\21; and 'HIS Information', 1 Dec. 1947, IDFA 900\52\\56.
278. 'Ibrahim' to Palmah HQ, 'Subject: Report on Reconnaissance in Jaffa on 5.12.47', HA 73\98.

279. HIS reports from 2 Dec. 1947, KMA-PA 101-45,46, 47 and 50; and 6th Airborne Division Logbook, entry for 3 Dec. 1947, PRO WO 275–52.

280. See 'Schedule' of events appended by V. Fox-Strangways, Chief Secretary's Office, Government of Palestine, to Jewish Agency, 8 Dec. 1947, CZA S25-4148; and sheet from Haganah logbook, c. 8 Dec. 1947, HA 73\98.

281. Undated unsigned Haganah intelligence logsheet, from around 11 Dec. 1947, HA 73\98.

282. 'HIS Information', 15 Dec. 1947, HA 105\61.

283. For example, untitled logbook entry from c. 4 Dec. 1947, HA 73\98.

284. Golan, *Transformation*, 78–79.

285. 'HIS Information', 9 Dec. 1947, IDFA 900\52\\58.

286. HIS, 'Subject: Jaffa', 25 Dec. 1947, HA 105\72.

287. Untitled, unsigned report, 17 Dec. 1947, CZA S25-9208; and Arab Division, 'In the Arab Camp', 28 Dec. 1947, CZA S25-9051.

288. '01203' to HIS-AD, 2 Jan. 1948, HA 105\23 aleph.

289. Arab Division, 'In the Arab Camp', 28 Dec. 1947, CZA S25-9051; and Golan, *Transformation*, 79.

290. 'Information from Jaffa . . . 23.12.47', 5 Jan. 1948, HA 105\215 aleph.

291. 'In the Arab Camp', 1 Feb. 1948, IDFA 128\51\\71.

292. Golan, *Transformation*, 76–77.

293. 'Zarhi Says', 9 Dec. 1947, IDFA 481\49\\62.

294. 'HIS Information', 10 Dec. 1947, IDFA 900\52\\58.

295. 'Arye', 'The Situation in Jaffa', 11 Dec. 1947, CZA S25-4011.

296. '01203' to HIS-AD, 2 Jan. 1948, HA 105\23 aleph.

297. '01203' to HIS-AD, 2 Jan. 1948, HA 105\23 aleph.

298. 'Arye', 11 Dec. 1947, CZA S25-4011.

299. Entry for 10 Dec. 1947, DBG-YH I, 35.

300. Arab Division JA-PD, 'In the Arab Camp', 14 Dec. 1947, CZA S25–9046; and 'Peh' to Sasson, 18 Jan. 1948, CZA S25-3569.

301. HIS, 'Subject: Meeting of Bat-Yam Representatives with Arab Representatives to Agree on Peace', 19 Dec. 1947, HA 105\72.

302. 'Shiloni' to chief of HNS, 4 Jan.1948, HA 80\105\1 (Moshe Svirsky papers).

303. 'Protocol of the Third Meeting on Arab Affair on 23.3.48', IDFA 8275\49\\126.

304. One HIS report stated: 'The economic situation [is] bad. The prices of vegetables and fruit are low. Eggs and chickens are also cheap, as Jaffa receives all the produce once sold to Tel Aviv' ('Hiram' to HIS-AD, 'Meetings in Transjordan', 26 Feb. 1948, HA 105\23 gimel).

305. HIS, 'Subject: In Jaffa', 25 Dec. 1947, HA 105\72; and Committee for Economic Defence, 'Information of the Arab Economy, Bulletin No. 8, Summary of Information from 5 to 20 April', 26 April 1948, HA 105\146.

306. 'Hiram' to HIS-AD, 26 Jan. 1948, HA 105\32 aleph.

307. Arab Division, 'In the Arab Public', 2 Mar. 1948, HA 105\100.

308. Committee for Economic Defence, 'Information about the Arab Economy, Bulletin No. 1', 11 April 1948, HA 105\146.

309. Committee for Economic Defence, 'Information about the Arab Economy, Bulletin No. 4', 10–13 April 1948, HA 105\146.

310. 'Zarhi says', 9 Dec. 1947, IDFA 481\49\\62; and HIS-AD, 'From the Yogev', 5 Jan. 1948, CZA S25-9051.

311. HIS-AD, 'From the Yogev', 5 Jan. 1948, CZA S25-9051.

312. 'Zarhi says', 9 Dec. 1947, IDFA 481\49\\62. Petrol prices soared.

313. 'HIS Information', 10 Dec. 1947, IDFA 900\52\\58.

314. '01203' to HIS0-AD, 2 Jan. 1948, HA 105\23 aleph. See also 'Shiloni' to chief of HNS, 4 Jan. 1948, HA 80\105\1 (Moshe Svirsky Papers).

315. Gelber, *Palestine*, 80.

316. It was of operations of this sort that Ben-Gurion said that 'I could not forget that we carried out the first [such explosions] . . . The Jews were the first to commit such a deed' (see Protocol of Meeting of Defence Committee, Ben-Gurion's statement, 24 Feb. 1948, CZA S25-9346).

317. 'Hapo'el Ha'aravi' to the Arab Division, JA-PD, 2 Feb. 1948, CZA S25-4066.

318. Unsigned but HIS, 'Information from Jaffa 16.1.48', HA 105\32 aleph.

319. '01203' to HIS-AD, 16 Jan. 1948, HA 105\23 aleph.

320. '01203' to HIS-AD, 16 Jan. 1948, HA 105\23 aleph.

321. 'Albert, 18.1.48', CZA S25-9007.

322. 'Peh' to Sasson, 18 Jan. 1948, CZA S25-3569.

323. Transcripts of tapped telephone conversations from Jaffa, JI IZL Papers, kaf-4, 8\9.

324. See 'Dafna' to 'Dromi-Tzuriel', 'Subject: A Pithy Survey of the Arab Camp in Our Area', 15 Mar. 1948, IDFA 8275\49\\136, for a summary of the development of the militias in Jaffa, and the relations between them.

325. 'Avner' to HIS-AD, 28 Mar. 1948, HA 105\257; and IDF History Branch, 'The ALA', 85, IDFA 1046\70\\182.

326. 'HIS Information', 8 Feb. 1948, IDFA 900\52\\58; and Hassan Salame, 'To Jaffa's Kind Inhabitants', 10 Feb. 1948, HA 105\23 bet.

327. 'Hashmonai' to 'Dromi', 2 Feb. 1948, IDFA 500\48\\60.

328. 'Protocol of Meeting on Arab Affairs, 1–2 January 1948', 38, 40, etc., KMA, Israel Galili Papers.

329. Entry for 7 Jan. 1948, DBG-YH I, 121; and *Political and Diplomatic Documents*, 333, Ben-Gurion to Shertok (New York), 12 Feb. 1948.

330. *In Enemy Eyes*, 32–33.

331. Arab Division, 'In the Arab Camp', 14 Dec. 1947, CZA S25-9046.

332. Entry for 9 Dec. 1947, DBG-YH I, 29.

333. 'Protocol of Meeting on Arab Affairs, 1–2 January 1948', KMA-IGP; and entry for 2 Jan. 1948, DBG-YH I 104. See also Ya'akobson ('Ben-Avi') to Ben-Gurion ('Amitai'), 'Siege of Jaffa', 4 Jan. 1948, DBGA.

334. Entry for 25 Jan. 1948, DBG-YH 184–85. Galili denied knowledge of the events Ya'akobson described.

335. Protocol of meeting of Defence Committee, 27 Jan. 1948, CZA S25-9345. See also Galili to Kiryati, 5 Mar. 1948, IDFA 481\49\\50.

336. 'Avram' to HIS-AD, 15 Feb. 1948, HA 105\23 bet; and 'Information from Jaffa . . . 16.2.48', 2 Mar. 1948, HA 105\32.

337. 'Report on the Operation of the "Centre", 13.3.48', IDFA 8275\49\\114.

338. 'Avner' to HIS-AD, 'The Attack on Abu Kabir and its Effect', 28 Mar. 1948, HA 105\32 aleph.

339. 'Na'im' to HIS-AD, 25 Mar. 1948, HA 105\32 aleph.
340. 'Avner' to HIS-AD, 28 Mar. 1948, HA 105\32 aleph.
341. 'Selection from Letters', 25 Apr. 1948, IDFA 500\48\\29. The names of the correspondent and recipient and the date of the letter are not given, only the HIS officer's summary of parts of the letter.
342. 'Avner' to HIS-AD, 29 Mar. 1948, IDFA 8275\49\\126.
343. Kiryati-'Dafna' to 'Dromi-Tzuriel', 15 Apr. 1948, IDFA 8275\49\\136; and 'Protocol of Arab Division Meeting on Thursday 22.4.48', CZA S25-9664.
344. Kiryati-'Dafna' to 'Dromi-Tzuriel', 15 Apr. 1948, IDFA 8275\49\\136.
345. See Golan, *Transformation*, 22.
346. Entry for 12 Jan. 1948, DBG-YH I, 141.
347. HIS, 'Subject: Doings in the Old City', 7 Jan. 1948, IDFA 500\48\\60; and 'Hashmonai' to 'Dromi', 7 Jan. 1948, IDFA 500\48\\5.
348. Unsigned, 'Subject: The Economic Situation in a Number of Arab Neighbourhoods', 15 Jan. 1948, IDFA 500\48\\60; and 'Hashmonai', 15 Jan. 1948, IDFA 500\48\\5.
349. Unsigned, 'Subject: The Feeling Among the Arabs', 15 Jan. 1948, IDFA 500\48\\60.
350. 'Hashmonai', 17 Jan. 1948, IDFA 500\48\\5; and Unsigned, 'Subject: Food Supplies in the Arab Sector', 17 Jan. 1948, IDFA 500\48\\60.
351. Unsigned, 'Subject: Shortage of Bread among the Arabs', 20 Jan. 1948, IDFA 500\48\\60.
352. 'Hashmonai' to 'Dromi', 17 Jan. 1948, IDFA 500\48\\60.
353. 'Hashmonai' to 'Aka' and 'Levanon, 31 Jan. 1948, IDFA 500\48\\60.
354. Unsigned, 'Subject: The Situation in the Old City', 1 Feb. 1948, IDFA 500\48\\60.
355. Unsigned, 'Subject: Conversation between Khalidi and the High Commissioner', IDFA 500\48\\60. For example of report on Arab train robbery, see 'Tiroshi', 'Subject: Train Robbery Between Taibe and Farun', 25 Dec. 1947, HA 105\23, and '02122' to HIS-AD, 'Subject: Train Robberies', 31 Dec. 1947, HA 105\23.
356. Unsigned, 'Subject: Letter of Complaint to the Inspector of Foods about Bread Arrangements in the Old City', undated, IDFA 500\48\\60.
357. Unsigned, 'Well-founded Information (from 7.2.48)', IDFA 500\48\\60.
358. Unsigned, 'Subject: In the Greek Colony', 1 Feb. 1948, IDFA 500\48\\60.
359. Unsigned, 'Subject: Groups of Thieves Inside the "National Guard"', 4 Feb. 1948, IDFA 500\48\\60.
360. Unsigned, 'Well-founded Information from 13.2.48', IDFA 500\48\\60.
361. Unsigned, 'HIS-AD Information 4.3.48', IDFA 922\75\\1205.
362. Unsigned, 'The Situation in the Arab Neighbourhoods in the Southern Parts of the City (Summary of Information from 21.3.48)', IDFA 5254\49\\75.
363. Pages from an HIS summary of the Arab Economy during Nov. 1947–May 1948, HA 119\105.
364. Committee for Economic Defence, 'Transport, Bulletin No. 2', HA 105\146.
365. Committee for Economic Defence, 'Information About the Arab Economy, Bulletin No. 1', HA 105\146.
366. HIS-AD, 'On the Situation in the City and its Environs', 30 Nov. 1947, HA 73\98.

367. 'Hamami' to 'Yehoshua', 1 Dec. 1947, CZA S25-9210.

368. '00004' to HIS-AD, 'Subject: Arab Preparations', 30 Nov. 1947, HA 73\98.

369. Unsigned, 'Schedule', undated, CZA S25-9210; and 'The Jerusalem Information Bureau' (i.e., Haganah HQ Jerusalem) to Jerusalem Haganah members, 10 Dec. 1947, CZA S25-9210.

370. Haganah logbook entry for 2 Dec. 1947, CZA S25-9210.

371. 'To the Members in the Bases', 3 Dec. 1947, CZA S25-9210.

372. Haganah logbook entry for 3 Dec. 1947, CZA S25-9210.

373. 'To Our Members in the Bases', 3 Dec. 1947, CZA S25-9210.

374. Haganah logbook entries for 4 Dec. 1947, CZA S25-9210.

375. Haganah logbook, entry for 4 Dec. 1947, CZA S25-9210.

376. Jerusalem Haganah, 'Summary of Information for 4.12.47', CZA S25-9210.

377. Unsigned, 'Report on the Situation in the Old City from 5-14.12.1947', IDFA 481\49\\23.

378. For example, 'Hashmonai', 'Subject: Report for 28-29.12.47', IDFA 500\48\\56.

379. Haganah Jerusalem District, 'Bulletin No. 15', 10 Dec. 1947, CZA S25-9210; and Haganah Jerusalem District, 'Bulletin No. 16', 11 Dec. 1947, HA 105\61.

380. 'Bulletin No. 17', 11 Dec. 1947, HA 105\61.

381. For example, 'Zohar' to 'Yitzhak', 'Subject: Combat Patrol to Lifta', 16 Dec. 1947, IDFA 553\50\\100.

382. For example, 'Tzadik' to 'Hashmonai', 30 Dec. 1947, IDFA 500\48\\61; and 'Hashmonai' to 'Ben-Yehuda', 'Subject: Report – 29-3.12.47', undated, IDFA 500\48\\56.

383. 'Following is Report As Given by Gavriel', 29 Dec. 1947, HA 105\23.

384. '00004' to HIS-AD, 2 Jan. 1948, IDFA 500\48\\60.

385. '02204' to HIS-AD, 31 Dec. 1947, IDFA 500\48\\60.

386. HIS-AD, '[Arab] Emigration from December to the End of February', undated, HA 105\102.

387. 'Tzadik' to HIS-AD, 'Subject: Doings in Lifta', 15 Jan. 1948, HA 105\23.

388. Lisser to District OC, 22 Jan. 1948, IDFA 2644\49\\402.

389. 'Tzadik' to 'Hashmonai', 22 Jan. 1948, IDFA 500\48\\61.

390. 'Tzadik' to 'Ma"then' and 'Hashmonai' 'Report for 30.1.48', 30 Jan. 1948, IDFA 500\48\\61.

391. '02204' to HIS-AD, 'Subject: The Position of Lifta's Men,' 9 Feb. 1948, HA 105\32 aleph.

392. 'Shadmi' to 'Hashmonai', 24 Dec. 1947, IDFA 500\48\\61; and 'Hashmonai' to 'Ben-Yehuda', 'Subject: Report for 23-24.12.47', IDFA 500\48\\56.

393. 'Shadmi' to 'Hashmonai', 27 Dec. 1947, IDFA 500\48\\61.

394. 'Tzadik' to 'Hashmonai', 28 Dec. 1947, IDFA 500\48\\61; and 'Hashmonai' to 'Ben-Yehuda', 'Subject: Report on 27-28.12.47', IDFA 500\48\\56.

395. 'Shadmi' to 'Hashmonai', 14 Jan. 1948, IDFA 500\48\\61.

396. 'Hashmonai', 'Information', 2 Jan. 1948, IDFA 500\48\\60; and HIS-AD, 'Emigration from December Until the End of February', HA 105\102.

397. 'Subject Romema', unsigned, 23 Jan. 1948, IDFA 26605\49\\5; and 'Tzadik' to 'Hashmonai', 'Report for 4.2.48,' 4 Feb. 1948, IDFA 500\48\\61.
398. See Golan, *Transformation*, 24.
399. Entry for 20 Jan. 1948, DBG-YH I, 165.
400. British Army HQ, 'Fortnightly Intelligence Newsletter', 16 Jan. 1948, PRO WO275-64; 'CID Summary of Events', 17 Jan. 1948, PRO CO537-3855; and 'Hashmonai' to 'Shadmi', 18 Jan. 1948, IDFA 500\48\\60. 'Tzadik' to 'Hashmonai', 'Addition to the Daily Report . . .', 17 Jan. 1948, IDFA 500\48\\61 hints at this.
401. 'Tzadik' to 'Mat"hen' and 'Hashmonai', 15 Jan. 1948, IDFA 500\48\\61.
402. 'Tzadik' to 'Hashmonai', 19 Jan. 1948, IDFA 500\48\\61.
403. 'Tzadik' to 'Mat"hen' and 'Hashmonai', 17 Jan. 1948; 'Tzadik' to 'Mat"hen' and 'Hashmonai', 'Addition to Daily Report . . .', 17 Jan. 1948, IDFA 500\48\\61; 'Tzadik' to 'Mat"hen' and 'Hashmonai', 18 Jan. 1948; 'Tzadik' to 'Hashmonai', 19 Jan. 1948; and 'Tzadik' to 'Hashmonai', 20 Jan. 1948 – all in IDFA 500\48\\61.
404. 'Tzadik' to 'Mat"hen' and 'Hashmonai', 19 Jan. 1948, and 'Tzadik' to 'Hashmonai', 20 Jan. 1948 – both in IDFA 500\48\\61.
405. 'Tzadik' to 'Hashmonai', 21 Jan. 198, IDFA 500\48\\61.
406. 'Falastin', 28 Jan. 1948, CZA S25-9271.
407. 'Hashmonai', untitled, 3 Jan. 1948, IDFA 2605\49\\3.
408. 'Tzadik' to 'Hashmonai', 'Information', 20 Jan. 1948, IDFA 500\48\\61.
409. Unsigned, 'Subject: The Atmosphere and Events Among the Christian Arabs', 9 Feb. 1948, IDFA 500\48\\60.
410. Entry for 20 Jan. 1948, DBG-YH I, 165.
411. HIS, 'Well-founded Information from 10.2.48', undated, IDFA 500\48\\60; and Milstein, *War*, III, 152.
412. 'Tzadik' to 'Hashmonai', 'Report for 10.2.48', 10.2.48, IDFA 500\48\\61.
413. 'HIS, 'Well-founded Information from 13.2.48', and '90004' to 'Aluka', 'Well-founded Information from 11 Feb. 1948', undated – both in IDFA 500\48\\60. A later British report has the loudspeaker van moving through Talbiyeh on '12 February', reportedly after a Jewish woman had been shot in the neighbourhood (British Army HQ, 'Fortnightly Intelligence Newsletter', 27 Feb. 1948, PRO WO 275-64).
414. HIS, 'Well-founded Information from 13.2.48', IDFA 500\48\\60; and HIS, 'Well-founded Information (from 12.2.48)', IDFA 500\48\\5.
415. HIS, 'Well-founded Arab Information from 21.2.48', IDFA 500\48\\5.
416. 'Hashmonai' to 'Dromi', 22 Feb. 1948, IDFA 500\48\\60.
417. HIS, 'Well-founded Arab Information from 19.2.48', IDFA 500\48\\5.
418. 'Tzadik' to 'Hashmonai' and 'Moriah', 26 April 1948, IDFA 553\50\\25.
419. 'Hashmonai', 'Information', 15 Jan. 1948, IDFA 500\48\\5.
420. Jerusalem Haganah, 'Bulletin No. 16', 11 Dec. 1948, HA 105\61; and, unsigned, 'Subject: Houses Evacuated for Purpose of Sniping', 9 Feb. 1948, IDFA 500\48\\60.
421. Unsigned, 'Subject: Evacuation of Arab Houses Next to Talpiyot', 4 Feb. 1948, IDFA 500\48\\60.
422. 'Well-founded Information from 13.2.48', and 'Hashmonai' to 'Dromi', 22 Feb. 1948 – both in IDFA 500\48\\60.

423. 'Well-founded Arab Information from 16.2.48', IDFA 500\48\\5.
424. 'Hashmonai', 'Information', 2 Jan. 1948, IDFA 500\48\\60; 'HIS-AD Information 6.1.48', HA 105\23; and 'Hashmonai', 'Information', 12 Jan. 1948, IDFA 500\48\\60.
425. 'Hashmonai' report, 2 Jan. 1948, IDFA 500\48\\60; and 'HIS Information 6.1.48', HA 105\23.
426. 'Shadmi' to 'Zohar', 'Operational Order,' 12 Jan. 1948, and 'Zohar' to 'Shadmi', 'Report on Execution', 13 Jan. 1948 – both in IDFA 500\48\\4.
427. 'Tzadik' to 'Hashmonai', 15 Jan. 1948, IDFA 500\48\\61.
428. 'Shadmi' to 'Hashmonai', 14 Jan. 1948, and 'Tzadik' to 'Hashmonai', 16 Jan. 1948 – both in IDFA 500\48\\61.
429. 'Hashmonai', 12 Jan. 1948, IDFA 500\48\\60.
430. 'Tzadik' to 'Mat"hen' and 'Hashmonai', 30 Jan. 1948, IDFA 500\48\\61.
431. 'Tzadik' to 'Hashmonai', 30 Jan. 1948, IDFA 500\48\\61. See also 'Hashmonai' to 'Dromi', 'Subject: Arab Reinforcement for the Southern Parts of the City', undated but c. 21 Feb. 1948, IDFA 500\48\\60.
432. 'Hashmonai' to 'Moriah', 'Annexes to Information Summary No. 131 2.4.48', IDFA 2605\49\\2.
433. 'Hamami' to 'Yehoshua', 1 Dec. 1947, CZA S25-9210; '00004' to HIS-AD, 'Subject: The [Arab] Registering of the Jewish Inhabitants of Qatamon', 2 Dec. 1947, CZA S25-9210; and Haganah logbook entry for 15 Dec. 1947, CZA S25-9210.
434. Jerusalem Haganah HQ, 'Bulletin No. 15', 10 Dec. 1947, CZA S25-9210.
435. Unsigned, untitled report (in English) 4 Jan. 1948, CZA S25-4147; and 'HIS Information', 4 Jan. 1948, IDFA 900\52\\58.
436. 'Tzadik' to 'Hashmonai', etc., 'Report on the Demolition of the Semiramis Hotel . . .', 5 Jan. 1948, IDFA 500\48\\61. Shaham, who commanded the operation, later said that its aim was, in part, to halt Jewish flight from the mixed neighbourhoods and to precipitate Arab flight from them (Milstein, *War*, III, 77).
437. 'Tzadik' to 'Hashmonai, 'Subject: Hotel Semiramis', 7 Jan. 1948, IDFA 500\48\\60; and Milstein, *War*, III, 73–78.
438. Public Information Office, 'Press Release No. 8', 6 Jan. 1948, CZA S25-4013.
439. Cunningham to Secretary of State, 7 Jan. 1948, PRO FO 816\115.
440. 'Statement by the Jewish Agency for Palestine', 6 Jan. 1948, CZA S25-4013.
441. Ben-Gurion to Cunningham, 8 Jan. 1948, CZA S25-4013.
442. Unsigned, 'Subject: The Feelings in Qatamon After the Explosion', 7 Jan. 1948, IDFA 500\48\\60.
443. Untitled, unsigned HIS report, 5 Jan. 1948, IDFA 2605\49\\3. See also 'Through Yosef, deputy CO Area 4 . . . ', Hebrew translation of what seems a British intelligence report, 5 Jan. 1948, IDFA 2605\49\\3.
444. Arab Division, 'Summary of Information about Hotel Semiramis . . .', 8 Jan. 1948, CZA S25-4013.
445. 'HIS Information', 7 Jan. 1948, IDFA 900\52\\58.
446. HIS, 'The Situation in the Arab Neighbourhoods in the Southern Part of Town (Summary of Information from 21.3.48)', IDFA 5254\49\\75.
447. Quoted in Krystall, 'The Fall of the New City 1947–1950', 100.

448. 'Survey of the Arab Neighbourhoods of Southern Jerusalem', 29 Feb. 1948, IDFA 2605\49\\3.
449. Unsigned, 'The Qatamon Affair', undated, IDFA 500\48\\54.
450. 'Hashmonai' to 'Moriah', 'Annexes to Information Summary No. 131, 2.4.48', IDFA 2605\49\\2; and 'The Situation of the Arab Neighbourhoods of the Southern Part of the City (Summary of Information from 21.3.48)', IDFA 5254\49\\75.
451. Sakakini, *Diary*, 231.
452. Sakakini, *Diary*, 231–32.
453. Sakakini, *Diary*, 235.
454. Unsigned, 'The Situation in the Arab Neighbourhoods in the Southern Part of the City (Summary of Information from 21.3.48)', undated but from late Feb. 1948, IDFA 5354\49\\75. Krystall, 'The Fall of the New City 1947–1950', makes no mention of these internal divisions as an important factor in the exodus from Jerusalem.
455. 'Na'im' to HIS-AD, 29 Dec. 1947, HA 105\215 aleph. It is worth remembering that various villages referred to in Haganah records as abandoned during December 1947 – March 1948 were subsequently either fully or partially re-populated, only to be finally abandoned at a later date.
456. '01227' to HIS-AD, 'Subject: Reprisal Against the Village of Qazaza', 22 Dec, 1947, IDFA 481\49\\62; and Qazaza village file, HA 105\136.
457. IDF-GS\Operations Logbook, entry for 16 July 1948, IDFA 922\75\\1176.
458. '01122' to HIS-AD, 'Subject: Miscellaneous Information', 2 Dec. 1947, IDFA 6400\49\\66.
459. 'Ben-Ari' to Kiryati, 'From the Logbook – Court 4', undated, HA 73\98.
460. 'Tiroshi' to HIS-AD, 'Subject: Khirbet 'Azzun', 23 Dec. 1947, HA 105\23.
461. 'Khirbet 'Azzun-Tabsar', 18 Dec. 1941, HA 8\195.
462. '01112' to HIS-AD, 27 Jan. 1948, IDFA 6400\49\\66; and 'Tiroshi (Eitan)' to HIS-AD, 19 Feb. 1948, HA 105\72.
463. HIS-AD, 'The Migratory Movement . . .', 30 June 1948' 30 June 1948, HHA-ACP 10.95.13 (1).
464. '01122' to HIS-AD, 'Subject: Arab al Balawina', 16 Dec. 1947, IDFA 6400\49\\66; and HIS-AD 'Arab al Balawina', summer 1943, IDFA 1627\94\\231.
465. '01122' to HIS-AD, 'Subject: Miscellaneous Information', 2 Dec. 1947, IDFA 6400\49\\66.
466. HIS-AD, 'The Migratory Movement . . .', 30 June 1948, HHA-AC 10.95.13 (1).
467. HIS-AD to Galili, 1 Dec. 1947, HA 73\98. The village was composed of two parts – Jammasin al Gharbi and Jammasin al Sharqi.
468. 'Avram', 9 Jan. 1948, HA 105\23.
469. Reconnaisance squad to Third Battalion, 2 Jan. 1948, IDFA 6647\49\\13.
470. 'Avram', 8 Jan. 1948, HA 105\23.
471. 'Avram', 9 Jan. 1948, HA 105\23.
472. 'Tiroshi' to HIS-AD, 17 Mar. 1948, HA 105\257.
473. Kiryati to 'the Engineer', 15 Jan. 1947, IDFA 8275\49\\126.
474. HIS-AD to 'Dan', 'Hillel', 1 Dec. 1947, HA 105\61.
475. 'HIS-AD Information 2-3-4.1.48,' 5 Jan., 1948, HA 105\61.

476. 'Tsfoni' to 'Kiryati', 10 Feb. 1948, IDFA 8275\49\\138; and 'Tsfoni' to 'Kiryati', 23 Feb. 1948, HA 105\72.
477. 'Avram' to HIS-AD, 11 Feb. 1948, HA 105\72; and 'Tiroshi (Aran)', to HIS-AD, 29 Feb. 1948, HA 105\72.
478. 'Tiroshi (Aran)' to HIS-AD, 9 Mar. 1948, HA 105\257.
479. 'Tiroshi (Aran)' to HIS-AD, 9 Mar. 1948, HA 105\257.
480. Alexandroni HQ to first and second battalions, 10 Mar. 1948, IDFA 2687\49\\35.
481. Alexandroni HQ to OCs second and third battalions, etc., 14 March 1948, IDFA 2323\49\\5.
482. Uriah Shavit and Jalal Bana, 'The Palestinian Dream, the Israeli Nightmare', *Haaretz* magazine, 6 July 2001.
483. This is implied in Alexandroni to Haganah CGS, 25 Mar. 1948, IDFA 6127\49\\93.
484. HIS-AD, 'The Migratory Movement . . .', 30 June 1948, HHA-ACP 10.95.13 (1).
485. Tel Aviv Haganah intelligence logsheet, 22 March 1948, HA 105\62.
486. 'Protocol of Meeting No. 3 on Arab Affairs on 23.3.48', IDFA 8275\49\\126.
487. HGS to brigade OCs, etc., 24 Mar. 1948, IDFA 922\75\1219. See also Galili, 'Meeting of HNS', 22 Mar. 1948, IDFA 481\49\\64, in which 'the [continued] protection of Sheikh Muwannis' is explicitly mentioned.
488. 'Gur' to 'Etzioni', 7 Apr. 1948, IDFA 5254\49\\148.
489. Galili, 'Meeting of HNS', 29 Mar. 1948, IDFA 481\49\\64.
490. 'Tiroshi (Aran)' to HIS-AD, 31 Mar. 1948, HA 105\257.
491. 'Tiroshi (Aran)' to HIS-AD, 'Subject: The Evacuation of 'Arab Abu Kishk by its Inhabitants', 31 Mar. 1948, HA 105\257.
492. Protocol of meeting of Defence Committee, 1 Apr. 1948, CZA S25-9348.
493. 'Tiroshi (HIS-AD, 6 Apr. 1948, HA 105\257. See also Kan'ane and 'Abd al Hadi, 'Abu Kishk'.
494. HIS-AD, 'The Migratory Movement . . .', 30 June 1948, HHA-ACP 10.95.13 (1).
495. 'Tiroshi (Allon)' to HIS-AD, 1 Apr. 1948, HA 105\257; and 'Tiroshi (Aran)' to HIS-AD, 31 Mar. 1948, HA 105\257.
496. 'Tiroshi (Allon)' to HIS-AD, 12 Apr. 1948, HA 105\257.
497. 'Tiroshi (Aran)' to HIS-AD, 11 Apr. 1948, HA 105\257.
498. On the Sharon beduin tribes, see HIS, 'On the Beduin Tribes of the Sharon Sub-district', 1 Mar. 1944, IDFA 1627\94\\231; and '1113' to HIS-AD, 'Subject: Comments on the List of Beduin Tribes in the Sharon Sub-district from 1.3.44', 10 Apr. 1944, HA 8\206.
499. '01122' to HIS-AD, 16 Dec. 1947, IDFA 6400\49\\66; and HIS-AD, 'The Migratory Movement . . .', 30 June 1948, HHA-ACP 10.95.13 (1).
500. HIS-AD, 'Migration from December to the End of February', undated, HA 105\102.
501. HIS-AD, 'Migration from December to the End of February', HA 105\102.
502. HIS-AD, 'Migration from December to the End of February', HA 105\1902.
503. '01112' to HIS-AD, 9 Feb. 1948, IDFA 6400\49\\66.
504. HIS-AD, 'The Migratory Movement . . .', 30 June 1948, HHA-ACP 10.95.13 (1).
505. 'Tiroshi (Aran)' to HIS-AD, 19 Mar. 1948, HA 105\257, mentions members of the Sawarka and Hijazi tribes in this context.

506. HIS-AD, 'The Migratory Movement . . .', 30 June 1948, HHA-ACP 10.95.13 (1).
507. 'Testimony of Arye Bachar', interviewed 24 July 1957, JI IZL papers, kaf-4, 7\7.
508. 'Tiroshi (Eitan)' to HIS-AD, 30 Mar. 1948, IDFA 6400\49\\66; and Rafael Ruppin, letter to the editor, Haaretz, 11 Apr. 1999.
509. 'Tiroshi (Dror)' to HIS-AD, 18 Feb. 1948, IDFA 6400\49\\66.
510. 'Tiroshi (Dror)' to HIS-AD, 24 Mar. 1948, IDFA 2506\49\\85. Alexandroni complained that the Palmah attack had been 'contrary to the general lines that we follow as the basis of our relations with the Arabs' (Alexandroni to CGS, 25 Mar. 1948, IDFA 6127\49\\93).
511. Palestine Post, 28 Mar. 1948.
512. 'Yavne' to HIS-AD, 8 Apr. 1948, HA 105\257.
513. 'Summary of Meeting of Arab Affairs Advisers in Netanya 9.5.48', IDFA 6127\49\\109.
514. HIS-AD, 'The Migratory Movement . . .', 30 Jun. 1948, HHA-ACP 10.95.13 (1).
515. HIS-AD, 'Migration from December Until the end of February', undated, HA 105\102.
516. 'Tiroshi (Aran)' to HIS-AD, 20 Apr. 1948, HA 105\257.
517. HIS-AD, 'The Migratory Movement . . .', 30 June 1948, HHA-ACP 10.95.13 (1).
518. Danin to Sasson, 13 Jan. 1948, CZA S25-9007.
519. '01112' to HIS-AD, 12 Jan. 1948, HA 105\23 aleph.
520. '02112' to HIS-AD, 1 Feb. 1948, HA 105\358.
521. Palmah HQ to 'Boaz', 3 Feb. 1948, IDFA 922\75\1025; and Galili statement, protocol of meeting of Mapam Political Committee, 5 Feb. 1948, 66.90 (1).
522. 'Amon' to Palmah HQ, 10 Feb. 1948, IDFA 922\75\\1211.
523. Palmah HQ to HGS, 20 Feb. 1948, IDFA 922\75\\1214.
524. Wagman, mukhtar Sdot-Yam, to 'Reuven', undated, IDFA 2687\49\\35.
525. Cohen to Levite and Riftin, 13 Mar. 1948, HHA 10.95.11 (21).
526. '01112' to HIS-AD, 22 Dec. 1947, IDFA 6400\49\\66.
527. HIS-AD, 'Migration from December until the end of February', undated, HA 105\102; and HIS-AD, 'The Migratory Movement . . .', 30 June 1948, HHA-ACP 10.95.13 (1).
528. 'Tiroshi (Eitan)' to HIS-AD, 6 Mar. 1948, HA 105\257.
529. HIS-AD, 'Qumya', early 1942, HA 105\225.
530. Weitz to Granovsky, 31 Mar. 1948, CZA A202–217 (Avraham Granott Papers).
531. 'Binyamin' to Golani, 31 Mar. 1948, IDFA 128\51\\71. See also Yanai, Toldot Ein Harod, I, 281.
532. Weitz to Granovsky, 31 Mar. 1948, CZA A202–217.
533. Entry for 11 Jan. 1948, Weitz, Diary, III, 223.
534. Entry for 20 Feb. 1948, Weitz, Diary, III, 239–40.
535. Entry for 26 Mar. 1948, Weitz, Diary, III, 256–57; and interview with Eliezer Be'eri (Bauer), Kibbutz Hazore'a, Apr. 1984.
536. Entry for 26 Mar. 1948, Weitz, Diary, III, 256–57. See also Morris, 'Yosef Weitz and the Transfer Committees, 1948–1949'.
537. Entries for 31 Mar. and 2 Apr. 1948, Weitz, Diary, III, 260–61.

538. Entry for 26 Mar. 1948, Weitz, *Diary*, III, 256–57. Tira's inhabitants had left, on 15 Apr., after receiving 'friendly Jewish advice' (HIS-AD, 'The Migratory Movement . . .', 30 June 1948, HHA 10.95.13 (1)).
539. Palmah HQ to HGS, 'News', 18 Jan. 194, IDFA 922\75\\1066; Palmah HQ to HGS, 'News', 19 Jan. 1948, IDFA 922\75\\1066; and 'Eitan' to 'Ali', 'Report on the Mansurat al Kheit Operation', 19 Jan. 1948, IDFA 922\75\\1224.
540. Allon to HGS, 'Daily Report', 13 Mar. 1948, IDFA 922\75\\1066; and Allon to HGS, 'Daily Report', 17 Mar. 1948, HA 105\62.
541. MacMillan to Eliezer Kaplan, 22 Mar. 1948, CZA S25-7721; and entry for 22 Mar. 1948, YND.
542. 'Mitzpa' to HIS-AD, 29 Mar. 1948, HA105\257.
543. HIS-AD, 'The Migratory Movement . . .', 30 Jun. 1948, HHA-ACP 10.95.13 (1).
544. 'Yavne' to HIS-AD, 4 Jan. 1948, HA 105\215 aleph; and 'Hashmonai' to 'Moriah', 'Concentration of Information No. 104', 7 Mar. 1948, IDFA 2605\49\\2; HIS, 'Annexes to Information Concentration No. 125', 29 Mar. 948, IDFA 2605\49\\2; and HIS-AD, 'The Migratory Movement . . .', 30 Jun. 1948, HHA-ACP 10.95.13 (1).
545. 'Hashmonai' to 'Dromi', 15 Feb. 1948, IDFA 500\48\\60.
546. 'On Events in the Negev', 22 March 1948, CZA S25-3569. The report is signed 'RA, 7 Mar. 1948'.
547. H.L. Gurney, chief secretary, Government of Palestine, to Ben-Gurion, 15 Dec. 1947; and Ben-Gurion to Gurney, 23 Dec. 1947, both in CZA S25-4148.
548. 'Yoske' to Sarig, 30 July 1948, IDFA 1676\51\\12. A key passage in the report has been censored out by IDFA officials.
549. Gelber, *Palestine*, 7; and Gabbay, *Political Study*, 66. Gelber points out that already during World War I, 'many thousands' of Palestinians had fled to Syria to avoid Ottoman conscription; flight was something of a tradition.
550. *Behind the Screen*, 50.
551. A hint of this is afforded by the (possibly true) report on 21 Dec. 1947 in the Syrian newspaper *Al Ayyam* that Damascus and Beirut had asked the AHC to influence the Palestinians along their borders not to flee to Syria and Lebanon but to stay put and fight (see Arab Division, 'Information on the Arab Military Preparations', 9 Jan. 1948, CZA S25-3999).
552. Gabbay, *Political Study*, 92; and Nimrod, 'Hamahapach', *Al Hamishmar* (Hotam), 5 Apr. 1985.
553. Gelber, *Palestine*, 77.
554. Arab Division report, 24 March 1948, citing the Arab newspapers *Al-Masri* and *Al-Ahram*, HA 105\257.
555. Unsigned but HIS, 'Subject: Report on What Happened in Haifa on Tuesday 23.3', 24 Mar. 1948, IDFA 5942\49\\23.
556. 'Na'im', 'Subject: Details from a Talk with Dr. Dajani', 24 Dec. 1947, HA 105\215 aleph.
557. '02204' to HIS-AD, 'Subject: A Tendency by the Arabs to Leave the Country', 15 Jan. 1948, HA 105\215 aleph. See also '02104' to HIS-AD, 14 Jan. 1948, HA 105\215 aleph.

558. British Military HQ, Palestine, 'Fortnightly Intelligence Newsletter', 30 Jan. 1948, PRO WO 275-64.

559. '00004' to HIS-AD, 'In the Arab Public', 29 Jan. 1948, HA 105\23 bet. Such Haganah broadcasts continued, because in late March we find the head of the Histadrut Arab Department, Agassi, complaining about them. 'Our broadcasts heaped contempt on the Arabs who fled . . . as if we are interested in them remaining in the country and fighting against us!' (Agassi to Sasson, Shimoni and Arazi, 28 Mar. 1948, CZA S25-9188.

560. HIS, 'Information Circular', c. 21 Jan. 1948, IDFA 500\48\\60.

561. 'Elkana' to Ben-Gurion ('Amitai'), 19 Feb. 1948, DBG Archive.

562. Gelber, *Palestine*, 77.

563. 'Hashmonai', 'Subject: Doing Among the Arabs', 12 Jan. 1948, IDFA 500\48\\60.

564. 'Hashmonai,' 'Subject: Demographic Changes in Jerusalem', 25 Jan. 1948, IDFA 500\48\\60.

565. Unsigned, 'The Situation in the Arab Neighbourhoods in the Southern Part of the City (Summary of Information from 21 March 1948)', IDFA 5254\49\\75.

566. 'Yavne', 23 March 1948, HA 105\257.

567. HIS, 'Reliable Information from 13.2.48', IDFA 500\48\\5.

568. HIS, 'Reliable Arab Information from 21.2.48', IDFA 500\48\\5.

569. 'Hashmonai,' 'Information', 22 Feb. 1948, IDFA 500\48\\5.

570. IDF History Branch, 'The Arab Liberation Army, 31.12.1947–23.9.1955', 7, IDFA 1046\70\\182.

571. HIS-AD, 'Subject: Report on Events in Haifa on Friday 23.1.48', 25 Jan. 1948, IDFA 5942\49\\23.

572. 'HIS-AD information 9.2.1948', IDFA 922\75\\1205.

573. 'Na'im' to HIS-AD, 3 Mar. 1948, HA 105\257.

574. HIS-AD translation of Tulkarm NC Communiqué of 27 Feb. 1948, HA 105\102.

575. Alexandroni HQ, 'Sarkas, General Survey', 11 Mar. 1948, IDFA 6400\49\\66. The report mentions that the NC had twice arranged that horses stolen by local Arabs during the previous weeks be returned to their Jewish owners – this in the middle of a war between the two communities!

576. 'Tiroshi' to HIS-AD, 14 Mar.1948, IDFA 661\69\\36.

577. Unsigned, 'Subject: The Anger of the Inhabitants of Beit Safafa Concerning the Entry into their Village and Attacks on Mekor-Hayim by the Gangs', 28 Jan. 1948, IDFA 500\48\\5; and part of untitled report, 'Yavne', 9 Mar. 1948, HA 105\257.

578. '01122' to HIS-AD, 2 Dec. 1947, IDFA 6400\49\\66.

579. '02112' to HIS-AD, 9 Feb. 1948, IDFA 6400\49\\66.

580. '02122' to HIS-AD, 10 Dec. 1947, IDFA 6400\49\\66.

581. 'Naim' to HIS-AD, 22 Feb. 1948, HA 105\72.

582. Husseini to NC of Tiberias, undated but from Mar. 1948, HA 105\257.

583. 'Yavne' to HIS-AD, 18 Mar. 1948, conveying the main points of the British censor's report on Husseini's letter of 8 Mar. 1948 from Cairo to the Jerusalem NC. The Jerusalem HIS got hold of a copy of the censor's

report but not of the original letter. I have not found a copy of the letter itself (see also 'Avner' to HIS-AD, 19 Mar. 1948, and excerpt from report by 'Yavne', 21 Mar. 1948 – both in HA 105\257).

584. 'Mitzpa' to HIS-AD, 29 Mar. 1948, and two reports by 'Yavne', 30 March 1948, all in HA 105\257. One of the 'Yavne' reports said that in Jerusalem, women, too, were being forced to apply for exit permits.

585. 'Hiram' to HIS-AD, 31 Mar. 1948, HA 105\257.

586. Brief report, possibly HIS, 28 Mar. 1948, HA 105\257.

587. HIS, 'In the Arab Camp', 5 Apr. 1948, IDFA 661\69\\36.

588. Quoted in Gabbay, *Political Study*, 66.

589. HIS-AD, 'The Migratory Movement . . .', 30 June 1948, HHA-ACP 10.95.13 (1).

4 | The second wave: the mass exodus, April–June 1948

　　The Yishuv looked to the end of March with foreboding: Its back was to the wall in almost every sense. Politically, the United States appeared to be withdrawing from its earlier commitment to partition, and was pressing for 'trusteeship' – an extension of foreign rule – after 15 May. Militarily, the Palestinian campaign along the roads, interdicting Jewish convoys, was slowly strangling West Jerusalem and threatening the existence of clusters of outlying settlements. The Galilee Panhandle settlements could be reached only via the Jordan Valley road and the Nahariya–Upper Galilee road; both were dominated by Arab villages. Nahariya and the kibbutzim of Western Galilee were themselves cut off from Jewish Haifa by Acre and a string of Arab villages. Haifa itself could not be reached from Tel Aviv via the main coast road as a chain of Arab villages dominated its northern stretch. The veteran Mapam kibbutz, Mishmar Ha'emek, which sat astride the main potential route of advance from the 'Triangle' to Haifa, was itself surrounded by Arab villages. To the south, in the Hebron Hills, the four kibbutzim of the Etzion Bloc were under siege, and the 20-odd settlements of the Negev were intermittently blockaded, with their vital water pipeline continuously sabotaged. Three large Jewish convoys, the Yehiam Convoy, the Nabi Daniel Convoy and the Khulda Convoy, were ambushed and destroyed during the last week of March, with the loss of more than 100 Haganah troops and the bulk of the Haganah's armoured truck fleet. The British evacuation, which would remove the last vestige of law and order in the cities and on the roads, was only weeks away, and the neighbouring Arab states were mobilising to intervene. The Yishuv was struggling for its life; an invasion by the Arab states could deliver the *coup de grâce*.

　　It was with this situation and prospect in mind that the Haganah chiefs, in early March, produced 'Tochnit Dalet' (Plan D), a blueprint for securing the emergent Jewish state and the blocs of settlements outside the state's territory against the expected invasion on or after 15 May. The battle against the militias and foreign irregulars had first to be won if there was to be a chance of defeating the invading armies. To win the battle of the roads, the Haganah had to pacify the villages and towns that dominated them and served as bases of belligerency: Pacification meant the villages' surrender or depopulation and destruction. The essence of the plan was the clearing of hostile and potentially hostile forces out of the interior of the territory of the prospective Jewish State, establishing territorial continuity between the major concentrations of Jewish population and securing the future State's borders before, and in anticipation of, the invasion. The Haganah regarded almost all the villages as actively or potentially hostile.

Plan D's architects, headed by OC Operations Yadin, did not know whether the British would withdraw piecemeal and gradually from various areas of the country during the months and weeks before 15 May or whether they would pull out abruptly and *en masse* on or just before that date. In either case, Yadin envisaged activating the plan in the week before 15 May. However, the military realities of Arab attack, blocked lines of communication and besieged settlements, and gradual, early British withdrawal from large areas prompted the HGS to bring forward its timetable. Plan D's piecemeal implementation over April–May was to follow hard on the heels of successive British military pullouts from each district. Most of the operations were prompted by specific Arab attacks or threats. The Haganah units generally followed the strategic and tactical guidelines set down in the plan; but, in part, the operations were also dictated by the specific requirements of situation and peril. Plan D augured a quick end to the civil and guerrilla war between the thoroughly intermixed populations and a switch to the straightforward or almost straightforward conventional warfare that was inaugurated by the Arab invasion of 15–16 May.

Plan D was not a political blueprint for the expulsion of Palestine's Arabs:[1] It was governed by military considerations and geared to achieving military ends. But, given the nature of the war and the admixture of populations, securing the interior of the Jewish State and its borders in practice meant the depopulation and destruction of the villages that hosted the hostile militias and irregulars.

The plan called for 'operations against enemy settlements which are in the rear of, within or near our defense lines, with the aim of preventing their use as bases for an active armed force'. Given Palestine's size and the nature of the war, almost every village in or near the territory of the prospective Jewish state sat astride a main road or a border area or was located on or near one of the Arab armies' potential axes of advance. Plan D provided for the conquest and permanent occupation, or levelling, of villages and towns. It instructed that the villages should be surrounded and searched for weapons and irregulars. In the event of resistance, the armed forces in the village should be destroyed and the inhabitants expelled. In the event of non-resistance, the village should be disarmed and garrisoned. Some hostile villages were to be destroyed '([by] burning, demolition and mining of the ruins) – especially . . . villages that we are unable to permanently control'. The Haganah wanted to preclude their renewed use as anti-Yishuv bases.[2]

The plan gave each brigade discretion in its treatment of villages in its zone of operations. Each brigade was instructed:

> In the conquest of villages in your area, you will determine – whether to cleanse or destroy them – in consultation with your Arab affairs advisers and HIS officers . . . You are permitted to restrict – insofar as you are able – cleansing, conquest and destruction operations of enemy villages in your area.[3]

The plan was neither understood nor used by the senior field officers as a blanket instruction for the expulsion of 'the Arabs'. But, in providing for the expulsion or destruction of villages that had resisted or might threaten the Yishuv, it constituted a strategic–doctrinal basis and *carte blanche* for expulsions by front, brigade, district and battalion commanders (who in each case argued military necessity) and it gave commanders, *post facto*, formal, persuasive cover for their actions. However, during April–June, relatively few commanders faced the moral dilemma of having to carry out the expulsion clauses. Townspeople and villagers usually fled their homes before or during battle and Haganah commanders rarely had to decide about, or issue, expulsion orders (though they almost invariably prevented inhabitants, who had initially fled, from returning home after the dust of battle had settled).

In effect, Plan D was carried out during the eight weeks following 2 April. But most of the units mounting these offensives and counteroffensives were unaware that they were, in fact, carrying out parts of the grand design; most thought in terms of their own, local problems and perils, and their amelioration. Only the Alexandroni Brigade, responsible for the Coastal Plain from just north of Tel Aviv to just south of Haifa, appears from the start to have regarded its offensive operations, starting in early April, as parts of Plan D. In fact, the brigade explicitly ordered its battalions, during the first week of April 'to complete [the implementation] of this plan during the week following 8.4.'[4] Elsewhere, Haganah brigades unleashed offensives and counter-offensives in the spirit of Plan D without quite realising that this was what they were doing. But in Operation Nahshon (2–3 April – 20 April), in the Jerusalem Corridor, and, to the north, in the battles of Mishmar Ha'emek (4–15 April), Ramat Yohanan (12–16 April), Arab Tiberias (16–18 April) and Arab Haifa (21–22 April), Operation Yiftah, in eastern Galilee (15 April – 15 May), and Operation Ben-Ami (parts I and II), in western Galilee

(13–22 May), the Haganah, for the first time, systematically conquered and emptied of inhabitants (and often levelled) whole clusters of villages, clearing lines of communication and border areas.

Plan D aside, there is no trace of any decision-making by the Yishuv's or Haganah's supreme bodies before early April in favour of a blanket, national policy of 'expelling the Arabs'. Had such a decision in principle been taken by the JAE, the Defence Committee, the HNS or the HGS, it would have left traces in the documentation. Nor – perhaps surprisingly, in retrospect – is there evidence, with the exception of one or two important but isolated statements by Ben-Gurion, of any general expectation in the Yishuv of a mass Arab exodus from the Jewish part of Palestine. Such an exodus may have been regarded by most Yishuv leaders as desirable; but until early April, it was not regarded as likely or imminent. When it did occur, it surprised even the most optimistic and hardline Yishuv executives, including such a leading advocate of transfer as Yosef Weitz. On 22 April 1948, he visited Haifa, witnessed the start of the mass flight from the city, and wondered about 'the reason . . . Eating away at my innards are fears . . . that perhaps a plot is being hatched [between the British and the Arabs] against us . . . Maybe the evacuation will facilitate the war against us.' The following day, he wrote: 'Something in my unconscious is frightened by this flight.'[5] A few weeks later, Ben-Gurion told his cabinet: 'Acre has fallen and not many Arabs have remained in it. This phenomenon is difficult to understand. Yesterday I was in Jaffa – I don't understand how they left such a city . . .'[6] Ben-Gurion was especially surprised by the rural evacuations: '. . . the assumption [among us] was that a village cannot be moved from its place, but the fact is that Arab villages were evacuated also where there was no danger. Sheikh Muwannis [for example] was not imperiled and nonetheless was evacuated.'[7]

But a vital strategic change occurred during the first half of April: Clear traces of an expulsion policy on both national and local levels with respect to certain key districts and localities and a general 'atmosophere of transfer' are detectable in statements made by Zionist officials and officers. They are discernable, too, in the actions of Haganah units around the country. A vital shift occurred in the mindset of the political and military leadership. During 4–9 April, Ben-Gurion and the HGS, under the impact of the dire situation of Jewish Jerusalem and the ALA attack on Mishmar Ha'emek, and under pressure from settlements and local commanders, decided, in conformity with the general guidelines of Plan D, to clear out and destroy the clusters of hostile or potentially hostile villages dominating vital axes. The decision may have been reached, initially, *ad hoc* and only in relation to two specific areas – the coast road and the Jerusalem–Tel Aviv road – or it may have been reached in principle, in relation to all the areas earmarked for Jewish sovereignty. We don't know. But in any event, a policy of clearing out Arab communities sitting astride or near vital routes and along some borders was insti-tuted. Orders went out from HGS to the relevant units to drive out and, if necessary, expel the remaining communities along the Tel Aviv–Haifa axis, the Jenin–Haifa road (around Mishmar Ha'emek) and along the Jerusalem–Tel Aviv road. Exceptions were made only of al Fureidis and 'Arab al Ghawarina (Jisr Zarqa) on the Tel Aviv–Haifa road and Abu Ghosh on the Tel Aviv–Jerusalem road. During the following months, though no overall, general directive of expulsion was ever issued by the governing political and military bodies, various officers and units adopted, and implemented, an expulsory policy and carried out individ-ual expulsions. As one IDF intelligence officer coyly put it: 'There is an opinion that we must step up the eviction of Arabs from the territory of the State of Israel as it renders Arab administrative functioning far more difficult and, as well, the morale of the population declines with each new wave of refugees.'[8]

This vital shift in thinking is starkly illustrated in the documented delib-erations of the Haganah Arab affairs advisers in the central (Alexandroni) area of operations. Meeting on 31 March near Netanya, the advisers focused on protecting abandoned property against Jewish looting and determined guidelines for the harvest and sale of crops from abandoned groves and fields. The harvest of grain crops was to be postponed for a fortnight. 'Meanwhile, it will become clear, possibly, in what cases Arab owners will [be allowed to] come to reap [them] themselves. The deci-sion about how to treat such reapers is postponed until the second [i.e., next] meeting.' The advisers further decided to 'clear away' abandoned beduin tents and huts, lest they serve as sleeping places for 'robbers and suspects.' In general, the decision about the movement back into the area of Arabs who had left was postponed until the next meeting (the local OCs were ordered to set up roadblocks to 'check' incoming Arabs, implying that all or some would be permitted to enter). Should a unit, for military reasons, have to set up positions on Arab-owned lands, the owners should be 'told and promised' that there 'is no intention to harm their property [or their rights over it].' Lastly, a decision regarding the possible displacement of tenant-farmers from Jewish-owned lands was postponed, pending talks with the JNF. In other words, at the end of March, the advisers were still unclear about future relations with the local Arabs and the implication was that the status quo – with Arabs continuing to live in the Jewish areas or moving back into them – was to be maintained.[9]

By 6 April, when the advisers met again, the policy had substantially changed. 'An explicit order was issued that Arabs were not to be allowed into the area to reap [grain crops]', and those 'who had evacuated the area were not to be allowed back . . .', it was decided. The settlements should harvest the abandoned Arab crops. Arabs were to be 'advised not to move about the evacuated area and our inability to vouch for their safety should be explained to them kindly'. The advisers concluded that 'in general the direction [i.e., the intention] is to evict [hakivun hu lefanot] the Arabs from the Jewish area of the brigade'. As to tenant farmers, the meeting euphemistically resolved 'to accept' into Jewish hands at this time the lands leased out or owned by Jews – presumably meaning to evict the tenant farmers, after due compensation.[10] The advisers' instructions were disseminated among Alexandroni's units.[11] The following week, the advisers discussed the fate of a number of specific communities: The Arabs returning to Wadi Faliq, west of Even Yehuda, had been ordered 'evicted'; the inhabitants of Khirbet 'Azzun (Tabsar) had been 'warned that it was best that they leave'. The Arabs of Khirbet Beit Lid were 'expected to leave in a day or two' and the movement of Arabs in the (Jewish) town of Hadera was about to be stopped.[12] Three days later, an HIS officer less guardedly explained what happened to Khirbet Beit Lid: 'After the order was received – to expel all the Arabs still in the [Alexandroni] area – these Arabs were informed (Khirbet Beit Lid, etc.) and all left the area.'[13]

Similar orders went out during the course of Operation Nahshon (see below), between 2–3 and 20 April, as the Haganah battled to break the siege of Jerusalem. At first, Galili merely empowered the Haganah 'to take control of the villages along the Jerusalem–Sha'ar Hagai road if they have been abandoned' and if the British didn't interfere.[14] Ten days later, Galili expanded this, ordering 'to surround and harass [into flight] the villages whose inhabitants had not [yet] evacuated'.[15] On 18 April, Palmah OC Allon, cabled HGS\Operations: 'It is clear to me that we should not continue sending out convoys [to Jerusalem] until we increase our attacks . . . on most enemy bases [i.e., villages] in order to destroy what can be [destroyed], demoralise him [i.e., the Arabs] further, disrupt his organisation and cause a wandering of refugees [ligrom lindidat plitim] and withdrawal of armed [irregulars].'[16]

But not only the Haganah was empowered to decide on the eviction of Arab villagers. On 13 April HGS informed the brigades that the Committee for Arab Property, chaired by Machnes, was 'empowered to decide . . . regarding the movement of Arabs in the Jewish area and . . . the eviction [pinui] of Arab villages not in battle'.[17] Ben-Gurion rubber-stamped this authorisation three weeks later at a meeting with his Arab affairs advisers. It was agreed that 'the Arab Affairs Department [sic] has permission to decide on the removal [siluko] of an Arab village that hinders the Yishuv's plans or is provocative'.[18]

On 4 May, Ben-Gurion, in a public speech, spoke of the 'great ease' with which the Arab masses had fled their towns and villages (while the Yishuv, to date, had not abandoned a single settlement). 'History has now shown', he said, 'who [i.e., which people] is really bound to this land and for whom this land is nothing but a luxury, to be easily abandoned.'[19] But Zionist agency had considerably contributed to the Arabs' demoralisation. During April, the HGS's 'Psychological War-fare Department' had prepared and recorded six speeches, which were broadcast time and again by the Haganah's radio station and loud-speaker vans. One, entitled 'For Whom Are You Fighting?', harped on the flight of the urban elites. 'You are here, in the killing fields, but they – have fled the country. They sit in hotels in Damascus and Egypt . . . Where today is Jamal Husseini, where is Emile Ghawry? . . . Enjoying life in the cabarets of Beirut, with the girls and the dancers . . .' Another broadcast spoke of the foreign irregulars who embroiled the villages in hostilities and then abandoned them to Jewish depredation. 'When we interdict transportation . . . who stays hungry? . . . And if you abandon a village, leave it and go, whose property is destroyed . . .?' None of the recordings called upon the Arabs to flee.[20] But they were desiged to cause demoralisation – and HGS\Operations proposed to 'exploit' this demoralisation (it didn't say how).[21]

Alongside the mainstream 'atmosphere of transfer' and the Ha-ganah's general guideline and tendency to drive out Arabs and de-stroy villages along main roads and border areas, there surfaced during April–June a secondary tendency or counter-policy – to leave in place friendly or surrendering Arab communities. This tendency, which never became official Yishuv or Haganah policy and only infrequently guided the executive agencies in their operations, centred around the person of Bechor Shitrit, from 15 May Israel's minister of police and minority af-fairs, and his Minority Ministry officials. Mapam's Arab Department and certain Mapam kibbutzim also periodically acted as spoilers, curtailing the unfettered activation of the mainstream tendency.

Already on 22 April, the authorities – probably the JA-PD Arab Division – issued a set of formal guidelines relating to the occupation of surrendering villages: 'In the course of events, we may face the phe-nomenon of surrendering villages or individuals who demand [Haganah] protection and the right to stay in the Jewish area.' If the appellants live 'in the border area or front line they must be moved to the rear', where they could be properly guarded, states the guideline. Once transferred inland, their freedom of movement would have to be restricted and they should not be allowed contact with other Arabs, for reasons of intelli-gence. The Haganah was cautioned that 'in every case of an approach to receive Jewish protection [hasut], it must be carefully weighed whether the Arabs can be left in place or [have to be] transferred to the rear'.[22] However, these guidelines were generally not taken seriously by Haganah units, though the inhabitants of a handful of surrendering vil-lages at this time were ultimately allowed to remain.

Less than three weeks later, on 10 May, Shitrit submitted a mem-orandum to the People's Administration (the JAE's successor as the Yishuv's 'Cabinet'), within days to become the 'Provisional Government of Israel'. It appears that the memorandum was never debated by that body, which had its hands full preparing for the declaration of statehood and the impending invasion. The document was entitled 'Memorandum of the Ministry for Minority Affairs, Subject: The Arab Problem'. The Zionist leaders had long announced their desire to live in peace with their neighbours and to give them 'equal civil rights', wrote Shitrit. The Jewish people, which had suffered centuries of oppression, would be judged according to how it treated its own minority. It was incumbent upon the new state to protect the property abandoned by the Arabs who had fled and 'to maintain fair and proper relations with those who had stayed or who will want to stay among us or return [to live] among us'. Shitrit acknowledged that 'criminal deeds' had been committed in places captured by the Yishuv; he alluded specifically to looting. But the Zionist leadership had to look to the future and had to 'restrain our evil drives'.

Shitrit demanded that matters relating to Arab property and existing communities be placed under his jurisdiction, including 'the evacuation' of villages, 'the return of Arabs to their places', and the 'cooption [of Arabs] in government institutions and in the state's economy if circumstances allow'. Close cooperation must be instituted with the defence forces.[23]

IDFA files contain a second document produced at this time, possibly also by Shitrit or his officials, detailing the requisite behaviour of the military upon conquering an Arab towns and villages. The memorandum called for the immediate cooption into the staff of the IDF governor of any occupied zone a Minority Ministry official. Contact should immediately be established with the local Arab authorities; outsiders and combatants should be arrested and arms, fuel and vehicles confiscated. The authorities should provide the inhabitants with food and medical care, if necessary. 'It must be remembered that cooperation with the local population will save on manpower needed for other operations', states the memorandum. Places of worship and holy sites should be protected. The memorandum drew a sharp distinction between sites within the partition borders and communities outside them. Within the Jewish state, 'governors', not 'military governors', should be appointed.[24]

The assumptions underlying these memoranda were that Israel would not oppose the continued presence within the state of (peaceful) Arab communities, that there would be a sizable minority, and that Israel would be open to a return of Arab refugees. But this was not, and not to be, the policy of the mainstream leadership. However, neither did Ben-Gurion, the People's Administration\Provisional Government nor the Haganah\IDF GS formally adopt or enunciate a contrary policy. So Shitrit was left believing, or partly believing, that his guidelines were acceptable to Ben-Gurion and his colleagues – and briefly and haphazardly acted upon them. But the decisive institutions of state – the Haganah\IDF, the intelligence services, the kibbutz movements – as we shall see, acted in a contrary manner, promoting the Arab exodus in a variety of ways. It took Shitrit months to catch on and, reluctantly, follow suit.

Shitrit was only marginally effective in imposing his benign will, as the Haganah\IDF moved from conquest to conquest. By and large, in the countryside, military commanders were unhappy about leaving in place Arab communities, whom they would have to garrison, guard against and protect from Jewish depredation. So they normally didn't. But in a handful of towns, on the other hand, where part of the population stayed put (Jaffa, Acre, Nazareth), Shitrit's desires and guidelines were partially followed: Arab affairs administrators were added to the military governors' staffs, food and medical care were provided, and looting was eventually curtailed and then eradicated. Similarly, Mapam officials, backed by Shitrit, were instrumental in forcing the army to leave in place a handful of Arab rural communities, including Jisr az Zarqa and Fureidis. In its addendum to Plan D, issued on 11 May, HGS\Operations provided for the garrisoning of conquered villages and towns and establishing 'a special apparatus to manage [civilian] affairs in these territories' – implying an expectation that Arab communities would remain in place. Nowhere is there an instruction to expel 'the Arabs' nor is the evacuation of the inhabitants assumed.[25] Here, too, one can feel Shitrit's impress.

But ultimately, the atmosphere of transfer, as we shall see, prevailed through April–June: Most communities attacked were evacuated and where no spontaneous evacuation occurred, communities more often than not were expelled. Throughout, Arabs who had fled were prevented from returning to their homes. In some areas, villages that surrendered were disarmed – and then expelled; in others, Haganah (and IZL and LHI) units refused to accept surrender, triggering departure. But, still, because of the absence of a clear, central expulsive policy order, different units behaved differently. The Giv'ati, Harel and Yiftah brigades almost invariably ascertained that no Arab inhabitants remained in areas they had just conquered; the Golani Brigade, on the other hand, acted with far less consistency.

The policy shift during the first half of April also affected behaviour toward abandoned property, a term by then relating to whole urban neighbourhoods and dozens of villages, with their houses and lands. The first major problem faced by the authorities was looting, most often carried out by a village's or neighbourhood's Jewish neighbours. Initially, the HGS worried about specific villages and tracts of land, such as those in the area between the Yarkon River and Herzliya,[26] and instructed each brigade to supervise the property left in its own zone of operations through appointed inspectors of abandoned property.[27] But soon it was felt that the problem had to be tackled in a systematic, 'national' manner. In mid-March, David Horowitz had been appointed Eliezer Kaplan's representative in the matter. (Within weeks, Kaplan was to be Israel's first finance minister and Horowitz, his director general.)[28] And at the end of March, Galili had appointed the Committee for Arab Property, consisting of Machnes, Gwirtz and Danin.[29]

On 1 April, the committee, chaired by Gwirtz, sent out a circular notifying all and sundry of its functions and powers; the focus was exploiting Arab property for Jewish needs and uses rather than protecting it. Gwirtz instructed the recipients – Haganah commanders and local authorities – to inform the committee 'within a week' about 'the Arab property in your area', including categories of ownership (absentee landlords, *fellahin*, beduin, etc.), and to supply the names of Jews who had been given power of attorney by Arabs to manage their properties.[30] The committee began organising the Jewish harvest of abandoned fields and the prevention of Arab harvesting[31] and the systematic registration of types of abandoned property.[32] In the course of April, the somewhat hesitant prevention of Arab cultivation and organisation of Jewish harvesting of abandoned fields became systematic, as reflected in the deliberations of Alexandroni's Arab affairs advisers.[33] Galili ordered all the brigades to cooperate with the committee and informed them that 'the committee . . . is authorised to give you orders concerning . . . behaviour regarding Arab property'. The committee, as noted, was authorised to decide on the expulsion of specific villages.[34] The committee stepped up its activities in May and June as the crops ripened; it toured the country, meeting regional councils and apportioning the fields for harvest to the settlements, who often vied for the right and the profit therefrom.[35]

But given the chaotic civil war situation and the embryonic nature and powers of the new institutions of state, Haganah (and civilian) behaviour in each locality regarding abandoned property was not all the committee hoped it would be; pillage and vandalism continued. In early May, Horowitz resigned in disgust, charging that the committee was 'without influence on the course of events'. He was appalled by the looting; he may also have been put off by expulsions and the razing of villages.[36]

During the second half of May, the Committee for Arab Property became a 'department', initially in the Minority Affairs Ministry and, later, within the Office of the Custodian for Abandoned (later, Absentees') Property in the Finance Ministry. Gwirtz became departmental director. In retrospect, while partially successful in organising the harvest, the committee\department ultimately failed to prevent the vandalisation and pillage of Arab houses. And the fate – expulsion, destruction, etc. – of villages in effect remained the purview of Ben-Gurion and the military.

The society against which the offensives of Plan D were to be unleashed, had, as we have seen, undergone months of strain and corrosion. Palestinian arms, supplemented by the steady stream of foreign volunteers, had partially succeeded in wearing down the Haganah and had severely curbed Jewish use of the roads. But while many Jewish settlements remained under semi-permanent siege, the Arabs had failed to capture any, and not for lack of trying. Worse, Jewish ambushes and roadblocks had in turn isolated many villages and there was a deep sense of siege and vulnerability in the two main Arab centres, Haifa and Jaffa. The flight of the middle and upper classes from these towns and Jerusalem during the previous months had severely undermined morale; so had the gradual breakdown of law and order, which stemmed from the influx of the foreign volunteers and the devolution, and expected end, of British government. The Palestinians, unlike the Yishuv, failed to establish effective self-governance as the British pulled out.

The process of disintegration accelerated in April. Policemen ran off with their weapons; officials stopped coming to work. The irregulars stole property, molested women and intimidated the population, and, at the same time, were militarily ineffective; the population lost confidence in their ability to beat off, let alone defeat, the Haganah. Moreover, the Palestinians sense of 'national' isolation from the surrounding Arab world was continually reinforced by the Arab states' refusal to intervene in Palestine before 15 May and by their continuous rejection of requests for arms. Food and fuel shortages, price rises and widespread unemployment fuelled the demoralisation.

The villages generally fared better than the towns. They were more or less economically autarkic and not all areas of the country were engulfed or seriously affected by the conflagration. However, most, in one way or another, were affected by what happened in the towns, to which they looked for leadership, information and support. And in Jaffa's environs, the Jerusalem Corridor, eastern Galilee and the Negev, the villagers were directly caught up in the fighting, sustaining Haganah attacks and losses. The general slide into lawlessness, fears for the harvest and of the Haganah and the IZL, and concern about what would happen when the British left all affected the villagers.

The Haganah's April offensives caught the Arab states and the AHC by surprise; so did the mass exodus they precipitated. For several weeks, the Arab world failed to react to the uprooting – until the exodus from Haifa (22 April – early May). Given the poor communications and the enveloping fog of battle, it probably took some days to learn of, and understand, what was happening, especially in the countryside. Perhaps some of the states' leaders feared to make too much of the exodus lest they stoke up public pressure to invade even before the British withdrawal. In terms of propaganda value, and as *a priori* justification for their contemplated invasion, nothing suited better than the exodus, which could be – and was – presented to the world as a deliberate expulsion of the Palestinians by the Jews. And, alternatively, if there were uncoerced evacuations, surely they demonstrated – again to the benefit of Arab propaganda – that Arabs were unwilling to live under Jewish rule, making nonsense of the minority provisions in the partition resolution. In any case, no one regarded the exodus as permanent; surely the refugees would within weeks return, in the wake of pan-Arab invasion or British compulsion or UN intercession?

Whatever the reasoning and attitudes of the Arab states' leaders, I have found no contemporary evidence to show that either they or the Mufti ordered or directly encouraged the mass exodus of April–May. As to the Palestinian leaders, it may be worth noting that for decades their policy had been to hold fast to the soil and to resist the eviction and displacement of communities. But two qualifications are necessary. During April, the AHC and some NCs stepped up their pressure on villages in various areas and in some towns to send away women, children and the old to safety, and in some areas there was compliance. And in several areas, Arab military or political leaders ordered the complete evacuation of villages.

During April, the irregulars and at least some of the NCs, apparently at the behest of the AHC, continued to promote, either out of inertia or in line with reiterated policy, the departure from combat and potential combat zones of women, children and the old. Ben-Gurion took note – and explained (regarding Coastal Plain villages): 'Possibly it is being done because of pressure from the gangs' commanders out of Arab strategic needs: Women and children are moved out and fighting gangs are moved in.'[37]

HIS reported on 17 April that there was 'a general order' to remove the women and children from the neighbourhoods bordering Jewish areas in Jerusalem.[38] On 22 April, the Jerusalem NC, citing the AHC circular of 8 March, ordered its neighbourhood branches (Sheikh Jarrah, Wadi Joz, Musrara, Qatamon and others) to move out their women, children and old people 'to places more distant, away from the dangers'. The NC warned that resistance to this order would be seen as 'an obstacle to the Holy War . . . and would hamper their actions in these neighbourhoods'.[39] Already on 5 April the seam neighbourhood of Musrara evacuated most of its women and children to Jericho;[40] around 19 April, the women and children were reported to have evacuated Wadi Joz.[41] Similar evacuations took place from other towns. Some women and children reportedly evacuated Jaffa by sea.[42] Beisan, near the Jordanian border, was ordered by the Arab Legion in early May to evacuate its women and children, possibly in preparation for the pan-Arab invasion,[43] and on 9 May HIS reported the ongoing evacuation.[44]

The evacuation of dependents was even more pronounced in the countryside. Most of the villages around Jerusalem appear to have evacuated their women and children during late March – early May.[45] Many women and children were moved from Qastal to Suba and Beit Surik at the end of March.[46] Kamal Erikat, a band leader, was reported to have demanded that Beit Naqquba, too, should evacuate 'the families, to Imwas' – but the villagers were unwilling and dragged their feet.[47] Beit Hanina, to the north of the city, had emptied of women and children as 300 Iraqi irregulars had moved in.[48] Qaluniya, near Qastal, was emptied of women and children around 10 April, just before it fell to the Haganah.[49] Suba, too, sent out its women and children at this time.[50] On 11 April, Qalandiya, north of Jerusalem, completely evacuated in January but later re-populated, was reportedly sending away most of its women and children.[51] Most or all of Shu'fat's women and children were gone by the end of April.[52] Al Maliha, southwest of Jerusalem, was also reported evacuating its women and children (to Walaja) as was 'Ein Karim (to Beit Jala and Bethlehem).[53] The women and children were removed from Beit Iksa, west of the city, to make room for 200 Iraqis.[54] At the same time, Isawiya was reported to have evacuated its women and children on orders from 'the gangs.'[55] The women and children of Abu Dis, a-Tur and al 'Eizariya, three village suburbs east of Jerusalem, had been emptied of women and children to make way for Iraqi irregulars.[56] Apparently, all this happened in compliance with a general order 'to evacuate the women and children from all the villages in the Jerusalem area, so that they would not hamper [offensive] operations'.[57]

The pattern was similar to the west and north. On 8 April, HIS-AD reported the start of the evacuation of women and children from Sarafand al Kharab, near Ramle, probably because of pressure by foreign irregulars.[58] Majdal Yaba, in the Ramle District, was also reported evacuating women and children for fear of Haganah assault.[59] In the Jezreel Valley, Zir'in evacuated its women and children following a Haganah raid in early May.[60] In Eastern Galilee, Dawwara and 'Abisiyya were ordered to remove their women and children to make room for irregulars.[61] The fall of Arab Haifa on 21–22 April appears to have triggered evacuations of women and children from many nearby villages.[62] On 24 April, the ALA ordered the inhabitants of Fureidis, south of Haifa, to evacuate their women and children, 'and make ready to evacuate [the village] completely'.[63] A few kilometres to the north, the women and children of Tira were evacuated with the help of the Arab Legion to Neuherrdorf, near Haifa, and later to Jordan.[64] Similarly, dependents had been evacuated from Khirbet as Sarkas, near Hadera (to Baqa al Gharbiya and Jatt).[65] The women and children of Qannir were evacuated starting 22 April on 'orders from on high'.[66] In early May, Umm al Zinat was reported empty of women and children.[67] North of Haifa, Kabri was completely evacuated.[68] A few days earlier, the Arab communities around Rosh Pina, in Eastern Galilee, were ordered to evacuate their women and children, the men staying to guard the sites.[69]

In most cases, the evacuation of the dependents proved permanent – as this was followed shortly after by Haganah\IDF conquest and complete evacuation and destruction. But in some cases, the evacuations were brief, triggered by fears of imminent Jewish attack; once the fear subsided, women and children would return. In 'Iraq Suweidan, for example, in the northern Negev approaches, women and children were reported to have been evacuated in early May for one night, only to return the following day.[70]

The invasion by the Arab states prompted fresh evacuations of dependents by communities fearful that they, too, would now be engulfed in war. For example, Qastina reportedly sent away its women and children around 15 May (but they returned from Tel as Safi after discovering that that there was insufficient water in the host village).[71]

Evacuations of women and children continued, but with much less frequency, during the second half of the war – by which time the Arabs should have understood that it was detrimental to their interests. In late June – early July, for example, the ALA ordered the evacuation of women and children from Ma'lul and Mujeidil, apparently to make room for incoming ALA contingents and in preparation for anticipated offensive operations.[72] Ma'lul and Mujeidil sent their children and womenfolk to Nazareth; a similar evacuation apparently took place in the other villages in the area.[73] Regarding Ma'lul, the ALA was apparently angered by the villagers' declaration that they would cooperate with any government in control, and would not participate in fighting. ALA troops beat villagers and killed cattle and sheep – causing a panic flight.[74] On 24 June, 'Arab Mazarib and 'Arab Sa'ida, two Jezreel Valley beduin tribes, packed up and moved out following a 'grave warning from the [ALA] headquarters in Nazareth'.[75] On 7 July, Qawuqji's officers in 'Illut ordered the villagers to evacuate their women and children[76] and the following day, obviously in preparation for the renewal of hostilities, at the end of the First Truce, Qawuqji ordered all villagers in the Nazareth area henceforth 'to sleep outside their villages'.[77] The beduins encamped on the southern slopes of Mount Tabor, near Dabburiyya, were ordered 'to move their tents northwards, into the hills'.[78] A month later, during the Second Truce, Qawuqji ordered the inhabitants of Kafr Manda to evacuate their village, then under IDF control, preparatory to attacking it,[79] and a month later, a similar order was issued by the ALA to the villagers of Majd al Kurum, for similar reasons.[80] Still later, elsewhere, the women and children of Deir Aiyub, near Latrun, were sent inland.[81] And on 31 October, the villagers of Dimra, near Gaza, reportedly evacuated their women and children, probably in response to the nearby IDF advance.[82]

During April–May, some two dozen villages were completely evacuated as a result of orders by local Arab commanders, governments or the AHC, mostly for pre-invasion military reasons. 'Arab al Satariyya, near Ramle, was ordered 'from Ramle' – either by the NC or local commanders – to completely evacuate by 30 April. The inhabitants of Beit Dajan left at the same time and Iraqi irregulars moved into the village.[83] HIS reported that Arabs in Haifa were saying that 'all the villages between

Haifa and Tel Aviv had orders from the general Arab headquarters [sic] to evacuate their villages as soon as possible in preparation for the general [Arab] invasion'.[84] More specifically, and probably more accurately, it was reported in mid-May that 'small villages' south of Haifa had been ordered to evacuate 'and move to a distant area' while the menfolk were instructed to move to 'the villages designated as concentration areas' (i.e., 'Ein Ghazal-Ijzim-Jab'a).[85] On 11–12 May, the villages of Shu'fat, Beit Hanina, al Jib, Judeira, Bir Nabala and Rafat, in the Ramallah area, were completely evacuated at the command of the Arab Legion.[86] The Legion also ordered 'all the inhabitants' of East Jerusalem's central neighbourhoods outside the Old City to move into the Old City. Many of 'Ein Karim's Christian families also moved to the Old City, on 'the advice' of the local commander.[87] Isawiya had already been evacuated, at AHC command, on 30 March. On 20 May the villagers of al Dahi, Nein, Tamra, Kafr Misr, al Tira, Taiyiba and Na'ura, all near Mount Gilbo'a, were ordered to leave by Arab irregular forces (who apparently feared that they intended to throw in their lot with the Yishuv);[88] a few weeks earlier, the 'irregulars' headquarters' – meaning, apparently, the AHC – probably for similar reasons, ordered the evacuation of nearby Sirin, 'Ulam, Hadatha and Ma'dhar.[89]

Farther to the north, there was apparently a Syrian order to Arabs living along the Palestine–Syria border to pull out in preparation for the pan-Arab invasion.[90] The inhabitants of Nuqeib ('Arab Argibat), on the eastern shore of the Sea of Galilee, traditionally friendly with Kibbutz 'Ein-Gev, were pressured by the Syrians to evacuate but held off for a few days.[91] At the end of April, after a Haganah raid on Samakh, the Argibat began to evacuate, fearing the Jews. A Haganah emissary asked them to stay put.[92] But in mid-May, with the pan-Arab invasion only hours away, things changed. On 13–14 May, the Haganah demanded that the village accept Jewish rule and turn over its weapons; the villagers preferred not to and evacuated the next day; the kibbutz then demolished their houses.[93] A fortnight later, on 27 May, the Haganah expelled the Persian Zickrallah family, who owned a large farm just south of 'Ein Gev, and their Arab hands, some 30 souls all told, half of them children. 'In war there is no room for sentiment', it was explained in 'Ein Gev's logbook. They were ferried to Tiberias, where the Haganah put them up in a hotel. Subsequently they were resettled in Acre.[94]

Until the last week of April, the AHC and the Arab governments, at least publicly, did not seem to be unduly perturbed by the exodus. 'Azzam Pasha, secretary general of the Arab League, to be sure, in April used the flight and the massacre at Deir Yassin (see below) to drive home anti-Zionist propaganda points, but there seems to have been no feeling that something momentous was happening. The Arab states did nothing: *en large*, they acted neither to aggravate the exodus nor to stem it.[95]

The AHC during April and May was probably driven by a set of contradictory interests. On the one hand, its members – almost to a man out of Palestine by the end of April – were unhappy at the sight of the steady dissolution and emigration of their society. The exodus dashed their hopes of a successful Palestinian resistance to the Yishuv. On the other hand, led by the Mufti, by late April they understood that all now depended on the intervention of the Arab states. Husseini well knew the essential fickleness of the Arab leaders, and understood that Egypt's Farouk, Jordan's Abdullah, Lebanon's Prime Minister Riad Solh and the rest were not overly eager to do battle in Palestine. Husseini may well have reasoned, as 15 May approached, that the bigger the tragedy, the greater would be the pressure – by public opinion at home, by the other states and by the demands of Arab 'honour' – on these leaders to abide by their commitment to intervene. Nothing would bind them to their word like a great Palestinian disaster. Moreover, the AHC was unhappy at the prospect of Arab communities surrendering and accepting Jewish rule. Pulled hither and thither by such considerations, during April and the first half of May Husseini and the AHC remained largely silent about the unfolding exodus.

Given the lack of clear direction from the Arab states and the AHC, the burden of decision-making fell mainly on the shoulders of local leaders, both civil and military. It is largely to the local leadership, therefore, that one must look for decision-making concerning staying or leaving by this or that Arab community during April 1948. Local leaders may have been motivated in part by what they thought the AHC would want them to decide, as in Haifa on 22 April, but in general, they were left to their own devices.

In most cases, the NCs during April–May acted to curb flight from their localities, especially of army-aged males. In Jerusalem, in late April the NC ordered militiamen to stop vehicles with fleeing inhabitants and to haul them back,[96] and issued the following communiqué:

> There are people sowing false rumours and as a result [have] forced some Arabs to leave the city . . . These rumours help the enemy in our midst . . . The committee declares herewith that the state of Arab defences in the towns is relatively strong, and it demands of the citizens not to pay attention to the false rumours and to stay in their places.[97]

The committee also resolved to punish satellite villages from which there was unauthorised flight; the villagers were ordered to 'stay in place and not leave'.[98] In mid-May, as the Haganah occupied areas in central Jerusalem and threatened the Old City, masses of Arabs assembled in front of the NC building, demanding permits to leave. NC officials 'refused' and armed men were sent after vehicles fleeing the town without permits.[99]

Haifa's NC acted similarly. The chairman appealed to NC members who had left to return[100] and threatened shopkeepers who had left that it would revoke their licenses.[101] Jaffa's NC tried to halt flight by imposing fines and threatening property confiscation. Departing families were forced to pay special taxes.[102] The efforts to halt the evacuation seem to have ended with the IZL attack of 25–27 April (see below).

In some of the smaller towns, too, the NCs made efforts to stem the tide. In early April, Sidqi al Tabari was 'making desperate efforts to bring back' those who had fled Tiberias, HIS reported.[103] Arabs who had fled to al Hama 'were ordered back and, in fact, returned'.[104] In Beisan, adult males were prevented by NC order from leaving town and, indeed, guard duty on the perimeters was increased 'out of fear of flight from the city'.[105] The fall of Arab Haifa had promoted demoralisation and flight and the Beisan 'NC had made efforts to curb the flight, but was unsuccessful despite the acts of violence against the departees . . . But the adult males are not allowed to leave . . .'[106]

There is also substantial evidence that in various rural areas, neighbouring NCs, ALA and local commanders, and mukhtars made serious efforts during April–June to curtail flight (alongside fewer instances, in other places, to promote flight). At al Bira, next to Ramallah, foreign irregulars prevented locals from leaving.[107] In Burayr, in the Gaza District, the foreign irregulars' commander tried to stem flight.[108] In Lydda, an Iraqi officer was reported at the end of April to have forced, at gunpoint, fleeing villagers to return.[109] Similarly, the Marshad family from Sindiyana was forced to return home by ALA officers.[110] North of Gaza, Majdal's militiamen forced villagers fleeing neighbouring Beit Daras to return.[111] Indeed, a few days later, Majdal's NC ordered the inhabitants of Barqa, Batani al Gharbi and Batani al Sharqi, Yasur, Beit Daras and the three Sawafir villages (Gharbiya, Shamaliya and Sharqiya) not to flee, 'on pain of punishment'. The militiamen manning the roadblocks around Majdal and Gaza were ordered not to allow any of these villagers to enter with belongings. The inhabitants of Yibna were also ordered to stay put.[112] In early May, Shakib Wahab, a senior ALA officer, forbade Shafa 'Amr's inhabitants from leaving the town. But some succeeded, reported HIS, after paying a P£100 bribe.[113] The would-be leavers were apparently threatened that their homes would be expropriated.[114] At the start of May, Sabbarin was ordered by its larger neighbour, Umm al Fahm, not to evacuate.[115] To the northwest, the remaining inhabitants of Tira were forbidden by the ALA to leave;[116] again, the irregulars brandished the threat of confiscation.[117]

During the First Truce, as well, there were irregulars' commanders who ordered villagers to stay put; this happened in mid-June in the area south of Ramle[118] and at Tarshiha and Lubya in the Galilee (on Qawuqji's orders).[119] During the Second Truce, Qawuqji was reported to have left small contingents in the Galilee villages 'from Maghar to Malikiya to make sure the villagers did not flee out of fear'.[120]

At the end of March, Qawuqji had told the mukhtar of Kafr Saba, near Kafr Qasim, that 'places of habitation should not be abandoned, so long as there were proper relations with [neighbouring] Jews. At the same time, Arabs who had evacuated their homes without reason were spoken of angrily.'[121] But by early May, the inhabitants, feeling under Jewish military threat, were ready to leave. They were ordered by the ALA to stay put.[122] When, at last, the village was attacked, on 13 May, the inhabitants fled. At the exit from town, the Syrian ALA commander extorted P£5 from each departee.[123]

A few days before, perhaps under the cumulative impact of the fall of Arab Haifa and the mass evacuation of Jaffa, ALA headquarters in Ramallah issued a blanket proscription against flight. The Arab states, too, suddenly awakened to the problem. Already in late April, the Haganah noted that Abdullah was pressing beduin refugees from the Beit Shean Valley to return home.[124] On 5–6 May, the ALA, in radio broadcasts and newspapers, forbade Ramallah area villagers from leaving their homes: The homes of fleeing villagers would be demolished and their fields confiscated. Inhabitants who had fled were ordered to return.[125] Jordan endorsed the order. According to the Haganah, the population of Ramallah was about to take flight, so the ALA was blocking the roads out: 'The Arab military leaders are trying to stem the flood of refugees and are taking stern and ruthless measures against them', reported the Haganah. On 5 May, Radio Jerusalem and Damascus Radio broadcast the ALA orders to those who had fled to 'return within three days'.[126] Haganah Radio, capitalising on the order, on 6 May broadcast that 'in an endeavour to put a stop to the flight . . . the Arab command has issued a statement warning that . . . any Arab leaving . . . will be severely punished'.[127]

During 5–15 May, King 'Abdullah, 'Azzam Pasha, and, more hesitantly, the AHC, in semi-coordinated fashion issued similar announcements designed to halt the flight and induce refugees to return. A special appeal, also promoted by the British Mandate authorities, was directed at the refugees from Haifa. On 15 May, Faiz Idrisi, the AHC's 'inspector for public safety', issued orders to Palestinian militiamen to fight against 'the Fifth Column and the rumour-mongers, who are causing the flight of the Arab population'. On 10–11 May, the AHC called on officials, doctors and engineers who had left to return and on 14–15 May, repeating the call, warned that officials who did not return would lose their 'moral right to hold these administrative jobs in the future'. Arab governments began to bar entry to the refugees – for example, along the Lebanese border.[128]

By the end of May, with their armies fully committed, the Arab states (and the AHC) put pressure on the refugee communities encamped along Palestine's frontiers to go home. According to monitored Arab broadcasts, the AHC was arguing that 'most of the [abandoned] villages had been made safe thanks to Arab victories'.[129] However, the sudden pan-Arab concern came too late, was never enunciated as official policy and was never translated into systematic action. Moreover, the Arab League Political Committee persisted in prodding member states to 'grant asylum . . . to women, children and the elderly' (while urging them to bar adult males).[130] Having failed to halt the mass exodus at birth, the states proved powerless to curb its momentum, let alone reverse the process. Perhaps more forceful efforts would also have been of little avail – given the Palestinian fear of the Jews, stemming from actual Haganah, IZL and LHI operations, reinforced by Arab radio broadcasts over the previous months, which highlighted real and alleged Jewish atrocities. Little could have induced those who had fled to head back. In any event, by late May – early June the Arab leaders were preoccupied with their armies' performance, inter-Arab feuding and the anti-Zionist diplomatic struggle in the United Nations, London and Washington, rather than with the refugees. By mid-June, when the First Truce took effect and the Arab states were at last able to turn their gaze away from the battlefields, conditions had radically changed. The borders had become continuous front lines with free-fire zones separating the armies, and the victorious Yishuv was resolved to bar a return. Thus, the pressure by some of the Arab countries to push the refugees back across the borders, reported by IDF intelligence in early June, had little effect.[131] And by August, indeed, the AHC was arguing against the repatriation of the refugees lest this would represent 'recognition of the State of Israel' and place repatriates at the mercy of the Jewish authorities.[132] But in the main, what the Arabs states, the AHC, the ALA, the NCs and the various militias did or did not do during April–June to promote or stifle the exodus was only of secondary importance; the prime movers throughout were the Yishuv and its military organisations. It was their operations that were to prove the major precipitants to flight. To understand what happened, it is necessary to examine in detail what occurred in the field. I shall focus on the main towns and on key operations in the countryside. I shall start with the towns because their fall and the exodus of their populations helped trigger the exodus from the countryside.

THE CITIES

Tiberias

The first Arab urban community to fall was that of Tiberias, the mixed town (6,000 Jews, 4,000 Arabs) on the western shore of the Sea of Galilee, which sat astride the north–south road linking the settlements in the Galilee Panhandle with those in the lower Jordan Valley. The UN partition resolution had included Tiberias in the Jewish State.

On 4 December 1947, a leading notable, Sheikh Naif Tabari – the Tabaris, originating in Ajlun, Transjordan, were the town's most prosperous and respected family[133] – initiated talks with local Jewish leaders to conclude a local 'peace pact'.[134] Nonetheless, Arab families, fearing trouble, began to leave their homes, some moving to purely Arab neighbourhoods and others, such as the small Shi'ite community, leaving town altogether.[135] Jewish families also fled the predominantly Arab 'Old City'; by early February 1948, only a quarter of the Old City's Jews were still in place (with the abandoned flats being filled by Arab evacuees from Jewish neighbourhoods) – and the remaining Jews threatened to leave if Haganah protection was not forthcoming. (They also demanded that the Haganah order those who had left the Old City to return and those still in the area, to stay put.)[136]

The Tabaris, who controlled the NC, consistently stymied efforts by hotheaded youngsters to unleash hostilities[137] and preached peaceful coexistence.[138] Yosef Nahmani, one of the Jewish community leaders and head of the JNF office in eastern Galilee, confirmed that they sought continued peace though Jewish youngsters were continually provoking the Arabs, which could lead to an 'explosion' and 'a disaster', he warned. The town's Sephardi Jews, according to Nahmani, 'tended to boastfulness and self-praise just like the Arabs'. He told of the incident on 4 February, in which three drunken 'oriental' Jews went down to the Old City, met and cursed some Arab guards, a fracas broke out, an Arab lightly wounded one of the Jews and the Haganah retaliated with grenades and light weapons (but no one was hit). That night or the following day, the NC, led by Sidqi Tabari, met with the town's Jewish leaders, including Mayor Shimon Dahan, and concluded a non-belligerency agreement.[139] But both the 'mindless' local Haganah commanders, according to Nahmani, and the shabab, according to the HIS, were unhappy with the pact.[140] Nonetheless, quiet was restored and one visiting HIS-AD operative was struck by how Arabs, including beduin, moved about freely in the Jewish markets, rode on Jewish buses, and conducted commerce with Jews, as if the two communities 'know or hear nothing of what is happening between the Jews and the Arabs in the rest of the country'.[141]

The fragile truce collapsed in mid-March. Shooting erupted in downtown Tiberias on the 12th, apparently following efforts by Jewish policemen to disarm Arabs. The fighting went on intermittently for three days and the leaders of the two communities met in the town hall on 14 March. The Arabs charged that the Jews had provoked the shooting and Nahmani, in his heart (and diary), 'endorsed the Arabs' charges'.[142] Quiet resumed, with Israel Galili apparently endorsing the new pact: 'It's good that you've done this', he told the Tiberias Jewish leaders, 'because we have plenty of fronts and we would rather not spread ourselves [too thin].'[143] Additional Jews fled the Old City and the Haganah, tried to put a stop to the exodus.[144] The ALA's OC in the Galilee, Adib Shishakli, wanted to take over the defense of Arab Tiberias – but the NC, preferring calm, rejected the offer.[145] Nonetheless, a small contingent of outside irregulars took up positions in the Arab quarters in late March or early April. By the second half of March, Haganah operations had caused food shortages, resulting in sharp price rises ('even of fish'), followed by the closure of 'most [Arab] shops'.[146]

The (final) battle of Tiberias began on 8–9 April, when shooting once again erupted in the downtown area. On 10 April the Haganah bombarded 'the Arab population [i.e., residential area]' with mortars.[147] The British tried to mediate a truce but failed. On the 12th, a company of the 12th Battalion, Golani Brigade, attacked and captured the small tenant farmer village of Khirbet Nasir ad Din and the Sheikh Qaddumi hilltop above it, overlooking Tiberias, cutting the city off from Lubya and Nazareth, the major Arab centres to the west. The orders were 'to destroy the enemy concentration' in the village. During the four-hour skirmish, in which the Haganah met unexpected resistance, most of the population fled to Tiberias, and the village was occupied. The Haganah recorded 22 Arabs killed, six wounded and three captured (Haganah casualties were two lightly wounded).[148] The Arabs subsequently alleged that 'there had been a second Deir Yassin'[149] in Nasir ad Din – and, indeed, some non-combatants, including women and children, were killed.[150] The arrival of the Nasir ad Din refugees helped to undermine the morale of Arab Tiberias.[151] Nahmani reacted by jotting down in his diary:

> I cannot justify this action by the Haganah. I don't know whether there was justification for the assault and the killing of so many Arabs. The flight of the women and children of the village in panic made a bad impression on me.[152]

The British had not intervened in Nasir ad Din. The Haganah decided to pacify Arab Tiberias, which blocked the road to the Galilee Panhandle settlements.[153] On the night of 16\17 April, units of Golani and the Palmah's 3rd Battalion, freshly introduced into Tiberias, attacked in the Old City, using mortars and dynamite, blowing up eight houses. The attack caused 'great panic'. Arab notables apparently sued for a truce but the Haganah commanders refused to negotiate; they wanted a surrender.[154] The Arabs appealed to the British to lift the Haganah siege on the Old City and to extend their protection to the Arab neighbourhoods. The British said that they intended to evacuate the town within days and could offer no protection beyond 22 April. The Arab notables 'agreed to evacuate', perhaps at British suggestion.[155] Already on 17 April, Arabs – including members of the Tabari family – had begun to stream out of the town 'in panic' and local clergymen asked the British to help the population 'to leave Tiberias'.[156] Colonel Anderson, the ranking British officer, reportedly informed Jewish representatives that they would be leaving in a few days, that they were unwilling to guarantee the Arabs' safety after their departure and that 'in order to assure the Arabs' safety, it had been decided to evacuate the Arabs from the town'.[157]

On 21 April, an HIS-AD officer reported that one of Tiberias's militia leaders, Subhi Shahin Anqush, had left Tiberias on 17 April and had returned the following day 'with a large number of buses from various Arab [transport] companies in Nazareth'. This might indicate that the idea of a complete evacuation had germinated on 17 April – rather than at British suggestion on 18 April.[158] It was Shahin, according to the HIS officer, who had made sure, using 'threats and force', that the evacuation of Tiberias would be complete after some 700 inhabitants had initially wanted to raise 'the white flag' and stay put.[159]

The evacuation of Tiberias clearly exercised the Yishuv military (and perhaps, political) leaders and, to most, came as a surprise. One Golani intelligence officer was sufficiently intrigued, or perturbed, to write during the following days a two-page analysis and explanation entitled 'Why the Arabs had Evacuated Tiberias'. Strikingly, he made no mention at all of Arab orders (or even rumours of orders) from 'outside' or 'from on high' or of advice by the British, as the cause of the exodus. It was, he explained, the end result of a cumulative process of demoralisation. The exodus, which, he argues, began immediately after Nasir ad Din, was caused by (a) a sense of military weakness, stemming from the diffusion of power among three separate, and often rival, militias; (b) economic conditions, worsened by Haganah control of the access roads into town, and price rises; (c) societal 'rottenness' and the flight of the leaders; (d) the non-arrival of reinforcements from the hinterland; (e) the steadfastness of the Haganah contingent in the Old City, which held on, despite British threats and Arab siege and harassment; (f) the fall of Nasir ad Din and the demoralisation caused by the arrival of its refugees, with their 'imaginative oriental stories' of Jewish atrocities; and (g) the successful Haganah offensive of 16–18 April, which had included the demolition of the Tiberias Hotel.[160]

In any event, at around noon on 18 April, a de facto truce took hold and the British imposed a four-hour curfew. They (and private Arab entrepreneurs) brought in dozens of buses and trucks, the inhabitants boarded, and the vehicles, under British escort, headed for Nazareth. Some families, in cars, drove southward, toward Jordan. The Jewish population observed the exodus of their former neighbours from windows and balconies.[161] 'The [British] Army is evacuating all the Arabs from Tiberias; there is a chance', reported the Palmah's 3rd Battalion, 'that Tiberias tomorrow will be empty of Arabs.'[162] That evening, a Golani patrol reported: 'We have completed a reconnaissance of the whole of the lower city. There are no strangers [i.e., Arabs] on the site.' The unit reported that it was guarding Arab shops and homes against looting. 'Our morale is high.'[163]

But within hours, 'the Jewish mob descended upon [the evacuated areas] and began to pillage the shops . . . The looting was halted by the armed intervention of the Jewish police . . .'[164] HIS-AD reported that both Jewish residents and Haganah soldiers participated in the 'robbery, on a large scale. There were disgusting incidents of robbery by commanders and disputes among people who fought over the loot.' The looting continued intermittently during the following days and several malefactors were arrested;[165] a number were seriously injured by Haganah troops. In one incident, a Haganah man shot a Sephardi looter (who later died). The largely Sephardi townspeople remarked 'that the Ashkenazis shoot only Sephardis . . .'. Looting was resumed on 22 April, when the Haganah and the police completely lost control.[166] Nahmani jotted down in his diary:

> Groups of dozens of Jews walked about pillaging from the Arab houses and shops . . . The Haganah people hadn't the strength to control the mob after they themselves had given a bad example . . . [It was as if] there was a contest between the different Haganah platoons stationed in Migdal, Genossar, Yavniel, 'Ein Gev, who came in cars and boats and loaded all sorts of goods [such as] refrigerators, beds, etc. . . . Quite naturally the Jewish masses in Tiberias wanted to do likewise . . . Old men and women, regardless of age . . . religious [and non-religious], all are busy with robbery . . . Shame covers my face . . .[167]

With Haganah agreement, a few Arabs returned to Tiberias under British escort on 21–22 April to retrieve property.[168]

The Jewish troops had not been ordered to expel the Arab inhabitants, nor had they done so. Indeed, they had not expected the population to leave. At the same time, once the decision had been taken and once the evacuation was under way, at no point did the Haganah act to stop it. During the night of 18\19 April, the Jewish community leaders printed a proclamation explaining what had happened. They wrote that the Arabs had started the hostilities, the Haganah had responded, and the Arabs had decided to leave. 'We did not deprive the Arab inhabitants of their homes', read the poster. The leaflet enjoined the Jews not to lay hands on Arab property as 'the day will come when the Arab inhabitants will return to their homes . . .'.[169]

Three days later, Jamal Husseini informed the UN that the Jews had 'compelled the Arab population to leave Tiberias'. Years later, the OC of the Golani Brigade obliquely concurred when he recalled that the brigade's conquest of the key Arab military position in the town had 'forced the Arab inhabitants to evacuate'.[170] On the other hand, Elias Koussa, a Haifa Arab lawyer, in 1949 charged that 'the British authorities forcibly transported the Arab inhabitants [of Tiberias] *en masse* to [sic] Transjordan.' Instead of forcefully restoring order in the town, as was their 'duty,' they had 'compelled the Arabs to abandon their homes and belongings and seek refuge in the contiguous Arab territory'.[171] However, to judge from the evidence, the decision to evacuate Tiberias was taken jointly by the local Arab leaders and the British military authorities. It is possible that the idea of evacuation, under British protection, was first suggested by British officers – but it was the Arab notables who had decided whether to stay or go. The British unwillingness – actually, inability – to offer long-term protection and their announcement of impending withdrawal probably acted as spurs. The flight, before and at the start of the battle, of leading Tiberias notables, the real and alleged events at Nasir ad Din (reinforced by news of the massacre, a week before, in Deir Yassin) and the Haganah conquest on 10 April of the village of al Manara, to the south, cutting the road to Jordan, all probably contributed to the exodus.[172]

Within days, the fall of Arab Tiberias and the evacuation of its inhabitants sparked the evacuation of a string of villages around the lake. The beduin sub-tribe of 'Arab al Qadish (of the 'Arab al Dalaika), encamped near Poriya, south of the town, left under Haganah escort (which they requested) on 19 April, moving to Samakh and Jordan.[173] The Syrian shop owners in Samakh, south of the town, fled on or just before 22 April;[174] and truckloads of women and children were seen leaving the village on 24 April. Women and children were also seen leaving Lubya.[175] The remaining inhabitants of al 'Ubeidiya, southwest of the Sea of Galilee, departed on 21 April.[176] The inhabitants of Majdal, a lakeside village north of Tiberias, evacuated their homes after being 'persuaded by the headmen of [neighbouring Jewish] Migdal and Genossar'; the villagers were paid P£200 for eight rifles, ammunition and a bus they handed over – and were transported to the Jordanian border in Jewish buses.[177] The fall of Arab Tiberias no doubt helped in the work of 'persuasion'. Jewish persuasion also precipitated the evacuation of neighbouring Ghuweir Abu Shusha.[178] Al Samra, at the southern end of the lake, was also partially evacuated in response to the fall of Tiberias, as were Kafr Sabt and Shajara.[179]

Haifa

The fall and exodus of Arab Haifa were among the major events of the war. The departure of the town's Arabs, who before the war had numbered 65,000, by itself accounted for some 10 per cent of the Arab refugee total. The fall of, and flight from, Haifa, given the city's pivotal political, administrative and economic role, was a major direct and indirect precipitant of the subsequent exodus from elsewhere in the North and other areas of the country, including Jaffa.

The mass exodus of 21 April – early May must be seen against the backdrop of the gradual evacuation of the city by some 20,000–30,000 of its inhabitants, including most of the middle and upper classes, over December 1947 – early April 1948; most NC members and municipal councillors, and their families, were among the departees. Haifa was especially vulnerable to the gradual closure of the Mandate Government camps, installations and offices, which sharply increased unemployment during March–April.[180] This, and the months of skirmishing, bombings, food shortages (especially of flour and bread) and sense of isolation from the Arab hinterland, had combined to steadily unnerve the remaining population.[181]

During the first week of April, Palmah intelligence reported, 150 Arabs were leaving a day.[182] Sometime during the first half of April, NC chairman Rashid al Haj Ibrahim, left, apparently after quarrelling with the new militia commander, the Lebanese Druse officer Amin 'Izz a Din Nabahani.[183] Haganah intelligence reported that 'more than 100' militiamen, mostly Syrians and Iraqis, who had failed to receive their wages, left during the third week of April.[184] The Haganah's successes during the previous days against the ALA in the battles of Mishmar Ha'emek and Ramat Yohanan, a few miles to the southeast, no doubt also left their mark. By 21 April, when the Haganah launched its onslaught, the remaining population was in great measure primed for evacuation.

According to the British GOC North Sector, Major General Hugh Stockwell, the final battle was triggered by the Arab irregulars, who in mid-April

> went over to the offensive in many quarters . . . with the object tactically to push forward from two salients, Wadi Nisnas and Wadi Salib, to get astride . . . the main Jewish thoroughfare in Hadar Hacarmel, and . . . to strengthen the personal positions of both Amin Bey 'Izz a Din and Yunis Nafa'a,

their two commanders.[185] On 16 April, Arab fire killed four Jews and wounded five. Starting that day, the Arabs 'stepped up their use of mortars', reported the Haganah.[186]

The Haganah had intended to leave Haifa till last, in light of the continued, large British presence in the city and the fact that the city was crucial to the British withdrawal from Palestine, slated for completion on 15 May: The Haganah was far from eager to tangle with them. But the Arab pressure in mid-April, which culminated in the abrupt British troop redeployment out of the 'seam' areas on 21 April, and Arab fire early that morning against Jewish traffic in Wadi Rushmiya and elsewhere,[187] forced the Carmeli Brigade's hand.

Plan D called for the consolidation of the Jewish hold on the mixed cities by

> gaining control of all government property and services, the expulsion of the Arabs from the mixed districts and even from certain [all-Arab] neighbourhoods that endanger our lines of communication in these cities or that serve as staging grounds for attack. Also [Plan D called for] the sealing off of the Arab population – in a part of the city that will be surrounded by our forces.

The plan assigned the neutralisation of Arab Haifa to the Carmeli Brigade, which was specifically instructed

> to conquer and take control of Elijah's Cave, the Old City, the German Colony, Jaffa Street, the old and new commercial districts, Nazareth Street, Wadi Rushmiya, the 'shacks neighbourhood' [i.e., Ard al Ghamal] and [the village of] Balad al Sheikh.[188]

Throughout the crisis, Stockwell was primarily motivated by the desire to assure the safety of his troops and to guarantee that the British withdrawal from Palestine – most of it through Haifa port – should not be impeded. He was particularly concerned about the security of the harbour, the railway lines and the oil refinery. Lastly, he was interested in maintaining peace between the Jews and Arabs.[189] Stockwell was throughout aware that Haifa had been earmarked by the UN for the Jewish state and that the Carmeli Brigade was stronger than its Arab foes. He may also have had greater sympathy for the Zionist cause. In mid-March, in a meeting with the JA-PD representative in the city, Harry Beilin, and the powerful Mapai Party local branch boss, Abba Khoushi (Schneller), he apparently expressed a wish 'to cooperate with [the Jews] in such a way that Haifa will be handed over to the Jews as a clean city'. A few days later, Beilin took Stockwell to Kibbutz Mishmar Ha'emek, where they had lunch, and he was 'very [favourably] impressed'.[190]

In mid-April, Stockwell had spoken with Jewish and Arab officers and urged them to step down their attacks. Both sides gave him 'vague and useless promises'. The Arab provocations of mid-April had persuaded Carmeli Brigade, which had persuaded Haganah HQ, of the need for 'a major operation'.[191] On the afternoon of 19 April, Khoushi, accompanied by Beilin, sounded out Stockwell on the British attitude to a possible 'major [Haganah] offensive'. According to Stockwell, Khoushi said that the Jewish position was 'no longer tolerable' and that Hadar Hacarmel was 'being threatened by the Arab offensive'. Stockwell warned that a major Jewish offensive would be 'most unwise'. Khoushi reported back to Tel Aviv and the idea of a Haganah push in Haifa was temporarily shelved. But Stockwell, perhaps partly on the basis of the conversation with Khoushi, was convinced that a 'major clash' was imminent. He believed that with the 'slender forces' at his command in the city, he would be unable to stop the fighting and that his troops would suffer casualties. He decided that of the three courses open to him – 'to maintain my present dispositions in Haifa and Eastern Galilee', 'to concentrate the Eastern Galilee force in Haifa', and 'to retain my present dispositions in Eastern Galilee and to redeploy my forces in Haifa, whereby I could secure certain routes and areas vital to me and safeguard as far as possible my troops' – the third course was the most attractive.

He ordered his troops, the First Guards Brigade and auxiliary units, to redeploy 'by first light on 21 April' and move out of their downtown positions and along the seam between the Jewish and Arab districts. The redeployment was effected by 06:00 hours. Immediately, firefights erupted between Jews and Arabs for possession of the buildings evacuated by the British along the front lines.[192] According to Beilin, Stockwell had in effect said: 'The flag is down, may the best man win.'[193]

According to Nimr al Khatib, in 'the early morning' of 21 April a British officer had informed the NC of the 'impending' British redeployment.[194] Similar informal notice may have been given to the Haganah. More formally, Stockwell at 10:00 hours summoned Jewish and, subsequently, Arab leaders and handed them a prepared statement announcing the redeployment, which had already been completed. He asked both to end the hostilities and vaguely promised British assistance in maintaining peace and order. At the same time, he said that the British security forces would refrain from involvement in the clashes.[195]

The sudden British redeployment triggered a hurried consultation in Carmeli headquarters. During the morning and early afternoon *Mivtza Bi'ur Hametz* (Operation Passover Cleansing) was hammered out. In part, it was based on a plan drawn up in late March, *Pe'ulat Misparayim* (Operation Scissors), which had provided for a multi-pronged assault on militia positions and the neutralisation of the irregulars' power to disrupt traffic and life in the Jewish neighbourhoods. The objective of Scissors was to damage and shock rather than to conquer; Operation Passover Cleansing aimed at 'breaking the enemy' by simultaneous assault from several directions, 'to open communications to the Lower City [i.e., the downtown area and the port] and to gain control of Wadi Rushmiya in order to safeguard the link between Haifa and the north . . .'.[196] The planning did not call for, or anticipate, the conquest of most of Arab Haifa; the Carmeli commanders, led by brigade OC Moshe Carmel, deemed such an objective over-ambitious and probably unattainable, because of Arab strength and possible British intervention.

Before the planning of Passover Cleansing was completed, a platoon was sent to take the Building of the Committee of the Arab Eastern Districts, known as Najada House, which dominated the Rushmiya Bridge and the eastern approach to Haifa. Arab efforts to recapture the house and desperate Jewish attempts through the day and night to reinforce the remnants of the besieged platoon inside turned into a pitched battle for the Halissa and Wadi Rushmiya districts, the ultimate Jewish victory assuring an open link between Jewish Haifa and the settlements to the east and north. It was the hardest and longest fought engagement that day and, in retrospect, can be seen as having been decisive.

As the Haganah relief column, supported by mortar barrages, fought its way to Najada House, the Arab militia in Halissa broke and fled, and the bulk of the population of Halissa and Wadi Rushmiya fled in its wake northwestwards, towards Wadi Salib and the downtown area. The arrival of the panic-stricken and battered refugees during the night of 21\22 April could not have failed to instill in the inhabitants of the central Arab neighbourhoods similar feelings of panic and dread while offering them a precedent and model of behaviour.

The relief column finally reached Najada House at 09:00 hours, 22 April. Hours before, during the night, three other Haganah companies, one of them Palmah, and an independent platoon, had launched simultaneous assaults on the main Arab defensive positions in downtown Haifa, along Stanton Street, against the Railway Offices Building (Khuri House) in Wadi Nisnas, the telephone exchange and the Arab City Militia headquarters, overlooking the Old Marketplace.[197] In preparation for the assault, around midnight 21\22 April, the Haganah had let loose with a 15-minute, 50-round barrage of heavy mortars on the lower city, triggering 'great panic . . . and the mass exodus began'. Further barrages were released periodically during the night and in the morning of 22 April. By the early afternoon, the attacks had broken the back of Arab resistance. Hours earlier, at 09:00, 22 April, Haganah units had reached Hamra Square and found it deserted: 'All was desolate, the shops closed, no traffic . . . only several sick old Arab men and women moved about, confused.'[198]

Just before, at 06:00, a mass of Arabs had rushed into the harbour, and by 13:00 some 6,000 had boarded boats and set sail for Acre. A Palmah scout, who had been in the (Arab) Lower City during the battle, later reported:

> [I saw] people with belongings running toward the harbour and their faces spoke confusion. I met an old man sitting on some steps and crying. I asked him why he was crying and he replied that he had lost his six children and his wife and did not know [where] they were. I quieted him down and told him that he mustn't cry so long as he knew nothing [of their fate]. It was quite possible, I said, that the wife and children were transported to Acre but he continued to cry. I took him to the hotel . . . [and] gave him P£2 and he fell asleep. Meanwhile, people [i.e., refugees] arrived from Halissa . . .[199]

The panic-stricken rush of inhabitants from the Lower City into the harbour was later described by Nimr al Khatib:

Suddenly a rumour spread that the British army in the port area had declared its readiness to safeguard the life of anyone who reached the port and left the city. A mad rush to the port gates began. Man trampled on fellow man and woman [trampled on] her children. The boats in the harbour quickly filled up and there is no doubt that that was the cause of the capsizing of many of them.[200]

A British intelligence officer provided a description of the scene at the harbour entrance a few hours later:

During the morning [the Jews], were continually shooting down on all Arabs who moved both in Wadi Nisnas and the Old City. This included completely indiscriminate and revolting machinegun fire, mortar fire and sniping on women and children sheltering in churches and attempting to get out . . . through the gates into the docks. . . . The 40 RM. CDO. [i.e., Royal Marine Commando] who control the docks . . . sent the Arabs through in batches but there was considerable congestion outside the East Gate of hysterical and terrified Arab women and children and old people on whom the Jews opened up mercilessly with fire. Two [Royal Marine] officers were seriously wounded . . .[201]

By late afternoon, 22 April, Carmeli Brigade was reporting:

The Arab HQ is empty. They do not answer the telephones . . . The Arab hospitals are full of dead and wounded. Corpses and wounded lie in the streets and are not collected for lack of organisation and sanitary means; panic in the Arab street is great . . .[202]

The Haganah command issued orders to the troops to treat places of worship with respect, especially mosques, and to refrain from looting.[203]

Throughout, the Haganah made effective use of Arabic language broadcasts and loudspeaker vans. Haganah Radio announced that 'the day of judgement had arrived' and called on the inhabitants to 'kick out the foreign criminals' and to 'move away from every house and street, from every neighbourhood, occupied by the foreign criminals'. The Haganah broadcasts called on the populace to 'evacuate the women, the children and the old immediately, and send them to a safe haven'.[204] The vans announced that the Haganah had gained control of all approaches to the city and no reinforcements could reach the embattled militiamen, and called on the Arabs to lay down their arms, urging the irregulars 'from Syria, Transjordan and Iraq' to 'return to [their] families'.[205]

Jewish tactics in the battle were designed to stun and quickly overpower opposition; demoralisation was a primary aim. It was deemed just as important to the outcome as the physical destruction of the Arab units. The mortar barrages and the psychological warfare broadcasts and announcements, and the tactics employed by the infantry companies, advancing from house to house, were all geared to this goal. The orders of Carmeli's 22nd Battalion were 'to kill every [adult male] Arab encountered' and to set alight with firebombs 'all objectives that can be set alight. I am sending you posters in Arabic; disperse on route.'[206] The British estimated that in the battle for Haifa some '2,000' Arab militiamen were set against '400 trained Jews backed by an indeterminate number of reserves'. The estimate of Arab combatants seems excessive; of Jewish troops, on the low side. But the key factors were not numbers or firepower but topography, organisation, command and control, and determination and morale (which was firmly linked to the element of surprise). Haifa's Arabs entered the battle largely demoralised and psychologically unprepared, and without a clear objective. The Arabs, stated one British intelligence eve of battle report, 'freely admit that the Jews are too strong for them at present'. The Haifa militiamen were poorly trained and armed. The repeated requests from Damascus and the AHC over the previous months for reinforcements and arms had been mostly ignored or turned down.

> The hurried departure of Ahmad Bey Khalil, [the city's] Chief Magistrate and only remaining AHC representative in Haifa, for the Lebanon by sea on 21 April is a very significant illustration of the opinion of the local Arabs as to the outcome of any extensive Jewish operations at present,

stated British intelligence.[207] Stockwell's post facto report concurred: 'I think local Arab opinion felt that the Jews would gain control if in fact they launched their offensive.' He, too, underlined the Arabs' sense of isolation and vulnerability.[208]

Khalil's flight early on 21 April was not merely illustrative of low morale. Taken together with the flight that day and the next of many of the other remaining Arab leaders, it was one of its main causes. Khalil was followed in the early afternoon by Amin Bey 'Izz a Din, the town militia OC. Yunis Nafa'a, his deputy, a former Haifa sanitation inspector, fled the city and country early on 22 April.[209] The departure of the senior commanders was probably known almost immediately to the militia officer corps, to many of the militia rank and file and, within hours, to the community in general; Haganah broadcasts made sure of that.[210] Towards the end of April, one branch of British intelligence assessed that 'the hasty flight of Amin Bey 'Izz a Din . . . [was] probably the greatest single factor' in the demoralisation of the Arab community.[211] This was also the judgement of the High Commissioner. On 26 April, Cunningham devoted a whole telegram to Colonial Secretary Creech-Jones on the flight of the leaders from Haifa and Jaffa.[212] The British view was succinctly expressed on 6 May: 'The desertion of their leaders and the sight of so much cowardice in high places completely unnerved the [Arab] inhabitants [of Haifa].'[213] American diplomats sent Washington similar reports: 'The Arab Higher Command all [reportedly] left Haifa some hours before the battle took place.' Vice-consul Lippincott was comprehensively contemptuous of the Arab performance: 'The Haifa Arab, particularly the Christian

Arab . . . generally speaking . . . is a coward and he is not the least bit interested in going out to fight his country's battles.'[214]

In the battle for Haifa, the Arabs suffered 100–150 dead and probably a greater number of wounded.[215] The Haganah suffered 14–16 dead and about 50 wounded.[216]

Against the backdrop of militia collapse and mass flight, early on the morning of 22 April members of the NC asked to see Stockwell with 'a view to . . . obtaining a truce with the Jews'. Stockwell contacted lawyer Ya'akov Salomon, the Haganah liaison, and asked to know the Jewish 'terms [for an Arab] surrender'. Carmel was astounded; the Arabs, though strongly pressed, did not appear on the verge of collapse. The situation did not seem to warrant surrender 'and the idea of our complete conquest of all of Haifa still appeared so fantastic as to be incomprehensible'. Nonetheless, Carmel jotted down terms and sent them to Stockwell, 'who . . . said that he thought they were fair . . . and the Arabs would accept them . . .'.[217]

The Arab appeal to Stockwell followed a gathering of notables during the night of 21\22 April in the house of banker Farid Sa'ad, an NC member. The notables, who constituted themselves as the 'Haifa Arab Emergency Committee', drafted a document stating that the Arabs held Stockwell responsible and appealed to the British commander 'to stop the massacre of Arabs' by intervening or, alternatively, by allowing Arab reinforcements into the city.[218]

There are two versions of what transpired at the subsequent meeting with Stockwell, at 10:00 hours, 22 April. Present were Cyril Marriott, the British Consul-General-designate in Haifa, and Sa'ad, Victor Khayyat (a businessman and Spain's honorary consul in the city), lawyer Elias Koussa, Haifa District Court Judge Anis Nasr and NC member George Mu'ammar. The Arab version is that the delegation straightforwardly asked Stockwell to stop the Haganah or to allow in Arab reinforcements. Stockwell refused, saying that the Arabs must accept 'the principle of the truce' (i.e., surrender). The Arabs demanded that Stockwell put this in writing. Stockwell and the 'Emergency Committee' then signed a statement saying that he had replied to an Arab appeal to intervene by saying that he was

> not prepared to clash with either of the two contesting parties and that he would not allow the Arab armed forces to enter the town . . . He was only prepared to act as a peace intermediary if the Arabs accepted in principle the condition of the truce.

The Arabs then asked to hear the Haganah truce conditions.[219]

The contemporary British descriptions of the proceedings are somewhat different, stressing not the appeals to Stockwell to intervene or allow in reinforcements, but the Arab readiness for a truce based on a recognition that the battle was already lost. In their reports, neither

Stockwell nor Marriott mentioned that Stockwell had signed a document. According to the British reports, the Arabs merely sought Stockwell's help in obtaining a truce, but the delegation feared that some might see this as a treacherous surrender. Hence, they wanted the onus to fall on the British. Stockwell had to be manoeuvred into declaring that the Arabs had been 'forced' to accept a truce. The Arabs would ask the British to fight the Haganah or allow in reinforcements; Stockwell would refuse; and the Emergency Committee, bowing to *force majeure*, would accede to the truce terms. This, at least, is how Stockwell viewed the meeting. 'They felt that they in no way were empowered to ask for a truce, but that if they were covered by me, they might go ahead.' The general recorded that the Arabs 'wanted [him] to say' that he would not intervene against the Haganah or allow in Arab reinforcements. Stockwell did as he was asked: He stated that he could not intervene or allow in reinforcements.[220] From the Stockwell and Marriott reports it emerges that the interests and views of the British and the Arab notables dovetailed that morning. Both feared, and opposed, a renewal of major fighting; both understood that the Arabs had lost; both feared that the arrival of Arab reinforcements would not tip the scales but merely cause additional bloodshed; both wanted a truce. And Stockwell was willing to 'play along'.

The Arabs then asked to see the Haganah terms. Stockwell presented them and the notables left to talk it over in Khayyat's home. They agreed to meet British and Jewish representatives at the town hall at 16:00 hours. Apparently, they felt that immediate acceptance would open them to charges of betrayal. Through the Syrian consul, Thabet al Aris, who had a radio transmitter, they attempted to contact the Arab League Military Committee in Damascus and the Syrians for instructions. But Damascus failed to respond.[221] Instead, Damascus activated the Lebanese Government, which summoned the British Minister in Beirut, Houstoun Boswall, to complain of British inaction against 'Jewish aggression'. At the same time, the Syrian president, Shukri al Quwatli, flanked by his senior ministers, hauled in the British Minister, Philip Broadmead, and read him two telegrams by al Aris. The telegrams described the Jewish offensive and warned of 'a massacre of innocents'. The president charged that the British were 'doing nothing' and implicitly threatened Syrian intervention. Broadmead warned him against taking 'stupid action'.[222]

Broadmead left but was immediately summoned back, and Quwatli, saying he was 'bewildered', showed him a further cable from al Aris, who related that Stockwell had rejected the notables' appeal for intervention or to allow in reinforcements. They sought 'instructions' in preparation for the town hall meeting. Quwatli said that he was 'very nervous' about Syrian public opinion and asked Broadmead 'what instructions he [Quwatli] could send. What did I [Broadmead] suggest?' Broadmead said he did not know the facts and urged moderation, and then asked London for 'something' that would 'calm [Quwatli's] mind'.[223] Quwatli had no idea what to instruct Haifa's remaining Arabs: To surrender? To reject the Haganah terms? To stay put and accept Jewish sovereignty? To evacuate the city? Each option was acutely problematic. So he simply refrained from responding.

Meanwhile, Stockwell reviewed the Haganah terms, was 'not entirely satisfied', and sent for the Jewish representatives. Beilin, Salomon, and Mordechai Makleff, OC Operations of the Carmeli Brigade, arrived and, after discussion, accepted Stockwell's amendments. The final version called for the disarming of the Arab community (with the arms going to the British authorities who only on 15 May would transfer them to the Haganah); the deportation of all foreign Arab males of military age; the removal of all Arab roadblocks; the arrest of European Nazis found in Arab ranks; a 24-hour curfew in the Arab neighbourhoods to assure 'complete disarming'; freedom for

each person in Haifa . . . to carry on with his business and way of life. Arabs will carry on their work as equal and free citizens of Haifa and will enjoy all services along with the other members of the community.[224]

British armoured cars then ferried the Arab leaders to the town hall; the Jews arrived on their own steam. The British were represented by Stockwell, Marriott, and a handful of senior officers; the Jews by mayor Shabtai Levy, Salomon, Makleff, and a number of officials; and the Arabs by Khayyat, Sa'ad, Koussa, Anis Nasr, Muhammad Abu Zayyad (a businessman), Mu'ammar, and Sheikh Abdul Rahman Murad, head of the Muslim Brotherhood in Haifa. Outside, the Haganah slowly pushed its units into the downtown districts while keeping up a sporadic mortar barrage, 'to keep up the pressure' on the remaining militiamen and the notables in the town hall.[225] According to Stockwell and Marriott, both delegations 'unanimously agreed' to a ceasefire, which amounted to an Arab surrender. Mayor Levy opened by declaring that 'members of both communities in Haifa should live in peace and friendship together'. Stockwell read out the Haganah terms. A discussion ensued: The Arabs wished to retain licensed arms and asked that the curfew and house-to-house searches to be conducted by the British rather than the Haganah. They also 'objected most strongly' to recording on paper the eventual handover of the Arab arms to the Haganah. 'This was evidently to protect themselves against the displeasure of the AHE [i.e., AHC]', commented Stockwell.[226] The Jews insisted that the clause remain, as formulated, but agreed to compromise on most other issues. The Arabs 'haggled over every word', recorded Beilin.[227]

Stockwell thought that the Jewish representatives had been 'conciliatory'. Marriott, who was soon to turn fiercely anti-Israeli, was even more emphatic. 'The Jewish delegation', he wrote, 'made a good impression by their magnanimity in victory, the moderation of their truce terms, and their readiness to accede to the modifications demanded by General Stockwell.' Marriott described Levy as a man of 'courage and character . . . warm-hearted and friendly', whose 'main concern is the peace and prosperity of Haifa'. He thought Salomon 'not without personality and a sense of humour – at least when he is on the winning side'. As to P. Woolfe-Rebuck, a Haganah liaison officer, he 'speaks with what is known as an Oxford accent but is not devoid of brains'. On the other hand, the Arab delegation 'made a lamentable impression'. The force of this judgement is underlined by Marriott's description of himself as one whose

> experiences of Jews was gained in Rumania (where one knew that if there were a dirty house in a village it was the Jew's); in New York (where they were rarely met in decent society but were regarded in business circles as kikes and shysters); and in South America (where many of the leading families, though now Catholics, trace their descent from escapers from the Holy Inquisition).

The Arab, for Marriott, newly arrived in the Middle East, 'was a romantic figure living in the open air and spending much of his life on camel-back or riding blood-horses'. But at the town hall they thoroughly failed to meet his expectations, save for Murad, whom Marriott described as 'a simple man . . . who, I am sure, in the absence of a Jihad, desires peace'. Khayyat was 'obviously, not to say ostentatiously, wealthy and is said still to own a shop in Fifth Avenue, New York, where objets d'art are dealt in'. Sa'ad struck Marriott as 'a hard business man' with an obvious dislike of the British. 'The only word to describe Mr. Elias Koussa is revolting', wrote the consul.

> He suffers from having an artificial eye which fits so poorly that, in his moments of excitement, it rolls up, leaving but the thinnest rim of brown iris showing. He is a lawyer and I would neither employ him nor wish to see him representing the other side.

Marriott did not take kindly to Koussa's declaration that while the Arabs had lost one round, there would be others.[228]

The meeting recessed at 17:30 hours, the Arabs asking for 24 hours in which to consider the terms. The Jews demurred. At the GOC's insistence, it was agreed that the Arabs would have an hour. The delegates reassembled at 19:15, with the Arabs – now consisting only of Christian notables, the Muslims, Abu Zayyad and Murad, staying away – stating

> that they were not in a position to sign a truce, as they had no control over the Arab military elements in the town and that . . . they could not fulfill the terms of the truce, even if they were to sign. They then said as an alternative that the Arab population wished to evacuate Haifa . . . man, woman and child.[229]

The Jewish and British officials were surprised, even shocked. Levy appealed 'very passionately . . . and begged [the Arabs] to reconsider'. He said that they should not leave the city 'where they had lived for hundreds of years, where their forefathers were buried and where, for so long, they had lived in peace and brotherhood with the Jews'. But the Arabs said they 'had no choice'.[230] According to Carmel, who was briefed on the meeting by Makleff, Stockwell 'went pale' when he heard the Arabs' decision, and also appealed to them to reconsider and not make 'such a grave mistake'. He urged them to accept the terms: 'Don't destroy your lives needlessly', he said. He then turned to Makleff, and asked: 'What have you to say?' Makleff replied: 'It's up to them [i.e., the Arabs] to decide.'[231] Salomon, in his recollection of events, wrote that he also appealed to the Arabs to reconsider, but to no avail.[232]

Israeli chroniclers of these events subsequently asserted that the Haifa Arab leadership on 22 April had been ordered by the AHC to evacuate the city. Carmel wrote that sometime after 22 April,

> we learned that during the intermission [in the meeting, the Arabs] had contacted the AHC and asked for instructions. The Mufti's orders had been to leave the city and not to accept conditions of surrender from the Jews, as the invasion by the Arab armies was close and the whole country would fall into [Arab] hands.[233]

Some Jewish officials, flustered by the unexpected exodus from Haifa, at the time believed that it was part of a comprehensive Arab or Anglo-Arab plot, which also accounted for the mass flight from other parts of Palestine in late April.[234] On 23 April Sasson cabled Shertok, who was in New York:

> Mass flight of Arabs now witnessed here there Palestine, as Tiberias, Haifa, elsewhere, is apparently not consequence of mere fear and weakness. Flight is organised by followers of Husseinites and outcarried cooperation foreign 'fighters' with object: (1) Vilifying Jews and describing them as expellants who are out outdrive Arabs from territory Jew[ish] State. (2) Compelling Arab States intervene by sending regular armies. (3) Create in Arab world and world opinion in general impression that such invasion undertaken for rescue persecuted Pal[estinians].

Sasson also asserted that the flight of the Arab commanders at the start of each battle was part of the plot to 'spread chaos, panic' among the Arabs, leading to flight.[235]

However, if Sasson meant that the exodus was orchestrated or ordered from outside Palestine, the weight of the evidence suggests that this is incorrect. As we have seen, the local notables had tried and failed to obtain instructions from Damascus. Damascus preferred silence. Nor is there any persuasive evidence that orders came from Husseini or the AHC. Haifa's Arabs were simply left to decide on their own[236] and it is probable that the local Husseini-supporting, Muslim notables – perhaps doing what they thought the AHC\Husseini would have wanted them to do – intimidated and ordered their fellow Christian notables gathered at the town hall after 19:00, 22 April, to reject a truce or anything smacking of surrender and acquiescence in Jewish rule, and to opt for evacuation. No doubt, the shadow of 1936–1939 and the memories of Husseini terrorism against Opposition\Christian figures loomed large in their minds.

But if the weight of the evidence suggests that the initial order to evacuate had come from the local leadership, there is a surfeit of evidence that the AHC and its local supporters endorsed it *ex post facto* during the following days, egging on the continuing evacuation. On 25 April, Lippincott, reported: 'Local Mufti dominated Arab leaders urge all Arabs leave city . . .', and added the following day: 'Reportedly AHC ordering all Arabs leave.'[237] British observers concurred. Cunningham on 25 April reported to Creech-Jones: 'British authorities at Haifa have formed the impression that total evacuation is being urged on the Haifa Arabs from higher Arab quarters and that the townsfolk themselves are against it.' The Sixth Airborne Division was more explicit:

> Probable reason for Arab Higher Executive [i.e., AHC] ordering Arabs to evacuate Haifa is to avoid possibility of Haifa Arabs being used as hostages in future operations after May 15. Arabs have also threatened to bomb Haifa from the air.

British military headquarters Middle East similarly referred to 'the evacuation of Haifa by the AHC . . . who . . . have encouraged the population to evacuate . . . greatly embarrass[ing] the Jews'.[238] Most of the remaining Arab leaders also encouraged the remaining townspeople to leave (perhaps assuring them that they would soon be returning in the wake of victorious Arab armies, but I have found no evidence of this). The urgings were in the form of threats, warnings and horrific rumours. The cumulative effect of these rumours in inducing flight cannot be exaggerated.

> Most widespread was a rumour that Arabs remaining in Haifa would be taken as hostages by the Jews in the event of future Arab attacks on other Jewish areas. And an effective piece of propaganda with its implied threat of Arab retribution when the Arabs recapture the town, is that people remaining in Haifa acknowledged tacitly that they believe in the principle of the Jewish State. It is alleged that Victor Khayyat is responsible for these reports

said one British intelligence unit. But for these 'rumours and propaganda spread by the National Committee members remaining in the town', many of the Arabs 'would not have evacuated Haifa' over 22–28 April, according to the British Army's 257 and 317 Field Security Section.[239]

As late as 29 April, NC members were reported to be 'for the most part' encouraging the Arabs to leave. An exception may have been Farid Sa'ad, who told Lippincott that NC members were telling the population 'to use their own judgement as to whether they should stay or leave'.[240] But most members of the Emergency Committee were busy both encouraging departure and organising the convoys out. Indeed, when a Haganah roadblock stopped a 3–4 truck convoy bound for Nazareth, the committee complained that the British weren't living up to their promise of 22–23 April to assist the evacuation.[241]

Haganah intelligence also monitored what was happening: 'The Arabs in Haifa relate that they have received an order from the AHC to leave Haifa as soon as possible, and not to cooperate with the Jews.'[242]

The present Haifa Arab leadership, while speaking to our people of bringing life back to normal, their practical policy is to do the maximum to speed up the evacuation . . . Higher Arab circles relate that they have received explicit instructions to evacuate the Arabs of Haifa. The reason for this is not clear to us . . . The [Arab] masses explain the order to evacuate Haifa as stemming from [the prospect that] Transjordanian forces intend to commit wholesale massacre. (Artillery, airplanes, and so on).[243]

HIS reported that Arab residents were receiving 'threatening letters' in which they were ordered to leave; otherwise they would 'be considered traitors and condemned to death'.[244]

HIS periodically described the mechanics of the AHC encouragement of the exodus. On 25 April 'Hiram' reported that on the afternoon of 23 (or 24) April, Salomon and Mu'ammar jointly went to 'refugees' in Abbas Street and urged women, children and men aged over 40 'to return to their homes'. The refugees were about to return home when Sheikh Murad and another Muslim figure appeared on the scene. Murad, according to HIS, told the refugees:

The Arab Legion has volunteered to give 200 trucks to take the refugees to a safe place outside Haifa, where they will be housed and given food and clothes aplenty and all without payment, and he threatened that if they stayed in Haifa, the Jews would kill them and not spare their women and children.

The crowd changed its mind and many made their way to the evacuation point in the harbour.[245]

The notables' announcement of evacuation on the evening of 22 April was not a bolt from the blue. Tens of thousands of Arabs, including most of the city's middle and upper classes, had departed during December 1947 – early April 1948. On 21–22 April, the notables had the fresh example of Arab Tiberias before their eyes. And by the evening of 22 April, thousands had already voted with their feet, first by fleeing in a panicky rush to the city centre from the embattled, outlying neighbourhoods, and then by fleeing to the harbour and the boats to Acre. Thus, the evacuees had shown their leaders the way out of the strait bounded on the one side by continued – and hopeless – battle and on the other, by (treacherous) acceptance of Jewish rule.

The Haganah mortar attacks of 21–22 April were primarily designed to break Arab morale in order to bring about a swift collapse of resistance and speedy surrender. There is no evidence that the commanders involved hoped or expected that it would lead to mass evacuation (though events in Tiberias four days before must have been prominent in their minds). But clearly the offensive, and especially the mortaring, precipitated the exodus. The three-inch mortars 'opened up on the market square [where there was] a great crowd . . . a great panic took hold. The multitude burst into the port, pushed aside the policemen, charged the boats and began fleeing the town', as the official Haganah history later put it.[246]

Some 15,000 Arabs probably evacuated Haifa during 21–22 April. Most of them left by sea and land to Acre and Lebanon well before the notables had announced the decision to evacuate. By nightfall, 22 April, there were still some 30,000–40,000 Arabs in the town (the Emergency Committee spoke of '37,000'[247]). Stockwell had agreed to assist their evacuation. From 23 April, four Royal Navy Z-Craft and a small fleet of lorries and armoured car escorts, began to ferry the departees to Acre. The Z-Craft, operating until 28 April, shuttled across Haifa Bay while the lorries, in convoys, went up the coast road through successive Haganah, British and Arab checkpoints. Dozens of Egyptian families left Haifa for Alexandria on a chartered schooner and Syrian nationals sailed to Beirut on another boat. At the same time, the Emergency Committee and Arab entrepreneurs each day organised private convoys of lorries, escorted by the British, which took out hundreds of families to Acre, Nazareth, Jenin and Nablus.[248] As late as 11 May, HIS was reporting that 'the Arab evacuation of Haifa was continuing'. Though some refugees briefly returned, usually to see what was happening to their property or to collect something they had left behind, they generally left a day or two later.[249] But 'several hundred' returned permanently during the first half of May, mostly from among the employees of the refinery and other government institutions.[250]

At the beginning of the mass evacuation, Arab leaders even appealed to the Jewish authorities for help in organising the departure as the British, they complained, were not supplying enough transport. Beilin responded enthusiastically: 'I said that we would be more than happy to give them all the assistance they require.'[251]

However, Beilin, at this stage, was unrepresentative of the local Jewish leadership that, for the most part, was clearly embarrassed and uneasy about the exodus. Several municipal (and, apparently, Haganah) figures during 22–28 April tried to persuade Arabs to stay. One Jewish officer was reported by HIS to be 'conducting propaganda among the refugees in the Abbas area not to leave'.[252] Salomon later recalled that on the morning of 23 April, he had gone to Abbas Street and Wadi Nisnas, after receiving 'instructions . . . to go to the Arab quarters and appeal to the Arabs not to leave'. He did not say who issued the instructions – the Haganah, Shabtai Levy, or someone else – but noted that he was accompanied by 'a Haganah officer'. Despite warnings from his friends that it was still dangerous, Salomon 'went from street to street and told the Arabs . . . not to leave. [But] the net result was that during that day and the next few days many Arabs left . . .'[253] The man who accompanied Salomon may have been Tuvia Lishansky, a senior HIS officer. Lishansky later recalled 'a feeling of discomfort . . . As soon as we capture a city . . . the Arabs leave it. What will the world say? No doubt they will say – "such are the Jews, Arabs cannot live under their rule".' Lishansky recalled trying to persuade the Arabs to stay.[254] These efforts did not go unnoticed. On 25 April, Baghdad Radio reported that 'the Haganah is trying to persuade [the Arabs] to stay in Haifa'.[255] And on 28 April, the British police were still reporting: 'The Jews are . . . making every effort to persuade the Arab populace to remain and settle back into their normal lives . . .'[256]

British military intelligence concurred:

The Arab evacuation is now almost complete. The Jews have been making extensive efforts to prevent wholesale evacuation, but their propaganda appears to have had very little effect. [In trying to check the Arab exodus, the Haganah] in several cases [had resorted] to actual intervention . . . Appeals have been made on the [Jewish] radio and in the press, urging Arabs to remain in the town; the Haganah issued a pamphlet along these lines and the Histadrut, in a similar publication, appealed to those Arabs previously members of their organisation [sic], to return. On the whole, [however] Arabs remain indifferent to this propaganda.[257]

According to Lippincott, quoting Farid Sa'ad, the Haifa Jewish leaders had 'organised a large propaganda campaign to persuade Arabs to return'. But the Arabs no longer trusted the Jews, said Sa'ad.[258] *The Times* correspondent in the city noticed the same thing: 'The Jews wish the Arabs to settle down again to normal routine but the evacuation continues . . . Most of the Arabs seem to feel there is nothing to stay for now.'[259] Christian priests and nuns were also reportedly appealing to (Christian) Arabs to stay.[260]

Both the British, including Cunningham, and Lippincott believed, at least initially, that the Jews of Haifa wanted the Arabs to stay mainly for economic reasons. The Jews feared 'for the economic future of the town' once its Arab working class had departed, reported the High Commissioner.[261] More explicitly, Lippincott wrote that unless the Jews succeeded in persuading the Arabs to stay or return, 'acute labour short-age will occur'.[262] (The Jews also wanted the Arabs to stay 'for political reasons, to show democratic treatment', thought Lippincott.[263]) British units reported that 'the Jews are being forced to man the factories and places of essential work with their own people where Arabs worked be-fore and this is proving most unsatisfactory for them as Arab labour was much cheaper'.[264]

But the Haganah was not averse to seeing the Arabs evacuate, as illustrated by Makleff's 'no comment' response to Stockwell's question about the evacuation announcement at the town hall meeting on 22 April. Illustration can also be found in the Haifa Haganah's second com-muniqué, issued on 22 April. The communiqué, distributed about town as a poster, speaks of the ongoing destruction of the 'Arab gangs' and the penetration by Haganah units of the Arab neighbourhoods. The troops (and the Jewish civilian population) were ordered to respect 'the Arabs' holy places: Every effort will be made not to enter mosques, not to fire from them, and not to house soldiers in them.' The communiqué also forbade looting of 'the abandoned Arab property . . . [which would] when the time came, be returned to its lawful owners . . .'. But nowhere did it ask or advise the populace to stay, stop fleeing or return.[265] Indeed, the HIS assessment in the days following the start of the mass exodus was: 'Following the steps taken by our people in Haifa, our propaganda and admonitions, many Arabs fled by boat and other craft to Acre.'[266] Carmel's commanders were keenly aware that an exodus would solve the brigade's main problem – how to secure Jewish Haifa with very lim-ited forces against attack by forces from outside the town while having to deploy a large number of troops inside to guard against insurrection by a large, potentially hostile Arab population.[267]

However, according to most British observers in the days after 22 April, the picture was simple: The Jews were interested in the Arabs staying and the local Arab leadership was bent on a complete exodus. The only exception noted by the British was the IZL, which moved into part of downtown Haifa on 23 April. IZL policy, wrote 1st Battalion Cold-stream guards, 'was to promote a further rush of armed forces into the Suq and other places where Arabs were still living . . . to force the issue by creating more refugees and a new wave of terror'.[268]

But the situation in Haifa between 23 April and early May was con-fused and complex. The British, restricted to semi-isolated enclaves and bent on only one thing – to get out safely – failed to note the full spectrum of events. Initial Jewish attitudes towards the Arab evacuation changed within days; and what Jewish liaison officers told their British contacts did not always conform with the realities on the ground or with those quickly changing attitudes. The local Jewish civilian leadership initially sincerely wanted the Arabs to stay (and made a point of letting the British see this). But the offensive of 21–22 April had delivered the Arab neighbourhoods into Haganah hands, relegating the civil leaders to the sidelines and for almost a fortnight rendering them relatively ineffectual in all that concerned the treatment of the Arab population. At the same time, the attitude of some of these local leaders radically changed as they took stock of the historic opportunity afforded by the exodus – to turn Haifa permanently into a Jewish city. As one knowledgeable Jewish observer put it a month later, 'a different wind [began to] blow. It was good without Arabs, it was easier. Everything changed within a week.'[269] At the same time, the Haganah commanders from the first understood that an Arab evacuation would greatly ease their strategic situation and workload.

The British withdrawal from downtown Haifa on 21 April and the Jewish victory left the Haganah in control of the Arab areas until 3 May. During this time Carmeli's relatively meagre forces, still worried about the possible intervention of Arab forces from outside, had to conduct a complex security operation in conditions of extreme disorder: To sift through tens of thousands of frightened Arabs in abandoned and semi-abandoned, war-ravaged districts for ex-combatants and arms, and to clear the area of unexploded projectiles and mines. All this had to be done quickly, while thousands of refugees were on the move out of the city, in order to free the battalions for defensive or offensive operations. At the same time, the Jewish authorities had to provide food and restore basic services for the remaining Arabs, whose infrastructure and services had collapsed. The provision of bread and water was a major problem.

The Haganah security operation – involving curfews, searches, interrogations and the incarceration of young adult males[270] – took about a week and perforce included a great deal of arbitrary behaviour and unpleasantness. The Arab inhabitants were removed from homes or streets, their houses were carefully searched, and they were then allowed back – women and children first, and then the menfolk, after interrogation. The operation progressed slowly, involving unintended hardships for the inhabitants. And the situation lent itself to excesses such as looting, intimidation and beatings. The British – and the Haganah – generally preferred, with only partial justification, to attribute all these excesses to the IZL. The looting and vandalisation of Arab property, which continued into May, 'stood in contradiction to the official declarations appealing to the Arabs to return to Haifa', as well as to the 'spirit of Israel', complained the Haifa Jewish Chamber of Commerce and Industry.[271] What was happening was described at the meeting of Jewish and Arab local leaders on 25 April. The meeting was called to find ways to ease the situation of the city's Arabs and to assist those who wanted to leave. The sense of the meeting, and of the statements of the Jewish participants, was against the Arab exodus, but none of the Jewish participants, who included Levy, Salomon, Beilin and Dayan, explicitly renewed the appeal to stay. That morning, the Haganah had firmly driven the IZL out of Wadi Nisnas, where they had ignored Haganah warnings and committed 'organised looting';[272] at least one IZL man was seriously wounded in a firefight. Looters had pillaged, according to one report, 'two churches' and a medical clinic, taking 'pianos, refrigerators and cars'.[273] The condition of the Arab population, according to George Mu'ammar, remained 'catastrophic' and was 'getting worse'. The Haganah troops, he complained, had not allowed him to distribute flour among the thousands temporarily encamped in the marketplace. (The Arab bakeries had all closed down on 21–22 April.) Looting and robbery, he said, were rampant. The Haganah searched Arab shops – breaking open their shutters, leaving them prey to Jewish and Arab looters. 'Houses in Wadi Nisnas had been completely looted. Was that the Jews' intention in Haifa?' asked Mu'ammar. He added that one Arab notable, Sulayman Qataran, had been beaten up that morning; other Arabs had been robbed during identity checks. 'If our people had [previously] considered staying in the city, that thinking has been severely undermined', concluded Mu'ammar.

Another Arab participant, George Tawil, recalled that at the previous meeting, on 23 April, he had said that 'if there were suitable conditions' the Arabs should stay. Tawil added that after the meeting, he had 'tried to persuade our people to stay. But I must sadly say that the Haganah command has been harsh, if not to use a stronger word.' He told the participants about a Haganah search of his house and said: 'I have reached the conclusion that I will leave the city if I am to live [here] a life of humiliation.'[274] After 4–5 days of Haganah rule, 'the Arabs were not interested in staying', an American diplomat reportedly told the Haganah. 'They fear belligerent acts by the Arab institutions. And they are unsure about the Jews' attitude toward them.'[275]

Without perhaps fully understanding what was happening, the Arabs were describing what amounted to a temporary rupture between the local Jewish civil and military authorities, which reflected, and was part of, the similar, larger rupture between these authorities that characterised much of the Yishuv's policy-making and actions through the war. In Haifa, for days, the civilian authorities were saying one thing and the Haganah was doing something quite different. Moreover, Haganah units in the field acted inconsistently and in a manner often unintelligible to the Arab population. The Arabs, who had coexisted with Jewish civilians for decades, were unaccustomed to Jewish military behaviour or rule, which was only lifted on 3 May.[276] The Arabs did not grasp the essential powerlessness of the civilian authorities during the previous fortnight. This lack of comprehension underlies the dialogue at the 25 April meeting. Victor Khayyat complained that the Arabs were being prevented from returning to their homes, which were being searched. He charged that this was contrary to the promises given by the civilian leaders two days before.

At that meeting, Salomon had assured the Arabs that 'orders have already been issued by the Haganah command that the old, women and children could that very evening return to their homes'.[277] Nevertheless, on 25 April Arabs were still being barred from their homes. Khayyat described the situation as 'shameful and opprobrious to the Jewish community'. Pinhas Margolin, a municipal councillor, assured the Arabs that matters would 'soon' be put right. But Nasr commented: 'By the time you take control of the situation, there won't be one Arab left in Haifa.'

HIS officer Tuvia Arazi assured the participants, in the name of the Haganah, that 'we are making a supreme effort to bring things back to normal . . . Bad things have happened', he conceded, but

> the Haganah command has issued sharp orders [against robbery] and it is possible that robbers will be shot . . . Women, the old and children should return home . . . [but] they cannot return to all places at once, because first of all the city must be cleared of Arab bombs. And this is for the good of the Arabs themselves.[278]

Unknown to the Jewish leaders, the Emergency Committee that day renewed its appeal to the British to intervene. They asked Stockwell to reimpose British rule in downtown Haifa to assure 'peace and order'. Above all, the committee sought 'the removal of members of Jewish armed forces from Arab quarters'. This, they argued, would restore Arab confidence, 'minimising the number of Arab evacuees [a curious argument, given the fact that committee members were themselves promoting the exodus]'.[279] The duplicity of members of the Emergency Committee continued into mid-May, when Khayyat emerged as the Arab community's dominant figure. Carmeli reported that he was continuing to promote evacuation by 'reducing' the bread ration issued by the warehouses under his control (while profiting from this).[280]

By 27–28 April, there was a substantial improvement in conditions in the Arab quarters. Most of those still in the city had been allowed to return to their homes, although martial law remained in force. They needed special travel passes, obtainable only after a long wait in a queue and close questioning, to move from neighbourhood to neighbourhood. There was no electricity in most Arab areas (and, hence, Arabs could not hear radio), no Arabic newspapers, no buses, and Arabs were not allowed to drive cars – the Haganah arguing that the IZL might confiscate them. Arrests and house searches were common. Aharon Cohen said that whether the Arab population of Haifa increased, remained stable or decreased depended in large measure on 'the policy of the Jewish institutions' despite the continuing appeals by the Arab notables to complete the evacuation.[281] On 28 April, the Histadrut published an appeal, in Hebrew and Arabic, to Haifa's Arabs to resume the coexistence with the Jews and stay:

> Do not destroy your homes . . . and lose your sources of income and bring upon yourselves disaster by evacuation . . . The Haifa Workers Council and the Histadrut advise you, for your own good, to stay . . . and return to your regular work.[282]

But most Arabs were not responding. British police reported long queues waiting in the harbour for places on boats to Acre: 'Some families have lived and sleep on the quaysides for several days waiting a chance to get away.'[283] But in the days following the resumption of civilian rule, the situation did not much improve. The Committee for Arab Property and Golda Meir, the acting head of the JA-PD, appointed a local committee of Jews to care for the remaining Arabs and look after Arab property. A joint meeting of Meir, the Committee for Arab Property and the newly appointed local committee resolved 'to treat the remaining Arab inhabitants as citizens with equal rights'. The local committee spawned a host of well-meaning sub-committees ('Committee for Prisoners and Detainees', 'Committee for Supervision of Holy Places', and others).[284]

But nothing seems to have changed. Carmeli reported at the end of the first week of May:

> The Arabs of Haifa are in despair. No one knows what to do. Most of the Christians are waiting for the government salaries and think of leaving. Anyone staying is regarded as a traitor. In town, sanitary conditions are terrible. Most of the houses have been broken into and robbed. There are still corpses [lying about] . . .

Arabs were also leaving out of fear that the Arab armies would take the city and punish them for treason.[285] A small number of families apparently returned to the city – encouraged by the British authorities – after temporarily shifting to Acre.[286] But on 10 May, the Israel Communist Party charged that Haifa's remaining '4,000' Arabs for the most part still lacked running water and electricity, garbage had not been collected and had piled up on sidewalks, the looting of Arab property continued, many shops remained closed, employment offices had not opened, and, with the tight curbs on freedom of movement, the Arab inhabitants lived in 'a prison regime'.[287]

Conditions in the Arab neighbourhoods during the week following the Haganah offensive of 21–22 April had more or less reflected the normal dislocations and exigencies of war, but they were exacerbated by the general military and political situation in Palestine and by particular local circumstances – the continuing mass evacuation, the continued British control of parts of the city, the presence of Arab Legion units in camps around the city, the continuing possibility of Arab attack from without and the breakdown of municipal services and government. Haganah actions to consolidate its hold on Arab Haifa were characterised by the natural arbitrariness and harshness of military rule, and certainly contributed to the steady exodus.

But were Haganah actions, over 23 April – early May, motivated by a calculated aim to egg on the evacuation? At the level of Carmeli head-quarters, no orders, as far as we know, were ever issued to the troops to act in a manner that would precipitate flight. Rather the contrary. Strict, if somewhat belated, orders were issued forbidding looting, and leaflets calling on the Arabs to remain calm and return to work – if not explicitly to stay in the city – were distributed.[288] But if this was official policy, there was certainly also an undercurrent of expulsive thinking, akin to the IZL approach. Many in the Haganah cannot but have been struck by the thought that the exodus was 'good for the Jews' and must be encouraged. A trace of such thinking in Carmeli headquarters can be discerned in Yosef Weitz's diary entries for 22–24 April, which he spent in Haifa. 'I think that this [flight prone] state of mind [among the Arabs] should be exploited, and [we should] press the other inhabitants not to surrender [but to leave]. We must establish our state', he jotted down on 22 April. On 24 April, he went to see Carmel's adjutant, who informed him that the nearby Arab villages of Balad ash Sheikh and Yajur were being evacuated by their inhabitants and that Acre had been 'shaken'. 'I was happy to hear from him that this line was being adopted by the [Haganah] command, [that is] to frighten the Arabs so long as flight-inducing fear was upon them.'[289] There was a dovetailing here of Jewish interests, as perceived by Weitz and likeminded Yishuv figures, with the wishes of the local Arab leaders and the AHC, who believed that the exodus from the city would serve the Palestinian cause (or, at least, that the non-departure of the inhabitants would serve the Zionist cause). Weitz, it appears, had struck a responsive chord in Carmeli headquarters. It made simple military as well as political sense: Haifa without Arabs was more easily defended and less problematic than Haifa with a large minority.

In the days following 21–22 April, the Haganah moved to safeguard the Jewish hold on the city by securing its approaches and by opening up routes to the clusters of settlements to the south, north and east. The exit to the north and east was dominated by the large village of Balad al Sheikh and its two satellites, Yajur and Hawassa; the southern exit was dominated by Tira, whose population had been considerably bolstered by refugees from Haifa.

The Haganah attacked Balad ash Sheikh on 24 April and Tira during the following two days. Whether the Haganah intended to trigger the evacuation of Balad al Sheikh is unclear, but the method of attack and the subsequent Jewish–Arab–British negotiations seem to have been designed to achieve it. That, at least, was the understanding of the British observers involved.

Balad al Sheikh and neighbouring Hawassa had been partially evac-uated after the Haganahs retaliatory strike on 31 December 1947–1 January 1948.[290] The withdrawal in early April of an Arab Legion unit that had garrisoned the village led to an abandonment of the houses on its southeastern periphery, the inhabitants moving to the village centre.[291] By then, most of Hawassa's inhabitants had evacuated their homes.[292] A week or two later, most of Yajur's inhabitants departed in response to reports of the Deir Yassin Massacre. By late April, both satellite villages were inhabited mainly by irregulars.[293] The fall of Arab Haifa apparently triggered a major evacuation of women and children from Balad al Sheikh: The villagers expected to come under Haganah attack, reported British observers.[294]

During the early morning hours of 24 April, Haganah units surrounded the village and at 05:00 hours, possibly after unsuccessfully demanding that the village surrender its weapons, opened up with three-inch mortars and machine-guns. Many adult males fled, 'leaving women and children behind'. There was 'virtually no reply' from the village, reported a British unit which reached the scene an hour later and imposed a ceasefire. At the meeting that followed of Haganah, Arab and British representative in the Nesher cement factory, the Haganah demanded that the villagers surrender their arms. The Arabs handed over '22 old and useless rifles' and a Sten Gun and asked for a truce (in another version, 'asked for Haganah protection'.[295]). A few hours before, an HIS agent had told the mukhtar of Hawassa that he 'was not interested in the evacuation of the village', but being allowed to stay was conditional on a complete handover of weaponry.[296] The three villages were given until 14:00. The headmen apparently asked the British to intervene. The British then either advised[297] or ordered[298] the villagers to prepare to evacuate Balad al Sheikh (and perhaps the two satellites) and 20 British Army lorries drove into the village. The remaining inhabitants were warned that the Haganah intended 'to bomb' the site and they boarded the vehicles. The convoy left, heading for Nazareth under British escort. By afternoon, the three villages were almost completely emptied.[299] On 29 April, HIS reported that some 30 families were still left in Hawassa, 20 in Balad al Sheikh and 20 in Yajur.[300] These, too, eventually drifted off or were expelled.

There can be no doubt that the fall of Arab Haifa and the news of the exodus of its inhabitants had thoroughly unnerved the inhabitants at all three sites as well as provided them with a model of behaviour. Haganah and British pressures appear to have helped them make up their minds.[301]

Tira, which for months had interdicted traffic along the Tel Aviv – Haifa road, was lightly attacked by the Haganah on the night of 21–22 April, 'to prevent assistance being given to the Haifa Arabs', as a British report put it.[302] This caused a spontaneous evacuation of women and children.[303] At dawn on 25 April, the Haganah briefly mortared Tira[304] and in the early hours of 26 April launched a strong attack, apparently with the aim of conquest, using mortars and machineguns. An infantry company reached the eastern outskirts and conquered positions on the Carmel slopes overlooking the village – but were apparently halted by fire from British units. During the lull that followed, an 'orderly evacuation' to Acre of the village's non-combatants, in Arab Legion trucks and buses, took place, though the young adult males stayed on. Simultaneously, Khirbet Damun, to the south, surrendered without a fight and was garrisoned by the Haganah; the inhabitants, for the moment, remained in place and were provided with special passes.[305] In early May, the British arranged a further, orderly evacuation from Tira, of 600 inhabitants, to Jenin and Nablus.[306] Hundreds of men stayed on, however, successfully defending the village until July, when it fell to the IDF and was completely evacuated.

Meanwhile, on the night of 25\26 April, the Haganah mounted an harassing raid against Acre, which was inundated by refugees from Haifa, hitting the town with mortars and machineguns, demolishing three houses in the village suburb of Manshiya and briefly conquering Tel al Fukhar, that dominated the town from the east. Mortar rounds landed on Acre Prison, triggering a mass prisoner escape. British troops intervened and fired at neighbouring Kibbutz Ein Hamifratz, a Haganah base, and at Tel al Fukhar, and the Haganah withdrew.[307] The raid caused panic and flight from the town.[308] The general assessment of First Battalion Coldstream Guards was that the Jews wanted to open up the approach roads to Haifa and would 'likely . . . continue mortaring and shelling around Haifa to create an evacuation of the [Arab] population'.[309]

The fall of Haifa had a resounding effect in the north but also elsewhere in the country. In Lydda, a day of mourning was declared and most shops closed to mark 'the great massacre' [sic].[310] Carmeli reported the evacuation of women and children from villages around Haifa.[311] The Jewish Agency summarised: 'The evacuation of Haifa' (along with the conquest of Tiberias) was 'a turning point', which 'greatly influenced the morale of the Arabs in the country and abroad . . .'[312]

In mid-May, some 4,000 Arabs were left in Haifa; the largest and, in terms of influence on the departure of other communities, perhaps the most significant exodus of the war was over. Haifa had become a Jewish city. Within weeks, the Jewish authorities carried out two major urban projects: The concentration of Haifa's remaining Arab inhabitants in two downtown neighbourhoods; and the systematic destruction of Arab housing in a number of areas.

The concentration, undertaken for both reasons of security (the war was still on and the Arabs, a potential Fifth Column, could more easily be supervised if restricted) and immigrant absorption (from summer 1948 there was a growing, dire need for housing in which to accommodate incoming Jewish immigrants), was ordered by Northern Front OC General Moshe Carmel on 28 June 1948, two days before the scheduled pullout of the last British troops from their enclaves in and around Haifa (Ramat David air base, the Kurdani camps complex, the Peninsular Barracks in Bat Galim, the harbour area and several camps on the Carmel, including Stella Maris). Implementation was to take place immediately. The concentration of the Arabs in Wadi Nisnas and Wadi Salib, according to Carmel, was prefigured in 'Plan D' [*kefi hamesuman beTochnit Dalet*]. Carmel explained the need for the operation wholly in strategic-military terms (housing needs are not mentioned).[313] On 1 July, OC Haifa District ordered his units to evict the Arabs from 'the French Carmel, the German Colony, etc.' to Wadi Nisnas and Wadi Salib, to be completed by 5 July.[314] The Haifa Arab Emergency Committee (Khayyat, Shihadeh Shalah, Tewfiq Tubi, and Nablus Farah) were called in, objected, and eventually were persuaded to help carry out the concentration; the army had threatened to use force if there was no cooperation.[315] The transfer began on 3 July.[316] The Arabs were concentrated in Wadi Nisnas and in a small number of houses in Abbas Street, their numbers not requiring additional housing in Wadi Salib (which was left empty for Jewish habitation). Minority Affairs Ministry officials raised various obstacles[317] as did Christian clerics,[318] but within days the operation was completed. By mid-July HIS-AD was able to report: 'The great majority of the Arabs of Haifa have been concentrated in Wadi Nisnas, in line with Plan D.'[319]

Within days of the fall of Arab Haifa, the municipality's Technical and Urban Development departments, in cooperation with the IDF's city commander, Ya'akov Lublini, formulated a proposal, for 'immediate implementation', for the renovation of large downtown areas and thoroughfares. Headed by an epigraph from *Ecclesiastes* (III\3), 'A time for . . .', the 'Memorandum on Urgent Improvement Works in Haifa' begins:

> 1. The exodus of the Arab population of Haifa and the almost complete evacuation of the Lower City, and of the Arab neighbourhoods between it and Hadar Hacarmel, affords an exceptional opportunity for improvement works connected to destruction. These works can fundamentally correct the security conditions, the road network and the sanitary situation of the city. The fact that the buildings earmarked for demolition have meanwhile suffered substantially from the ravages of the hostilities and are condemned for destruction according to [municipal] by-laws regarding dangerous buildings facilitate and provide an additional cause to carry out the required work.

Given the situation, the renovative work was urgent:

> The fact that in recent days a start has been made in settling [Jewish] immigrants, [Jewish] refugees [from elsewhere in Palestine] and institutions [of state] in empty areas of the city and the realisation that the city cannot long remain desolate and empty in face of the waves of immigration that we all expect and of the return of many of the Arabs who abandoned Haifa, should energise us to carry out all the necessary actions without delay.

Most of the buildings designated for destruction had already been marked out in various prewar plans; others were illegally built structures. The memorandum's authors argued for urgency both because such an opportunity 'might not recur in our time' and because it would be cheaper, in terms of expected compensation suits, to carry out the demolitions swiftly: 'One may assume as well that for lack of evidence, not many suits for compensation will be launched.' The detailed list of buildings earmarked for destruction included 46 'small houses' in the Vardiya neighbourhood, which endangered Jewish traffic and health (lack of sewage); 15 buildings between Ibn Gavirol and Herzl streets; 17 buildings in Ibn Rushd Street; 214 buildings on King George V Street – and the destruction of the shanty neighbourhoods In Wadi Rushmiya and Hawassa.[320]

On 16 June, Ben-Gurion met with Uriel Friedland, a factory manager and senior Haifa Haganah officer, and urged that the project be taken in hand 'immediately with the [final] British evacuation'.[321] IDF Planning Branch immediately ordered the start of the demolitions –

> to insure a convenient and safe route . . . between Hadar Hacarmel and the industrial part [of the city] and the *krayot* [i.e., the northern suburbs], to safeguard the route to the harbour, and to reduce the manpower needed now for guard duty in the city.[322]

The demolitions got under way in the third week of July, just after the start of the Second Truce, which freed IDF units, including engineers, for the task. The remaining Arab notables immediately complained, adding that they had not been consulted or compensated.[323] Mayor Levy responded that he did not know who was responsible or why the demolitions were taking place and disclaimed financial liability; he was worried that the municipality would be sued. For months, the legal basis of the operation was unclear. On 1 September, Shitrit brought up the subject in the Cabinet. Ben-Gurion parried with a deceitful evasion, saying that the matter was the responsibility of the official responsible for the occupied territories.[324]

Meanwhile, Levy was brought around, persuaded by Interior Minister Gruenbaum of the necessity, and benefit of the operation – designated by the IDF 'Operation Shikmona'. And his mind was laid to rest on the compensation issue; Gruenbaum explained that the operation was military rather than civilian, so compensation was not required by law.[325] With fits and starts, the demolitions continued through the summer and were apparently completed in October.[326]

Jaffa

During the early morning hours of 25 April, the IZL launched what was to be its major offensive of the war – the assault on Jaffa, the largest Arab city in Palestine. According to Gurney, the Arabs 'attach[ed] more value to Jaffa on historical and sentimental grounds than to any other Palestine town except Jerusalem.'[327] In the partition plan, Jaffa had been designated an Arab-ruled enclave in the Jewish-dominated Coastal Plain; its condition and functioning during the war's first months was in great measure determined by this geography. Some two thirds of its prewar population of 70,000–80,000 was still in place at the start of the final battle,[328] as were some 80 British soldiers, with armoured cars.[329] But the inhabitants knew that the British were about to leave and could not protect them beyond 14–15 May.

Through the civil war, the Haganah believed that there was no need to frontally assault Jaffa. While firing from the town occasionally disturbed south Tel Aviv, it posed no strategic threat. The Haganah felt that the inhabitants' sense of isolation and the realities of siege would eventually bring it to its knees; it would fall like a ripe plum the moment the British withdrew. Plan D did not call for the conquest of Jaffa but rather for penning in its population and conquering its suburbs of Manshiya, Abu Kabir and Tel al Rish.[330] The Haganah planners failed completely to anticipate, let alone plan for, the exodus of the population.

But the Haganah was not to have the decisive say. Since the start of April, when the Haganah went over to the offensive, the IZL had been looking for a major objective, partly to demonstrate that the Haganah was not the Yishuv's only effective military force. Political calculations obtruded.[331] Begin had considered East Jerusalem, the 'Triangle', the Hills of Menashe, southeast of Haifa, and Jaffa. On 23–24 April, the IZL leaders decided on Jaffa, which they viewed as a 'cancer' in the Jewish body politic and as the scourge of Tel Aviv, the IZL's power base.

The equivalent of six infantry companies were assembled and, of overwhelming importance, as we shall see, two three-inch mortars – stolen from the British in 1946 – were taken out of hiding, along with a plentiful supply of bombs. In the early morning hours of 25 April the IZL struck, attacking the Manshiya quarter at the northern end of Jaffa; the aim was to drive through the quarter's southern end to the sea, severing it from the town. If all went well, Jaffa itself was then to be attacked. The assault was to be accompanied by a mortar barrage on Manshiya and downtown Jaffa.

Jaffa was already thoroughly demoralised; its population felt 'insecure . . . and hopeless'.[332] There had been weeks of Haganah retaliatory strikes, which had included mortaring.[333] In late April, food, apart from flour, was still plentiful. But there were serious fuel shortages and skyrocketing prices, telephone lines were generally down[334] and transportation to and from the city had almost ceased. Most of the city's middle and upper classes had already left; its militias were fragmented and unruly, unemployment was rife, commerce had broken down, and bankruptcies had mounted.[335] The day before the assault, many had rushed to the banks and withdrawn deposits; within hours, they had run out of money and closed their doors.[336]

On 25 April, the IZL force, advancing from house to house, encountered strong resistance and the assault on Manshiya stalled. Regrouping and changing tactics, the attack was renewed and on 27 April, the IZL broke through and reached the sea, after suffering some 40 dead and twice that number wounded. Manshiya's inhabitants, under infantry and mortar attack, fled southwards to the 'Ajami and Jibalya quarters.

But of even greater consequence than the assault on Manshiya was the simultaneous, almost ceaseless, three-day mortaring of Ajami and other areas of central Jaffa; the prison and central post office were hit, as were King George and Butrus streets.[337] The fall of Arab Haifa and its exodus added to Jaffa's demoralisation.[338] According to Nimr al Khatib, Jaffa's Arabs felt that 'now their turn had come'.[339] The ground assault and the incessant mortaring broke the back of civilian morale and military resistance.

Writing shortly after the battle, Begin claimed that the mortarmen were ordered to avoid hitting 'hospitals, religious sites' and consulates.[340] But as the IZL's fire control and ranging were at best amateur, even if restrictions had been imposed, they would have been meaningless. In any case, the objectives of the three-day barrage, in which 20 tons of ordnance were delivered, were clear: 'To prevent constant military traffic in the city, to break the spirit of the enemy troops, [and] to cause chaos among the civilian population in order to create a mass flight', is how Amihai Paglin, the IZL head of operations, put it in his pre-attack briefing. The mortars were aimed roughly at 'the port area, the Clock Square, the prison, King George Boulevard and 'Ajami'.[341] Cunningham wrote a few days later: 'It should be made clear that IZL attack with mortars was indiscriminate and designed to create panic among the civilian inhabitants.'[342] And, indeed, most of the casualties were civilians, according to Haganah intelligence.[343] Jacques De Reynier, the Red Cross representative in Palestine, described the panic that took hold of Jaffa's medical staff:

> Soon the flight started. In the hospital, the drivers of cars and ambulances took their vehicles, collected their families and fled without the slightest regard to their duty. Many of the . . . nurses and even doctors left the hospital [only] with the clothes they had on and ran to the countryside.[344]

An IZL intelligence report from 28 April, based on interrogations of captured POWs, states:

> Our shells . . . fell on many central sites near the post office, near the municipality . . . and near the port. A coffee shop in the vegetable market

was hit and tens of gang members [i.e., irregulars] were killed and injured. The prisoners who fell into our hands know of more than 200 hit in the barrage . . . The barrage stopped the movement of buses to Jaffa and in it and paralyzed completely the supply of food to the city and in it. Hotels turned into hospitals. The shelling caused great panic. The port filled up with masses of refugees and the boarding of boats took place in confusion.

The Manshiya police force, added the report, fled, abandoning the population.[345]

It is probable that Jaffa's inhabitants at some point in the battle learned that it was the IZL attacking them and that this was a contributing factor to the exodus; Deir Yassin had taken place a fortnight before and was fresh in everyone's mind. IZL spokesmen subsequently asserted that this was a major factor in the inhabitants' precipitate exodus.[346]

In any event, the major result of the attack on Jaffa was the precipitation of mass flight, from the harbour and by road, usually under British escort, eastward toward the West Bank and southward toward Gaza. In the wake of the attack, shops and markets closed, traffic ceased, and injured and dead piled up in the streets, hospitals and hotels; almost no doctors and nurses remained. Lack of fuel hampered the shipment of the wounded to Nablus.[347] By 8 May, only one doctor and one nurse remained in the main, government hospital.[348] From 1 May, HIS reported a succession of convoys, loaded with families and furniture, departing the town.[349]

According to British observers, a major cause of the exodus, as from Haifa and Tiberias, was the flight of the local leaders before and during the battle. Even before the battle, Jaffa, far more than the other towns, was characterised by disunity of command. In April there were seven distinct, different and in part rival power centres, which had overlapping responsibilities: The municipality, the NC, Rafiq Tamimi (the Mufti's representative), the Najada, the local militia and its command, the various non-local irregular units and the separate commander appointed by the Arab League Military Committee. The IZL attack encountered disunity and triggered dissolution, and the leaders fled. 'It is pathetic to see how the [Jaffa] Arabs have been deserted by their leaders', recorded Gurney.[350] Cunningham, pointing directly to the leaders' flight as a precipitant of the mass flight, reported that the mayor, Heikal, had gone on 'four days' leave' in mid-April and had not yet returned, and that half the NC had left.[351] The War Office, not completely accurately, informed senior British Cabinet ministers on 29 April that 'all Arab Leaders have left and town appears dead'.[352]

At the end of April, Shertok, in an address to the UN General Assembly, charged that in both Tiberias and Jaffa 'the mass evacuation had been dictated by Arab commanders as a political and military demonstration . . . The Arab command ordered the people to leave.' With regard to Jaffa, there is little evidence for this assertion;[353] rather, an obverse process seems to have occurred. The shelling 'had produced results beyond expectation'. It had 'caused dread and fear among the inhabitants', precipitating flight.[354] The flight of the inhabitants had, in turn, led to a collapse of the irregular formations, who then also took to their heels.[355]

The IZL assault on Jaffa, following hard upon the fall of Arab Haifa, had placed the British in a difficult position, eventually sparking a minor crisis in Whitehall. Arab leaders in Palestine and outside blamed the British for what had happened in Haifa: they claimed that Stockwell had conspired with the Haganah, or at least had played into Jewish hands, by his sudden redeployment of troops out of the city centre; that he had prevented the entry of Arab reinforcements; that he had failed to halt the Haganah offensive, which, the Arabs alleged, had included 'massacres'; and that he had promoted the truce, which was effectively a surrender. In general, the Arabs argued that Britain was officially and legally in control of Palestine until 15 May and should have acted accordingly.[356]

Cunningham, Stockwell and the War Office rejected the charges. As the War Office succinctly put it:

> After defeat at Haifa[,] in order to excuse their own ineptitude, Arab leaders accused us of helping Jews and hindering Arabs although it was actually due to inefficient and cowardly behaviour of Arab Military Leaders and their refusal to follow our advice and to restrain themselves. Consequently[,] Anglo-Arab relations have considerably deteriorated.[357]

This deterioration, which took place against the backdrop of the impending withdrawal from Palestine, was acutely felt in Whitehall, and led directly to a clash between Bevin and the army chiefs and to British intervention in the battle for Jaffa. The Foreign Office felt that the Haifa episode had undermined Britain's position throughout the Arab world. On the evening of 22 April, the Chief of the Imperial General Staff (CIGS), Field Marshal Montogmery, was summoned to 10 Downing Street, where he was apparently forced to admit that he had not been kept posted by his generals about events in Haifa. Bevin 'became very worked up; he said 23,000 [sic] Arabs had been killed and the situation was catastrophic'. Montgomery said he would try to ascertain what was happening.[358]

The Prime Minister, Clement Attlee, Bevin and Montgomery reconvened the following morning at 10 Downing Street, with Bevin, according to the Field Marshal, 'even more agitated'. Bevin thought the army should have stopped the Haganah: 'The massacre of the Arabs had put him in an impossible position with all the Arab states.' Bevin concluded his attack by saying that 'he had been let down by the Army'.[359] Montgomery, according to his own account, demanded that Bevin retract the charge, formally complained to Defence Minister A. B. Alexander, and attacked Bevin's handling of the Palestine crisis, saying that the Foreign Secretary was 'now . . . trying to make the Army the scapegoat'. Montgomery, according to his account, threatened to resign and make disclosures in the House of Lords. 'This fairly put the cat among the pigeons', he recalled, and Alexander and Attlee were forced to summon a further meeting at 10 Downing Street on 7 May.

As things turned out, Montgomery got little joy. Attlee thought that Montgomery was making a major issue out of 'a phrase in the course of . . . a discussion' and criticised the army's lack of up-to-date information. Bevin 'still felt' that the Army should 'not have lost control over the perimeter of Haifa and allowed so many Arabs to be driven out . . .'. According to Montgomery, the meeting ended on a light note, with everyone present 'laughing . . . Attlee handled the situation beautifully; and it was impossible to be angry with Ernie Bevin for long.' But Montgomery received no apology, and both Stockwell and Marriott (the latter for supporting Stockwell) were long to remain the butts of Foreign Office criticism.[360]

Whitehall squabbling aside, the chief upshot of Haifa was to be forceful British intervention in Jaffa. Its aim was to 'compensate' for Britain's alleged role in Haifa and to restore the prestige and goodwill lost in the Arab world. When the first news of the IZL attack reached London, Bevin 'got very excited . . . and [instructed] the CIGS . . . to . . . see to it that the Jews did not manage to occupy Jaffa or, if they did, were immediately turned out'. Such was Bevin's fear of a re-enactment of Haifa that he had bypassed normal channels (the Defence Minister and High Commissioner) in trying to get the army to act.[361] On 27 April, the British military – who had no direct lines to the IZL – informed Tel Aviv Mayor Yisrael Rokah and the HIS that they intended to 'save Jaffa for the Arabs at all costs, especially in the light of the fact that the Jews had conquered Haifa'.[362]

The following day, the British went into action. Some 4,500 troops, with tanks, moved into the city; Spitfires swooped overhead and fired some bursts; warships anchored in Jaffa harbour; and British mortars shelled IZL positions. In tripartite negotiations between Britain, the Haganah and the IZL, the British demanded the IZL's withdrawal from Manshiya. On 30 April, agreement was reached, the IZL withdrew – after blowing up the local police fort – and British troops were left in control of the city. Haganah intelligence reported that the IZL had left behind 'badly mutilated . . . Arab corpses'[363] and that the British were looting the abandoned houses.[364]

According to Begin, the British troops initially tried to stem the exodus. They

> tried to calm the terrified inhabitants of Jaffa . . . and . . . repeatedly announced that they would defend Jaffa with all their military strength. But all their soothing efforts came to nought . . . Nothing could have prevented the complete evacuation of the town.[365]

One reason the British were unsuccessful was Mivtza Hametz (Operation Hametz), the Haganah's offensive during 28–30 April against a cluster of villages just east of Jaffa. The aim was the conquest of Yahudiya, Kafr 'Ana, Sakiya, Kheiriya, Salame, Yazur, Beit Dajan and the suburb village of Tel al Rish, which afforded Jaffa a (precarious) connection to the Arab hinterland to the east (Lydda and Ramle). According to the HGS's preparatory order, the objective was 'the complete surrounding and cutting off' of Jaffa and 'opening the way [to Jewish forces] to Lydda'. No explicit mention was made of the prospective treatment of the villages' inhabitants though the order generally spoke of 'cleansing the area [*tihur hashetah*]'.[366] But the final operational order stated: 'Civilian inhabitants of places conquered would be permitted to leave after they are searched for weapons.' It cautioned the troops against harming women and children 'insofar as possible' and against looting and 'undisciplined acts [*maasei hefkerut*], robbery, or harming holy places'. Prisoners, it instructed, were to be moved to the brigade HQs.[367]

During 28–30 April, the Haganah took Kheiriya, Saqiya, Salama and Yazur – the first three without a fight. HIS attributed the non-resistance of the inhabitants to the prior defeat of Arab arms in Tiberias, Haifa, Ramat Yohanan and Mishmar Ha'emek: 'It is clear that the inhabitants have no stomach for war and . . . would willingly return to their villages and accept Jewish protection.'[368] Yahudiya and Kafr 'Ana were not attacked and Tel al Rish was briefly taken but abandoned under counterattack. The inhabitants and militiamen of all the villages (including Kafr 'Ana and Yahudiya)[369] panicked and fled with the approach of the Haganah columns or as rounds began to fall. In Kheiriya, Alexandroni's 32nd Battalion found and buried the bodies of four adult males and three women and briefly detained a handful of men, women and children.[370] Two of the adult male detainees were promptly executed, charged with having killed a Haganah man.[371] When Ben-Gurion visited Salama on 30 April, he encountered 'only one old blind woman'.[372] A day or two later, hooligans from Tel Aviv's Hatikva Quarter torched several buildings.[373] Under British pressure, Yazur was abandoned by the Haganah – but only after its alleyways and buildings had been mined.[374]

The swift collapse of resistance in Jaffa's rural hinterland and the flight of the villages' inhabitants was attributed by the IZL and the Haganah in large measure to the IZL assault on Manshiya and the demoralisation and exodus of Jaffa's inhabitants. In turn, however, the fall of these villages further undermined the morale of the 15,000–25,000 inhabitants still left in the town;[375] it was completely cut off and any possibility of Arab military relief had vanished. The rural hinterland that had supplied the town's food was no more.[376]

In Jaffa, confusion reigned. Alongside a brigade of British troops, Arab irregulars arrived from Ramle; they reportedly tried to stem the exodus or at least of army-aged males.[377] On or just before 8 May, the AHC ordered municipal officials to stay at their posts.[378] But at the same time militiamen were fleeing the city[379] and local leaders pleaded with the British to arrange the evacuation of some of the remaining inhabitants 'by sea . . . to Beirut'. Others sought British help in leaving through Haganah lines. Alexandroni Brigade OC Dan Even agreed and thousands more left.[380] All understood that the British presence was temporary: 'We are in a weak position in attempting to discourage evacuation because whatever counter-operation we might take against the Jews, we cannot guarantee safety of Arabs in a fortnight's time', reported Cunningham.[381]

By 8 May, Jaffa was almost a ghost town, with convoys of evacuees departing daily, its streets dominated by British soldiers and looting militia gangs. Bands of robbers pillaged the town's warehouses, often after bribing British guards.[382] Only some 5,000 inhabitants remained, many of them 'ill, poor, handicapped and old'.[383] Kiryati's intelligence officer provided a concise portrait of the dying city:

> In Jaffa – complete anarchy and collapse. The mayor [Heikal] has fled the city. All the municipal departments, banks and the government hospital have shut down . . . The court buildings are being evacuated. The postal offices have been occupied by the British Army. The robbery and looting continue. Armed irregulars – apparently Iraqis – break into shops and steal food from the port area. [British] soldiers too appear to be taking part in the robbery. Food and fuel supplies are disastrous.[384]

Cunningham wrote that 'nearly all councillors and members of National Committee have fled'. The remaining notables apparently hoped that the Jews would take over and restore order – but were afraid to say so publicly.[385] Nimr al Khatib wrote that the ALA contingent, headed by Michel al Issa, which arrived at the end of April, 'acted as if the town was theirs, and began to rob people and loot their houses. People's lives became worthless and women's honour was defiled. This prompted many inhabitants to leave . . .'[386] Cunningham concluded that 'Jaffa is the fruit of the premature military action against which the Arab Governments have been repeatedly warned and that further premature action on their part will only add to the sufferings of the Arabs of Palestine . . .'.[387]

On 11 May, Mayor Heikal, writing from his Philadelphia Hotel room in Amman, asked the British to prevent Jewish occupation of Jaffa.[388] But the day before, Kiryati had issued its 'preparatory order' for 'Operation Dror', the impending takeover of the town – which included detailed instructions for the imposition of a curfew, the screening of the remaining inhabitants and their eventual concentration in one or two neighbourhoods, the detention of ex-combatants, the prevention of looting and the protection of religious sites.[389] On 12 May, the members of the 'Jaffa Arab Emergency Committee' – Amin Andraus, Salah al Nazer and Ahmad Abu Laban – crossed into Tel Aviv and met Kiryati officers to smooth the way for the Jewish takeover and discuss terms. Kiryati OC Michael Ben-Gal promised that the occupation would be light-handed and there would be 'no military trials or acts of vengeance'; the Haganah would only arrest persons deemed a threat to peace. Andraus asked: 'What about those who recently left Jaffa and wish to return. Will they be allowed to return . . .?' Ben-Gal answered: 'We agree that every citizen of Jaffa who wishes to return, we will check the matter in consultation with them [i.e., the Emergency Committee] and in line with municipal records [proving that the person in question] was in fact an inhabitant of the city. If there is no special reason to think him dangerous, we will not prevent his return . . .'[390] At the follow-up meeting the next day, Ben-Gal reiterated that 'we wish to help the residents of Jaffa who wish to return but in this matter there will be a need to make some arrangement so that they will be able to return. The intention of the clause is that inhabitants will be able to return . . .'[391] In the 'Agreement' that was signed, Ben-Gal committed the Haganah to abide by 'the Geneva Convention and all International Laws and Usages of War'; the Arab signatories endorsed the 'instructions' the brigadier was about to issue. The 'Instructions to the Arab Population by the Commander of the Haganah, Tel Aviv District, given on 13th May 1948' included the handover of all arms and the punishment of those not complying, the screening of all adult males, and the internment of 'criminals or persons suspected of being a danger to the peace'. Lastly, Ben-Gal stated that adult males wishing to return would be individually screened, implying that women and children could return to Jaffa without such screening.[392]

On 13 May, Kiryati issued the operational order for 'Operation Dror'[393] and on 14 May Haganah units, accompanied by token IZL forces, occupied Jaffa in an orderly, uncontested deployment. Kiryati issued a special 'order of the day': 'Jaffa is almost empty of inhabitants. We have promised to allow the inhabitants to live peacefully, with respect, and each of us must abide by this promise.'[394] Yitzhak Chizik was appointed military governor. On 18 May, Ben-Gurion visited the town and commented: 'I couldn't understand: Why did the inhabitants . . . leave?'[395]

Chizik did his best to protect the population – a quick census registered some 4,100 inhabitants – from the occupying troops: He stationed guards outside public buildings, organised Military Police patrols, and ordered homes and businesses that had been checked to be secured against looters and vandals. But the following days saw a great deal of unpleasantness, and some brutal behaviour, vis-á-vis the occupied population, which was arbitrarily pushed about, screened, and concentrated in one or two areas behind barbed wire fences, and its property vandalised, looted and robbed. Troops briefly used inhabitants for forced, unpaid labour.[396]

On 25 May, 15 Arab men were found dead in the Jibalya neighbourhood, near the waterfront: All had been shot and four had on them ID cards issued by the Military Governor's office, indicating that they – and probably all 15 – had been killed after the Haganah had occupied the town. Three doctors who examined the bodies two days later determined that they had been shot a week or so before.[397] On 14 or 15 May, a 12-year-old girl was raped by two Haganah soldiers;[398] there were also a number of attempted rapes. There was widespread institutional and private looting by Haganah and IZL troops and Tel Aviv citizens who infiltrated the town, there was robbery on the roads by patrolling Jewish troops (with 'watches, rings, cash, etc.' taken) and there was widespread vandalisation of property. In general, the inhabitants complained, they were 'being incessantly molested'.[399] The looting was so bad that Chizik appealed directly to Ben-Gurion, who on 22 May ordered the IZL and the Haganah to obey Chizik's instructions.[400] A senior Kiryati officer, Zvi Aurbach, made a point of washing his hands of any responsibility for property in Jaffa.[401] On 25 May, one official reported: 'During the whole day I walked about the streets . . . I saw soldiers, civilians, military police, battalion police, looting, robbing, while breaking through doors and walls . . .'[402]

A few days later, Chizik was able to report that the situation had improved: individual looting had been largely curtailed, though institutional looting, with official permits, was still continuing.[403] There was so much looting that IDF CGS Dori, exasperated, on 23 June wrote Ben-Gal: 'I want to know once and for all: Can you put Jaffa's affairs in order . . . or not . . . I must, *en fin*, draw conclusions from this.' Dori gave him two days.[404]

A month earlier, a senior IDF officer – possibly Ben-Gal – had told the Red Cross that he was aware of all the 'incidents' that had occurred, including the rape, and assured him that those responsible had been put on trial. He added that this was his fourth war and that conditions in Jaffa, compared to the terrible things he had seen elsewhere, were 'like paradise'.[405] But few if any trials had actually occurred. On 21 June Chizik complained that 'despite the many cases of soldiers being caught stealing . . . I have not yet received a single report showing a verdict against any of the perpetrators'. Chizik, clearly, believed that no one had actually been punished.[406]

The situation gradually improved, but Jaffa's Arabs remained objects of depredation by undisciplined soldiers. For weeks, the chief miscreants appear to have been naval personnel. At the end of July, Jaffa's military commander repeatedly complained that navy soldiers had broken into several homes, beaten the owners and robbed them.[407] A few days later, a catholic church was broken into and silver chalices and crucifixes were stolen. The CGS, incensed, ordered that the perpetrators be found and 'severely' punished.[408] Eighteen naval personnel were arrested and some goods were recovered.[409] The harassment and vandalisation of Arabs and Arab property in Jaffa appears to have ended in August.

THE SMALL TOWNS

On 16 April, the British evacuated Safad and on 28 April, nearby Rosh Pina. On 21 April, three days after the exodus from Tiberias, Palmah OC Allon flew in to review the situation. The following day he recommended to Yadin and Galili launching a series of operations, in line with Plan D, that would brace the area for the expected Arab invasion. He recommended 'the harassment of Beit Shean [i.e., Beisan] in order to increase the flight from it . . . [and] the harassment of Arab Safad in order to speed up its evacuation.' Both were sensitive border towns – Beisan was five kilometres from Jordan and Safad 12 kilometres from Syria – and Allon did not want to leave Palestinian population centres immediately behind what would be HIS front lines.[410]

Safad

Immediately after presenting these recommendations, Allon was appointed OC of the campaign to take control of Eastern Galilee, eventually codenamed Mivtza Yiftah (Operation Yiftah). The conquest of the Arab part of Safad was the linchpin of the campaign. With 10,000–12,000 Arabs, almost all Muslims, and 1,500 Jews, Safad, the ancient Mishnaic and Kabbalistic centre, was Eastern Galilee's major ALA and anti-Zionist base.[411]

Safad's Arabs were militarily weak and disorganised.[412] At the end of November 1947, the Arab inhabitants had been described by a Palmah scout as edgy; there was 'fear of the Jews' and the better educated were 'depressed'.[413] The partition resolution's inclusion of Safad in the Jewish State area had sorely dented local morale. Nonetheless, Husseini's supporters embarked on violence. On 13 December they had shot dead, in the Arab market, Haganah intelligence agent Nissim Mizrahi. The Haganah retaliated by killing three Arabs.[414] During the following months, there were periodic exchanges of fire and Haganah raiding in the surrounding countryside. On 2\3 January, the Palmah blew up the house of Subhi al Khidra, the local Husseini leader.[415]

Safad's Arab militia was commanded by Ihsan Kam al Maz, a Syrian officer apparently attached to the ALA. He was replaced in mid-April by Sari Fnaish, and his deputy, Amin al Jmai'an, two Jordanian ALA officers. Though both of Safad's communities suffered a measure of isolation and siege, there were no food shortages and civil life continued unimpaired. There was no noticeable flight of population before late April.[416]

On 16 April, the British evacuated their two bases in town, handing them over to irregulars, who then attacked the Jewish Quarter but were beaten off. The Haganah lobbed a Davidka mortar bomb into the Arab area, where it killed '13 Arabs, most of them children'. This triggered panic and despondency.[417] During 16–18 April, Palmah and ALA units moved in to beef up the respective militias, and the two sides continued to trade fire. But arguments over turf immediately broke out between the ALA and local militia officers. During the following days, many Syrian and Jordanian volunteers left.[418] This divisiveness may have triggered some civilian flight, with one ALA commander threatening the departees that their property would be confiscated and their homes demolished.[419]

The final battle began on 1 May, when the Palmah's 3rd Battalion conquered the neighbouring villages of 'Ein al Zeitun and Biriyya, closing the route to town from the north and partially relieving the siege of the Jewish Quarter. In 1929, 'Ein al Zeitun villagers had killed several settlers in neighbouring 'Ein Zeitim and, along with the inhabitants of Biriyya,[420] had been very active in 1936–1939.[421] On 2\3 January 1948, the village had been raided by the Haganah, who blew up several houses, killing a number of Arabs.[422] 'Ein al Zeitun served as a base for attacks against Jewish traffic and 'Ein Zeitim. During the assault on 1 May, the 700–800-strong Safad Arab militia did nothing to help the two villages.

As usual, the early morning attack on 'Ein al Zeitun began with a mortar barrage; it was followed by a ground assault by two platoons. Within an hour, 'the village of murderers was in our hands', recalled Elad Peled, the OC of Jewish Safad. Palmah losses were one dead and six wounded. The Palmah took 30–100 prisoners.[423] Another platoon conquered Biriyya. While some of 'Ein al Zeitun's inhabitants fled during the mortaring, many women, children and old men stayed put and were rounded up and expelled, with shots fired over their heads to speed them on their way.[424] The next day, several villagers tried to return to 'Ein al Zeitun, perhaps to collect belongings, but were fired upon and fled; one was apparently killed.[425]

One Yiftah HQ report says that '30' Arab prisoners were 'transferred to Golani [Brigade]'.[426] But a day or two later, two Palmah soldiers, on Third Battalion OC Moshe Kelman's orders, murdered several dozen prisoners, probably including young men from 'Ein al Zeitun, in the gully between 'Ein al Zeitun and Safad.[427]

During 1–2 May, Palmah sappers blew up and burned houses in the village with the dual aim, according to one participant, Gavriel (Gabbi)

Cohen, of 'destroying an enemy base and of undermining the morale of the Arab inhabitants of Safad', who witnessed the leveling of the village across the wadi.[428] According to Peled, the Palmahniks were drunk and 'blind' with the victory, and proceeded to vandalise property and blow up houses. The Jews of Safad, watching from afar, were 'happy', seeing in it vengeance for what the Arabs of 'Ein al Zeitun 'had done to the Jews of Safad and 'Ein Zeitim' in 1929 and 1936–1939.[429]

The conquest of 'Ein al Zeitun and Biriyya, which opened the way for Palmah reinforcement of Safad, mortally undermined the morale of the town's Arab population. The inhabitants were already perturbed by the news of Deir Yassin and the fall of Arab Tiberias and Haifa, and by the evacuation of the inhabitants of Ja'una, to the east, and Ghuweir Abu Shusha, to the southeast. Indeed, several prominent families left either just before or just after 1 May.[430] On 2 May, the bulk of the Palmah's Third Battalion reached the Jewish Quarter – and immediately let loose with a mortar barrage on the Arab neighbourhoods: 'Panic took hold of the Safad inhabitants, and long columns of Arabs began to leave the town in the direction of Meirun' and eastward, toward the Jordan River.[431] That day, Haganah radio announced, prematurely, that 'Safad is being evacuated by its Arab population'. British intelligence also noted the start of the evacuation, attributing it to the general demoralisation precipitated by the fall of Arab Tiberias and Haifa.[432]

The first Palmah ground attack on Arab Safad took place on 6 May. The Third Battalion failed to take the main objective, the citadel, which dominated the Arab quarters, but 'terrified' the population sufficiently to prompt further flight, urgent appeals for outside help and an effort to obtain a truce. Allon turned down the overture.[433] Despite their success, the Arab militiamen and inhabitants were in a state of 'panic'.[434]

The plight of Arab Safad triggered a wave of protests in the Arab world. 'Azzam Pasha accurately described the aim of Plan D, of which Operation Yiftah was a part, when he said: The

> Jews were following a perfectly clear and ruthless plan . . . They were now drawing [driving?] out the inhabitants of Arab villages along the Syrian and Lebanese frontiers, particularly places on the roads by which Arab regular forces could enter the country. In particular, Acre and Safad were in very great danger of Jewish occupation. It was obvious that if this continued, the Arab armies would have great difficulty in even entering Palestine after May 15.[435]

Broadmead was warned by the Syrians that the

> situation at Safad was desperate and that unless there was immediate [British] intervention there would be second Deir Yassin . . . If massacre took place, Syria would be blamed throughout the Arab world for not having intervened.[436]

The minister's cable elicited from London a response similar to that following the IZL attack on Jaffa. Colonial Secretary Creech-Jones, presumably after consulting with Bevin, authorised Cunningham to intervene militarily to prevent a Jewish victory:

> The Arab states are clearly most concerned at the possibility of an Arab disaster and it is of the greatest importance to our relations with them to avoid anything of this kind. Such a disaster would almost certainly involve the entry of forces of Arab states into Palestine before the end of the Mandate. If you would in your judgement warrant it[,] you and the G.O.C. are authorised to use all practical means including air action to restore the situation.'[437]

But the Haganah attack failed and the British did not intervene.

Nor, indeed, did the British – now less than a week away from the end of the Mandate – intervene against the second and final Haganah attack, which began on the evening of 9 May, with a mortar barrage on key sites. A few hours later, early on 10 May, the Palmah's First Battalion conquered the village of 'Akbara, two and a half kilometres south of town. Many of the villagers had already fled, under the impact of Deir Yassin and the fall of 'Ein al Zeitun.[438] The operation was designed to block reinforcements reaching Safad from the south and 'to create among the Arabs of Safad a feeling that they were about to be surrounded and would be unable to flee'. The Palmah blew up the village.[439] The fall and destruction of 'Akbara without doubt undermined morale in Safad – as did the mortar barrage. Indeed, some of the inhabitants apparently believed that the bombs fired from the Haganah's home-made 'Davidka' mortar were 'atom' bombs, both because of their tremendous noise and great flash on explosion and because an unusual downpour occurred that night and the next day.[440] Following the barrage, Palmah infantry, in bitter fighting, took the citadel, Beit Shalva and the police fort, Safad's three dominant buildings. The irregulars, despite support from ALA artillery based at Meirun, began to flee. Through 10 May, Haganah mortars continued to pound the Arab neighbourhoods,[441] causing 'fires in the market area and in the fuel dumps, which exploded. Chaos afflicted the town and with screams and yells flight began from the whole Arab area . . .' A dawn patrol by a Haganah reconnaissance aircraft revealed 'thousands of refugees streaming by foot toward Meirun and a concentration of several hundred refugees near 'Ein a Tina, west of Safad', reported Yiftah HQ.[442] It was later reported that some of the commanders had 'advised' the inhabitants to flee.[443] The Palmah 'intentionally left open the exit routes for the population to "facilitate" their exodus . . . The 12,000 refugees (some estimate 15,000) . . . were a heavy burden on the Arab war effort', recalled Allon.[444] According to one report, a 120-strong column of ALA reinforcements made its way to Safad – and met the stream of departing inhabitants, 'loaded down with parcels, women carrying their children in their arms, some going by foot, others on ass and donkey-back'. The encounter surely did little for the troops' morale – and most reportedly fled Safad hours after arriving.[445] The Haganah also apparently dropped a handful of makeshift bombs from reconnaissance aircraft and fired some mortar rounds at or near the columns of refugees to speed them on their way.[446]

On 11 May, the Palmah troops secured the now empty Arab quarters, confiscated 'goods that could serve the combat units', and sealed off the area against looters.[447] Meanwhile, Safad's Jews went 'wild with joy and danced and sang in the streets'.[448]

A major cause of the collapse of Arab resistance and the exodus was the absence and\or flight of militia commanders. On 11 May, fleeing irregulars complained of 'the treachery of their commanders who fled at the start of the battle'.[449] Fnaish and Kam al Maz had been at loggerheads for weeks. Between 2 and 8 May, Jmai'an was away in Damascus and Amman. On 9 May, Fnaish, a former Arab Legion officer apparently cashiered for embezzlement, and hired by the ALA,[450] quit and left for Damascus, apparently on orders from King Abdullah. Jmai'an, upon returning from Amman on 8 May, told the townspeople that he had been ordered to pull out his Jordanian volunteers as Safad was in the Lebanese–Syrian area of control. Jmai'an pulled out at 01:00 hours on 10 May, just hours into the final Palmah offensive. Moreover, Adib Shishakli, the ALA regional battalion commander, was not in town during the battle; nor was Kam al Maz, who appears to have left just before 1 May.[451]

The Palmah troops scouring the abandoned quarters found about 100 Muslims, 'with an average age of 80', according to Safad's newly appointed military governor, Avraham Hanochi, of Kibbutz Ayelet Hashahar. They were expelled to Lebanon later that month.[452] Only 34–36 Christian Arabs remained. Distancing themselves from the 'the Arabs who had migrated', they pleaded to stay on, under Jewish rule[453] and, initially, refused to budge.[454] HIS saw them as an intelligence risk and recommended their transfer to Haifa.[455] On 13 June, this last remnant of the Arab community was shipped to Haifa and deposited in two convents – Les Filles de la Charité de la Sacré Cour and Les Dames de Nazareth – with the Arab Affairs Committee of Haifa providing some of the maintenance costs. The matter caused a bureaucratic wrangle, with the Foreign Ministry demanding that the IDF allow them back to Safad 'to improve our relations with our minorities'. The ministry was also worried about the effect that the eviction might have on relations with the churches. But the army refused.[456] Shertok, uncharacteristically, persisted. His stand, as conveyed by his aide-de-camp Yehoshafat Harkabi, was that while Israel absolutely refused 'to accept back Arab refugees from outside Israel, we must behave towards the Arabs inside the country with greater moderation. Through this will be tested our ability to govern the Arab minority.' Shertok, supported by the Minority Affairs Ministry, demanded that at least some of the Christians be allowed back.[457] But, against the backdrop of the start of the settlement of new Jewish immigrants in the abandoned quarters, the army rejected the request. The Safad group remained in Haifa, welfare cases maintained by the municipality, local Arabs and the Haifa convents. Of this group three were in their eighties and six in their seventies. By spring 1949, three had died, five were hospitalised and two women had become demented, according to Marriott.[458]

The fall of Arab Safad severely undermined morale in the surrounding hinterland. The day after, HIS reported that the inhabitants of Ras al Ahmar, Jish, Safsaf, Teitaba, Qaddita and Sa'sa 'had decided to abandon their villages if the Arabs of Safad surrender'.[459]

Beisan (Beit Shean)

The Beit Shean (Beisan) Valley, with the Arab town of Beisan (pop. 5,000) at its centre (on the site of Biblical Beit Shean, where the Philistines displayed the body of King Saul, after his defeat and death on Mount Gilbo'a), was viewed by HGS as a probable point of entry for Jordanian forces invading Palestine. Allon's recommendation of 22 April, that the town be conquered and its population harassed into flight, reflected Haganah thinking on the eve of the invasion and conformed with the general guidelines of Plan D. There was also strong pressure from local settlements to eject the Arabs from the town and its environs. On 4 May, a delegation of settlers from the Beit Shean and Jezreel valleys journeyed to Tel Aviv to persuade the Yishuv leaders to move against Beisan. At one of their meetings, the delegation warned that Arab Legion troops had moved into the town and were fortifying it. The settlers urged Yosef Weitz to press the Haganah to attack. Weitz, agreeing, responded: 'The emptying of the valley [of Arabs] is the order of the day.' That night, Weitz talked to Shkolnik, who agreed that the Haganah had to attack.[460]

The town was surrounded on all sides by Jewish settlements. During March–April, Arab vehicles heading for Beisan were often interdicted, and electricity and telephone lines were intermittently down. By early May, fuel prices had skyrocketed. Jewish sabotage of the water mains proved particularly disruptive. Beisan was raided by the Palmah in mid-February and several houses were demolished;[461] the Arab League Military Committee had sent Ahmad al Jayusi to organise the militia. On 18 March, he complained of lack of arms and ammunition.[462] A Mandate official, Ismail al Faruqi, controlled a second force, consisting of 60 policemen. Jayusi, Faruqi and the NC were constantly at loggerheads.[463] News of the fall of Arab Tiberias and Haifa precipitated a partial exodus, which the NC tried unsuccessfully to stop. The Haganah takeover of the Gesher police fort, to the north, on 27 April further undermined morale.[464] From 28 April, when the Golani Brigade took control of the nearby British Army camp (and the Arab militiamen occupied the town's police fort), the Haganah placed Beisan under intermittent siege.[465] The ALA managed to reinforce the town with 150–200 irregulars.[466] But most of the women and children were evacuated, to Nablus, Tubas and Jordan. Adult males were not allowed to leave.[467] There was a shortage of doctors and medicines.[468]

On the night of 10\11 May, Golani units occupied Beisan's two main satellite villages, Farwana and al Ashrafiya, the inhabitants fleeing to Jordan as the troops approached. Haganah sappers began to blow up the houses. The following night, Golani units mortared Beisan and stormed Tel al Husn, a hill dominating the town from the north. Faruqi appears to have fled that night, taking with him P£9,000 of tax revenues.[469] During the fight for Tel al Husn, a Haganah officer telephoned the Beisan militia HQ and 'advised' surrender. A militia officer responded defiantly. But following the hill's fall, the Arabs repeatedly pleaded with the Haganah for a ceasefire. The Haganah agreed and at a meeting on the morning of 12 May, presented terms – surrender of weapons and expulsion of foreign irregulars.[470] The Arabs apparently were 'told that any inhabitant wishing to stay . . . could do so';[471] those wishing to leave were offered safe passage. The notables – Hanna Nimri, Hashim al Solh and Mayor Rashad Darwish – said they had to obtain agreement from the HQ in Nablus (or Jenin) and a delegation left for the Triangle. Meanwhile, the ALA troops and most of the inhabitants fled, mainly to Jordan. The notables announced the town's surrender and Israeli troops moved in the next day.[472]

Some 1,000–1,200 inhabitants initially remained,[473] much to Weitz's chagrin.[474] The Haganah provided them with water and food.[475] Martial law and a curfew were imposed, arms were collected, and a committee of local Jewish settlers was appointed to oversee property and life in the town. Shmuel Govrin, of Kibbutz Kfar Ruppin, was appointed civilian governor. An Arab police force was appointed.[476]

But the presence of this concentration of Arabs just behind the lines and the constant coming and going of Beisan residents and former residents – who plundered the abandoned houses – troubled Haganah commanders. They sought and obtained authority, probably from HGS, to expel the remaining inhabitants. 'There was a danger that the inhabitants would revolt in the rear, when they felt a change in the military situation in favour of the [Arab] invaders, [so within days] an order was given to evict the inhabitants from the city'. Most were apparently expelled around 15 May across the Jordan.[477]

Govrin later recalled:

> . . . I received an order to clear the town of Arabs, we went from house to house and we told the [townspeople] with loudhailers that they had to leave by the following morning. They were very frightened. There were no vehicles there and I had to order them to go by foot to the Sheikh Hussein Bridge, and to throw them across. It was hard seeing the old people with the bundles, the women and the children. A difficult eviction– not brutal, but difficult . . . I gave them food. The last to leave was a priest . . . Suddenly the town had emptied, had turned into a ghost town surrounded by mines.[478]

An HIS-AD agent, 'Giora', visited Beisan on 18 May and reported the town 'completely empty', but for some 300 persons, many of them Muslims. Jewish inspectors had pinned yellow tags on shop doors to signify that they had been checked; Arab inspectors wandered around with yellow armbands. 'Giora' commented that both reminded him of the 'mark of shame' which he 'wished to avoid'. But the officer was pleasantly received by the local Qadi and Mayor Rashad, who both praised the governor's behaviour. But Rashad appeared 'very depressed', 'Giora' commented.[479] On 28 May the remaining inhabitants were given the choice of transfer to Jordan or Nazareth (at the time also outside Jewish territory). The majority, perhaps Christians, preferred Nazareth, to which the IDF trucked them the same day.[480] Beisan had reverted to being Beit Shean.

To keep it Jewish, the Haganah began systematically to mine the approaches and alleyways, to prevent infiltration back. On 10 June, a Haganah commander reported that on the previous night marauding Arabs (and dogs and donkeys) had set off no less than 11 mines, with a commensurate loss of life and injuries.[481] The returning exiles, who also torched and vandalised buildings,[482] were motivated by hunger and poverty.[483]

Influenced by the exodus from the town and pressured by the Haganah, the remaining Arabs, mostly beduin, of the Beit Shean Valley left for Jordan or the Jenin area. The inhabitants of the villages of al Hamidiya, north of town, and al Samiriya, to the south, also fled the country, on 12 May.[484] (Hamidiya had received orders 'from the irregulars' headquarters' to evacuate already on 30 March – but had not complied.)[485] What Weitz and the local settlements had wanted had come to pass. 'For the first time . . . the Beit Shean Valley had become a purely Jewish valley,' wrote David Yizhar, one of the contributors to the official history of Golani's 1948 campaigns.[486]

Acre

Acre, a town of some 12,000–15,000, had been destined in the partition resolution for Arab sovereignty. But from the start, the inhabitants had feared Jewish attack. As in Haifa, most members of the NC, including the mayor, Hussein Halifi, had opposed attacks on Jewish neighbours or traffic, fearing reprisals. But local and foreign irregulars flouted him.[487] On 20 January, members of the NC visited al Sumeiriya, to the north, and cautioned the villagers not to clash with their neighbours, Regba and Shavei Zion, arguing that the Jews could cut the Acre–Lebanon road.[488] Halifi asked the British police to mediate a local ceasefire.[489] But Jewish ambushes outside Acre eventually triggered retaliation by militiamen, in which a Jewish driver was killed. The cycle of violence resulted in the departure from town of 'several families'.[490] In the second half of March, Haganah forces effectively isolated Acre by blowing up a series of bridges, preventing people from going to work and causing an increase in crimes against property.[491] HIS reported that there was no flour to be had, until a large shipment arrived on 8 April. But there were plenty of meat and vegetables.[492] The NC again sought a truce.[493]

The battle for and exodus from Haifa severely disrupted life in Acre. For a fortnight there was almost complete chaos. The Haganah cut off the town's water and electricity and prices skyrocketed. Fuel and flour were in short supply. The NC asked the government for flour. Acre turned overnight into a major refugee way-station and absorption centre. The NC supplied temporary accommodation and free food from emergency stocks.[494] The Haganah attack on 25\26 April, with mortars falling in the town centre, thoroughly unnerved the inhabitants, even though only two were wounded and four houses damaged (and the prison population, 'except the lunatics', escaped).[495] On 26 April, one inhabitant wrote:

> . . . Most [of the population] has left or is about to leave. We may go to Beirut. The preparations for evacuation . . . pertain to all classes: The rich, the middle, and the poor – they are all preparing to leave and are selling everything they can. Following the evacuation of Haifa, Hawassa and Balad al Sheikh . . . the population of Acre has risen to [sic] 50,000 and there is terrible tension in the town.[496]

Haganah intelligence noted the appalling conditions, with refugees sleeping in the mosques and 'in the streets and coffee shops'.[497] The situation was chaotic: The rich had fled, local government had broken down and the town was in the hands of four vying militia groups (headed by Khalil al Kalas, Mahmoud al Saffuri, Musa al Najami, and Ahmad al Tubi).[498] There were 'unemployment, fear, filth and hunger', wrote Carmel.[499] At the end of April, the ALA sent in reinforcements – which further unnerved the population, which saw this as an augury of impending battle.[500]

The fall of Haifa and its repercussions prompted the British to seek to prevent the fall of Acre (as of Jaffa) before their scheduled pullout. At the end of April, the British repeatedly intervened to frustrate Jewish attacks on the town. But the exodus to Lebanon continued. During the first days of May, the British withdrew from the camps around town as part of the pullback into the Haifa enclave, increasing unemployment, which further undermined local morale.[501]

A further precipitant to flight was the outbreak of typhoid (possibly caused, directly or indirectly, by Haganah actions, which forced the inhabitants to dig unsanitary wells).[502] At the end of April, British observers had predicted an outbreak of disease in the overcrowded town.[503] Cunningham feared 'a very large number of cases' of typhoid. Indeed, in early May conditions were such that many refugees wanted to return to Haifa, but were being prevented, according to the British, by 'strong [anti-return Arab] propaganda'. At the same time, Cunningham, the Haganah and the Haifa civil authorities thought such a return from Acre 'inadvisable' precisely because of fear of an epidemic.[504] But the outbreak was contained. HIS estimated that 'the panic that arose following the rumours of the spread of the epidemic' was more important in generating flight than the cases themselves.[505]

By 5–7 May, the situation appears to have stabilised. According to the British, the population was down to '8,000',[506] many of the Haifa refugees having moved on, to Lebanon. Others had been moved off the streets into public buildings; and food distribution was running smoothly. But there was still no electricity or fuel.[507]

Fear of impending Jewish attack and conquest, and the collapse and departure of Acre's leadership helped energise the exodus. The mayor apparently fled (to Lebanon) on 11 May, the local militia commander announced his departure the same day or just after, and most of the NC had already left.[508]

The Haganah offensive in Western Galilee, called Operation Ben-Ami (see below), began on 13 May; Acre fell on 17–18 May. The town's new militia commander, Yunis Naf'a (perhaps accompanied by another Haifa veteran, Amin 'Izz a Din), fled with his troops by boat to Lebanon on 14 May.[509] The inhabitants were reported ready, indeed eager, to surrender but a new commander, with a band of 70 irregulars, appeared on the scene, Mahmoud al Saffuri, and organised the defense of the Old City.[510] During 13–14 May, Haganah ground columns and seaborne units bypassed Acre and captured the Arab villages and positions, including Tel al Fukhar, immediately north and east of the town. Acre was completely surrounded, with no hope of outside relief.

Al Saffuri and his men fled on 16 May.[511] The Haganah that night unleashed a mortar barrage on the militia positions.[512] As Carmeli infantry advanced, an armoured car mounting a loudhailer, in a psychological warfare ploy, predicted the imminent fall of the town and declared that the choice was surrender or suicide. On 17 May, during a lull in the fighting, Carmel sent a POW across the lines with the message that 'we will destroy you to the last man' if the fight continued and demanded surrender.[513] Towards evening, the assault was renewed and the Haganah took the strategic police fort on the northern edge of town;

Carmeli boats machine-gunned the town from the sea. 'Panic took hold in the town and terrible shrieks were heard coming from it', Carmel later related; resistance collapsed. Around midnight, a group of notables and religious leaders emerged from the Old City and asked to surrender the town unconditionally. Carmel presented the usual terms – the handover of arms, the screening of all adult males, and acceptance of Israeli rule. Carmel promised that 'all the local Arabs could stay . . . and carry on with their normal lives'.[514] The Arabs agreed, and early on 18 May, Haganah troops marched in. The Israelis had lost altogether six dead and eight seriously wounded.[515]

The town had been ravaged: There were 'corpses everywhere' (about '60'), and many of the remaining 5,000 population were non-local – refugees from Haifa, Syrian labourers, Egyptians, Sudanese. There were about 50 cases of typhoid. 'Sanitary conditions were appalling', observed an HIS officer. The Haganah organised the re-opening of the water mains and the collection of the corpses; shops and bakeries were opened.[516] Assisted by Arab notables, the Haganah collected arms and radio sets.[517] A military administration was set up, headed by Major Rehav'am Amir, and looting and abuse of the inhabitants were curtailed (though one priest later charged, exaggerating, that for the first fortnight 'there had been rape, pillage and terrorisation of the community' and 'we seemed to be under the Nazis').[518] The only serious atrocity recorded was the rape-murder of a girl and the murder of her father.[519] A nightlong curfew was imposed, the Haganah searched from house to house looking for weapons and ex-irregulars. No expulsion orders were issued and no pressure was exercised on the townspeople to leave.[520] On 25 May the Haganah began shifting families that lived outside the walls into Acre's walled Old City, 'the easier to keep an eye on them'.[521] The head of HIS in the north, 'Hiram', recommended that the refugees – about two thirds of the town's inhabitants – be expelled.[522] Another officer, 'Giora', reported on his unit's work – screening combatants and handing out permits, among other tasks – and stated: 'I don't know what the policy is and if a policy has yet been determined with respect to the treatment [of the local population]'. Meanwhile, he was turning down requests from Haifa refugees to return home.[523]

In the weeks after the conquest, a Red Cross representative described Acre's Arabs as living under a 'regime of terror', with economic life paralysed.[524] An HIS officer said the town was 'almost dead'[525] and the Israel Communist Party daily, *Al Ittihad*, said that Acre's population was living 'in a cage' and being exploited by the collaborationist notables who had remained.[526]

During the First Truce (11 June), the front between the Haganah/IDF and the ALA stretched along a line 7–10 kilometres to the east of Acre. As the truce neared its end and renewed hostilities loomed, IDF Northern Front sought to evict the inhabitants of Acre, either to Jaffa or across the border. The IDF did not want a large Arab civilian concentration just behind its lines and lacked the manpower to oversee and provide for the inhabitants. The army asked the Foreign Ministry's opinion. Ya'akov Shimoni, acting head of the Middle East Department, turned to Foreign Minister Shertok. Shertok, recorded Shimoni, 'had no objection in principle to the transfer of [Acre's] Arab inhabitants to another place (Jaffa), in order to free our soldiers . . .'. But who would care for them? Shimoni approached Shitrit.[527] Shitrit was upset: This was the first he had heard of a possible eviction of Acre's inhabitants – and, after all, they were part of his 'constituency'. Indeed, there was a standing IDF-GS order (of 6 July, see below), he informed Shimoni, that no inhabitants

> were to be uprooted . . . without a written order from the Defence Minister . . . So long as the Defence Minister has not . . . issued a written order, the local army authorities must not evacuate a complete town and cause suffering, wandering and upset to women, children and the old.

The population could not be evicted. Nor, he added, could Jaffa serve as a dumping ground for transferees. And his ministry could not care for their maintenance. Lastly, Jaffa's empty houses were needed for resettling Jews.[528]

And Shitrit did not limit himself to argumentation; he sought and obtained the powerful support of Finance Minister Kaplan. Kaplan called the eviction proposal 'strange'.[529] Shitrit had made a stand and, in effect, dared Ben-Gurion to issue an explicit transfer order. Ben-Gurion backed down and shelved the idea. It is worth noting that throughout 1948, Ben-Gurion had always avoided personally issuing explicit expulsion or transfer orders.

THE COUNTRYSIDE

During the exodus from the countryside, Weitz visited the area around Kibbutz Mishmar Ha'emek. He found the Arab villages 'in ruins. No one has remained. The houses and huts are completely destroyed . . . Among the ruins echoed the cries of an abandoned chicken, and a miserable and orphaned ass strayed along the village paths.' Why did the Arabs leave?

> Out of a psychosis of fear . . . Village after village was abandoned in a panic that cannot be explained . . . The villages of the Coastal Plain are steadily emptying. Between Tel Aviv and Hadera, you won't find today a single Arab. During the past days multitudes left the large villages around Tel Aviv.

It was for the good. Weitz reasoned that 'the very presence of many refugees among the Arabs weakens their position and brings nearer our victory'.[530]

Like the exodus from the towns, the evacuation of the countryside in April–June closely followed, and was largely precipitated by, Jewish offensives. The exodus almost completely followed the sequence of Jewish attacks in each area, but it was Arab military pressure in key areas that forced the Haganah prematurely to launch these offensives, which, in retrospect, were to be seen as the beginning of the implementation of Plan D, and which involved for the first time the conquest and permanent occupation of swathes of territory and the eviction of clusters of Arab communities.

OPERATION NAHSHON

During December 1947 – March 1948, irregulars and militiamen from the villages dominating the eastern half of the Tel Aviv – Jerusalem road (including Deir Muheisin, Beit Mahsir, Suba, al Qastal and Qaluniya) had intermittently attacked Jewish traffic to and from Jerusalem. By late March, Jewish Jerusalem, despite occasional British intervention, was under siege, its 100,000 inhabitants sorely pressed for food, fuel and munitions.

On the night of 31 March – 1 April, Ben-Gurion and the HGS decided that the Haganah's first priority was to relieve the pressure on Jerusalem. Representatives of Jerusalem's Jews had appealed to the JA for 'real action'. The community was 'already hungry and if, heaven forbid, their morale should break there was a danger of a general collapse of the Haganah front line'.[531] At Ben-Gurion's insistence, a force of 1,500 troops was mobilised for the largest Jewish offensive to date. The objective was to push several large convoys through to Jerusalem. Strategically speaking, as a senior Haganah officer later put it, Nahshon marked the transitional stage between the prior, defensive, 'policing' approach of safeguarding Jewish convoys by manning them with guards and the 'military' approach of protecting the convoys by conquering and holding the routes themselves and the heights dominating them.[532] In the course of Nahshon, which lasted two weeks, the Haganah groped its way to a new strategy.

Giv'ati Brigade OC Shimon Avidan was appointed OC Operation Nahshon. A profound hesitancy imbues his initial operational orders. His first, of 2 April, speaks of merely placing 'ambushes' near Arab villages that served as militia bases in order to prevent irregulars from reaching and attacking the convoys.[533] But the 'real' operational order, of 3 or 4 April, is also equivocal about the objectives. The preamble states that 'all the Arab villages along the [Khulda–Jerusalem] axis were to be treated as enemy assembly or jump-off bases'. (Plan D had specified that villages so defined, if offering resistance, should be destroyed and their inhabitants expelled.) The Nahshon orders called, during the first stage of the operation, for the conquest of three Arab villages at the western entrance to the Jerusalem corridor – Deir Muheisin, Khulda and Seidun. But elsewhere, the order spoke only of setting up ambushes or hilltop positions near villages (such as Saris and Beit Thul), to prevent their militiamen from reaching the road or the evacuated British Army base at Wadi Sarar.[534] The order aptly reflected the ambiguity that briefly prevailed in the high command with respect to the treatment of Arab villages. On 2 April, Galili had spoken of a shift from a diffuse defence to a concentrated offence, with the Haganah embarking on 'operations of conquest and occupation'.[535] But on 5 April, he succinctly wrote: 'An order [has been issued] to take control of the villages from Jerusalem to Sha'ar Hagai [*bab al wad*] if the villages have been abandoned [by their inhabitants] and if a clash with the [British] Army [can be avoided].'[536] And the day before, Yadin, OC Haganah\Operations, was empowered to instruct the Nahshon troops 'to try so far as possible to take up positions near villages and not to conquer them. If no such possibility exists – then conquer them.'[537] Yadin was still perturbed by the notion of conquering villages and queried his political masters. Galili responded:

> 1) If securing the Jerusalem road requires that our units take control of villages whose inhabitants have abandoned them – it must be done.
> 2) Regarding villages not abandoned by their inhabitants and that securing the road requires that they be isolated and surrounded and intimidated by our units – it should be done.

If the British Army intervened and ordered the Haganah to evacuate villages, the Haganah should use delaying tactics – but ultimately, it must comply.[538] Underlying these equivocations was fear of British intervention.

Operation Nahshon began, in effect, with the Palmah Fourth Battalion's unopposed conquest of al Qastal on the night of 2\3 April. The village, which dominated the approach to Jerusalem, had for weeks been involved in hostilities. On 16 March it was raided by Palmah troops. On 1 April, militiamen attacked Jewish positions around Motza. Haganah counter-fire and fear of assault resulted in the flight that night of almost all of Qastal's inhabitants. The Haganah feared that foreign irregulars would occupy the village, so Palmah troops moved in in the early hours of 3 April.[539] The troops were instructed that 'if there is no opposition, do not to blow up the village's houses'. This conformed to the Plan D guideline not to destroy villages that offered no resistance. The commander at the site appealed against the order, saying that leaving the houses intact made 'the defence of the place difficult'.[540] But permission to raze the village was not granted; the local Palmah company commander, Uri Ben-Ari, was subsequently to define the non-demolition of the village as 'a decisive mistake'.[541] And, indeed, on 8 April, the site was retaken by Arab irregulars following repeated assaults; among the dozens of Arabs killed was 'Abd al Qadir al Husseini, the Palestinian Jerusalem District

OC, who was shot while walking toward a Palmah-held house during a lull in the fighting.[542] The 'mistake' – of not demolishing Qastal after its initial conquest – was rectified on 9 April, after the village fell to a renewed Palmah attack: 'The blowing up of all the houses not needed for defence of the site was immediately begun', reported the commander.[543]

The lesson of Qastal was extended to other sites. On 11 April Palmah units conquered neighbouring Qaluniya, whose inhabitants had fled on 2 April. The village was held by foreign irregulars. The attackers were ordered to kill everyone they found and to blow up the village. Some Arabs may have died in the attack; others, it would appear, possibly including two Egyptians, an Iraqi and an Englishman (identified by the Palmah as 'Taylor?') found at the site, were captured and executed. Haganah units spent that day and the next blowing up the village. The demolition, involving some 55 houses in all, 'made a great impression in the area . . .'.[544] A western journalist accompanied the troops:

> When I left, sappers were blowing up the houses. One after another, the solid stone buildings . . . exploded and crashed. Within sight of Jerusalem I still heard the explosions rolling through the hills; and in between, somewhere in the lonely distance, still rose the half-hearted barking of the village dog.[545]

On 6 April – the official start of Nahshon – Khulda and Deir Muheisin fell to Haganah forces. After the battles for Qastal, the hesitancy regarding the fate of the villages gave way to a growingly definite resolution, with an appropriate shift in the terminology employed. By 10 April, Haganah orders explicitly called for the 'liquidation' [hisul] of villages.[546] By 14 April, Operation Nahshon HQ, within the context of 'cleansing [tihur]' operations, generally ordered 'the continuation of intimidation and cleansing activities as a first stage in operations [geared to] the destruction and conquest of enemy forces and bases [i.e., villages]'. The order posited the 'blowing up' of the enemy 'bases' of 'al Qubeib, 'Aqir, Biddu, Beit Surik, Beit Iksa, Beit Mahsir and Suba', and Ramle.[547] On 15 April, Nahshon HQ issued a series of specific orders: Battalion 2 was ordered 'to attack with the aim of annihilation and destruction and arson [litkof bimegamat hashmada veheres vehatzata]' the village of Beit Suriq.[548] Battalion 1 was ordered to attack 'with the aim of annihilation and destruction and temporary occupation' the village of Beit Jiz and to destroy 'at least seven houses' in al Qubeib.[549] Battalion 3 was ordered to annihilate and destroy the village of Sajad.[550] On 16 April, Nahshon forces conquered and blew up Saris, 'including [the] mosque and school', before withdrawing.[551] The operation in effect ended with raids on Biddu and Beit Surik on 19–20 April and the levelling of (Arab) Khulda by bulldozers on 20 April.

Operation Nahshon was a strategic watershed, characterised by an intention and effort to clear a whole area, permanently, of hostile or potentially hostile villages. The destruction of the Jerusalem Corridor villages both symbolized and finalized the change in Haganah strategy. The change was epitomised in the successive orders regarding Qastal: The Etzioni Brigade order, of 2 April, not to destroy the village if there was no resistance, was superceded by the orders of 8–10 to level the village (and neighbouring Qaluniya). In practice, the Plan D provision to leave intact non-resisting villages was superceded by the decision to destroy villages in strategic areas or along crucial routes regardless of whether or not they were resisting. The Qastal episode had powerfully and expensively demonstrated why the harsher course had to be adopted; intact villages could quickly revert to becoming Arab bases. Initially, the architects of Nahshon, mindful of possible British intervention, had thought of securing the road by occupying positions on dominant hillsides and in abandoned villages and by positioning ambushes near villages from which militia bands might strike. But mid-way through the operation, HGS and Nahshon HQ changed strategy, ordering the occupation and destruction of villages that were or might represent a threat to the convoys. Indeed, from 9–10 April onwards, the emphasis of Nahshon HQ orders was on levelling villages. Levelling villages, of course, assumed the evacuation or expulsion of their inhabitants – and assured that they, and irregulars, would have nowhere to return to.

The strategic change represented by the evolving nature of the Operation Nahshon orders had a wider significance. If, at the start of the war, the Yishuv had been (reluctantly) willing to countenance a Jewish State with a large, peaceful Arab minority, by April the Haganah's thinking had radically changed: The toll on Jewish life and security in the battle of the roads and the dire prospect of pan-Arab invasion had left the Yishuv with very narrow margins of safety. It could not afford to leave pockets of actively or potentially hostile Arabs behind its lines. This was certainly true regarding vital roads and areas such as the Jerusalem Corridor. No comprehensive expulsion directive was ever issued; no hard and fast orders went out to front, brigade and battalion commanders to expel 'the Arabs' or level 'the Arab villages'. But the demographic by-product and implications of the implementation of Plan D were understood and accepted by the majority of Haganah commanders at this juncture, when the Yishuv faced, and knew it faced, a life and death struggle. The gloves had to be, and were, taken off. The process of taking off the gloves is embodied in the shift in Nahshon orders from hesitancy (3–6 April) to village levelling, expulsive resolve (8–15 April).

Operation Nahshon was partially successful. It briefly opened the Tel Aviv – Jerusalem road and enabled the Haganah to push through three large supply convoys to the besieged city. But the hills and some villages were quickly reinvested by irregulars and the door to Jerusalem once again slammed shut. So Nahshon was followed, in the second half of April and in May, by operations Harel, Yevussi and Maccabi, all aimed at re-securing and widening the Jewish-held corridor and wresting from Arab control further areas in and around Jerusalem. The units involved were ordered to raid or occupy and destroy a swathe of neighbour-hoods and villages north and west of the city centre, including Shu'fat, Sheikh Jarrah, Nabi Samwil, Beit Iksa, Beit Hanina and Beit Mahsir. The HGS operational order for 'Yevussi − Stage A' called for the 'conquest and destruction' (kibush vehashmada) of Sheikh Jarrah and Shu'fat, respectively a north Jerusalem neighbourhood and a satellite village to its north.[552] The scope of the operation was expanded in the Harel Brigade's orders to its battalions to take and hold the small hilltop vil-lage of Nabi Samwil, and to destroy Shu'fat and the village of Beit Iksa, all north-northwest of Jerusalem, and possibly also the neighbouring village of Beit Hanina.[553] On 22 April, Palmah units duly attacked, occu-pied and partially demolished Shu'fat and Beit Iksa;[554] on 24 April, they attacked and partially demolished Sheikh Jarrah.[555]

But, ironically, it was not the Haganah's Operation Nahshon and its follow-ups but a small IZL–LHI operation − undertaken with the reluctant, qualified consent of the Haganah[556] − which had the most lasting effect of any single event of the war in precipitating the Palestinian exodus. On 9 April, 80 IZL and 40 LHI troopers, for part of the battle supported by Haganah machine-gunners from nearby Givat Shaul and two Palmah ar-moured car squads,[557] attacked and took Deir Yassin, which, as we have seen, had signed a non-belligerency pact with its Jewish neighbours and repeatedly had barred entry to foreign irregulars. The operation loosely meshed with the Nahshon objective of securing the western approaches to Jerusalem.

The attackers encountered unexpectedly strong resistance and, be-ing relatively inexperienced, suffered four dead and several dozen wounded before pacifying the village after a full day of fighting. The units had advanced from house to house, lobbing grenades and spraying the interiors with fire, in the routine procedure of house-to-house combat.[558] They blew up several houses with explosives.[559] The attackers shot down individuals and families as they left their homes and fled down alleyways.[560] They apparently also rounded up villagers, who included militiamen and unarmed civilians of both sexes, and murdered them, and executed prisoners in a nearby quarry. On 12 April, HIS OC in Jerusalem, Yitzhak Levy, reported:

> The conquest of the village was carried out with great cruelty. Whole families − women, old people, children − were killed . . . Some of the prisoners moved to places of detention, including women and children, were murdered viciously by their captors.[561]

The following day he added: 'LHI members tell of the barbaric behaviour of the IZL toward the prisoners and the dead. They also relate that the IZL men raped a number of Arab girls and murdered them afterward (we don't know if this is true).'[562] The HIS operative on the spot, Mordechai Gichon, reported on 10 April:

> Their [i.e., the IZL?] commander says that the [initial] order was: To take prisoner the adult males and to send the women and children to Motza. In the afternoon [of 9 April], the order was changed and became to kill all the prisoners . . . The adult males were taken to town in trucks and paraded in the city streets, then taken back to the site and killed with rifle and machine-gun fire. Before they [i.e., other inhabitants] were put on the trucks, the IZL and LHI men . . . took from them all the jewelry and stole their money. The behaviour toward them was especially barbaric [and included] kicks, shoves with rifle butts, spitting and cursing (people from Givat Shaul took part in the torture).

Gichon reported that the HIS's 'regular informer', 'the mukhtar's son', was 'executed [in front of his mother and sisters] after being taken prisoner'.[563] Meir Pa'il, a Palmah intelligence officer who claimed to have spent part of the afternoon of 9 April in Deir Yassin as a 'guest' of the LHI, reported on 10 April:

> In the quarry near Givat Shaul I saw the five Arabs they had paraded in the streets of the city. They had been murdered and were lying one on top of the other . . . I saw with my own eyes several families [that had been] murdered with their women, children and old people, their corpses were lying on top of each other . . . The dissidents were going about the village robbing and stealing everything: Chickens, radio sets, sugar, money, gold and more . . . Each dissident walked about the village dirty with blood and proud of the number of persons he had killed. Their lack of education and intelligence as compared to our soldiers [i.e., the Haganah] was apparent . . . In one of the houses at the centre of the village were assembled some 200 women and small children. The women sat quietly and didn't utter a word. When I arrived, the 'commander' explained that they intended to kill all of them. [But] in the evening I heard that the women and children had been transported and released in Musrara.[564]

Several inhabitants, who had hidden or pretended to be dead, were apparently killed by LHI men on 10 or 11 April.[565]

Altogether about 100–120 villagers died that day.[566] The IZL and LHI troops subsequently transported the remaining villagers in trucks in a victory parade through west Jerusalem before dumping them in the Musrara Quarter, outside the Old City walls.[567] The weight of the evidence suggests that the dissidents did not go in with the intention of committing a massacre but lost their heads during the protracted combat. But from the first, the IZL's intention had been to expel the inhabitants.

The massacre was immediately condemned by the mainstream Jewish authorities, including the Haganah,[568] the Chief Rabbinate,[569] and the JA; the agency also sent a letter of condemnation, apology and condolence to King Abdullah.[570]

News of what had happened immediately reached the Mandate authorities, the Arab states and the West through the survivors who reached east Jerusalem, and Zionist and Red Cross officials. For days and weeks thereafter, the Arab media broadcast the tale of horror and atrocity as a means of rallying public opinion and governments against the Yishuv.[571] Cunningham wrote that 'the bitterness resulting from the massacre has produced an atmosphere in which local Arabs are little inclined to call off hostilities'. The massacre and the way it was trumpeted in the Arab media added to the pressure on the Arab states' leaders to aid the embattled Palestinians and hardened their resolve to invade Palestine. The news had aroused great public indignation – which the leaders were unable to ignore. However, the most important immediate effect of the massacre and of the media atrocity campaign that followed was to trigger and promote fear and further panic flight from Palestine's villages and towns.[572] Later, in trying to justify their actions, the IZL latched onto this side-effect of Deir Yassin: It had promoted

> terror and dread among the Arabs in all the villages around; in al Maliha, Qaluniya and Beit Iksa a panic flight began that facilitates the renewal of road communications . . . between the capital [Jerusalem] and the rest of the country.[573]

On 14 April, an IZL radio broadcast repeated the message: The surrounding villages had been evacuated because of Deir Yassin. 'In one blow we changed the strategic situation of our capital', boasted the organisation.[574] A few months later, the LHI declared: 'Everybody knows that it was Deir Yassin that struck terror into the hearts of the Arab masses and caused their stampede . . .'[575] Begin, who denied that civilians had been massacred, later recalled that the 'Arab propaganda' campaign had sowed fear among the Arabs and 'the legend was worth half a dozen battalions to the forces of Israel . . . Panic overwhelmed the Arabs of Eretz Yisrael . . . [It] helped us in particular in . . . Tiberias and the conquest of Haifa.'[576]

IZL leaders may have had an interest, then and later, in exaggerating the panic-generating effects of Deir Yassin, but they were certainly not far off the mark. In the Jerusalem Corridor area, the effect was certainly immediate and profound. Haganah intelligence reported on 14 April that the episode was 'the talk of the Old City' and the horrors were being amplified and exaggerated in the Arab retelling.[577] More specifically, HIS reported that 'fear of Deir Yassin' had fallen upon the village of al Fureidis, which immediately appealed to the Haifa NC for arms.[578] In Beit Iksa, Deir Yassin had triggered 'fright' and the start of evacuation.[579] The same happened in al Maliha,[580] and the villagers of Fajja, near Petah Tikva, and Mansura, near Ramle, contacted their Jewish neighbours and promised quiet.[581] In Yajur, near Haifa, the inhabitants decided to evacuate and their neighbours in Balad al Sheikh and Hawassa sought advice from Haifa's leadership.[582] In Haifa, noted Ben-Gurion, news of Deir Yassin had propelled Muslims into flight.[583] Khirbet 'Azzun, in the Coastal Plain, was evacuated because of 'the inability to guarantee that what happened in Deir Yassin wouldn't also happen here.'[584] The British noted that the Haganah, whether or not involved in Deir Yassin, had 'profited from it. The violence used so impressed Arabs all over the country that an attack by Haganah on Saris met with no opposition whatsoever.'[585] More generally, in May and June Mapam's leaders assessed that Deir Yassin had been one of the two pivotal events in the exodus of Palestine's Arabs (the other was the fall of Arab Haifa).[586] This, more or less, was also the judgement of HIS-AD, which, in its mid-war report on the causes and nature of the exodus, defined Deir Yassin as a 'decisive accelerating factor' (*gorem mezarez machri'a*) in the general evacuation. 'Deir Yassin . . . greatly influenced the thinking of the Arab', especially in the centre and south of the country, it stated.[587]

THE BATTLE OF MISHMAR HA'EMEK

The battle of Mishmar Ha'emek, over 4–15 April, was initiated by Qawuqji's ALA. It began as a desperate Jewish defence and turned into a Haganah counteroffensive conforming with Plan D guidelines. The available evidence indicates that here, for the first time, Ben-Gurion explicitly sanctioned the expulsion of Arabs from a whole area of Palestine (though, as we shall see, the expulsion was largely preempted by mass flight sparked by the fighting).

The battle began on 4 April when the ALA shelled and attempted to take Mishmar Ha'emek, the Mapam (Hashomer Hatza'ir) kibbutz which sat astride the Jenin–Haifa road, which the Haganah commanders regarded as one of the most likely routes for a major Arab attack on the Yishuv on or after 15 May. The kibbutz members, backed by Haganah reinforcements, beat off the attack. The subsequent shelling in which much of the kibbutz was destroyed was stopped by a British column that arrived on the scene. The ALA attack, especially after its failure, was viewed with trepidation and distaste by at least some local Arabs. The locals were also 'frightened of [the ALA] and do what they are told. The officers of the ALA treat the locals like dirt', reported one British officer.[588]

On 7 April, the ALA agreed to cease fire for 24 hours and called on the kibbutz to surrender its weapons and submit to Arab rule. During the ceasefire, the kibbutz evacuated its children.[589] At the same time, the

Arab commanders – and the British intermediary – demanded that the Jews promise 'not to take reprisals against local villages' or traffic.[590] The kibbutz responded that it would not attack the neighbouring villages but could not vouch for Haganah forces outside. In any case, the kibbutz leaders said, they needed to consult Tel Aviv.[591] A few hours later they added: 'The men of Mishmar [Ha'emek] have agreed to nothing.'[592]

Meanwhile, on 8 or 9 April, as the HGS hastily began to organise a counteroffensive, a delegation of Mishmar Ha'emek leaders came to Ben-Gurion and, according to Ben-Gurion,

> said that it was imperative to expel the Arabs [in the area] and to burn the villages. For me, the matter was very difficult. [But] they said that they were not sure [the kibbutz could hold out] if the villages remained intact and [if] the Arab inhabitants were not expelled, for they [i.e., the villagers] would [later] attack them and burn mothers and children.

Ben-Gurion related this story in July, within the context of polemics with Mapam, which was accusing him of implementing a policy of expulsion. He charged the Mapam leaders with hypocrisy, arguing that during Mishmar Ha'emek they had come to realise that ideology (i.e., Jewish–Arab brotherhood) was one thing and strategic necessity another. 'They faced a cruel reality . . . [and] saw that there was [only] one way and that was to expel the Arab villagers and burn the villages. And they did this. And they were the first to do this.'[593]

In reality, HGS began thinking of destroying the villages around the kibbutz shortly after Qawuqji launched his attack. On 5 April, HGS\Operations instructed the Golani Brigade: 'You must tell the following villages . . . that we cannot assure their safety and security, and that they must evacuate forthwith.' Among the four villages named were Abu Shusha, next to Mishmar Ha'emek, and Daliyat al Ruha and Rihaniya, 4–5 kilometres to the west-northwest.[594]

Ben-Gurion and HGS decided to reject the ALA proposal, to mount a comprehensive counterattack, and to drive the ALA and the Arab inhabitants out of the area and level their villages, permanently removing the threat to Mishmar Ha'emek and denying an invading force from Jenin easy passage to Haifa. On 8–9 April, Yitzhak Sadeh, the Palmah's founder, was dispatched to head the ragtag collection of units mustered for the counteroffensive. In the planning session for the counteroffensive at Kibbutz Hazore'a, the assembled officers spoke specifically of 'cleansing' Abu Shusha and nearby Abu Zureiq.

Initially, in the counteroffensive, Haganah units took a village (at night), partially destroyed it and left in the morning (in deference to Qawuqji's artillery capabilities). But from midday 10 April, the Haganah took and permanently occupied villages.[595] The bulk of the Arab inhabitants fled before or during each attack. The villages were then razed and the remaining inhabitants expelled toward Jenin.

In the course of the battle, ALA units – demoralised by reports of Deir Yassin and the death of 'Abd al Qadir al Husseini[596] – often retreated first, abandoning the villagers.[597] Al Ghubayya al Tahta, al Ghubayya al Fawqa and Khirbet Beit Ras were raided by Haganah forces on 8–9 April and blown up piecemeal during the following days.[598] On 9 April, Haganah units raided Abu Shusha; most of the villagers had already fled.[599] Those who had remained behind were expelled. The village was partially razed. On the night of 11\12 April Palmah units took al Kafrin, which was found empty, and Abu Zureiq, where some 15 adult males and some 200 women and children were taken captive, and occupied Abu Shusha. Some 30 of Kafrin's houses were blown up that day and some of Abu Zureiq's houses were blown up that night.[600] The women and children of Abu Zureiq were expelled.[601] The last houses in Abu Zureiq were demolished by 15 April.[602] During the night of 12\13 April, Palmah units occupied Ghubayya al Fawqa and attacked al Mansi and al Naghnaghiya, southeast of Mishmar Ha'emek.[603] Mansi and Naghnaghiya were evacuated by the Arabs on 15 April.[604] The villages were blown up during the following days. According to the Mishmar Ha'emek logbook, by 15 April, 'all the villages in the area [more or less] as far as the eye can see [had] been evacuated'.[605] Most of the villagers reached the Jenin area and sheltered in makeshift tents.[606] They appealed to the AHC:

> Thousands of poor women and children from the villages of Abu Zureiq and Mansi and Ghubayya and Kafrin and other places near the colony of Mishmar Ha'emek, whose houses the Jews have destroyed and whose babies and old people [the Jews] have killed, are now in the villages around Jenin without help and dying of hunger. We ask you to repair the situation . . . and do everything to quickly send forces of vengeance against the Jews and restore us to our lands.[607]

The battle of Mishmar Ha'emek was over. But there were some follow-up operations. On the night of 15\16 April, Palmah units raided and blew up much of the large village of al Lajjun. 'The area between our bases [in Ramot Menashe] and the Wadi 'Ara road is [now] empty of Arabs', reported Palmah HQ on 16 April.[608] On 19 April, a Palmah unit held a built-up area combat exercise in Kafrin. At the end of the training session, the village was leveled.[609]

The battle of Mishmar Ha'emek had left a bitter taste in the mouths of some of the local kibbutzniks. On 14 April, Eliezer Bauer (Be'eri), a Middle East scholar and member of Hazore'a (Mapam), dispatched a pained letter to senior Mapam defence figures:

> Of course in a cruel war such as we are engaged in, one cannot act with kid gloves. But there are still rules in war which a civilised people tries to follow . . . [Bauer focused on events in Abu Zureiq a day or two earlier.] When the village was conquered, the villagers tried to escape

and save themselves by fleeing to the fields of the [Jezreel] Valley. Forces from the nearby settlements sortied out and outflanked them. There were exchanges of fire in which several of these Arabs were killed. Others surrendered or were captured unarmed. Most were killed [i.e., murdered]. And these were not gang members as was later written in [the Mapam daily] *Al Hamishmar* but defenceless, beaten peasants. Only members of my kibbutz [Hazore'a] took prisoners . . . Also in the village, when adult males were discovered hiding hours after the end of the battle – they were killed . . . It is said that there were also cases of rape, but it is possible that this is only one of those made-up tales of 'heroism' that soldiers are prone to. Afterwards, all the village's houses and the well were blown up . . . Of the property in the houses and the farm animals left without minders, they took what they could: One took a kettle for coffee, another a horse, a third a cow . . . One may understand and justify, if they took cows from the village for Mishmar Ha'emek for example, or if soldiers who conquered the village would slaughter and fry chickens for themselves. But if every farmer from a nearby moshava [the allusion is to Yoqne'am] takes part in looting, that is nothing but theft . . .

Bauer called on the Mapam leaders to make sure that the troops were ordered to abide by the Geneva Conventions.[610]

Bauer's letter, and the events described, were roundly discussed in the general members' meetings at Hazore'a on 18 and 20 April. One member, Yosef Shatil, spoke out against the looting; another, 'Arnon', said he was not happy with what had happened to Abu Zureiq and nearby Qira wa Qamun; 'Fritzie' condemned the cruel treatment meted out to the prisoners at Abu Zureiq. But Fritzie added, at the second meeting, that the members should refrain from 'argument about transfer'.[611]

Though here and there irregulars had fought bravely, Weitz rather accurately described what had happened around Mishmar Ha'emek and what was happening nationwide:

Our army is steadily conquering Arab villages and their inhabitants are afraid and flee like mice. You have no idea what happened in the Arab villages. It is enough that during the night several shells whistle overhead and they flee for their lives. Villages are steadily emptying, and if we continue on this course – and we shall certainly do so as our strength increases – then tens of villages will empty of their inhabitants. This time these self-confident ones, too, will feel what it is like to be refugees. Maybe they will understand us.[612]

An epilogue to the battle was provided by the IZL, whose units from Zikhron Ya'akov, Hadera, Binyamina and Netanya on 12 May attacked and cleared the last Arab villages in the Hills of Menashe, overlooking Mishmar Ha'emek from the west. The dissidents attacked Sabbarin, al Sindiyana, Bureika, Khubbeiza and Umm al Shauf. Many villagers had fled during the previous weeks.[613] Sabbarin had been ordered by Umm al Fahm's leaders to stay put.[614] But most of the remaining villagers fled as the Jewish forces approached and laid down mortar fire. At Sindiyana, whose inhabitants continued until early May 1948 to work in Zikhron Ya'akov and which had barred Syrian irregulars,[615] the mukhtar and some 300 inhabitants stayed put and raised a white flag. A few days before they had proposed to their Jewish neighbours that they jointly 'stage' a Jewish attack on themselves, which would enable them to surrender honourably.[616] Nonetheless, they were driven out. At Sabbarin, where the IZL met resistance, the villagers fled after 20 died in the firefight; an IZL armoured car fired at the fleeing villagers. More than one hundred old people, women and children, who had stayed, were held for a few days behind barbed wire, and then expelled to Umm al Fahm, in Arab-held territory to the southeast. An IZL officer at Umm al Shauf later recalled searching a column of refugees and finding a pistol and rifle. The troops detained seven young adult males and sent the rest of the column on its way. The troops demanded to know who the weapons belonged to. When the detainees refused to own up, the IZL men threatened them with death. When no one owned up, the IZL officers held 'a field court martial . . . which sentenced the seven to death'. The seven were executed.[617]

The villagers of Umm al Zinat, just north of Rihaniya, had remained peaceful during the civil war and had hosted no foreign irregulars. Following the Arab defeat at Mishmar Ha'emek and the fall of Arab Haifa, some villagers had fled.[618] By 7 May, some 400 adult males remained.[619] Golani units took the village on 15 May[620] and found it empty, but for the mukhtar, Yusuf al Isa, and a dozen or so adult males. Golani ordered them out, along with the remaining women and children.[621] In early August, Haganah troops scoured the village, with orders to kill males and expel females. The soldiers captured a number of males, executed at least two, and expelled several women.[622]

Qannir, near Sabbarin, was abandoned by most of its women and children, apparently on orders from Arab authorities, on 22–24 April.[623] On 9 May, Alexandroni troops raided the village, killed four Arabs and blew up 55 houses;[624] the remaining population probably fled.

THE BATTLE OF RAMAT YOHANAN

As the battle of Mishmar Ha'emek raged to the south, an ALA battalion took up positions in Shafa 'Amr, Khirbet Kasayir and Hawsha, about 10 kilometres east of Haifa, and intermittently attacked Jewish traffic and settlements, including Ramat Yohanan;[625] perhaps Qawuqji wished to take pressure off the Mishmar Ha'emek area. The Carmeli Brigade was ordered to take Hawsha and Khirbet Kasayir which it did on the morning of 16 April. The inhabitants fled. The Carmeli units then beat off repeated, courageous but ineffective counterattacks by the ALA's Druse Battalion, commanded by Shakib Wahab, and then levelled the two villages and destroyed satellite hamlets, including Khirbet Sasa.[626] The ALA defeat resulted in mass flight from Shafa 'Amr[627] and, no doubt, helped demoralize the Arabs of Haifa, who were about to face Carmeli's troops.

THE COASTAL PLAIN

As we have seen, most of the Arabs of the Coastal Plain north of Tel Aviv evacuated their homes and villages during the preceding months. April and May witnessed the completion of that exodus, save for several isolated villages that were allowed to remain (Jisr Zarqa and Fureidis) or were conquered by the IDF only in July (Tira, 'Ein Ghazal, Jab'a and Ijzim). The April–May evacuations were prompted by a sense of vulnerability and weakness, fear of attack, and actual attacks, pressure and expulsion orders, as well as pressure by Arab irregulars commanders.

As we have seen, the new Haganah policy in the area, of clearing out the Arab inhabitants, was enunciated at the meeting of Alexandroni Brigade's Arab affairs advisers on 6 April.[628] The Arabs remaining in Khirbet 'Azzun (Tabsar), near Ra'anana, had been ordered by the Haganah on 3 April to leave and departed on 16 April.[629] The inhabitants of the small village of Bayyarat Hannun, south of Netanya, left at the start of April.[630] The remaining beduin around Hadera – the 'Arab al Fuqara, 'Arab an Nufei'at and 'Arab al Dumeira – were all ordered to leave on 10 April;[631] the Nufeiat left by the 13th.[632] A similar order was issued on 15 April by the Haganah to the inhabitants of Khirbet as Sarkas, a friendly Circassian community east of Hadera that had three times defied AHC orders to evacuate its women and children.[633] The evacuation of the village's women and children took place on 20–22 April.[634] The men probably left a few days later. At this time, the inhabitants of Khirbet Zalafa and Khirbet Manshiya, south of Hadera, also evacuated eastwards, apparently after reaching an agreement with Haganah representatives that Jewish settlements would safeguard their property and allow them to return after the war. In the case of Khirbet Manshiya, the local HIS officer, Aharon Braverman, of Kibbutz 'Ein Hahoresh, it seems pleaded with the villagers to stay and accept Haganah protection, but to no avail. On the other hand, the traditionally-hostile inhabitants of Khirbet Zalafa, were not asked to stay and were probably pressured to leave.[635] The inhabitants of Khirbet Beit Lid, east of Netanya, whose inhabitants had fled and returned to their homes in mid-December 1947, had been ordered by the Haganah to evacuate in early April and by the 16th had departed.[636]

The inhabitants of the large village of Miska, northeast of Qalqilya, had enjoyed a special dispensation and in early April were allowed to stay.[637] But on the 19th, after sniping from the village and several

Haganah dead, the headman of neighbouring Kibbutz Ramat Hakovesh ordered the inhabitants 'to depart within two hours'. The order was softened by members of the Committee for Arab Property, who proposed, instead, that the villagers hand over their arms, accept Jewish rule, and move inland, to Khirbet al Zababida, inside the Jewish area. But they refused and opted for evacuation eastwards. On 20–21 April, the villagers departed, as described in one Yishuv logbook: 'That day and the next the movement of motor vehicles, donkeys and camels from Miska to Tira did not cease.' Haganah troops moved in on the evening of the 21st.[638]

Back in early March 1948, Tawfiq Abu Kishk had succeeded in mediating a nonaggression pact between the Arab village of Biyar Adas and neighbouring Magdiel, northeast of Ramatayim.[639] But LHI gunmen, firing from Magdiel, repeatedly broke the ceasefire[640] and many families departed, the menfolk returning only in the daytime to cultivate the fields.[641] By 12 April the village had been evacuated.[642] A few days later, a few kilometres to the south, the small village of Jaramla was evacuated 'out of fear of Jewish assault'.[643] In early April, in view of the impending harvest, the large village of Fajja, bordering on Petah Tikva, had sued for a truce with its Jewish neighbours.[644] But the inhabitants were under pressure from the ALA, which demanded that they sever their ties with the Jews[645] and contribute 'volunteers' for the 'gangs'. The mukhtar, Abdullah al Haj, was reluctant, fearing retaliation,[646] and was interrogated by the ALA commanders in Ras al 'Ein.[647] The villagers evacuated just after 10 April, but a handful returned a few days later, to mount guard.[648] They were fearful both of the ALA and the Jews, who periodically pillaged the empty houses.[649] The Haganah regarded the Arabs who remained 'a bothersome factor' and decided on the complete evacuation of the village, as well as of the nearby hamlet Nabi Thari.[650] Abdullah al Haj, meanwhile, was regarded as a traitor and arrested and 'severely tortured' by the ALA.[651] In the end, on 15 May, the Haganah used psychological warfare and warnings (ta'amulat lahash) to drive out the remaining inhabitants of Fajja.[652]

By the beginning of May, few Arabs were left in the Coastal Plain. Alexandroni's Arab affairs experts, in preparation for the declaration of statehood and the expected pan-Arab invasion, on 9 May decided to immediately 'expel or subdue' the villages of Kafr Saba, al Tira, Qaqun, Qalansuwa and Tantura.[653]

Tira and Qalansuwa were not conquered (and were transferred to Israeli sovereignty only in May 1949, as part of the Israeli–Jordanian armistice agreement). But on 13 May Alexandroni units took Kafr Saba, prompting a mass evacuation. The village had lived in 'dread' of Haganah assault for some time, and was guarded by a small ALA detachment.[654] Nonetheless, the attack caught them by surprise and triggered a 'panic flight'. The local Syrian ALA commander stood at the exit to the village and extorted P£5 from each evacuee.[655] Nine old men and women, incapable of speedy flight or of paying up, were left in the village[656] and were later expelled. Due to this panic-bearing influx and to Israeli harassing attacks, Qalqilya was almost completely (albeit only temporarily) evacuated and many notables fled Tulkarm.[657]

Tantura, a large coastal village south of Haifa, was conquered by Alexandroni's 33rd Battalion on the night of 22\23 May. The village had served as a channel for supplies, via the sea, for a swathe of villages in the area, including 'Ein Ghazal and Jaba. The morale of the population plummeted following the fall of Arab Haifa and the arrival of refugees from Haifa and, earlier, from Qisarya and 'Arab al Bara. By early May, the population was reported to be ready to surrender if attacked or presented with an ultimatum – but not to hand over their arms.[658] But was the Haganah really interested in Tantura's surrender – and 'leaving the inhabitants in place?' asked the local HIS-AD officer.[659] Flight from the village began in early May after a local man killed a Jew and was in turn killed.[660] Many left by boat for Tyre. At the last minute – probably prompted by the start of the pan-Arab attack on Israel and the failure of the Haganah to offer them terms – the villagers (along with those of 'Ein Ghazal, Jab'a and Ijzim) decided to 'stay . . . and fight'.[661] The villagers worked on fortifications, laying mines on the approach roads; inhabitants of hamlets in the area were ordered to concentrate in, and help defend, Tantura and Ijzim.[662]

Alexandroni HQ issued the operational order for the attack on 22 May; no mention was made of the prospective fate of the civilian inhabitants[663] – though there can be little doubt that the troops went in with the intention of driving out the inhabitants. The village was not offered the option to surrender quietly. The attack began that night with a barrage of machine-gun fire; infantry companies then moved in simultaneously from north, east and south, with a naval vessel blocking escape from the sea. The villagers offered serious resistance but the battle was over by 08:00, 23 May. Dozens of villagers were killed. The initial report spoke of '300 adult male prisoners' and '200 women and children'.[664]

As usual, the fall of the village was followed by looting by settlers from nearby, and Haganah efforts to stop it. One search recovered 'one carpet, one gramophone . . . one basket with cucumbers, one goat . . .'.[665] There was also widespread destruction of property.[666] For days, the village and its environs remained strewn with human and animal corpses, creating a health hazard.[667]

Some of the villagers fled to Arab-held territory. Hundreds of others, mostly women and children, were moved to al Fureidis, an Arab village to the east that had earlier surrendered, where hundreds of Tantura refugees were already encamped. On 31 May, Minority Affairs Minister Shitrit asked Ben-Gurion whether to expel these women and children, as maintaining them in Fureidis was a problem.[668] HIS-AD also applied pressure; the Tantura evictees were leaking intelligence to neighbour-ing, unconquered, villages and there were problems of overcrowding and sanitation.[669] Ben-Gurion's reply, if any, is unknown. But on 18 June, some 1,000 Tantura 'women, children and old Arabs' (together with '80' detainees from elsewhere) were expelled from Fureidis to Iraqi-held Tulkarm in Samaria.[670] Another 200 women and children, probably with menfolk still in Israeli detention, stayed on in Fureidis.[671]

Among the smaller villages near Tantura evacuated in early May were Kafr Lam and Sarafand.[672] By mid-May, some of the villagers had re-turned. On 15 May Carmeli troops occupied the two villages and briefly garrisoned them.[673] Two days later, Carmeli raided al Mazar, four kilo-metres northeast of Sarafand, with the aim of 'rendering [the village] unworthy of use'. The troops encountered 10–20 Arabs, who ran away, and then proceeded to 'burn what could be burned'.[674] But within days some of the villagers were back.[675] The three villages were re-occupied and finally cleared only in mid-July (see below).

Qaqun, northwest of Tulkarm, was attacked and conquered by Alexandroni units on the night of 4\5 June. The operational order did not say what was to be done with the inhabitants, but repeatedly spoke of 'cleaning' or 'clearing' the village.[676] The attack was preceded by an artillery barrage that precipitated the evacuation of most of the inhabi-tants to nearby groves.[677] Only a few local militiamen and several dozen Iraqi Army soldiers remained to fight and they were rapidly overwhelmed by the Alexandroni infantry.[678]

OPERATION YIFTAH (MIVTZA YIFTAH)

During the second half of April and in May, as part of Plan D, the Haganah secured the border from Metula to the Sea of Galilee in expectation of the Syrian invasion. In the course of Operation Yiftah, as it was eventually called, the Arab population of eastern Galilee – earmarked for Jewish sovereignty in the partition resolution – was evicted.

In the operational order, the objective was defined as 'gaining con-trol of the Tel-Hai area and its consolidation in preparation for invasion from outside'. The order made no mention of policy toward the civilian population.[679]

The campaign, in effect, began with two failed Palmah assaults, on 15 and 20 April, on the Nabi Yusha police fort on the southwestern end of the Galilee Panhandle. HGS then appointed Yigal Allon to take charge. He had the equivalent of two undermanned battalions; he faced dozens of Arab villages, the town of Safad and highly permeable bor-ders with Syria and Lebanon. To judge from his report of 22 April and his subsequent actions, Allon concluded that completely clearing the area of Arabs was necessary to secure the frontier.[680] But the Palmah had to wait for the British evacuation of the area. The British handed some local police forts and camps to the Arabs, but on 27–28 April, Palmah units occupied the camps and forts in Mahanayim and around Rosh Pina.[681] Allon was far from optimistic about the military situation.[682] However, under the impact of the fall of Arab Haifa and the prospect of pan-Arab invasion, which portended fullscale hostilities, Arab morale was collapsing. During 20–22 April, Arab commanders ordered women and children to evacuate al Dawwara and al 'Abisiyya, two large pan-handle villages,[683] and there was a general evacuation by Maghrebi villagers and beduin tribesmen in the area west and south of Lake Hula. Among those who reportedly left were 'Arab al Zubeid and most of the inhabitants of 'Ulmaniya, Husseiniya, Kirad al Baqqara and Kirad al Ghannama, and Khisas.[684]

Before Allon could complete his preparations, local militiamen and ir-regulars based in Syria and Lebanon, on 1 May unsuccessfully attacked Ramot Naftali, Kibbutz Dan, Kibbutz Kfar Szold and Kibbutz Lehavot Habashan in the panhandle.[685] The villagers of neighbouring al Madahil, Khirbet al 'Aziziyat, Khiyam al Walid, al Hamra, Ghuraba and (partially) al Muftakhira feared reprisals or being caught in a crossfire and fled.[686] The Syrian authorities or local commanders that day and the next ordered the villages around Rosh Pina to send away their women and children.[687] The inhabitants of the Shi'ite village of Hunin, who had for years main-tained good relations with Jewish neighbours and bad relations with Sunni Safad, were ordered to evacuate within six days – apparently by Arab, perhaps Lebanese, authorities.[688] A fortnight later a Palmah raid on the village resulted in the flight of most of the inhabitants.[689] (About 400 remained. Shitrit thought that Israel should foster special relations with the (Palestinian) Shi'ites,[690] but the army thought otherwise. Dur-ing the summer four village women were raped and murdered by IDF soldiers.[691] In August, some inhabitants were forced by the IDF to flee; the remainder fled the following month, after an IDF raid in which 20 were killed and 20 buildings demolished.)[692]

On 2 May, Allon launched his operation, conquering 'Ein al Zeitun and Biriya (see above), and intimidating with mortar barrages the villages of Fir'im, Qabba'a and Mughr al Kheit, northeast of Safad, precipitating a mass evacuation. The villagers had periodically hit Jewish traffic be-tween Rosh Pina and Ayelet Hashahar.[693]

In his report of 22 April, Allon had recommended, among other things, 'an attempt to clear out the beduin encamped between the Jordan [River], and Jubb Yusuf and the Sea of Galilee'. With Safad now targeted, this sub-operation became imperative.[694] On 4 May, Allon launched Operation Broom (Mivtza Matate). The nomadic and semi-settled in-habitants – al Qudeiriya, 'Arab as Samakiya, 'Arab as Suyyad, 'Arab al Shamalina and the Zanghariya – had for months harassed Jewish traffic between Tiberias and Rosh Pina. Operation Yiftah HQ defined the ob-jectives as '(a) the destruction of bases of the enemy . . . (b) to destroy points of assembly for invading forces from the east [and] (c) to join the lower and upper Galilee with a relatively wide and safe strip' of continuous, Jewish territory. The order to the company commanders stated that Zanghariya and Tabigha, and the 'Arab al Shamalina, should be attacked, 'their inhabitants expelled and the[ir] houses blown up'. Friendly Arabs and churches 'should on no account be harmed'.[695]

The operation, preceded by mortaring, was carried out by the Palmah's First Battalion with help from Alexandroni and local Haganah units. They 'blew up most of the houses and burned the tents of Kedar' between Tabigha and the Buteiha, where the Jordan enters the sea; some 15 Arabs were killed and the rest fled to Syria.[696] The following day, Palmah sappers methodically blew up more than 50 houses in Zanghariya and other villages in the area.[697] A catholic priest, Boniface Bittelmeier, of Tabigha, described what he saw and heard:

> When I just finished blessing the bread there was a terrible explosion in Tabigha. We rushed out and saw pillars of smoke rising skyward. House after house was bombed and torched, then matters proceeded toward the Jordan. All was bombed, the tents and the huts were burned. All day there were explosions, and smoke and fire were visible; in the evening the 'victors' returned with trucks loaded with cattle. What they couldn't take they shot . . . The mother of Big Awad and Old Dahan were killed. The hospice, the Church of the Bread and the Fishes, and the home of Kassim Shihadeh were not hit.[698]

The Syrians informed the British that the operation had created a further 2,000 refugees.[699] As 'Azzam Pasha had understood and predicted, Allon was 'driving out the inhabitants' from areas 'on or near roads by which Arab regular forces could enter the country . . . The Arab armies would have the greatest difficulty in even entering Palestine after May 15th.'[700]

According to Allon, Operation Broom had a 'tremendous psychological impact' on Safad and the Hula Valley villages, and paved the way for their conquest and the flight of their inhabitants.[701] In turn, the fall of Arab Safad precipitated (along with fears of the impending invasion) the abandonment of a string of nearby villages, including Ja'una, Deishum, Dhahiriya, Abil al Qamah, Zuq al Tahtani, Shawqa al Tahta, Qaddita, Sammui, al Khalisa, and al Na'ima.[702] Many of the inhabitants of Meirun, west of Safad, probably left at this time.[703] Safad's fall also helped Allon in the biggest psychological warfare operation of the war:

> The echo . . . carried far . . . The confidence of thousands of Arabs of the Hula [Valley] was shaken . . . We had only five days left . . . until 15 May. We regarded it as imperative to cleanse the interior of the Galilee and create Jewish territorial continuity in the whole of Upper Galilee. The protracted battles reduced our forces, and we faced major tasks in blocking the invasion routes. We, therefore, looked for a means that would not oblige

us to use force to drive out the tens of thousands of hostile Arabs left in the Galilee and who, in the event of an invasion, could strike at us from behind. We tried to utilise a stratagem that exploited the [Arab] defeats in Safad and in the area cleared by [Operation] Broom – a stratagem that worked wonderfully.

I gathered the Jewish mukhtars, who had ties with the different Arab villages, and I asked them to whisper in the ears of several Arabs that giant Jewish reinforcements had reached the Galilee and were about to clean out the villages of the Hula, [and] to advise them, as friends, to flee while they could. And the rumour spread throughout the Hula that the time had come to flee. The flight encompassed tens of thousands. The stratagem fully achieved its objective . . . and we were able to deploy ourselves in face of the [prospective] invaders along the borders, without fear for our rear.[704]

Allon's men also distributed a flier, advising those who wished to avoid harm to leave 'with their women and children'.[705] One Palmah commander, perhaps Allon, later summarised what had occurred:

The only joint operation between the Jews and the Arabs was the evacuation by the Arabs of the Hula area. Orders from abroad [i.e., apparently Syria] for the evacuation of the whole area by the Arabs were buttressed by a whispering campaign by our intelligence services.[706]

HIS-AD estimated that '18%' of the exodus from the panhandle was due to the 'whispering campaign'. It attributed the final exodus from Qeitiya, Lazzaza, Zuq al Fauqani, al Manshiya, Khisas, al Mansura, Dawwara, al 'Abisiyya, Beisamun and Mallaha – all in the second half of May – at least in part, to that campaign.[707]

Several panhandle villages were evacuated for other reasons. According to IDF intelligence, the inhabitants of Khalisa evacuated the area on 11 May after the Haganah turned down their request for an 'agreement'. (The fall of Arab Safad the day before no doubt also had an effect.) The inhabitants of al Salihiya left on 25 May for a similar reason: 'They wanted negotiations [with us]. We did not show up. [They became] afraid.' The village traditionally was 'friendly' towards the Yishuv.[708] The inhabitants of nearby al Buweiziya evacuated along with Khalisa. The remaining inhabitants of Zawiya left under more dramatic circumstances: The village was mortared and raided on 19 May by the 11th Battalion, whose orders were 'to conquer the village . . . to destroy it and to expel the inhabitants'. The village was destroyed.[709] Fir'im, to which inhabitants had begun to return, was torched on 22 May.[710] 'Ammuqa, Qabba'a, Marus, al Malikiya and Qadas were all finally evacuated at the end of May as a result of Haganah attack.[711]

During late May, hungry refugees from eastern Galilee began to drift back – to Muftakhira, Hamra, Zuq al Tahtani, Salihiya, 'Abisiyya and Fir'im, mainly to harvest crops; many erected huts in the swamplands outside their original villages from which they could reach their crops while remaining relatively inaccessible to Israeli patrols. The Haganah acted to curb this and persuade the returnees to leave Palestine.[712] On 24 May, the Palmah began the 'systematic torching of the villages of the Hula [Valley]'.[713]

By late June, HIS was able to report (somewhat inaccurately) that

> all the Arab villages in the Safad area as far [northwestward] as Sa'sa were empty and the inhabitants have not returned . . . In the Hula [Valley] all the villages were empty apart from the Hula swamp area and Ghuraba and Darbashiya, where there were concentrations of Arab refugees . . . The whole area from Mei Marom [i.e., Lake Hula] to the Sea of Galilee east of the main Tiberias–Metula road was clear of its Arab inhabitants, as were [certain areas west of the road].[714]

In all, the traumatic effect of the fall of the regional 'capital', Safad, Jewish attacks and a general fear of being caught up in a crossfire were probably more significant as causes of demoralisation and departure than the deliberate whispering campaign; or, put another way, the psychological warfare ploys were effective because they came on top of the other factors, which included orders for partial or full evacuation by local commanders and the Syrians. The picture that emerges from the IDF intelligence analysis of June 1948 of the evacuation is more complex than Allon's subsequent recollection – that the exodus was simply the result of the orchestrated whispering campaign.

OPERATION BEN-'AMI (MIVTZA BEN-'AMI)

The last major Haganah operation launched before the termination of the Mandate, in line with Plan D's provision for securing blocks of settlements outside the partition borders, was Carmeli's thrust up Western Galilee to the Lebanese border. Called Operation Ben-'Ami, the offensive, carried out in two stages between 13 and 22 May, saw the capture of all the villages along the coast road from just south of Acre to Rosh Haniqra-al Bassa and a few to the east of the road, and the flight of almost all their inhabitants. The operation's main aim was to resupply and reinforce the settlements in Western Galilee – Nahariya and a number of kibbutzim – to extricate noncombatants, in view of the impending pan-Arab invasion, and, in general, to secure permanent Jewish control of the area. The orders specifically called for the conquest and demolition of the main targeted villages, al Bassa, al Zib and al Sumeiriya,[715] but did not explicitly refer to the prospective fate of the region's Arab inhabitants. In all likelihood, Carmel, who commanded Ben-'Ami, desired a complete evacuation.

The villages had been badly shaken by the Palmah raid on al Kabri, on the night of January 31\1 February, in which the house of the main, Husseini-affiliated notable, Fares Sirhan, was demolished.[716] Sirhan and his family fled to Lebanon.[717] Zib, Ghabisiya, Umm al Faraj, Kabri, al Nahar, Sheikh Daoud and Kuweikat reportedly expressed interest in a mutual non-aggression pact with the Haganah.[718] But attacks on Jewish traffic resumed shortly thereafter.

In late April, the Haganah prepared an initial blueprint for an operation called 'Operation Ehud', which provided for attacks on Kabri, Nahar, Bassa and Zib, 'the destruction of the gangs [and] the menfolk, [and] destruction of property'.[719] This served as a basis for the operational order for Ben-'Ami. By the start of the operation, under the impact of events in Haifa and Safad, there was significant flight from the area; Kabri and al Mazra'a were reported completely abandoned; and Acre, by most of its inhabitants.[720]

Ben-'Ami was launched on the evening of 13 May, with a column of Carmeli armoured cars and trucks pushing northward along the coast road while a squadron of boats dropped off companies at points along the way. Sumeiriya fell before dawn. The attackers left the village's eastern side open to allow flight – and the villagers used it as the first mortars began to fall. Many had left earlier, demoralised by previous Arab defeats and lack of assistance from the ALA.[721] The village was immediately demolished.[722] Zib and Bassa fell hours later. Zib had been militantly anti-Zionist; mortared and fearful of Jewish vengeance, the villagers fled during the battle.[723] Most of Bassa's women and children had fled to Lebanon during the previous weeks. Villagers later complained that upon capturing Bassa, the Haganah had executed a handful of youngsters[724] and there (as in Sumeiriya and Zib) had molested or violated a number of women.[725] During the following days, about 100 old people and Christians, were transferred from Bassa to Mazra'a, as were a handful of people from Zib. Mazra'a became a collection point for 'remainders' from the region's villages and was to remain the only Arab community near the coast in western Galilee.[726]

The fall of the villages undermined the morale of Acre; the town fell on 17–18 May (see above). In turn, Acre's fall shook the remaining villages, which Carmeli decided to take during the following days, in what was designated 'Operation Ben-'Ami – Stage 2'. The operational order, of 19 May, instructed Carmeli's 21st Battalion to break through to and supply Kibbutz Yehi'am and to 'attack with the aim of conquest, the killing of adult males, destruction and torching', Kabri, Nahar and Umm al Faraj.[727] The following day, Carmeli sought approval from HGS\Operations;[728] approval was given. On 20–21 May, Carmeli attacked Umm al Faraj, Kabri, al Tell and Nahar, all to the east of Nahariya, and then demolished them. Carmel wanted both to punish the villagers, especially of Zib and Kabri, for past misdemeanors, and to make sure they would never return.[729] In Kabri, a number of villagers were apparently executed by the troops.[730]

The last village to fall in stage two of Ben-'Ami was al Ghabisiya, south of Kabri. The villagers, who had helped the Haganah during the first months of the war, formally surrendered but Carmeli troops entered the village with guns blazing, killing a handful; six more appear to have been selected and executed in a nearby ditch after the conquest, apparently in revenge for alleged participation in the ambush of the 'Yehiam Convoy', in March 1948, in which 47 Haganah men had died.[731] During the following months, some villagers resettled in their homes with IDF permission – but they were expelled in January 1950.[732]

THE SOUTH, APRIL–JUNE 1948

In the south, the Haganah and, later, the IDF, remained on the defensive throughout the period. No major offensives were undertaken and, from the Egyptian invasion of 15 May, the Negev and Giv'ati brigades had their hands more or less full averting a Jewish collapse. However, both brigades mounted sporadic, local attacks on the peripheries of their zones, usually with specific tactical aims, to facilitate defence against expected or continuing Egyptian advances. These attacks, especially those east of Majdal (Ashkelon) and Isdud by Giv'ati, caused the flight of tens of thousands of local inhabitants.

Plan D's guidelines to the Giv'ati Brigade gave Lt. Col. Avidan wide discretion. In order to stabilise his lines, the plan stated 'you will determine alone, in consultation with your Arab affairs advisers and Intelligence Service officers, [which] villages in your zone should be occupied, cleansed or destroyed'.[733] During May – early June, before and after the invasion, Avidan moved to expand his area of control westwards and southwards.

In mid-December 1947 and again in February 1948, Muhammad Mustafa Mussa, the mukhtar of the large village of 'Aqir, south of Rehovot, sought to conclude a non-belligerency agreement with neighbouring 'Eqron and tried to restrain hotheaded youngsters and irregulars from attacking Jewish traffic. An agreement was signed on 9 February.[734] But the village notables were under constant pressure from the Ramle NC to demonstrate belligerency, avoid contact with the Jews, and host foreign irregulars. The villagers generally managed to keep out of trouble but occasionally blocked Jewish traffic.[735] The takeover in mid-April by Haganah forces of the nearby abandoned British camp near Kfar Bilu cut off 'Aqir from Ramle and caused trepidation in the village.[736] The mukhtar tried to renew the agreement.[737]

On 4 May, Giv'ati troops – apparently with prior, secret agreement with at least some village notables – surrounded and entered 'Aqir and demanded the surrender of weapons. Four villagers were killed and five injured in the operation. '60–70' rifles, a Bren Gun and some pistols were handed over.[738] A British patrol appeared on the scene and the Jews withdrew, apparently after some looting. But believing that the villagers were holding back, the withdrawing troops took with them six or eight Arabs hostages 'for interrogation . . . and to trade for the release of [a Haganah] informer [in Arab hands]'.[739] The Haganah promised to release them when the remaining weapons were surrendered. The villagers agreed and Mussa signed a letter to this effect.[740] But almost all of 'Aqir's inhabitants left that day, moving to Yibna and al Mughar; they apparently feared that they would be branded traitors for surrendering. Giv'ati threatened to execute the hostages if the arms were not forthcoming.[741]

On 7 May, Giv'ati re-entered the village, where only several dozen inhabitants remained, and blew up two houses.[742] Within weeks, the villagers who had remained were expelled – an act that sparked a flurry of protests in Mapam, which over the years had had contacts with a small group of village leftists who were willing to live in peace with the Yishuv.[743]

A similar arms collection operation was conducted by Giv'ati troops in Qatra, four kilometres west of 'Aqir, on 5–6 May, but without an actual attack. About 60 weapons were handed over – but a Jewish officer was shot and killed (either by an Arab or friendly fire) while searching (or looting) one of the houses. Three Arabs were taken hostage and Giv'ati demanded the name of the killer, and the handover of foreign irregulars and additional weapons.[744] The Haganah reoccupied the village and the inhabitants were either intimidated into flight or expelled on 17 May, as the Egyptian army drew near.[745]

Both operations were characterised by looting and brutal behaviour. The HIS officer who accompanied the troops later highlighted several problems, including the lack of clear orders regarding behaviour, the absence of a POW camp for detainees, and looting.[746] More explicitly, the brigade's official history states that after these operations, the brigade HQ acted to 'curtail the instinct to loot and maltreat prisoners [hit'alelut beshvuyim]'. Henceforth, only HIS officers were to interrogate prisoners.[747]

The inhabitants of 'Arab Abu Fadl ('Arab al Satariyya), northwest of Ramle, were unenthusiastic about assisting the Husseinis but felt trapped between the Haganah, which demanded neutrality or submission, and the nearby commanders of Ramle, who urged belligerence. Families began to leave in December 1947. In late April 1948, the mukhtar, Sheikh Salim, appealed for Haganah protection.[748] But before the Haganah could respond, the authorities in Ramle, perhaps sensing that treachery was afoot, ordered the villagers to evacuate.[749] By 9 May, 'Arab al Satarriya (along with the nearby village of Bir Salim) evacuated.[750]

That day, the clearing of the southern end of Giv'ati's zone of operations, in anticipation of invasion, began in earnest with the launching of 'Operation Lightning' (*Mivtza Barak*). The objective was

> to deny the enemy a base for future operations . . . by creating general panic and breaking his morale. The aim is to force the Arab inhabitants 'to move' . . . It can be assumed that delivering a blow to one or more of these [population] centres [i.e., Majdal, Isdud or Yibna] will cause the wandering [i.e., exodus] of the inhabitants of the smaller settlements in the area. This possibility is likely especially in view of the wave of panic that recently swept over [the Arabs of] the country.

The operational order to the 52nd and 53rd battalions initially targeted the villages of Bash-shit and Beit Daras. In apparent partial contradiction to the spirit of the preamble, the villages were to be surrounded and called upon to surrender and relinquish their arms. If they declined, they were to be mortared and stormed. In the case of Beit Daras, if it resisted, it was to be 'destroyed . . . and dealt with in the manner of scorched earth'.[751] In a follow-up order, issued on the evening of 10 May, the 54th battalion and auxiliary Palmah forces were to subdue Batani al Sharqi and neighbouring Batani al Gharbi 'with the same means used vis-à-vis 'Aqir, Bash-shit and Beit Daras'.[752]

Giv'ati's attacks created the desired exodus. Mortaring almost invariably preceded each ground assault. Beit Daras had already been severely hit in a Haganah retaliatory strike on 20–21 April, when about 100 villagers were killed and wounded and many fled to Majdal, but some were forced by the irregulars in Majdal to return to Beit Daras.[753] On 10–11 May, Giv'ati attacked Beit Daras for the last time. The villagers offered serious resistance and suffered some 50 casualties. Subsequently, 'many houses were blown up and torched, and wells and granaries were sabotaged'. Throughout the area there was 'mass evacuation';[754] villagers fled from Ibdis, Julis and Beit Affa.[755] That night, Sawafir Shamaliya and Bash-shit were also taken, after a serious fight; here too houses were blown up.[756] During 10–12 May, units of the Ephraim sub-district, apparently without success, repeatedly mortared and raided Nabi Rubin, with the aim of forcing evacuation.[757] The attack on Beit Daras also triggered flight from neighbouring Batani al Sharqi. When Giv'ati troops entered the village on 11 May, they found it empty but for a few old people. The rest had departed 'in line with the instructions of the mukhtars', related one of the old people. Giv'ati troops 'executed four of the remaining Arabs on the instructions of OC 54th Battalion', HIS dryly reported.[758] Barqa was occupied on 12 May.[759]

On 13 May, Giv'ati launched the second stage of Barak, codenamed 'Operation Maccabi'. Abu Shusha, southeast of Ramle, was mortared on 13\14 May and then stormed by units of the 51st and 54th battalions; some inhabitants fled and houses were blown up.[760] But many inhabitants apparently remained. On 19 May, a nearby Arab Legion unit reported that 'the Jews . . . were killing [Abu Shusha] villagers'. A day later, Giv'ati reported that some 30 Arabs had been killed during the 13\14 May assault though the Arabs claimed that 'more than 70' had died. The Giv'ati report may have been an oblique way of referring to killings after 14 May.[761] On 21 May, Arab authorities in Ramle informed the Red Cross that 'the Jews had committed barbaric acts' in Abu Shusha and called for Red Cross intervention.[762] One Haganah soldier twice attempted to rape a 20-year-old woman prisoner.[763] Abu Shusha's remaining inhabitants were expelled, apparently on 21 May.[764]

During the attack on Abu Shusha, nearby Na'na was surrounded and disarmed after 11 of its notables were taken hostage.[765] Many of the villagers appear to have left. But they began returning on 17 May.[766] During the First Truce, Israeli local commanders lobbied for the inhabitants' removal, arguing that they were a security risk.[767] On 12 June, the day after the start of the truce, the IDF occupied the village.[768] During the following days, the villagers were ordered to leave or intimidated into flight.[769]

As part of Operation Maccabi, al Qubab, northwest of Latrun, was attacked and conquered on 15 May.[770] Mughar, southwest of 'Aqir, was also taken, by Giv'ati's 53rd Battalion, that day. The troops found only a 'small number of old people and women'.[771]

On 18 May, Giv'ati's 51st Battalion captured − for the second time − Sawafir al Sharqiyya and adjoining Sawafir al Gharbiyya. The (typical) operational order had instructed 'C' Company, 51st Battalion,

> to expel the enemy from the villages . . . to clean the front line . . . To conquer the villages, to cleanse them of inhabitants (women and children should [also] be expelled), to take several prisoners . . . [and] to burn the greatest possible number of houses.[772]

Both villages were found almost completely abandoned. The troops blew up and torched several houses. But after they withdrew, villagers returned and fired at Israeli convoys. One Giv'ati commander commented:

> The problem of conquering the villages: Because of a lack of appropriate equipment to destroy or occupy the villages conquered in difficult battles, we are forced to leave them after a few hours. So it was in 'Aqir, Bash-shit, Beit Daras and the Sawafirs. [We] must demand from the commanders . . . to seriously consider the continued occupation and to prepare in advance the bulldozers, petrol and explosives.[773]

By late June, both Sawafir al Gharbiyya and Sawafir al Sharqiyya were once again 'full of Arabs'.[774]

The problem of leaving conquered villages both ungarrisoned and intact, with villagers simply returning after the Haganah had left, continued to plague Giv'ati. On 23 May, for example, HIS-AD reported that the Sawafir villagers, and those of nearby Beit Daras, Jaladiya, Summeil, and Juseir, slept at night in the fields and returned to the villages to work during the days.[775] Nonetheless, the Haganah attacks, the flight of inhabitants and the partial destruction of the villages drove the inhabitants to despair[776] and contributed to their eventual permanent exodus.

In coordination with Giv'ati's local pushes southwards, the besieged Palmah Negev Brigade during May carried out a number of small pushes northwards and eastwards. Burayr, northeast of Gaza, was taken on 12–13 May. Its inhabitants fled to Gaza. The 9th Battalion troops killed a large number of villagers, apparently executing dozens of army-age males. They appear also to have raped and murdered a teenage girl.[777] The same day, the inhabitants of neighbouring Sumsum and Najd, to the west, were driven out. In Sumsum the occupying troops found only a handful of old people. They blew up five houses and warned that if the village's weapons were not handed over the following day, they would blow up the rest.[778] But inhabitants repeatedly returned to the village, either to resettle or to cultivate crops. At the end of May, a Negev Brigade unit, with orders to expel 'the Arabs from Sumsum and Burayr and burn their granaries and fields', swept through the villages, encountering resistance in Sumsum, and killed '5' (or, according to another report, '20') and blew up granaries and a well.[779] The troops returned to Sumsum yet again, on 9 or 10 June, again burning houses and skirmishing with Arabs.[780]

The inhabitants of Huleiqat and Kaukaba, to the north, fled westwards in mid-May under the impact of the fall of Burayr.[781] A fortnight later, on the night of 27\28 May, Negev Brigade units raided al Muharraqa and Kaufakha, south of Burayr, driving out or expelling their inhabitants.[782] The villagers of Kaufakha had earlier repeatedly asked to surrender, accept Jewish rule and be allowed to stay, to no avail.[783] The Haganah generally regarded such requests as insincere or untrustworthy; with the Egyptian army nearby, it was felt that it was better not to take a chance.

Beit Tima, north of Burayr, was conquered by the Negev Brigade's 7th Battalion on 30\31 May; some 20 Arabs were killed, and the granary and a well were destroyed.[784] On 31 May, the brigade expelled the villagers of Huj, seven kilometres south of Burayr, to the Gaza Strip. Huj had traditionally been friendly; in 1946, its inhabitants had hidden Haganah men from a British dragnet. In mid-December 1947, while on a visit to Gaza, the mukhtar and his brother were shot dead by a mob that accused them of 'collaboration'.[785] But at the end of May 1948, given the proximity of the advancing Egyptian column, the Negev Brigade decided to expel the inhabitants – and then looted and blew up their houses.[786]

To the north, near Rehovot, on 26–27 May Giv'ati took al Qubeiba and the nearby, semi-abandoned village of Zarnuqa. Zarnuqa was considered 'friendly' as it was economically dependent on wages earned in cultivating Jewish-owned orange groves.[787] In early December 1947, the villagers had sought a non-belligerency pact with Rehovot[788] but it appears never to have been formalized. In April 1948, a contingent of irregulars moved in. With the Egyptian invasion on 15 May, the war drew near. One of Zarnuqa's clans, Dar Shurbaji, wanted the village to surrender its weapons and accept Haganah protection. The others argued against and the village evacuated most of its old people, women and children to nearby Yibna. The Shurbajis stayed on along with several dozen armed menfolk from the two other clans.[789]

The Giv'ati attack on the village on 27 May kicked off with a mortar barrage.[790] The troops then moved in. A graphic description of what happened next was sent to the Mapam daily, *Al Hamishmar*:

> The soldier told me how one of the soldiers opened a door and fired a Sten at an old man, an old woman and a child in one burst, how they took the Arabs . . . out of all the houses and stood [them] in the sun all day – in thirst and hunger until they surrendered 40 rifles . . . The Arabs had [previously] claimed that they hadn't [weapons, and] in the end they were expelled from the village towards Yibna.

The Arabs protested that they were being driven towards their enemies, anti-Zionist Arabs whom they, in Zarnuqa, had not allowed into their village, 'but this did not help, and, screaming and crying, they left . . .'.[791]

Altogether, six inhabitants (three men and two women and a girl) were killed and 22 taken prisoner.[792] The following day the inhabitants came back, relating that the Yibnaites had driven them off as 'unredeemable traitors unworthy of hospitality'. The returnees watched the Jewish troops and neighbouring settlers ransack their homes. Then, for the second time, they were ordered to leave. Zarnuqa's houses were demolished in June.[793]

In the following days, Giv'ati captured several more villages, including Julis (27 May and, again, on 11 June), Juseir (11 June) and Yibna. Giv'ati was 'interested in the evacuation' of the large village of Yibna, as the official history put it.[794] A contingent of Iraqi volunteers had moved in in mid-March. On 30 March some two dozen villagers were killed in a Haganah reprisal.[795] On 21 April the Iraqi village commander, Abdul Razek, was arrested in Jaffa after getting drunk and shooting two Arabs.[796]

Units of Giv'ati's 51st and 57th battalions conquered Yibna on 5 June. The operational order spoke of 'completing the cleansing of the area of enemy fighting elements'.[797] Most of Yibna's population had fled to Isdud on 27 May after the fall of Qubeiba and Zarnuqa – but armed males had been forced back by Isdud's militiamen.[798] After mortaring and a brief firefight, the Giv'ati units found Yibna deserted 'save for some old Arab men and women', who were sent packing.[799] The sand dunes south of the town were covered with refugees fleeing toward Isdud; Giv'ati artillery fired at them 'to increase [their] panic'.[800]

Summarising its operations between '15 May and 2 June', Giv'ati HQ wrote two months later: While leaving one battalion as a screen to face the advancing Egyptians, 'the rest of the battalions were deployed in two defense lines and [employed] in cleansing the internal area, a cleansing that was carried out to completion [*bi'ur hamerhav hapnimi, bi'ur shebutza 'ad tom*]'.[801]

The Negev Brigade, for its part, was ordered by IDF GS\Operations on the eve of the First Truce 'to create facts of political importance' and 'to "clean" all the Arab villages that were occupied by the Egyptian military force'. The reference was, specifically to the villages of Julis and Yasur, which were to be occupied 'several hours' before the start of the truce (to assure that the Egyptians would have no time, before the truce took effect, to recapture them).[802]

But Haganah\IDF behaviour in various parts of the country was not monolithic. The Giv'ati and Negev brigades tended to expel communities near their front lines against the backdrop of the approach or proximity of the invading Egyptians, whom HGS for weeks believed to be far stronger than they were. But Golani's and Carmeli's operations were anything but uniform in character or effect. On 16 May, hours after Iraqi and Syrian troops invaded, Golani captured the villages of 'Indur and Kaukab al Hawa. At 'Indur (biblical 'Ein Dor, home of the witch), most of the inhabitants probably fled at the start of the battle and several who were captured and '[later] tried to escape' were shot. Three rifles were captured. The commander briefly left a small garrison in place and, he reported, 'the [remaining] population is being transferred in the direction of Nazareth'.[803] A fortnight later, on 7 June, a large Golani patrol, mounted on an armoured car and three buses, swept through 'Indur, where it encountered 'no foreign force' and blew up two houses. Moving on, the force entered the large village of Tamra, where it found only women and children (the men had fled as the column approached). The troops demanded that the villagers hand over their arms – or 'depart . . . within half an hour'. But the commander relented and gave them several days. The patrol moved on to Kafr Misr, where it managed to surprise the menfolk. The commander demanded that their arms be delivered up within half an hour – or all the menfolk would have to leave. The villagers handed over eight rifles and promised to deliver several more the following day. 'The inhabitants asked permission to continue the harvest and to [be able to] move freely to Nazareth. I said that they would receive an answer after they delivered the arms.' The patrol then drove to Na'ura, south of Tamra. Most of the males had left and the mukhtar said that he would give up the arms to two local officers. The commander opined that 'there is no need to expel these inhabitants but to reach an agreement with them after they deliver up their arms'.[804]

But other Golani troops behaved differently (if also somewhat erratically). A few days earlier, on 4 June, two platoons of Golani's 12th

('Barak') Battalion, commanded by Haim Levakov and mounted on three trucks and a jeep, swept through the villages of Hadatha, 'Ulam, Sirin, and Ma'dhar, some10 kilometres west-southwest of Samakh. In Hadatha, 'Ulam and Ma'dhar, the force found a handful of Arabs busy with the harvest. All had written permission to stay. In Sirin they found about 100 inhabitants. The troops checked identity cards, searched for weapons (finding only some knives) and left; no hostile irregulars were found and the inhabitants were left in place – though the battalion's intelligence officer, in his report, recommended that 'the Arabs should be ejected from the area, the young men should be arrested, and the crops confiscated . . .'.[805]

A half a century later, one of the Israeli participants, Victor 'Oved, described this or a similar patrol:

> On one of the hot summer days as part of the effort to clear areas of hostile Arabs, we set out at midnight to check a number of Arab villages above Ramat Yavniel . . . We approached . . . on foot . . . From a distance we began to smell the special smell of the Arab village, to hear the chickens and the braying of donkeys . . . and the barking of tens of dogs. In a number of minutes we're on the outskirts . . . dozens of villagers . . . start screaming: The Jews have come . . . The mukhtar is summoned to the commander and is given an order to evacuate the village in reasonable time. Thus we moved from village to village and carried out a meticulous search from house to house, but without success. At the last and largest village, the mukhtar was given an order as in the other villages, to prevent the entry of hostile enemy forces.

As the Israeli force was about to leave, an Arab approached the commander, 'began to kiss his hands and feet', and complained that during the search, a batch of bank notes had disappeared from the pocket of a coat that had been hanging in his house. The commander announced to the assembled platoons that the force would not move out until the money was returned and that the culprit would not be punished. Suddenly, the money was dropped on the floor. The villager was given back his money and he then kissed the commander's feet and hands 'again and again . . . We return to base satisfied but with a bitter taste.' Soon afterwards, according to 'Oved, the villagers left, taking whatever they could with them, including livestock, 'doors [and] windows . . . During [the subsequent] fighting, this area was quiet and this saved the IDF a lot of troops and, of course, unnecessary clashes.'[806]

In another operation, three days later, on 7 June, a platoon of 'Barak' troops, commanded by Yitzhak Shusterman, mounted on a bus and a jeep, raided Danna, al Bira, Kafra, Yubla, Jabbul, and al Murassas, north-northwest of Beisan. The troops first passed through al Taiyiba and a satellite community at Jabl Tirat al Harb, northeast of Moledet – Arab communities that had been allowed to stay. The troops then took up a position on a high point on the outskirts of each designated village, starting with Danna, lobbed a few two-inch mortar rounds into its centre and then moved in and searched it. Danna, al Bira, Kafra, Yubla and al Murassas were all found empty. At Jabbul, the troops encountered harvesters, who ran off. 'Our troops opened fire but hit no [one].' Arabs also fled from the village itself. 'Our men burned their crops and set alight several houses.' The platoon then returned to base.[807] IDF GS\Operations summarised: 'There were violent patrols [*siyurim alimim*] in Lower Galilee villages. The Arabs [are?] leaving and the farmers who returned to their places were expelled.'[808]

On the night of 10\11 June, on the eve of the start of the First Truce, a Golani unit attacked and occupied the village of Faqqu'a, ten kilometres west of Beisan, drove out its inhabitants and blew up some 30 houses.[809] To the north, Golani's 14th Battalion was ordered to take Lubya, west of Tiberias, and 'to expel its inhabitants' – but met heavy resistance and failed to take the village.[810] To the west, Carmeli units on the night of 5\6 June took the villages of al Makr and Judeida, east of Acre, after a brief firefight. The troops were ordered to 'confiscate weapons and if there is strong resistance [by Judeida] . . . to destroy it, but if it submits, to act nicely'. The same was to apply to al Makr. In effect both villages surrendered and gave up their arms. Some Muslims fled Makr but the bulk of the inhabitants at both sites were allowed to stay. Around Judeida, the Israeli troops killed nine Arabs: Five prisoners, taken before the operation began, were killed by a guard who 'thought that they were escaping (so he claimed)'; two more were shot to prevent them from telling enemy forces where the IDF had planted a mine; and two others were killed when a caravan 'of donkeys and camels' approaching the village was ambushed as the operation began.[811]

From the foregoing, it appears that Golani and Carmeli had no overall, monolithic guideline about how to relate to Arab communities behind and along the front lines (save to disarm them): Some units expelled villagers or made sure that villages stayed empty, while others merely occupied or searched and disarmed them. Unlike in Giv'ati's zone of operations, arms confiscation operations did not invariably result in expulsion. And while some communities initially left in place were subsequently expelled, other communities were left in place permanently and these large Muslim villages remain to this day (al Makr, Judeida and others).

CONCLUSION

From the foregoing, it emerges that the main, second wave of the exodus, resulting in 250,000–300,000 refugees, was not the result of a general, predetermined Yishuv policy. The exodus of April–May caught the Yishuv leadership by surprise, though it was immediately seen as a phenomenon to be exploited. As Galili put it on 11 May:

> Up to 15 May and after 15 May we must continue to implement the plan of military operations [i.e., Plan D] . . . which did not take into account the collapse and flight of Arab settlements following the route in Haifa . . . [But] this collapse facilitates our tasks.[812]

A major shift in attitudes towards Arab communities can be discerned in the Haganah and among civilian executives during the first half of April, when, reeling from the blows of the battle for the roads, the Yishuv braced for the expected Arab invasion. The Plan D guidelines, formulated in early March, to a certain degree already embodied this new orientation. Their essence was that the rear areas of the State's territory and its main roads had to be secured, and that this was best done by driving out hostile or potentially hostile communities and destroying swathes of villages. During the first half of April, Ben-Gurion and the HGS approved a series of offensives – in effect, counterattacks (Operation Nahshon and the operations around Mishmar Ha'emek) – embodying these guidelines. During the following weeks, Haganah and IZL offensives in Haifa, Jaffa, and eastern and western Galilee precipitated a mass exodus.

During its first months, the exodus was regarded by the Arab states and the AHC as a passing phenomenon of no particular consequence. Palestinian leaders and commanders struggled against it, unsuccessfully. The transformation of the exodus in April into a massive demographic upheaval caught the AHC and the Arab states largely unawares and caused great embarrassment: It highlighted the AHC's (and the Palestinians') weakness and the Arab states' inability, so long as the Mandate lasted, to intervene. At the same time, it propelled these states closer to the invasion about which they were largely unenthusiastic. There is no evidence that the Arab states and the AHC wanted a mass exodus or issued blanket orders or appeals to flee. At the same time, the AHC and the Arab states often encouraged villagers (and, in some places, townspeople) to send their women, children and old people out of harm's way. Local political and military leaders also ordered some villages to evacuate in order to forestall their (treacherous) acceptance of Jewish rule. In certain areas (around Jerusalem, and along the Syrian border), the Arab states ordered villages to uproot for strategic reasons.

The picture that emerges is complex and varied, differing widely from place to place and week to week. In trying to elucidate patterns, it is necessary to distinguish between the towns and the countryside.

The evacuation of the towns during April–May must be seen as the culmination of a series of processes and events and against the backdrop of the basic weaknesses of Palestinian society: The Arab inhabitants of Haifa, Jaffa, Tiberias and, to a lesser extent, Safad, Beisan and Acre had for months suffered from a collapse of administration and law and order, difficulties of communications and supplies, isolation, siege, skirmishing and intermittent harassment at the hands of Jewish troops. In the case of Jaffa, Haifa and Jerusalem, the steady exodus of the middle and upper classes over December 1947 – March 1948 considerably demoralised the remaining inhabitants and provided a model for their own departure once conditions became intolerable. The urban masses (and the *fellahin*) had traditionally looked to the notability for leadership.

A major factor in the exodus from the towns was the earlier fall of and exodus from other towns. The exodus from Arab Tiberias served as a pointer and model for Haifa's Arab leaders on the eve of their own decision to evacuate. It also undermined morale in Safad. Even more telling were the fall and exodus of Arab Haifa: These strongly affected the inhabitants of Jaffa, and also radiated defeatism throughout the north, affecting Safad, Beisan and Acre. If mighty Haifa could fall and be uprooted, how could relatively unarmed, small communities hope to hold out? Moreover, the exodus from the towns demoralised the surrounding hinterland. The fall of Tiberias had resulted in the exodus of villages along the Sea of Galilee shoreline (Ghuweir Abu Shusha and others), and the collapse of Jaffa had a similar effect on such villages as Salama, Yazur and Kheiriya.

In turn, the defeat of, and exodus from, hinterland villages served to undermine morale in the towns. The townspeople felt, and were, cut off. The fall of Khirbet Nasir ad Din undermined morale in Tiberias; the fall of Salama and other satellite villages contributed to the exodus from Jaffa; the fall of Biriya and 'Ein al Zeitun affected Safad; and the fall of the Western Galilee villages precipitated the collapse of Acre.

The 'atrocity factor' certainly fuelled the process. What happened, or allegedly happened, at Nasser ad Din demoralized Arab Tiberias. In a more general way, the massacre at Deir Yassin, and the exaggerated descriptions broadcast on Arab radio stations for weeks undermined morale throughout Palestine, especially in the countryside.

A major factor in the urban exodus was the dissolution and flight of the local civil and military leadership just before and during the final battles. The flight of the Tabaris from Tiberias; the flight of the NC and the commanders from Arab Haifa just before and during the battle; the flight of Jaffa's leaders during and after the IZL assault; and the departure from Safad and Beisan of prominent local families and commanders – all contributed to the mass exodus from each town and its hinterland.

In the villages, there was normally no flight of leaders before or during attack. Except for those evacuated earlier by women and children, villages were by and large abandoned at one go; the mukhtar and the militia usually left together with the remaining male population.

Undoubtedly, as was understood by IDF intelligence, the most important single factor in the exodus of April–June was Jewish attack. This is demonstrated clearly by the fact that each exodus occurred during or in the immediate wake of military assault. No town was abandoned by the bulk of its population before the main Haganah\IZL assault. In the countryside, while many of the villages were abandoned during Haganah\IZL attacks and because of them, other villages were evacuated as a result of Jewish attacks on neighbouring villages or towns; they feared that they would be next.

In general, Haganah operational orders for attacks on towns did not call for the expulsion or eviction of the civilian population. But from early April, operational orders for attacks on villages and clusters of villages more often than not called for the destruction of villages and, implicitly or explicitly, expulsion. And, no doubt, the spectacle of panicky flight served to whet the appetites of Haganah commanders and, perhaps, the HGS as well. Like Ben-Gurion, they realised that a transfer of the prospective large minority out of the emergent Jewish State had begun and that with very little extra effort and nudging, it could be expanded. The temptation proved very strong, for solid military and political reasons.

By and large, when it came to ejecting Arab communities, Haganah commanders exercised greater independence and forcefulness in the countryside than in the towns. This was due partly to the greater distance from headquarters, where senior officers and officials, as exemplified by Ben-Gurion, were reluctant to openly order or endorse expulsions, and partly, to the guidelines set down in Plan D, which enabled local commanders to expel and level villages but made no provision for wholesale expulsions from towns.

During April–June, a time factor clearly influenced Haganah behaviour. The closer drew the 15 May British withdrawal deadline and the prospect of invasion by the Arab states, the readier became commanders to resort to 'cleansing' operations and expulsions to rid their rear areas, main roads, and prospective front lines of hostile and potentially hostile civilian concentrations. After 15 May, the threat and presence of the Arab regular armies near the Yishuv's population centers dictated a play-safe policy of taking no chances with communities to the rear; hence, the Giv'ati Brigade's expulsions in May–June near Rehovot. In general, however, the swift collapse of almost all the Palestinian and foreign irregular formations and of civilian morale, and the spontaneous panic and flight of most communities meant that Jewish commanders almost invariably did not have to face the dilemma of expelling: Most villages were completely or almost completely empty by the time they were conquered.

ENDNOTES

1. Khalidi, 'Plan Dalet . . .'; Pappe, *Making*, 54–55, 89–94; and Masalha, 'The Historical Roots . . .', 43–44 – argue the opposite, to my mind contrary to the evidence.
2. HGS, 'Tochnit Dalet', 10 Mar. 1948, IDFA 922\75\\949, IDFA 922\75\\595 and IDFA 2687\49\\35.
3. HGS, 'Tochnit Dalet', 10 Mar. 1948, IDFA 922\75\\595 and 922\75\\949, for Giv'ati and Alexandroni brigades.
4. See Operations Officer, Alexandroni, to battalions 31, 32, 33 and 34,? April 1948 (apparently 5\6 April), IDFA 2687\49\\35.
5. Entries for 22 and 23 Apr. 1948, Weitz, *Diary*, III, 272.
6. Protocol of Cabinet meeting, 19 May 1948, ISA. See also Sharett's statement of 'surprise' in protocol of Cabinet meeting, 20 June 1948, ISA.
7. Protocol of Cabinet meeting, 8 Jun. 1948, ISA. But it is worth noting that a week later, Ben-Gurion affirmed that 'the Arab flight' came to him as 'no surprise' (protocol of Cabinet meeting, 16 June 1948, ISA).
8. IDF GS\Intelligence to 'Conrad', 'Summary of Information from Northern Front', 3 June 1948, IDFA 922\75\\1044.
9. 'Summary of the Meeting of the Advisers on Arab Affairs in Camp Dora 31.3.48', IDFA 4663\49\\125.
10. 'Summary of the Meeting of the Arab Affairs Advisers in Dora Camp 6.4.48', IDFA 4663\49\\125.
11. 'Naftali' to zone OCs, 18 Apr. 1948, IDFA 4663\49\\46.
12. 'Summary of the Meeting of the Arab Affairs Advisers in Dora Camp 13.4.48', IDFA 4663\49\\125.
13. 'Tiroshi (Dror)' to HIS-AD, 16 Apr. 1948, HA 105\257.
14. Galili, 'Meeting of HNS, 5.4.', IDFA 481\49\\64.
15. Galili to Yadin, 15 Apr. 1948, IDFA 661\69\\45.
16. Allon to HGS\Operations, 18 Apr. 1948, IDFA 196\71\\83. From April on, Haganah\IDF documents often use the word *plitim* (refugees) as a synonym for Arab inhabitants.
17. HGS to brigades, 13 Apr. 1948, IDFA 922\75\\1219.
18. 'Summary of a Meeting with "Amitai", 6 May 1948', DBGA.
19. Ben-Gurion, *As Israel Fights*, 100. A slightly different version appears in DBG-YH II, 387.
20. Unsigned, 'Hebrew Translation of Record-Posters in Arabic [Nos.] 1–6', undated, IDFA 1196\52\\1.
21. HGS\Operations\5 to brigades, 16 Apr. 1948, IDFA 922\75\\1206.
22. Unsigned, 'Assumptions [i.e., Guidelines? Concerning] Behaviour Toward Surrendering Villages', 22 Apr. 1948, HA 80\774\7 (Zvi Aurbach Papers). This document reached the Haganah's Arab affairs advisers and is referred to in 'Summary: Meeting of the Arab Affairs Advisers in Netanya 25.4.48', IDFA 2506\49\\91.
23. Shitrit, 'Memorandum of the Ministry for Minority Affairs', 10 May 1948, ISA, Labour Ministry, 6178\2924. The memorandum was apparently produced at Ben-Gurion's suggestion after Machnes came to him and complained of

Haganah behaviour in the occupied areas (entry for 6 May 1948, Ben-Gurion Diary).

24. Unsigned, 'Definition of the [Requisite] Behaviour in Managing Arab Towns and Villages to be Conquered by the Military', undated but stamped 'received 16 May 1948', IDFA 6127\49\\109.

25. HGS\Operations, 'Chapter 1. – General', 11 May 1948, IDFA 2384\50\\9.

26. Chief of HGS to Alexandroni, 23 Mar. 1948, IDFA 481\49\\50.

27. Alexandroni to sub-district OCs (mafanim), 2 Mar. 1948, IDFA 4663\49\\84; Alexandroni to sub-district OCs, 15 Mar. 1948, IDFA 2506\49\\91; Alexandroni to battalions, etc., 28 Mar. 1948, IDFA 922\75\\1211; Naftali to heads of councils and headmen, 30 Mar. 1948, IDFA 4663\49\\84; and Hadari to district OCs, 23 Mar. 1948, IDFA 244\51\\81.

28. Protocol of meeting of Defence Committee, 16 Mar. 1948, CZA S25–9347.

29. Galili to Gwirtz, Danin, Machnes, 26 Mar. 1948, and HGS to brigades, 29 Mar. 1948, both in IDFA 481\49\\50.

30. Gwirtz to ?, 1 Apr. 1948, IDFA 2506\49\\91.

31. Gwirtz to ?, 1 April 1948, 'Subject: Sdot Tvuah', IDFA 2506\49\\91.

32. 'Yaakobi' to Giv'ati, 28 Apr. 1948, IDFA 1041\49\\7.

33. 'Summary of Meeting of the Arab Affairs Advisers in Camp Dora 31.3.48'; 'Summary of Meeting of the Arab Affairs Advisers in Camp Dora 6.4.48; and 'Summary of Meeting of the Arab Affairs Advisers in Camp Dora 13.4.48', – all in IDFA 4663\49\\125; 'Summary, Meeting of the Arab Affairs Advisers in Netanya 25.4.48', IDFA 2506\49\\91; and 'Summary of Meeting of the Arab Affairs Advisers in Netanya 9.5.48', IDFA 6127\49\\109.

34. Galili to brigades, 13 Apr. 1948, HA 73\169.

35. See Morris, 'The Harvest of 1948 . . .'; and OC Kinneret sub-district to 'Reuven', 30 May 1948, IDFA 1096\49\\51.

36. Horowitz to Ben-Gurion, 2 May 1948, IDFA 6127\49\\109.

37. Ben-Gurion, *As Israel Fights*, 87–88, text of Ben-Gurion's speech to Zionist Actions Committee, 6 Apr. 1948.

38. 'Yavne', 'Arab Information from 17.4.48', IDFA 500\48\\55.

39. Tahsin Kamal, Defence and Security Dept., NC, Jerusalem, to secretaries of neighbourhood committees, 22 Apr. 1948, ISA FM2570\11.

40. 'Hashmonai', 'Arab Information from 5 April 1948', IDFA 500\48\\55.

41. 'Hashmonai' to 'Moriah', 'Annexes to Information Summary No. 182.', c. 19 Apr. 1948, IDFA 2605\49\\2.

42. Unsigned, untitled segment of HIS report, 22 Apr. 1948, HA 105\257.

43. Entry for 4 May 1948, CZA A246–13, 2373.

44. 'Tzuri' (Levi Avrahami, OC HIS Northern Front) to HIS-AD, 'Miscellaneous Intelligence', 9 May 1948, IDFA 1196\52\\1.

45. HIS, 'Daily Summary', 3 May 1948, IDFA 900\52\\58.

46. 'Peretz' to 'Hashmonai', 'Subject: Information from the Motza Area', 30 Mar. 1948, IDFA 500\48\\29; and unsigned, 'Qastal', 3 Apr. 1948, IDFA 5545\49\\114.

47. 'Yavne to HIS-AD, 6 Apr. 1948, HA 105\257.

48. 'Hashmonai' to 'Michmash', 'Annexes to Information Summary No. 143', 8 Apr. 1948, IDFA 4944\49\\499.

49. 'Yavne' to HIS-AD, 10 Apr. 1948, HA 105\257.

50. 'Arab Intelligence from 28.4.48', IDFA 500\48\\55.
51. 'Yavne' to HIS-AD, 11 Apr. 1948, HA 105\257.
52. Unsigned, 'Shu'fat', 29 Apr. 1948, IDFA 196\71\\83; and 'Hashmonai' to 'Michmash', 'Summary of Intelligence No. 205, 29.4.48', IDFA 4944\49\\499.
53. 'Yavne' to HIS-AD, 15 Apr. 1948, HA 105\257; and unsigned, 'Arab Intelligence from 20.4.48', IDFA 500\48\\55.
54. Untitled, unsigned intelligence report, 18 Apr. 1948, IDFA 5545\49\\114.
55. 'Yavne' to HIS-AD, 19 Apr. 1948, HA 105\257.
56. 'Summary of Intelligence for Alexandroni Brigade (11.5.48), No. 8', IDFA 2506\49\\80; and 'HIS Intelligence, Daily Summary', 7 May 1948, HA 105\94.
57. 'Yavne to District OC, 'Urgent Arab Intelligence from 20.4.48', IDFA 500\48\\55.
58. 'Na'im (Na'aman)' to HIS-AD, 8 Apr. 1948, HA 105\257.
59. 'Summary of Information for Alexandroni Brigade (11.5.48), No. 8', IDFA 2506\49\\80.
60. 'Tzuri (Shaanan)' to HIS-AD, 7 May 1948, HA 105\92.
61. 'Oded' to Golani, 20 Apr. 1948, IDFA 128\51\\50.
62. Unsigned, 'Carmeli Brigade Summary of Intelligence No. 3 for 7.5.48', IDFA 273\52\\2.
63. 'Tiroshi (Eitan)' to HIS-AD, 2 May 1948, HA 105\217.
64. 'Hiram', untitled, 22 Apr. 1948, HA 105\257; and 'Hiram' to HIS-AD, 27 Apr. 1948, HA 105\257; and Alexandroni, 'Bulletin No. 34', 9 Jun. 1948, IDFA 2323\49\\6.
65. 'Tiroshi (Eitan)' to HIS-AD, 22 Apr. 1948, HA 105\257.
66. 'Tiroshi (Eitan)' to HIS-AD, 29 Apr. 1948, HA 105\257.
67. 'Summary of Intelligence for Alexandroni Brigade (11.5.48), No. 8', IDFA 2506\49\\80.
68. HIS, 'Intelligence, Daily Summary', 7 May 1948, HA 105\94.
69. 'Yiftah' to HGS, Yadin, etc., 2 May 1948, IDFA 128\51\\50.
70. 'Yovev', untitled, 8 May 1948, HA 105\217.
71. HIS-AD, Qastina village file, entry for 19 May 1948, HA 105\134.
72. 'Tzuri (Leshem)' to HIS-AD, 26 June 1948, HA 105\127 aleph; and 'Hiram' to HIS-AD, 'Subject: The Journey of the Wife of Ma'luli to Beirut', 4 July 1948, HA 105\127 aleph.
73. 'Tzuri (Leshem)' to HIS-AD, 7 July 1948, IDFA 7249\49\\138.
74. 'Hiram' to IDF Intelligence Service, 3 Aug. 1948, IDFA 7249\49\\138.
75. Golani\Intelligence, 'Intelligence', 27 Jun. 1948, IDFA 1096\49\\64.
76. 'Tzuri (Leshem)' to HIS-AD, 11 July 1948, HA 105\127 aleph.
77. 'Tzuri (Leshem)' to HIS-AD, 7 July 1948, IDFA 7249\49\\138.
78. 'Tzuri (Shaanan)' to HIS-AD, 11 July 1948, IDFA 7249\49\\138.
79. 'Giora' to 'Utz', 17 Aug. 1948, IDFA 7249\49\\138.
80. 'Tzuri (Yosef)' to IDF Intelligence Service, 19 Sept. 1948, IDFA 7249\49\\138.
81. Intelligence officer, 6th Battalion, 'page No. 387, No. 576', undated but late Aug. 1948, IDFA 1046\70\\417.
82. Yiftah intelligence logbook, entry for 31 Oct. 1948, IDFA 922\75\\1230.

83. 54th Battalion to Giv'ati, 'Subject: Summary for 29.4.48', 30 Apr. 1948, IDFA 1041\49\\18.
84. 'Hiram' to HIS, 30 Apr. 1948, HA 105\257.
85. Alexandroni, 'Bulletin No.12', 18 May 1948, IDFA 2323\49\\6.
86. 'Yeruham' to HIS-AD, 13 May 1948, HA 105\217.
87. Unsigned, 'Arab Intelligence from 13.5.48', IDFA 5254\49\\75.
88. HIS-AD, 'The Migratory Movement . . .', 30 June 1948, HHA-ACP 10.95.13 (1).
89. 'Mitzpa' to HIS-AD, 6 Apr. 1948, HA 105\257.
90. 'Yiftah' to HGS, etc., 2 May 1948, IDFA 128\51\\50.
91. 'Tzuri' to HIS-AD, 10 May 1948, IDFA 1196\52\\1.
92. 'Tzuri' to HIS-AD, 'Subject: Miscellaneous Information from Samakh and the Area', 27 Apr. 1948, HA 105\92 bet.
93. Unsigned, 'Ein-Gev. [Testimony] Taken from Ezra Klopfeny, 9.10.48', IDFA 1235\52\\1. See also *Ein Gev in the War*, 35.
94. Unsigned, 'Ein-Gev, [Testimony] Taken 4.7.48, from Zili Diter, OC "Persian" Sector', IDFA 1235\52\\1; *Ein Gev in the War*, 34 and 71; and Yitah, MAM, to Military Governor, Western Galilee, 26 Oct. 1948, and Hassan Zickrallah to OC Acre, 20 Oct. 1948, both in IDFA 922\52\\564.
95. The former Prime Minister of Syria, Khalid al 'Azm, in his memoirs *Mudhakkirat Khalid al 'Azm*, I, 386, wrote: 'We brought destruction upon 1 million Arab refugees by calling upon them and pleading with them repeatedly to leave their lands and homes and factories.' (I am grateful to Dr Gideon Weigart of Jerusalem for this reference.) But I have found no contemporary evidence of such blanket, official 'calls', by any Arab government. And I have found no evidence that the Palestinians or any substantial group left because they heard such 'calls' or orders from outside Arab leaders. The only, minor, exceptions to this are the traces (mentioned above) of the order, apparently by the Syrians, to some of the inhabitants of Eastern Galilee to leave a few days prior to, and in preparation for, the invasion of 15–16 May. This order affected at most several thousand Palestinians and, in any case, 'dovetailed' with Haganah efforts to drive out the population in this area (see treatment below of 'Operation Yiftah').

It is possible that it is to this order that al 'Azm was referring. Or, as is most probable, he inserted the passage to make some point within the context of inter-Arab polemics (i.e., blaming fellow Arab leaders for the exodus).

Had blanket orders to leave been issued by the outside Arab leaders, including the exiled Palestinian leaders – via radio broadcasts or in any other public manner – traces of them would certainly have surfaced in the contemporary documentation produced by the Yishuv's\Israel's military and civilian institutions, the Mandate Government, and British and American diplomatic legations in the area. The Yishuv's intelligence agencies – HIS and its successor organisation, the IDF's Intelligence Service, and the Arab Division of the JA-PD, and its successor bodies, the Middle East Affairs, Research and Political departments of the Israel Foreign Ministry – as well as Western intelligence agencies all monitored Arab radio broadcasts and attended to the announcements of the Arab leaders. But no Jewish or

British or American intelligence or diplomatic report from the critical period, December 1947 – July 1948, quotes from or even refers to such orders.

The BBC for years monitored Arab radio broadcasts. In the early 1970s, John Zimmerman checked the BBC monitoring reports to see whether they referred to broadcast Arab orders to evacuate. In 1973–1974 he published 'Radio Propaganda in the Arab-Israeli War 1948'. He found no such broadcasts, only reports of broadcasts describing the evacuation of women and children from a handful of sites.

In his article, 'The New Historians', Shabtai Tebeth quotes from an HIS-AD report of 27 April 1948 as follows: '[There are] rumours that an order was issued by the AHC in Jerusalem to evacuate the Arab inhabitants of several sites in the country, as the Arab governments want to send strong forces of tanks and aircraft and to bomb all the country's cities, and do not wish to harm the Arab inhabitants. [They are] advising the Arab inhabitants to flee the country as soon as possible and after its conquest by the Arab governments they will bring back the Arab inhabitants as conquerors.' I have never seen the document. But if it exists, and reads as quoted, then it is the only contemporary document that has surfaced referring in some way to a general order to evacuate. However, HIS never again referred, in any document, to these rumoured 'orders' – and would have had they been verified. And the Yishuv's spokesmen would no doubt have made use of such a monitored order or orders, if only to rebut Arab charges, in the UN and elsewhere, that the Yishuv was conducting a policy of expulsion vis-à-vis the Palestinians. Had the HIS or any other Yishuv body had the text of a blanket Arab order to evacuate or solid references to such an order, it would without doubt have brandished and broadcast them to high heaven. But the Yishuv never did.

As well, it is worth noting that the quoted document refers explicitly to 'rumours'; speaks of the AHC 'in Jerusalem' – not to the real AHC centre of power, Husseini's villa outside Cairo; and seems to be speaking of the evacuation 'of several sites', not of a blanket order 'to Palestine's Arabs'. But as with most rumours, there was a grain of truth in them: There was one major site where the AHC had certainly pressed at this time for continued civilian evacuation – Haifa. Several sources, including British intelligence, at the end of April, referred to reports and 'rumours' of AHC orders to Haifa's Arabs to continue their evacuation, as it was to be targeted by Arab bombers on invasion day (see below). These rumours originating in Haifa were in all likelihood the source of the HIS report of 27 Apr.

96. 'Hashmonai' to ?, 'Intelligence Summary No. 184, 25.4.48', IDFA 5254\49\\75.
97. 'Daily Monitoring Report, No. 20', undated but referring to 25–26 Apr. 1948, IDFA 4944\49\\617.
98. 'Yavne' to HIS-AD, 19 Apr. 1948, HA 105\257.
99. 'Arab Intelligence from 18.5.48', 19 May 1948, IDFA 500\48\\55.
100. 'Hiram' to HIS-AD, 5 Apr. 1948, HA 105\102.
101. The Committee for Economic Defence, 'Information About the Arab Economy, Bulletin No. 3', 13 Apr. 1948, HA 105\146.
102. 'Avner' to HIS-AD, 18 Apr. 1948, HA 105\257.

103. 'Tzefa' (Tuvia Lishansky, senior HIS officer), untitled, 6 Apr. 1948, HA 105\257.
104. 'Tzuri' to Golani, 'General Survey for Months of March, April 1948', 3 May 1948, IDFA 1196\52\\1.
105. 'Tzuri', untitled, 29 Apr. 1948, HA 105\257.
106. 'Tzuri' to Golani, 'General Survey for Months of March, April 1948', 3 May 1948, IDFA 1196\52\\1.
107. 'Hashmonai' to 'Michmash', 'Annexes to Summary of Intelligence No. 143, 8.4.48', IDFA 4944\49\\499.
108. 'Yovev' to HIS-AD, 20 Apr. 1948, HA 105\128.
109. 'Tiroshi (Aran)' to HIS-AD, 28 Apr. 1948, HA 105\257.
110. 'Tiroshi (Eitan)' to HIS-AD, 29 Apr. 1948, HA 105\257.
111. 'Doron (Elitzur)' to HIS-AD, 3 May 1948, HA 105\102.
112. 'HIS Intelligence 12.5.48', IDFA 922\75\\1205.
113. 'Hiram' to HIS-AD, 5 May 1948, HA 105\217.
114. 'Summary of Carmeli Brigade Intelligence No. 3 for 7.5.48', IDFA 273\52\\5.
115. 'Tzuri (Barkan)' to HIS-AD, 9 May 1948, IDFA 1196\52\\1.
116. Alexandroni, 'Bulletin No. 6',? May 1948, IDFA 2323\49\\6.
117. 'Summary of Carmeli Brigade Intelligence No. 5 for 24.5.48', IDFA128\51\\71.
118. IDFA-GS Logbook, entry for 16 June 1948, IDFA 922\75\\1176.
119. HIS radio interception, Majd al Kurum to Tarshiha and Lubya (Qawuqji to 'Omar Fasil al Rami), 16 June 1948, HA 105\217.
120. 'Tzuri (Uri)' to HIS-AD, 22 July 1948, IDFA 7249\49\\138.
121. 'Tiroshi (Allon)' to HIS-AD, 31 Mar. 1948, HA 105–257.
122. 'Tiroshi (Allon)' to HIS-AD, 4 May 1948, HA 105\127.
123. Alexandroni, 'Bulletin No. 12', 18 May 1948, IDFA 2323\49\\6.
124. Entry for 26 Apr. 1948, Weitz, *Diary*, III, 273.
125. Unsigned, untitled, undated HIS report, HA 105\217; and Alexandroni, 'Bulletin No. 1', 7 May 1948, IDFA 2323\49\\5.
126. Text of broadcast of Kol Hamagen Ha'ivri (Haganah Radio), Jerusalem, 5 May 1948, CZA S25–8918; 'Information about the Arabs of Palestine (According to Arab Radio Transmissions, 6–7 May 1948)', CZA S25-9045; and 'Daily Monitoring Report No. 28,' 6 May 1948, DBGA.
127. Text of broadcast by Kol Hamagen Ha'ivri, 6 May 1948, CZA S25-8918.
128. Aharon Cohen, 'Our Arab Policy in the Middle of the War', 10 May 1948, HHA-ACP 10.95.10 (4); Aharon Cohen, 'In Face of the Arab Evacuation', summer 1948, HHA-ACP 10.95.11 (8); 'HIS Information', 13 May 1948, KMA-PA 100\MemVavDalet\3-158; and 'Information about the Arabs of Palestine (from Arab Broadcasts, 10–11 May)', and 'Information about the Arabs of Palestine (from Arab Broadcasts, 14–15 May)', both in CZA S25-9045.
129. 'Arab Broadcasts', 6–7 June 1948, CZA S25-9047; and Israel Foreign Ministry, 'In the Arab Public', 26 May 1948, KMA-PA 100\Mem Vav Dalet\1-5. See also Zagorsky to Harzfeld, 2 June 1948, LA 235 IV, 2251 bet, on Arab pressures on evacuees from the Beisan Valley to return.
130. The committee's 26 May reiteration of policy is quoted in Gelber, *Palestine*, 258.

131. For example, see Israel Foreign Ministry, 'In the Arab Public', 11 June 1948, regarding Syria and the Arabs of the Hula Valley; or *Tree and Sword*, 228, on the Arabs of Lubya.
132. Gelber, *Palestine*, 265.
133. HIS, 'The Tabari Family,' undated but stamped 'received 29 Apr. 1941', HA 105\222. Naif is said to have successfully led a band of Arab irregulars in the 1936–1939 rebellion.
134. 'Tzefa' to HIS-AD, 9 Dec. 1947, HA 105\72.
135. 'Tzefa' to HIS-AD, 'Subject: Arab Families leaving their Apartments', 22 Dec. 1947, HA 105\215 aleph; and 'Tzefa' to HIS-AD, 9 Dec. 1947, HA 105\195.
136. 'The Committee of the Jewish Residents of the Old City of Tiberias to the Defence Committee', Tiberias, 8 Feb. 1948, CZA S25-4147. See also Entry for 10 Feb. 1948, DBG-YH I, 227.
137. 'HIS Intelligence, Daily Summary', 23 Dec. 1947, HA 105\61.
138. 'Tzefa' to HIS-AD, 29 Dec. 1947, HA 105\23; and Major Ben-Zion and Y. Ben-Arye, IDF History Branch, 'Testimony of Major Schusterman', 22 Mar. 1957, IDFA 922\75\\943.
139. Entry for 4 Feb. 1948, YND; and Nahmani to Yosef Weitz, 10 Feb. 1948, CZA S25-7721.
140. Nahmani to Weitz, 10 Feb. 1948, CZA S250-7721; and 'Mitzpa (Hava)' to HIS-ASD, 16 Feb. 1948, HA 105\54 aleph.
141. 'Hiram' to HIS-AD, 22 Feb. 1948, HA 105\54 aleph.
142. *Tree and Sword*, 109; and YND, entry for 14 Mar. 1948. See also Sami Khalil al Tabari, Tiberias NC, to head of the Division for National Guidance, AHC, Cairo, undated but from c. 17 Mar. 1948, HA 105\32 aleph.
143. M. Hildsheimer and Yael Avital, 'Interview with Moshe Weiss (Tzahar)', head of the Tiberias Jews' Situation Committee in 1948, 18 Jan. 1982, Tiberias Municipal Archive. See also Tzahar, 'Historians . . .', 204, for a later, different version of the meeting with Galili.
144. Stefan to Yadin, 14 Mar. 1948, and HGS\Operations to Golani, 17 Mar. 1948, both in IDFA 67\51\\677.
145. 'Mitzpa (Hava)' to HIS-AD, 23 Mar. 1948, HA 105\257.
146. 'Tzuri' to Golani, 3 May 1948, 'General Survey for the Months of March, April 1948', IDFA 1196\52\\1.
147. 'Optik' to Golani, 'No. 2', 10 Apr. 1948, and Optik to Golani, 10 Apr. 1948, both in IDFA 128\51\\18.
148. 'Kna'ani', 'Report on the Nasir a Din Operation', 12 Apr. 1948, IDFA 922\75\\1025.
149. HIS Intelligence, Daily Summary', 18 Apr. 1948, IDFA 900\52\\58. 'Deir Yassin' meant massacre.
150. In Ben-Zion and Ben-Aryeh, IDF History Branch, 'Testimony Taken from Amos Mukadi (Brandstetter) about His Activities in the Golani Brigade during the War of Independence', 22 Mar. 1957, IDFA 922\75\\943, Mukadi recalled that some 'gang' members tried to escape from the site by hiding behind fleeing women. 'My men did not know what to do . . . And then I gave an order to fire at anyone trying to escape even if this leads to hitting the women. Otherwise there was no way of destroying the gang members. As a result, a number of women were killed . . . [That] night Radio Damascus

announced that the Jews had repeated the Deir Yassin deed. Incidentally, I think that one of the things that broke the Arabs of Tiberias so quickly was that the Arabs themselves published and exaggerated [the story] in connection with Nasir al Din and this led to the flight of the Arabs of Tiberias.'

151. Divisional Logbook, 6th Airborne Division, entry for 12 Apr. 1948, PRO WO 275-54; and Nazzal, *Exodus*, 29 (who misdates the attack '10 April 1948'). The AHC misdated the attack '14 April 1948' (see AHC memorandum, 26 July 1948, PRO CO 733-487\2).

152. Entry for 12 Apr. 1948, YND.

153. 'Oded' to Golani, Palmah, 13 Apr. 1948, IDFA 922\75\\1208.

154. 'Written Testimony of David Khidra, A Resident of Tiberias', undated, Tiberias Municipal Archive; Tiberias to ?, 17 April 1948, 22:45 hours, IDFA 128\51\\50; and entry for 17 Apr. 1948, YND.

155. MILPAL to ?, 19 April, IDFA 900\52\\43; and Ben-Zion and Ben-Aryeh, 'Testimony of Major Schusterman', 22 Mar. 1957, IDFA 922\75\\943. Schusterman, who commanded the 12th Battalion's 'C' Company in Tiberias in April 1948, is quoted as saying: 'British feelers regarding an evacuation of the city began. The British commander proposed to the Arabs to evacuate the city.' But another Haganah commander, the deputy OC of 12th Battalion, Yitzhak Broshi, remembered things differently: 'The British Commander showed up and announced that the Arabs were asking to evacuate the town . . . [The British] in the end offered their help in the evacuation . . .' (see Ben-Zion, Y. Ben-Aryeh and Avigdor Kirchner, 'Summary of Meeting with Yitzhak Broshi, deputy OC 12th Battalion in War of Independence', 13 Mar. 1957, IDFA 922\75\\943).

156. Tiberias to ?, 17 April, 1948, IDFA 128\51\\50; 'Tzuri (Hava)' to HIS-AD, 20 Apr. 1948, HA 105\257; and 'Tzuri' to HIS-AD, 24 Apr. 1948, HA 105\92 bet.

157. Nazzal, *Exodus*, 29–30; Moshe Tzahar interview, Tiberias Municipal Archive; and Divisional Logbook, 6th Airborne Division, entry for 18 Apr. 1948, PRO WO 275-54. According to Tzahar, the news of the Arab evacuation came to him as a 'shock' and he protested to Anderson against the evacuation but the British 'did not relent'. Tzahar then asked Anderson to summon the Arab leaders to try to persuade them to reconsider. Anderson answered: 'There are no longer leaders [here]. They have fled.' Tzahar's recollection (Tzahar interview, Tiberias Municipal Archive and in Tzahar, 'Historians . . .', 207–208) is not corroborated by any contemporary document, and lacks credibility. Golan, *Transformation*, 22, implies that in April, the British adopted a policy of 'encouraging the evacuation of ethnic enclaves'. I have seen no hard evidence of such a 'policy' ever having been adopted, though there is evidence that such thinking may have underpinned specific commanders' decisions in certain areas at certain times (possibly in Tiberias, possibly also vis-à-vis Kibbutz Mishmar Ha'emek earlier in April (see below)). Tzahar's recollection is that the decision by the Arabs to abandon Tiberias was taken by the local leadership either in consultation with the British authorities or at their suggestion. But there are contemporary reports suggesting that the town's Arabs received an order from outside – from the AHC? The Nazareth NC? The Arab League in Damascus? – to leave. One HIS-AD report states: 'From various Arab and

[British] military sources it has become known that the Arabs in the place received orders to leave Tiberias' ('Tzuri (Hava)' to HIS-AD, 20 Apr. 1948, HA 105\257). See also 'Tzuri (Hava)' to HIS-AD, 'Subject: Miscellaneous Reports on the Evacuation of Tiberias', 21 Apr. 1948, HA 105\257, reporting that the order to evacuate had come 'from on high' (*higi'a migavoha*).

158. 'Tzuri (Hava)' to HIS-AD, 'Subject: Miscellaneous Reports from Tiberias,' 21 Apr. 1948, HA 105\257.

159. 'Tzuri' to HIS-AD, 24 Apr. 1948, HA 105\92 bet. 'Tzuri' ('Tzuri (Hava)' to HIS-AD, 21 Apr. 1948, HA 105\257) also reported that most of the families had reached northern Jordan – the Tabaris' place of origin – where the government provided them with tents. A town crier was going about Irbid announcing that the Jews of Tiberias 'had raped Arab women . . . Great propaganda is being carried out using the incidents of rape to stir up the masses who believe [the reports].' (I have seen no other reference to rape in any document relating to Tiberias.) He also reported that Sidqi Tabari, in Damascus, was put on trial on charges of taking a bribe – of P £3,000 – from the Jews for agreeing to 'the truce' (of mid-March ?); rumours of this alleged bribe – and that Naif Tabari and Rashid Tabari had also received bribes – had been rife in Tiberias before the final battle. It was alleged that Tiberias's inhabitants had learnt of these bribes and that this is what had led to the Tabaris' flight before 18 April.

160. 12th Battalion\Intelligence to Golani Brigade\Intelligence, ? April 1948, IDFA 128\51\\18. On 4 Sept 1955, the daily *Falastin* published a highly imaginative report on 'The Fall of Tiberias', including among the reasons: 'Intrigues by the Mandate forces and the influx into their [i.e., the Arab militia] camps of Jewish lasses, where they held "red night" parties.' As to the Arab evacuation, the article accuses neither the British nor the Jews, and implies that the inhabitants fled on their own volition (see IDFA 922\75\\695).

161. Entry for 18 Apr. 1948, YND.

162. Palmah HQ to HGS, 18 Apr. 1948, IDFA 922\75\\1066.

163. 'Shimon' to Golani, 18 Apr. 1948, 18:15 hours, IDFA 128\51\\50.

164. Entry for 18 Apr. 1948, YND.

165. 'Tzuri (Hava)' to HIS-AD, 20 Apr. 1948, HA 105\257.

166. 'Tzuri (Hava)' to HIS-AD, 25 Apr. 1948, HA 105\92 bet.

167. Entries for 21 and 22 Apr. 1948, YND. Tzahar, 'Historians . . .', 211, recalled: 'The whole police force of the Hebrew government was activated only in order to protect the Arab property. It is possible that in the first two days [after the Jewish victory] there were isolated incidents of robbery [i.e., looting], but this is light years away from [maintaining that there was] a mass assault on Arab property.' His memoirs are littered with such erroneous apologetics.

168. 'Tzuri (Hava)' to HIS-AD, 25 Apr. 1948, HA 105\92 bet.

169. Presidium of the Community Committee, Temporary Situation Committee, untitled proclamation, 19 Apr. 1948, Tiberias Municipal Archive.

170. Colonial Secretary (New York) to Cunningham, 24 Apr. 1948, SAMECA CP III\4\23; and *Tree and Sword*, 9.

171. E.N. Koussa, letter to editor, *The Palestine Post*, 6 Feb. 1949.

172. HIS-AD, 'The Migratory Movement . . .', 30 Jun. 1948, HHA-ACP 10.95.13 (1), succinctly explains the causes of the Tiberias exodus thus: 'Our

operations [i.e., Haganah assault], lack of leaders on the spot. The rich fled earlier.'

173. 12th Battalion to Golani, 19 Apr. 1948, IDFA 128\51\\50; and 'Tzuri (Khokh)' to HIS-AD, 21 Apr. 1948, HA 105\257. In a letter to the editor (*Haaretz*, 11 Apr. 1999), David 'Iron recalls that the tribe's mukhtar, Diab al Ibrahim, told his Jewish neighbours that he had received an order originating in the AHC to evacuate the site and this precipitated the evacuation. Contrariwise, the deputy OC of 12th Battalion, Broshi (Ben-Zion, Kirschner, and Ben-Aryeh, 'Summary of Meeting with Yitzhak Broshi . . .', 13 Mar. 1957, IDFA 922\75\\943), earlier recalled that 'Arab al Qadish were evacuated under Haganah pressure.

174. 'Tzuri (Khoch)' to HIS-AD, 22 Apr. 1948, HA 105\257.

175. Golani Brigade Logbook, entry for 24 Apr. 1948, IDFA 665\51\\1. See also 'The Fall of Tiberias', *Falastin*, 4 Sept. 1955, in IDFA 922\75\\ 695.

176. 'Tzuri (Fawzi)' to HIS-AD, 21 Apr. 1948, HA 105\257; and Golani Brigade Logbook, entry for 22 Apr. 1948, IDFA 665\51\\1.

177. Golani Brigade Logbook, entry for 22 Apr. 1948, IDFA 665\51\\1; and 'Tzuri' to HIS-AD, 23 Apr. 1948, HA 105\257. The action by the headman of Genossar was apparently ordered by 12th Battalion headquarters (Ben-Zion, Kirschner and Ben-Aryeh, 'Summary of Meeting with Yitzhak Broshi . . .', 13 Mar. 1957, IDFA 922\75\\943).

178. 'Tzuri (Kochva)' to HIS-AD, 'Subject: Ghuweir Abu Shusha', 24 June 1948, HA 105\226.

179. HIS-AD, 'The Migratory Movement . . .', 30 Jun. 1948, HHA-ACP 10.95.13 (1).

180. Committee for Economic Defence, 'Information from the Arab Economy, Bulletin No. 4', 10–13 Apr. 1948, HA 105\146.

181. 'Hiram' to 'Jeremiah', 1 Apr. 1948, IDFA 5942\49\\23; and 'Hiram' to HIS-AD, 4 Apr. 1948, HA 105\257.

182. Unsigned, 'Report on "Shahar" Patrol', 10 Apr. 1948, HA 105\257.

183. 'Hiram' to HIS-AD. 19 Apr. 1948, HA 105\257. Goren, 'Haifa', 183, misdates his departure '17 Apr. 1948.'

184. 'Hiram' to HIS-AD, 20 Apr. 1948, HA 105\257.

185. Stockwell, 'Report by GOC North Sector Major General H.C. Stockwell CB, CBE, DSO, Leading Up to, and After, the Arab-Jewish Clashes in Haifa on 21–22 April 1948', (henceforward 'Stockwell Report'), 24 April 1948, SAMECA CP V/4/102. See also Cyril Marriott (Haifa) to Bevin, 26 Apr. 1948, a 17-page letter that in the main reproduces the 'Stockwell Report' (henceforward 'Marriott Report'). See also Cunningham to Secretary of State, 23 Apr. 1948, SAMECA CP III/4/15, and Henry Gurney, 'Palestine Postscript', the Chief Secretary's unpublished diary, 73–74 (SAMECA, Gurney Papers), which concurs with the Stockwell-Marriott view of what precipitated the Haganah offensive. Gurney, no friend of Zionism, wrote: 'It became clear today that the Jewish offensive at Haifa was staged as a direct consequence of four days' continuous Arab attacks. The Arabs have played right into [Jewish] hands.'

186. 'Segal' to all divisions, 'Summary of Intelligence in the District from Friday 16.4.48 14:00 hours Until Sunday 18.4.48 08:00 Hours', IDFA 7353\49\\46.

187. Unsigned but Carmeli, 'Addition to Daily Report 20.4.48 14:00 Hours for 21.4.48 08:00', and Carmeli to HGS\Operations, 'Report for 21.4.48', both in IDFA 7353\49\\46.
188. Pa'il, *Haganah*, 310–11; and HGS\Operations, 'Plan D', IDFA 933\75\\949 (see especially sub-clause 3 ('Definition of Functions') gimel ('Consolidation in the Big Cities') 3).
189. Harry Beilin to JA-PD, 1 April 1948, CZA S25-10555.
190. Beilin to JA-PD, 1 Apr. 1948, CZA S25-10555.
191. Beilin, 'Operation Haifa', 25 Apr. 1948, CZA S25-10584.
192. 'Stockwell Report', SAMECA CP V\4\102.
193. Beilin, 'Operation Haifa', 25 Apr. 1948, CZA S25-10584.
194. *In Enemy Eyes*, 21.
195. NorthSec [i.e., GOC North Sector] to 1st Guards Brigade, CRAFORCE, etc., 21 Apr. 1948, 18:45 hours, PRO WO 275–62.
196. Eshel, *Battles*, 347–49; and Carmel, *Battles*, 86–87.
197. Unsigned, 'Addition to Daily Report 21.4 14:00 hours, Summary of Information Up to 22.4 08:00', IDFA 7353\49\\46.
198. 'Yosef', 'The Conquest of Haifa', HA 80\54\1, a good summary of the battle, produced by a Carmeli HQ officer a few days after its end. Regarding the mortar barrage, see also Mandate Government Press Office communiqué, 22 Apr. 1948, 12:45 hours, CZA S25-7721; and protocol of 'Meeting of Mista'arabim' in Giv'at Hashlosha, '10 Apr. 1969, quoting from a report by 'Havakuk', written c.23 Apr. 1948, on how the mortaring and the Haganah ground assault felt from the Arab side, HA 25\12.
199. Protocol of 'Meeting of Mista'arabim', quoting from 'Havakuk' report, HA 25\12.
200. *In Enemy Eyes*, 23–24.
201. Tactical HQ, 1st Battalion, Coldstream Guards, 'Battalion Sitrep', 22 Apr. 1948, 16:30 hours, PRO WO 261-297. The Guards Brigade OC was later injured in the arm by a 'Jewish sniper' as he headed a column of ambulances trying to collect Arab wounded.
202. Unsigned but Carmeli, 'Summary of Information on the Enemy 22.4.48', undated but from afternoon of 22 Apr. 1948', IDFA 7353\49\\46; and 'Yosef', 'The Conquest of Haifa', HA 80\54\1.
203. Haganah HQ, Haifa District, '(poster) 'Haganah OC Announcement No. 2', 22 Apr. 1948, HA 105\92.
204. 'Yosef', 'The Conquest of Haifa', HA 80\54\1; and *The Times* (London), 22 Apr. 1948.
205. Carmel, *Battles*, 104; and Eshel, *Battles*, 375.
206. Eshel, *Battles*, 356.
207. '257 and 317 Field Security Section Weekly Report No. 2 for Week Ending 21 April 1949', PRO WO 275–79.
208. 'Stockwell Report', SAMECA CP V\4\102.
209. Carmeli HQ, 'Addition to Daily Report 21.4 14:00 Hours, Summary of Information Up to 22.4 08:00 Hours', IDFA 7353\49\\46; and 'Hiram' to HIS-AD, 'Subject: Yunis Nafa'a', 28 Apr. 1948, HA 105\257. By early May, Arabs in Haifa were saying that Nafa'a had received a P£ 100,000 bribe 'from the Jews to hand over the city of Haifa' ('Hiram' to HIS-AD, 5 May 1948, HA 105\92). One HIS agent reported that the Arabs thought that their

commanders had 'betrayed' them and fled like 'mice'. Had they stayed, the Arabs could have held out, they said ('Hiram' to HIS-AD, 'Subject: Feelings', 25 Apr. 1948, HA 105\257).

210. Khalidi, 'The Fall of Haifa', argues that the departure of the militia chiefs did not affect general Arab morale and remained unknown to the townspeople. This is contrary to logic. On 22 Apr., Kol Hamagen Ha'ivri broadcast: 'Why did . . . Yunis Nafa'a take his family with him to Beirut? Do you know that he has rented a flat there . . .?' (Eshel, *Battles*, 375).

211. '257 and 317 Field Security Section Weekly Report No. 3 for the Week Ending 28 April 1948', PRO WO 275–79.

212. Cunningham to Creech-Jones, 26 Apr. 1948, SAMECA CP III\4\71.

213. British Army HQ, Palestine, 'Fortnightly Intelligence Newsletter No. 67', 6 May 1948, PRO WO 275–64. In their reports, Stockwell and Marriott called the flight of the leaders 'significant' in explaining the swift Arab collapse. Khalidi, 'Fall', explains that 'Izz a Din had merely wanted to report in person on the situation (and, presumably, plead for reinforcements); had left before the shooting started; and was 'guilty of miscalculation', not cowardice. However, it appears that 'Izz a Din actually left the city at 13:00 hours, 21 April, after the shooting had started – and when he should have understood that the decisive battle had begun.

214. Lippincott (Haifa) to Secretary of State, 23 Apr. 1948 (two cables), NA RG 84, Haifa Consulate Classified Records 1948, 800 – Political Affairs.

215. 'Stockwell Report', SAMECA CP V\4\102; and '[Mandate Government] Haifa District Summary of Battle Headquarters Dated 22.4.48', IDFA 900\52\\24.

216. Cunningham to Secretary of State, 23 Apr. 1948, 11:00 hours, SAMECA CP III\4\15; and 'Stockwell Report', SAMECA CP V\4\102.

217. 'Stockwell Report', SAMECA CP V\4\102; and Carmel, *Battles*, 104–105. Throughout the negotiation, the Haganah referred to 'surrender terms' while the British and Arabs referred to 'truce terms'. All meant the same thing, and knew it.

218. Khalidi, 'Fall'; 'Stockwell Report', SAMECA CP V\4\102; and Goren, 'Haifa', 187.

219. Khalidi, 'Fall'; and Goren, 'Haifa', 187–88.

220. 'Stockwell Report', SAMECA CP V\4\102; and Goren, 'Haifa', 187–88.

221. Khalidi, 'Fall'; Goren, 'Haifa', 188; and Assaf, *History*, 331–32 (giving text of letter from Koussa to *Jewish Observer and Middle East Review*, 1 Sept. 1959).

222. Broadmead to FO, 22 Apr. 1948, 11:58 hours, PRO CO 537–3901.

223. Broadmead to FO, 22 Apr. 1948, 15:14 hours, PRO CO 537–3901. At the same time, 'Azzam Pasha, who had been shown copies of the consul's telegrams, complained to the British ambassador in Cairo, Roy Campbell, of the 'continuing' Jewish 'massacres' of 'Arab population, including women and children'. (He was lying; there had been no 'massacres'.) He threatened intervention by the Arab armies (Campbell to FO, 22 Apr. 1948, 21:07 hours, PRO CO 537–3901).

224. 'Stockwell Report', SAMECA CP V\4\102, reproducing the original Haganah terms and the Stockwell-amended version.

225. Carmel, *Battles*, 105–106.

226. 'Stockwell Report', SAMECA CP V\4\102; and 'Marriott Report', PRO FO 371-68505.

227. Beilin, 'Operation Haifa', 25 Apr. 1948, CZA S25 10584.

228. 'Marriott Report', PRO FO 371-68505; and 'Stockwell Report', SAMECA CP V\4\102. See also Marriott to FO, 23 Apr. 1948, PRO FO 371-68544.

229. 'Stockwell Report', SAMECA CP V\4\102; Marriott Report', PRO FO 371–68505; and Beilin, 'Operation Haifa', 25 Apr. 1948, CZA S25-10584.

230. Beilin, 'Operation Haifa', 25 Apr. 1948, CZA S 25-10584; and Carmel, *Battles*, 107. Neither Stockwell nor Marriott mention Levy's appeal.

231. Carmel, *Battles*, 107.

232. Salomon to Political Department, Foreign Ministry, 1 Apr. 1949, ISA FM 2401\11. Salomon recalled that Makleff also tried to reassure the Arabs that they could stay in Haifa, but this is not supported elsewhere and is implicitly contradicted in Carmel's memoir. On the other hand, Jewish Agency radio broadcasts at this time assured the Haifa Arabs that the Jews had no intention of expelling them and emphasized that the city's best interest lay in continued co-existence; but they did not explicitly call upon the Arabs to stay or, if already outside the town, to return (see Gelber, *Palestine*, 107).

233. Carmel, *Battles*, 107. The earliest version of the 'AHC orders' explanation of the evacuation of Haifa is contained in the JA spokesman's announcement of 23 Apr. that the exodus had been 'carried out deliberately by the Arabs to besmirch the Jews, to influence the Arab governments to send more help and to clear the ground for an attack by regular Arab forces later'. The statement was quoted in *The Times* (London, 24 Apr. 1948). *The Times* correspondent, incidentally, disagreed, commenting that 'the simplest, most human explanation is that the Arabs have fled out of pure disorder'.

The Haifa Arab Emergency Committee report of 30 April 1948 (ISA 437\940\4–69) makes no reference to any orders reaching them from outside during the consultations in Khayyat's house. Goren, 'Haifa', 189, maintains that during the intermission in the town hall meeting, the notables, receiving no instructions from Damascus, had telephoned Beirut, 'where then apparently sat the Mufti or his senior representative . . . From Beirut they were given an explicit order to leave the city.' Goren bases himself on the transcripts of interviews conducted in the early 1970s by HA personnel with Ephraim Alroi and Aharon Kremer, two HIS wire-tappers. They claimed to have heard and recorded the conversation – but could not say, admits Goren, who was speaking on either side of the telephone line. Alroi, according to Goren, proceeded to the town hall to inform Salomon and the Haifa Haganah's Arab affairs adviser, Naftali Lifshitz, of the conversation. But there is no supporting contemporary documentation for any of this – no reference in any document from 1948 to the Beirut–Haifa conversation, to an order from Beirut on 22 April to evacuate, or to a conversation between Alroi and Salomon or Lifshitz. Indeed, in later interviews and writings, neither Salomon nor Lifshitz ever mentioned such an order or such a conversation (and, surely, they would have had they occurred). On the contrary, Salomon's letter of 1 Apr. 1949 says that he was told on 22 Apr.

1948 by the Arab delegation members, after the dispersal of the meeting at the town hall, 'that they had instructions not to sign the truce . . . as this would mean certain death at the hands of their own people . . . and that it was quite clear that no Christian could do anything which might displease the Muslims. Whilst, therefore, they would remain in town, as they thought that that would be best in their own interests, they had to advise the Arabs [i.e., the population at large] to leave.' The implication seems to be that the Christian members of the delegation had been intimidated and instructed by their Muslim partners, who had absented themselves from the second part of the town hall meeting, not to sign the truce and to advise the townspeople to evacuate (ISA FM 2401\11). David Ariel's memorandum, 'The Arab States and the Refugee Problem', Notebook A,' 7 Oct. 1951, ISA FM 2566\13, reproduces the letter from the Emergency Committee (Khayyat, Sa'ad, Koussa, Nasr, Mu'ammar) to Stockwell, 23 April 1948, in which they 'reiterate . . . that . . . the removal of the Arab inhabitants from the town is voluntary and is being carried out at our request'. Khayyat later told an HIS officer or informant: 'There are rumours that the Mufti, the AHC, ordered the Arabs to leave the city. There is no truth to these rumours' ('Hiram' to HIS-AD, 'Subject: The Flight of the Arabs from Haifa', 28 May 1948, HA 105\257).

234. Entries for 22 and 23 Apr. 1948, Weitz, *Diary*, III, 272; Levin, *Jerusalem*, 90, entry for 23 Apr. 1948: 'There is something eerie in the way the Arabs are running . . .'; and Efraim Harari (ed.), *The Tel of the Winds*, Ilana to Levavi and Elah, Passover, 1948: 'It is a bit suspicious – as if they (the British) are doing us dirty.'

235. Sasson to Shertok, 23 Apr. 1948, *Political and Diplomatic Documents*, 670.

236. It is worth noting that neither Stockwell nor Marriott, in their reports, as much as hinted that the delegation in the town hall had been under instructions from Damascus or the AHC. Moreover, HIS, in 'The Migratory Movement . . .', 30 June 1948 (HHA ACP 95.10.13 (1)), attributed the flight to the Haganah onslaught and conquest of Haifa, and made no allusion to orders from outside.

237. Lippincott to Secretary of State, 25 Apr. 1948, and Lippincott to Secretary of State, 26 Apr. 1948, both in NA RG 84, Haifa Consulate, Classified Records 1948, 800 – Political Affairs.

238. Cunningham to Secretary of State, 25 Apr. 1948, SAMECA CP III\4\52; Secretary of State (London) to Kirkbride, 27 Apr. 1948, PRO FO 816\118; 6th Airborne Division Logbook, entry for 4 May 1948, PRO WO 275-54; and British Military HQ Middle East to certain British Cabinet Ministers, 'Extract from ME Daily Sitrep No. 147', 4 May 1948, PRO CO 537-3875.

239. '257 and 317 FS Section Weekly Report No. 3, for Week Ending 28 April 1948', PRO WO 275-79.

240. 1st Battalion Coldstream Guards, 'Battalion Sitrep No. 20', 29 Apr. 1948, PRO WO 261-297; Lippincott to Secretary of State, 26 Apr. 1948, and Lippincott to Secretary of State, 29 Apr. 1948, both in NA RG 84, Haifa Consulate, Classified Records 1948, 800 – Political Affairs.

241. Annex by Farid Sa'ad and Elias Koussa to Haifa Arab Emergency Committee report of 30 April 1948, in Ariel, 'The Arab States . . .', ISA FM 2566\13.

242. 'Hiram' to HIS-AD, 'Subject: The Order of the AHC to the Arabs of Haifa', 28 Apr. 1948, HA 105\257.

243. 'Hiram' to HIS-AD, 'Subject: The Question of the Evacuation of Haifa's Arabs', 28 Apr. 1948, HA 105\257. These two reports appear, given their dates, context and wording, to be referring to an order issued not on 21–22 April but days later, well into the evacuation.

244. 'Hiram' to HIS-AD, 'Subject: The Arabs Returning to Haifa', 28 Apr. 1948, HA 105\257.

245. 'Hiram' to HIS-AD, 'Subject: The State of the Arabs in Abbas Street', 25 Apr. 1948, HA 105\257. Ahmad Bey Khalil later wrote to Solomon that 'I can never forgive those who advised the people to leave Haifa. They should have remained there. Unfortunately, neither Rashid [Haj Ibrahim] nor I were there to stand for [i.e., against] this view' (Khalil (Amman) to Solomon, 9 June 1948, HA 105\127 aleph).

246. Eshel, *Battles*, 365.

247. Sa'ad and Koussa, appendix to committee report of 30 Apr. 1948, ISA 437\940\4-69.

248. Tactical HQ, 1st Battalion Coldstream Guards, 'Battalion Sitrep No. 18', 26 Apr. 1948, PRO WO 261–297; and '257 and 317 FS Section Weekly Report No. 3, for Week Ending 28 Apr. 1948', PRO WO 275–79.

249. 'Hiram' to Jeremiah, 11 May 1948, IDFA 5942\49\\23.

250. 'Hiram' to ?, 16 May 1948, IDFA 7249\49\\152.

251. Beilin, 'Operation Haifa', 25 Apr. 1948, CZA S25–10584.

252. 'Hiram' to HIS-AD, 'Subject: The State of the Arabs in Abbas St.', 25 Apr. 1948, HA 105\257. The document refers to this happening on the afternoon of '22.4' – but this is highly unlikely.

253. Salomon to JA-PD, 1 Apr. 1949, ISA FM 2401\11.

254. Eshel, *Battles*, 376–77.

255. 'Daily Monitoring Page, No. 20, (including summary of world radio station broadcasts in the 48 hours ending at 09:00 on 26.4.48)', IDFA 4944\49\\617.

256. A.J. Bidmead, superintendent, CID, Haifa, 28 Apr. 1948, IDFA 900\52\\25.

257. '257 and 317 FS Section Weekly Report No. 4, for Week Ending 5 May 1948', PRO WO 275–79. This report seems to be referring to the days immediately after the 22 April. By 4–5 May, the Haganah and, indeed, the civil authorities were no longer interested in Arabs staying in or returning to Haifa.

258. Lippincott to Secretary of State, 29 Apr. 1948, NA RG 84, Haifa Consulate, Classified Records 1948, 800 – Political Affairs.

259. Report datelined 'Haifa, 25 April', *The Times* (London), 26 Apr. 1948.

260. 'Hiram' to HIS-AD, 27 Apr. 1948, HA 105\257; and 'Hiram' to HIS-AD, 'Subject: Attitude of the Nuns to the Arab Exodus', 27 Apr. 1948, HA 105\193 bet.

261. High Commissioner to Secretary of State, 25 Apr. 1948, SAMECA CP III\4\52.

262. Lippincott to Department, 25 Apr. 1948, NA RG 84, Haifa Consulate, Classified Records, 1948, 800 – Political Affairs.

263. Lippincott to Department, 26 Apr. 1948, NA RG 84, Haifa Consulate, Classified Records 1948, 800 – Political Affairs.

264. Tactical HQ, 1st Battalion Coldstream Guards, 'Battalion Sitrep No. 18', 27 Apr. 1948, PRO WO 261–297.

265. Haganah Haifa District OC, 'Announcement of the Commander of the Haganah, No. 2', 22 Apr. 1948, HA 105\92.

266. 'Hiram' to HIS-AD, 25 Apr. 1948, HA 105\31, quoted in Gelber, *Palestine*, 105.

267. Carmel, *Battles*, 107. Following the exodus from Haifa, both Arab and left-wing Jewish leaders blamed the British for the evacuation. The Arab states, the AHC and Haifa Arab community leaders all charged that Stockwell's precipitate withdrawal of troops from the Arab – Jewish front lines, coupled with his refusal to intervene against the Haganah and his prevention of entry of Arab reinforcements, all 'forced' the Arabs to decide on flight. Aharon Cohen went further: 'It was the English who had advised the Arabs to leave [Haifa].' He added that, during the battle, 'and while the Haganah people were calming the Arabs . . . the British . . . advised them to "flee to the port, where the British Army would protect them"'. He also noted the 'alacrity' with which the British supplied the evacuees with transport and escorts (Cohen, 'Our Arab Policy in the Midst of the War', 10 May 1948, HHA ACP 10.95.10 (4); and Cohen to Prof. Ernst Simon, 25 Apr. 1948, HHA ACP 10.95.10 (4)). But I have found no other evidence to support this contention, of 'British advice'. Rather, Stockwell on 22 April had advised the opposite. British troops did allow Arabs, pressing at the gates, into the port area – but this was to protect them and to enable them to flee by boat, if they wished.

268. Tactical HQ, 1st Battalion Coldstream Guards, 'Battalion Sitrep No. 18', 25 Apr. 1948, PRO WO 261–297; and 'Marriott Report', PRO FO 371-68505. Marriott hinted that at a meeting of Arab and Jewish leaders on 25 April, the Jews had used 'threats'. But in the same breath, he said that the Arab leaders continued to stress that the evacuation was 'voluntary'.

269. Protocol of meeting of Mapam Political Committee, statement by P. Alonim, 26 May 1948, HHA 66.90 (1).

270. Carmeli\Operations to 'Bar-Kochba' and 'Hadari', 23 April 1948, IDFA 6680\49\\4.

271. Jewish Chamber of Commerce and Industry, Haifa, to Situation Committee, Haifa, 18 May 1948, ISA FM 2564\9.

272. Unsigned but Carmeli, 'Report for 26.4.48', IDFA 7353\49\\46.

273. 'Hiram' to HIS-AD, 27 Apr. 1948, HA 105\92.

274. 'Protocol of the Meeting of 25 April 1948', HMA 1374.

275. 'Hiram' to HIS-AD, 27 Apr. 1948, HA 105\92.

276. Eshel, *Battles*, 379.

277. 'Protocol of Meeting of 23 April 1948', HMA 1374.

278. 'Protocol of the Meeting of 25 April 1948', HMA 1374.

279. Emergency Committee (signed Khayyat, Sa'ad, Koussa, Mu'ammar and Nasr) to GOC North Sector, 25 Apr. 1948, HMA 1374.

280. 'Summary of Carmeli Brigade Information No.4, 17.5.48', IDFA128\51\\71.

281. Cohen to Secretariat of Mapam Centre, 28 Apr. 1948, HHA-ACP 10.95.10 (4).

282. 'An Appeal by the Haifa Workers Council', 28 Apr. 1948, IDFA 481\49\\62.
283. Bidmead, CID, Haifa, 28 Apr. 1948, IDFA 900\52\\25. Ironically, Bidmead also reported the capture by the Royal Navy of two Haganah ships filled with illegal Jewish immigrants and their arrival in Haifa, where the illegals were transferred to the 'Empire Comfort' and 'Empire Rest' for onward shipment that day to detention camps in Cyprus. The arrivals and departures from the same harbour that day of Jewish illegal immigrants or refugees and outward-bound Arab refugees must have been a sight.
284. A. Hoter-Yishai, 'Summary of Things Said . . . (On 2.5.48)', and Hoter-Yishai, 'Protocol No. 1 of the Committee for the Affairs of Haifa's Arabs', undated, both in CZA S25-9193.
285. 'Summary of Carmeli Brigade Information No. 1, from 1.5 to 5.5', 5 May 1948, IDFA 273\52\\5.
286. 'Hiram' to HIS-AD, 28 Apr. 1948, 'Subject: Arabs Leaving and Returning', HA 105\257; 'Summary of Carmeli Brigade Information No. 1, from 1.5 to 5.5', 5 May 1948, IDFA 273\52\\5; and High Commissioner to Secretary of State, 5 May 1948, PRO FO 8126\119. Cunningham mistakenly reported that: 'The Jews at [sic] Haifa are anxious that the Arabs should now return . . . At Tiberias the Jews would welcome the Arabs back . . .'
287. ICP, 'The Situation in Haifa Two Weeks after the Conquest of the Arab Parts of the City by the Haganah', 10 May 1948, and Cisling to Cabinet, 20 May 1948, both in ISA AM 20 aleph.
288. Tactical HQ, 1st Battalion Coldstream Guards, 'Battalion Sitrep No. 19', 27 Apr. 1948, PRO WO 261–297. The unit reported that it had picked up a leaflet signed by 'Chief of Haganah', in Arabic, stating: 'All those who have left the Wadi Nisnas and Wadi Salib areas must return to their homes immediately, open their shops and start work. We will ensure that they are safe.'
289. Entries for 22–24 Apr. 1948, CZA A246-13, 2364–65.
290. 'Hiram' to HIS-AD, 'Subject: Balad al Sheikh', 7 Jan. 1948, HA 105\32 aleph.
291. 'Hiram' to HIS-AD, undated but probably from 5 Apr. 1948, HA 105\257.
292. 'HIS-AD Intelligence 5.4.48', IDFA 922\75\\1205.
293. 'Hiram' to HIS-AD, 'Subject: The Evacuation from Yajur', 18 Apr. 1948, HA 105\257.
294. Entry for 22 Apr. 1948, 6th Airborne Division Logbook, PRO WO 275-54.
295. 'Hiram' to HIS-AD, 'Subject: The Request of the Arabs of Balad al Sheikh', 27 Apr. 1948, HA 105\54.
296. 'Hiram (Kafri)' to HIS-AD, 'Subject: Report on the Evacuation of Hawassa and Balad al Sheikh on Sabbath 24.4.48', 27 Apr. 1948, HA 105\257.
297. 'Yosef', 'The Conquest of Haifa', undated but from late April 1948, HA 80\54\1 (Moshe Gat papers).
298. 'Hiram (Kafri)' to HIS-AD, 'Subject: Report on the Evacuation . . .', 27 Apr. 1948, HA 105\257.
299. 'Hiram (Kafri)' to HIS-AD, 'Subject: Report on the Evacuation . . .', 27 Apr. 1948, HA 105\257.
300. 'Hiram' to HIS-AD, 29 Apr. 1948, HA 105\257.

301. 'Summary of [British] Battle Headquarters Diary for 23rd [sic] April, 1948', IDFA 900\52\\24; entry for 24 Apr. 1948, 6th Airborne Division Logbook, PRO WO 275-54; 6th Airborne Division, North Sector Sitrep, 24 Apr. 1948, PRO WO 275-66; '257 and 317 FS Section, Weekly Report for Week Ending 28 Apr. 1948', PRO WO 275-79; and HIS-AD, 'The Migratory Movement . . .', 30 Jun. 1948, HHA-ACP 10.95.13 (1). Aharon Cohen later asserted that the villagers had evacuated 'on British advice' and 'contrary to Haganah advice' ('Cohen, 'Our Arab Policy in the Midst of the War', 10 May 1948, HHA-ACP 10.95.10 (4)). A contemporary HIS-AD report ('Hiram' to HIS-AD, 'Subject: British Propaganda to Increase the Arab Evacuation', 25 Apr. 1948, HA 105\257) confirms Cohen's first assertion: 'On 24.4 between 11:00 and 13:00 the British Army conducted comprehensive propaganda designed to speed up the Arab evacuation from . . . Balad ash Sheikh . . . Hawassa and Yajur . . . The British propaganda points to the great robbery that the Jews may carry out.' It is probable that the British officers in Balad al Sheikh that morning thought that an Arab evacuation, modelled on the ongoing exodus from Haifa, was the best solution and made this clear to the villagers. But I have seen no other source that claims that the Haganah advised against evacuation. Probably at this point there was a dovetailing of British, Haganah and Arab desires – all, for different reasons, were keen on a speedy Arab evacuation.
302. Unsigned, '[Mandate Government] Haifa District Summary of Battle Headquarters Dated 22.4.48', IDFA900\52\\24.
303. Unsigned but Carmeli Brigade, 'Addition to Daily Report 21.4 14:00 hours, Summary of Information Up to 22.4 08:00 hours', IDFA 7353\49\\46.
304. 'Summary of [British] Battle Headquarters Diary Dated 25th April, 1948', IDFA 900\52\\24.
305. Unsigned but Carmeli, 'Report for 26.4.48', IDFA 7353\49\\46; 'Hiram' to HIS-AD, 'Subject: Events in Haifa on Monday 26.4', 27 Apr. 1948, HA 105\257; and Mobile Garrison Battalion\Intelligence Officer to battalion CO, 28 Apr. 1948, IDFA 7249\49\\\130. Part of the last document – a handwritten minute by 'Maxi', the battalion CO, of 29 Apr. – has been blacked out by IDFA censors: 'Maxi' probably recommended the inhabitants' expulsion.
306. North Sector to MILPAL, 1st Guards Brigade, etc., 5 May 1948, PRO WO 275-62.
307. Unsigned but Carmeli, 'Report for 26.4.48', IDFA 7353\49\\46; and 'Summary of [British] Battle Headquarters Diary Dated 25th April, 1948', IDFA 900\52\\24.
308. 'Summary of Carmeli Brigade Information No.3 for 7.5.48', IDFA 273\52\\5.
309. 1st Battalion Coldstream Guards, 'Battalion Sitrep No. 20', 29 Apr 1948, PRO WO 261–297.
310. 'Tiroshi (Aran)' to HIS-AD, 27 Apr. 1948, HA 105\31.
311. 'Summary of Carmeli Brigade Information No. 3 for 7.5.48', IDFA 273\52\\5.
312. JA-PD Arab Division, 'In the Arab Public', 5 May 1948, HA 105\100.
313. Carmel to Carmeli Brigade, 28 Jun. 1948, IDFA 260\51\\4.

314. OC Haifa District to area OCs, IDFA 244\51\\104.
315. City Intelligence Officer to OC City, 2 July 1948, IDFA 5492\49\\3.
316. City Intelligence Officer to OC City, 3 July 1948, IDFA 5492\49\\3.
317. OC Carmeli to IDF GS\Operations, 3 July 1948, IDFA 2315\50\\15.
318. Sommerville to Marriott, 20 July 1948, and Marriott to Sommerville, 20 July 1948, both in HA 105\193 bet.
319. 'Hiram' to IDF IS, 15 July 1948, HA 105\260. For more on the concentration, see Morris, *1948 and After*, rev. ed., 215–37.
320. Unsigned, 'Memorandum on Urgent Improvement Works in Haifa', undated but with covering letter from Friedland (Shilon) to Ben-Gurion, 11 June 1948, IDFA 782\65\\1186. The letter is minuted in Ben-Gurion's hand: 'Haifa's institutions must make sure not to miss the opportunity.'
321. Entry for 16 June 1948, DBG-YH, 522. The last British forces in Palestine, in the Haifa enclave, withdrew on 30 June 1948.
322. IDF\OC Planning Division to ?, 16 Jun. 1948, IDFA 260\51\\54.
323. Khayyat to Minority Affairs Minister, 25 July 1948, ISA MAM 298\82; and Koussa to S. Levy, 21 July 1948, HMA 556.
324. 'Decisions of the Provisional Government', 1 Sep. 1948, KMA-ACP 9.9.1. Haifa was not 'occupied territory' and, in any case, Ben-Gurion, as defence minister, was responsible for the OC Military Government in the Occupied Territories, Gen. Elimelekh Avner.
325. Levy to Gruenbaum, 8 Sept. 1948, HMA 556.
326. IDF GS\OC Planning Division to Lublini ('Hadari'), 13 Aug. 1948, IDFA 260\51\\54; and IDF GS\Operations to ?, 27 Sept. 1948, and OC Northern Front to IDF GS\Planning Division, 30 Sept. 1948, both in IDFA 260\51\\3. For further information on 'Shikmona', see Morris, *1948 and After*, rev. ed., 230–37.
327. Gurney, 'Palestine', 84.
328. On 22 Apr., Ya'akov Shimoni of the JA-PD Arab Division said that Jaffa was 'half-empty' ('Protocol of Meeting of the Arab Division on Thursday 22.4.48,' CZA S25-9664) but this was mere guesswork.
329. Unsigned Haganah or HIS Jaffa area 'Logbook', 27 Apr. 1948, IDFA 922\75\\949.
330. STH III, part 2, 1474–75.
331. 'HIS Information, Daily Summary', 29 Apr. 1948, IDFA 900\52\\58.
332. 'Avner' to HIS-AD, 'On Events in Jaffa from the Attack on Her. A General Survey', 6 May 1948, HA 105\92 aleph.
333. See, for example, 'Avner' to HIS-AD, 27 Apr. 1948, HA 105\31, on the mortaring of Jaffa on 23 Apr., which hit the telephone exchange and the area of the central post office, and had 'great effect in increasing anarchy in Jaffa' and promoting flight.
334. Committee for Economic Defence, 'Information on the Arab Economy, Bulletin No. 4', 10–13 Apr. 1948, HA 105\146.
335. Committee for Economic Defence, 'Information on the Arab Economy, Bulleting No. 7', 18–20 Apr. 19048, HA 105\146.
336. 'Avner' to HIS-AD, 'Events in Jaffa from the Attack on Her. A General Survey', 6 May 1948, HA 105\92 aleph. See also pages from a summary report produced probably by the Committee for Economic Defence, undated but probably from May 1948, HA 105\119.

337. Haganah, 'Logbook' for Jaffa area, 27 Apr. 1948, IDFA 922\75\\949.
338. 'Avner' to HIS-AD, 27 Apr. 1948, HA 105\31.
339. *In Enemy Eyes*, 33–34.
340. Begin, 'The Conquest of Jaffa', a 46-page report, written in May or June 1948, 24, JI, IZL, kaf-4, 8\1.
341. Lazar, *Conquest*, 124 and 126.
342. Cunningham to Secretary of State, 3 May 1948, SAMECA CP III\5\43. Nimr al Khatib (*In Enemy Eyes*, 33–34), says that in three days, '2,000' mortar bombs fell on Jaffa.
343. Haganah 'Logbook' for Jaffa area, 27 Apr. 1948, IDFA 922\75\\949.
344. Quoted in Gabbay, *Political Study*, 90.
345. Unsigned, 'Summary of the Interrogation of the Manshiya PoWs from 28 April 1948', JI, IZL, kaf-8, 8\8; and 'Miscellaneous (Events in Jaffa, from Prisoner Interrogations by "Ham")', 28 Apr. 1948, IDFA 8275\49\\136.
346. Begin, 'The Conquest of Jaffa', 25, JI, IZL, kaf-4, 8\1.
347. 'Kiryati-Dafna' to fronts, 'Summary for Night of 29-30.4.48', 30 Apr. 1948; 'Kiryati-Dafna' to fronts, 'Summary: 291100-291720', 30 Apr. 1948; and 'Kiryati-Dafna' to fronts, 'Summary . . . 300800–300915', all in IDFA 8275\49\\130; and unsigned, 'Feelings 30.4.48, Jaffa', HA 73\98.
348. 'Avner' to HIS-AD, 'Events in Jaffa 18:45, 7.5.48 – 10:00, 8.5.48', IDFA 8275\49\\162.
349. See, for example, unsigned, 'Movement from Jaffa', 1 May 1948, IDFA 8275\49\\162; Kiryati, intelligence officer, to 'Prat', 'Daily Summary from 30\1800 until 1\1800', HA 105\94; and unsigned, 'Movement from Jaffa', 3 May 1948, IDFA 8275\49\\162.
350. Gurney, 'Palestine', 84.
351. HC to Secretary of State, 26 Apr. 1948, SAMECA CP III\4\71.
352. WO to PS to Prime Minister, etc., 'Extract from Middle East Special Situation Report 29 April 1948', 29 Apr. 1948, PRO CO 537-3875.
353. Shertok speech to UN General Assembly, undated but probably 27 Apr. 1948, ISA FM 2451\13. Shertok was no doubt, at least in part, basing himself on Sasson's cable of 23 Apr., cited above. A year later, on the basis of talks with Jaffa, Ramle and Lydda refugees in the Gaza Strip, representatives of the Quakers' refugee relief agency, the American Friends Service Committee, told an American intelligence officer that at least some of the refugees were saying that they had 'fled against their wills because their leaders told them they must do so or be considered traitors, and if they fled they could return in a few months' (Col. B.C. Anirus, 'Intelligence Report', 1 May 1949, NA RG 84, Tel Aviv Embassy, Classified Records 1949, 571 – Palestine Refugee Relief). However, I have found no evidence from Haganah, Western or Arab sources corroborating this explanation for the exodus from Jaffa. It is possible that some Jaffa militia officers recommended or ordered flight; but there is no evidence of such a general order, from inside or outside the town.
354. Lazar, *Conquest*, 138.
355. Unsigned, 'Operation of Conquest', undated, four-page IZL military report, and Begin, 'The Conquest of Jaffa', undated, both in JI, IZL, kaf-4, 8\1.
356. 'Fortnightly Intelligence Newsletter No. 67 Issued by HQ British Troops Palestine', 6 May 1948, PRO WO 275-64, quotes an Iraqi Cabinet

Minister as saying that Britain 'has purposely engineered Jewish domination in Haifa as an integral part of its programme for Palestine'. See
also '257 and 317 FS Section Weekly Report No. 3, for Week Ending 28
April 1948', PRO WO 275-79; Secretary of State to High Commissioner,
22 Apr. 1948, SAMECA CP III\3\136; Secretary of State to High Commissioner, 23 Apr. 1948, SAMECA CP III\4\6; Secretary of State to High
Commissioner, 23 Apr. 1948, SAMECA CP III\4\7; and Secretary of State
to High Commissioner, 23 Apr. 1948, SAMECA CP III\4\23.

357. WO to PS of PM, PS of Foreign Secretary, etc., 'Extract from Middle East
Special Situation Report 29 April 1948', 29 Apr. 1948, PRO CO 537-3875.

358. Montgomery, *Memoirs*, 473–74.

359. 'Note of a Meeting Held at 10 Downing Street at 5:15 p.m. on Friday 7th
May 1948,' 7 May 1948, PRO CAB 127–341.

360. Ibid.; Montgomery, *Memoirs*, 474; and minutes attached to PRO FO 371-
68544 E5102\4\31G.

361. Minute by W.A.C. Mathieson, 4 May 1948, PRO CO 537-3870. Cunningham in fact had acted before receiving word or orders from Bevin, as he
made clear in his angry telegram of 30 April (Cunningham to Secretary of
State, etc., PRO CO 537-3870).

362. Montgomery, *Memoirs*, 473; STH III, part 2, 1552; and Haganah 'Logbook',
27 Apr. 1948, IDFA 922\75\\949. In the last document, a British brigadier
is quoted as telling an HIS officer, 'Avner', that the British would preserve
Jaffa from Jewish attack for 'about three weeks'; the army would then leave
the town and 'then it was no longer the brigadier's concern'.

363. 'Kiryati – Intelligence' to 'Prat', 'Daily Summary from 30\1800 until 1\1800',
2 May 1948, HA 105\94.

364. 'Kiryati-Dafna' to 'fronts', 4 May 1948, IDFA 8275\49\\136.

365. Begin, 'The Conquest of Jaffa', JI, IZL kaf 4, 8\1; and Lazar, *Conquest*,
138.

366. HGS\Operations to Alexandroni, etc., 'Orders for Operation "Hametz",'
26 Apr. 1948, IDFA 6647\49\\15.

367. Operation Hametz HQ to Giv'ati, etc., 27 Apr. 1948, 14:00 hours, IDFA
67\51\\677. See also Alexandroni to battalions, 27 Apr. 1948, IDFA
922\75\\949.

368. Alexandroni to brigades, etc., 8 May 1948, IDFA 2323\49\\6.

369. 'Tiroshi' to HIS-AD, 3 May 1948, HA 105\127.

370. B Company to OC 32nd Battalion, 29 Apr. 1948, IDFA 6647\49\\15; and
'Tiroshi' to HIS-AD, 2 May 1948, HA 105\54 aleph.

371. 'Tiroshi' to HIS-AD, 2 April 1948, HA 105\54 aleph.

372. Entry for 30 Apr. 1948, DBG-YH II, 377.

373. Unsigned logbook entry, '2.5.48,' HA 105\94.

374. HGS\Operations, 'Summary of Hametz Operations', 2 May 1948, IDFA
2687\49\\35.

375. Unsigned, 'Latest Reports from the Front', 28 Apr. 1948, 12:00 hours, HA
48\3, states: 'In Jaffa there is great panic . . . [because of Operation
Hametz].'

376. STH III, part 2, 1553 and 1574–75.

377. HGS\Operations, 'Summary of Operation Hametz', 2 May 1948, IDFA
922\75\\949.

378. 'Avner' to HIS-AD, 8 May 1948, IDFA 8275\49\162.

379. Kiryati\Intelligence, 'Daily Summary from 30\18:00 until 1\18:00', HA 105\94.

380. HC to Secretary of State, 1 May 1948, SAMECA CP III\5\26.

381. HC to Secretary of State, 3 May 1948, SAMECA CP III\5\43.

382. 'Tiroshi' to HIS-AD, 11 May 1948, IDFA 6400\49\\66.

383. Unsigned but Kiryati\intelligence, 'Events in Jaffa in the Week Ending on 9.5.48', IDFA 8275\49\\136.

384. Kiryati\Intelligence Officer, to 'Dromi' (?), 'Daily Summary from 03\1800 until 04\18:00,' 4 May 1948, HA 73\98.

385. HC to Secretary of State, 5 May 1948, SAMECA CP III\5\92; and Gurney, 'Palestine', 94.

386. *In Enemy Eyes*, 34.

387. HC to Secretary of State, 5 May 1948, PRO FO 816\119.

388. Heikal to Kirkbride, 11 May 1948, PRO FO 816\119.

389. Kiryati\Operations, 'Preparatory Order for Operation Dror', 10 May 1948, IDFA 321\48\\100.

390. 'Protocol of Meeting Between the Commander of the Haganah in Tel Aviv and his Aides and Representatives of the Inhabitants of Jaffa, in Tel Aviv, on 12 May 1948', IDFA 321\48\\97.

391. 'Second Meeting Between the Haganah OC in Tel Aviv and the Representatives of the Jaffa Emergency Committee in Tel Aviv on 13 May 1948, at 10:45 hours', IDFA 321\48\\97.

392. Texts of 'Agreement' and 'Instructions . . .', HA 55\31.

393. 'Operational Order for Operation Dror', 13 May 1948; and Kiryati, 'The Organisation of the Identification Detention Compounds and the Prisoner Holding Spaces', 13 May 1948, both in IDFA 321\48\\100.

394. Kiryati, 'Special Order of the Day with Jaffa's Capture', 14 May 1948, IDFA 321\48\\97.

395. Entry for 18 May 1948, DBG-YH II, 438.

396. Chizik to Shitrit, 1 June 1948, and Y. Harkabi, 'Summary of Memorandum Regarding Mr. Chizik's Meeting with Mr. de Reynier and Mr. Gouy of the Red Cross on 22.6.1948', both in ISA FM 2564\9.

397. Nicola Saba, Jaffa Emergency Committee, 'Note', 27 May 1948; Dr. M. Mishalany, Dr. G. Ayoub and Dr. H. Pharaon, 'Report on the Bodies that were found Dead [sic] on Jabalieh Area of Jaffa on 25.5.48 and Examined by Us on 27.5.48'; 'Second Memorandum Submitted by the Emergency Committee of Jaffa Protesting Against the Irregular Activities of the Jewish Forces in Jaffa Area', 28 May 1948 – all in ISA FM 2406\2; and Chizik, 'Minutes of a Meeting Held on the 31.5.48 between the Military Governor of Jaffa and Mr. Robert Gee [sic] of the International Red Cross', ISA FM 2564\9. In mid-July, the Emergency Committee claimed that '20' Arabs had been killed by Israelis since the start of the occupation (Gelber, *Independence and Nakba*, Chap. 15).

398. Military Governor's Office, Jaffa, 'Summary, 15.5.48', IDFA 321\48\\97. There may have been additional, unreported cases.

399. Emergency Committee to representative of Commander Tel Aviv District, 22 May 1948 (Ref. No. 7); Emergency Committee to representative of commander Haganah Tel Aviv District, 22 May 1948 (Ref. No. 5); Emergency

Committee to representative Haganah Tel Aviv District OC, 22 May 1948 (Ref. No. 6); and Emergency Committee to representative of the 'International Red Cross Organisation', Tel Aviv, 21 May 1948 – all in ISA FM 2564\9; and illegible signature, 'Report on Actions to Prevent Thefts from Manshiya', 20 May 1948, IDFA 8275\49\\136. This last report, by a Haganah officer, describes the pillage of Manshiya on 18 May by 'hordes of women, children and men [from Tel Aviv] . . . Chairs, cupboards, and other furniture, household and kitchen utensils, sheets, pillows, bedware, and more [were taken].' The platoon led by the signatory stopped the looting and confiscated the loot, firing shots in the air and occasionally throwing stun grenades. Chizik later confirmed, 'I am sorry to say . . . [that] most of the Arabs' complaints are true' (Chizik to Shitrit, 1 June 1948, ISA FM 2564\9).

400. Ben-Gurion to Chizik, 22 May 1948, IDFA 121\50\\183; and Ben-Gurion to OC IZL troops, Jaffa, 22 May 1948, IDFA 321\48\\97.
401. 'Shiloni' to Kiryati, 23 May 1948, HA 80\774\7.
402. Y. Gefen to minister of police and Arab affairs, 25 May 1948, ISA MAM 306\77.
403. Chizik to Shitrit, 1 June 1948, ISA FM 2564\9.
404. CGS to Kiryati, 23 June 1948, IDFA 481\49\\143.
405. Kiryati to CGS, 25 May 1948, IDFA 6127\49\\161.
406. Chizik to OC Military Forces Jaffa, 21 June 1948, IDFA 6127\49\\161.
407. OC Military Forces Jaffa to Kiryati Brigade HQ, 28 July 1948, IDFA 6127\49\\161.
408. CGS to Navy (Gershon Zak), 2 Aug. 1948; and minute, dated 13 Aug., about undated letter from security officer to OC military forces Jaffa, both in IDFA 6127\49\\161.
409. Military Governor Jaffa, 'Weekly Report on the Activities of the Jaffa Military Governor from 25 July until 5 August 1948', (sic) 4 Aug. 1948, IDFA 580\56\\252.
410. Allon to Yadin and Galili, 22 Apr. 1948, KMA-PA 170–44.
411. For Safad, see HIS-AD, 'Safad Questionnaire', 30 Oct. 1941, HA 8\193. The following pages focus on Safad; Operation Yiftah is dealt with below.
412. 'Abasi, 'Safad . . .', 313–321.
413. 'Ibrahim' to PS, 2 Dec.1947, HA 73\98.
414. 'Abasi, 'Safad . . .', 328.
415. Palmah, 'Logbook of Operations', undated, entry for 3 Jan. 1948, IDFA 661\69\\36.
416. 'Tzuri' to Golani, 'General Survey for Months of March, April 1948', 3 May 1948, IDFA 1196\52\\1.
417. 'Tzuri' to HIS-AD, 1 June 1948, HA 105\222; and 'Tzuri (Dori)' to HIS-AD, 2 July 1948, HA 105\127 aleph.
418. 'Abasi, 'Safad . . .', 346.
419. 'Abasi, 'Safad . . .', 347.
420. HIS-AD, 'Biriya', 1942, HA 105\226.
421. HIS-AD, 'Ein Zeitun', 9 Aug. 1942, HA 105\226.
422. 'Itamar' to 'Ali', 'Report on the Attack on 'Ein Zeitun', 21 Jan. 1948, IDFA 922\75\\1224.

423. Unsigned, 'Information, Third Battalion', 08:00, 1 May [1948], IDFA 922\75\\1224; *Book of the Palmah*, II, 303–304; and Peled, 'Conquest of Safad', 24 Apr. 1949, HA Peh-222\2, 68. The first document gives both '30' and '100' for the number of prisoners taken.

424. Nazzal, *Exodus*, 35–36.

425. 'Yiftah' to HGS, Yadin, etc., 2 May 1948, 21:00 hours, IDFA 128\51\\50; Nazzal, *Exodus*, 36–37; and *Book of the Palmah*, II, 304.

426. 'Yiftah', 'Daily Report Continuation', undated but from 1 or 2 May 1948, IDFA 128\51\\50.

427. Ben-Yehuda, *Ropes*, 243–48. Nazzal, *Exodus*, 36, quotes refugees from 'Ein al Zeitun, interviewed in Lebanon in the early 1970s, who implied that '37' youngsters from the village had been massacred. Ben-Yehuda graphically describes the prelude to, and aftermath of, the slaughter. She did not witness the slaughter itself, in which as many as 70 may have died. According to Ben-Yehuda, Kelman's company COs all refused to massacre the prisoners or to allow their men to do it. In the end, Kelman found two 'broken' men, who did not belong to the fighting formations, and who claimed that they had previously suffered at Arab hands, to do the killing. Subsequently, he assigned Ben-Yehuda to untie the hands of the dead as a Red Cross visit to the area was expected. Several villagers were apparently shot by the Palmah in 'Ein Zeitun on 1 May immediately after the village's conquest. The Syrians subsequently charged that 'women had been raped' (Broadmead (Damascus) to Kirkbride (Amman), 4 May 1948, PRO FO 816\119). The massacre in the wadi and the deaths in the village may have been the source of the AHC's apparently false charge, lodged with the UN in July, that after the fall of the village, the Haganah troops had 'herded women and children into [the village] mosque and blew it up' ('AHC Memorandum on Jewish Atrocities', 26 July 1948, PRO CO 733-487\2). But a massacre there was. According to Emmanuel ('Mano') Friedman, the Israeli Minority Affairs Ministry representative in the Galilee, the troops killed '40 prisoners on the main road [to Safad]' (unsigned, 'Visit of the Minority Affairs and Police Minister in Kfar Giladi, 29.7.48', HA 105\260). Presumably, these were the men killed in the wadi.

428. *Book of the Palmah*, II, 279 and 304; 'Information, 3rd Battalion', IDFA 922\75\\1224; and Broadmead to Kirkbride, 4 May 1948, PRO FO 816\119.

429. Peled, 'The Conquest of Safad', HA Peh-222\2.

430. 'Tzuri (Dori)' to HIS-AD, 2 Jul. 1948, HA 105\127 aleph.

431. *Book of the Palmah*, II, 324; and 'Yiftah' to HGS, Yadin, etc., 2 May 1948, 21:00 hours, IDFA 128\51\\50.

432. Kol Hamagen Ha'ivri broadcast, in English, 2 May 1948, CZA S25-8918; and 'Fortnightly Intelligence Newsletter No. 67 Issued by HQ British Troops in Palestine (for the Period . . . 19 April – 3 May 1948)', 6 May 1948, PRO WO 275–64.

433. *Book of the Palmah*, II, 283–284 and 304–306; and 'Yiftah' to Palmah HQ, Golani, etc. 6 May 1948, 15:45 hours, IDFA 128\51\\50.

434. 'Abasi, 'Safad', 353.

435. Broadmead to HC, 5 May 1948, SAMECA CP III\5\102.

436. Broadmead to FO, 6 May 1948, PRO FO 371-68548.
437. Creech-Jones to HC, 6 May 1948, SAMECA CP III\5\119.
438. Nazzal, *Exodus*, 44.
439. 'Yiftah' to Golani, 10 May 1948, 13:20 hours, IDFA 128\51\\50.
440. 'Tzuri' to HIS-AD, 'Subject: Events in Safad After its Conquest', 1 June 1948, HA 105\222.
441. 'Abasi quotes Kelman as saying that the mortaring was designed to 'cause panic' among the inhabitants ('Abasi, 'Safad . . .', 359).
442. Yiftah HQ to Palmah HQ, 'Report on Operation', 10 May 1948, IDFA 922\75\\1066; and 'Yiftah' to Golani, 10 May 1948, 13:20 hrs, and 'Yiftah' to Palmah HQ, etc., 10 May 1948, 22:30 hrs, both in IDFA 128\51\\50.
443. 'Tzuri' to HIS-AD, 1 June 1948, HA 105\222.
444. *Book of the Palmah*, II, 285.
445. 'Tzuri (Dori)' to HIS-AD, 2 July 1948, HA 105\127 aleph.
446. 'Abasi, 'Safad . . .', 360, quoting Kelman.
447. 'Yiftah HQ, 'Daily Report', 11 May 1948, 20:00 hrs., IDFA 922\75\\1082.
448. Peled, 'The Conquest of Safad', HA 222\2.
449. 'Report of Patrol in Syria and Lebanon – 7–12.5.48 – by Two "Shahar" Men', IDFA 922\75\\1082.
450. 'Tzuri (Dori)' to HIS-AD, 2 Jul. 1948, HA 105\127 aleph.
451. *In Enemy Eyes*, 37; Nazzal, *Exodus*, 16 and 41; and 'Tzuri (Dori)' to HIS-AD, 2 July 1948, HA 105\127 aleph. 'Tzuri' reported that Safad refugees were saying that Fnaish had received money from the Zionists and had deliberately brought about the defeat.
452. 'A Meeting in Safad', 29 July 1948, ISA MAM 310\33; entry for 7 June 1948, DBG-YH II, 494; and 'Tzuri' to HIS-AD, 1 June 1948, HA 105\222. According to 'Tzuri', only one Muslim was allowed to remain in Safad, Mustafa Dalasi, a land-owner from Biriya, who enjoyed 'special privileges'.
453. George Nuni to Safad Area OC, 17 May 1948, HA 105\222.
454. 'Tzuri' to HIS-AD, 1 June 1948, HA 105\222.
455. 'Tzuri (Dori)' to HIS-AD, 11 June 1948, HA 105\260.
456. Carmel to IDF\GS, 14 Aug. 1948, IDFA 260\51\\4.
457. Avraham Ye'eli to Shabtai Levy, 11 June 1948, HMA 13784; Foreign Ministry to IDF-GS, 11 July 1948, ISA FM 2402\29; Harkabi to IDF\Operations, 18 Aug. 1948, ISA FM 2464\10; and Moshe Yitah to Levy, 9 Aug. 1948, HMA 1374.
458. Weitz to Ben-Gurion, 11 Sep. 1948, in Weitz, *Diary*, III, 340; and Marriott to Foreign Secretary, 23 April 1949, PRO FO 371-75198 E5810.
459. 'Tzuri (Dori)' to HIS-AD, 12 May 1948, HA 105\127.
460. Entry for 4 May 1948, CZA A246-13, 2373.
461. Palmah HQ to HGS, 'Daily Report', 17 Feb. 1948, IDFA922\75\\1066.
462. IDF History Branch, 'ALA,' IDFA 1046\70\\182.
463. Al Jayusi (?) to OC ALA, 14 Apr. 1948, HA 105\127 aleph.
464. 'Tzuri' to Golani, 'General Survey . . .', 3 May 1948, IDFA 1196\52\\1.
465. Golani to HGS, etc., 28 Apr. 1948, IDFA 128\51\\50.
466. 'Tzuri' to HIS-AD, 9 May 1948, IDFA 1196\52\\1.
467. 'Tzuri' to Golani, 'General Survey . . .', 3 May 1948, IDFA 1196\52\\1.
468. 'Tzuri' to Golani, 10 May 1948, HA 105\237.

469. 'Giora' to 'Utz', 19 May 1948, HA 105\92 bet.
470. 'Tzuri' to HIS-AD, 'Subject: The Battle for Beisan', 14 May 1948, HA 105\92 bet.
471. Unsigned, 'Events on 12.5.48', HA 105\94.
472. *Tree and Sword*, 144–46; and Nazzal, *Exodus*, 49.
473. Golani to Yadin, 12 May 1948, IDFA 922\75\\1025; and Golani Brigade Logbook, entry for 12 May 1948, IDFA 665\51\\1.
474. Entry for 12 May 1948, CZA A246-13, 2385.
475. Unsigned, 'Events on 12.5.48', HA 105\94.
476. Golani to Yadin, 12 May 1948, IDFA 922\75\\1025; and 'Tektz', 'In Occupied Beisan', 2 July 1948, *Tsror Michtavim*, KMA.
477. *Tree and Sword*, 146; and Nazzal, *Exodus*, 49.
478. Dalia Karpel, 'I am Ready to Run After a Picture a Great Distance', *Haaretz*, 28 October 1994. See also the recollection of another soldier who participated in the expulsion, Yitzhak (Izzi) Goldstein, 'The Partisan Sinyatovsky', *Al Hamishmar*, 15 October 1978.
479. 'Giora' to 'Utz', 19 May 1948, HA 105\92 bet.
480. Shitrit to Defence Minister and Foreign Minister, 16 Sep. 1948, ISA FM 2564\18; and 'Tektz', 'In Occupied Beisan', *Tsror Michtavim*, KMA.
481. 'Tzipori' to Golani and Carmeli, 10 June 1948, IDFA 128\51\\32.
482. Golani OC to IDF GS, 7 July 1948, IDFA 922\75\\1025; and 'Tzuri (Paltiel)' to IDF Intelligence Service, 1 Aug. 1948, HA 105\260.
483. Intelligence Officer, 13th Battalion, to Golani\Intelligence, 25 July 1948, IDFA128\51\\71; and Committee for Abandoned Property, Gilbo'a Area, to Sub-District OC, 29 July 1948, IDFA 6127\49\\109.
484. HIS-AD, 'The Migratory Movement . . .', 30 June 1948, HHA-ACP 10.95.13 (1).
485. 'Mitzpa' to HIS-AD, 6 Apr. 1948, HA 105\257.
486. *Tree and Sword*, 146.
487. 'Hiram (Nahari)' to HIS–AD, 28 Dec. 1947, HA 105\23; and '01011' to HIS-AD, 26 Jan. 1948, HA 105\72.
488. '01011' to HIS-AD, 26 Jan. 948, HA 105\72.
489. Unsigned but HIS-AD, 'Report on Events in Haifa on Saturday 7.2.48', 9 Feb. 1948, IDFA 5942\49\\23.
490. 'Hiram' to HIS-AD, 12 Feb. 1948, HA 105\23 bet.
491. 'HIS Information, Daily Summary', 7 Apr. 1948, HA 105\62.
492. Committee for Economic Defence, 'Information on the Arab Economy, Bulletin No. 1', 11 Apr. 1948, HA 105\146; and Committee for Economic Defence, 'Information on the Arab Economy, Bulletin No. 5', 14–16 Apr. 1948, HA 105\146.
493. Carmeli HQ to HGS\Operations, 'Weekly Report on Events in the Area between [sic] 20.3–26.3', 31 March 1948, IDFA 7353\49\\46.
494. Committee for Economic Defence, 'Information on the Arab Economy, Bulletin No. 9', 28 Apr. 1948, HA 105\146.
495. Divisional Police HQ, to Harry [Beilin?], 26 Apr. 1948, HA 105\92 bet.
496. ? to Munir Effendi Nur, 16 Apr. 1948, HA 105\252.
497. 'Hiram' to HIS-AD, 29 Apr. 1948, HA 105\31; and 'HIS Information', 28 Apr. 1948, KMA-PA 100\MemVavDalet\2–102; and HIS Information, Daily Summary', 28 Apr. 1948, HA 105\62. HIS reported that the Lebanese

were preventing the refugees from reaching Beirut, halting them in Tyre and Sidon.

498. 'Hiram' to HIS-AD, 'From Ma'aluli who Returned from Acre and Shafa-'Amr on 30.4.48', HA 105\127.

499. Carmel, *Battles*, 151–53.

500. 'Hiram' to HIS-AD, 6 May 1948, HA 105\237.

501. 'Hiram' to HIS-AD, 6 May 1948, HA 105\237.

502. 'Hiram', 7 May 1948, HA 105\237.

503. '257 and 317 FS Section Weekly Report No. 3 for Week Ending 28 April 1948', PRO WO 275–79.

504. HC to Secretary of State, 5 May 1948, SAMECA CP III\5\92; 'North Sector Sitrep', 5 May 1948, PRO WO 261–297; and 'Extract from Middle East Daily Situation Report No. 153', 7 May 1948, PRO CO 537–3875. Even the AHC was worried – it ordered doctors who had left to return to Acre (Committee for Economic Defence, 'Information on the Arab Economy, Bulletin No. 11', 11 May 1948, HA 105\146).

505. HIS-AD, 'The Migratory Movement . . .', 30 June 1948, HHA-ACP 10.95.13 (1).

506. 'Hiram' to HIS-AD, 11 May 1948, HA 105\54.

507. 'Hiram' to HIS-AD, 6 May 1948, HA 105\237; and 'Hiram', 7 May 1948, HA 105\237.

508. *In Enemy Eyes*, 41–42; and 'Hiram', 11 May 1948, HA 105\237.

509. IDF History Branch, 'The ALA,' IDFA 1046\70\\182; and 'Hiram' to HIS-AD, 21 May 1948, HA 105\92 bet.

510. 'Hiram' to HIS-AD, 21 May 1948, HA 105\92 bet.

511. 'Hiram' to HIS-AD, 21 May 1948, HA 105\92 bet.

512. Carmeli to HGS\Operations, 17 May 1948, IDFA 922\75\\1025.

513. Carmel, 'To the Notables of Acre', 17 May 1948, IDFA 922\75\\1025.

514. Untitled terms of surrender, signed by Haganah officer and Albert Rock, Ahmad Effendi Abdu, Mitkal Zreir, Ahmad Adlumi, etc., 18 May 1948, 01:40 hrs., and covering note Carmel to HGS, 19 May 1948, both in 922\75\\1022.

515. Carmel to HGS\Operations, 18 May 1948, IDFA 922\75\\1022.

516. 'Hiram' to HIS-AD, 21 May 1948, HA 105\92 bet.

517. 'Hiram' to HIS-AD, 9 June 1948, HA 105\92 bet.

518. Marie Syrkin, 'Preliminary Report on Holy Places', undated but from Sep. 1948, IDFA 922\52\\563.

519. ? to Prime Minister, 2 Dec. 1948, and General Avissar, president, Military Supreme Court, to CGS, 20 Dec. 1948, both in IDFA 121\50\\165.

520. Carmel, *Battles*, 151–62.

521. 'Hiram' to HIS-AD, 25 May 1948, HA 105\252.

522. 'Hiram' to HIS-AD, 30 May 1948, HA 105\252.

523. 'Hiram' to HIS-AD, 31 May 1948, conveying report from 'Giora', HA 105\252.

524. Comité International de la Croix Rouge, 'Rapport No. 9', 6 June 1948, HA 105\260.

525. 'Hiram' to HIS-AD, 9 June 1948, HA 105\92 bet.

526. Unsigned, 'State of Affairs in Acre', 25 Oct. 1948, IDFA 922\52\\563.

527. Shimoni to Shitrit, 13 July 1948, ISA MAM 307\10.

528. Shitrit to Shimoni, 19 July 1948, ISA MAM 307\10.

529. Kaplan to Shitrit, 20 July 1948, ISA MAM 307\10.

530. Entry for 2 May 1948, Weitz, *Diary*, III, 275–76.

531. Haim Solomon to Bernard Joseph, JA, 29 Mar. 1948, IDFA 500\48\\54.

532. Haim Laskov, 'Operations of the 7th Brigade, 22.3.48–22.7.48', undated but from late 1950s, 35, IDFA 1046\70\\56.

533. Unsigned, 'Operational Order for Operation Nahshon', 2 Apr. 1948, IDFA 47\53\\2. This may have been merely an undistributed draft.

534. Nahshon Corps HQ to battalions A, B, C, 'Operational Orders', ? Apr. 1948, IDFA 922\75\\1233.

535. *Book of the Palmah*, II, 189.

536. Galili, 'Meeting of National Staff 5\4', 5 Apr. 1948, IDFA 481\49\\64.

537. Unsigned, 'The Meeting of Heads of [HGS] Divisions, 4.4.48', IDFA 481\49\\18.

538. Galili to Yadin, ? Apr. 1948, IDFA 661\69\\45. (It appears to read '15' April – but '5' April is more likely.) The words 'and intimidated', possibly shorthand for 'intimidated to cause their inhabitants to flee', were added by hand. Of course, once the inhabitants were intimidated into flight, then guideline '(1)' would apply.

539. Haganah logbook of cables, for 30 March-3 Apr. 1948, IDFA 500\48\\54.

540. Unsigned, 'The Conquest of the Qastal 3.4.48', IDFA 661\69\\45.

541. Ben-Ari, 'Report on Reinforcing the Qastal', 7 [sic, should be 8] Apr. 1948, IDFA 661\69\\45.

542. 'Abd al Qadir's death is described in Logbook of Haganah cables, entry for 8 Apr. 1948, IDFA 500\48\\54. 'Nimrod', Etzioni Brigade, 'Report on the Battles of the Qastal,' 25 Apr. 1948, IDFA 500\48\\54, gives the Etzioni view of the battles, highly critical of the Palmah. 'Nimrod' writes that the Palmah on 2–3 Apr. merely wanted to 'destroy' Qastal while Etzioni had wanted to occupy the village.

543. Unsigned, 'The Second Conquest of the Qastal 9.4.48', IDFA 922\75\\1233.

544. Unsigned, 'Report on the Capture of Qaluniya', 11 Apr. 1948, IDFA 922\75\\1233. The report dryly records: 'While blowing up one of the houses, cries of "Help", in English, were heard.' See also HC to Secretary of State, 17 April 1948, SAMECA CP III\3\91.

545. Levin, *Jerusalem*, 66–67.

546. Nahshon Corps HQ to Battalions 1, 2, 3, 'Operational Orders', 10 Apr. 1948, IDFA 922\75\\1233, ordered the 'liquidation' of two villages, codenamed 'Milano' and 'Sheffield'. Perhaps the villages were Beit Jiz and Khirbet Deir 'Amr. See also Nahshon to Battalion 2, ? Apr. 1948, IDFA 661\69\\45.

547. Nahshon Corps HQ, 'Framework for Corps' Operations', 14 Apr. 1948, IDFA 661\69\\45. See also Nahshon to Battalions 1,2,3, intelligence, 14 Apr. 1948, IDFA 661\69\\45.

548. Nahshon Corps HQ to Battalion 2, 15 Apr. 1948, IDFA 236\53\\1. The order also appears in IDFA 661\69\\45, but here IDFA censors have deleted the words 'with the aim of annihilation and destruction and arson'.

549. Nahshon HQ to Battalion 1, IDFA 236\53\\1.

550. Nahshon Corps HQ to Battalion 3, 15 Apr. 1948, IDFA 661\69\\45. In this document, the IDFA censor has deleted key words – but they appear in

Nahshon HQ to 52nd Battalion, 15 Apr. 1948, IDFA 236\53\\1, relating to the planned operation against Sajad.

551. Major ?, [British Army, Palestine] General Staff, 'SouthPal' to List 'D', undated, IDFA 900\52\\43; and Etzioni to HGS, Yadin, 16 Apr. 1948, IDFA 196\71\\83.

552. ? to 'Yevussi', 'Operation Yevussi Stage A', undated, IDFA 922\75\\1233; and Yadin to Yevussi and Harel and Etzioni brigade HQs, 'Document', 19 Apr. 1948, IDFA 661\69\\45.

553. Harel Corps HQ to Battalions 1, 2, etc., 22 Apr. 1948, IDFA 922\75\\1233.

554. Palmah HQ to HGS, 23 Apr. 1948, IDFA 922\75\\1066.

555. Palmah HQ to HGS, 25 Apr. 1948, IDFA 922\75\\1066.

556. District OC to 'Yitzhak' etc., 7 Apr. 1948, IDFA 500\48\\29.

557. D Company OC, 4th Battalion, to Jerusalem District OC, 11 Apr. 1948, IDFA 4944\49\\584.

558. Niv, *Battles*, VI, 83.

559. Niv, *Battles*, VI, 83–86.

560. Milstein, *History*, IV, 380–81, gives the recollections in this connection of an IZL participant.

561. 'Yavne' to HIS-AD, 12 Apr. 1948, IDFA 5254\49\\372.

562. 'Yavne' to HIS, 13 Apr. 1948, IDFA 5254\49\\372.

563. 'Eliezer' to 'Tzadik', etc., 'Report on the Conquest of Deir Yassin', 10 Apr. 1948, IDFA 500\48\\56. See also Kanane and Zeitawi, 'The Village of Deir Yassin', 53–57, based on interviews with Deir Yassin refugees. In many particulars, the interviews, conducted in the 1980s, substantiate what appears in the contemporary Haganah documentation.

564. 'Avraham' (Pa'il) to Jerusalem District OC, 10 Apr. 1948, in HGS\Operations\Intelligence to Haganah corps, 'Lessons from the Dissidents' Operation in Deir Yassin', '12.2.48' [sic, probably should be 12.5.48 or 12.6.48], HA 20\253. This seems to be an abridged version of Pa'il's original report, which IDFA refuses to open to researchers. Milstein claims that Pa'il was not in Deir Yassin on 9 Apr. (Milstein, *History*, IV, 366 and 378, and interview with author, 18 Aug. 2001). Milstein argues that there was no organised, largescale massacre in Deir Yassin and that various HIS reports were doctored by their authors or their superiors to exaggerate the atrocities and blacken the dissident organisations' name within the context of Yishuv political in-fighting (see Milstein, *History*, IV, 382–88). But Milstein admits that whole families were gunned down in the course of the fighting.

   Part of Pa'il's report is apparently reinforced by a report by two Jewish doctors, who found five male bodies in a house by the village quarry (Dr Z. Avigdori and Dr A. Druyan, 'Report on Visit to Deir Yassin on 12.4.1948', 18 Apr. 1948, IDFA 500\48\\54).

565. 'Yavne' to HIS-AD, 12 Apr. 1948, IDFA 5254\49\\372.

566. 'Yavne', 'Urgent Arab Information, 10.4.48', 11 Apr. 1948, IDFA 5254\49\\75. Haganah, British and Arab officials subsequently broadcast that '254' Arabs had died – each exaggerating the number for his own reasons. The number seems to have originated with Mordechai Ra'anan, the IZL OC in Jerusalem, who on the morning of 10 April told reporters, untruthfully, that 'so far, 254 Arab bodies have been counted' (Milstein,

History, IV, 369 and 376). In the 1980s, Palestinian anthropologist Sharif Kanane, of Beir Zeit University, investigated the issue and emerged with a tally of '110–120' killed (Yizhar Beer, 'The Hidden Villages', *Kol Ha'ir*, Jerusalem, 25 Nov.1988) in the fighting and subsequent executions.

567. 'Yavne' to District OC, 'Urgent Arab Information from 9.4.48', 9 Apr. 1948, IDFA 5254\49\\75; Dr. S. Shereshevsky to the 'HQ', Jerusalem, 11 Apr. 1948, IDFA 5254\49\\372; and Levine, *Jerusalem*, 57, entry for 9 Apr. 1948.

568. Haganah HQ, 'Statement on Deir Yassin,' *Haaretz* and *Davar*, 12 Apr. 1948.

569. Isaac Herzog and Ben-Zion Uziel, chief rabbis of Palestine, 12 Apr. 1948, CZA S25–4147.

570. Jewish Agency to King Abdullah, 12 Apr. 1948, ISA, *Political and Diplomatic Documents*, 625–626.

571. For example, extract of Haganah or JA monitoring report of articles in *Falastin*, 10–11 Apr. 1948, HA 105\31.

572. HC to Secretary of State, 17 Apr. 1948, SAMECA CP III\3\91; HC to Kirkbride, 25 Apr. 1948, SAMECA CP III\4\48; and US Legation (Damascus) to Secretary of State, 3 May 1948, NA RG84, Jerusalem Consulate, Classified Records 1948, 800-Syria. See also Larry Collins Papers, Georgetown University Library, LC interview with Hazem Nusseibi, May 1968, recalling the statement he had issued along with Husayn Khalidi and Tabet Khalidi: 'We fell into their [i.e., the Zionist] trap. We weren't sure the Arab armies for all their talk were really going to come. We thought to shock the population of the Arab countries to stir pressures against their governments. We did, but we also unfortunately stirred our own population to fear. It had a traumatic effect. We committed a fatal error, and set the stage for the refugee problem.'

573. IZL, 'Announcement on the Deir Yassin Affair', c. 12 Apr. 1948, IDFA 5254\49\\372.

574. Text of Kol Zion Halohemet broadcast, 14 Apr.1948, JI, IZL, kaf-4, 8\13.

575. LHI, 'Daily Press Bulletin No. 33', Tel Aviv, 30 Aug. 1948.

576. Begin, *Revolt*, 164.

577. 'HIS Information', 14 Apr. 1948, KMA-PA 100\MemVavDalet\3–126.

578. 'Hiram' to 'Jeremiah', 15 Apr. 1948, IDFA 5942\49\\23.

579. 'Yavne' to HIS-AD, 15 Apr. 1948, HA 105\257.

580. Unsigned, untitled report, 16 Apr. 1948, IDFA 2504\49\\4.

581. 'Yovev' to HIS-AD, 17 Apr. 1948, and 'Tiroshi (Aran)' to HIS-AD, 19 Apr. 1948, both in HA 105\54 aleph.

582. 'Hiram' to HIS-AD, 18 Apr. 1948, HA 105\257.

583. Entry for 1 May 1948, DBG-YH II, 378.

584. 'Tiroshi (Alon)' to HIS-AD, 20 Apr. 1948, HA 105\257.

585. British Army HQ Palestine, 'Fortnightly Intelligence Newsletter, 21 April 1948', PRO WO 275–64.

586. Cohen, 'In Face of the Arab Evacuation', 20 May 1948, HHA-ACP 10.95.11 (8); statement by Hazan, protocol of meeting of Mapam Political Committee, 26 May 1948, HHA 66.90 (1); and statement by Cohen, protocol of meeting of Mapam Political Committee, 15 June 1948, HHA 66.90 (1).

587. HIS-AD, 'The Migratory Movement . . .', 30 Jun. 1948, HHA-ACP 10.95.13 (1).
588. 'Report on the Negotiations over the Mishmar Ha'emek Fighting by Lt. Col. A. Peel, Commanding 3rd The King's Own Hussars', 12 Apr. 1948, PRO WO 275–48.
589. 'Tzuri' to HIS-AD, 'The Battle of Mishmar Ha'emek', 8 May 1948, HA 105\127; and *Mishmar Ha'emek in the War*, 15–16.
590. Logbook, 6th Airborne Division, entry for 7 Apr. 1948, PRO WO 275–54; and 'Report on the Negotiations . . .', 12 Apr. 1948, PRO WO 275–48; and Golani to Galili, etc., 8 Apr. 1948, 17:45 hrs., IDFA 128\51\\50.
591. Golani to Galili, 8 Apr. 1948, 17:45 hrs., IDFA 128\51\\50; and Yehuda (Lovka) Ivzori, 'Mishmar Ha'emeq Sits Next to the Road from Haifa to Jenin', undated, Mishmar Ha'emek Archive 3.64\24.
592. Golani to Galili, 8 Apr. 1948, 21:30 hrs, IDFA 128\51\\50.
593. Protocol of meeting of Mapai Centre, 24 July 1948, LPA 23 aleph\48. Presumably, Ya'akov Hazan and Mordechai Bentov were members of the 'delegation'; both were in Tel Aviv on 8–10 Apr. attending, with Ben-Gurion, the meeting of the Zionist Actions Committee. Zeev Tzahor, in the worst tradition of official Zionist historiography (*Hazan*, 184–185), omits mention of the affair, and, instead, writes that Mishmar Ha'emek's members were 'embarrassed' by the Haganah assault on their friendly neighbour, Abu Shusha, and 'did not strain themselves' to prevent the expulsion. Of Hazan he writes, merely, that he 'ignored the expulsion of his neighbours'.

   The expulsion around Mishmar Ha'emek was repeatedly referred to in Mapam-Mapai polemics during the following months. For example, the Mapai-affiliated Gordonia–Maccabi Hatza'ir kibbutz movement, in 'Bulletin Gimel', Circular no. 3, 17 September (Ihud Hakibbutzim Archive, 111\2), charged: 'Mishmar Ha'emek was the first to demand the destruction of the Arab villages around it.' Gordonia leader Pinhas Lubianker (Lavon) put it somewhat differently. At a meeting of the Zionist Actions Committee on 23 August 1948, he said that 'when the Arab inhabitants around [his kibbutz] Khulda and around Mishmar Ha'emek were ejected for security reasons, neither the inhabitants of Mishmar Ha'emek nor of Khulda objected. Because Mishmar Ha'emek knew and Khulda knew that if they [were allowed to] stay during wartime, surrounded by three–four Arab villages, they would not be safe' (protocol of meeting of Zionist Actions Committee, 23 Aug. 1948, CZA S25–323).
594. HGS\Operations to Golani, 5 Apr. 1948, IDFA 922\75\\1025.
595. Yadin to Golani, 10 Apr. 1948, IDFA 128\51\\50.
596. 'Tzuri' to HIS-AD, 'The Battle of Mishmar Ha'emek', 8 May 1948, HA 105\127.
597. 'Tiroshi (Yosef)' to HIS-AD, 16 Apr. 1948, HA 105\257.
598. Golani to Carmeli and Golani HQ, 9 Apr. 1948, IDFA 128\51\\50; and Palmah HQ to HGS, 'Daily Report,' 10 Apr. 1948, IDFA 922\75\\1066.
599. Palmah HQ to HGS, 'Daily Report', 9 Apr. 1948, IDFA 922\75\\1066; and Golani to Golani HQ, undated, IDFA 128\51\\50.
600. Palmah HQ to HGS, 'Daily Report', 12 Apr. 1948, IDFA 922\75\\1214.
601. Golani to HGS, etc., 12 Apr. 1948, IDFA 128\51\\50.

602. Palmah HQ to HGS, 'Daily Report', 15 Apr. 19048, IDFA 922\75\\1066.
603. Palmah HQ to HGS, 'Daily Report', 13 Apr. 1948, IDFA 922\75\\1066.
604. Palmah to HGS, 'Daily Report', 15 Apr. 1948, IDFA 922\75\\1066.
605. 'Logbook of the battle', entry for 15 Apr. 1948, IDFA 1058\52\\1. The log-book records that two girls found hiding in Abu Zureiq were taken for treatment to Hazore'a.
606. 'Tzuri (Barkan)' to HIS-AD, 'Subject: The Interrogation of Ali al Bahut – Mansi Village', 27 Apr. 1948, HA 105\54 aleph. Among the refugees it was rumoured that '15,000–40,000' Russian troops were fighting alongside the Jews.
607. 'Tzuri', 19 Apr. 1948, HA 105\31.
608. Palmah HQ to HGS, 'Daily Report', 16 Apr. 1948, IDFA 922\75\\1214.
609. Palmah HQ to HGS, 'Daily Report', 19 Apr. 1948, IDFA 922\75\\1214.
610. Bauer to Galili, Moshe Mann, Baruch Rabinov, and Ya'akov Riftin, 14 Apr. 1948, Eliezer Bauer (Be'eri) Papers.
611. Protocols of kibbutz meetings, 18 and 20 April 1948, Kibbutz Hazore'a Archive; and Ofek, 'The Relations Between Hazore'a and the Villages of Qira and Abu Zureiq during the years 1936–1948'.
612. Weitz to Rema, 21 Apr. 1948, Weitz, *Diary*, III, 271.
613. For example, 'HIS-AD Information 29.4.48', IDFA 922\75\\1205, regarding Burayka.
614. 'Tzuri (Barkan)' to HIS-AD, 9 May 1948, IDFA 1196\52\\1.
615. 'Hiram' to HIS-AD, 2 May 1948, HA 105\217; 'Tiroshi (Eitan)' to HIS-AD, 14 March 1948, IDFA 6400\49\\66; and Alexandroni HQ, 'Bulletin No. 7', 13 May 1948, IDFA 2323\49\\6.
616. Alexandroni HQ, 'Alexandroni Brigade Bulletin No. 9 – 15.5.48', IDFA 922\75\\949.
617. 'Testimony of Moshe Nesher (Wagner)', an IZL officer, JI IZLP, kaf-4, 7\8. Niv, *Battles*, VI, 131–32, writes that Sindiyana's inhabitants 'were allowed to leave eastwards'.
618. 'HIS-AD Information 29.4.48', IDFA 922\75\\1205.
619. 'Summary of Carmeli Brigade Information No. 3 for 7.5.48', IDFA 273\52\\5.
620. Entry for 15 May 1948, HGS\Operations Logbook, IDFA 922\75\\1176.
621. 'Tzuri (Barkan)' to HIS-AD, 4 June 1948, HA 105\92 bet.
622. OC A Company, 'Shlosnitzki', 5 Aug. 1948, IDFA 128\51\\32.
623. 'Tiroshi (Eitan)' to HIS-AD, 29 Apr. 1948, HA 105\257; and 'HIS-AD Information 29.4.48', IDFA 922\75\\1205.
624. 'Tiroshi (Eitan)' to HIS-AD, 3 May 1948, IDFA 6400\49\\66; and Logbook, entry for 9 May 1948, IDFA 665\51\\1.
625. Shakib Wahab to ALA HQ ? (probably 16) Apr. 1948, HA 105\127.
626. Shakib Wahab to OC ALA, 17 Apr. 1948, HA 105\127; and Carmeli to HGS\Operations, 'Daily Report 22.4.48'; Carmeli to HGS\Operations, 'Daily Report 19.4.48'; and unsigned but probably Carmeli HQ, 'Report on the Battle of Ramat Yohanan', undated, all three in IDFA 7353\49\\46.
627. 'Segal' to all Divisions, 'Summary of Information Concerning the Area from Friday 16.4.48 14:00 hrs. until Sunday 18.4.48 08:00', IDFA 7353\49\\46.
628. 'Summary of the Meeting of the Arab Affairs Advisers in Dora Camp 6.4.48', IDFA 4663\49\\125.

629. 'Summary of the Meeting of the Arab Affairs Advisers, Camp Dora, 13.4.48', IDFA 4663\49\\125; and 'Tiroshi (Alon)' to HIS-AD, 20 Apr. 1948, HA 105\257. The Haganah told the villagers that they had to go because it couldn't guarantee that 'another Deir Yassin would not occur here as well'.

630. 'Tiroshi (Dror)' to HIS-AD, 9 Apr. 1948, HA 105\257.

631. HIS-AD, 'The Migratory Movement . . .', 30 June 1948, HHA-ACP 10.95.13 (1).

632. 'Summary of the Meeting of the Arab Affairs Advisers, Camp Dora, 13.4.48', IDFA 4663\49\\125.

633. Alexandroni HQ, 'Sarkas', 11 Mar. 1948, IDFA 6400\49\\66.

634. HIS-AD, 'The Migratory Movement . . .', 30 June 1948, HHA-ACP 10.95.13 (1); and 'Tiroshi (Eitan)' to HIS-AD, 20 Apr. 1948, and 'Tiroshi (Eitan)' to HIS-AD, 22 Apr. 1948, both in IDFA 6400\49\\66.

635. HIS-AD, 'The Migratory Movement . . .', 30 June 1948, HHA-ACP 10.95.13 (1); and interview with Aharon Braverman (Bar-On), 10 Nov. 1985, 'Ein Hahoresh.

636. 'Summary of the Meeting of the Arab Affairs Advisers Dora Camp 13.4.48', IDFA 4663\49\\125; and 'Tiroshi (Dror)' to HIS-AD, 16 Apr. 1948, HA 105\257.

637. 'Summary of the Meeting of the Arab Affairs Advisers in Camp Dora, 6.4.48', IDFA 4663\49\\125.

638. 'Tiroshi (Alon)' to HIS-AD, 27 Apr. 1948, HA 105\257; 'Summary, Meeting of the Arab Affairs Advisers in Netanya 25.4.48', IDFA 2506\49\\91; and page from logbook, perhaps of Ramat Hakovesh's security officer, IDFA 922\75\\949. See also Hativat Alexandroni, 102–104, and Kanane and al Ka'abi, 'Al Miska'.

639. 'Tiroshi (Aran)' to HIS-AD, 9 Mar. 1948, HA 105\54 aleph.

640. 'Tiroshi (Alon)' to HIS-AD, 2 Apr. 1948, HA 105\257.

641. 'Tiroshi (Alon)' to HIS-AD, 6 Apr. 1948, HA 105\257.

642. 'Tiroshi (Alon)' to HIS-AD, 12 Apr. 1948, HA 105\257.

643. 'Tiroshi (Aran)' to HIS-AD, 20 Apr. 1948, HA 105\257.

644. 'Tiroshi (Aran)' to HIS-AD, 7 Apr. 1948, HA 105\54 aleph.

645. 'Tiroshi (Aran)' to HIS-AD, 'Subject: The Village of Fajja was Evacuated by its Inhabitants', 14 Apr. 1948, HA 105\257.

646. 'Tiroshi (Aran)' to HIS-AD, 8 Apr. 1948, HA 105\257.

647. 'Tiroshi (Aran)' to HIS-AD, 'Subject: The Mukhtar of Fajja', 14 Apr. 1948, HA 105\257.

648. 'Tiroshi (Aran)' to HIS-AD, 15 Apr. 1948, HA105\257.

649. 'Tiroshi (Aran)' to HIS-AD, 3 May 1948, HA 105\92 aleph.

650. 'Summary, Meeting of the Arab Affairs Advisers in Netanya 25.4.48', IDFA 2506\49\\91; and 'Summary of the Meeting of Arab Affairs Advisers in Netanya, 9.5.48', IDFA 6127\49\\109.

651. 'Tiroshi (Aran)' to HIS-AD, 12 May 1948, HA 105\217.

652. HIS-AD, 'The Migratory Movement . . .', 30 June 1948, HHA-ACP 10.95.13 (1).

653. 'Summary of the Meeting of the Arab Affairs Advisers in Netanya, 9.5.48', IDFA 6127\49\\109.

654. 'Tiroshi (Alon)' to HIS-AD, 11 May 1948, HA 105\127.

655. Alexandroni Intelligence Officer, 'Information, the Attak on Arab Kafr Saba on 13.5', IDFA 922\75\\949. See also Kanane and Ka'abi, 'Kafr Saba', 56–59.

656. 'Tiroshi (Alon)' to HIS-AD, 17 May 1948, HA 105\54 aleph. See also *Hativat Alexandroni*, 194–207.

657. Alexandroni, [sic] 42nd Battalion [should be 32nd], 'Brigade Bulletin', 21 June 1948, IDFA 922\75\\949.

658. 'Tiroshi (Eitan)' to HIS-AD, 'Tantura', and 'Tiroshi (Eitan)' to HIS-AD, 'Subject: The Village of Tantura', 6 May 1948, both in HA 105\54 aleph; and Alexandroni HQ, 'Bulletin No. 6',? May 1948, IDFA 2323\49\\6.

659. 'Tiroshi (Eitan)' to HIS-AD, 'The Village of Tantura', 6 May 1948, HA 105\54 aleph; and 'Tiroshi' to Alexandroni, 10 May 1948, IDFA 922\75\\949.

660. Unsigned, 'Brigade Bulletin', 7 May 1948, IDFA 922\75\\949.

661. Unsigned, 'Summary of Information for Alexandroni Brigade (18.5.48)', IDFA 2506\49\\85.

662. Alexandroni HQ, 'Information Circular: The preparations for Attack in the Villages of Tantura, 'Ein Ghazal, Ijzim and Jab'a', 22 May 1948, IDFA 922\75\\949.

663. Alexandroni CO, 'Operational Order', 22 May 1948, IDFA 922\75\\949.

664. Unsigned, 'Short Report on Tantura Operation' undated, IDFA 922\75\\949; and 'Ya'akov B.', in the name of deputy OC 'A' Company, 'Report on Operation Namal', 26 May 1948, IDFA 6647\49\\13. See also *Hativat Alexandroni*, 31–32 and 220–230, which claims that Tantura was offered the option of surrendering and staying.

665. Sub-sub-district (hevel) 1 OC, Zikhron Ya'akov, to sub-district (nafa) OC, 29 May 1948, IDFA 4663\49\\46.

666. IDF CGS to Alexandroni, 1 June 1948, IDFA 481\49\\143. The CGS used the term '*khabala*', meaning sabotage. Alexandroni responded that it stemmed from 'the enthusiasm of victory' (Alexandroni to IDF GS\Operations, 2 June 1948, IDFA 2687\49\\35).

667. Sub-sub-district 1 OC to sub-district OC, 31 May and 1 June 1948, both in IDFA 4663\49\\46.

668. Shitrit to Ben-Gurion, 31 May 1948, ISA MAM 302\48.

669. 'Tiroshi (Eitan)' to HIS-AD, 7 (?) May 1948, HA 105\260.

670. A. Goldfarb, Alexandroni Adjutant, to Alexandroni\Operations, 16 June 1948, IDFA 2506\49\\91; 'Tiroshi (Eitan)' to HIS-AD, 22 June 1948, HA 105\260; and Courvoisier, Red Cross, Tel Aviv, to Red Cross Delegate, Nablus, undated but from 16 or 17 June 1948, HA 105\260.

671. In March 1998, an Israeli student, Theodor ('Teddy') Katz, submitted a 211-page MA thesis – 'The Exodus of the Arabs from the Villages at the Foot of the Southern Carmel in 1948' – to Haifa University, which the university authorities subsequently approved, giving him a 97. The thesis dealt with two villages, Tantura and Umm al Zinat, and maintained that dozens, and perhaps as many as 250, of Tantura's inhabitants were massacred by Alexandroni troops after its conquest. Katz based his findings on interviews conducted in the 1990s with former inhabitants. He also interviewed Alexandroni veterans. On 21 Jan. 2000 the Israeli daily *Ma'ariv* published an article, 'The Massacre at Tantura', by Amir Gilat, based on

Katz's thesis and independent interviews with former Tantura inhabitants and Alexandroni veterans. The Arab witnesses again alleged a massacre; the veterans denied there had been one. Katz unearthed no Haganah or IDF document alleging or referring to a massacre – or any contemporary Arab or western document to this effect. The charge of massacre was based solely on oral testimony. And the few Alexandroni veterans whom Katz had alleged had admitted that a massacre had taken place, or had hinted that atrocities had taken place, subsequently denied that they had said any such thing.

In April 2000, a group of Alexandroni, 33rd Battalion, veterans sued Katz for libel in the Tel Aviv District Court (*Haaretz*, 30 Apr. 2000.) After the prosecuting lawyers demonstrated that some of Katz's transcriptions of taped interviews with Alexandroni veterans were inaccurate, Katz agreed to apologise and agreed that there was no basis for the massacre charge. The court adopted Katz's recantation as its ruling. (*Haaretz*, 22 December 2000.) But Katz then reneged, withdrew his recantation, and appealed against the ruling to Israel's Supreme Court. In 2001–2002, Israeli historian Ilan Pappe published 'The Tantura Case in Israel: The Katz Research and Trial' (*Journal of Palestine Studies*, Vol. 30\3, Spring 2001, 19–39) and 'The Katz Affair and Tantura: History, Historiography, Law and Academia' (*Tei'oriya U'vikoret* 20, spring 2002, 191–217), defending Katz's work. Meanwhile, Haifa University withdrew its approval of the thesis and asked Katz to revise and re-submit it. Katz resubmitted the thesis – now some 500 pages long – and the university appointed five anonymous examiners – who rejected the thesis (three gave it failing marks, two, passing marks). Opting for a 'compromise', the university then decided to award Katz a non-research (meaning second-class) MA degree. The university's ruling is currently being appealed by Katz's department, the Middle East Studies Department. (Whatever its outcome, the Katz case highlights the ineluctable fragility of historiography based on oral testimony.)

In light of the available evidence, it is doubtful whether there was a massacre at Tantura. Katz amassed a number of interviews with or written statements from Tantura refugees who claimed, some 50 years after the event, that there had been a massacre. For example, 'Adnan 'Aqab Yihiya, described (in 2000) how Jewish troops, after the battle, had selected 40 young adult males, taken them to the cemetery, forced them to dig graves, and then executed 24 of them. A similar story appeared in Nimr al Khatib, *Disaster*, 204–205.

But the fact that the Alexandroni veterans were willing to go to court to clear their names (and that of their unit) implies certainty that no massacre had occurred (or at least a near certainty that no credible witness would come forward and testify to the contrary). Even more tellingly, immediately after her arrival in the West Bank, a refugee from Tantura complained 'that the Jews raped women in addition to [committing] acts of robbery, theft and arson'. The report was carried on (East) Jerusalem and Ramallah radio stations (unsigned, 'Palestine in Arab Radio Broadcasts, 21–22.6.48', HA 105\88; and extract from radio monitoring report, unsigned, 'Jerusalem 16:00', 21 June 1948, HA 105\92 aleph). Had there been a massacre, would not the woman who had complained of rapes, theft and arson have thrown in, for good measure, the massacre as well? Would not the Arab radio stations have broadcast news of the massacre? In summer 1948, the refugees from Palestine were eager to tell and retell tales of Jewish viciousness (if only to justify their headlong flight), and Arab propagandists were eager to lay their hands on, and broadcast, such tales. Surely reports of such a largescale massacre, had there been one, would have been bound to surface? Yet in the course of 1948, only one atrocity report regarding Tantura ever surfaced – the one quoted above, relating to rapes (and robbery, theft and arson); but not a word about a massacre or a series of massacres.

On the other hand, there is evidence that Alexandroni troops that day here and there executed POWs. Moreover, CGS to OC Alexandroni of 1 June 1948, complaining of acts of 'sabotage' [habala] after the conquest of the village, may have been a euphemistic reference to a massacre.

A few days after the conquest of Tantura, Ya'akov Epstein, of Zikhron Ya'akov, the Ministry for Minority Affairs' man in the moshava and its long-standing liaison with Tantura, prepared a report. He had arrived in the village minutes or hours after the completion of the conquest, on the morning of 23 May. He reported that he had seen bodies everywhere – 'in the [village] outskirts, in the streets, in the alleys, in the village houses' – and had had a hand in organising their burial. But he had made no mention of a recently completed or ongoing massacre of any sort. On the contrary, he had seen women and children and adult males sitting on the shore and had moved among them in order to identify, at the Haganah's request, any possible strangers. And he had asked the Alexandroni commander to see to it that villagers were removed from the site and not allowed to remain lest 'vengeful' Haganah troops attack them. But he had made no mention of a massacre or of allegations of a massacre (handwritten draft and typed reports by Epstein, probably written respectively in May and late June, Zikhron Ya'akov Archive).

Lastly, a refugee from Tantura, Mahmoud al Yihiya Yihiya, in August 1998 (Dar al Shara, Damascus) published a book on his village, entitled Al Tantura, in which he desribed the battle and named the village dead, 52 in all, from May 1948 (pp. 117–126 and 143–146). He made no mention of a massacre. It is probable that some of the 52 were unarmed villagers killed in the course of the battle; but this is a far cry from the dozens or hundreds Katz and his Arab 'witnesses' claimed were massacred.

In the absence of documentary proof to the contrary, the silences of the plaintive women refugees who reached the West Bank in June 1948, of Epstein (in May and June 1948) and of Yihiya concerning a largescale massacre must strike the historian as outstandingly odd if a massacre had indeed taken place.

672. Unsigned, 'Precis of Information for Alexandroni Brigade (11.5.48), No. 8', IDFA 2506\49\\80.
673. Intellligence Officer, mobile garrison battalion, to 'Baruch', 17 May 1948, IDFA 244\51\\38.
674. B Company to OC Mobile Garrison Battalion, 'Report on Al Mazar Operation, 17.5.48', IDFA 5942\49\\32.
675. 'Carmeli Brigade Information No. 5 for 24.5.48', IDFA 128\51\\71.

676. Alexandroni, 'Operational order for Operation Kipa', 3 June 1948, IDFA 922\75\\949. Previously, HGS\Operations had ordered Alexandroni 'to conquer and destroy' Qaqun (along with al Tira and Qalansuwa) but this had not been carried out (see HGS\Operations to Alexandroni, 12 May 1948, IDFA 922\75\\949).

677. 'Abd al Rahim 'Abd al Madur, 'The Village of Qaqun', 94–95.

678. Unsigned, 'The course of Operation Kipa', IDFA 922\75\\949; and 'Report on Operation Kipa (from the Combat HQ)', undated, IDFA 922\75\\949.

679. HGS\Operations\1 to Allon, 'Operation Yiftah Order', 25 Apr. 1948, IDFA 67\51\\677.

680. Allon to Yadin and Galili, 22 Apr. 1948, KMA-PA 170–44.

681. Palmah HQ to HGS, 'Daily Report', 29 Apr. 1948, IDFA 922\75\\1066.

682. 'Yiftah' to Galili, etc., 29 Apr. 1948, IDFA 128\51\\50.

683. 'Oded' to Golani, 20 Apr. 1948, IDFA 128\51\\50.

684. HIS-AD, 'The Migratory Movement . . .', 30 June 1948, HHA-ACP 10.95.13 (1); and 'HIS Information, Daily Summary', 25 Apr. 1948, IDFA 900\52\\58. The inhabitants of the two Kirads returned to Israel at the end of the war only to be finally expelled, mostly to Syria, in 1956.

685. 'Yiftah' to HGS, etc., 2 May 1948, IDFA 128\51\\50.

686. HIS-AD, 'The Migratory Movement . . .', 30 June 1948, HHA-ACP 10.95.13 (1).

687. Yiftah to HGS, etc., 2 May 1948, 21:00 hrs., IDFA 128\51\\50.

688. Palmah HQ to HGS, 'Daily Report', 8 May 1948, IDFA 922\75\\1066.

689. Palmah HQ to HGS, 'Daily Report', 23 May 1948, IDFA 922\75\\1066.

690. Shitrit to Ben-Gurion and Sharett, 13 Aug. 1948, ISA FM 2564\9.

691. 'Visit of the Minority Affairs and Police Minister in Kfar Gil'adi 29.7.48', HA 105\260.

692. Foreign Ministry, Middle East Dept., 'Clashes on the Lebanese Border', 15 Sept. 1948, and Foreign Ministry, Middle East Dept., 'Village of Hunin', 21 Sep. 1948, both in ISA FM2564\9; and Ehrlich, *Lebanon*, 277–83.

693. Palmah HQ to HGS, 'Daily Report', 2 May 1948, IDFA 922\75\\1044; and Yiftah HQ to HGS\Operations 3, 1 May 1948, IDFA 922\75\\1082.

694. Allon to Galili and Yadin, 22 Apr. 1948, KMA-PA 170–44.

695. *Beineinu*, no. 13, 9 May 1948, KMA 2–20\aleph; and Yosef Ulitzky, 'Operation Yiftah for the Liberation of the Galilee', HHA 5.18 (2).

696. Palmah HQ to HGS, 'Daily Report', 4 May 1948, 19:30 hrs., IDFA 922\75\\1066; and Palmah HQ to HGS, 'Daily Report', 4 May 1948, 20:00 hrs., IDFA 922\75\\1082.

697. Palmah HQ to HGS, 'Daily Report', 6 May 1948, IDFA 922\75\\1066.

698. 'Tzuri (Cochba)' to HIS, 'A Letter Sent by the Priest Boniface . . .', 4 June 1948, HA 105\92.

699. Broadmead to FO, 4 May 1948, PRO FO 816\119. Some of the Zanghariya later returned and were expelled again (unsigned, untitled, undated report, probably by GSS in 1949 or early 1950s, IDFA 1627\94\\231.)

700. Broadmead to Kirkbride, 5 May 1948, PRO FO 816\119.

701. *Book of the Palmah*, II, 281.

702. HIS-AD, 'The Migratory Movement . . .', 30 June 1948, HHA-ACP 10.95.13 (1).

703. On 28\29 May, Haganah forces raided the village, causing at least tempo-rary flight (First Platoon, 'A' Company, to 'A' Company, 29 May 1948, IDFA 128\51\\32).

704. *Book of the Palmah*, II, 286. See also Palmah HQ to HGS, 'Daily Report', 15 May 1948, IDFA 922\75\\1066; Beineinu, no. 15, 20 May 1948, KMA-PA 2–20\aleph; and interview with Mula Cohen in 'Al Nakba', a documentary produced and directed by Benny Brunner.

705. Hebrew translation of flier, dated 14 May 1948, and accompanying let-ter, 'Tzuri (Drori)' to HIS-AD, 16 May 1948, HA 105\54 aleph. See also Alexandroni HQ, 'Bulletin No. 17', 23 May 1948, IDFA 2323\49\\6.

706. Unsigned, untitled, undated report on Haganah deployment in Galilee in first half of May, KMA-PA 109\gimel 1–4.

707. HIS-AD, 'The Migratory Movement . . .', 30 June 1948, HHA-ACP 10.95.13 (1). Allon's account (*Book of the Palmah*, II, 286) implies that the whispering campaign worked instantly on or before 15 May (as does Palmah HQ to HGS, 'Daily Report', 15 May 1948, IDFA 128\51\\50) whereas the HIS-AD report, in detailed fashion, brackets the flight due to the psychological warfare between 19 and 25 May. The HIS-AD dates are probably more reliable – but it is possible that the whispering campaign was initiated between 11 and 15 May.

708. HIS-AD, 'The Migratory Movement . . .', 30 June 1948, HHA-ACP 10.95.13 (1).

709. 'Daniel', 11th Battalion, 'Report on Zawiya Operation 19.5.48', IDFA 128\51\\32.

710. Palmah HQ to HGS, 'Daily Report', 23 May 1948, IDFA 922\75\\1066.

711. HIS-AD, 'The Migratory Movement . . .', 30 June 1948, HHA-ACP 10.95.113 (1); and (relating to Qadas) Yiftah HQ to HGS, 15 May 1948, IDFA 922\75\\1066.

712. 9th Brigade Logbook, part 3, 14.5.48–31.5.48', entries for 18 and 25 May and 8 June 1948, IDFA1046\70\\9; unsigned to 'Tzuri', 'Yiftah' and 'Oded', 25 May 1948, 922\75\\1082; and Yiftah HQ, 'Daily Report', 22 May 1948, IDFA 922\75\\1082.

713. Palmah HQ to HGS, 'Daily Report', 24 May 1948, IDFA 922\75\\1066; and HGS\Operations\Intelligence, 'Daily Report on the North-Eastern Front 25 [May], 20:00', IDFA 922\75\\1044.

714. 'Tzuri (Drori)' to HIS-AD, 21 June 1948, HA 105\127.

715. 'Zmiri', 'Report on my Visit to Northern Front', 14 May 1948, IDFA 2384\50\\9. The conquest of Acre itself, of course, was the linchpin of the operation (see above).

716. 'Levanoni' to battalions, 'Report on Events in the Brigade's Area during the Month 11.1.48–13.2.48', IDFA 128\51\\71; and Palmah HQ to HGS, 1 Feb. 1948, IDFA 922\75\\1066.

717. 'Hiram (Amikam)' to HIS-AD, 17 Feb. 1948, HA 105\23 bet.

718. Unsigned, 'Conversation with Abu Muhammad (Rabah)', 4 Feb. 1948, CZA S25–4000.

719. Carmeli, 'Operation Ehud' ? Apr. 1948, IDFA 5942\49\\53.

720. 'HIS Information, Daily Summary', 9 May 1948, IDFA 900\52\\58; and 'Hiram' to HIS-AD, 'The Strangers, their Location and Strength in the Acre-Nahariya Area', date indecipherable but mid-May 1948, HA 105\127.

721. Eshel, *Carmeli*, 166; Nazzal, *Exodus*, 52–54; and Carmel, *Battles*, 120–47.

722. Carmeli, 'Operation Ben-Ami', 15 May 1948, IDFA 2687\49\\35; and ? to HIS-AD, 'Arab Cables from 16.5', 17 May 1948, HA 105\252.

723. Eshel, *Carmeli*, 167; and Nazzal, *Exodus*, 55–57.

724. Nazzal, *Exodus*, 58.

725. 'Hiram' to HIS-AD, 19 May 1948, HA 105\92 aleph.

726. Eshel, *Carmeli*, 168–69; Nazzal, *Exodus*, 47–59; 'Protocol of the Meeting of the Ministerial Committee for Abandoned Property', 31 Dec. 1948, ISA FM 2401\21 aleph; and Nahariya district officer, 'Notes on a Tour of the Village of al Mazra'a', undated, ISA MAM 302\93.

727. Carmeli to 'Eitan', etc. 'Operation Ben-'Ami – Stage 2', 19 May 1948, IDFA 6680\49\\5.

728. Carmeli HQ to HGS\Operations, 20 May 1948, IDFA 6680\49\\5.

729. Eshel, *Carmeli*, 173; entry for 22 May 1948, Weitz, *Diary*, III, 290; and LPA, protocol of meeting of Mapai Bureau, 1 June 1948, statement by M. Yaffe.

730. Nazzal, *Exodus*, 62.

731. *Al Hamishmar*, 30 Jan., and 5 and 6, and 21 Feb. 1950, articles by Yirmiyahu Shmueli.

732. *Judgements of the High Court of Justice*, IX, 692; and Moshe Perlman, letter to the editor, and response by Yirmiyahu Shmueli, *Al Hamishmar*, 22 Feb. 1950.

733. Ayalon, *War of Independence*, 485.

734. 'Na'im' to HIS-AD, 9 Feb. 1948, HA 105\54 aleph.

735. HIS, 'Aqir village file, entries for 16 Dec. 1947, 4 and 23 Jan. 1948 and 10 Feb. 1948 and 14 Mar. 1948, HA 105\134.

736. Excerpt from unsigned HIS report, 18 Apr. 1948, HA 105\257.

737. 'Doron (Naaman)' to HIS-AD, 22 Apr. 1948, HA 105\54 aleph.

738. 'Doron' to HIS-AD, 'Operation Helem', 6 May 1948, HA 105\92 aleph; 'Doron (Shevah)' to HIS-AD, 'From the 'Aqir Operations', 9 May 1948, HA 105\92 aleph; and HIS, 'Aqir village file, entry for 6 May 1948, HA 105\134.

739. 'Doron' to HIS-AD, 'Assessment of Operation Helem', 7 May 1948, HA 105\92 aleph.

740. Muhammad Mustafa Mussa, 'Letter of Commitment', 5 May 1948 and 'Doron' to HIS-AD, 'Aqir', 9 May 1948, both in HA 105\54 aleph.

741. 52nd Battalion, 'Daily Report from 10:00 hours 4.5 until 10:00 hours 5.5', and 52nd Battalion, 'Daily Report from 10:00 hours 5.5 to 10:00 hours 6.5', both in IDFA 1041\49\\12; and Ayalon, *War of Independence*, 523–24.

742. 52nd Battalion, 'Daily Report from 10:00 hours, 6.5 until 10:00, 7.5', IDFA 1041\49\\12.

743. Protocol of meeting of Mapam's Political Committee, 15 June 1948, HHA 66.90 (1); and statement by Erem at meeting of Mapam defence activists, 26 July 1948, HHA 10.18.

744. 'Doron' to HIS, 'The Village of Qatra', 9 May 1948, HA 105\92 aleph; and 'Doron (Elitzur)' to HIS-AD, 'The Conquest of Qatra', 12 May 1948, HA 105\92 aleph.

745. HIS-AD, 'The Migratory Movement . . .', 30 June 1948, HHA-ACP, 10.95.13 (1).

746. 'Doron' to HIS, 'Assessment of Operation Helem', 7 May 1948, HA105\92 aleph.
747. Ayalon, *War of Independence*, 526. It would appear that one or more of those who had died in 'Aqir had been murdered.
748. Doron (Shevah) to HIS-AD, 27 Apr. 1948, HA 105\54 aleph; and HIS, 'Arab al Satariyya village file, HA 105\134.
749. 54th Battalion to Giv'ati HQ, 'Daily Summary for 29.4.48', 30 Apr. 1948, IDFA 1041\49\\18.
750. HIS-AD, 'The Migratory Movement . . .', 30 June 1948, HHA-ACP 10.95.13 (1).
751. Giv'ati HQ, 'Operation "Barak" – General Instructions', ? May 1948, IDFA 7011\49\\5.
752. Giv'ati HQ to battalions 51, 52, etc., 10 May 1948, IDFA 7011\49\\5.
753. 'Doron (Elitzur)' to HIS-AD, 'The Beit Daras Operation', 25 Apr. 1948, HA 105\92 aleph; and HIS, Beit Daras village file, HA 105\243.
754. Giv'ati HQ to HGS\Operations, 11 May 1948, IDFA 922\75\\1017; 'Doron (Elitzur)' to HIS-AD, 13 May 1948, HA 105\92 aleph; and entry for 12 May 1948, DBG-YH, I, 411.
755. 'Doron (Elitzur)' to HIS-AD, 'The Beit Daras Operation', 18 May 1948, HA 105\31.
756. Giv'ati to HGS\Operations, 11 May 1948, IDFA 922\75\\1017.
757. 'Ephraim' Sub-district to 'Ya'akov', 'Report on Harassment Operation in "Rubin"', 13 May 1948, IDFA 1041\49\\7.
758. 'Doron (Elitzur)' to HIS-AD, 'Batani Sharqi', 13 May 1948, HA 105\92 aleph; and HIS, Batani al Sharqi village file, entries for 12 and 13 May 1948, HA 105\243.
759. Ayalon, *Egyptian Invader*, 82. HIS-AD, 'The Migratory Movement . . .', 30 June 1948, HHA-ACP 10.95.13 (1) says '13 May 1948.'
760. Ayalon, *War of Independence*, 459–60.
761. 'Doron' to HIS-AD, 'Tapping Legion Radios', 20 May 1948, and 'Doron (Maoz)' to HIS-AD, 'The Operation in the Village of Abu Shusha', 20 May 1948, both in HA 105\92 aleph. The official Giv'ati history uncharacteristically notes (Ayalon, *War of Independence*, 460) that the conquering (Giv'ati) units were immediately replaced by militiamen from Kibbutz Gezer who were themselves replaced by Kiryati Brigade troops – the implication being that if a massacre took place, it was not carried out by Giv'ati.
762. Ramle police station to Red Cross delegation, 21 May 1948, apparently the text of a HIS radio intercept, HA 105\31.
763. 'Doron (Maoz)' to HIS-AD, 'The Interrogation of Women Prisoners in the Village of Abu Shusha', 24 Jun. 1948, HA 105\92 aleph.
764. 'Doron (Maoz)' to HIS-AD, 'Weapons and Ammunition from the Village of Abu Shusha, and Prisoners', 21 May 1948, HA 105\92 aleph.
765. Ayalon, *War of Independence*, 460.
766. HIS, Na'na village file, entries for 14 and 17 May 1948, HA 105\134.
767. Shaul Fogel, 'Report on the Attack on Gezer on 10.6.48', 13 Jun. 1948, IDFA 7011\49\\1.
768. Mahmud al Rifai, Lydda, to 'Ramallah', 16 June 1948, a radio intercept, HA 105\92 aleph.

769. HIS-AD, 'The Migratory Movement . . .', 30 June 1948, HHA-ACP 10.95.13 (1).
770. Giv'ati, 'The Brigade's Operations', a list, IDFA 922\75\\900. The Israelis then moved out and the site was re-occupied by irregulars. It was recaptured by the Yiftah Brigade on 5\6 June 1948. The Palmah reported that four Arabs 'were liquidated with knives' and some 20 others were captured (Palmah HQ, 'Daily Report', 6 June 1948, IDFA 922\75\\1215).
771. 'Doron (Elitzur)' to HIS-AD, 'The Conquest of Mughar', 18 May 1948, IDFA 922\75\\1025; and Ayalon, *Egyptian Invader*, 82.
772. 51st Battalion HQ to 'C' Company, 'Operational Order "Medina" ', 17 May 1948, IDFA 170\51\\49.
773. 'Doron' to HIS-AD, 'The Conquest of the Sawafirs', 19 May 1948, HA 105\92 aleph.
774. HIS, Sawafir al Gharbiyya village file, entry for 23 June 1948, and HIS, Sawafir al Sharqiyya village file, entry for 23 June 1948, both in HA 105\134.
775. 'Doron (Elitzur)' to HIS-AD, 23 May 1948, HA 105\31.
776. 'Report on Eavesdropping on Arab Transmissions on 18.5.48', HA 105\92 aleph.
777. Giv'ati, *Desert and Fire*, 45–47; and Rami Rosen, 'Col. G. Speaks Out', *Haaretz*, 16 September 1994. Moshe Giv'ati described a battle followed by a massacre. Rosen interviewed a number of elderly Haganah participants. All resisted the word 'massacre' (*tevakh*) but admitted to 'killings' (*hereg*). Or as Simha Shiloni, one of them, put it: 'I don't think one can call what happened there a "massacre" . . . But in effect what happened was a liquidation [*hisul*] of some of the adult males captured with arms.'
778. 'Ephraim' to Sarig, 'Summary for 14.5.48', IDFA 922\75\\1220; and HGS\Operations Logbook, entry for 14 May 1948, IDFA 922\75\\1176.
779. 'Yisrael', 'Report of the Search through Burayr and Sumsum', 2 Jun. 1948, IDFA 2090\50\\10; unsigned, 'Daily Report for 31.5.48', IDFA 922\75\\1220; and HGS Logbook, entry for 1 June 1948, IDFA 922\75\\1176.
780. Unsigned, 'Daily Summary – 11.6.48', IDFA 922\75\\1220.
781. HIS-AD, 'The Migratory Movement . . .', 30 Jun. 1948, HHA-ACP 10.95.13 (1).
782. Palmah HQ, 'Daily Report', 28 May 1948, IDFA 922\75\\1066; Sergei to Palmah HQ, 28 May 1948, KMA-PA 105 – 123; and Kan'ane and Almadani, '*Kaufakha*', 42–44.
783. Arye Farda, Ya'akov Gavri, and Eliezer Frisch, the headmen of Dorot, Nir-Am and Ruhama, to Ben-Gurion, 4 Aug. 1948, ISA FM 2564\9.
784. Palmah HQ, 'Daily Report', 31 May 1948, IDFA 922\75\\1066. The village, which was subsequently conquered by the Egyptian Army, was finally re-captured on 18 October (IDF GS\Operations Logbook, entry for 18 Oct. 1948, IDFA 922\75\\1176).
785. 6th Airborne Division Logbook, entry for 15 Dec. 1947, PRO WO 275–52.
786. Palmah HQ, 'Daily Report', 31 May 1948, IDFA 922\75\\1214; 'Oded' to Palmah HQ, 1 Jun. 1948, KMA-PA 105–122; and Farda, Gavri and Frisch to Ben-Gurion, 4 Aug. 1948, ISA FM 2564\9. The three kibbutz headmen complained about the treatment meted out to Huj. Ben-Gurion responded

(Ben-Gurion to headmen of Dorot, Nir-Am and Ruhama, 29 Aug. 1948, DBG Archive, Correspondence) that: 'I hope that the HQ will pay attention to what you say, and will avoid such unjust and unjustified actions in the future, and will set right these things in so far as possible with respect to the past.' But Ben-Gurion avoided a specific condemnation of the expulsion and did not instruct the IDF to let the villagers return or to safeguard their property.

787. 'Na'im (Naaman)' to HIS-AD, 'Report on Zarnuqa', 30 Mar. 1948, HA 105\228.

788. HIS, Zarnuqa village file, entry for 4 Dec. 1947, HA 105\243.

789. HIS, Zarnuqa village file, entry for 10 May 1948, HA 105\243; and 'Doron (Shevah)' to HIS-AD, 10 May 1948, HA 105\217.

790. Ayalon, *War of Independence*, 595–97.

791. 'S.K.' to the editors, *Al Hamishmar*, undated but from early June, HHA-ACP 10.95.10 (4). 'S.K.' wrote that the letter was not for publication but to prompt Mapam's leaders to do something; the Haganah was turning friendly Arabs into enemies. See also Cisling's statement at Cabinet meeting, 20 June 1948, KMA-ACP 9.9.1.

792. HIS, Zarnuqa village file, entries for 26 and 30 May 1948, HA 105\243; and 'Doron' to HIS-AD, 30 May 1948, HA 105\92 aleph.

793. 'S.K.' to editors of *Al Hamishmar*, undated, HHA-ACP 10.95.10 (4); and Cisling statement in Cabinet meeting 20 June 1948, KMA-ACP 9.9.1.

794. HIS, Yibna village file, entry for 9 Sep. 1947, HA 105\134; and Ayalon, *War of Independence*, 598.

795. HIS, Yibna village file, entries for 15 March and 4 April 1948, HA 105\134; and 'Na'im (Elitzur)' to HIS-AD, 1 Apr. 1948, HA 105\92 aleph.

796. 'Doron (Naaman)' to HIS-AD, 3 May 1948, HA 105\217.

797. Ayalon, *Egyptian Invader*, 143.

798. Unsigned, 'The Interrogation of Mahmud Ruzi (interrogated on 31.5)', and covering note 'Doron' to HIS-AD, 2 June 1948, HA 105\217.

799. Ayalon, *Egyptian Invader*, 143–47; and 'Testimony of Yosef Zekzer ('Yeshurun'),' JI, IZL, kaf-4, 7\12.

800. Unsigned, 'Report on Observations and Information for 5.6.48', IDFA 2323\49\\6.

801. Giv'ati, 'The Southern Front – Assessment, Conclusions and Proposals', 2 August 1948, IDFA 957\51\\16.

802. IDF GS\Operations to Giv'ati and Sarig, 9 June 1948, IDFA 957\51\\16.

803. 'Dror' to Golani HQ, 17 May 1948, IDFA 128\51\\50; and Assaf Leshem to author, 22 May 1998.

804. Unsigned, 'Report on Search\Patrol Operation in the Villages', undated, IDFA 128\51\\32; and IDF GS Operations Logbook, entry for 8 June 1948, IDFA 922\75\\1176.

805. 'Barak' Intelligence Officer, 'Report on Search\Patrol Operation in the Villages: Ma'dhar, Hadatha, 'Ulam, Sirin', 3 [sic, should be 4?] June 1948, IDFA 128\51\\32.

806. 'Oved, 'The Evacuation\Eviction from Villages in Ramat Yavniel [*pinui kfarim miramat yavniel*]' *Kokhav Hatzafon*, 21 Nov. 1997. A further 'Barak' report, from 5 June, possibly describing the operation recalled by 'Oved', states: 'The [remaining] inhabitants were expelled with [live]

fire. The granaries were set alight [and] tens of houses were blown up . . . Inhabitants were pushed to Wadi Bira [just south of Sirin]' ('Barak' to Golani, 5 June 1948, IDFA 128\51\\50). Ma'dhar, Hadatha, 'Ulam, and Sirin were all permanently depopulated that summer.

807. 'Barak' Intelligence Officer to Golani Intelligence Officer, 'Report on Search\Patrol [*srika*] in the Villages: Danna, al Bira, Kafra, Jabbul, Yubla, Murassas', 8 June 1948, IDFA 128\51\\32.

808. IDF GS operations logbook, entry for 8 June 1948, IDFA 922\75\\1176.

809. 'Tzipori' to Golani HQ, 11 Jun. 1948, IDFA 128\51\\32.

810. 'Dror', 'Report on the Lubiya-Sejera Operation', undated, IDFA 665\51\\2.

811. OC 'B' Company, Mobile Battalion ('Naftali'), 'Report on Acre [Area] Operations on Night of 5\6.6.48', IDFA 5942\49\\10.

812. Protocol of meeting of Mapam Centre, 11 May 1948, HHA 68.90 (1).

5 | Deciding against a return of the refugees, April–December 1948

The exodus confronted the Yishuv with a major problem: Whether or not to allow those who had fled or been expelled to return. Already during the spring, refugees in various localities began pressing to return. Local Haganah and civic leaders had to decide, without having national guidelines, whether to allow this – and almost invariably ruled against.[1] In May, the Arab states, led by Jordan, began clamouring for a refugee return. From early summer, the Yishuv's leaders came under intense international pressure – spearheaded first by Count Folke Bernadotte, the Swedish United Nations Mediator for Palestine, and later by the United States – to repatriate the refugees. At the same time, the government was subjected to lobbying by army and local authorities in various parts of the country to bar a refugee return. In mid-June the Cabinet discussed the matter and a consensus emerged to prevent a return, at least so long as the hostilities continued. The consensus turned into a formal Cabinet decision in July. Without doubt, this was one of the most important decisions taken by the new State in its first formative months.

The decision, taken against the backdrop of the pan-Arab invasion and the intensification of the fighting, had crystallised over April–June. Already in early April, as the Haganah switched to the offensive, local commanders and Arab affairs advisers in predominantly Jewish areas decided to bar a return to their areas. For example, Alexandroni's Arab affairs advisers, responsible for a large section of the coastal plain, formally decided 'not to allow the return of the Arabs who evacuated the area'. They were driven mainly by calculations of Jewish security, but also by a desire to protect the Arabs from Jewish depredations and by considerations of economic advantage (preventing a refugee return to harvest crops would translate into Jewish economic gain).[2]

The mass exodus from Haifa and Jaffa in late April and early May focused minds in the Jewish leadership regarding a possible return.

Golda Myerson (Meir), the acting head of the JA-PD, visited Arab Haifa a few days after its conquest. She reported on 6 May:

> It is a dreadful thing to see the dead city. Next to the port I found children, women, the old, waiting for a way to leave. I entered the houses, there were houses where the coffee and pita bread were left on the table, and I could not avoid [thinking] that this, indeed, had been the picture in many Jewish towns [i.e., in Europe, during World War II]'.

The situation, she said, 'raised many questions'. Should the Jews

> make an effort to bring the Arabs back to Haifa, or not [?] Meanwhile, so long as it is not decided differently, we have decided on a number of rules, and these include: We won't go to Acre or Nazareth to bring back the Arabs. But, at the same time, our behaviour should be such that if, because of it, they come back – [then] let them come back. We shouldn't behave badly with the Arabs [who remained] so that others [who fled] won't return.[3]

A few days later, Myerson spoke about the issue within the context of general policy toward Palestine's Arabs. She told the Mapai Central Committee that the Jews could not treat villagers who had fled because they did not want to fight the Yishuv, 'such as [those of] Sheikh Muwannis', in the same way as hostile villagers. But while implying that she thought 'friendly' villagers should be allowed back, Myerson avoided saying so outright. Rather, she posed questions:

> What are we to do with the villages . . . abandoned by friends? . . . Are we prepared to preserve these villages in order that their inhabitants might return, or do we want to wipe out every trace that there had been a village on the site?

She then turned to Haifa:

> I am not among those extremists – and there are such, and I applaud them, who want to do everything that can be done in order to bring back the Arabs. I say I am not willing to make extraordinary arrangements to bring back Arabs.

The question remained of how the Yishuv should behave toward those who had remained. Ill-treatment might both prompt those who had remained to leave and discourage those who had left from returning – 'and we would [then] be rid of the lot of them'. She concluded by saying that the party and, by implication, the Yishuv, had entered the war without a clear policy regarding Palestine's Arabs. She called for a comprehensive discussion of the 'Arab Question' in the central committee.[4] But the call went unheeded.

Myerson's line was an amplification of the policy sketched by Ben-Gurion during his visit to Haifa on 1 May: The Jews should treat the remaining Arabs 'with civil and human equality' but 'it is not our job to worry about the return of [those who had fled]'. Clearly, neither he nor Myerson was interested in their return (though Myerson implied that she was willing to make an exception of 'friendly' Arabs). Ben-Gurion had already said as much back in early February, specifically regarding the depopulated Arab neighbourhoods of west Jerusalem.[5]

The crystallisation in the national leadership of the policy against a return was heralded on 25 April – as the exodus from Haifa and Jaffa was under way – in a cable from Shertok, in New York, to his officials in Tel Aviv: 'Suggest consider issue warning Arabs now evacuating [that they] cannot be assured of return.'[6]

Pressure for a return began to build up in early May as, for their part, the Arab leaders began to contemplate the political, economic, and military implications of the exodus. At a meeting in Amman on 2 May, Arab officials and notables from Haifa agreed that 'the Arabs should return to Haifa'. There was, apparently, coordination with the British as the following day, the British Army removed several Haganah roadblocks in the town and took up positions in the abandoned Arab neighbourhoods. Immediately afterward, 'Azzam Pasha, 'Abdullah and Qawuqji all issued well-publicised calls to the refugees to return, while the Mandate Government proclaimed, on 6 May: 'In the view of the Government, the Arabs can feel completely safe in Haifa.'[7] The day before, 'Abdullah had called on 'every man of strength and wisdom, every young person of power and faith, who has left the country [i.e., Palestine], let him return to the dear spot. No one should remain outside the country except the rich and the old.' 'Abdullah went on to thank 'those of you . . . who have remained where they are in spite of the tyranny now prevailing', and went out of his way to cite the JA condemnation of the Deir Yassin Massacre.[8] By the end of the month, HIS-AD was reporting that 'in the Arab states the pressure on the refugees to return' was 'building up'.[9]

This joint Arab–British effort, aiming at a general repatriation and not only to Haifa, came to nought. The Haganah was not allowing Arabs to return and, given the continued fighting and confusion on the ground, the call to return may not have generated much enthusiasm among the refugees themselves. In Haifa itself, where initially the local Jewish civilian leadership had not been averse to a return, a major change of heart took place. One participant (expressing the general view) in a meeting of local officials in Haifa's town hall on 6 June, put it this way: 'There are no sentiments in war . . . Better to cause them injustice than that [we suffer] a disaster . . . We have no interest in their returning.'[10]

The talk and diplomatic movement in May surrounding a possible return helped trigger the consolidation in Israel of an effective, if loosely coordinated, lobby against repatriation. The lobby consisted of local authorities, the kibbutz movements, the settlement departments of the National Institutions, Haganah commanders and influential figures such as Yosef Weitz and Ezra Danin.

Weitz regarded the exodus, which he had helped to promote in a number of places, as an implementation, albeit unplanned and largely spontaneous, of the transfer schemes of the late 1930s and early and mid-1940s, which had envisaged the movement of the Arab minority out of the future Jewish State so that it would be homogeneous, politically stable and secure against subversion from within. He and his colleagues realised that, for Israel's sake, the exodus must be expanded by nudging or propelling more Arab communities into flight and the post-exodus status quo consolidated and shored up. A return would endanger the Jewish State. Weitz considered that the matter was sufficiently important to merit the establishment of a special state body to supervise what he defined as the 'retroactive transfer'. During March and April, Weitz energetically sought political backing and help to implement the transfer. From May, Weitz pressed Ben-Gurion and Shertok to set up a 'Transfer Committee', preferably with himself at its head, to oversee 'transfer policy', which in the main was to focus on measures that would assure that there would be no return. More guardedly, the committee was also to advise the political leadership and the Haganah on further population displacements.

The first unofficial Transfer Committee – composed of Weitz, Danin and Sasson, now head of the Middle East Affairs Department of the Foreign Ministry – came into being at the end of May, following Danin's agreement to join and Shertok's 28 May unofficial sanction of the committee's existence and goals.

In mid-May, Danin resigned from the Committee for Arab Property. Danin wrote Weitz that what was needed was 'an institution whose role will be . . . to seek ways to carry out the transfer of the Arab population at this opportunity when it has left its normal place of residence'. Danin thought that Christian organisations could be found, acting under the rubric of helping the refugees, which would assist in their resettlement in the Arab countries. 'Let us not waste the fact that a large Arab population has moved from its home, and achieving such a thing would be very difficult in normal times', he wrote. To prevent a refugee return 'they must be confronted with *faits accomplis*'. Among the *faits accomplis* Danin proposed were the destruction of Arab houses, 'settling Jews in all the area evacuated' and expropriating Arab property.[11]

On 28 May, Weitz went to Shertok and proposed that the Cabinet appoint himself, Sasson and Danin as a Transfer Committee 'to hammer out a plan of action designed [to achieve] the goal of transfer'. Shertok, according to Weitz, congratulated him on his initiative and agreed that the 'momentum [of Arab flight] must be exploited and turned into an accomplished fact'.[12] On 30 May, Weitz met Finance Minister Kaplan, number three in the Mapai hierarchy, and, according to Weitz, received his blessing.[13] That day, the Transfer Committee met for its first working session, and Weitz began preparing a draft proposal for its activities.

But official authorisation by Ben-Gurion and\or the full Cabinet continued to elude him. Nonetheless, from the beginning of June, with JNF funds and personnel, the committee set about razing villages in various areas. On 5 June, Weitz, armed with a three-page memorandum, signed by himself, Danin and Sasson, entitled 'Retroactive Transfer, A Scheme for the Solution of the Arab Question in the State of Israel', went to see Ben-Gurion.

The memorandum stated that the war had unexpectedly brought about 'the uprooting of masses [of Arabs] from their towns and villages and their flight out of the area of Israel . . . This process may continue as the war continues and our army advances.' The war and the exodus had so deepened Arab enmity 'as perhaps to make impossible the existence of hundreds of thousands of Arabs in the State of Israel and the existence of the state with hundreds of thousands of inhabitants who bear that hatred'. Israel, therefore, 'must be inhabited largely by Jews, so that there will be in it very few non-Jews.' 'The uprooting of the Arabs should be seen as a solution to the Arab question . . . and, in line with this, it must from now on be directed according to a calculated plan geared toward the goal of "retroactive transfer".'

To consolidate and amplify the transfer, the committee proposed:

'(1) Preventing the Arabs from returning to their places.
(2) [Extending] help to the Arabs to be absorbed in other places.'

Regarding the first guideline, the committee proposed:

(1) Destruction of villages as much as possible during military operations.
(2) Prevention of any cultivation of land by them [i.e., the Arabs], including reaping, collection [of crops], picking [olives] and so on . . .
(3) Settlement of Jews in a number of villages and towns so that no "vacuum" is created.
(4) Enacting legislation [geared to barring a return].
(5) [Making] propaganda [aimed at non-return].

The committee proposed that it oversee the destruction of villages and the renovation of certain sites for Jewish settlement, negotiate the purchase of Arab land, prepare legislation for expropriation and negotiate the resettlement of the refugees in Arab countries.[14]

Weitz recorded that Ben-Gurion 'agreed to the whole line' but thought that the Yishuv should first set in train the destruction of the villages, establish Jewish settlements and prevent Arab cultivation, and only later worry about the organised resettlement of the refugees in the Arab countries. Ben-Gurion agreed to the idea of a supervisory committee but was opposed to Weitz's 'temporary committee'. At the same time, he approved the start of organised destruction by the committee of the villages, about which Weitz had informed him.[15]

According to Ben-Gurion's account of the meeting, he had approved the establishment of a committee to oversee 'the cleaning up [nikui] of the Arab settlements, cultivation of [Arab fields] and their settlement [by Jews]', and the creation of labour battalions to carry out this work'. Nowhere did he explicitly refer to the destruction of villages or the prevention of a refugee return.[16]

The following day, 6 June, Weitz wrote Ben-Gurion:

> I . . . take the liberty of setting down your answer to the scheme proposal I submitted to you, that: A) You will call a meeting immediately to discuss [the scheme] and to appoint a committee . . . B) You agree that the actions marked in clauses 1, 2 [i.e., the destruction of villages and the prevention of Arab cultivation] . . . begin immediately.

Weitz continued: 'In line with this, I have given an order to begin [these operations] in different parts of the Galilee, the Beit Shean Valley, the Hills of Ephraim and Samaria.'[17] Weitz, of course, was covering himself. He sensed that on this sensitive subject, Ben-Gurion might prefer not to commit anything to paper, and he did not want to leave himself open to charges that he had acted without authorisation. Probably he also wanted to prod Ben-Gurion to set up the committee.

Then, using his JNF branch offices, Weitz set in motion the levelling of a handful of villages (al Mughar, near Gedera, Fajja, near Petah Tikva, Biyar Adas, near Magdiel, Beit Dajan, east of Tel Aviv, Miska, near Ramat Hakovesh, Sumeiriya, near Acre, Buteimat and Sabbarin, southeast of Haifa). His agents toured the countryside to determine which other villages should be destroyed or preserved and renovated for future Jewish settlement. He remained hopeful that official Cabinet-level endorsement of his actions would be forthcoming and that an official letter of appointment would be issued for the Transfer Committee.

But, at least initially, Weitz was unaware that his semi-covert activities had been noted by Mapam and that Mapam, together with Shitrit, had launched a counter-campaign to halt the destruction of the villages and to resist the atmosphere of transfer of which this destruction was a manifestation. This campaign was probably at least in part responsible for Weitz's inability to obtain formal, Cabinet-level authorisation for the Transfer Committee. At the beginning of July, Weitz suspended the destruction operations, effectively terminating the activities of the first, unofficial, self-appointed Transfer Committee.

But by then, the government decision to oppose a refugee return was all but formalised (in this sense, Weitz's efforts had been fruitful). Initially there had been polyphony and dissidence. On 23 May, Shitrit had told his Cabinet colleagues:

> A great many of them still have giant assets [in the country] . . . and they will no doubt return. I do not believe that they have acquiesced in the idea of [permanently] leaving . . . It will be sufficient to demonstrate [our] goodwill for [them] to begin to return . . . If they return – and in my opinion they will certainly return – we must find a way [to make sure] that there will

be no discrimination [against the returnees] regarding education, health and religion . . .[18]

Justice Minister Felix Rosenblueth (Pinhas Rosen) had spoken out against transfer and criticised 'the plunder of [Arab] property' and the destruction of villages as designed to prevent a refugee return.[19] And on 29 May the official state radio station, Kol Yisrael (the Voice of Israel), had proclaimed that Israel would allow a refugee return.[20]

Weitz had notified Foreign Minister Shertok of the broadcast and Shertok had minuted his director general, Walter Eytan:

> We must avoid unequivocal statements on this matter. For the moment, only [use] a negative formulation. That is, so long as the war continues, there should be no talk of allowing a return. [But don't let it appear] from our statements that at the war's end, they will be allowed back. Let us keep open every option.[21]

Shertok was reflecting the gist of what had been tentatively decided five days earlier, on 1 June. Shertok, Shitrit, Cabinet Secretary Zeev Sharef, Minority Affairs Ministry Director General Gad Machnes, and Sasson had discussed the issue and, in Ben-Gurion's terse diary phrase, concluded that the Arabs 'were not to be helped to return' and that the IDF commanders 'were to be issued with the appropriate orders'.[22] At the full Cabinet meeting that day, Ben-Gurion and his colleagues tackled the problem obliquely while referring to the question of freedom of movement across the front lines if a truce was concluded. 'We have no real interest in freedom of movement', declared the prime minister; it would enable refugees to return to the empty villages along the Jerusalem – Tel Aviv road. Agriculture Minister Aharon Cisling put it more directly:

> Freedom of movement along the roads will be reflected in [i.e., will result in] the return of Arabs to the villages . . . There are more than 100 Arab settlements in our hands; the possibility of the return of Arabs to them during the truce is a great danger.

His fellow Mapam minister, Mordechai Bentov, agreed.[23]

The political leadership was on the way to reaching a firm strategic-political decision against a refugee return. Meanwhile, the army was instructed to stymie the return on the ground. On 9 June and 11 June, front-line units were instructed to bar villagers from harvesting crops or entering 'the areas in our hands'.[24] Two days later, on 13 June, Oded Brigade HQ ordered its battalions 'to take every possible measure to prevent' a return and thus 'we will prevent tactical and political complications down the road'.[25]

Weitz and his colleagues were not the only anti-return lobbyists in the arena. Others were hard at work during the crucial days before and during the First Truce (11 June–8 July) pressing the Cabinet not to succumb to international or internal political pressures. From around the country, local leaders demanded that the government bar a return. The more distant from the centre of Jewish population or isolated the settlement, and the more vulnerable, the stronger was the clamour against a return.

In the first days of June, the notables of the Safad Jewish community attempted to appeal directly to the Cabinet. They journeyed to Tel Aviv and got as far as Shlomo Kaddar, the Principal Assistant at the Cabinet Secretariat. He reported that they had demanded that the government bar a return, set up a ring of Jewish settlements around the town and settle Jews in Safad's abandoned houses. 'The Jewish community will not be able to withstand the pressure of the returning Arabs, especially in view [of the fact] that most of the Arab property in Safad has been stolen and plundered since the Arabs left', they said. If the Arabs were allowed to return, the Jewish community would leave, they warned. A similar message was conveyed by Safad's leaders to a visiting delegation of Yishuv officials on 5 July. If Jewish settlers were not brought to Safad, then it were best that 'the Arab houses . . . be destroyed and blown up lest the Arabs have somewhere to return to'.[26] If the Jews did not quickly fill the abandoned villages, they would be 'filled with returning Arabs with hatred in their hearts', Weitz concluded after visiting the Safad area.[27]

A similar note was struck by Ephraim Vizhensky, secretary of the Western Galilee Settlements Block Committee and a member of Kibbutz Evron, in a letter to Cisling. Western Galilee 'no longer [has] an Arab population'. There was a need 'to exploit the situation which [has] arisen . . . [and] immediately to establish [new Jewish] settlements' in the area to assure its 'Judaization'.[28] At the same time, a delegation of local Western Galilee leaders arrived in Tel Aviv seeking audience with ministers. They got as far as the Cabinet Secretariat, where they said

> that a return to the status quo ante and a return of the Arabs were unthinkable. If the Arabs returned, they [i.e., the Jews] would leave [the area] . . . If they stay put, then it is on condition that the Arabs do not return and that the area be incorporated in the Jewish State.[29]

Similar petitions arrived from other parts of the country. On 2 June, Shmuel Zagorsky, the inspector of Arab property in the Gilbo'a area, urged Avraham Harzfeld to promote the establishment of new settlements in the Beit Shean Valley as a means of preventing a refugee return.

> I am fearful that the Arabs of the area will return to these areas and that we will lose the immediate opportunity to set up new settlements. For my part, I have done all in my power to close the way back to the Arabs, but pressure by them to return is already being felt,

he warned.[30]

The input of the military lobby may have weighed even more heavily with the Cabinet. IDF intelligence regarded the prospect of a mass refugee return as a major threat to the war effort. As the First Truce approached, local commanders began to press GS\Operations for guidelines. 'Waiting for exact instructions regarding the ceasefire, for fear of a return of Arabs to the villages', 'Oded' of Northern Front radioed on 2 June.[31] 'The problem of the return of the refugees is increasing', Northern Front radioed six days later.[32] On 16 June, the head of the IDF Intelligence Service wrote to Reuven Shiloah, the director of the Foreign Ministry's Political Division:

> There is a growing movement by the Palestinian villagers who fled to the neighbouring countries [to] return now, during the days of the [First Truce]. There is a serious danger [that returning villagers] will fortify themselves in their villages behind our front lines, and with the resumption of warfare, will constitute at least a [potential] Fifth Column, if not active hostile concentrations.

If nothing was done, there was a danger that at the end of the truce, the IDF would have 'to set aside considerable forces again to clean up the rear and the lines of communication'.[33] Some officers thought that the piecemeal refugee return was part of a deliberate policy by the Arab states with clear political and economic goals.[34]

Officials from government departments also weighed in. At the start of the First Truce, the Foreign Ministry's Middle East Department noted the Arab leaders' calls for the return to Palestine of 'the 300,000 refugees'. Already, a trickle of refugees had infiltrated back. The department conjectured that a major reason for this return was the desire 'to harvest the [summer] crops . . . The Arabs in their places of wandering are suffering from real hunger.' But this harvest-geared return, the department warned, could

> in time bring in its wake [re-]settlement in the villages, something which might seriously endanger many of our achievements during the first six months of the war. It is not for nothing that Arab spokesmen are . . . demanding the return . . . [of the refugees], because this would not only ease their burden but weigh us down considerably.[35]

Shertok, the main Cabinet patron of Weitz's Transfer Committee, in a letter to the chairman of the World Jewish Congress, Nahum Goldmann, explained the primary consideration behind the crystallising policy against a refugee return:

> The most spectacular event in the contemporary history of Palestine – more spectacular in a sense than the creation of the Jewish State – is the wholesale evacuation of its Arab population . . . The reversion to the status quo ante is unthinkable. The opportunities which the present position open up for a lasting and radical solution of the most vexing problem of the Jewish State [i.e., the large Arab minority] are so far-reaching as to take

one's breath away. Even if a certain backwash is unavoidable, we must make the most of the momentous chance with which history has presented us so swiftly and so unexpectedly.[36]

Matters came to a head in mid-June. The institution of the truce had stilled the guns along the front lines, posing the physical possibility of a refugee return. A trickle of refugees began making their way back to villages and towns. At the same time, the truce enabled the Arab states to ponder the enormous burden that they had unexpectedly incurred; solving the refugee problem became a major policy goal. Similarly, as the dust of battle temporarily settled, the international community at last took note. Public opinion in the West began to mobilize and refugee relief drives were inaugurated. The newly appointed Mediator, Bernadotte, who in World War II had worked on refugee assistance, having successfully orchestrated the inauguration of the truce made clear his intention to focus on a final settlement, in which a solution to the refugee problem would, it was believed in Tel Aviv, figure prominently.[37] He was due back in Israel on 17 June.

The Cabinet met on 16 June. In a forceful speech, Ben-Gurion set out his views, which were to serve as the basis of the consensus that emerged. 'I do not accept the version [i.e., policy] that [we] should encourage their return', he said, in an obvious response to the resolution of Mapam's Political Committee the day before, to support the return of 'peace-minded' refugees at the end of the war.[38] 'I believe', said Ben-Gurion, 'we should prevent their return . . . We must settle Jaffa, Jaffa will become a Jewish city . . . [Beisan and Abu Kabir must not be resettled with Arabs.] To allow the return of the Arabs to Jaffa would be . . . foolish.' If the Arabs were allowed to return 'and the war is renewed, our chances of ending the war as we wish to end it will be reduced . . . Meanwhile, we must prevent at all costs their return', he said, and, leaving no doubt in the ministers' minds about his views on the ultimate fate of the refugees, he added: 'I will be for them not returning also after the war.' He added that he favoured a 'treaty' between Israel and the Arab states and said that the Turkish-Greek experience proved that it was possible: They were

> enemies for more than four hundred years – and after the last war in which the Turks won and expelled the Greeks from Anatolia – they became friends and signed a treaty of peace, and it is also possible between us and the Arabs.[39]

(Ben-Gurion, incidentally, had always had a hard spot for Jaffa. When arriving in Palestine as a new immigrant in 1906, he had landed at Jaffa and been horrified by the filth.[40] In 1936, three months into the Arab Revolt, he jotted down in his diary:

> Jaffa's destruction, the town and the port, will happen, and it is good that it will happen . . . This town, which fattened on Jewish immigration and

settlement, deserves to be demolished as [i.e., because] it swings an axe over the heads of its builders and feeders [i.e., the Jews of Tel Aviv]. If Jaffa goes to hell I will not participate in its grief.[41])

Shertok spoke against a return with equal vehemence. A return to the status quo ante was inconceivable. Jaffa, a 'Fifth Column' and 'pest' in the heart of Israel, must not revert to becoming an 'Arab city'. Israel had managed to 'clear of Arabs' a continuous line from Tel Aviv to Romema, in west Jerusalem. Most of the country was now clear of Arabs. There was now

> a need [for the government] to explain [to the Israeli public] the enormous importance of this [demographic] change in terms of [possibilities of Jewish] settlement and security, and in terms of the solidity of the state structure and [of] the solution of crucial social and political problems that cast their shadow over the whole future of the state. Had anyone arisen among us and said that one day we should expel all of them – that would have been madness. But if this happened in the course of the turbulence of war, a war that the Arab people declared against us, and because of Arab flight – then that is one of those revolutionary changes after which [the clock of] history cannot be turned back, as it did not turn back after the [sic] Syrian-Greek [i.e., should be Turkish-Greek] war, [or] after the war in Czechoslovakia . . . which caused revolutionary changes, in the social or ethnic composition in those countries . . . The aggressive enemy brought this about and the blood is on his head and he must bear [the consequences] and all the lands and the houses that remained . . . all are spoils of war . . . all this is just compensation for the [Jewish] blood spilled, for the destruction [of Jewish property] . . . This compensation is natural . . .

Nonetheless, Shertok felt that Israel must be ready to pay compensation for the land 'and this would facilitate the [refugees'] resettlement in other countries'. But 'this is [i.e., must be] our policy: That they are not returning', he said.[42]

Cisling said that 'at this time [i.e., during the war] we must not give the Arabs back even a shoelace. If I have reservations it is only about places where we left [Arabs in place] and we shouldn't have, because this endangers peace.' At the same time, he warned that the refugees would breed hatred toward Israel in their places of exile in the Arab world. 'They will carry in their breasts the desire for revenge and for a return . . . This orientation, of prohibiting a return of the Arabs . . . will be to our detriment.'[43] He implied, though did not say explicitly, that the refugees should be allowed back after the war – but added that the villagers of Qumiya, which overlooked his own home in the Jezreel Valley kibbutz of 'Ein Harod, should not be allowed back.[44]

No formal vote was taken or resolution passed by the ministers. But the line advocated by Ben-Gurion and Shertok – that the refugees should not be allowed back – had now become Israeli policy. Orders immediately went out down the IDF chains of command to bar the return of refugees.[45] During the following weeks, again and again orders reached the brigades manning the lines to prevent a return, 'also with live fire'.[46] The military's opposition to a return was to remain firm and consistent through the summer. On 14 August, IDF OC Operations (and acting chief of staff) Yadin wrote to Shertok:

> Because of the spread of diseases among the Arab refugees, I propose that [we] declare a quarantine on all our conquered areas. We will thus be able to more strongly oppose the demand for the return . . . and all infiltration by Arabs [back] into the abandoned villages – in addition to our opposition [to a return] on understandable military and political grounds.[47]

In the diplomatic arena, this policy was given a somewhat less definitive, more flexible countenance. At their meeting on 17 June, Bernadotte asked Shertok whether Israel would allow back 'the 300,000' refugees 'and would their proprietary rights be respected?' Shertok responded that 'they certainly could not return so long as the war was on'[48] or, alternatively, that 'the question could not be discussed while the war was on' and that the government had not yet 'fixed its policy on the ultimate settlement of the matter'. Shertok added that Arab 'proprietary rights would certainly be respected'.[49]

Shertok appeared to leave open the possibility that Israel might allow back the refugees after the war. This clearly eased the task of Israeli officials meeting with United Nations and American representatives. But it seems to have been the product less of diplomatic expediency than of the exigencies of coalition politics and the need to maintain national unity in wartime. The nettle in the garden was Mapam, Mapai's chief coalition partner in the Provisional Government. Mapam opposed transfer and endorsed the right of 'peace-loving' refugees to return after the war. Had Ben-Gurion definitively closed the door to the possibility of a return, a coalition crisis would have ensued, undermining national unity and isolating Mapai in the Cabinet, where Ben-Gurion would have been left, embarrassingly, with only non-socialist and religious parties as partners. Moreover, the top echelons of both the military and, to a lesser degree, the civil bureaucracies of the new state were heavily manned by Mapam cadres.

During the summer, Mapam's Political Committee, after weeks of debate, at last formulated the party's Arab policy. The party – as its co-leader Meir Ya'ari said – was agreeable to deferring a refugee return until the termination of hostilities,[50] but it opposed 'the intention [megama] to expel the Arabs from the areas of the emerging Jewish State' and proposed that the Cabinet issue a call to peace-minded Arabs 'to stay in their places'. As to the Arabs already in exile, the party declared: 'The Cabinet . . . should [announce] that with the return of peace they should return to a life of peace, honour and productivity . . . The property of the returnees . . . will be restored to them.'[51]

Meanwhile, as refugees began to cross truce lines to reach their homes and fields, spokesmen for the remaining, much diminished Arab communities within Israel began to press for specific measures of repatriation, with special pleading on behalf of Haifa, Jaffa and Christian refugees. These appeals sparked repeated – and illuminating – debates within the Israeli bureaucracies.

On 26–27 June, the Greek Catholic Archbishop of Haifa, George Hakim, back from a visit to Beirut and meetings with refugees, met with Haifa lawyer Ya'akov Salomon and then with Shitrit, Machnes and Sasson. He pleaded that Israel allow back at least Christians from Haifa. 'We were frank with him', Shitrit reported, 'and we asked him if the return of Christian Arabs to Haifa, without Muslims, would not damage Muslim-Christian unity.' The Archbishop responded that he was not troubled by this and, in any case, would not publicly appear as seeking only a return of Christians. But both on local and national levels, Hakim met only with 'no's.[52]

Appeals on behalf of Jaffa's refugees also began to reach the authorities, within weeks of their exodus. The petitions, presented by the remaining notables, were anchored in the surrender agreement signed with the Haganah in mid-May. That agreement had stated that those wishing to leave were free to do so;

> likewise, any male Arab who left Jaffa and wishes to return to Jaffa may apply for a permit to do so. Permits will be granted after their bona fides has been proven, provided that the [city] commander of the Haganah is convinced that the applicants will not . . . constitute a threat to peace and security.[53]

The notables thus had good grounds for their appeal to allow back refugees, men, women and children.[54] Yitzhak Chizik, the town's military governor, passed on the appeal to Shitrit, with a covering letter: 'You will certainly recall', he wrote, 'that in Clause 8 of the surrender agreement it states that every Arab who left Jaffa and wishes to come back, can do so by submitting a request, on condition, of course, that their presence here [in Jaffa] will not constitute a security risk.'[55]

Chizik's letter triggered a debate in the upper reaches of the government. Shitrit wrote to Ben-Gurion and Shertok that similar appeals were reaching him from Haifa.[56] Replying for Ben-Gurion, Shlomo Kaddar wrote:

> I have been asked to tell you that the prime minister is opposed to the return of the Arab inhabitants to their places so long as the war continues and so long as the enemy stands at our gates. Only the full Cabinet, the prime minister believes, can decide on a change of approach.[57]

Shertok, for his part, passed on Shitrit's letter to Yehoshua Palmon for comment. Palmon, perhaps to Shertok's surprise, proposed:

> I think that we should adopt a public posture that we do not oppose the return of the Arab inhabitants of Jaffa, and even to announce this in a [radio] broadcast to the Arabs – but, in practice, their return should be contingent on certain conditions and restrictions.

Palmon thought that the returnees should be asked to sign a loyalty oath and fill out detailed questionnaires. This, he argued, 'would leave in our hands complete supervision of their actual return. We shall have the ability to let back mainly [non-Moslems] . . . something that could be of use [to us] in the future.'[58]

But Palmon's letter drew a blunter rejoinder from Ya'akov Shimoni, the acting director of the Foreign Ministry's Middle East Affairs Department. Shimoni was prepared to allow exceptions in special cases of hardship. But in general he supported the 'no return during the war' line.[59] Shertok came down solidly behind Shimoni, adding: 'I fear a loosening of the reins . . . Permission [to return] should be forthcoming only in a limited number of special cases.'[60]

But Israel's main problem was to be not the uncoordinated, individual or communal Arab attempts to return or requests to return but the increasing international pressure, spearheaded by Bernadotte, for Israeli agreement to a mass repatriation. After several rounds of meetings with Israeli and Arab leaders, Bernadotte, on 27 June, demanded that Israel recognise 'the right of the residents of Palestine who, because of conditions created by the conflict there, have left their normal places of abode, to return to their homes without restriction and to regain possession of their property'.[61] The Israelis responded on 5 July, rejecting Bernadotte's other 'suggestions', that Palestine and Jordan be joined in economic 'Union', that immigration to Israel be subject to that Union's – or UN – jurisdiction, that Jerusalem be given over to Arab rule, and that – in Shertok's phrase – a settlement be 'imposed' from the outside on the parties rather than reached through direct negotiations 'between the interested parties'. (Bernadotte had not explicitly made this last 'suggestion'.) Tergiversating, the Israeli reply did not specifically refer to the demand that Israel recognise the 'right of return', but suggested somewhat vaguely that the Mediator should reconsider his 'whole approach to the [Palestine] problem'.[62]

But the refugee problem could not be dismissed by a sleight of hand, and the Israeli Cabinet understood that Bernadotte's 'suggestion' would eventually have to be directly addressed. By the second half of July the United States, too, was pressing for an Israeli answer. In the course of July – when another 100,000 or so Arabs became refugees (see below) – the Cabinet hammered out the official line.

Yet even before the final formulation was agreed upon, Shertok in-structed his diplomats as follows:

> Our policy: 1) Arab exodus direct result folly aggression organized by Arab states . . . 2) No question allowing Arabs return while state of war continuing, as would mean introduction Fifth Column, provision bases for enemies from outside and dislocation law and order inside. Exceptions only in favour special deserving cases compassionate grounds, subject [to] security screening . . . 4) Question Arab return can be decided only as part peace settlement with Arab State[s] and in context its terms, when question [of] confiscation property Jews [in] neighbouring countries and their future will also be raised. 5) Arabs remaining [in] Israel [to be] unmo-lested and receive due care from State as regards services.[63]

The Cabinet consensus of mid-June had thus undergone a significant reshaping. The Cabinet had formally resolved against a return during the hostilities, leaving open the possibility of a reconsideration of the matter at war's end. But Shertok was now saying that there would be no return during the war and reconsideration and a solution of the problem only within the framework of talks aimed at a general peace settlement and with a linkage to the confiscation of the property, and the fate, of the Jewish communities in the Arab world. Thus links were forged between (a) a full-fledged peace settlement and Israeli willingness to consider a return, making the refugees a bargaining counter in Israel's quest for recognition and peace in the region, and (b) the fate of the refugees and that of the Jews in the Arab states.[64]

Dr Leo Kohn, Shertok's veteran Political Adviser, may have been al-luding to this policy shift when he wrote on 22 July that 'as far as I know, our attitude on this question has hardened in recent months'. Kohn an-ticipated that Bernadotte would continue to press the refugee issue,[65] and, indeed, Bernadotte raised the matter again when he met Shertok on 26 July. Shertok responded that there could be no return during the hostilities and that the problem could be reconsidered thereafter 'in the context of a general peace settlement'.[66]

It was this meeting that triggered the final Israeli Cabinet discus-sion, and resolution, on 28 July. Shertok described his meeting with Bernadotte. Bernadotte had spoken of '300,000–350,000' refugees, living in poverty and deprivation. Assistance had to be organised, but 'the most effective assistance would be their return . . . to their places'. Who, argued the Swede, knows better than the Jews the tribulations of dis-placement? The Germans, he added by way of illustration, had allowed displaced Frenchmen to return to their homes 'without waiting for the end of [the Second World] War'. Bernadotte recalled that Shertok had once told UN Secretary General Trygve Lie that displaced Arabs would be allowed to return home. Shertok responded (so he told his Cabinet colleagues) that he may once have said this, but it was under different circumstances, when there were only a handful of refugees. But since then, 'circumstances have radically changed'. The matter should not be treated, or resolved, solely on a humanitarian basis – 'it is a matter for political and military calculation'. Moreover, long-term humanitarian considerations may indicate that resettlement in the Arab countries may well be the best solution, as with the Greek–Turkish population exchanges. Shertok told the Mediator that there could be no return during the war – such a return would be a 'warlike measure' against us, 'the introduction of a Fifth Column . . . and of an explosive to blow us up from within'. But Bernadotte, according to Shertok, stuck to his guns and 'showed little flexibility': Indeed, he pointed out that a population of long standing had been uprooted and was being replaced by new Jewish immigrants.

To his fellow ministers Shertok now proposed the following formula:

> We cannot agree to a mass return of Arab refugees so long as the war continues. We are ready to discuss exceptional cases, be it involving extraordinary suffering or special privilege – each case on an individual basis.

Bernadotte, said Shertok, had argued that the 'world would not understand' Israel's position. He, Shertok, disagreed: 'The world, which understood the uprooting of the Sudeten [Germans] from Czechoslovakia, would also understand this.' Moreover, the Arab states were demanding that Israel pay for the upkeep of the refugees in their places of exile. Shertok suggested that Israel demand compensation from the Arab states for the destruction and expenditure inflicted on the Yishuv by the war they had launched. Ben-Gurion seconded the motion. Interior Minister Grunbaum endorsed the Shertok–Ben-Gurion line: No return during the war. Shitrit agreed, but supported the return to their homes of refugees still inside Israeli-held territory – such as refugees from Jaffa living in Lydda. Peretz Bernstein, minister of commerce and industry, agreed with Shitrit. Ultra-orthodox Social Welfare Minister Yitzhak Meir Levin wasn't so sure about flatly rejecting the call for a refugee return: 'Every gentile has a bit of anti-Semitism in him, but we may yet need the Mediator's [good will].' Levin, supporting Immigration and Health Minister Moshe Shapira, called for allowing a partial return, of women and children. But the Ben-Gurion–Shertok line won the day. At the end of the meeting the Cabinet decided, by nine votes to two, that 'so long as the war continues there is no agreement to the return of the refugees'.[67]

The Mediator, unhappy with Shertok's position, that same day submitted a strongly worded 'Note', suggesting that Israel accept the principle that 'from among those who may desire to do so, a limited number . . . and especially those formerly living in Jaffa and Haifa, be permitted to return to their homes'. Bernadotte seemed to have resigned himself to Israel's rejection of a blanket return before war's end and accepted the principle of differentiation, on security grounds, between army-age males and 'others'.[68] Bernadotte sought to wedge open the door, however slightly. He was unsuccessful. Kohn drafted a proposal for a response:

Present Arab outcry for return of refugees is move in warfare. Purposes are not, or not merely, humanitarian but desire to get rid of incubus, saddle Israel with it, introduce explosive element into Israel, eliminate sources of menacing bitterness from their own midst . . .

And Kohn divined the chink in Bernadotte's argument, the special pleading for the Jaffa and Haifa exiles. 'Is suffering of those from other towns or from villages less acute, or are they less deserving?' he asked.[69] Kohn's view was that the existence of the refugee problem, on balance, benefited Israel. For the Arab states, the refugees were 'the greatest inconvenience'; for Israel 'at the present moment [they are] our most valuable bargaining asset'. But Kohn realized that they were also a strong card for the Arabs 'in the councils of the UN and among world opinion generally'.[70]

On 1 August, Shertok replied to Bernadotte's 'Note'. Israel, he wrote, was 'not unmindful of the plight of the Arabs . . . Our own people has suffered too much from similar tribulations for us to be indifferent to their hardships.' But Israel could not agree to readmission: It would 'prejudice Israel's rights and positions'. Shertok then took up Kohn's line, asking why Bernadotte had seen fit to plead for special treatment for the exiles of Jaffa and Haifa. The Foreign Minister concluded by saying that while Israel might reconsider the issue at war's end, it was not now in a position 'to re-admit the Arabs who fled . . . on any substantial scale'.[71]

From Israel's point of view, Shertok's use of the phrase 'on any substantial scale' was a bad mistake. The Mediator latched on to it four days later, at their next meeting. If Israel was unwilling, at present, to contemplate a 'substantial' return, how about an insubstantial one – and Bernadotte suggested several categories that might be allowed back immediately: 'Refugees [from] territory controlled by Israeli forces' but lying outside the partition borders Jewish State, 'citrus farmer[s] . . . whose villages . . . are intact . . . [those] for whom employment is available . . . [and] special cases on humanitarian grounds'. Shertok riposted that 'only in exceptional cases would we allow people to come back . . . We are against whole categories of people returning while the war is on.'[72]

Over the following weeks, as the pressures on Israel – internal and external Arab, UN and American – mounted, the Cabinet again and again discussed the problem. The discussions were usually prompted by specific UN or American demarches. Each time the Cabinet re-endorsed the thrust of the decision of 28 July.

Kohn pinpointed Israel's main potential problem – the United States, not Bernadotte. Kohn surmised that the growing American concern was a result of pressure by American ambassadors in Muslim countries, who were arguing that the 'pauperized, embittered' exiles were a seedbed for 'communist revolution' in the host countries, and that it was best that the refugees return to Palestine.[73] Israel's chief fear was that Washington would soon openly back the Mediator's position. American diplomats were already bluntly describing – even to Israelis – Israel's positions as 'rigid and uncompromising'.[74] They had begun to sense that Israel was never going to allow the refugees back. 'There is little if any possibility of Arabs returning to their homes in Israel or Jewish-occupied Palestine', wrote the American Consul General in Jerusalem, John MacDonald. He described the conditions of those camped out near Jericho and Ramallah as 'not yet desperate' but predicted that they would be 'completely destitute' and highly vulnerable to the elements when winter came.[75] Jefferson Patterson, the American chargé d'affaires in Cairo, reported that the International Committee of the Red Cross had supplied information 'indicating that there may be little prospect for the several hundred thousand Arab refugees from Palestine to return to their former homes'.[76]

The resolve of Israel's leaders and public against a return of refugees hardened daily. But the leaders realised that while this resolve would itself be a major factor in shaping the outcome, the ultimate issue would depend also on external factors – especially on the amount and character of international, particularly American, pressure. As Ben-Gurion put it: 'We do not know if this [i.e., the outcome] will depend on us.'[77]

Bernadotte felt Israel was showing 'every sign of having a swelled head.' It seemed to him

> an anomaly that the Israeli Government should advance as an argument for the establishment of their state the plight of Jewish refugees and to demand the immediate immigration [to Israel] of [Jewish] displaced persons at the same time that they refused to recognize the existence of the Arab refugees which they had created.

And the abandoned Arab property – the 'loot' – was simply being distributed among the new Jewish immigrants, reported one American diplomat.[78]

John Reedman, the special representative in Palestine of the United Nations Secretary General, gave Israeli officials an idea of how things stood with pro-Israeli international opinion. He said he understood Israel's opposition to a mass return but suggested that 'a trickle' could be allowed back. Alternatively, Israel could at least announce its intention 'to solve the refugee problem after a final peace settlement'.[79] Bernadotte was blunter when he met Shertok two days later, on 10 August. Israel was 'driving too hard a bargain', he said, and its 'stock was dropping' in the international community (business images with an anti-Semitic undertone that were bound to set off alarm bells in Shertok's mind).[80]

Shertok reported that Bernadotte had asked for an Israeli 'gesture'. He had replied, he told the Cabinet, that perhaps it would raise Israel's stock

> among idealists and the naive, but not among men of action . . . And the rulers in the world at this time are not idealists but men of action. They would say that the Jews are fools – they hold an important card and are discarding it [to no purpose] . . . Bernadotte laughed and did not respond.

Shertok told his colleagues that he had said that

> the Arab minority in our state should be made as small as possible . . . If there was a large Arab minority . . . as much as we would pamper them, they would charge us with discrimination, and these charges would serve as a pretext for intervention by the Arab states in our affairs.

On the other hand, for these states, three hundred thousand refugees were but 'a drop in the ocean', and easily assimilable. 'Bernadotte thanked me for the explanation.'[81]

Only one dissenting voice emerged from the higher reaches of Israeli officialdom, that of Eliahu Sasson, the peripatetic director of the Foreign Ministry's Middle East Affairs Department. Sasson, a Syrian-born Arabist with a liberal outlook, wrote to Shertok:

> I would advise reconsidering the refugee problem . . . I do not by this advice mean, heaven forbid, the return of all the refugees. No, and again no. My meaning is to the return of a small part of them, 40 to 50 thousand, over a long period . . . [starting] immediately, to silence a lot of people in the next meeting of the UN [General Assembly].[82]

Through late 1948 – early 1949, Sasson was to remain a consistent (and isolated) advocate of this position. He was prompted both by a desire to brighten Israel's image in the West and to facilitate peace (he resided for much of this time in Paris, where he tried to initiate secret talks with Arab leaders).[83]

Just how isolated Sasson was is clear from a policy meeting called by Ben-Gurion on 18 August. The meeting was prompted by problems arising out of the need to cultivate and expropriate Arab lands, pressure by Bernadotte and the impending arrival of the first United States Representative (later Ambassador) to Tel Aviv, James McDonald.

The meeting was attended by the country's senior political leaders (without Mapam) and senior political and Arab affairs officials. The participants included Ben-Gurion, Shertok, Shitrit, Kaplan, David Horowitz, director general of the Finance Ministry, Machnes, Weitz, Danin and Zalman Lifshitz, the cartographer and adviser on land matters to Ben-Gurion, Palmon, soon-to-be the prime minister's adviser on Arab affairs, Shimoni and Shiloah, the liaison between the Foreign Ministry and the defence establishment, General Elimelech Avner, OC Military Government in the Conquered Territories, and Kaddar. The sense of the meeting

was summed up by Shimoni the following day: 'The view of the participants was unanimous, and the will to do everything possible to prevent
the return of the refugees was shared by all.'[84]

According to Weitz, Shertok opened the discussion by posing the
problem 'with clarity'. Ben-Gurion, according to Weitz, then confused
the issue by straying into the question of the fate of the abandoned
Arab lands. David Hacohen, an intelligence officer and Mapai stalwart,
proposed that Jews be settled on these lands. Horowitz agreed, but
proposed the sale of Arab property to private individuals ('one can sell
[it] to Jews in America'), with the proceeds going to the original owners as
compensation. 'The solution [should not be] the prevention [of an Arab
return] by force but through a commercial transaction', said Horowitz.
Kaplan objected to the destruction of the villages, and said that Jewish
settlement on Arab lands presented a serious problem of principle 'if
[we] are speaking of more than [temporary] cultivation'.[85] (Shimoni wrote
about the Finance Ministry's representatives that while all at the meeting
were agreed that it was best that the refugees not be allowed to return,
'Kaplan and [Horowitz] were more conservative and careful regarding
[the means] that could be used immediately and principally regarding
the fate of Arab property'.[86])

Weitz then managed to steer the talk back to what he regarded as
the cardinal issue: Should the Arabs be allowed to return?

> If the policy we want is that they should not be allowed to return, [then]
> there is no need to cultivate land beyond what is needed for our existence.
> It is possible that Jews should be settled in some villages and that there are
> villages that should be destroyed so that they do not attract their refugees
> to return. What can be bought [from Arabs] should be bought . . . [But]
> first we must set policy: Arabs who abandoned [their homes] should not
> [be allowed to] return.

He also recommended that plans be developed for the resettlement
of the refugees in the Arab countries. Hacohen agreed. Israel should
'reap, plough, settle on [Arab] land – until they understand that they will
not be allowed to return'.

Ben-Gurion's own thinking was clear. 'We must start out', he said,
'from an assumption, of how to help those who will not return, whatever their number (and we want them to be as numerous as possible),
to resettle abroad.'[87] According to Danin's recollection a month later,
Ben-Gurion had not allowed 'any alternative' opinion – such as to allow
the return of '20,000 or 50,000 or 100,000 refugees; of families of adult
males who had stayed here; whether to bring [i.e., allow] back property owners; whether to allow back [refugees] according to communal
differences [i.e., Christians], etc.' – to be broached.[88]

Weitz (once again) proposed the appointment of a non-governmental
authority to formulate a 'plan for the transfer of the Arabs and

their resettlement'.[89] Although no formal decision was reached, a committee – the second and official Transfer Committee – with far narrower terms of reference than Weitz had originally sought, was at last appointed by Ben-Gurion.[90]

The 18 August gathering at the Prime Minister's Office had been defined as 'consultative'. The participants had been united on the need to bar a return and there was general, if not complete, agreement as to the means to be used to attain this end – destruction of villages, settlement in other sites and on abandoned lands, cultivation of Arab fields, purchase and expropriation of Arab lands, and the use of propaganda to persuade the refugees that they would not be allowed back. The same day, orders went out to all IDF units to prevent 'with all means' the return of refugees.[91]

On 22 August, Shertok explained the government's position to Zionism's elder statesman and president of the Provisional Council of State, Chaim Weizmann:

> With regard to the refugees, we are determined to be adamant while the war lasts. Once the return tide starts, it will be impossible to stem it, and it will prove our undoing. As for the future, we are equally determined – without, for the time being, formally closing the door to any eventuality – to explore all possibilities of getting rid, once and for all, of the huge Arab minority which originally threatened us. What can be achieved in this period of storm and stress will be quite unattainable once conditions are stabilised. A group of people from among our senior officers [i.e., the Transfer Committee] has already started working on the study of resettlement possibilities [for the refugees] in other countries . . . What such permanent resettlement of 'Israeli' Arabs in the neighbouring territories will mean in terms of making land available in Israel for the settlement of our own people requires no emphasis.[92]

Serious American pressure over the plight of the refugees began to be felt only in late August. Israel's representative in Washington, Eliahu Epstein (Elath), reported: 'American public opinion gradually being undermined . . . All hostile forces unite in publicizing and shedding crocodile tears regarding plight Arab refugees.'[93] America's representative, McDonald, met Ben-Gurion for the first time on 20 August and warned that the United States was contemplating measures on the refugee question that would prove unpalatable to Israel, and that Washington might even be prepared to impose sanctions to enforce its will. Ben-Gurion replied that Israel would not compromise on its 'security and independence.' Returning the refugees, 'so long as an invading army' was on Israeli soil, was hazardous. 'We could not allow back one who hates [us], even if sanctions were imposed on us', he concluded.[94]

Israel's two senior diplomats in the United States were recalled for consultations and in early September briefed the Cabinet. Epstein quoted Robert Lovett, the deputy secretary of state, as saying that the refugees constituted a 'severe problem', public opinion-wise, though he 'did not make any threats'.[95] Abba Eban, the Israeli observer (soon ambassador) at the United Nations, said that Britain had failed to mobilize the United Nations 'to act' in support of a refugee return.[96]

A specific American initiative was launched in early September, with the submission to Tel Aviv of 'suggestions' to facilitate the peace process. Western Galilee (in Israeli hands since mid-May but originally allotted to the Palestine Arab State) should go to Israel and a 'large portion of desert land' in the Negev (still largely in Egyptian hands but allotted to the Jewish State) should go to the Arabs (implicitly, to Jordan) and the problem of Jerusalem should be solved on the basis of 'internationalization' (or anything else acceptable to both the Jews and the Arabs). Moreover, Washington said very hesitantly, it 'would like the Israeli government to consider some constructive measures for the alleviation of Arab refugee distress.'[97]

Ben-Gurion, Shertok and McDonald met on 8 September to discuss the 'suggestions'. Ben-Gurion left it to Shertok to deliver the response on the refugee question. '[Shertok] said that we were [willing] to consider the return of individual refugees now, and the return of part of the refugees after the war, on condition that most of the refugees would be settled in Arab countries with our help.' This marked a substantial softening of Israel's official and public position, but McDonald apparently failed to realise this. He asked whether 'the door is shut' to discussing the matter and Ben-Gurion responded: 'In my opinion, the door is not shut − if we discuss the arrangement of a solid, stable peace with the Arabs. As part of such an arrangement, one can discuss anything.'[98] Briefing the Cabinet later that day, Shertok said that it was 'unclear' whether the Americans had presented their *démarche* (the 'suggestions') off their own bat or whether they had been put up to it by 'someone' else.[99]

But if in private, with the newly arrived Americans, Ben-Gurion and Shertok were exhibiting or appearing to exhibit flexibility, Israel's official and public stance continued to conform with July's Cabinet decision. On 12 September, the Cabinet approved Shertok's draft instructions to the Israel delegation to the United Nations General Assembly. The instructions, dated 10 September, read:

> No return before the end of the war save for individual cases; a final solution to the refugee problem as part of a general settlement when peace comes. In informal conversations, the delegation will explain that it were better that the problem be solved by settling the refugees in the neighbouring countries than by returning them to the State of Israel − for their own good, for the good of the neighbouring countries, for the good of Israel and for the good of [future] Israeli relations with her neighbours.

No mention was made of possible Israeli readiness to allow back a portion of the refugees.[100] In Cabinet, Shertok stressed the widespread ignorance regarding 'Iraq's dire need for workers, [and its] vast settlement projects that were not implemented because of lack of manpower'. Cisling objected to the 'instructions', calling for an addendum stating that Israel 'will be ready to discuss the return of refugees' following the withdrawal of the Arab armies from Palestine. Bentov supported Cisling, adding that Israel should allow the refugees to return to their places or, alternatively, to the areas vacated by the Arab armies when they leave Palestine. Shapira agreed (and argued that the Arabs would, in any case, never agree to withdraw their armies so a refugee return would never materialise). Ben-Gurion, surprisingly, said that Israeli officials should privately explain to Israel's 'friends' that if direct Israeli–Arab negotiations became possible,

> and through this we brought about peace – we would bring [allow?] back the refugees. [But] if the Arabs continue their war against us, even if it is a non-active war [i.e., a cold war], and do not want peace – the return of the refugees is a weapon against us; [as] leaving refugees with them – is our weapon.

The ministers then voted. By seven votes to three, it was decided 'not to discuss the return of the refugees until a peace settlement'.[101]

The first round of the diplomatic battle over the refugees climaxed on 20 September, with the publication of Bernadotte's report on his mediation efforts. The report had been completed on 16 September, the day before the Mediator's assassination at the hands of LHI (Stern Gang) terrorists in Jerusalem. In it, Bernadotte strongly supported the right of the refugees to return to their homes 'at the earliest practical date'. No 'just and complete' settlement was possible, the Mediator wrote, if the right of return was not recognised.

> It would be an offence against the principles of elemental justice if these innocent victims of the conflict were denied the right to return to their homes while Jewish immigrants flow into Palestine and, indeed, at least offer the threat of permanent replacement of the Arab refugees,

he wrote. At the same time, however, Bernadotte was fully aware that the radically changed and changing circumstances in Israel (including the immigrant influx) strongly militated against a mass return. 'It must not be supposed', he wrote,

> that the establishment of the right of refugees to return . . . provides solution of the problem. The vast majority of the refugees may no longer have homes to return to and their re-establishment in the State of Israel presents an economic and social problem of special complexity.[102]

The Israeli response to the report, which contained guidelines for a general settlement of the conflict, was tailored to suit the highly embarrassing and vulnerable diplomatic position in which Tel Aviv found itself. The Mediator had been murdered by – albeit dissident – Israelis and his report included proposals, such as handing over the Negev to the Arabs, which were anathema to Tel Aviv. The circumstances required contrition and caution – but without saying anything that could later be construed as concrete concessions. In its response on 23 September, Tel Aviv, on the refugee issue, simply ignored the Mediator's call for recognition of the right of return.[103]

Meanwhile, a new wave of *ad hoc* appeals from exiled communities to be allowed back reached Shitrit. Shitrit generally referred them to Ben-Gurion, the IDF and Shertok for a ruling. By nature and politically a softliner, Shitrit, by the end of August, had more or less come around to Ben-Gurion's and Shertok's view. Allowing any Arabs back might serve as a precedent and might constitute a security problem. As Machnes, his director general, put it: 'Over time, views have changed, and now the Minority Affairs Ministry is doing all in its power to prevent the Arabs who have gone from returning to the country.'[104]

A major debate, in which the various arguments re-surfaced, erupted over the refugees from Huj, near the Gaza Strip. Its inhabitants had been expelled eastwards, to Dimra, on 31 May (see above). Nothing was to demonstrate so convincingly the inflexibility of the crystallising Israeli resolve against a return.

In September, the exiles, noting that the Second Truce (19 July–15 October 1948) was holding and that the area around Huj was quiet, appealed to Israel to allow them back. The appeal, as usual, made the rounds of the bureaucracies – the IDF, the Military Government, the Foreign Ministry Middle East Affairs Department and the Minority Affairs Ministry. Shimoni wrote that the Huj appeal deserved 'special treatment' because the inhabitants had been 'loyal collaborators', 'because they had not fled but had been expelled', and because they had not wandered far afield and were still living near the village. His department, therefore, in view of 'the commonly held opinion that an injustice had been done', would be willing to recommend that the IDF permit the villagers to return to Israeli territory, not necessarily to Huj itself but rather to another 'abandoned village'.

But, Shimoni added: 'The problem of precedents arises. If we allow them [to return], hundreds and thousands of others may perhaps come, each with his own good reasons [to be allowed back].' So he concluded his qualified recommendation by writing that 'if the Defence Ministry could find a way' to prevent the Huj case from becoming a precedent, 'then we withdraw our opposition [to a return] in this particular case'.[105]

Shitrit found Shimoni's reservations irksome. He wrote that he did 'not believe that allowing some . . . to return would [necessarily] serve as a precedent'. After all, there was a firm Cabinet decision that so long as the war continued, 'there could be no talk of a return . . .'. So if the Middle East Affairs Department supported allowing the return of the inhabitants of Huj, 'there will be no opposition on our part', he wrote. But Shitrit, too, thought that the villagers would have to be resettled 'inside' Israel rather than in their home village, which was near the front lines.[106]

But these (hesitant) recommendations proved unavailing. The defence authorities overruled Shitrit and Shimoni, and the inhabitants of Huj, whether because of arguments of security or precedent, were never allowed back. The flare-up of hostilities between Israel and Egypt a few weeks after this exchange sealed the fate of the villagers.

The post-Bernadotte months were dominated by the reverberations of the report or 'plan' he had left behind, and by the growing awareness, abroad as well as among the Israeli public, of the solidity and inflexibility of Israel's resolve to bar a return.[107] In this respect, Bernadotte's murder worked to Israel's advantage: He had made the solution of the refugee problem, including the principle of the right of return, a personal issue and goal. His successor, Acting Mediator, Ralph Bunche, displayed far less determination in pursuing the matter.

On 27 September, a senior Israeli diplomat, Michael Comay, apprised the Israel Delegation to the United Nations General Assembly meeting in Paris of his meetings on 23–24 September in Haifa with Bunche and two of his aides, Reedman and Paul Mohn. While the United Nations' officials had reiterated Bernadotte's commitment to securing recognition of the right of return, 'they were all of the opinion that for the most part the Arabs did not want to go back and live under Jewish domination'. he reported. The middle-class exiles were definitely unenthusiastic about returning, and some of the villagers who wanted to return would, once back, no doubt 'drift off again when they saw some of the things that were alleged to be going on in Israel, such as destruction of villages and taking over of land'. Comay reported that, according to Reedman, Bernadotte had first thought in terms of a general return 'but had retreated from this position when he came to realise the deep-rooted and permanent complications'. Bernadotte, in the end, had sought only a partial return, for political and humanitarian reasons – agreeing that the main solution must be found through organised resettlement in the Arab countries.[108]

Henceforward, while lip-service was still occasionally paid to the concept of 'the right of return', and while the General Assembly, in December, endorsed the refugees' 'right of return' in Resolution 194 (see below), the international community was to focus more and more on the necessity, desirability and possibility of a partial repatriation coupled with the re-settlement of the bulk of the refugees in Arab lands. Israel, it would later be seen, had successfully rebuffed the pressures for a mass return.

Within Israel, the continued state of war had been decisive in the crystallisation of the decision to bar a return. The hostilities facilitated the task of those like Ben-Gurion, Weitz and Shertok, who, from early on, realised and argued that to be established securely and remain secure, the newfound state had to have as small as possible an Arab minority.

The political argument against having a 40 per cent Arab minority inter-meshed with the strategic argument against retaining or bringing back hundreds of thousands of Arabs who would or might constitute a Fifth Column. The fighting provided both the opportunity and the reason for creating or at least maintaining an Arab-free country.

A mass return of refugees would have created grave problems for all the Israeli agencies prospectively involved in their repatriation – the IDF, the police, the civilian bureaucracies and the Jewish settlements – at a time when their energies and resources were being strained to capacity by the war and by the influx of masses of Jewish immigrants.

To this, as the weeks and months passed, were added the 'positive' arguments of the Yishuv's settlement and immigration absorption bodies. To expand (and it had to expand to meet the needs of the burgeoning Jewish population), Jewish agriculture had to have the abandoned lands. Jewish settlements, in general, needed more land. And the immigrants (and the many more potential immigrants) required land and houses. Moreover, some of the immigrants who reached Israel in 1948–1949 and, more so, during the 1950s, hailed from Arab countries (Yemen, Iraq, Morocco) – enabling the Israeli leaders, with some justification and logic, to view what had happened as an (unplanned, uncoordinated) 'exchange of population'. Hundreds of thousands of Arabs had left Palestine, losing almost all their belongings, and hundreds of thousands of Jews had left their native, Muslim countries, generally leaving their property behind. History had created an equation that helped Israel rebuff efforts and pressures for Palestinian refugee repatriation.

The political decision to bar a return had matured over April–June, had become official policy in July, and had been repeatedly reaffirmed by the Cabinet in August and September. It was reaffirmed at various levels of government over the following months as successive communities of exiles asked to be allowed back. During the second half of 1948 and the first half of 1949, developments on the ground worked to harden the status quo and certify the refugeedom of Palestine's Arabs.

ENDNOTES

1. See, for example, entry for 26 Mar. 1948, Weitz, *Diary*, III, 257, describing a meeting between Yosef Weitz and local leaders from the Beit Shean and Jezreel valleys in which a consensus emerged against allowing a return.
2. Unsigned, 'Summary of the Meeting of the Arab Affairs Advisers in Dora Camp 6.4.48', IDFA 2506\49\\91; and unsigned, 'Summary of Meeting of the Arab Affairs Advisers, Camp Dora 13.4.1948', IDFA 4663\49\\125.
3. Protocol of meeting of JAE, 6 May 1948, CZA 45\2.
4. Protocol of meeting of Mapai Central Committee, 11 May 1948, LPA 48\23 aleph.

5. Entry for 1 May 1948, DBG-YH I, 382; and Ben-Gurion, *As Israel Fights*, 68–69, text of 7 Feb. 1948 speech at meeting of Mapai Council. Indeed, there is evidence that on his visit to Haifa on 1 May, Ben-Gurion went further. Hearing that the Mapai boss in the city, Abba Khoushi, was trying to persuade Arabs to stay, Ben-Gurion is said to have remarked: 'Doesn't he have anything more important to do?' (Nimrod, 'Patterns . . .' 268).

6. Shertok to Zaslani (Shiloah), 25 Apr. 1948, *Political and Diplomatic Documents*, 674.

7. Cohen, 'Our Arab Policy in the Midst of the War', 10 May 1948, HHA-ACP 10.95.10 (4).

8. 'A Call from His Majesty King 'Abdullah to the Arab People of Palestine on Behalf of the Arab League', as carried in *Al Nasr*, an Amman daily, 5 May 1948, NA Record Group 84, US Consulate General, Jerusalem, Classified Records 1948, 800 – Political Affairs.

9. Middle East Department, Israel Foreign Ministry, 'In the Arab Public', 28 May 1948, IDFA 4944\49\\504.

10. Protocol of meeting in Haifa, 6 Jun. 1948, ISA MAM 303\41.

11. Danin to Weitz, 18 May 1948, Yosef Weitz Papers, Institute for the Study of Settlement (Rehovot). For a full examination of Weitz's transfer activities and the 'Transfer Committees' see Morris, 'Yosef Weitz . . .'.

12. 'M.S.' (Moshe Shertok), '[Talk] with Yosef Weitz', 28 May 1948, ISA FM 2564\20.

13. Entry for 30 May 1948, Wietz, *Diary*, III, 294.

14. Weitz, Sasson, Danin, 'Retroactive Transfer . . .' undated but from early June, ISA FM 2564\19.

15. Entry for 5 June 1948, CZA A246-13, 2411.

16. Entry for 5 June 1948, DBG-YH II, 487.

17. Weitz to Ben-Gurion, 6 June 1948, ISA FM 2564\19.

18. Protocol of Cabinet meeting of 23 May 1948, ISA.

19. Heller, *Birth*, 192.

20. Shertok to Eytan, 6 June 1948, ISA FM 2444\19.

21. Shertok to Eytan, 6 June 1948, ISA FM 2444\19.

22. Entry for 1 June 1948, DBG-YH II, 477.

23. Protocol of Cabinet meeting, 1 June1948, ISA.

24. Levi, IDF OC Jezreel Valley District, to area commanders, 9 June 1948, HHA-ACP 10.95.10 (5); and Ya'akobi to Ephraim, Gershon, 11 June 1948, IDFA 410\54\\104.

25. Oded\Operations to battalions, 13 June 1948, IDFA 6309\49\\2.

26. Kaddar to Sharef, 3 June 1948, ISA FM 2345\10; unsigned, 'Report on a Visit to Safad of the Committee for Abandoned Property, 5 July 1948', ISA AM aleph\19\aleph; and Safad Workers Council, 'Memorandum for Consolidating Safad after Its Liberation', undated, IDFA 782\65\\1189.

27. Entry for 3 June 1948, Weitz, *Diary*, III, 297.

28. Vizhensky to Cisling, 3 June 1948, ISA AM 5\kof.

29. Protocol of Meeting of Mapai Secretariat, statement by Shertok, 13 June 1948, LPA.

30. Zagorsky to Harzfeld, 2 June 1948, LA 235 IV, 2251 bet. See also unsigned, 'The Visit of the Minister of Minority Affairs and Police in Kfar Gil'adi, 29.7.48', HA 105\260.

31. IDF GS\Operations logbook, entry for 2 June 1948, IDFA 922\75\\1176.
32. IDF GS\Operations logbook, entry for 8 June 1948, IDFA 922\75\\1176.
33. OC, IDF Intelligence Service, to Shiloah, 16 June 1948, ISA FM 2426\9.
34. See, for example, Oded\Operations to battalions, 13 June 1948, IDFA 6309\49\\2.
35. Israel Foreign Ministry Middle East Department, 'In the Arab Public', 11 June 1948, ISA FM 2570\6.
36. Shertok (Tel Aviv) to Goldmann (London), 15 June 1948, ISA, *Documents* I, 163. Shertok said similar things the following day in Cabinet (see protocol of Cabinet meeting, 16 June 1948, ISA). He also defined the Arab exodus as 'the most surprising thing' that had happened in the course of the war. Ben-Gurion, on the other hand, said that he had not been surprised by the exodus but that he had been 'bitterly' surprised by the 'ethical failures' of the Yishuv. He was referring to the looting.
37. Shertok to Goldmann, 15 June 1948, ISA, *Documents* I, 162–63.
38. Protocol of the meeting of Mapam Political Committee, 15 June 1948, HHA 66.90 (1); and Secretariat of Mapam Centre, 'Our Policy Towards the Arabs During the War (Decisions of the Political Committee of 15.6.48)', 23 June 1948, HHA-ACP 10.95.11 (1).
39. The full version of Ben-Gurion's important speech is inaccessible. In the version open at the ISA, six long, paragraph-size passages (as well as the odd sentence) have been blanked out by internal censors. Over the years, Ben-Gurion himself published two abridged versions, in *As Israel Fights*, 127–31, and in *The Resurgent State of Israel*, I, 165–68. In 1982, Gershon Rivlin and Elhanan Orren, published a third abridged version, in DBG-YH, II, 524–26. The quotations in this paragraph intermix passages from the published versions and the ISA protocol. Only once the ISA opens the full protocol will we know everything that was said, and in its proper order.
40. Morris, *Righteous Victims*, 44–45.
41. Ben-Gurion's diary, 11 July 1936, quoted in Segev, *One Palestine, Complete*, 383.
42. Protocol of Cabinet meeting, 16 June 1948, ISA.
43. Protocol of Cabinet meeting, 16 June 1948, ISA.
44. This passage was censored out in the ISA protocols – but appears in the KMA, 9\9\3.
45. For example, see Nahum [Golan], OC Golani, to 'Shimon', 'Binyamin', and 'Levi', 16 June 1948, IDFA 1096\49\51: 'On no account should Arabs be allowed during the truce to return to areas from which they have been ejected.'
46. For example, see Rabin, Operation Dani HQ, to Harel, Yiftah, Kiryati and 8th brigades, 19 July 1948, KMA-PA 141–419; and Giv'ati to battalions, 24 July 1948, IDFA 922\75\\899.
47. Yadin to Shertok, 14 Aug. 1948, ISA FM 2444\19.
48. Protocol of Cabinet meeting, 20 June 1948, ISA.
49. Eytan, 'Meetings: M. Shertok-Count Bernadotte and Assistants, Tel Aviv, 17 and 18 June 1948', ISA 2466\2.
50. Ya'ari, 'If You Go to War' (speech delivered on 14 June 1948 at seminar for IDF recruits), 'Kibbutz Artzi Movement Fact-Sheet', No. 274\43, 8 Aug. 1948, HHA.

51. Secretariat of Mapam Centre, 'Our Policy Towards the Arabs During the War (Decisions of the Mapam Political Committee, 15 June 1948)', 23 June 1948, HHA-ACP 10.95.11 (1).

52. Salomon, 'Details of a Conversation with Archbishop Georgius Hakim on Saturday, 26 June 1948', and Shitrit to Ben-Gurion, 6 July 1948, both in ISA FM 2563\21; and protocol of Cabinet meeting, 2 July 1948, ISA.

53. 'Instructions to the Arab Population by the Commander of the Haganah, Tel Aviv District, Given on 13th May 1948', and appended 'Agreement', 13 May 1948, signed by Michael Rabinovich (Ben-Gal), OC Haganah Tel Aviv District, and Ahmed Effendi Abu Laban, Salah Effendi al Nazar, Amin Effendi Andraus, and Ahmad Effendi Abdul Rahim, HA 55\31. It was because of this agreement that Danin urged the IDF to stop signing surrender agreements with conquered communities (Danin to Shertok, 28 July 1948, ISA FM 2564\5).

54. Nicola Saba, Jaffa Emergency Committee, to representative of OC Haganah [sic], Tel Aviv District, 26 June 1948, ISA FM 2564\9.

55. Chizik to Shitrit, 27 June 1948, ISA FM 2566\15.

56. Shitrit to Ben-Gurion and Shertok, 30 June 1948, ISA FM 2566\15.

57. Kaddar to Shitrit, 5 July 1948, ISA MAM 307\49.

58. Palmon to Shertok, 6 July 1948, ISA FM 2566\15.

59. Shimoni to Shertok, 'Comments on the Attached Memorandum by Yehoshua Palmon, in Answer to a Letter by Mr Shitrit on the Jaffa [Emergency] Committee Regarding the Return of Jaffa's Arab Residents', 7 July 1948, ISA FM 2566\15.

60. Shimoni to Palmon and Shiloah,12 July 1948, quoting Shertok's minuted reaction to Palmon's proposals.

61. 'Appendix' to Bernadotte (Rhodes) to Shertok, 27 June 1948, *Documents* I, 230–34. Bernadotte also suggested that the Negev, in whole or in part, be included in 'Arab territory' and Western Galilee in 'Jewish territory.' Bernadotte's letter and 'Appendix', rather undiplomatically, nowhere referred to 'Israel', the 'Government of Israel' or the 'State of Israel' but rather to 'Palestine' and 'your Government'.

62. Shertok to Bernadotte, 5 July 1948, *Documents* I, 262–64. In an interview in *The New York Herald Tribune* of 21 June, Sasson had said that there would be no return of refugees except as part of a peace agreement with the Arab states; restitution for confiscated Arab property would be linked to compensation for Jewish property confiscated in Arab countries; and any return would be selective. Moreover, the Arabs left in Israel were free to leave. This was a new formulation of Israel's position, and Israel's delegation at the United Nations, prodded by the Americans, sought clarification from Tel Aviv (Comay to Shertok, 19 July 1948, *Documents* I, 353 and footnote 2). It was partly to end such unauthorised, 'rogue' responses by its diplomats that the Israeli Cabinet that month sat down to definitively define and formalize its policy on the refugee issue.

63. Shertok to Comay, 22 July 1948, *Documents* I, 374.

64. The linkage between the fate of the refugees and the Jewish communities in the Arab world had first been established at the Cabinet meeting of 2 July 1948. Justice Minister Rosen had said that an 'exchange of population', if

proposed by the United States and Britain – Palestinian Arabs moving to the Arab world and Jews moving out of the Arab countries to Israel – would be 'wonderful' (but if this was not agreed, Israel should not adopt a policy of barring a refugee return). Shitrit, too, had thought that an exchange of population would be 'good for the Arabs' as well as for Israel (protocol of Cabinet meeting of 2 July 1948, ISA. Censors have blanked out a large passage from Shitrit's statement). Such an exchange would 'free us of a large minority and also give us the possibility of bringing [to Israel] Jews from the oriental countries', Shitrit added two days later (protocol of Cabinet meeting, 4 July 1948, ISA).

65. Kohn to Shertok, 22 July 1948, ISA FM 2444\19.
66. 'Meeting: M. Shertok – Count Bernadotte and Assistants, Tel Aviv, 26 July 1948', *Documents* I, 409–14.
67. Protocol of Cabinet meeting, 28 July 1948, ISA. What exactly Shapira proposed is unclear as ISA censors have blanked out a passage in his speech.
68. Bernadotte, 'Note from the Mediator to be Submitted to the Consideration of the Provisional Government of Israel on the Subject of Arab Refugees', 28 July 1948, ISA FM 2444\19.
69. Kohn, 'Lines for a Reply to Mediator on Return of Refugees', undated, ISA FM 2444\19.
70. Kohn, 'Note on Walter Eytan's Memorandum', 27 July 1948, *Documents* I, 415–16.
71. Shertok to Bernadotte, 1 Aug. 1948, *Documents* I, 441–44.
72. 'Meeting: M. Shertok and Members of the Staff of the Ministry for Foreign Affairs with Count Bernadotte and His Associates', Tel Aviv, 5 Aug. 1948, *Documents* I, 465–87.
73. Kohn to Shertok, 5 Aug. 1948, ISA FM 2444\19.
74. Ross (New York) to Secretary of State, 30 July 1948, NA 501 BB. Palestine\7–3048.
75. MacDonald to Secretary of State, 27 July 1948, NA RG 84, Consulate General Jerusalem, Classified Records 1948, 800 – Refugees.
76. Patterson to Secretary of State, 29 July 1948, NA RG 84, Haifa Consulate, Classified Records 1948, 800 – Political Affairs.
77. Protocol of meeting of Mapai Central Committee, 24 July 1948, LPA48\23. Ben-Gurion's statement was revealing about his attitude to Palestine's Arabs: 'I doubt whether they deserve respect as we do. Because we did not flee *en masse*. [And] so far no Arab Einstein has arisen and [they] have not created what we have built in this country and [they] have not fought as we are fighting . . . We are dealing here with a collective murderer.'
78. Patterson (Cairo) to Secretary of State, 5 Aug. 1948, NA 501 BB. Palestine\8-548.
79. David Horowitz, 'Meeting: D. Horowitz-J. Reedman, Tel Aviv, 8 August 1948', ISA FM 2425\1.
80. 'Meeting: M. Shertok-Count Bernadotte, Jerusalem, 10 August 1948', *Documents* I, 501–506.
81. Protocol of Cabinet meeting, 11 Aug. 1948, ISA.
82. Precis of a letter from Sasson (Paris) to Shertok (Tel Aviv), 13 Aug. 1948, ISA FM 2451\13.

83. See Shimoni (Tel Aviv) to Sasson (Paris), 16 Sep. 1948; and Sasson (Paris) to Danin, 29 Nov. 1948, both in ISA FM 3749\1; and entry for 14 Dec. 1948, Weitz, *Diary*, III, 365. For Sasson's activities in Paris, see Cohen-Shany, *Operation Paris*, 73–120.

84. Shimoni (Tel Aviv) to Sasson (Paris), 19 Aug. 1948, ISA FM 2570\11.

85. Shimoni, 'Precis of Things Said at a Meeting in the Office of the Prime Minister about the Problem of the Arab Refugees and their Return, 18 August 1948'; ISA FM 2444\19. See also entry for 18 Aug. 1948, DBG-YH II, 652–54; entry for 18 Aug. 1948, Weitz, *Diary*, III, 331; and Shimoni to Sasson, 19 Aug. 1948, ISA FM 2570\11.

86. Shimoni to Sasson, 19 Aug. 1948, ISA FM 2570\11.

87. Shimoni, 'Precis . . .', 18 Aug. 1948, ISA FM 2444\19.

88. Danin (Tel Aviv) to Sasson (Paris), 22 Sep. 1948, ISA FM 2570\11.

89. Entry for 18 Aug. 1948, Weitz, *Diary*, III, 331.

90. See Morris, 'Yosef Weitz . . .'.

91. Yadin to brigades, 18 Aug. 1948, IDFA 2687\49\\35.

92. Shertok (Tel Aviv) to Weizmann (Montreaux), 20 July\22 August 1948, *Documents* I, 369.

93. Epstein (Washington) to Shertok, 24\26 Aug. 1948, *Documents* I, 549–551.

94. Entry for 20 Aug. 1948, DBG-YH III, 657.

95. Protocol of Cabinet meeting, 1 Sep. 1948, ISA. Shitrit asked Elath: 'Did you not draw a comparison between our [Jewish] refugees and the Arab refugees? . . . Did they [i.e., you] not mention the empty spaces in the Arab countries in connection with the refugee problem?' Elath: 'I said: Our refugees are victims of Hitler, while the Arab refugees are victims of their own leaders. I told them what happened in Haifa and other places . . . In my opinion, it would not have been wise to speak of the empty spaces in the Arab states.'

96. Protocol of Cabinet meeting, 5 Sep. 1948, ISA.

97. 'Statement Delivered by James McDonald at a meeting with M. Shertok, Tel Aviv, 6 September 1948', *Documents* I, 570–71.

98. Entry for 8 Sep. 1948, DBG-YH II, 677.

99. Protocol of Cabinet meeting, 8 Sep. 1948, ISA.

100. Foreign Minister to Cabinet members, 'Instructions to the Israeli Delegation to the UN General Assembly', 10 Sep. 1948, appended to protocol of Cabinet meeting, 12 Sep. 1948, ISA. See also Shimoni (Tel Aviv) to Sasson (Paris), 16 Sep. 1948, ISA FM 3749\1.

101. Protocol of Cabinet meeting, 12 Sep. 1948, ISA. Ben-Gurion's stated agreement to allow the return of all the refugees within the framework of a comprehensive peace settlement must be seen as tactical; by September 1948 he thought it extremely unlikely that the Arabs would agree to such a settlement.

102. Bernadotte, 'Progress Report of the UN Mediator on Palestine', 16 Sep. 1948, ISA FM 2527\9.

103. 'Statement by the Spokesman of the Government of Israel', Tel Aviv, 23 Sep. 1948, *Documents* I, 626–27.

104. Protocol of Meeting of Ministerial Committee on Abandoned Property, 27 Aug. 1948, ISA FM 2564\13. See also Shitrit to Ben-Gurion and

Shertok, 16 Aug. 1948; Shimoni to Foreign Ministry Political Division, 21 Sep. 1948; and Shitrit to Foreign Ministry Middle East Affairs Department, 26 Sep. 1948 – all in ISA FM 2564\18.

105. Shimoni to Foreign Ministry Political Division, 21 Sep. 1948, ISA FM 2564\18.

106. Shitrit to Foreign Ministry Middle East Affairs Department, 26 Sep. 1948, ISA FM 2564\18.

107. Even Weizmann, a traditional softliner, agreed or had been brought round to agreeing, with Weitz's inflexible opposition to a return (entry for 9 Dec. 1948, Weitz, *Diary*, III, 363).

108. M. Comay, 'Note on Discussions of M.S. Comay with Bunche, Reedman and Mohn – Haifa, 23rd and 24th September 1948', to Israel Delegation to UN General Assembly, Paris, 27 Sep. 1948, *Documents* I, 640–44.

6 Blocking a return

In the course of 1948 and the first half of 1949, a number of processes definitively changed the physical and demographic face of Palestine. Taken collectively, they steadily rendered the possibility of a mass refugee return more and more remote until, by mid-1949, it became virtually inconceivable. These processes were the gradual destruction of the abandoned Arab villages, the cultivation or destruction of Arab fields and the share-out of the Arab lands to Jewish settlements, the establishment of new settlements, on abandoned lands and sites and the settlement of Jewish immigrants in empty Arab housing in the countryside and in urban neighbourhoods. Taken together, they assured that the refugees would have nowhere, and nothing, to return to.

These processes occurred under the protective carapace of the Haganah\IDF's periodically reiterated policy of preventing the return of refugees across the lines, including by fire, and of the repeated bouts of warfare between the Israeli and Arab armies, which effectively curtailed the movement of civilians near the often fluid front lines. At the same time, these processes were natural and integral, major elements in the overall consolidation of the State of Israel. They were not, at least initially, geared or primarily geared to blocking the return of the refugees. They began in order to meet certain basic needs of the new State. Some of the processes, such as the destruction of the villages and the establishment of new settlements along the borders, were dictated in large part by immediate military needs. Others were due to basic economic requirements – the kibbutzim's need for more land, the Yishuv's growing need for more agricultural produce, the new immigrants' need for housing. But, taken together, these processes substantially contributed, and were understood by the Yishuv's leaders to contribute, to definitively preventing a refugee return.

THE DESTRUCTION OF THE ARAB VILLAGES

About 400 villages and towns were depopulated in the course of the war and its immediate aftermath. By mid-1949, the majority of these sites were either completely or partly in ruins and uninhabitable.

Some of the desolation was caused during abandonment and, later, by the ravages of time and the elements. Some of the destruction was the result of warfare – villages were mortared, shelled and occasionally bombed from the air, and houses were often destroyed to clear fields of fire immediately after conquest. In general, however, the Jewish forces, which were short of artillery and bombers, especially before July 1948, caused little destruction during the actual fighting. Most of the destruction was due to vandalism and looting, and to deliberate demolition, with explosives, bulldozers and occasionally hand tools, by Haganah and IDF units or neighbouring Jewish settlements in the days, weeks and months after their conquest. We shall trace the evolution of this process in the following pages.

The destruction of the villages can be said to have begun with, and stemmed naturally from, pre-war British Mandate antiterrorist policy and Haganah retaliatory policy. In punishing Arab terrorists and irregulars during the 1936–1939 rebellion and in the countdown to 30 November 1947, both the British and the Haganah destroyed houses, in towns and villages. Destroying the house of a guerrilla fighter or terrorist or their accomplices was regarded as just punishment and as a deterrent. The British[1] meted out the punishment in open and orderly fashion; the Haganah, usually in clandestine nighttime raids. On 20 May 1947, for example, a Palmah unit blew up a coffee house in Fajja after the murder of two Jews in Petah Tikva; in August, a Haganah unit blew up a house, suspected of being a terrorist headquarters, in the Abu Laban orchard, outside Tel Aviv.[2]

During the countdown to the 1948 War, the destruction of Arab houses was formalised as a legitimate retaliatory measure in a succession of HGS plans setting out the guidelines for operations if and when the Yishuv was attacked by the Palestinians. The Haganah's 'Plan B', finalised in September 1945, provided only vaguely for 'the sabotage or destruction of [Arab] installations' in retaliatory attacks. (The plan assumed that as during the Revolt, the British Army would assist in the defense of the Yishuv.)[3] Its successor, 'Plan C', of May 1946 (which assumed British neutrality in the imminent Arab-Jewish hostilities), provided in detailed fashion for retaliatory strikes against economic and infrastructure targets '(water [works], flour mills, etc.)' and, more generally,

> against villages, [urban] neighbourhoods and farms, serving as bases for Arab armed forces . . . by arson or explosion. If the aim was general

punishment – the torching of everything possible and the demolition [with explosives] of the houses of inciters or [their] accomplices [was to be carried out].

The plan provided, 'in certain cases,' for the demolition of 'club-houses, coffee-shops, assembly [halls] . . . after removing the people from them'. The Haganah was further instructed to sabotage 'the property' of Palestinian political and military leaders, 'inciters' and militants.[4]

After the start of hostilities, the dynamiting of houses and parts of villages became a major component of most Haganah retaliatory strikes. The operational orders for the strikes almost invariably contained an order to blow up one or several houses (as well as to kill 'adult males' or 'armed irregulars'). On 9 December 1947, units of the Giv'ati Brigade blew up a house (the orders were 'two houses') in the village of Karatiyya. Two nights later, Haganah units blew up a house in Haifa's Wadi Rushmiya neighbourhood.[5] The Palmah orders in the raid on Khisas, in the Galilee Panhandle, on 18 December 1947, included the demolition of two specific houses – and these, in fact, were destroyed.[6] On 19 December, in response to the murder of a Jew, Haganah units partially destroyed the home of the mukhtar of Qazaza, 'Abdullah Abu Sabah.[7] On 26 December, the Etzioni Brigade blew up several houses in the village of Silwan, a suburb of East Jerusalem, and three more houses the following night in the village of Yalu.[8] On 4 January 1948, Etzioni blew up the Semiramis Hotel in Jerusalem's Qatamon neighbourhood.[9] The theoretical underpinning of the destruction of individual houses in retaliatory strikes was reformulated in an HGS directive of 18 January 1948. Targeted for destruction were 'houses serving as concentration points, supply depots and training sites' for irregulars as well as residential houses, economic targets, and public buildings.[10]

As the fighting gained in intensity, so did the efficiency and destructiveness of Haganah raids. Through January, February and March, the raiders destroyed houses and parts of villages that harboured or were suspected of harbouring hostile militiamen and irregulars. In one exceptional reprisal – against 'Arab Suqrir (see above) – the orders were to destroy the whole village, and this was done.[11] But while the main aim of the raids was cautionary and punitive, they often, almost inevitably, led to the evacuation of families. The destruction of houses had a major demoralising effect in each village attacked (and sometimes on neighbouring villages). In January and February, Palmah raiders destroyed houses in Yazur and Salama, east of Jaffa. The operational orders for Salama were typical. They stated:

> The villagers do not express opposition to the actions of the gangs and a great many of the youth even provide [the irregulars with] active cooperation . . . The aim is . . . to attack the northern part of the village . . . to cause deaths, to blow up houses and to burn everything possible.

A qualification stated: 'Efforts should be made to avoid harming women and children.'[12]

In mid-January, the Palmah raided the village of Mansurat al Kheit, north of the Sea of Galilee, and 'houses and shacks were set alight'.[13] The Haganah was not alone in adopting this tactic. On the night of 14 January, LHI troops destroyed three houses in East Jerusalem's Sheikh Jarrah quarter.[14] In March, the Palmah's 3rd Battalion raided the village of al Husseiniya, near Lake Hula in Upper Galilee. The battalion blew up five houses and killed several dozen villagers and 'the village was completely evacuated'.[15] Later that month, Palmah units blew up or torched 'a number of houses' in the village of Sandala, north of Jenin,[16] and 15 houses in the village of Qa'un.[17]

The demolition of houses was so basic a component of Haganah retaliatory strategy that in mid-February, when the organisation's officer in charge of education and propaganda suggested issuing an order-of-the-day to all Haganah members outlining the organisation's achievements in the first three months of hostilities, he proposed that it 'contain a summary of casualties we inflicted on the enemy in dead and wounded' and 'the number of houses (bases of murderers) and bridges we blew up and destroyed'.[18] The Arabs took note of the Haganah policy of destroying houses, but, according to Ezra Danin, the Mufti's men were dismissive, saying 'that the Jews don't know how to fight – therefore [instead] they destroy houses'.[19]

The Haganah strategy of aggressive defence, consisting mainly of fighting off attackers on the perimeters of settlements peppered with occasional retaliatory strikes, gave way in April to an offensive strategy, in line with 'Plan D', of conquest and permanent occupation of Arab sites. In the section in its preamble regarding 'consolidating defence systems and obstacles', the plan provided for the 'destruction of villages (burning, blowing up and mining the ruins)' that the Haganah was incapable of permanently controlling and that might be used as bases for Arab forces.[20]

As the HGS directive of 18 January had provided the doctrinal foundation for the destruction of individual houses in reprisal raids, so Plan D supplied the doctrinal underpinning for the post-March leveling of whole villages and clusters of villages. The passage from the January directive to the March plan paralleled the growing scale of the war as well as its increased brutality. The directive had sought to pinpoint 'guilty', individual targets (such as houses of terrorists); Plan D, on the other hand, consigned to collective destruction whole hostile and potentially hostile villages. However, the degree to which Plan D's provision for destroying villages was implemented in different sectors over April–June 1948 depended largely on the local military situation (i.e., Arab resistance and topography), the mindset of individual Israeli commanders, and the availability to Haganah units of dynamite, bulldozers and manpower.

During the Haganah offensives of April and May, swathes of Arab villages were partly or completely destroyed – in the Jerusalem Corridor, around Mishmar Ha'emek, and in Eastern and Western Galilee. The destruction of most of the sites was governed by the cogent military consideration that, should they be left intact, irregulars or, come the expected invasion, Arab regular troops, would reoccupy and use them as bases for future attacks. An almost instant example of this problem was provided at Qastal in early April (see chapter 4). The Haganah lacked the manpower to garrison each abandoned village and supervise and curtail the activities of communities that remained along and behind the front lines.

During the April–May fighting in the Jerusalem Corridor (operations 'Nahshon', 'Harel', 'Yevusi' and 'Maccabi'), Palmah units more or less systematically levelled Qastal, Qaluniya and Khulda, and largely or partly destroyed the villages of Beit Surik, Biddu, Shu'fat, Beit Iksa, and Beit Mahsir and the Jerusalem neighbourhood of Sheik Jarrah.[21] The destruction of these sites reflected the changed military situation and the resultant change of mood, perception and policy among the Yishuv's leaders. During the first months of hostilities, the Haganah, while battling the Arab irregulars for control of, or freedom of passage along, the roads, determined its strategy, operations and, to a degree, tactics in line with the political framework and constraints of the partition resolution – that is, a Jewish State within partition borders and with a substantial Arab minority. But the lack of a quick and favourable resolution to the battle of the roads in February–March 1948, and the increasingly certain and ominous prospect of an invasion by the Arab states' armies radically altered the military situation. Bases – i.e., villages – which were filled with irregulars, or had harboured irregulars, or which might do so in the immediate future, could no longer be tolerated in strategic areas (such as the Jerusalem Corridor, through which ran the road from Tel Aviv, the lifeline to the city's besieged Jews).

The original operational order for Nahshon, issued on 4 or 5 April, had included no instructions to destroy villages in the Jerusalem Corridor.[22] But sometime during the second week of April, as a component of the in-principle decision to expel the hostile inhabitants in vital areas, Ben-Gurion and the HGS, prompted by the Battle of Mishmar Ha'emek, agreed to, or initiated and ordered, the destruction of the conquered villages to assure that they would not again constitute a threat to the Yishuv. The second stage, follow-up order by Operation Nahshon HQ, dated 10 April, spoke of the conquest and destruction or 'liquidation' [hisul] of specific villages (while still refraining from a blanket order to demolish all conquered villages).[23] But on 14 April, Nahshon HQ issued guidelines to its units

> to continue harrassing and cleansing operations as a first stage [i.e., preliminary] to the destruction and conquest of enemy forces and their bases . . . [We should deliver] strong blows against and blow up main enemy bases.[24]

The 'bases' referred to, of course, were villages. Nahshon HQ followed this up with a general order to destroy the villages.[25] These orders were followed by specific directives to various units to attack – and destroy – specific villages (Qubab, Beit Jiz, Beit Surik, Sajad, and Qazaza).[26] In the wake of Nahshon, units were directed, in the same spirit, to destroy villages as part of their raiding *modus operandi*. For example, on 23 April, Palmah units raided Shu'fat and Beit Iksa 'with the aim of destruction'. In Shu'fat, the raiders blew up eight buildings before withdrawing; in Beit Iksa, much of the village was blown up or torched.[27]

At the same time, southeast of Haifa, following Qawuqji's abortive assault on Mishmar Ha'emek, the counterattacking Haganah units, with the assistance of local settlers, systematically destroyed the surrounding villages. On 9 April, Golani units informed the brigade HQ and Carmeli Brigade HQ: 'Our forces are fighting in . . . Mansi . . . [and] are in Ghubiyya al Fawqa and [Khirbet] Beit Ras . . . We are preparing to destroy the villages when we evacuate them.'[28] That night, Palmah forces destroyed Ghubiyya al Fawqa.[29] On the night of 11 April, the Palmah's First Battalion entered and blew up 30 houses in al Kafrin and houses in nearby Abu Shusha.[30] On 15 April the last of Abu Zureiq's houses was demolished.[31] Khirbet Beit Ras, al Mansi and al Naghnaghiya, to the southeast, were also levelled.[32] Lajjun, south of the kibbutz, was demolished on the night of 15–16 April.[33] One empty village was destroyed as part of a Haganah training exercise. Palmah headquarters informed the Haganah General Staff on 19 April: 'Yesterday company exercises in fighting in built-up areas took place south and east of Mishmar Ha'emek. At the end of the exercises, the village of al Kafrin was blown up completely.'[34] The destruction of the villages around Mishmar Ha'emek and in the Jerusalem Corridor were the first regional razing operations of the war, born of local military imperatives admixed with a measure of vengefulness.

A policy of destroying villages as part and parcel of operations was to characterise Haganah attacks through April–May in other areas and most offensive operational orders included instructions to destroy all or part of the targeted villages. For example, on 19 April Palmah HQ ordered First Battalion OC Dan Lanner 'to destroy enemy bases in al Mazar, Nuris and Zir'in [in the Jezreel Valley] . . . Comment: With the capture of Zir'in, most of the village's houses must be destroyed while [some] should be left intact for accommodation and defence.'[35] In the northern Negev, on 4 April, Haim Bar-Lev, a company commander, reported to OC Negev Brigade Nahum Sarig on an Arab mine attack on a patrol and on the reprisal in the Shu'ut area that followed. A Palmah unit in two armoured cars had destroyed 'nine bedouin lay-bys and . . . one mud hut . . . The mud hut was destroyed by a blow from an armoured car going backwards. It is worth noting that this seems very efficient and one blow completely demolished the mudhut', reported Bar-Lev.

Operation Yiftah in late April–May was characterised by similar demolition of the conquered villages in eastern Galilee. The Yiftah Logbook entry for 4 May reads: 'The operation is going according to plan and at 9:00 o'clock the units reached their objectives as, on the way, they blow up all the houses and burn all the beduin tents.'[36] Two weeks later, Company D of the 11th Battalion reported that, in line with the orders to 'destroy' the village of Zawiya, its platoons had blown up two houses with explosives and used Molotov cocktails on the rest, before 'a tractor began working on the [final] destruction of the houses . . . The village was destroyed [*hakfar hushmad*]', concluded the report.[37] On 24 May, Operation Yiftah HQ reported: 'We have begun the systematic burning of the [Lake] Hula [area] villages.'[38]

Similar destructiveness characterised the conquest of the villages of Western Galilee in Operation Ben-'Ami in mid- and late May. At the start of the operation, the HGS's observer accompanying the troops reported:

> Two companies . . . are attacking . . . al Bassa with the aim of blowing up the village . . . Two [other] companies . . . are attacking al Zib with the aim of blowing up the village . . . [Another] company will attack Sumeiriya with the aim of destroying the village.[39]

The next day, Carmeli HQ informed HGS\Operations that Bassa and Sumeiriya had been 'blown up completely'.[40] The operational order for stage two of the operation read: 'The objective . . . To attack with the aim of conquest, the killing of adult males, [and] the destruction and torching of the villages of Kabri, Umm al Faraj and al Nahar.'[41] During the following days, the orders were implemented.

The destruction of the villages went to the heart of the political dilemma faced by Yishuv left-wingers, who believed in the possibility of, or at least hoped for, Jewish–Arab coexistence. Was the destruction dictated by military imperatives or was it, at least in part, politically motivated, with all the implications that this entailed, they asked. Already in early May, Mapam's Aharon Cohen wrote that 'a policy of eviction' was being implemented. The Yishuv had insufficient troops to garrison every conquered village, so a policy had been adopted of 'blowing up villages so that [Arabs] would not return'.[42] On 10 May, Cohen completed a six-page memorandum entitled 'Our Arab Policy in the Midst of the War', which he circulated among Mapam Political Committee members in advance of the committees debate on the party's Arab policy. He attacked what he saw as an emergent policy of transfer. He added:

> The complete destruction of captured villages is not always carried out only because of 'lack of sufficient forces to maintain a garrison' or only so 'that the gangs [i.e., irregulars] will not be able to return there' so long as the war continues.[43]

However, the assessment of Marxist Mapamniks, that the destruction of the villages was a main component of a politically motivated policy of transfer being implemented by the Haganah–Mapai leaders was probably a few weeks premature. Until June, it was perceived strategic–military necessity that underlay the Haganah's destruction of the villages. There may have been local, isolated cases of destruction – in the Beit Shean Valley, in the northern Negev approaches and in the Sharon – where other reasons obtruded or were dominant: The desire to settle a score with aggressive neighbours or a wish to appropriate lands or a politically based desire to see as few Arabs as possible in the emergent Jewish State. Such considerations certainly guided some of the activities of Yosef Weitz's circle over March–May 1948.[44] But primarily, until early June, the destruction of the villages was carried out by the Haganah with clear military motives – to deny bases and refuge to hostile irregulars and militiamen, to prevent a return of irregulars to strategic sites and to avoid the emergence of a Fifth Column in areas already cleared of Arabs.

The mass exodus of April and early May 1948 and the imminence of the invasion focused Jewish minds wonderfully. During May, ideas about how to consolidate and give permanence to the Palestinian exile began to crystallise in the minds of Yishuv officials, and the destruction of the villages was immediately perceived as a primary means of achieving this aim. The destruction of the villages became a major political enterprise. Henceforward, while on the local level the military continued to destroy villages for military reasons, major figures in the Yishuv sought the destruction of the villages with a primarily political rather than military objective in mind.

The thrust of this enterprise was to prevent a return; its principal guidelines were to mature in the Transfer Committee's deliberations in late May and June 1948. They were augured in Danin's letter to Weitz of 18 May.[45] On 4 June, the three members of the 'self-appointed' Transfer Committee – Weitz, Danin and Sasson – discussed the 'miracle' of the Arab exodus. The question was 'how to make it permanent'. The answer, according to the committee, was to prevent a return by destroying villages and by renovating and settling Jews in other villages. Weitz agreed to allocate IL 5,000 from JNF funds 'to begin destruction and renovation activities in the Beit Shean Valley, near 'Ein Hashofet [the Ramot Menashe area] and in the Sharon [the Coastal Plain]'.[46]

The next day, 5 June, Weitz, armed with the committee's proposal, 'Retroactive Transfer, a Scheme for the Solution of the Arab Question in the State of Israel', saw Ben-Gurion. One of the main recommendations was the destruction of the abandoned villages.[47] According to Weitz, Ben-Gurion agreed to the proposed policy, including the destruction of villages, the settlement of abandoned sites and the prevention of Arab cultivation of fields, though he had reservations about Weitz's 'temporary committee' Nevertheless, Weitz informed the Prime Minister that he had 'already given orders to begin here and there destroying villages and [Ben-Gurion] approved this. I left it at that', Weitz recorded.[48]

The following day, 6 June, Weitz sent Ben-Gurion a list of the abandoned villages, and a covering note stating that at their meeting, Ben-Gurion had agreed to the start of the destruction operations: 'In line with this, I have given an order to begin [these operations] in different parts of the Galilee, in the Beit Shean Valley, in the Hills of Ephraim and in Samaria [that is, the Hefer Valley].'[49]

There was no reply from Ben-Gurion, but, at this stage, Weitz was not deterred by the lack of formal authorisation. On 7 June, Weitz and Danin discussed the campaign, and Weitz recorded:

> Preparations are under way for action in the villages. We have brought in [Yoav] Zuckerman, who will act in his area [i.e., around Gedera, southeast of Tel Aviv]. The questions are many: The town of Beit Shean, to leave it alone completely . . . and Acre and Jaffa? And Qaqun?[50]

With most able-bodied men conscripted, with most equipment, such as tractors, in use by the army and in agriculture, and with dynamite in short supply, Weitz had a problem organising what amounted to a giant demolition project. But he had his 'personal' JNF apparatus at hand, the network of regional JNF offices and workers, and a web of land-purchasing agents and intelligence and settlement contacts around the country.

On 10 June, Weitz sent two officials, Asher Bobritzky and Moshe Berger, to tour the Coastal Plain to determine which empty villages should be destroyed and which renovated and settled with Jews. Berger's activities were approved by and coordinated with the IDF. The same day, Zuckerman informed Weitz that he had made arrangements for the destruction of the village of al Mughar, which was to begin the next day.[51]

On 13 June, Weitz travelled to the Jezreel and Beit Shean valleys, where he met with local leaders and IDF officers. He recorded that he found agreement to his programme of 'destruction, renovation and settlement'. It can be assumed that he advised or ordered those he talked with to go ahead.[52] On 14 June, Danin informed Weitz of the progress in the destruction of Fajja and Zuckerman gave a progress report on the destruction of al Mughar.[53] The following day, Weitz went to look for himself and recorded:

> Three tractors are completing its destruction. I was surprised that nothing moved in me at the sight... Not regret and not hatred, as [if] this is the way of the world... The dwellers of these mud-houses did not want us to exist here.[54]

Almost certainly on the basis of a progress report from Weitz, Ben-Gurion, on 16 June, partially summarised the destruction of villages to date:

> [Al] Mughar, Fajja, Biyar Adas have been destroyed. [Destruction is proceeding in] Miska, Beit Dajan (east of Tel Aviv), in [the] Hula [Valley], [in] Hawassa near Haifa, al Sumeiriya near Acre and Ja'tun [perhaps Khirbet Jattun] near Nahariya, Manshiya... near Acre. Daliyat ar Ruha has been destroyed and work is about to begin at [al] Buteimat and Sabbarin.[55]

Through June, Weitz pressed the national leadership to officially adopt his proposals and sanction the Transfer Committee. Ben-Gurion prevaricated. He was happy that the work was going ahead but could not, for a variety of reasons, bring himself to openly support the policy or Weitz's activities. Weitz grew frustrated and wary. By the end of June, the wind had gone out of his self-appointed committee. 'There are no tools and no materials' with which to continue the work of demolition, he recorded.[56]

But the problem went deeper. How could he and his committee take upon themselves such politically momentous actions without clear-cut endorsement from the political leadership? Weitz had nothing in writing. He got cold feet. Angry and frustrated, he at last gave orders to cease work.[57]

Unknown to Weitz, word of his committee's activities had quickly trickled out, generating anger and dissent on the Left; the army's separate but complementary demolition activities in the villages were also noted. Opposition to the destruction quickly crystallised in Mapam and in the cabinet. The item 'destruction of Arab villages' – for discussion or response – appears on the Cabinet agenda on 16, 20, 23, 27 and 30 June.[58]

Agriculture Minister Cisling spoke at length on 16 June. He differentiated between 'destruction during battle' – citing the case of Qastal – and destruction afterwards – citing the destruction of Beisan. Destruction during battle

> is one thing. But [if a site is destroyed] a month later, in cold blood, out of political calculation... that is another thing altogether... This course [of destroying villages] will not reduce the number of Arabs who will return to the Land of Israel. It will [only] increase the number of [our] enemies.

Cisling charged that Ben-Gurion was 'responsible'.[59]

Four days later, Shitrit raised the question of the 'destruction of al Qubeiba and Zarnuqa'. Ben-Gurion promised to investigate.[60] The question had been prompted by a letter sent a month before by Gwirtz, director of the Arab (or Absentee) Property Department. He had written to the Giv'ati Brigade complaining about the destruction in the two villages. He said it was motivated by 'vandalism':

Machinery was destroyed, farm animals were killed, houses and granaries were torched that could have been of benefit to the army itself and the state's treasury . . . The soldiers should be told that when they destroy Arab property without need, they are harming state property, not the Arabs . . .[61]

On 23 June, Ben-Gurion asked the army to investigate.[62] The army denied that the villages had been 'completely levelled' but conceded that some destruction had occurred during conquest.[63]

Be that as it may, the destruction of the villages growingly encountered 'economic' opposition, spearheaded by Gwirtz: It made no sense in terms of the country's economic problems and needs. Already on 26 May he wrote to HGS: 'Groups of sappers are blowing up Arab houses, sometimes during conquest, and sometimes merely in exercises.' Occasionally, military necessity may be the explanation. 'But in many cases they destroy houses indiscriminately solely out of feelings of revenge, thus denying us the use of these buildings, which we need and will need.' Gwirtz proposed that the army issue an order against blowing up buildings 'not out of military necessity' and consult his department about the demolitions in the course of exercises. In any case, things of value, such as machinery, should be first removed from buildings slated for destruction.[64]

HGS responded by instructing all the brigades as follows:

1. The blowing up of Arab houses, if it is urgent and necessary for operational reasons, must be carried out immediately without taking into account other needs . . . 2. If the destruction is not urgent, [the troops] must try to remove from the houses destined for destruction the machinery (if there is any) or anything else . . . that can be of use to us. 3. It is prohibited to blow up Arab houses out of feelings of revenge. This harms us in several ways and mainly leads to a waste of explosives and [needless] destruction of property.

HGS instructed the troops to consult Gwirtz's department when possible about destroying buildings during exercises.[65] A fortnight later, IDF-GS-HGS's succesor issued a further order to curtail the 'tendency to destroy Arab property, especially machinery and vehicles . . .'. Interestingly, the order failed to explicitly prohibit the destruction of *houses*.[66]

The vandalisation and destruction of the villages continued. On 4 July, Cisling complained: 'The army had received orders to destroy houses in the Arab villages in my area [i.e., the Jezreel Valley].' He said that he did not know who was the source of the order and asked that all units be instructed that villages should not be destroyed in future without express orders from Ben-Gurion himself.[67] Meanwhile, hitting the nail on the head, Gwirtz again complained: Why the wanton destruction? '[I am] ready to accept the premise that we do not want the return of the Arabs to these villages.' But why not first extract some benefit (by removing doors, frames, tiles and the like)?[68] Gwirtz had an ally in JNF chairman Granovsky (Granott), who berated (his subordinate) Weitz '[regarding] the negative and dangerous phenomenon of the destruction of the villages'.[69]

This cumulative pressure against the destruction of the villages and what some saw as a policy of expulsion resulted in the IDF-GS's blanket order, at Ben-Gurion's instruction, of 6 July, stating:

> Outside of the actual time of combat, it is forbidden to destroy, burn and demolish Arab towns and villages [and] to expel Arab inhabitants . . . without special permission or an explicit instruction from the minister of defence in each case.[70]

By then, Weitz had suspended his destructive operations. He and his colleagues had accounted directly for only a handful of villages, and perhaps for a dozen more through 'advice' and 'instructions'. But his continuous lobbying, arguments and actions had constituted a major factor in the crystallisation among the Yishuv's leaders of the policy against a return, with a focus on the necessity of immediately destroying the empty villages (or alternatively filling them with Jewish settlers). Weitz, arguing clearly and acting with speed and determination, had shown the way.

Paradoxically, his activities had contributed to Ben-Gurion's difficulties in implementing the Transfer Committee's programme. The destruction of villages during or after conquest by the IDF could always be explained away on grounds of military necessity. Civilian critics, however august their positions, had difficulty in assailing the army's motives and actions. Who was Cisling to say whether a local commander's decision to destroy a certain village lacked military merit? But the simultaneous and similar activities of a shadowy, apparently unauthorised civilian group – clearly motivated by political considerations – placed a question mark beside the motives of the military when doing the same things.

However, the political and economic pressures – by the Mapam ministers, occasionally augmented by Shitrit and others, and by Gwirtz, and eventually supported by Finance Minister Kaplan – and the order of 6 July without doubt to some degree curtailed demolition operations. IDF operational orders for the capture of towns and villages from July onwards only occasionally explicitly ordered the destruction of the sites (in contrast with the routinely 'destructive' operational orders from mid-April until mid-June). More often than not – as in the general directives for operations Dekel and Dani in July and operations Yoav and Hiram in October[71] – the subject was simply not addressed, and it was left to the discretion of field commanders to do as they wished, some obeying the 6 July directive and others disobeying it and destroying or expelling inhabitants apparently without Ben-Gurion's prior agreement (though, let it be quickly stressed, no Israeli officer was ever punished for violating the 6 July prohibitions).

IDF units continued to raze villages, with Ben-Gurion's tacit approval – and Mapam's leaders, themselves under pressure from left-wing stalwarts, kept up the barrage of criticism and questions,[72] which Ben-Gurion usually parried by claiming ignorance or asking the critics to supply more 'facts' or give him time to investigate. At the cabinet meeting of 14 July, hard on the IDF expulsion of the inhabitants of Lydda and Ramle (see below), Cisling angrily (and very unusually) retorted: 'I will not make do with the answer that you [Ben-Gurion] don't know who destroyed [certain villages].' Ben-Gurion responded that he could not be expected 'to send men to seek out destroyed villages'.[73]

The continued pressure of the dissident ministers bore institutional fruit at the Cabinet meeting of 21 July. It was resolved that jurisdiction over the abandoned villages henceforward would reside with the Ministerial Committee for Abandoned Property, which had been set up earlier that month. But the committee was to prove, at least initially, something of a hollow reed. As Kaplan told his committee colleagues: 'In practice, [the Finance Ministry and the Custodian for Abandoned Property] have no control over the situation, and the army does as it sees fit.' Kaplan charged that his representative 'was not even allowed [by the IDF] to enter occupied territory [so] how can he be responsible for property . . .?'[74] Indeed, that summer, Ben-Gurion himself 'ordered the General Staff to prepare a list of 109 villages recommended for destruction'. In the end, he approved the destruction of 76 of the sites.[75]

After the start of the Second Truce, on 19 July, IDF units continued to destroy villages in various parts of the country. But it had become increasingly difficult. A ministerial committee was now, at least formally, responsible for the villages. Moreover, when the guns were silent, as they were until mid-October, the argument of 'military necessity' sounded a bit hollow. Lastly, the growing influx of Jewish immigrants had begun to focus attention on housing needs and possibilities. The contradiction between destroying villages and preserving property for Jewish use quickly pushed itself to the fore. Even military units began to take note. In mid-August, for example, Golani Brigade HQ instructed its sub-units to stop burning 'granaries with hay . . . in the [abandoned] Arab villages' as these were needed by 'the [Jewish] settlements'.[76] Special interest groups, such as archeologists, also began to complain, calling for curbs on IDF destructiveness.[77] Thus, on 7 October, Haifa

District HQ ordered the 123rd Battalion to stop all demolition activities in 'Qisarya [Caesarea], Atlit, Kafr Lam and Tiberias'; all contained Roman or Crusader ruins.[78]

The IDF now occasionally felt compelled to apply to the ministerial committee for permission to destroy villages. On 13 September, Ben-Gurion asked the committee for permission to destroy a cluster of villages in the central area (though he said he was doing so on behalf of OC Central Front, General Ayalon). Ayalon, he said, had written to him that

> because of a lack of manpower to occupy the area [in depth] . . . there was a need to partially destroy the following villages: 1. al Safiriya, 2. al Haditha 3. 'Innaba, 4. Daniyal, 5. Jimzu, 6. Kafr 'Ana, 7. al Yahudiya, 8. Barfiliya, 9. al Barriya, 10. al Qubab, 11. Beit Nabala, 12. Deir Sharif [should be Deir Tarif], 13. al Tira, 14. Qula.

Ben-Gurion feared opposition so instead of submitting the request to the full committee when it convened, he wrote to each member individually, asking that they respond in writing: 'I will wait for your answer for three days . . . Lack of response will be regarded as consent.' Cisling, used to the prime minister's tricks, wrote back insisting that the committee be convened.[79] Ben-Gurion backed down and the demolitions were suspended. The committee decided that it would tour the sites and decide per each village – though it gave the IDF the go-ahead in relation to Deir Tarif, Qubab, Qula, and Beit Nabala 'if [Ayalon] deems it urgent and necessary'.[80]

During 1948, Ben-Gurion consistently distanced himself in public from the destruction of villages as, more generally, from any linkage to the expulsion of Arabs. He was probably driven more by concern for his image in history and the image of the new State than by fears for coalition unity. Indeed, Ben-Gurion occasionally seems to have deliberately tried to put future historians off the scent. Thus on 27 October – a day filled with important happenings and meetings – he found time to insert in his diary the following: 'Tonight our army entered Beit Jibrin [west of Hebron] . . . Yigal [Allon, OC Southern Front] asked [permission] to blow up some of the houses. I responded negatively.'[81] Usually, however, he chose the path of omission. For example, his lengthy entry on the 18 August meeting on the question of a refugee return, in which several participants expatiated on the need to destroy the villages, simply omits any mention of the subject.[82]

But Mapam's leaders were not fooled.

> The method of destruction *vis-à-vis* the abandoned Arab village is continuing . . . It is difficult to be free of the impression that there is a guiding hand, for whom the possibility that the Arabs will have nowhere to return to, or for what, is unproblematic,

BLOCKING A RETURN | 355

stated a circular of the Mapam-affiliated Kibbutz Artzi kibbutz movement to its members serving in the IDF.[83] 'Ben-Gurion', according to Aharon Cohen,

> orders the destruction of villages without strategic need... In the ruling [i.e., Mapai] circles there is an inclination to erase more than one hundred Arab villages... Will our state be built on the destruction of Arab settlements?

he asked. Zvi Lurie called for legislation to prevent the demolitions. 'There is a group of people in the Defence Ministry who are busy "improving the landscape"', he charged.[84]

Through the second half of 1948, the IDF, under Ben-Gurion's tutelage, continued to destroy Arab villages, usually during or just after battle, occasionally, weeks and months after. The ministerial committee was not usually approached for permission.[85] The destruction stemmed from immediate military needs, as in Operation Dani, and from long-term political considerations. On 10 July, for example, Operation Dani HQ ordered the Yiftah and 8th brigades to blow up most of 'Innaba and Tira, north of Deir Tarif', while leaving a few houses intact to accommodate a small garrison.[86] Headquarters dispatched 50 sappers 'to destroy the village[s]'.[87] A few hours later, Yiftah Brigade reported that its units had conquered Kharruba and (sic) 'Khirbet al Kumeisa' (probably al Kunaiyisa). 'After blowing up the houses and cleaning up the village [sic] – our troops occupied strongpoints overlooking the village', reported the brigade.[88] The following day, Dani headquarters ordered Yiftah 'to dig in in every place captured and to destroy every house not intended for occupation [by IDF troops]'.[89]

During the Second Truce, from 19 July until 15 October, the army continued to destroy abandoned villages in piecemeal fashion, usually for reasons that were described as military. In the centre of the country, for example, in September most of the village and monastery of Deir Rafat were blown up. In the Negev and northern Negev approaches, where the IDF and the Egyptian army were strung out in an uneasy truce, with a handful of Jewish settlements more or less besieged behind Egyptian lines, raiding continued, with villagers expelled and villages demolished, as happened to al Muharraqa on 16 August[90] and to the small beduin villages and encampments east of the line al 'Imara-Tze'elim in the last days of September and the first days of October.[91]

The demolition of villages occasionally encountered local opposition, usually from Hashomer Hatza'ir kibbutzim. Sha'ar Ha'amakim, Aharon Cohen's kibbutz, for example, campaigned against Golani's intention to blow up neighbouring 'Arab Zubeidat, a traditionally friendly village.[92] Labour Minister Bentov even raised the matter in Cabinet. Ben-Gurion denied all: 'No permission was given [by me] to any commander to destroy houses.' He promised to investigate.[93] The commotion stirred up by Sha'ar Ha'amakim and Mapam stayed the advance of the bulldozers for several months. However, it was not sufficient to persuade the authorities to allow the return of the villagers, and, in the absence of a return, the village was doomed.[94]

In the south, several kibbutzim took up the cause of the friendly village of Huj, protesting against the vandalisation of its houses.[95] Yitzhak Avira, an old-time HIS officer and member of Kibbutz Ashdot Ya'akov, in the Jordan Valley, in late July protested against the destruction of the villages and policy toward the Arabs in general. He wrote Ezra Danin that

> recently a view has come to prevail among us that the Arabs are nothing. 'Every Arab is a murderer,' 'all of them should be slaughtered,' 'all the villages that are conquered should be burned'...I...see a danger in the prevalence of an attitude that everything of theirs should be murdered, destroyed and made to vanish.

Danin answered:

> War is complicated and lacking in sentimentality. If the commanders believe that by destruction, murder and human suffering they will reach their goal more quickly – I would not stand in their way. If we do not hurry up and do [things] – our enemies will do these things to us.[96]

Some Mapam members in government service also tried to stem the tide of destruction. Moshe Erem, a member of the party's Political Committee and a senior official in the Minority Affairs Ministry, tried to halt the destruction of some of the villages – 'Innaba, al Barriya and Barfiliya – listed in September for demolition by General Ayalon. Erem understood the army's desire to level the sites 'to prevent infiltration', but he regarded as 'simplistic' the assumption that 'demolished villages would not attract refugees and would, therefore, reduce the influx of [Arab] refugees ... It is the land rather than the buildings which attracts [them]', he wrote.[97]

But dissident kibbutzim and bureaucrats were the exception. The great majority of settlements and officials supported the destruction. Benny Marshak, of Kibbutz Giv'at Hashlosha and the 'Education Officer' of the Palmah, was representative. He frequently spoke in favour of the destruction of (usually hostile) clusters of abandoned villages, including those in the Jerusalem Corridor.[98]

Other kibbutzniks demanded – and often themselves carried out – the destruction of neighbouring villages for local (and selfish) reasons. On 27 July, Alexander Prag of Kibbutz Beit Zera complained of the destruction of villages and the takeover of lands in the Jordan Valley, south of the Sea of Galilee, by the local Settlements Block Committee, led by Ben-Zion Israeli.[99] Prag's complaint reached Ya'akov Peterzil, a Mapam activist, who wrote to Cisling, Bentov and Erem: 'Once again, proof is given that behind the government's back, action is taken aimed at destroying Arab villages and expropriating their lands.'[100]

To the south, in the Beit Shean Valley, pressure built up in September in the kibbutzim to level a cluster of villages. In a letter which was probably addressed to Aharon Cohen, a veteran local leader, Nahum Hurwitz, of Kfar Gil'adi, appealed for permission to destroy al Hamidiya, Kaukab al Hawa, Jabbul and al Bira, on the high ground north of the valley. (At the same time, he criticised the continuing destruction of a cluster of other villages – Na'ura, al Taiyiba, Danna, al Murassas, Yubla and Kafra – which, he thought, would be willing to cooperate with the Yishuv and 'allocate part of their lands for our settlement [purposes]'.)[101]

The hand of Weitz and his Transfer Committee can be traced in the work of demolition some miles to the north. The following complaint reached Mapam's leaders:

> The destruction of the Arab villages has been going on for some months now. We are on the Syrian border and there is a danger that the Arabs will use [the villages] for military operations if they get a chance. But I spoke to a number of members from [Kibbutz] Ma'ayan Baruch and nearby kib-butzim and I got the impression that there exists the possibility that there is a desire to destroy the villages and [the Arabs'] houses so that it will be impossible for the Arabs to return to them. A week ago a represen-tative of the JNF [possibly Yosef Nahmani] came to visit. He saw that in the village of al Sanbariya . . . several houses were still standing, albeit without roofs. He told the secretariat of the kibbutz to destroy the houses immediately and he said openly that this will enable us to take the village's lands, because the Arabs won't be able to return there. I am sorry to say the kibbutz agreed immediately without thinking about what they were doing.[102]

Through the summer and autumn of 1948, Weitz and his associates were active in dispensing this type of advice and instruction, indirectly carrying out the task they had abandoned at the end of June.

Over September–October, however, a gradual but important shift oc-curred in the views of executives charged with the fate of the villages. They began to think more in terms of renovation and Jewish settlement than destruction. Two major factors contributed. The first, clearly, was the growing awareness that the threat of a refugee return had dimin-ished. The First and Second truces saw the IDF in control of firm front lines and in most areas able to bar significant infiltration. Politically, the Yishuv had for the moment staved off international pressures to allow a return. Secondly, the legal immigration of Jews into Israel, renewed with the lifting of the British naval blockade in May, began to assume mass proportions. By autumn 1948, it was clear that the country faced a major housing problem; it was necessary to salvage rather than de-stroy houses.

Complaints began to reach the various economic and settlement agencies about needless destruction of housing, especially from low-level officials responsible for abandoned property. Reuven Gordon, the inspector of abandoned property responsible for Isdud, on 14 December complained that

> a week ago [soldiers] from the army began to destroy the buildings . . . Of course, if the army has an order, they carry it out, but I ask, can't they find a [i.e., another] solution . . . [as] these villages near Rehovot can be used to house new immigrants.[103]

From October–November, important officials – including supporters of transfer – began to battle openly against further demolitions. In late November, Weitz records, two of his officials, one of them Nahmani, complained that 'the army continues to destroy villages in the Galilee, which we are interested in [settling]'.[104] Weitz himself, the following month, during a visit to Western Galilee, voiced apparent regret at some of the destruction. The village of Zib had been 'completely levelled and I now wonder if it was good that it was destroyed and would it not have been a greater revenge had we now settled Jews in the village houses'. Weitz reflected that the empty houses were

> good for the settlement of [our Jewish] brothers, who have wandered for generation upon generation, refugees . . . steeped in suffering and sorrow, as they, at last, find a roof over their heads . . . This was [the reason for] our war.[105]

In early November, Finance Minister Kaplan complained about the rumoured destruction of villages in the wake of the IDF conquest of upper central Galilee in Operation Hiram. 'Every possibility of accommodating [immigrants] must be exploited and a general order must be issued to the army not to destroy houses without a reason.' Some 20,000 immigrants, in need of housing, were living in tent camps, Kaplan complained.[106]

During the second half of the war and in the months that followed, the authorities also destroyed parts of three urban sites – the old city of Tiberias and, to a much smaller extent, downtown Jaffa and Haifa.

In January 1950, Shitrit complained: 'Old Tiberias was demolished without Cabinet consent [lo 'al da'at hamemshala].'[107] He was referring to the destruction of the old city of (his native) Tiberias – before the war the old city had housed 2,500 Arabs and 1,000 Jews – that was begun shortly after the start of the First Truce and ended in 1949. In the course of March – early April 1948, almost all the Jews had left the old city; and when Tiberias fell to the Haganah, on 18 April, the whole Arab population, including that of the old city, cleared out. The Haganah then prevented the old city's Jewish inhabitants from returning to their homes, arguing that they were no longer habitable. Golani HQ, apparently together with the Jewish municipal authorities, decided to destroy the old city. Underlying the decision was a desire to renovate the downtown area as well as to facilitate the building of a militarily important highway through the town to link the lower Jordan Valley to the Galilee Panhandle. The IDF, assisted by the municipal engineering department, began the systematic destruction of the old city in July. But protests by former Jewish residents, who had been promised no compensation, and a lack of dynamite led to a suspension of the work at the end of August.[108] Yadin, under pressure from the 'archeological lobby' (including the newly formed Antiquities Department of the Israeli Government), formally halted the demolitions on 28 September.[109] During the following months, IDF Planning Division looked into the matter and decided to continue to destroy the abandoned houses, Jewish and Arab, which were in disrepair. Demolitions were renewed in January 1949. In February, Nahmani, who played a leading role in the operation, jotted down: 'My plan is being implemented despite the interference of the townspeople . . . I had to instruct the sappers to be careful in the destruction of houses near the churches . . .'[110] In March, Ben-Gurion paid a visit and thought the ongoing destruction excessive. Altogether, 477 houses of the old city's 696 were destroyed.

In July 1949, Shitrit raised the matter in Cabinet but was reassured that the Jews who had moved out of the old city, along with a handful of new immigrants, had been given alternative accommodation in abandoned Arab housing in newer parts of town.[111]

Jaffa was occupied by the Haganah in mid-May 1948. In early June, the Cabinet decided to destroy parts of Abu Kabir[112] and a few weeks later, Tel Aviv municipality decided to immediately complete the destruction of Manshiya, which had been badly damaged in the IZL offensive of late April 1948. Manshiya was systematically levelled during July–September.[113] Destruction of houses in the old city of Jaffa (al-Kal'a) began a year later, in mid-September 1949. The plan to demolish 'the whole of the old city' was set in motion by the municipality because 'these buildings, because of their instability, endanger the lives of their occupants or their health because of the rampant conditions'.[114] But the operation immediately encountered opposition from the Custodian for Absentees Property and Antiquities Department. Shmuel Yevin, the department's director, demanded a halt until a committee of experts, including archeologists, would determine what could or should be destroyed.[115] During the following years, as piecemeal destruction went forward, a succession of interdepartmental committees reviewed the demolitions and limited their scope in order to preserve antiquities and to assure housing for new immigrants.[116]

During the rest of 1948, and through 1949 and the early 1950s, the destruction of abandoned sites, usually already partially demolished, continued. By then, the threat of a return had disappeared and the destruction was part of the process of clearing areas and renovating houses for Jewish cultivation or habitation rather than directed against would-be returnees.

The exact chronology and quantification of the amount of destruction of each village in the course of 1948 and during the following years is impossible to trace. Nor is it possible accurately to quantify and distinguish between the amounts of destruction for strictly military reasons, from political motives or for economic reasons, especially as much of the destruction resulted from a combination of reasons and the protagonists involved were variously motivated.[117]

TAKEOVER AND ALLOCATION OF ABANDONED LANDS, 1948–1949

A question related to, but distinct from, the problem of destroying or renovating the villages was the fate of the abandoned lands. Ben-Gurion provided an early clue to his attitude in an address to the Mapai Council on 7 February. He spoke of the need for a substantial Jewish presence in the Jerusalem Corridor. Someone interjected: 'We have no [Jewish-owned] land there.' Ben-Gurion: 'The war will give us the land. The concepts of "ours" and "not ours" are only concepts for peacetime, and during war they lose their meaning.'[118]

In a similar vein, he asked Weitz whether the JNF was ready to buy 'from him' land at P£25 a dunam. Weitz replied: 'If the land is Arab [-owned] and we will receive the deed of property and possession then we will buy. Then he [i.e., Ben-Gurion] laughed and said: Deed of property – no, possession – yes.' The next day, Weitz and Granovsky lunched with Ben-Gurion, who restated his

> plan... Our army will conquer the Negev, will take the land into its hands and will sell it to the JNF at P£ 20–25 per dunam. And there is a source... of millions [of pounds]. Granovsky responded jokingly that we are not living in the Middle Ages and the army does not steal land. After the war the beduins [of the Negev] will return to their place – if they leave at all – and will get [back] their land.[119]

A week later, Ben-Gurion suggested to Weitz that he divest himself of 'conventional notions... In the Negev we will not buy land. We will conquer it. You are forgetting that we are at war.'[120]

Of course, Ben-Gurion was thinking ahead – and not only about the Negev. The White Paper of 1939 had almost completely blocked Jewish land purchases, asphyxiating the kibbutzim and blocking Jewish regional development. In 1947, Jews (i.e., the JNF, the PICA and private landholders) owned some seven per cent (i.e., 1.775 million dunams) of Palestine's total of 26.4 million dunams of land. The partition resolution had earmarked some 55 per cent of Palestine for the Jewish State; most of it was not Jewish owned. But war was war and, if won, as Ben-Gurion saw things, it would solve the State's land problem.

The Jewish takeover of Arab lands began with the *ad hoc*, more or less spontaneous reaping of crops in abandoned fields by settlers in the spring of 1948. The summer crop ripened first in the Negev, and it was here that Jewish harvesting of Arab fields began. On 21 March, in the first documented incident of its kind, kibbutzniks from Kfar Darom, near Gaza, reportedly began reaping wheat adjacent to their own fields. Arab militiamen retaliated by firing on the settlement and British troops intervened, ordering the Arabs to cease firing and the Jews 'to stop reaping the grass'.[121]

Weitz, as chairman of the Negev Committee the de facto administrator of the Negev, linked Jewish harvesting of Arab fields to Jewish claims for war damages. He wrote to Nahum Sarig, OC Negev Brigade, which guarded the Negev settlements and the roads and water pipeline between them, that

> until a [national level] decision was taken regarding the Arab wheat crop in the area – the committee believes that our settlements in the Negev, whose fields were destroyed by their Arab neighbours, will receive compensation by [way of] reaping the fields of the saboteurs to the [same] extent that their own fields were damaged.[122]

Sarig thought otherwise. On 8 May he informed the kibbutzim in his jurisdiction that 'all the crops reaped by the settlements will remain the property of the [Brigade] HQ and the settlements have no right to use them'.

As the summer crop ripened and as the exodus gained momentum, Jewish harvesting of Arab fields spread to other parts of the country. During late April and early May, as requests from settlements and regional councils to harvest abandoned fields poured into the Arab Property Committee, Gwirtz began to organise the cultivation. In coordination with the settlements block committees, he allocated the fields to the settlements. Gwirtz's committee regarded the abandoned crop as State property and sold the right to reap it to farmers and settlements. The embryonic State needed the money as well as the extra grain. The reaping was 'crucial to the war effort', wrote Gwirtz.[123]

The mechanics of the harvest were described at a meeting between local leaders in the Galilee Panhandle and Machnes and Gwirtz on 5 June. The local leaders, who included Emmanuel ('Mano') Friedman of Rosh Pina, reported that

> when the Arabs left... they took all their moveable possessions... All the villages from Metula to the Sea of Galilee... were evacuated. The urgent problem now was the reaping... We [i.e., the Arab Property Committee] demanded that the settlements institute mutual help... Now they are completing [the reaping of] the Jewish fields and in a few days' time [they] will turn to the Arabs' fields... Apart from the Nabi Yusha–al Malikiya–Kadesh Naftali [Qadas] area, there are about 12,000 dunams of wheat and 3,000

dunams of barley. It was agreed that the buyer of the seeds would be the purchasing organisation of the Upper Galilee settlements. The question arose regarding the [war-]damaged settlements, who demanded that they be given compensation from among Arab fields. They were told to ask for compensation from the minister of finance.[124]

Not everywhere were things so well organised. Many settlements, without institutional authorisation or permission, took the initiative and harvested abandoned fields – and avoided payment to the government. In June and July, Gwirtz sent out a spate of angry notes to settlements, demanding that they conclude agreements with his department. 'I heard with bewilderment and sorrow,' he wrote to Kibbutz Ma'ayan Zvi, 'that [your] members . . . are stealing vegetables in the eastern fields of Tantura. Don't your members have a more honourable way to spend their time . . .?'[125] Gwirtz regarded such unauthorised harvesting as part of the widespread looting of Arab property. And, inevitably, disputes broke out between settlements over the right to cultivate specific abandoned fields.[126]

By the beginning of July, the reaping of the summer crop in the abandoned fields was nearing completion. Several objectives were achieved, according to Gwirtz: '(A) We added 6–7,000 tons of grain to the Yishuv's economy. (B) We denied them to those fighting against us. (C) We earned more than I£ 100,000 for the Treasury.'[127]

During May, the organised reaping of the abandoned fields dovetailed with the emergent Haganah strategy of preventing Arabs from reaping and of destroying Arab fields that, for military or logistical reasons, could not be harvested by Jewish farmers. While before May, burning Arab crops was mainly a Haganah means of retaliation for Arab attacks, during May–June the destruction of the fields hardened into a set policy designed to demoralise the villagers, hurt them economically and, perhaps, precipitate their exodus. Certainly, it served to sever the *fellah* physically and psychologically from his land. The prevention of Arab harvesting, especially near the front lines, was seen by the Yishuv's leaders as one element in the battle against a refugee return. The IDF\GS repeatedly ordered the brigades to prevent Arab harvesting with light arms fire. The burning of Arab fields inaccessible to Jewish cultivation and the prevention of Arab harvesting continued around the country through 1948.[128]

Meanwhile, the cultivation by the settlements of the abandoned lands gave rise to possessive urges. For decades, the Mandatory Government and Arab nationalists had blocked Jewish acquisition of Arab lands. The settlements had felt choked for land. The sudden exodus seemed to hold out a solution. The settlements were being asked to temporarily cultivate the abandoned fields; it was but a short step to thinking in terms of permanent possession. Such thinking began to surface as early as late April.

The concept of 'compensation' for war damage offered a morally 'soft' entry point to acquiring abandoned lands. Kibbutz Mishmar Hasharon, in the Coastal Plain, wrote twice to the Arab Property Committee listing the war damage it had suffered at Arab hands (3,400 dunams of wheat and barley burned), requesting compensation. The kibbutz pointedly referred in this connection to 400 dunams of Arab land between Kfar Yona and Ge'ulim and another 80 dunams near Shuweiqa, implying a desire for more than temporary possession.[129]

The line between requesting the right of (temporary) cultivation and requesting permanent possession of a tract of land was almost imperceptibly crossed during May. A request from one settlement rapidly triggered requests from neighbouring settlements, prompted perhaps by a natural instinct to follow suit or fear of being left out by the land-dispensing institutions. Thus, for example, Kibbutz Sdeh Nehemia (Huliyot), in the Hula Valley, objecting to a land-allocation proposal they had seen, wrote to Harzfeld asking, somewhat shamefacedly, for 1,700 dunams of the lands of al 'Abisiyya.[130]

While some settlements in spring 1948 were already inching towards the idea of permanent acquisition, the thrust of individual requests and institutional activity over April–June was *ad hoc* and hand to mouth – to reap the largely abandoned summer crop so that it would not go to waste. This done, the settlements and agricultural institutions began to look to the future. The question of what was to happen to the abandoned lands was inexorably linked to the wider, political question – of a refugee return. A decision against a return would facilitate permanent possession.

The cultivation of the abandoned tracts over the summer built up and reinforced resistance to a refugee return. The farmers grew attached to 'their' new lands. The settlements delighted in the newly won expanses for economic reasons; and they relished the sense of security engendered by the permanent departure of their often belligerent neighbours. The settlers emerged as a powerful interest group in the struggle against a return.

Already in June, settlements began petitioning the State institutions for formal leaseholds on abandoned fields;[131] by late July, they were formally applying for permanent possession. The Tel Mond Settlements Block Committee wrote the Agricultural Centre that it was interested in 'receiving in perpetuity' two tracts of Arab land (near Tulkarm and al Taiyiba). Kibbutz Neve-Yam on the Mediterranean asked for the lands of neighbouring Sarafand; the Arab departure had 'opened up the possibility of a radical solution which once and for all could give us sufficient land for the development of [our] settlement'. Mishmeret, in the Coastal Plain, asked for permanent possession of lands belonging to Tira. Kibbutz 'Ein Harod asked for the lands of neighbouring Qumiya. Kvutzat (Kibbutz) Schiller applied for the lands of Zarnuqa and Mughar, southeast of Rehovot – 'to be transferred into our hands in perpetuity as a supplement to our land allocation'. Kibbutz Genossar, on the shores of the Sea of Galilee, asked for a permanent 'supplement' to their land allocation from neighbouring fields, arguing war damages. The Mapam-affiliated kibbutz pointed out that the lands they coveted were not owned by *fellahin* but by effendis. The veteran *moshava* Nahalal, in the western Jezreel Valley, asked for some 700 dunams of land belonging to the (still inhabited) village of 'Illut. There was a danger, wrote Nahalal, that a new village would at some point be established on this land: 'It seems to us that the time is now ripe to transfer this land to permanent Jewish possession.'[132]

But, as Gwirtz pointed out, there was as yet no legal basis for such transfers.[133] On 30 June, the Provisional Government had issued Emergency Regulations (Cultivation of Abandoned Lands) empowering itself to declare any depopulated conquered Arab area 'abandoned'. The government could then impose any 'existing law' on the area or 'regulate regulations as [it] sees fit', including 'confiscation of property'.[134] But the ordinance, according to legal experts, while covering 'confiscation' of property, failed to relate to leasing. During the following months, the Ministerial Committee for Abandoned Property and the justice and agriculture ministries hammered out the appropriate legal measure, opting in the end for an administrative order rather than legislation. The 'Emergency Regulations Relating to Absentees Property' were published by the government on 12 December, giving the Agriculture Ministry control or possession (*khazaka*) of the lands.[135] The insufficiency of the regulations, and the possible illegality of some of the operations being carried out in their name, drew strong criticism, culminating in the detailed analysis of 18 March 1949 by the Prime Minister's Adviser on Land Affairs, Zalman Lifshitz.[136] Legal deliberations on these matters dragged on until the passage in 1950 of the Absentees Property Law.

But in the summer of 1948, a major quarrel over the fate of the abandoned lands developed between the government and the JNF, which hitherto had been the official purchaser, proprietor and dispenser of almost all land in the Yishuv. It was the JNF that leased agricultural lands to the settlements. The impending 'annexation' of vast tracts of Arab land and its dispensation to settlements by the government promised a radical, indeed revolutionary, change and threatened the JNF's *raison d'être*.

By mid-May, Weitz was certain that the refugees 'would not return' and that this would lead to 'a complete territorial revolution . . . The state was destined to expropriate . . . their land.'[137] But Weitz felt threatened on two fronts: Within the JNF directorate, there was serious opposition in principle to the expropriation of Arab lands. And that expropriation, under whatever legal cover, threatened to leave the JNF, and Weitz, out in the cold. Weitz therefore campaigned to persuade the government to transfer to JNF custodianship or sell outright to the JNF over 300,000 dunams of arable Arab land that the JNF had long sought to purchase. After months of negotiation, the government agreed to JNF control of this land, according it the right to lease the lands to the settlements or, at least, to exercise control over the Agriculture Ministry's leasing arrangements.[138]

Meanwhile, against the backdrop of the hardening government resolve never to allow back the refugees, the Agriculture Ministry, in early August 1948 set up the interdepartmental 'Committee for the Cultivation of the Abandoned Lands' to oversee and coordinate the leasing. The Ministerial Committee for Abandoned Property had decided to put their cultivation on a formal, orderly and relatively long-term basis. The Committee for Cultivation usually dealt with the regional councils and settlement block committees; occasionally, it dealt directly with individual settlements.[139]

From early August 1948, the Agriculture Ministry and the JNF began leasing the abandoned fields to the settlements, for periods of six months to a year. The initiative often came from the authorities; more often, from below, from the settlements themselves. Word of the establishment of the Committee for Cultivation itself generated many leasing requests. Some of the settlements needed, and requested, government funding to cover the purchase of seeds for the sowing of the winter crop.

The regional settlement block committees drew up proposals for the distribution of fields among their settlements. Inevitably, some settlements regarded the proposals as inequitable or illogical. Kibbutz Mishmar Ha'emek, for example, remonstrated with the Jezreel Valley Settlement Block Committee, demanding 'several hundred additional dunams of sorghum', arguing war damages.[140] But, generally, as we have seen, government officials during the summer of 1948 rejected the compensation argument as a basis for claims to Arab land.[141]

Through August–September, the authorities were flooded with leasing requests. Given the novelty of the enterprise and of the new State's bureaucratic machinery, the settlements often did not know which was the right body to turn to; on occasion, neither did the institutions involved.[142]

The *ad hoc*, often spontaneous harvesting of the abandoned crops of spring and early summer of 1948 had within weeks led to feelings – on both the national and local levels – of acquisitiveness. Land long coveted before the war had become land temporarily cultivated. Temporary cultivation led to a desire for permanent possession. The agricultural cycle itself reinforced the drift of political and demographic change. The harvesting of the summer crop left the fields ready for sowing the winter crop, but this meant large-scale investment of funds and workdays – which made sense only if harvesting the winter crop was assured. Such assurance – to the extent that there can be any certainties in wartime – could be vouchsafed only by long-term leasing. (Almost all agricultural land in the pre-1948 Yishuv was leased out by the JNF to the settlements for 49 or 99 years.) The one-year leases of autumn 1948 were a way-station on the road to such long-term leases and to the 'equalisation' of the status of the abandoned lands with pre-1948 JNF lands.

During September and October, the authorities leased tens of thousands of dunams of abandoned lands to settlements and farmers. The leasing arrangements were coordinated with the Office of the Custodian for Abandoned (or Absentees) Property. The leases were for no more than one year because of the fluid political situation and because of the authorities' desire to retain full powers to carry out a definitive distribution of the lands, should they remain in Jewish hands, at a later date. Moreover, the government and the JNF had to consider equitable distribution between existing settlements and the need to set aside land for the establishment of new settlements.

By 10 October, the Agriculture Ministry had formally leased or approved the leasing for cultivation of 320,000 dunams of abandoned land, and ministry Secretary Avraham Hanochi expected that another 80,000 would soon be approved for Jewish cultivation. However, he told Cisling, not all the leased tracts would in fact be cultivated as the settlements lacked manpower and equipment (both were still mobilised by the IDF).[143]

For the most part, the leasing of the abandoned lands, despite the rush, proceeded smoothly, and their cultivation – usually meaning the sowing of the winter crop – began immediately. But in various places, the hasty distribution, coupled with the duplication of functions engendered by the involvement of three leasing bodies (Agriculture Ministry, Custodian and JNF), their local representatives and a myriad of lobbying bodies with semi-official status, such as the Agricultural Centre, the settlement block committees, farmers' associations, etc., led to inequities and complaints.

A major complaint by private and cooperative (*moshava* and *moshav*) farmers was discrimination in favour of the kibbutzim, the collective settlements. For example, Menahem Berger, a farmer from Pardes Hana, complained that he had signed a leasing agreement with a local inspector for abandoned property (attached to the Custodian's office) for 250 dunams of abandoned land belonging to Baqa al Gharbiya. 'After the kibbutzim in the area found out, they activated all the factors [i.e., bodies concerned] to dispossess me...and, under pressure from the Agricultural Centre, the Ministry of Agriculture decided' to deprive Berger of 125 dunams, which were transferred to the kibbutzim 'Ein Shemer, Gan Hashomron and Ma'anit. Berger, according to the complaint, was left with a tract 'in a remote corner'.[144] In the north, the *moshava* Migdal, next to the Sea of Galilee, complained that while 'we have suffered from an acute lack of land for years...we know that [the nearby kibbutzim] Genossar, Hukok and Hahoshlim have received large tracts' of neighbouring abandoned lands, and 'only we have been discriminated against, and have not received one extra foot of land'. After investigation, the Agriculture Ministry agreed to lease the settlement one tract (of unspecified size). In the second round of leasing, in summer–autumn 1949, Migdal shared with Genossar the substantial lands of Ghuweir Abu Shusha.[145]

A similar problem arose a few kilometres to the southwest between the *moshava* Ilaniya (Sejera) and Moshav Sharona. Ilaniya had been besieged and devastated in the early months of the war. It demanded compensation and had been allocated 350 dunams of the lands of Kafr Sabt, 'our destroyers'. But the farmers of Sharona, 'off their own bat, had ploughed and sowed this land . . . displaying very saddening covetousness . . . [and] had taken over the land by force'. Ilaniya demanded ministry intervention. The authorities ordered the Sharona farmers off the land.[146]

Better off than Migdal and Sejera was Kibbutz Tel-Yitzhak, in the Coastal Plain, which had a powerful political backer in the person of Interior Minister Yitzhak Gruenbaum. Gruenbaum was the leader of the General Zionists Party; Tel-Yitzhak was founded by the party's labour organisation, Ha'oved Hatzioni. The Tel Mond Settlement Block Committee had allocated nearby *wakf* lands to a number of neighbouring *moshavim*. The kibbutz appealed to Gruenbaum, who, on 9 November, warned the Agriculture Ministry that a 'land dispute' was in the offing, which might disturb 'the public peace', a matter which fell within his jurisdiction as Minister of Interior. The kibbutz was duly allocated part of the lands of Birket Ramadan.[147]

There were also disputes over lands between kibbutzim, though they usually managed to solve them between themselves, without recourse to adjudication by the authorities. And by and large the kibbutzim did well. For example, the kibbutzim of the Hefer Valley, around Hadera, by December 1948 had received about 15,000 dunams out of the 21,000 dunams of abandoned land in the area (though kibbutzim constituted only a quarter of the 22 settlements among which these lands were distributed).[148]

By the start of 1949, the first wave of leasing was over. By mid-March, some 680,000 dunams had been leased to settlements and farmers in the Galilee, Jezreel Valley, Samaria, Judea and the northern Negev approaches, of which about 280,000 had been sown with winter crops.[149]

However, the leasing mechanism was cumbersome and legally and politically problematic; the confiscation and allocation of Arab-owned lands, some of them in territory earmarked by the UN for Palestinian Arab sovereignty, was probably inconsistent with international law. The December 1948 Absentees Property Regulations cleared away the obstacles to a more efficient arrangement, one which had been on Ben-Gurion's mind since February. Why should the State not sell the land to the JNF, which would lease it out to the settlements? The State would thus earn a large sum of money and be divested of the complex and politically irksome management of the abandoned lands.

It is possible that Ben-Gurion was also affected by the 11 December 1948 passage in the UN General Assembly of Resolution 194, which effectively endorsed the refugees' 'right of return', if they so wished, and, at the same time, established the Palestine Conciliation Commission (PCC), empowered to mediate and facilitate peace between Israel and the Arabs, a settlement that might include a refugee return. The resolution thus threatened, at least in theory, to impose or usher in a refugee return, which may have helped persuade Ben-Gurion to speed up the settlement of the abandoned villages and lands.[150] On 18 December, Ben-Gurion informed Weitz that the government had decided to sell the JNF a million dunams at cheap prices; it would use the money to establish new settlements.[151] Three days later, Ben-Gurion broached the idea more formally over lunch with Weitz, Granovsky, Kaplan and Eshkol: The JNF would buy from the state one million dunams, paying I£10 per dunam on account. If Israel ended up paying the Arab owners more than this in compensation, the JNF would pay the state another I£20 per dunam. The JNF representatives questioned the legality of the deal. Ben-Gurion responded that they had to stop thinking in 'pre-State' terms. The diners reached agreement in principle.[152] On 27 January 1949, Ben-Gurion and Kaplan summarised the terms[153] and, the following day a letter from Ben-Gurion and Kaplan informed Weitz of the implementation of the sale. The JNF proceeded to lease out the land, mostly for new settlements.[154]

By spring and early summer 1949, most of the leases signed the previous year had expired. A new leasing campaign began, adding one million dunams to Jewish agriculture. The ministry pressed the settlements to cultivate more and more land, an expansion made possible by the demobilisation of troops and the influx of immigrants. The ministry anticipated leasing a further one million dunams during the second half of 1949.[155]

Weitz graphically described the Yishuv's sense of an agrarian revolution transforming the country: During the Mandate years, the JNF had purchased land 'crumb by crumb'.

But now, a great change has taken place before our eyes. The spirit of Israel, in a giant thrust, has burst through the obstacles, and has conquered the keys to the land, and the road to fulfillment has been freed from its bonds and its guardians-enemies. Now, only now, the hour has come for making carefully considered [regional] plans . . . The abandoned lands will never return to their absentee owners.[156]

The leases of summer 1949 were generally for one year. The political–geographical status quo had not yet formally congealed. The authorities wanted to retain full control of the lands until their ultimate disposition was agreed upon and until they were politically and legally 'ripe' for leasing for 49 or 99 years. Regional planning and the need to set aside a great deal of land for new settlements were paramount considerations. The leasing correspondence was characterised by fears among the officials that the veteran settlements were becoming overly attached to the lands they had been temporarily given to cultivate.[157]

ESTABLISHMENT OF NEW SETTLEMENTS, 1948–1949

There were 279 Jewish settlements in Palestine on 29 November 1947. Mapai's settlement experts – 'the Committee for Settlement and Irrigation Matters' – met during December and January 1948 to hammer out a plan for agricultural settlement and development in the emergent Jewish State. On 17 February 1948 the committee presented the party's Central Committee with a plan for 1949–1951 based on the purchase, from Arabs, of 320,000 dunams of land and the establishment of 162 new settlements geared to securing the new State's northern borders and developing the arid south. It was assumed that Arabs would sell the JNF land and that the modernisation of agriculture among the Israeli Arabs would enable more Arabs to subsist on less land; everybody would benefit.[158]

As things turned out, the country was engulfed in war, much of the Arabs' land was conquered by the Yishuv, and a giant settlement venture, its start delayed by the hostilities and substantially different from that envisioned by the party stalwarts, was soon under weigh. About 135 new settlements were established between the start of the hostilities in November 1947 and the end of August 1949; 112 of them had gone up by June – 51 in the north (between Ijzim and the Lebanese border), 27 in the south and 34 in the coastal plain and Jerusalem Corridor.[159] Most were established on Arab-owned land and dozens were established on territory earmarked by the UN partition resolution for the Palestine Arab State.

The establishment of new, mainly agricultural, settlements lay at the core of Zionist ideology and the Zionist enterprise: The settlements embodied the drive to free the new Jew from the coils of mercantilism and a lower middle class existence by once again, as 2,000 years ago, mating him to the soil. Working the land was at once the symbol and fulfillment of nationalist Jewish aspirations. But agricultural settlement was not only a matter of ideology. The settlements, mostly kibbutzim, had expanded and deepened the Jewish hold on parts of Palestine, gradually making more of the country 'Jewish', or at least not *Judenrein*. In the successive partition plans, the presence of clusters of settlements determined what would constitute the areas of future Jewish statehood. Settlements ultimately meant sovereignty. Each new settlement or cluster staked out a claim to a new area. Linked to this was their military–strategic value and staying power; over the decades the settlements stymied marauders and irregulars.

Nothing demonstrated the settlements' political import and military significance more than the partition resolution and the subsequent months of hostilities. The partition plan largely followed the pattern of settlement/population distribution around Palestine. Areas with no, or practically no, Jewish settlements (except for the Negev) were automatically assigned to Arab sovereignty. In the first months of the fighting, the areas of Jewish strength and control overlapped the areas of concentrated settlement.

The partition resolution, at once reluctantly and enthusiastically accepted by the Yishuv's leaders, left outside the Jewish state-to-be several clusters of settlements – the Etzion Bloc in the southern West Bank, the settlements in Western Galilee, and several settlements immediately north and east of Jerusalem – and forbade, at least for a transition period, Jewish settlement in the areas earmarked for Arab statehood.

But as the hostilities turned into full-scale war, attitudes in the Yishuv to the partition resolution and settlement changed. The partition plan was a peacetime solution to the Palestine problem; the war undermined its 'sanctity'. As we have seen, already in early February 1948 Ben-Gurion spoke of the need to establish settlements in the Jerusalem Corridor (an Arab-owned and -populated area earmarked for Arab sovereignty).[160] Shkolnik (Eshkol) called for the establishment of settlements, particularly in the Negev, as a response to Arab violence and as a means of reinforcing Jewish territorial claims.[161] Ben-Gurion laid out his demographic-settlement strategy in broad *realpolitik* strokes:

> Security [considerations] require a different [demographic] distribution of the Yishuv . . . We shall move tens of thousands of people northward and southward . . . [and] settle them . . . The Negev must be strengthened with people, arms, fortifications . . .[162]

The settlements, he explained, were a tool in the armed struggle and 'a string of points [i.e., settlements]' should be set up in the Negev, the Beit Shean Valley and in the Galilee. But he acknowledged two problems: The Yishuv lacked funds and manpower, and not everyone understood the vital importance of establishing settlements in the midst of war.[163] But he did. On the brink of the Haganah offensives of April 1948, and to consolidate the expected victories, Ben-Gurion said:

We shall enter the empty villages and settle in them. The war will also bring with it favourable internal changes in the internal constitution of the Yishuv; tens of thousands will move to less populated centres [i.e., districts] – to the Negev, the Galilee and the area of Jerusalem. We shall cure the Jewish body. In peacetime we would not have been able to do this.

Ben-Gurion had outlined two major characteristics of the settlement drive of the following months: Settlement of the abandoned villages and settlement in areas thinly populated by Jews (Western Galilee, Upper Galilee, the Jerusalem Corridor).[164] Indeed, Ben-Gurion argued that real victory was contingent on the settlement drive:

> We will not be able to win the war if we do not, during the war, populate Upper and Lower, Eastern and Western Galilee, the Negev and the Jerusalem area, even if only in an artificial way, in a military way.

This, of course, entailed at least a measure of displacement of the Arab population from these areas.[165]

Preliminary discussions concerning the organisation of these new settlement ventures took place at the end of March.[166] A 'Committee for New Settlement' was established by the HNS. On 7 April, Yadin informed Galili that the committee had agreed on a plan for 34 settlements on sites recommended by Weitz, 27 of them on JNF land and two on Arab-owned land.[167] But the Yishuv's limited resources, ongoing battles (Operation Nahshon and the struggle for Mishmar Ha'emek) and perhaps political considerations prompted a curtailment of the plan. On 12 April, Galili reported that the committee, for now, was proposing '8' settlements: '[in] Beit Mahsir, Saris, Khirbet ad Duweir, Kafr Misr, Khirbet Manshiya, Tantura, Burayr, [and] Mis [in the Galilee Panhandle].'[168] None of these sites was yet in Yishuv hands and some were Arab-owned and still inhabited. The following day, Galili set the ball in motion, asking Weitz to see to the establishment of these settlements 'as soon as possible'.[169]

The Haganah command was itself under pressure from the field commanders. Immediately after hearing of the settlement committee's decision, Allon cabled HGS to 'speed up the establishment' of the outpost at Burayr, 'which will help us in securing out transportation to the Negev'.[170] Galili reassured Allon that Weitz 'has already spoken to Sergei [i.e., Nahum Sarig] in the matter' and the relevant quartermaster had already been appropriately instructed.[171] On the night of 18\19 April, the new outpost – eventually named Kibbutz Brur Hayil – was established near the village of Burayr (which harassed the Jewish construction workers with light weapons fire[172] and was attacked and conquered by the Haganah a month later (see above)). A few hours earlier, on 17 April, the Haganah had occupied the German Templar colonies of Waldheim and Beit Lahm (Galileean Bethlehem); the following day, settlers moved into the latter site, making it the first settlement established during the war.[173] (The lobbying by local commanders for the establishment of settlements in their areas of control was to continue through the war. OC Galilee District, for example, in September pressed Yehoshua Eshel, Mishael Shaham's successor as IDF Settlement Officer, to help establish a settlement at the confluence of the Jordan River and the northern end of the Sea of Galilee, near Tabigha.[174] Commanders also tried to influence the exact siting of the new settlements.[175])

On 22 April, the Haganah command, agreed to provide the manpower and equipment to set up five new settlements, all on Jewish-owned (or non-Arab) land – at Khirbet ad Duweir, Kafr Misr, Ma'lul, Ashrafiya and Daliyat ar Ruha.[176]

Daliyat ar Ruha, southeast of Haifa, was inhabited by Arab tenant farmers. Already in March, Weitz had started pressing the Haganah and local settlers to displace tenant farmers in the area and to set up new settlements. Simultaneously, local kibbutz leaders in the Beit Shean Valley had demanded the establishment of a settlement in their area 'as a means of freeing our land [from Arabs] and preventing the return of beduins who had fled to Transjordan'.[177]

On 28 April, HGS appointed a general staff officer, Mishael Shechter (Shaham) ('Azarya'), to oversee the new settlement ventures.[178] He was to work with the JA Settlement Department, the Agricultural Centre and the JNF. Once they had agreed to establish a new settlement, the kibbutz and *moshav* movements were approached to supply the manpower. The movements began to jockey among themselves for the best sites and established kibbutzim worried that good tracts would go to new settlements.[179] A variety of tensions and subterranean struggles developed.

But Weitz and Harzfeld had other worries. They were depressed by the tardiness of the settlement process. April turned into May and dozens of Arab villages were being abandoned – and nothing much was happening in terms of new settlement. Weitz felt that key players – such as Kaplan – were shirking decisions and a great opportunity for reconfiguring the country was being missed. Weitz himself was under pressure from local lobbyists, like the two Jordan Valley representatives, who on 3 May told him that their area had emptied of Arabs – 'Samakh, al 'Ubeidiya, Samra [on the southern shore of the Sea of Galilee]. Now was the time to act in setting up settlements. They demanded the establishment of settlements at Khirbet ad Duweir and Samra.'[180]

Once the major campaigns of April 1948 against the irregulars and ALA had ended, with Haganah victories, the settlement enterprise began to pick up steam. Weitz and Harzfeld met Ben-Gurion and Shkolnik on 7 May and, again, on 9 May, the second meeting attended by Yadin. The focus remained settlement on Jewish-owned land and within the Jewish State partition borders. Weitz hammered out a new 42-settlement plan, which Harzfeld presented to the Mapai Central Committee: 'There are now 24 sites [all within the partition borders] . . . that we can actually settle tomorrow . . . Apart from the settlement value [of such new settlements], there are also security . . . [considerations] pushing and motivating us.' The other 18 sites, said Harzfeld, were being considered for settlement for security reasons – eight of them (in the Corridor and in Western Galilee, on Arab-owned land) outside the partition borders.[181]

But Shaham was already formulating a far more ambitious plan, covering 82 sites, with the aim of 'consolidating our borders'. His plan was 'based on the partition proposal with appropriate changes to determine borders more comfortable for the defence of the Jewish State, alongside the changes that have occurred as a result of our military activity and the flight of the Arab population . . .' He ruled that 'there was a necessity and unrepeatable opportunity in the near future to determine facts on the ground which any political solution in the future will not be able to ignore. Making these *faits accomplis* will have a major influence in facilitating our military actions and consolidating our conquests.' The war, he stressed, had opened up a new method of acquiring land – not, as previously, by purchase but 'through military conquest'. The aim of the planned settlement enterprise, he wrote, was to 'create borders' according to the partition resolution but also to 'correct them in line with strategic needs' and 'the inclusion [in the State] of settlement blocks left outside the State area'; and 'the opening of a permanent, safe road and . . . corridor to Jerusalem'. Most of the settlements were to be established on Jewish-owned land but settlements were also to be established on German-owned, State and Arab-owned lands.[182]

In planning these settlement ventures, officials were already thinking in terms of the expected mass influx of immigrants. As Haim Gvati, of the Agricultural Centre, put it:

> The establishment of the state and the opening of the gates to large immigration in the not distant future obliges us to plan for agricultural settlement with momentum and with a scope which we never anticipated until now.[183]

But the Yishuv lacked the wherewithal and energy to embark on these giant settlement projects as independence and the pan-Arab invasion loomed.[184] Moreover, as with expulsions and the destruction of villages, criticism of the planned settlement drive quickly surfaced. Mapam's Ya'akov Hazan warned against settling on lands owned by *fellahin* (though he agreed to settlement on effendi-owned land). Other Mapam leaders were more critical. 'Should we [really] use this moment of opportunity when the Arabs have fled in order to create settlement facts?' asked party stalwart Ya'akov Amit.[185]

The advent in mid-June of the First Truce galvanised the settlement lobbyists and executives: At last, some of the Yishuv's resources could be diverted from war-making. Moreover, the ceasefire raised the prospect of Arab infiltration back to the villages; the establishment of settlements would help neutralize the danger. (As described in chapter 5, this was the line used by Weitz with Ben-Gurion, and by the Safad Jewish community notables, Ephraim Vizhensky and other local leaders with anyone who would listen.) Ben-Gurion was in favour. But he stressed that, unlike in the past, this settlement enterprise – which must be carried out quickly and massively – should not be accompanied by publicity: 'The damage [that could be caused by publicity] outweighs the possible gains . . . This time we must maintain silence.'[186]

On 21 June Weitz, Harzfeld, Yehuda Horin, director of the JA Settlement Department, and Ra'anan Weitz, Yosef Weitz's son and the department's secretary, formulated a new, stopgap 19-settlement plan. Only two of the proposed settlements were outside the partition plan state and most were on Jewish-owned land.[187]

Meanwhile, settlements began to go up, perhaps not quite as fast and on as much non-Jewish land as Weitz and Harzfeld would have liked; but things were definitely moving. Less than a handful of settlements had been set up in May – at Waldheim and Shomrat in the north and in Burayr (Brur Hayil) in the south. More than twice as many were founded in June – Hahotrim (at Neuherrdorf on 7 June), Reshafim and Sheluhot (10 June), Nahsholim (at Tantura, 14 June), 'Ein Dor (on Kafr Misr lands, in the Galilee, 14 June), Netzer-Sereni (at Bir Salim, east of Ramle, 20 June), Timurim (on Ma'lul lands, in the Galilee, 21 June) and at Kfar Yavetz (a Coastal Plain *moshav* that was abandoned at the start of the war and resettled on 29 June).[188] Most were established on Jewish-owned land but, from the start, also contained abandoned Arab land. Three of the settlements – at Beit Lahm, Bir Salim and Waldheim – were set up on German-owned lands. Five of the June settlements (and one from May) were settled by Mapam groups. The new settlers, many of them soldiers, were warned, for fear of disease, not to move into the existing houses, not to use the toilets but 'to dig new ones', to use well water only after sterilisation, and to kill stray dogs.[189] The exact location of the new settlements was determined in consultations between the army, the executives of the civilian settlement agencies (principally Yosef Weitz) and local civilian leaders.[190]

Five new settlements went up in July, all on Jewish-owned lands and within the partition borders.[191] But pressure was building for settlement on Arab-owned lands within and beyond the partition lines. The IDF victories in mid-July contributed by adding territory outside the partition borders that, to be retained, it was felt, would quickly have to be settled.[192] On 19 July, Ben-Gurion jotted down in his diary that empty villages would have to be destroyed and that the abandoned sites should be settled.[193] Two days later, Shkolnik called for the establishment 'within one or two days' of four new settlements in the Jerusalem Corridor (before the arrival of UN truce inspectors, who might view new settlements as truce violations). Weitz and Harzfeld agreed, but JNF chairman Granovsky 'doubted the legality of settlement on Arab land'. Weitz also anticipated opposition from Cisling and Bentov.[194]

Two days later, meeting with Ben-Gurion, Weitz asked for decisions in principle whether the Yishuv should establish settlements beyond the partition borders, whether settlements should be set up on Arab-owned lands and, if so, should differentiation be made between the various types of Arab-owned lands (land owned by foreigners, by effendis and by *fellahin*). Ben-Gurion avoided a direct response but advocated the immediate establishment of '10–12' new settlements in the Corridor and in the Lydda–Ramle area (all outside the partition borders). He agreed that 'military victories [should be] translated into political achievement'.[195]

On 28 July, Weitz, Harzfeld and Horin presented Ben-Gurion with a revised plan (new conquests necessitated upgrading old plans), calling for the establishment of 21 settlements mostly on Arab-owned lands in the Corridor, the Lydda–Ramle area and Western Galilee.[196] Weitz explained the plan to the JNF directorate on 16 August. Granovsky, performing a *volte face*, highlighted the plan's 'strategic-political' importance. He stressed that the Yishuv would only expropriate some Arab land, so-called 'surplus' land. The rest, 'with their houses and trees,' would be left untouched and set aside for the *fellahin* and tenant farmers 'for when they return'. Then the Yishuv would pay the returnees for the expropriated land and help the Arabs modernize and shift from 'extensive' to 'intensive' agriculture so that less land would produce more crops.[197]

Mapam's leaders had adopted the 'surplus lands' formula – first worked out and enunciated by Weitz in January[198] – in July. In mid-July, Cisling had spoken of the need for 'development' schemes that would enable the Arabs to return. Haim Kafri, a local Mapam figure from the Hefer Valley, a fortnight later explained that through 'agrarian reform' and 'intensification' of cultivation, it was possible both to set aside tracts from the abandoned lands for the Arabs to return to and to embark, at the same time, on a 'giant' Jewish settlement drive.[199]

The '21-settlement' plan forced Mapam to face the ideological problem of settlement on Arab-owned land and on land earmarked for Arab sovereignty. The party supported continued Jewish–Arab co-existence and the return of the refugees. But the kibbutzim, of both the party's Hashomer Hatza'ir and Ahdut Ha'avodah wings, favoured the establishment of new settlements and the expansion of existing ones as well as expanding Jewish agriculture. On both local and national levels, the establishment of new settlements, both inside and outside the partition borders, was seen as serving security and strategic interests. The 'surplus lands' formula pointed the way to both having one's cake and eating it: Strategic and agricultural-territorial interests could be safeguarded while at the same time lands could be set aside for a possible refugee return. In any case, the Arabs were to be compensated for the lands expropriated. Hence, it was to be 'development for the benefit of both peoples', as Hazan described it; or, 'we must fight for development and against eviction [of Arabs]', said party co-leader Ya'ari. Mapam had found a formula that seemed to marry strategic and economic expediency with principle.[200]

During the first weeks of August, Eshel and Ben-Gurion engineered a major change in the '21-settlement' plan, pressing the need for a block of new settlements in the south.[201] On 20 August, the settlement executives submitted the revised plan: It provided for 32 settlements on JNF, State and Arab-owned lands. They stressed that settlement on Arab land would be only on sites where there was sufficient land both for the new settlement and the sustenance of the original inhabitants, should they return. The 32 were: (Arab) Khulda (eventually Kibbutz Mishmar-David), Khirbet Beit Far (Tal-Shahar), Beit Jiz (Kibbutz Harel), Beit Susin (Taoz), Sar'a (Kibbutz Tzor'a), Beit Mahsir (Beit Meir) and Saris (Shoresh), Kasla (Kesalon) and Khirbet Deir 'Amr (Giv'at Yearim/Eitanim) – in the Jerusalem Corridor; Wilhelma (Bnei Atarot, Mahane Yisrael and Be'erot Yitzhak), al Haditha (Beit Nehemia), Khirbet Zakariya/Jimzu (Gimzo) and Khirbet al Kunaisiya/al Qubab (Mishmar-Ayalon and Kfar Bin-Nun) – in the Lydda-Ramle area; Qazaza-Amuriya (Tirosh), al Kheima (Kibbutz Revadim), Barqusiya-Summeil (Segula and Nahala), Zeita (Kibbutz Gal-on), Hatta (Revaha), Karatiya (Otzem or Komemiut), Jaladiya (Zerah'ya/Shafir) and Bash-shit (Meishar/Asoret/Zekher-Dov/Shdeima/ Kfar Mordechai) – in the northern Negev approaches; al Birwa (Ahihud/Kibbutz Yas'ur), 'Amqa ('Amqa), Khirbet Shifiya ('Ein Ya'akov/Kibbutz Ga'aton), Khirbet Jalil (Goren), I'ribbin, al Bassa (Shlomi) and Sumeiriya (Kibutz Lohamei Hagetaot/Regba) – in Western Galilee; and Nimrin (northwest of Kibbutz Lavi) and 'Eilabun – in eastern Galilee.

Some of the proposed sites, such as 'Eilabun, were not yet in Israeli hands. Almost all were aptly described as 'strategic sites' as they were located along the front lines established in late summer 1948 opposite the Jordanian, Egyptian and Lebanese armies. All but five lay outside the partition borders. The settlements were to be on 120,000 dunams of land, of which 23,000 were Jewish-owned; most were on Arab private land (58,000 dunams) and *wakf* lands. According to Kaplan, the settlements were primarily designed to secure the road to Jerusalem and to enhance Israel's grip on Western Galilee. Shitrit thought the plan involved no 'wrong-doing' as the original landowners were to be compensated. Cisling supported the plan for 'security' reasons and reiterated the 'surplus lands' formula.[202]

The political shift from the new settlement ventures of June–July to those planned in August is clear: The midsummer settlements had been established mainly on Jewish-owned land and within the partition plan borders; those established in August – Kibbutz Sa'ar, north of Nahariya, on 6 August; Be'erot Yitzhak, Bnei Atarot and Mahane Yisrael, on the lands of Wilhelma, on 7–9 August; Kibbutz Yiftah, on the lands of Blida, in the Galilee Panhandle, on 18 August; Nordiya, at Khirbet Beit Lid in the Coastal Plain, on 1 August; Kibbutz Yizra'el, near Zir'in, in the Jezreel Valley, on 20 August; and Udim, in Wadi Faliq south of Netanya, on 29 August[203] – were mostly on non-Jewish-owned land but inside the partition state borders; and those planned in August for the following weeks and months were almost all outside the partition borders and almost completely based on expropriation of Arab- and German-owned land.[204] Most of the 32 settlements fortified Israel's new borders and staked out claims to the newly conquered areas of Western Galilee, the Jerusalem Corridor and the Lydda–Ramle district.

But these planned settlements did not solve the problem of the 'vacuum' in the rear areas created by the exodus. In September, thinking matured regarding a 'second series'. On the 11th, Weitz submitted to Ben-Gurion a proposal for settling '150' empty villages whose lands would be expropriated by the government and sold to the JNF. Ben-Gurion rejected the idea of formal expropriation and sale to the JNF as legally problematic – but did not reject the core of the proposal, to settle the villages.[205] Eshel, too, began to look to the filling of the empty spaces behind the lines, 'to consolidate the access to [the front lines]', and in early October he set out a list of sites that 'had been prepared for settlement' the previous month.[206] But in autumn 1948 the Yishuv lacked the resources to immediately implement even the 32-settlement plan in full. As Eshel put it:

> The weak link in the establishment of new settlements on a very wide scale remains the question of manpower... [Moreover] the difficulties in building fortifications for the new settlements are still not small, especially [due to the lack of] heavy equipment.[207]

During the following months, attitudes against a return hardened. The 'surplus lands' concept provided a smokescreen behind which those who opposed a return – Ben-Gurion, Sharett, Weitz and many in Mapam – were able, without disturbing the national consensus, to implement a settlement policy whose effect (and, in part, purpose) was to bar any possibility of a return. This was understood in Mapam, where Ya'ari acknowledged that if the implementation was in the hands of the anti-return majority, then the 'surplus lands' concept was all so much hot air. 'They want to sweep under the carpet the problem of the return... by [espousing] theories of planning and development', he said.[208] Mapam's posture, or postures, remained clear: Theoretically, the party was troubled and divided; in practice, it was as forward as any in participating in the settlement drive, on Arab-owned lands and within and outside the partition borders. As Kibbutz Artzi member Shlomo Rosen put it: 'We have no choice; we must contribute our share towards the defensive settlement along the borders, despite our doubts about the intentions of those at the helm . . .'[209]

Settlement policy was a barometer of general attitudes towards a return. In mid-November, Kaplan noted that most of the new settlements were to be established on 'Arab[-owned] lands', some on the actual sites of Arab villages. Cisling observed, critically, but with a touch of resignation, that previously the settlements had been slated for establishment near, but not on the site of, the villages, 'for the contingency that the Arabs who would return would be able to [re-]settle there . . . Now there are the problems of [determining] the border and [so we speak of] settling in the Arab village.'[210]

Without doubt, for a time, Mapam's ideological line, bolstered by occasional support from Kaplan and Shitrit, affected settlement policy and temporarily curbed settlement on village sites, theoretically assuring their preservation for possible return and resettlement (though, to be sure, settlement was mainly curtailed during those war-torn months by a lack of resources). But the where and when of settlement was also politically affected in another way, connected with the definition of the state's final frontiers. International talk of Israel ceding the Negev – based on Bernadotte's recommendations – renewed interest in settling the area. From New York, the Israeli representative to the UN, Abba Eban, in late October pressed for 'constructive [settlement] action' – though Allon, then OC Southern Front, according to Ben-Gurion, considered the military situation too 'difficult' to contemplate such endeavours in the immediate future.[211] But IDF conquests at the end of the month and in early November in Operation Hiram in the Galilee and in the appendages to Operation Yoav in the south brought matters to a head, necessitating immediate action to consolidate Israel's hold on the newly acquired territories and finalise the borders. Kaplan said that the army had to free soldiers to settle sites along and below the Lebanese border (such as Tarbikha and Suruh) and along the new front lines in the south (such as Beit Jibrin and Hirbiya).[212] This reflected the thrust of Eshel's memorandum of early November projecting settlement trends during the following months. He wrote of the need for a series of '10–12' settlements along the Lebanese border and '5–6' more in the southwest (the Majdal–Hirbiya area) as well as near crucial Negev road junctions and in the Jerusalem Corridor.[213] The dust of battle had barely settled but the Israeli leadership was determined to incorporate the newly won territories (some outside the partition plan borders) and 'to Judaise the [northern] border area'.[214] In this last sense, the settlement enterprise was merely the obverse side of the border-clearing operations (see below) that denuded the frontier areas of their original Arab inhabitants.

But Eshel's memorandum was merely an *hors d'ouvre*; the *entrée*, a giant settlement plan, comprehending the new border and interior areas, was already in the works. During October – early November Ra'anan and Yosef Weitz, Eshel, and Gvati toured the country. On 17 November they submitted a new 96-settlement plan – 40 in Upper Galilee, 8 in the Jerusalem Corridor, 40 in the Negev and its approaches, and 8 on the Mediterranean coast. Ra'anan Weitz wrote: 'Wherever conditions make it necessary, the new settlement should be established [on the site of] the existing village' – a practice avoided almost completely in the first series of settlements. No mention was made of 'surplus lands'.[215]

But political objections, financial and manpower constraints and specific reservations – as Yadin had regarding seven of the sites at the western end of the Jerusalem Corridor[216] – ate away at the ambitious plan. To begin with, Cisling took offence at the omission of the Agriculture Ministry in the plan's formulation.[217] Then at the Committee of Directorates of the National Institutions on 3 and 10 December, Kaplan and, apparently, Cisling opposed the plan's provision for settlement on the village sites (some of which were still inhabited), and Kaplan reiterated the need to set aside a 'territorial reserve' for returning Arabs. Weitz, annoyed, commented: 'Many of the ministers were worrying more about [re-]settling the Arabs than settling the Jews.' Weitz feared that, if there was a delay in implementation, 'many Arab will manage to infiltrate back to their villages'. Nonetheless, the plan was halved and on 7 December the JNF directorate endorsed the establishment of 41 settlements – and with the stipulation that lands be set aside for returnees. The plan, 'with qualifications', was then approved by the Committee of Directorates[218] and, on 17 December, by the Ministerial Committee for Abandoned Property, which ruled that land should be left for returning Arabs and that settlement on actual village sites should be avoided, unless security considerations dictated otherwise. A strip 8–10 kilometres deep along all the borders was to be exempted from these stipulations.[219]

What occurred during September–December 1948 was a complex dialectic between the demands of existing settlements for more land and the State's need to establish new settlements along its borders and fill the empty interior areas for reasons of immigrant absorption, security and border-determination; the available resources of a society at war; the thrust and parry of party political considerations; criticism and potential criticism of Israeli policies by the outside world; and a variety of contradictory ideological imperatives. But the bottom line, as it were, comes through starkly in a conversation between Yosef Weitz and Ben-Gurion – the ultimate fount of authority and policy – on 18 December. Weitz asked whether, in planning settlements, 'surplus land' should still be set aside for a return. Ben-Gurion replied: 'Not along the borders, and in each village we will take everything, as per our settlement needs. We will not let the Arabs back.'[220] In the end, the months of moralising breast-beating about 'surplus lands' amounted to no more than a hill of beans.

A major factor propelling the settlement enterprise at the end of 1948 and the beginning of 1949 was the flood of new immigrants. Once the initial stock of adequate accommodations in the cities had been filled (see below), the country's leaders looked to the rural hinterland as one vast absorption site. As Ben-Gurion put it in mid-December 1948:

> . . . The problem of housing has become more difficult. I believe, we will have to house immigrants in the Galilee villages, this is necessary because of the lack of [urban] apartments . . . The Galilee settlements can accommodate a large number of immigrants . . . this is not only a matter of solving the housing problem, but this is [important] in itself. There is a phenomenon of largescale infiltration by Arab soldiers, and there is a fear that a new war will erupt . . . There is a need, therefore, to settle a lot of Jews there and to cultivate the lands. There is a lot of water in the Galilee, and there is a need to increase the means of sustenance [i.e., food production] in the country. It is possible to settle tens of thousands of Jews in the Galilee [villages] . . . [This will] greatly change the situation security wise.[221]

Settling immigrants in the empty Galilee villages thus contributed to housing the homeless, increasing the food supply, and barring infiltration and raised obstacles to future Arab attack.

In the course of September–December 1948 and January 1949, the bulk of the 32-settlement plan approved in August was carried out (though the hostilities in October–December caused delays). In September 1948, five new settlements were established – Kibbutz Gazit (Kibbutz Artzi, 10 September) at Tira, in Eastern Galilee; Bariya Bet (Hapoel Hamizrahi, 21 September) at Barriya, southeast of Ramle; Kibbutz Hagoshrim (Kibbutz Me'uhad, 26 September) in the Galilee Panhandle, next to the abandoned village of Khisas; Beit Meir (Hano'ar Hatzioni, 27 September) at Beit Mahsir, in the Corridor; and 'Amelim (Hever Hakvutzot, 30 September) at Abu Shusha, southeast of Ramle. Another five were established in October – Kibbutz Ga'aton (Kibbutz Artzi, 8 October) at Khirbet Shifiya, in Western Galilee; Kesalon (Herut, 11 October) at Kasla, Kibbutz Tzova (Kibbutz Me'uhad, 19 October) at Suba, Kibbutz Eretz-Yisrael Yod-Gimel, Gizo (Kibbutz Artzi, 27 October) at Beit Susin, and Tal-Boqer (later Tal-Shahar) (the Moshav Movement, 27 October), at Khirbet Beit Far, all in the Jerusalem Corridor.

Only one new settlement was added in November, Kibbutz Revadim (Kibbutz Artzi, 20 November) at al Kheima, at the western end of the Corridor. In December, three new settlements were established – Bustan Hagalil (1 December) on the lands of Sumeiriya, in Western Galilee; Kibbutz Misgav-David (later changed to Mishmar-David, Hever Hakvutzot, 7 December) at Khulda, at the western end of the Corridor; and Kibbutz Tzor'a (Kibbutz Me'uhad, 7 December) at Sar'a, in the Jerusalem Corridor.

In January 1949, 11 new settlements were established, some from the list of 32 and others from the new 41-settlement plan – Habonim (later called Beit Ha'emek, Kibbutz Me'uhad, 4 January) at Kuweikat, in Western Galilee; Netiva (Poalei Agudat Yisrael, 4 January) at Mukheizin, south of Rehovot; Kibbutz Yas'ur (Kibbutz Artzi, 6 January) at Birwa, northeast of Haifa; Kfar Rosh Hanikra (Hever Hakvutzot, 6 January) near Bassa, in Western Galilee; Hashahar (later called Sifsufa, Hapoel Hamizrahi, 11 January) at Safsaf, northwest of Safad; Mavki'im (Ha'oved Hatzioni, 12 January) at Barbara, just south of Majdal (Ashkelon), north of the Gaza Strip; Kibbutz Sasa (Kibbutz Artzi, 13 January) at Sa'sa in Upper Galilee; Kibbutz Kabri (Hever Hakvutzot, 18 January) at Kabri in Western Galilee; Kibbutz Lohamei Hageta'ot (Kibbutz Me'uhad, 27 January) on the lands of Sumeiriya in Western Galilee; Beit Ha'arava (later Kibbutz Gesher Haziv, 27 January) at Zib in Western Galilee; and Yosef Kaplan (later Kibbutz Meggido, Kibbutz Artzi, 27 January) at Lajjun, at the western edge of the Jezreel Valley.

The bulk of the new settlements were kibbutzim, established mostly by veteran Israelis, usually from the established kibbutzim or the Palmah. But growingly, settlements, such as at Tarshiha, Bassa and Safsaf in the north and 'Aqir, Yavne (Yibna) and Majdal (Ashkelon) in the south,[222] were established by new immigrants. These new settlements were in fact called 'absorption settlements' (*hityashvuyot klita*) and Eshel deemed them, given their size, 'the principal factor in the Judaisation of whole areas'.[223] Some were cooperative settlements (*moshavim)* and were to be fostered by, and to join, the Moshav Movement, affiliated with Mapai. The movement had traditionally seen itself as the object of discrimination by the settlement institutions and the kibbutz movements, largely affiliates of Mapam. The kibbutz movements criticised the settlement institutions' aim to settle immigrants who had no agricultural expertise or military knowhow in settlements along or not far from the borders.[224] But Weitz and Eshkol were unmoved. At the start of January 1949, the settlement agencies drew up a plan for 69 settlements, to be established by June. 51 were to be set up by demobilised soldiers and veteran settlement groups (*gar'inim*) and 18 by new immigrants. In fact, by June 1949, 54 had been established, 24 by veteran settlement groups, 9 by demobilised soldiers and 24 by new immigrants. In line with the changing demographic realities, the immigrants constituted a larger proportion of the new settlers than originally envisioned. And most of the settlements were wholly or partly established on Arab-owned land. This process was facilitated by the January 1949 general elections; in the subsequent coalition-making, Mapam was dropped from the government and lost control of the Agriculture Ministry.[225] The ministry reverted to Mapai control, under Dov Yosef. By mid-June 1949, Eshel wrote, the whole northern border area had been Judaised through the 'absorption settlements' – *moshavim* and development towns – such as at 'Tarshiha, Suhmata, Deir al Qasi, Tarbikha, Meirun, Sammu'i, Safsaf, Ras al Ahmar'.[226]

In April 1949, the JA Settlement Department began planning a new series of settlements, based almost solely on new 'olim, of whom '200,000' were slated for the agricultural sector, to be settled largely in moshavim, largely on abandoned Arab land. The plan was published on 14 June and was entitled 'Proposal for New Settlements and for the Absorption of 'Olim in the Hityashvut [Agricultural Settlements] – Series B'. 83 settlements were planned, but only about half that number, 42, were actually established by the target date, the end of September. The settlements established in the following months, up to March 1950, were largely immigrant settlements or demobilised soldiers' settlements with a contingent of immigrant families.[227] But, ideological debates aside, few of the settlements were established on actual village sites; the original infrastructure – houses, roads and pavements, waterworks – was deemed inadequate. It proved easier to simply level the villages and build completely new settlements on the site or nearby. By September 1949, settlers had moved into original, Arab housing in only 27 of the 131 settlements established.[228]

ABSORPTION AND SETTLEMENT OF NEW IMMIGRANTS, 1948 – EARLY 1949

Almost all the settlements established during 1948 were founded by pioneering youth groups (gar'inim) drawn from the socialist youth movements of Palestine or their affiliates in the Diaspora; many, such as the new settlements in the Jerusalem Corridor and Kibbutz Yiftah in the Galilee, were settled by groups on active duty as part of, or at the end of, their military service, often from the Palmah brigades. Almost all were founded as – and remained – kibbutzim. Almost invariably, they settled outside the perimeter of abandoned villages (though often on Arab-owned lands).

Most of the settlements established in 1949 were something else altogether. To be sure, several dozen new kibbutzim were founded. But the old Yishuv's human resources for further pioneering settlement had been almost exhausted by the settlement enterprise of 1948, war losses and the needs of the State bureaucracies for high-calibre personnel. The bulk of the settlers of 1949 were 'olim, who poured into the country from May 1948. (One hundred and forty-three thousand 'olim arrived between 14 May 1948 and 9 February 1949;[229] some 700,000 arrived between May 1948 and December 1951.) There was mutuality and reciprocity in the process: The state needed to fill the empty villages; and the immigrants needed a roof over their heads and work – with agriculture, for which not all were qualified, requiring the least investment and offering the most immediate prospects of a return. Ben-Gurion, as we have seen, was also keen on dispersing the (Jewish) population; his experience in London during the Blitz had persuaded him of the vulnerability of heavily populated urban hubs. And, of course, agriculture had to be expanded to feed the rapidly growing population. The bulk of the sites in the 41-settlement plan, like the overwhelming majority of all the sites settled in 1949, were filled with new immigrants – from Europe, survivors of Hitler's death camps, and from the Middle East and North Africa.

To settle the new immigrants – invariably indigent and mostly without Hebrew and, often, without skills – in the abandoned villages and urban neighbourhoods either directly or after a sojourn in transit camps (ma'abarot) seemed natural and appropriate. Few of the 'olim were suited to the ideologically inspired but materially rigorous demands of the collectivist lifestyle of the kibbutz; almost all were settled in cooperative or semi-private farming villages (moshavim) or in towns.

In February 1948, the immigration absorption authorities anticipated that the first wave of immigrants, ending in September–October 1949, would consist of some 150,000. They believed that this would necessitate 'the construction of more than 60,000 rooms'; they were thinking, at this time, of 'construction' rather than conquest and confiscation of Arab housing.[230] But the projections fell short of reality: By autumn 1949, more than 200,000 had arrived. Moreover, the Yishuv's mobilisation of resources and energies for the war effort, the creation of an internal (Jewish) 'refugee' problem during the hostilities, and the destruction of settlements and housing in the fighting further curtailed the authorities' ability to accommodate the immigrant influx. One upshot was the establishment of the transit camps, which housed (routinely in squalor) tens of thousands of immigrants, most of them Jews from Muslim and Eastern European countries. (Ma'abarot existed until the early 1960s though most were dismantled in the mid-1950s.) The other was the abrupt settlement of immigrants in abandoned villages and towns.

The accommodation of immigrants in abandoned housing began in 1948, in the towns rather than the countryside. It began almost immediately with the flight of Arab families from mixed and Arab districts in the mixed cities. Perhaps a first trace of the policy can be found in Ben-Gurion's instructions to the newly appointed Haganah commander in Jerusalem, David Shaltiel, at the end of January 1948. Some Arab neighbourhoods in west Jerusalem had already been abandoned. Ben-Gurion ordered Shaltiel 'to settle Jews in every house in abandoned, half-Arab neighbourhood[s], such as Romema'.[231]

It was Weitz's original Transfer Committee that first proposed that the government adopt, as part of a multi-faceted programme to bar a refugee return, the settlement of immigrants in abandoned Arab housing. In his letter to Weitz of 18 May, Danin recommended 'settling Jews in all the abandoned area'.[232] The committee's proposals in early June included 'the settlement of Jews in a number of villages and cities to prevent a "vacuum"', to which, according to Weitz, Ben-Gurion agreed.[233] That month, during his tours around the country, Weitz instructed or advised local leaders to settle immigrants in empty villages, and pressed the government to endorse this.[234]

The first mass settlement of immigrants in Arab housing occurred in the centre of the country, in Jaffa and Haifa, where the largest – and most modern – concentrations of abandoned houses were to be found. The settlement of 'olim in the empty neighbourhoods was facilitated by their proximity to existing Jewish municipal services and infrastructure. The process began in late May. Foreign Minister Shertok (Sharett) ordered Giora Yoseftal, head of the JA's Absorption Division, to ready housing in Jaffa (and the nearby abandoned village of Salama) for Jewish immigrants.[235]

The road to the settlement of immigrants in the abandoned houses was paved by the preliminary settlement of Jews – mainly from the urban 'seam' neighbourhoods and from endangered rural communities – who had been displaced from their homes by the war. In the Tel Aviv area, an abandoned Arab house in Summeil was the first to be confiscated, on 11 December 1947, by the Tel Aviv Municipality for use as a school and home for Jewish children displaced from their homes by the fighting and initially quartered in a tent encampment near the village.[236] Displaced Jewish families, or 'refugees', moved into Jammasin and Summeil in large numbers toward the end of January 1948, soon after these villages were completely abandoned. The move was initiated by a local Haganah commander who lacked troops to properly garrison the villages and felt that the introduction of Jews would 'close a gap' in Tel Aviv's defences. By the end of February, there were 170–180 families in Jammasin.[237] By mid-April, 200 families had been moved into neighbouring Sheikh Muwannis, whose population had fled a fortnight before.[238] By late May, 135 families had been settled in Salama,[239] conquered by the IDF at the end of April. By February 1949, when Jammasin was incorporated into the Tel Aviv municipal area, the village had more than 1,000 Jewish inhabitants. That month, without JA authorisation though with backing from the Custodian for Absentees Property, immigrant families began to move into Kheiriya,[240] to the east of Tel Aviv. Immigrants began to settle in neighbouring Yazur in November 1948, their number reaching 1,700 by the end of April 1949.[241] That month, settlers began to move into Saqiya (Or-Yehuda) and in June, nearby Kafr 'Ana was also settled'.[242] During September–October 1948, some 4,000 immigrants settled in Yahudiya (Yehud).[243]

Some of the first Jews to move into abandoned housing in Jaffa had themselves been displaced from homes in Jaffa earlier in the fighting.[244]

By early May 1948, there were '18,000' Jewish 'refugees' living in Tel Aviv.[245] At first, Ben-Gurion agreed to Jewish settlement only in part of Jaffa, where some 4,000 Arabs had remained (mostly in the 'Ajami neighbourhood). On 19 May, six days after the Haganah had occupied the town, Ben-Gurion instructed the military to set aside the German Colony neighbourhood, south of Manshiya, for displaced Jews. On 16 June, he told the Cabinet that Jaffa was to become a 'Jewish city' and that Arabs had to be barred from returning to it.[246] By the beginning of July, some 150 immigrant and displaced families had been settled near or in the German Colony. Soldiers' families also began appealing to the authorities for accommodation. Early that month Immigration Minister Moshe Shapira asked Ben-Gurion to open further areas of Jaffa – Jibalya and houses east of King George Boulevard – for Jewish settlement; he expected that the British release of Jewish detainees from the camps in Cyprus would result in a flood of new immigrants. He spoke of readying '2,000 apartments'. Ben-Gurion agreed.[247] Finance Minister Kaplan more generally spoke of 'exploiting the housing possibilities that have opened up as a result of the development of the war. We want now to introduce another 2,000 families to Haifa and 1,000 families to Jaffa.'[248] The requested '2,000 housing units' were immediately set aside by Jaffa's military governor, Yitzhak Chizik, though initially there was a problem with the water supply in some areas.[249] Cabinet Secretary Sharef then put in for '600 [additional] rooms' to house government officials; the Nuz'ha Quarter was earmarked for this purpose. Soldiers and social affairs officers of various IDF units, especially the Kiryati Brigade, also continued to press for housing.[250] By the end of September, '2,400' Jewish families had settled in Jaffa.[251] Meanwhile, during July–September, the IDF and Tel Aviv Municipality completed the destruction of Manshiya, whose housing and infrastructure had been damaged in the April fighting and after.[252]

On 25 July, Chizik resigned. Since May, he had been battling IDF units and civilian agencies, vandals and private looters to protect Jaffa's abandoned property. He may have been unhappy with the settlement of Jews in the abandoned houses,[253] which effectively barred the road to a refugee return. Ben-Gurion appointed lawyer Meir Laniado in his stead.[254] Laniado was ordered 'to evict the [remaining] Arabs from the places where Jews were to be settled'.[255]

Laniado summoned Jaffa's Arab Emergency Committee to inform them of the settlement plans. He argued that there were 'many empty flats in Jaffa ... [and] we need to settle families in them ... From the humane perspective we cannot leave [Jewish] people homeless and leave an unlimited number of flats [in Jaffa] empty.' Laniado asked the notables for their cooperation. The notables asked whether the settlement enterprise would result in 'the transfer of [Arab] families from place to place'. Laniado responded:

To be sure there would be special areas for Jews and [special] areas for Arabs and there would have to be transfers but we would make sure that the transfers would be carried out in line with their advice taking account of the number of persons, the type of family, etc.[256]

The following day the notables returned and 'energetically voiced their opposition to any sort of [Jewish] settlement [in Jaffa]'. Laniado said that the order was irrevocable but assured them that the Arabs moved would receive accommodation at least as good as what they were losing and in any case, as a result of the transfer, would end up living with their own people.[257]

The Israeli officials spent the following fortnight planning the concentration of the remaining Arabs in part of the 'Ajami neighbourhood and the settlement of immigrants in the rest of the town. The concentration of the Arab families was carried out during the second and third weeks of August.[258]

The operation caused waves. Erem, head of the Minority Affairs Ministry's Department for Promotion and Ordering of Relations between the Jews and the Minorities, complained to Shitrit that a barbed wire fence was going to be set up between the Arab area and the surrounding, soon-to-be Jewish, neighbourhoods, creating a 'ghetto, raising among us many awful associations'; and access from the Arab area to the sea was to be barred 'for security reasons'. Erem argued that Israel was 'planting poisonous seeds, unnecessarily and without cause or purpose'.[259]

Shitrit went to Jaffa to discuss the town's affairs with Laniado and the Arab notables. The latter 'complained bitterly' about the concentration and house-transfer plans. The minister responded that it was a security matter but that the transferees would be properly accommodated. 'I succeeded in persuading them', he informed Ben-Gurion. He added that some houses must be held in reserve for (extraordinary) refugees who would be allowed back and that a few 'old people, notables and those favoured' would be allowed to remain in homes outside the concentration area. Shitrit explained that these people had said they would rather die than be moved to live in

company that, though Arab, was undesirable to them, as the vast majority of those who had remained in Jaffa were from among the poor, among whom were Egyptians whose hygienic conditions [i.e., habits] were very poor . . .[260]

By 12 August, about 50 Arab families had been moved to the concentration area or moved about within it, and about 800 Jewish – mostly immigrant – families had been settled in the town, overwhelmingly in Manshiya and the German Colony.[261] Another 150 Arab families were moved into the concentration area during the following days. Many of the families were happy with the transfer as they ended up with better housing, wrote Laniado.[262]

But 11 families that remained outside the concentration area, in the Jewish or soon-to-be Jewish areas, remained a problem. IDF Tel Aviv District demanded that they too be moved. Shitrit (successfully) resisted this, saying that he had given them his word.[263]

The start of massive Jewish settlement was delayed by the need to concentrate the Arabs and by poor infrastructure; many of the houses needed renovation. It was additionally plagued by a three-way struggle over the allocation of the housing – between the Immigration Ministry, representing the needs of the new immigrants; the defence establishment, which sought housing for soldiers' families and military units, and other government agencies; and private individuals, some of them soldiers and soldiers' relatives, who sought to take over flats and houses for personal use or gain. The struggle, which was reproduced in Jerusalem and Haifa, resulted in a great deal of confusion; in Jaffa, for months, the situation bordered on anarchy.

The immigrants' needs were pressing; but the army believed that its needs took precedence and should be met first.[264] It reserved '400' housing units and then another '900' for soldiers and their families and for the use of military units.[265] But during the first week of August, impatient 'olim, uncomfortably quartered in schools and other public buildings, spontaneously began to 'invade' and seize apartments in Jaffa. Soldiers who had been promised housing became worried, but Dov Shafrir, the Custodian for Absentees' Property, insisted that they wait until the flats could be allocated in an orderly fashion, after renovation. By contrast, the Absorption Ministry encouraged 'olim to take over flats, including in areas reserved for soldiers' families, and on 1 September ministry officials organised a veritable 'invasion' by hundreds of 'olim of houses earmarked for troops and their families.[266] Immigrant families received Immigration Ministry permits to take over specific apartments. 'Akiva Persitz, the Defence Ministry official in charge of requisitioning Arab property, saw 'people dragging objects in carts from place to place'.[267] He immediately set in motion, not quite inadvertently, a 'counter-invasion' by soldiers' families in the Jibalya neighbourhood. On 8–10, September Naval and 34th Battalion units moved into the 'Ajami 'ghetto' area and seized apartments; the Second Truce (19 July–15 October) had freed many soldiers from front line duties. Officers feared clashes between the various units.[268] The 8th Brigade also sent in troops – 'with full webbing accompanied by armoured cars and signals [equipment], as is customary in embarking on any military operation' – to guard houses against 'invasion' by immigrants and to safeguard houses for its own soldiers' families. One officer intervened and persuaded the troops to take off their helmets and dispense with the armoured cars.

Troops appear to have intermittently fired into the air to frighten off invasive immigrants and rival units and into nearby cemeteries, damaging 'crosses and tombstones'.[269] Meanwhile, soldiers' families promised housing began to move into apartments, some without proper authorisation. Disputes erupted between these families and soldiers assigned to guard buildings against 'invaders', of whatever ilk. An officer trying to sort things out was beaten by a fellow officer whose family had moved into a flat.[270] Shafrir demanded that Yoseftal order the *'olim* to move out[271] and complained to the Cabinet that the Immigration Ministry had launched the settlement drive 'without our knowledge and behind our back'.[272]

The upshot was that IDF CGS Dori ordered an internal investigation of the military's part in the affair while government and JA officials tried to hammer out an equitable shareout of the real estate. IDF Adjutant General Hoter-Ishai presented his findings on 15 and 17 September, in two reports.[273] But even before these were in, Ben-Gurion condemned the troops' 'running wild [*hishtolelut*] and abuse of weapons and power' and called for 'severe' and 'maximal punishment (by which I mean a reduction in rank to private and imprisonment)' of the culprits.[274] Meanwhile, on 12 September the officials agreed to turn back the clock to the pre-'invasion' share-out arrangements.[275] The army was ordered to clear Jaffa, quarter by quarter, of all the 'invaders' and 'counter-invaders' and then to redistribute and resettle the soldiers, immigrants and officials in line with the agreed quotas.[276] Dori, for his part, ordered the trial and punishment of a number of officers, including the deputy OC of the 8th Brigade's 89th Battalion.[277]

But while some sort of order was restored, 'invasions' by troops, soldiers' families and immigrants continued for months; neither Ben-Gurion's anger, nor investigations, nor interdepartmental agreements seemed to help. On 15 September, for example, troops of the 89th Battalion took over a house in Jibalya and forcibly evicted a group of young women affiliated to the Mizrahi Party. At the same time, a group of Air Force soldiers ejected 41st Battalion troops from another house.[278] A week later, Ben-Gurion again met officials to discuss ways to curb the 'invasions'.[279] But nothing helped. An IDF investigation the following month found that hundreds of flats earmarked for soldiers were still occupied by immigrants and flats earmarked for officials were still occupied by the army. The CGS ordered that the situation be rectified,[280] and Assa'el Ben-David, the chief IDF social and cultural affairs officer, managed to free several dozen apartments for officials but in the meantime, he discovered, more apartments were invaded by the families of soldiers and immigrants. On 19 October Ben-David organised a mixed police and IDF force to evict squatters from certain buildings in the Nuz'ha Quarter. The squatters resisted and force 'and patience' had to be exercised. Three out of four targeted houses were eventually cleared. But Ben-David then discovered that Jaffa's military governor, aided by police, had evicted soldiers' families from other homes that he,

Ben-David, had only recently assigned them. The removal by the IDF of roadblocks at the entrances to Jaffa instituted in September hadn't helped. 'The multiplicity of authorities makes difficult, indeed, renders impossible, accomplishing the mission', Ben-David concluded.[281] This was also Sharef's judgement:

> The time has come to conclude and inform you of our complete failure in solving the problem of housing for government officials and offices in Jaffa. I believe that it is no longer possible to fix matters and I must inform the government officials (some 400 families) that they have no prospect of receiving a flat . . .

He charged that neither the immigration absorption agencies nor the army had fulfilled their promises. 'I have no [further] proposals, as everything I could propose I already have, without result', he wrote the Cabinet and the CGS.[282] On 8 December Ben-Gurion again ordered the IDF to stop the soldiers' 'invasions' of flats and houses in the abandoned areas.[283] Yet two days later a group of soldiers from the 92nd Battalion, 'armed with machine-guns, rifles and submachine-guns' and with authorisation from Ben-David, took over a house, 'to house their families', inside a compound controlled by the 141st Battalion.[284] The constant pressure to obtain and free houses and rooms for various uses and agencies also resulted in the at least temporary eviction of additional Arabs resident outside the 'ghetto'.[285]

Jaffa was thus anarchically settled by 'invasions and counter-invasions' by immigrants, soldiers and others, summarised a disgusted Shafrir in March 1949. Occasionally, 'invaders' roughly evicted Arabs and at least some houses went to veteran Israelis with the right connections.[286] In April–August 1950, Jaffa ceased to exist as a separate municipal entity and Tel Aviv officially changed its name to 'Tel Aviv-Jaffa'.[287]

As with Jaffa, the concentration of Haifa's remaining 4,000 Arabs in the Wadi Nisnas neighbourhood and on Abbas Street in the beginning of July facilitated the settlement of 'olim in the town's empty neighbourhoods.[288] Between 1 January and 1 August 1948, 51,000 'olim had entered the country. The hostilities had 'greatly facilitated' their absorption, said Finance Minister Kaplan, as 'because of the war, thousands of flats had come into our hands. 12,000 people, and some say 13,000, had moved into Haifa alone since [the town's] liberation . . . Haifa [authorities] demand another 20,000 . . .'[289] The absorption of the immigrants in Haifa was more orderly than in Jaffa though here, too, there were periodic 'invasions' by military personnel – as occurred on 7 April 1949, when soldiers of the 7th and 9th brigades took over about a dozen apparently empty flats in the upmarket Abbas Street with the aim of housing in them handicapped ex-soldiers from the 7th, 9th and 11th brigades. The initiative for the 'operation' had come from David Adler, chairman of the Haifa District Handicapped Committee, who had approached the brigades and asked for help in procuring housing for some 150 handicapped veterans who were living in hotels and could no longer pay their bills. The military police swiftly intervened and ordered the troops out – but many of the handicapped refused to leave and remained.[290]

In the towns as in the countryside, settlement followed relatively hard on the heels of IDF conquest. Less than six weeks after the capture of Ramle, OC Military Government, General Avner, asked Ben-Gurion about settling new immigrants in the town. He complained that Shertok and Kaplan were opposed for political reasons.[291] The ministers' objections prevailed for a time, bolstered apparently by the IDF's reluctance to have masses of 'olim settle so near the front. But the needs of the new State were inexorable. Yoseftal predicted a housing crisis. He asked that the IDF 'free' housing and estimated that there was accommodation for 2,000 families in Ramle and Lydda.[292] On 5 November the Ministerial Committee for Abandoned Property at last discussed Ramle, as

> the country is in a bad way in connection with the continuing arrival of new immigrants. Every possibility of accommodation should be exploited and the army should be given a general instruction not to destroy houses without cause . . . There are 20,000 in ma'abarot,

said Kaplan.[293] On 14 November some 300 'olim moved into Ramle's empty houses,[294] and by March 1950, there were 8,600 Jews in the town.[295] In December 1948, Ben-Gurion removed the ban on settlement in Lydda, and 'olim began to move in at the end of the month.[296] By March 1950, the town had 8,400 Jewish settlers.[297]

Acre, where some 5,000 Arabs had remained, was settled more quickly. At first, the local military commander – who was worried about Arab–Jewish relations – blocked the move, and Shitrit, wary of a repetition in Acre of what had happened in Jaffa, counselled prudence.[298] Indeed, at one point in July, the army had recommended the transfer of the town's remaining Arabs to Jaffa – but the ministers had rejected the idea.[299] The inter-ethnic law and order problem was sorted out and on 18 September, Shitrit, Avner, Shafrir and Ben-Gurion decided to go ahead.[300] The first batch of immigrants were settled on 6 October 1948.[301] During October, 'more than 100' immigrant families settled in the town. The military governor, Major Rehav'am 'Amir, insisted that no more be sent so long as adequate police and other services were not in place. 'The delays in the opening of a medical clinic, the operation of sanitation workers in the streets, and the opening of a school and kindergarten are extremely worrying', he wrote.[302] Nevertheless, by 22 November Acre had 2,000 Jews.[303] But all was not well. Settlers frequently broke into the homes and offices of 71st Battalion troops stationed in the town and stole furniture and clothing. And, as in Jaffa, the immigrants forcibly 'invaded' homes and gardens. The battalion's OC threatened to 'take independent measures' if the problem was not dealt with.[304] By the end April 1950, Acre had 4,200 Jews.[305]

The decision to settle immigrants in Safad's abandoned Arab quarters was in part prompted by petitions during June–July 1948 by the local community elders, who feared an Arab return.[306] But the town lacked adequate infrastructure and employment possibilities and the settlement was delayed. But by early November, it was reported that about 1,000 immigrants had moved in. By March 1950, more than 3,000 had settled in Safad.[307]

On 5 December 1948, the Ministerial Committee for Abandoned Property approved the settlement of Beersheba, conquered on 21 October, but the army resisted.[308] Ben-Gurion intervened, ordering Southern Front headquarters to free 'half the town'. But infrastructure problems delayed implementation. The first 17 immigrant families settled in Beersheba on 23 February 1949. Plans provided for some 3,000 settlers by the end of the year.[309]

On 31 December 1948, the Ministerial Committee for Abandoned Property decided to settle new immigrants in the (still) Arab-populated town of Majdal (Ashkelon), conquered in early November. Avner ruled that a police force had first to be set up and the JA had first to provide municipal and social services. The local military governor would then control the pace of settlement.[310] The first male settlers moved in in the first half of March and whole families during the following fortnight.[311] By the end of April 1949, the town had 300 Jewish settlers (alongside the remaining 2,500 Arabs).[312] In July, the authorities began settling demobilised soldiers and their families. In December, the authorities constricted the Arab 'ghetto' area in order to free more housing for soldiers' families. By January 1950, Majdal had 3,000 Jewish inhabitants, 2,000 of them new immigrants.[313] The transfer in 1950 of the remaining Arab population to the Gaza Strip (and, in small numbers, to Lydda and Ramle) freed further housing for Jewish settlement (see below).

Beisan was first settled with immigrants at the end of April 1949. By April 1950, Beit Shean (as it was called once again) had 2,000 settlers.[314]

In Jerusalem, Jewish families displaced from their homes by the fighting moved into abandoned Arab houses already in January 1948. One HIS report described the movement into 'Mamoud's house by many Jewish residents' as 'apparently the beginning of Jewish settlement activity in [the] Romema [neighbourhood]'.[315] Curiously, initially, the local Jewish neighbourhood committee (in and around Romema) reached agreement with some departing Arab home-owners to pay them rent. The committee then moved in Jewish families who had fled from the seam neighbourhood of Nahalat Yitzhak.[316] But displaced Jews were not always happy to be moved into Arab housing, which was sometimes inferior or too near the front line. At the end of January 1948, for example, the authorities had forcibly to move 35 families displaced from Nahalat Yitzhak and Beit Yisrael into the just-abandoned Arab houses of Sheikh Badr.[317] In February–March, Jewish 'refugees' from front-line Yemin Moshe were resettled in empty houses in Lifta. By the beginning of May, some 5,000 Jewish inhabitants had left Jerusalem altogether and another 3,400 were internally displaced; some of these, at least temporarily, were resettled in empty Arab housing; others moved into empty Arab housing without authorisation, sometimes receiving 'retroactive' permission.[318] During May–June, Qatamon, just captured by the Haganah, was settled with 1,400 Jews expelled by the Arab Legion from the Jewish Quarter of the Old City, which had fallen to the Jordanians on 28 May. The neighbourhood was also filled (temporarily) with women and children who had been evacuated from front-line kibbutzim in the Jerusalem Corridor; Lifta was settled with Jewish 'refugees' from the settlement of 'Atarot, which had also fallen to the Jordanians.[319] The following months, especially during summer and autumn 1948, were characterised by 'invasions' of empty Arab houses by long-suffering displaced Jerusalem Jews and soldiers' families, especially in Qatamon, which the authorities proved unable to halt and, usually retroactively resigned themselves to. Here, as in Jaffa, the 'invasions' were often sanctioned, if not initiated, by IDF social affairs officers trying to solve the problem of housing homeless soldiers' families.[320]

The massive settlement of 'olim in the abandoned Arab districts of Jerusalem began about 2–3 months after it had begun in Jaffa and Haifa, probably due to a mix of political, security and economic considerations. The city was split roughly in half, with the IDF holding the western side and the Jordanians holding the eastern districts (with small Egyptian contingents on the southern edge of the city). In the partition plan, Jerusalem had been designated an international enclave and for various reasons, some of them religious, there was acute sensitivity among the western powers and in the Muslim world to what happened in the city. As well, the city remained a war zone, with the two sides occasionally trading shells and bullets until November. And the fighting had undermined the city's in any case weak economy, making it less able to sustain new immigrants. On the other hand, the Israeli government had an interest in settling as many Jews as possible in the abandoned districts both to 'Judaise' them and to assure that Israel retained them in any settlement. The signing of the Israeli–Jordanian ceasefire agreement on 30 November 1948 changed matters to some degree; it made available for settlement a great many abandoned houses in hitherto unsafe front line areas.[321]

The authorities began settling 'olim in Jerusalem's abandoned Arab areas – especially in the German Colony – in September.[322] In December 1948, some 150 families were settled in 'Ein Karim, an

Arab village to the west of the city which was later incorporated in the municipal area.[323] By the end of March 1949, some 4,200 *'olim* had been settled in the city, mainly in the German Colony, Bak'a and 'Ein Karim.[324]

Frontier demarcation considerations played a role in Israeli decision-making concerning settlement in Jerusalem's neighbourhoods. In mid-March 1949, the military governor of Jewish Jerusalem, Colonel Moshe Dayan, demanded that 'civilians' be settled immediately in the southern neighbourhoods of Talpiyot, Ramat Rachel (a war-ravaged kibbutz, on the southern edge of the city) and Abu Tor because if a United Nations-chaired mixed armistice commission team visited the neighbourhoods 'and finds [them] empty of civilians, there will be United Nations pressure [on us] to evacuate the area'.[325]

By the end of May, it appears that all of west Jerusalem's former Arab neighbourhoods had been at least partially settled by Jews, most of them *'olim.* An Interior Ministry official reported that the Musrara (later Morasha) neighbourhood was being settled with *'olim* from Muslim countries, and that Abu Tor also had to be settled 'if Israel wanted to hold onto it'.[326]

During the summer of 1949, several hundred *'olim* from Eastern Europe were settled in Deir Yassin, despite a protest to Ben-Gurion by several leading intellectuals, including Martin Buber and 'Akiva Ernst Simon. They wrote that while aware of the suffering of the *'olim* and of their need for housing, they did not think that Deir Yassin was

> the appropriate place . . . The Deir Yassin episode is a black stain on the honour of the Jewish people . . . It is better for the time being to leave the land of Deir Yassin uncultivated and the houses of Deir Yassin unoccupied, rather than to carry out an action whose symbolic importance vastly outweighs its practical benefit. The settlement of Deir Yassin, if carried out a mere year after the crime, and within the regular settlement framework, will constitute something like . . . approbation of the slaughter.

The intellectuals asked that the village be left empty and desolate, as 'a terrible and tragic symbol . . . and a warning sign to our people that no practical or military necessity will ever justify such terrible murders from which the nation does not want to benefit'. Ben-Gurion failed to reply, despite reminders, and 'Givat Shaul Bet', as it came to be called, was duly established on the site, with several Cabinet ministers, the two chief rabbis and Jerusalem's mayor attending the dedication ceremony.[327]

The settlement of *'olim* in the abandoned villages began in the last months of 1948, as the momentum of settlement by pioneers began to run out and after most of the housing potential of the towns was exhausted. An initial recommendation to settle *'olim* in the villages (usually in the existing Arab houses) was submitted to the Military

Government Committee on 23 September 1948. General Avner named as suitable the villages of 'Aqir, Sarafand al Kharab, Beit Dajan, Yahudiya, Zarnuqa, Kafr 'Ana and Abu Kishk (all in the Tel Aviv–Rehovot–Ramle triangle).[328]

No less pressing than the new immigrants' need for housing was the State's need to fill the newly conquered territories, lest the absence of a civilian population undermine Israel's territorial claims in future negotiations. Weitz proposed immediately settling 36 abandoned sites in the Galilee: 'This emptiness, besides leaving a stamp of desolation [which can be attributed to] the Israeli army, serves as a weak point for the return of the Arab refugees ... by way of infiltration.' Natural erosion was quickly destroying the villages – while Israel faced the problem of accommodating tens of thousands of 'olim.[329] On 23 December, Ben-Gurion instructed immigration absorption chief Yoseftal to send 'ten thousand 'olim' to the Galilee villages.[330]

But there was political opposition. Mapam's views were expressed clearly by Pinhas Ger, a member of Kibbutz Ma'anit: 'As Zionists, we never thought of settling a Jewish 'oleh in the house of the expelled Arab. It is the right of the Arabs who were expelled or fled to return to the Land of Israel. And the [problem of] Jewish 'aliya should not be solved at the expense of Arab housing.'[331] When Avner proposed that 'olim be settled in the northern border villages of Bassa, Deir al Qasi and Tarshiha (some 700 Arabs still lived in the latter site), Cisling asked that the decision be postponed. The militarily useful settlement of pioneers, who knew how to use weapons, was one thing; putting in untrained 'olim was quite another.[332] General Avner complained to Ben-Gurion about Cisling's stand and tactics and the Prime Minister brought the matter for decision to the Cabinet on 9 January 1949. The prime minister said the immigrant housing situation was 'catastrophic'. A majority, supporting Ben-Gurion, voted 'to encourage introducing 'olim into all the abandoned villages in the Galilee'.[333]

Cisling's objection to the settlement of 'olim in the Galilee villages may not have been motivated solely by political considerations. Perhaps, it was also an expression of the growing antagonism of the two Mapam-affiliated kibbutz associations to the settlement of 'olim in the countryside. The kibbutzim had no problem with the settlement of 'olim in the cities or with absorbing a small proportion of them in the kibbutzim themselves. But massive settlement of the 'olim on the land in moshavim posed a threat to the kibbutz movements' domination of agriculture and to the collectives' standing in the Yishuv. The growth of the moshavim could not but proportionally reduce the national and political influence of the kibbutzim and might well – if the moshavim proved successful – threaten the kibbutzim ideologically as well. Furthermore, land allocated to moshavim in the end meant less land for kibbutzim.

Weitz, who emerged as a powerful proponent of the agricultural settlement of *'olim,* marvelled at the kibbutzniks' inability to see that sending the *'olim* to the abandoned villages 'is the basic way to turn them into farmers'. The kibbutzniks, felt Weitz, feared that the *'olim* would adopt the *moshav* form of settlement. 'But is collectivism *[kibbutziut]* the goal or the means [to consolidate] the State [of Israel]?' he asked. He suggested that the *kibbutzim* also opposed the new *'olim* settlements out of fear that kibbutzniks would leave their collectives and move to *moshavim.* In any case, there was no other way to quickly fill the abandoned villages, he believed.[334]

The usually subterranean antagonism between *kibbutzim* and the *'olim* settlements occasionally surfaced in open violence – usually over land. Kibbutz 'Amelim-Gezer, at the western end of the Jerusalem Corridor, for example, in July 1949 complained that the settlers at al Qubab were preventing them from ploughing lands they had received from the Agriculture Ministry.[335]

A further problem arose out of some *'olim'*s lack of motivation. Unskilled in agriculture and preferring the seeming comforts of town, some *'olim* simply abandoned newly settled sites, as occurred at al Barriya (settled in September 1948), near Ramle.[336] In general, however, the *'olim* settlements took root, if only because life in a transit camp was the only alternative for most.

In April 1949, Yoseftal reported that of '190,000' *'olim* who had arrived since the establishment of the State, 110,000 had been settled in abandoned Arab houses. Most had been settled in the former Arab neighbourhoods of Jaffa and the mixed towns; 16,000 had been settled in towns (Ramle, Lydda, Acre); and 18,800 in the abandoned villages.[337] By May, the number of *'olim* settled in abandoned villages had risen to 25,000.[338] By 27 May, new *'olim* had been settled in 21 abandoned villages – including Masmiya al Kabira, 'Aqir, Zarnuqa, Yibna and Qatra, in the south; Ijzim and 'Ein Hawd, in the Coastal Plain; Tarshiha, Safsaf and Tarbikha in the Galilee; and Deir Tarif, near Lydda. Another six villages, including Deir Yassin, were slated for settlement in the following days.[339]

The first immigrants moved into 'Aqir in early December 1948; by April their number had reached 1,000.[340] Neighbouring Yibna (Yavne) was first settled at the end of December 1948; by January 1950, its population numbered 1,500.[341] Tira, south of Haifa, was first settled with immigrants in February 1949; by April it contained 2,000 settlers.[342] Khalisa was settled by a small group of immigrants (from Yemen) in August 1949. Initially designed by the JA Settlement Department as an agricultural settlement, it eventually became a development town (Kiryat Shmona).[343] Over the following months, with the towns saturated, dozens more abandoned villages were similarly filled with *'olim* as the new state struggled desperately to house the influx of immigrants.

ENDNOTES

1. For descriptions of British house demolitions, see Eyal, *Arab Revolt*, 109–13, et al.
2. STH III, part 2, 1333–36.
3. Messer, *Plans*, 104.
4. Messer, *Plans*, 118–20.
5. Unsigned list of Haganah operations, entries for 9 and 11 Dec. 1947, IDFA 6127\49\\93.
6. 'Pinhas' to 'Ali', 'Report on the Khisas Operation', 22 Dec. 1947, and entry for 18 Dec. 1947, Palmah Third Battalion logbook, both in IDFA 922\75\\ 1224.
7. '01227' to HIS-AD, 'Reprisal Against the Village of Qazaza', 22 Dec. 1947, IDFA 481\49\\62.
8. Unsigned, 'Our Reprisal Operations', undated but from January 1948, IDFA 481\49\\23.
9. HGS\Operations, 'Report on Operations', undated but from mid-January 1948, IDFA 481\49\\23.
10. HGS\Operations to OCs brigades, city HQs, and Palmah, 'Instructions For Planning Operations', 18 Jan. 1948, IDFA 1196\52\\1.
11. 'Uri' to sub-commanders, 'Operational Order', 20 Jan. 1948, IDFA 1041\ 49\\9; and '00007' to HIS-AD, 'Reprisal Against Abu Suwayrih', 26 Jan. 1948, HA 105\32.
12. Battalion OC to platoons, etc., 'Operational Order', undated but from early Jan. 1948, and unsigned, 'Report on Salama Operation', 3 Jan. 1948, both in IDFA 922\75\\1213.
13. Page ('5') from Palmah HQ logbook, entry for 17 Jan. 1948, IDFA 661\ 69\\36.
14. 'Hashmonai' to Shadmi, 'Information Wrap-up', 20 Jan. 1948, IDFA 500\ 48\\60.
15. Palmah HQ to HGS, 'Daily Report', 13 Mar. 1948, IDFA 922\75\\1066; and Palmah HQ to HGS, 'Daily Report', 17 Mar. 1948, HA 105\62.
16. Palmah HQ to HGS, 'Daily Report', 28 Mar. 1948, IDFA 922\75\\1066.
17. Palmah HQ to HGS, 'Daily Report', 24 Mar. 1948, IDFA 922\75\\1214.
18. 'Information' (Zeevi) to Galili, 16 Feb. 1948, IDFA 481\49\\35.
19. Entry for 19 Feb. 1948, DBG-YH I, 253–55.
20. HGS\Operations, 'Plan D – 10 March 1948', IDFA 922\75\\595.
21. Unsigned, 'Report on the Conquest of Qaluniya', 11 Apr. 1948, IDFA 922\ 75\\1233; Palmah HQ to HGS, 'Daily Report', 20 Apr. 1948, IDFA 922\75\\ 1066; Palmah HQ to HGS, 'Daily Report', 21 Apr. 1948, IDFA 922\75\\1214; entry for 21 Apr. 1948, DBG-YH I, 361; entry for 20 Apr. 1948, 6th Airborne Division Logbook, PRO WO 275–54; D Company to First Battalion, 'Report – Shu'fat', 26 Apr. 1948, KMA-PA 130–76; Palmah HQ to HGS, 'Daily Report', 23 Apr. 1948, KMA-PA 109 gimel-155; entry for 23 Apr. 1948, DBG-YH I, 366; entry for 11 May 1948, Harel Brigade logbook, KMA-PA 131–13; and 'Benny' to 'Yerubaal', 'Harel Report up to 110745', 11 May 1948, IDFA 6127\49\\93.
22. Rather, the order spoke of setting up ambushes outside villages to prevent irregulars from approaching the Tel Aviv-Jerusalem road and of 'conquering'

'the Deir Mukheizin-Khulda-Saidun triangle' (see Nahshon Forces HQ, 'Operational Orders', ? [4 or 5] Apr. 1948, IDFA 47\53\\2).

23. Operation Nahshon HQ, 'Operational Orders', 10 Apr. 1948, IDFA 922\75\\1233.

24. Operation Nahshon HQ, 'Framework for the Forces' Operations (Continuation of Operation Nahshon)', 14 Apr. 1948, IDFA 66\69\\45.

25. Nahshon HQ to Battalions 1,2,3, etc., 14 Apr. 1948, IDFA 661\69\\\45.

26. Nahshon HQ to Battalion 1, 'Operational Order', 15 Apr. 1948, IDFA 661\69\\45; Nahshon Forces HQ to Battalion 2, 'Operational Orders', 15 Apr. 1948, IDFA 236\53\\1; Nahshon Forces HQ to Battalion ?, 'Operational Order', 15 Apr. 1948, IDFA 661\69\\45; and Nahshon Forces HQ to Battalion 52, 'Summary of Conversation between Nahshon\Operations and Yourself', 15 Apr. 1948, IDFA 236\53\\1.

27. Palmah HQ, 'Daily Report', 23 Apr. 1948, IDFA 922\75\\1214.

28. Golani to Carmeli, 9 Apr. 1948, IDFA 128\51\\50.

29. Palmah HQ to HGS, 'Daily Report', 10 Apr. 1948, IDFA 922\75\\1066.

30. Palmah HQ to HGS, 'Daily Report', 12 Apr. 1048, IDFA 922\75\\1214.

31. Palmah HQ to HGS, 'Daily Report', 15 Apr. 1948, IDFA 922\75\\1066.

32. 'CID Summary of Events (Appendix B, Haifa Area)' 15 Apr. 1948, PRO CO 537–3856; Yiftah Logbook, KMA-PA 120–1 aleph; and entry for 17 Apr. 1948, 6th Airborne Division Logbook, PRO WO 275–54.

33. Palmah HQ to HGS, 16 Apr. 1948, IDFA 922\75\\1066.

34. Palmah HQ to HGS, 'Daily Report', 19 Apr. 1948, IDFA 922\75\\1066

35. Palmah HQ to 'Hagai', 19 Apr. 1948, KMA-PA 107–186.

36. Yiftah logbook, as quoted in *Beineinu*, No. 13, 9 May 1948, KMA 2 aleph\20.

37. Company D to 11th Battalion HQ, 'Report on the Zawiya Operation 19.5.48', IDFA 1012\49\\102.

38. Yiftah to Palmah HQ, 24 May 1948, IDFA 922\75\\1216.

39. 'Zamiri', 'Report on my Visit to Northern Front', 14 May 1948, IDFA 2384\50\\9.

40. Carmeli to HGS\Operations, 15 May 1948, IDFA 957\51\\61.

41. Carmeli HQ to 'Eitan', 'Tzidoni', 'Hadari', etc., 'Operation Ben-'Ami – Part 2', 19 May 1948, IDFA 6680\49\\5.

42. Untitled handwritten notes, unsigned but by Cohen, 6 May 1948, HHA-ACP 10.95.10 (4).

43. Cohen, 'Our Arab Policy in the Midst of the War', 10 May 1948, HHA-ACP 10.95.10 (4).

44. Morris, 'Yosef Weitz . . .'.

45. Danin to Weitz, 18 May 1948, Yosef Weitz Papers, Institute for the Study of Settlement, Rehovot.

46. Entry for 4 June 1948, CZA A246, 2410. On 10 June the JNF directorate formally allocated 10,000 pounds for Weitz's use 'to cover eviction expenses' (entry for 10 June 1948, Weitz, *Diary*, III, 301).

47. Weitz, Danin and Sasson, 'Retroactive Transfer, a Scheme for the Solution of the Arab Question in the State of Israel', undated but from early June 1948, ISA FM 2564\19.

48. Entry for 5 June 1948, Weitz diary, CZA A246-13, 2411; and entry for 5 June 1948, DBG-YH II, 487. Golan, *Transformation*, 209–12, argues that

Ben-Gurion rejected Weitz's transfer proposals including its centerpiece, the destruction of the villages – but at the same time notes the Haganah\IDF policy of systematically destroying villages after conquest, which Ben-Gurion knew about and, in some cases, authorised. There is a contradiction here that Golan fails to address.

49. Weitz to Ben-Gurion, 6 June 1948, ISA FM 2564\19.
50. Entry for 7 June 1948, CZA A246-13, 2412.
51. Entry for 10 June 1948, CZA A246-13, 2415; Shitrit to Ben-Gurion, 23 June 1948, ISA MAM 307 gimel\33, complaining of Berger's activities; Bobritzky to Jewish Agency Settlement Department, 21 June 1948, LA 235 IV, 2060 aleph, listing which villages he recommended for destruction and which for renovation; and Kiryati to deputy brigade OC, etc., '"The Treatment [*tipul*]" of Arab Property', 13 June 1948, IDFA 1277\49\\11. The last document stated that 'Mr Berger' had been appointed by 'the authorised institutions' as the coordinator of 'special actions "to deal with" the abandoned Arab villages. He must be given all help and cooperation . . . The brigade HQ and the brigade engineers service HQ will direct the operation, in cooperation with Mr Berger.'
52. Entry for 13 June 1948, Weitz, *Diary*, III, 301.
53. Entry for 14 June 1948, CZA A246-13, 2418.
54. Entry for 15 June 1948, Weitz, *Diary*, III, 303.
55. Entry for 16 June 1948, DBG-YH II, 523–24.
56. Entry for 25 June 1948, CZA A246-13, 2425.
57. Entry for 1 July 1948, Weitz, *Diary*, III, 310.
58. Agendas of the meetings of the Provisional Government of Israel, 16, 20, 23, 27, and 30 June 1048, KMA-AZP 9\9\1.
59. Cisling's statement in Cabinet, 16 June 1948, KMA-AZP 9\9\3; and Cisling to Ben-Gurion, 16 June 1948, ISA FM 2401\21 aleph. The destruction of Beisan apparently surprised Ben-Gurion. He cabled Golani Brigade HQ: 'Ask Avraham Yoffe [a battalion OC] is it true that he burned down the town of Beit Shean in whole or in part, and on whose instructions did he do this?' (defence minister to Golani, 18 June 1948, DBG Archive, Correspondence). Apparently he received no satisfactory answer – for on 5 July, General Zvi Ayalon, writing in the name of the CGS, cabled Golani: 'I have heard a rumour that Beit Shean was burned and destroyed . . . If the rumour is true – inform me in what circumstances this happened and who gave the order . . .' OC Golani Brigade responded: 'Apart from a few houses destroyed during the conquest of Beit Shean, our people did not carry out destruction operations . . . The fires that occurred in the town were set by enemy units (gangs) who penetrated the town with the aim of robbery, destruction, sabotage and arson' (Ayalon to Golani, 5 July 1948, and Golani to IDF\GS, 7 July 1948, both in IDFA 922\75\\1025). Three weeks later, Ben-Gurion wrote Cisling, quoting (or misquoting) Golani's response to Ayalon: 'Apart from houses destroyed or burned during the conquest of Beit Shean by Avraham Yoffe's battalion, no acts of destruction were carried out by our soldiers. It is known that the fires that occurred in the town were set by groups of Arabs who had infiltrated the town after its capture' (protocol of Cabinet meeting, 25 July 1948, Ben-Gurion's statement, ISA. See also protocol of Cabinet meeting, 1 Aug. 1948, ISA).

60. 'Decisions of the Provisional Government Meeting', 20 June 1948, KMA-AZP 9\9\1. The relevant passage in this Cabinet meeting, deposited at the ISA, has been blanked out by censors.
61. Gwirtz's letter is in Giv'ati HQ to battalions 51, 52, 53, 54, 55 and 58, 2 June 1948, IDFA 6127\49\\109.
62. Ben-Gurion to Sukenik (Yadin), 23 June 1948, IDFA 2315\50\\15.
63. Giv'ati to IDF\GS\Operations\Intelligence, 2 July 1948, and OC Operations (Yadin) to Ben-Gurion, 8 July 1948, both in IDFA 2315\50\\15.
64. Gwirtz to HGS, 26 May 1948, IDFA 6127\49\\109.
65. HGS to brigades, 30 May 1948, IDFA 481\49\\142.
66. IDF-GS to brigades, 14 June 1948, IDFA 481\49\\143. It is possible that this order represents a reconsideration of the 30 May order that sought to curtail the destruction of Arab housing; perhaps in the interim HGS had been persuaded, perhaps by the start of the First Truce and upsurge of efforts by Arabs to cross the front lines and to return to their homes, that the destruction of Arab housing was, in principle, positive and beneficial and should not be restrained.
67. Cisling's statement at Cabinet meeting of 4 July 1948, KMA-AZP 9\9\3.
68. Gwirtz to Shitrit, 23 June 1948, and Gwirtz, 'Report for the Month of June', undated but arrived at Agriculture Ministry on 7 July 1948, both in ISA AM gimel\19\aleph.
69. Entries for 28 June and 1 July 1948, Weitz, *Diary*, III, 309 and 310.
70. Ayalon to OCs brigades, battalions, districts, etc., 6 July 1948, KMA-AZP 9\9\1.
71. Northern Front HQ, 'Operations Brosh and Dekel', 6 July 1948, IDFA 4858\49\\495; 7th Brigade Tactical HQ, 'Operation Dekel', 8 July 1948, IDFA 1137\49\\84; GS\Operations, Southern Front, 'Operation Larlar [Dani]', 26 June 1948, IDFA 922\75\\1237; and Kiryati Brigade HQ, 'Operational Order – Operation Dani', 8 July 1948, IDFA 6450\49\\98; Northern Front, to brigades, etc., 'Operational Order "Hiram"', 26 Oct. 1948, IDFA854\52\\321; IDF Galilee District to Battalion 101, etc., 26 Oct. 1948, IDFA 1096\49\\65; and Giv'ati Brigade HQ, 'Operational Order Yoav', 11 Oct. 1948, IDFA 922\75\\899.

   On the other hand, the operational order for 'Operation An-Far', Southern Front's operation against the Egyptian Army south of Rehovot, specifically called for 'the liquidation of Arab villages within the ['Ajjur-Tel a Safi-Majdal] area' (Giv'ati Brigade HQ, 'An-Far Operations', 7 July 1948, IDFA 7011\49\\1).
72. Zvi Lurie to Ben-Gurion and Shitrit, 13 July 1948, ISA MAM 304\76; Lurie to Ben-Tov, etc., 26 July 1948, KMA-ACP 8\8 aleph\11; protocol of meeting of Mapam defence activists, statement by Moshe Erem, 26 July 1948, HHA 10.18; and Lurie to Ben-Gurion 3 Aug. 1948, KMA-ACP 8\8 aleph\11.
73. Cisling's and Ben-Gurion's statements at Cabinet meeting of 14 July 1948, KMA-ACP 9\9\3; and 'Decisions of the Provisional Government', 14 July 1948, KMA-ACP 9\9\1. The ISA censors have blanked out long passages from the protocols of that day's debate.
74. 'Protocol of the meeting of the Ministerial Committee for Abandoned Property, 26 July 1948', ISA FM 2401\21 aleph.
75. Gelber, *Palestine*, 284.

76. Golani HQ to battalion and sub-district OCs, 16 Aug. 1948, IDFA 1678\51\\11.
77. See, for example, Shmuel Yevin, director of Department of Antiquities, to Shamir, engineers officer, Yarden Battalion, 23 Sep. 1948, IDFA 260\51\2, regarding Tiberias.
78. Haifa District HQ to 123rd Battalion, 7 Oct. 1948, IDFA 200716\49\\1.
79. Ben-Gurion to Cisling, 13 Sep. 1948, and Cisling to Ben-Gurion, 15 Sep. 1948, both in KMA-ACP 9\9\4.
80. Gen. Avner to IDF CGS, 1 Oct. 1948, IDFA 2433\50\\11.
81. Entry for 27 Oct. 1948, DBG-YH III, 778.
82. Entry for 18 Aug. 1948, DBG-YH II, 652–54. Compare to Weitz's diary entry – Weitz, *Diary*, III, 331 – and Ya'akov Shimoni's protocol of the meeting (see Chap. 5). Ben-Gurion exercised tight self-censorship as he penned his diary entries.
83. Secretariat of the Actions Committee, Kibbutz Artzi, 'Letter to the Mobilised No. 3', 25 Aug. 1948, HHA 11.18.
84. Protocol of meeting of Mapam Political Committee, 19 Aug. 1948, HHA 66.90 (1).
85. For example, see Harel Brigade HQ\Intelligence, 'Daily Report for 22 October', 23 Oct. 1948, IDFA 4775\49\3, for the destruction of Beit Nattif and Deiraban, at the western end of the Jerusalem Corridor; and Beit Horon Battalion to 6th Brigade\Operations, 23 Nov. 1948, IDFA 6774\49\\119, for the destruction of Beit Thul, north of Saris (also in the corridor).
86. Lifshitz\Dani HQ to OC engineers, sappers (Yiftah Brigade), 08:35, 10 July 1948, IDFA 922\75\\1234; and Lishitz\Dani HQ to OC engineers, 8th Brigade, 10 July 1948, KMA-PA 141–54.
87. Lifshitz to Yiftah HQ, 11:30, 10 July 1948, IDFA 922\75\\1234.
88. Yiftah to Dani HQ, 21:15 hours, 10 July 1948, IDFA 922\75\\1237.
89. Lifshitz\Dani HQ, to Yiftah HQ, 09:40, 11 July 1948, IDFA 922\75\\1234.
90. Report on the period 11 Aug.–11 Sep. 1948, diary of Israel Livertovsky, JNF files, 501–4.
91. Report on period 14 Sep.–12 Oct. 1948, diary of Israel Livertovsky, JNF files, 501-4; and Palmah daily reports to IDF-GS for 1 and 4 Oct. 1948, KMA-PA 120\1\39-bet and 42.
92. Sha'ar Ha'amakim to defence minister and minister of finance, 4 Aug. 1948, HHA-ACP 10.95.10 (4); Sha'ar Ha'amakim to Golani HQ, 8 Aug. 1948, HHA-ACP 10.95.10 (5); and protocol of meeting of Mapam Political Committee, statements by Ya'ari and Cohen, 19 Aug. 1948, HHA 66.90 (1).
93. 'Decisions of the Provisional Government', 8 Aug. 1948, KMA ACP 9\9\1.
94. Maj. Elisha Sulz to Sha'ar Ha'amakim, 14 Oct. 1948, and Gad Machnes to Sha'ar Ha'amakim, 22 Oct. 1948, both in HHA-ACP 10.95.10 (6).
95. Farda (from Dorot), Gavri (Nir-'Am), and Frisch (Ruhama) to prime minister, 4 Aug. 1948, ISA FM 2564\9.
96. Avira to Danin, 29 July 1948, and Danin to Avira, 16 Aug. 1948, both in ISA FM 2570\11.
97. Erem to Shitrit, ? Oct. 1948, HHA-ACP 10.95.39 (2).
98. For example, see protocol of meeting of Mapam defence activists, 26 July 1948, HHA 10.18.
99. Prag to Ya'ari, 27 July 1948, HHA-MYP 7.95.3-(2) bet.

100. Peterzil to Cisling, Bentov and Erem, 2 Aug. 1948, KMA-ACP 8\8 aleph\11.
101. Hurwitz to ?, ? Sep. 1948, HHA-ACP 10.95.10 (6).
102. Peterzil to Erem, Bentov, Hazan and Cisling, 10 Aug. 1948, quoting an extract from an undated letter from Faivel Cohen, of Ma'ayan Baruch, to Peterzil, HHA-ACP 10.95.10 (5).
103. Gordon to *Davar* editorial board, 14 Dec. 1948, IDFA 1292\51\\68.
104. Entry for 23 Nov. 1948, CZA A246-14, 2530.
105. Entry for 18 Dec. 1948, Weitz, *Diary*, III, 367. Weitz's reference to 'revenge' in this case probably also had a personal aspect: One of his sons, Yehiam, was killed during a Palmah raid in 1946 on the al Zib bridge.
106. 'Protocol of the Meeting of the Ministerial Committee for Abandoned Property, 5 Nov. 1948', ISA FM 2401\21 aleph.
107. Protocol of Cabinet meeting of 10 Jan. 1950, ISA.
108. See YND, entries for 27 July and 16 and 31 Aug. 1948, and Rabbis Abulafia, David Yeluz, etc. to prime minister, undated, IDFA 580\56\\625.
109. Yadin to OC Northern Front, 28 Sept. 1948, IDFA 2384\50\\1. He also ordered a halt to destruction in Kafr Lam, Atlit and Qisarya. See also B. Meisler, Shmuel Yevin and Emmanuel Ben-Dor, 'Report on the Visit of E. Ben-Dor, S. Yevin and B. Meisler in the North of the Country from 22 July until 2 August', IDFA 2315\50\\15; and Shmuel Yevin, director, Antiquities Department, to Shamir, Engineers Officer, Yarden Battalion, 23 Sep. 1948 and appended Ya'akov Finkerfeld, 'List of Buildings in Need of Protection against Destruction in Tiberias'; Lt. Gustav Landau, deputy city officer, to Ben-Dor, Antiquities Dept., 18 Jan. 1949; Ruth Amiran, Antiquities Dept. to Landau, 13 Feb. 1949; Amiran to Landau, 18 Mar. 1949, etc. – all in Antiquities Authority Archive (AAA), peh\Tiberias\1.
110. YND, entries for 6,18 and 28 Feb. 1948.
111. Golan, *Transformation*, 163–65.
112. Golan, *Transformation*, 93.
113. Golan, *Transformation*, 94.
114. Brutzkus, Planning Division, Tel Aviv Municipality, to Dr. Altman, tourism adviser to prime minister, 25 Oct. 1949, AAA peh\Yaffo\2; and H. Reizel, inspector of absentees' property, Jaffa, to director of Antiquities Department, 30 Sep. 1949, AAA, peh\Yaffo\2.
115. Unsigned, 'From the Logbook', entry for 18 Sep. [1949]; and S. Yevin to Custodian for Absentees Property, 19 Sep. 1949, both in AAA, peh\Yaffo\2.
116. See correspondence, protocols and memoranda in AAA peh\Yaffo – Administrative, and peh\Yaffo\2. For the destruction of parts of Haifa, see Chapter 4.
117. Golan, *Transformation*, 243–46, dates 'the start of the systematic destruction [of the Arab villages]' to July 1949, when the head of the Public Works Department instructed the Jerusalem and Tel Aviv district engineers to see to the destruction of 41 villages in the Jerusalem Corridor and the south. The destruction encountered opposition from various quarters, primarily on the grounds that material and housing useful for Jewish settlement was being destroyed needlessly. But the destruction continued, by fits and starts, as the settlement agencies generally ruled that the housing earmarked for destruction was unfit for Jews.

118. Ben-Gurion, *As Israel Fights*, 71.
119. Entries for 3 and 4 Feb. 1948, Weitz, *Diary*, III, 232–33.
120. Entry for 10 Feb. 1948, Weitz, *Diary*, III, 235.
121. 'CID Summary of Events (of 21 March 1948),' 23 Mar. 1948, PRO CO 537-3857. For a fuller treatment of 'the battle of the crops', see Morris, 'The Harvest of 1948 . . .'.
122. Negev Committee to Sarig, 4 May 1948, Weitz, *Diary*, III, Appendix 1, 377.
123. 'Things Said at a Meeting of the Settlements Block Committee in Tel Aviv, 26 May 1948', Arab (later Minority) Affairs Ministry, LA 235 IV, 2251 bet; and unsigned but Gwirtz, 'Report of the Arab Property Department at the End of May 1948', undated, ISA MAM 303\41.
124. Unsigned, 'Summary of the Meeting with the Arab Property Committee in the Tel Hai District, 5 June 1948', ISA AM aleph\19\aleph. For the allocation of Arab fields and their cultivation around Hadera, see Samaria Settlements Block Committee, 'Circular [No. 11]', 24 May 1948, LA 235 IV, 2082\aleph.
125. Gwirtz to Ma'ayan Zvi, 3 June 1948, LA 235 IV, 2251\bet.
126. For example, see Z. Stein (Tsur) and V. Wilder, Agricultural Centre, to Kibbutz Ramat Hakovesh and Kibbutz Mishmar Hasharon, 19 May 1948, LA 235 IV, 2251\bet.
127. Gwirtz, 'Report [of the Arab Property Department] for the Month of June 1948', undated but received at the Agriculture Ministry on 7 July 1948, ISA AM aleph\19\gimel (part 1).
128. For more, see Morris, 'The Harvest of 1948 . . .'.
129. Weitz to Machnes, 2 May 1948, LA 235 IV, 2251\bet.
130. Sdeh Nehemia to Harzfeld, 18 May 1948, LA 235 IV, 2179. Neighbouring Kibbutz Manara made a similar request for the lands of Qadas, 'suitable for winter crops' (implying an interest in more than ephemeral cultivation (see Gvati to members of the committee responsible for Arab property in Upper Galilee, 2 June 1948, LA 235 IV, 2251\bet)).
131. Gwirtz to finance minister, 29 June 1948, ISA AM gimel\19 aleph (part 1).
132. Tel Mond Settlements Block Committee to Agricultural Centre, 15 July 1948; 'Mishmeret' to Agricultural Centre, 29 July 1948; Kibbutz Neve-Yam to Agricultural Centre, 3 Aug. 1948; Kibbutz 'Ein Harod to Agricultural Centre, 10 Aug. 1948; Kvutzat Schiller to Agricultural Centre, 23 Aug. 1948; Kibbutz Genossar to Agricultural Centre, 8 Aug. 1948; and Nahalal and Kishon Regional Council to?, 8 Aug. 1948 – all in LA 235 IV, 2251; Nahalal and Kishon Regional Council to Settlement Department of Agricultural Centre, 8 Aug. 1948, LA 235 IV, 2088; and Golan, *Transformation*, 214, for similar requests by Kvutzat 'Ayanot (Ramat David) and Kfar A"zar.
133. Gwirtz to finance minister, 29 June 1948, and Gwirtz, 'Report [of the Arab (Abandoned) Property Department] for the Month of June 1948', both in ISA AM gimel\19 aleph (part 1).
134. 'Protocol of the Meeting of the Ministerial Committee for Abandoned Property, 13 July 1948', ISA FM 2401\21 aleph; and Lifshitz (Lif), 'The Legal Settlement of Absentees Property for Purposes of Settlement, Housing and Economic Reconstruction', 18 Mar. 1949, ISA FM 2401\21 bet.

135. 'Cabinet Announcement – Emergency Regulations . . .', 26 Nov. 1948, ISA AM gimel\19\aleph (part 1), 2185\gimel; and Lifshitz, 'The Legal Settlement . . .', 18 Mar. 1949, ISA FM 2401\21 bet.

136. Lifshitz, 'The Legal Settlement . . .', 18 Mar. 1949; Lifshitz to prime minister, etc., 30 Mar. 1949; and 'Summary of a Meeting Held on 1 May 1949 in the Prime Minister's Office', undated, – all in ISA FM 2401\21 bet.

137. Entry for 20 May 1948, Weitz, *Diary*, III, 288.

138. Protocol of meeting of JNF directorate, 7 July 1948, CZA KKL 10; JNF to Provisional Government of Israel, 28 July 1948, ISA AM bet\19\aleph, 2185\gimel; Weitz to Shafrir, 28 July 1948, ISA AM gimel\19\aleph (part 1); Weitz to agriculture minister, 29 Aug. 1948, and Cisling to JNF, 14 Oct. 1948, both in ISA AM gimel\19\aleph (part 1), 2185\gimel; and entry for 17 Aug. 1948, CZA A246-13, 2464-65.

139. Hirsch, deputy director general of Agriculture Ministry, to the Organisation of Cooperative Settlements, 8 Aug. 1948, and Organisation of Cooperative Settlements to Hirsch, 11 Aug. 1948, both in ISA AM bet\19\aleph, 2185\gimel.

140. Mishmar Ha'emek to Carmeli (Kibbutz Genigar), 9 Aug. 1948, Mishmar Ha'emek Archive, 3.64\5.

141. For example, see Gwirtz to the Committee for the Displaced Population and the Reconstruction of the Settlements, 7 July 1948, for a rejection of Kibbutz Negba's compensation claims, LA 235 IV, 2251 bet. Negba had been almost completely levelled by the Egyptian Army.

142. For examples, see Creative Cooperative Farmers Association Yoqne'am Ltd. to Government of Israel, (sic) Agriculture Department, 6 Aug. 1948; Kibbutz Sha'ar Hagolan to Agriculture Ministry, 16 Aug. 1948; Schechter, Agriculture Ministry, to Custodian for Abandoned Property, 19 Aug. 1948; Tsur (Stein), Agricultural Centre, to Hanochi, Agriculture Ministry, 22 Nov. 1948, referring to the receipt of a letter of 1 Aug. 1948 from Kibbutz Beit Keshet; Southern Sharon (Settlements) Block (Committee) to Agriculture Ministry, 26 Aug. 1948 – all in ISA AM gimel\19\aleph (part 1), 2185\gimel; and Shomron Jewish Settlement Block Committee to Agriculture Ministry and Custodian for Abandoned Property, 1 Sep. 1948, ISA AM gimel\19\aleph (part 3).

143. Hanochi to agriculture minister, 10 Oct. 1948, ISA AM aleph\19\gimel (part 1). See also Golan, *Transformation*, 219–20.

144. Berger to Haim Halperin, director general of the Agriculture Ministry, 29 Oct. 1948, and Hanochi to Berger, 8 Nov. 1948 – both in ISA AM aleph\19\gimel (part 1).

145. Migdal to Hanochi, 12 Dec. 1948, and Reuven Aloni, Agriculture Ministry, to Migdal, 21 Dec. 1948 – both in ISA AM aleph\19\gimel (part 2); and Agriculture Ministry to Migdal, 21 July 1949, ISA AM aleph\19\gimel (part 3).

146. Shmuel Zimmerman, the Moshava Sejera Council, to Agriculture Ministry, Abandoned Lands Department, undated (but received '16 December 1948'), and Aloni to Moshav Sharona, 17 Dec. 1948 – both in ISA AM aleph\ 19\gimel (part 2).

147. Gruenbaum to finance and agriculture ministers, 9 Nov. 1948, ISA AM aleph\19\gimel (part 1); and Hanochi to Tel Mond Settlement Block

Committee, 14 Nov. 1948, and Hanochi to the Even-Yehuda Council, 2 June 1949 – both in ISA AM aleph\19\gimel (part 3).

148. For a typical wrangle between two kibbutzim, Ma'abarot and Mishmar Hasharon, see Mishmar Hasharon to Settlement Department, Agricultural Centre, 25 July 1948, LA 235 IV, 1695; Mishmar Hasharon to Hakal, 25 Nov. 1948, and Hanochi to Mishmar Hasharon, 13 Dec. 1948 – all in ISA AM aleph\19\gimel (part 2); and Hefer Valley Regional Council to Lebovsky, Agriculture Ministry, 7 Dec. 1948, ISA AM aleph\19\gimel (part 3).

149. Agriculture Ministry to prime minister, 22 Mar. 1949, ISA AM 210\11.

150. Golan, *Transformation*, 224–25, suggests this linkage but offers no documentary proof.

151. Entry for 18 Dec. 1948, Weitz, *Diary*, III, 366; and entry for 18 Dec. 1948, DBG-YH III, 885.

152. Entry for 21 Dec. 1948, DBG-YH, 892; and entry for 21 Dec. 1948, Weitz, *Diary*, III, 369.

153. Golan, *Transformation*, 226.

154. Entry for 9 Jan. 1949, Weitz, *Diary*, IV, 9; and protocol of meeting of JNF directorate, 8 Mar. 1949, CZA KKL 10. Golan, *Transformation*, 227, suggests that the sale – which reduced the Agriculture Ministry's control of lands and the establishment of new settlements – was partly motivated by Ben-Gurion's (and Mapai's) desire to curb Mapam's and the Mapam-affiliated kibbutzim's grip on the agricultural sector and, ultimately, electoral clout. Without doubt, the sale enhanced Mapai's control over new settlements and made the new immigrant-settlers beholden to Mapai and its officials.

155. Protocols of meetings of the Committee for Agricultural and Settlement Development, 12 and 26 July 1949, and appended statistics ('Estimate of the Sown Area of the State', 'The Areas of Irrigated Fields in the Jewish (Agricultural) Economy', and 'Summary of Area of Abandoned Land Leased by the Agriculture Ministry'), ISA AM 29\7.

156. Weitz, 'To Settle New Lands', 1949, ISA AM 29\7.

157. For example, see JA Settlement Department to Northern District (Office), undated but received at Agriculture Ministry, 3 July 1949, ISA AM aleph\19\gimel (part 3).

158. Mapai, 'Settlement and Irrigation . . .'.

159. Lists of settlements established by the end of May 1949, IDFA 756\61\\ 128.

160. Ben-Gurion, *As Israel Fights*, 70–71.

161. Protocol of meeting of Defence Committee, 3 Feb. 1948, CZA S25-9346. But Yosef Sapir, of the General Zionists, objected: 'I have never seen a war in which two [sic, three] things are done simultaneously, construction, settlement, fighting . . .' Ben-Gurion interjected: 'I have!'

162. Protocol of meeting of Defence Committee, 10 Feb. 1948, CZA S25-9346.

163. Protocol of meeting of Mapai Secretariat, 20 Mar. 1948, LPA 24\48.

164. Protocol of joint meeting of Mapai Secretariat, the secretariat of the (Mapai-affiliated) Ihud Hakvutzot kibbutz movement and the Mapai faction in the Zionist Actions Committee, 4 Apr. 1948, LPA 24\48.

165. Ben-Gurion, *As Israel Fights*, 86–87 and 92, Ben-Gurion before the Zionist Actions Committee, 6 Apr. 1948.
166. Entry for 31 Mar. 1948, Weitz, *Diary*, III, 260.
167. Golan, *Transformation*, 206.
168. 'Meeting of the National Command 12.4', IDFA 481\49\\64.
169. Galili to Weitz, 13 Apr. 1948, Yosef Weitz Papers, Institute for the Study of Settlement.
170. OC Palmah to HGS, 12 Apr. 1948, IDFA 922\75\\1219. See also OC Carmeli to Weitz, 19 May 1948, IDFA 6680\49\\5, pressing for the establishment of a settlement on the German Templar lands at Neuherrdorf, near Tira, which would 'help us in our aim of gaining control of the Haifa-Zikhron Ya'akov road . . .'; and the correspondence on the settlement of Tantura in late May–early June 1948 (IDFA 2506\49\\80).
171. Galili to Palmah HQ, 18 Apr. 1948, IDFA 922\75\\1223.
172. Palmah HQ, 'Daily Report', 20 Apr. 1948, IDFA 922\75\\1214.
173. Entries for 17–18 Apr. 1948, Weitz, *Diary*, III, 268; and entry for 27 Oct. 1948, DBG-YH III, 778.
174. OC Galilee District to Eshel, 16 Sep. 1948, IDFA 548\51\\87. Eshel, in turn, pressed for the establishment of settlements at nearby Zangariya and on lands previously occupied by 'Arab Shamalina (Eshel to General Staff Division, 28 Sep. 1948, IDFA 756\61\\128, and Eshel to Eshkol, 28 Oct. 1948, both in IDFA 782\65\\1186).
175. See, for example, Carmel to General Staff Division, 3 Oct. 1948, IDFA 548\51\\87.
176. Entry for 22 Apr. 1948, Weitz, *Diary*, III, 271–72.
177. Entry for 26 Mar. 1948, Weitz, *Diary*, III, 256–57. This is the first documented linkage between the establishment of new settlements and the prevention of a return. Two settlements, the kibbutzim Sheluhot and Reshafim, were established in the valley, on Ashrafiya lands, on 10 June 1948. Kibbutz Ramot Menashe was founded on the lands of Daliyat ar Ruha on 31 July 1948.
178. Galili to brigades, etc., 28 Apr. 1948, IDFA 1242\52\\1. Shaham was replaced at the start of June by Yehoshua ('Izik') Eshel (see 'Izik' to Shkolnik, 2 June 1948, IDFA 782\65\\1186).
179. See, for example, Yoman Hamazkirut, Hakkibutz Ha'artzi, 28 June 1948, HHA, record of deliberations of secretariart of the Kibbutz Artzi on 18 Apr. 1948.
180. Entry for 3 May 1948, CZA A246-13, 2372.
181. Entry for 7 May 1948, DBG-YH I, 309; entry for 9 May 1948, Weitz, *Diary* III, 280–81; and protocol of meeting of Mapai Central Committee, 12 May 1948, LPA 23 aleph\48.
182. Shaham to HGS, hand-written 'Proposal to Consolidate Our Borders and Establish Conquest Settlements [*nekudot kibosh*]', undated, IDFA 1242\52\\1. It is not clear whether this proposal was presented to the HGS or was merely an unsubmitted draft.
183. Gvati, 'Socialist Agriculture and the Mass Immigration', *Molad*, 1, Nos. 2–3 (May–June 1948), 103–107.
184. Golan, *Transformation*, 208.

185. Protocol of meeting of Mapam Political Committee, 26 May 1948, HHA 66.90 (1).
186. Protocol of meeting of Cabinet, 14 June 1948, ISA. In fact, the 'silence' was such that the Cabinet was not consulted or, for weeks, informed about the establishment and location of new settlements (see protocol of Cabinet meeting of 11 Aug. 1948, ISA, in which Agriculture Minister (!) Cisling complained and Ben-Gurion soothed him by promising that he would give him a list of new settlements and a map detailing their location).
187. Golan, *Transformation*, 212.
188. 'A List of New Settlements from the Start of Hostilities in the Country', ISA AM kof\5. See also Eshel, 'Report for Month of June 1948', 2 July 1948, and accompanying letter, Eshel to Shkolnik, 4 July 1948, IDFA 782\65\\1186. Eshel says that Beit Lahm and Waldheim were settled respectively on 21 and 22 June 1948 – thus falling within, and aggrandising, his tenure as IDF Settlement Officer. None of the settlements were established in the Negev and Weitz, chairman of the Negev Committee, was extremely upset. On 5 July he gave vent to his frustration in a bitter letter to Shkolnik (he signed off: 'Yours with great anger, Yosef Weitz' (IDFA 782\65\\1186)).
189. OC Ephraim Area to sub-areas, etc., 23 June 1948, IDFA 410\54\\144.
190. For example, OC IDF Planning Division to Weitz, ? June 1948, IDFA 756\61\\128, regarding Kafr Misr and nearby Tira; Planning Division\ Settlement Officer to Alexandroni Brigade, 30 June 1948, and Deputy OC Alexandroni Brigade to Settlement Officer, 5 July 1948, both in IDFA 2506\49\\80, regarding the establishment of another outpost near Kfar Yavetz; and Eshel to Deputy OC Alexandroni Brigade, 28 June 1948, and Deputy OC Alexandroni Brigade to Eshel, 3 July 1948, both in IDFA 2506\49\\80, regarding the establishment of a settlement at Nahal Zarqa (near Tantura). During the following weeks, Eshel was to rail that he was being sidelined and ignored (by Weitz, Shkolnik, etc.) (Eshel to Shkolnik, 16 Aug. 1948, IDFA 782\65\\1186).
191. The settlements were Habonim (later renamed Kfar Hanassi) at Mansurat al Kheit, on the Jordan River (2 July); Yesodot, southeast of 'Aqir (6 July); Regavim, at Buteimat (6 July); Hagilbo'a-Zera'im, near 'Ein Harod (20 July); and Kibbutz Ramot-Menashe (31 July).
192. For example, Eshel wrote: 'In light of the conquests carried out this month – most of the time was spent determining settlements in the direction of Jerusalem [i.e., the Jerusalem Corridor] and in Upper Galilee' ('The Sites Where Settlements were Established this Month (July 1948)', undated, IDFA 782\65\\1186).
193. Entry for 19 July 1948, DBG-YH II, 603.
194. Entry for 21 July 1948, Weitz, *Diary*, III, 318–19. Another problem was funds. In late July IDF Planning Division informed Ben-Gurion that it had spent the whole I£ 400,000 allocation for settlement and that a further I£ 800,000 was needed if several dozen settlements were to be established during the Second Truce in the Jerusalem Corridor, the Negev and the Galilee (IDF Planning Division to defence minister, 21 July 1948, IDFA 756\61\\128).
195. Entry for 23 July 1948, Weitz, *Diary*, III, 319; and entry for 23 July 1948, DBG-YH II, 618.

196. 'Proposal for New Settlements by the Agricultural Settlements Committee of the National Institutions . . .', 28 July 1948, KMA-ACP 8\4 aleph; Eshel to defence minister, 6 Aug. 1948, KMA-ACP 8\4 aleph; and protocol of meeting of Mapai Central Committee, Harzfeld statement, 9 Aug. 1948, LPA 23 aleph\48.

197. Protocol of meeting of JNF directorate, 16 August 1948, CZA KKL 10.

198. Golan, *Transformation*, 215.

199. Protocol of meeting of Mapam Central Committee, 15–16 July 1948, HHA 68.9 (1); and protocol of meeting of Mapam defense activists, 26 July 1948, HHA 10.18.

200. Protocol of meeting of Mapam Political Committee, 19 Aug. 1948, HHA 66.90 (1).

201. Golan, *Transformation*,, 215–216.

202. Settlement Committee of the National Institutions (Weitz, Harzfeld, Horin) to defence minister, 20 Aug. 1948, ISA AM kof\5; 'Protocol of the Meeting of the Ministerial Committee for Abandoned Property', 20 Aug. 1948, and 'Protocol of the Meeting of the Ministerial Committee for Abandoned Property', 27 Aug. 1948, both in ISA FM ISA FM 2564\13; and entry for 23 Aug. 1948, Weitz, *Diary*, III, 334.

203. Eshel gives a somewhat different list – of settlements whose establishment 'was prepared' in August. He names 13 sites – including Tzor'a (Sar'a), Tzuba, Kasla, Beit Mahsir, Gezer (Abu Shusha – 'Amelim), Arab Khulda and Latrun-Beit Jiz in the Corridor and Tira (Wadi Bira) (Eshel, 'Sites Prepared for Settlement in August 1948', undated but with covering note Eshel to defence minister, 5 Sep. 1948, IDFA 782\65\\1186).

204. Golan, *Transformation*, 220, points to 'the end of August' as the moment in which 'a major change occurs in the permanent transfer of Arab lands to Jewish hands'. He links this to Ben-Gurion's appointment of Eshkol (Shkolnik) as director of the JA Settlement Department.

205. Weitz to Ben-Gurion, 11 Sep. 1948, and entry for 11 Sep. 1948, Weitz, *Diary*, III, 340–343; and Golan, *Transformation*, 220–221.

206. Eshel, 'Report [for] September 1948', 8 Oct. 1948, IDFA 2433\50\\11. Interestingly, under pressure of the Mapam ministers (especially Cisling), Eshel noted the need to set aside lands for a possible return of refugees. Eshkol objected to Eshel's description of what had been accomplished and what was still needed; he argued that at least one crucial, front line zone, the Jerusalem Corridor, had not yet been properly settled. So, it was premature to shift the focus from the border areas to the interior (Eshkol to Eshel, 14 Oct. 1948, IDFA 782\65\\1186).

207. Eshel, 'Report [for] September 1948', to defence minister, etc., 8 Oct. 1948, ISA AM kof\5.

208. Protocol of meeting of Actions Committee of the Kibbutz Artzi, 4 Nov. 1948, HHA 5.10.5 (2).

209. 'Report from the Meeting of the Kibbutz Artzi-Hashomer Hatza'ir Council', Nahariya, 10–12 Dec. 1948, Yediot Hakkibutz Haartzi, No. 278 (1), Jan. 1949, HHA.

210. Protocol of Cabinet meeting, 18 Nov. 1948, ISA.

211. Protocol of Cabinet meeting, 31 Oct. 1948, ISA.

212. Protocol of Cabinet meeting, 18 Nov. 1948, ISA.

213. Eshel to defence minister, etc., 'Settlement Trends in the Coming Months', 8 Nov. 1948, IDFA 782\65\\1186. Some of the sites along the Lebanese border were settled in Jan. 1949.

214. Eshel, 'Report and Summary for the Months of November 1948 – January 1949', and accompanying letter Eshel to defence minister, 18 Feb. 1949, IDFA 756\61\\128.

215. Ra'anan Weitz memorandum to Ministerial Committee for Abandoned Property, 30 Nov. 1948, KMA-ACP 4, aleph\8.

216. Yadin to CGS, 30 Nov. 1948, and CGS's aide de camp to OC Military Government, 8 Dec. 1948, both in IDFA 121\50\\223.

217. Golan, *Transformation*, 222.

218. Protocol of meeting of JNF directorate, 7 Dec. 1948, CZA KKL 10; and entries for 3 and 10 Dec. 1948, Weitz, *Diary*, III, 360 and 364.

219. 'Protocol of the Meeting of the Ministerial Committee for Abandoned Property, 17 December 1948', ISA FM 2401\21 aleph.

220. Entries for 18–19 Dec. 1948, Weitz, *Diary*, III, 366 and 369. Weitz also recorded Shitrit at last agreeing to the establishment of settlements on actual village sites and Kaplan agreeing to the 'free use of the villages' for settlement (entry for 4 Dec. 1948, CZA A246-14, 2540; protocol of meeting of Committee of Directorates of the National Institutions, 11 Dec. 1948, in Weitz, *Diary*, III, 401; and entry for 24 Dec. 1948, CZA A246-14, 2558).

   Golan, *Transformation*, 224 and elsewhere, describes a more monolithic reality in which Kaplan, Shitrit and the Mapam ministers consistently clung to liberal and socialist principles and consistently strove to assure the possibility of a refugee return by insisting on the 'surplus lands' formula and by prohibiting settlement on village sites. Similarly, he argues that Ben-Gurion, while in his heart supporting the settlement officials' desire to settle actual village sites and take over all of the lands, was cognisant of the damage this could cause Israel's foreign relations and used Kaplan to neutralise these officials. Golan also seems unaware of the deep ambiguity in Mapam's formal espousal of a refugee return, an ambiguity that characterised Cisling's thinking and actions through the second half of 1948.

   Golan, *Transformation*, 224–225, suggests that Ben-Gurion's assertions on 18 Dec. were prompted by UN General Assembly Resolution 194, which endorsed the refugees' right of return. Golan says that the resolution forced Ben-Gurion to make up his mind – to bar a return and to use the villages and lands in a way that would help bar such a return, primarily through rapid settlement. But, as has been shown, Ben-Gurion had made up his mind to bar a return months before (certainly by 16 June) and had periodically signaled his support for settling the villages and lands partly with this in mind. I would suggest that the UN resolution in principle changed nothing in Ben-Gurion's thinking – though it probably served as an additional spur to speed up the settlement enterprise.

221. Protocol of Israel Cabinet meeting, 19 Dec. 1948, ISA. See Major E. Oren to OC General Staff Division\Planning Department, ? Aug. 1949, IDFA 756\61\\128, analysing the security value of the new border settlements.

222. Eshel, 'Report and Summary for the Months of November 1948-January 1949', and accompanying letter, Eshel to defence minister, 18 Feb. 1949,

IDFA 756\61\\128; and Major El'ad Peled, Northern Front, to brigades, etc., 21 Jan. 1949, IDFA 4858\49\\434.

223. Eshel, 'Report and Summary for the Months of November 1948–January 1949', IDFA 756\61\\128.

224. Golan, *Transformation*, 227–29.

225. Golan, *Transformation*, 231–32.

226. Eshel, 'Yearly Report, from 15.6.48 to 15.6.49', ? June 1949, IDFA 756\61\\128. Eshel expected another '100' settlements to go up during the following year (from mid-June 1949 to mid-June 1950), with 25 of these 'completing the Judaisation of the Jerusalem Corridor . . . and the areas opposite the Triangle.'

227. Golan, *Transformation*, 236–237.

228. Golan, *Transformation*, 238. And some of these were subsequently abandoned as the new settlements were re-established at nearby sites.

229. Entry for 10 Feb. 1949, DBG-YH III, 969.

230. Jewish Agency Immigration Department, 'Information of the Immigration Department', 18 Feb. 1948, CZA S53-526\dalet.

231. Entry for 31 Jan. 1948, DBG-YH I, 197. It is likely that Ben-Gurion was thinking specifically of displaced or 'refugee' Jews, forced out of their original homes by the fighting, rather than of new immigrants, few of whom were arriving in the country at this time. But it is possible that he was already thinking of immigrants as well.

232. Danin to Weitz, 18 May 1948, Yosef Weitz Papers, Institute for Settlement Research, Rehovot.

233. Weitz, Danin and Sasson, 'Retroactive Transfer, A Scheme for the Solution of the Arab Question in the State of Israel', undated, ISA FM 2564\19.

234. For instance, see entry for 13 and 15 June 1948, Weitz, *Diary*, III, 301–302.

235. Yoseftal to the Coordinator of the Census for Popular Service (*sherut la'am*), 23 May 1948, IDFA 6127\49\\161.

236. Golan, *Transformation*, 81.

237. Golan, *Transformation*, 81.

238. Golan, *Transformation*, 83.

239. Golan, *Transformation*, 88.

240. Golan, *Transformation*, 139.

241. Golan, *Transformation*, 141.

242. Golan, *Transformation*, 144 and 147.

243. Golan, *Transformation*, 148.

244. Untitled testimony by 'Akiva Perseitz, chairman of the Confiscation Committee, undated but from Sep. 1948, IDFA 121\50\\204.

245. Golan, *Transformation*, 87.

246. Protocol of Cabinet meeting, 16 June 1948, ISA.

247. Shapira to Ben-Gurion, 2 July 1948, and Ben-Gurion minute, 14 July 1948, both in IDFA 6127\49\\161.

248. Protocol of meeting of Mapai Secretariat, 5 July 1948, LPA 24\48.

249. Chizik, 'Monthly Report on the Governance of Jaffa', undated but stamped 'received 18 July 1948', IDFA 6127\49\\161.

250. Typescript of Persitz testimony, IDFA 121\50\\204.

251. Golan, *Transformation*, 91.

252. Golan, *Transformation*, 93–94.
253. Typescript of testimony by Giora Persitz, IDFA 121\50\\204.
254. Entry for 25 July 1948, DBG-YH II, 622.
255. Laniado, 'Weekly Report No. 2, 5–12 August 1948', 13 Aug. 1948, IDFA 580\56\\252.
256. Laniado to defence minister, etc., 27 July 1948, IDFA580\56\\252. Gelber, (forthcoming) *Independence and Nakba*, Chap. 15, argues that the decision to concentrate the remaining Arabs in the 'Ajami quarter was taken on security grounds, after several weapons were found in the office of the Emergency Committee and elsewhere and after its members were placed under house arrest. My feeling is that the need for housing played a greater role.
257. Laniado to Defence and minorities and police ministers, 28 July 1948, IDFA 580\56\\252; and Laniado, 'Weekly Report on the Activities of Jaffa's Military Governor from 25 July to 5 August 1948', 4 Aug. 1948, IDFA 580\56\\252.
258. Laniado, 'Weekly Report No. 3 . . . 13–20 August 1948', 21 Aug. 1948, ISA MAM 306\77.
259. Erem to Shitrit, 11 Aug. 1948, ISA FM 2564\9. Erem was skeptical about the defence establishment's explanation, that the fence was designed to protect the Arabs from Jewish vandals and robbers.
260. Shitrit to prime minister, 13 Aug. 1948, ISA FM 2564\9.
261. Laniado, 'Weekly Report No. 2 . . . 5–12 August 1948', 13 Aug. 1948, IDFA 580\56\\252.
262. Laniado, 'Weekly Report No. 3 . . . 13–20 August 1948', 21 Aug. 1948, ISA MAM 306\77; and Laniado to foreign minister, 23 Aug. 1948, ISA FM 2564\9.
263. Tel Aviv District HQ to Military Governor Jaffa, 28 Aug. 1948, and Shitrit to General Avner, 9 Sep. 1948, both in ISA FM 2564\9.
264. Persitz to Shafrir, 30 Aug. 1948, IDFA 121\50\\204.
265. Typescript of testimony by Persitz, IDFA 121\50\\204.
266. Hoter-Ishai to CGS, 15 Sep. 1948, IDFA 121\50\\204. See also Golan, *Transformation*, 98–99.
267. Typescript of testimony by Persitz, IDFA 121\50\204.
268. OC Military Government to CGS, 13 Sep. 1948, IDFA 121\50\\183.
269. 'Affidavit' by Battalion 141 officer, IDFA 121\50\\205.
270. 'Testimony of the Social and Cultural Affairs Brigade Officer of 8th Brigade, Ya'akov Burstein', undated, IDFA 121\50\\204.
271. Shafrir to Yoseftal, 1 Sep. 1948, IDFA 121\54\\204.
272. Shafrir to Cabinet Secretariat, 2 Sep. 1948, IDFA 121\50\\204.
273. Hoter-Ishai to CGS, 15 Sep. 1948, IDFA 121\50\\204; and Hoter-Ishai to CGS, 17 Sep. 1948, IDFA 121\50\\205.
274. Ben-Gurion to Dori, 13 Sep. 1948, IDFA 121\50\\183. As usual, Ben-Gurion was incensed about (a variant of) looting – in contrast with his silence or leniency regarding Hagana\IDF atrocities against civilians and PoWs (see below).
275. Typescript of testimony by Persitz, IDFA 121\50\\204.
276. Sharef to prime minister, 13 Sep. 1948, and Ben-Gurion to CGS, 13 Sep. 1948, both in IDFA 121\50\\183.

277. Dori to OC 8th Brigade, 23 September 1948, and Dori to OC Central Front, ? September 1948, both in IDFA 121\50\\\183.
278. 'Testimony' by 141st Battalion officer, IDFA 121\50\\\205.
279. Zvi Maimon, 'Memorandum of a Meeting Attended by Prime Minister D. Ben-Gurion', 22 Sep. 1948, IDFA 121\50\\\183.
280. Assa'el Ben-David, 'Report on Activities to Set Right the Housing of Soldiers' Families in Jaffa', 11 Oct. 1948, IDFA 121\50\\\183.
281. 'Report B Concerning Activities to Set Right the Housing of Soldiers' Families in Jaffa', undated but from late Oct. 1948, IDFA 121\50\\\183.
282. Sharef to prime minister, Cabinet ministers and CGS, 11 Nov. 1948, IDFA 121\50\\\183.
283. Major Nehemiah Argov, the defence minister's aide de camp, to the CGS, 8 Dec. 1948, IDFA 121\50\\\223.
284. Moshe Nakdimon, OC 141st Battalion, to Military Government, 13 Dec. 1948, IDFA 121\50\\\223. On 28 Feb. 1949, Dori once again issued a general order, to all units, to curb 'invasions' of abandoned housing, warning (again) that 'severe' measures would be taken against malefactors (IDFA 1292\51\\\68).
285. See, for example, the case of two old Arab women 'occupying five rooms' evicted at the start of 1949 – though they appear to have been reinstated afterwards in part of the house (Laniado, 'Weekly Report No. 23, 24, 25, and 26', 7 Feb. 1949, IDFA 580\56\\\252).
286. Shafrir to prime minister, 24 Mar. 1949, ISA PMO 5440; and Shafrir, 'Report on the Activities [of the Custodian for Absentees Property] Until 31 March 1949', 18 Apr. 1949, ISA AM 210\05.
287. Golan, *Transformation*, 131.
288. See Morris, 'The Concentration . . . July 1948'.
289. Protocol of meeting of Mapai Central Committee, 9 Aug. 1948, LPA 23 aleph\48; and entry for 11 Sep. 1948, Weitz, *Diary*, III, 346.
290. Military Police Haifa District to OC Haifa District, 7 Apr. 1949, and 'Statement by 72518 – Adler David Yosef . . . Herzl Street 46, Haifa', undated, both in IDFA 260\51\\\64.
291. Entry for 26 Aug. 1948, DBG-YH II, 662.
292. Protocol of meeting of JAE, 20 Oct. 1948, CZA 46\1.
293. Protocol of meeting of Ministerial Committee for Abandoned Property, 5 Nov. 1948, ISA FM 2401\21 aleph.
294. Military Governor of Ramle and Lydda, 'Report of the [Military] Government Activities in the Ramle Lydda Area during 10.10.1948–15.11.1948', 19 Nov. 1948, IDFA 1860\50\\\30.
295. Golan, *Transformation*, 154.
296. 'Decisions of the Meeting of the Six Ministers for Arab Affairs, 5 December 1948', and protocol of meeting of Ministerial Committee for Abandoned Property, 17 Dec. 1948, both in ISA FM 2401\21 aleph.
297. Golan, *Transformation*, 154.
298. Protocol of meeting of the Military Government Committee, 9 Sep. 1948, ISA FM 2564\11; and protocol of meeting of Ministerial Committee for Abandoned Property, 10 Sep. 1948, ISA FM 2564\13.
299. Golan, *Transformation*, 177.
300. Entry for 18 Sep. 1948, DBG-YH II, 701.

301. Golan, *Transformation*, 178.
302. 'Amir to JA Absorption Division in Acre [sic], 24 Oct. 1948, IDFA 922\52\\563.
303. Entry for 22 Nov. 1948, DBG-YH III, 839.
304. OC 71st Battalion to Military Governor of Acre, 16 Nov. 1948, IDFA 922\52\\563.
305. Golan, *Transformation*, 178.
306. See Chap. 5.
307. Golan, *Transformation*, 167–68.
308. 'Decisions of the Meeting of the Six Ministers for Arab Affairs, 2 December 1948', ISA FM 2401\21 aleph; and entry for 8 Dec. 1948, Weitz, *Diary*, III, 363.
309. Entry for 23 Dec. 1948, DBG-YH, III, 897; and entry for 23 Feb. 1949, Weitz, *Diary*, IV, 14.
310. Avner to Military Governor Majdal, ? Jan. 1949, IDFA 1292\51\\68. Elsewhere, Avner defined the military governors' powers in the settlement of former Arab towns or mixed towns as 'determining the areas of [Jewish] settlement, [determining the uses of empty Arab buildings] (residence, shops, industry, etc.) and determining the pace of settlement' (Avner to military governor Jaffa, etc., 31 Jan. 1949, IDFA 1292\51\\68).
311. Morris, *Correcting*, 152.
312. Golan, *Transformation*, 190.
313. Golan, *Transformation*, 191–192.
314. Golan, *Transformation*, 175–176.
315. Unsigned, 'The Subject: Romema', 16 Jan. 1948, IDFA 2605\49\\5.
316. Golan, *Transformation*, 26.
317. Golan, *Transformation*, 26.
318. Golan, *Transformation*, 27–29. By war's end, about 35,000 of Jerusalem's Jewish inhabitants – about one-third of the total Jewish population – had been displaced by the fighting, many of them leaving town, and many others moving to other – mostly abandoned Arab – housing inside the city. By comparison, in the course of the war about 30,000 of Jerusalem's Arabs were displaced. This figure included 'the majority of the Arab population living outside the Old City walls' (Golan, *Transformation*, 51).
319. Golan, *Transformation*, 36.
320. Golan, *Transformation*, 46–47.
321. Golan, *Transformation*, 47.
322. Golan, *Transformation*, 41–42.
323. Entry for 23 Dec. 1948, DBG-YH III, 897; and Schechter to Bergman, 20 Dec. 1948, ISA AM aleph\19\gimel (part 3).
324. Golan, *Transformation*, 42. Compare this to 35,000 'olim settled in Jaffa by this time and 24,000 in Haifa.
325. Dayan to Eytan, 15 Mar. 1949, ISA FM 2431\2.
326. Avraham Bergman (Biran) to Foreign Ministry, 25 May 1949, ISA FM 2431\4.
327. Buber, Simon, W.D. Senator (former member of the JAE), and H.Y. Roth (philosophy professor and former Hebrew University Rector) to Ben-Gurion, 6 June 1949; and Tom Segev, *First Israelis*, 100–103. Eventually, some of Deir Yassin's houses were used as a mental hospital.

328. Protocol of Meeting of Military Government Committee, 23 Sep. 1948, ISA FM 2564\11.
329. Weitz, 'Proposal for a Plan to Settle 'Olim in Upper Galilee (In Outline)', 21 Dec. 1948, KMA-ACP 4, aleph\8.
330. Entry for 23 Dec. 1948, DBG-YH III, 897.
331. 'Report from the Meeting of the Kibbutz Artzi-Hashomer Hatza'ir Council', Nahariya, 10–12 Dec. 1948, HHA, Yediot Hakkibutz Ha'artzi-Hashomer Hatza'ir, No. 278 (1).
332. Protocol of the meeting of the Ministerial Committee for Abandoned Property, 31 Dec. 1948, ISA FM 2401\21 aleph.
333. Entry for 4 Jan. 1948, DBG-YH III, 926; and protocol of Cabinet meeting, 9 Jan. 1949, ISA.
334. Entry for 13 Jan. 1949, and entry for 2 Mar. 1949, Weitz, *Diary*, IV, 4 and 15; and Weitz to 'Rema', 15 Jan. 1949, and Weitz to 'Rema', 7 Mar. 1949, Weitz, *Diary*, IV, 5 and 16.
335. Gwirtz, Agricultural Workers Organisation, to Agriculture Ministry, 26 June 1949; Agriculture Ministry to Custodian for Absentees Property, 5 July 1949; Custodian for Absentees' Property to Agriculture Ministry, 17 July 1949; Aloni to Custodian, 24 July 1949; Aloni to JA Settlement Department, 24 July 1949; and A. Bobritzky, JA Settlement Department, to Aloni, 24 July 1949 – all in ISA AM aleph\19\gimel.
336. Entry for 24 June 1949, Weitz, *Diary*, IV, 36.
337. 'A Consultation About Immigration Absorption (in the [Mapai] Party)', 22 Apr. 1949, ISA, Finance Ministry Papers, 10\1\9.
338. General Avner, 'Report of the Committee Probing the Problems of the Military Government and Its Future', 3 May 1949, ISA FM 2401\19.
339. JA Settlement Department to Gershon Zack, Prime Minister's Bureau, 27 May 1949, ISA PMO 5559\gimel.
340. Golan, *Transformation*, 185.
341. Golan, *Transformation*, 187–188.
342. Golan, *Transformation*, 181.
343. Golan, *Transformation*, 173.

7

The third wave: the Ten Days (9–18 July) and the Second Truce (18 July–15 October)

The First Truce ended on 8 July, with the Egyptian army initiating battle in the south. The following day the IDF went on the offensive in the northern and central fronts. In its subsequent counter-offensive in the south, codenamed 'Mivtza An-Far' (Operation Anti-Farouq), the IDF failed to establish a corridor from the Jewish-controlled Coastal Plain to the 20-odd, besieged Negev settlements but, together with the Negev Brigade, managed to expand its hold in the northern Negev approaches and overrun clusters of villages, including Masmiya al Kabira, al Tina, Qazaza, Tel as Safi, Qastina, Jaladiya, Juseir and Hatta, thinning the Egyptian army's line of fortifications from Majdal (Ashkelon) to the Hebron Hills (via Faluja and Beit Jibrin). In the north, in 'Mivtza Dekel' (Operation Palm Tree), the IDF conquered parts of the Galilee, including the towns of Shafa 'Amr and Nazareth.

But the IDF's main effort was in the centre, where 'Operation Dani' was designed to fully open and secure the length of the Tel Aviv–Jerusalem road and to push back the Arab Legion from the vicinity of Tel Aviv by conquering the towns of Lydda and Ramle and, later, Latrun and Ramallah. Operation Dani attained only its first objectives, with the IDF conquering the Lydda–Ramle plain, including Lydda (today, Ben-Gurion) International Airport.

The IDF operations of 9–18 July, triggered by the Arabs' unwillingness to prolong the 30-day truce and, in the south, by the Egyptians' pre-emptive offensive, created a major new wave of refugees, who fled primarily to Jordanian-held eastern Palestine, and to Upper Galilee, Lebanon and the Egyptian-held Gaza Strip.

Just before the start of the 'Ten Days', as this round of hostilities was to be called in Israeli historiography, Ben-Gurion instructed the IDF to issue a general order to all units concerning behaviour towards Arab communities. Signed by General Ayalon 'in the name of the Chief of Staff', it stated:

Outside the actual time of fighting, it is forbidden to destroy, burn or demolish Arab cities and villages, to expel Arab inhabitants from villages,
neighbourhoods and cities, and to uproot inhabitants from their places
without special permission or explicit order from the Defence Minister in
each specific case. Anyone violating this order will be put on trial.[1]

The order was a grudging response to left-wing political pressure, and,
at least in the higher echelons of the IDF, may have been understood
as such, rather than as a reflection of Ben-Gurion's or the CGS's real
thinking. However, it reached all large formations and headquarters,
and presented at least a formal obstacle to the deliberate precipitation
of mass flight and the unauthorised destruction of villages.[2]

During the 'Ten Days', Ben-Gurion and the IDF were largely left on
their own to decide and execute policy towards conquered communities,
without interference or instruction by the Cabinet or the ministries. That
policy, as shall be seen, was inconsistent, circumstantial and haphazard.
The upshot – different results in different places – was determined by
a combination of factors, chief of which were the religious and ethnic
identity of the conquered populations, specific local strategic and tactical
considerations and circumstances, Ben-Gurion's views on the cases
brought, or of interest, to him, the amount and quality of resistance
offered in each area, and the character and proclivities of particular
IDF commanders. The result was that the Ramle–Lydda and Tel as
Safi areas were almost completely emptied of their Arab populations
while in Western and Lower Galilee the bulk of the Christian and Druse
inhabitants as well as many Muslims stayed put and were allowed to
remain in place.

THE NORTH

The operational orders for Mivtza Dekel spoke of 'attacking . . .
Qawuqji's forces' – the Arab Liberation Army units in Western Galilee
and in and around Nazareth – and 'completely destroying' them. No explicit mention was made of how the overrun civilian population was to
be treated.[3]

But the civilians were already under pressure, by Qawuqji, even before the start of Dekel on 9 July, at least to partially evacuate their homes.
Already on 24 June, soldiers garrisoning Ma'lul and Mujeidil instructed
the villagers 'to evacuate all their women and children [with] all their
property'. The beduin tribes 'Arab Muzeirib and 'Arab Jamuis were similarly instructed. (The beduin were also ordered to send their young
men to Ma'lul to join Qawuqji's forces – but 'they refused for fear of
their Jewish neighbours'.) The Muzeirib and a neighbouring tribe apparently packed up and evacuated the area that night.[4] Qawuqji anticipated an end to the truce and the resumption of hostilities and appears

to have believed that evacuating dependents from the villages would serve his purposes. Indeed, a day or two before the resumption of the fighting, Qawuqji's headquarters instructed all the inhabitants of the villages 'around Nazareth' to 'sleep outside the[ir] villages', starting on the night of 8 July. The villagers of 'Illut, west of the town, were reported on 7 July to have begun leaving; the departees included the mukhtar and several other notables.[5] That day, 'all the women and children' of Mujeidil and Ma'lul were reported to have been moved to Nazareth, and the same was happening 'in the rest of the villages in the area'.[6] The ALA was not alone at this time in instructing inhabitants to evacuate villages in Lower Galilee that were potential combat zones: during the first week of July, the residents of Nein and Tamra were urged by relatives already in Nazareth 'to immediately end the harvest . . . and leave for Nazareth . . .'.[7]

The first stage of Mivtza Dekel, during 8–14 July, saw the 7th Brigade and the 21st Battalion of the Carmeli Brigade advance eastwards from the Acre–Nahariya area into the western Galilee's hill-country, capturing the villages of 'Amqa (Muslim), Kuweikat (Muslim), Kafr Yasif (Muslim and Christian), Abu Sinan (Druse and Christian), Julis (Druse) and al Makr (Christian and Muslim) and then, further to the south, I'billin (Christian and Muslim) and Shafa 'Amr (Muslim, Christian and Druse).

Prior to this, the Druse collectively had decided to part company with the Muslims and Christians. Already on 23 June, the Druse notables of Abu Sinan, Julis and Yarka had decided to stay out of the hostilities.[8] Along with the notables in other Druse villages, they were also determined to stay put (as, in less uniform and organised fashion, were many Christian villagers). Muslim villagers, on the other hand, were by and large determined to resist and to evacuate should they fall under Israeli control. Apparently, this was also what the IDF commanders involved wanted. Dov Yirmiya, a company commander in the 21st Battalion, recalled the attack on Kuweikat thus: 'I don't know whether the artillery softening up of the village caused casualties but the psychological effect was achieved and the village's non-combatant inhabitants fled before we began the assault.' A few of the inhabitants had participated in the Yehiam Convoy battle and massacre of 28 March, and this, a fact known to the Israeli commanders, may have been a factor in unleashing the relatively strong barrage on Kuweikat. Certainly the inhabitants feared retribution, which contributed to their panicky departure. Some of the villagers had already left in June, after an earlier, abortive IDF attack. ALA officers apparently told the villagers during the First Truce to prepare defences and not to send away their women, children and old; it was probably felt that leaving them in the village would bolster the militiamen's staying power. On 9 July, the IDF appealed to the village to surrender, but the *mukhtar*, probably fearing a charge of treason by the ALA, refused. That night, the Carmeli Brigade let loose with artillery. One inhabitant later recalled:

> We were awakened by the loudest noise we had ever heard, shells exploding . . . the whole village was in panic . . . women were screaming, children were crying . . . Most of the villagers began to flee with their pyjamas on. The wife of Qassim Ahmad Sa'id fled carrying a pillow in her arms instead of her child.

The village militiamen quickly followed, some of them going to 'Amqa, whose inhabitants also fled following an IDF artillery barrage on their own village. The handful of Kuweikat villagers – mostly old people – who stayed put when the village fell were apparently expelled to neighbouring Abu Sinan. The Druse of Abu Sinan subsequently refused to give most of them shelter and they moved on into Upper Galilee and Lebanon.[9]

Elsewhere, the IDF refrained from serious use of artillery, and the Druse and Christian inhabitants remained, while many Muslim inhabitants fled. The Druse villagers, according to OC Northern Front Carmel, often helped the Israelis beforehand with intelligence and greeted the conquering columns with song, dance and animal sacrifices.[10] Most of the Muslims fled mainly out of fear of Israeli retaliation for having supported or assisted Qawuqji's troops.

At Shafa 'Amr, Israeli–Druse cooperation peaked, with IDF intelligence agents and Druse emissaries repeatedly meeting during the days before the assault and arranging a sham Druse resistance and surrender. Early on 14 July, after a heavy artillery barrage on the Muslim quarter and military positions, the entering 7th Brigade found the town almost completely empty of Muslims. Most had fled to Saffuriya, to the east.[11]

The arrival of thousands of Shafa 'Amr refugees in Saffuriya on 14–15 July severely undermined morale in the host village. IDF aircraft bombed Saffuriya on the night of 15 July, apparently killing a few inhabitants and causing panic; the villagers were not prepared for air attack. The village was also hit by artillery. The mass evacuation began, the villagers initially moving to nearby gullies and orchards. Though sought, no help came from the ALA in Nazareth, and the Saffuriya militiamen, despairing, on 16 July joined their families and fled northwards, mostly to Lebanon. A small number – about 100, mostly old people – stayed put.[12] During the following days IDF sappers blew up 30 houses.[13] Later, the remaining handful were joined by hundreds of infiltrating returnees and by December, according to the IDF, there were 450 people in the village;[14] 550 by early January 1949. Later that month, Northern Front expelled them all to 'Illut.[15]

Those remaining in Mujeidil were apparently driven out toward Nazareth.[16] Of the villages captured in the second stage of Dekel, only Mujeidil, Ma'lul, ar Ruweis and Damun were completely emptied of inhabitants and, later, along with Saffuriya, leveled. It is worth noting that four of these villages were completely or overwhelmingly Muslim and that at least Saffuriya and Mujeidil had strongly supported Qawuqji and had a history of anti-Yishuv behaviour (prominently during 1936–1939). Some of them, especially Saffuriya, put up strong resistance to the IDF advance. In all the other villages captured in the second phase of Operation Dekel and where the IDF had encountered no, or no serious, resistance, at least a core of inhabitants stayed put (usually by clan, some clans preferring to depart, some to stay), and these villages exist to this day.

Most observers at the time believed that the IDF, in Dekel, had roughly drawn a distinction between Muslims on the one hand and Druse and Christians on the other. Yitzhak Avira, an old-time HIS hand and something of an Arabist, wrote about this in critical terms to Danin. Avira noted the 'cleansing [of the area] of Muslims and a softer attitude towards Christians . . . [and] Druse'. He related that he had visited Shafa 'Amr and had seen 'wanted' Christians and Druse who 'not only walked about freely, but also had on their faces joy at the misfortune of the Muslims who had been expelled'. Avira warned of the 'danger' of assuming that Christians and Druse were 'kosher' while Muslims were 'non-kosher'. He conceded that the Muslims were 'our serious enemies, especially the Husseini [supporters]', but added that some Druse and Christians were also dangerous and untrustworthy.[17]

Overwhelmingly Christian Nazareth from the first was earmarked for special treatment because of its importance to the Christian world. On the eve of the attack, there was 'great fear' and 'panic' in the town. An IDF bombing raid, though causing no casualties, apparently jolted local morale, triggering flight by those 'with means'.[18] People were sleeping 'outside their homes', it was reported. While the inhabitants were unwilling to resist and turn their town into a battlefield, the ALA was trying to prevent the inhabitants from fleeing, according to IDF intelligence.[19] But many left nonetheless.[20]

The order for the conquest of Nazareth (and several neighbouring villages) – codenamed 'Mivtza Ya'ar' (Operation Forest) – made no mention of how the town's civilians were to be treated.[21] But on 15 July, the day before Nazareth fell, Ben-Gurion ordered the army to prepare a special administrative task force to take over and run the town smoothly and to issue warnings against the desecration of 'monasteries and churches' (mosques were not mentioned) and against looting. Soldiers caught looting should be fired upon, 'with machine-guns, mercilessly', Ben-Gurion instructed.[22] The order was transmitted down the ranks and was strictly obeyed. Carmel instructed the Carmeli, Golani and 7th brigades not to loot and not to damage churches in the 'cradle of Christianity, holy to many millions'.[23] Golani's OC, Nahum Golan (Spiegel), explained: 'Because of its importance to the Christian world – the behaviour of the occupation forces in the town could serve as a factor in determining the prestige of the young state abroad.'[24] Even the property of those who had fled Nazareth was treated more diffidently than elsewhere.[25]

On 16 July, units of the Golani and 7th brigades occupied the town, suffering one soldier wounded (the Arabs had 16 dead).[26] As the troops entered, the ALA units fled – and 'immediately, white flags appeared on most of Nazareth's buildings . . . A real wave of joy engulfed the city, joy mixed with dread regarding what was about to happen.' The inhabitants, according to IDF intelligence, were happy at the departure of the 'tyranny and humiliation . . . beating, cursing, shooting and detentions' they had suffered at the hands of the Palestinian irregulars, headed by Tawfiq Ibrahim ('Abu Ibrahim') and, subsequently (and to a lesser degree), at the hands of the ALA's Iraqi soldiery. But they were filled with dread lest 'the reports that they had received about the Jews' behaviour in [other] conquered areas' be confirmed, 'especially [those regarding] . . . rape . . . in Acre and Ramle'. But the inhabitants were quickly reassured by the Israelis' benign behaviour. The locals handed over their arms and 'a general atmosphere of cooperation prevailed among all classes'. The few incidents of robbery did not mar the proceedings. By the second day, 'the markets and shops were open and the streets filled with people. It was evident that the inhabitants, who had suffered from a severe lack of food, were hoping to see us as saviours in this respect.'[27]

On the evening of 16 July the remaining notables and Haim Laskov, OC Operation Dekel, signed an instrument of surrender. Combatants were to surrender and arms were to be handed over. The mayor was to remain in place and 'the Government of Israel . . . recognised the equal civil rights of all the inhabitants of Nazareth as of all the citizens of Israel without attention to religion, race or language'.[28]

Yet the following day, 17 July, the army issued an expulsion order. According to Ben-Gurion, it was Carmel, the front commander, who had given the order 'to uproot all the inhabitants of Nazareth;[29] according to Colonel Ben Dunkelman, the Canadian commander of 7th Brigade, the order had come from Laskov, his immediate superior.[30] Hours earlier, Laskov had appointed Dunkelman military governor of Nazareth. But Dunkelman was 'shocked and horrified' and refused to carry out the order,[31] forcing Laskov to obtain higher sanction. Laskov asked IDF General Staff for a ruling: 'Tell me immediately, urgently, whether to expel [leharhik] the inhabitants from the city of Nazareth. In my view all, save for clerics, should be expelled.'[32] The matter was referred to Ben-Gurion, who vetoed the proposal. 'According to the order of the defence minister, the inhabitants of Nazareth should not be expelled', the Golani Brigade was told that evening.[33] Meanwhile, Laskov appointed another officer as military governor, in Dunkelman's stead.

The townspeople were unaware of these goings on and quickly settled down to life under the Israelis. Indeed, the situation was so good that villagers from the surrounding area poured in.[34] Shimoni, of the Foreign Ministry, urged the military governor to 'demand that the church leaders and the Muslims' send a cable to the Pope and other 'appropriate addresses' affirming the Jews' 'good behaviour toward the holy places'.[35] To prevent depredations against the Arab citizenry, on 22 July the IDF declared the town off limits 'to all soldiers' save those with special permits.[36]

In the days following its conquest, Nazareth contained about 15,000 inhabitants and 20,000 refugees. An Arab informant reported that all told about '30,000' people had fled the town and the surrounding villages, most of them going to Lebanon. In Bint Jbail, in southern Lebanon, the joke was that the locals were renting out to the refugees shady spots under fig trees for P£25. The refugees' situation, in terms of food, was reportedly 'very bad'. Lebanon had tried to bar entry to refugees unless they had with them at least P£100. During the following weeks, refugees in large numbers were infiltrating through IDF lines back to Nazareth,[37] while villagers who had initially fled to Nazareth – from Shafa 'Amr, Kafr Kanna, Dabburiyya, etc. – were being allowed to return to their villages.

Why most of Nazareth's inhabitants, despite the battle around them, had stayed put was explained – in part inadvertently – by Shitrit after he visited the town. No doubt, Qawuqji's prevention of flight from the city just before and on 15 July played a part. Moreover, the inhabitants' maltreatment by the ALA and the fact that the town's mayor, Yusuf Bek al Fahum, and other municipal councilors, along with much of the municipal bureaucracy and the 170 policemen, had stayed, discounting fears of expected Jewish atrocities and retribution, had also contributed. The occupying troops had generally behaved well. A Minority Affairs Ministry official, Elisha Sulz, rather than a military man, had quickly (on 18 July) been appointed military governor, and had been advised by Chizik, former military governor of Jaffa, on how to behave.

During his visit, Shitrit had also instructed Sulz on behaviour towards the population: to get the search for weapons over quickly, and to open the shops and renew normal life as soon as possible. The minister asked that a judge be appointed, the municipality and post office be reactivated and measures be taken against the spread of infection and epidemics. And Shitrit told the Cabinet that 'the army must be given strict instructions to [continue to] behave well and fairly towards the inhabitants of the town because of the great political importance of the city in the eyes of the world'.

The thousands who had nonetheless fled the town immediately after conquest had done so, according to Shitrit, because they had believed 'spurious and counterfeit Arab propaganda . . . about atrocities by Jews, who cut off hands with axes, break legs and rape women, etc.'. Some 200 of the Fahum clan had fled to Lebanon, he said, 'mainly out of fear of rape of women'. Sulz later reported that most of those who had fled had been Qawuqji collaborators.[38] But during the following weeks, as some refugees, evading Arab and Israeli roadblocks, were making their way back to Nazareth, Muslims were continuing to leave the town – at the rate of 10 families a day, and growing, according to one IDF intelligence informant.[39]

During Dekel's second stage, over 15–18 July, units of the 7th Brigade captured ar Ruweis (Muslim), Damun (mostly Muslim), Kabul (Muslim), Sh'ab (Muslim), Tamra (Muslim), Mi'ar (Muslim), Kaukab (Muslim) and Kafr Manda (Muslim), while other units captured the villages around Nazareth, including Ma'lul (Christian and Muslim), Yafia (Muslim and Christian), 'Illut (Muslim), ar Reina (Muslim and Christian), Kafr Kanna (Muslim and Christian), Rummana (Muslim), 'Uzeir (Muslim), Tur'an (Muslim and Christian) and Bu'eina (Muslim) (as well as Mujeidil and Saffuriya, both Muslim).

Events followed a pattern similar to that in the first stage of the operation. Either with the approach of the IDF columns or after the pre- liminary artillery barrage or during the skirmish on the outskirts, most Muslim villagers fled, eastwards and northwards. The earlier Arab loss of Acre and the villages to the east, and, later, Nazareth, Mujeidil and Saffuriya, severely undermined Muslim morale. Where there were sub- stantial Christian communities, the IDF expected and encountered less resistance and, consequently, used less artillery fire – and the inhabi- tants by and large stayed put. The inhabitants of several largely Muslim villages – such as Dabburiyya and Iksal – who stayed and offered no resistance were not molested when the IDF moved in.

The conquest of towns and villages both inside and outside the parti- tion plan Jewish state had raised a general problem of governance: how was Israel to behave toward its Arab citizens, how were they to be cared for, watched over and governed? Until July, the leadership had taken an *ad hoc* approach, appointing military governors for each conquered town; these had felt out and established their powers while dealing with the day-to-day problems that arose *vis-à-vis* the population and other state agencies (especially the IDF and Minority Affairs Ministry). But the conquest of three towns outside the partition borders, Nazareth and, a few days earlier, Lydda and Ramle, highlighted and exacerbated the gen- eral questions, which Ben-Gurion had formulated two months before:

> There is a need to determine rules regarding a conquered city . . . Who rules it: The [military] commander or an appointed governor . . . What will be his powers . . . *vis-à-vis* the inhabitants [and] their property? . . . Should Arabs be expelled? . . . What is the rule regarding Arabs who stay? . . . Who looks after those who stay?[40]

Uniformity – a policy – had to be established in the treatment of Arab communities and areas incorporated into the state and a central guiding hand had to control and supervise that treatment. On 21 July 1948, the Ministerial Committee for Abandoned Property decided on the establishment of a 'Military Government Department' in the Defence Ministry and Ben-Gurion decided to appoint Elimelekh Avner (Zelikovich), a veteran Haganah officer, as its director, with the rank of general. Avner spent the following weeks studying the subject, touring the conquered towns and meeting military governors and officials. In mid-August, he received and accepted his commission. Initially, four military 'governorates' came under his jurisdiction: Western Galilee (Acre), which included Haifa; Galilee (Nazareth); Jaffa; and Lydda-Ramle. Others (Majdal and Negev (Beersheba)) were added as the southern coastal plain and the northern Negev were brought under Israeli control in October–November. With the help of attached IDF units, the governors ruled the communities, imposing curfews, handing out residency and travel permits, organising municipal services, dispensing food and health care to the needy, establishing schools and kindergartens, and organising search operations for infiltrating refugees and their expulsion. As part of the Defence Ministry, the Military Government was directly subordinate to the defence minister in matters of policy, but in terms of daily functioning – manpower, equipment, and operations – it operated as a military unit under IDF\GS supervision. Partly for this reason, as well as because of their bifurcated tasks, a lack of clarity characterised the authorities' treatment of the Arab communities during the following months, with continuous clashes over powers and areas of jurisdiction between the IDF, the Military Government and the Minority Affairs Ministry.[41]

The fall of Nazareth and its satellite villages was a formidable blow to the morale of the rest of the rural population in Lower Galilee; most of the surrounding villages fell to the IDF without a fight and the inhabitants were left in place. Dekel operational orders contained no instructions to expel. The first to fall was 'Illut, just west of Nazareth, on 16 July. The available documentation does not paint a clear picture of what exactly happened. The villagers may (or may not) have resisted the conquering force, Golani's 13th Battalion. Some 15 inhabitants were killed that day and the inhabitants fled, according to one Golani report. Two days later, after the force left, the inhabitants began to return. An IDF patrol ordered the returnees to leave. At the end of July, troops surrounded the village and, during a 'search and identification' operation, shot and killed 'about 10' inhabitants – 'while trying to escape', according to a Golani Brigade report.[42] The report was written in response to a complaint sent to Ben-Gurion about the troops' behaviour. The unnamed complainant wrote (confusedly) that '46 ['Illut] youngsters' had been detained 'and taken to an unknown destination. Some of these people were found dead in the hills on 3.8.1948 by Arab shepherds. That day, 14 of the prisoners were murdered in the olive grove near 'Illut in the presence of the villagers – women and children.'[43] But the villagers were not expelled (and 'Illut today has a population of 5,800 Muslims).

Another atrocity occurred in Kafr Manda, a village on the edge of the area occupied in Dekel that was to change hands repeatedly. The initial occupying force 'behaved well', disarming the population. Thereafter, IDF patrols from time to time visited the village. Then, apparently in August, an ALA force moved in and, maltreating the remaining inhabitants, forced them to build fortifications and supply the troops with water and food. The ALA was peeved at the villagers' surrender to the IDF. One day, an IDF force attacked the village, the ALA fled and the inhabitants took refuge in the mosque. 'A Jewish officer named Shlomo came to the mosque and pulled out some 20 young men and led them to the spring, where he stood them in a line [and] pulled out two and executed them.' The Israelis – apparently angered by the villagers' help to the ALA – then left and the village was again occupied by the ALA, finally falling into Israeli hands in October.[44]

But 'Illut and Kafr Manda were exceptional. Most of the villages fell without battle and without atrocities or expulsions. On 17 July, Daburriyya and Iksal and the beduin tribe of 'Arab al Zbeih ('Arab al Shibli), all at the foot of Mount Tabor, surrendered without a fight and handed over their weapons.[45] Many of Daburriyya's young men were detained as POWs and three houses were blown up in retaliation for the murder of two Jewish girls earlier in the war.[46] That day, the villagers of Tamra, ar Ruweis, Damun, Mi'ar, Sh'ab and Majd al Kurum informed the IDF of their readiness to surrender.[47] The 7th Brigade occupied Damun and ar Ruweis on 18 July while Golani occupied the villages of Tur'an, Hittin, Mashhad, Kafr Kanna, and Nimrin. Tamra and Sh'ab were occupied, without a fight, the following day, as was Mi'ar following a firefight. The village of 'Ein Mahal was also occupied, the elders signing an instrument of surrender in which they agreed that those who had fled the village could not return on pain of execution, and their property was declared forfeit.[48]

Sakhnin surrendered on 20 July, its notables having asked the IDF to occupy the village. An IDF patrol drove in, was handed 15 rifles, and then left. But before a permanent garrison could be installed, Qawuqji's troops surrounded the village, exchanged fire with the locals, killing several, and took control.[49] Neighbouring Deir Hanna and 'Arraba, which also sought to surrender, were not occupied and all three remained in Arab hands until their conquest by the IDF in Operation Hiram at the end of October.[50]

THE CENTRE

For the IDF, Operation Dani was the linchpin of the 'Ten Days'. The aim was to relieve the pressure on semi-besieged Jerusalem, secure the length of the Tel Aviv–Jerusalem road and neutralise the perceived threat to Tel Aviv from the Arab Legion, whose forward units, in Lydda and Ramle, were less than 20 kilometres away.

From the start of the war, militiamen from Ramle and Lydda had attacked Jewish traffic on nearby roads. Jewish retaliatory strikes, such as that by the Haganah, on 10 December 1947, in which 15 empty Arab vehicles, including two buses, were destroyed in a parking lot in Ramle and two guards were killed,[51] and the IZL's bomb attack, on 18 February 1948, in Ramle's market, in which seven died and two dozen were injured,[52] eroded Arab morale. So did the massacre, apparently by the IZL, of ten Arab workers (one of them a woman) in the groves near 'Arab al Satariyya ('Arab al Fadl), near Ramle, in late February 1948.[53] The notables of both Lydda and Ramle, after the initial bouts of violence, generally tried to keep the peace and keep local militants in check, but were only sporadically successful.[54] By early May, there was mass flight from Ramle, which suffered from periodic cut-offs of water and electricity and a shortage of fuel.[55] Militiamen on Ramle's outskirts were reportedly preventing young males from leaving town, though women, children and the old were allowed to go.[56] On 30 May, the IDF's embryonic air force briefly bombed Ramle and Lydda, killing three and injuring at least 11 persons.[57] All of this took a toll on morale.

Even before the First Truce, IDF\GS and Ben-Gurion had begun to think offensively *vis-à-vis* the two towns. The Kiryati Brigade, responsible for Tel Aviv, in late May reported that the Arabs had a 'substantial force concentrated (including armour and apparently also artillery) in the Ramle-Lydda-[Lydda] Airport-Wilhelma-Beit Nabala line' and the idea that they might 'break out in the direction of Tel Aviv' had to be taken into account.[58] On 30 May, Ben-Gurion told his generals that the two towns 'might serve as bases for attack on Tel Aviv' and other settlements. Their conquest by the IDF would gain new territory for the state, release forces tied down in the defense of Tel Aviv and the highway to Jerusalem, and sever Arab transportation lines. While the Arab Legion in fact had only one, defensively-oriented company (about 120–150 soldiers) in Lydda and Ramle together, and a second-line company at Beit Nabala to the north, IDF intelligence and Operation Dani OC General Yigal Allon believed at the start of the offensive that they faced a far stronger Legion force and one whose deployment was potentially aggressive, posing a threat to Tel Aviv itself.[59]

Allon was appointed OC Operation Dani only on 7 July, some 48 hours before battle was joined. Neither his operational orders for Dani, nor the operational orders for Operation Ludar and Operation LRLR, earlier plans upon which Dani was based, dealt with the prospective fate of the civilian population of the two towns and the surrounding villages.[60] But during May–June, Ben-Gurion appears to have developed an obsession regarding Lydda and Ramle, partly because they sat astride the Tel Aviv–Jerusalem road and, ultimately, threatened Jewish Jerusalem, partly because of their proximity, and threat, to Tel Aviv. Repeatedly he jotted down in his diary that Lydda and Ramle had to be 'destroyed':[61] In mid-June, he spoke in Cabinet of the need to remove 'these two thorns' in the Yishuv's side.[62]

In July 1948, the two towns together had a population of roughly 50,000–70,000, of whom 20,000 or so were refugees from Jaffa and its environs. The inhabitants had some reason for confidence: the towns lay outside the partition plan Jewish state and the presence in them of Arab Legion troops implied a commitment by King Abdullah to their defence. (Conversely, the withdrawal of these Legionnaires during 11–13 July was to have a devastating effect on morale.) Unlike Haifa or Jaffa (where the feeling of isolation and siege had been severe), the two towns were contiguous with the heavily Arab-populated hinterland of the West Bank. And there had been the month of quiet during the First Truce. 'The civilian population has not left the towns, and they do not believe that we will succeed in conquering the two towns because they are well-fortified', an IDF intelligence officer concluded on 28 June.[63]

But there were also serious demoralising factors. There had been two (unsuccessful) Jewish ground attacks on Ramle on the nights of 21–22 May and 24–25 May and the Haganah air arm bombing of the towns a few days later. Taken together, the two towns had been put on notice. As well, the protracted presence in the towns of thousands of refugees from areas already conquered by the Jews must certainly have had a destabilising effect. The refugees were hungry and short of money; braving possible IDF fire, they made foraging raids into the fields in no-man's land 'to gather the stalks of wheat and vegetables'. Moreover, the towns had suffered from severe unemployment since the start of the hostilities (many had been employed in Jewish settlements) and from occasional food shortages, which had triggered sharp price increases. Some wealthy families had fled to the Triangle or Jordan during the previous months.[64] Operation Dani, which involved four IDF brigades and began on the night of 9 July, was swiftly to complete the demoralisation of the towns and, within days, to result in the almost complete exodus of their inhabitants eastward.

From the start, the operations against Lydda and Ramle were designed to induce civilian panic and flight – as a means of precipitating military collapse and possibly also as an end itself. After the initial air attacks on the towns, Operation Dani headquarters at 11:30 hours, 10 July, informed IDF\GS: there was 'a general and serious [civilian] flight from Ramle. There is great value in continuing the bombing.'[65] During the afternoon, the headquarters asked General Staff for renewed bombing, and informed one of the brigades: 'Flight from the town of Ramle of women, the old and children is to be facilitated. The [military age] males are to be detained.'[66]

The bombing and shelling of 10 July were successful. The following day, Yiftah Brigade's intelligence officer reported: 'The bombing from the air and artillery [shelling] of Lydda and Ramle caused flight and panic among the civilians [and] a readiness to surrender.' That day, Operation Dani HQ repeatedly asked for further bombing, 'including [with] incendiaries'.[67] Civilian morale (and the military will to resist) was further dented by the raid on late afternoon 11 July of the 89th Battalion (commanded by Lt. Colonel Moshe Dayan) on Lydda and along the Lydda–Ramle road. Two of the battalion's companies, mounted on an armoured car, jeeps, scout cars and half-tracks, drove through Lydda from east to west spraying machine-gun fire at anything that moved, and then proceeded southwards, shooting up militia outposts along the Lydda–Ramle road, reaching Ramle's train station on the town's northeastern edge, before returning to their starting point at Ben Shemen. The battalion suffered six dead and 21 wounded – but killed and wounded dozens of Arabs (perhaps as many as 200).[68] One of Dayan's troopers, 'Gideon', was some months later to describe what he saw and felt that day:

> [My] jeep made the turn and here at the . . . entrance to the house opposite stands an Arab girl, stands and screams with eyes filled with fear and dread. She is all torn and dripping blood – she is certainly wounded. Around her on the ground lie the corpses of her family. Still quivering, death has not yet redeemed them from their pain. Next to her is a bundle of rags – her mother, hand outstretched trying to draw her into the house. And the girl understands nothing . . . Did I fire at her? . . . But why these thoughts, for we are in the midst of battle, in the midst of conquest of the town. The enemy is at every corner. Every one is an enemy. Kill! Destroy! Murder! Otherwise you will be murdered and will not conquer the town. What [feeling] did this lone girl stir within you? Continue to shoot! Move forward! . . . Where does this desire to murder come from? What, because your friend . . . was killed or wounded, you have lost your humanity and you kill and destroy? Yes! . . . I kill every one who belongs to the enemy camp: man, woman, old person, child. And I am not deterred.[69]

To judge from this description, the battalion's death-dispensing dash through Lydda combined elements of a battle and a massacre. Some months later, in November, Natan Alterman, Israel's most celebrated poet, was to portray the operation in a condemnatory, moralistic poem.[70] Be that as it may, the battalion's hour-long expedition certainly shook morale in Lydda (and probably in Ramle).

How many civilians fled Lydda and Ramle over 10–11 July, before the capture of the towns, is unclear. Dani HQ reported 'serious general flight' from Ramle already on the morning of 10 July.[71] The flight gained momentum during the night of 11–12 July, after the withdrawal from Ramle of the Arab Legion company based there. Yiftah HQ had apparently initiated contact on 10 July with Ramle's notables to bring about a surrender.[72] The following day, IDF aircraft dropped leaflets on the two towns calling for surrender: 'Whoever resists – will die. He who chooses life will surrender.' The notables of Ramle were instructed to proceed by foot to the village of Barriya holding aloft a white flag; Lydda's notables were told to go Jimzo.[73] During the night of 11–12 July, a delegation of Ramle notables – Isma'in Nakhas, Haret Haji, Hussam al Khairi, and Imada Khouri – reached Barriya and were ferried to Yiftah Brigade HQ at Kibbutz Na'an, where the following morning they signed a formal instrument of surrender.[74] The document stated that all arms and 'all strangers in the town' would be handed over to the army; 'all non-military age inhabitants . . . would be allowed to leave town should they wish to'; 'the lives and peace of the inhabitants would be guaranteed if their representatives . . . will cooperate with the army'.[75] Kiryati Brigade's 42nd Battalion entered Ramle later that morning and imposed a curfew.

In Lydda, where no formal surrender was signed, events took a more violent turn. The Yiftah Brigade's 3rd Battalion fought its way into town on the evening of 11 July, hard on the heels of the 89th Battalion's blitz. Supported by a company from the brigade's 1st Battalion, the 3rd Battalion took up positions in the town centre. A small force of Legionnaires and irregulars continued to hold out at the police fort on the southern edge of town. 'Groups of old and young, women and children streamed down the streets in a great display of submissiveness, bearing white flags, and entered of their own free will the detention compounds we arranged in the mosque and church – Muslims and Christians separately.' Soon, the two sites were overflowing: 'There was a need to let the women and children go and to collect only the adult males.' A curfew was imposed, by which time only a few thousand males were in detention.[76]

The calm in Lydda was shattered at 11:30 hours, 12 July, when two or three Legion armoured cars, commanded by Lt. Hamadallah al 'Abdullah, either lost or on reconnaissance or seeking a missing officer, entered the town. A firefight erupted and, eventually, the armoured cars withdrew.[77] But the noise of the skirmish sparked sniping by armed Lydda townspeople against the occupying troops; some townspeople probably believed that the Legion was counter-attacking and tried to assist.[78]

The 300–400 Israeli troops in the town, dispersed in semi-isolated pockets in the midst of thousands of hostile townspeople, some still armed, felt threatened, vulnerable and angry: they had understood that the town had surrendered. 3rd Battalion OC Moshe Kelman ordered the troops to suppress the sniping – which Israeli and Arab historians and chroniclers, for different reasons, were later to describe as an 'uprising' – with the utmost severity. The troops were told to shoot at 'any clear target' or, alternatively, at anyone 'seen on the streets'.[79] At 13:15, Yiftah HQ informed Dani HQ: 'Battles have erupted in Lydda. We have hit an armoured car with a two-pounder [gun] and killed many Arabs. There are still exchanges of fire in the town. We have taken many wounded.'[80]

Some townspeople, shut up in their houses under curfew, took fright at the sound of shooting outside, perhaps believing that a massacre was in progress. They rushed into the streets – and were cut down by Israeli fire. Some of the soldiers also fired and lobbed grenades into houses from which snipers were suspected to be operating. In the confusion, dozens of unarmed detainees in one mosque compound, the Dahaimash Mosque, in the town centre, were shot and killed. Apparently, some of them tried to break out and escape, perhaps fearing that they would be massacred. IDF troops threw grenades and apparently fired PIAT (bazooka) rockets into the compound.[81]

By 13:30, it was all over. The IDF had lost three–four dead and about a dozen wounded. Yeruham Cohen, an intelligence officer at Operation Dani headquarters, later described the scene:

> The inhabitants of the town became panic-stricken. They feared that . . . the IDF troops would take revenge on them. It was a horrible, earsplitting scene. Women wailed at the top of their voices and old men said prayers, as if they saw their own deaths before their eyes.[82]

Yiftah's fire caused 'some 250 dead . . . and many wounded'.[83] The ratio of Arab to Israeli casualties was hardly consistent with the descriptions of what had happened as an 'uprising' or battle. In any event, the Israeli officers in charge were later to regard the suppression of the 'uprising' (and the subsequent expulsion of the townspeople) as a dismal episode in Yiftah's history. 'There is no doubt that the Lydda–Ramle affair and the flight of the inhabitants, the uprising and the expulsion [geirush] that followed cut deep grooves in all who underwent [these experiences]', Yiftah Brigade OC Mula Cohen was to write.[84] These events were accompanied and followed by a great deal of looting.

The Third Battalion was withdrawn from Lydda on the night of 13–14 July and, along with the brigade's other battalions, spent the following day in a 'soul-searching gathering' in the Ben Shemen Wood, where they were berated by Cohen and forced to hand over their loot, which was subsequently thrown onto a large bonfire and destroyed.[85] But the looting of the empty houses of Ramle and Lydda by groups of troops continued, apparently, for weeks.[86]

While some IDF officers began advising people in Lydda to leave the town already during the morning of 12 July,[87] before the outbreak of the shooting, the mass exodus from both towns, which began a few hours later, must be seen against the backdrop of the massacre. The shooting in the centre of Lydda also sealed the fate of the inhabitants of Ramle. As the outbreak of sniping had scared the Third Battalion, so, apparently, it had shaken Operation Dani HQ, where, during the previous hours, it was believed that the two towns were securely in IDF hands. The unexpected eruption highlighted the threat of a Jordanian counter-attack accompanied by a mass uprising by a large Arab population behind Israeli lines, as Allon's brigades continued their push eastwards, towards the operation's second-stage objectives, Latrun and Ramallah. The shooting focused minds at Operation Dani HQ at Yazur. A strong desire to depopulate the two towns already existed; the shooting seemed to offer the justification and opportunity for what the bombings and artillery barrages, insubstantial by World War II standards, had in the main failed to achieve.

Ben-Gurion was at Yazur that afternoon. According to the best account of the meeting, at which Yadin, Ayalon and Allon, Israel Galili and Lt Colonel Yitzhak Rabin, chief of operations of Operation Dani (and of the Palmah), were present, someone, possibly Allon, after hearing of the outbreak in Lydda, proposed expelling the inhabitants of the two towns. Ben-Gurion said nothing, and no decision was taken. Then Ben-Gurion, Allon and Rabin stepped outside for a cigarette. Allon reportedly asked: 'What shall we do with the Arabs?' Ben-Gurion responded with a dismissive, energetic gesture with his hand and said: 'Expel them [garesh otam].'[88]

Within minutes, at 13:30 hours, just as the shooting was dying down, Operation Dani HQ issued the following order to Yiftah Brigade HQ:

1. The inhabitants of Lydda must be expelled quickly without attention to age. They should be directed towards Beit Nabala. Yiftah [Brigade HQ] must determine the method and inform [Operation] Dani HQ and 8th Brigade HQ.
2. Implement immediately.

The order was signed 'Yitzhak R[abin].'[89] A similar order, concerning Ramle, was apparently communicated to Kiryati Brigade headquarters at the same time. An echo of that order is to be found in a cable the following day from Kiryati Brigade HQ to its officer in charge of Ramle, Zvi Aurbach:

1. In light of the deployment of 42nd Battalion out of Ramle – you must take [over responsibility] for the defence of the town, the transfer of the prisoners [to PoW camps] and the emptying of the town of its inhabitants.
2. You must continue the sorting out of the inhabitants, and send the army-age males to a prisoner of war camp. The old, women and children will be transported by vehicle to al Qubab and will be moved across the lines – [and] from there will continue on foot . . .[90]

Already during the afternoon of 12 July, Kiryati officers began organising transport to ferry Ramle's inhabitants toward Arab Legion lines. Local, confiscated Arab transport and the brigade's own vehicles proved insufficient. During the night of 12–13 July, Kiryati OC Ben-Gal radioed General Staff\Operations for more vehicles.[91] Meanwhile, during the afternoon and evening of 12 July, thousands of Ramle's inhabitants streamed out of the town, on foot and in trucks and buses. In Lydda, with the troops recovering from the afternoon's shooting and burying the corpses, and the inhabitants under curfew shut away in their homes, the expulsion order was not immediately implemented. During the night of 12–13 July, two companies from Kiryati's 42nd Battalion arrived in Lydda to reinforce the 3rd Battalion.

During the afternoon of 12 July, a spanner was thrown in the works in the person of Minority Affairs Minister Shitrit. He arrived in Ramle – and almost halted the exodus from both towns before it was well under way.

The Cabinet had been told nothing of the expulsion orders. Shitrit, as was his wont, had arrived in Ramle to look over his new 'constituency'; after all, he was responsible for the Arab minority. He was shocked by what he heard and saw: Kiryati troops were in the midst of preparations to expel the inhabitants. Ben-Gal told him that 'in line with an order from . . . Paicovitch [i.e., Allon], the IDF was about to take prisoner all males of military age, and the rest of the inhabitants – men, women and children – were to be taken beyond [*sic*] the border and left to their fate'. The army 'intends to deal in the same way' with the inhabitants of Lydda, Shitrit reported.[92] Upset and angry, Shitrit returned to Tel Aviv and went to Shertok, reporting on what he had heard. Shertok rushed to Ben-Gurion and the two men hammered out a set of policy guidelines for IDF behaviour towards the population of Lydda and Ramle. Ben-Gurion apparently failed to inform Shertok (or Shitrit) that he had been the source of the original expulsion orders; perhaps he denied that any had been issued.

Shertok then wrote to Shitrit explaining what had been agreed. The guidelines reached between Shertok and Ben-Gurion, according to Shertok's letter to Shitrit of 13 July, were:

1. It should be publicly announced in the two towns that whoever wants to leave – will be allowed to do so.
2. A warning must be issued that anyone remaining behind does so on his own responsibility, and the Israeli authorities are not obliged to supply him with food.
3. Women, children, the old and the sick must on no account be forced to leave [the] town[s].
4. The monasteries and churches must not be harmed.

Shertok appeared to believe that he had averted the expulsion – but he wasn't certain. His letter ended with a caveat: 'We all know how difficult it is to overcome [base] instincts during conquest. But I hope the aforementioned policy will be carried out.'[93]

True to his word, Ben-Gurion passed on (a variant of) these guidelines to General Staff\Operations, which transmitted them to Operation Dani headquarters at 23:30 hours, 12 July, in somewhat abridged form:

1. All are free to leave, apart from those who will be detained.
2. To warn that we are not responsible for feeding those who remain.
3. Not to force women, the sick, children and the old to go\walk [*lalechet* – a possibly deliberate ambiguity].
4. Not to touch monasteries and churches.
5. Searches without vandalism.
6. No robbery.'[94]

But Ben-Gurion, clearly, was saying different things to different people over 12–13 July. Finance Minister Kaplan, for instance, said that Ben-Gurion had told him – either late on 12 July or early 13 July – that the orders were that 'the young male inhabitants [of Ramle and Lydda] were to be taken prisoner. The rest of the inhabitants were to be encouraged to leave the place [*yesh le'oded la'azov et hamakom*], but whoever stayed – Israel would have to take care of his maintenance.'[95]

Shitrit came away from his meeting with Shertok and his reading of Shertok's letter of 13 July believing that he had averted a wholesale expulsion. He was wrong. During 13–14 July, the townspeople of both Ramle and Lydda were ordered and 'encouraged' to leave. At the same time, the inhabitants – especially of Lydda – probably needed little such 'encouragement.' Within a 72-hour period, they had undergone the shock of battle and unexpected conquest by the Jews, abandonment by the Arab Legion, a slaughter, a curfew with house-to-house searches, a round-up of able-bodied males and the separation of families, lack of food and medical attention, the flight of relatives, continuous isolation in their homes and general dread of the future. News of what had happened in Lydda probably reached Ramle, three kilometres away, almost immediately, causing fright. During the night of 12–13 July, many of the remaining inhabitants of the towns probably decided that it would be best not to live under Jewish rule. The fall of the Lydda police fort on the morning of 13 July, may, for some, have clinched the issue.

Thus, at this point, there was dovetailing, as it were, of Jewish and Arab interests and wishes – an IDF bent on expelling, and preparing the expulsion of, the population and a population ready, perhaps even eager, to move to Arab-held territory. There remained, however, one problem: the detained able-bodied Ramle and Lydda menfolk, whom their parents, women and children were loath to abandon. The stage was set for the 'deal' struck on the morning of 13 July and for the mass evacuation that followed.

The 'deal' was apparently reached in 'negotiations' between IDF intelligence officer Shmarya Guttman and other Palmah officers and some Lydda notables. The IDF said they wanted everyone to leave. The Arab notables said there could be no exodus so long as thousands of townspeople (many of them heads of families) were incarcerated in detention centres. The officers agreed to release the detainees if all the inhabitants left. The notables assented. Guttman then proceeded to the mosque, where his announcement that the detainees could leave was greeted with cries of joy. Town criers and IDF soldiers went about the town announcing that the inhabitants were about to leave and instructed them where to muster for the departure.[96]

The bulk of the exodus from Ramle and Lydda took place on 13 July. Many from Ramle were trucked and bussed out by Kiryati to al Qubab, from where they made their way on foot to Legion-held Latrun and Salbit. Others walked all the way. The 43rd Battalion's intelligence officer described it thus:

> The transfer of the [sic] refugees began at 17:30 hours. Most of the refugees are moving along the main street on the Jerusalem Road . . . From there the refugees were transported in vehicles on the Jerusalem Road to a point some 700 metres from al Qubab and sent on foot to Beit Tina [i.e., al Tina] and Salbit.[97]

All Lydda's inhabitants walked, making their way to Beit Nabala and Barfiliya.

To judge from IDF signals on 13 July, the commanders involved understood that what was happening was an expulsion rather than a spontaneous exodus. Operation Dani HQ informed General Staff/Operations at 11:35 hours: 'Lydda police fort has been captured. [The troops] are busy expelling the inhabitants ['oskim begeirush hatoshavim].' At the same time, the HQ informed Yiftah, Kiryati and 8th brigades that 'enemy resistance in Ramle and Lydda has ended. The eviction [pinui] of the inhabitants . . . has begun.'[98] Dani HQ apparently expected the removal of Lydda's inhabitants to have been completed by the evening. At 18:15 hours, the headquarters queried Yiftah Brigade: 'Has the removal of the population [hotza'at ha'ochlosiah] of Lydda been completed?'[99]

Through 12–14 July, some Yiftah and Kiryati soldiers remained unaware of the expulsion orders and may have believed that they were witnessing a spontaneous or semi-spontaneous exodus. The apparent eagerness of some of the inhabitants to leave seemed to support this. Moreover, IDF announcements to the populations were sometimes informative and instructive rather than imperative in tone: 'You will assemble at such and such points', 'you will walk towards Beit Nabala', and so on. Indeed, most of the soldiers involved probably had no need to say anything; the inhabitants understood what was expected of them. In Lydda, however, some were ordered to 'get out' by soldiers who went from house to house.

All the Israelis who witnessed these events agreed that the exodus, under a hot July sun, was an extended episode of suffering, especially for the Lydda refugees. Some were stripped by soldiers of their valuables as they left town or at checkpoints along the way.[100] Guttman subsequently described the trek:

A multitude of inhabitants walked one after another. Women walked burdened with packages and sacks on their heads. Mothers dragged children after them . . . Occasionally, [IDF] warning shots were heard . . . Occasionally, you encountered a piercing look from one of the youngsters . . . in the column, and the look said: 'We have not yet surrendered. We shall return to fight you.'

For Guttman, an archaeologist, the spectacle conjured up 'the memory of the exile of Israel [at Roman hands, two thousand years before]'; the town, he added, looked like 'after a pogrom'.[101]

One Israeli soldier (probably 3rd Battalion), from Kibbutz 'Ein Harod, a few weeks after the event recorded his vivid impressions of the refugees' thirst and hunger, of how 'children got lost' and of how a child fell into a well and drowned, ignored, as his fellow refugees fought each other to draw water.[102] Another soldier described the spoor left by the slow-shuffling columns, 'to begin with [jettisoning] utensils and furniture and in the end, bodies of men, women and children, scattered along the way'. Quite a few refugees died on the road east – from exhaustion, dehydration and disease – before reaching temporary rest near and in Ramallah. Muhammad Nimr al Khatib, working from hearsay, put the Lydda refugee death toll during the trek eastward at '335'; Arab Legion OC John Glubb, more carefully wrote that 'nobody will ever know how many children died'.[103]

The creation of the refugee columns, which for days cluttered the roads eastward, may have been one of the motives for the expulsion decision. The military thinking was simple and cogent: the IDF had just taken its two primary objectives and had, for the moment, run out of offensive steam. The Legion was expected to counter-attack (through Budrus, Jimzu, Ni'lin and Latrun). Cluttering the main axes, deep into Arab territory, with human flotsam would severely hamper the Legion. And, inevitably, the large, new wave of refugees would sap Jordanian resources at a crucial moment. An IDF logbook noted on 15 July:

The refugees from Lydda and Ramle are causing the Arab Legion great problems. There are acute problems of housing and supplies . . . In this case, the Legion is interested in giving all possible help to the refugees as the Arab public is complaining that the Legion was unforthcoming in assisting Ramle and Lydda.[104]

A Palmah report, probably written by Allon soon after, stated that the exodus, beside relieving Tel Aviv of a potential, long-term threat, had 'clogged the Legion's routes of advance' and had foisted upon the Jordanians the problem of 'maintaining another 45,000 souls . . . Moreover, the phenomenon of the flight of tens of thousands will no doubt cause demoralisation in every Arab area [the refugees] reach . . . This victory will yet have great effect on other sectors.'[105] Ben-Gurion, in his wonted oblique manner, also referred to the strategic benefits: 'The Arab Legion cables that on the road from Lydda and Ramle some 30,000 refugees are on the move, who are angry with the Legion. They demand bread. They must be transferred to Transjordan. In Transjordan there are anti-government demonstrations.'[106]

In the policy debate in Mapam during the following weeks, there was criticism of Allon's use of the refugee columns to achieve strategic aims. Party co-leader, Meir Ya'ari, said:

> Many of us are losing their [human] image . . . How easily they speak of how it is possible and permissible to take women, children and old men and to fill the roads with them because such is the imperative of strategy. And this we say, the members of Hashomer Hatza'ir, who remember who used this means against our people during the [Second World] war . . . I am appalled.[107]

On 14 July, the IDF informed Ben-Gurion that 'not one Arab inhabitant remained in Ramle and Lydda' – or so he told his Cabinet colleagues that day.[108] In truth, several hundred inhabitants remained, mostly old and sick, and a handful of Christians, including clerics. The situation in Lydda – where 'about 100' remained – was initially far worse than in Ramle: 'There is still no supply of water in the town. The dirt and filth threaten the health of both the inhabitants and the army.' A Minority Affairs Ministry official recommended moving the inhabitants to Jaffa – or 'enabling [them] to resume normal life'.[109] Over the following months, hundreds of Arabs infiltrated back into the two towns, their population swelling to some 2,000 by mid-October.[110] Meanwhile, Lydda and Ramle were settled with new immigrants and became overwhelmingly Jewish towns.

Providing basic services and food for the remaining Arab inhabitants was to burden the second-line, territorial units that replaced the 3rd and 42nd battalions in the days after the conquest. So did the presence of hundreds of unburied corpses littering Lydda's streets and houses and the road between Lydda and Ramle during 12–15 July. Initially, at least, the corpses posed a political problem: as the new (Kiryati) military governor of Ramle put it: 'The [scheduled] visit by the Red Cross tomorrow is too early and must be delayed.'[111] When at last the visit was finalised, for 15:00, 14 July, Dani HQ instructed Kiryati to 'by then evacuate all the [sic] refugees [and] to get rid of the corpses . . .'.[112] But the problem was still unresolved on 15 July: Dr Klaus Dreyer (Ya'akov Dror), of the IDF Medical Corps, complained to General Staff\Operations that there were still unburied bodies in Lydda 'and neighbouring fields' and that they were a health hazard and a 'moral and aesthetic' issue. The Medical Corps hadn't the wherewithal to deal with them. He asked General Staff\Operations to find the trucks and personnel, including 'some tens of [Arab] civilians from the towns themselves', to solve the problem.[113] Presumably, the corpses were then buried.

The fall of Lydda and Ramle and the exodus of their inhabitants were to shake Jordan. Demonstrations erupted in Amman and other towns on both sides of the river, with the Legion – and particularly its British commanders – being charged, by Palestinians and outside Arab leaders, with 'abandoning' the towns if not actually colluding with the Zionists in their demise.[114] Even among the some 2,400 local militiamen and army-age adults detained by the IDF in the towns there was 'great bitterness' toward the Legion and King Abdullah, 'who receives money from the British'.[115] The arrival in Ramallah – population 10,000 – of as many as '70,000' refugees severely undermined civilian morale. The acting mayor, Hana Khalaf, appealed to the king to order them to leave the town: they 'are dispersed in the town streets, most of them poor, they suffer from great want of basic goods and water and pose a serious threat to health'. Abdullah advised 'patience'.[116] The British consul-general in Jerusalem reported a similar state of affairs in Nablus and Bethlehem.[117] The fall of Ramle and Lydda and the expulsions were to haunt Abdullah (and Glubb) for months. Indeed, when Israeli–Jordanian negotiations resumed at the end of 1948 – early 1949, a principal Jordanian demand was that the towns be returned to Jordanian sovereignty or, at the least, that their inhabitants be allowed to return home.

During 9–13 July, Operation Dani forces also overran the villages around Ramle and Lydda. The intention, from the first, was to depopulate them. On 10 July Yiftah Brigade HQ informed Dani HQ: 'Our forces are clearing the 'Innaba-Jimzu-Daniyal area and are torching everything that can be burned.' Several hours later, Yiftah HQ added: 'Kharruba, Khirbet al Kumeisa [have been captured]. After blowing up the houses and clearing the village[s] – our men occupied outposts above the villages.'[118] A few hours earlier, the Engineers Officer in Dani HQ informed the Yiftah Brigade that he was sending '50 sappers' to 'destroy the village' of 'Innaba. And Lifshitz added: 'Most of the buildings of the village of 'Innaba should be blown up. Leave a minimum of buildings and for-tify them for two [IDF garrison] companies.'[119] The following day, Yiftah informed Dani HQ that its forces had conquered Jimzu and Daniyal and were 'busy clearing the villages and blowing up the houses ['*oskot beti-hur hakfarim u'fitzutz habatim*].'[120] That day, Lifshitz issued the following general instruction to the Yiftah Brigade: 'In all the places you have con-quered you should . . . destroy every house that you do not intend to garrison.'[121] Demolition, of course, presupposed depopulation.

Meanwhile, to the east, as part of Operation Dani, the Palmah Harel Brigade and elements of the Jerusalem-based Etzioni Brigade launched a number of local attacks aimed at expanding the Jewish-held corridor to Jerusalem and at relieving the pressure on the city's western and southern neighbourhoods. On 15 July, Etzioni captured part of the vil-lage of Beit Safafa, which was abandoned (temporarily) by most of its inhabitants. Further to the east, on 14–15 July, IZL and LHI units took

the already semi-abandoned village of al Maliha, held by irregulars.[122]
The large village of 'Ein Karim, partially evacuated in April following the
attack on Deir Yassin two kilometres to the north, was abandoned by
its civilian inhabitants on 10–11 July and, on 14–16 July, by its militiamen after Jewish forces captured two dominating hilltops, Khirbet Beit
Mazmil and Khirbet al Hamama, and shelled the village. During its last
days, 'Ein Karim suffered from severe food shortages.[123]

A few kilometres to the west, Harel Brigade units expanded the corridor southwards, on 13–14 July taking the chain of small villages of
Suba, Sataf, Khirbet al Lawz, Deir 'Amr, 'Aqqur, and Sar'a (held by the
Egyptians), and on 17–18 July, Kasla, Ishwa', 'Islin, Deir Rafat and 'Artuf.
Most of the inhabitants of these villages, who had been on the front line
since April, had already left the area. Much of the remaining population
fled with the approach of the Harel columns and with the start of the
mortar barrages. The handful of people who remained at each site were
expelled.[124]

At the end of Operation Dani, on 19 July, Dani HQ instructed the
Harel, Yiftah, 8th and Kiryati brigades 'to prevent the return of the Arab
inhabitants to their conquered towns and villages *also with live fire*'.[125]

THE SOUTH

During the 'Ten Days', the IDF invested its main energies in the north and
centre of the country. In the south, the Negev and Giv'ati brigades tried –
and failed – to establish a secure corridor between the Negev settlements enclave and the Jewish-held areas of the Coastal Plain. But Giv'ati
succeeded in substantially expanding its area of control southwards and
eastwards, conquering areas in the northern Negev approaches and in
the western Hebron District foothills.

Giv'ati OC Shimon Avidan clearly intended to precipitate the flight of
the Arab population of the area, bounded by Qazaza, Jilya, Idnibba and
Mughallis in the east, Masmiya al Kabira and Qastina in the west, and
Hatta and Beit 'Affa in the south. A preparatory order for the conquest
of Masmiya al Kabira, Masmiya al Saghira, al Tina, Qastina and Tall al
Turmus was produced by Giv'ati's 51st Battalion during the First Truce,
on 29 June. It spoke of the 'liquidation' (*hisul*) of the two Masmiya villages
and conquering and 'cleansing' (*bi'ur*) the rest.[126] On 5 July the brigade
HQ discussed and outlined its plans for the 'Ten Days' and two days later
Avidan issued operational instructions. The order was to expedite 'the
liquidation [*hisul*] of Arab villages inside this area'. The 51st Battalion
was ordered to take the large village of Tel as Safi and 'to destroy the
enemy's fighting force and . . . to destroy, to kill and to expel [*lehashmid,
laharog u'legaresh*] refugees encamped in the area, in order to prevent
enemy infiltration from the east to this important position'. The nature of
the written order and, presumably, the accompanying oral explanations,

probably left little doubt in the battalion OCs minds that Avidan wanted the area cleared of inhabitants.[127]

Operation An-Far was unleashed on the night of 8–9 July, hours after the Egyptians broke the First Truce. The area covered by Avidan's order was overrun during 8–11 July, with most of the population fleeing before the IDF columns reached each village. Tel as Safi was captured in the early morning hours of 9 July. Laying down a barrage of mortar and machine-gun fire, the 51st Battalion approached from the north and west. After taking the *tel* itself, the IDF fired on the houses down the slope 'increasing the mass flight, which was accompanied by screams of fear . . .'. According to the official IDF historian, the fall of this key village 'caused the mass flight of more than 10,000 Arabs from the area who saw themselves cut off . . .' from Egyptian and irregular Arab forces to the east and south.[128] Beit 'Affa, 'Ibdis, Tall al Turmus and the village of 'Iraq Suwaydan all fell on 8–9 July, the villagers fleeing as IDF troops approached or attacked; local rumour had it that the Israeli troops had dealt with the inhabitants of Beit 'Affa 'as they had dealt with Deir Yassin'.[129] The village of Karatiya was harassed by machine-gun fire and abandoned by its inhabitants.[130] During 12–15 July, Giv'ati units raided and harassed a number of other villages, including 'Ajjur, Deir al Dubban, and Summeil, and conquered Bi'lin and Barqusya, which were both found empty. The last two were put to the torch, 'to the extent possible'.[131] Reporting on these operations, the brigade's 'Combat Page', penned by the vengeful poet Abba Kovner, a former anti-Nazi partisan and Hashomer Hatza'ir stalwart, declared:

> Suddenly, the ground was soft [under the wheels of the jeeps of 'Samson's Foxes', Giv'ati's commando unit] – bodies! Tens of bodies under their wheels. The driver was put off: human beings under his wheels! [But] wait a minute. He remembered [Kibbutz] Negba [and] Beit Daras [in both, Arab troops had killed Jews] – and he ran them over! Do not be deterred, sons: murderous dogs – their punishment is blood! And the more you run over bloody dogs, the more you will love the *beautiful*, the *good*, and *liberty*.[132]

On 16 July, Giv'ati HQ informed General Staff\Operations that 'our forces have entered the villages of Qazaza, Kheima, Jilya, 'Idnibba, Mughallis, expelled the inhabitants, [and] blown up and torched a number of houses. The area is at the moment clear of Arabs.'[133]

The Giv'ati operations during the 'Ten Days' precipitated the final evacuation of the villages of Masmiya al Kabir, Masmiya as Saghira, al Tina, al Kheima, 'Idnibba, Mughallis, Jilya, Qazaza, Sajad, Tall al Turmus, Jaladiya, Summeil, Zeita, Bi'lin, Barqusya and Tel as Safi, and a number of hamlets and beduin encampments. Most of the villagers fled to the Hebron Hills, with a small minority, from the Masmiya area, passing through Israeli-held territory to the Gaza Strip.

OPERATIONS DURING THE SECOND TRUCE, JULY–OCTOBER 1948

During the three months between the start of the Second Truce on 19 July and the renewal of hostilities on 15 October, the IDF carried out a number of operations designed to clear its rear and front line areas of actively or potentially hostile concentrations of Arab population.

One such concentration was the cluster of half a dozen villages along the northern section of the Tel Aviv–Haifa road. Early in the 'Ten Days', the IDF had decided to conquer Tira, a large village that blocked traffic on the road, just south of Haifa; an earlier attempt, in late April, had failed but precipitated the evacuation of women and children.[134] The Arab Legion had persuaded the menfolk to stay on and protect the village.[135] The July operational order, which spoke of a local militia 'more than 800' strong, said nothing about the prospective fate of the civilian population.[136] Tira was attacked and fell on 16 July, some of the inhabitants fleeing to the Arab-held enclave to the south, the so-called 'Little Triangle', comprising the villages of Jab'a, Ijzim and 'Ein Ghazal.[137]

During 17–19 July, IDF units attacked and occupied the semi-abandoned villages south of Tira of Kafr Lam, Sarafand, 'Ein Haud and al Mazar (which had all been captured by the IDF in late May, left, and then reoccupied by Arab militiamen and civilians).[138] But the 'Little Triangle', some 20 kilometres south of Haifa, was to be the objective of the major rear-area 'clearing' operation of the Second Truce. For months, the villagers had sniped at Jewish vehicles on the vital coast road (while intermittently sending out peace feelers). With the fall of the village cluster to the north, the Little Triangle remained the only obstacle blocking Israeli traffic.

Back in early May, the 'Little Triangle' and Tira inhabitants had decided 'on no account to abandon the villages, to fight until the last man . . . .'.[139] Against the backdrop of the summer harvest, 'Ein Ghazal had made contact with neighbouring Zikhron Ya'akov to achieve a local truce.[140] Indeed, by mid-June there were substantial factions in all three villages interested in peace;[141] and a measure of *de facto* co-existence took shape. During the summer, the villages' agricultural produce was sold, via the Carmel Druse villages of Isfiya and Daliyat al Karmil, in (Jewish) Haifa.[142] At the same time, there was pressure from nearby settlements to uproot the villages.[143] In early July, the 'Little Triangle' inhabitants reportedly 'felt sure that they could hold out until the Arab victory'.[144] Their militiamen continued to snipe at Jewish traffic. On 8 July, Carmeli and Alexandroni units mounted an only partially successful retaliatory strike against militia positions overlooking the road.[145] On 14 July, the Israeli Cabinet briefly discussed the problem, with Finance Minister Kaplan pressing for a solution (for economic-infrastructure reasons). Ben-Gurion, with bigger things on his mind (operations Dani, Dekel and An-Far), was not particularly perturbed. There was no need to hurry.

> These villages are in our pocket [he said]. We can act against them also after the [reinstitution of the] truce. This will be a police action . . . They are not regarded as enemy forces as their area is ours [i.e., in Israel] and they are inhabitants of the state . . . [and] these villages do not represent a military danger.[146]

Nonetheless, on 17 July, as the 'Ten Days' drew to a close, the villagers were given an ultimatum – to surrender or evacuate. They refused and, the following day, in an immediate response to an attack on two Israeli drivers on the coast road (one body was found a fortnight later; the other body was never recovered[147]), poorly organised forces attacked the 'Little Triangle' militia positions while shelling the villages themselves with 65 mm cannon and mortars. The attackers were beaten off.[148] During the following days, the villages were intermittently shelled and bombed.[149] Many inhabitants fled and morale was reportedly 'low'.[150]

On 24 July, the IDF unleashed *Mivtza Shoter* (Operation Policeman) with the aim of conquering the 'Little Triangle' – or, as the order had it, of 'gaining control' of the coast road between Zikhron Ya'akov and Haifa 'and destroying all the enemy in the area'. No explicit mention was made of the fate of the inhabitants.[151] The assault ended on the morning of 26 July. The IDF used fighter-bombers and four infantry companies, accompanied by eight armoured cars and four batteries of light artillery and mortars. (Foreign Minister Shertok lied to the acting United Nations Mediator when he wrote, on 28 September 1948, that 'no planes were used'.[152]) The aircraft appear to have killed '37' or – in another account – 'about 100' of the inhabitants in strafing and bombing runs.[153] Jab'a and 'Ein Ghazal, where there was street fighting on 25 July, were found deserted after being subdued on the morning of the 26th. At Ijzim and nearby Khirbet Qumbaza, the IDF found hundreds of women, children and old people. About 100 militiamen were taken prisoner and 'more than 100' Arabs were killed. The IDF was impressed by the defenders' 'stiffnecked resistance'.[154] The mukhtar of Ijzim, Mahmud al Mahdi, signed an instrument of surrender at 12:00 hours, 26 July.[155] Most of the three villages' militiamen managed to flee to 'Ar'ara, to the east, after overcoming a series of IDF ambushes, to whom they lost 60 dead.[156]

Most of the villagers managed to reach the Iraqi-held areas of Wadi 'Ara and the northern West Bank. But many others initially came to rest in neighbouring Druse villages or in abandoned sites in Israeli-held territory. During the following days and weeks, Israel rounded them up and expelled them. On the morning of 28 July, '1,400 Arab women, children and old people' from Ijzim were transported by the IDF to the village of al Lajjun and then sent on their way, on foot, toward Jenin.[157] Another 24 were transferred to the West Bank the following day[158] and

480 more, who had initially encamped in Daliyat al Karmil, were transferred on 31 July.[159] Another 90 persons, mostly from Ijzim – '7 old men,
44 old women and 39 children' – were transferred from Isfiya to the West
Bank on 23 August.[160]

During the days after *Shoter*, the IDF blew up much of 'Ein Ghazal
and Jab'a. Arab spokesmen complained of Israeli brutality and atrocities.
Tawfiq Abul Huda, the Jordanian prime minister, cabled the UN that the
villagers were 'subjected to savage treatment of the cruelest kind known
to humanity. Masses were . . . forced to evacuate their homes . . .'[161]
Another complaint spoke of '4,000' dead or missing in Ijzim. On the
morning of 29 July, a team of UN observers, at Bernadotte's behest,
visited the village and found 'not one body'.[162] But they were not looking
hard. There were bodies in the villages, lying under rubble, in the outlying
militia outposts, and in the surrounding hills, of those strafed and shelled
by IDF aircraft and artillery, or killed in ambushes. According to one IDF
report, 'some 200 [Arab] bodies' were found in the Little Triangle.[163] IDF
teams buried them.[164]

The main atrocity story that surfaced was that IDF troops had burned
alive 28 Arabs.[165] Israel vehemently denied the allegation. The story may
have originated in the burning of 25–30 bodies 'in an advanced state of
decomposition' found near 'Ein Ghazal. For lack of timber, explained
Walter Eytan, the bodies were only partially consumed, and captured
villagers had been assigned to bury them.[166] 'Azzam Pasha had alleged
that most of the 28 had been refugees from Tira who had fled to the
'Little Triangle'. On 28 July, a United Nations observer visited the area
and, according to Bernadotte, found 'no evidence to support claims of
massacre'.[167]

However, Arab pressure resulted in a thorough UN investigation of
Shoter. Altogether, five teams were deployed and, basing themselves
largely on interviews with refugees from the three villages encamped in
the Jenin area, they worked out what had happened and compiled lists
of who was missing or killed. According to Bernadotte, Israel's assault
on the villages was 'unjustified . . . especially in view of the offer of the
Arab villagers to negotiate and the apparent Israeli failure fully to ex-
plore this offer'. Bernadotte condemned Israel's subsequent 'systematic
destruction' of 'Ein Ghazal and Jab'a and demanded, 'in the light of the
findings of the Board' of inquiry, that the inhabitants of all three villages
be allowed to return, with Israel restoring their damaged or demolished
houses. Bernadotte concluded by saying that altogether, 'the number
killed [in the three villages] could not have exceeded 130' and that 'no
great number were captured' (he was responding to the allegation that
'4,000' Arabs had been 'massacred' or 'captured').[168] The investigating
'Central Truce Supervision Board', chaired by W.E. Riley, a seconded US
Marine Corps Brigadier General who later became the first head of the
UN Truce Supervision Organisation in the Middle East, concluded that
'with the completion of the attack . . . all the inhabitants . . . were forced

to evacuate'. The investigators found no evidence that, in the days before the IDF assault, the villagers had violated the truce (that began on 18 July). The assault, on the other hand, had been a violation.[169]

The Israelis was unhappy with the UN findings and recommendations, insisting that the villagers had repeatedly attacked traffic during the First Truce and the 'Ten Days', and during the Second Truce had blocked traffic with stone barriers and blown up two bridges or culverts.[170] Shertok denied that the villagers had been expelled, stating that 'when the action commenced on the 24th July, only [a] few of the normal inhabitants were still in the villages'. He maintained that the destruction of houses in 'Ein Ghazal and Jab'a had been limited to 'buildings dominating the highway, as it was from them that firing had been directed at the traffic'. It was done 'to prevent the recurrence of such attacks . . .'. He rejected Acting Mediator Bunche's demand that the villagers be allowed to return.[171] Bunche, who had succeeded Bernadotte, replied that the inhabitants had been 'forced to evacuate' and two of the villages had been 'systematically destroyed'.[172] During early August, neighbouring Jewish settlers arrived in carts and looted the villages.[173] But some weeks later, the authorities allowed several Arab families, led by Mahmud al Mahdi, who is described in the Israeli documentation as 'a friend of the Yishuv' and had temporarily encamped at Daliyat al Karmil, to return and resettle in Ijzim. However, in late December 1948 – early 1949, these 'resettlers' were evicted by the IDF[174] and, during the following months, the three villages were settled by new Jewish immigrants.

The 'Ten Days' had greatly aggravated the refugee problem in the West Bank; many thousands of new refugees joined those created in earlier bouts of hostilities, especially in the area south of the Nablus–Tulkarm line. A vivid description of the situation is provided in an analysis from 22 July by Alexandroni's Arab affairs adviser, Shimshon Mashbetz. Initially, he wrote, the refugees were a source of income for Tulkarm, where they spent their money on provisions.

But later, their money ran out or the flow of destitute refugees increased and these served to pressure the public institutions and the national committee. So did the theft and harvest of fields belonging to the town and the neighbouring villages [by refugees] . . . In view of the situation, the Tulkarm Municipality was forced to house the refugees in the schools that had closed two months before and to feed them with rations, comprising about 400 grams per day of bread, a piece of cheese weighing 30–40 grams, or a similar portion of jam or uncooked potatoes per person, a portion that in normal circumstances is insufficient for a minimal existence . . . With the increase in the number of refugees and the reduction of job openings, especially with the end of the wheat harvest, the phenomenon of begging by women and children has become widespread, which is bad for morals, especially in Arab society. Begging by men who cannot find a day's work or who have no wife or do not want their wives to beg has also become not infrequent. Worsening the economic situation is the flight of prosperous people from the area to distant Arab centres in the country and abroad. Under normal circumstances, this would be a period of intense agricultural labour enlarging the cash flow which provides work for those in need. Not so this year, in this season. Large areas of [Arab] winter crops [i.e., such as wheat] remain across our lines [i.e., on the Israeli side of the line] and we are reaping them. And those in front of our lines [i.e., on the Arab side], some 500–600 metres distant, we do not allow them to approach . . . The same applies to summer crops (sorghum and watermelons). The relations between the locals and the refugees are not good mainly because of the custom of the beduin refugees to raid the [villagers'] fields and harvest them for their own use . . . [Moreover] since the start of the war the commerce in cattle with the Jews [has ended] . . . and the inhabitants who subsisted off this have lost their livelihood and cannot find an alternative source of income. The fuel situation is terrible . . .[175]

The institution of the Second Truce and the relative quiet that descended on the front lines tempted the refugees to try to return to their homes or, at least, to reap their crops along and behind the lines. Immediately after the start of the truce, IDF units on all the fronts were instructed to bar the way, including by use of live fire, to Arabs seeking to cross into Israeli territory, be it for resettlement, theft, smuggling, harvesting, sabotage or espionage.[176] Such instructions were periodically reissued.[177] The units were also instructed to scour the now-empty villages for infiltrators, to kill or expel them, and to patrol still-populated villages where illegal residents were to be identified, detained and expelled. Different units implemented these orders with varying degrees of efficiency, severity and consistency.

Pressure on the national-level leadership to act firmly against Arab infiltration was applied by settlements, especially in hard-hit areas like the Coastal Plain, which feared terrorism and theft; by officials who feared for the future of the new settlements; by IDF units deployed along the front lines, who saw the infiltrators as a security threat;[178] and by the police. On 29 August, Police Commissioner Yehezkeel Sahar wrote to Police Minister Shitrit:

There are organised groups of Arabs infiltrating between the [IDF] positions at night across the [truce] lines and stealing cows. Last week a farmer was even murdered, and there is no doubt that their successes in this area may open the way for the Arab military commanders to exploit this for tactical purposes . . . We see the matter as grave . . .

Shitrit passed the letter on to Ben-Gurion, adding his own cautions:

From [Sahar's] words you will realise that the Arab infiltration . . . is a very worrying phenomenon, undermining security in the country . . . In my tours around the country I have personally encountered this phenomen mainly in Upper Galilee and Beit Shean, where Arabs infiltrate nightly in their hundreds, steal and vandalize and do so with impunity.

The police, he argued, were under-budgeted, understaffed and ill-equipped, and only the army could solve the problem.[179]

But, contrary to the implication of Shitrit's letter, the army had been dealing with the problem – albeit without decisive success – since the end of the 'Ten Days'. A good example is provided by the Giv'ati Brigade, which took over the front line to the west of Bethlehem–Hebron just after the start of the Second Truce. Brigade HQ instructed its battalions 'to set up a supervisory network based on patrols [and] observation posts'. Most local Arabs 'had been expelled from their villages. [But] individuals were infiltrating and reaching their villages with the aim of regaining their possessions, concentrating [i.e., gathering] food and giving information to the enemy.'[180] This guideline was translated, down the chain of command, into specific instructions. The 51st Battalion, for example, cautioned its companies: 'With the start of the truce there is a fear of the return of the villagers to the conquered villages. Such a return could also be accompanied by the infiltration of a camouflaged enemy force.' The companies were instructed to prevent infiltration to Summeil, Barqusya, Bi'lin, Masmiya al Saghira, al Tina, Kheima, Idnibba, Jilya, Qazaza, and Mughallis. The orders specifically were to 'destroy' any 'armed force' encountered and to 'expel . . . unarmed villagers'.[181] On 19 July, even before this order was issued, a jeep-mounted 51st Battalion patrol visited al Kheima, Jilya, Qazaza, Mughallis and Idnibba to make sure that they were empty. Near Kheima, they encountered a group of Arabs in a grove of carob trees, refugees from the Masmiya villages and 'Ajjur. 'They were warned . . . that if anyone entered areas under our control – they would be killed. They promised to obey and were released.' A similar warning was issued to a group found near Jilya. Another patrol, which clashed that day with armed infiltrators at Summeil (killing one and wounding another), issued the same caution to refugees it encountered.[182] During the following days, patrols expelled refugees near Tel as Safi, al Tina, and Mughallis, apparently killing three of those initially detained.[183] At Tel as Safi, the previous occupying battalion had left its replacement, the 53rd Battalion, with an unwelcome 'present' – 'fourteen Arab males, aged over sixty, four of them handicapped, and six old Arab women, all blind, and eight toddlers.' The 53rd's intelligence officer complained that they should not have been left this 'inheritance' and requested the use of a 'vehicle' to solve the 'problem' (presumably by expulsion).[184]

A few days later, the 53rd Battalion's intelligence officer reported Arabs returning to Barqusya and Bi'lin, 'to harvest sorghum and resettle', and asked the neighbouring 54th Battalion to torch the villages. He also asked brigade HQ for permission to torch al Tina and al Kheima.[185] Al Kheima (and nearby al Mukheizin) were duly attacked and torched on 6 August. A week later, a Giv'ati patrol re-visited Idnibba, Mughallis, Jilya, Qazaza and Sajd, killing a handful of Arabs in a number of clashes.[186]

Perhaps the most extensive rear-area Second Truce 'cleansing' operation was carried out by Giv'ati around Yibna-'Arab Suqrir-Nabi Rubin, an area of sand dunes north of the Egyptian Army's area of control. Two earlier planned operations in the area, at the end of July and in early August, either failed to materialise or failed to do the trick.[187] On 24 August, Giv'ati HQ issued the order for Mivtza Nikayon (Operation Cleaning), aimed at 'cleansing [letaher]' the area between Wadi Suqrir, Wadi Rubin, the Mediterranean coast and the railway tracks between Ashdod (Isdud) and Yibna. Armed units in the area were to be destroyed and civilians expelled.[188] The operation took place on 28 August; only part of the designated area was dealt with, due to a shortage of manpower. The troops – of the 55th Battalion, the brigade Cavalry Unit, Samson's Foxes and the 1st Territorial Corps – destroyed 'most of the stone houses and the [wooden] shacks were torched; [and] killed 10 Arabs, wounded three and captured 3'. The troops killed about 20 camels, cows and mules. There were no IDF casualties. One of the troops described the operation in great detail. He wrote that they set out with a feeling of 'merriment' ['alitzut]. Later, they captured several 'fear-filled, shocked' Arabs whose 'miserable appearance caused mixed feelings of contempt and pity'. The soldiers sat around discussing whether or not to kill them. In the end, after deciding, in half-jest, that they should not be killed but turned into 'drawers of water and hewers of wood' – as Joshua had done three thousand years before with his Gibeonite prisoners – the troops fed them bread and cheese and gave them water. It emerged from IDF interrogation of the captives that the refugees encountered were from Yibna, Zarnuqa and Qubeiba, were encamped around Majdal, and were trying to reap their fields. 'The hunger rampant among the refugees forces them to endanger themselves [and] penetrate our area', opened the full IDF report on the operation.[189]

Similar behind-the-lines 'cleansing' operations took place elsewhere. In the north, Northern Front set in motion Mivtza Matate (Operation Broom), aimed at detaining potentially troublesome army-age males and collecting arms from recently occupied western and lower Galilee villages and Acre.[190] The detentions appear to have been brief and ad hoc, with the aim of forcing the villagers to cough up hidden arms.[191]

Elsewhere in the north, on 8 August a company of the Golani Brigade scoured the village of Umm al Zinat and the wadi to its east, in the Hills of Menashe, 'to seek out and destroy the enemy'. The IDF believed that refugees from the 'Little Triangle' were encamped there.[192] Outside the village, the company discovered a handful of Arabs fleeing along the road to Daliyat al Rawha. It chased them, firing; one Arab was killed and another wounded. The company then searched the wadi and discovered another group of Arabs. One man was apprehended, briefly interrogated 'and shot' (the report does not say why). The company moved on to Umm al Daraj, where it encountered another group, including women. They said they were Druse 'and [i.e., so] we did nothing to them'.[193] Another Golani unit ambushed a group of Arabs as they entered the abandoned village of Hittin – 'to extract their belongings' – chasing them off and, in the process, killing some men and pack animals.[194]

On 10 September, units of the Galilee District's 103rd Battalion scoured the hamlet of al Qudeiriya (Sheikh al Rumi), just south of Safad, where Arabs had reoccupied several houses and set up a tent encampment. The soldiers crept up on the tents and opened fire, causing panic and a number of casualties. But the Arabs returned fire, driving off the soldiers, who had three lightly wounded and two MIAs. The 103rd reported killing '32'.[195] Three nights later, Northern Front sent in a second IDF force which took the village and blew it up.[196]

In the northern Negev, the Yiftah Brigade regularly scoured the villages and encampments in its area. On 20 September, the 3rd Battalion was ordered to put an end to infiltration to al Muharraqa and Kaufakha by ambushing and killing those trying to enter the villages.[197] Two days later, the battalion searched the villages, detained four persons and blew up houses. A number of 'old residents', regarded as 'innocuous', were allowed to stay.[198]

During the Second Truce, IDF outposts and patrols regularly harassed harvesters between front line positions, behind the lines and in no man's land, to a depth of 500–600 metres – though the phenomenon was not as widespread as during the First Truce, when the harvest had been at its height.[199] The policy often involved destroying structures used by harvesters for storage or sleep.

In the north, in early August an IDF intelligence officer recommended mining a path near Kafr Misr and 'destroying' the lean-tos of the Sabarja tribe used by infiltrators trying to gather 'a little wheat or sorghum' from Kafr Misr's (and neighbouring (Jewish) Moledet's) fields.[200] A few days later the Jezreel Battalion (Golani) reported that one of its patrols had encountered 'groups of Arab women working fields' near the abandoned village of al Mujeidil: 'I [squad OC Shalom Lipman] ordered the machine-gun to fire three bursts over their heads, to drive them off. They fled in the direction of the olive grove . . .' But after the patrol left, the Arabs returned. The patrol came back and encountered 'a group of Arab men and women . . . I opened fire at them and as a result one Arab man died and one Arab man and one woman were injured. In the two incidents, I expended altogether 31 bullets.' The following day, 6 August, the same patrol encountered two Arab funeral processions. The commander remarked dryly that 'one can assume that one of yesterday's wounded died'. A day or two later, the patrol again encountered 'a large group of Arab women in the fields of Mujeidil. When we approached them to drive them off, an Arab male [was found] hiding near them, [and] he was executed by us. The women were warned not to return to this area of

Mujeidil.' The company commander's comment, appended to the squad OC's report, was: 'Arab women repeatedly attempt to return to Mujeidil, and they are usually accompanied by men. I gave firm orders to stymie every attempt [*lehasel kol nisayon*] to return to the area of the village of Mujeidil and to act with determination.'[201] On 2 August, an ambush set by 'C' Company, 13th Battalion, near Saffuriya, encountered a group of Arabs – possibly intent on harvesting – and opened fire, killing 'four women and three men'.[202]

Another execution was reported a fortnight later by a patrol in the Negev. The force, probably belonging to the Negev Brigade, mined paths east and south of the Rkaik Bridge near Kibbutz Mishmar Hanegev. An Arab caravan with camels appeared on the scene. 'We opened fire at close quarters. Some of the camels were killed and the Arabs, exploiting the darkness, fled.' Later, the patrol ambushed two more caravans, killing additional camels – altogether killing some 20 camels. All the caravans were carrying wheat and barley. The patrol took prisoner 'an Arab suspect. He couldn't explain what he was doing in the area. He claimed to come from Nablus. [He] was executed because there was no possibility of transferring him to base.'[203] Some miles to the north, Giv'ati's 52nd Battalion reported sending out a patrol to the fields of the abandoned villages of Sawafir, Jaladiya and Beit 'Affa, where 'a large number of Arabs were seen reaping . . . Most . . . were women and old men.' The patrol killed eight Arabs and detained three – two men and a child – 'who were taken for questioning'.[204]

Between 18 July and 15 October, the IDF also mounted sporadic 'clearing' operations to drive away concentrations of refugees who had temporarily encamped near the front lines. For example, immediately after the end of Operation Dani, on 21 July, Kiryati Brigade troops at 'Outpost 219', on the eastern edge of the conquered area, expelled 'masses of refugees'.[205]

Meanwhile, inside and on the peripheries of the Jewish Negev settlements enclave, the Negev Brigade continued harassing the Arab inhabitants and beduin tribes. On 16 August, the brigade carried out a full-scale clearing operation in the Kaufakha–al Muharraqa area. 'The villages' inhabitants and [beduin] concentrations in the area were dispersed and expelled. A number of houses were blown up. Muharraqa and the houses of Sheikh 'Ukbi . . . were mined.'[206] Elsewhere in the Negev, Yiftah 51st and 53rd battalions were ordered 'to cleanse [*letaher*] the areas [between Tkuma and 'Imara-Tze'elim and between 'Alumim and Beersheba and between Hatzerim and Mishmar Hanegev] of the enemy [i.e., unfriendly beduin tribes] and to destroy his possessions by burning and sabotage and to [confiscate and] concentrate his flocks in 'Imara as well as to blow up his wells in the area north of Hatzerim'. The operation was mounted because Arab marauders had blown up a Jewish water pipeline and mined roads.[207] Five days later, the 1st Battalion duly reported that 'all the Arabs [in these areas] have been expelled, save for one friendly tribe',[208] and their livestock was confiscated.

Unusually, these particular 'cleansing' operations were criticised both by the Foreign Ministry and some local settlement leaders. Shimoni described them as 'contrary to the instructions of the Foreign Minister', who, for political reasons, was urging Israeli utilisation of the Negev beduin. A few weeks earlier, the *mukhtars* of the kibbutzim Dorot, Nir-'Am and Ruhama had complained to Ben-Gurion that the army had 'destroyed houses, robbed sheep, cattle and horses, and burned fields' belonging to local beduins who had 'throughout maintained a benign neutrality and helped us actively in our war by supplying information'.[209] There were also (ineffectual) political waves: Shitrit asked Ben-Gurion in Cabinet: 'Is it true that we are throwing out the beduin on our Negev borders?' To which the prime minister responded, evasively: 'You should properly ask this during question time. But as you have raised the matter, I must say that, *au contraire*, there are plans to organise [i.e., induct] the beduin in the IDF.'[210]

With his penchant for hyperbole and lies, on 4 August Haj Amin al Husseini complained, more than two weeks into the truce, that 'for two weeks now . . . the Jews have continued with their attacks on the Arab villages and outposts in all areas. Stormy battles are continuing in the villages of Sataf, Deiraban, Beit Jimal, Ras Abu 'Amr, 'Aqqur, and 'Artuf . . .'[211] But there was an element of truth in the charge. Periodically through the Second Truce, the IDF raided Arab villages across the lines, in Arab-held territory, moving in and killing local militiamen and civilians, blowing up houses and then withdrawing. Yigal Yadin explained: 'The lack of operations on our part during the truce prompts the Arab irregular forces to acts of robbery, infiltration, etc. Therefore, ambushes and light raids [*pshitot kalot*] against the border villages should be organised.'[212] The aim was usually retaliation and deterrence.

Such raiding took place mainly in the northern and southern fronts. In the south, for example, the village of Zikrin was raided on 6 August, two 53rd Battalion squads lobbing grenades and torching three or four houses. About ten adult males, two children and a woman were killed (the last three, 'accidentally [i.e., unintentionally]'); the IDF suffered one soldier lightly injured.[213] Further to the south, already on 22 July, the Negev Brigade raided the village of Shu'ut, inhabited at the time only by a small force of militiamen, with the aim of destroying houses and killing inhabitants, mainly in retaliation for the killing of six Israelis by the villagers back in December 1947.[214] Two months later, Yiftah Brigade units again raided Shu'ut, killing 'a number of Arabs' and blowing up 'close to 30 houses'.[215] In the north, Carmeli Brigade troops in early September raided the semi-abandoned village of Hunin – the largest of the seven Shi'ite villages in the Galilee – reportedly killing about 20 and blowing up 20 buildings, including the mosque,[216] despite assurances, the previous month, by the local notables that they were willing to live in peace as a minority under Jewish rule.[217] The village's 400 remaining inhabitants were apparently expelled to Lebanon in the second half of August and, finally, with the raid in early September.[218] On the night of 17–18 September, Northern Front forces took the village of Marus, north of Safad. Several Arabs were killed or wounded and the village was completely demolished. The IDF suffered one dead and one wounded.[219]

While in general this pattern during the Second Truce of 'cleansing' the rear areas along strategic routes or near the front lines prevailed, exceptions were made of a handful of communities, which were left in place, such as Abu Ghosh, west of Jerusalem, and al Fureidis and 'Arab al Ghawarina (Jisr az Zarqa) in the Coastal Plain.[220] In the north, while some beduins (such as the 'Arab al Heib) were moved into the interior, Arab communities near or not far from the front lines generally were not moved or expelled during the Second Truce.

Altogether, the Israeli offensives of the 'Ten Days' and the subsequent clearing operations probably sent something over 100,000 Arabs into exile in Jordanian-held eastern Palestine, the Gaza Strip, Lebanon and the Upper Galilee pocket held by Qawuqji's ALA.

ENDNOTES

1. Z. Ayalon in the name of the CGS to OCs brigades, battalions, etc., 6 July 1948, KMA-ACP 9\9\1.
2. See, for example, CGS to 'Larlar' HQ, 13 July 1948, IDFA 481\49\\144, complaining that he had heard that OC Harel Brigade had 'given an order to the Arabs of Abu Gosh to evacuate.' The CGS reiterated that such orders required the explicit authorisation of the defence minister, in line with the order of 6 July.
3. See Moshe Carmel, OC Northern Front, to Oded, Golani, Carmeli, etc., 'Operation[s] "Brosh" and "Dekel"', 6 July 1948, IDFA 4858\49\\495, and 'Operation Commander' 7th Brigade Tac. HQ, to 21, 71 and 73 battalions, etc. 'Operation "Dekel"', 8 July 1948, IDFA 1137\49\\84. But it is worth noting that in the first document, the IDF's Haifa District ('Hadari') is instructed to 'systematically harass' the Arab villages south of Haifa and eventually 'to completely cleanse these villages of the enemy'. It is unclear whether what was meant was the complete depopulation of the villages or merely ridding them of combatants (though the first meaning seems more likely).
4. 'Tzuri (Leshem)' to Tene (Ayin), 26 June 1948, (two messages), both in IDFA 7249\49\\138. See also 'Tzuri (Shaanan)' to Tene (Ayin), 11 July 1948, IDFA 7249\49\\138.
5. 'Tzuri (Leshem)' to Tene (Ayin), 7 July 1948, IDFA 7249\49\\138. See also 'Tzuri (Leshem)' to Tene (Ayin), 11 July 1948, IDFA 7249\49\\138. Villagers from Iksal were also reported evacuating at around this time (see 'Tzuri (Shaanan)' to Tene (Ayin), 11 July 1948, IDFA 7249\49\\138.
6. 'Tzuri (Leshem)' to Tene (Ayin), 7 July 1948, IDFA 7249\49\\138.
7. 'Tzuri' to Golani, 8 July 1948, IDFA 7429\49\\138.

8. Parsons, *Druze*, 86.
9. Eshel, *Carmeli*, 210; and Nazzal, *Exodus*, 71–74.
10. Carmel, *Battles*, 199–200.
11. Parsons, *Druze* 77–85; Carmel, *Battles*, 202–203; and Gelber, 'Druze and Jews in the War of 1948', 236.
12. Nazzal, *Exodus*, 74–77; and Erem at meeting of Mapam defense activists, 26 July 1948, HHA 10.18.
13. Intelligence Officer, 13th Battalion, to Golani\Intelligence, 24 July 1948, IDFA 128\51\\32.
14. Military Governor, Nazareth, to operations officers, Northern Front, 21 Dec. 1948, IDFA 260\51\\3.
15. P. Weinstein, operations officer, 9th Brigade, to Battalion 91, etc., 4 Jan. 1949, IDFA 6309\49\\3; and 9th Brigade HQ to Northern Front\Intelligence, etc., 7 Jan. 1949, IDFA 1012\49\\72.
16. Kamen, 'After the Disaster', 48. Some 1,200 refugees from Mujeidil were reportedly in Nazareth at the end of July.
17. Avira to Danin, 29 July 1948, ISA FM 2570\11. The word 'expelled' (*gurshu*) was often used loosely by Israelis during 1948. It was quite often assumed by non-participants that a given community of Arabs had been expelled when, in fact, it had evacuated before Israeli forces had arrived. The desire to see the Arabs depart often triggered the assumption that commanders – who presumably shared the same desire – had acted overtly to obtain that result when this was not true. But most of 1948's displaced Arabs were indeed 'expellees' in the sense that almost all were prevented from returning after they had left their villages and towns before or during their conquest.
18. 'Tzuri (Shaanan)' to Tene (Ayin), 14 July 1948, IDFA 7249\49\\138.
19. Report by 'Yehuda', Golani Brigade Intelligence Officer, 15 July 1948, IDFA 7249\49\\138. See also 'Appendix A, Information About Operation "Ya'ar"', at end of 'Operational Order for Operation "Ya'ar"', Combat HQ 7th Brigade, 15 July 1948, IDFA 7249\49\\115.
20. 'War Logbook', 7th Brigade, entry for 16 July 1948, IDFA 721\72\\310. See also 12th Battalion to Golani Brigade HQ, 16 July 1948, IDFA 128\51\\50, which relates how the battalion fired on the columns of refugees from Nazareth to Tur'an.
21. OC Operation, 'Operational Order for Operation Ya'ar', 15 July 1948, IDFA 82\54\\260.
22. Ben-Gurion to Yadin, etc., 15 July 1948, IDFA 922\75\\1025.
23. Carmel, 'Order of the Day for 16 July 1948', IDFA 2384\50\\1.
24. Eshel, *Carmeli*, 218; and Anon., *Tree and Sword*, 23 and 275.
25. Entry for 17 July 1948, DBG-YH II, 598.
26. 'Aryeh', Intelligence Officer, 7th Brigade, 'Report on Conquest of Nazareth', to General Staff\Operations, Carmeli Brigade HQ, etc., 17 July 1948, IDFA 82\54\\260.
27. 'Tzuri (Leshem)' to Tene\Da'at (Ayin), 19 July 1948, HA 105\92 bet. About the behaviour of the Palestinian irregulars in Nazareth during June–July, see 'Hiram' to Da'at (Ayin), 'Interrogation of [. . .] from Tulkarm', 3 August 1948, IDFA 7249\49\\138. (The person's name was blacked out by IDFA censors.)

28. 'Terms of Surrender of the City of Nazareth to the Army of Israel', 16 July 1948, IDFA 2315\50\\15.
29. Entry for 18 July 1948, DBG-YH II, 599. Carmel later denied that he had issued any such order (Gabi Bashan, 'Carmel Doesn't Get Bored', *Al Hamishmar*, 9 May 1989).
30. Peretz Kidron, 'Truth Whereby Nations Live', 86–87. But clearly, Laskov would not have issued such an order off his own bat. It had either been initiated by Carmel, his superior, or at least received Carmel's endorsement.
31. Kidron, 'Truth Whereby Nations Live', 86–87.
32. Combat HQ 7th Brigade to General Staff, 14:30 hrs, 17 July 1948, IDFA 922\75\\1025.
33. 'Yirmiyahu' to Golani, 18:30 hours, 17 July 1948, IDFA 1281\51\\50. Earlier, Ben-Gurion had handwritten his decision on the 14:30 hours cable itself: 'Do not expel people from Nazareth' (*al tarhiku anashim minatzrat*). Interestingly, however, Bar-Zohar (*Ben-Gurion*, II, 776) records that when Ben-Gurion later visited the town, he 'looked around in astonishment and asked . . . : "Why so many Arabs? Why did you [i.e., the IDF] not expel them?"'
34. 'Tzuri (Leshem)' to IDF Intelligence Service and Foreign Ministry Political Department, 21 July 1948, IDFA 7249\49\\138.
35. Shimoni to Yadin, 21 July 1948, IDFA 2384\50\\1.
36. Northern Front to Golani, 22 July 1948, IDFA 5205\49\\1.
37. 'Tzuri (Paltiel)' to Da'at (Ayin), 29 July 1948, HA 105\92bet.
38. Shitrit to Cabinet members, 'Report of the Visit of the Minority Affairs Minister in Nazareth on 19 July 1948', 23 July 1948, ISA JM 5756 gimel\4820; and Sulz, 'Report on the Activities of the Military Government in Nazareth and [its Surrounding] District for the Three Months 17 July–17 October 1948', undated, ISA FM 2564\11. The number of Nazareth inhabitants who fled is uncertain; most appear to have been Muslims and people who had helped the ALA. One American diplomat serving in the north had put the number at 'approximately 500' (see Randolph Roberts, vice-consul, Haifa, to Secretary of State, 30 July 1948, NA RG 84, Haifa Consulate, Classified Records 800 – Political Affairs (General)). But a more reasonable estimate would be 4,000–5,000, based on the probable pre-conquest population figure of 17,000 and a 17,000 figure (comprising remaining local inhabitants and some 4,500 from elsewhere) at the end of 1948 (see Kamen, 'After the Catastrophe', 47–48).
39. 'Tzuri (Yosef)' to 'Da'at', 31 August 1948, IDFA 7249\49\\138.
40. Entry for 8 May 1948, DBG-YH I, 399.
41. Gelber, *Independence and Nakba*, Chap. 15.
42. Golan to OC Northern Front, 4 Sep. 1948, IDFA 260\51\\54.
43. Unsigned, undated report headed 'Copy', IDFA 5205\49\\1 and attached letter OC Northern Front to Golani, 2 Sep. 1948, IDFA 5205\49\\1. The writer also complained of a 'search and identification' operation in Nazareth on 4 Aug. 1948, in which, he alleged, 180 persons were detained. One Arab was bitten in the leg by a dog. The detainees were afraid that they would be treated like the villagers at 'Illut. Golan denied that anything untoward had happened in Nazareth (Golan to OC Northern Front, 4 Sep. 1948, IDFA 260\51\\54). IDF intelligence later reported that one 'Illut villager, Muhammad Ibrahim Shihade, was wont to sit in Nazareth cafes and

speak about 'the atrocity' (Combat Intelligence Service, Haifa District, to General Staff\Intelligence, 29 Aug. 1948, IDFA 7149\49\\138). Israeli oral testimony has it that on the day of 'Illut's capture, the IDF left a squad to garrison the village. The villagers attacked the squad killing or wounding a number of troopers. The remaining soldiers fled to the main road where they flagged down an IDF jeep unit – which promptly entered the village firing in all directions. The following day, a 13th Battalion unit entered the village, rounded up the young adult males, and selected and executed 'about 45'. See also Gelber, *Palestine*, 165–66.

44. Intelligence Officer, Northern Front, to Intelligence Officer, 13th Battalion, 29 Aug. 1948, IDFA 260\51\\4; and 'Ma'ami (Paltiel)' to 'Da'at (Ayin)', 10 Oct. 1948, IDFA 715\49\\16. Another document (Intelligence officer, 13th Battalion, to Golani\Intelligence, 2 Aug. 1948, IDFA 128\51\\71) reports that an IDF patrol, after entering Kafr Manda, saw 'Arabs fleeing . . . in various directions. They were given an order to come back. They did not obey and so they were fired upon. Six were killed and others fled.' It is unclear whether these documents deal with the same incident or two separate incidents. That an atrocity occurred is clear from Northern Front, intelligence officer, to intelligence officer, 13th Battalion, 29 Aug., IDFA 260\51\\4, which reads: 'Carry out an investigation and send me a detailed report regarding the bahaviour of a certain unit in your battalion, which belonged previously to the IZL, during its handling of Arab civilians. I was told of two incidents: (A) Their behaviour in Kafr Manda, during our entry the last time . . .'

45. Golani Intelligence Officer, 'Summary from Noon 17.7.48 until 24:00 hours', IDFA 128\51\\84; Golani\Intelligence, 'Daily Summary', 18 July 1948, IDFA 128\51\\84; and 12th Battalion, 'Conditions of Surrender of the Village of Dabburiyya', 17 July 1948, IDFA 2315\50\\15.

46. 'Testimony of Reuven Ron, Company CO, 12th Battalion, during the War of Independence About . . .', 23 Mar. 1957, IDFA 922\75\\943.

47. Combat HQ 7th Brigade, 'Operation "Hatzlaha" [Following] Operation Dekel', 17 July 1948, IDFA 7249\49\\115.

48. 'Instrument of Surrender for the Village of 'Ein Mahal', 18 July 1948, IDFA 2315\50\\15 (signed by 'Abd al Qadir al Dib, Nimr Qassem, Habib 'Adalla, and Muhammad Hassan 'Aluwan).

49. 'Tzuri (Paltiel)' to 'Da'at (Ayin)', 29 July 1948, IDFA 7249\49\\138; and Shmuel Toledano in the name of OC Operations\Intelligence to Reuven Shiloah and Baruch, 28 July 1948, and 'Conditions of Surrender of the Village of Sakhnin which was Occupied Today at 15:40', 20 July 1948, both in IDFA 2168\50\\86. A number of Sakhnin notables were subsequently tried by the ALA and sentenced to death – and at least one, Sheikh Ibrahim al 'Abdullah, was executed ('Tzuri (Yosef)' to 'Da'at (Ayin)', 10 August 1948, and 'Tzuri (Yosef)' to 'Da'at (Ayin)', 15 August 1948, both in IDFA 7249\49\\138).

50. IDF Operations Logbook, entry for 21 July 1948, IDFA 922\75\\1176.

51. 'Report on Ramle Operation', unsigned, undated but probably from 11 Dec. 1947, IDFA 922\75\\1213.

52. 'Na'im (Na'aman)' to HIS-AD, 'The Bomb in Ramle', 24 Feb. 1948 (two reports, with the same heading), both in HA 105\358; and *Haaretz*, 19 Feb. 1948.

53. 'Na'im' to HIS-AD, 'Murder of Arabs in Rehovot', 24 Feb. 1948, HA 105\358.

54. See, for example, 'Na'im (Na'aman)' to HIS-AD, 3 Mar. 1948, HA 105\257, which speaks of Ramle notables continuing to maintain commercial ties with neighbouring Jews, and unsigned, 'The Conversation of Ben Shemen's Mukhtar with the Mayor of Lydda (Muhammad Kiali) and with the Commander of Lydda and Its Environs (Shihadeh Hassuni) On the Telephone. The Telephone Conversation Took Place on 1.1.48', undated, CZA S-25\4147.

55. Kiryati-Dafna to Natani, 4 May 1948, IDFA 8275\49\\162.

56. 'Avner' to HIS-AD, 7 May 1948, HA 105\217.

57. HIS-AD, 31 May 1948, intercepted messages from the mayors of Ramle and Lydda to the 'heads of the Egyptian Army, etc.', HA 105\92 aleph.

58. Kiryati\Operations, 'Operational Order "Irgun"', 26 May 1948, IDFA 1277\49\\11; and Kiryati\Operations, 'Operational Order for Operation "Yahad"', 30 May 1948, IDFA 1277\49\\11.

59. Entry for 30 May 1948, DBG-YH II, 468; and Orren, On the Road, 66–67 and 299, footnotes 29–30. Kiryati HQ believed that there were '500–600' Legionnaires and '400' beduin volunteers from Transjordan as well as 'about 500' local militiamen in Ramle and 'about 650' Legionnaires, '300' beduin, and 'about 1,000' local militiamen in Lydda on the eve of Operation Dani (see Alexandroni, 'Bulletin No. 55', 7 July 1948, IDFA 2323\49\\6).

60. General Staff\Operations, 'Operation "Larlar"', 26 June 1948, IDFA 922\75\\1237; Kiryati HQ. 'Operational Order – Operation "Dani"', 8 July 1948, IDFA 6450\49\\98; and 8th Brigade HQ, 'Operational Order 1. Aleph', 8 July 1948, IDFA 6450\49\\98.

61. See entries for 11 and 24 May and 4 June 1948, DBG-YH, I, 410 and DBG-YH II, 453 and 485 respectively.

62. See protocol of Cabinet meeting, 16 June 1948, ISA. Ben-Gurion referred to the 'two thorns' – and added a further comment that ISA officials saw fit to censor (perhaps he had explicitly called for expelling the towns' populations).

63. 'Intelligence Service Information', 31 May 1948, KMA-PA 100\Mod\3-171; and Kiryati Brigade Intelligence Officer, 'Summary of Information on the Enemy Toward the End of the Truce in the Ramle-Lydda Front and Environs', 28 June 1948, KMA-PA 141–535.

64. See reports from 'The Arab Labourer', codename of an Arab agent working for the JA-PD, CZA S25-4066; and Kiryati Brigade Intelligence Officer, 'Summary of Information on the Enemy Toward the End of the Truce in the Ramle-Lydda Front and Environs', 28 June 1948, KMA-PA 141–535.

65. Dani HQ to General Staff, 10 July 1948, IDFA 922\75\\1235.

66. 'Malka' to 'Tziporen', 10 July 1948, 16:00 hours, IDFA 922\75\\1237.

67. Yiftah Brigade Intelligence Officer to Dani HQ, 11 July 1948, KMA-PA 120–91; Dani HQ to General Staff\Operations, 11 July 1948, KMA-PA 141–105; and Dani HQ to General Staff\Operations, 11 July 1948, KMA-PA 141–109.

68. Kadish, Sela, Golan, Conquest, 36. Third Battalion\Intelligence at the end of the campaign put Arab casualties in Lydda on 11 July at 'about 40 dead and a large number of wounded' – but it is not clear whether these were caused only by Third Battalion actions or by the Third and 89th battalions combined (3rd Battalion Intelligence, 'Comprehensive Report of Third

Battalion Activities from Friday 9.7 until Sunday 18.7', 19 July 1948, IDFA 922\75\\1237).

69. Quoted in Kadish, Sela and Golan *Conquest*, 143–44.
70. Alterman, 'On This' (*al zot*), *The Seventh Column*, II, 24–26.
71. Dani HQ to General Staff, 10 July 1948, IDFA 922\75\\1235.
72. Yiftah HQ\Intelligence to Dani HQ, 8th Brigade HQ, etc., 11 July 1948, IDFA 922\75\\1237.
73. Dani HQ\Intelligence to General Staff\Intelligence, etc., 11 July 1948, IDFA 922\75\\1237.
74. 'Telephone message from Dani [HQ]', 12 July 1948, 10:30 hours, IDFA 922\75\\1235.
75. 'Terms of Surrender of the Town of Ramle,' 12 July 1948, IDFA 2315\50\\60.
76. Unsigned, printed page describing events in Lydda on 11–12 July 1948, IDFA 922\75\\1237.
77. 1st Battalion HQ to chief of staff, Arab Legion, 'Following are the memoirs of 1st Battalion Officer Arshid Marshud on the Battles of the 1st Battalion in Palestine', 9 Dec. 1948, IDFA 922\75\\693.
78. It is unclear how many armed townspeople joined the fray. Kadish, Sela and Golan (*Conquest*, 44) quote the 3rd Battalion's OC Kelman, who spoke, years later, of fire being opened up by 'thousands of weapons'. This is nonsense. Probably no more than several dozen townspeople participated in the (brief) firefight.
79. See *Book of the Palmah* II, 571 and 717; and 3rd Battalion\Intelligence, 'Comprehensive Report of the Activities of the Third Battalion from Friday 9.7 until Sunday 18.7', IDFA 922\75\\1237.
80. Yiftah HQ to Dani HQ, 13:15 hours, 12 July 1948, IDFA 922\75\\1237.
81. Orren, *On the Road*, 110; 'Avi-Yiftah' (Shmarya Guttman), 'Lydda', 456; and interview with Eldad Avidar , in 'Al-Nakba' (1998), a documentary film produced and directed by Benny Brunner. Kadish, Sela and Golan, *Conquest*, 45–46, maintain that not a massacre but a battle took place in the 'small' mosque between armed Arabs and the Palmah troops, who used PIATs to suppress them. But they acknowledge that some of those killed in the mosque compound were unarmed 'old people, women and children'.
82. Cohen, *By Light*, 160.
83. *Book of the Palmah* II, 565; Third Battalion Intelligence Officer, 'Report from 11 [sic – should be 14] of July – Action in Lydda', 14 July 1948, IDFA 922\75\\1237; and 3rd Battalion Intelligence, 'Comprehensive Report of the Activities of the Third Battalion from Friday 9.7 until Sunday 18.7', 19 July 1948, IDFA 922\75\\1237
84. Mula Cohen in *Book of the Palmah* II, 810 and 885. In his autobiography (*To Give*), 141–46, published more than forty years later, Cohen was to write more ambivalently about what had happened: on the one hand, he wrote that 'we decided to place the Arabs of Lydda between our forces and the Arab Legion forces [i.e., to move the town's population eastward]' and spoke explicitly of 'the expulsion'. On the other, he wrote that the population of Lydda 'went voluntarily' and 'the inhabitants of Ramle also asked to leave.' To judge from the amount of space Cohen devoted to the subject, it clearly troubled him toward the end of his life.

85. Kadish, Sela and Golan, *Conquest*, 49–53; and Cohen, *To Give*, 146.
86. See for example, the governor of Lydda and Ramle to 8th Brigade HQ, 30 July 1948, IDFA 6450\49\\40, complaining of a raid by brigade troops on a house in Ramle on 28 July, in which they blew open a safe. Apparently, soldiers were tried for looting in Ramle months afterwards (see military district prosecutor, 'File No. 388\48', undated, concerning the trial of a soldier for looting a radio in Ramle, IDFA 6450\49\\40).
87. 'Avi-Yiftah', 'Lydda', 455.
88. Bar-Zohar, *Ben-Gurion*, II, 775. Bar-Zohar cites an interview with Rabin as the source. Itzchaki, *Latrun*, II, 394, says that Ben-Gurion did not say 'Expel them' but merely made a gesture meaning 'expel them'. Itzchaki, who was director of the archive at IDF General Staff\History Branch, adds: 'Allon and Rabin then . . . decided that it was crucial to expel the inhabitants.' See also Kidron, 'Truth . . .', 91–92, which quotes a censorially deleted passage from Rabin's autobiography, in which he recalled the meeting and said that Ben-Gurion merely made a gesture whose meaning was 'Drive them out'. Kadish, Sela, Golan, *Conquest*, 46–47, leave vague the authorship of the decision to expel. They state that Ben-Gurion's hand gesture 'was interpreted as saying "expel them"'. And they add: 'On the night of 12\13 July, it was decided at Dani HQ to apply pressure on the population to leave.' Surprisingly, they make no mention of, and do not cite, the explicit order from Operation Dani HQ (Yitzhak Rabin) to Yiftah HQ, of 13:30 hours, 12 July, cited below, to expel the population of Lydda.
89. IDFA has copies of two versions of the order, which are identical save that one refers to Lydda, Beit Naballah and 8th Brigade by their codenames ('Orbali', 'Baruch' and 'Shesek', respectively) and the other, in which these appear *en clair*, is signed 'Yitzhak R.' (respectively in IDFA 922\75\\1237 and 922\75\\1234). Allon later denied that Ben-Gurion or he himself had issued an expulsion order or, indeed, that there had been an expulsion. Rather, he said the order to the civilian population to evacuate the two towns had come from the Arab Legion (see *Al Hamishmar*, 25 Oct. 1979, news page article reproducing some of what Allon had said on a Kol Yisrael radio interview the day before).
90. Kiryati HQ to Aurbach, Tel Aviv District HQ (Mishmar), etc., 14:50 hours, 13 July 1948, HA 80\774\12 (Zvi Aurbach Papers). See also Kiryati HQ to Hail Mishmar HQ Ramle – Shiloni, 19:15 hours, 13 July 1948, HA 80\774\12.
91. Orren, *On the Road*, 124.
92. Unsigned, but perhaps by Shitrit, 'A Report of the Minister's Visit to Ramle on 12 July 1948', 13 July 1948, ISA FM 2564\10. The report was addressed to Ben-Gurion and other ministers.
93. Foreign Minister to Minority Affairs Minister, 13 July 1948, ISA FM 2564\10.
94. General Staff\Operations to Operation Dani HQ, 23:30 hours, 12 July 1948, KMA-PA 142–3. See also Dani HQ\Operations to Forward HQ Yiftah and Kiryati brigades, 00:35 hours, 13 July 1948, IDFA 922\75\\1237.
95. Kaplan's statement, 'Protocol of the Meeting of the Ministerial Committee for Abandoned Property', 13 July 1948, ISA FM 2401\21 aleph. Shitrit said at the meeting that the soldiers were busy looting Ramle and that Shertok had told him that 'all the inhabitants who wished to remain in their places

would be allowed to do so on condition that the State of Israel did not take upon itself [i.e., was not burdened with] their maintenance. Those wishing to leave would be allowed to do so.'

96. See 'Avi-Yiftah', 'Lydda', 458–60. Guttman's memoir, published in the Ahdut Ha'avoda journal *Mibifnim* in November 1948, is the only evidence I have found describing this 'negotiation'. Guttman was a member of Na'an, an Ahdut Ha'avoda (and Galili's) kibbutz – and no doubt exercised some self-censorship in writing the memoir, published while the war was still raging. There may also have been external censorship. The deal struck by Guttman, involving the release of army-age males, appears to have caused consternation among his superiors. At 18:15 hours, 13 July, Dani HQ (meaning Allon) cabled Yiftah HQ: '1. Tell me immediately: Have the Lydda prisoners been released and who authorised this?' (IDFA 922\75\\1234).

97. Intelligence Officer, 43rd Battalion, to OC 43rd Battalion, 13 July 1948, IDFA 922\75\\1237. It is worth noting that IDF radio traffic began to refer to the inhabitants of Ramle and Lydda as 'refugees' (*plitim*) even before they had left the towns; the issue of the expulsion orders had sufficed to change their status from inhabitants to refugees.

98. Dani HQ to General Staff\Operations, 13 July 1948, KMA-PA 141–516; Dani HQ to Yiftah, Kiryati and 8th brigades, 13 July 1948, KMA-PA 141–597; and Dani HQ to Kiryati Brigade, 13 July 1948, KMA-PA 142–133.

99. Dani HQ to Yiftah HQ, 18:15 hours, 13 July 1948, IDFA 922\75\\1234.

100. Aharon Cohen to Allon, 12 Oct. 1948, and Allon to Cohen, 31 Oct. 1948, both in HHA-ACP 10.95.10 (6); Winifred A. Coate (Amman) to 'Mabel', 30 July 1948, SAMECA JEM LXXXII\1; and Cisling statement at Cabinet meeting, 21 July 1948, KMA-AZP 9\9\3.

101. 'Avi-Yiftah', 'Lydda,' 460–61.

102. *Tzror Michtavim*, 5 Aug. 1948, KMA.

103. *Book of the Palmah* II, 718; *In Enemy Eyes*, 36; and Glubb, *Soldier*, 162.

104. Logbook – possibly Giv'ati Brigade – entry for 15 July 1948, IDFA 922\75\\1226.

105. Untitled, undated, printed report, signed, 'Yigal', KMA-PA 142–51.

106. Entry for 15 July 1948, DBG-YH II, 589.

107. Ya'ari speech, 12 Dec. 1948, protocol of meeting of Kibbutz Artzi Council, 10–12 Dec. 1948, HHA 5.20.5 (4).

108. Protocol of Cabinet meeting, 14 July 1948, ISA.

109. Gwirtz, Department for Arab Property, to Minister for Minority Affairs, 21 July 1948, ISA MAM 297\5gimel.

110. For example, military governor of Ramle-Lydda, 'Monthly Report on the Activities of the Military Governor of Ramle-Lydda and on the General Situation in this Area', Oct. 1948, IDFA 1860\50\\30. The report put the population of Ramle at '960', Lydda '580' and the Lydda train station, '450'. See also Erem to Hagler, deputy military governor Lydda-Ramle, 17 Sep. 1948, MAM 297\5. Kadish, Sela and Golan, *Conquest*, 49, basing themselves on these later figures, argue – apologetically – that in July the IDF had carried out only a 'partial' expulsion (presumably morally less reprehensible than a full expulsion).

111. Kiryati to Dani, 19:15 hours, 13 July 1948, IDFA 922\75\\1235; and Dani HQ to Kiryati, undated but from 13 July 1948, IDFA 922\75\\1234.

112. Rabin, Dani HQ, to Kiryati, 01:05 hours, 14 July 1948, IDFA 922\75\\1234.
113. Dreyer, Medical Corps, Operation Dani HQ, to General Staff\'Operations, etc., 15 July 1948, IDFA 2417\50\\59.
114. See Morris, *Road to Jerusalem*, 172–81, for further details. See also 'Hiram' to 'Da'at (Ayin)', 'Visit to Amman, Irbid, Nablus', 17 July 1948, ISA FM 2569\13.
115. Haim Werfel to Ya'akov Shimoni, 22 July 1948, HA 105\260.
116. 'Da'at (Ayin)', 'From Monitoring the Legion Wavelength,' 21 July 1948, Khalaf to Abdullah, undated, and, Abdullah to Khalaf, undated, ISA FM 2569\13.
117. Jerusalem consulate to FO, 25 July 1948, PRO FO 816\139.
118. Yiftah HQ to Dani HQ, undated, and Yiftah HQ to Dani HQ, 21:15 hours, 10 July 1948, both in IDFA 922\75\\1237.
119. Lifshitz, Dani HQ, to Yiftah HQ, 11:30 hours, 10 July 1948, and Lifshitz, Dani HQ, to Yiftah HQ, 23:35 hours, 10 July 1948, both in IDFA 922\75\\1234.
120. Yiftah HQ\Intelligence to Dani HQ, etc., 11 July 1948, IDFA 922\75\\1237.
121. Lifshitz, Dani HQ, to Yiftah, 09:40 hours, 11 July 1948, IDFA 922\75\\1234.
122. 'Yeruham', 'Arab Information (from 14.7.48)', 15 July 1948, HA 105\127aleph.
123. Entries for 10 and 11 July 1948, General Staff\Operations Logbook, IDFA 922\75\\1176; and Mordechai Abir, 'The Local Arab Factor in the War of Independence (Jerusalem Area)', 18–19, IDFA 1046\70\\185; and Yeruham, 'Arab Information (from 14.7.48)', 15 July 1948, HA 105\127aleph.
124. The capture of Suba and Deir 'Amr is sketchily described in *Book of the Palmah* II, 580–81.
125. Yitzhak R[abin], Dani HQ to Harel, Yiftah, etc., 19 July 1948, IDFA 922\75\\1235 (emphasis in the original).
126. 51st Battalion, 'Operational Order for "David and Goliath"', 29 June 1948, IDFA 7011\49\\5.
127. Giv'ati, 'Operation An-Far', 7 July 1948, IDFA 7011\49\\1. Ayalon, *Invader*, 227-28, gives a laundered version of the order – which I (unfortunately) used in the original edition of *The Birth*.
128. Ayalon, *Invader*, 254.
129. Pages of IDF logbook, possibly Giv'ati Brigade's, entry for 9 July 1948, IDFA 922\75\\1226; and Ayalon, *Invader*, 247–49. Beit 'Affa was immediately retaken by the Egyptians, and retaken again by Giv'ati on 15 July 1948. For Tel al Turmus's fall on 9 July (found empty by the entering IDF patrol), see 'Mati', OC B Company, to 51st Battalion HQ, 9 July 1948, IDFA 170\51\\49.
130. Giv'ati HQ to (?) General Staff\Operations, 09:45 hours, ? July 1948, IDFA 922\75\\908.
131. Intelligence officer, 51st Battalion, to Giv'ati HQ\Intelligence, 12 July 1948, and Intelligence Officer, 51st Battalion, ? July 1948, both in IDFA 1041\49\\12. For Summeil and Deir al Dubban, see 51st Battalion, Intelligence officer, to Giv'ati HQ\Intelligence, 15 July 1948, IDFA 1041\49\\12.
132. Giv'ati Brigade, 'Combat Page', 14 July 1948, IDFA 6127\49\\118.

133. Giv'ati HQ to General Staff\Operations, 20:50 hours, 16 July 1948, IDFA 922\75\\1176. See also Giv'ati Brigade, 'Combat Page', 16 July 1948, IDFA 6127\49\\118.

134. Unsigned, 'Addition to Daily Report 21.4, 14:00 hours, summary of Information until 22.4, 08:00 hours', undated, IDFA 7353\49\\46; and unsigned, untitled intelligence report, 27 April 1948, HA 105\257. Many families returned to the village at the end of April and early May.

135. 'Segal', 'Summary of Information, Carmeli Brigade, No. 2, 6.5.48', IDFA 1196\52\\1.

136. A. 'Akaviya, OC Haifa, 'Operational Order – Operation Ring', 12 or 13 July 1948 (both dates appear on the document), IDFA 240\54\\2.

137. 'Hiram' to 'Da'at (Ayin)', 'Interrogation of Tira Prisoners', 17 July 1948, HA 105\92bet; and IDF General Staff\Operations Logbook, entry for 16 July 1948, IDFA 922\75\\1176. Descriptions, from 1942, of Jab'a, Ijzim and 'Ein Ghazal, are in HIS village files, HA 105\224.

138. Intelligence Officer, Northern Front HQ, 'Summary of Enemy Forces' Activities in Northern Front's Area Between Truce and Truce, from 9.7.48 until 27.7.48', 1 Aug. 1948, IDFA 352\53\\28. For Kafr Lam and Sarafand, see Intelligence Officer, Carmeli Brigade, 'Daily Report for 18.7 (up to 08:00 hours)', 18 July 1948, IDFA 5492\49\\3; and untitled IDF prisoner interrogation report, 31 July 1948, IDFA 4663\49\\46. For 'Ein Haud, see also A. 'Akaviya, OC Haifa, 'Operational Order – Operation Gizum', 17 July 1948, IDFA 240\54\\2; and Slyomovics, Memory, 99–102.

139. 'Tiroshi (Eitan)' to HIS-AD, 2 May 1948, IDFA 6400\49\\66. But, at the same time, another HIS officer provided a contrary appreciation: 'With the fall of Haifa there was a meeting in Ijzim attended by men from the Arab Carmel [Range] villages. The general opinion was – to surrender . . . Only the men of the small village of Jab'a . . . decided to fight . . .' ('Hiram' to HIS-AD, 3 May 1948, HA 105\31). In the end, bolstered by contingents of Iraqi and Syrian irregulars, the villagers decided against surrender.

140. 'Tiroshi (Eitan)' to HIS-AD, 7 June 1948 and appended letter from 'Ein Ghazal Village Committee to Mukhtar of Zikhron Ya'akov, 3 June 1948, HA 105\260.

141. 'Tiroshi (from Hiram)' to Alexandroni, 10 June 1948, IDFA 922\75\\949.

142. 'Hiram' to HIS-AD, 14 June 1948, HA 105\237.

143. Galili to Yadin 21 June 1948, IDFA 481\49\\143.

144. 'Hiram' to 'Tene (Ayin)', 'A Visit to Ijzim by Our Informant Anton on 1–2.7.48', 4 July 1948, HA 105\127aleph.

145. Unsigned, 'Report of a Reprisal Against 'Ein Ghazal on 8\7', undated, IDFA 5492\49\\3; and unsigned, 'A Reprisal,' undated, IDFA 922\75\\949.

146. Protocol of Cabinet meeting, 14 July 1948, ISA.

147. General Staff\Staff Division\Baruch to Foreign Minister, 17 Sep. 1948, IDFA 2168\50\\86.

148. OC Haifa, 'Report on Jab'a-'Ein Ghazal Operation', 19 July 1948, IDFA 5492\49\\3.

149. Naif Halif, 'Statement' (taken by UN observers), 30 July 1948, ISA FM 2427\1.

150. Carmeli HQ, Intelligence Officer, to Northern Front HQ, etc., 'Daily Report 20.7.48', undated, IDFA 5492\49\\3.

151. 'Bentz', 'Operational Order for Operation "Shoter"', 24 July 1948, IDFA 352\53\\28.
152. Shertok to Bunche, 28 Sep. 1948, ISA FM 2426\12.
153. Unsigned, 'The Jab'a-'Ein Ghazal-Ijzim Operation According to Arab Sources', undated, IDFA 922\75\\949; and Hadari\Operations to Northern Front\Intelligence, 30 July 1948, IDFA 5942\49\\3.
154. IDF General Staff\Operations Logbook, entries for 25–26 July 1948, IDFA 922\75\\1176; 'Moshe', 33rd Battalion, to Alexandroni Brigade HQ, 'Report on Operation "Shoter"', 27 July 1948, IDFA 922\75\\949; and Intelligence Officer, Northern Front HQ, to General Staff\Intelligence, etc., 'Report for 27.7.48, 08:00 hours', undated, IDFA 922\75\\1094.
155. Hadari, Intelligence Officer, 'Report on the Cleansing Operation in the Little Enclave Near Haifa on 25–26.7.48 by 3rd Brigade', undated, IDFA 5492\49\\3.
156. Unsigned, 'The Jab'a-'Ein Ghazal-Ijzim Operation, According to Arab Sources', undated, IDFA 922\75\'\949.
157. Hadari\Operations to Northern Front\Intelligence, 29 July 1948, IDFA 200716\49\\122.
158. Hadari\Operations to Northern Front\Intelligence, 31 July 1948, IDFA 200716\49\\122.
159. Hadari\Operations to Northern Front\Intelligence, 1 Aug. 1948, IDFA 5492\49\\3.
160. Haifa District HQ\Operations\Intelligence to OC Haifa District, etc., 24 Aug. 1948, IDFA 244\51\\129.
161. Bunche (Rhodes) to Reedman (Tel Aviv), 31 July 1948, IDFA 2315\50\\15.
162. Hadari\Operations to Northern Front\Intelligence, 30 July 1948, IDFA 5942\49\\3.
163. Northern Front HQ, 'Summary of Enemy Forces' Activities in the Northern Front Area Between Truce and Truce From 9.7.48 until 27.7.48', 1 Aug. 1948, IDFA 352\53\\28.
164. See, for example, Hadari\Operations to Northern Front\Intelligence, 3 Aug. 1948, IDFA 5492\49\\3, for the burial on 2 Aug. of '8 bodies' at and around 'Ein Ghazal.
165. 'Tzuri (Yosef)' to 'Da'at (Ayin)', 15 Aug. 1948, IDFA 7249\49\\138.
166. Eytan to Paul Mohn, political adviser to chief of staff, UN HQ Observer Group, Haifa, 8 Sep. 1948, ISA FM 2426\11.
167. Kuniholm (Beirut) to Secretary of State, 2 Aug. 1948, and Bernadotte to 'Azzam Pasha, 29 July 1948, both in NA 501 BB. Palestine\8-248. But there is an enigmatic, partly censored document that indicates that something amiss had indeed occurred (see Baruch Komarov, OC liaison with the UN, to IDF Manpower Division 3–PoWs, 11 Nov. 1948, IDFA 2168\50\\86). The document refers to an ongoing IDF 'trial' concerning the '28'. The full story will probably emerge only when IDFA fully opens its documents. During 1948, UN observers questioned two persons in Sidon who claimed to have survived the 'massacre', but deemed their testimony contradictory (see Gelber, *Palestine*, 164).
168. Bernadotte to Shertok, 9 Sep. 1948, ISA FM 2426\11.
169. Riley, Central Truce Supervision Board, 'Name of Case: Villages of 'Ein Ghazal, Ijzim and Jab'a', 8 Sep. 1948, ISA FM 2426\11. The '130' the

Board and Bernadotte reported as killed or missing (or captured) were all from the three village communities. Presumably, there were additional dead from among the many hundreds of refugees (from Tantura, Tira, etc.) who had reached and encamped in the 'Little Triangle' during May–July and from among the non-local irregulars who had beefed up the local militias.

During the UN investigation, IDF General Staff attempted to verify how many villagers were being held as prisoners of war. The OC PoWs Department, Central PoW Camp No. 1, responded that no villagers were being held as PoWs – but there were a number of PoWs who had been in the villages (irregulars? refugees from elsewhere?) when they were captured (OC POWs Department to General Staff, 15 Aug. (or Sep.) 1948, IDFA 2168\50\\86).

170. General Staff\Staff Division\Baruch to Foreign Minister, 17 Sep. 1948, IDFA 2168\50\\86; and Shertok to Bunche, 28 Sep. 1948, ISA FM 2426\12.
171. Shertok to Bunche, 28 Sep. 1948, ISA FM 2426\12.
172. Bunche to Shertok, 14 Nov. 1948, ISA FM 2426\13.
173. Hadari\Operations to Northern Front\Intelligence, 11 Aug. 1948, IDFA 244\51\\129.
174. Shitrit to director of MAM office, Haifa, 30 Nov. 1948, ISA FM 2564\9; OC Haifa District to Battalion 23, etc., 22 December 1948, and operations officer, Haifa District, to Military Governor, Western Galilee, 14 Jan. 1949, both in IDFA 200176\49\\24;
175. Alexandroni to Minority Affairs Minister, General Staff\Intelligence, etc., 'The Feeling Among the Inhabitants in the Tulkarm Area as Emerging from Interrogation of Prisoners on 14, 16 and 18.7.48', 22 July 1948, IDFA 2506\49\\85.
176. For example, Rabin, Dani HQ, to Harel, Yiftah, Kiryati and 8th Brigades, 19 July 1948, KMA-PA 141–419.
177. See, for example, 51st Battalion to companies 'B', 'C', etc., 26 July 1948, IDFA 170\51\\49, and Ephraim District to the district company, 25 July 1948: 'I repeat and stress that no resident of the empty Arab villages is to be allowed back to his village. You must use all means, including the harshest, to prevent this.'
178. Morris, *Border Wars*, 32–34, 99, 111–17, 128–29, etc.
179. Sahar to Police Minister, 29 Aug. 1948, and Police Minister to Defence Minister, 6 Sep. 1948, both in IDFA 121\50\\183.
180. Giv'ati HQ to 54th Battalion, ? (possibly 19) July 1948, IDFA 1041\49\\12.
181. OC 51st Battalion to 'C' Company, etc., 20 July 1948, IDFA 922\75\\899.
182. 51st Battalion\Intelligence to Giv'ati HQ\Intelligence, 19 July 1948, IDFA 1041\49\\12.
183. 5th (Giv'ati) Brigade, untitled logbook page, entries for 21–25 July 1948, IDFA 922\75\\899. The entry for 21 July is partly whited out by IDFA censors. The missing passage deals with the fate of the three detainees.
184. Intelligence Officer, 53rd Battalion, to Giv'ati HQ\Intelligence, 24 July 1948, IDFA 1041\49\\12.

185. 53rd Battalion, intelligence officer, to Giv'ati HQ\intelligence, and 54th Battalion\intelligence, 5 August 1948, both in IDFA 1041\49\\18.

186. 5th (Giv'ati) Brigade Logbook, entries for 6 and 13 Aug. 1948, IDFA 922\75\\899.

187. See Battalion 55 to 'A' Company, etc., 'Operational Order 53\19,' 27 July 1948, and Giv'ati HQ to Cavalry Unit, 51st Battalion, etc., 'Operational Order', 4 Aug. 1948, both in IDFA 7011\49\\5.

188. OC Giv'ati Brigade to 55th Battalion, etc., 24 Aug. 1948, IDFA 7011\49\\5.

189. Intelligence Officer, 55th Battalion, to Giv'ati\Operations, 'Report on Operation "Nikayon"', 29 Aug. 1948, IDFA 922\75\\899; and Giv'ati\Intelligence to Navy\Department of Coastal Protection, 4 Sep. 1948, IDFA 1041\49\\9. Ayalon, *Invader*, 364–68, writes that the ten Arabs were killed while 'trying to escape'.

190. 7th Brigade HQ, "Operational Order "Matate"', 30 July 1948, IDFA 82\554\\260.

191. 'Yisrael' to Tzidoni, 8 Aug. 1948, IDFA 5492\49\\3, and operations officer, 'Operation Matate, Operational Order', undated, IDFA 1137\49\\44, concerning the village of Damun, in western Galilee; and, concerning Kabul, 'Avinoam' OC southern area, Tzidoni, to OC Tzidoni District, 'Report from a Visit to Kabul on 7.8.48,' IDFA 1137\49\\44.

192. Alexandroni HQ to General Staff\Staff Division, 2 Aug. 1948, IDFA 2506\49\\83.

193. Shlosnizki, OC 1st Company, to Jezreel Battalion HQ, 5 Aug. 1948, IDFA 128\51\\32. In his summary, Shlosinsky speaks of 'the Arabs who were interrogated before they were killed' – but later speaks of 'two' Arabs killed altogether in the operation.

194. 'Yehuda', Golani Brigade\Intelligence, 'Daily Summary 25–26.8,' IDFA 1096\49\\64.

195. 103rd Battalion\Intelligence, to OC Galilee District, 'Report on Search Operation Around al Qudeiriya 10.9.48,' 19 Sep. 1948, IDFA 128\51\\34.

196. 2nd (Carmeli) Brigade, intelligence officer, to Intelligence\HQ 312, 'Daily Report up to 13 [Sep.] 08:00 hours', 13 September 1948, IDFA 6680\49\\107.

197. Yiftah\Operations to 3rd Battalion, 22 Sep. 1948, IDFA 922\75\\1227.

198. 3rd Battalion\Intelligence to Yiftah HQ\Intelligence, 27 Sep. 1948, IDFA 922\75\\1227.

199. Alexandroni to Minority Affairs Minister, General Staff\Intelligence, etc., 'The Feelings Among the Inhabitants of the Tulkarm Area as Emerging from Interrogation of Prisoners from 14, 16 and 18.7.1948', 22 July 1948, IDFA 2506\49\\85. See also Morris, 'The Harvest of 1948 . . .', 682–83.

200. 'Tzuri (Paltiel)' to 'Da'at (Ayin)', 5 Aug. 1948, IDFA 7249\49\\138.

201. Jezreel Battalion HQ to Golani\Intelligence, 8 Aug. 1948, IDFA 128\51\\32. The report says that the execution occurred on '3.8.48' – but this would seem to be an error: It should probably have read '7.8.48.' The use of the word *lehasel* – literally, to liquidate – is indicative. Also typical is the shift to a passive mode when reporting the execution.

202. 13th Battalion, intelligence officer, to Golani\Intelligence, 2 Aug. 1948, IDFA 128\51\\71. Interestingly, the brigade intelligence officer, in his

subsequent report, 'reduced' these casualty figures to '3 Arab males killed and a number of Arabs wounded' – omitting mention of the four dead Arab women ('Yisrael' in the name of the brigade intelligence officer, Golani Brigade, 'Daily Summary', 3 Aug. 1948, IDFA 1096\49\\64).

203. Unsigned but probably by Negev Brigade, 'Daily Summary for 24.8.48', IDFA 922\75\\1220.

204. 52nd Battalion to Giv'ati\Intelligence, 25 Aug. 1948, IDFA 1041\49\\12.

205. Kiryati\Operations to Dani HQ, 11:45 hours, 21 July 1948, IDFA 922\75\\1235, and Rabin, Dani HQ to General Staff\Operations, 13:30 hours, 21 July 1948, IDFA 922\75\\1234.

206. Israel Livertovsky diary, 15 Sep. 1948, 'The Events of 11 August–11 September 1948', JNF files 501–4; and Negev Brigade, 83.

207. Yiftah\Operations to 1st and 2nd battalions, etc., 30 Sep. 1948, IDFA 922\75\\1227.

208. 1st Battalion\Intelligence to Yiftah\Intelligence, etc., 'Daily Report [3–4.10.48]', 4 Oct. 1948, IDFA 922\75\\1225.; and Yiftah\Intelligence to General Staff, 5 Oct. 1948, IDFA 922\75\\1216.

209. Shimoni to Foreign Ministry Political Department, 10 Oct. 1948, ISA FM 2564\10; and Arye Farda (Dorot), Ya'akov Gavri (Nir-Am) and Eliezer Frisch (Ruhama) to Prime Minister, 4 Aug. 1948, ISA FM 2564\9.

210. Protocol of Cabinet meeting, 6 Oct. 1948, ISA.

211. SVT (Damascus) to SVB (Cairo), 4 Aug. 1948 (an IDF intelligence intercept), HA 105\104.

212. Yadin, General Staff\Operations Division, 8 Sep. 1948, IDFA 957\51\\16.

213. Intelligence officer, 53rd Battalion, to Giv'ati\Intelligence, 7 Aug. 1948, IDFA 1041\49\\18.

214. Yoske (Jerry) to Sergei, 30 July 1948, IDFA 1676\51\\12.

215. Yiftah\Intelligence, 'Daily Report 17.9.48', IDFA 922\75\\1216.

216. Israel Foreign Ministry, Middle East Department, 'Hostilities on the Lebanese Border', 15 Sep. 1948, and Foreign Ministry, Middle East Department, 'Hunin Village', 21 Sep. 1948, citing Beirut newspaper reports, both in ISA FM 2564\9. The bulk of the inhabitants had fled to Lebanon during Operation Yiftah, in May.

217. Shitrit to Prime Minister and Foreign Minister, 'The Inhabitants of Hunin', 13 Aug. 1948, ISA FM 2564\9. A few weeks earlier, Oded Brigade troops had raped and murdered four village women (see unsigned, 'The Visit of the Minority Affairs and Police Minister [Shitrit] in Kfar Gila'di', 29 July 1948, HA 105\260). Shitrit had supported accepting the Hunin notables' overture for economic and political reasons, looking to good relations with south Lebanon's Shi'ite community.

218. Ehrlich, *Lebanon*, 282.

219. 'Uri' in the name of the intelligence officer, Northern Front, 'Daily Report for 18.9.48, 08:00 hours', IDFA 6680\49\\107.

220. See Morris, 'Why Four Villages Remained . . .' in Morris, *1948 and After*, 257–84.

8

The fourth wave: the battles and exodus of October–November 1948

Bernadotte's report of 16 September, proposing the award of the Negev to the Arabs in exchange for Jewish sovereignty over Western Galilee, compelled the Israeli political and military leadership to focus attention on the south, where the surrounded, poorly supplied enclave of less than two dozen settlements was cut off from the core of the Yishuv by Egyptian forces holding the Majdal–Faluja–Beit Jibrin–Hebron axis. Contrary to the truce terms, the Egyptians refused to allow Israeli supply of the enclave by land. The threat of an award of the Negev to the Arabs, the untenable geo-military situation and the plight of the besieged settlements made the breakdown of the truce, in the absence of a political settlement, inevitable. In early October, the Cabinet approved an Israeli offensive to link up with the enclave and to rout the Egyptian army. The IDF deployed elements of four brigades (amounting to 12–14 battalions) and, on 15 October, a supply convoy was sent in. The Egyptians, as expected, opened fire, providing a *casus belli.* The IDF immediately launched Operation Yoav, originally named 'Operation Ten Plagues,' which lasted, with its appendages, until 9 November. During the three weeks of fighting, the IDF overran much of the southern coastal strip, including the small towns of Isdud, Hamama and al Majdal; Beersheba, the Negev's 'capital'; Beit Jibrin, in the Hebron foothills; 'Ajjur, in the Judean Hills; and several dozen smaller villages, including Beit Tima, Qauqaba, Barbara, Hirbiya, al Qubeiba and Dawayima, between the Mediterranean and Hebron. The inhabitants fled or were expelled, mainly to the Gaza Strip but also eastward, into the Hebron Hills. Simultaneously, in a complementary series of attacks, the Harel and Etzioni brigades (operations 'Yekev' and 'Hahar', 19–22 October) captured from the Egyptians a string of Judean Hills' villages – Beit Nattif, Zakariya, Deiraban, Beit Jimal and others – south of the Tel Aviv – Jerusalem road, widening the Jewish-held corridor to the holy city. Thousands of inhabitants fled to the Hebron Hills.

In the north, Qawuqji's ALA similarly provoked the Israeli conquest of the remainder of the Galilee when its units, on 22 October, stormed the Sheikh 'Abbad hilltop position, overlooking Kibbutz Manara, and opened fire on Israeli traffic. Elements of four Israeli brigades, with auxiliary units, totalling 11–12 battalions, responded on 28 October, and within 60 hours, in Operation Hiram, conquered the Upper Galilee pocket bounded by the villages of Yanuh and Majd al Kurum in the west, 'Eilabun, Deir Hanna and Sakhnin in the south, Farradiya, Qaddita, Alma and al Malikiya in the east, and the Lebanese border to the north. The pocket, according to Israeli estimates, contained 50,000–60,000 Arabs, comprising local inhabitants and refugees from other areas.[1] Tens of thousands fled, almost all to Lebanon, during the offensive and its aftermath.

Just after the start of the fighting in the south, and before the offensive in the Galilee, Riftin, one of Mapam's two political secretaries, asked Ben-Gurion what would be the fate of the Arab inhabitants should the IDF overrun additional populated areas. 'I was told that strict orders had been issued not to cause "unhappy punctures" and that preparations had been made for [setting up] local administration[s]', Riftin related.[2] But Ben-Gurion's answer had been vague and misleading. On 26 September, he had told the Cabinet that, should the fighting be renewed in the north, the Galilee would become 'clean' (naki) and 'empty' (reik) of Arabs, and had implied that he had been assured of this by his generals. The Prime Minister had been responding to a statement/question by Sharett, who, addressing the Bernadotte proposal that Israel be awarded the Galilee, had implied that it were better that Israel should not take over the Galilee pocket as it was 'filled with Arabs' – 'we are definitely not getting the Galilee empty, we are getting it full' – including refugees from Western and Eastern Galilee bent on returning to their villages.[3] On 21 October, when Ezra Danin, in a tête-à-tête with Ben-Gurion, tabled the Foreign Ministry Arabists' pet project at the time of setting up a Palestinian puppet state in the West Bank, the prime minister had impatiently declared that he was not interested in new 'adventures' and that 'the Arabs of the Land of Israel [i.e., Palestine] have only one function left – to run away'.[4] Ten days later, at the end of Operation Hiram, Ben-Gurion visited the Galilee and talked with OC Northern Front, General Moshe Carmel. In his diary, Ben-Gurion described the exodus from the newly-conquered Galilee pocket and jotted down: '. . . and many more will flee.' It is unclear whether Ben-Gurion was quoting Carmel or making his own prediction – but, without doubt, both men shared the same hope.[5] It was an attitude shared by many key figures in the Israeli military and civil bureaucracies. Shimoni, of the Foreign Ministry, for example, that month informed a Tel Aviv travel agency that 'we view favourably the migration of Arabs out of the country, and we would recommend assisting them to make it as easy for them as possible'. Weitz, on hearing from Moshe Berger of the start of Operation Hiram, on 29 October penned a note to Yadin urging that the army expel the 'refugees' from the newly–conquered areas.[6]

This attitude was not converted into or embodied in formal government or even IDF General Staff policy. Neither before, during nor immediately after Yoav and Hiram did the Cabinet or any of its committees decide or instruct the IDF to drive out the Arab population from the areas it was about to conquer or had conquered. Nor, as far as the available evidence shows, did the heads of the defence establishment – Ben-Gurion, IDF CGS Dori or Yadin – issue any general orders to the advancing brigades to expel or otherwise harm the civilian populations.

But, clearly, the OCs of northern and southern fronts, respectively Moshe Carmel and Yigal Allon, both hoped and acted to clear their areas of Arab communities. Both were affiliated to Ahdut Ha'avoda and its leader, Yitzhak Tabenkin, a major proponent of transfer in the Israeli political arena. In the north, at 07:30, 31 October, with the start of the ceasefire scheduled for 11:00, Carmel ordered his brigades and district OCs 'to continue in the cleansing operations inside the Galilee'.[7] A few hours later, at 10:00 hours, Carmel honed his order as follows: 'Do all in your power for a quick and immediate cleansing [tihur] of the conquered areas of all the hostile elements in line with the orders that have been issued[.] The inhabitants of the areas conquered should be assisted to leave.' The order was apparently issued while Carmel and Ben-Gurion – who had come to visit – were meeting in Nazareth, or minutes after their meeting; one may assume that it was authorised, if not actually authored, by the prime minister.[9] Ten days later, Carmel repeated this order, in a somewhat watered down version: '[We] should continue to assist the inhabitants who wish to leave the areas we have conquered. This matter is urgent and should be expedited quickly.'[10]

In the south, Allon, in the course of Operation Yoav and its aftermath, apparently never issued such general orders, in writing (at any rate, none have surfaced in the archives). But he most certainly passed on expulsive guidelines orally – and, indeed, almost no Arabs remained in the towns and villages conquered in that campaign. But whereas Allon acted with determination and consistency, and with almost complete success, Carmel, perhaps impeded by moral and political considerations and recalcitrant subordinates, displayed irresolution and belatedness, and many of the Arab communities overrun in Hiram remained in place.

On both fronts, to be sure, most IDF soldiers and officers at this stage in the war were happy – for military and political reasons – to see Arab civilians along their path of advance take flight. Many were also ready to expel communities and some, as we shall see, were even willing to commit atrocities, perhaps in part to induce flight. The exodus, all understood, vastly simplified things. But, as we shall also see, different units acted in different ways, their disparate behaviour governed by the political outlook and character of their commanders, their 'collective outlook', circumstances of topography and battle, and the religion and political or military affiliations of the communities encountered.

THE SOUTH

In all his previous campaigns Yigal Allon had left no Arab communities in his wake: So it had been in Operation Yiftah in eastern Galilee in the spring, so it had been in Operation Dani in July. Nothing was said in the operational order for Operation Yoav about the prospective fate of the communities to be overrun[11] – but Allon, the OC, no doubt let his officers know what he wanted and most probably they knew (and agreed with) what he wanted without explicit instruction.

The inhabitants of the areas conquered in Yoav were nervous and largely demoralised before the battle was joined. They were Muslim almost to a man. Small towns (or oversized villages) like Isdud, Majdal and Hamama contained fairly large refugee populations that had fled from areas to the north in the spring and summer. They had been living under unsympathetic, coercive Egyptian military rule since May. The Egyptians were inefficient and often heavy-handed and were regarded by many locals as foreigner occupiers; they were perennially short of supplies and not generous with them with the locals, whose fields, in many cases, had been ravaged or rendered inaccessible by the hostilities. Moreover, during the long Second Truce, the locals understood that the stalemate would soon be broken, that they would be on the firing line, and that the Egyptian army was weak. They feared the flail of war and dreaded Jewish conquest and rule; they, too, had heard of Deir Yassin.

The IDF of October–November 1948 was radically different from the Israeli army of even three months before. It had – and deployed with telling effect – a small number of bombers and fighters, batteries of field artillery and mortars, and tanks (in small numbers). Operation Yoav began on 15–16 October, with bombing and strafing attacks on Beersheba, Gaza, Majdal, Hamama, Barbara, Isdud, Beit Hanun, Dimra, Hirbiya, al Jura, Deir Suneid, Faluja and Beit Jibrin. While by World War II standards these attacks were pinpricks and not particularly accurate, most of the affected communities had never experienced air attack and were not built for it, either psychologically or in terms of shelters and ground defences. Artillery was also used far more extensively than in any previous IDF campaign, though it was generally directed against Egyptian and militia positions.

The aerial and artillery bombardment and the ground attacks of 15–19 October in the central area, where the IDF broke through the strong Egyptian defences and linked up with the besieged Negev enclave, caused (at least temporarily) mass civilian flight from Faluja and

'Iraq al Manshiya, according to 5th Brigade intelligence.[12] There was also flight from Beit Tima, Hulayqat and Kawkaba (which were already largely empty). There had generally been no need for expulsions; the locals had simply fled in face of the approaching Israeli columns.

In the second wave of advances, over 19–24 October, the Harel Brigade, in Operation Hahar, captured Deiraban, Beit 'Itab, Sufla, Beit Jimal, Beit Nattif, Zakariya, and Bureij.[13] Most of the population fled southwards, towards Bethlehem and Hebron. At Beit Nattif – 'the village of the murderers of the 35 [members of the Palmah relief column sent to the Etzion Bloc in January 1948], the attackers of the Etzion Bloc and the destroyers of [the] Jewish [settlement of] Har-Tuv' – the inhabitants 'fled for their lives', as one Palmah report put it. The Palmahniks then blew up the village and Deir al Hawa, to the north.[14]

A Palmah account, by a woman soldier, Aviva Rabinowitz, of Kibbutz Kabri, of a patrol in the Hebron Hills, near al Jab'a, in the wake of the Harel offensive, illustrates the immediate fate and condition of the refugees from these hilltop villages:

> Scattered in the gully, sitting in craters and caves . . . [were] dozens of refugees . . . We surprised them. A cry of fear cut through the air . . . They began to praise us and dispense compliments about the Jewish army, the State of Israel. With what obsequiousness! Old men bowing, genuflecting, kissing our feet and begging for mercy; young men standing with bowed heads and helpless . . . We tried to persuade them to flee towards Hebron. We fired several shots in the air – and the people were indifferent. 'Better that we die here than return [to Egyptian-held territory] to die at the hands of the Egyptians.' We fired again. No one moved. Tiredness and hunger deprived them of any will to live and of any human dignity. These are the Arabs of the Hebron Hills, and it is possible that this youngster, or that man, shed the blood of the 35 or looted the Etzion Bloc [after its fall in May] – but can one take revenge here? You can fight against people of your own worth, but against this 'human dust'? We turned back and returned [to our base] . . . That evening, for the first time during the whole war, I felt I was tired. My soul has grown weary of this war.[15]

The Giv'ati Brigade, meanwhile, pushed northeastwards, conquering the villages of Kidna (Kudna), Zikrin, Ra'na, Deir ad Dubban and 'Ajjur, in the Hebron and Judean foothills. Here too most of the population fled before the troops arrived; those who remained were expelled eastwards. In Jordan, there was fear that the IDF would push further eastwards, into the hills, precipitating 'another mass of refugees . . . which this country could neither accommodate nor feed . . . The people are very frightened.'[16]

On 21 October, the 8th Brigade's 89th Battalion and the Negev Brigade's 7th and 9th battalions conquered Beersheba. The operational order had called for the 'conquest of Beersheba, occupation of outposts around it, [and] demolition of most of the town' – but did not state explicitly what was to be done with the inhabitants.[17] Mass flight from the town had begun already on 19 October, by foot and in buses, mainly toward Hebron, following repeated IAF bombing raids on the night of 18\19 October.[18] The town was bombed again, repeatedly, the following night,[19] precipitating further flight.[20]

Many of the wealthier inhabitants had left the town weeks and months before, beginning in April–May.[21] The exodus continued during and immediately after the conquest, some fleeing toward Gaza. The conquest was accompanied by the execution of a handful of Egyptian POWs,[22] and wholesale looting by individuals and military units.[23]

In Beersheba, the IDF had captured about 120 Egyptian soldiers. The remaining population, some 200 adult males and 150 women and children, were temporarily housed in the town's police fort. A few days later, apparently on 25 October, the women and children, 'together with several dozen old men and cripples', were trucked to the border with Gaza and shoved across.[24] The Egyptian PoWs were sent to prisoner of war camps in the north and the remaining able-bodied adult males, about 120 in number, were put to work in cleaning and other menial chores. They were treated like POWs and housed in the mosque.[25] Complaints reached IDF\GS that they were supplying the Egyptian Army with intelligence. Yadin ordered that they be removed from Beersheba.[26] Some were apparently transferred to POW camps and others to Egyptian-held Majdal or Gaza. Ben-Gurion and Shafrir, the Custodian of Absentees Property, were greatly annoyed by the looting.[27] On 30 October, Ben-Gurion visited Beersheba. According to Galili, Allon asked the Prime Minister (or, perhaps, Gad Machnes, the director general of the Minority Affairs Ministry, who accompanied Ben-Gurion): 'Why have you come?' – and added: 'There are no longer minorities [i.e., Arabs] in Beersheba.' Machnes responded, according to Galili: 'We have come to expel the Arabs. Yigal, rely on me.' But the Arabs, as Allon pointed out, were already gone.[28]

Many had gone to Gaza, where the condition of the refugees was described two months later by an American observer:

> Gaza is an unattractive little Arab town with an original population of about 25,000. It now has, in addition, about 60,000 refugees. They pack sidewalks, take up the vacant lots and the public market, occupy barnyards, and generally seem to fill in every empty space which the town might have had. They live in churches, mosques, schools and public buildings . . . These people receive no relief ration . . . [as they are] recently arrived . . .

A few kilometres to the south, the observer visited Bureij,

> a former British Army camp now housing 13,500 refugees . . . All . . . are under cover, either in UN tents or in patched-up army huts. We went into one Army building . . . about 50 feet wide and 120 feet long. There must

have been 800 people in the place. They had staked out little cubicles for themselves using rags or flattened gasoline tins . . . Everyone was very dirty and cold. In one cubicle we saw a group of ten people ranging in age from infancy to about seventy, looking at an old woman on the floor who had just died . . . The people in Bureij are now getting two and a half kilos of flour per person every ten days . . .'[29]

On 23 October, the guns fell silent in the south as another UN-imposed ceasefire took effect. But within days, truce violations triggered a succession of IDF 'nibbles' at Egyptian-occupied areas, with the IDF occupying additional villages, including Beit Jibrin, al Qubeiba and Dawayima, in the Hebron foothills, and Isdud and Hamama along the coast. Yadin outlined the aims of these operations as 'softening up the surrounded enemy forces' and 'the achievement of tactical advantages'. He also ordered the launching of 'psychological warfare operations' and instructed the units 'to deal with the civilian [populations]'.[30] Yadin did not elaborate but presumably the intention was to frighten civilian communities into flight. However, in advance of the start of these 'tactical' operations, Allon issued guidelines to his brigades and district officers about behaviour in the newly-occupied areas: 'Do not harm the population in the conquered Arab towns and villages . . . [Do] not participate in looting . . . Holy sites (places of worship, monasteries, graveyards, etc.) must not be harmed . . .'[31]

In the east, panic flight from Beit Jibrin (and Beit Nattif) began already on 19 October, following IAF bombing,[32] and continued following a raid on the neighbouring police fort on the night of 24\25 October. On the 27th, IDF units took Beit Jibrin and its police fort. At the same time, a few kilometres to the north, the villagers of 'Ajjur, captured on the 24th, asked permission to return, in conformity with flyers previously dropped by the IAF in the area that had promised that 'peace-loving Arabs would be allowed to stay, like the Arabs in Haifa and Nazareth'. The villagers were told by Giv'ati's 54th Battalion that they would be allowed back if they handed over '40' Bren Guns and '200' rifles and were given until 30 October to respond.[33] The villagers failed to produce the weapons and were not allowed back.

There was apparently also flight from Tarqumiya – which the IDF was expected to attack next – towards Hebron. In Hebron itself there was panic, and Abdullah issued assurances that, not as with Ramle and Lydda, he would defend the town. Kirkbride, the British minister to Jordan, reported that the 'principal' fear was that another wave of refugees, from Hebron, Bethlehem and the surrounding villages, would inundate (east) Jordan. Abdullah sent Legion units to Bethlehem and Hebron, where the Egyptian units, cut off by the loss of Beersheba and the severing of the Majdal-Beit Jibrin road, were on the verge of collapse. Had he not done so, according to Kirkbride, 'the majority of the local population . . . would have left their homes'. Already, he commented, 'the number of refugees . . . dependent on Transjordan is as disastrous as a military defeat'.[34] As it was, according to IDF intelligence, Hebron's rich were taking flight, lacking confidence in the Legion's ability to defend the town.[35] On 30 October, indeed, it was reported that the Legion had blocked entry to Hebron to refugees fleeing the Beit Jibrin–Tarqumiya area[36] and, a few days later, the Hebron NC was reported taking measures to deter flight from the town.[37]

Hundreds of the refugees who made their way up the hills towards Hebron were from al Dawayima, a large village whose core clan, the Ahdibs, traced their origins to the Muslim conquest and settlement of Palestine in the seventh century. Before 1948, the Ahdibs were aligned with the 'Opposition'; the village was regarded by the HIS as 'very friendly'.[38]

Dawayima was captured by companies of the 89th Battalion, Eighth Brigade, who encountered only 'light resistance', on 29 October.[39] The troops, mounted on half-tracks, first laid down a mortar and machinegun barrage and then stormed in, machine-guns blazing.[40] Villagers were gunned down inside houses, in the alleyways and on the surrounding slopes as they fled:

> As we got up on the roofs, we saw Arabs running about in the alleyways [below]. We opened fire on them . . . From our high position we saw a vast plain stretching eastward . . . and the plain was covered by thousands of fleeing Arabs . . . The machineguns began to chatter and the flight turned into a rout.[41]

The houses of Dawayima, later wrote one 89th Battalion veteran,

> were filled with the loot of the Etzion Bloc . . . The Jewish fighters who attacked Dawayima knew that . . . the blood of those slaughtered cries out for revenge; and that the men of Dawayima were among those who took part in the massacre . . . [in] the Etzion Bloc.[42]

The refugees who reached Hebron, according to Yiftah Brigade intelligence, informed UN observers that 'the Jews had repeated the Deir Yassin massacre in Dawayima', and Arab officials demanded an investigation.[43] The Egyptian garrison in Bethlehem cabled Egypt that 'the Jews had massacred 500 men, women and children'.[44] The American consul-general in Jerusalem reported that '500 to 1,000' Arabs had reportedly been 'lined up and killed by machinegun fire' after the capture of the village.[45] Word of the massacre swiftly reached the Israeli authorities. Ben-Gurion, quoting General Avner, briefly referred in his diary to 'rumours' that the army had 'slaughtered (?) about 70–80 persons'.[46] One version of what happened was provided by an Israeli soldier to a Mapam member, who transmitted the information to Eliezer Peri, the editor of the party daily *Al Hamishmar* and a member of the party's Political Committee. The party member, 'Sh.' (possibly Shabtai)

Kaplan, described the witness as 'one of our people, an intellectual, 100 per cent reliable'. The village, wrote Kaplan, had been held by Arab 'irregulars' and was captured by the 89th Battalion without a fight. 'The first [wave] of conquerors killed about 80 to 100 [male] Arabs, women and children. The children they killed by breaking their heads with sticks. There was not a house without dead', wrote Kaplan. Kaplan's informant, who arrived immediately afterward in the second wave, reported that the men and women who remained were then shut away in houses 'without food and water'. Sappers arrived to blow up the houses.

> One commander ordered a sapper to put two old women in a certain house . . . and blow it up . . . The sapper refused . . . The commander then ordered his men to put in the old women and the evil deed was done. One soldier boasted that he had raped a woman and then shot her. One woman, with a newborn baby in her arms, was employed to clean the courtyard where the soldiers ate. She worked a day or two. In the end they shot her and her baby.

The soldier, according to Kaplan, said that

> cultured officers . . . had turned into base murderers and this not in the heat of battle . . . but out of a system of expulsion and destruction. The less Arabs remained – the better. This principle is the political motor for the expulsions and the atrocities.

Kaplan understood that Mapam was in a bind. The matter could not be publicised; it would harm the State and Mapam would be blamed. But he demanded that the party 'raise a shout' in internal debate, launch an investigation and establish disciplinary machinery in the army.[47]

Unknown to Kaplan, a number of parallel investigations were under way, the first initiated by Allon himself. On 3 November, Allon cabled OC Eighth Brigade, General Yitzhak Sadeh – his mentor, the founder and first commander of the Palmah – to check the 'rumours' that the 89th Battalion had 'killed many tens of prisoners on the day of the conquest of al Dawayima', and to respond.[48] (Two days later, perhaps worried about a UN investigation, Allon ordered Sadeh to instruct the unit 'that is accused of murdering Arab civilians at Dawayima to go to the village and bury with their own hands the corpses of those murdered'.)[49] On 4 November, Yadin informed Dori that there had recently been 'a number of incidents like Deir Yassin' – he apparently named Dawayima – and recommended an investigation.[50] The following day, Dori appointed Isser Be'eri, the commander of the IDF Intelligence Service – HIS-AD's successor organisation – to investigate, and on 13 and 18 November he submitted his interim and final reports. Be'eri concluded that about 80 inhabitants had been killed during the 89th Battalion's conquest of the site and another '22' had been subsequently captured and murdered. He recommended that the platoon OC who had carried out the massacre (and had confessed) be tried.[51] (Later Arab reports also tended to 'downgrade' the massacre: On 7 November, for example, Haj Amin al Husseini was informed by West Bank AHC officials Rafiq Tamimi and Munir Abu Fadl that the initial reports had been 'exaggerated'; one report spoke of only '27' villagers killed from one Dawayima clan.[52])

On 7 November, a team of UN observers visited the site. They found several demolished buildings and one corpse but no evidence of a massacre. Nonetheless, they assumed – presumably on the basis of previously heard oral testimony by Arab survivors – that a massacre had taken place.[53] No one, it appears, was ever tried or punished, Be'eri's recommendation notwithstanding.[54] News of the massacre no doubt reached the village communities in the western Hebron and Judean foothills, possibly precipitating further flight.

To the west, on the Mediterranean coast, the bulk of the population of Isdud (Ashdod) fled along with the retreating Egyptian forces before the Israeli conquest of the town on 28 October. The Egyptians had apparently ordered or strongly advised the inhabitants to leave but several hundred had opted to stay. These had greeted the arriving troops with white flags. The IDF immediately appointed one 'Sergeant Sasson Gottlieb' military governor. The inhabitants 'asked [the IDF] for permission to stay'.[55] Permission was granted – but then, almost immediately, the decision was reversed by Southern Front HQ and the inhabitants were expelled southwards.[56] The same day, the IDF entered the large village of Hamama, which was reported 'full of refugees' from Isdud and elsewhere.[57] The inhabitants and the refugees were probably expelled southward. An IAF reconnaissance patrol reported 'a vast stream of refugees, with cattle, sheep, mules and wagons, is spotted flowing along the whole coastline between Isdud and Gaza'.[58]

The events in the villages and towns along the coast were summarised by the Yiftah Brigade's Intelligence Officer on 2 November. The IDF operations had caused 'despair among the local inhabitants'. The locals were certain the Jews would win. 'Our air force had made a tremendous impact. It was a surprise for them to see squadrons of Jewish aircraft rule the skies.' He reported that, initially, after the air raids, the townspeople of Gaza had fled the town to the dunes and beaches but had returned a few days later.[59] The flight from the coastal towns increased following the Israeli navy shelling of Gaza (17 October) and Majdal (21 October). Hundreds were reportedly hit in Gaza, near the train station. Majdal was bombed twice on the night of 19\20 October.[60] In Majdal, indeed, the attacks precipitated popular demonstrations against the Egyptian Army for its inability to defend them.

A senior Egyptian official, Mustafa al Sawaf, in charge of the civil administration in the Egyptian-held areas, on 20 October had issued a flyer denouncing the Palestinians' penchant for flight:

> Why do I see the people confused in their thoughts, packing to leave, wandering long distances to countries that are not theirs, abandoning their towns in haste . . . rushing to flee, leaving behind their lands, cities, homes, and relatives, going south, where there is no haven or sanctuary . . . Don't you have it in you, noble Arab sons, to end this wandering? Remember the bitter fate of winter, when rain and cold will come.

Sawaf, who addressed the flyer to the inhabitants of Gaza, said that the Egyptian Army would protect them.[61] The mayor of Gaza apparently made a similar pronouncement: He called on the inhabitants to stay put even if the IDF occupied the town.[62] But Gaza was not overrun.

However, Majdal, a few miles to the north, was. Much of the population had evacuated after the start of Operation Yoav, under the impact of the aerial and naval bombardment.[63] The Egyptian brigade headquarters had departed for Gaza already on 19 October, and part of the town garrison left on the 30th. No doubt these pullouts helped undermine civilian morale. On 31 October, for example, the intelligence officer of the 55th Battalion reported that '293' trucks – 62 of them 'packed with civilians' – seven taxis, 21 jeeps and nine motorcycles had departed southwards that day.[64] The last Egyptian troops left just after noon on 4 November. A few hours later, at 19:30 hours, a Giv'ati reconnaissance unit entered Majdal.[65] Giv'ati's operational orders were to occupy and search; nothing was said of the fate of the civilian population.[66] The troops were greeted by 11 elders who asked to surrender the town; five were taken to HQ for questioning and then returned home.[67] About 200 inhabitants, mostly women and children, had remained and another 1,000 waited in the dunes around, hoping to be allowed home.[68] The main Giv'ati force entered the town the following morning, 5 November. The troops 'behaved well', according to an accompanying intelligence officer: There was practically no looting and there were no attacks on the population. Posters were pasted that morning on the town walls, 'in Hebrew and Yiddish', warning against improper behaviour. But 'the behaviour of the population was, as usual in such cases, fawning and obsequious', reported an intelligence officer. The IDF sent out criers to beckon those hiding in the dunes and orchards to come home.[69] During the following days, hundreds streamed back into town. On 28 November Yadin ordered Southern Front to conduct a census to determine who had legal rights of residency 'and to free the place of [i.e., expel] everyone who was not there on the day of conquest'.[70] On 1 December, Southern Front carried out the order, identifying and expelling from Majdal to the Gaza Strip 'about 500 refugees'.[71]

The upshot of the October–November battles in the south was that the Gaza Strip's refugee population jumped from the pre-Yoav figure of less than 100,000 to '230,000', according to an official of the United Nations

Refugee Relief Project, F.G. Beard. Beard reported that the condition of these refugees 'def[ies] description . . . Almost all of them are living in the open . . . [and are] receiving no regular rations of food . . . There are no sanitary facilities . . . and conditions of horrifying filth exist.' Beard said the Egyptian Army and the Arab Higher Refugee Council had been 'grossly negligent in their handling of the situation'.[72]

THE NORTH

In the north, the IDF's 60-hour campaign, Operation Hiram, precipitated major civilian flight from the Upper Galilee pocket held by Qawuqji's forces. Many fled before the approaching battle; some were expelled; many others, to be out of harm's way, initially left their villages for nearby gullies, orchards and caves. In many cases, Israeli units barred their return or encouraged them to move on to Lebanon. Some may have decided not to return to live under Israeli rule. Of the area's estimated 50,000–60,000 population (locals and refugees) before 28 October, more than half ended up in Lebanon. On 31 October, Ben-Gurion recorded that roughly half the pocket's villagers had fled, and a few days later, the army estimated that only some 12,000–15,000 inhabitants had remained,[73] lending credence to the later reports that 'more than 50,000 new refugees' had reached Lebanon as a result of Hiram.[74]

The operation kicked off on the night of 28\29 October, Northern Front fielding elements of Carmeli (Second), Golani (First), the Seventh and Oded (Ninth) brigades against the central-upper Galilee pocket held by the ALA, beefed up by a Syrian Army battalion (which included a contingent of Moroccan Army volunteers). The operational order was 'to destroy the enemy in the central Galilee "pocket", to occupy the whole of the Galilee and to establish the defence line on the country's northern border'. No mention was made of the prospective fate of the inhabitants and the refugees encamped in their midst, and there were no instructions to expel anyone.[75]

The offensive was preceded by intermittent bombing raids that began on 22 October, with concentrated attacks, by B-17s and C-47s (Dakotas converted to ground-support use), on the main villages of Tarshiha, Jish and Sa'sa. The most intensive round of bombing was on the night of 29\30 October, with 13 missions against seven villages, with 21 tons of bombs dropped.[76] The bombing of Tarshiha that night killed 24 and buried 60 more under rubble, and triggered mass flight.[77]

The main initial thrust was by Seventh Brigade advancing from Safad northwards, early on 29 October taking Qaddita and Meirun and then Safsaf and Jish.[78] From Jish, its 72nd and 79th battalions pushed westward, taking Sa'sa, and then northeastward, taking Kafr Bir'im, Saliha and, on the afternoon of 30 October, al Malikiya. A third battalion, the 71st, advanced westward, taking Ras al Ahmar, Rihaniya, Alma and, in the afternoon of 30 October, Deishum.[79] In the 79th Battalion's report, the battles for Safsaf and Jish were described as 'difficult' and 'cruel' (achzari).[80] Gershon Gil'ad, Northern Front's intelligence officer, reported that '150–200' Arabs, 'including a number of civilians', died in the battle for Jish.[81] At the same time, Golani units, pushing northward from Lubya, early on 30 October took 'Eilabun and Maghar and then veered westward, taking Rama, Beit Jann and Suhmata, meeting the 123rd Battalion, Haifa District, coming from the west, at Majd al Kurum.[82] To the north, Ninth Brigade (battalions 11, 91 and 92) on the morning of 30 October took Tarshiha,[83] Hurfeish, Fassuta,[84] Mansura, Tarbikha and Iqrit, meeting Seventh Brigade forces at Sa'sa.[85] The Carmeli Brigade, held in reserve in the Galilee Panhandle, on 30–31 October crossed the international frontier westward and conquered a string of 15 villages from Bleida to Kafr Qila and Qantara in southeastern Lebanon.

Repeatedly during the operation, Northern Front ordered the units to issue strict prohibitions against looting.[86] No such prohibitions were issued regarding expulsions (or, for that matter, the killing of civilians and POWs[87]). Regarding expulsions, rather the opposite, as we have seen: On 31 October Northern Front instructed all units 'to assist' the inhabitants 'to leave'. But that order came too late, reaching almost all the units after they had completed their initial sweeps and conquests. (The follow-up order, of 10 November, came even later.) It was one thing to order units before they had set out, before they had overrun villages, to expel inhabitants in the midst of battle and conquest; it was quite another to instruct them, after the shooting had died down, to go back and expel communities they had already overrun and left in place. Moreover, the order of 31 October was couched in euphemistic, non-imperative terms, avoiding the verb 'to expel' (legaresh); this left commanders with a great deal of discretion. As none, subsequently, were held to account for expelling anyone, so no one was tried or reprimanded for failing to expel (so far as the available records show).[88]

The demographic upshot of the operation followed a clear, though by no means systematic, religious-ethnic pattern: Most of the Muslims in the pocket fled to Lebanon while most of the pocket's Christian population remained where they were.[89] Almost all the Druse and Circassian inhabitants remained. Thus, despite the fact that no clear guidelines were issued to the commanders of the advancing IDF columns about how to treat each religious or ethnic group, what emerged roughly conformed to a pattern as if such 'instinctive' guidelines had been followed by both the IDF and the different conquered communities.

At the same time, the demographic outcome generally corresponded to the circumstances of the military advance. Roughly, villages which had put up a stiff fight against IDF units were depopulated: Their inhabitants, fearing retribution, or declining to live under Jewish rule, fled or, in some cases, were expelled. The inhabitants of villages that surrendered quietly generally stayed put and usually were not harmed or expelled by the IDF. They did not fear (or little feared) retribution. This apparently was the main reason why the inhabitants of the half-Muslim, half-Christian village of Fassuta decided to stay: 'The majority argued that the Jews had no reason to vent their wrath on Fassuta', which had not fought against the Haganah or the IDF. Only a few fled to Lebanon.[90] The facts of resistance or peaceful surrender, moreover, roughly corresponded to the religious-ethnic divide. In general, wholly or largely Muslim villages tended to put up a fight or to support units of Qawuqji's army that fought. But there were Muslim villages that surrendered without a fight. Christian villagers tended to surrender without a fight or without assisting Qawuqji. In mixed villages where the IDF encountered resistance, such as Tarshiha and Jish, the Christians by and large stayed put while the Muslims fled or were forced to leave. Druse and Circassian villagers nowhere resisted the IDF advance (except in (Druse) Yanuh).

A bald Minority Affairs Ministry list from this time of 'Villages that Surrendered and [Villages that] were Conquered [after Resistance] Outside the State of Israel [i.e., outside the partition borders]' underlines the connection between resistance and depopulation in Operation Hiram. The villages listed as 'surrendering' are al Bi'na (Muslim), Kaukab (Muslim), Kafr Manda (Muslim), Sakhnin (Muslim), 'Arraba (Muslim), Deir Hanna (Muslim), Maghar (Druse), Jish (Muslim–Christian), Rihaniya (Circassian–Muslim) and 'Alma (Muslim). Of these, only 'Alma was uprooted and expelled. Many of the inhabitants of the rest of the villages (mostly Muslims) fled northwards but the remaining population in each was left *in situ* and not uprooted. The villages, except for 'Alma, exist to this day. The villages that resisted are listed as 'Eilabun (mostly Christian), Farradiya (Muslim), Meirun (Muslim), Sammu'i (Muslim), Safsaf (Muslim), and al Malikiya (Muslim). All were depopulated – either by flight or by partial flight plus expulsion. None – except 'Eilabun, where the inhabitants were allowed back – exist today.[91]

Apart from these general patterns, the campaign was characterised by vagaries of time and place. Much depended on the circumstances surrounding the capture of a given village and on the character of middle-echelon IDF commanders. The history of each village, whether in the past 'friendly' or hostile towards the Yishuv, also affected IDF (and the villagers' own) behaviour as, apparently, did its behaviour after being conquered: In all the villages, the IDF assembled the villagers, sorted out non-locals from locals and young adult males from the old, women and children and usually sent for questioning or to PoW camps the non-local and local army-age males. The units also collected the villages' arms. Some villages were more cooperative than others in these detention and arms collection sweeps.

A few days later, Shimoni defined what had happened in the Galilee:

> The attitude towards the Arab inhabitants of the Galilee and to the refugees [there] . . . was accidental/haphazard [*mikri*] and different from place to place in accordance with this or that commander's initiative or this or that official's . . . Here [inhabitants] were expelled, there, left in place; here, the surrender of villages was accepted . . . there [the IDF] refused to accept surrender; here, [the IDF] discriminated in favour of the Christians, and there [the IDF] behaved towards the Christians and the Moslems in the same way . . .; here, refugees who fled in the first instance under shock of conquest were allowed back to their places, there, [they] were not allowed [back].

Apparently, Shimoni did not know of Carmel's expulsion order of 31 October. Nor, in this description, did he give sufficient weight to the general discrimination in favour of Christian and Druse villagers, a handful of exceptions notwithstanding.

Prior to Hiram, the Foreign Ministry Middle East Department had advised the IDF

> to try during conquest [to make sure] that no Arab inhabitants remain in the Galilee and certainly that no refugees from other places remain there. Truth to tell, concerning the attitude to the Christian [Arabs] and the problem of whether to discriminate in their favour and to leave them in their villages, clear instructions were not given [by the IDF command?] and we did not express an opinion.

The Middle East Department, complained Shimoni, had simply not been informed that the operation was about to be launched and, hence, had not had time to work out 'an accurate plan'.[92]

A few days later, in a plaintive report to Foreign Ministry Director General Eytan, Shimoni was to write, after visiting the Galilee and talking to Hiram commanders:

> From all the commanders we talked to we heard that during the operations . . . they had had no clear instructions, no clear line, concerning behaviour towards the Arabs in the conquered areas – expulsion of the inhabitants or leaving them in place; harsh or 'soft' behaviour; discrimination in favour of Christians or not; a special attitude towards Maronites; a special attitude towards Matawalis [Shi'ites].

Shimoni added that he had no doubt that some of the atrocities committed would not have taken place 'had the conquering army had a clear and positive line of behaviour'. In general, Shimoni complained, the Ministry's opinion was not often elicited by the IDF, sometimes failed to reach the appropriate commanders and almost always was never taken into account during operations.[93]

Following the end of Hiram, a great deal of haphazardness continued to characterise IDF behaviour in the Galilee. For example, al Rama, a mainly Christian village with a substantial Druse minority and some Muslims, was overrun without a fight by Golani on 30 October. The following day, another unit – probably the 91st Battalion – entered the village and expelled its almost 1,000 Christian and Muslim inhabitants, on pain of death. The Druse were allowed to stay.[94] The unit remained in the village until 5 November. The following day, the Christians, who had camped out in nearby caves and *wadis*, returned to their homes. The return was no doubt facilitated by the intervention of Ben Dunkelman (Binyamin Ben-David), OC Seventh Brigade, who had cabled Carmel on the morning of 2 November:

> I protest against the eviction of Christians from the village of Rama and its environs. We saw Christians at [i.e., from] Rama in the fields thirsty for water and suffering from robbery. Other brigades expelled Christians from villages that did not resist and surrendered to our forces. I suggest that you issue an order to return the Christians to their villages.[95]

The expulsion was probably ordered because one of the town's leading Christians, Father Yakub al Hanna, had loudly supported Qawuqji. There may also have been local Druse pressure on the IDF to expel the Christians.

In a number of villages, IDF troops separated resident refugees from villagers and expelled them. Such was the fate of refugees, including a group from Ghuweir Abu Shusha, who had fled to Rama at the end of April.[96] One former Ghuweir resident, who was at Rama on 31 October, decades later described what happened:

> The people in Rama were ordered to assemble at the centre of the village. A Jewish soldier stood on top of a rise and addressed us. He ordered the Druse present . . . to go back to their homes . . . Then he ordered the rest of us to leave to Lebanon . . . Although I was given permission to stay by my friend, Abu Musa [a Jewish officer], I could not remain without the rest of my tribe who were forced to flee.

Unlike the Rama Christian community, these non-residents did not remain in the area but moved off to Lebanon.[97]

Similar events took place in al Bi'na, next to Majd al Kurum. The ALA abandoned Bi'na (two thirds Muslim, one third Christian) and neighbouring Deir al Asad (Muslim) on 29 October. The following day, a delegation of notables from the two villages formally surrendered to the IDF. Golani troops occupied the villages on the morning of 31 October. The inhabitants assembled in Bi'na's square and 100 weapons were handed over. The troops then randomly selected four young men, two from Bi'na and two from Deir al Assad, took them to a nearby olive grove and executed them. Some 270 of the men were hauled off to a POW camp while the rest of the population was briefly expelled in the direction of Rama and the villages were thoroughly looted. A few days later, the villagers were allowed back. On 5 November, an IDF unit arrived and blew up three houses in Deir al Asad and torched another in Bi'na.[98]

But before the villagers were temporarily driven out, the refugees in their midst were identified, separated and permanently expelled. A refugee from Sha'b later recalled that at first

> the Jews grouped us with the other [Bi'na] villagers, separating us [only] from our women. We remained all day in the village courtyard . . . we were thirsty and hungry . . . It was almost night . . . [The] Bi'na mukhtar asked the Jews to permit us to stay overnight . . . rather than travel [northwards] at night with our old men, women and children. The Jews rejected the mukhtar's request and gave us [i.e., the refugees] half an hour to leave . . . When half an hour passed, the Jews began to fire in the air . . . they injured my nine-year-old son in the knee. We walked a few hours until we reached Sajur . . . We were terrified, the road was full of people in every direction you looked . . . all in a hurry to get to Lebanon.

A few days later, after a brief stay in the Druse village of Beit Jann, they reached Lebanon.[99]

Some Muslim villages with an anti-Yishuv past, such as Majd al Kurum, were not uprooted. Majd al Kurum was conquered on 30 October. About one-third of its inhabitants left the night before the IDF's 123rd Battalion arrived, after the ALA garrison began to withdraw. The local ALA commander apparently advised the young men and women of the village to leave with him. According to one inhabitant's recollection, about 100–120 families left that night: 'We did not want to take any risks and decided to leave to Lebanon.' Those who stayed, according to Nazzal, did so 'because they were too old and were "afraid of dying in a strange land" . . . [or feared] they would starve' or out of a general fatalism.[100] A curfew was imposed and the inhabitants reluctantly handed over 20 rifles and then, 'after additional pressure and threats', another 15 rifles. The village mukhtar, Haj 'Abd, 'displayed a lot of *hutzpa* during the handover of the weapons . . . There is a lot of open obstructionism . . .', reported the occupying unit. Some of the young adults had fled to the hills. The following day, the 123rd was replaced by the 122nd Battalion.[101] The IDF suspected that the villagers were holding back arms. On 5 November, the mukhtar was ordered to hand over the remaining arms. He responded that there were no more arms and, in any case, the 25–35 minutes allotted were insufficient. The soldiers selected five men and, according to a UN report, 'lined them up alongside a wall next to the water pump and shot them'. The soldiers then searched the houses, killing another four inhabitants, including two women, in the process. They confiscated 275 sheep and goats and blew up the mukhtar's house before leaving the village.[102] But the villagers did not leave and were not expelled.

The haphazardness of what occurred is underlined by the case of Mi'ilya, a Christian village whose militia had fought alongside the ALA against the Oded Brigade. During the previous months the villagers had decided not to allow any villagers to flee to Lebanon. When the battle was lost, on 31 October, almost all the inhabitants left, some crossing to Lebanon. But during the following days, the local IDF commanders allowed all those who had fled to return, one of the few such cases during the 1948 war.[103]

At Tarshiha, the population had long feared Israeli retribution, given their role in the destruction of the Yehiam Convoy on 28 March, when 47 Haganah men were killed. The IDF ground assault of 29 October was preceded by a short aerial bombardment and an artillery barrage. Most of the Muslims fled with the ALA garrison that morning, before the Oded troops arrived. The village's Christians by and large stayed and were not expelled.[104] Much to the chagrin of the IDF, a few weeks later inhabitants were busy infiltrating back. 'Tarshiha is slipping through our fingers as an empty settlement ready to absorb Jewish [settlers]', warned Major 'Amir, military governor of Western Galilee.[105]

Christian villages, traditionally friendly or not unfriendly towards the Yishuv, were generally left in peace. An exception was 'Eilabun, a mainly Maronite community, which fell to Golani's 12th Battalion on 30 October after a battle on its outskirts with the ALA, in which the Israelis suffered six injured and four armoured cars knocked out.[106] The villagers hung out white flags and the Israelis were welcomed by four priests. The inhabitants huddled inside the churches while the priests surrendered the village. But the troops were angered by the battle just concluded and by reports of a procession in the village, a month before, in which a large number of inhabitants had participated, in which the heads of two IDF soldiers who had gone missing after the attack on 12 September on a nearby hilltop – 'Outpost 213'[107] – were carried through the streets, or by the actual discovery in a house of one of the rotting heads.

What happened next is described in a letter from the village elders to Shitrit: The villagers were ordered to assemble in the square. While assembling, one villager was killed and another wounded by IDF fire.

Then the commander selected 12 young men[108] and sent them to another place, then he ordered that the assembled inhabitants be led to [the neighbouring village of] Maghar and the priest asked him to leave the women and babies and to take only the men, but he refused, and led the assembled inhabitants – some 800 in number – to Maghar preceded by military vehicles . . . He himself stayed on with another two soldiers until they killed the 12 young men in the streets of the village and then they joined the army going to Maghar . . . He led them to Farradiya. When they reached Kafr 'Inan they were joined by an armoured car that fired upon them . . . killing one of the old men, Sam'an ash Shoufani, 60 years old, and injuring three women . . . At Farradiya [the soldiers] robbed the inhabitants of I£ 500 and the women of their jewelry, and took 42 youngsters and sent them to a detention camp, and the rest the next day were led to Meirun, and afterwards to the Lebanese border. During this whole time they were given food only once. Imagine then how the babies screamed and the cries of the pregnant and weaning mothers.

Subsequently, troops looted 'Eilabun.[109]

Not all the villagers were taken on the trek to Lebanon. The four priests were allowed to stay. Hundreds fled to nearby gullies, caves and villages, and during the following days and weeks infiltrated back. The affair exercised the various Israeli bureaucracies for months, partly because the 'Eilabun case was taken up and pleaded persistently by Israeli and Lebanese Christian clergymen. The villagers asked to be allowed back and receive Israeli citizenship. They denied responsibility for severing the soldiers' heads, blaming one Fawzi al Mansur of Jenin, a sergeant in Qawuqji's army.[110]

The affair sparked a guilty conscience and sympathy within the Israeli establishment. Shitrit ruled that former inhabitants still living within Israeli-held territory must be allowed back to the village. But Major Sulz, Military Governor of the Nazareth District, responded that the army would not allow them back. He asserted, ambiguously, that 'Eilabun had been 'evacuated either voluntarily or with a measure of compulsion'. A fortnight later, he elaborated, mendaciously: 'The village was captured after a fierce fight and its inhabitants had fled.' The Foreign Ministry opined that even if an 'injustice' had been committed, 'injustices of war cannot be put right during the war itself'.[111]

However, Shitrit, supported by Mapam's leaders and egged on by the village notables and priests, persisted. Cisling suggested that the matter be discussed in Cabinet. Shitrit requested that the villagers be granted citizenship (relieving them of the fear of deportation as illegal infiltrees), that the 'Eilabun detainees be released and that the villagers be supplied with provisions.[112] Within weeks, Shitrit was supported by General Carmel, who wrote that 'in light of the arguments [about their mistreatment]' and of the fact that the area was not earmarked for Jewish settlement, the inhabitants should be left in place 'and accepted as citizens'.[113] Within weeks, the inhabitants received citizenship and provisions, and the detainees were released. At the same time, Shitrit, as Minister of Police, persuaded Yadin, to initiate an investigation of the massacre.[114] During the summer of 1949, the 'Eilabun exiles in Lebanon who wished to return were allowed to do so, as part of an agreement between Palmon, head of the Arab Section of the Political Department of the Foreign Ministry, and Archbishop Hakim, concerning the return of several thousand Galilee Christians in exchange for that cleric's future goodwill towards the Jewish State. Hundreds returned to 'Eilabun.[115]

The abortive attack on 'Outpost 213', bizarrely enough, triggered a second atrocity four days after the first massacre. On 2 November, two squads of the 103rd Battalion were sent on a search operation to Khirbet Wa'ra as Sauda, a village inhabited by the 'Arab al Mawasi beduins, three kilometres east of the outpost. While one squad kept guard over the villagers, the other – led by Lt. Haim Hayun, veteran of the September assault – climbed up to the outpost, where it discovered 'the bones of the soldiers lost in the previous action'. The bodies were 'headless'. The troops then torched the village (and presumably expelled the inhabitants), taking with them to their HQ in Maghar 19 adult males. There, the prisoners were sorted out and 14 were determined to have 'taken part in enemy activity against our army'. They were taken away and 'liquidated' (*huslu*). The remaining five were transferred to a POW camp.[116]

'Eilabun and 'Arab al Mawasi were only two of the atrocities committed by the IDF during Hiram, which saw the biggest concentration of atrocities of the 1948 war. Some served to precipitate and enhance flight; some, as in 'Eilabun, were part and parcel of an expulsion operation; but in other places, the population remained *in situ* and expulsion did not follow atrocities.

Details about most the atrocities remain sketchy; most of the relevant IDF and Israel Justice Ministry documentation – including the reports of various committees of inquiry – remain classified. But there is some accessible, civilian documentation – and a few military documents have escaped the censorial sieve. It emerges that the main massacres occurred in Saliha, Safsaf, Jish and the (Lebanese) village of Hule, between 30 October and 2 November.[117] In the first three villages, Seventh Brigade troops were responsible. At Saliha it appears that troops blew up a house, possibly the village mosque, killing 60–94 persons who had been crowded into it.[118] In Safsaf, troops shot and then dumped into a well 50–70 villagers and POWs.[119] In Jish, the troops apparently murdered about 10 Moroccan POWs (who had served with the Syrian Army) and a number of civilians, including, apparently, four Maronite Christians, and a woman and her baby.[120] In Hule, just west of the Galilee Panhandle, a company commander and a sergeant of the Carmeli Brigade's 22nd Battalion shot some three dozen captured Lebanese soldiers and peasants and then demolished a house on top of them, killing all.[121] Civilians appear to have been murdered in Sa'sa as well.[122]

The atrocities clearly embarrassed the IDF and civilian officials, who were soon forced to respond to Arab and UN charges in various forums. The main response was a flat or qualified denial that atrocities had taken place.[123] But this was not always sufficient. As Lt Colonel Baruch Komarov, responsible for IDF liaison with the UN observer corps, put it:

Atrocities committed in the Galilee have not been covered and are still visible to the eye of visitors. In a number of places the corpses have not been buried.[124] This makes a difficult impression on the UN observers, and they, certainly, will blacken our names in the Security Council. It appears that there was negligence on this score by Northern Front . . . In [certain] villages the inhabitants dared to accuse us [in front of visiting UN personnel] of murder and robbery.[125]

He was apparently thinking specifically of Majd al Kurum, where the inhabitants, during a UN observers visit on 11 November, charged the IDF with 'atrocities [involving] robbery and murder'.[126]

These atrocities, mostly committed against Muslims, no doubt precipitated the flight of communities on the path of the IDF advance. A community already nervous at the prospect of assault and probable conquest would doubtless have been driven to panic by news, possibly embellished by exaggeration, of atrocities in a neighbouring village. What happened at Safsaf and Jish no doubt reached the villagers of Ras al Ahmar, 'Alma, Deishum and al Malikiya hours before the Seventh Brigade's columns. These villages, apart from 'Alma, seem to have been completely or largely empty when the IDF arrived. If the memory of a former inhabitant of Sa'sa is to be believed, the Safsaf atrocity, rather than the battle for Sa'sa, was what precipitated the exodus from the village.[127]

But the atrocities were limited in size, scope and time. And as, immediately after Hiram, movement by inhabitants between villages was curtailed, news of massacres probably moved slowly. Moreover, atrocities did not occur in many, perhaps most, of the villages captured. In most, the primary causes of flight were those that had precipitated previous waves: Fear of being caught up and hurt in battle, fear of the conquerors and of revenge for past misdeeds or affiliations, a general fear of the future and of life under Jewish rule, and confusion and shock.

A year or so after Hiram, Moshe Carmel described the panic flight of some of the villagers:

They abandon the villages of their birth and that of their ancestors and go into exile . . . Women, children, babies, donkeys – everything moves, in silence and grief, northwards, without looking to right or left. Wife does not find her husband and child does not find his father . . . no one knows the goal of his trek. Many possessions are scattered by the paths; the more the refugees walk, the more tired they grow – and they throw away what they had tried to save on their way into exile. Suddenly, every object seems to them petty, superfluous, unimportant as against the chasing fear and the urge to save life and limb.

I saw a boy aged eight walking northwards pushing along two asses in front of him. His father and brother had died in the battle and his mother was lost. I saw a woman holding a two-week-old baby in her right arm and a baby two years old in her left arm and a four-year-old girl following in her wake, clutching at her dress.

[Near Sa'sa] I saw suddenly by the roadside a tall man, bent over, scraping with his fingernails in the hard, rocky soil. I stopped. I saw a small hollow in the ground, dug out by hand, with fingernails, under an olive tree. The man laid down the body of a baby who had died in the arms of his mother, and covered it with soil and small stones. [Near Tarshiha, Carmel saw a 16-year-old] sitting by the roadside, naked as the day he was born and smiling at our passing car.

Carmel described how some of the Israeli soldiers, regarding the refugee columns with astonishment and shock and 'with great sadness', went down into the *wadis* and gave the refugees bread and tea. 'I knew [of] a unit in which no soldier ate anything that day because all [the food] sent it by the company kitchen was taken down to the *wadi*', he recalled.[128]

But usually, it appears, IDF behaviour in the days after Hiram was less humane. In general, the units along the Lebanese border made sure that the refugee columns continued on their way to Lebanon and often prevented with live fire any attempt to return to Israeli territory. And in the interior of the Galilee, the IDF made sure that villages that had been depopulated would stay empty. For example, on 3 November the 11th Battalion reported that a squadron of its armoured cars had encountered 'columns of refugees returning [to Israel] from Lebanon' on the Sa'sa-Malikiya road. 'A number of bursts were fired at them and they vanished.'[129] The following day, Golani's 14th Battalion described a patrol by a squadron of jeeps east of the 'Eilabun-Maghar road. The patrol spotted a new 15-tent beduin encampment.

When we approached the tents, several Arabs were seen fleeing to the [nearby] *wadis*. We found only women and old people . . . It looked as if [the group] had returned here only today. In line with the order not to allow Muslim inhabitants to return, we told them that they must leave. We did not use force.

The patrol then drove to Farradiya, north of Maghar. They spotted groups of 'women and old people', their belongings piled up on mules, leaving the village. 'They said they were going to Lebanon, but it is possible that they were going to their menfolk in the hills.' Inside Farradiya, the patrol encountered three IDF Druse soldiers 'collecting loot. I think that they are responsible for the sudden departure [of the Muslims] from the village . . .'[130] A 91st Battalion patrol on 10 November encountered a group of refugees walking toward Lebanon between Deir al Qasi and Mansura. One of them refused to say where he was from – and was 'shot and killed trying to escape'.[131] In Ras al Ahmar, an 11th Battalion patrol that day found 'a number of women and children'. They were sent on their way to Lebanon 'with a warning not to return'.[132] The following day, another 11th Battalion patrol encountered a group of

'30' refugees returning to Saliha 'and expelled them northwards'.[133] When Battalion 103 around 12 November took over responsibility for the Maghar–'Eilabun area, it was instructed to 'carry out harassing operations' – meaning, apparently, vis-à-vis civilian Arab concentrations.[134] Israeli policy during November was embodied in an (unsigned) minute to an 11th Battalion report: '[You] must expel and harm the returning refugees.'[135]

But behaviour toward inhabited villages was different. Here, IDF units rounded up and detained army-age males and collected weapons; usually there were no expulsions. On 9 November, for example a 40-man contingent of the 123rd Battalion surrounded and then entered Kafr Manda in search of weapons and Arab 'gang' members. Five young men were arrersted. At first, the detainess

> displayed *hutzpa* and denied [that they were 'gang' members or hiding weapons]. [But] under pressure and threats, the mukhtar began to talk to [the detainees] [and] a few of those interrogated showed willingness to show us the hiding place of the weapons. Several were sent under guard and by 20:00 they had brought back 6 rifles and ammunition. One of the Arabs . . . was killed when he tried to escape.

It is worth noting that the IDF did not expel or, apparently, otherwise punish the villagers who had harboured the irregulars and their weapons.[136]

By mid-November, once the dust of battle had settled, the Military Government in the Occupied Territories was demanding that Northern Front hand over control of the internal areas of the Galilee. General Avner wrote that already on 11 November, Yadin had assured him that 'these areas would be handed over in the coming days'. The events in Majd al Kurum had only highlighted the need to transfer authority from the regular army to the Military Government. Or as Komarov put it: 'The situation in the central Galilee is awful, and causes us great [diplomatic–political] harm. The [UN] observers are still [out there and] gunning for us. Please rush the transfer of governance.' Yadin minuted: 'Write the Military Government that they can immediately receive control of the Galilee areas in coordination with OC Northern Front.'[137]

But it was precisely the chaotic situation – with IDF troops having committed atrocities, inhabitants streaming out of the country and from Lebanon back into Israel, ex-irregulars on the loose and hiding in the villages, and arms caches still undiscovered in many places – that prevented Carmel from handing over the area, he explained later that month. He would be happy to transfer control 'the moment it was possible in light of security [considerations]'.[138]

Carmel was responding to a sharp protest by Avner following Northern Front's distribution of a letter to military governors and units outlining requisite behaviour towards Druse and Christian inhabitants. The letter stated that it had been decided that the Druse were to be allowed to keep their weapons, which needed to be registered. The letter went on to state that Christian and Druse who had been transferred from their villages inland should be told that this was 'a temporary measure for security reasons' and when 'things got better, their return to their villages would be considered'. Lastly, inhabitants who had left the country should be prevented from returning. Northern Front specifically stipulated that the military governors were responsible for the implementation of this order.[139] Avner was particularly annoyed by Carmel's instructions to the military governors – who were nominally under his, Avner's, authority.[140]

No doubt, in the background was Avner's anger at the postponement of the transfer of central Galilee into his own hands – and over the memorandum entitled 'The Organisation of Rule in the Conquered Territory. General Guidelines', dated 16 November, which had been issued by Ninth Brigade, no doubt with Carmel's explicit approval, which also instructed the military governors about behaviour in the occupied territories. The Ninth Brigade, assisted by battalions 122 and 123, had been empowered at the start of November, to take over the areas of central Galilee which were about to be evacuated by the Seventh and First brigades. The memorandum dealt with the carrying out of a census, rules pertaining to movement by the inhabitants, carrying arms, search and detention operations, curfews and roadblocks. The military governors and army units were instructed to 'limit to the maximum' the movement of inhabitants from place to place; 'to shoot any citizen' violating the curfew orders; and to forbid the carrying of weapons.[141]

Rule over central Galilee was at last transferred to the Military Government in the first half of December. Before taking on the offered post of military governor, Lt Colonel Emmanuel Markovsky (Mor) toured the area and met the regional military governors and IDF unit OCs. He reported on what he found (apparently to Dori) in the following terms:

> The population in many places has grown greatly since the end of hostilities [as a result of infiltration back] . . . No effective means have been adopted . . . to prevent infiltration and the increase of the population . . . In the rural areas the population does not feel any existing, orderly government that can prevent it from doing what it wants . . .

He concluded that the military governors control only two towns, Acre and Nazareth, 'and the whole of the Galilee is in effect without effective government'. Markovsky saw his main task as 'preventing the increase in the size of the population by preventing the possibility of infiltration back and effective supervision [i.e., prevention] of resettlement in the abandoned or semi-abandoned villages'.[142]

Ben-Gurion's views were also fairly clear. Soon after Hiram, he travelled to Tiberias for a holiday weekend. He jotted down in his diary: '. . . [it's] almost unbelievable: On the way from Tel Aviv to Tiberias there are almost no Arabs.'[143] The passage echoed, almost word for word, his thoughts in February (see above), when he had travelled from

Tel Aviv through west Jerusalem to the Jewish Agency building, encountering no Arabs on the way. But then his observation had expressed a mixture of astonishment and satisfaction; now, it was pure satisfaction.

The Hiram atrocities, like a brushfire, triggered rumours and reports, accurate and inaccurate, that sped up and down the various IDF chains of command and sideways, through Arab survivors and conscience-stricken soldiers, to civilian officials and party politicians. Key in the transmission of the rumours and reports were Arab radio broadcasts and complaints and old HIS hands and kibbutz mukhtars in the Galilee, such Emmanuel Friedman, of Rosh Pina, and Benjamin Shapira, of Kibbutz 'Amir.[144] By 4 November, Yadin had heard of the atrocities committed by the 89th Battalion in Dawayima and by the Seventh Brigade in the Galilee, and was demanding an investigation.[145] A handful of internal IDF investigations were set in motion. These were quickly followed by what was slated to be a major, external probe by the country's attorney-general, Ya'akov Shimshon Shapira. Until then, through the war Ben-Gurion had consistently protected and defended the men in uniform and their actions against all outside criticism and investigation (save in the matter of looting). Maltreatment of civilians and POWs went almost completely uninvestigated and unpunished: It was a war for survival and the Haganah and IDF had to be allowed to get on with the job. And all were aware that the Arabs, viewed as barbaric and mendacious, had (a) launched the war and (b) had themselves committed countless atrocities before 1948 and a number of major ones during the war (which, needless to say, they had never apologised for, investigated, or atoned for through punishment of the guilty). So they were to blame for what had happened.

But by Hiram, it was no longer, palpably, a war for survival, from Israel's perspective; the danger to the State's existence, at least in the short term, had passed. And the October–November atrocities were simply too concentrated, widespread and severe to be ignored. Even Ben-Gurion could no longer keep the lid on. On 12 November, Major Emmanuel Yalan (Vilensky) was appointed by Be'eri (at Dori's behest) to investigate what had happened in Safsaf, Jish, Sa'sa and 'Eilabun (and Kafr Bir'im, whose inhabitants were about to be expelled). A week earlier, Haim Laskov, the IDF's new head of training, began investigating what had happened at Saliha; already on 7 and 8 November he had begun questioning 79th Battalion officers.[146] At about the same time, an IDF Intelligence Service\Field Security unit cursorily investigated the atrocities and submitted a report. On 16 November, Laskov presented CGS Dori with a 'file' – apparently of depositions though it may also have contained a report with conclusions – concerning Saliha, which the CGS duly passed on to the Defence Minister.[147] Meanwhile, Yalan questioned 79th Battalion senior officers[148] and on the 18th submitted a very confused and undefinitive report of his own. Yalan concluded that the atrocities were committed deliberately and with aforethought, mainly in order to promote flight and secondarily as expressions of revenge. It may have been the inadequacy of Yalan's report that prompted Carmel to appoint, on 20 November, yet another investigative team to look into Northern Front's atrocities. The team was composed of Captain Nahum Segal, Captain Moshe Taflas and First Lieutenant Isser Perlman. It was instructed to start work on 22 November and submit its findings – on 'the accuracy of the rumours regarding the atrocities committed in the course of Operation "Hiram"', as the letter of appointment put it – by the 25th.[149] The team questioned 79th Battalion officers – 'regarding atrocities in Jish and Safsaf' – on 24 November.[150] At the end of November, it submitted an interim report which determined, according to Carmel, that 'there is a basis for charging soldiers and officers for committing unjustified killings outside the framework of military necessity, in Safsaf, Jish and Saliha'. Carmel ordered the Front's adjutant-general to 'immediately' put these people on trial – and informed the CGS that one officer, presumably Captain Shmuel Lahis, a company OC, was to be tried on 2 December for the massacre in Hule. Meanwhile, the investigative team continued work.[151]

The atrocities, given their number and lethality, almost inevitably generated political fallout. But as not a word about them was published in the media, probably due to a combination of internal and external censorship,[152] the fallout was limited to closed meetings of senior political bodies, such as the Cabinet and Mapam's Political Committee. Large parts of the Cabinet meetings of November and December were devoted to the atrocities and their repercussions.[153] At the Cabinet meeting of 7 November, the criticism was led off by Immigration and Health Minister Shapira. He was followed by Interior Minister Gruenbaum and Justice Minister Rosenblueth. Labour and Construction Minister Bentov also spoke up. Mapai's ministers apparently kept their peace, but Ben-Gurion beat a tactical retreat. The Cabinet appointed a three-man (Bentov, Rosenblueth and Shapira) ministerial committee of inquiry to investigate 'the army's deeds in the conquered territories'. Bentov later reported that only Ben-Gurion and Sharett appeared not to have been 'shocked' by what had happened.[154]

The atrocities, and the start of the ministerial probe, were discussed in Mapam's executive bodies on 11 November. The party faced its usual problem: Ideologically, it was motivated to lead the clamour; in practice, caution had to be exercised as its 'own' generals, party members Sadeh and Carmel, were involved if not implicated. Aharon Cohen demanded that the party set up its own, internal inquiry. Benny Marshak asked that the party executives – he was referring to Cisling – refrain from using the phrase 'Nazi actions' and said that the Palmah had already tried a number of soldiers for killing Arabs not during battle. Riftin asserted that there was 'no connection' between the atrocities and the expulsion of Arabs (in effect, justifying the expulsions while condemning the atrocities). He called for death sentences for those guilty of atrocities. Galili warned against 'rushing to attribute responsibility to our officer comrades' before investigation. But Bentov feared that the soldiers would decline to testify before the ministerial committee and that the ministers lacked an effective investigative apparatus. The Political Committee decided to hold formal 'clarification' sessions with the Mapam officers involved and to urge its members to testify before the ministerial committee.[155]

The doings – or, more accurately, the non-doings – of the ministerial 'Committee of Three' preoccupied the Cabinet and some of the political parties for weeks. On 12 November, Kaplan, urged the three – in light of details he had heard about what had happened in the Galilee – to push on with their work.[156] But the committee encountered evasiveness, delays and silence from the IDF; the officers refused to cooperate and testify. Rosenblueth and Shapira complained to Ben-Gurion and demanded wider powers; Ben-Gurion refused.[157] The committee then raised the matter in Cabinet, on 14 November. Rosenblueth asked for increased powers, to be anchored in new emergency regulations; Gruenbaum suggested that a senior IDF officer be added to the committee and that the defence minister issue an order compelling all officers summoned to appear before the committee 'and answer all questions'. Ben-Gurion parried manipulatively by taking the committee to task for doing nothing and wasting a week; '[and] after a week it is much harder to investigate than immediately after a deed', he added. He turned down Rosenblueth's proposal that the committee be given judicial powers and avoided response to the suggestion that he issue an order compelling officers to cooperate. The exchange led to a further week's delay.[158] Three days later, in the Cabinet meeting of 17 November, Cisling charged that for over half a year, Ben-Gurion had avoided the problem of Jewish behaviour toward the Arabs, had pleaded ignorance of abuses and had consistently deflected criticism of the army. Cisling referred to a letter he had received about the atrocities – possibly Shabtai Kaplan's on Dawayima – and declared: 'I couldn't sleep all night . . . This is something that determines the character of the nation . . . Jews too have committed Nazi acts.' Cisling agreed that outwardly Israel, to preserve its good name and image, must admit nothing; but the matter must be thoroughly investigated, he insisted. Dori, said Cisling, had repeatedly postponed appearing before the 'Committee of Three', arguing that he did not yet have the information required, while a subordinate officer had delayed appearing on the grounds that the committee should first hear the CGS.[159]

The Cabinet, at Ben-Gurion's insistence, refused to increase the committee's powers and Shapira resigned (from the committee). Ben-Gurion then proposed that the committee be replaced by a one-man probe, and accompanied this with a statement apparently threatening, or implying a threat of, resignation from the Defence Ministry if he did not get his way. The ministers caved in and voted that 'the Prime Minister investigate the charges concerning the army's behaviour . . .'.[160] Ben-Gurion appointed Attorney-General Ya'akov Shimshon Shapira as sole investigator, and proposed that three IDF officers help him. Ben-Gurion's letter of instruction to Shapira read:

> You are requested herein . . . to investigate if there were depredations [p'gi'ot] by . . . the army against Arab inhabitants in the Galilee and the South, not in conformity with the accepted rules of war . . . What were the attacks . . .? To what degree was the army command, low and high, responsible for these acts, and to what degree was the existing discipline in the army responsible for this and what should be done to rectify matters and to punish the guilty?

Ben-Gurion added that orders would be issued to the troops to provide all the necessary evidence and aid to the investigation.[161] In consequence, on 25 November, Carmel issued a stern warning to his troops against further atrocities and ordered 'every battalion' OC to 'help uncover the atrocities and put the criminals on trial'. He said the battalion OCs were 'personally responsible' for bringing the perpetrators to justice.[162]

In a masterly political stroke, Ben-Gurion then switched from a manipulative, stonewalling defence to the offensive, outflanking Mapam on its own turf. On 21 November, he wrote to the nation's leading poet, Natan Alterman, praising his poem 'Al Zot' (on this). The poem, critical of the atrocities, had appeared in the Histadrut daily, Davar, two days before. Ben-Gurion requested the poet's permission for the Defence Ministry to reprint and distribute it throughout the IDF. The poem, apparently about the 89th Battalion's July raid on Lydda, was duly reprinted and distributed, along with Ben-Gurion's letter to Alterman. Ben-Gurion later read out the poem at a meeting of the Provisional Council of State. The poem describes a young, jeep-mounted soldier 'trying out' his machine-gun on an old Arab in a street in a conquered town. More generally, it castigates 'the insensitivity of the Jewish public' to the atrocities. Its publication in Davar was an 'event.'[163]

On 5 December, Ben-Gurion submitted the Attorney General's (bland, unilluminating) report to the Cabinet and promised that the IDF was continuing its own investigations. The Cabinet set up a standing committee of five ministers to continue probing past IDF misdeeds and to look into future ones, should these occur, and a second committee to formulate guidelines geared to preventing atrocities.[164]

The major outcome of the simultaneous Mapam, IDF and Shapira investigations was the publication in the IDF of strict rules on the treatment of civilians.[165] On 23 December, Ben-Gurion instructed General Avner to take severe measures to protect the inhabitants of the Gaza Strip – which the Prime Minister believed was about to fall into Israeli hands – and to avoid expulsions ('The policy [is] – to leave the inhabitants in place, to prevent any attempt at robbery').[166] A few days before, on 17 December, Allon, just before the start of Operation Horev, which he commanded and in which the IDF conquered Abu Ageila and reached the outskirts of El Arish, issued a detailed appendix to the operational orders setting out guidelines for the treatment of captured soldiers and overrun civilian populations. The preamble referred to the 'disgraceful incidents' that had occurred in the past. The appendix stated that the IDF should take prisoners where possible (rather than kill them); 'unjustified killing of civilians will be regarded as murder . . . Torture of placid civilians will be dealt with sharply; Arab populations must not be expelled except with special permission from the Front Combat HQ.' The appendix ordered commanders of brigades and districts to issue 'special orders' to all units in this connection. All battalion commanders were instructed to sign a special form declaring that 'they had received these orders and would abide by them'. The brigade and district commanders were ordered to react to any infringement publicly and with extreme severity. Similar orders reached all large IDF formations during the winter.[167]

CONCLUSION

The primary aims of operations Yoav and Hiram were to destroy enemy formations – the Egyptian army in the south and Qawuqji's ALA in the central Galilee – and to conquer additional territory, giving the Jewish State greater strategic depth. The operational orders, as in nearly all IDF offensives, did not refer to the Arab civilian population. It was probably assumed by the colonels and generals, on both fronts, that once again there would be mass, spontaneous flight. But brigade, battalion and company commanders, by October–November 1948, generally shared the view that it was best that the State contain as few Arabs as possible, and both front commanders were clearly bent on driving out the population in the area they were conquering. At the same time, the Arabs in both areas had for months lived with the fear of an impending Israeli onslaught and of the treatment they might receive at Israeli hands. Many, perhaps most, expected to be driven out, or worse.

Hence, when the offensives were unleashed, there was a 'coalescence' of Jewish and Arab expectations, which led, especially in the south, to spontaneous flight by most of the inhabitants. And, on both fronts, IDF units 'nudged' Arabs into flight and expelled communities.

However, there were major differences. In the south, the OC, Allon, was known to want 'Arab-clean' areas along his line of advance; such had been his policy in Eastern Galilee in April–May and in Lydda-Ramle in July. His subordinates usually acted in accordance. Moreover, the nature of the battle in the south, involving two large armies and the use of relatively strong firepower affected civilian morale. Moreover, the inhabitants were almost uniformly Muslim, had for months suffered serious material privations and had had a difficult, unhappy time under the Egyptians. At the same time, the shock entailed by the Egyptian army's abrupt collapse and retreat was probably far greater than that experienced in the Galilee with the demise of the ALA (never regarded by anyone – Jew or Arab – as a serious force). In some areas, retreating Egyptian units urged communities to retreat with them. Due to these factors, the exodus to the Gaza Strip and, to a lesser extent, to the Hebron Hills in Operation Yoav was almost complete (Arab civilians remained only in Majdal, Faluja and Iraq al Manshiya).

In the Galilee, the picture was far more circumstantial and complex. There, there was no clear IDF policy and Carmel displayed hesitancy and ambivalence. And Carmel's officers sensed this. Previously, Carmel – in Haifa and Acre in April–May and in Nazareth in July – had left thousands of Arabs in place. And the Galilee, with its patchwork of communities, including many Druse and Christians, was different. In October, different communities, like different IDF officers, acted differently. Druse and Christian villages by and large offered no or less resistance and had no, or less of a, history of anti-Zionist militancy and, hence, expected, and received, 'better' treatment. Muslim villages often had a history of pro-Husseini activism and, in 1948, often resisted and expected, and received, worse treatment. In mixed villages, such as Tarshiha and Jish, Christians remained while Muslims fled. Often, non-resisting Muslims stayed put and were left in peace (as happened, for example, in 'Arraba and Deir Hanna). Expulsions, where they occurred, were usually at the initiative of local commanders and were linked to resistance during Hiram. In the end, Carmel issued a softly worded expulsion order ('assist the inhabitants to leave'). But it came too late to affect a systematic outcome.

To the foregoing must be added the 'atrocity factor', which played a major role in precipitating flight from several clusters of Galilee villages and from Dawayima in the south. In the north, the atrocities appear largely to have been premeditated rather than spontaneous outbreaks of vengeful impulses by undisciplined troops; company OCs, and perhaps battalion OCs, gave the orders. They appear to have felt that they were carrying out the wishes of Northern Front HQ. The atrocities were largely limited to Muslims.

This said, about 30–50 per cent of the Galilee pocket's inhabitants stayed and were left in place during and immediately after Operation Hiram.

From the Arab side, there were several factors that generated greater 'staying power' in the Galilee than in the south. Firstly, the traditional non-belligerency toward the Yishuv of the Christians and Druse meant that they had less fear of Israeli conquest. Secondly, before October 1948, the war had not severely affected the lives of the inhabitants. There had been little Haganah/IDF harassment and, in most places, no major food shortages. And the presence of Qawuqji's troops may have been less irksome (except in the Christian villages) than that of the Egyptians in the south. It is likely, too, that the conquest of the Galilee pocket by the IDF had been expected by the inhabitants and had been less of a shock than the rout of the Egyptian Army and the conquest of the northern Negev and lower coastal plain in Yoav had been to that area's inhabitants. Moreover, Operation Hiram was very swift, extending to less than 60 hours; many inhabitants probably found that they had been overrun by the IDF before they could make up their minds whether or not to flee. As well, flight from Galilee villages to Lebanon usually involved the unappealing prospect of a long trek through physically difficult – mountainous, rocky and shrub-strewn – terrain (dissimilar from the generally flat and barer south).[168] Lastly, the IDF had deployed in the Galilee far less firepower than in the South.

Together, operations Hiram and Yoav and their appendages precipitated the flight of roughly 200,000–230,000 Arabs.

ENDNOTES

1. Entry for 31 Oct. 1948, DBG-YH III, 788–89; and entry for 31 Oct. 1948, CZA A246-14, 2512.
2. Protocol of meeting of Political Committee, Mapam, 21 Oct. 1948, HHA 66.90 (1).
3. Protocol of Cabinet meeting, 26 Sep. 1948, ISA, for Sharett's statement. The relevant part of Ben-Gurion's statement, from which I have cited, has been blacked out by ISA censors and is unavailable for public scrutiny.
4. Protocol of Cabinet meeting, 26 Sep. 1948, ISA; Danin to Sasson (Paris), 24 Oct. 1948, ISA FM 2570\11; and entry for 21 Oct. 1948, DBG-YH III, 759.
5. Entry for 31 Oct. 1948, DBG-YH III, 788–789.
6. Shimoni to management of Peltours, 26 Oct. 1948, ISA FM 2564\10; and entries for 29 and 31 Oct. 1948, CZA A246-14, 2511-2512. As we have seen, 'inhabitants' and 'refugees' were often used interchangeably.
7. Northern Front to brigades, districts, 4th Field Battalion, 07:30 hours, 31 Oct. 1948, IDFA 715\49\\3. See also Nahum Golan to Combat HQ 1st Brigade, 09:30 hours, 31 Oct. 1948, IDFA 128\51\\50.
8. Carmel to brigades and districts, 10:00 hours, 31 Oct. 1948, IDFA 715\49\\3. Northern Front HQ issued a variant of this order (Carmel to brigades and districts, 31 Oct. 1948, IDFA 2289\50\\165), apparently at 09:00, with slightly, but significantly, different wording: 'The inhabitants who have left the conquered areas should be assisted. The matter is most urgent.' This doesn't make sense and appears to have been mistakenly phrased – and therefore was followed up and superceded by the cable of '10:00' hrs. The '10:00' version was repeated by OC Golani Brigade to his Combat HQ (1st Brigade to Combat HQ 1st Brigade, 11:30 hours, 31 Oct. 1948, IDFA 128\51\\50).

The Druse, incidentally, were, in advance, exempted from the consequences of Carmel's 10:00 hrs. order: At 00:30 hours, 31 October, hours before the first order was issued, the troops were specifically ordered 'to behave nicely toward the Druse' (OC Golani Brigade to Combat HQ 1st Brigade, 31 Oct. 1948, IDFA 128\51\\50). A few days later, on 10 November, Ben-Gurion, at a meeting with General Avner, specifically singled out the Druse, Maronites and Circassians for favoured treatment. He jotted down in his diary: 'Regarding the Druse (18 villages, approximately 12,000 [souls]) I advised to set up a "national" [i.e., ethnic] council (millet) . . . Regarding the Maronites – to behave with friendliness. The Circassians should also be brought closer [i.e., embraced as friends].' (entry for 10 Nov. 1948, DBG-YH III, 807).

9. Entry for 31 Oct. 1948, DBG-YH III, 788–89, for visit and meeting. Ben-Gurion had jotted down: '[From] all the villages where we fought – the villagers fled, but many more will flee.'

10. 'A' Front to 2nd and 9th brigades, 09:30 hours, 10 Nov. 1948, IDFA 4858\49\\495.

11. 5th Brigade to 51, 52, 53, 54, 55 battalions, etc., 'Operational Order "Yoav"', 11 Oct. 1948, IDFA 922\75\\899. The 'general objective' [hakavana] was defined as: 'The defeat of the Egyptian force in 'D' [Southern] Front's area.' The specfic objectives were defined as 'breaking up . . . the enemy forces', opening up the way to the Negev, and conquering Faluja, Majdal and Gaza.

12. 5th Brigade\Intelligence, 'Summary of Activities 16-17.10.48', 18 Oct. 1948, IDFA 922\75\\900.

13. For the conquest of Deiraban, Deir al Hawa and Beit Jimal, see Intelligence Officer, Jerusalem Area, 'The Conquest of Deiraban, Deir al Hawa and Beit Jimal', 21 Oct. 1948, IDFA 6308\49\\141; and 5th Battalion, Harel Brigade\Intelligence, 'Summary of the Battalion Battles in the Deiraban Beit Jimal Area', 1 Nov. 1948, IDFA 922\75\\1233.

14. *Book of the Palmah* II, 646 and 652.

15. 'Aviva R.', 'In the Hebron Hills', in *Book of the Palmah* II, 656.

16. Kirkbride (Amman) to Secretary of State, 21 Oct. 1948, PRO FO 816\131.

17. Combat HQ 12th Brigade\Operations, to battalions 7, 9, 88 and 82, etc., 'Operational Order for Operation "Moshe"', 20 Oct. 1948, IDFA 6308\49\\10. Two engineers companies were specifically instructed to 'prepare the demolition of the town, apart from the main streets.'

18. 12th Brigade\Intelligence, 'Daily Activities Report 20\21.10.48', 22 Oct. 1948, IDFA 6308\49\\141.

19. IDF General Staff\Operations logbook, entry for 20 Oct. 1948, IDFA 922\75\\1176.

20. Major Michael Hanegbi, Negev Military Governor, to General Avner, OC Military Government, 'Following is a Report on the Conquest of the Town of Beersheba and the Situation in It During the First Days', 31 Oct. 1948, IDFA 121\50\\223.

21. Untitled, brief HIS report, 19 Apr. 1948, HA 105\257; and untitled brief HIS report, 10 May 1948, HA 105\257.

22. Giv'ati, *Desert and Fire*, 226.

23. HQ Military Government in the Occupied Areas, to CGS, 27 Oct. 1948, IDFA 121\50\\223; Hanegbi to Avner, 'Following is a Report on the Conquest . . .', 31 Oct. 1948, IDFA 121\50\\223; and Giv'ati, *Desert and Fire*, 228.

24. Nahum Sarig, the commander of the Negev Brigade, later related that he had given the remaining '120' civilians the choice of staying (albeit living among

unsympathetic Israeli soldiers), going to Hebron, or moving to Gaza. All, he said, opted for Gaza – and he organised their transport. One woman was mistakenly shot and killed by a soldier as they reached the border (Yehuda Koren, 'I Never Wanted to be a Soldier', *Haaretz*, 27 Apr. 1990).

25. Hanegbi to Avner, 'Following is a Report on the Conquest . . .', 31 Oct. 1948, IDFA 121\50\\223.

26. Yadin to Avner, 3 Dec. 1948, IDFA 922\75\\1025; and Avner to Yadin, 7 Dec. 1948, IDFA 2433\50\\11.

27. Entry for 27 Oct. 1948, DBG-YH III, 780; and 'Protocol of the Meeting of the Ministerial Committee for Abandoned Property', 5 Nov. 1948, ISA FM 2401\21aleph.

28. Aharon Cohen, handwritten notes from the meeting of the Political Committee, Mapam, 11 Nov. 1948, HHA-ACP 10.95.10 (6).

29. John Devine to Ambassador Griffis, 'Gaza Trip', 13 Dec. 1948, AFSC Archive – Foreign Service 1948.

30. Yadin to 'D' [Southern] Front, CGS, etc., 'Proposal for Operation 'Peten'', 27 Oct. 1948, IDFA 6127\49\\93.

31. OC Southern Front to brigades, etc., 27 October 1948, IDFA 1046\70\\434.

32. IDF General Staff\Operations logbook, entry for 19 October 1948, IDFA 922\75\\1176.

33. 5th Brigade\Intelligence to Southern Front\Intelligence, 27 October 1948, IDFA 1041\49\\4. The demand for 40 Bren Guns was probably designed to stymie a return: A village was lucky if it had more than one such machine-gun – and to purchase 40 would have been well beyond the means of the 'Ajjur refugees (even if 40 were on the market in the Bethlehem area, which is unlikely).

34. Kirkbride to Secretary of State, 21 Oct. 1948, PRO FO 371-68689; and Kirkbride to FO, 25 Oct. 1948, PRO CAB 21-1922.

35. Yiftah Brigade\Intelligence, 'Daily Intelligence Summary', (second page), 31 Oct. 1948, IDFA 922\75\\1216.

36. IDF General Staff\Operations logbook, entry for 30 Oct. 1948, IDFA 922\75\\1176.

37. 12th Brigade\Intelligence, 'Daily Intelligence Summary 4.11.48', 4 Nov. 1948, IDFA 6308\49\\141.

38. HIS, Dawayima village file, undated but probably from 1942, HA 201\8.

39. Southern Front, untitled report, 16:30 hours, 29 Oct. 1948, IDFA 922\75\\1017; and IDF General Staff\Operations logbook, entry for 29 Oct. 1948, IDFA 922\75\\1176. Isser Be'eri's report on the atrocity at Dawayima (see below) described serious resistance.

40. Avraham Vered, one of the 89th Battalion troopers, later wrote a memoir, recalling: 'Our fire was strong and deadly. We knew that we were coming to the Hebron Hills. We remembered 1929 [when inhabitants of Hebron and nearby villages massacred, without provocation, 66 members of Hebron's Jewish community in a two-day pogrom] and the Etzion Bloc [which was captured in May 1948 by Arab Legion troops, assisted by hundreds of villagers from the surrounding area. Some 125 of the Bloc's defenders were massacred during their surrender or just after (see Morris, *Road to Jerusalem*, 138–40)]. Here no order was given to cease fire. The belts of bullets were emptied and filled [again] . . .' (Vered, *Bush*, 225–230).

41. Vered, *Southern Front*, 185.
42. Vered, *Southern Front*, 184.
43. Unidentified IDF logbook, entry for 31 Oct. 1948, IDFA 922\75\\1230. In an interview during the late 1990s, Vered denied that there had been a massacre at Dawayima. On the other hand, journalist Yoela Har-Shefi (*Hadashot*, 24 and 26 Aug. 1948), interviewed some of the survivors, who claimed that there had been massacres in a number of sites in and near the village. Some Arab witnesses maintained that the IDF units chased after the fleeing inhabitants and massacred groups of them in their hiding places in the hills. Some of those killed may have been refugees from al Qubeiba, captured by the 89th Battalion on 28 October, who had fled to Dawayima.
44. 12th Brigade\Intelligence, 'Daily Intelligence Report 4.11.48', 4 November 1948, IDFA 6308\49\\141.
45. Burdett to Secretary of State, 16 November 1948, NA RG 84, US Consulate General Jerusalem, Classified Records 800 – Palestine. This report, and others like it, were most probably based on rumours rather than first-hand accounts or investigation.
46. Entry for 10 Nov. 1948, DBG-YH III, 807.
47. Kaplan to Peri, 8 Nov. 1948, KMA-AZP 6\6\4. Kaplan's informant appears to have based himself largely or completely on hearsay and not to have witnessed any of the alleged atrocities.
48. Allon to Sadeh, 3 Nov. 1948, KMA-PA 124–177.
49. Dror, *Sadeh*, 409. Unknown to Allon, the 89th Battalion had already 'cleaned up' Dawayima, and gotten rid of the bodies, on 1 Nov. 1948 (Dror, *Sadeh*, 409).
50. Yadin to CGS, 4 Nov. 1948, IDFA 121\50\\167. The sites of the two incidents to be investigated have been whited out by the IDFA censor – but one of them, it says, is connected to '8th Brigade', which must mean Dawayima.
51. Gelber, *Palestine*, 209. Gelber had access to Be'eri's reports and appended sheets of testimony. These all remain classified in the IDF Intelligence Division Archive.
52. Gelber, *Palestine*, 209.
53. Antras to Consul General de France, Jerusalem, 'Rapports', 6 Jan. 1949, UNA DAG\13.3.1:4, 'Daily Reports from Chef de la Mission des Observateurs Francais'. Antras concluded from his assessment of a number of incidents (Dawayima, Majd al Kurum, 'Eilabun (see below), etc.) that Israeli policy aimed at 'the elimination of the Arab population of Israel.'
54. In Mapam, the leaders took umbrage at the imputation that one of their own, the legendary Sadeh, was culpable. Galili said: 'It was contemptible and strange to cast blame on Yitzhak Sadeh.' The responsibility lay with the 89th Battalion, 'where many were from the LHI, Frenchmen, Moroccans, prone to bad behaviour'. Benny Marshak, the Palmah's education officer (or 'commissar'), said: 'The LHI are to blame.' (Cohen, handwritten notes on the meeting of Mapam's Political Committee, 11 Nov. 1948, HHA-ACP 10.95.10 (6); and protocol of the meeting of the Political Committee, Mapam, 11 Nov. 1948, HHA 66.90 (1)).
55. 5th Brigade\Intelligence, 'Summary of Activities 26-27.10.48,' IDFA 922\75\\900. Some reports put the number of remaining inhabitants at '300'.

56. Rehovot Base, Intelligence Service 3, to Intelligence Service 3 HQ, 31 Oct. 1948, and Rehovot Base, Intelligence Service 3, to Intelligence Service 3 HQ, 8 Nov. 1948, both in IDFA 922\75\\1017; 'Protocol of the Meeting of the Ministerial Committee for Abandoned Property', 5 Nov. 1948, ISA FM 2401\21aleph; and entry for 29 Oct. 1948, Weitz, *Diary*, III, 349. The Rehovot Base intelligence officer complained, in his report of 31 Oct., of the 'lack of clarity regarding [requisite] behaviour toward civilian inhabitants.'

57. Yiftah Brigade\Intelligence, 'Daily Intelligence Report No. 17', 28 Oct. 1948, IDFA 922\75\\1216.

58. IDF General Staff\Operations logbook, entry for 28 Oct. 1948, IDFA 922\75\\1176.

59. Yiftah Brigade\Intelligence, 'Daily Intelligence Report No. 18', 2 Nov. 1948, KMA-PA 109dalet-132.

60. IDF General Staff\Operations logbook, entry for 20 Oct. 1948, IDFA 922\75\\1176.

61. Intelligence Officer, Negev District, 20 Nov. 1948, enclosing Sawaf to 'respected inhabitants of Gaza', 9 Nov. 1948, IDFA 922\75\\1025.

62. Handwritten notes by Aharon Cohen from the meeting of Mapam's Political Committee, 11 Nov. 1948, HHA-ACP 10.95.10 (6).

63. See, for example, IDF General Staff logbook entries for 19, 20 and 21 Oct. 1948, IDFA 922\75\\1176.

64. 55th Battalion\Intelligence Officer, to 5th Brigade\Intelligence, 31 Oct. 1948, IDFA 1041\49\\18.

65. 5th Brigade\Intelligence, 'Summary of Activities 3-4.11.48', 5 Nov. 1948, IDFA 715\49\\16.

66. 5th Brigade to battalions 51, 52, etc., 'Operational Order "Maga"', 4 Nov. 1948, IDFA 6308\49\\141.

67. 5th Brigade\Intelligence, 'Summary of Activities 3-4.11.48', 5 Nov. 1948, IDFA 715\49\\16.

68. IDF-GS\Operations logbook, entry for 5 Nov. 1948, IDFA 922\75\\1176.

69. Rehovot Base, Intelligence Service 3, to OC Southern Front, 'Report on the Entry into Majdal', 7 Nov. 1948, IDFA 922\75\\1017. According to Galili, reporting to Mapam's leaders, Southern Front had ordered Giv'ati to expel Majdal's inhabitants but, for some reason, the order was not implemented (Aharon Cohen, notes taken at meeting of Political Committee, Mapam, 11 Nov. 1948, HHA-ACP 10.95.10 (6)).

70. Yadin to Southern Front, 28 Nov. 1948, IDFA 401\52\\12. See also Coastal District HQ to Battalion 151, etc., 'Operational Order No. 42', 30 Nov. 1948, IDFA 401\52\\12.

71. Southern Front\Operations to General Staff\Operations, 8 Dec. 1948, IDFA 922\75\\1025. A small segment of the letter has been whited out by IDFA censors.

72. Patterson (Cairo) to Secretary of State, 16 Nov. 1948, NA 501 BB. Palestine\11-1648.

73. Entry for 31 Oct. 1948, DBG-YH III, 788–89; 'Protocol of the Meeting of the Ministerial Committee for Abandoned Property', 5 Nov. 1948, ISA FM 2401\21aleph; and Keeley (Damascus) to Secretary of State, 4 Nov. 1948, NA 501 BB. Palestine\11-448. Or as Ben-Gurion told his ministers on 31 Oct.: '. . . according to [Northern] Front's estimate . . . in this pocket there

were about 60 thousand Arabs and many of them were refugees. Of these so far about 30 thousand have fled . . . The flight is still continuing . . .' (protocol of Cabinet meeting, 31 October 1948, ISA).

74. Intelligence Service 1, 'Daily Intelligence Report', 11 Nov. 1948, IDFA 5942\49\\72.

75. Northern Front to brigades, districts, etc., 'Operational Order "Hiram"', 26 Oct. 1948, IDFA 854\52\\321. It is worth noting that, similarly, brigade operational orders also omitted any mention of what was to be done with the inhabitants (see 9th Brigade to Battalion 91, etc., 'Operational Order "Hiram No. 1"', 27 Oct. 1948, IDFA 352\53\\28, which, however, did vaguely instruct the units, after conquering Tarshiha, 'to cleanse' the area to the east in the second stage; and 7th Brigade HQ, 'Operational Order "Hiram B"', 26 Oct. 1948, IDFA 854\52\\321).

Let me add that the original Front draft order for Hiram, from mid–Sep., described the objective as 'the cleansing [*tihur*] of central Galilee and the destruction of the enemy force in it' (Northern Front to brigades, districts, etc, 'Operational Order "Snir", "Hiram", [and] "Yehoshafat"', ? Sep. 1948, IDFA 2289\50\\277). And the original draft version of one district HQ order, Haifa District HQ, 'Operational Order No. 2, "Hiram"', 16 Sep. 1948, IDFA 240\54\\2, instructed its three battalions, after the initial conquest stage, to 'help Battalion 71 in the operations to cleanse Western Galilee'. Later in the order, under the heading 'Administration,' the instructions were 'not to harm the Druse villages'. As to the treatment of the 'Arabs', IDFA censors have blacked out the crucial line – which may include instructions to expel.

76. Chief of Air Intelligence to CGS, etc., 1 Nov. 1948, and 'Summary of Estimates of Results of IAF Bombing in Operation "Hiram" for the Liberation of the Galilee', 28 Feb. 1949, both in IDFA 600137\51\\941.

77. Intelligence Officer, Northern Area, to Intelligence Service 1, etc., 30 Oct. 1948, IDFA 7249\49\\138.

78. 79th Battalion combat logbook, entry for 30 Oct. 1948, IDFA 721\72\\298.

79. 71st Battalion\Intelligence Officer, to OC 71st Battalion, etc., 'Report on the Activities of the Battalion in Operations "Hiram" and "Atzmon" on 27.10.48-1.11.48,' 8 Nov. 1948, IDFA 1094\49\\77.

80. 79th Battalion HQ to 7th Brigade HQ, etc., 'Report on Operation "Hiram 2"', 1 Nov. 1948, IDFA 2289\50\\277; and Emmanuel Sharon, 'Operation Hiram – Battalion 79', IDFA 1046\70\\6.

81. Gil'ad, 'Intelligence Report on Operation "Hiram" (28.10-31.10)', 21 Nov. 1948, IDFA 715\49\\15.

82. The surrender of Majd al Kurum is described in Battalion 123\Intelligence, to Haifa District HQ\Intelligence, etc., 31 Oct. 1948, IDFA 200716\49\\45.

83. 'A' Company, 91st Battalion, to OC 91st Battalion, etc., 'Operation Report – Conquest of Tarshiha', 9 Nov. 1948, IDFA 715\49\\3.

84. OC 11th Battalion to OC 9th Brigade, 'Report on Operation of Assault Company – Operation "Hiram"', 4 Nov. 1948, IDFA 715\49\\3, for the surrender of Fassuta.

85. 9th Brigade, 'Report on Operation "Hiram"', undated, IDFA 715\49\\9.

86. See, for example, Northern Front to brigades and districts, 08:15 hours, 30 Oct. 1948, IDFA 128\51\\50; 7th Brigade Logbook, entry for 08:45, 30 Oct.

1948, IDFA 721\72\\310; and Battalion 123 to 'A' Company, etc., 31 Oct. 1948, IDFA 200716\49\\1.

87. Even after the spate of atrocities committed during Operation Hiram (see below), the authorities were more concerned with the phenomenon of looting, as disruptive of IDF discipline, than with murder. For example, an IDF Intelligence Service report from early December 1948 stated: 'Every battalion carries out searches and expulsions. There were cases of . . . execution [of Arabs] by the military, on the basis of informing by villagers. . . . The patrolling soldiers continue to carry out robbery and confiscation . . .' But the report concluded: 'We have passed on details about the cases of robbery and looting for treatment by the military police, which investigates such matters.' The cases of murder appear not to have been referred for investigation (Kidron, Intelligence Service, to OC Northern Front, 2 Dec. 1948, IDFA 260\51\\2).

88. For a fuller discussion of Carmel's orders of 31 Oct. and 10 Nov., see Morris, *Correcting*, 141–48. These pages, among other things, survey Maj. Yitzhak Moda'i's analysis of Operation Hiram, written for the IDF in the mid-1950s ('Operation Hiram', undated, IDFA 922\75\\189), and his explanation of why Northern Front did not carry out a systematic policy of expulsion.

89. Entry for 6 Nov. 1948, Weitz, *Diary*, III, 353.

90. Shoufani, 'Fall of a Village', 113.

91. Unsigned, 'Villages that Surrendered and [Villages that were] Conquered [after Resistance] Outside the State of Israel', 17 Nov. 1948, ISA MAM 302\114. The list does not include any of the villages – all Muslim – from which the population fled before the IDF arrived or some of the Muslim villages which did not surrender and from which the remaining inhabitants were expelled (such as Saliha and Sa'sa). Nor does it include some of the Christian and Druse villages that surrendered (such as Kafr Bir'im and Hurfeish). Moreover, in Jish the ALA troops, perhaps assisted by the local Muslims, resisted. But the village was not uprooted (though its Muslims fled). However, the list gives a rough idea of the inter-relationship between surrender and staying put, and resistance and depopulation in Operation Hiram.

92. Shimoni to Sasson (Paris), 12 Nov. 1948, ISA FM 2570\11.

93. Shimoni to Eytan, 'On Problems of Policy in the Galilee and on the Northern Border and on the Link Between the Foreign Ministry and the Army Staff', 18 Nov. 1948, ISA FM 186\17.

94. Antras to consul general of France, Jerusalem, 'Rapports', 6 Jan. 1949, Annex 2, Captain Perrosier, 'Notes sur les Procédés d'Elimination des Arabes Chretiens et Musulmans par Les Juifs en Galilee', undated, UNA DAG\13.3.1:4; and Nazzal, *Exodus*, 32–33.

95. 7th Brigade HW Combat Logbook, entry for 10:00 hours, 2 Nov. 1948, IDFA 721\72\\310.

96. For what happened at Ghuweir, see 'Tzuri (Kochba)' to HIS-AD, 'The Village of Ghuweir Abu Shusha', 24 June 1948, HA 105\226.

97. Nazzal, *Exodus*, 32–33; unsigned, letter from Nazareth to prime minister and minority affairs minister, 6 Apr. 1949, IDFA 1308\50\\485; and M. Yitah, Haifa, to MAM, 16 May 1948, ISA MAM 299\78.

98. Antras to consul general of France, Jerusalem, 'Rapports', 6 Jan. 1949, UNA DAG\13.3.1:4, Annex 3, 'Rapport Date du 16 Novembre 1948 par le Lieutenant Colonel Sore (FA) Adjoint A B.3', reporting on a UN investigative team visit to Deir al Asad and al Bi'na on 16 Nov. 1948. It is possible that Golani's treatment of the two villages was directly inspired by Carmel's order of 31 Oct. 1948.

99. Nazzal, *Exodus*, 89–90.

100. Nazzal, *Exodus*, 92.

101. Intelligence officer, Battalion 123, to Haifa District\Intelligence, 31 October 1948, IDFA 200716\49\\45.

102. Antras to Consul General de France, Jerusalem, 'Rapports', Annex 4 – consisting of two reports, 'Rapport de l'adjutant Pallemans lors de la visite faite a Majd al Kurum', undated but reporting on a visit on 11 Nov. 1948, and 'Rapport Special adresse au Chef d'Etat Major par l'Observateur Capitaine David Penson', 13 Nov. 1948 – UNA DAG 13\3.3.1:4; and 'Statement by UN Observer Major Stewart M.F. Luce (US Army)' to Chief of Staff, Haifa, 13 Nov. 1948, UNA DAG 13\3.3.1:11.

103. Shoufani, 'Fall of a Village', 121.

104. Nazzal, *Exodus*, 96–97; and IDF, *War of Independence*, 323–324.

105. 'Amir to Northern Front Intelligence Officer, 27 Nov. 1948, IDFA 240\54\\112.

106. 1st Brigade to Northern Front, 12:30 hours, 30 Oct. 1948, IDFA 128\51\\50.

107. The action is described in 'Form of Recommendation for Award of Citation', dealing with Lt. Haim Hayun, who had led the abortive attack on the outpost, IDFA 1096\49\\65; and unsigned, untitled IDF intelligence report (probably by Intelligence Officer, Northern Area, to Intelligence Service 1, etc.), undated but probably from 17 Sep. 1948, stating that the two soldiers had been taken alive, slaughtered, mutilated and then decapitated by men of the neighbouring 'Arab al Mawasi tribe. One of the heads had been taken to 'Eilabun, the other to Maghar (IDFA 7249\49\\138).

108. Four or five of the men were non-locals and seven were villagers (12th Battalion intelligence officer, 'Report on Hostile Behaviour by the Clergy', undated, IDFA 2168\50\\86).

109. Faraj Diab Surur, mukhtar of 'Eilabun, Father Yukha Daud Almualim and other village priests, to Minority Affairs Minister, 21 Jan. 1949, ISA FM 2564\10; and 12th Battalion intelligence officer, 'Report on Hostile Behaviour of the Clergy', undated, IDFA 2168\50\\86. Nahmani (entry for 6 Nov. 1948, YND) briefly describes the massacre and expulsion but mistakenly speaks of 'thirty' killed in 'Farradiya and 'Eilabun'. I have seen no other evidence of a mass killing in Farradiya. See also 'Spector' to Baruch, 'Report No. 29', 12 Nov. 1948, IDFA 1261\49\\4, for an IDF denial of the 'Eilabun massacre to UN officers.

110. 'Extraits d'une lettre de S.B. Patriarche a S.E. Mgr Hakim', 8 Nov. 1948, and Hakim to Tuvia Arazi (Paris), 12 Nov. 1948, both in ISA FM 2563\22; Father Basilius Laham (Nazareth) to the Military Governor, Nazareth, 15 Nov. 1948, ISA FM 2564\18; 'Eilabun notables to Minority Affairs Minister, 25 Jan. 1949, ISA FM 2564\10; and 'Eilabun notables to Interior Minister, 21 Jan. 1949, ISA MAM 302\80.

111. Shitrit to Sulz, 28 Nov. 1948, and Sulz to Shitrit, 12 Dec. 1948, both in ISA MAM 302\80; and Sulz to Military Government HQ, 30 Dec. 1948, Yadin to Foreign Ministry, 7 Dec. 1948, and Shimoni to Yadin, 10 Dec. 1948, all in ISA FM 2564\18.
112. Cisling to Prime Minister, Minority Affairs Minister, etc., 4 Feb. 1949, and Shitrit to Ben-Gurion, 8 Feb. 1948, both in ISA MAM 302\80.
113. Carmel to CGS, 28 Feb. 1949, IDFA 260\51\\91. General Avner, OC Military Government, took a hard line, advising the Defence Minister not to give them citizenship as it would serve as a precedent and encourage infiltration, which the Military Government was trying to thwart (Avner to Defence Minister's Bureau, 17 Mar. 1949, IDFA 1308\50\\485).
114. Police Minister to Defence Minister, 18 Apr. 1949, and Major Ezra 'Omer, adjutant to CGS, to OC Northern Front, 23 May 1949, both in ISA MAM 302\80.
115. 'Mr. Palmon's Commitment in the Name of the Government [of the State of Israel],' 10 June 1949, ISA FM 2563\22.
116. First Sergeant 'Moshe', 103rd Battalion, 'C' Company, 'Report On a Search Operation in the Area of "Arab al Mawasi" Outpost 213. Presented by Platoon OC Haim Hayun,' 2 Nov. 1948, IDFA 1096\49\\65.
117. The subsequent Justice Ministry-IDF investigations of the atrocities in the Galilee appear to have limited themselves to the events in these four villages (Gelber, *Palestine*, 226).
118. Yosef Nahmani, in his diary (entry for 6 Nov. 1948, YND), refers to '60–70' men and women murdered after they 'had raised a white flag'. Aharon Cohen (handwritten notes from Mapam Political Committee meeting, 11 Nov. 1948, HHA-ACP 10.95.10 (6)), has Galili (or Moshe Erem) speak of '94 in Saliha blown up in a house'.
119. Entry for 6 Nov. 1948, YND, HAHH speaks of '50–60 fellahs'; Aharon Cohen (handwritten notes from meeting of Mapam Political Committee meeting, 11 Nov. 1948, HHA-ACP 10.95.10 (6)), quoting Galili or Erem, speaks of '52 adult males' tied together and dropped into a well and of three cases of rape, including of a 14-year-old girl. Nahmani also mentions several cases of rape and 'a number of dead women'. Nahmani heard the details from Emmanuel Friedman, the old HIS-AD hand and MAM representative in eastern Galilee; it is possible that the facts described in Cohen's notes also originated with Friedman. It is possible that some of those dumped in the well had died during the bombing of and battle for Safsaf and only a minority were murdered after the battle. Arab oral testimony from the early 1970s, as recorded by Nazzal (*Exodus*, 93–95), more or less corroborates the contemporaneous Jewish documentation. According to Nazzal, the soldiers raped four women and blindfolded and executed 'about 70' men. 'The soldiers [then] took their bodies and threw them on the cement covering of the village spring.' Soldiers who came afterwards assured the remaining villagers that they would not be harmed further – but the villagers fled to Lebanon.
120. Again, it is unclear how many people were actually massacred in Jish after its capture. As in Safsaf, both civilians and soldiers died during the hard-fought battles; additional civilians and POWs were killed afterward. Cohen (handwritten notes from meeting of Mapam Political Committee,

11 Nov. 1948, HHA-ACP 10.95.10 (6)) wrote: 'Jish – woman and her baby killed. Another 11 [murdered?] . . .' It is worth noting that the initial IDF intelligence report after the capture of Safsaf and Jish spoke of the capture of '150–200 prisoners' (Gershon Gil'ad, '"Hiram" Report Activities 'B' 290800-292000', undated, IDFA 7249\49\\170). The next report, written a day later, (Gil'ad, '"Hiram" Report Activities 'C' – 292000-300800', undated, IDFA 7249\49\\170) states: 'The number of prisoners given in report Activities 'B' is based on a mistake. [Only] a small number of prisoners is in our hands.'

121. 'Khirbet Lahis', *Ha'olam Haze*, 1 Mar. 1978; Ehrlich, *Lebanon*, 214 and 622, footnote 18, which says that, according to Lebanese sources, '58' persons were massacred in the village; and interview with Dov Yirmiya, 1987. Lt. Shmuel Lahis, the company OC, was tried and convicted in a military court in 1949 and given a seven-year sentence. On appeal, the Supreme Military Court reduced the sentence to one year, which he served as an open prisoner in an IDF base. In 1955, Israel's President Yitzhak Ben-Zvi, on Defence Minister Ben-Gurion's recommendation, pardoned Lahis, who thus emerged with a clean record. Lahis, a lawyer, went on to become director general of the Jewish Agency.

122. Moshe Carmel, interviewed in 1985, recalled that he had seen evidence of killings in the village shortly after its capture. The report by Emmanuel Yalan (Vilensky) (see below) says that some civilians, including cripples, may have been killed after the village was conquered.

123. For examples, see Spector to Baruch, 'Report No. 29', 12 Nov. 1948, IDFA 1261\49\\4, in which the IDF liaison officer, Spector, reports to his commander, Komarov: 'In relation to the 13 killed [in 'Eilabun], I proved [sic] that the army was not in the village at the time . . .'; and Schnorrman to Baruch, 17 Nov. 1948, IDFA 1261\49\\4.

124. The corpses were seen by IDF Medical Corps personnel as a health hazard (unsigned, 'Report on a Tour By the Inspector of the Department of Preventive Medicine, Prof. G.G. Mar, on 4.11.48', IDFA 1085\52\\203, complaining of unburied corpses in Saliha).

125. Komarov to Yadin, 16 Nov. 1948, IDFA 2168\50\\86.

126. Komarov to Northern Front, etc., 13 Nov. 1948, IDFA 2168\50\\86. See also Schnorrman to Baruch [Komarov], 17 Nov. 1948, IDFA 1261\49\\4. Reports of these atrocities spread far and wide – but with telling distortions. A month after Hiram, the Anglican bishop of Jerusalem wrote to the head of the Church: '. . . I heard ugly stories of mass executions in the northern frontier villages. But these were, I think, done in the heat of the actual fighting, and one of my own priests assured me that the mass executions were the work of Druses and not of Jews' (Bishop of Jerusalem to Archbishop of Canterbury, 8 Dec. 1948, SAMECA JEM LXXII\1).

127. Sayigh, *Palestinians*, 92.

128. Carmel, *Battles*, 275–76.

129. 11th Battalion\Intelligence to 9th Brigade\Intelligence, 3 Nov. 1948, IDFA 1012\49\\71.

130. 14th Battalion intelligence officer to OC 14th Battalion, 4 Nov. 1948, IDFA 128\51\\71. The Druse may have been civilians from Maghar.

131. 91st Battalion to 9th Brigade\Operations, etc., 12 Nov. 1948, IDFA 1012\ 49\\75.
132. 11th Battalion\Intelligence to 9th Brigade\Operations, etc., 11 Nov. 1948, IDFA 1012\49\\71.
133. 11th Battalion\Intelligence to 9th Brigade\Operations, 12 Nov. 1948, IDFA 1012\49\\71.
134. Operations Officer Galilee District to Northern Front, 12 Nov. 1948, IDFA 548\51\\87.
135. 11th Battalion to 9th Brigade\Operations, 24 Nov. 1948, IDFA 1012\ 49\\71.
136. R.T. Kashtan to intelligence officer, Battalion 123, 'Operation Report,' 9 Nov. 1948, IDFA 200716\49\\45.
137. Military Government HQ to General Staff Division\Baruch, 16 Nov. 1948, and undated minutes on the letter by Baruch Komarov and (apparently) Yadin, IDFA 2433\50\\11.
138. Carmel to Military Government HQ, 28 (?) Nov. 1948, IDFA 121\50\\223. See also Gelber, *Independence and Nakba*, Chap. 15.
139. Operations officer, Northern Front, to Military Governor Western Galilee, Military Governor Eastern Galilee, etc., 'Behaviour Toward the Population'. 18 Nov. 1948, IDFA 1860\50\\60.
140. Avner to Carmel, 22 Nov. 1948, IDFA 1860\50\\60.
141. P. Weinstein, 9th Brigade, to Military Governor Acre, etc., 16 Nov. 1948, IDFA 128\51\\34. This is apparently a copy of a memorandum that was sent out by Northern Front HQ.
142. Markovsky to Ya'akov [Dori ?], undated but from early Dec. 1948, IDFA 121\50\\223.
143. Entry for 3 Dec. 1948, DBG-YH, 863.
144. On 8 Nov. 1948, Shapira wrote Isser Be'eri, head of the IDF Intelligence Service, that IDF troops had murdered '82' men, women and children, in Saliha; 42 in Safsaf; 52 in Hule; and at least four Maronite Christians in Jish.
145. Yadin to CGS, 4 Nov. 1948, IDFA 121\50\\167.
146. 79th Battalion logbook, entries for 7 and 8 Nov. 1948, IDFA 721\72\\298. Laskov had commanded the battalion earlier in the war.
147. Dori to Defence Minister, 16 Nov. 1948, and Laskov to CGS, 17 Nov. 1948, both in IDFA 121\50\\226. The contents of the file remain classified.
148. 79th Battalion logbook, entry for 16 Nov. 1948, IDFA 721\72\\298.
149. (Draft) Northern Front HQ to OC 7th Brigade, etc., 20 Nov. 1948, IDFA 2289\50\\165; and 9th Brigade to OC 11th Battalion, 28 Nov. 1948, IDFA 6309\49\\3.
150. 79th Battalion logbook, entry for 24 Nov. 1948, IDFA 721\72\\298.
151. Carmel to Dori, 1 (?) December 1948, IDFA 260\51\\3. Carmel mistakenly writes that the trial was due to begin on '2.11'. It appears that no soldiers apart from Lahis were ever put on trial. Lahis was tried because of the insistence of his immediate superior, the deputy OC of the 22nd Battalion, Dov Yirmiya.
152. Indeed, the first time most of these atrocities (Saliha, Safsaf, Jish, 'Eilabun, etc.) were publicised in Israel and the West was in the first version of this book (in 1988).

153. The dozens of pages of protocols of Cabinet meetings during these two months in which the atrocities and the investigations were discussed have been whited out by ISA censors and remain closed to researchers indefinitely.

154. 'Decisions of the Provisional Government', 7 Nov. 1948, KMA-ACP 9\9\1; protocol of the meeting of the Political Committee of Mapam, 11 Nov. 1948, HHA 66.90 (1); and DBG-YH 809, entry for 10 Nov. 1948. Ben-Gurion wrote: 'Shitrit handed me shocking material about atrocities by several soldiers in the Galilee. The matter must be investigated fully and, this time, the guilty must be punished, so that [all] will hear and fear.'

155. Protocol of meeting of Mapam Political Committee, 11 Nov. 1948, HHA 60.90 (10); and handwritten notes by Aharon Cohen from meeting of Political Committee, 11 Nov. 1948, HHA-ACP 10.95.10 (6).

156. Kaplan to Bentov, Rosenblueth and Shapira, 12 Nov. 1948, ISA Labour Ministry, 6178\2924.

157. Entry for 12 Nov. 1948, DBG-YH III, 820.

158. Protocol of Cabinet meeting, 14 Nov. 1948, ISA. Rosenblueth prepared a draft of the required regulation – 'Emergency Laws (Ministerial Committee for Investigating the Condition of the Arabs in the State), 1948' (ISA Labour Ministry, 6178\2924).

159. Transcript of Cisling's statement at Cabinet meeting, 17 Nov. 1948, KMA-ACP 9\9\3.

160. 'Decisions of the Provisional Government, 17 Nov. 1948', ISA.

161. DBG to Ya'akov Shimshon Shapira, 19 Nov. 1948, DBG Archive, Correspondence. Among the three proposed was Yalan.

162. Carmel to brigade, district and battalion OCs, 25 Nov. 1948, IDFA 1137\49\\84.

163. Entry for 21 Nov. 1948, DBG-YH III, 835–36, reproducing the text of the letter – which compares the power of Alterman's poem to that of an armoured column – and the poem itself.

164. 'Decisions of the Provisional Government', 5 Dec. 1948, KMA-ACP 9\9\1. It is unclear whether Shapira actually conducted or orchestrated any investigation. Shapira's report (in ISA Justice Ministry, 25\1\0) and the Cabinet discussions of the report remain classified.

The 5-member committee established on 5 Dec. apparently met once or twice in the following weeks – but seems not to have conducted any investigations.

165. It appears that while some soldiers may have been reprimanded, Ben-Gurion made sure that no one was actually jailed for taking part in the atrocities. Clearly, the avoidance of trials and real punishment was geared to keeping the whole subject under wraps and preserving the IDF's and Israel's good name. But perhaps there was more at stake. Perhaps there was a fear that were the matter brought to the courts, soldiers and officers might point fingers up the chain of command, implicating brigade OCs, Carmel and perhaps even Ben-Gurion himself. What exactly transpired between Ben-Gurion and Carmel in Nazareth on 31 Oct. is uncertain, but it is possible that a full opening of the can of worms would have led to revelations about Ben-Gurion's role in the expulsion orders and, indirectly, in the atrocities that were, at least in part, connected with them.

166. Entry for 23 Dec. 1948, DBG-YH III, 896. Yosef Weitz, incidentally, got wind of Ben-Gurion's anti-expulsion guideline to Avner concerning the Gaza Strip and sent Ben-Gurion a note questioning the decision (entries for 30 and 31 Dec. 1948, CZA A246-14, 2560-61; and Weitz to Ben-Gurion, 31 Dec. 1948, Yosef Weitz Papers (Rehovot)).

167. Yigal Allon, 'A Special Appendix to Operational Orders Operation Horev', 17 Dec. 1948, KMA-PA 34-3aleph.

168. This point is made in Moda'i, 'Operation Hiram', undated but from mid-1950s, IDFA 922\75\\189.

9 | Clearing the borders: expulsions and population transfers, November 1948–1950

In the weeks and months after the termination of hostilities, the Israeli authorities adopted a policy of clearing the new borders of Arab Communities. Some were transferred inland, to Israeli Arab villages in the interior; others were expelled across the border. The policy, which matured *ad hoc* and haphazardly, was motivated mainly by military considerations: The borders were long and highly penetrable. Along the frontiers of the newly conquered territories there were few, if any, Jewish settlements. Arab border villages could serve as way-stations and bases for hostile irregulars, spies and illegal returnees. In the event of renewed war, the villages could serve as soft entry points for invading armies.

At the same time, IDF, police and GSS units repeatedly scoured the populated, semi-populated and empty villages in the interior to root out illegal infiltrees and returnees. Some, such as Farradiya, sat astride strategic routes; almost all, given the State's size and shape, were themselves relatively close to the borders. In one or two cases – *vide* Faluja and 'Iraq al Manshiya in the south – the authorities expelled whole villages from sites in the interior. In general, throughout this period, the political desire to have as few Arabs as possible in the Jewish State and the need for empty villages to house new immigrants meshed with the strategic desire to achieve 'Arab-clear' frontiers and secure internal lines of communication. It was the IDF that set the policy in motion, with the civil and political authorities often giving approval after the fact.

THE NORTH

A week after Operation Hiram, Carmel, with General Staff consent, decided to clear the Israeli side of the Israeli–Lebanese border of villages. On 10 November, he instructed the Ninth and Second brigades: 'A strip five kilometres deep behind the border with Lebanon must be empty of [Arab] inhabitants . . .'[1]

The border-clearing began a few days before. On 7 November, the Ninth Brigade ordered 'all the inhabitants of . . . Iqrit', about three kilometres south of the frontier, to evacuate their village – 'except the priest' – the following day and move to Rama, 'for reasons of public security'.[2] They were told that their removal was for 15 days.[3] Simultaneously, orders were issued to the remaining inhabitants of neighbouring Tarbikha (Shi'ite) and its two satellite hamlets, Suruh (Sunni) and Nabi Rubin (Sunni), to leave for Lebanon, which most did. Iqrit's inhabitants, about 600 in number,[4] began to move to Rama, about 20 kilometres to the southeast, inside Israel a few days later, assisted by the IDF. Iqrit was inhabited solely by Greek Catholics and had surrendered to 'Oded Brigade troops without a fight, indeed, welcomed them as 'liberators', with bread and salt,[5] on 30 October.[6]

On 10 November, Northern Front sent out the blanket order to clear the Lebanese border and, during the following months, the policy was to be implemented in staggered fashion along Israel's other borders. It is unclear whether Carmel received specific prior support for the policy from Ben-Gurion or whether he simply drew on the blanket authorisation he apparently received from the prime minister at their meeting on 31 October. On 24 November, the Cabinet retroactively endorsed the Lebanese border-clearing operation.[7]

Unlike earlier transfers, these evictions were carried out with a soft touch: The villagers were given days in which to move out and were usually allowed to take their property with them, in organized fashion. Some, such as Iqrit's Christians, were transferred inland rather than kicked across the border (of course, filling up Rama's empty Muslim-owned houses served the additional purpose of obstructing the return of Muslims).

But a transfer it was. By 12 November, the clearing operations along the length of the Rosh Hanikra–Malikiya line were in full swing. Northern Front\Intelligence reported: 'The evacuation [*pinui*] of the villages in the Galilee along a line parallel to the frontier is being completed.'[8] The following day, 13 November, the inhabitants of Kafr Bir'im (Maronites) and al Mansura (Maronites), to the east of Iqrit, were also ordered to leave – and to trek to Lebanon.[9] They were given a day or two. The Ninth Brigade units were told to expect a 'large wave' of refugees on the 15th: 'Make sure that this wave will move northward [i.e., to Lebanon] only and not return to the interior of the State', the battalions were instructed.[10] The remaining (Maronite) inhabitants of Jish were also ordered to go but managed, through the intercession of Shitrit and Yitzhak Ben-Zvi, a senior Mapai figure, to have the order rescinded.[11]

The inhabitants of Bir'im were also told that they were being moved out temporarily and would eventually be allowed back. This may well have been a ruse designed to facilitate a quick, unresisting departure[12] (though the junior officers dealing with the inhabitants may not have known this); Carmel's blanket order, as formulated, had been open-ended. The inhabitants were instructed to take some of their posses-sions and food supplies with them and to leave the rest. A handful of adult males were initially allowed to stay on to protect property. About 300 villagers crossed to Rmaich in Lebanon while the remaining 700 encamped in nearby caves and gullies, on the Israeli side. In the follow-ing days, three villagers crossing into Lebanon were apparently killed by ALA men and seven children died of exposure.[13]

The evacuation from Bir'im began on 13 November. Apparently there was some confusion; many 'didn't know where to go' and asked a passing IDF patrol.[14] As late as 23 November, there were inhabitants still in Bir'im, waiting to move.[15] As in most villages through 1948, at Iqrit, Suruh, Tarbikha and Nabi Rubin some remainders – 'old women, old men and children', incapable of walking – had stayed on. On 22 December, the IDF decided once and for all to 'cleanse' these villages. Units of the 92nd Battalion, Ninth Brigade, conducted a house-to-house sweep, and collected and trucked out the remaining villagers, who in-cluded 'women more than 100 years old'.[16]

On 20 November, Minority Affairs Minister Shitrit visited the area and refugees from Bir'im pleaded with him to be allowed back to their homes: He ordered that those living in the gullies around the village be allowed to temporarily move to Jish, into the homes of Muslims who had left. A few days later, the IDF gave permission to the Bir'im refugees in Lebanon to return, but to Jish.[17] 'Mano' Friedman organised their 'return' to Jish. But lack of transport and accommodation left some, at least temporarily, stranded in Rmaich.[18]

Then, on 15–16 November, the expulsions came to an abrupt stop – even before all the designated villages had been emptied.[19] On 15 November, IDF Galilee District HQ ordered its battalions 'to immedi-ately stop evicting the inhabitants from the occupied villages and freeze the existing situation'.[20] The following day, Ben-Gurion met with Dori and Carmel. Carmel, according to Ben-Gurion's diary entry, explained that he had 'had . . . to expel the border villages southward for military reasons . . . [But] he was [now] ready to freeze the situation – not to expel any more, and not to allow [those expelled] to return . . .' Ben-Gurion agreed, and added: 'As to the Christians in Kafr Bir'im and other villages, [Carmel] should announce that we will willingly discuss their return, once the border was secure.'[21] Why Ben-Gurion put a stop to the northern border-clearing operation, and why specifically on 15–16 November, is unclear. Of course, by then almost all of what had been planned had been implemented; only Fassuta (Christians), Jish (Maronites), Rihaniya (Circassians), Mi'ilya (Christians), and Jurdiye (Muslim), within the 5–7-kilometre-deep strip, were not uprooted, the last because its beduin inhabitants, the 'Arab al 'Aramshe, were deemed 'friendly'. Perhaps the ongoing ruckus over the October–November atrocities, which were linked, in various ways, to expulsions, also stayed Ben-Gurion's hand; he was facing enough criticism in Cabinet as it was. He was particularly worried about pressure from Mapam, itself in turmoil over the atrocities, and Immigration Minister Shapira.[22] And then there were the pro-Christian lobbyists, Shitrit and Ben-Zvi, as well as pressure from clerics in Lebanon, all militating against the evictions. (A few days later Shitrit was to complain that 'villages were being uprooted' without his knowledge and that General Avner had done nothing to prevent the atrocities (and, perhaps, the expulsions).)[23]

Initially, in the border-clearing, the IDF had not drawn much of a distinction between Christians and Muslims;[24] all (save, of course, Druse and Circassians) were ordered uprooted. The IDF had asked the Foreign Ministry for its opinion – but before it could be given, the army had gone ahead and expelled Muslims and Christians indiscriminately. (Shimoni felt that Maronite communities, if they had to be uprooted, should be transferred inland rather than to Lebanon.)[25] But as the operation unfolded, input from officers such as Dunkelman and government officials, including Shimoni, and intercession by Christian clerics, gradually tilted Northern Front toward a more benign and discriminating attitude toward the Christians. Hence, the expulsion from Jish was frustrated and Bir'im's (and 'Eilabun's) exiles in Lebanon were allowed back; hence, Northern Front's guidelines of 18 November concerning behaviour toward the Galilee's inhabitants. The guidelines had left open the possibility of a return home of Christian (and Druse) villagers transferred inland; no mention was made in them of Muslims.[26]

During the last months of 1948 and the first months of 1949 there was constant infiltration of refugees from Lebanon back to the villages. As with other sites, so with Bir'im, the authorities feared that, through infiltration, the village would soon fill up and cease to be 'abandoned'.[27] In June 1949, they removed the last Arabs from Bir'im – the ten original guards and a handful who had joined them – and transferred them to Jish.[28] At the same time, a group of Jews settled in Bir'im's houses (in August 1950 they moved to a permanent site, designated Kibbutz Bar'am, on the village's lands) – 'and members of this kibbutz began to behave toward our property and our land as if they were the true owners', the villagers later complained.[29]

On 27 April 1949, the government issued regulations, based on the Mandatory Emergency Regulations, empowering the defence minister to declare a border area a 'security zone', enabling him to bar anyone from entry. In September, the Lebanese border area was declared such a zone.[30] This legalised the previous months' operations.

For decades thereafter, the refugees of Bir'im (in Jish and Lebanon), Iqrit (in Rama) and Mansura (in Lebanon) pleaded with Israel to be permitted to return to their homes. They were supported by Shitrit and Ben-Zvi, president of Israel from 1952 to 1963. They also appealed to the High Court of Justice. On 31 July 1951, the High Court ruled in favour of the return of the Iqrit refugees to their village. But the IDF continued to obstruct a return. As to Bir'im, in 25 February 1952 the High Court ruled in favour of the state, though it allowed that the initial eviction had not been completely legal. Here, too, the IDF continued to block a return and new settlements were established on the two villages' lands. The settlements joined the IDF and GSS in lobbying against a return. The defense establishment argued that a return would harm border security, pave the way for infiltrators and serve as a precedent; the settlements, that a return, or an endorsement of the refugees' claims to lands, would undermine their existence. During 1949–1953, natural erosion, the settlers and the IDF gradually levelled the villages. On 24 December 1951 – Christmas eve – the IDF razed what remained of Iqrit with explosives; on 16 and 17 September 1953, using fighter-bombers and sappers, the IDF leveled Bir'im. In Iqrit, only the church was left standing, in Bir'im, the ancient synagogue. Since then, no one has returned to the two sites.

The case of Bir'im, Iqrit and Mansura illustrates how deep was the IDF's determination from November 1948 onward to create and maintain a northern border 'security belt' clear of Arabs. That determination quickly spread to the civilian institutions of state, particularly those concerned with immigrant absorption and settlement. Immediately after Hiram, Weitz and other executives began planning settlements in the border strip and exempted them from the 'surplus lands' requirement; indeed, in their planning, they tended to 'widen' the strip to a depth of 10–15 kilometres. However, Kaplan and Cisling, while accepting the IDF's arguments, insisted that the evictees should be properly and comfortably resettled. Only Minority Affairs Ministry director general Machnes opposed the principle of an Arab-less border strip.[31]

The expulsions and transfers of the first half of November had only partially cleared the strip. The IDF still wanted the job completed and the strip populated only with Jews. On 15 January 1949, Northern Front informed the General Staff that Fassuta, Jish and Bir'im – where '20 inhabitants' were still in place – remained, and said: 'We are today looking for a possibility to move them to central Galilee, we ask that you sanction this operation.'[32] The request was rejected. OC Military Government pointed out that on 21 November 1948, the Cabinet had appointed a committee charged with deciding whether 'to move Arabs from place to place'; such decision-making, henceforward, was no longer the prerogative of the IDF.[33] A similar fate met the Western Galilee Military Governor's 'most urgent' demand in October 1949 to evict the inhabitants of Jurdiye, most of whom, he argued, would 'agree to move to Lebanon'.[34]

But for months, IDF and GSS attention focused on Tarshiha, the largest village in the area (though, strictly speaking, beyond the ken as it was situated 9–10 kilometres south of the border). Most of its original 4,000–5,000 inhabitants (4/5 Muslims) had fled during Hiram. By December 1948, the village had some 700 inhabitants, 600 of them Christians, a minority of them infiltrees (inhabitants who had fled the country and then infiltrated back). The settlement authorities wanted the abandoned housing for immigrants; the military viewed settlement in the village as 'very important', as only 12 per cent of the Galilee's population at this time was Jewish.[35] Their main fear was that, if left partially empty, the village would fill up with returnees. The villagers, for their part, lived in continuous fear of expulsion, and periodically sent delegations to plead with Israeli officials. Shitrit repeatedly interceded with Ben-Gurion and 'saved' them.[36]

But the military periodically raided the full and half-empty Galilee villages to weed out illegal returnees, dubbed 'infiltrators'. The authorities did not recognise the legality of residence of anyone not registered during the October–November 1948 census and not in possession of an identity card or military pass. Anyone who had left the country before the census and was not registered and in possession of a card or pass was regarded as an 'absentee'. If he subsequently infiltrated back into the country (including to his home village), he was regarded as an 'illegal' and could be summarily deported. In the course of 1949, the IDF repeatedly raided the villages, sorted out legal from illegal residents and, usually, expelled returnees.

The IDF raid on 16 January on Tarshiha was typical:

> The Israeli army formed a cordon around the village and imposed a curfew. All males over 16 years were gathered in the village square. Here they were questioned by a panel of 8 Israelis . . . In all, 33 heads of families and 101 family members . . . were arrested and deported.

Apparently, officers also informally told the legally resident inhabitants that it would be in their interest to leave as well. Representatives in Israel of the AFSC (Quakers), Don Peretz and Ray Hartsough, who visited Tarshiha soon after, believed that the 'concerted' Israeli campaign against infiltrees and those who harboured them seemed to be directed at making 'room for new Jewish immigrants. It is their belief that the Jews plan to make of Tarshiha a completely Jewish town.' Some 300 Jewish immigrants moved into the abandoned houses over February and March and the dispersed Arab families were concentrated in one area.[37]

Following the 16 January operation, the authorities 'concluded that the inhabitants [of Tarshiha] should be moved in part to neighbouring Mi'ilya and the majority to Majd al Kurum and [they wished] to completely empty the place'. But UN and Christian clerical intercession prevented the eviction.[38] One IDF intelligence officer pointed to a worrying phenomenon: The (until then submissive) locals had handed the authorities petitions, 'formulated . . . by the Communists . . .', in which they threatened to mount 'passive resistance in the event of a transfer. This is the first announcement [i.e., instance] until now of organised resistance by the Arab population in our area.'[39]

On 21 January, General Avner proposed that the inhabitants of Tarshiha be transferred to Mi'ilya, but political objections blocked a final decision. Matters hung fire. In March, Weitz lamented that it would be good, 'if only it were possible,' to empty the village so that '1,000 [Jewish] families' could move in. But it was not possible: 'The prime minister is against dealing with transfers at the moment, [and] this from an international [political] viewpoint,' explained one of Ben-Gurion's aides, Zalman Lifshitz. He proposed 'to try to persuade [the inhabitants] to move.'[40] There were also internal objections. One official explained, in a private letter to Rehav'am 'Amir that 'we . . . have no right or authority to order the inhabitants of the place . . . to leave (unless they agree to this, on their own volition, and this is unlikely).' They are 'citizens,' he argued, and, as such, 'the State must protect their rights.' No 'security' or 'moral' arguments could justify their transfer. He assumed, he wrote, that 'all or most' of his fellow members on the Committee for Transferring Arabs from Place to Place shared his view.[41]

But the defence establishment wanted Tarshiha cleared. In light of the political obstructions, it opted for suasion rather than coercion. The pressure on the Arab inhabitants increased after the first Jewish families moved in. On 5 June, Jewish officials met with the local Arab leaders and, according to the AFSC representatives, said that the Arabs would have to move out. 'The Arabs refused.' The Jewish officials said that the village's '115' illegal inhabitants would be expelled from the country – unless the infiltrees and the remaining '600' legal residents agreed to move to other villages or Acre.[42] But the inhabitants stayed put.

For months the defence establishment continued to toy with the idea of a completely Arab-free northern border strip. Towards the end of 1949, a new plan surfaced to expel the inhabitants of 'Fassuta, Tarshiha, Mi'ilya, Jish, Hurfeish, [and] Rihaniya' (as well as of Zakariya and Majdal in the south). But objections by the Foreign Ministry (and perhaps others) frustrated adoption and implementation.[43]

But another cluster of northern border villages failed to gain the attention and protection of foreign interlopers – and the upshot was their transfer southward, to the interior of the Galilee. This transfer, in mid-1949, triggered an inter-departmental correspondence and, for the first time, (brief) public criticism and debate. At midnight, 5\6 June 1949, the remaining inhabitants of Khisas and Qeitiya, at the northern end of the Galilee panhandle, and of Ja'una, near Rosh Pina, were surrounded by IDF units, forced into trucks 'with brutality . . . kicks, curses and maltreatment' (in the words of Mapam Knesset Member and *Al Hamishmar* editor Eliezer Peri), and dumped on a sun-scorched hillside near 'Akbara, just south of Safad. The 55 Khisas villagers complained that they had been 'forced with their own hands to destroy their dwellings,' had been treated like 'cattle,' and their wives and children were 'wandering in the wilderness [near 'Akbara] thirsty and hungry'.[44]

Pressure to eject the remaining Arabs from Khisas had been building for months. Atiya Juwayid and his clan had for years provided services for the HIS and the JNF; Arabs from neighbouring Qeitiya had also apparently been of service to the JNF. But in February–March 1949, Jewish settlers and officers of the IDF Galilee District (Battalion 102) began pressing for eviction. The complaints related to general security in the area and intelligence being passed to the Syrians. Avraham Weingrad, the secretary of the neighbourting kibbutz, Ma'ayan Baruch, wrote to the army:

> This village is next to the Syrian border and the presence of Arabs there seriously endangers the security of our settlement. They also constitute a constant danger to our transportation . . . Therefore, we ask that you do all in your power to have them evicted from this village.[45]

Battalion 102 was sympathetic but passed the buck: 'I hope that by action on your part we will be able to reduce the movement of Arabs in your area and prompt the institutions [i.e., authorities] to deal appropriately with this problem.'[46] In April, Ninth Brigade intelligence weighed in: ' . . . the villagers see every movement of our army [in the area] . . . I see no good [reason] why this village should not be moved inland. There is no doubt that this village is a source of information for the enemy.'[47]

The IDF moved on 5 June.[48] The evictions sparked outrage in various quarters. 'This is shameful and disgraceful . . . Brutality . . . Woe to a state that treads such an immoral path,' Yosef Nahmani jotted down in his diary.[49] Nahmani, a friend of Ben-Gurion's, for decades had enjoyed good relations with Khisas's Arabs, who had helped him in land purchases.[50] Mapam's leaders also criticised the operation. Ben-Gurion responded that he found the military's reasons for the eviction 'sufficient'. Mapai's Yosef Sprinzak, the speaker of the Knesset, sarcastically criticised the government over the operation and the post-operation explanations.[51] *Ha'aretz*, the leading independent daily newpaper, also criticised Ben-Gurion's justifications as 'not very convincing'. The newspaper conceded the army's right to move Arabs out of 'border areas', but such evictees must be adequately resettled, with land, houses and food. The editorial argued that this was sheer common sense as well as humanity, since to create a class of deprived and dispossessed Arabs would play into the hands of subversives bent on 'undermining . . . the State'.[52] The June evictions moved American chargé d'affaires in Tel Aviv Richard Ford to reflect pessimistically about the fate of Israel's

Arab minority: 'The unhappy spectacle presents itself of some scores of thousands of aimless people "walking about in thistle fields" until they either decide to shake the ancestral dust of Israel from their heels or just merely die.'[53] Conditions at 'Akbara, a dumping spot for 'remainders' from various eastern Galilee villages, were to remain bad for years.[54]

A last border problem remained in the north: A string of villagers in eastern Galilee, in the area that became the Demilitarised Zone (DMZ) along the Israeli–Syrian border. Their presence and property were formally protected by the provisions of the Israeli–Syrian General Armistice Agreement (Article V) of 20 July 1949.[55] Nonetheless, for a combination of military, economic and agricultural reasons, Israel wanted the inhabitants of Kirad al Baqqara, Kirad al Ghannama, Nuqeib, al Samra, and al Hama, numbering about 2,200 in all, to move, or move back, to Syria. The military suspected them of helping Syrian intelligence. The DMZ inhabitants remained in the main loyal 'Syrians' and, under Syrian pressure, refused to recognise the legitimacy of Israeli rule. In case of renewed hostilities, they could prove strategically useful to the Syrians. As it was, Jewish settlers and police suspected the villagers of stealing cattle, trespassing and other criminal or troublesome behaviour.[56] And, of course, the settlement agencies and settlers coveted their lands.

Most of the villagers, including from Samra[57] and Nuqeib,[58] had fled or been expelled to Syria during April and early May 1948. Some of the population returned following the Syrian invasion of 16 May. More returned following the signing of the Israeli–Syrian General Armistice Agreement. During the following months, using a combination of stick and carrot – economic and police pressures and 'petty persecution', and economic incentives – Israel gradually evicted the inhabitants of Samra and Khirbet al Duweir. Small beduin encampments, such as that at Khirbet al Muntar, east of Rosh Pina, were periodically visited by IDF patrols and, ultimately, expelled.[59] The two Kirads, though subjected to the same treatment, received UN protection and were only removed to Syria in the course of the 1956 war, though some had earlier been moved to, and permanently settled in, Sh'ab, near Acre.[60]

Immediately after Hiram, the Israeli authorities, parallel to the start of the border-clearing operations, put their minds to the problem of the populated, semi-populated and empty Arab villages in the interior of the Galilee, to all of which refugees were returning. The fear was that with the worsening winter weather[61] and the refugees' steady pauperisation, the influx would increase and empty and semi-populated villages would fill up anew, ultimately increasing the State's Arab minority and the security problems thus engendered. Ben-Gurion personally authorised the expulsion of the infiltrating returnees at a meeting with General Avner at the beginning of 1949.[62] Ben-Gurion was later to say that he viewed the infiltration problem 'through the barrel of a gun'.[63]

From mid-December 1948 onward, the IDF periodically mounted massive sweeps in the Galilee villages to root out returnees and expel them. Perhaps the first was *Mivtza Magrefa* (Operation Rake), planned at meetings between officers of the Ninth Brigade, Haifa District HQ, Military Government Western Galilee, and Intelligence Service Department 3. The operational order, of 21 December, called for the scouring of 25 'abandoned' villages, some along the Lebanese border (Iqrit, Tarbikha, Suruh, Nabi Rubin, Fassuta) and the rest in the interior of Western Galilee (Ghabisiya, Kuweikat, 'Amqa, Birwa, Sh'ab, Mi'ar, etc.), 'to make sure that Arabs haven't infiltrated back. At the end of the operation all these villages must remain completely abandoned.'[64] During the following days, Ninth Brigade units scoured 17 of the villages. One village, Sh'ab, was found inhabited and 'its inhabitants were expelled on foot [though] one may assume that they will return'. All the rest were found empty, save for guards, with permits, left to protect property.[65]

At the same time, the Ninth Brigade was ordered to mount a similar operation in Shafa 'Amr. The orders were to surround the village, impose a curfew, round up the inhabitants, identify the infiltrees and arrest and expel them, while 'causing a minimum of discomfort to the [permanent] inhabitants'. The executing unit, the 92nd Battalion, was also ordered to find hidden arms and 'to expel across the border [several] local inhabitants as ordered by Intelligence Service 3'.[66] The battalion, assisted by officers of the Military Government and Intelligence Service, mounted the operation on 27 December. 42 infiltrators were identified and expelled to the West Bank and five 'suspects' were transported to a POW camp for further interrogation.[67] During January 1949, the IDF expelled in similar operations almost 1,000 Arabs and transferred another 128 to other villages inside the country.[68]

One of the villages that had been earmarked for cleansing in *Magrefa* was the Western Galilee village of Umm al Faraj, overrun by the Haganah in May 1948, its population driven out. But the Ninth Brigade apparently didn't get to it in December and by February 1949, it was filling with returnees.[69] The civil authorities were particularly worried as the site was slated for imminent settlement: They asked the military 'to take all the necessary steps to cleanse the village'.[70] The operation took place at the end of March: The IDF Druse unit, Battalion 300, rounded up and expelled 62 persons to the West Bank; ten adult males, with an unknown number of dependents, were transferred to al Mazra'a, the village south of Nahariya that had become the collection point for the 'remainders' from Western Galilee's emptied villages. One family, the Aslans, were allowed to remain as caretakers.[71] But infiltrators continued to return. On 28 July, in a repeat operation, Battalion 300 raided the village and expelled 60 to the West Bank. Again, the Aslans, and perhaps some others with permits, were allowed to remain[72] but they were all removed some months later.

A similar problem developed in nearby Zib, just north of Nahariya. There, too, a family – numbering 13 souls – had been left to guard property. But, as one Israeli official put it, 'they should be moved at the earliest opportunity to an Arab settlement, otherwise they will serve as a nucleus for . . . groups of infiltrators arriving as a result of the improving weather conditions'.[73] A settlers' lobby – the members of the newly established kibbutz, Gesher Haziv (set up on Zib lands) – joined in:

> In our view, the time has come to sort out the affairs [i.e., problem] of the Arabs in our area. Even before we moved here, we pointed out to the military governor in Acre the danger stemming from the presence of Arabs in the village of al Zib, such a small distance from the [Lebanese] border [i.e., about six kilometres]. Despite the repeated promises by the office of the military governor, nothing has been done so far to move out the Arabs.[74]

Eventually, the inhabitants were cleared out and the village was razed.

Following *Magrefa*, there were periodic sweeps, usually targeting single villages. On 6 January, IDF troops swept Deir al Asad and Bi'na, expelling from them, respectively, 62 and four infiltrators; on 15 January, 28 were expelled from Mi'ilya; on 20 February, 32 were expelled from Tamra; on 1 March, 250 were expelled from Kafr Yasif; on 8 March, 79 were expelled from Sh'ab; on 10 March, 62 were expelled from Nahf; on 25 March, 27 adult males and a number of family members, were expelled from Rama; on 29 March, 250 were expelled from Abu Sinan; on 31 March, 43 adult males and some dependents were expelled from Kabul.[75] The expellees were invariably trucked to the West Bank.

But a problem arose, as IDF officers were quick to note: After being shoved into the West Bank, many expellees infiltrated back. The operations officer of the Ninth Brigade explained:

> . . . the system of expelling infiltrators to the Triangle is not very effective . . . The unit bringing the deportees lets them off the vehicles and sends them toward the border, and leaves the place. There is no one there to make sure that they will not return. In most cases the refugees move several kilometres across the border, wait until sunset and infiltrate back during the night.[76]

Another officer thought he had a solution, after pointing out that 'almost all' those expelled – all adult males – from one village, 'Ibillin, had since returned: 'We have not yet heard of any case in which a whole family of expellees has returned. It is clear, therefore, that the expulsion of whole families better assures their non-return.'[77]

The longest lasting problem of this sort in Western Galilee was the village of al Ghabisiya, initially conquered in May 1948, in Operation Ben-'Ami. Some inhabitants had fled, others had been expelled.[78] During the first months of the war, the villagers had helped the Haganah with ammunition, weapons and intelligence, though the authorities concluded that some villagers had participated in the attack on the Yehiam Convoy, in late March 1948.[79] The inhabitants had temporarily resettled in neighbouring Abu Sinan, Yarka and Kafr Yasif, where they were registered in the census of October–November. The villagers pleaded to be allowed to return home. Some were given permission; others infiltrated back and resettled illegally. On 24 January 1950, the Military Government ordered all the villagers to leave within 48 hours, and they complied. The authorities had not prepared alternative accommodation and the expellees moved temporarily to abandoned houses in nearby Sheikh Daoud. Eventually, many were resettled in Mazra'a.

The expulsion raised a hue and cry in Mapam, which condemned Ben-Gurion and the army.[80] But the regional Jewish settlements bloc, in which Mapam kibbutzim were dominant, publicly endorsed the eviction: 'The action of the Military Government was routine and very understandable and there is no basis for the newspaper reports' references to "the unhappinness of the settlements" regarding the matter itself.' One of the Mapam kibbutzim, Evron, was cultivating 1,500 dunams of Ghabisiya land, as Captain Krasnansky, of the Military Government, was quick to point out. The committee resolved that the 'Arabs of Ghabisiya should on no account be allowed to return to their village'. In its press release, the committee mildly criticised the operation's timing, given the 'difficult winter conditions . . .'[81] The publication of the committee's views confounded Mapam's leaders and the editors of the party's daily, *Al Hamishmar*, which was critical of the expulsion, and led to a spat with Mapai's daily, *Davar*, which alleged that Mapam was behaving hypocritically.[82] Some months later, a few Ghabisiya refugees resettled in the village. They were arrested, tried in a military court and sentenced to several months in prison and given fines.[83]

To the east, pressure built up during December 1948 and January 1949 to evict the remaining and resettled Arabs in Saffuriya, near Nazareth, and in Farradiya and neighbouring Kafr 'Inan, southwest of Safad. Shitrit said that infiltration back to villages was increasing and that if the phenomenon was not halted, Israel would have to 'conquer the Galilee anew'. Major Sulz, the regional military governor, proposed that the returnees in Farradiya and Kafr 'Inan be moved to Tur'an while those in Saffuriya be moved to neighbouring al Reina. The Committee for Transferring Arabs from Place to Place on 15 December 1948 endorsed Sulz's proposal but bureaucratic footdragging followed.[84]

Saffuriya, a large Muslim village with a history of anti-Yishuv activity, had almost completely emptied in July 1948; perhaps some '80' old people had been left behind.[85] Some of the remaining inhabitants were expelled in September but over the following months hundreds infiltrated back. The Jewish authorities feared that if the infiltrees were left untouched, the village would soon return to its pre-war population of 4,000.

Besides, neighbouring settlements coveted Saffuriya lands. One senior official put it bluntly in November: 'Next to Nazareth is a village . . . whose distant lands are needed for our settlements. Perhaps they can be given another place.' By early January 1949, there were some 550 Arabs in place. Northern Front ordered their eviction[86] and on the 7th, 14 were expelled across the border and the rest ordered to leave for 'Illut.[87] Many apparently moved to Nazareth and 'Illut; the rest went to al Reina and Kafr Kanna. In February, Saffuriya's lands were distributed among neighbouring settlements: Kibbutz Sdeh Nahum got 1,500 dunams, Kibbutz Heftzi-Bah, 1,000. Later that year, Kibbutz Hasolelim received 3,795 dunams.[88]

A similar situation developed in Farradiya and Kafr 'Inan. Like Saffuriya, both were officially designated 'abandoned villages' (*kfarim netushim*) but were gradually filling up. In January, the IDF expelled '54' and moved another '128' inhabitants to other villages inside Israel.[89] But the two villages filled up again. On 4 February, units of the 79th Battalion surrounded Farradiya and Kafr 'Inan and expelled 45 'infiltrators' to the West Bank and transferred the rest, about 200, who had permits, 'almost all old men, women and children', to Majd al Kurum.[90] But some apparently returned. By mid-February, there were about '100' back in residence, according to the IDF. The two villages were again scoured and emptied, some going to other villages in Israel and the rest to the West Bank.[91] The Military Government said the evictions had been necessary to assure 'security, law and order'.[92]

The search and expulsion operations in the Galilee continued during the following months.[93] The IDF growingly pressured permanent inhabitants, especially mukhtars, to inform on infiltrators and assist them in identification. The mukhtars routinely complied.[94]

THE SOUTH

In the south, in the wake of Operation Yoav, the army's operations combined features of border-clearing and internal 'cleansing', and nowhere was this clearer than in the area roughly between Majdal and the northern edge of the Gaza Strip. As we have seen, at the end of November 1948, about 500 refugees were expelled from Majdal itself to the Gaza Strip.[95] At the same time, Coastal Plain District troops carried out sweeps in the villages around and to the south of Majdal. The orders to the battalions and the engineers platoon were to expel to Gaza 'the Arab refugees' from 'Hamama, al Jura, Khirbet Khisas [misnamed 'Khirbet Khazaz'], Ni'ilya, al Jiyya, Barbara, Beit Jirja, Hirbiya and Deir Suneid' and 'to prevent their return by destroying the villages'. The paths leading to the villages were to be mined. The troops were enjoined to carry out the operation 'with determination, accuracy and energy' while curbing 'any undesirable deviation' from norms.[96]

The operation took place on 30 November. The troops found 'not a living soul' in Isdud, Hamama, al Jura, Beit Jirja, and Hirbiya and 'about 150 persons' in Ni'ilya and neighbouring Khirbet Khisas, and 'about 40' in Barbara and al Jiyya, 'composed of women, old men and children', who offered no resistance. They were expelled to Egyptian-held Beit Hanun, in the northern Gaza Strip, though 'several tens of old men, blind women, etc., and a number of children belonging to them' were allowed to remain (where exactly is unclear). The troops also found eight young men, who were sent to a POW camp. But the destruction of the villages was not completed, due to the dampness of the mud houses and insufficient explosives. Coastal Plain District HQ promised Southern Front to complete the operation, and to check Deir Suneid, in the future.[97]

A similar operation was mounted by the district troops in the eastern area of its jurisdiction. The order called for 'the cleansing of the area west of the Beit Jibrin-Har Tuv road . . . of Arab inhabitants [*tihur hashetah . . . meochlosiya 'aravit*]'. The Arabs encountered were to be 'dispersed' or taken captive.[98]

A few kilometres to the north, the Palmah's 4th Battalion (Harel Brigade) on 5 November raided the area south of Beit Nattif. At Khirbet Umm al Lauz, one platoon encountered dozens of refugees with flocks moving westwards, into Israel. 'The platoon . . . ordered them to get out' and confiscated a flock of 65 goats, a camel and an ass. The following day, a platoon sent to 'expel refugees' found some 150 at Khirbet Umm Burj. The unit expelled about 100, apparently injuring some of them. Initially, the Fourth Battalion reported, the refugees were unresponsive to threats and refused to move eastwards. Some even asked 'to live under "Shertok's [*sic*] rule"'. But the raids ultimately proved persuasive, and the refugees eventually moved off. A raid on al Jab'a on the night of 5\6 November, in which some 15 houses were blown up, led to a temporary evacuation of the village. A few kilometres to the south, the Fifth Brigade raided three southern West Bank border villages – Idna, Khirbet Beit 'Awwa and Khirbet Sikka – apparently with the aim of pushing the inhabitants eastward. In Idna, the raiders blew up a house and in Khirbet Sikka, after driving out the inhabitants, blew up about 20 houses. At Khirbet Beit 'Awwa the raiders were driven off but they blew up some buildings in nearby Khirbet Beit al Meis.[99]

During the following months, Southern Front was successful in preventing refugees from returning to the villages. In contrast with Northern Front, Yigal Allon, OC Southern Front, had completely driven out the local population during Operation Yoav and no fully or semi-populated villages were left behind his front lines (save for Majdal and Egyptian-held Faluja and 'Iraq al Manshiya in the Faluja Pocket). There were no recurrent, large-scale cat-and-mouse games as occurred in the north. So, while large-scale infiltration continued, aimed at retrieving possessions, smuggling, theft, harvest and the like, the infiltrators found it almost impossible to resettle or gain permanent footholds in the villages; there was no local population to assist them or among which they could disappear. When, five months later, in April 1949, Coastal District troops carried out a sweep in a dozen or so villages west of the southern West Bank, almost all were found completely empty and in the rest the troops encountered only a handful of adult male infiltrators, not whole families. There was no need to mount complex operations involving large numbers of troops and prolonged identification checks; everyone encountered, it was understood, was an infiltrator. In Deir ad Dubban, the troops killed three Arabs 'trying to escape' and captured two. Some camels and donkeys also were killed. Two Arabs managed to escape from Zikrin. Another Arab was shot dead in Sajad. That was it. The villages were essentially, unproblematically, empty.[100]

Not so the grey area along the southern West Bank's border, where the Israeli and Jordanian lines were ill-defined and where the two states jockeyed for tactical advantage and position in the run-up to the signing of the Israel–Jordan General Armistice Agreement and the future border demarcation. Here were temporarily encamped concentrations of refugees driven out from the villages to the west as well as village communities that Israel wanted to uproot.

> The many khirbot [ruins or satellite hamlets, in Arabic khurab] spread in the no man's land east of the Beit Jibrin-'Ajjur road constitute hiding places for refugees and infiltrators. Enemy scouts also use them as observation points and hideouts . . .,

explained one IDF intelligence report.[101] On the night of 7\8 March 1949, the Third Brigade troops occupied a series of hilltops northeast and southeast of Beit Jibrin, including Khirbet Umm Burj, and hilltops overlooking Khirbet Sikka and Khirbet Beit Mirsim.[102] 'Many villagers in the area fled for their lives [toward Hebron and Dura]', IDF intelligence reported.[103] More ambitiously, on 11 March the IDF mounted a series of major pushes eastward, to 'create facts' on the ground in advance of the UN survey of the Jordanian and Israeli positions scheduled for later that day.[104] The aim was to gain a little more, or tactically advantageous, territory and to drive concentrations of Arabs eastwards. But Israeli liaison officers took pains to persuade UN observers that the clashes were the result of Arab incursions and attacks:

> Arab civilians with their herds go into a valley where the pastures are good . . . five kilometres west of Surif. Some of these Arabs even go between the Israeli positions with their herds. Normally, the local [IDF] commander orders small arms fire directed above their heads to scare them away. When they remain near the Israeli positions, the local commander sends out patrols to take prisoner all men of [military] age . . . This is why nine Arab civilians were taken to a prisoners camp on

> 11 March . . . The local commander stated that on 11 March . . . [Arab]
> irregulars infiltrated . . . at . . . Khirbet Jubeil Naqqar, directing rifle fire
> at . . . [an IDF] position . . . [and] two mortar rounds coming from Khirbet
> 'Illin were directed at the Israeli position . . . On 13 March . . . a group of
> 25 Arab irregulars advanced from [Khirbet] Ghuraba to the Israeli position
> at Khirbet al Hamam.[105]

In reality, the Israeli troops were ordered, in a well-organised, concerted operation, to take al Qabu, Khirbet Sanasin (southwest of Wadi
Fukin), al Jab'a, and Khirbet al Hamam, even if it involved battling the
Jordanians.[106] The Fourth Brigade troops took several of these hilltops
(and one or two besides, including Khirbet Jubeil Naqqar and Sheikh
Madh-kur[107]) and went on, during the following days, to take and clear
of Arabs a series of hilltops northeast and southeast of Dawayima (including Muntar al Joza) and east of Deir Nakh-khas. Khirbet Sikka was
apparently occupied on 16 March and Khirbet Beit 'Awwa on 19–20
March. The force, which included half-tracks, used machine-guns and
mortars and killed 'about 10 Arabs and five camels' and drove off groups
of Arabs and confiscated flocks.[108] The orders were to 'hit every [adult
male] Arab spotted in the area [but] not to harm women and children'.[109]
A UN report, based on testimony by the expellees, described what happened at Khirbet Beit 'Awwa:

> On . . . 19 March they heard machingun fire all around . . . Women and
> children began to cry . . . An [IDF] sergeant and about 25 soldiers . . .
> picked out three notables . . . and . . . told [them] that the inhabitants of
> [Khirbet] Beit 'Awwa would be authorized [i.e., allowed] to stay there and
> cultivate part of their fields if they provided cows and sheep to the Jewish
> troops. The three notables agreed . . . But [the next day] the same Jewish
> sergeant arrived with 50 soldiers and ordered the people to leave within
> two hours . . . 1,800 Arab civilians, old men and women included, left the
> village with only a small part of their belongings . . . For the time being
> part of them are sheltered in caves between Beit 'Awwa and Dura, some
> have fled towards Hebron.

Altogether, according to the UN, the IDF overran '35 or 36' *khurab* and
beduin encampments adjacent to no man's land, expelling the inhabitants eastward. One UN report put the number of those expelled toward
Dura during March at '7,000'.[110] But within days, UN intervention persuaded Israel to withdraw from some of the *khurab*, including Khirbet
Sikka and Khirbet Beit 'Awwa, and the inhabitants trickled back.

Following the signing of the armistice agreement on 3 April, a question mark arose regarding a number of villages on the southern edge
of the Jerusalem Corridor. Refugees had gradually returned to both al
Walaja and al Qabu, which were in Israeli territory, and the IDF wanted
them empty. On 1 May, Israeli troops raided them, and the inhabitants
fled and the troops blew up their houses.[111] A few weeks later, the IDF

raided the village of Wadi Fukin, on the Jordanian side of the border and expelled its inhabitants. The village had been at least partially abandoned during the war and for months was in no man's land, both sides claiming that their troops – during March–April 1949 – had occupied or patrolled it.[112] It had been partially inhabited during the winter months and 'completely inhabited' during the spring, according to a UN observer. But most of the houses had been demolished.[113] Around 14 April, in accordance with the territorial provisions of the armistice accord, the Jordanians had withdrawn from Wadi Fukin, though the inhabitants had remained.[114] In July, the IDF drove out the villagers, claiming that they were infiltrees.[115] On 31 August, the Israel–Jordan MAC ruled that Israel must allow the inhabitants to return, the UN chairman casting the deciding vote.[116] The inhabitants returned and, ultimately, the village was transferred to Jordanian sovereignty.

The longest lasting of the Arab communities in the southern Jerusalem Corridor area was Zakariya. The village was conquered by the 54th Battalion, Fifth Brigade, on 23 October 1948; it was 'almost empty', most of the inhabitants having temporarily fled to nearby hills.[117] The soldiers executed two of the inhabitants.[118] In December, the IDF had swept the village and expelled the 40-odd 'old men and women' found there to the West Bank.[119] But the village filled up again. In March 1949, pressing for the eviction of the remaining '145 or so' inhabitants, the Interior Ministry official in charge of the Jerusalem District pointed out that 'in the village there are many good houses, and it is possible to accommodate in them several hundred new immigrants'.[120] In January 1950, Ben-Gurion, on vacation in Tiberias, met with Sharett, Weitz and other officials and decided to evict the Arabs of Zakariya (along with those from several other sites) '[but] without coercion'. Land-owners who wished to leave the country would be bought out.[121] The health and food situation in the village was appalling.[122] One intelligence report stated: 'Among the 160 inhabitants of the village today, only about 20 are able to work, all the rest are sick, blind or infected. The dirt and desolation in the village is great and the sanitary situation is indescribable.' The officer recommended transferring the registered inhabitants to a site inside the country and the infiltrees, and potential troublemakers, to the West Bank.[123] On 19 March, General Staff\Operations approved 'the transfer of the Arabs of Zakariya to the towns of Lydda and Ramle'.[124] On 9 June, they were evicted, some preferring resettlement in Ramle and Lydda; others, perhaps the majority, opted for the West Bank, where they ended up in the Deheishe Refugee Camp near Bethlehem.[125]

Further to the south, three major problems remained. One was the Faluja Pocket (today, the site of the Israeli town of Kiryat Gat), where some 4,000 Egyptian troops had been left stranded and surrounded by the IDF between late October 1948 and late February 1949. Inside the pocket were two large villages with civilian inhabitants, Faluja and

'Iraq al Manshiya, with a combined population of over 3,100: More than 2,000 were locals and the rest, refugees from elsewhere in Palestine. On 24 February, Israel and Egypt signed an armistice agreement. Two days later the besieged troops (who included Egypt's future president, Gamal 'Abdel Nasser), along with some of the refugees, departed for Egypt. But most of the civilians remained and were placed under Military Government rule, with nightly curfews and severe restrictions on movement. The Egyptians had insisted that the armistice agreement explicitly guarantee their safety.[126] In the appended exchange of letters, Israel agreed that

> those of the civilian population who may wish to remain in Al Faluja and 'Iraq al Manshiya are to be permitted to do so . . . All of these civilians shall be fully secure in their persons, abodes, property and personal effects.[127]

But within days Israel went back on its word. Southern Front's soldiers mounted a short, sharp, well-orchestrated campaign of low-key violence and psychological warfare designed to intimidate the inhabitants into flight. According to one villager's recollection, the Jews 'created a situation of terror, entered the houses and beat the people with rifle butts'.[128] Contemporary United Nations and Quakers documents support this description. The UN Mediator, Ralph Bunche, quoting UN observers on the spot, complained that 'Arab civilians . . . at Al Faluja have been beaten and robbed by Israeli soldiers and . . . there have been some cases of attempted rape'.[129] The Quaker team (Ray Hartsough and Delbert Replogle), who were at Faluja between 26 February and 6 March assessing the civilians' food and medical needs, kept a diary. On 3 March they wrote that 'about half the people of Faluja plan to remain'. But at 'Iraq al Manshiya, the acting *mukhtar* told them that 'the people had been much molested by the frequent shooting, by being told that they would be killed if they did not go to Hebron, and by the Jews breaking into their homes and stealing things'. On March 4, 02:30 hours, they recorded: 'The worst barrage of shooting we had heard all week – about 300 rounds by a machinegun within a hundred yards of where we were sleeping . . .' And at 06:30 hours: 'The boy living in one of the rooms of our compound brought a man into the room where I was sleeping. His eye was bloody and he had other wounds on his face and ear . . . He had been beaten by "the Jahoudy".' The Quaker and UN observers complained to an Israeli officer. He reportedly replied: 'They had some new recruits stationed there and . . . new recruits are the same the world over. When they get hold of a gun they want to shoot and shoot and shoot.' And at 09:00 hours:

> Jane Smith [one of the Quaker party] has bandaged six men. The worst case was a man with two bloody eyes, a torn ear, and a face pounded until it was blue . . . A young Arab told me: 'We could not sleep last night because

of much shooting and because the Israeli soldiers came into the homes and tried to "make into" the Arab women.' I asked: 'Did they succeed?' He answered: 'No, because the women could be heard screaming and the men would run to chase the Israel soldiers away . . . They asked when the trucks would go to Hebron because all the people in Faluja wanted to go to Hebron.[130]

The Quakers said that the Arabs now wanted to leave but that sincere reassurances by Israeli officials could still persuade the Arabs to stay. No such reassurances were forthcoming.[131] The intimidation operation was orchestrated by Rabin, Allon's head of operations.[132] Yadin dismissed the United Nations complaints of Israeli intimidation as 'exaggerated'.[133] But Sharett, wary of the international repercussions and, especially, of the possible effect on Israeli–Egyptian relations, and angered by the IDF actions, that lacked Cabinet authorisation and were carried out behind his back, was not easily appeased. He let fly at IDF CGS Dori in most uncharacteristic language. 'The IDF's actions', he wrote, threw into question

> our sincerity as a party to an international agreement . . . One may assume that Egypt in this matter will display special sensitivity as her forces saw themselves as responsible for the fate of these civilian inhabitants. There are also grounds to fear that any attack by us on the people of these two villages may be reflected in the attitude of the Cairo Government toward the Jews of Egypt.

The Foreign Minister pointed out that Israel was encountering difficulties at the United Nations, where it was seeking membership,

> over the question of our responsibility for the Arab refugee problem. We argue that we are not responsible . . . From this perspective, the sincerity of our professions is tested by our behaviour in these villages . . . Every intentional pressure aimed at uprooting [these Arabs] is tantamount to a planned act of eviction on our part.

Sharett added that in addition to the overt violence displayed by the soldiers, the IDF was busy conducting covertly

> a 'whispering propaganda' campaign among the Arabs, threatening them with attacks and acts of vengeance by the army, which the civilian authorities will be powerless to prevent. This whispering propaganda (*ta'amulat lahash*) is not being done of itself. There is no doubt that here there is a calculated action aimed at increasing the number of those going to the Hebron Hills as if of their own free will, and, if possible, to bring about the evacuation of the whole civilian population of [the pocket].

Sharett called the army's actions 'an unauthorised initiative by the local command in a matter relating to Israeli government policy'.[134] Allon admitted (to Yadin) only that his troops had 'beaten three Arabs . . .

There is no truth to the observers' announcement about abuse/cruelty [hit'aleluf], etc. I investigated this personally.'[135]

The decision to intimidate into flight the inhabitants of the two villages was probably taken by Allon after a meeting with Yosef Weitz on 28 February (and probably after getting agreement from Ben-Gurion).[136] A few months before, Weitz and Ben-Gurion had agreed on the need to drive out, by intimidation, Arab communities along the Faluja–Majdal axis.[137] Ben-Gurion may also have approved the action as Faluja had become a symbol of Egyptian military fortitude and courage; the expulsion of the inhabitants that army had protected would no doubt dent its reputation.[138] On 28 February, Allon asked the General Staff for permission to evict the inhabitants. He argued that they were near the West Bank border and could serve as way stations for infiltrators, spies and guerrilla fighters, and that they sat astride a strategic crossroads. 'I am certain that with the right argumentation and real help in transporting their property across the border we can persuade them to evacuate the villages voluntarily (in relative terms, of course)', he argued. If, for international-political reasons, it was decided not 'to encourage' their departure from Israeli territory, '[I] recommend to transfer them inland . . .'. Allon said the matter was 'urgent'.[139] That day, he issued an order declaring the two villages closed to unauthorised personnel, effectively sealing off the area from busybodies.[140] General Staff Division apparently approved Allon's request, probably adding a caution concerning the visibility of the means employed.[141]

The fright inflicted on the pocket's civilians in the first days of March sufficed to persuade most of them to opt for the 'Jordanian solution'. They left for Hebron in a series of Red Cross-organised convoys. Faluja's inhabitants all seem to have left in the first half of March; 'Iraq al Manshiya's left over the following weeks. Several incidents appear to have helped them make up their minds. On 18 March, an IDF patrol intercepted a group of Arabs who apparently had sneaked into Faluja to collect grain they had left behind and killed two of them. The following night the troops encountered another group of Arabs and fired on them, 'probably hitting a number'. The following day, 19 March, IDF sentries shot and killed two Arabs outside 'Iraq al Manshiya.[142] On 27 March, two soldiers robbed an Arab woman of a calf. The woman complained to UN observers, saying that the calf's mother would die if the calf were not returned. An IDF officer investigated the charge, found it well-founded and recommended that the soldiers be 'severely punished'.[143] The last of 'Iraq al Manshiya's inhabitants – numbering '1,160' souls, along with '86' donkeys, '22' cows and '2' horses – left, in six convoys, during 21–22 April.[144] Five days later, Rabin ordered the demolition of Faluja and Iraq al Manshiya (and a string of other villages).[145]

Subsequently, Israeli officials, sometimes feigning outrage, were not completely frank about what had happened. Foreign Ministry

Director General Eytan, for instance, told the United States Ambassador, McDonald, that Israel had broadcast 'repeated reassuring notices' to the Faluja and 'Iraq al Manshiya Arabs to stay put. However, the local inhabitants had acted 'as if they smelled a rat' and abandoned their homes. Eytan described the Arabs, in this connection, as 'primitive [and] rumour-ridden'. Alternately, when admitting that intimidation had occurred, Israeli officials put the blame on local initiatives and unruly local commanders.[146]

A second major problem in the south, as seen from the Israeli perspective, was the beduin tribes concentrated in the northern Negev. The Israeli leadership was split on the issue. There were two basic approaches. The army's approach, at least initially, was that the beduin were congenitally unreliable and unruly, had sided with the Arabs during the war and, given the chance, would do so again. As well, they were incorrigible smugglers and thieves. It was best that they clear or be cleared out of the area. A more nuanced approach was adopted by various Arabists, who differentiated between 'good' and 'bad' beduin. The 'bad' ones should be ejected. But the 'good' ones – and beduins naturally tended to accept and display loyalty towards those in power – could be harnessed to serve the state, particularly in the form of an *in situ* border guard.[147]

During Operation Yoav, many had moved off, some into Sinai, to be out of harm's way. Afterwards, for more than a month, the authorities pondered the problem, undecided. At the end of October, following the clear IDF victory, a number of chieftains – led by Sheikh Suleiman al Huzeil – asked to meet the newly-appointed military governor of the Negev, Michael Hanegbi:[148] They wanted to know 'what would be their future'.[149] Ben-Gurion told his fellow ministers that he favoured 'a peace pact with all the tribes', implying that they would be allowed to stay. But 'the locals', he said – presumably he meant settlers and IDF units in the area – were opposed. So meanwhile, he said, the beduin would not be allowed 'to return to their places'.[150] On 3 November, Southern Front ordered that the beduin within a radius of 10 kilometres of Beersheba be expelled. The IDF was concerned about infiltration into town and intelligence the beduin might give the Egyptians; there was also sniping at Israeli traffic on the road between Beersheba and Bir 'Asluj, to the south.[151] The following day, the Ninth Battalion carried out the 'cleansing' operation, killing a number of 'suspicious Arabs' and expelling one tribe.[152] But beyond the 10-kilometre limit, and perhaps even inside that radius, the number of nomads steadily grew as more and more returned, reported Hanegbi.[153]

On 2 November, Hanegbi and other officers met al Huzeil and several other traditionally friendly chieftains. The army, it appeared, wanted 'to push back the beduin as much as possible from the [Beersheba] area, far into the desert'. Some officers suggested that the tribes voluntarily move 'into Transjordan'.[154] The Foreign Ministry, previously more conciliatory, now bowed to the military, but suggested that Israel offer compensation to the departees.[155] But the local Minority Affairs Ministry representative, Ya'acov Berdichevsky, thought the tribes could be usefully turned into a border guard.[156]

As the Israeli bureaucracies tergiversated, the tribes' economic situation deteriorated. They were unable to reach their cereal stocks, which were stored near Beersheba. There was real 'hunger' and infiltration into Beersheba 'to steal food.' Some tribes demanded that Israel 'recognise them as citizens of the state'. Hanegbi and his officers 'brushed them off with [empty] promises'. But he agreed that most of the beduin had been neutral during the war and had rejected Egyptian pressures to help the invaders; and some beduin had actively helped the Jews. Hanegbi began vigorously lobbying that Israel take the beduin under its wing. He argued that there were only '8–10,000'[157] 'friendlies' and, dispersed over a large area, they represented 'no danger to our plans, in terms both of security and development'. Accepting them as citizens would also look good vis-à-vis the outside world, he argued. The Foreign Ministry came round to Hanegbi's way of thinking: It began to regard a well publicised ceremony in which the beduin sheikhs declared allegiance to the Jewish state as a boon to Israel's efforts to parry international demands that it give up its claim to the Negev (most of which was still in Arab hands).[158] The IDF Negev Brigade, too, began to come round. On 25 November, OC Nahum Sarig informed his Seventh Battalion that 'the tribal heads' desire to accept Israeli protection . . . was politically important' and enjoined the battalion not to harm the tribes or their property.[159]

A ceremony of sorts duly took place on 18 November. Sixteen sheikhs offered to submit to Jewish rule and formally requested permission to stay. The officials did not respond, except to ask for the request in writing.[160] Weitz feared that important settlement and agricultural interests were being sacrificed for short-term political gain. He wrote Ben-Gurion that it was best that the beduin were not around. But, 'if political requirements' compelled leaving them in Israel, then they should be 'concentrated' in a specific, limited area.[161]

It was Weitz's line of retreat that was eventually adopted. On 25 November, Ben-Gurion met with his top Arab affairs and military advisers, including Yadin and Avner. Allon and Hanegbi favoured allowing loyal beduins to stay – but to concentrate them in an area east of Beersheba, far from the border. Shimoni asked: 'If [we] assume that reducing the number of Arabs [in Israel] is good for us – why [make an exception of] the beduin?' Weitz argued that leaving the beduin in place would result in a host of problems. ('[W]e will have to care for [their] food, camels, rice. We will have to worry about protecting them . . . If we formulate a development plan for the Negev – they will be in the way.')

Ben-Gurion ruled that military rather than political or agricultural considerations should determine policy. The decision was left in the hands of the IDF.[162]

Five days later, on 30 November, the Allon–Weitz approach became official policy. IDF General Staff Division, together with Weitz and Allon, decided to leave 'the friendly beduin', in three tribal concentrations, two between Beersheba and Dawayima and the third north of Nevatim-Kurnub. Beduin youngsters would be inducted in the IDF.[163]

But before the 'friendly' beduin could be moved to the new concentration areas (soon to be known as *eizor hasayig* or the limited or fenced area), Israel launched Operation Horev. Between 22 December and 7 January 1949, the IDF drove the Egyptian Army out of the western Negev and surrounded most of it in the Gaza Strip. Its annihilation, in a matter of days, was only averted by forceful Anglo-American diplomatic intervention, which led to a ceasefire and Egyptian agreement to armistice talks, previously taboo, with Israel.

The new conquests resulted in the incorporation of thousands of additional beduin and to renewed movement by beduin from Sinai into the Negev. Additional tribes, including the 'Azazme, most of which had supported the Egyptians during the war, now asked for Israeli protection (*khasut*) and to pledge allegiance.[164] A few months later, during Operation 'Uvda, in early March 1949, when two IDF columns swept southwards from Beersheba and occupied the central and southern Negev down to the Gulf of 'Aqaba (Gulf of Eilat), the troops were ordered 'to expel all the beduin who had not accepted IDF protection [*khasut*] . . .'.[165] It is unclear whether any, indeed, were expelled though additional beduin certainly came under Israeli control.

During 1949, thousands of beduin living south and west of Beersheba were moved to the concentration areas east and northeast of town.[166] But elsewhere in the Negev the paucity of security forces, the relative vastness of the area and the beduins' migratory habits meant that Israel was left with a major and continuing problem. In January, the head of the Military Government reported 'a massive flow' of beduins back to Israeli-held territory; the beduins felt 'that there was no government or supervision'.[167] Some engaged in smuggling, theft,[168] inter-tribal raiding and, occasionally, sabotage.[169] Periodically, after incidents, Israeli forces swept parts of the northern Negev, destroyed houses and tents,[170] and expelled tribes and sub-tribes.[171] A major expulsion to the West Bank took place in early November, with some 1,500–2,500 beduins being pushed across the border south of Hebron. The expulsion was triggered by the murder, a few days before, of five members of Kibbutz Mishmar Hanegev. The troops first separated the men from the women, searched for arms, and then informed the assembled tribe that Israel was refusing to grant them protection and that they must leave the state within

24 hours.[172] A similar expulsion occurred on 2 September 1950, when, according to the United Nations, some 4,000 beduin were reportedly driven into Egyptian-held Sinai. Israel said the true figure was in 'the hundreds' and that they were 'infiltrees'.[173]

During 1949, the status of the beduins granted protection – initially numbering some '10,000' – remained precarious. Many had been given Israeli citizenship and ID cards; others had not. Their number continuously grew. By mid-1950, according to the IDF, there were '35,000' in the Negev, '20,000' of them protected.[174] Yehoshu'a Palmon, the prime minister's adviser on Arab affairs, wanted to restrict the number getting citizenship. He wrote: 'In my opinion one must keep down as much as possible the number with permanent [ID] cards and to give the majority of those recently registered [only] temporary residence permits.'[175] But the military in the Negev, no doubt with Hanegbi prodding them, sought to clarify the situation and bring closure to the problem. All the beduin given protection should be treated as 'citizens of Israel', wrote the Negev District HQ.[176] Most apparently were.

The last major problem in the south was the Arab concentration in al Majdal (Ashkelon), whose pre-war population had been around 10,000. Almost all had fled their homes in October–November 1948. By early 1949, due to infiltrating returnees and refugees from the area, the town had more than 2,000 inhabitants; by the end of the year, the number had swelled to '2,600'.[177] The Arab inhabitants were placed under military government, concentrated and sealed off with barbed wire and IDF guards in a small, built-up area commonly known as the 'ghetto'.[178] In December 1948, the authorities approved the settlement in the town of 3,000 Jews; hundreds of families moved in during 1949. Outright eviction of the Arabs was ruled out for political reasons but the settlement authorities wanted more space and houses.[179]

Already in January 1949, Allon urged the General Staff to approve the transfer of the registered Arab inhabitants inland, to Isdud or Yibna, and the rest to the Gaza Strip. The town was 'too close to the [Egyptian] front lines . . . [and] served as a base for enemy infiltration and for small hostile actions . . .'.[180] But Ben-Gurion turned down the request 'for the time being'.[181] When Moshe Dayan became OC Southern Command, in early November 1949, he renewed the campaign. On 14 November, Dayan submitted a detailed proposal for the transfer of the Arabs to sites inside Israel. He repeated Allon's arguments and added that a port city for the Negev was to be built in Majdal.[182] The IDF CGS approved, adding that the town served as a way station for Arabs infiltrating to Jaffa and Ramle and 'the Arab inhabitants of Majdal hope for the return of Arab rule to their city'.[183] In December, Ben-Gurion agreed[184] and on 14 January 1950 the matter was decided, with the stipulation that the transfer 'should be carried out without coercion'.[185]

The matter was not brought before the Cabinet, and it is not clear when and how Southern Command switched the prospective refugees' destination from sites inside Israel to the Egyptian-ruled Gaza Strip. What is clear is that during the following months, the authorities, spearheaded by Major Yehoshu'a Varbin, the military governor of Majdal, employing carrots and sticks, applied subtle and not-so-subtle pressure, and offered incentives, to obtain the population's evacuation. Israel's trade union federation, the Histadrut, and the Israel Communist Party tried unsuccessfully to stem or limit the transfer. Many, perhaps most, of Majdal's Arabs, who were and felt isolated, wanted to rejoin their families, who had fled during 1948 to the Gaza Strip. The Israelis bolstered this with oppressive restrictions on movement and employment and a readiness to exchange Israeli pounds for Palestine pounds (used in the Gaza Strip) at favourable rates. During February–March 1950, more than 100 Arabs were transported from Majdal to the Gaza Strip. But the transfer formally began on 14 June, when IDF trucks moved '38' inhabitants to the Gaza border. During the following months, Majdal's Arabs were gradually trucked to the Strip; at the same time, about 200 refugees, originally from Qatra, were transferred inland, to Ramle. The last two transports left for Gaza and Lydda on 12 and 13 October. At last, Dayan and Varbin had achieved an Arab-free Majdal (or Ashkelon, as it was to be renamed). The last transports were of families who had sought to remain in Israel and a measure of coercion – of the sort used in Faluja and 'Iraq al Manshiya – had had to be employed (shots during the night, selective arrests of local leaders, IDF soldiers banging on doors with rifle butts and shouting 'get out, go to Gaza').[186] Majdal was the last big post-1948 transfer operation.

THE CENTRE

Few Arab villagers were left on the Israeli side of the ceasefire lines separating the new State and the areas held by Jordan and the Iraqi forces in the Triangle when the major bouts of fighting ended in central Palestine in mid-1948. Most of the empty pre-1948 villages were demolished by the IDF to render the sites unattractive to would-be returnees. Along the front lines, the army continuously harassed Arab cultivators and barred infiltrators; Israel, for both military and political reasons, wanted as few Arabs inside the country, behind the lines, as possible, and feared saboteurs and spies. The purpose of most of the infiltrations was agricultural or to return home or theft; very few were terroristic.[187] But there was sporadic terrorism. A cluster of terrorist infiltrations at the end of 1948 triggered the first of the post-war IDF retaliatory strikes, on the night of 2\3 January 1949, against the Iraqi-held village of Tira, northwest of Qalqilya, and neighbouring military positions.[188]

The Israeli–Jordanian armistice agreement of 3 April 1949 provided for minor frontier changes, with a few small areas (in the Beisan Valley and southwest of the Hebron Hills) being transferred from Israel to Jordan, and two larger strips, along Wadi 'Ara and between Baqa al Gharbiya and Kafr Qasim, being ceded to Israel. In the secret negotiations with Abdullah and his emissaries, Israel had demanded that the Arabs cede territory to widen Israel's vulnerable Coastal Plain 'waist' and almost openly threatened military action if Jordan did not accede. Abdullah feared that a renewal of full-scale war would lose him all of the West Bank. The British *chargé d'affaires* in Amman, Christopher Pirie-Gordon, compared Abdullah's cession of territory under military threat to Czech President Hacha's capitulation to Hitler in March 1939.[189] Abdullah and the British feared that the cession, which involved handing over 15–16 villages to Israeli rule, would precipitate a new wave of refugees, 12,000–13,000 strong. It was to guard against this that Article VI, clause 6, of the Israel–Jordan armistice agreement explicitly protected the villagers against expulsion and expropriation.[190]

But the Americans, British and Jordanians suspected that Israel, following the Arab withdrawal from the ceded areas scheduled for May, would engineer the departure of the villagers (à la Faluja and 'Iraq al Manshiya). The British Consul-General in Jerusalem Sir Hugh Dow, for instance, thought that the United Nations Relief for Palestine Refugees 'would do well to prepare for a further 20,000 [refugees] . . . [They] will almost certainly be driven out on some pretext or other.'[191] US Secretary of State Dean Acheson instructed McDonald to propose to the Israeli government to issue public reassurances to the villagers that they would be well treated.[192] At the same time, the withdrawing Jordanians themselves took steps to allay the villagers' fears. Brigadier Ahmad Bey Khalil, the Jordanian military governor of the Triangle (formerly of Haifa), pleaded with Israeli representatives that Tel Aviv broadcast assurances 'by wireless that [the civilians] would come to no harm should they remain in Israel . . . He . . . begged that no incidents occur that would discourage Arabs . . . to remain in Israel.' IDF intelligence reported (and advised?) from mid-April that the Arabs 'live in great fear of our "barbarity" and it would take little to persuade them to abandon their lands'.[193]

Israel reassured the United States that nothing would happen to the villagers. Tel Aviv did not want to jeopardise the cession or damage relations with Washington. Eytan told McDonald that Tel Aviv was 'keenly anxious' for the villagers to stay as Israel did not wish to further aggravate the refugee situation and that if these villagers were to stay, it would serve as proof 'to the world that [the] mass exodus [from] other [previously] captured areas was more [the] fault [of the] hysterical Arabs . . . than [of the] occupying forces'. Eytan said that the troops who would take over the ceded areas were being thoroughly briefed about how to behave.[194] A fortnight later, McDonald conveyed Acheson's and Truman's concern directly to Sharett. The Ambassador asked that Israel reassure the inhabitants and cautioned that harming them might damage the continuing secret Israeli–Jordanian peace negotiations. Sharett told McDonald that all would be well.[195] But Sharett's thinking in fact took another tack altogether:

> We have inherited a number of important villages in the Sharon and Shomron and I imagine that the intention will be to be rid of them [i.e., the inhabitants], as these sites are on the border. Security interest[s] dictate to be rid of them. [But] the matter [in light of the American diplomatic warnings] is very complicated.[106]

The cession passed relatively smoothly. There were almost no expulsions or transfers or untoward pressures. Indeed, in advance of the entry of the troops, Carmel, OC Northern Front – responsible for Wadi 'Ara – had specifically instructed: 'The explicit desire of the state of Israel is that no soldier will harm the Arab population . . . All . . . are obliged to careful and kind behaviour . . . in the areas passing under our control . . .' Violators would be severely punished, he warned.[197] Identical orders were issued by OC 16th Brigade, which took over the Kafr Qasim area.[198]

The troops began to move in on 6 May; the inhabitants generally greeted them 'with joy and blessings'.[199] In Qalansuwa, the new military governor, 'it was rumoured', threatened the inhabitants with 'expulsion' if they did not hand over a certain number of rifles and machineguns. The frightened villagers went to Tulkarm and bought some weapons – but on the way back encountered a Legion patrol and some people died in the ensuing skirmish. The Israeli troops apparently evicted a number of families from isolated homes southwest of Qalqilya (Pardes Ha'otzar and Nabi Yamin) and north of Taiyiba (Fardisiya).[200]

But these were exceptions. Political considerations – generated by the repeated American warnings against the backdrop of the deadlocked Lausanne Conference – prevailed over the military's desire for Arabless border areas. Apparently it was felt that there was no 'clean' way to 'persuade' the Arabs to leave. The inhabitants of the main villages – Baqa al Gharbiya, al Taiyiba, Qalansuwa, Kafr Qasim, al Tira and the Wadi 'Ara villages – did not budge and were allowed to stay. As Sharett put it on 28 July:

> This time . . . the Arabs learned the lesson; they are not running away. [And] it is not possible in every place to arrange what some of our boys engineered in Faluja [where] they chased away the Arabs after we signed an . . . international commitment . . . There were warnings from the UN and the US in this matter . . . [There were] at least 25–30,000 . . . whom we could not uproot.'[201]

But an exception was made of the refugees living in and around the villages. For example, 1,200–1,500 such refugees[202] living in and around Baqa al Gharbiya on the night of 27 June were 'forcefully and brutally' (in Sharett's phrase)[203] pushed across the border into the Triangle.

The Israel–Jordan MAC, chaired by the United Nations, investigated the incident during the following months. Israel argued that the armistice agreement protected only local inhabitants, not refugees temporarily resident in the ceded areas and that, in any case, it was the Baqa al Gharbiya *mukhtar* rather than the Israelis who had ordered them out. In September, the MAC – meaning its United Nations chairman – ruled in favour of the Israeli interpretation (save regarding 36 of the expellees, who were deemed permanent inhabitants who had been wrongfully expelled).

Not unnaturally, given the character of his relationship with the Israeli authorities, the *mukhtar* confirmed the Israeli arguments. He testified that

> the village council decided for economic reasons [that the village] could not maintain the many refugees . . . and [therefore] told them to leave. No order to do this had been received from the Israeli military governor or from any other Israeli official. In certain cases, when refugees did not agree to leave, the *mukhtar* told them that this was an order from of the [Israeli] governor . . . (despite the fact that such an order had not been issued by the governor).[204]

One Israeli analysis later explained that the refugees had left 'under pressure from the local inhabitants' because they had been a burden, in terms of accommodation and employment, 'they had stolen from the local inhabitants, they had stolen from the Jewish neighbours [in neighbouring settlements], [and they had] been engaged in smuggling'. The presence of the refugees, as the Baqa al Gharbiya notables saw things, had undermined the development of good relations between their village and the Israeli authorities.[205]

While the commission's decision hung in the balance, Israel made it clear that, if forced to take the expellees back, they, the refugees, 'would regret it' (in Dayan's phrase). General Riley, the United Nations chief of observers in Palestine, privately described this as 'typical' of Israel's use of threats during negotiations.[206] At the same time, clandestinely, Israeli intelligence mounted a campaign to persuade the expellees now in the Triangle not to agree to return. 'We are busy spreading rumours among the Arab refugees', Dayan wrote to Sharett,

> that whoever is returned to Israel will not receive assistance from the Red Cross . . . [and] would be returning against the wishes of the Israeli government [and, therefore,] there is no chance that he would return one day to his [original] land. We therefore hope that . . . most of them will refuse to return.

In other words, IDF intelligence had disseminated the rumour that there would one day be a mass refugee repatriation but that those Baqa expellees returning 'prematurely' and against Israel's wishes would 'suffer for it'. The expellees duly told the UN investigators that they were not eager to return. Friedlander, Dayan's deputy on the MAC, observed that 'these rumours . . . are easily accepted by the Arabs . . .'.[207]

The 'pro-Israel' vote at the MAC meeting on 15–16 September was influenced at least in part by the Israeli threat of mistreatment of the refugees should they be repatriated to Israel.[208] But the matter didn't end there: The Jordanian government, which had to host the refugees, now took up their cause. A special Jordanian–Israeli committee continued to discuss the matter, Israel ultimately agreeing to take back several dozen. The Israelis argued that the problem was that the inhabitants of Baqa were loath to take the refugees back.[209]

The case of the Baqa refugees was not unique (even if it alone 'benefited' from thorough documentation). In the course of the takeover of the ceded central area, the authorities evicted to the West Bank thousands of additional refugees who were temporarily living in and near the main villages. As in the case of Baqa, the evictions were carried out by remote control or proxies. The Military Government

> informed the [permanent] inhabitants that they must not employ the refugees, [must] raise difficulties in housing them and refuse to accept their children into the schools. . . . The government would regard it favourably if they [i.e., the inhabitants] pressured them to leave the area. The inhabitants took the hint and acted accordingly and within a fortnight close to 8,500 refugees left the area.[210]

One last matter remained: The dozens of small inhabited border-hugging sites (*khurab*) in Wadi 'Ara and the 'Little Triangle' (as the ceded area from Baqa al Gharbiya to Kafr Qasim was now designated). The population in each *khirbe* ranged from 13 to 250 souls. Between May and November 1949, the authorities gradually and systematically transferred most of the *khurab* inhabitants in the southern area (Kafr Qasim-Baqa al Gharbiya) to the large, neighbouring villages (inside Israel). The operation was carried out 'mainly' for security reasons, Major Goel Levitzky, of the Military Government, explained.[211]

IDF General Staff\Operations approved the depopulation of the *khurab* but instructed that 'an effort should be made to carry out the eviction without force'. But if force proved necessary, the Military Government was authorised to use it.[212] By December, there remained about two dozen such sites (with some 1,500 inhabitants altogether) – two near Jaljuliya (Kafr Bara and Khirbet Khureish), eight near Baqa al Gharbiya and Qaqun (including Khirbet al Jalama, Khirbet Ashayir, Khirbet Ibthan, Khirbet ash Sheikh Meisar, Khirbet Bir al Isyar, and Khirbet al Yamma), two near 'Ara, and 11 around Umm al Fahm (including Khirbet Salim, 'Ein Ibrahim, 'Iraq ash Shabab, Khirbet al Biyar and Qasr Sharayi). The regional Military Government officers proposed that the inhabitants be transferred, along with the inhabitants of the Israeli half of the village of Barta'a (with 450 inhabitants), to the neighbouring, large villages (Umm al Fahm, Baqa al Gharbiya) in two stages, first the ones closer to the border, then the ones further inland. The officers were mainly troubled by the *khurab*'s facilitation of 'infiltration [and] espionage'.[213] Most of the sites were emptied during the following months. One of the largest ones, Khirbet al Jalama, with about 225 inhabitants, was emptied on 1 March 1950, but the inhabitants petitioned the High Court of Justice, which in June 1952 ruled in their favour, authorising their return. But before they were able to, members of Kibbutz Lehavot Haviva (Mapam), who had settled on the *khirbe*'s lands, on 11 August 1953 blew up the remaining Arab houses. The kibbutzniks said they had been ordered by the army to carry out the demolition and the IDF had given them funds for this purpose. The army denied this. Be that as it may, the destruction assured that the inhabitants would never return to the site.[214]

The clearing of the borders of Arab communities following the hostilities was initiated by the IDF but, like the expulsions of the months before, was curbed by limitations imposed by the civilian leadership and was never carried out consistently or comprehensively.

Even the initial border-clearing operation in the north in November 1948, which set as its goal an Arab-free strip at least five kilometres deep, was carried out without consistency or political logic. Maronite communities such as Kafr Bir'im and Mansura were evicted while Muslims in Tarshiha and Fassuta were allowed to stay. Intervention by 'softhearted' Israeli leaders, such as Shitrit and Ben-Zvi, succeeded in halting some evictions and expulsions. Consideration of future Jewish–Druse, Jewish–Circassian and Jewish–Christian relations, as well as fears for Israel's image abroad, played a decisive role in mobilising the various civilian bureaucracies against undifferentiating, wholesale expulsions and, in some cases, changed expulsion to Lebanon to eventual resettlement inside Israel.

In terms of the army's independence in expelling or evicting Arab communities, November 1948 marked a watershed. The Lebanese border operation was ordered by OC Northern Front, probably after receiving clearance from Ben-Gurion. It was not weighed or debated in advance by any civilian political body. Thereafter, the IDF almost never acted alone and independently; it sought and had to obtain approval and decisions from the supreme civilian authorities, be it the full Cabinet or one or more of the various ministerial and inter-departmental committees. The IDF's opinions and needs, which defined in great measure Israel's security requirements, continued to carry great weight in decision-making councils. But they were not always decisive and the army ceased to act alone.

The army wanted Arab-free strips along all of Israel's frontiers. It failed to achieve such a strip on the Lebanese border (Rihaniya, Jish, Hurfeish, Fassuta, Tarshiha and Mi'ilya remained) as it was to fail – even more decisively – along the armistice line with Jordan, west of the Triangle. With respect to the villages ceded by Jordan in spring-summer 1949, international political considerations outweighed the security arguments. Given the state of Israeli–United Nations and Israeli–United States relations against the backdrop of the Lausanne talks, Israel's leaders found that they could not allow themselves the luxury of causing the type of friction a new wave of expulsions would have generated. The American warnings on this score had been explicit. The fact that peace talks were proceeding intermittently with King Abdullah and that Tel Aviv still hoped for a breakthrough no doubt also influenced decision-making.

In this sense, the very success of the intimidation operation in Faluja and 'Iraq al Manshiya in early March 1949, which precipitated the flight of 3,000 or so villagers, proved counterproductive. It put the Arabs, the United Nations and the United States on alert against a repeat performance along the border with the Triangle, where there were many more Arabs.

But where politics did not interfere, the army's desire for Arab-clear borders was generally decisive. Arab villages along the border meant problems in terms of infiltration, espionage and sabotage. When the villages were semi-abandoned, as was generally the case, it meant a continuous return and resettlement in the empty houses, thus consolidating the Arab presence in the area and increasing their numbers in the country. To this was added the interest of the Jewish agricultural and settlement bodies in more land and settlement sites and the interest of the various government ministries (health, finance, minorities) to be rid of the burden of economically problematic, desolate, semi-abandoned villages. These interests generally dovetailed.

The period November 1948 – March 1949 saw a gradual shift of emphasis from expulsion out of the country to eviction from one site to another inside Israel: What could be done without penalty during hostilities became increasingly more difficult to engineer in the following months of truce and armistice. There was still a desire to see Arabs leave the country and occasionally this was achieved (as at Faluja and Majdal), albeit through persuasion, selective intimidation, psychological pressure and financial inducement. The expulsion of the Baqa al Gharbiya refugees was a classic of the genre, with the order being channelled through the local *mukhtar*. But generally, political circumstances ruled out brute expulsions. Eviction and transfer of communities from one site to another inside Israel was seen as more palatable and more easily achieved.

Side by side with the border-clearing operations Israel also mounted recurrent sweeps in the villages in the interior designed to root out illegal returnees and to 'shut down' minimally inhabited villages (such Umm al Faraj and Bir'im after November 1948). The aim was to keep down the Arab population as well as to curtail various types of trouble that infiltrators augured. In a narrow sense, political, demographic, agricultural and economic considerations rather than military needs seem to have been decisive. The presence of Arabs in a half-empty village, given the circumstances, meant that the village would probably soon fill out with returnees. Completely depopulating the village and levelling it or filling the houses with Jewish settlers meant that infiltrators would have that many less sites to return to. In complementary fashion, filling out half-empty Arab villages (as happened at Tur'an, Mazra'a and Sha'b) with the evicted population of other villages meant that these host villages would be 'full up' and unable to accommodate many infiltrees.

Excluding the Negev beduin, it is probable that the number of Arabs kicked out of, or persuaded to leave, the country in the border-clearing operations and in the internal anti-infiltration sweeps during 1948–1950 was around 20,000. If one includes expelled northern Negev beduin, the total may have been as high as 30,000–40,000.

ENDNOTES

1. Northern Front to 9th and 2nd brigades, 09:30 hours, 10 Nov. 1948, IDFA 4858\49\\495. While this initial order spoke of 'five' kilometres, in practice there was a measure of flexibility to the policy. Two months later, Major El'ad Peled wrote, 'in the name of OC Northern Front': 'After the conquest of the Galilee, we ruled that citizens-inhabitants would be evacuated from an area 5–7 kilometres [deep] along the Lebanese border in order to facilitate border security and prevent infiltration' (Peled to General Staff\Staff Division, 15 Jan. 1949, IDFA 1860\50\\60).
2. Intelligence officer, 9th Brigade, 'Order', 7 Nov. 1948, IDFA 715\49\\16.
3. Oussetzky-Lazar, 'Iqrit and Bir'im', 8–9.
4. Oussetzky-Lazar, 'Iqrit and Bir'im', 8.
5. Ehrlich, *Lebanon*, 312; and Oussetzky-Lazar, 'Iqrit and Bir'im', 8.
6. 'Temporary Surrender Instrument', signed by four notables, undated, HA 55\31.
7. 'Decisions of the Meeting of the Provisional Government', 24 Nov. 1848, KMA-ACP 9\9\1; and private information.
8. Quoted in Ehrlich, *Lebanon*, 310.
9. Oussetzky-Lazar, 'Iqrit and Bir'im', 9.
10. Intelligence officer, 9th Brigade, to all battalions, 22:00 hours, 14 Nov. 1948, IDFA 7249\49\\286.
11. Segev, *First Israelis*, 73; and Shimoni to Eytan, 'On Problems of Policy in the Galilee and Northern Border . . .', 18 Nov. 1948, ISA FM 186\17.

12. An intelligence report from this period (Aharon Schweig, 'Weekly Report on Arab Affairs', 5 Dec. 1948, IDFA 240\54\\383) states: 'The Maronite Christians etc. uprooted from the Northern border to some villages were told by the army that they were being transferred to the new places only temporarily. This was, of course, only a sweetener to facilitate their transfer [*glulat hamtaka leha'avaratam*], but they are still awaiting their return to their places. It is desirable to inform them that it is better that they begin to cultivate the abandoned fields in their new places so that they have what to eat in the next season and that they not become a burden upon the State.'

13. Unsigned, untitled memorandum (missing first page) on Kafr Bir'im, undated but probably from late summer 1950, IDFA 848\91\\105; Shitrit to defence minister, 2 Dec. 1948, ISA FM 2564\9; and unsigned, 'Instructions Regarding Behaviour Toward the Arabs of Kafr Bir'im', 24 Nov. 1948, IDFA 7249\49\\286.

14. 11th Battalion\Intelligence to 9th Brigade\Operations, etc., 14 Nov. 1948, IDFA 1012\49\\71.

15. 11th Battalion\Intelligence to 9th Brigade\Operations, etc., 24 Nov. 1948, IDFA 1012\49\\71.

16. 92nd Battalion, 'Activities Report No. 97', 24 Dec. 1948, IDFA 4859\49\\32.

17. Unsigned, 'Instructions Regarding Behaviour Toward the Arabs of Kafr Bir'im', 24 Nov. 1948, IDFA 7249\49\\286.

18. Minority Affairs Ministry office, Safad, 'Weekly Report for Week 25–30 November 1948', undated, ISA MAM 302\73; Shitrit to Ben-Gurion, 2 Dec. 1948, ISA FM 2564\9; and Ben-Zvi to Ben-Gurion, 14 Oct. 1949, ISA FM 2570\1.

19. Peled ('in the name of OC Northern Front') to General Staff\Staff Division, 15 Jan. 1949, IDFA 1860\50\\60, complained that the 'evacuation . . . had been almost completed' when the CGS's halt order arrived. The inhabitants of Fassuta and Jish (600 Maronites) and 20 inhabitants of Bir'im remained in place.

20. Quoted in Ehrlich, *Lebanon*, 310. Ehrlich conjectures that the freeze was imposed by Ben-Gurion.

21. Entry for 16 Nov. 1948, DBG-YH III, 828. The passage would seem to imply that Carmel had decided on the border-clearing policy and operation without Ben-Gurion's knowledge or approval – and that might be why Ben-Gurion inserted it in his diary. He did the same in Cabinet. He told the ministers that, the week before, he had 'demanded' that Carmel stop the expulsions (see protocol of Cabinet meeting, 24 Nov. 1948, ISA). But it seems unlikely that Carmel would have decided to expel to Lebanon the inhabitants of a string of villages, including Christians, off his own bat, without Ben-Gurion's explicit permission. Such an expulsion would have been contrary to the Ben-Gurion–Ayalon directive of 6 July 1948. It is possible, however, that Carmel felt that he did not need any further permissions, beyond what he had received from Ben-Gurion on 31 October.

Ben-Gurion's diary entry raises the problem of when exactly the freeze order was issued. The quoted Haifa District order of the 15th implies that it was already in place, and being acted upon, before the Ben-Gurion–Carmel meeting of the 16th.

22. On 24 Nov. 1948, Shapira tabled a question about the plight of Bir'im's refugees. Ben-Gurion avoided a clear reply (protocol of Cabinet meeting, 24 Nov. 1948, ISA).

23. Entry for 19 Nov. 1948, DBG-YH III, 832.

24. This was the gist of Shimoni's complaint in Shimoni to Sasson, 12 Nov. 1948, ISA FM 2570\11, and Shimoni to Eytan, 18 Nov. 1948, ISA FM 186\17. See also Ehrlich, *Lebanon*, 313–14.

25. Shimoni to Eytan, 'On Problems of Policy . . .'; 18 Nov. 1948, ISA FM 186\17.

26. Northern Front Operations officer to Military Governor Western Galilee, etc., 'Behaviour toward Inhabitants', 18 Nov. 1948, IDFA 4858\49\\495.

27. For example, see 9th Brigade HQ\Intelligence to Military Governor Galilee District, 6 Feb. 1949, IDFA 922\52\\194.

28. Untitled (first page missing) memorandum on Bir'im, IDFA 848\91\\105.

29. Bir'im notables to the director of the Arab Affairs Department, Interior Ministry, 4 July 1949, IDFA 922\52\\194.

30. Oussetzky-Lazar, 'Iqrit and Bir'im', 15.

31. Protocol of meeting of JNF directorate, 7 Dec. 1948, CZA KKL 10; entry for 10 Dec. 1948, Weitz, *Diary*, III, 364 (and protocols of meetings of Committee of Directorates of the National Institutions, reproduced on 399 and 401); protocol of meeting of Ministerial Committee for Abandoned Property, 17 Dec. 1948, ISA FM 2401\21aleph; and entry for 2 Jan. 1949, Weitz, *Diary*, III, 4.

32. Peled, 'in the name of OC Northern Front', to General Staff\Staff Division, 15 Jan. 1949, IDFA 1860\50\\60.

33. Military Government HQ to OC Northern Front, 27 Jan. 1949, IDFA 1860\50\\60. The decision to establish the committee may well have been triggered by the northern border evictions, which angered many in Mapam.

34. Captain Yisrael Krasnansky, Military Government Western Galilee and Haifa District, to Military Government HQ, 24 Oct. 1949, IDFA 922\52\\183.

35. Protocol of meeting of Ministerial Committee for Abandoned Property, 31 Dec. 1948, ISA FM 2401\21aleph.

36. See, for example, Yitah to Shitrit, 18 Jan. 1949; Yitah to Major 'Amir, 18 Jan. 1949; and Shitrit to Yitah, undated – all in ISA MAM 1319\42.

37. Thomas Bloodworth Jr., vice-consul, Haifa, to Secretary of State, 'Report of an Interview with Representatives of the AFSC', 7 June 1949, with enclosure: Charles Freeman, AFSC, 'Report on Evacuation of Residents from the Town of Tarshiha', 25 Mar. 1949, NA RG 84, Haifa Consulate, Classified Records, 350 – Political Affairs, 1949; and ? to Foreign Ministry, 25 Jan. 1949, a complaint about expulsions from Shafa 'Amr, Tarshiha and Mi'ilya. The expellees complained that the troops had robbed them before pushing them across the border. According to Giora Zeid, MAM, the 25 expelled from Mi'ilya were 'suspected of . . . passing information to the enemy' (Yitah to T. Ashbal, MAM, 14 Mar. 1949, ISA MAM 1319\40).

38. 'Zvi K.', Intelligence Service 3, Haifa Base, 'Weekly Summary for Department "Ayin" (16.1.49–23.1.49)', undated, IDFA 240\54\\383.

39. 'Zvi K.' 'Weekly Report for Department "Ayin" (23.1.49–30.1.49)', undated but with accompanying letter Intelligence Service 3, Haifa Base, to Military Governor Western Galilee, 6 Feb. 1949, IDFA 922\52\\1277.

40. 'Protocol of the Seventh Meeting of the Committee for Transferring Arabs from Place to Place', 21 Jan. 1949; and 'Protocol of the Tenth Meeting of the Committee for Transferring Arabs', 20 Mar. 1949 – both in ISA MAM 1322\22. The inter-departmental committee, set up in Nov. 1948, was chaired by Shitrit.

41. ? to 'Amir, 6 Mar. 1949, IDFA 922\52\\1334.

42. Thomas Bloodworth Jr. to Secretary of State, 'Developments in Israeli Controlled Arab Sections of Galilee', 10 June 1949, NA RG 84, Haifa Consulate, Classified Records 350 – Political Affairs, 1949; and unsigned, 'A Report on the Visit of Archbishop Hakim to Tarshiha', undated, ISA FM 2563\22.

43. Eytan to Sharett (New York), 4 Dec. 1949, ISA FM 2402\29.

44. Sheikh Attiya Juwayid to the Justice Minister, 'In the Name of the Oppressed', 9 June 1949, ISA JM 5667\25\gimel; and Haaretz, 7 Aug. 1949.

45. A. Weingrad to Galilee District Battalion 102, undated but from Feb. or early Mar. 1949, IDFA 170\54\\41. See also Hasson Goldberg to regions officer [Battalion] 102, 3 Feb. 1949; and Hasson Goldberg to regions officer [Battalion] 102, 10 Mar. 1949 – both in IDFA 170\54\\41.

46. Regions HQ Rosh Pina, Galilee District, to security officer [Goldberg], Ma'ayan Baruch, 12 Mar. 1949, IDFA 170\54\\41.

47. Security Officer, Intelligence Department 3, 9th Brigade, to Northern Front, Intelligence Department 3, 10 Apr. 1949, IDFA 1012\49\\72.

48. The evictions were investigated and are described in Lt. Colonel Baruch Rabinov to CGS, 'Report on the Investigation about the Transfer of the Arabs of the Villages of Khisas, Ja'una, Qeitiya', 30 Aug. 1949, HHA, Baruch Rabinov Papers.

49. Entry for 8 June 1949, HA-YND.

50. See Morris, 1948 and After, (rev. ed. 1994), Chapter V.

51. Protocol of meeting of Knesset Defence and Foreign Relations Committee, 29 June 1949, ISA, Defence and Foreign Relations Committee, 7561\4-aleph.

52. Ha'aretz, 7 Aug. 1949.

53. Richard Ford to Secretary of State, 11 Aug. 1949, NA RG 84, Tel Aviv Embassy, Dec. #571, Classified Records 1949.

54. The Khisas Arabs, assisted by Nahmani, were eventually moved from 'Akbara to a site of their own, in Wadi Hamam, northwest of Tiberias.

55. ISA, Documents, III, 725.

56. See, for example, Moshe Belhorn, Tiberias District Police HQ, to IDF, 5 Aug. 1949, ISA FM 2433\4.

57. Golani Brigade\Intelligence, 'The List of Arab Villages in Our Hands Conquered by the 12th Battalion', 25 June 1948, HA 105\114.

58. 'Ein Gev. Testimony of Ezra Klupfer', undated, IDFA 1235\52\\1.

59. See, for example, OC 8th Platoon to OC 'C' Company, 17 March 1949, IDFA 721\72\\389.

60. See E.L.M. Burns, Between Arab, 115-18. For more on Kirad al Baqqara and Kirad al Ghannama, see Morris, Birth, 353, note 24. See also Morris, Border Wars, 378-79.

61. See, for example, Military Governor Western Galilee to Northern Front HQ, 9 Nov. 1948, IDFA 260\51\\2.

62. Avner to defence minister, ? Feb. 1949, IDFA 1308\50\\485; and entry for 4 Jan. 1949, DBG–YH III, 926.

63. Protocol of meeting of Knesset Defence and Foreign Affairs Committee, 6 June 1949, ISA, Defence and Foreign Affairs Committee, 7561\3-aleph.

64. Haifa District HQ, 'Operational Order "Magrefa"', 21 Dec. 1948, IDFA 715\49\\16.

65. Intelligence officer 9th Brigade to Northern Front\Intelligence, etc., 'Weekly Report for 18.12.48–25.12.48', 25 Dec. 1948, IDFA 1012\49\\72.

66. 9th Brigade to 92nd Battalion, etc., ? Dec. 1948, IDFA 6309\49\\2.

67. Lt. Menahem Ziselman to Northern Front, 'Report on Operation "Zikuk"', 28 Dec. 1948, IDFA 260\51\\54. *Zikuk* is Hebrew for purification\refining.

68. Avner to defence minister, ? Feb. 1949, IDFA 1308\50\\485.

69. Intelligence officer, Military Government Western Galilee, to Military Governor Western Galilee, 2 Feb. 1949, IDFA 922\52\\820.

70. Nahariya District Officer to Military Governor Western Galilee, 22 Feb. 1949, IDFA 922\52\\820.

71. Intelligence officer, Western Galilee Military Government, to Military Governor Western Galilee, 'Report on Activities in the Western Galilee', 1 June 1949, IDFA 922\52\\183.

72. Intelligence officer, Battalion 300, to General Staff\Operations, 28 July 1949, IDFA 721\72\\859.

73. Representative of Israeli administration in Tarshiha to the military governor, 20 Mar. 1949, IDFA 922\52\\820.

74. The letter is quoted in Wendor, Nahariya District officer, to Major 'Amir, 11 Apr. 1949, IDFA 922\52\\820. A similar letter was sent by Kibbutz Ramat Yohanan to 'Amir complaining of 'Arab families who have resettled in [neighbouring] Hosha' – Ramat Yohanan to 'Amir, 24 Feb. 1949, IDFA 922\52\\1277.

75. Intelligence officer, Military Government Western Galilee, to military governor, Western Galilee, 1 June 1949, 'Report on Activities in Western Galilee', IDFA 922\52\\183.

76. Major Pinhas Weinstein to Northern Front\Operations, 13 Apr. 1949.

77. 'Zvi K.', Intelligence Service 3, Haifa Base, 'Weekly Report of Department "Ayin" (23.1.49–30.1.49)', IDFA 922\52\\1277. See also Intelligence Service 3, Haifa Base, to Military Governor, Western Galilee, "Ibillin Expellees Who have Returned to Their Village', 15 Feb. 1949, IDFA 922\52\\820, which recommended that the six persons named be expelled again, 'this time with their families and belongings'.

78. Captain Y. Krasnansky, security officer, Military Government Western Galilee, to Lt. Colonel Mor, 1 Mar. 1950, IDFA 1860\50\\60; and Special Correspondent, 'The Arabs of Ghabisiya in Western Galilee Were Forced to Leave their Homes,' *Al Hamishmar*, 30 Jan. 1950.

79. Western Galilee Settlements Bloc Committee, 'Communiqué . . . Regarding Ghabisiya . . . 27.2.50,' IDFA 1860\50\\60; and Special Correspondent (Yirmiyahu Shmueli, of Kibbutz Evron), 'The Arabs of Ghabisiya in Western Galilee Were Forced to Leave their Homes', *Al Hamishmar*, 30 Jan. 1950.

80. Unsigned, draft of a Knesset motion calling for the establishment of a committee of inquiry to probe the Ghabisiya (and Farradiya and Kafr 'Inan)

expulsions, undated, IDFA 1860\50\\60. It seems that the matter was never brought up in the Knesset plenum.

81. Western Galilee Settlements Bloc Committee, 'Communiqué . . . Regarding . . . Ghabisiya . . . 27.2.50', and Krasnansky to Mor, 1 Mar. 1950, both in IDFA 1860\50\\60.

82. See *Al Hamishmar* editorial, 'More on the Affair of the Arabs of Ghabisiya', 6 Feb. 1950.

83. Gershon Czerniak to IDF CGS, 11 Oct. 1951; Colonel Moyal, IDF Advocate-General, to head of Public Relations Branch, Defence Ministry, 21 Oct. 1951; and Moyal to CGS, 25 Oct. 1951 – all in IDFA 1559\52\\113.

84. Unsigned memorandum, possibly by Yosef Weitz, 'Transfer of Arab Population', undated but probably from Dec. 1948, ISA MAM 297\59; Sulz to Military Government HQ, 11 Jan. 1949, ISA MAM 308\38; and 'Protocol of the Third Meeting of the Committee for Transferring Arabs', 15 Dec. 1948, MAM 1322\22.

85. Military Governor Nazareth to Northern Front\Operations officer, 4 Dec. 1948, IDFA 260\51\\3.

86. Operations officer, 9th Brigade, to Battalion 91, etc., 4 Jan. 1949, IDFA 6309\49\\3.

87. Ninth Brigade\Intelligence to Northern Front\Intelligence, 7 Jan. 1949, IDFA 1012\49\\72.

88. A report on a tour of Arab villages in the Galilee by a representative of the Muslim Department, Ministry of Religious Affairs, 15–17 Dec. 1948, ISA MAM 307 gimel\41; 'Protocol of the First Meeting of the Committee for Transferring Arabs', 30 Nov. 1948, ISA MAM 1322\22; MAM office, Nazareth, to Shitrit, 13 Jan. 1949, ISA MAM 302\97; Kamen, 'After the Catastrophe', 32; Hanochi to the directors of the Anglo-Palestine Bank, 17 and 23 Feb. 1949, both in ISA AM gimel\19\aleph (part 2); and Agriculture Ministry, 'List of the Lands Leased for Cultivation for 1949\50 by 31 Oct. 1949', ISA AM aleph\19\aleph.

89. Avner to defence minister,? Feb. 1949, IDFA 1308\50\\485.

90. Military Government, Northern Front, to 79th Battalion, etc., 31 Jan. 1949, IDFA 1289\50\\277; and Intelligence Service 3, Haifa Base, 'Report to the Arab Department (30.1.49–6.2.49)', IDFA.

91. OC 79th Battalion to 'B' and 'C' companies, etc., 21 February 1949, IDFA 2289\50\\277; and Kamen, 'After the Catastrophe', 32.

92. 'Report of the Committee Probing the Problems of the Military Government and Its Future,' 3 May 1949, ISA FM 2401\19.

93. See, for example, Captain Shimon Oslander, 192nd Battalion, to Military Government HQ Northern Front, 14 June 1949, IDFA 922\52\\820; Krasnansky to Military Government Western Galilee, 6 July 1949, IDFA 922\52\\820; Krasnansky to HQ Military Government, 8 Nov. 1949, IDFA 741\72\\843; and Dov Yirmiya, Battalion 300, to OC Northern Command, 23 Nov. 1949, IDFA 922\52\\183.

94. See, for example, Krasnansky to Military Governor, Western Galilee, 8 June 1949, IDFA 922\52\\820.

95. Yadin to Southern Front, 28 Nov. 1948, and Coastal Plain District HQ to Battalion 151, etc., 30 Nov. 1948, both in IDFA 401\52\\12; and Southern Front\Operations to General Staff Division, 8 Dec. 1948, IDFA 922\75\\1025.

96. Coastal Plain District HQ to battalions 151 and '1 Volunteers', etc., 19:55 hours, 25 Nov. 1948, IDFA 6308\49\\141.

97. Coastal Plain HQ to Southern Front\Operations, 30 Nov. 1948, IDFA 1978\50\\1; and Southern Front\Operations to General Staff Division, 2 Dec. 1948, IDFA 922\75\\1025.

98. Coastal Plain District HQ to 89th Battalion, 17 Nov. 1948, IDFA 401\52\\12.

99. Fifty-first Battalion\Intelligence to Fifth Brigade\Intelligence, 29 Nov. 1948, IDFA 1041\49\\12; and Fifth Brigade\Intelligence, 'Summary of Activity 27–28.11.48', 29 Nov. 1948, IDFA 922\75\\1017.

100. Coastal Plain District HQ, 'Report on Sweep on 26.4.49', IDFA 2539\50\\14.

101. Fourth Brigade\Intelligence, 'Intelligence Annex to Operation Order 1\50 [for] Operation "Open Eyes"', 5 Mar. 1949, IDFA 863\50\\362.

102. Fourth Brigade\Operations to OC 44th Battalion, etc, "Operational Order 1\50 Operation "Open Eyes"', 5 Mar. 1949, IDFA 863\50\\362; and General Staff Division\Intelligence\1, 'Activity Report No. 47', 8 Mar. 1949, IDFA 401\52\\68.

103. General Staff Division\Intelligence\1, 'Daily Intelligence Report', 11 Mar. 1949, IDFA 401\52\\68.

104. Fourth Brigade\Operations to OCs 44th, 42nd and 145th brigades, etc, 'Operational Order 49\3', 10 Mar. 1949, IDFA 922\75\\949; and Major Simon to Col. Coverdale, 30 Aug. 1949, ISA FM 2431\7.

105. Lt Colonel Robin and W.O. van Wassenhove, UNMO Tel Aviv, to Tel Aviv Field Observers Group, 14 Mar. 1949, UNA DAG-13\3.3.1:18.

106. Fourth Brigade\Operations to OCs 44th Battalion, 42nd Battalion, etc., 'Operation Order 49\3', 10 Mar. 1949, IDFA 922\75\\949.

107. Major Simon to Col. Coverdale, 30 Aug. 1949, ISA FM 2431\7.

108. Shakliar to Southern Front HQ\Operations, "Report on Operation "Control"', 21 Mar. 1949, IDFA 2539\50\\15. A similar raid was carried out northeast of Dawayima on 20 Apr. 1949 (see Southern Front\Intelligence, 'Report on Sweep by 8th Battalion on 20.4.49', 24 Apr. 1949, IDFA 1062\53\\63).

109. Lt Col. Yishayahu Shakliar, Seventh Brigade, to OC 9th Battalion, 19 Mar. 1949, IDFA 2539\50\\15.

110. Simon and Vermeersch, 'Investigation Report', 24 Mar. 1949, UNA DAG-13\3.3.1:18. See also Col. Nickerson, deputy chief of staff, UNTSO, to Bunche, 23 Mar. 1949, UNA DAG-13\3.3.1:18.

111. General Staff Division\Intelligence\1, 'Activities Report No. 53', 2 May 1949, IDFA 880\49\\202.

112. Lt Col. Bergeon to chairman Jordan-Israel MAC, 28 Aug. 1949; and Lt Col. Bergeon to chairman, Jordan-Israel MAC, 29 Aug. 1949, both in ISA FM 2431\7. It would appear that the Israeli claim was a lie (see Major J.A.P. Simon to Col. G.B. Coverdale, IJMAC, 30 Aug. 1949, ISA FM 2431\7).

113. Lt Col. Bergeon to chairman Jordan–Israel MAC, 29 Aug. 1949, ISA FM 2431\7.

114. Simon to Coverdale, 30 Aug. 1949, ISA FM 2431\7.

115. Central Command\Operations to General Staff Division\Baruch, 5 July 1949, IDFA 1000\52\\7; and Major Ramati to S.M.9 (3), 'MAC Meeting

Held at Mandelbaum Gate on Wednesday 31st August 49 at 11:00 Hours', undated, ISA FM 2431\7.

116. Ramati to Intelligence Service 9 (3), 'MAC Meeting . . . 31st August . . .', ISA FM 2431\7.

117. Fifty-second Battalion\Intelligence to Fifth Brigade\Intelligence, ? Oct. 1948, IDFA 1041\49\\12; and Fifth Brigade\Intelligence, 'Summary of Activity', 24 Oct. 1948, IDFA 922\75\\900.

118. Statement by 'S. Mahmoud,' a refugee from Zakariya, in 'Al-Nakba', film by Benny Brunner.

119. Fourth Brigade\Intelligence, 'Daily Summary 18.12.48', 19 Dec. 1948, IDFA 6647\49\\48.

120. A. Bergman to 'the Government Committee for Settling Dispossessed Arabs', 16 Mar. 1949, ISA MAM 307\44; and Interior Ministry to Government Committee for the Settlement of Arab Refugees (inside Israel), 22 Mar. 1949, ISA MAM 307\44.

121. Entry for 14 Jan. 1950, Weitz, *Diary*, IV, 69.

122. Unsigned, 'Report on the Health Situation in the village of Zakariya, 14 Feb. 1950', ISA AM 2166 gimel\642.

123. Unsigned, 'Zakariya Village', undated, HA 8\201.

124. Prolov, OC Operations Department, to OC Military Government, 19 Mar. 1950, IDFA 2539\50\\14.

125. Interview with Mordechai Bar-On, the officer in charge of the eviction, 1999; and Palmon to British Commonwealth Department, Israel Foreign Ministry, 18 Oct. 1950, ISA FM 2402\11.

126. Eytan (Rhodes) to Sharett, 20 Feb. 1949, in ISA, *Documents* III, 257; and ibid., 257, note 143\1.

127. ISA, *Documents* III, 702–703,

128. Kan'ane and Madani, 'Faluja', 77.

129. Bunche to Shiloah, 4 Mar. 1949, ISA FM 2431\1

130. 'Visit of the Quaker Team to Faluja Feb. 26 to March 6th, Reported by Ray Hartsough, Edited by Corrinne Hardesty', undated, AFSCA – Foreign Service 1949, Palestinians – Faluja.

131. Bloodworth to Secretary of State, 7 June 1949, NA RG 84, Haifa Consulate, Classified Records 350 – Political Affairs 1949; and Department of International Institutions, Israel Foreign Ministry, to Director General, 13 Mar. 1949, ISA FM 2477\3. The Arab media alleged mendaciously that 'Men, women and children have been murdered in Faluja by the Jews' – the exaggeration, as usual, undermining the credibility of their complaints (All Palestine Government, Ministry of Foreign Affairs report, 19 Mar. 1949, PRO FO 371–75455).

132. The relevant cables – Allon ordering Rabin to carry out the operation and Rabin's subsequent report on the operation – remain classified in IDFA.

133. Yadin to Shiloah (Rhodes), 4 Mar. 1949, ISA FM 2431\1.

134. Sharett to Dori, 6 Mar. 1949, ISA FM 2425\7.

135. Allon to OC General Staff Division, 5 Mar. 1949, IDFA 1046\70\\434.

136. Entry for 28 Feb. 1949, Weitz, *Diary*, IV, 15; and Y. Berdichevsky to Machnes, 3 Mar. 1949, ISA MAM 297\60.

137. Entry for 22 and 26 Sep. 1948, Weitz, *Diary*, III, 343-44; and entry for 26 Sep. 1948, DBG-YH III, 721.

138. Entry for 6 Jan. 1949, DBG–YH III, 931. Faluja had become 'the Egyptian Tel-Hai', he wrote.
139. Allon to OC General Staff Division, 28 Feb. 1949, IDFA 1046\70\\434. Another cable (Allon to General Staff, 18:00 hours, 1 Mar. 1949), in the same file and probably dealing with the same matter, remains classified (as is Allon to General Staff, 10:45 hours, 5 Mar. 1949).
140. Allon to 1st, 3rd, 8th and 12th brigades, etc., 28 Feb. 1949, IDFA 6308\49\\16. But Allon explained this step to the General Staff by saying that he was doing it to protect the inhabitants from Israeli revenge attacks as a rumour was going around that villagers from 'Iraq al Manshiya had murdered three 3rd Brigade POWs (Allon to General Staff Division, 28 Feb. 1949, IDFA 1046\70\\434).
141. The relevant cable remains classified but the fact that Allon had to 'explain' what had happened, including the admission that three inhabitants had, indeed, been beaten, points to the contingent nature of the permission he had received from IDF General Staff.
142. A. Shefak to General Avner, 20 Mar. 1949, IDFA 1292\51\\68. Shefak thought that the sentries in 'Iraq al Manshiya had been too quick on the trigger.
143. Shefak to OC 141st Battalion, 29 Mar. 1949, IDFA 1292\51\\68.
144. Captain P. Levanon to HQ Military Government, 'Report on the Evacuation of 'Iraq al Manshiya', 24 Apr. 1949, IDFA 1292\51\\68; Major Amos Horev, 'Report of Southern Front HQ on the Evacuation of the Villagers of Faluja and 'Iraq al Manshiya', 1 June 1949, ISA FM 2426\5; and Zuckerman to HQ Military Government, 22 Apr. 1949, IDFA 1292\51\\68.
145. Rabin to 3rd Brigade, 26 Apr. 1949, IDFA 979\51\\17.
146. Report on the meeting between Ben-Gurion and the PCC, 7 Apr. 1949, ISA FM 2451\13; MacDonald to Secretary of State, 11 Apr. 1949, NA RG 84, Tel Aviv Embassy, Classified Records 1949, 350 – Israel; MacDonald to Secretary of State, 12 Apr. 1949, NA RG 84, Tel Aviv Embassy General Records 1949, 321.9 – Israel-Transjordan; MacDonald to Secretary of State, 2 May 1949, NA RG 84, Tel Aviv Embassy Classified Records; and protocol of meeting of Mapai Knesset Faction and Secretariat, statement by Sharett, 28 July 1949, LPA 2-11\1\1.
147. Shimoni to Political Department, 14 Oct. 1948, ISA FM 2564\10; and Shimoni to Sasson (Paris), 2 Nov. 1948, ISA FM 2570\11.
148. Hanegbi to General Avner, 'Following is a Report on the Conquest of the Town of Beersheba and the Situation in It During the First Days', 31 Oct. 1948, IDFA 121\50\\223.
149. Southern Front\Intelligence, 'Meeting of Intelligence Officers 16.11.48', undated, IDFA 1041\49\\17.
150. Protocol of Cabinet Meeting, 31 October 1948, ISA.
151. Negev Brigade to 9th Battalion, etc., 3 November 1948, IDFA 6298\49\\21.
152. 12th Brigade\Intelligence, 'Daily Intelligence Report – 6.11.48', 6 November 1948, IDFA 6308\49\\141.
153. Hanegbi to Avner, 'Weekly Activities Report 9-15.11.49', 18 November 1948, IDFA 721\72\\841.
154. Hanegbi, 'Report on the Meeting with the Beduin Sheikhs, 2 November 1948', 5 Nov. 1948, ISA MAM 297\60.

155. Shimoni to Sasson (Paris), 2 Nov. 1948, ISA FM 2570\11.

156. Berdichevsky to Machnes, 4 Nov. 1948, ISA MAM 297\60.

157. Estimates varied: Hanegbi to Avner, 'Weekly Activities . . .', 18 Nov. 1948, IDFA 721\72\\841, said '8–10,000'. But other IDF officers spoke at this time of '15–20,000,' with their number increasing and expected to reach '30,000 who can claim that they were at least neutral' during the war (see Southern Front\Intelligence, 'Meeting of Intelligence Officers 16.11.48', undated, IDFA 1041\49\\17).

158. Hanegbi to Avner, 'Weekly Activities . . .', 18 Nov. 1948, IDFA 721\72\\841; and Southern Front\Intelligence, 'Meeting of Intelligence Officers 16.11.48', IDFA 1041\49\\17.

159. 12th Brigade HQ to 7th Battalion, 25 Nov. 1948, IDFA 834\53\\380. Much to Sarig's anger, his troops continued to confiscate beduin flocks (see 12th Brigade HQ to 7th Brigade and Military Prosecutor, 17 Dec. 1948, IDFA 834\53\\380).

160. Entry for 30 Nov. 1948, segment of logbook of the Military Government HQ, IDFA 721\72\\841.

161. Entry for 18 Nov. 1948, CZA A246-14, 2526; entry for 19 Nov. 1948, DBG-YH III, 832; Weitz to Ben-Gurion, 19 Nov. 1948, Weitz Papers; and Shimoni to Sasson (Paris), 23 Nov. 1948, ISA FM 2570\11.

162. Entry for 25 Nov. 1948, DBG-YH III, 844-45; entry for 25 Nov. 1948, Weitz, *Diary*, III, 357.

163. Yadin to CGS, 3 Dec. 1948, IDFA 121\50\\223. There is a minute on the letter which reads: 'CGS, BG does not approve the summary [i.e., guidelines]. Nehemiah [Argov, Ben-Gurion's aide de camp], 9.12[.48]'. What Ben-Gurion objected to – or how the guidelines were subsequently revised, if at all – is unclear.

164. Hanegbi to Military Government HQ, 7 Jan. 1949, IDFA 834\53\\380.

165. Southern Front HQ\Operations to 1st, 3rd and 12th brigades, 'Operational Order "Uvda"', 1 Mar. 1949, IDFA 6308\49\\146.

166. Entry for 30 Nov. 1948, Weitz, *Diary*, III, 359; entry for 28 Jan. 1949, Weitz, *Diary*, III, 9; and Berdichevsky to Minority Affairs Ministry, 20 Feb. 1949, ISA MAM 297\60.

167. Avner to defence minister, etc., c.7 January 1949, IDFA 2433\50\\11.

168. For example, see 'Frisch', security officer, military governor, the Negev, 28 Feb. 1949, IDFA 834\53\\245.

169. For example, see 1st Brigade to 19th Battalion, 15 Jan. 1949, IDFA 128\51\\58.

170. For example, see Frisch to military governor, the Negev, 28 Feb. 1949, IDFA 834\53\\245.

171. See, for example, Allon to CGS, 17 June 1949, IDFA 1046\70\\434, for a planned expulsion of infiltrating tribes south of 'Auja al Khafir; and Avraham Shemesh to Negev military governor, undated but from Oct. 1949, IDFA 721\72\\843, for a description of the expulsion of the 'Ukbi tribe.

172. Shemesh to military governor, the Negev, undated but from early Nov. 1949, IDFA 721\72\\843; Negev District\Intelligence to Southern Command\Operations, 15 Nov. 1949, IDFA 2539\50\\14; A. Cadogan to FO, 21 Nov. 1949, and FO to UK Delegation UN, 26 Nov. 1949, both in PRO FO 371-75354 E14040\1017\31; Hugh Dow (Jerusalem) to FO,

24 Nov. 1949, Kirkbride (Amman) to FO, 24 Nov. 1949, and Knox Helm (Tel Aviv) to FO, 24 Nov. 1949 – all in PRO FO 371-75355

173. Israel Foreign Ministry, 'Information for the Israeli Missions Abroad: General Riley's Statement on Expulsion of Beduins [and] Israel's Reaction', 22 Sep. 1950, ISA FM 2402\12.

174. Negev District\Intelligence, 'Beduins – Protected Tribes', July 1950, IDFA 1627\94\\231. Earlier, in Jan. 1950, the military estimated that there were altogether in the Negev '18,000' beduin (see 'Protocol [of meeting of] Secondary Coordinating Committee from 25.1.50', IDFA 100243\52\\6).

175. Palmon to Military Government HQ, etc., 18 Dec. 1949, IDFA 100243\52\\3.

176. Negev District\Intelligence, 'Beduins – Protected Tribes', July 1950, IDFA 1627\94\\231.

177. Dayan to CGS, 14 Nov. 1949, IDFA 2539\50\\14.

178. See, for example, 'in the name of Rabbi Dr Abraham Deutsch', chief inspector of Agudat Yisrael schools, to Y. Slipper, Jewish Agency, Tel Aviv, 30 Jan. 1950, Ashkelon Municipal Archive, 37.

179. 'Protocol of the Ninth Meeting of the Committee for Transferring [Arabs]', 25 Feb. 1949, ISA MAM 1322\22; and entry for 23 Feb. 1949, CZA A246-14, 2584-85.

180. Allon to CGS, 26 Jan. 1949, IDFA 922\75\\1025.

181. Unsigned but probably by Moshe Sasson, Israel Foreign Ministry Middle East Affairs Department, 'Regarding the Matter of the Emptying of Migdal-Gad [i.e., Majdal] of Its Arab Inhabitants', 22 Oct. 1950, ISA FM 2436\5; and CGS's aide de camp to General Avner, 30 Jan. 1949, Avner to CGS's Bureau, 27 Feb. 1949, and CGS to Allon, ? Mar. 1949 – all three in IDFA 1308\50\\485.

182. Dayan to CGS, 14 Nov. 1949, IDFA 2539\50\\14.

183. Unsigned, 'Regarding the Emptying . . .', 22 Oct. 1950, ISA FM 2436\5.

184. Eytan (Tel Aviv) to Sharett (New York), 4 Dec. 1949, ISA FM 2402\29.

185. Entry for 14 Jan. 1950, CZA A246-15; and E.N. Mul to Burstein, 25 Oct. 1950, LA (Lavon) IV-219-163.

186. Mul to Burstein, 25 Oct. 1950, LA (Lavon) IV-219-163; and unsigned memorandum (but probably by Mul), 'For the Majdal Logbook', undated, LA (Lavon) IV-219-163. For the full story, see Morris, *Correcting*, 149–174 and, an earlier version, Morris, *1948 and After* (1994 ed.), chapter 10.

187. For example, see Central Front HQ to General Staff Division, 'Infiltration', 6 Mar. 1949, IDFA 880\49\\205, which details 59 cases of theft, 11 of attempted theft, two murders and two kidnappings during Dec. 1948 and Jan.-Feb. 1949 in Central Front's area.

188. Battalion 52\Intelligence to 5th Brigade\Intelligence, 'Summary of Activity for Night of 2\3.1', 3 Jan. 1949, IDFA 1041\49\\12; and Battalion 405, 'A' Battery, to Operations Officer\Artillery Corps, etc., 'Operation Report No. 3', undated, IDFA 880\49\\205.

189. Pirie-Gordon to FO, 24 Mar. 1949, PRO FO 371-75386 E3844\1095\31; FO to UK embassy, Washington, 24 Mar. 1949, PRO FO 371-75386 E3824\1095\31; Eytan to Sharett (New York), 23–24 Mar. 1949, *Documents* III, 468-74; and Stabler (Amman) to Secretary of State, 23 Mar. 1949, NA 501 BB. Palestine\3-2349.

190. Stabler (Amman) to Secretary of State, 23 Mar. 1949, NA 501 BB. Palestine\3–2349; Eytan to Sharett, 23–24 Mar. 1949, *Documents* III, 473; Pirie-Gordon to FO, 23 Mar. 1949, PRO FO 371-75386 E3824\1095\31; and Pirie-Gordon to FO, 24 Mar. 1949, PRO FO 371-75386 E3844\1095\31.

191. Dow to FO, 4 Apr. 1949, PRO FO 371-75424 E4458\1821\31.

192. Acheson to US Embassy, Tel Aviv, 4 Apr. 1949, NA RG 84, Tel Aviv Embassy, General Records 1949, 321.9 – Israel-Transjordan.

193. Unsigned but probably by Major Yehoshafat Harkabi, Sharett's military adviser, 'Secret: Intelligence Report', 19 Apr. 1949, ISA FM 2431\4.

194. McDonald to Secretary of State, 12 Apr. 1949, NA RG 84, Tel Aviv Embassy, General Records 1949, 321.9 – Israel-Transjordan.

195. McDonald to Secretary of State, 26 Apr. 1949, NA RG 84, Tel Aviv Embassy, Classified Records 1949, 350 – Israel.

196. Protocol of 'Meeting of the Secretariat of [Mapai Knesset] Faction with our Cabinet Ministers', 26 Apr. 1949, LPA 2, 11\1\6.

197. Carmel, 'Order of the Day for Operation 'Short-Cut'', 16 May 1949, IDFA 260\51\\64. The operational order itself also forbade any harm to the inhabitants' property and persons (see Northern Front to 7th Brigade, etc., 'Operational Order – "Short-Cut"', 14 May 1949, IDFA 4858\49\\495). See also Carmel, Northern Command, 'Order of the Day for Operation "Gilbo'a"', 15 July 1949, IDFA 260\51\\64.

198. Lt Col. Mishael Schechter [Shaham], 'Order of OC 16th Brigade', to all units, undated but c. 18 May 1949, IDFA 4775\49\\7.

199. Central Front HQ, 'Daily Intelligence Report A\91-93', 8 May 1948, IDFA 880\49\\202.

200. Central Front to Lt. Col. Moshe Dayan, 10 May 1949, IDFA 880\49\\202.

201. 'Protocol of the Meeting of the [Mapai Knesset] Faction and the Secretariat', 28 July 1949, LPA 2, 11\1\1.

202. Israel had been aware of the presence in the area of groups of refugees who hoped that, when the area was ceded to Israel, they, once inside Israel, would be able to go back to their original villages (see General Staff Division\Intelligence Department 3, to 7th Brigade\Operations, etc., 15 May 1949, IDFA 880\49\\202).

203. 'Protocol of the Meeting of the Faction and the Secretariat', 28 July 1949, LPA 2, 11\1\1. A few weeks earlier, Sharett had spoken less critically of the expulsion: 'A while ago', he told his fellow ministers, 'we arranged that the Arabs in the [Little] Triangle would push out of their midst some 1,300 persons . . .' (protocol of Cabinet meeting, 5 July 1949, ISA).

204. Capt. Arye Friedlander (Shalev) to Military Intelligence 9, 5 Aug. 1949. The Jordanians argued that the mukhtar was 'a spokesman for the Israeli Government'. The Israelis involved, including Dayan and Sharett, in internal correspondence almost invariably referred to the 1,200–1,500 as 'expellees' (*megorashim*). Without doubt, the Israelis had instructed the mukhtar to order the refugees to leave.

205. Unsigned (possibly Yehoshu'a Palmon), 'Details about the Exodus of the 1344 Refugees who had Lived in and around Baqa al Gharbiya', undated; Dayan to foreign minister, 3 July 1949; and Dayan to defence minister, etc., 30 June 1949 – all in ISA FM 2431\4.

206. Ramati to IDF Intelligence Department, 'Special Committee Meeting Held at Mandelbaum Gate – 11:00 hrs., 10 August 1949', ISA FM 2431\7; and Burdett (Jerusalem) to Secretary of State, 15 Aug. 1949, NA 501 BB, Palestine\8–1549.
207. Dayan to foreign minister, etc., 11 Aug. 1949; and Friedlander to Dayan, 26 Aug. 1949 – both in ISA FM 2431\7.
208. Burdett (Jerusalem) to Secretary of State, 17 Sep. 1949, NA RG 84, Tel Aviv Embassy, Classified Records 1949, 321.9 – Israel.
209. Tuvia Arazi and A. Baram, Special Committee on the Baqa al Gharbiya Refugees, 'Summary of Third Meeting in Jerusalem on 21.11.49', IDFA 100243\52\\6.
210. Military Government Central Area, 'Protocol of Coordinating Meeting of Elements Active in the Central Area', 4 Dec. 1949, IDFA 741\72\\843.
211. Military governor central area, 'Protocol of Coordinating Meeting of Elements Active in Central Area', undated but from Nov. 1949, IDFA 721\72\\843.
212. Lt Col. Israel Ber to OC Military Government, 15 Nov. 1949, IDFA 721\72\\843.
213. Major Levitzky, Military Government Central Area, to OC Military Government, 18 Dec. 1949, IDFA 741\72\\843. Levitzky thought that ideally all the Arab villagers along the border should be transferred inland.
214. Y. Yekutieli to acting prime minister's secretary, 17 Dec. 1953, ISA FM 2401\19 aleph.

10 | Solving the refugee problem, December 1948 – September 1949

THE PALESTINE CONCILIATION COMMISSION AND LAUSANNE I: STALEMATE

International efforts at the end of 1948 and during the first half of 1949 to solve the refugee problem proceeded along two crisscrossing avenues – one, as conducted by agencies of the United Nations, primarily the Palestine Conciliation Commission (PCC), and the other, as conducted by the Great Powers, meaning, primarily, the United States. Both sets of efforts were guided in large measure by Bernadotte's testament, the interim report of mid-September 1948, and its 'doctrinal' postulate that the right of the refugee to return to his home and land was absolute and should be recognised by all parties. This postulate was enshrined two months after the Mediator's death in UN General Assembly Resolution 194, of 11 December 1948. The resolution stated that 'the refugees wishing to return to their homes and live at peace with their neighbours should be permitted to do so at the earliest practicable date'. (The resolution also offered those 'choosing not to return' the alternative of 'compensation'.) The PCC, set up by the resolution, was instructed to facilitate the 'repatriation' of those wishing to return.

The absolute nature of the return provision was immediately and almost universally qualified, in the minds of Western observers, by the appreciation that Israel would not allow a mass return and that many refugees might not wish to return to live under Jewish rule. It was understood by the powers, and by Bernadotte himself already from late summer 1948, that the bulk of the refugees would not be repatriated. The solution to the problem, therefore, would have to rest mainly on organised 'resettlement' in areas and countries outside Israel, a matter vaguely addressed in Resolution 194.

The decision in principle, not to allow a return, taken in Tel Aviv in summer 1948, hardened into an iron resolve during the following months. Israel, beside arguing strategic necessity by claiming (quite reasonably) that returning refugees would constitute a Fifth Column, pointed unabashedly to the changed physical realities on the ground. In presenting the case for resettlement in the Arab states, two top Israeli officials, Michael Comay and Zalman Lifshitz, wrote in March 1949: 'During the war and the Arab exodus, the basis of their economic life crumbled away. Moveable property . . . has disappeared. Livestock has been slaughtered or sold. Thousands of town and village dwellings have been destroyed in the course of the fighting or in order to deny their use to enemy forces . . . And of those which remain habitable, most are serving as temporary homes for [Jewish] immigrants.'[1]

Israeli Foreign Ministry Director General Eytan shortly afterwards wrote in the same vein to Claude de Boisanger, the French chairman of the PCC:

> The war that was fought in Palestine was bitter and destructive, and it would be doing the refugees a disservice to let them persist in the belief that if they returned, they would find their homes or shops or fields intact. In certain cases, it would be difficult for them even to identify the sites upon which their villages once stood.

Eytan added that masses of immigrants had poured into the country and their absorption

> might have been impossible altogether if the houses abandoned by the Arabs had not stood empty. As it was, the government took advantage of this vacant accommodation . . . Generally, it can be said that any Arab house that survived the impact of the war . . . now shelters a Jewish family. There can be no return to the status quo ante.[2]

But the Arab states refused to absorb the refugees. Over the second half of 1948, the Arabs united in thrusting the refugee problem to the top of the agenda. They demanded repatriation and linked all progress towards a resolution of the conflict to Israeli agreement to a return. United Nations and United States efforts to organise Israeli–Arab peace talks were dashed on the rocks of Arab insistence on, and Israeli resistance to, a return. Arab policy on this score was bolstered by a genuine economic inability to properly absorb hundreds of thousands of refugees and by fear of the refugees as a major potential subversive element vis-à-vis their own regimes. The western governments, fed by alarmed diplomats in the field and fired by global Cold War concerns, concurred that the masses of disgruntled refugees were potential tools of Communism and posed a threat to the pro-western host governments.

The Arab states appeared to be in a no-lose situation. Israeli refusal to take back the refugees, leaving them in misery, would turn world opinion and perhaps western governments against the Jewish State on humanitarian grounds. Israeli agreement to take back all or many of the refugees would result in the political and demographic destabilisation of the Jewish State, with clear military implications. All of Israel's leaders appreciated this: The refugees had become a 'political weapon against the Jews'.[3]

But conversely, for Tel Aviv, the refugees also constituted a political tool by means of which Israel might prise peace and recognition out of a reluctant, rejectionist Arab world. As the months passed and the prospects of peace grew increasingly dim, Israel hesitantly brandished the refugees as a carrot in the multilateral negotiations. (Indeed, Israel had little else, save hard-won territory, to offer in exchange for peace.) Tel Aviv would accept back a small number of refugees if the Arabs agreed to direct negotiations leading to peace.

It is against this backdrop of policy and calculation that the two-track efforts of the United Nations and United States in the first half of 1949 to solve the Middle East conflict in general and the refugee problem in particular must be seen.

The December 1948 UN resolution had asserted the 'right of return'; Bernadotte had insisted on it; the Arabs would agree to nothing less; and the western powers had supported the resolution. But could Israel be persuaded to accede?

On the whole, western diplomats in the Middle East thought not. William Burdett, the United States Consul-General in Jerusalem, saw the promulgation of the Absentees Property Ordinance in Tel Aviv in December 1948 as effectively a rejoinder to the resolution.

> Together with settlement of new Jewish immigrants . . . new Ordinance considered further indication PGI [i.e., Provisional Government of Israel] intends not rpt not permit return sizeable number Arab refugees.

Burdett warned that this would solve Israel's Arab minority problem but would also 'perpetuate refugee problem'.[4] Sir Rafael Cilento, the director of the UN Refugee Relief Project, the precursor of UNRWA, told British officials the same thing. Israel was unwilling to take back most or a large number of the refugees; resettlement in the Arab countries was the only realistic option.[5] The US representative in Jidda, Saudi Arabia, agreed, albeit reasoning somewhat differently:

> There can be no question of returning large numbers of Arabs to Israeli territory. It is inevitable that they would be treated as second-class citizens . . . A new large dissident minority in a Near Eastern state is certainly not something to be sought after.

J. Rives Childs thought – independently, but along the same lines as Israel's leaders – that resettlement of the refugees 'principally in Iraq and possibly Syria' would be the best solution.[6]

But the Arab states refused to absorb the exiles. The impasse pushed the United States and the PCC towards a solution based on Arab agreement to absorb, with western aid, most of the refugees coupled with Israeli agreement to the repatriation of the remaining several hundred thousand.

From the first Ambassador McDonald and Burdett thought Israeli agreement to such a massive (if still partial) repatriation unlikely, if not inconceivable. Moreover, Burdett doubted, given Israel's major economic problems, whether Tel Aviv would agree to pay the refugees substantial compensation. Politically, security in the region would best be served by refugee resettlement in the Arab countries, principally in the Arab-held parts of Palestine and in Transjordan.

> Since the US has supported the establishment of a Jewish State, it should insist on a homogeneous one which will have the best possible chance of stability. Return of the refugees would create a continuing 'minority problem' and form a constant temptation both for uprisings and intervention by neighbouring Arab states,

he wrote. But he acknowledged that, in the absence of organised, systematic absorption and resettlement in the Arab countries, the refugees represented a subversive 'opportunity' on which the USSR 'may capitalize'.[7]

Mark Ethridge, the Southern Baptist appointed by Truman to the PCC, quickly understood that the developing impasse over the refugees was lethal to any possibility of peace. Ethridge thought Shertok's attitude – that the refugees were 'essentially unassimilable' in Israel and should all be resettled in the Arab world – 'inhuman'. Israel's views in this context, he said, were 'similar to those which I heard Hitler express in Germany in 1933. It [sic] might be described as anti-Semitism toward the Arabs.' At the same time, he believed that 'it might be wise in long run to resettle greater portion Arab refugees in neighbouring Arab states'.[8]

Ethridge, like everyone attuned to the Arab position, soon realised that the refugee problem was the 'immediate key to peace negotiations if not to peace' itself. The Arab states were united around the proposition that a start to the solution of the refugee problem must precede meaningful negotiations for a settlement. The outlines of a compromise were clear: The Arabs, Ethridge felt, had to reduce their demand for complete repatriation and Israel had to abandon its opposition to a substantial partial repatriation. Both sides were treating the refugees 'as [a] political pawn'. By the end of February 1949, Ethridge felt that there was need of 'a generous Israeli gesture' – that is, a statement agreeing to a return of a large number of refugees and an immediate start to repatriation. This would break the 'Arab psychosis' and enable movement towards a compromise. (This assumed sincere Arab interest in a compromise that included the continued existence of the Jewish State.) Ethridge asked the State Department to 'encourage' Israel to make the gesture and the

Arabs to respond favourably. The idea of a redemptive Israeli 'gesture' as the key to peace was to characterise all Ethridge's work on the PCC during the frustrating weeks ahead. The lack of such a gesture had 'prejudiced whole cause of peaceful settlement', Ethridge wrote in March. He dismissed as 'rubbish' Shertok's insistence that Israel could not make such a gesture or specify the number of refugees it might be willing to take back.

On 14 March, Shertok wrote Ethridge that while the main solution to the refugee problem must rest on resettlement in the Arab countries, Israel might, under certain circumstances, admit a 'certain proportion', though this would depend on the 'kind of peace' that emerged. But Ethridge sought a precise and public commitment. Six weeks of PCC efforts had failed to elicit any concrete concessions. Ethridge pressed Washington to 'urge' Tel Aviv to make the required 'gesture'.[9]

Sharett (Shertok) put it bluntly at a meeting with Acheson in Washington on 22 March: The Israeli government 'could not possibly make such a commitment' before negotiations began and, in any case, 'it was out of the question to consider the possibility of repatriation of any substantial numbers of the refugees'.[10] The Arabs, for their part, appear to have insisted, at the Arab League foreign ministers' meeting with the PCC in Beirut the day before, on the refugees' 'right of return' – while continuing to reject the UN partition resolution of 1947 and recognition of Israel.[11]

What to do about the refugees had been debated within the American administration since late summer 1948. The establishment and peregrinations of the PCC had in a sense taken the pressure off Washington. The PCC had to be given a chance; parallel American activities might jeopardise the commission's prospects of success. And perhaps the PCC might achieve something before Washington was forced into armtwisting in Tel Aviv or the Arab capitals. But Israeli and Arab inflexibility, the PCC's lack of success and Ethridge's constant importunings (often in personal letters to his friend, President Truman), by the end of March caused a change of tone and approach in Washington, especially in contacts with Israel. Ambassador McDonald's 'soft' line was temporarily abandoned.

The joint communication on 29 March from Ethridge and George McGhee, Special Assistant to Acheson, appears to have been decisive with Truman and the Secretary of State. Sent after the meeting with the Arab leaders in Beirut, the letter reflected the growing desperation of the American policy-makers. Ethridge and McGhee forcefully argued that without 'maximum possible repatriation', there was no hope of Arab absorption of a substantial number of refugees. Resettlement in the Arab countries would be a long and arduous process, contrary to the wishes of the host countries and of the refugees themselves, would lay the seeds of future economic and political difficulties and would provide 'lasting monuments [to] UN and US failure'. Repatriation, on the other hand, could be accomplished quickly and far more cheaply. However, taking account of Israel's military, political and economic objections to total repatriation, the two officials concluded that Israel must be pressed to repatriate at least '250,000', from the areas conquered by the IDF outside the Jewish State partition borders. The rest of the refugees, it was implied, should be resettled in the Arab countries.[12]

Washington was fired into action. McDonald 'informally' pressed that Israel agree to take back the 250,000 from the conquered areas.[13] On 5 April, Acheson and Sharett met in New York. Acheson performed with unwonted bluntness, deploying the 'big gun' of presidential displeasure. Truman, he said, was greatly concerned about the plight of the refugees, who numbered, he said, some '800,000'.

> While it can be understood that repatriation of all of these refugees is not a practical solution, nevertheless we anticipate that a considerable number must be repatriated if a solution is to be found. The president is particularly anxious that an impasse not develop on this subject, with one side refusing to negotiate for a final settlement until a solution is found for refugees and the other side refusing to take steps to solve the refugee question until there is a final settlement.

The President, said Acheson, felt the time was ripe for an Israeli gesture – a statement of readiness to allow back 'say a fourth of the refugees'. Such a gesture would 'make it possible for the President to continue his strong and warm support for Israel and efforts being made by its government to establish its new political and economic structure on a firm basis'. The threat was clear.

Sharett responded reflexively, questioning the refugee numbers offered by Acheson, rejecting the distinction between the 1947 partition boundaries and those carved out by the IDF, and rejecting a mass refugee return as a threat to Israel's homogeneity.[14]

But PCC–American pressure slowly wore down Israeli obduracy. An early sign appeared in Shertok's contacts over February–March 1949 with the second Transfer Committee (Weitz, Danin and Lifshitz), appointed by Ben-Gurion at the end of August 1948 to plan the refugees' organised resettlement in the Arab states. On 11 February 1949, Shertok informed the Committee that he had told the PCC that Israel would not allow a return. Israel, he agreed, had to persuade American and Arab public opinion that there could and would be no return. A month later, however, while asking the committee for a more detailed proposal on the possibilities of funding and resettling the refugees in Arab countries, Sharett requested that the three prepare

> an absolutely secret plan for the event that the Cabinet feels itself compelled to agree to a return of part of the refugees to Israel. This plan must determine the maximal dimensions of the return . . . the method of selecting the returnees and . . . the areas and villages that can be resettled.

A plan was apparently prepared.[15]

Ben-Gurion himself hinted at a new-fangled flexibility at his meeting with the PCC in Tel Aviv on 7 April. He said: '. . . it is desirable that the refugees be resettled in the Arab states. But I do not discount the possibility that we might contribute [to the solution] by settling part of them in our [country].' But Ben-Gurion denied 'emphatically that Israel had expelled the Arabs . . . The State of Israel expelled nobody and will never do it', he said. PCC chairman de Boisanger seemed to agree, noting that 'no Arab maintained [before the PCC] that he had been expelled from the country. The refugees said they had fled from fear, because of the preparations for war, as thousands fled from France in 1940.' Ben-Gurion thanked de Boisanger for 'admitting' that the Yishuv had not expelled the Arabs or harassed them out of the country and explained that the Arab leaders were responsible for the exodus:

> It was an organised plan, part of the Arab attack plan, a plan worked out by the Arab leaders, British agents and others . . . [They] advised the Arabs to leave in order to facilitate the plans they hatched against us. Take Tiberias, for example. We were attacked, the Haganah counterattacked, but asked the Arabs who were there to stay; but they left. We did not ask them to go, we did not expel them and we are unwilling to bear the responsibility for their departure. The responsibility is the Arab states' and their leaders.[16]

Vague statements about a readiness to repatriate some of the refugees served the practical purpose of parrying PCC–American pressures. But the Yishuv's desire to take back refugees had in no way increased; if it depended on Tel Aviv, there would be no returnees.

Meanwhile, the PCC was affected by growing gloom. In late March and early April, de Boisanger, Ethridge and Huseyin Cait Yalcin, the Turkish PCC representative, concluded that their Middle East shuttle was fruitless. Yalcin, 'disgruntled' chiefly with the United States, explained it this way:

> Nobody was strong enough or sufficiently determined to deter the Jews from doing anything they wanted to do . . . [US] diplomatists and officials seemed [not] to have the courage to tell the truth about the Jews unless they were within sight of retirement.

Yalcin added that before joining the PCC, he had 'always had a soft spot for the Jews . . . a universally oppressed people'. Now, according to his British interlocutor, he was 'definitely anti-Semitic'.[17]

The PCC took two steps to try to break the logjam: It set up a Technical Committee on Refugees to work out 'measures . . . for the implementation of the provisions of the [11 December 1948 UN] resolution', meaning to find out how many refugees there were, how many wished to be repatriated and how many to stay in Arab countries, and how these could be economically 'rehabilitated'; and called an international conference at Lausanne where, under PCC chairmanship, the parties could discuss the range of issues – refugees, Jerusalem, borders, recognition – and hammer out a comprehensive peace settlement.[18] After months of fruitless labour, the PCC reasoned that nothing could be lost by a conference and that it might manoeuvre Arabs and Jews towards compromise, neither party wishing to lay itself open to a charge of torpedoing the gathering. Ethridge demanded complementary, forceful American pressure on Israel.

Israel's policy-makers met to define the country's positions. The meetings were attended by Ben-Gurion, Sharett, Yadin, Eytan (who was to head the delegation to Lausanne), members of the Transfer Committee, and other senior officials, including Sasson, who was to be Eytan's second in command. The refugee problem received scant attention, few of the participants anticipating that the Arab delegations intended to push it immediately to the top of the agenda. When Shiloah, director of the Foreign Ministry's Political Division, commented: 'We have still almost not touched upon the question of the refugees', no one took him up and the discussion on border problems continued. Only Leo Kohn, Sharett's Political Adviser, who did not participate in the meetings, predicted that the Arabs would categorically demand that the refugees receive top billing. Kohn advised that the delegation stress the security threat which a mass return would pose and cited the Sudeten problem as a telling and useful comparison: 'Now that the exodus of the Arabs from our country has taken place, what moral right have those who fully endorsed the expulsion of the Sudeten Germans from Czechoslovakia to demand that we readmit these Arabs?'[19]

Yadin and, implicitly, Ben-Gurion rejected compromise on repatriation. Yadin lumped together the issues of 'the refugees and the [State's final] borders'.

> My opinion is that we must say, with all cruelty: The refugee problem is no concern of the Land [sic] of Israel . . . We must say openly: If they [i.e., the Arabs] want war – let them continue [pressing us] on the refugee problem . . . It can be explained to them that the refugees in their countries bring them only benefit.

Ben-Gurion was more oblique. He stressed that Israel's primary concern and need at the moment was the absorption of new Jewish immigrants: 'This encompasses all the historical needs of the state.' Immigrants and their absorption were the key to Israel's security. In this context, the implication was that repatriation of Arabs would preclude the absorption of Jews.

Lifshitz and Comay described a recent meeting with Ethridge. Lifshitz said that Ethridge believed that Israel had expelled the Arabs. Ethridge had told the two Israelis of his encounter with a column of some 200 refugees just pushed by Israel across the Lebanese border and warned against repetition of such expulsions. Ethridge called for Israel to repatriate 250,000. Comay had responded that Israel had enough

Arabs ('130,000'). Ethridge had concluded, correctly, that 'Israel does not intend to take back one refugee more than she is forced to'.

Ethridge was incensed by the denials by Ben-Gurion and Comay of any Israeli responsibility for the creation of the refugee problem, as he put it, 'in face of Jaffa, Deir Yassin, Haifa and all reports that come to us from refugee organisations that new refugees are being created every day by repression and terrorism'. Ethridge added that Arab propaganda was ineffective as compared with the Israeli public relations machine and said that had the Arabs a 'tenth of the genius at it, they would rouse public opinion to where it would engulf Israel in a wave of indignation'.

The upshot of the consultative meetings in Tel Aviv was a reiteration of the traditional line – no substantial repatriation, no 'gesture' and no statement on the number of returnees Israel might be willing to take back within the framework of a settlement.[20]

The lack of movement in the Israeli position was brought home to Ethridge at a meeting with Ben-Gurion in Tiberias (which, in his cable, Ethridge called 'Siberias') on 18 April. Ben-Gurion treated Ethridge to an extended analysis of British misdemeanours in the Middle East since 1917 and to a lecture on how the United States 'should declare its second independence of [the] British Foreign Office'. On the refugees, Ben-Gurion gave not an inch. He made no mention of a possible Israeli 'gesture'. Resettlement in the Arab countries was the 'only logical answer', he said. Israel 'cannot and will not accept return Arab refugees to Israeli territory', on grounds both of security and economics. Israel, said Ben-Gurion, would compensate the refugee *fellahin* for their land, would provide advice on resettlement in the Arab countries and would allow back a few refugees within the family reunion scheme.

The meeting appropriately crowned the months of fruitless PCC shuttling. Ethridge rushed off a cable to Acheson asking to be relieved of his post. The PCC could not solve the refugee problem, he wrote; only American pressure could facilitate a solution. He did not look to the prospective meeting at Lausanne with great hope.[21]

Ethridge's resignation threat elicited a reaffirmation of the American position favouring substantial repatriation and a plea by the Secretary of State and the President that he soldier on, at least for a while longer. Acheson wrote that the United States Government 'is not disposed to change policy because of Israeli intransigence'; Truman wrote that he was 'rather disgruntled with the manner in which the Jews are approaching the refugee problem'. Truman and Acheson both personally pressed Israeli officials at the end of April to soften its stance.[22] Ethridge agreed to stay on, probably hoping that at Lausanne the United States would at last bring its full weight to bear on Israel.

On the eve of the convocation, Acheson instructed his missions in the Arab world to press for greater flexibility all around. Washington asked London to make similar representations to the Arab governments.

Acheson reiterated American support for the 'principle of repatriation' alongside the need to obtain Arab agreement to 'resettlement [of] those not desiring repatriation'.[23]

The delegations gathered at Lausanne at the end of April. But the PCC's effort to bring the parties to formal face-to-face negotiations failed; the Arabs refused (though Arab and Jewish officials met often and secretly for informal discussions). The refugees represented the major, initial and insuperable sticking point.

The Arab delegations arrived united in the demand that Israel declare acceptance of the principle of repatriation before they would agree to negotiate peace. Eytan, in response, mouthed only a pious plea for the refugees' 'permanent settlement and rehabilitation'. The Israeli delegation, he said, had 'come prepared to tackle [the refugee problem] with sincerity and above all in the spirit of realism'. 'Realism' meant no repatriation.

Privately, however, Eytan acknowledged that Israel's opening positions were inadequate. He wrote Sharett:

> I think the time has come for us to realise that mere words will not carry us much further towards peace . . . A statement such as that which I issued [at the press conference] this afternoon is interpreted by everyone as yet another attempt by us to shirk the real issues.

Israel, in Ethridge's view, 'had grown arrogant' on military and politcal successes, and was 'unwilling to [meaningfully] negotiate'. Ethridge was pessimistic, believing that Ben-Gurion alone determined policy and Ben-Gurion's attitude was 'negative . . . towards the [PCC], [toward Ethridge] himself, to the negotiations, [and] to the various problems which had to be solved'.[24]

The PCC, the delegations and the Great Power representatives got down to work. The Commission met this or that delegation; then met with the other side, conveying the first delegation's views. Then the second delegation's responses would be submitted to the first delegation, and so on. Behind the scenes, PCC members and Great Power representatives met privately to cajole, blandish or pressure members of the delegations. Occasionally, Sasson would meet privately (often in Paris) with this or that Arab official. Earlier, Eytan had candidly described Sasson's prospective role; he and Shiloah had opposed the original proposal that Sasson be appointed head of the delegation. Rather, wrote Eytan,

> we see his role as that of an ideal liaison officer between our delegation and the Arabs, making contacts, speaking soft words into Arab ears, formulating difficult matters in a way which may make it easier for the Arabs to swallow them, etc. etc.[25]

Through the spring and summer, Israel and Jordan conducted parallel, direct peace negotiations. Sharett met King Abdullah on 5 May 1949.

They discussed borders, recognition, access for Jordan to the Mediterranean and refugees. Amman linked the refugee and territorial questions: The more occupied territory Israel would be willing to cede, the
more refugees Jordan would be willing to absorb and resettle. Abdullah
was primarily interested in Lydda and Ramle, but Israel was unwilling to
give up territory. Indeed, it sought further land (Tulkarm and Qalqilya).
Nothing came of the talks though, in Tel Aviv's view, the Jordanians were
'most anxious' to make peace.[26]

At the same time, Sasson held informal talks at Lausanne with a
Palestinian refugee delegation, headed by Muhammad Nimr al Hawari,
the Jaffa lawyer who had commanded the *Najjada*. Hawari proposed
that Israel agree to the repatriation of 400,000, who would live in peace
with Israel and act as a 'peace bridge' between Israel and the Arab
states. On the other hand, he argued, if the masses of refugees continued to live stateless and impoverished along Israel's borders, they
would cause the Jewish State nothing but grief. This – not a return –
was precisely what the Mufti and Abdullah wanted, argued Hawari. The
Arab states did not want the refugees and would not assimilate them.
Nothing came of the talks. Hawari returned to Ramallah, 'desperate and
depressed'.[27]

At Lausanne, no progress was achieved in May. The impasse hardened. The Arabs demanded Israeli agreement to the principle of full
repatriation and a start to actual repatriation before substantive peace
talks could begin. Israel insisted that resettlement in the Arab states
was the inevitable core of a solution and that Israel might agree to an
indeterminate but small measure of repatriation within the framework
of a final peace settlement. Israel refused to throw out numbers. Eytan
described the situation as 'one vast vicious circle'. Only the introduction
of some 'entirely new element' could offer an exit.[28]

Whether by Israeli design or American misunderstanding and wishful
thinking (or, as is probable, by an admixture of the two), while things
at Lausanne were at a standstill, Israeli diplomats in the United States
signalled a more moderate line. Abba Eban, Israel's representative to
the United Nations, on 5 May told the United Nations Ad Hoc Political
Committee at Lake Success that Israel 'does not reject' the principle of
repatriation.[29]

Eagerly awaiting such a sign of flexibility on this cardinal issue, United
States policy-makers jumped for joy. Acheson took Eban to mean that
Israel had formally accepted the principle of repatriation, and cabled
as much to all and sundry.[30] Eliahu Elath, the Israeli Ambassador
to Washington, provided further grounds for optimism by telling the
Americans that Israel feels that 'both repatriation and resettlement are
required for solution of problem'. But the Israelis refused to talk numbers. Acheson believed that Israel would be more specific after it was
assured that the Arabs would integrate the remainder of the refugees

and that 'outside' financial assistance for such resettlement would be vouchsafed.[31]

But, of course, Israel had not accepted the principle of repatriation, whatever its emissaries were hinting or were understood to have said. But for weeks thereafter, American policy-makers referred to Israel's acceptance of the principle of repatriation. Israeli officials, such as Eban, found this amusing – and advantageous to Israel.[32]

This proved to be only a temporary semi-comic interlude. In truth, apart from fleeting moments of self-delusion, American policymakers understood that Israel remained set against repatriation and that this was a major obstacle to progress. Hence, Truman intervened personally at the end of May, sending a forceful, minatory message to Ben-Gurion, conveying 'grave' American concern. Washington, to no avail, had repeatedly asked Israel to accept 'the principle of substantial repatriation and the immediate beginnings of repatriation on a reasonable scale . . . The US Government', wrote Truman, 'does not . . . regard the present attitude of the Israeli government as being consistent with the principles upon which U.S. support [of Israel] has been based.' Israel's stand endangered the prospects of solving the conflict: Its attitude 'must inevitably lead to a rupture in [the Lausanne] conversations'.[33]

Sharett responded in Ben-Gurion's name that Washington had 'misunderstood' Israel's position. Israel had accepted the principle of a negotiated peace embedded in Resolution 194. But the Arabs had refused to negotiate in good faith – indeed, even to meet the Israelis or to negotiate peace. As to the refugees, the Jews had never intended to expel them:

> What produced the Arab exodus was the war on Israel. The exodus was partly spontaneous, partly decreed from above by Arab leaders and commanders . . . The refugees are members of an aggressor-group defeated in a war of its own making. History does not record any case of large-scale repatriation after such experience.

The economic, demographic and social conditions in Palestine had meanwhile changed: '. . . The wheel of history cannot be turned back . . . Israel cannot in the name of humanitarianism be driven to commit suicide', though it was willing to assist in the refugees' resettlement elsewhere, to provide compensation and to 'reunite families separated by the war . . . So long as the Arab states do not evince any readiness even to discuss peace, any significant measure of repatriation is clearly impracticable.'[34]

American and PCC pressures on Israel increased as the prospect for a settlement dimmed. Ethridge's resignation accurately reflected the situation and his personal sense of frustration. The PCC and Ethridge, as the Israelis saw it, were obsessed with 'one point, and one point only' – Israel's refusal to accept the principle of repatriation. Eytan described

Ethridge as a 'fundamentally decent, fair-minded person, the best type of Southern liberal'. But Ethridge felt that he had been 'snubbed' in Tel Aviv and regarded the Israelis as dishonest, unethical and legalistic. He was returning to the United States 'thoroughly disgruntled', an attitude Eytan expected Ethridge to pass on to Truman. Ethridge had regarded Israel's bland response of 8 June to Truman's message of 29 May as 'impertinent', 'a declaration of intellectual warfare against the US'. He was unimpressed by Israel's hint of possible agreement to 'significant' repatriation after the Arabs agreed to peace. Ethridge, according to Eytan, had remained 'fair-minded enough' to see that the Arabs were being 'unrealistic' over repatriation. But, to achieve 'immediate peace', Israel had to agree to repatriate 200,000 refugees and to give the Arabs 'part of the Southern Negev', Ethridge felt, according to Eytan.[35]

At the end of June, the Lausanne talks were recessed for three weeks, the PCC aiming to allow the two sides to utilise the break to contemplate the logjam and the prospect of failure, and to come up with concessions on refugees and territory.

Through June and early July, the policymakers in Tel Aviv agonised, understanding that continued blanket stonewalling would inevitably lead to the collapse of the conference, with Israel possibly figuring as chief culprit. The refugee problem 'seems in many ways to have become now the central problem of our foreign affairs', wrote Teddy Kollek, one of Ben-Gurion's aides. (He was in London, trying, among other things, to interest British businessmen, including Sir Marcus Sieff, in financing development projects in the Middle East that could employ Palestinian refugees.) Kollek urged Tel Aviv to take 'positive action', by which he may have meant that Israel should agree to a limited measure of repatriation.[36] The problem was to find a concession or 'gesture' whose implementation could cause Israel least damage while sufficing to relieve or reduce American and PCC pressure and to transfer the ball to the Arab court. The solution adopted was the '100,000 Offer'.

THE GAZA PLAN INTERLUDE

But before Israel made the '100,000 Offer', another possible solution surfaced, which was intermittently to magnetise diplomatic effort for months. Given the realities of mid-1949, the 'Gaza Plan' was a mirage, but it riveted the attention of policy-makers in Washington and, to a far lesser extent, in Tel Aviv and London, and held out the promise of a miraculous deliverance.

Simply and initially, the plan was that the Gaza Strip – occupied by the Egyptian army since May 1948 – should be transferred to Israeli sovereignty along with its relatively large local and refugee populations. While gaining a strategic piece of real estate, Israel would thus be considered to have done its bit for refugee repatriation. In most American and British readings of the plan, the refugees in the Strip, after the transfer, were to be allowed to return to their towns and villages of origin. In a revised version, Israel, in addition to absorbing the Strip's populations, was expected to give either Egypt or Jordan (or both) territorial compensation for the Strip, probably in the southern Negev. Discussion of the plan, even after all hope of its implementation had vanished, continued through the summer, playing a counterpoint to the American and PCC main efforts to induce Israel to agree to substantial 'front door' repatriation and the Arabs, to organised refugee resettlement in their own countries.

In Operation Horev, between 22 December 1948 and 6 January 1949, the IDF had attempted to destroy the Egyptian army in the Strip and to conquer the area. The operation had involved a deep thrust into Sinai by IDF armoured columns but was only partially successful. An internationally imposed ceasefire, on 7 January, halted the onslaught in mid-stride. The Egyptian forces managed (barely) to hold onto most of the Strip. With the IDF withdrawal from Sinai back to the international frontier, under Great Power pressure, the Egyptians re-established their lines of communications and supply with the Strip, and it remained in their hands.

But the position of the extended, semi-beleaguered Egyptian army remained highly uncomfortable during the following months. And, international relief efforts notwithstanding, the Strip's 200,000–250,000 refugees, whom Egypt did not want to absorb and Israel refused to take back, constituted a giant burden for the Egyptian authorities. Was holding onto the Strip worth the candle?

By March, according to Israeli officials, the Egyptians thought not. Sasson, who was in constant touch with them in Paris, believed that Egypt wanted to evacuate the Strip. Sharett feared that Egypt would try to transfer the Strip to the Jordanians. Mapai Knesset Member David Hocohen suggested that it would be worth Israel's while to take over the area, even if it meant enlarging the State's Arab minority. Sharett, while mindful of the price, thought that Israel would gain a strategic piece of real estate and 'could portray the absorption of 100,000 [sic] refugees as a major contribution . . . to the solution of the refugee problem as a whole and to free itself once and for all of UN pressure in this regard'.[37]

The idea was formally debated in the consultative meetings in April in preparation for Lausanne. On 12 April, Sasson said that there were in the Strip altogether some '140,000' Arabs; the mooted figure of '240,000' was an exaggeration. Yadin said that an Israeli takeover of the Strip under present conditions would be a 'catastrophe'. There were three possibilities, he said: Turning the Strip into some form of autonomous Egyptian–Israeli protectorate, which he considered 'the ideal solution'; incorporation in Israel; or 'that the Arabs in the area will go somewhere else and we will receive the territory'.[38]

No decision was taken. Ethridge, reporting from Jerusalem on 13 April, thought that Israel would not take the Strip – which, he said, contained '230,000' refugees and '100,000' locals – if it meant absorbing its entire population. But, as Ethridge learned a few days later, Ben-Gurion quite clearly favoured Israeli absorption of the Strip, with (and despite) its population. Ben-Gurion even seems to have suggested that the Gaza refugees would be allowed to return to their original villages.[39]

The idea of the Gaza Plan meshed with the peace plan then being secretly negotiated with Abdullah. Abdullah stressed Jordan's need for an outlet to the sea via Gaza or Acre. The transfer by Egypt – unfriendly to Jordan – of the Strip to Israel could facilitate the conclusion of a deal which included Jordanian access to the Mediterranean through Gaza, though there was a school of thought in Tel Aviv that opposed 'conspiring' with Abdullah against Egypt.[40]

Matters were clarified somewhat on 22 April at the last consultative meeting before Lausanne. Sasson, eager to conclude a deal with Abdullah, backed the transfer of the Strip to Jordan. Ben-Gurion cautioned against rushing into a decision, but Shiloah rejoined that the matter would surely be raised in the impending negotiations. Ben-Gurion responded that if the Strip was transferred to Israel, 'we would not refuse [it], and then of course we would take it with all its inhabitants. We will not expel them.' But Shiloah, unlike Sasson, was worried that Egypt might agree to transfer Gaza to Jordan in a deal against which Israel would be powerless. Shiloah opposed such a transfer because – if the West Bank was eventually linked to the Strip by a land corridor, as Jordan was demanding – it would 'sever' the Negev from the rest of Israel. Sharett argued that the war had made the Yishuv's leaders think too much in terms of territory and too little in terms of population: 'We are drunk with victory [and] territorial conquests.' He opposed having to 'swallow 150,000' Arabs and argued against both Israeli incorporation of and joint Israeli–Egyptian condominium over the Strip. The moment Israel became responsible, the Strip's refugees would press to be allowed to return to their original homes. Lifshitz, of the Transfer Committee, also opposed Israeli incorporation though pressed for Israeli annexation of Qalqilya and Tulkarm, which had 'only 20,000 Arabs'. Like Shiloah, Sharett opposed a Jordanian takeover of the Strip.[41]

Ethridge was enthusiastic about the Gaza idea, which he began calling a 'plan'. He saw it as a 'back door' method of achieving a measure of repatriation and of getting the Lausanne peace ball rolling. Ethridge told Eytan that he was

> sure the Egyptians did not want to keep it and he personally was in favour of giving it to Israel . . . [if] the refugees went with it. He felt that by accepting those refugees, estimated at 150–200,000, [Israel] would be making [its] contribution towards the solution of the refugee problem.[42]

But were the Egyptians amenable? An initial indication was provided in early May. Egypt would rather give the Strip to Israel than to Jordan, said a Jordanian official in Lausanne. But it was more likely that Egypt would prefer to hold onto the Strip 'and give it to nobody'.[43]

A cable on 2 May from Eytan to Tel Aviv brought matters to a head. The Cabinet met the next day and decided that 'if the incorporation of the Gaza district into Israel with all its population is proposed, our response will be positive'. Sharett had argued against, saying that Israel had not 'matured sufficiently to absorb three hundred thousand Arabs. I see it as a catastrophe [*ani ro'eh zot ke'sho'ah*].' But Ben-Gurion, mobilising geo-political and strategic arguments, brought the majority around. In the vote, Sharett abstained.[44] On 20 May, after informing Ethridge that Israel would 'demand' the Strip but would not press the demand 'if Egypt said no', Israel formally proposed to the PCC that she be given the Strip and said that '[we] would be prepared to accept . . . all Arabs at present located in the Gaza area, whether inhabitants or refugees, as citizens of Israel'. Tel Aviv committed itself to their 'resettlement and rehabilitation', reiterating the proposal on 29 and 31 May.[45]

Israel felt that by accepting Gaza's local and refugee populations, as well as a handful of refugees under the family reunion scheme – coupled with its existing Arab citizens – it would have an Arab minority roughly equal in number to the Arab minority it would have had under the 1947 UN partition scheme and it 'would have discharged its full obligation' towards solving the refugee problem. 'The proposal is an earnest of the great lengths to which the Government of Israel is prepared to go in helping to solve the problem that is central to all our discussions', Eytan wrote de Boisanger. Israel linked acceptance of Gaza and its refugees to large-scale international aid to cover the entailed costs.[46]

But from Washington's perspective, which took account of projected Arab sensibilities, the plan could not be so simple as mere Israeli incorporation of the Strip. While the United States regarded the refugee problem and its potential solution as the 'overriding factor in determining eventual disposition Gaza Strip', Washington was prepared to approve the incorporation only if achieved with full Egyptian consent 'and provided [that] territorial compensation [is] made to Egypt . . . if Egypt desires such compensation'. Washington added that Israel would have to provide iron-clad assurances and guarantees that the Gaza locals and refugees would enjoy full rights and protection; the fear was of a repeat 'Faluja'. There was also chariness in Washington about footing the Gaza refugees' resettlement bill.

The feeling of the United States Embassy in Cairo was that the Egyptian Government 'might well be willing [to] cede [the] Gaza Strip' if Israel 'assumed refugee burden' and that Arab League Secretary General 'Azzam was similarly minded. But the Egyptians, the embassy felt, would probably 'reserve final decision' until formal peace negotiations took place, using Gaza as a 'bargaining point'.[47]

Ethridge correctly gauged the Israeli position. He thought that the plan was Israel's only real and, possibly, last significant offer: 'If she cannot have Gaza Strip, she will take only small number refugees.' Only the Gaza Plan, Ethridge believed, held out the promise of Israeli acceptance of a substantial repatriation.[48]

The Israeli Government had given only scant publicity to its decision to incorporate the Strip with its population. The Cabinet feared a strong public reaction against the plan, especially from the Right. The plan had been approved only reluctantly and under the mistaken belief that the Strip contained substantially fewer than 200,000–250,000 refugees.[49] The lack of a positive Egyptian response after 20 May had further eaten away at Israeli enthusiasm.

The official caginess about Israel's acceptance of the plan stretched to covering the plan's origin, which was to become the focus of a minor, and somewhat bizarre, diplomatic scuffle. The scuffle was unwittingly provoked by Ambassador McDonald who, on 31 May, quoting an Israeli Foreign Ministry official, cabled that the plan had been first 'suggested' by Ethridge to Eytan. However, a few days later, Eban said that it had been Egypt's Mohammed 'Abd al-Mun'im Mustafa, head of delegation at the armistice talks, who 'had first raised question of Israel taking over Gaza Strip', in Rhodes, in late February; only subsequently, on 30 April at Lausanne, had Ethridge made the suggestion to Eytan. Meanwhile, in Tel Aviv, according to British Ambassador Knox Helm, the Israeli Government denied initiating any formal Gaza proposal, saying that the PCC had 'put forward' the proposal. The Egyptians, for their part, denied that they had first suggested the idea.

But Ethridge was unwilling to shoulder the burdens of paternity. 'It is clear from the record', he wrote, that it had been Ben-Gurion at their meeting in Tiberias on 18 April, who had first proposed the kernel of the Gaza Plan. (Sharett subsequently disclaimed that the plan had been conceived at Tiberias.) And through June, Ethridge went out of his way to repudiate authorship. He believed that Eytan's official publication of the proposal on 20 May had for the present 'torpedoed' any possibility of progress in the matter.[50]

The dispute about the origin of the plan was not motivated by a penchant for accuracy so much as by political calculation. Egypt, having just lost a war with Israel, could not allow itself to appear eager or willing to cede the only chunk of Palestine it had won to the Jews while helping them get off the hook on the refugee issue. Israel, for reasons of internal unity and diplomacy, could neither appear as the fount of the idea nor overeager to lay its hands on the Strip, lest its eagerness put off the Egyptians. Moreover, Israeli conception of, or eagerness about, the plan implied that Israel was willing and able to absorb some 200,000–250,000 refugees. If the plan fell through, American and United Nations pressure for a 'gesture' of repatriation could be expected to be renewed, citing Israel's eagerness and expressed ability to take in a large number of refugees. (This, indeed, happened.) Ethridge, for his part, apparently did not wish to be seen as the author of a plan that promised to enlarge the State of Israel or, alternatively, that failed to fly. By early June, in addition to denying authorship, Ethridge began linking an Egyptian cession of the Strip to territorial compensation by Israel.[51] Ethridge's reluctance to be identified with the plan grew as Egyptian opposition to it crystallised and as its prospects of implementation diminished. No one wanted to be identified with a nonstarter.

The American linkage of an Egyptian cession of the Strip to territorial compensation in the Negev (possibly at the northern end of the Gulf of 'Aqaba) was not manifest in the early multilateral contacts on the matter. Its appearance in late May or early June probably owed much to the seeming Egyptian disinterest in the original proposal and, possibly, also to British signals favouring Israeli–Egyptian 'reciprocity', stemming from an imperial interest in obtaining a land-bridge between the British-ruled Suez Canal and Jordan–Iraq, where British troops were stationed and which were linked by defence treaties to London.[52] The United States concurred with the British view that it was in the West's interests to maintain a territorially continuous Arab world, with a land-bridge across the Negev between Egypt and Jordan.

From the start, Cairo opposed the Gaza Plan: In the circumstances, it implied a separate peace with Israel. 'Not only would Egypt not give up the Gaza district but [it] would firmly demand the southern Negev', the Egyptian delegation head at Lausanne, 'Abd al Mun'im Mustafa, told Sasson on 1 June.[53] 'The Egyptian Government', Cairo told Washington a few days later, 'regarded the proposal as "cheap barter." [The Egyptian ambassador to Washington] characterised the offer as that of exchanging human lives for territory.' Or, as Arab representatives put it to a British official at Lausanne, 'it is wrong to bargain territory against refugees', and that if the Israelis wanted the Strip, they should compensate the Arabs in kind (that is, with territory).[54]

Egypt's lack of enthusiasm did not kill the plan, if only because it was the only thing on the market in May and June. Taking stock of the Egyptian response, Ben-Gurion agreed, on 6 June, to compensate Egypt with a similarly sized strip of territory along the border in the northwestern Negev. But Ben-Gurion 'doubted whether this proposal would win the Arabs' heart'.

When Eytan put it to 'Abd al Mun'im Mustafa a few days later, the Egyptian 'didn't think much of the idea'. 'And I [Eytan] don't think the Egyptian Government will. Why should Egypt give up the fertile Gaza belt in return for a wilderness somewhere between Rafa and 'Auja?' he reasoned.[55] But the United States still felt that the plan was 'perhaps the key that would unlock whole problem'. It sought to engineer a formal, face-to-face Israeli–Egyptian negotiation, in which some form of the Gaza Plan would figure large. Israel agreed, proposing New York as the venue,[56] but Egypt demurred. Washington appealed to Britain to help persuade Egypt to negotiate.[57]

Eban was appointed to lead the projected talks with the Egyptians. He said a successful outcome would 'break [the] back of refugee problem', which all saw as the nemesis of Lausanne, but he acknowledged that Egypt might face serious internal and inter-Arab problems if it agreed to cede territory to Israel. He apparently saw the United States playing some sort of mediating role but Acheson rejected the idea.[58]

Washington, explaining Egyptian tardiness in taking up the Plan, said that Israel had handled the matter clumsily, 'always [stressing] . . . the territorial rather than the refugee aspect, which, of course, made it harder for the Egyptian negotiators to accept'. Eban agreed.[59]

The introduction by the United States of the idea of Israeli territorial 'compensation' was largely conceived to offset the territory-for-refugees 'barter' image of the original proposal. The Americans pushed the compensation theme to such an extent that the Egyptians believed, or pretended to believe, that the United States would not allow Egypt to withdraw from the Strip without compensation. Mainstream Israeli thinking held that agreement to absorb several hundred thousand Arabs was a sufficient *quid pro quo* for the Strip though it was willing to compensate Egypt with a chunk of the barren Negev if that was what Egyptian pride (and peace) demanded.[60]

In July, during the Lausanne recess, the Eastern Department of the Foreign Office, at the behest of Bevin, formulated a revised plan for a comprehensive settlement in which the Gaza Plan figured as a prominent element; it included the idea of compensation. Britain thought a breakthrough over Gaza essential if Lausanne was to succeed: Israel would get the Strip if it compensated 'the Arabs' with territory and if 'safeguards' were instituted concerning Israel's future treatment of the Gaza refugees, including allowing them to return to their original homes.

Britain interwove in the plan the original Israeli core with other ideas for a territorial–political solution then floating about at Lausanne. The thrust of the British plan was to assure the interests of its Hashemite client State, Jordan, rather than of Egypt: 'If the . . . compensation . . . were to be in the form of the award to Jordan or Jordan and Egypt of part or whole of the Southern Negev, thus providing a land bridge between Egypt and Jordan', Israel must receive freedom of access to the Red Sea. The Arabs, similarly, must receive access to the Mediterranean through 'Gaza and Haifa', stated the plan. 'If another solution were adopted for the Southern Negev, there should nonetheless be guaranteed freedom of communication and access across it between Egypt and Jordan.' The plan also called for incorporation into Jordan of the Arab Legion-held West Bank, partition of Jerusalem with international supervision of the Holy Places, the sharing by Israel and the Arab states of the waters of the Jordan and Yarmuk rivers, and the establishment of a free port at Haifa, through which Iraqi oil could be exported.[61]

Acheson agreed to the bulk of the British proposal. The State Department understood that territorial 'land communication' between Jordan and Egypt was of major importance to the Arab states and agreed both to the partition of Jerusalem and the desirability of the incorporation of 'Arab [eastern] Palestine in Jordan'. (Ethridge, incidentally, had long stressed that for the Arabs, the provision of a land-bridge between Egypt and Jordan was a major political point, not merely 'a satisfaction of strategic concepts'. The Arab world needed territorial continuity; a 'wedge' in the form of a completely Jewish-held Negev would make for 'eternal friction' in the region.) Washington understood that the establishment of a land corridor between Jordan and Egypt was also a major British interest. Washington concurred that the Gaza Plan, more than anything else, held out hope of major achievement at Lausanne. As McGhee put it: Israeli incorporation of the Strip and its '230,000 refugees' is 'the most important of all the things to be aimed at. It was more important even than the exact nature of the territorial settlement [between Israel and the Arab states].' If Israel and Egypt agreed, 'the Arabs might be brought to resettle the remainder of the refugees'.[62]

Sir John Troutbeck, head of the regional British intelligence centre in Cairo, the British Middle East Office, had only one major objection to the evolving joint Anglo-American stand: The territorial compensation must be made to Egypt, not Jordan.

> We should bear in mind [Egyptian] susceptibilities which, though childish, are nonetheless real . . . The Gaza Strip . . . does represent for the Egyptians the only asset they have got out of the campaign . . . They would not regard it as compensation to see the southern Negeb go to Jordan.[63]

What had started as a limited Israeli initiative had become a comprehensive, joint Anglo–American démarche. The two western powers separately but simultaneously approached the Egyptian government with the proposal. The American chargé d'affaires, Jefferson Patterson, felt that if 'suitable' territorial compensation were offered, 'the Egyptians might be able to get away with it'. The Egyptian forces in the Strip, he said, were 'rather jittery' and felt strategically exposed and isolated, and 'this might dispose them to get rid of the strip against territorial compensation'. And Cairo did not want the refugees.

But the Egyptians took an obstreperous tack. The Egyptian Prime Minister, while complaining of the refugee burden, reacted 'with some bitterness to the US proposal for cession of the Gaza Strip to Israel'.[64] At Lausanne, the Egyptians said they 'could not discuss Gaza proposal. Showed complete indifference fate Gaza refugees who were international and Jewish responsibility.' In Cairo, the Egyptians denounced the plan as a 'forerunner of Israeli aggression against Gaza and Arabs expressed surprise US should "lend itself" to such schemes'.

The Egyptians questioned America's impartiality and Patterson gained the impression that if the United States continued 'to play up merits of Gaza Plan, which are invisible to Arab eyes, Egypt may begin regard US as accomplice of Israeli aggression'. Egypt officially rejected the plan on 29 July. The Egyptian Foreign Ministry contended that the plan could serve only the interests of Israel, which was 'making use' of the refugee question to extend its boundaries. The Egyptians ignored the offer of territorial compensation and asserted the refugees' right of return.[65]

By July, Israel was having deep second thoughts about the plan, and not only because of the compensation element. Officially, Tel Aviv remained willing to go through with it, as initially conceived – incorporation in 'exchange' for agreement to absorb the Strip's population. But over the months, the sceptics had gained the upper hand. Israel had agreed to the territory–population trade-off, explained Sharett, in the belief that the Strip contained '150–180,000 Arabs'. But this 'assumption . . . turned out to be incorrect'. Israel now believed there were some 211,000 refugees and 65,000 locals in the Strip; it could not absorb such a total. Also, Israel feared that other refugees, now in Lebanon, Syria and Transjordan, would move to the Strip before its incorporation in the hope of using it as a springboard from which to return to their homes. Israel, he said, must specify the maximum number of Arabs it was willing to take back with the Strip; otherwise, in practice, the commitment would be open-ended. In early August, Sharett, Ben-Gurion, Kaplan and Lifshitz met and decided on a '200,000' ceiling. Israeli diplomats were instructed to 'mention' in conversation that Israel would not take back 'an unlimited number' of Gaza refugees.[66]

As to territorial compensation, Sharett instructed his diplomats to 'vigorously' reject the idea. But he added:

> If things reach a practical stage and it appears necessary to abandon the completely rejectionist stance, it would be possible to discuss border corrections/changes in the northern Negev, both in the east and in the west, that is, in favour of both Transjordan and Egypt, but on no account [will we be willing to discuss] any concession [i.e., cession] in the southern part of the Negev, including Eilat.

(Eytan, incidentally, objected to this. He argued in favour of a cession in the southern Negev, if it brought peace with Egypt, and dismissed Eilat's strategic importance.) Sharett thought that Israel might have to decide whether to agree to take the full '300,000' Arabs in Gaza in 'exchange' for the Strip but without making any territorial compensation, or to agree to take part of the Strip's population *and* to make territorial compensation. In the end, thought Sharett, perhaps the status quo in Gaza was best left as it was.[67]

American and Israeli officials continued to discuss the plan through July. But for all practical purposes, it had died with the Egyptian veto.

The rest was mere shadow-boxing. During the following weeks, the Americans occasionally hinted at the plan in meetings with Egyptian officials, but Egyptian opposition remained unwavering. The Gaza Plan was dead.[68]

THE PCC AND LAUSANNE II: THE '100,000 OFFER' AND THE COLLAPSE OF THE TALKS

At a meeting between Ethridge and Eytan in Lausanne at the end of May, Eytan had reaffirmed Israel's readiness to incorporate the Strip and absorb its population. Ethridge had responded that what the PCC lacked was clarification of how many refugees Israel would be willing to take back 'if she did not get Gaza Strip'.[69]

Since autumn 1948, Israel had intermittently indicated in private conversations that it might agree to take back a substantial number of refugees within the context of a final peace settlement and on condition that the Arab states committed themselves to absorbing and resettling the bulk of the refugees. What was needed, felt the United States and the PCC, was a public and firm Israeli declaration of intent regarding repatriation which would specify the numbers the Jewish State would be ready to take back coupled, if possible, with an immediate start to repatriation. The Americans and the PCC felt that such a 'gesture' might soften the Arabs and, perhaps, induce a matching commitment to absorb the bulk of the refugees.

Through May, the United States pressed Israel to make the 'gesture'. State Department officials, such as McGhee, took heart from the occasional report that the Israeli leaders were seriously considering a substantial repatriation and that a plan had been, or was being, drawn up to repatriate as many as '300,000 or 350,000 refugees'. Ambassador McDonald believed that 'intensive consideration was being . . . given . . . in Tel Aviv to the repatriation of a large number of Arab refugees'. But Burdett and Ethridge, who suspected McDonald of pro-Zionist sympathies, were unconvinced, and believed that Tel Aviv would resist any repatriation as hard as possible.[70]

Lausanne dragged on unpromisingly as the bright hope of the Gaza Plan rapidly faded. The Americans stepped up their demand for a 'gesture', Israel's readiness to incorporate the Strip, indeed, being cited in support.

> US Government greatly disturbed over present Israeli attitude refugee question . . . This attitude . . . difficult [to] reconcile with Gaza Strip proposal, which represents firm admission on part [of] Israel [of] its ability [to] assume responsibility 230,000 refugees plus 80,000 normal residents area.

If Israel was able and willing to absorb the 300,000 Arabs of Gaza, how could it argue an inability and unwillingness to take in a smaller number outside the context of the Gaza Plan?[71]

Ethridge, retiring from the fray, primarily blamed Israel for the Lausanne impasse. Tel Aviv was 'steadfastly' refusing to make concessions. Ethridge took a high moral tone:

> Israel was a state created upon an ethical concept and should rest upon an ethical base. Her attitude toward refugees is morally reprehensible and politically short-sighted. She has no security that does not rest in friendliness with her neighbours.

He felt, in summation, that 'there never has been a time in the life of the [Palestine Conciliation] Commission when a generous and far-sighted attitude on the part of the Jews would not have unlocked peace'.[72]

Israel's position, according to Israeli diplomats in the United States, was also affecting American public opinion, until then solidly pro-Israel. The Israel Consul General in New York, Arthur Lourie, transmitted a copy of a letter from American journalist Drew Pearson, which Lourie said 'expressed . . . anxieties . . . characteristic of a large section of American opinion on whose support we have hitherto been able to count'. Pearson had written that 'in preventing Arab refugees from returning to their native land, the Jews may be subject to the same kind of criticism for which I and others have criticised intolerant Gentiles . . . Now we have a situation in which the Jews have done to others what Hitler, in a sense, did to them!'[73] Eban on 22 June assessed that the impasse was leading to a major rupture in Israeli–American relations:

> We face crisis not comparable previous occasions. Careful attempt being made alienate President from us nearer success than ever before, owing humanitarian aspect refugee situation and his firm belief gesture our part is necessary condition persuade Arabs [to agree to] resettlement and Congress vote funds. We may have face choice between some compromise principle non-return before peace and far-reaching rift USA.[74]

Sasson's assessment of the situation in Lausanne did not differ greatly from Ethridge's. Sasson wrote, in mid-June, that he was sorry he had come. The city was beautiful, the climate temperate, the hotel (the Beau Rivage) luxurious. But the delegation had come to make peace and, after two months, had advanced 'not one step' towards its goal. Moreover, he wrote, 'there is no chance of such progress in the future even if we decide to sit in Lausanne for several more months . . . The Lausanne talks are fruitless and are destined to fail.'

Sasson explained – and his order of priorities is worth noting – that:

> Firstly, the Jews believe that it is possible to achieve peace without [paying] any price, maximal or minimal. They want to achieve (a) Arab surrender of all the areas occupied today by Israel, (b) Arab agreement to absorb

all the refugees in the neighbouring [Arab] states, (c) Arab agreement to rectification of the present frontiers in the centre, south and Jerusalem area in favour of Israel only . . . etc., etc.

The refugees, wrote Sasson, had become

a scapegoat. No one pays attention to them, no one listens to their demands, explanations and suggestions. But . . . all use their problem for purposes which have almost no connection to the aspirations of the refugees themselves.

For example, while all the Arab states demanded the refugees' repatriation, in practice none of them, 'save Lebanon', wanted this. Jordan and Syria wanted to hold on to their refugees in order to receive international relief aid; the Egyptians wanted the problem to remain in order to destabilise Jordan and Israel.

Nor was Israel concerned about the refugees, he wrote. Israel was 'determined not to accept them back . . . come hell or high water'. Sasson himself believed that, in essence, this attitude was correct but thought that Israel should demonstrate flexibility and statesmanship by favourably considering a proposal brought to him by the refugees' representatives at Lausanne, which called for Israeli annexation of the Gaza Strip and the area now known as the 'West Bank', while granting these territories autonomy and absorbing in Israel proper 100,000 refugees. Sasson felt that such a plan could achieve for Israel the complete withdrawal from Palestine of the Arab armies and the 'complete resolution of the Palestine question', and possibly also hasten peace between Israel and the Arab states.[75]

The intense American and PCC pressure on Israel over the early summer bore minor fruit in the form of the 'Family Reunion Programme', announced by Sharett in the Knesset on 15 June. Israel would 'consider favourably' requests by Israeli Arab citizens to allow back 'their wives and young children' – meaning 'sons below the age of 15 and unmarried daughters'. Israel proposed that special posts be set up on the frontiers with Egypt, Jordan and Lebanon (no armistice agreement had yet been signed with Syria) through which the reunions could be accomplished.

Israeli officials widely described and trumpeted the scheme as a 'broad measure easing the lot of Arab families disrupted as a result of the war'. But, in fact, the scheme eased the lot of only a handful of families. During the following months, according to Israel Foreign Ministry figures, 1,329 requests were received pertaining to 3,957 refugees. Tel Aviv issued 3,113 entry permits. By 20 September 1951, a total of 1,965 refugees had made use of the permits and returned to Israeli territory.[76]

If meant as a sop to the United States and the PCC and as a means of neutralising western pressure for repatriation, the family reunion scheme was not a major success.[77] The United States and the PCC wanted a grand 'gesture', not a trickle of returnees. The acting American representative at Lausanne, Raymond Hare, on 23 June delivered a strong 'verbal' communication 'from the US Government' to Eytan, expressing Washington's 'disappointment' in the lack of Israeli compliance with the refugee provision of Resolution 194. 'USA emphatic that responsibility for refugee solution rests squarely on Israel and Arabs, and nowhere else . . . Israel causing delay in refugee solution.'[78] The United States awaited a 'gesture'.

The seeds of such a 'gesture' had long been hibernating in the soil of Tel Aviv. Already in August 1948, Sasson had recommended that Israel consider allowing a return of '40–50,000' refugees and to start repatriating them 'immediately.' (He said he sought to neutralise the expected pressure on Israel at the impending meeting of the United Nations General Assembly in Paris.)[79] In mid-April 1949, with America demanding that Israel agree to repatriate 250,000, Sasson implied that Israel could perhaps take back '150,000'.[80]

Until summer 1949, Sasson's advice had been consistently rejected. But by late June, the cumulative pressure was proving irresistible. Sharett enjoined Ben-Gurion to agree to publicly declare that Israel would accept '25,000' refugees through the reunion scheme. Moreover, Sharett informed Eban on 25 June, 'am weighing whether [to] urge Government [to] agree [that we] should add 50,000 as further maximum contribution without Gaza . . . Will this pacify U.S.[,] turn scales our favour?'[81]

On 5 July, Sharett proposed to the Cabinet that Israel publicly declare its readiness to absorb '100,000' refugees in exchange for peace. This number, he said, would include the '25,000' refugees who had already returned to the country illegally and some '10,000' who would return within the family reunion scheme. Most of the ministers supported Sharett. But Ben-Gurion objected, arguing that the number would not mollify Washington or satisfy the Arabs. He also argued, on security grounds, against re-absorbing so large a number. Agriculture Minister Dov Yosef was more adamant: 'I oppose the return of even a single refugee.' Sharett, who did not want to push through a major decision opposed by the Prime Minister and fellow Mapai stalwarts, then proposed, by way of compromise, that the Cabinet merely authorise him to sound out the Americans as to whether an Israeli announcement of readiness to take back 100,000 would indeed reduce or neutralise the pressure on Tel Aviv. The ministers agreed, and Sharett was empowered to make the 100,000 offer if, indeed, the feelers to Washington resulted in an encouraging response.[82]

The Israeli leadership had concluded that there must be some 'give' if Israeli–American relations were not to be strained to the breaking point. Sharett later explained the Cabinet's vote thus:

The attempt to resurrect the Lausanne Conference is necessary also because of the urgent need to ease the tension which has been created
between us and the United States. This tension has surfaced especially
[over] the refugee problem, whose non-solution serves as an obstacle in
the whole [Lausanne] negotiation.[83]

During the following days, the State Department and White House
were indirectly, and then directly, sounded out on the prospective announcement of readiness to take back 100,000 refugees. The United
States was first informed on 15 July of Israel's decision in principle to let
back a specific number. Ambassador McDonald had already heard that
the Cabinet 'was toying with the idea of an offer of 100,000'.[84]

On 27 July, Sharett told the Transfer Committee of the Cabinet's decision. He asked the committee to produce a plan for absorbing and
resettling the refugees in Israel. Weitz and Danin argued against the decision, calling it a 'catastrophe'. Lifshitz backed Sharett. Sharett added
that if the committee studied the matter and ruled that there was no way
Israel could absorb the refugees, 'then the Cabinet would [just] have to
accept this view'. Weitz, Danin and Lifshitz accepted the task but on condition that the Cabinet agreed to decide nothing without first considering
their views.[85]

The Israeli feelers about the '100,000 Offer' met with a mixed recep-
tion in Washington. Eban's impression on 8 July was that the '100,000'
announcement 'would have very deep impression', to judge from a talk
with McGhee and Hare. But Andrew Cordier, a senior aide to the United
Nations Secretary General, reported that the Americans regarded the
'figure [as] too low'.[86] On 26 July, Acheson reiterated the American demand that Israel absorb some 250,000 – bringing its Arab population up
to 400,000, or roughly the number of Arabs who would have lived in the
Jewish State under the 1947 partition plan.[87]

But President Truman's was the decisive reaction. John Hilldring, a
Truman aide, reported after a conversation with the President on 18 July
that Truman was 'extremely pleased . . . thinks 100,000 offer may break
deadlock'.[88]

The United States was officially informed on 28 July of Israel's readiness to take back 100,000 refugees after there was an overall refugee
resettlement plan and after there was 'evidence' of 'real progress' towards a peace settlement. Elath said that day that Israel had taken the
decision in order 'to demonstrate [its] cooperation with the U.S.' and to
contribute its share to a solution of the refugee problem, and 'in spite
of the fact that Israeli security and economic experts had considered
the proposed decision as disastrous'. Elath said the figure included
'infiltrees' already inside Israel as well as those returning through the
reunion scheme. Sharett, informing McDonald, stressed that 100,000

was the limit, bringing Israel's Arab minority 'far beyond margin of safety by all known security standards'.[89]

The State Department did not immediately react to the '100,000 Offer'. Perhaps Acheson wanted to see how the Arabs would react. And, as perhaps anticipated, the Arabs immediately and flatly rejected the offer. But, unofficially, some Arab officials at Lausanne now hinted at a willingness to accept less than full repatriation. Israel, they said, should take back '340,000' refugees from the conquered territories (outside the partition borders), and repatriate another '100,000' from inside partition plan Israel. The Arab states, with international aid, would then absorb the remaining '410,000'.[90]

Meanwhile, the publication of the '100,000 Offer' caused a major political explosion in Tel Aviv. There was enormous opposition to it within Mapai. Hapo'el Hamizrahi, the General Zionists and Herut all vigorously opposed the offer.

> The Progressives were silent, and the press interpreted their silence as a silent protest . . . Mapam's acknowledgement in weak language of the justice of the act . . . was buried and blurred completely in the wave of rage in which the government was swept for surrendering to 'imperialist pressure',

Sharett reported.

Eban felt that the offer 'represents a very considerable effort in advance of public opinion in [Israel].' Acheson's view was similar: 'Israel . . . has allowed public opinion to develop . . . to such an extent that it is almost impossible for [the] Israeli Government to make substantial concessions re refugees and territory.'[91]

A major debate took place in Mapai on 28 July. The party's Knesset faction leader, Meir Grabovsky (Argov), put the case against the offer succinctly: 'No one wanted . . . and anticipated that the Arabs would leave', he said. But events produced a 'more or less homogeneous [Jewish] state, and now to double the number of Arabs without any certain recompense . . . [should be seen] as one of the fatal mistakes destroying the security of the state . . . We will face a Fifth Column.' Israel would have a minority problem like that 'in the Balkans'.

Sharett called Grabovsky's attack 'illogical'. Grabovsky had supported the incorporation of the Gaza Strip with its population; how could he now oppose absorbing '65–70,000' refugees? The figure contained Sharett's second point: The '100,000 Offer' was not exactly what it seemed. Israel intended to deduct from the figure the 'illegal' infiltrees and the 'legal' returnees (family reunions and special deals, such as with the 'Eilabun and Kafr Bir'im's villagers). There were some 25,000 infiltrees and thousands more of special-case returnees, according to Sharett – hence, '65–70,000'.

But Sharett's main defence was historical. In the beginning, he said, referring to spring 1948,

> there was among us an assumption that the uprooting of these Arabs was temporary . . . and it was [accepted as] natural that the Arab would return to his village . . . When the Foreign Ministry began speaking publicly against a return . . . it was first of all trying to consolidate [Israeli] public opinion against such a return . . . As time passed, the public understood . . . that . . . there would be a catastrophe if there was a return . . . and this policy [against a return] crystallised. It produced decisive results. If now they speak seriously in England and the US of resettlement [of the refugees] in other countries – it is a [result] of this absolute emphasis . . . on our part.

But now the Lausanne cart was in the mud and Israel was being asked to help pull it out: The '100,000 Offer' was the necessary upshot.[92]

The internal Mapai debate continued on 1 August (just before the Knesset plenum debated the offer). Opposition was bitter. As Knesset Member Assaf Vilkomitz ('Ami) put it, 'there will be too large an Arab minority'. Knesset Member Shlomo Lavi (Levkovich) called the offer 'a grave mistake'. Knesset Member Eliahu Carmeli (Lulu) said that bringing back the refugees would create 'not a Fifth but a First Column. I am not willing to take back even one Arab, not even one *goy* [i.e., non-Jew]. I want the Jewish state to be wholly Jewish.' Moshe Dayan's father, Knesset Member Shmuel Dayan, another Mapai old-timer, opposed any return, 'even in exchange for peace. What will this formal peace give us?' Knesset Member Ze'ev Herring argued that allowing back '100,000' would generate further pressure and waves of returnees.

Sharett, stung by the lack of backbench support, told Carmeli that he 'envied' his willingness to live 'in isolation not only from the Orient [i.e., within the Middle East] but also from the whole world.' Sharett stressed that questions of peace, world public opinion, and relations with other countries were important, and that the '100,000 Offer' served an important function in these contexts. 'Comrade Carmeli knows only one thing, that [the] Arabs are a terrible people and that we must uproot them.'

Sharett announced that while there would be no Knesset vote on the offer, the Government 'should be interested in being attacked in the Knesset on this question . . . It is important that the uneasiness of the Mapai members in this matter be expressed.' Sharett's thinking was clear: The more widespread and vicious the internal opposition, the easier it would be for Israel to 'sell' to the United States and the PCC the offer as final and as 'the limit of possible concession'. And, indeed, Sharett instructed his diplomats in this vein: To play up the Government's difficulties in selling the offer to the parties and the public. 100,000, clearly, was the absolute ceiling.[93] In the noisy Knesset plenum debate that followed, Sharett assured the members that the offer would not be binding except as part of a general peace settlement.

'It must be [made] clear to Paul Porter [Ethridge's successor as United States representative on the PCC] that anything further cannot be dreamed of . . . Explain to Porter', Sharett cabled the new head of the Israeli delegation to Lausanne, Reuven Shiloah, 'that our proposal generated grave opposition internally, including in Mapai, and we only with difficulty in a five-hour debate succeeded in calming the storm in the faction . . . Any further concession will destroy the Government's standing.' Sharett added that if the Arabs failed to 'latch onto' the Israeli offer Immediately, pressure would surface, which the Cabinet would be unable to withstand, to withdraw it. The proposal was being made on a 'take it or leave it' basis. Sharett suggested that the United States counsel the Arabs to take it. He repeatedly referred to the mood of the Israeli public.[94]

Sharett believed that the storm over the offer had 'slightly undermined' his personal political standing but that it had helped to 'sell' the proposal abroad. In any case, he tended to believe that the Lausanne talks would collapse, in which event the '100,000 Offer' would never have to be implemented.[95]

Needless to say, the Arab rejection of the '100,000 Offer' did not overly displease Israel. In general, its leaders were not unhappy with the no-war, no-peace situation. In mid-July, Ben-Gurion described Eban's thinking thus:

He sees no need to run after peace. An armistice is sufficient for us; if we run after peace – the Arabs will demand of us a price – [in the coin of] borders [i.e., border rectification] or refugees or both. We will [i.e., can afford to] wait a few years.

In jotting this down in his diary, Ben-Gurion seemed to be conveying his own thinking as well.[96]

And this was also how Acheson assessed Israeli thinking:

Israel prefers . . . status quo . . . Objectives [of Tel Aviv Government] appear to be (1) Absorption of almost all Arab refugees by Arab states and (2) de facto recognition of armistic lines as boundaries.[97]

Israel formally informed the PCC of its readiness to take back '100,000' refugees on 3 August, making it conditional on 'retaining all present territory' and on the freedom to resettle the returnees where it saw fit. The PCC, considering the offer 'unsatisfactory', informally transmitted it to the Arab delegations. The Arabs reacted as expected. One Arab diplomat told Porter the offer was a 'mere propaganda scheme and [the] Jews [are] either at your feet or [at your] throat'. The offer was rejected as 'less than token'. The Arabs maintained that there were '1,000,000' refugees and that 'Jews cannot oppose return large number refugees on economic ground while encouraging mass immigration of Jews [to Israel]'. But Jordan and Syria, making a concession, informed the PCC that they would be able to absorb 'such refugees as might not return to their homes'. Egypt and Lebanon, more vaguely, said that they could absorb 'numbers of refugees'.

Burdett, like the Arabs at Lausanne, immediately dismissed the proposal, along with the family reunion scheme, as a 'sham' designed to frustrate American and United Nations efforts to get Israel to agree to more substantial repatriation. He believed that 'in large part', the Knesset debate and the press campaign against the '100,000' were geared to foreign consumption. The American Embassy in Tel Aviv, on the other hand, stressed the 'genuineness' of the internal opposition to the offer. It explained:

> Conditioned by a long build-up in the Hebrew press, in the Knesset and by Government leaders themselves, which had as its theme the utter undesirability of taking back any Arab refugees whatsoever, the people of this country were hardly prepared for a reversal in policy.

No Israeli, 'from Prime Minister down wishes see single Arab brought back if can possibly be avoided'.[98]

The United States did not think that the Israeli offer 'provide[d] suitable basis for contributing to solution of Arab refugee question'. The offer was 'not satisfactory', Acheson wrote.[99]

But Israel was immovable; 100,000 was the ceiling. By mid-August, all the participants understood that Lausanne had failed. Even Shiloah was 'worried [and] tense'. Sharett reassured him that the Israeli offer had 'vastly improved' Israel's 'tactical position vis-à-vis UN and Arabs.' But Shiloah, like Eytan and Sasson before him, knew that Lausanne was going nowhere. The Arab rejection of the Gaza Plan and of the '100,000 Offer' and Israel's rejection of complete repatriation and withdrawal to the partition plan borders left, in Acheson's phrase, 'no real basis for conciliation'. By the end of August, it was all over. The participants raised their hands, having achieved nothing, and indefinitely suspended the conference. The delegations returned home in September. The PCC continued to churn out reports on the Palestine refugee problem into the 1950s.[100]

But meanwhile, in August 1949, the PCC and the United States made one last more or less coordinated effort. Politics had clearly failed. So they tried an indirect approach, economics. The upshot was Washington's 'McGhee Plan' and the PCC's Economic Survey Mission. Both were geared to finding an economic solution to the refugee problem. The American policymakers focused on a grand economic development scheme for the Middle East, a regional Marshall Plan, which would bring the Arab states into the American orbit against the backdrop of the Cold War, push these states forward economically and, possibly, solve the refugee problem by well-funded, organised resettlement in the Arab states. The scheme was known as the 'McGhee Plan'.

Meanwhile, the Technical Committee on Refugees, created by the PCC on 14 June 1949 to report on the scope and nature of the refugee problem, on 20 August submitted its findings. The committee found that there were '711,000' bona fide refugees, and that the higher number of international relief recipients (totalling close to one million) was the result of 'duplication of ration cards' and the inclusion 'of persons who, although not displaced, are destitute'. It recommended that a thorough census be conducted. The committee found that an 'overwhelming' number of refugees wished to return to their homes but that Israel was blocking repatriation. The committee opined that 'the clock cannot be turned back', especially in view of the increase of the Yishuv by '50 per cent' since the Palestinian exodus; immigrants were pouring into Israel at the rate of '800 a day'. The committee surveyed employment possibilities and mooted regional development projects of benefit to the refugees.[101]

Even before the Technical Committee's report was in, the PCC and the United States set in motion the creation of the Economic Survey Mission (ESM), whose focus was regional development projects that could employ the refugees. The ESM, headed by Gordon Clapp, was formally set up on 23 August, as (like the Technical Committee) a subsidiary body of the PCC under Resolution 194. Washington understood that the projects' funding would be mainly American and the underlying assumption was a solution based on resettlement in the Arab countries rather than repatriation.[102] The ESM, based in Beirut, began touring the region in mid-September and presented an interim report to the PCC and General Assembly in December.

The ESM was only one of a number of economic and diplomatic devices which were invented over 1949–1956 to keep the refugee problem alive and on the international agenda. Like those of the Technical Committee before it, its findings and recommendations had no effect on anything. The refugees had been, and remained, a political problem; economic amelioration had to be preceded by political settlement.

As time passed, the status quo and Arab and Israeli policies hardened and calcified. The mass influx of immigrants into Israel steadily obviated any possibility of mass refugee repatriation. Only the destruction of the Jewish State and the death or expulsion of its population could have made a mass refugee return physically possible. From the Arab side, resettlement in the Arab countries remained through the years a clear possibility, though one requiring a vast amount of Western capital. But the Arab states objected to such resettlement mainly for political reasons. They regarded repatriation as the 'just' solution and, incidentally, as one that could help undermine the Jewish State, to whose continued existence they objected. The Arab states were also eager to be rid of the refugee burden for internal reasons, fearing the refugees' potential as a restive Fifth Column. Meanwhile, while Israel blocked repatriation, the refugees' presence and misery served as a useful political weapon against Israel.

In retrospect, it appeared that at Lausanne was lost the best and perhaps only chance for a solution of the refugee problem, if not for the achievement of a comprehensive Middle East settlement. But the basic incompatibility of the initial starting positions and the unwillingness of the two sides to move, and to move quickly, towards a compromise – born of Arab rejectionism and a deep feeling of humiliation, and of Israeli drunkenness with victory and physical needs determined largely by the Jewish refugee influx – doomed the 'conference' from the start. American pressure on both sides, lacking a sharp, determined cutting edge, failed to budge sufficiently either Jew or Arab. The '100,000 Offer' was a classic of too little, too late. The Gaza Plan, given Egypt's defeat in the war, the just-ended territorial expansion of the Jewish State and Egyptian–Jordanian rivalries, was a nonstarter; Egypt alone may have agreed to it, but not as part of an Arab coalition generally guided by its most extreme constituents (the key to Arab political group dynamics).

So Lausanne ended on 12 September without result, setting the seal on the refugee problem. It was probably the last chance of peacefully resolving the Middle East conflict.

ENDNOTES

1. Comay and Lifshitz, 'The Arab Refugee Problem', 16 Mar. 1949, ISA FM 2431\13.
2. Eytan to de Boisanger (Lausanne), 25 May 1949, ISA FM 2447\2. De Boisanger months earlier had independently arrived at the same conclusion (see H. Beeley to H. Ashley Clarke (Paris), 4 Jan. 1949, PRO FO 371–75346 E39\1017\31).
3. Mark Ethridge (Beirut), the American member of the PCC, to Secretary of State, 29 Mar. 1949, NA 501 BB. Palestine\3-2849.
4. Burdett to Secretary of State, 23 Dec. 1948, NA RG 84, Jerusalem Consulate, Classified Records 1948, 800 Israel.
5. C. Waterlow, minute on 'Resettlement of Arab Refugees', 5 Jan. 1949, and minute by F. B. A. Rundall, 11 Jan. 1949, PRO FO 371-75417 E263\1821\31.
6. American Legation, Jidda to Secretary of State, 21 Jan. 1949, NA 501 BB. Palestine\1-2149.
7. Burdett to Secretary of State, 5 Feb. 1949, NA 501 BB. Palestine\2-549, and Burdett to Secretary of State, 9 Feb. 1949, NA 501 BB. Palestine\2-949. Burdett was no friend of Zionism and was highly critical of Israeli policies (often clashing over them with McDonald, who was pro-Zionist).
8. Burdett to Secretary of State, 8 Feb. 1949, and Ethridge to Secretary of State, 8 Feb. 1949 – both in NA 501 BB. Palestine\2-849.

9. Ethridge to Acheson, 28 Feb. 1949, NA 501 BB. Palestine\2–2849; Ethridge (Beirut) to Secretary of State, 29 Mar. 1949, NA 501 BB. Palestine\3-2949; Ethridge (Jerusalem) to Secretary of State, 14 Mar. 1949, NA 501 BB. Palestine\3-1449; Ethridge (Jerusalem) to Dean Rusk (Washington), 14 Mar. 1948, NA 501 BB. Palestine\3-1449; Satherthwaite, director of Office of Near Eastern and African Affairs, State Department, to Secretary of State, 16 Mar. 1949, NA 501 bb. Palestine\3-1649; and Caplan, *Diplomacy*, III, 62–64.

10. 'Memorandum of Conversation', 22 Mar. 1949, NA 501 BB. Palestine\3-2249.

11. Caplan, *Diplomacy*, III, 66.

12. Ethridge and McGhee (Beirut) to Secretary of State, 29 Mar. 1949, NA 501 BB. Palestine\3-2949.

13. 'Protocol of A Consultative Meeting Concerning the Peace Negotiations with the Arab States, 12 April 1949', ISA FM 2447\3.

14. 'Memorandum of Conversation', 5 Apr. 1949, New York, NA 501 BB. Palestine\4-549.

15. Entry for 11 Feb. 1949, Weitz, *Diary*, IV, 11; and Shertok to Weitz, Lifshitz and Danin, 14 Mar. 1949, ISA FM 2444\19.

16. 'Meeting of the PCC and Ben-Gurion', 7 Apr. 1949, ISA FM 2451\13; and 'Meeting of the Conciliation Commission with the Prime Minister and Ministry for Foreign Affairs Staff (Tel Aviv, 7 April 1949)', ISA, *Documents* II, 555–62. When Ethridge complained that there were reports that 'irresponsible elements in Israel' were continuing to expel Arabs, Ben-Gurion replied: 'We are responsible for our citizens. There are no "irresponsible elements". If it is true that Arabs are [still] being expelled by irresponsible people – please help us to catch these people. We will bring them to trial and punish them severely. We are responsible for all that happens in our State and will not stand for such deeds.'

17. Houstoun Boswall (Beirut) to Foreign Office, 1 Apr. 1949, PRO FO 371-75349 E4281\1017\31.

18. PCC communiqué, Beirut, 5 Apr. 1949, ISA FM 2444\19.

19. 'Protocol of Consultative Meeting in Advance of Lausanne', 19 Apr. 1949, ISA FM 2447\3; and 'Note on the Arab Refugee Problem', Leo Kohn to Gershon Hirsh (Avner) and Sharett, 24 Apr. 1949, ISA FM 2444\19.

20. 'Protocol of Consultative Meeting in Advance of Lausanne', 19 Apr. 1949, ISA FM 2447\3.

21. Ethridge (Jerusalem) to Acheson, 19 Apr. 1949, NA 501 BB. Palestine\4-1949; and Ethridge (Jerusalem) to Secretary of State, 20 April 1949, NA 501 BB. Palestine\4-2049.

22. Acheson to Ethridge, 20 Apr. 1949, NA 501 BB. Palestine\4-2049; and Truman to Ethridge, 29 Apr. 1949, NA 501 BB. Palestine\4-2949.

23. Acheson to Certain American Diplomatic and Consular Officers, 29 Apr. 1949, NA 501 BB. Palestine\4-2949.

24. Memorandum on Walter Eytan press conference at Lausanne, 30 Apr. 1949, ISA FM 2447\7; Eytan to Sharett, 30 Apr. l949, ISA FM 2447\6; and Hirsh to Sharett, 1 May 1949, ISA FM 2447\6.

25. Eytan (Tel Aviv) to Sharett (New York), 10 Apr. 1949, ISA FM 2447\2.

26. 'Sharett-Abdullah Conversation, 5 May 1949', ISA FM 2451\13; ISA, *Documents*, IV, 33–7, Sharett, 'Meeting: M. Sharett-King Abdullah (Shuneh,

5 May 1949)', 9 May 1949; and Eytan to Sharett, 21 June 1949, ISA FM 2447\1.

27. 'Extract from a Letter by Muhammad Nimr al Hawari to . . .', undated, ISA FM 2444\19; and Sasson (Lausanne) to Sharett, 17 Aug. 1949, ISA FM 2447\13.

28. Eytan (Lausanne) to Sharett, 9 May 1949, ISA FM 2447\6.

29. 'Mr A. Eban's Statement on the Arab Refugee Question Before the Ad Hoc Political Committee at Lake Success on 5th May 1949 in Connection with Application of Israel for Admission to Membership in the United Nations', ISA FM 2444\19.

30. Acheson to US Legation, Amman, 16 May 1949, NA 501 BB. Palestine\5-1695.

31. Acheson to Ethridge, 19 May 1949, NA 501 BB. Palestine\5–1949.

32. Eban (New York) to Eytan (Lausanne), 24 June 1949, ISA FM 2444\19.

33. Truman to Ben-Gurion, 29 May 1949, ISA FM 2451\13.

34. Sharett to McDonald, 8 June 1949, ISA, *Documents* IV, 107–11.

35. Eytan (Lausanne) to Sharett, 13 June 1949, ISA FM 2447\6; Eytan to Eban (New York), 9 June 1949, ISA FM 2447\6; Gideon Rafael to Eban, 22 June 1949, ISA FM 2414\26 aleph; and Eytan to Sharett, 13 June 1949, ISA FM 2447\2.

36. Kollek to Sharett, 10 June 1949, ISA FM 2444\19.

37. Sharett to Eytan, 15 Mar. 1949, ISA FM 174\2 aleph.

38. 'Protocol of a Consultation at the Prime Minister's Office on the Arab Refugee Problem, 12 April 1949', ISA FM 2447\3.

39. Ethridge to Acheson, 13 Apr. 1949, NA 501 BB. Palestine\4-1349; Ethridge to Acheson, 20 Apr. 1949, NA 501 BB. Palestine\4-2049; and Eytan (Lausanne) to Sharett, 30 Apr. 1949, ISA FM 2447\6.

40. 'Protocol of a Consultative Meeting Concerning Peace Negotiations with the Arab States, 19 April 1949', ISA FM 2447\3.

41. 'Protocol of a Consultative Meeting Concerning Peace Negotiations with the Arab States (Lausanne), 22 April 1949', ISA FM 2447\3.

42. Eytan (Lausanne) to Sharett, 30 Apr. 1949, ISA FM 2447\6. In contacts with Israelis, Ethridge tended to 'reduce' the number of refugees in the Strip, the better to sell the plan to Tel Aviv. The usual American estimate at the time was 225,000.

43. Ethridge to Acheson, 9 May 1949, NA 501 BB. Palestine\5–949.

44. Protocol of Cabinet meeting, 3 May 1949, ISA.

45. Ethridge to Secretary of State, 20 May 1949, NA 501 BB. Palestine\5-2049, and McDonald to Secretary of State, 31 May 1949, NA 501 BB. Palestine\5-3149; 'Memorandum transmitted by the PCC to the Arab delegations summarising proposals made by Israel on May 20', 23 May 1949, ISA FM 2447\2; Eytan to de Boisanger, 29 May 1949, ISA FM 2447\1; and Eytan to de Boisanger, 31 May 1949, ISA FM 2447\2.

46. Ethridge to Secretary of State, 28 May 1949, NA 501 BB. Palestine\5-2849; and ISA, *Documents* IV, 74–5, W. Eytan (Lausanne) to C. de Boisanger, 29 May 1949.

47. Acting Secretary of State James Webb to US Delegation, Lausanne, 28 May 1949, NA 501 BB. Palestine\5-2849; and ISA, *Documents* IV, 72–3, Rafael (New York) to Sharett, 27 May 1949. Rafael wrote: '[State] Department

(my guess [Dean] Rusk) doubts sincerity our offer accept Gaza refugees, believes that after annexation Strip [Israel] will have [the refugees] leave like Faluja Pocket inhabitants.'

48. Ethridge to Secretary of State, 2 June 1949, NA 501 BB. Palestine\6-249.
49. Burdett (Jerusalem) to Secretary of State, 16 June 1949, NA RG 84, Tel Aviv Embassy, Classified Records 1949, 321.1 Israel–Transjordan, reporting on a conversation with Moshe Dayan, Military Governor of Jerusalem. The head of the opposition Revisionist (Herut Party) camp, Menachem Begin, was also unenthusiastic about the plan (see 'Memorandum of Conversation' between Ambassador McDonald, First Secretary Knox and Begin, Tel Aviv, 14 June 1949, NA RG 84, Tel Aviv Embassy, Classified Records 1949, 321.9 – Israel).
50. McDonald to Secretary of State, 31 May 1949, NA 501 BB. Palestine\5-3149; McDonald to Secretary of State, 23 June 1949, NA 501 BB. Palestine\6-2349; Ross (US Delegation to United Nations) to Secretary of State, 1 June 1949, NA 501 BB. Palestine\6-149; Webb to Ethridge, 1 June 1949, NA 501 BB. Palestine\6-149; Ross to Secretary of State, 10 June 1949, NA 501 BB. Palestine\6-1049; Helm to Foreign Office, 2 June 1949, PRO FO 371–75350 46832\1017\31; Ethridge to Secretary of State, 2 June 1949, NA 501 BB. Palestine\6-249; Ethridge (Paris) to Secretary of State, 12 June 1949, NA 501 BB. Palestine\6-1249; 'Memorandum of Conversation, Webb, Ethridge, Eban, Shiloah and others, Washington, 17 June 1949, NA 501 BB. Palestine\6-1749; McDonald to Secretary of State, 22 June 1949, NA 501 BB. Palestine\6-2249; and Sir O. Franks (Washington) to Foreign Office, 6 June 1949, PRO FO 371-75350 E7011\1017\31.
51. Ethridge (Paris) to Secretary of State, 12 June 1949, NA 501 BB. Palestine\6-1249.
52. For the British interest in the Strip's future, see H. Beeley memorandum of 9 July 1949, PRO FO 371–75350 E8393/1017/3. A dominant school of thought in the Foreign Office explained Israel's acceptance of the Gaza Plan as motivated by the need for cheap Arab labour: Israel, contrary to its public protestations, argued the British officials, wanted the return of a substantial number of refugees. The British Ambassador to Tel Aviv, Knox Helm, wrote (very wrongheadedly) on 10 June 1949: 'My objective reasoning leads me to the conclusion that the Israelis never wanted the Arabs to leave and that, in spite of their propaganda, they wish in their innermost hearts that they had them or many of them back . . . The Arabs provided cheap and good labour . . . The Jews, in spite of all their publicity, do not take to farming [sic] . . . Thus Israel seems to me to need the Arabs. But it would want them as the tillers of the soil, the hewers of wood and the drawers of water.' William Strang, the Permanent Under-Secretary of State at the Foreign Office, minuted on 7 July: 'The Israelis' offer to accept the refugees in the Gaza area must, as you say, reflect a feeling on the part of Israel that she can make some use of these Arabs. It seemed at the time unlikely that the Gaza Strip in itself would be worth the price of looking after the refugees if they were to be a complete burden' (Helm to Michael Wright (Foreign Office), 10 June 1949, and Strang minute, 7 July 1949, both in PRO FO 371–7542, E74651821/31). Even Hugh Dow, the British Consul General in Jerusalem, agreed, though he took issue with Helm about what had happened in 1948. He wrote to

Wright that 'it cannot be sustained that "the Israelis never wanted the Arabs to leave" . . . The immediate advantages to the Jews of the Arab migration are patent enough. It offered an unexpected solution to the security problem . . . it gave them new lands for Jewish settlement; it offered a great alleviation of the housing problem created by the influx of new immigrants', and so on. But Dow then agreed with Helm that the Jewish leadership now, in mid-1949 – was having second thoughts and saw that the 'wholesale expulsion of the Arabs was great mistake . . . Helm's remarks about the poverty of Jewish agriculture are illuminating.' Dow agreed that the Jews now wanted a substantial return of refugees to place the Jewish economy 'on a sound basis' of cheap labour (Dow to Wright, 27 June 1949, PRO FO 371–75432 E8231).

53. Sasson (Lausanne) to Sharett, 1 June 1949, ISA, *Documents* IV, 86.
54. 'Memorandum of Conversation', Acting Secretary of State James Webb and other American officials and Egyptian Ambassador to Washington Kamil Abdul Rahim, Washington, 10 June 1949, NA 501 BB. Palestine\6-1049; and, memorandum by Michael Wright on his talk on 1 July 1949, at Lausanne, with Ray Hare, the acting US representative to the PCC, 1 July 1949, PRO Fo 371–75350 E8393/1017/31.
55. Eytan (Lausanne) to Sharett, 30 June 1949, ISA, *Documents* IV, 186–87, 187 footnote 3.
56. Eban (New York) to Sharett, 4 July 1949, ISA, *Documents* IV, 204 footnote 1.
57. McDonald to Secretary of State, 22 June 1949, NA 501 BB. Palestine\6-2249; Acheson to US Embassy, Tel Aviv, 25 June 1949, NA 501 BB. Palestine\6-2549; Acheson to US Embassy, Tel Aviv, 2 July 1949, NA RG 84, Tel Aviv Embassy, Classified Records 1949, 321.9 – Israel-Egypt.
58. Warren Austin, US representative to the United Nations, to Secretary of State, 6 July 1949, NA 501 BB. Palestine\7-649; and Acheson to US Delegation to United Nations, 6 July 1949, NA 501 BB. Palestine\7-649.
59. British Embassy, Washington DC, to Eastern Department, Foreign Office, 12 July 1949, PRO FO 371-75350 E8707; and 'Memorandum of Conversation', Eban, McGhee and Hare, Washington DC, 7 July 1949, NA 501 BB. Palestine\7-749.
60. Sasson (Lausanne) to Ziama Zeligson (Shmuel Divon) (Tel Aviv), 16 June 1949 ISA FM 3749\2; and Eytan to Sharett, 30 July 1949, ISA FM 2447\6.
61. 'Suggested Basis for a New Approach by the Conciliation Commission to the Parties on their Resumption of Work on the 18th of July', Eastern Department, Foreign Office, 9 July 1949, PRO FO 371-75350 E8393\1017\31.
62. Acheson to US Embassy, London, 13 July 1949, NA 501 BB. Palestine\7-1349; Hoyer Millar, UK Embassy, Washington DC, to Foreign Office, 14 July 1949, PRO FO 371–75350 E8636\1017\31; and Ethridge (Lausanne) to Secretary of State, 12 June 1949, NA 501 BB. Palestine\6-1249.
63. Foreign Office to UK Embassy, Washington, 16 July 1949, PRO FO 371–75350 E8636/1017/31; and, J. Troutbeck (BMEO Cairo) to Foreign Office, 16 July 1949, PRO FO 371–75350 E8704/1017/31.
64. A. Mayall, UK Embassy, Cairo, to G.L. Clutton, African Department, Foreign Office, 19 July 1949, PRO FO 371–75351 E9059/1017/31.

65. Acheson to US Embassy, Tel Aviv, 19 July 1949, NA RG 84, Tel Aviv Embassy, Classified Records 1949, 321.9–Israel–Egypt; Rockwell (Lausanne) to Secretary of State, 20 July 1949, NA 501 BB. Palestine\7-2049; Acheson to US Embassy, Tel Aviv, 22 July 1949, NA RG 84, Tel Aviv Embassy, Classified Records, 1949, 321.9 Israel–Egypt; and Acheson to US Embassy, Tel Aviv, 29 July 1949, NA RG 84, Tel Aviv Embassy, Classified Records 1949, 321.9 Israel–Egypt.

66. Sharett to Sasson (Lausanne), 21 Aug. 1949, ISA FM 2447\1.

67. 'Guidelines for the Missions (briefing No. 3) the [Israel] Foreign Minister's Briefing to the Delegation to Lausanne', 25 July 1949, ISA FM 2447\2; Sharett to Shiloah and Sasson (Lausanne), 7 Aug. 1949, ISA FM 2447\5; entry for 27 July 1949, Weitz, *Diary*, IV, 42; Sharett's statement at meeting of Mapai Secretariat and parliamentary faction, 28 July 1949, LPA 2-11\1\1; Eytan to Sharett, 30 July 1949, ISA FM 2447\6; and 'Memorandum of Conversation', Elath, McGhee, Rusk, etc., Washington DC, 28 July 1949, NA 501 BB. Palestine\7-2849.

68. Acheson to US Embassy, Tel Aviv, 1 Aug. 1949, NA 501 BB. Palestine\8-149; Acheson to US Embassy, London, 1 Aug. 1949, NA 501 BB. Palestine\8-149; and Patterson (Cairo) to Secretary of State, 19 Sep. 1949, NA 501 BB. Palestine\9-1949.

69. Ethridge to Secretary of State, 28 May 1949, NA 501 BB. Palestine\5–2849.

70. Burdett (Jerusalem) to Secretary of State, 16 June 1949, NA RG 84, Tel Aviv Embassy, Classified Records 1949, 321.9 Israel–Transjordan; McDonald to Secretary of State, 31 May 1949, NA RG 84, Tel Aviv Embassy, Dec. #571, Classified Records 1949; McGhee (Washington) to McDonald, 24 May 1949, NA 501 BB. Palestine\5–2449; Ethridge (Lausanne) to Secretary of State, 2 June 1949, NA 501 BB. Palestine\6-249; and, McDonald to Secretary of State, 13 July 1949, NA 501 BB. Palestine\7-1349. See also, British Legation, Tel Aviv, to Eastern Department, Foreign Office, 5 Aug. 1949, PRO FO 371–75436 E9822/1821/31, for a report on alleged Israeli preparations to take back refugees.

71. Acting Secretary of State Webb to US Delegation, Lausanne, 14 June 1949, NA 501 BB. Palestine\6–1449; and Ethridge to Rusk, 15 June 1949, NA 501 BB. Palestine\6–1549.

72. Ethridge (Lausanne) to Secretary of State, 12 June 1949, NA 501BB. Palestine\6–1249; and Ethridge to Dean Rusk, 15 June 1949, NA 501 BB. Palestine\6–1549.

73. Arthur Lourie (New York) to Esther Herlitz (Tel Aviv), 6 July 1949, ISA FM 2444\19

74. Eban (New York) to Sharett, 22 June 1949, ISA, *Documents* IV, 150.

75. Sasson (Lausanne) to Zeligson, 16 June 1949, ISA FM 3749\2.

76. Information Services, Government of Israel, Foreign Press Division, 'Press Release No. 1', 7 July 1949, ISA FM 2451/17; and, 'An Extract from Information to the Israeli Missions Abroad,' undated, ISA FM 2451/17.

77. See, for example, UK Embassy, Washington, to Eastern Department, Foreign Office, 12 July 1949, PRO FO 371–75350 E8707/1821/31.

78. Eytan (Lausanne) to Sharett, 23 June 1949, ISA, *Documents* IV, 154–5.

79. A précis of a letter, Sasson (Paris) to Shertok (Tel Aviv), 13 Aug. 1948, ISA FM 2451/13.

80. 'Protocols of the Consultative Meeting in Advance of the Lausanne Conference, Tel Aviv,' 12 Apr. 1949, ISA FM 2447\3.
81. Sharett to Eban (New York), 25 June 1949, ISA, *Documents* IV, 176.
82. Protocol of Cabinet meeting, 5 July 1949, ISA; and 'Editorial Note' and Sharett to Eban (New York), 6 July 1949, ISA, *Documents* IV, 206–207.
83. 'Guidelines to the Missions Abroad, Briefing No. 3, the Foreign Minister's Briefing to the Lausanne Delegation', 25 July 1949, ISA FM 2444\19.
84. McDonald to Secretary of State, 20 July 1949, NA RG 84, Tel Aviv Embassy, Classified Records 1949, 321.9 Palestine Conciliation Commission. See also, Marriott (Haifa) to Foreign Office, 28 Apr. 1949, PRO FO 371–75425 E5343/1821/31; and Colin Crowe, UK Embassy, Tel Aviv, to B. A. B. Burrows, Eastern Department, Foreign Office, 19 July 1949, PRO FO 371–75434 E9296/1821/31, for President Weizmann's reference already in Apr. to a return of '100,000'. Perhaps it was thought that the number would have nostalgic appeal for President Truman, who in 1946 had demanded that Britain let into Palestine '100,000' World War II Jewish refugees; it was also a round, tidy number, not too small to be dismissible as insignificant.
85. Entry for 27 July 1949, Weitz, *Diary*, IV, 42.
86. Eban (New York) to Sharett, 8 July 1949, and Lourie and Rafael (New York) to Sharett, 12 July 1948, ISA, *Documents* IV, 211–12 and 218.
87. Acheson to US Delegation, Lausanne, 26 July 1949, NA 501 BB. Palestine\7–2649.
88. Lourie (New York) to Sharett, 19 July 1949, and Eban (New York) to Sharett, 27 July 1949, ISA, *Documents* IV, 227 and 257.
89. 'Memorandum of Conversation', Elath, Rusk, McGhee, etc., Washington DC, 28 July 1949, NA 501 BB. Palestine\7–2849; Porter (Lausanne) to Secretary of State, 28 July 1949, NA 501 BB. Palestine\7–2849; and, McDonald to Secretary of State, 28 July 1949, NA 501 BB. Palestine\7–2849.
90. Shiloah (Lausanne) to Sharett, 10 Aug. 1949, ISA FM 2447\1.
91. Sharett to M. Eliash, Israel Minister to London, 10 Aug. 1949, ISA FM 2412\26; Eban (New York) to Elath (Washington), 26 July 1949, ISA FM 2444\19; and Acheson to US diplomatic posts, 1 Aug. 1949, NA 501 BB. Palestine\8-149.
92. Protocol of meeting of Mapai Knesset Faction and Secretariat, 28 July l949, LPA 2-11\1\1.
93. Text of Sharett's Knesset speech, 1 Aug. 1949, ISA FM 2451\13; and protocol of Special Meeting of Mapai Secretariat and Knesset Faction, 1 Aug. 1949, LPA 2-11\1\1.
94. Sharett to Shiloah (Lausanne), 2 Aug. 1949, ISA FM 2451\13; and Sharett to Eliash (London), 10 Aug. 1949, ISA FM 2412\26.
95. Sharett to Eliash (London) 10 Aug. 1949, ISA FM 2412\26; and Sharett to Shiloah and Sasson (Lausanne), 7 Aug. 1949, ISA FM 2447\5.
96. Sharett to Eliash (London), 10 Aug. 1949, ISA FM 2412\26; Sharett to Shiloah and Sasson (Lausanne), 7 Aug. 1949, ISA FM 2447\5; and entry for 14 July 1949, DBG–YH III, 993.
97. Acheson to United States diplomatic posts, 1 August 1949, NA 501 BB. Palestine\8-149.
98. 'United Nations Conciliation Commission for Palestine: Fourth Progress Report to the Secretary General of the United Nations', 15 Sep. 1949, ISA FM

2447\4; Porter (Lausanne) to Secretary of State, 3 Aug. 1949, NA 501 BB. Palestine\8-349; Porter (Lausanne) to Secretary of State, 5 August 1949, NA 501 BB. Palestine\8-549; Rockwell (Lausanne) to Secretary of State, 16 Aug. 1949, NA 501 BB. Palestine\8-1649; Burdett (Jerusalem) to Secretary of State, 4 Aug. 1949, NA RG 84, Tel Aviv Embassy, Classified Records 1949, 571 – Palestine Refugee Relief; Burdett (Jerusalem) to Secretary of State, 12 August 1949, NA RG 84, Tel Aviv Embassy, Classified Records 1949, 321.9 – Israel; Richard Ford (chargé d'affaires, Tel Aviv) to Secretary of State, 9 Aug. 1949, NA RG 84, Tel Aviv Embassy, Classified Records 1949, 321.9 – Israel; Ford (Tel Aviv) to Secretary of State, 11 Aug. 1949, NA RG 84, Tel Aviv Embassy, Classified Records, Dec. #571, 1949; and Ford (Tel Aviv) to Secretary of State, 19 Aug. 1949, NA 501 BB. Palestine\8-1949.

99. Porter (Lausanne) to Secretary of State, 3 Aug. 1949, and Acheson to Porter (Lausanne), 9 Aug. 1949, both in NA RG 84, Tel Aviv Embassy, Classified Records 1949, 321. Israel; Acheson to US Delegation, Lausanne, 11 Aug. 1949, NA 50I BB. Palestine\8-1149; and 'Memorandum of Conversation', Elath, McGhee, Wilkins, etc., Washington DC, 18 Aug. I949, NA 50I BB. Palestine\8-1849.

100. Sharett to Shiloah (Lausanne), 10 Aug. 1949, ISA FM 2451\13; and Acheson to US Embassy, Tel Aviv, 16 Aug. 1949, NA RG 84, Tel Aviv Embassy, Classified Records 1949, 321.9 Israel.

101. 'Terms of Reference of the Technical Committee on Refugees', 14 June 1949, ISA FM 2444\19; and 'Report of the Technical Committee on Refugees to the Conciliation Commission', 20 Aug. 1949, ISA FM 2447\4.

102. Arthur Lourie, 'Report of Conversation Between Abe Feinberg and Paul Porter', 18 Aug. 1949, ISA FM 2447\5; 'Terms of Reference of the Economic Survey Mission', 1 Sep. 1949, ISA FM 2447\4; and 'United Nations Conciliation Commission for Palestine: Fourth Progress Report to the Secretary General of the United Nations', 15 Sep. 1949, ISA FM 2447\4.

Conclusion

The first Arab–Israeli war, of 1948, was launched by the Palestinian Arabs, who rejected the UN partition resolution and embarked on hostilities aimed at preventing the birth of Israel. That war and not design, Jewish or Arab, gave birth to the Palestinian refugee problem.

But the displacement of Arabs from Palestine or from the areas of Palestine that would become the Jewish State was inherent in Zionist ideology and, in microcosm, in Zionist praxis from the start of the enterprise. The piecemeal eviction of tenant farmers, albeit in relatively small numbers, during the first five decades of Zionist land purchase and settlement naturally stemmed from, and in a sense hinted at, the underlying thrust of the ideology, which was to turn an Arab-populated land into a State with an overwhelming Jewish majority. And the Zionist leaders' thinking about, and periodic endorsement of, 'transfer' during those decades – voluntary and agreed, if possible, but coerced if not – readied hearts and minds for the denouement of 1948 and its immediate aftermath, in which some 700,000 Arabs were displaced from their homes (though the majority remained in Palestine).

But there was no pre-war Zionist plan to expel 'the Arabs' from Palestine or the areas of the emergent Jewish State; and the Yishuv did not enter the war with a plan or policy of expulsion. Nor was the pre-war 'transfer' thinking ever translated, in the course of the war, into an agreed, systematic policy of expulsion. Hence, in the war's first four months, between the end of November 1947 and the end of March 1948, there were no preparations for mass expulsion and there were almost no cases of expulsion or the leveling of villages; hence, during the following ten months, Haganah and IDF units acted inconsistently, most units driving out Arab communities as a matter of course while others left (Muslim as well as Christian and Druse) villages and townspeople in place; and hence, at war's end, Israel emerged with a substantial Arab minority, of

150,000 (a minority that today numbers one million – and still constitutes (a restive and potentially explosive) one fifth of the State's population).

At the same time, largely as a result of Arab belligerence and the Yishuv's sense of siege, fragility and isolation, from early April 1948 on, 'transfer' was in the air and the departure of the Arabs was deeply desired on the local and national levels by the majority in the Yishuv, from Ben-Gurion down. And while this general will was never translated into systematic policy, a large number of Arabs were expelled, the frequency of expulsions and the expulsive resolve of the troops increasing following the pan-Arab invasion of mid-May 1948 that threatened the Yishuv with extinction. Yet, still, in July and again in October–November 1948, IDF troops continued to leave Arab communities in place; much depended on local circumstances and on the individual Israeli company, battalion and brigade commanders.

But if a measure of ambivalence and confusion attended Haganah\IDF treatment of Arab communities during and immediately after conquest, there was nothing ambiguous about Israeli policy, from summer 1948, toward those who had been displaced and had become refugees and toward those who were yet to be displaced, in future operations: Generally applied with resolution and, often, with brutality, the policy was to prevent a refugee return at all costs. And if, somehow, refugees succeeded in infiltrating back, they were routinely rounded up and expelled (though tens of thousands of 'infiltrators' ultimately succeeded in resettling and becoming Israeli citizens). In this sense, it may fairly be said that all 700,000 or so who ended up as refugees were compulsorily displaced or 'expelled'.

Yet it is also worth remembering that a large proportion of those who became refugees fled their towns and villages not under direct Israeli threat or duress. Tens of thousands – mostly from well-to-do and elite families – left the towns in the war's early months because of the withdrawal of the British administration, the war-filled chaos that followed and the prospect of Jewish rule. And, in the following months, hundreds of thousands fled not under Jewish orders or direct coercion though, to be sure, most sought to move out of harm's way as Zionist troops conquered town after town and district after district. And most probably believed that they would be returning home in a matter of months if not weeks, perhaps after the Arab armies had crushed Israel.

From the first, the AHC and the local National Committees opposed the exodus, especially of army-aged males, and made efforts to block it. But they were inefficient and, sometimes, half-hearted. And, at the same time, they actively promoted the depopulation of villages and towns. Many thousands of Arabs – women, children and old people, from villages around Jerusalem, the Coastal Plain and the Jezreel and Jordan valleys, and from various towns – left, well before battle was joined, as a result of advice and orders from local Arab commanders and officials, who feared for their safety and were concerned that their presence would hamper their militiamen in battle. Indeed, already months before the war the Arab states and the AHC had endorsed the removal of dependents from active and potential combat zones. And, starting in December 1947, Arab officers ordered the complete evacuation of specific villages in certain areas, lest their inhabitants 'treacherously' acquiesce in Israeli rule or hamper Arab military deployments. There can be no exaggerating the importance of these early, Arab-initiated evacuations in the demoralisation, and eventual exodus, of the remaining rural and urban populations.

The creation of the Palestinian refugee problem was almost inevitable, given the geographical intermixing of the Arab and Jewish populations in what is a minute country (10,000 sq. miles), the history of Arab–Jewish hostility over 1881–1947, the overwhelming opposition on both sides to a binational state, the outbreak and prolongation of the war for Israel's birth and survival, the major structural weaknesses of Palestinian Arab society, the depth of Arab animosity towards the Yishuv and Arab fears of falling under Jewish rule, and the Yishuv's fears of what would happen should the Arabs win or of what would befall a Jewish State born with a very large and hostile Arab minority.

The exodus unfolded in four or four and a half stages, closely linked to the development of the war itself. It began during December 1947-March 1948 – the first stage – with the departure of many of the country's upper and middle class families, especially from Haifa and Jaffa, towns destined to be in, or at the mercy of, the Jewish state-to-be, and from neighbourhoods of Jewish west Jerusalem. Flight proved infectious. Household followed household, neighbour, neighbour, street, street and neighbourhood, neighbourhood (as, later, village was to follow neighbouring village, in domino clusters). The prosperous and educated feared death or injury in the ever-spreading hostilities, the anarchy that attended the gradual withdrawal of the British administration and security forces, the brigandage and intimidation of the Arab militias and irregulars and, more vaguely but generally, the unknown, probably dark future that awaited them under Jewish or, indeed, Husseini rule. Some of these considerations, as well as a variety of direct and indirect military pressures, also caused during these months the evacuation of most of the Arab rural communities in the predominantly Jewish Coastal Plain.

Most of the upper and middle class families, who moved from Jaffa, Haifa, Jerusalem, Ramle, Acre and Tiberias to Damascus, Nablus, Amman, Beirut, Gaza and Cairo, probably thought their exile would be temporary. They had the financial wherewithal to tide them over; many had wealthy relatives and accommodation outside the country. The urban masses and the *fellahin,* however, had nowhere to go, certainly not in comfort. For most of them, flight meant instant destitution; it was not a course readily adopted. But the daily spectacle of abandonment by their 'betters,' with its concomitant progressive closure of businesses, shops, schools, law offices and medical clinics, and abandonment of public service posts, led to a steady attrition of morale, a cumulative sapping of faith and trust in the world around them: Their leaders were going or had gone; the British were packing. They were being left 'alone' to face the Zionist enemy.

Daily, week in, week out, over December 1947, January, February and March 1948, there were clashes along the 'seams' between the two communities in the mixed towns, ambushes in the fields and on the roads, sniping, machine-gun fire, bomb attacks and occasional mortaring. Problems of movement and communication, unemployment and food distribution intensified, especially in the towns, as the hostilities drew out. There is probably no accounting for the mass exodus that followed without understanding the prevalence and depth of the general sense of collapse, of 'falling apart' and of a centre that 'cannot hold', that permeated Arab Palestine, especially the towns, by April 1948. In many places, it would take very little to nudge the masses to pack up and flee.

Come the Haganah (and IZL–LHI) offensives and counteroffensives of April–June, the cumulative effect of the fears, deprivations, abandonment and depredations of the previous months, in both towns and villages, overcame the natural, basic reluctance to abandon home and property and flee. As Palestinian military power was swiftly and dramatically crushed and the Haganah demonstrated almost unchallenged superiority in successive battles, Arab morale cracked, giving way to general, blind, panic or a 'psychosis of flight',[1] as one IDF intelligence report put it. This was the second – and crucial – stage of the exodus. There is a clear, chronological, one-to-one correspondence between the Jewish offensives and the flight of the bulk of the population from each town and district attacked.

Often, the fall of villages harmed morale in neighbouring towns (vide the fall of Khirbet Nasir ad Din and Arab Tiberias). Similarly, the fall of the towns – Tiberias, Haifa, Jaffa, Beisan, Safad – and the flight of their population generated panic in the surrounding hinterlands: After Haifa, came flight from Balad al Sheikh and Hawassa; after Jaffa, Salama, Kheiriya and Yazur; after Safad, Dhahiriya Tahta, Sammu'i and Meirun. For decades the villagers had looked to the towns for leadership; now, they followed them into exile.

If Jewish attack directly and indirectly triggered most of the exodus up to June 1948, a small but significant proportion was due to direct expulsion orders and to psychological warfare ploys ('whispering propaganda') designed to intimidate people into flight. Several dozen villages were ordered or 'advised' by the Haganah to evacuate during

April–June. The expulsions were usually from areas considered strategically vital and in conformity with Plan D, which called for clear main lines of communications and border areas. But, in general, Haganah and IDF commanders were not forced to confront the moral dilemma posed by expulsion; most Arabs fled before and during battle, before the Israeli troops reached their homes and before the Israeli commanders were forced to confront the dilemma.

Moreover, during April–July, Arab commanders and the AHC ordered the evacuation of several dozen villages as well as the removal of dependents from dozens more. The invading Arab armies also occasionally ordered whole villages to depart, so as not to be in their way.

In April–May, and indeed, again in October–November, the 'atrocity factor' played a major role in flight from certain areas. Villagers and townspeople, prompted by the fear that the Jews, if victorious, would do to them what, in the reverse circumstances, victorious Arab fighters would most probably have done (and, occasionally, did, as in the Etzion Bloc in May) to the Jews, took to their heels.[2] The actual atrocities committed by the Jewish forces (primarily at Deir Yassin) reinforced such fears considerably, especially when magnified loudly and persistently in the Arab media for weeks thereafter. Apart from the 20-odd cases of massacre, Jewish troops often randomly killed individual prisoners of war, farm hands in the fields and the occasional villager who had stayed behind. Such actions could not but amplify flight. There were also several dozen cases of rape, a crime viewed with particular horror in Arab and Muslim societies. The fear of rape apparently figured large in the Arab imagination, and this may in part account for the despatch of women and girls out of active or potential combat zones and, in some measure, for the headlong flight of villages and urban neighbourhoods from April on.

To what extent was the exodus up to June 1948 a product of Yishuv or Arab policy?

To be sure, the Haganah's adoption and implementation during December 1947 – March 1948 of a retaliatory strategy against Arab militia bases – meaning villages and urban neighbourhoods – resulted in civilian flight. But the strategy, to judge from the documentation, was designed to punish, harm and deter militiamen, not to precipitate an exodus.

In early March, the prospect of pan-Arab invasion gave rise to Plan D. It accorded the Haganah brigade and battalion-level commanders *carte blanche* to completely clear vital areas of Arab population. Many villages served as bases for bands of irregulars; most had militias that periodically assisted the irregulars in attacks on settlements and convoys. During April–May, Haganah units, usually under orders from HGS, carried out elements of Plan D, each unit interpreting and implementing the plan as it saw fit in light of local circumstances. The Haganah offensives were in large measure responses to Arab attacks. In general, the Jewish commanders preferred to completely clear the vital roads and border areas of Arab communities – Allon in Eastern Galilee, Carmel around Haifa and in Western Galilee, Avidan in the south. Most villagers fled before or during the fighting. Those who stayed put were almost invariably expelled.

During April–June, neither the political nor military leaderships took a decision to expel 'the Arabs'. As far as the available evidence shows, the matter was never discussed in the supreme decision-making bodies. But it was understood by all concerned that, militarily, in the struggle to survive, the fewer Arabs remaining behind and along the front lines, the better and, politically, the fewer Arabs remaining in the Jewish State, the better. At each level of command and execution, Haganah officers, in those April–June days when the fate of the State hung in the balance, simply 'understood' what was required in order to survive. Even most Mapam officers – ideologically committed to coexistence with the Arabs – failed to 'adhere' to the party line: Conditions in the field, tactically and strategically, gave precedence to immediate survival-mindedness over the long-term desirability and ethos of coexistence.

The Arab leadership inside and outside Palestine probably helped precipitate flight in the sense that, while doctrinally opposed to the exodus, it was disunited and ineffectual, and had decided, from the start, on no fixed, uniform policy and gave the masses no consistent guidelines for behaviour, especially during the crucial month of April. The records are incomplete, but they show overwhelming confusion and disparate purpose, 'policy' and implementation changing from week to week and area to area. No guiding hand or central control is evident; no overarching 'policy' was manifest.

During the months before April 1948, especially in March, the flight of the middle and upper classes from the towns provoked condemnations from local NCs and the AHC (while NC members, and their families, were themselves busy fleeing their homes or already living abroad). But little was effectively done to prevent flight. And the surrounding Arab states did little, before late March, to block the entry of the evacuees into their territory. The rich and middle class arrived in Nablus, Amman, Beirut, and Cairo in a trickle and were not needy; it seemed to be merely a repeat of the exodus of 1936–1939. No Arab country effectively closed its borders though, at the end of March, Syria and Lebanon severely curtailed the issue of entry visas. The Husseinis were probably happy that many Opposition-linked families were leaving Palestine. The AHC, almost all its members already dispersed abroad, issued no forceful, blanket, public condemnations of the exodus, though occasionally it implored army-aged males to stand, or return, and fight.[3] At the local level, some NCs (in Haifa and Jerusalem, for example) and local commanders tried to stem the exodus, even setting up people's courts to try offenders and threatening confiscation of the departees' property. However, enforcement seems to have been weak and haphazard; the measures proved largely unavailing. And bribes could overwhelm any regulation. Militiamen and irregulars often had an interest in encouraging flight – they needed the houses for quarters and there was money to be made out of it (departees paid to have their empty homes 'protected', abandoned houses were looted, and money was extorted from departees).

Regarding April–May and the start of the main stage of the exodus, I have found no evidence to show that the AHC or the Arab leaders outside Palestine issued blanket instructions, by radio or otherwise, to the inhabitants to flee. However, in certain areas, women, children and old people continued to be evacuated and specific villages were instructed to leave, lock, stock and barrel. Moreover, it appears that Husseini supporters in certain areas ordered or encouraged flight out of political calculation, believing that they were doing what the AHC would want them to do. Haifa affords illustration. While it is unlikely that Husseini or AHC members from outside Palestine instructed the Haifa Arab leadership on 22 April to opt for evacuation rather than surrender, local Husseini supporters, led by Sheikh Murad, certainly did. They were probably motivated by fear that staying in Haifa would be interpreted as acquiescence in Jewish rule and 'treachery' and by the calculation that Palestinian misery, born of the exodus, would increase the pressure on the Arab states to intervene. Local and AHC leaders believed that the evacuation was temporary and that a mass return would soon follow. In any event, the AHC encouraged the continuing exodus after it had begun. The case of Haifa in late April – early May is supremely instructive about the ambivalence of the national and local Palestinian leaderships toward the exodus.

The Arab states, apart from appealing to the British to halt the Haganah offensives and charging that the Jews were expelling Palestine's Arabs, seem to have taken weeks to digest and understand what was happening. They did not appeal to the Palestinian masses to leave, but neither, in April, did they publicly enjoin the Palestinians to stay put. Perhaps the politicians in Damascus, Cairo and Amman, like Husseini, understood that they would need to justify their armed intervention – and the exodus, presented as a planned Zionist expulsion, afforded such justification.

But the dimensions and burden of the problem created by the exodus, falling necessarily and initially upon the shoulders of the host countries, quickly persuaded the Arab states – primarily Jordan – that it were best to halt the floodtide. The AHC, too, was apparently shocked by the ease and completeness of the exodus. Hence the spate of appeals to the Palestinians in early May by Jordan, the AHC and the ALA to stay put or, if already in exile, to return home. But, given the ongoing hostilities and the expectation of a dramatic increase in warfare along the fronts, the appeals had little effect: The refugees, who had just left active combat zones, were hardly minded to return to them, especially on the eve of the invasion. Besides, in most areas the Haganah physically barred a return. Later, after 15 May, the pan-Arab invasion and the widespread fighting made any thought of a return impracticable. At the same time, the invasion substantially increased the readiness of Haganah commanders to clear border areas of Arab communities. (And given the narrow, elongated shape of the new State, every area was in effect a border area.)

Already in April–May, on the local and national levels, the Yishuv's leaders began to contemplate the problem of a return: Should the refugees be allowed back? The approach of the First Truce in early June raised the problem as one of the major political and strategic issues facing the new State. The Arab states, on the local level on each front and in international forums, had begun pressing for Israel to allow back the refugees. And the UN Mediator, Bernadotte, had vigorously taken up the cause.

However, politically and militarily it was clear to most Israelis that a return would be disastrous. Militarily – and the war, all understood, was far from over – it would mean the introduction of a large, potential Fifth Column; politically, it would mean the reintroduction of a large, disruptive, Arab minority. The military commanders argued against a return; so did political common sense. Both were reinforced by strident anti-return lobbying by settlements around the country.

The mainstream national leaders, led by Ben-Gurion, had to confront the issue within two problematic political contexts – the international context of future Israeli–Arab relations, Israeli–United Nations relations and Israeli–United States relations, and the local context of a coalition government, in which the Mapam ministers (and, less insistently, other ministers) advocated future Jewish–Arab coexistence and a return of 'peace-minded' refugees after the war. Hence the Cabinet consensus of June–August 1948 was that there would be no return during the war and that the matter could be reconsidered after the hostilities. This left Israel's diplomats with room for manoeuvre and was sufficiently flexible to allow Mapam to stay in the government, leaving national unity intact.

On the practical level, from spring 1948, a series of developments on the ground increasingly precluded any possibility of a refugee return. These were an admixture of incidental, 'natural' processes and steps specifically designed to assure the impossibility of a return, including the gradual destruction of the abandoned villages, the destruction or cultivation and long-term takeover of Arab fields, the establishment of new settlements on Arab lands and the settlement of Jewish immigrants in abandoned villages and urban neighbourhoods.

The months between the end of the First Truce (8 July) and the signing of the Israeli–Arab armistice agreements in spring–summer 1949 were characterised by short, sharp Israeli offensives interspersed with long periods of ceasefire. In these offensives, the IDF beat the Jordanian and Egyptian armies and the ALA in the Galilee, and conquered large parts of the territory earmarked by the UN for a Palestine Arab state. During and after these battles in July, October–November and December 1948 – January 1949, something like 300,000 more Palestinians became refugees.

Again, there was no Cabinet or IDF General Staff-level decision to expel. Indeed, the July fighting (the 'Ten Days') – the third stage of the exodus – was preceded by an explicit IDF General Staff order to all units and corps to refrain from destruction of villages and expulsions without prior authorisation by the Defence Minister. The order was issued as a result of the cumulative political pressure during the summer by various softline ministers on Ben-Gurion and, perhaps, was never intended to be taken too seriously. In any event, it was largely ignored.

But the overarching operational orders for operations Dekel, Dani, Yoav and Hiram – the main July–November offensives that resulted in Arab displacement – did not include expulsory clauses. However, from July onwards, there was a growing readiness in the IDF units to expel. This was at least partly due to the feeling, encouraged by the mass exodus from Jewish-held areas to date, that an almost completely Jewish State was a realistic possibility. There were also powerful vengeful urges at play – revenge for the Palestinian onslaught on the Yishuv during December 1947 – March 1948, the pan-Arab invasion of May–June, and the massive Jewish losses. In short, the Palestinians were being punished for having forced upon the Yishuv the protracted, bitter war that had resulted in the death of one, and the maiming of two, in every 100 in the Jewish population. The Arabs had rejected partition and unleashed the dogs of war. In consequence, quite understandably, the Yishuv's leadership – left, centre and right – came to believe that leaving in place a large hostile Arab minority (or an Arab majority) inside the State would be suicidal. And driving out the Arabs, it emerged, was easy; generally they fled at the first whiff of grapeshot, their notables and commanders in the lead. Ben-Gurion said that this revealed a collective lack of backbone. In general, the advancing Haganah and IDF units were spared the need to face morally painful decisions to expel communities; to a large degree, Arab flight let the commanders off the moral hook, though, to be sure, many were subsequently, at the very least, troubled by the need to confront, and repel, would-be returnees.

The tendency of IDF units to expel civilians increased just as the pressures on the remaining Arabs by their leaders inside and outside Palestine to stay put grew and just as their motivation to stand fast increased. During the summer, the Arab governments intermittently tried to bar the entry of new refugees into their territory. The Palestinians were encouraged to stay in Palestine or to return to their homes. At the same time, those Palestinians still in their villages, hearing of the misery that was the lot of their exiled brethren and despairing of salvation and a reconquest of Palestine, generally preferred to stay put, despite the prospect of Israeli rule. After July, Arab resistance to flight was far greater than in the pre-July days. There was to be much less 'spontaneous' flight; villagers tended either to stay put or to leave under duress.

Ben-Gurion clearly wanted as few Arabs as possible in the Jewish State. From early on he hoped that they would flee. He hinted at this in February 1948 and said so explicitly in meetings in August, September and October. But no expulsion policy was ever enunciated and Ben-Gurion always refrained from issuing clear or written expulsion orders; he preferred that his generals 'understand' what he wanted. He probably wished to avoid going down in history as the 'great expeller' and he did not want his government to be blamed for a morally questionable policy. And he sought to preserve national unity in wartime.

But while there was no 'expulsion policy,' the July offensives were characterised by far more expulsions and, indeed, brutality than the first half of the war. Yet events varied from place to place. Ben-Gurion approved the largest expulsion of the war, from Lydda and Ramle, but, at the same time, IDF Northern Front, with Ben-Gurion's authorisation, left mostly-Christian Nazareth's population in place; the 'Christian factor' outgunned security and demographic concerns and was allowed to determine policy. And, in the centre of the country, three Arab villages sitting astride vital axes – Fureidis, Jisr az Zarka and Abu Ghosh – were allowed to stay, for economic and sentimental reasons.

Again, the IDF offensives in October–November – the fourth stage of the exodus – were marked by a measure of ambivalence in all that concerned the troops' treatment of overrun civilian populations. In the south ('Yoav'), where Allon was in command, almost no Arab civilians remained. Allon preferred Arab-clear rear areas and let his subordinates know what he wanted. In the north ('Hiram'), where Carmel was in charge, the picture was varied. Many Arabs declined to budge, contrary to Ben-Gurion's expectations. This was partly due to the fact that before October, the villagers had hardly been touched by the war or its privations. Again, Carmel's hesitant, inexplicit expulsion orders, issued after the battles were over, contributed. So did the varied demographic make-up of the central-upper Galilee pocket. The IDF generally related far more benignly to Christians and Druse than to Muslims. Most Christian and Druse villagers stayed put and were allowed to do so. Many of the Muslim villagers fled; others were expelled. But many other Muslims – in Deir Hanna, 'Arraba, Sakhnin, Majd al Kurum and other villages – stayed put, and were allowed to stay. Much depended on specific local factors.

During the following months, with the Cabinet in Tel Aviv gradually persuaded by Arab rhetoric and actions that the conflict would remain a central feature of the Middle East for many years, the IDF was autho- rised to clear Arab communities from Israel's long, winding and highly penetrable borders to a depth of 5–15 kilometres. The result may be seen as 'stage four and a half' of the exodus. One of the aims was to prevent infiltration of refugees back to their homes. The IDF was also afraid of sabotage and spying. Early November saw a wave of IDF expul- sions and transfers inland of villagers along the northern border. Some villagers, ordered out, were 'saved' by last-minute intervention by soft- line Israeli politicians. The following months and years saw other border areas cleared or partially cleared of Arab inhabitants.

In examining the causes of the Arab exodus from Palestine over 1947–1949, accurate quantification is impossible. I have tried to show that the exodus occurred in stages and that causation was multi-layered: A Haifa merchant did not leave only because of the weeks or months of sniping and bombings; or because business was getting bad; or because of intimidation and extortion by irregulars; or because he feared the col- lapse of law and order when the British left; or because he feared for his prospects and livelihood under Jewish rule. He left because of the ac- cumulation of all these factors. And the mass of Haifaites who fled in his wake, at the end of April – early May 1948, did not flee only as a result of the Arab militia collapse and Haganah conquest of 21–22 April. They fled because of the cumulative effect of the elite's departure, the snipings and bombings and material privations, unemplyment and chaos during the previous months; and because of their local leaders' instructions to leave, issued on 22 April; and because of the follow up orders by the AHC to continue departing; and because of IZL and Haganah activities and pressures during the days after the conquest; and because of the prospect of life under Jewish rule.

The situation was somewhat more clear-cut in the countryside. But there, too, multiple causation often applied. Take Qaluniya, near Jerusalem. There were months of hostilities in the area, intermit- tent shortages of supplies, severance of communications with Arab Jerusalem, lack of leadership or clear instructions about what to do or expect, lack of sustained help from outside, rumours of impending Jewish attack, Jewish attacks on neighbouring villages and reports of Jewish atrocities, and, finally, Jewish attack on Qaluniya itself (after most of the inhabitants had left). Again, evacuation was the end product of a cumulative process.

Even in the case of a Haganah or IDF expulsion order, the actual departure was often the result of a process rather than of that one act. Take Lydda, largely untouched by battle before July 1948. During the first months of the war, there was unemployment and skyrocketing prices, and the burden of armed irregulars. In April–May, thousands of refugees from Jaffa and its hinterland arrived in the town, camping out in courtyards and on the town's periphery. They brought demoralisation and sickness. Some wealthy families left. There were pinprick Haganah raids. There was uncertainty about Abdullah's commitment to the town's defence. In June, there was a feeling that Lydda's 'turn' was imminent. Then came the attack, with bombings and shelling, Arab Legion pullout, collapse of resistance, sniping, massacre – and expulsion orders. Lydda was evacuated.

What happened in Palestine/Israel over 1947–1949 was so complex and varied, the situation radically changing from date to date and place to place, that a single-cause explanation of the exodus from most sites is untenable. At most, one can say that certain causes were important in certain areas at certain times, with a general shift in the spring of 1948 from precedence of cumulative internal Arab factors – lack of leadership, economic problems, breakdown of law and order – to a primacy of external, compulsive causes: Haganah/IDF attacks and expulsions, fear of Jewish attacks and atrocities, lack of help from the Arab world and the AHC and a feeling of impotence and abandonment, and orders from Arab officials and commanders to leave. In general, throughout the war, the final and decisive precipitant to flight in most places was Haganah, IZL, LHI or IDF attack or the inhabitants' fear of imminent attack.

During the second half of 1948, international concern about the refugee problem mounted. Concern translated into pressure. This pressure, initiated by Bernadotte and the Arab states in the summer of 1948, increased as the months passed, as the number of refugees swelled, as their physical plight became more acute and as the discomfort of their Arab hosts grew. The problem moved to the forefront of every discussion of the Middle East crisis and the Arabs made their agreement to a settlement, nay, even to meaningful negotiations, with Israel contingent on a solution of the problem by repatriation.

From summer 1948, Bernadotte, and from the autumn, the United States, pressed Israel to agree to a substantial measure of repatriation as part of a comprehensive solution to the refugee problem and the conflict. In December, the UN General Assembly endorsed the (peace-minded) refugees' 'right of return'. But, as the abandoned villages fell into decrepitude or were bulldozed or settled, and as more Jewish immigrants poured into the country and were accommodated in abandoned Arab houses, the physical possibility of substantial repatriation grew more remote. Allowing back Arab refugees, Israel argued, would commensurately reduce Israel's ability to absorb Jewish refugees from Europe and the Middle East. Time worked against repatriation. Bernadotte and the United States wanted Israel to make a 'gesture' in the coin of repatriation, to get peace negotiations off the ground.

In the spring of 1949, the thinking about a 'gesture' matured into an American demand that Israel agree to take back 250,000, with the remaining refugees to be resettled in the neighbouring countries. America threatened and cajoled, but never with sufficient force or conviction to persuade Tel Aviv to accede.

In the spring, in a final major effort, the United Nations and United States engineered the Lausanne Peace Conference. Weeks and months of haggling over agenda and secondary problems led nowhere. The Arabs made all progress contingent on Israeli agreement to mass repatriation. Under American pressure, Tel Aviv reluctantly agreed, in July, to take back 65,000–70,000 refugees (the '100,000 Offer') as part of a comprehensive peace settlement. But by summer 1949, public and party political opinion in Israel – in part, due to conditioning by the government – had so hardened against a return that even this minimal offer was greeted by a storm of public protest and howls within Mapai. In any case, the sincerity of the Israeli offer was never tested; the Arabs rejected it out of hand. The United States, too, regarded it as insufficient; as too little, too late.

The insufficiency of the '100,000 Offer', the Arab states' continuing rejectionism, their unwillingness to accept and concede defeat and their inability to publicly agree to absorb and resettle most of the refugees if Israel agreed to repatriate the rest, the Egyptian rejection of the 'Gaza Plan', and America's unwillingness or inability to apply persuasive pressure on Israel and the Arab states to compromise – all meant that the Arab–Israeli impasse would remain and that Palestine's displaced Arabs would remain refugees, to be utilised during the following years by the Arab states as a powerful political and propaganda tool against Israel. The memory or vicarious memory of 1948 and the subsequent decades of humiliation and deprivation in the refugee camps would ultimately turn generations of Palestinians into potential or active terrorists and the 'Palestinian problem' into one of the world's most intractable. And at the core of that problem remain the refugees.

ENDNOTES

1. HIS-AD, 'The Emigration . . . 1.12.47-1.6.48', 30 June 1948, HHA-ACP 10.95.13 (1).
2. Aharon Cohen, no enemy of the Arabs, at the time quoted two observations. An English sergeant told an American newsman on the day of Jaffa's surrender: 'The Arabs were frightened to death when they imagined to themselves that the Jews would do to them half of what they would have done to the Jews were the situation reversed'; and an educated Haifa Arab said, according to Cohen: 'The Arabs always thought that they [themselves] were a primitive, wild and uncivilised people, capable of anything, while the Jews [they thought] were a civilised people, able to restrain their impulses. But in face of the Deir

Yassin atrocity, [the Arabs] began to think that this was not exactly the picture. And because at that time [i.e., April] the Jews were winning the military struggle, the flight began' (Cohen, 'In Face of the Arab Evacuation', undated but late May 1948, HHA-ACP 10.95.11 (8), published in *Ahdut Ha'avodah*, June 1948).

3. HIS-AD, 'The Emigration . . . 1.12.47-1.6.48', 30 June 1948, HHA-ACP 10.95.13 (1).

Appendix I

THE NUMBER OF PALESTINIAN REFUGEES

Over the years, a minor point of dispute between Israel and the Arab states has been the number of Palestinian Arabs who became refugees during and as a result of the 1948 war. From 1949 onwards, Arab officials spoke of a total of 900,000 or one million. Israeli spokesmen, in public, usually referred to 'about 520,000'.[1] The United Nations Economic Survey Mission and the United Nations Relief and Works Agency for Palestine Refugees in the Near East (UNRWA) put the figure at 726,000.[2]

Other estimates ranged between the Israeli and Arab figures. For example, the British, in February 1949, thought that there were 810,000, of whom 210,000 were in the Gaza Strip, 320,000 in the West Bank and 280,000 in Lebanon, Syria and Jordan (East Bank).[3] The director general of the Israel Foreign Ministry, Walter Eytan, in a private letter in late 1950 referred to the UNRWA registration in 1949 of 726,000 as 'meticulous' but thought that 'the real number was close to 800,000'.[4] However, officially, Israel stuck to the low figure of 520,000–530,000. The reason was simple:

> If people . . . became accustomed to the large figure and we are eventually obliged to accept the return of the refugees, we may find it difficult, when faced with hordes of claimants, to convince the world that not all of these formerly lived in Israeli territory . . . It would, in any event, seem desirable to minimise the numbers . . . than otherwise.[5]

Israel sincerely believed that the Arab (and United Nations) figures were 'inflated'. This inflation, Sharett thought, stemmed from the inclusion of displaced persons from border areas outside Israeli territory and the inclusion of 'destitute people' who had preferred to jump onto the bandwagon of United Nations relief rather than stay at home impoverished. The refugees themselves tended to exaggerate their numbers (for example, by not registering deaths) in order to obtain more rations.[6] In August 1948, Sharett instructed his officials to obtain expert help in arriving at the real number of the refugees. The officials responded that the statisticians were 'at a loss' about how to work out the numbers and had themselves turned to the Foreign Ministry for figures.[7]

In mid-1949, Sharett asked Israel's Central Bureau of Statistics for an official estimate. On 2 June, the Bureau's Dr Helmut Meyuzam responded that 'the number of refugees was about 577,000'. The Bureau reached this figure by the following route: According to British Mandate estimates, the total number of non-Jewish inhabitants in the areas which became the Jewish State was 722,000 (including west Jerusalem). This included a six per cent exaggeration. Hence, the real number was probably 679,000. But at the end of the war there were about 102,000 Arabs left in Israel – hence 577,000 had become refugees.[8] (It was on this basis that the Israel Foreign Ministry reached the 520,000–530,000 total, arguing that about 30,000–40,000 refugees, who had infiltrated back into Israel since the November 1948 census that showed 102,000 Arabs in Israel, should be lopped off the 577,000 figure.) But Meyuzam had qualified his estimate by saying that in assessing the number of Arabs in the areas that became Israel (679,000), he had not taken into account 'illegal' Arab immigrants resident in Palestine or the beduin concentrations in the Negev, either left in place or in exile.

These points (among others) were taken up in a British analysis in September 1949. The Foreign Office concluded that the number of refugees was 'between 600,000 and 760,000'. This rather inconclusive conclusion, co-opting the extremes of the Foreign Office Research Department's estimate (600,000) and the PCC Technical Committee's 'maximum number' (766,000), was based on the following criticisms of the official Israeli estimate: It took no account of natural increase among the Palestine Arabs since 31 December 1947 (which was offset only in part by war casualties); it was incorrect in deducting six per cent from the Mandate total of about '725,000'; and it ignored the figure of '95,000' for the beduins, many of whom had become refugees. The thrust of the British analysis was that there were 711,000 bona fide refugees.[9]

Both Meyuzam and the British understood that there was no way accurately to assess the number of Arab illegals living in Palestine when the war broke out or to estimate the net difference between births and deaths during the war (the number of Palestinian war dead was unclear). And Meyuzam rightly implied that accurately assessing the number of beduin who had become refugees was impossible.

Because of these factors, it is impossible to arrive at a definite, persuasive estimate. My predilection would be to opt for the loose contemporary

British formula, that of 'between 600,000 and 760,000' refugees; but, if pressed, 700,000 is probably a fair estimate.

ENDNOTES

1. Comay to PCC Technical Committee on Refugees, 24 July 1949, ISA FM 2451\13; and Sharett to Elath (Washington), 31 July 1949, ISA FM 2444\19
2. Gabbay, *Political Study*, 175. Gabbay's own estimate (177) was 710,000. Gelber, *Palestine*, 272, citing UN sources, puts the number at '765,000', but this includes '47,000' 'internal' or 'domestic refugees' – i.e., Arabs displaced from their towns and villages who remained in Israeli territory. To my mind, these people and their descendents cannot properly be designated 'refugees'.
3. McNeil response to question by Brigadier Rayner, 16 Feb. 1949, PRO FO 371–75419 E2297\1821\31.
4. Eytan to Daniel Sirkis (*Hatzofe*), 10 Nov. 1950, CZA A340\24.
5. Lourie to Eytan, 11 Aug. 1948, ISA FM 2564\22.
6. Sharett to Elath (Washington), 31 July 1949, ISA FM 2444\19.
7. Shimoni to Eytan, 25 Aug. 1948 (with minute by Shertok), and Shimoni to Shertok, 2 Sep. 1948, both in ISA FM 2564\22.
8. H. Meyuzam to Asher Goren, Foreign Ministry, 2 June 1949, ISA FM 2444\19.
9. FO to UK Delegation UN (New York), 2 Sep. 1949, PRO FO 371–75436 E10083\1821\31.

Appendix II

BIOGRAPHICAL NOTES

Allon (Paicovitch), Yigal (1918–1980) b. Kfar Tavor, Palestine. Commander of the Palmah 1945–8. OC Operation Yiftah (April–May 1948), OC Operation Dani (July 1948) and OC Operation Yoav (October 1948). OC Southern Front September 1948–1949. Minister of Labour 1961–1968, Deputy Prime Minister, Foreign Minister 1974–1977.

Abdullah, Ibn Husayn (1882–1951) b. Mecca. Emir (1921–1946) and King (1946–1951) of Transjordan\Jordan.

Ben-Gurion (Gruen), David (1886–1973) b. Poland. Settled in Palestine 1906. Secretary-General of the Histadrut 1920–1935. Chairman of the Jewish Agency 1935 – May 1948. Leader of Mapai. Prime Minister and Minister of Defence of Israel 1948–1954, Prime Minister and Minister of Defence 1955–1963.

Carmel (Zalizky), Moshe (1911–2002) b. Minsk Mazowiecki, Poland. Settled in Palestine 1924. Member of Kibbutz Na'an. OC Haganah Haifa District 1947. OC Carmeli Brigade April–May 1948. OC Northern Front (Operation Dekel and Operation Hiram) July 1948–1950. Editor *Lamerhav* (Ahdut Ha'avodah's daily) 1960–1965, Minister of Transport 1955–1956, 1965–1969.

Cisling, Aharon (1901–1964) b. Russia. Settled in Palestine 1904. Member of Kibbutz 'Ein Harod. Ahdut Ha'avodah leader. Minister of Agriculture (Mapam) 1948–1949.

Cohen, Aharon (1910–1980) b. Bessarabia. Settled in Palestine 1937. Member of Kibbutz Sha'ar Ha'amakim. Director of Arab Department, Mapam and member of Mapam Political Committee, 1948–1949.

Cunningham, General Sir Alan Gordon (1887–1983) b. Dublin. GOC 8th Army 1941, last British High Commissioner in Palestine 1945 – May 1948.

Danin, Ezra (1903–1985) b. Jaffa. Senior officer of Haganah Intelligence Service (*Shai*)1936–1948. Official of Arab Division, JA-PD 1940–1948. Member of Arab Affairs Committee of the National Institutions 1940s. Member of first and second Transfer Committees and Senior Adviser on Arab Affairs to the Foreign Ministry 1948–1949. Orange-grower.

Eshkol (Shkolnik), Levi (1895–1969) b. Russia. Haganah Treasurer in 1940s. Deputy Minister of Defence 1948. Director Jewish Agency Land Settlement Department September 1948 – June 1963. Minister of Finance 1952–1963. Prime Minister 1963–1969.

Eytan (Ettinghausen), Walter (1910–2002) b. Munich. Settled in Palestine 1946. Director General, Israel Foreign Ministry 1948–1959. First head of Israel Delegation at Lausanne 1949. Israel Ambassador to France 1959–1970.

Galili, Israel (1910–1986) b. Ukraine. Settled in Palestine 1914. Founder member of Kibbutz Na'an, Ahdut Ha'avodah leader. Head of the Haganah National Staff 1946 – May 1948. Mapam leader 1948–1954. Cabinet Minister (Labour Party) (without portfolio, information) 1966–1977.

Hazan, Ya'akov (1899–1992) b. Poland. Member of Kibbutz Mishmar Ha'emek. Leader of Kibbutz Artzi and Mapam, 1948–1970s. Knesset Member 1949–1974.

al Husseini, 'Abd al Qadir (1907–1948) b. Jerusalem. Leader of Arab irregulars band, Jerusalem District 1936–9. Head of *al Jihad al Muqqadis* (Holy War) irregulars band 1947–1948. Killed in April 1948 in battle for Al Qastal.

al Husseini, Hajj Muhammad Amin (1895–1974) b. Jerusalem. President of Supreme Muslim Council 1921–1937. "Grand" Mufti of Jerusalem 1921–1948. President AHC 1936–1937. Worked for Nazi Germany 1941–1945. President AHC 1946–1948 and political leader of Palestine Arabs 1947–1949.

al Husseini, Jamal (1893?–1982) b. Jerusalem. Member of AHC1936–1937. Representative of AHC to United Nations 1947–1948.

Ibrahim, Rashid Hajj (?–?) Chairman of Haifa Arab National Committee 1947–1948.

Kaplan, Eliezer (1891–1952) b. Russia. Settled in Palestine 1923. Treasurer of the Jewish Agency 1933–1948. Finance Minister (Mapai) May 1948–1952.

al Khatib, Haj Mohammed Nimr (?–?) Preacher, leader of the Muslim Brotherhood in Palestine. Member of Haifa Arab National Committee 1947 – early 1948.

Khalidi, Dr Husayn Fakhri (1894–1962) b. Jerusalem. Mayor of Jerusalem 1934–1937. Founded Reform Party 1935. Member of AHC 1936–1937, 1946–1948. Only AHC member to stay in Palestine in 1948. Jordanian Cabinet Minister 1950s.

Machnes, Gad (1893–1954) b. Petah Tikva, Palestine. Leading orange-grower. Director General, Minority Affairs Ministry, 1948–1949.

Marriott, Cyril Herbert Alfred (1897–?) British Consular Service Officer. Consul General, Haifa, May 1948 – August 1949.

Meir (Myerson), Golda (1898–1975) b. Kiev, Russia. Director of Jewish Agency Political Department (in Jerusalem 1948), Mapai Knesset Member, Minister of Labour 1949–1956, Foreign Minister 1956–1965, Prime Minister 1969–1974

Rabin, Yitzhak (1922–1995) b. Jerusalem. Deputy Commander of the Palmah 1947–1948. OC Harel Brigade April–June 1948. OC operations Operation Dani July 1948. OC operations Southern Front September 1948 – March 1949. IDF Chief of General Staff 1964–1968. Prime Minister 1974–1977. Minister of Defence 1984–1990. Prime Minister 1992–1995.

Sasson, Elias (Eliahu) (1902–1978) b. Damascus. Settled in Palestine 1927. Director Arab Division of Political Department, Jewish Agency 1933–1948. Director Foreign Ministry Middle East Affairs Department 1948–1950. Member of first Transfer Committee 1948. Diplomat (Ambassador to Italy, Switzerland) 1950–1961. Minister of Posts 1961, Minister of Police 1966–1969.

Sharett (Shertok), Moshe (1894–1965) b. Ukraine. Settled in Palestine 1906. Director of the Jewish Agency's Political Department 1933 – May 1948. Foreign Minister (Mapai) May 1948–1954. Prime Minister 1954–1955. Foreign Minister 1955–1956. Chairman of Jewish Agency 1960–1965.

Shiloah (Zaslani), Reuven (1909–1959) b. Jerusalem. Haganah Intelligence Service officer. Official of Arab Division of Political Department,

Jewish Agency. Director Political Division, Foreign Ministry 1948–1949. Second head of Israel Delegation, Lausanne, 1949. Founder of the *Mossad* intelligence agency. Diplomat.

Shimoni, Ya'akov (1915–1996) b. Berlin. Settled in Palestine 1935. Official of Arab Division, Political Department, Jewish Agency 1941–1948. Deputy Director and Acting Director of Foreign Ministry Middle East Affairs Department May 1948–1949.

Shitrit, Bechor Shalom (1895–1967) b. Tiberias. Mandate police officer. Judge 1935. Chief Magistrate Lydda District 1945–1948. Minister of Minority Affairs and Police May 1948 – April 1949.

Tamimi, Rafiq (1890–1957) b. Nablus. School headmaster in Jaffa. Member of Arab Higher Committee 1947–1948. Head of Jaffa Arab National Committee 1948.

Weitz, Yosef (1890–1972) b. Poland. Settled in Palestine 1908. Director of Jewish National Fund Lands Department/Development Division 1932–1967. Member of Arab Affairs Committee of National Institutions 1940s. JNF Representative on the Committee of Directorates of the National Institutions 1940s. Chairman of first and second Transfer Committees 1948–1949. Chairman Negev Committee 1948. Member of JNF Directorate 1950–1967.

Yadin (Sukenik), Yigael (1917–1985) b. Jerusalem. OC Operations Haganah 1944 and 1947 – May 1948. OC Operations IDF June 1948–1949. IDF Chief of General Staff 1949–1952. Professor of Archaeology Hebrew University, Jerusalem 1963–1977. Deputy Prime Minister 1977–1981.

Bibliography

PRIMARY SOURCES

David Ben-Gurion Archives (DBG Archives), Sdeh Boqer, Israel

Central Zionist Archives (CZA) Jerusalem, Israel – papers of the Political Department of the Jewish Agency, protocols of the meetings of the Jewish Agency Executive and of the Jewish National Fund Directorate, Eliezer Granovsky Papers, manuscript notebooks of Yosef Weitz diary, etc.

Haganah Archive (HA) Tel Aviv

Hashomer Archive, Kfar Gil'adi, Israel – Yosef Nahmani Diary (YND)

Hashomer Hatza'ir Archive (HHA), Giv'at Haviva, Israel – papers of the Kibbutz Artzi, Mapam (Political Committee, Mapam Central Committee, etc. protocols), Aharon Cohen Papers (HHA–ACP), Meir Ya'ari Papers, etc.

Ihud Hakibbutzim Vehakvutsot Archive, Israel Kibbutz Hulda

Institute for Settlement Research – Rehovot – Yosef Weitz Papers

Israel Defence Forces and Defence Ministry Archive (IDFA) Giv'atayim, Israel

Israel State Archives (ISA) Jerusalem – papers of the Agriculture Ministry (AM), Foreign Ministry (FM), Justice Ministry (JM), Minority Affairs Ministry (MAM), Prime Minister's Office (PMO)

Jabotinsky Institute (JI) Tel Aviv – papers of the IZL, LHI, Revisionist Movement and Herut Party

Kibbutz Meuhad Archives (KMA), Ef'al, Israel – papers of the Kibbutz Meuhad (protocols of meetings of the movement and Ahdut Ha'avodah institutions), Aharon Cisling Papers (KMA–ACP), Palmah Archive (KMA–PA)

Labour Archive (LA) (Histadrut – Lavon Institute) – Tel Aviv

Labour Party Archives (LPA) – Beit Berl, Israel

National Archives (NA) – Washington DC – State Department Papers

Public Record Office (PRO) – London – papers of the Cabinet Office (CAB), Colonial Office (CO), Foreign Office (FO) and War Office (WO)

St Antony's College Middle East Centre Archive – Oxford, England – Alan Cunningham Papers (CP), Jerusalem and East Mission papers (JEM), etc.

United Nations Archive (UNA) – New York

Individual kibbutz archives – Mishmar Ha'emek, Ma'anit, Hazore'a (Eliezer Be'eri
Papers), etc.
Municipal archives in Israel – Haifa (HMA), Tiberias, Ashkelon

INTERVIEWS

Yigael Yadin, Yitzhak Ben-Aharon, Yehoshua Palmon, Ya'akov Shimoni,
Moshe Carmel, Eliezer Be'eri (Bauer), Binyamin Arnon, Aharon Bar-'Am
(Brawerman)

PUBLISHED PRIMARY SOURCES

Begin, Menachem, (Heb.) *In the Underground, Writings and Documents*, 4 vols.,
Tel Aviv, Hadar, 1959
Ben-Gurion, David, (Heb.) *As Israel Fights*, Tel Aviv, Mapai Press, 1952
—— (Heb.) *The Resurgent State of Israel*, 2 vols; Tel Aviv, Am Oved, 1969
—— (Heb.) *The War Diary, 1948–1949* (DBG-YH), 3 vols., eds. Gershon Rivlin
and Elhannan Orren, Tel Aviv Israel Defense Ministry Press, 1982
Israel State Archives/Central Zionist Archives, *Political and Diplomatic Docu-
ments, December 1947–May 1948*, ed. by Gedalia Yogev, Jerusalem, Israel
Government Press, 1980
Israel State Archives, *Documents on the Foreign Policy of the State of Israel,
May–September 1948*, Vol. I, ed. by Yehoshua Freundlich, Jerusalem, Israel
Government Press, 1981
Israel State Archives, *Documents on the Foreign Policy of the State of Israel,
October 1948–April 1949*, Vol. II, ed. by Yehoshua Freundlich, Jerusalem,
Israel Government Press, 1984
Israel State Archives, *Documents on the Foreign Policy of the State of Israel,
Armistice Negotiations with the Arab States, December 1948–July 1949*,
Vol. III, ed. by Yemima Rosenthal, Jerusalem, Israel Government Press,
1983
Israel State Archives, *Documents on the Foreign Policy of Israel,
May–December 1949*, Vol. IV, ed. by Yemima Rosenthal, Jerusalem, Israel
Government Press, 1986
Jabotinsky, Ze'ev, (Heb.) *Writings, On the Way to Statehood*, Jerusalem, Ari
Jabotinsky (Publishers), 1953.
Jewish Agency, *Twentieth Zionist Congress and the Fifth Session of the Jewish
Agency Council, 3–21 August 1937, A Stenographic Report*, Jerusalem,
Executive of the Zionist Organisation\Jewish Agency, 1938.
Mapai, (Heb.) *On the Problems of Settlement and Irrigation in the State*, May
1948.
Sharett (Shertok), Moshe, (Heb.) *Political Diary 1936–1942*, Tel Aviv, Am
Oved/Hasifriya Hatziyonit, 1976–1979.
Weitz, Yosef, (Heb.) *My Diary and Letters to the Children*, Vols. III and IV, Tel
Aviv, Massada, 1965.

SECONDARY WORKS

'Abasi, Mustafa, (Heb.) 'Safad During the Mandate; Social and Political Aspects',
Ph.D. thesis, Haifa University, 1999.

Anon. (Heb.), *The Alexandroni Brigade in the War of Independence*, eds. Gershon Rivlin and Zvi Sinai, Tel Aviv, IDF Press – Ma'arachot, 1964.

Anon. (Heb.), *The Book of the Palmah*, 2 Vols., ed. and compiled by Zerubavel Gilad together with Mati Megged, Tel Aviv, Kibbuu Meuhad Press, 1956.

Anon. (Heb.), *Behind the Screen, The Iraqi Parliamentary Inquiry on the War in Palestine*, Tel Aviv, Ma'arachot, 1954.

Anon. (Heb.), *The History of the Haganah*, (STH) 3 vols. sub-divided into eight books, ed. by Shaul Avigur, Yitzhak Ben-Zvi, Elazar Galili, Yehuda Slutzky, Ben-Zion Dinur and Gershon Rivlin, Tel Aviv, Am Oved, 1954–73.

Anon. (Heb.), *In Enemy Eyes, three Arab publications on the War of Independence* (Heb.) Tel Aviv, Israel Defence Forces, General Staff/History Branch, IDF Press–Ma'arachot, 1954. The book, translated into Hebrew by Captain S. Sabag, is composed of lengthy excerpts from Mohammed Nimr al Khatib, *Min Athar al Nakba, Kamel Ismail al Sharif, Al Ihwan al Muslemin fi Harb Falastin,* and Mohammed Ghussan, *Ma'arak Bab al Wad.*

Anon. (Heb.), *Mishmar Ha'emek in the War*, Tel Aviv, Sifriyat Poalim, 1950.

Anon. (Heb.), *Tree and Sword, the Route of Battle of the Golani Brigade*, collected and edited by Binyamin Etzioni, Tel Aviv, IDF Press – Ma'arachot, undated.

Anon. (Heb.), *'Ein Gev in the War: The Fortress at the Entrance to the Sea of Galilee*, Tel Aviv, Ma'arachot, 1950.

Anon. (Heb.), *The Negev Brigade during the War*, Tel Aviv, IDF Press – Ma'arachot, undated.

'Abd al Madur, 'Abd al Rahim, (Arab.) *The Village of Qaqun*, Bir Zeit University Press, 1994.

Assaf, Michael, (Heb.) *The History of the Awakening of the Arabs in Palestine and Their Flight*, Tel Aviv, Tarbut Vehinuch, 1967.

'Av, Nahum, (Heb.) *The Struggle for Tiberias, the First [City] Liberated in the War of Independence*, Tel Aviv, Ministry of Defence Press, 1991.

Avidar, Yosef, (Heb.) 'Plan D', in *Safra Veseifa*, No. 2, June 1978.

Ayalon, Avraham, (Heb.) *The Giv'ati Brigade in the War of Independence*, Tel Aviv, DF Press – Ma'arachot, 1959.

—— (Heb.), *The Giv'ati Brigade Opposite the Egyptian Invader*, Tel Aviv, IDF Press – Ma'arachot, 1963.

Al 'Azm, Khalid, (Arab.) *The Memoirs of Khalid al 'Azm*, Beirut, Dar al Mutahidda Lil-Nashr, 1973.

Banai (Mazal), Ya'akov, (Heb.) *Unknown Soldiers, the Book of LHI Operations*, Tel Aviv, Hug Yedidim, 1958.

Begin, Menachem, *The Revolt*, London, W.H. Allen 1964.

Ben-Artzi, Yoss, (Heb.) ' "To Conquer the State", Mapai's Settlement Plan in Advance of the Establishment of the State along Partition Borders', *Yahadut Zmanenu* 10, 1996.

Ben-Yehuda, Netiva (Heb.) *Passed the Ropes*, Jerusalem, Domino Press, 1985.

Bentov, Mordechai, (Heb.) *Days Tell*, Tel Aviv, Sifriyat Hapoalim, 1984.

Burns, E.L.M., *Between Arab and Israeli*, London, Harrap, 1962.

Caplan, Neil, *Futile Diplomacy, Vol. 3, The United Nations, the Great Powers and Middle East Peacemaking 1948–1954*, London, Frank Cass, 1997.

Carmel, Moshe, (Heb.) *Northern Battles*, Tel Aviv, IDF Press–Ma'arachot, 1949.

Carta's Atlas of Palestine From Zionism to Statehood, (Heb.) ed. by Jehuda Wallach, Jerusalem, Carta, 1972, 1974.

Carta's Historical Atlas of Israel, The First Years 1948–1961, (Heb.) ed. by Jehuda Wallach and Moshe Lissak, Jerusalem, Carta, 1978.

Cohen, Aharon, (Heb.) *Israel and the Arab World*, Tel Aviv, Sifriyat *Poalim*, 1964.

Cohen, Mula, (Heb.) *To Give and to Receive*, Personal Memoirs, Tel Aviv, Hakibbutz Hameuhad Publishing House, 2000.

Cohen, Yeroham, (Heb.) *By Light and in Darkness*, Amikam, Tel Aviv, 1969.

Cohen-Shany, Shmuel, (Heb.) *Operation Paris: International and Quiet Diplomacy in a New State*, Tel Aviv, Ramot-Tel Aviv University, 1994.

Dror, Zvika, (Heb.) *The Life and Times of Yitzhak Sadeh*, Tel Aviv, Hakkibutz Hameuhad Publishing House, 1996.

Ehrlich, (Heb.), *The Lebanon Tangle: The Policy of the Zionist Movement and the State of Israel towards Lebanon, 1918–1958*, Tel Aviv, IDF/Ministry of Defence Press, 2000.

Eshel, Zadok, (Heb.), *The Carmeli Brigade in the War of Independence*, Tel Aviv, Ma'arachot – IDF Press, 1973.

—— (Heb.) *The Haganah Battles in Haifa*, Tel Aviv, Ministry of Defence Press, 1978.

Eyal, Yigal, *The First Intifada, the Suppression of the Arab Revolt by the British Army, 1936–1939*, (Heb.) Tel Aviv, Ma'arachot\Defence Ministry Press, 1998.

Finkelstein, Norman, 'Myths, Old and New,' *Journal of Palestine Studies*, 81 (Autumn 1991).

Gabbay, Rony, *A Political Study of the Arab–Jewish Conflict: The Arab Refugee Problem (a Case Study)*, Geneva, Librairie E. Droz, and Paris, Librairie Minard, 1959.

Gelber, Yoav, (Heb.) *The Core of A Regular Jewish Army*, Jerusalem, Yad Ben-Zvi, 1986.

—— *Palestine 1948, War Escape, and the Emergence of the Palestinian Refugee Problem*, Brighton, Sussex Academic Press, 2001.

—— (Heb.) *Independence and Nakba* (forthcoming) (Chapter 15).

Giv'ati, Moshe, (Heb.) *In the Path of Desert and Fire, the History of the 9th Armored Battalion 1948–1984*, Tel Aviv, Ma'arachot\Defence Ministry Press, 1994.

Golan, Arnon, (Heb.) *Spatial Transformation – Result of War, the Former Arab Areas in the State of Israel 1948–1950*, Beersheba, Centre for Ben-Gurion's Heritage-Ben-Gurion University Press, 2001.

Goren, Tamir, (Heb.) 'Why did the Arab Inhabitants of Haifa Leave? An Examination of a Controversial Question', *Cathedra*, 80, June 1996.

Gorny, Yosef, *The British Labour Movement and Zionism, 1917–1948*, London, Frank Cass, 1983.

—— (Heb.) *The Arab Question and the Jewish Problem*, Tel Aviv, 'Am 'Oved, 1985.

Glubb, John, *A Soldier with the Arabs*, London, Hodder and Stoughton, 1957.

Grossman, David, (Heb.) *The Arab Village and Its Daughters, Processes in the Arab Settlement of Palestine in the Ottoman Period*, Jerusalem, Yad Ben-Zvi, 1994.

Harari, Ephraim, ed., *The Tel of the Winds, Letters from Home*, Kibbutz Hatzor, Shikma, no date (but ca.1986) (a book of letters).

Hasso, Frances, 'Modernity and Gender in Arab Accounts of the 1948 and 1967 Defeats', *International Journal of Middle East Studies*, 32, 2000.

Heller, Joseph, *The Birth of Israel, 1945–1949, Ben-Gurion and His Critics*, Gainesville, Florida University Press, 2000.

Horowitz, Dan, and Moshe Lissak, (Heb.) *The Origins of the Israeli Polity, the Political System of the Jewish Community in Palestine Under the Mandate*, Tel Aviv, 'Am 'Oved, 1977.

Israel Defence Forces, General Staff History Branch, (Heb.) *History of the War of Independence*, Tel Aviv, IDF Press – Ma'arachot, 1959.

Itzchaki, Arieh, (Heb.), *Latrun, the Battle for the Road to Jerusalem*, 2 vols., Jerusalem, Cana, 1982.

Kadish, Allon; Sela, Avraham; and Golan, Arnon, (Heb.) *The Conquest of Lydda, July 1948*, Tel Aviv, Haganah Archive\Ministry of Defence Press, 2000.

Kamen, Charles, (Heb.), 'After the Catastrophe: the Arabs in the State of Israel', in *Mahbarot Lemehkar U'lebikoret*, No. 10, 1985.

Kan'ane, Sharif, and Lubna 'Abd al Hadi, (Arab.), 'Abu Kishk', Bir Zeit, Bir Zeit University Press, 1990.

Kan'ane, Sharif, and Bassam al Ka'abi, (Arab.) 'Al Miska', Bir Zeit, Bir Zeit University Press, 1991.

—— (Arab.) 'Kafr Saba', Bir Zeit, Bir Zeit University Press, 1991.

Kan'ane, Sharif, and Nihad Zeitawi, (Arab.) 'The Village of Deir Yassin', Bir Zeit, Bir Zeit University Press, 1987.

Kan'ane, Sharif, and Rashad al Madani, (Arab.) 'Kaufakha', Bir Zeit, Bir Zeit University Press, 1990.

—— (Arab.) 'Faluja Village', Bir Zeit, Bir Zeit University Press, 1987.

Kark, Ruth, and Michal Oren-Nordheim, (Heb.) *Jerusalem and Its Environs, Quarters, Neighbourhoods and Villages 1800–1948*, Jerusalem, Akademon, 1995.

Katz, Shmuel, (Heb.) *Jabo, A Biography of Ze'ev Jabotinsky*, Tel Aviv, Dvir, 1993.

Katz, Teddy, (Heb.), 'The Exodus of the Arabs from Villages at the Foot of the Southern Carmel in 1948', Haifa University MA Thesis, March 1998.

Katz, Yossi, (Heb.) 'The Deliberations of the Jewish Agency Committee for Transfer of Population, 1937–1938', *Zion*, 2\53, 1988.

Khalidi, Walid, 'The Fall of Haifa', *Middle East Forum*, 35\10, December 1959.

—— 'Plan Dalet: Master Plan for the Conquest of Palestine', *Journal of Palestine Studies*, Autumn 1988.

(ed.) – *All that Remains: The Palestinian Villages Occupied and Depopulated by Israel in 1948*, Washington, DC, Institute for Palestine Studies, 1992.

Khatib, Muhammad Nimr al, *The Events of the Disaster or the Palestinian Disaster*, Beirut, Al Khay at Publishers, 1967 ed.

Kidron, Peretz, 'Truth Whereby Nations Live', in Christopher Hitchens and Edward Said, eds. *Blaming the Victims, Spurious Scholarship and the Palestinian Question*, London, Verso, 1988.

Kimche, Jon and David, *Both Sides of the Hill*, London, Secker and Warburg, 1960.

Krystall, Nathan, 'The Fall of the New City 1947–1950', in Salim Tamari, ed., *Jerusalem 1948: the Arab Neighbourhoods and their Fate in the War*, Jerusalem, Institute of Jerusalem Studies\Badil Resource Centre, 1999.

Lahav, Mordechai, (Heb.) *Fifty Years of the Palestinian Refugees, 1948–1999*, Israel, Rosh Tov, 2000.

Lazar (Litai), Haim, *The Conquest of Jaffa*, Tel Aviv, Shelah, 1951.

Lebel, Jennie, (Heb.) *Haj Amin and Berlin*, Tel Aviv, Technosdar, 1996.

Levenberg, Haim, *The Military Preparations of the Arab Community in Palestine, 1945–1948*, London, Frank Cass Ltd., 1993.

Levin, Harry, *Jerusalem Embattled, a Diary of the City Under Siege, March 25th, 1948 to July 18th, 1948*, London, Victor Gollancz Ltd., 1950.

Lorch, Netanel, *The Edge of the Sword, Israel's War of Independence, 1947–1949*, revised ed., Jerusalem, Masada Press, 1968.

Masalha, Nur, *Expulsion of the Palestinians, The Concept of 'Transfer" in Zionist Political Thought, 1882–1948*, Washington DC, Institute for Palestine Studies, 1992.

—— 'A Critique of Benny Morris', *Journal of Palestine Studies* 81, Vol. XXI\1, Autumn 1991.

—— 'The Historical Roots of the Palestinian Refugee Question,' in Naseer Aruri, ed., *Palestinian Refugees, the Right of Return*, London, Pluto Press, 2001.

Messer, Oded, (Heb.) *The Haganah's Operational Plans, 1937–1948*, Tag Publishing House, Israel, 1996.

Miller, Ylana, *Government and Society in Rural Palestine 1920–1946*, Austin, University of Texas Press, 1984.

Milstein, Uri, *History of Israel's War of Independence*, vols. 1–4, Lanham, Maryland, University Press of America, 1996–1998.

Montgomery of Alamein, Bernard, *Memoirs*, Collins, London, 1958.

Morris, Benny, *The Birth of the Palestinian Refugee Problem, 1947–1949*, Cambridge, Cambridge University Press, 1988.

—— *1948 and After: Israel and the Palestinians*, Oxford, Oxford University Press, (rev. ed.) 1994.

—— *Israel's Border Wars, 1949–1956*, Oxford, Oxford University Press, (rev. ed.) 1997.

—— *Righteous Victims, A History of the Zionist-Arab Conflict, 1881–1999*, New York, Knopf, 1999.

—— *The Road to Jerusalem: Glubb Pasha, Palestine and the Jews*, London, IB Tauris, 2002.

—— (Heb.) *Correcting a Mistake, Jews and Arabs in Palestine, 1936–1956*, Tel Aviv, 'Am 'Oved, 2000.

—— 'Haifa's Arabs: Displacement and Concentration, July 1948', *The Middle East Journal*, 42/2, Spring 1988.

—— 'The Harvest of 1948 and the Creation of the Palestinian Refugee Problem', *The Middle East Journal*, 40/4, Autumn 1986.

—— 'Yosef Weitz and the Transfer Committees, 1948–1949', *Middle Eastern Studies*, 22/4, October 1986.

—— 'Operation Dani and the Palestinian Exodus from Lydda and Ramle in 1948', *The Middle East Journal*, 40\1, Winter 1986.

Nazzal, Nafez, *The Palestinian Exodus from Galilee, 1948*, Beirut, The Institute for Palestine Studies, 1978.

Nimrod, Yoram, (Heb.), 'Patterns of Israeli-Arab Relations: The Formative Years 1947–1950', Hebrew University Ph.D. thesis, 1985.

Niv, David, (Heb.), *Battles of the IZL*, Vol. 6, Tel Aviv, Klausner Institute, 1980.

Orren, Elhannan, (Heb.), *On the Road to the City, Operation Dani*, Tel Aviv, IDF Press – Ma'arachot, 1976.

Oussetzky-Lazar, Sarah, (Heb.) 'Iqrit and Bir'im, the Full Story,' Report No. 10, Reports on the Arabs in Israel, Giv'at Haviva, Institute for Arab Studies\Institute for the Study of Peace, 1993.

Pa'il, Meir, (Heb.) *From the Haganah to the Israel Defence Forces*, Tel Aviv, Zmora, Bitan, Modan, 1979.

Pappe, Ilan, *The Making of the Arab-Israeli-Conflict 1947–1949*, London, IB Tauris, 1992.

—— 'The Tantura Case in Israel: The Katz Research and Trial', *Journal of Palestine Studies*, Vol. 30\3, Spring 2001.

—— (Heb.) 'The Katz Affair and Tantura: History, Historiography, Law and Academia', *Teioriya U'Vikoret* 20, Spring 2002.

Parsons, Laila, *The Druze between Palestine and Israel, 1947–1949*, Oxford, Macmillan\St Antony's, 2000.

Peretz, Don, *Israel and the Palestine Arabs*, Washington DC, The Middle East Institute, 1958.

Porath, Yehoshua, *The Emergence of the Palestinian–Arab National Movement 1918–1929*, London, Frank Cass, 1974.

—— *The Palestinian Arab National Movement 1929–1939*, London, Frank Cass, 1977.

Sakakini, Khalil al, (Heb.) *Such am I, Oh World, Diaries of Khalil al Sakakini*, Jerusalem, Keter, 1990.

Sayigh, Rosemary, *Palestinians: From Peasants to Revolutionaries*, London, Zed Press, 1979.

Schechtmann, Joseph, *Population Transfers in Asia*, NY, Hallsby Press, 1949.

Segev, Tom, (Heb.) *1949 – The First Israelis*, Domino Press, Jerusalem, 1984.

——*One Palestine, Complete, Jews and Arabs under the British Mandate*, New York, Metropolitan Books\Harry Holt, 2000.

Seikaly, May, *Haifa, Transformation of an Arab Society, 1918–1939*, London, IB Tauris, 1995.

Shaltiel, David, (Heb.) *Jerusalem 1948*, Tel Aviv, Defence Ministry Press, 1981.

Shapira, Anita, *Land and Power, The Zionist Resort to Force 1881–1948*, New York, Oxford University Press, 1992.

Shimoni, Ya'akov, (Heb.), *The Arabs of Palestine*, Tel Aviv, 'Am 'Oved, 1947.

Shoufani, Elias, 'The Fall of a Village', *Journal of Palestine Studies*, 1\4, 1972.

Simons, Chaim, *International Proposals for Transfer of Arabs from Palestine, 1895–1947*, Hoboken, NJ, Ktav Publishing House, 1988.

—— 'Supplement No. 1', Kiryat Arba, 1993.

Slyomovics, Susan, *The Object of Memory*, Philadelphia, University of Pennsylvania Press, 1998.

Stein, Kenneth, 'One Hundred Years of Social Change, the Creation of the Palestinian Refugee Problem', in Laurence Silberstein, ed., *New Perspectives on Israeli History, the Early Years*, New York, New York University Press, 1991.

Teveth, Shabtai, *Ben-Gurion and the Palestinian Arabs*, Oxford, Oxford University Press, 1985.

—— 'The Evolution of "Transfer" in Zionist Thinking', Occasional Papers, Tel Aviv, Moshe Dayan Centre, Tel Aviv University, May 1989.

—— (Heb.) 'The New Historians', *Ha'aretz*, 14.4.1989.

Tzahar, Moshe, (Heb.) 'Historians, Beware of Your Sources', *Alpayim* 13, 1996.

Tzahor, Ze'ev, (Heb.) *Hazan*, Jerusalem, Yad Ben-Zvi\Yad Ya'ari, 1997.

Vered, Avraham, (Heb.) *Burning Bush*, Tel Aviv, Tnufa Books, 1950.

—— (Heb.) *The Southern Front, Between Sinai and Hebron, from the Isolation of the Negev until the Defeat of the Invading Egyptian Army*, Tel Aviv, Yair Publishers, 1996.

Yihya, Mahmood al Yihya (Arab.), *Al Tantura*, Damascus, Dar al Shara, 1998.

Zimmerman, John, 'Radio Propaganda in the Arab-Israeli War of 1948', *Weiner Library Bulletin*, New Series, XXVII, nos. 30–31, 1–9.

Index

Other books in the series